D1622736

Transnational Management

Transnational Management

TEXT, CASES, AND READINGS IN CROSS-BORDER MANAGEMENT

SIXTH EDITION

Christopher A. Bartlett
Harvard Business School

Paul W. Beamish
Ivey Business School
The University of Western Ontario

McGraw-Hill Irwin

TRANSNATIONAL MANAGEMENT, SIXTH EDITION

Published by McGraw-Hill, a business unit of The McGraw-Hill Companies, Inc., 1221 Avenue of the Americas, New York, NY 10020. Copyright © 2011 by The McGraw-Hill Companies, Inc. All rights reserved. Previous editions © 2008, 2004, and 2000. No part of this publication may be reproduced or distributed in any form or by any means, or stored in a database or retrieval system, without the prior written consent of The McGraw-Hill Companies, Inc., including, but not limited to, in any network or other electronic storage or transmission, or broadcast for distance learning.

Some ancillaries, including electronic and print components, may not be available to customers outside the United States.

This book is printed on acid-free paper.

With respect to IVEY cases, Ivey Management Services prohibits any form of reproduction, storage or transmittal without its written permission. This material is not covered under authorization from any reproduction rights organization. To order copies or request permission to reproduce materials, contact Ivey Publishing, Ivey Management Services, c/o Richard Ivey School of Business, The University of Western Ontario, London, Ontario, Canada, N6A 3K7; phone (519) 661-3208, fax (519) 661-3882, email cases@ivey.uwo.ca
One time permission to reproduce Ivey cases granted by Ivey Management Services on 07/08/2009

The copyright on each case in this book unless otherwise noted is held by the President and Fellows of Harvard College and they are published herein by express permission. Cases may not be digitized, photocopied, or otherwise reproduced, posted, or transmitted without the permission of Harvard Business School Publishing. Permissions requests to use individual Harvard copyrighted cases should be directed to permissions@hbsp.harvard.edu

1 2 3 4 5 6 7 8 9 0 DOC/DOC 1 0 9 8 7 6 5 4 3 2 1 0

ISBN 978-0-07-813711-2
MHID 0-07-813711-X

Vice President & Editor-in-Chief: *Brent Gordon*
Vice President SEM, EDP/Central Publishing
  Services: *Kimberly Meriwether David*
Publisher: *Paul Ducham*
Sponsoring Editor: *Laura Spell*
Editorial Coordinator: *Jane Beck*
Marketing Manager: *Jaime Haltemann*
Project Manager: *Erin Melloy*
Design Coordinator: *Brenda A. Rolwes*

Cover Designer: *Studio Montage, St. Louis, MI*
USE Cover Image Credit: © *Photodisc*
  Collection/Getty Images
Production Supervisor: *Nicole Baumgartner*
Media Project Manager: *Suresh Babu*
Compositor: *S4Carlisle Publishing Services*
Typeface: *10/12 Times New Roman*
Printer: *R. R. Donnelley*

All credits appearing on page or at the end of the book are considered to be an extension of the copyright page.

Library of Congress Cataloging-in-Publication Data

Bartlett, Christopher A., 1943–
   Transnational management : text, cases, and readings in cross-border management /
Christopher A. Bartlett, Paul W. Beamish. -- 6th ed.
      p. cm.
    ISBN-13: 978-0-07-813711-2
    ISBN-10: 0-07-813711-X
    1. International business enterprises--Management. I. Beamish, Paul W.,
1953– II. Title.
  HD62.4.B365   2011
  658'.049--dc22
                           2009054449

www.mhhe.com

About the Authors

Christopher Bartlett   is the Thomas D. Casserly, Jr., Professor Emeritus of Business Administration at Harvard Graduate School of Business Administration. He received an economics degree from the University of Queensland, Australia, and both masters and doctorate degrees in business administration from Harvard University. Prior to his academic career, he was a marketing manager with Alcoa in Australia, a management consultant in McKinsey and Company's London office, and country general manager of Baxter Laboratories' subsidiary company in France.

He joined the faculty of Harvard Business School in 1979, and over the following 30 years his interests focused on strategic and organizational challenges confronting managers in multinational corporations and on the process of managing transformational change. While at HBS, he served as faculty chair of the International Senior Management Program, area head of the School's General Management Unit, faculty chairman of the Program for Global Leadership, and as chair of the Humanitarian Leadership Program.

He is the author or co-author of nine books, including *Managing Across Borders: The Transnational Solution* (coauthored with Sumantra Ghoshal), named by *Financial Times* as one of the 50 most influential business books of the century. *The Individualized Corporation,* his subsequent major research book with Ghoshal, was the winner of the Igor Ansoff Award for the best new work in strategic management and was named one of the Best Business Books for the Millennium by *Strategy+Business* magazine. Both books have been translated into over 10 foreign languages. His articles have appeared in journals such as *Harvard Business Review, Sloan Management Review, Strategic Management Journal, Academy of Management Review,* and *Journal of International Business Studies.* He has also researched and written over 100 case studies and teaching notes, and their sales of over 3 1/2 million copies make him the best-selling case author ever. He has been elected by his colleagues as a fellow of the Academy of Management, the Academy of International Business, the Strategic Management Society, and the World Economic Forum.

Paul Beamish   is the Donald Triggs Canada Research Chair in International Business at the Ivey Business School, University of Western Ontario. He is the author or coauthor of numerous books, articles, contributed chapters, and teaching cases. His articles have appeared in *Academy of Management Review, Academy of Management Journal, Strategic Management Journal, Journal of International Business Studies* (*JIBS*), *Organization Science,* and elsewhere. He has received best research awards from the Academy of Management and the Academy of International Business (AIB). In 1997 and 2003, he was recognized in the *Journal of International Management* as one of the top three contributors worldwide to the international strategic management literature in the previous decade. He served as Editor-in-Chief of *JIBS* from 1993–97. He worked for Procter & Gamble and Wilfrid Laurier University before joining Ivey's faculty in 1987.

He has supervised 25 doctoral dissertations, many involving international joint ventures and alliances. His consulting, management training, and joint venture facilitation activities have been in both the public and private sector.

At Ivey, he has taught in a variety of school programs, including the Executive MBA offered at its campus in Hong Kong. From 1999–2004, he served as Associate Dean of Research. He currently serves as Director of Ivey Publishing, the distributor of Ivey's collection of over 2,400 current cases; Ivey's Asian Management Institute (AMI); and the cross-enterprise center, Engaging Emerging Markets.

He is a Fellow of the Academy of International Business, Royal Society of Canada, and Asia Pacific Foundation of Canada.

Preface

■ ■ ■ ■ ■ ■ ■ ■ ■ ■ ■ ■ ■ ■ ■ ■ ■ ■

This book grew out of the authors' strongly held belief that the best international business research did more than capture the challenges, activities, perceptions, and best practices from the field. It also translated those findings into practical and relevant lessons for managers and students of management. Although one of the original authors, our late friend and colleague Sumantra Ghoshal, passed away six years ago, that founding philosophy fits very comfortably with his successor co-author on this volume, Paul Beamish, and lives on in this sixth edition.

In preparing this new edition, we have done all we can to ensure that the frameworks, concepts, and practical examples we have included are topical, relevant, and of importance to practitioners working in today's global business environment. We believe that those are the issues that are described in the case studies, illuminated by the articles, and embedded in the conceptual chapters that provide the framework for this course-long voyage in transnational management.

In the 20 years since the first edition of *Transnational Management* appeared, much has changed in the field of cross-border business management—new external demands have emerged, new strategic responses have been developed, new organizational capabilities have evolved, and new managerial competencies have become necessary. But old international hands will insist that these differences are largely superficial, and beyond such ongoing adjustments at the margin, the basics of managing a worldwide operation remain much as they have always been—understanding one's host country environment, being sensitive to cross-cultural differences, seeing the world as an integrated strategic reality, and being able to deal with the complexities of managing operations separated by the barriers of distance, language, time, and culture.

In many ways, both views are correct, and we are reminded of this with each revision of this volume, as we deal with conflicting pressures and demands that we must resolve with every new edition. On one hand we receive passionate input from teaching faculty anxious to keep up with the latest developments to keep the material fresh, reflecting the vibrancy of the field. But we also hear from those who recognize the importance of teaching the timeless international management issues that are often best captured in classic favorites. Based on input we received from the users of this text who are represented on our Editorial Advisory Board, we have sought to maintain this balance, retaining the most powerful existing cases and articles, while adding new material that captures the emerging issues that will keep courses fresh and students challenged. The end result is that, as in all previous editions, around half the cases and readings included in the sixth edition have been retained, and about half are new.

■ Distinguishing Characteristics of the MNE

What makes the study of the multinational enterprise (MNE) unique? The most fundamental distinction between a domestic company and an MNE derives from the social, political, and economic context in which each exists. The former operates in a single national environment where social and cultural norms, government regulations, customer tastes and preferences, and the economic and competitive context of a business tend to be fairly consistent. Although within-country local variations do exist for most of these factors, they are nowhere near as diverse or as conflicting as the differences in demands and pressures the MNE faces in its multiple host countries.

The one feature that categorically distinguishes these intercountry differences from the intracountry ones, however, is *sovereignty*.[1] Unlike the local or regional bodies, the nation-state generally represents the ultimate rule-making authority against whom no appeal is feasible. Consequently, the MNE faces an additional and unique element of risk: the political risk of operating in countries with different legal systems, social attitudes, and political philosophies regarding private property, corporate responsibility, and free enterprise.

A second major difference relates to competitive strategy. The purely domestic company can respond to competitive challenges only within the context of its single market; the MNE can, and often must, play a much more complex competitive game. Global-scale or cross-border sourcing may be necessary to achieve a competitive position, implying the need for complex international logistical coordination. Furthermore, on the global chessboard, effective competitive strategy might require that a competitive challenge in one country might call for a response in a different country—perhaps the competitor's home market. These are options and complexities a purely domestic company does not face.

Third, a purely domestic company can measure its performance in a single comparable unit—the local currency. Because currency values fluctuate against each other, however, the MNE is required to measure results with a flexible measuring stick. In addition, it is exposed to the economic risks associated with shifts in both nominal and real exchange rates.

Finally, the purely domestic company must manage an organizational structure and management systems that reflect its product and functional variety; the MNE organization is intrinsically more complex because it must provide for management control over its product, functional, *and* geographic diversity. Furthermore, the resolution of this three-way tension must be accomplished in an organization that is divided by barriers of distance and time and impeded by differences in language and culture.

The Management Challenge

Historically, the study of international business focused on the environmental forces, structures, and institutions that provided the context within which MNE managers had to operate. In such a macro approach, countries or industries rather than companies were the primary units of analysis. Reflecting the environment of its time, this traditional approach directed most attention to trade flows and the capital transfers that defined the foreign investment patterns.

---

[1] This difference is elaborated in J. N. Behrman and R. E. Gross, *International Business and Governments: Issues and Institutions* (Columbia: University of South Carolina Press, 1990). See also J. J. Boddewyn, "Political Aspects of MNE Theory," *Journal of International Business Studies* 19, no. 3 (1988), pp. 341–63.

During the 1970s and 1980s, a new perspective on the study of international management began to emerge, with a far greater emphasis on the MNE and management behavior rather than on global economic forces and international institutions. With the firms as the primary unit of analysis and management decisions as the key variables, these studies both highlighted and provided new insights into the management challenges associated with international operations.

This book builds on the company- and management-level perspective. More specifically, in order to make sense of the practice of managing the MNE, we tend to adopt a management perspective that views the world through the eyes of the executive who is in the thick of it—whether that is the CEO of the corporation, the global account manager, the country subsidiary manager, or the frontline business manager. The most powerful way to do this is to employ cases that require decisions to be made, and most of those in this book provide the reader not only with data on the business context but also with detailed information about the key actors, their roles, their responsibilities, and their personal motivations. In many instances, videos and follow-up cases lead to further insight.

It would be easy to build our structure around the traditional functions of the company—R&D, manufacturing, marketing, etc.—and many texts have done so. But we find such an approach limiting because almost all real-world problems cut across these functional boundaries. They require executives to understand all the disparate parts of the organization, and they demand integrative solutions that bring together, rather than divide, the people working in their traditional functional silos. So we have also chosen to focus on the core *organizational processes* that executives must create and manage—the entrepreneurial process (identifying and acting on new opportunities), the integrative learning process (linking and leveraging those pockets of entrepreneurial initiative), and the leadership process (articulating a vision and inspiring others to follow). This process perspective is sometimes more difficult to grasp than the compartmentalized functional view, but ultimately it provides a more fulfilling and realistic approach to the management of today's MNE.

By adopting the perspective of the MNE manager, however, we do not ignore the important and legitimate perspectives, interests, and influences of other key actors in the international operating environment. However, we do view the effects of these other key actors from the perspective of the company and focus on understanding how the various forces they influence shape the strategic, organizational, and operational tasks of MNE managers.

◼ The Structure of the Book

The book is divided into three parts (see figure on page xiii). **Part 1** consists of three chapters that examine the development of strategy in the MNE. In Chapter 1, we focus on the motivations that draw—or drive—companies abroad, the means by which they expand across borders, and the mind-sets of those who built the worldwide operations. Understanding what we call a company's "administrative heritage" is important because it shapes both the current configuration of assets and capabilities and the cognitive orientations of managers toward future growth—attitudes that can either enable or constrain such growth.

In Chapter 2, we examine the political, economic, and social forces that shape the business environment in which the MNE operates. In particular, the chapter explores the tension created by the political demands to be responsive to national differences, the economic pressures to be globally integrated, and the growing competitive need to develop and diffuse worldwide innovation and learning.

In Chapter 3, the focus shifts from the global business environment to MNEs' competitive responses to those external pressures. Building on the themes developed in Chapter 2, we examine the various approaches an MNE can use to generate competitive advantage in its international context. We identify three traditional strategic approaches—global, international, and multinational—each of which focuses on a different source of competitive advantage. We then go on to describe the transnational strategy, which combines the benefits of the other three models.

Part 2 changes the focus from the MNE's strategic imperatives to the organizational capabilities required to deliver them. Chapter 4 examines the organizational structures and systems that need to be put in place to be effective in a complex and dynamic world. Mirroring the three traditional strategic approaches, we explore three organizational models that all appear to be evolving toward the integrated network form required to manage transnational strategies.

Chapter 5 focuses on one of the most important processes to be developed in a transnational organization. The need to manage effective cross-border knowledge transfer and worldwide learning is creating additional organizational demands, and in this chapter, we explore how such processes are built and managed.

Then, in Chapter 6, we lift our organizational analysis up a level to examine the boundary-spanning structures and processes needed to create joint ventures, alliances, and interfirm networks in a global context. In this chapter, we explore how such partnerships can be built and managed to develop strategic capabilities that may not be available inside any single MNE.

Part 3 focuses on the management challenges of operating a successful MNE. In Chapter 7, the focus is on those who must implement the transnational strategies, operate within the integrated network organizations, and above all, deliver the results. This chapter allows us to look at the world through the eyes of frontline country subsidiary managers, and shows how their actions can have important implications for the competitiveness of the entire corporation.

Finally in Chapter 8, we ask some broad questions about the present and future role of the multinational enterprise in the global economy. The powerful forces unleashed by globalization have had a largely positive impact on economic and social development worldwide. But like all revolutions, the forces of changes have acted unevenly, and there have been casualties. As the divide between the "haves" and "have nots" expands, the challenge facing MNEs is to determine what role they can and should play in mitigating some of the unintended consequences of the globalization revolution. It is a challenge that should confront every current executive and be central to the task of the next generation of leadership in transnational companies.

■ Acknowledgments

Transnational Management has also benefited from the comments, suggestions, and insights provided by colleagues at the hundreds of institutions around the world that have adopted this book. In particular, we would like to acknowledge the role played by the Editorial Advisory Board (listed on page xii) who committed significant effort to providing a detailed critique of the fifth edition that helped us make decisions about what to include in this edition. We have also had extraordinary support from our colleagues in other institutions who have provided valuable feedback and suggestions for improvement. In particular, we would like to acknowledge Shih-Fen Chen, Jean-Louis Schaan and Charles Dhanaraj.

Next, we are extraordinarily grateful to the researchers and colleagues who have contributed new materials to this edition. In addition to our own case materials, new case studies have been provided by Rod White, Hari Bapuji, Bo Nielsen, Torben Pedersen, Jacob Pyndt, Jean-Louis Schaan, Andreas Schotter, Harry Lane, Jordan Siegel, John Quelch, Stefan Thomke, and Ashok Nimgade. Articles new to this edition and focused on important research have been contributed by Marcus Alexander, Harry Korine, Arindam K. Bhattacharya, David C. Michael, Pankaj Ghemawat, Jeanne Brett, Kristin Behfar, Mary C. Kern, Julian Birkinshaw, Cyril Bouquet, Tina C. Ambos, John Bessant, Rick Delbridge, and Thomas Donaldson.

We must also acknowledge the coordination task undertaken by our respective administrative assistants who worked over many months to coordinate the flow of manuscript documents back and forth among Boston, Sydney, and London, Ontario. To Jan Simmons and Mary Roberts, we give our heartfelt thanks for helping us through the long and arduous revision process. To Laura Hurst Spell, our sponsoring editor, Erin Melloy, our project manager, and Jane Beck, our editorial coordinator, at McGraw-Hill, as well as Jolynn Kilburg, our developmental editor at S4Carlisle Publishing Services, we thank you for your patience and tolerance through this long process and look forward to a long and productive working relationship.

Despite the best efforts of all the contributors, however, we must accept responsibility for the shortcomings of the book that remain. Our only hope is that they are outweighed by the value you find in these pages and the exciting challenges they represent in the constantly changing field of transnational management.

Christopher A. Bartlett
Paul W. Beamish

▪ Editorial Advisory Board

Our sincere thanks to the following faculty who provided detailed feedback and suggestions on the materials for this edition.

Name	School
Andrew H. Hageman, PhD	American InterContinental University
Axele Giroud	University of Manchester
Dr. Frank Borrmann	Universität Hamburg
Linda D. Clarke	Florida International University
Mohan V. Avvari	Nottingham University Business School
Dr. Susan Martin	University of Hertfordshire Business School

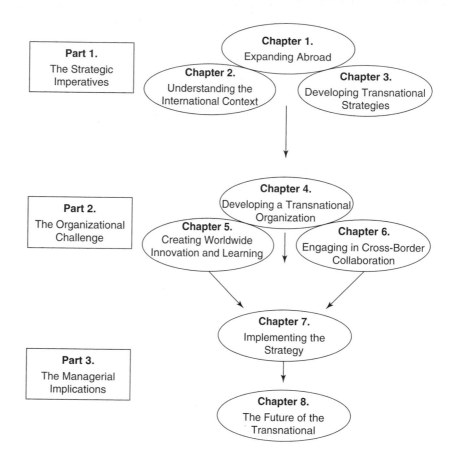

Part 1.
The Strategic Imperatives

Chapter 1.
Expanding Abroad

Chapter 2.
Understanding the International Context

Chapter 3.
Developing Transnational Strategies

Part 2.
The Organizational Challenge

Chapter 4.
Developing a Transnational Organization

Chapter 5.
Creating Worldwide Innovation and Learning

Chapter 6.
Engaging in Cross-Border Collaboration

Chapter 7.
Implementing the Strategy

Part 3.
The Managerial Implications

Chapter 8.
The Future of the Transnational

Table of Contents

Part 1 The Strategic Imperatives 1

Chapter 1

Expanding Abroad: Motivations, Means, and Mentalities *1*

Cases

1-1 Lincoln Electric 15
1-2 Jollibee Foods Corporation (A): International Expansion 34
1-3 Acer, Inc: Taiwan's Rampaging Dragon 53
1-4 Research in Motion: Managing Explosive Growth 68

Readings

1-1 The Tortuous Evolution of the Multinational Corporation 86
1-2 Distance Still Matters: The Hard Reality of Global Expansion 95
1-3 When You Shouldn't Go Global 105

Chapter 2

Understanding the International Context: Responding to Conflicting Environmental Forces *113*

Cases

2-1 Global Wine War 2009: New World versus Old 128
2-2 The Globalization of CEMEX 146
2-3 Mattel and the Toy Recalls (A)[1] 166

Readings

2-1 Culture and Organization 178
2-2 Clusters and the New Economics of Competition 195

Chapter 3

Developing Transnational Strategies: Building Layers of Competitive Advantage *210*

Cases

3-1 Marketing the "$100 Laptop" (A) 224
3-2 The Global Branding of Stella Artois 244
3-3 GE's Imagination Breakthroughs: The Evo Project 259

Readings

3-1 Managing Differences: The Central Challenge of Global Strategy 278
3-2 How Local Companies Keep Multinationals at Bay 290
3-3 Regional Strategies for Global Leadership 302

Part 2 The Organizational Challenge 314

Chapter 4

Developing a Transnational Organization: Managing Integration, Responsiveness, and Flexibility *314*

Cases

4-1   Philips versus Matsushita:
       Competing Strategic and
       Organizational Choices   331

4-2   ECCO A/S–Global Value Chain
       Management   348

4-3   World Vision International's AIDS
       Initiative: Challenging a Global
       Partnership   366

Readings

4-1   Managing Multicultural Teams   384

4-2   Managing Executive Attention in the
       Global Company   392

4-3   Matrix Management: Not a
       Structure, a Frame of Mind   400

Chapter 5

*Creating Worldwide Innovation
and Learning: Exploiting Cross-
Border Knowledge Management*   408

Cases

5-1   Siemens AG: Global
       Development Strategy (A)   419

5-2   P&G Japan: The SK-II
       Globalization Project   442

5-3   McKinsey & Company: Managing
       Knowledge and Learning   461

Readings

5-1   Building Effective R&D
       Capabilities Abroad   477

5-2   Connect and Develop: Inside
       Procter & Gamble's New Model
       for Innovation*   487

5-3   Finding, Forming, and Performing:
       Creating Networks for Discontinuous
       Innovation   496

Chapter 6

*Engaging in Cross-Border
Collaboration: Managing across
Corporate Boundaries*   510

Cases

6-1   Nora-Sakari: A Proposed
       JV in Malaysia (Revised)   525

6-2   Mahindra and Mahindra Ltd.—Farm
       Equipment Sector: Acquisition of
       Jiangling Tractor Company   538

6-3   Eli Lilly in India: Rethinking
       the Joint Venture Strategy   552

Readings

6-1   The Design and Management of
       International Joint Ventures   567

6-2   Collaborate with Your
       Competitors–and Win   580

Part 3   The Managerial Implications 588

Chapter 7

*Implementing the Strategy:
Building Multidimensional
Capabilities*   588

Cases

7-1   ING Insurance Asia/Pacific   601

7-2   BRL Hardy: Globalizing an
       Australian Wine Company   612

7-3   Silvio Napoli at Schindler India (A) 629

Readings

7-1   Local Memoirs of a Global Manager   645

7-2   Tap Your Subsidiaries for
       Global Reach   653

Chapter 8

The Future of the Transnational:
An Evolving Global Role   *662*

Cases

8-1   Hitting the Wall: Nike and
International Labor Practices   679

8-2   IKEA's Global Sourcing
Challenge: Indian Rugs and
Child Labor (A)   697

8-3   Killer Coke: The Campaign Against
Coca-Cola[1]   707

8-4   Genzyme's CSR Dilemma:
How to Play its HAND   725

Readings

8-1   Values in Tension: Ethics Away
from Home   743

8-2   Serving the World's Poor,
Profitably   754

Index   765

Expanding Abroad:
Motivations, Means, and Mentalities

▪ ▪ ▪ ▪ ▪ ▪ ▪ ▪ ▪ ▪ ▪ ▪ ▪ ▪ ▪ ▪ ▪ ▪

In this chapter, we look at a number of important questions that companies must resolve before taking the leap to operate outside their home environment. What market opportunities, sourcing advantages, or strategic imperatives drive their international expansion? By what means will they expand their overseas presence—through exports, licensing, joint ventures, wholly owned subsidiaries, or some other means? How will the attitudes, assumptions, and beliefs that they bring to their international ventures affect their chances of success? Before exploring these important questions, however, we first need to develop a definition of this entity—the multinational enterprise (MNE)—that we plan to study and develop some sense of its size and importance in the global economy.

This book focuses on the management challenges associated with developing the strategies, building the organizations, and managing the operations of companies whose activities stretch across national boundaries. Clearly, operating in an international rather than a domestic arena presents managers with many new opportunities. Having worldwide operations not only gives a company access to new markets and low-cost resources, but also opens up new sources of information and knowledge and broadens the options for strategic moves the company might make in competing with its domestic and international rivals. However, with all these new opportunities come the challenges of managing strategy, organization, and operations that are innately more complex, diverse, and uncertain.

Our starting point is to focus on the dominant vehicle of internationalization, the multinational enterprise (MNE), and briefly review its role and influence in the global economy.[1] Only after understanding the origins, interests, and objectives of this key actor will we be in a position to explore the strategies it pursues and the organization it develops to achieve them.

▪ [1]Such entities are referred to variously—and often interchangeably—as *multinational, international,* and *global enterprises.* (Note that we use the term "enterprise" rather than "corporation" because some of the cross-border entities we will examine are nonprofit organizations whose strategies and operations are every bit as complex as their corporate brethren's.) At the end of this chapter, we assign each of those terms—*multinational, international,* and *global*—specific meanings, but throughout the book, we adopt the widely used MNE abbreviation in a broader, more general sense to refer to all enterprises whose operations extend across national borders.

▨ The MNE: Definition, Scope, and Influence

An economic historian could trace the origins of international business back thousands of years to the seafaring traders of Greece and Egypt,[2] through the merchant traders of medieval Venice and the great British and Dutch trading companies of the 17th and 18th centuries. By the 19th century, the newly emerged capitalists in industrialized Europe began investing in the less-developed areas of the world (including the United States), but particularly within the vast empires held by Britain, France, Holland, and Germany.

Definition

In terms of the working definition we use, few if any of these entities through history could be called true MNEs. Most early traders would be excluded by our first qualification, which requires that an MNE have *substantial direct investment* in foreign countries, not just the trading relationships of an import–export business. Most of the companies that had established international operations in the 19th century would be excluded by our second criterion, which requires that they be engaged in the *active management* of these offshore assets rather than simply holding them in a passive investment portfolio.

Thus, though companies that source their raw materials offshore, license their technologies abroad, export their products into foreign markets, or even hold minor equity positions in overseas ventures without any management involvement may regard themselves as "international," by our definition, they are not true MNEs unless they have substantial, direct investment in foreign countries *and* actively manage and regard those operations as integral parts of the company, both strategically and organizationally.

Scope

According to our definition, the MNE is a recent phenomenon, with the vast majority developing only in the post–World War II years. However, the motivations for international expansion and the nature of MNEs' offshore activities have evolved significantly over this relatively short period, and we will explore some of these changes later in this chapter.

It is interesting to observe how the United Nations has changed its definition of the MNE as these companies have grown in size and importance.[3] In 1973, it defined such an enterprise as one "which controls assets, factories, mines, sales offices, and the like in two or more countries." By 1984, it had changed the definition to an enterprise (a) comprising entities in two or more countries, regardless of the legal form and fields of activity of those entities; (b) which operates under a system of decision making permitting coherent policies and a common strategy through one or more decision-making centers; and (c) in which the entities are so linked, by ownership or otherwise, that one or more of them may be able to exercise a significant influence over the activities of the others, in particular to share knowledge, resources, and responsibilities.

▮ [2]See Karl Moore and David Lewis, *The Origins of Globalization* (New York: Routledge, 2009).

▮ [3]The generic term for companies operating across national borders in most U.N. studies is *transnational corporation* (TNC). Because we use that term very specifically, we continue to define the general form of organizations with international operations as MNEs.

Table 1-1   Comparison of Top MNEs and Selected Countries: 2006

Company[†]	Value-Added (millions)	Rank	Country[‡]	Value-Added (millions)	Rank
ExxonMobil	111,724	1	United States	13,132,900	1
Royal Dutch/Shell	74,738	2	Japan	4,375,967	2
Toyota Motor	62,313	3	Germany	2,913,311	3
BP	54,829	4	Poland	341,670	24
Wal-Mart	54,094	5	Hungary	113,053	49
Chevron Corp	51,223	6	Morocco	65,637	56
Siemens	49,108	7	Tanzania	14,178	98
General Electric	49,073	8	Nepal	9,043	115
Ford Motor	41,429	9	Haiti	4,961	136
IBM	29,599	10	Burundi	903	166

Notes: "Value-added" refers to gross domestic product (GDP) for countries and to the sum of salaries, pretax profits, and depreciation and amortization for companies.
[†]Calculated from data from *World Investment Report 2008,* published by the United Nations, assuming the same value-added to sales ratios as in *World Investment Report 2000.* For Chevron Corp., the value-added is estimated by the authors.
[‡]Data are from *World Development Indicators,* published by the World Bank.

In essence, the changing definition highlights the importance of both strategic and organizational integration, and thereby, the *active, coordinated management* of operations located in different countries, as the key differentiating characteristic of an MNE. The resources committed to those units can take the form of skilled people or research equipment just as easily as plants and machinery or computer hardware. What really differentiates the MNE is that it creates an internal organization to carry out key cross-border tasks and transactions internally rather than depending on trade through the external markets, just as the companies in Table 1-1 do. This more recent U.N. definition also expands earlier assumptions of traditional ownership patterns to encompass a more varied set of financial, legal, and contractual relationships with different foreign affiliates. With this understanding, our definition of MNEs includes Intel, Unilever, and Samsung, but also Singapore Airlines, McKinsey & Company, and Starbucks.

MNE influence in the Global Economy

Most frequent international business travelers have had an experience like the following: She arrives on her British Airways flight, rents a Toyota at Hertz, and drives to the downtown Hilton Hotel. In her room, she flips on the Sony television and absent-mindedly gazes out at neon signs flashing "Coca-Cola," "Canon," and "BMW." The latest episode of *House* is flickering on the screen when room service delivers dinner along with the bottle of Perrier she ordered. All of a sudden, a feeling of disorientation engulfs her. Is she in Sydney, Singapore, Stockholm, or Seattle? Her surroundings and points of reference over the past few hours have provided few clues.

Such experiences, more than any data, provide the best indication of the enormous influence of MNEs in the global economy. As the cases and articles in this book show, few sectors of the economy and few firms—not even those that are purely domestic in their operations—are free from this pervasive influence. According to U.N. estimates, by 2008, the number of MNEs had risen to approximately 78,000, collectively managing at least 780,000 foreign affiliates. Total revenues were in the range of $20 trillion. The top 500 MNEs account for nearly 70 percent of world trade. Most of the world's automobiles, computers, and soft drinks are produced and marketed by MNEs.

Not all MNEs are large, but most large companies in the world are MNEs. Indeed, the largest 100 MNEs, excluding those in banking and finance, accounted for $9.2 trillion of total worldwide assets in 2006, of which $5.2 trillion was located outside their respective home countries.

A different perspective on their size and potential impact is provided in Table 1-1, which compares the overall value-added of several of the largest MNEs with the gross domestic products (GDPs) of selected countries. According to the *World Investment Report,* the measure of company value added (the sum of salaries, pretax profits, amortization, and depreciation) provides a more meaningful comparison with country GDP than simply looking at a company's gross revenues. By using this measure, it is clear that the world's largest MNEs are equivalent in their economic importance to medium-sized economies such as Chile, Hungary, or Pakistan and considerably more economically important than smaller or less developed economies such as Tanzania, Estonia, or Sri Lanka. They have considerable influence on the global economy, employ a high percentage of business graduates, and pose the most complex strategic and organizational challenges for their managers. For the same reasons, they provide the focus for much of our attention in this book.

■ The Motivations: Pushes and Pulls to Internationalize

What motivates companies to expand their operations internationally? Although occasionally the motives may be entirely idiosyncratic, such as the desire of the CEO to spend time in Mexico or link to old family ties in Europe, an extensive body of research suggests more systematic patterns.

Traditional Motivations

Among the earliest motivations that drove companies to invest abroad was the need to *secure key supplies*. Aluminum producers needed to ensure their supply of bauxite, tire companies went abroad to develop rubber plantations, and oil companies wanted to open new fields in Canada, the Middle East, and Venezuela. By the early part of this century, Standard Oil, Alcoa, Goodyear, Anaconda Copper, and International Nickel were among the largest of the emerging MNEs.

Another strong trigger for internationalization could be described as *market-seeking* behavior. This motivation was particularly strong for companies that had some intrinsic advantage, typically related to their technology or brand recognition, that gave them a competitive advantage in offshore markets. Their initial moves were often opportunistic, frequently originating with an unsolicited export order. However, many companies eventually realized that additional sales enabled them to exploit economies of scale and scope, thereby providing a source of competitive advantage over their domestic rivals. This market seeking was a particularly strong motive for some European multinationals whose small home markets were insufficient to support the volume-intensive manufacturing processes that were sweeping through industries from food and tobacco to chemicals and automobiles. Companies like Nestlé, Bayer, and Ford expanded internationally primarily in search of new markets.

Another traditional and important trigger of internationalization was the desire to *access low-cost factors* of production. Particularly as tariff barriers declined in the 1960s, the United States and many European countries, for which labor represented a major cost, found that their products were at a competitive disadvantage compared with imports. In response, a number of companies in clothing, electronics, household appliances, watch-making, and other such industries established offshore sourcing locations to produce components or even complete product lines. Soon it became clear that labor was not the only productive factor that could be sourced more economically overseas. For example, the availability of lower-cost capital (perhaps through a government investment subsidy) also became a strong force for internationalization.

These three motives (or two, if we ignore their historical differences and combine securing supplies and accessing low-cost factors into a single resource-seeking motive) were the main traditional driving force behind the overseas expansion of MNEs. The ways in which these motives interacted to push companies—particularly those from the United States—to become MNEs are captured in the well-known product cycle theory.[4]

This theory suggests that the starting point for an internationalization process is typically an innovation that a company creates in its home country. In the first phase of exploiting the development, the company—let's assume it is in the United States—builds production facilities in its home market not only because this is where its main customer base is located, but also because of the need to maintain close linkages between research and production in this phase of its development cycle. In this early stage, some demand also may be created in other developed countries—in European countries, for example—where consumer needs and market developments are similar to those of the United States. These requirements normally would be met with home production, thereby generating exports for the United States.

During this pre-MNE stage, firms would typically establish an export unit within the home office, to oversee the growing export levels. Committing to this sort of organizational structure would in turn typically lead to stronger performance than would treating exports simply as a part of the domestic business.[5]

As the product matures and production processes become standardized, the company enters a new stage. By this time, demand in the European countries may have become quite sizable, and export sales, originally a marginal side benefit, have become an important part of the revenues from the new business. Furthermore, competitors probably begin to see the growing demand for the new product as a potential opportunity to establish themselves in the markets served by exports. To prevent or counteract such competition

---

[4]Raymond Vernon, "International Investment and International Trade in the Product Cycle," *Quarterly Journal of Economics,* May 1966, pp. 190–207.

[5]Paul W. Beamish, Lambros Karavis, Anthony Goerzen, and Christopher Lane, "The Relationship Between Organizational Structure and Export Performance," *Management International Review* 39 (1999), pp. 37–54.

and to meet the foreign demand more effectively, the innovating company typically sets up production facilities in the importing countries, thereby making the transition from being an exporter to becoming a true MNE.

Finally, in the third stage, the product becomes highly standardized, and many competitors enter the business. Competition focuses on price and, therefore, on cost. This trend activates the resource-seeking motive, and the company moves production to low-wage, developing countries to meet the demands of its customers in the developed markets at a lower cost. In this final phase, the developing countries may become net exporters of the product while the developed countries become net importers.

Although the product cycle theory provided a useful way to describe much of the internationalization of the postwar decades,[6] by the 1980s, its explanatory power was beginning to wane, as Professor Vernon himself was quick to point out. As the international business environment became increasingly complex and sophisticated, companies developed a much richer rationale for their worldwide operations.

Emerging Motivations

Once MNEs had established international sales and production operations, their perceptions and strategic motivations gradually changed. Initially, the typical attitude was that the foreign operations were strategic and organizational appendages to the domestic business and should be managed opportunistically. Gradually, however, managers began to think about their strategy in a more integrated, worldwide sense. In this process, the forces that originally triggered their expansion overseas often became secondary to a new set of motivations that underlay their emerging global strategies.

The first such set of forces was the increasing *scale economies, ballooning R&D investments,* and *shortening product life cycles* that transformed many industries into global rather than national structures and made a worldwide scope of activities not a matter of choice, but an essential prerequisite for companies to survive in those businesses. These forces are described in detail in the next chapter.

A second factor that often became critical to a company's international strategy—though it was rarely the original motivating trigger—was its global *scanning and learning* capability.[7] A company drawn offshore to secure supplies of raw materials was more likely to become aware of alternative, low-cost production sources around the globe; a company tempted abroad by market opportunities was often exposed to new technologies or market needs that stimulated innovative product development. The very nature of an MNE's worldwide presence gave it a huge informational advantage that could result in it locating more efficient sources or more advanced product and process technologies.

---

[6]The record of international expansion of countries in the post–World War II era is quite consistent with the pattern suggested by the product cycle theory. For example, between 1950 and 1980, U.S. firms' direct foreign investment (DFI) increased from $11.8 billion to $200 billion. In the 1950s, much of this investment focused on neighboring countries in Latin America and Canada. By the early 1960s, attention had shifted to Europe, and the European Economic Community's share of U.S. firms' DFI increased from 16 percent in 1957 to 32 percent by 1966. Finally, in the 1970s, attention shifted to developing countries, whose share of U.S. firms' DFI grew from 18 percent in 1974 to 25 percent in 1980.

[7]This motivation is highlighted by Raymond Vernon in "Gone Are the Cash Cows of Yesteryear," *Harvard Business Review,* November–December 1980, pp. 150–55.

Thus, a company whose international strategy was triggered by a technological or marketing advantage could enhance that advantage through the scanning and learning potential inherent in its worldwide network of operations.

A third benefit that soon became evident was that being a multinational rather than a national company brought important advantages of *competitive positioning*. Certainly, the most controversial of the many global competitive strategic actions taken by MNEs in recent years have been those based on cross-subsidization of markets. For example, a Korean mobile phone producer could challenge a national company in Europe by subsidizing its European losses with funds from its profitable Asian or South American operations.

If the European company did not have strong positions in the Korean company's key Asian and South American markets, its competitive response could only be to defend its home market positions—typically by seeking government intervention or matching or offsetting the Korean challenger's competitive price reductions. Recognition of these competitive implications of multicountry operations led some companies to change the criteria for their international investment decisions to reflect not only market attractiveness or cost-efficiency choices, but also the leverage such investments provided over competitors.[8]

Although for the purposes of analysis—and to reflect some sense of historical development—the motives behind the expansion of MNEs have been reduced to a few distinct categories, it should be clear that companies were rarely driven by a single motivating force. More adaptable companies soon learned how to capitalize on the potential advantages available from their international operations—ensuring critical supplies, entering new markets, tapping low-cost factors of production, leveraging their global information access, and capitalizing on the competitive advantage of their multiple market positions—and began to use these strengths to play a new strategic game that we will describe in later chapters as *global chess*.

▪ The Means of Internationalization: Prerequisites and Processes

Having explored *why* an aspiring MNE wants to expand abroad (i.e., its motivation), we must now understand *how* it does so by exploring the means of internationalization. Beyond the desire to expand offshore, a company must possess certain competencies—attributes that we describe as prerequisites—if it is to succeed in overseas markets. It must then be able to implement its desire to expand abroad through a series of decisions and commitments that define the internationalization process.

Prerequisites for Internationalization

In each national market, a foreign company suffers from some disadvantages in comparison with local competitors, at least initially. Being more familiar with the national culture, industry structure, government requirements, and other aspects of doing business in that country, domestic companies have a huge natural advantage. Their existing relationships with relevant customers, suppliers, regulators, and so on, provide additional

---

▮ [8]These competitive aspects of global operations are discussed in detail in Chapter 3.

advantages that the foreign company must either match or counteract with some unique strategic capability. Most often, this countervailing strategic advantage comes from the MNE's superior knowledge or skills, which typically take the form of advanced technological expertise or specific marketing competencies. At other times, scale economies in R&D, production, or some other part of the value chain become the main source of the MNE's advantage over domestic firms. It is important to note, however, that the MNE cannot expect to succeed in the international environment unless it has some distinctive competency to overcome the liability of its foreignness.[9]

Such knowledge or scale-based strategic advantages are, by themselves, insufficient to justify the internationalization of operations. Often with much less effort, a company could sell or license its technology to foreign producers, franchise its brand name internationally, or sell its products abroad through general trading companies or local distributors, without having to set up its own offshore operations. This approach was explicitly adopted by RCA, which decided to aggressively license its extensive television and other patents to European and Japanese companies rather than set up its own international operations. The CEO argued that the safe return generated by license fees was preferable to the uncertainties and complexities of multinational management. The French multinational Thomson SA now owns the RCA trademark and licenses the name to other companies like Audiovox and TCL.

The other precondition for a company to become an MNE, therefore, is it must have the organizational capability to leverage its strategic assets more effectively through its own subsidiaries than through contractual relations with outside parties. If superior knowledge is the main source of an MNE's competitive advantage, for example, it must have an organizational system that provides better returns from extending and exploiting its knowledge through direct foreign operations than the return it could get by selling or licensing that knowledge.[10]

To summarize, three conditions must be met for the existence of an MNE. First, some foreign countries must offer certain location-specific advantages to provide the requisite *motivation* for the company to invest there. Second, the company must have some *strategic competencies* or ownership-specific advantages to counteract the disadvantages of its relative unfamiliarity with foreign markets. Third, it must possess some *organizational capabilities* to achieve better returns from leveraging its strategic strengths internally rather than through external market mechanisms such as contracts or licenses.[11] Understanding these prerequisites is important not only because they explain why MNEs exist but also, as we show in Chapter 3, because they help define the strategic options for competing in worldwide businesses.

---

[9]The need for such strategic advantages for a company to become an MNE is highlighted by the *market imperfections theory of MNEs*. For a comprehensive review of this theory, see Richard E. Caves, *Multinational Enterprise and Economic Analysis*, 2nd ed. (Cambridge: Cambridge University Press, 1996).

[10]The issue of organizational capability is the focus of what has come to be known as the *internalization theory of MNEs*. See Alan M. Rugman, "A New Theory of the Multinational Enterprise: Internalization versus Internalization," *Columbia Journal of World Business*, Spring 1982, pp. 54–61. For a more detailed exposition, see Peter J. Buckley and Mark Casson, *The Future of Multinational Enterprise* (London: MacMillan, 1976).

[11]These three conditions are highlighted in John Dunning's eclectic theory. See John H. Dunning and Sarianna M. Lundan, *Multinational Enterprises and the Global Economy*, 2nd ed. (Cheltenham, UK: Edward Elgar, 2008).

The Process of Internationalization

The process of developing these strategic and organizational attributes lies at the heart of the internationalization process through which a company builds its position in world markets. This process is rarely well thought out in advance, and it typically builds on a combination of rational analysis, opportunism, and pure luck. Nonetheless, it is still possible to discern some general patterns of behavior that firms typically follow.

The most well-known model for internationalization was developed during the 1970s by two Swedish academics based in Uppsala, who described foreign-market entry as a learning process.[12] The company makes an initial commitment of resources to the foreign market, and through this investment, it gains local market knowledge about customers, competitors, and regulatory conditions. On the basis of this market knowledge, the company is able to evaluate its current activities, the extent of its commitment to the market, and thus the opportunities for additional investment. It then makes a subsequent resource commitment, perhaps buying out its local distributor or investing in a local manufacturing plant, which allows it to develop additional market knowledge. Gradually, and through several cycles of investment, the company develops the necessary levels of local capability and market knowledge to become an effective competitor in the foreign country (see Figure 1-1).

Whereas many companies internationalize in the incremental approach depicted by the so-called Uppsala model, a great many do not.[13] Some companies invest in or acquire local partners to shortcut the process of building up local market knowledge. For example, Wal-Mart entered the United Kingdom by buying the supermarket chain ASDA rather than developing its own stores. Others minimize their local presence by subcontracting to local partners. Amazon.com has a business in Canada without a single Canadian employee—it manages its website from the United States, and it fulfills orders through the Canadian postal service. Cases such as these highlight the complexity of the decisions MNEs face in entering a foreign market.

One important set of factors is the assimilation of local market knowledge by the subsidiary unit, as suggested by the Uppsala model. Other, equally important factors to the

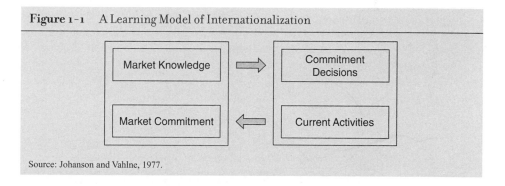

Figure 1-1   A Learning Model of Internationalization

Source: Johanson and Vahlne, 1977.

[12]Jan Johanson and Jan-Erik Vahlne, "The Internationalization Process of the Firm—A Model of Knowledge Development and Increasing Foreign Market Commitments," *Journal of International Business Studies* 88 (1977), pp. 23–32.

[13]Jonathan Calof and Paul W. Beamish, "Adapting to Foreign Markets: Explaining Internationalization," *International Business Review* 4 (1995), pp. 115–31.

MNE include its overall level of commitment to the foreign market in question, the required level of control of foreign operations, and the timing of its entry. To help make sense of these different factors, it is useful to think of the different modes of operating overseas in terms of two factors: the level of market commitment made and the level of control needed (see Figure 1-2).

Some companies internationalize by gradually moving up the scale, from exporting through joint venturing to direct foreign investment. Others, like Wal-Mart, prefer to move straight to the high-commitment–high-control mode of operating, in part because they are entering mature markets in which it would be very difficult to build a business from nothing. Still others choose to adopt a low-commitment–low-control mode, such as exporting or subcontracting. For example, Amazon.com is able to make this approach work in Canada because it retains control of its website from the United States and has secured a reliable local partner for order fulfillment. To be clear, none of these approaches is necessarily right or wrong, but they should be consistent with the overall strategic intentions and motivations of the MNE.

It is also important to emphasize that some firms are "born global," establishing significant international operations at or near their founding. Whether this is due to their internal orientation,[14] or the need to move quickly due to the nature of their product or services, such firms do not take such an incremental approach.

Similarly not all MNEs are large firms. By definition, most large MNEs started out small. Yet many small- and medium-sized enterprises (SMEs) retain such a size, while still

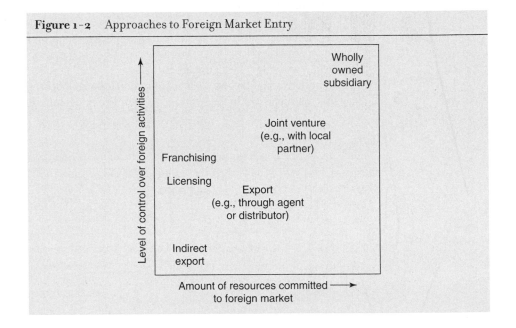

Figure 1-2   Approaches to Foreign Market Entry

[14]See Gary A. Knight and Tamar Cavusgil, "Innovation, Organizational Capabilities and the Born-Global Firm," *Journal of International Business Studies*, 35 (2004), pp. 124–41 and Daniel J. Isenberg, "The Global Entrepreneur," *Harvard Business Review*, December 2008.

being MNEs in their own right. Other SMEs, observing a positive impact on performance as a consequence of their FDI activity,[15] will grow.

The Evolving Mentality: International to Transnational

Even from this brief description of the changing motivations for and means of internationalization, it should be clear that a gradual evolution has occurred in the strategic role that foreign operations play in emerging MNEs. We can categorize this evolutionary pattern into four stages that reflect the way in which management thinking has developed over time as changes have occurred in both the international business environment and the MNE as a unique corporate form.

Although such a classification is necessarily generalized and somewhat arbitrary, it enables us to achieve two objectives. First, it highlights that for most MNEs, the objectives that initially induced management to go overseas evolve into a very different set of motivations over time, thereby progressively changing management attitudes and actions. Second, such a classification provides a specific language system that we use throughout this book to describe the very different strategic approaches adopted by various MNEs.[16]

International Mentality

In the earliest stages of internationalization, many MNE managers tend to think of the company's overseas operations as distant outposts whose main role is to support the domestic parent company in different ways, such as contributing incremental sales to the domestic manufacturing operations. We label this approach the *international* strategic mentality.

The *international* terminology derives directly from the international product cycle theory, which reflects many of the assumptions implicit in this approach. Products are developed for the domestic market and only subsequently sold abroad; technology and other knowledge are transferred from the parent company to the overseas operators; and offshore manufacturing represents a means to protect the company's home market. Companies with this mentality regard themselves fundamentally as domestic with some foreign appendages. Managers assigned to overseas operations may be selected because they happen to know a foreign language or have previously lived abroad. Decisions related to the foreign operations tend to be made in an opportunistic or ad hoc manner. Many firms at this stage will prefer to only enter countries where there is low "psychic distance" between it and the home market.

Multinational Mentality

The exposure of the organization to foreign environments and the growing importance of sales and profits from these sources gradually convince managers that international activities can provide opportunities of more than marginal significance. Increasingly,

[15]Jane Lu and Paul W. Beamish, "Internationalization and Performance of SMEs," *Strategic Management Journal* 22 (2001), pp. 565–86.

[16]It should be noted that the terms *international, multinational, global,* and *transnational* have been used very differently—and sometimes interchangeably—by various writers. We want to give each term a specific and different meaning and ask that readers put aside their previous usage of the terms—at least for the duration of our exposition.

they also realize that to leverage those opportunities, they must do more than ship out old equipment, technology, or product lines that had been developed for the home market. The success of local competitors in the foreign markets and the demands of host governments often accelerate the learning of companies that retain an unresponsive, international mentality for too long.

A *multinational* strategic mentality develops as managers begin to recognize and emphasize the differences among national markets and operating environments. Companies with this mentality adopt a more flexible approach to their international operations by modifying their products, strategies, and even management practices country by country. As they develop national companies that are increasingly sensitive and responsive to their local environments, these companies undertake a strategic approach that is literally multinational: Their strategy is built on the foundation of the multiple, nationally responsive strategies of the company's worldwide subsidiaries. In companies operating with such a multinational mentality, managers of foreign operations tend to be highly independent entrepreneurs, often nationals of the host country.

Using their local market knowledge and the parent company's willingness to invest in these growing opportunities, these entrepreneurial country managers often can build significant local growth and considerable independence from headquarters.

Global Mentality

Although the multinational mentality typically results in very responsive marketing approaches in the different national markets, it also gives rise to an inefficient manufacturing infrastructure within the company. Plants are built more to provide local marketing advantages or improve political relations than to maximize production efficiency. Similarly, the proliferation of products designed to meet local needs contributes to a general loss of efficiency in design, production, logistics, distribution, and other functional tasks.

In an operating environment of improving transportation and communication facilities and falling trade barriers, some companies adopt a very different strategic approach in their international operations. These companies think in terms of creating products for a world market and manufacturing them on a global scale in a few highly efficient plants, often at the corporate center.

We define this approach as a *classic global* strategy mentality, because it views the world, not just individual national markets, as its unit of analysis. The underlying assumption is that national tastes and preferences are more similar than different or that they can be made similar by providing customers with standardized products at adequate cost and with quality advantages over those national varieties they know. Managers with this global strategic approach subscribe to Professor Levitt's provocative argument in the mid-1980s that the future belongs to companies that make and sell "the same thing, the same way, everywhere."[17]

This strategic approach requires considerably more central coordination and control than the others and is typically associated with an organizational structure in which various product or business managers have worldwide responsibility. In such companies,

---

[17]See Theodore Levitt, "The Globalization of Markets," *Harvard Business Review,* May–June 1983, pp. 92–102.

research and development and manufacturing activities are typically managed from the headquarters, and most strategic decisions also take place at the center.

Transnational Mentality

In the closing decades of the 20th century, many of these global companies seemed invincible, chalking up overwhelming victories over not only local companies, but international and multinational competitors as well. Their success, however, created and strengthened a set of countervailing forces of localization.

To many host governments, for example, these global companies appeared to be a more powerful and thus more threatening version of earlier unresponsive companies with their unsophisticated international strategic mentality. Many host governments increased both the restrictions and the demands they placed on global companies, requiring them to invest in, transfer technology to, and meet local content requirements of the host countries.

Customers also contributed to this strengthening of localizing forces by rejecting homogenized global products and reasserting their national preferences—albeit without relaxing their expectations of high quality levels and low costs that global products had offered. Finally, the increasing volatility in the international economic and political environments, especially rapid changes in currency exchange rates, undermined the efficiency of such a centralized global approach.

As a result of these developments, many worldwide companies recognized that demands to be responsive to local market and political needs *and* pressures to develop global-scale competitive efficiency were simultaneous, if sometimes conflicting, imperatives.

In these conditions, the either/or attitude reflected in both the multinational and the global strategic mentalities became increasingly inappropriate. The emerging requirement was for companies to become more responsive to local needs while capturing the benefits of global efficiency—an approach to worldwide management that we call the *transnational* strategic mentality. The president of IBM has noted how the global integration of production allows the firm to reduce costs and access new skills and knowledge. But he adds a caveat about the challenge of adopting such an approach—"securing a supply of high value skills."[18]

In such companies, key activities and resources are neither centralized in the parent company nor so decentralized that each subsidiary can carry out its own tasks on a local-for-local basis. Instead, the resources and activities are dispersed but specialized, to achieve efficiency and flexibility at the same time. Furthermore, these dispersed resources are integrated into an interdependent network of worldwide operations.

In contrast to the global model, the transnational mentality recognizes the importance of flexible and responsive country-level operations—hence, the return of *national* into the terminology. And compared with the multinational approach, it provides for means to link and coordinate those operations to retain competitive effectiveness and economic efficiency, as is indicated by the prefix *trans*. The resulting need for intensive, organization-wide coordination and shared decision making implies that this is a much

---

[18]See Samuel J. Palmisano, "Global Integration and the Decline of the Multinational," *World Trade*, August 2006, p. 8.

more sophisticated and subtle approach to MNE management. In subsequent chapters, we will explore its strategic, organizational, and managerial implications.

It should be clear, however, that there is no inevitability in either the direction or the endpoint of this evolving strategic mentality in worldwide companies. Depending on the industry, the company's strategic position, the host countries' diverse needs, and a variety of other factors, a company might reasonably operate with any one of these strategic mentalities. More likely, bearing in mind that ours is an arbitrary classification, most companies probably exhibit some attributes of each of these different strategic approaches.[19]

Summary and Concluding Comments

This chapter provides the historical context of the nature of the MNE and introduces a number of important concepts on which subsequent chapters will build. In particular, we have described the evolving set of *motivations* that led companies to expand abroad in the first place; the *means* of expansion, as shaped by the processes of internationalization they followed; and the typical *mentalities* that they developed. Collectively, these motivations, means, and mentalities are the prime drivers of what we call a company's *administrative heritage,* the unique and deeply embedded structural, process, and cultural biases that play an important part in shaping every company's strategic and organizational capabilities.

Chapter 1 Readings

- In Reading 1-1, the now classic "The Tortuous Evolution of the Multinational Corporation," Perlmutter introduces the primary types of headquarters orientation toward subsidiaries: ethnocentric, polycentric, and geocentric, and the forces which move an organization toward—or away—from a geocentric mindset.
- In Reading 1-2, "Distance Still Matters: The Hard Reality of Global Expansion," Ghemawat introduces the CAGE distance framework. The intent of this cultural, administrative, geographic, and economic distance framework is to help managers understand which attributes create distance, and the impact on various industries.
- Reading 1-3, "When You Shouldn't Go Global," serves as a caution to organizations which might unwittingly jump on the globalization bandwagon. Alexander and Korine provide three questions to ask before going global: Are there potential benefits for our company? Do we have the necessary management skills? Will the costs outweigh the benefits?

All three readings are intended to underscore the motivations, means, and mentalities required to expand abroad.

---

[19]Professor Howard Perlmutter was perhaps the first to highlight the different strategic mentalities. See his article, "The Tortuous Evolution of the Multinational Corporation," *Columbia Journal of World Business,* January–February 1969, pp. 9–18, reproduced in the readings section of this chapter.

Case 1-1   Lincoln Electric

Jordan Siegel

Introduction

John Stropki, CEO of Lincoln Electric, returned home from Mumbai to company headquarters in Cleveland, having sampled the local Maharashtran delicacies while studying opportunities in the Indian market. From his vantage point in 2006, Stropki looked back on his company's more than 100 years in the welding equipment and consumables industry with pride, wondering whether a strong push into India should be the next step in his company's globalization. An India expansion had been considered for several years, but thus far the company had focused on growing its operations in China and elsewhere around the globe. If Stropki were to approve a significant allocation of resources toward an India expansion, he wondered what would be the best way to enter. He had a wealth of company lessons and experiences to apply to the India investment decision, as his company had had international operations since the 1940s, had struggled internationally in the late 1980s and early 1990s, and had gone on to regain its global competitive advantage in the late 1990s and early 2000s. During Stropki's tenure as CEO since 2004, the company had further expanded globally and by 2006 owned manufacturing operations in 19 countries across five continents.

Most recently, the company had enjoyed increasing success in China as a result of its aggressive expansion through both a joint venture and set of majority-owned plants. As Stropki opened the Cleveland newspaper to check the previous Sunday's Cleveland Browns score, he wondered how he could apply the lessons of the Chinese experience in particular, to India.

Welding Industry

Welding is a technique for joining pieces of metal by fusion through the application of concentrated heat. Virtually any two metal items can be joined by welding. Welding is also a supporting activity in most industrial activities, from the manufacture of construction equipment to machine tools, from pipelines to petrochemical complexes. The predominant method of welding is arc welding, where a welding power source generates electric current, which is used to create an electric arc, which then melts a filler metal used to create the bond between the two metal parts. The filler metal is in the form of a stick or wire electrode, and the electrode often has a series of chemical coatings and/or shielding gases designed to protect the welded metal from oxygen and nitrogen in the air and thus strengthen the bond. Electrodes are referred to as "consumables," and

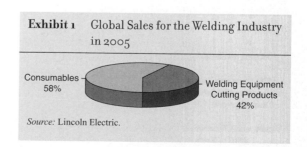

Exhibit 1   Global Sales for the Welding Industry in 2005

Consumables 58%

Welding Equipment Cutting Products 42%

Source: Lincoln Electric.

Exhibit 2   Geographic Pattern of Sales for the Global Welding Industry in 2005

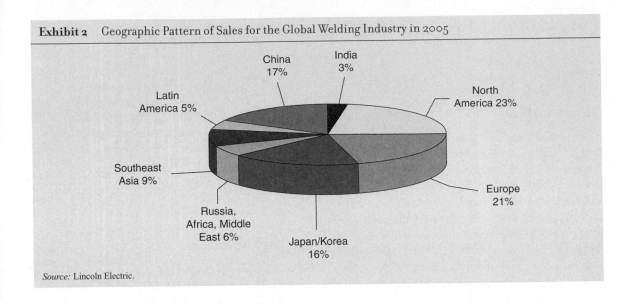

China 17%
India 3%
North America 23%
Latin America 5%
Southeast Asia 9%
Russia, Africa, Middle East 6%
Japan/Korea 16%
Europe 21%

Source: Lincoln Electric.

the power sources and related parts used to create the electric arc are referred to as "equipment."

As of 2005, the welding industry together with its associated metal-cutting technology was a $13 billion industry globally. As shown in **Exhibit 1,** 42% of welding industry sales came from equipment, whereas the remaining 58% came from sales of consumables. Welding products played a crucial role in the development of important structures around the world, such as bridges, oil-production facilities, and a range of other building, infrastructure, and commercial construction projects. As a result, the industry's growth rate in unit volume moved together with the global economic growth rate, which was predicted to be 3.0% in 2006.[1] The industry's growth in sales revenue could be even higher, as was the case in 2005 when growth was driven by high demand for welding products in China, India, and Eastern Europe. Customers included companies involved in general metal fabrication; infrastructure building including oil and gas pipelines

and platforms, buildings and bridges, and power generation; and transportation and defense industries (automotive/trucks, rail, ships and aerospace); equipment manufacturers in construction, farming and mining; and retail do-it-yourself (DIY). Sales were spread out across these various customer segments. As shown in **Exhibit 2,** sales were also spread geographically across the globe, with Asia responsible for 45% of global sales, followed by North America (23%) and Europe (21%).

Major Welding Competitors in 2006   In 2006 the global arc welding industry was seen as highly competitive. The industry was significantly fragmented, with more than a thousand companies producing equipment and consumables and the top six accounting for only 45% of the global market. **Exhibit 3** presents a visual comparison of the leading welding competitors by their level of revenue. Companies competed on the basis of price, brand preference, product quality, customer service, breadth of product offering, and technical expertise and innovation. In addition, because it was costly to ship welding products due to their weight, it was essential in this industry to set up a local or regional production presence to gain significant market share.

[1]"LINK Global Economic Outlook," Development Policy and Analysis Division, United Nations Department of Economic and Social Affairs, October 2005.

Exhibit 3   2005 Revenue for Largest Competitors in $13 Billion Welding Market

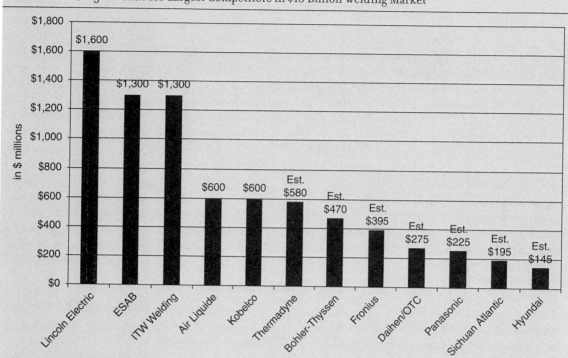

Sources: Data on individual companies came from public company releases and casewriter estimates based on publicly released financial statements. Sources for each company include: for ESAB, http://www.charterplc.com/charter/ar2005_links/ar2005.pdf; for ITW, http://library.corporateir.net/library/71/710/71064/items/175644/AnnualInvestorDayPartI.pdf; for AirLiquide, http://www.airliquide.com/file/stdpagetranslation/download-center-ra-en/2005-financial-report.pdf; for Kobelco, http://www.kobelco.co.kp; for Thermadyne, http://www.thermadyne. com/uplFiles/pressRelease/ThermadynePressReleasewithSchedules-July112006.pdf; for Bohler, http://www.kobelco.co.jp/ICSFiles/metafile/2006/01/27/annual2005comp.pdf; for Daihen, http://www.daihen.co.jp/gaiyou_e/gaimain.htm; for Panasonic, http://ir-site.panasonic.com/annual/2006/; for Fronius, http://www.fronius .com/; for Fronius, http://www. hypertherm.com/; for Sichuan Atlantic, http://www.chinaweld-atlantic.com/weldEn/introduction.htm; and for Hyundai, http://www.hdweld.co.kr/eng/company/introduce.asp.

The following is a brief description of Lincoln's key global competitors:[2]

[2]Data on individual companies are from public company releases and casewriter estimates based on publicly released financial statements. Sources for each company: for ESAB, http://www.charterplc.com/charter/ar2005_links/ar2005.pdf; for ITW, http://library.corporateir.net/library/71/710/71064/items/175644/AnnualInvestorDayPartI.pdf; for Air Liquide, http://www.airliquide.com/file/stdpagetranslation/download-center-ra-en/2005-financial-report.pdf; for Kobelco, http://www.kobelco.co.jp/ICSFiles/metafile/2006/01/27/annual2005comp.pdf; for Thermadyne, http://www.thermadyne.com/uplFiles/pressRelease/Thermadyne PressReleasewithSchedules-July112006.pdf; for Bohler, http://www.kobelco.co.jp/ICSFiles/metafile/2006/ 01/27/annual2005comp.pdf; for Daihen, http://www .daihen.co.jp/gaiyou_e/gaimain.htm; for Panasonic, http://ir-site .panasonic.com/annual/2006/; for Fronius, http://www.fronius.com/; for Fronius, http://www. hypertherm.com/; for Sichuan Atlantic, http://www.chinaweld-atlantic.com/weldEn/introduction.htm; and for Hyundai, http://www.hdweld.co.kr/eng/company/introduce.asp.

ESAB (Charter plc) – $1.3 billion, 2005 sales of welding and related equipment. ESAB, which represented some 75% of revenues of its parent company Charter, was a European-based company with a global presence. While ESAB was the number-three player in the United States, ESAB enjoyed market leadership in Europe, Brazil, Argentina, and India. In 2000, ESAB had agreed to be purchased by Lincoln Electric for $750 million plus the assumption of $300 million in ESAB's debt. Yet Lincoln Electric decided that same year not to go forward with the acquisition after antitrust and other issues arose in the due diligence process.

Illinois Tool Works (ITW) – $1.3 billion, 2005 revenues from welding products. ITW's parent company had sales of nearly $13 billion, with a diversified product line from over 700 business units including plastic and metal components, fasteners, industrial fluids, and adhesives. Additionally, ITW manufactured systems for consumer and industrial packaging, identification systems, industrial spray coating, and quality assurance equipment. ITW's two major welding subsidiaries included Hobart (acquired in 1996) and Miller (acquired in 1993). ITW was Lincoln's strongest U.S. competitor, and ITW maintained a U.S. market position in welding that was second to Lincoln. In U.S. welding equipment, however, ITW's market share was slightly higher than Lincoln's. Elsewhere around the world, Lincoln's welding equipment share was higher than ITW's. ITW did have a large Asian subsidiary named Tien Tai producing consumable products in Taiwan and China.

Air Liquide – $600 million, 2005 estimated sales derived from welding products. The main business of Air Liquide was industrial gases, but they also had a significant welding business in Europe. Their gas distribution business also provided natural leverage in sales of welding products.

Kobelco – $550–600 million, 2005 estimated sales derived from welding consumables. Kobe Steel, the parent company of Kobelco, was a leading Japanese steelmaker as well as a supplier of aluminum and copper products. Kobelco itself concentrated on welding consumables and enjoyed a dominant position in the Asia-Pacific region. Kobelco had also begun establishing a significant position in the China market through its joint venture with Panasonic.

Thermadyne Holding Corp. – $470 million, 2005 sales. Thermadyne was a primarily U.S.-focused manufacturer and also one that had its strongest market position in a specific niche (gas apparatus equipment), with good brand-name recognition for its "Victor" brand. Thermadyne's competitive position appeared constrained by its lack of product breadth, the limited liquidity of its shares in the public equity markets, and its excess debt level.

Lincoln Electric: Overview

Starting with a capital investment of only $200 in 1895, John C. Lincoln formed the Lincoln Electric Company to produce and sell electric motors that

Exhibit 4   Summaries of Lincoln Income Statements

	1986	1987	1988	1989	1990	1991	1992	1993	1994
INCOME STATEMENTS									
Net Sales	370.2	443.2	570.2	692.8	796.7	833.9	853.0	846.0	906.6
Cost of Goods Sold	245.4	279.4	361.0	441.3	510.5	521.8	553.1	532.8	556.3
Gross Profit	124.8	163.8	209.2	251.5	286.2	312.1	299.9	313.2	350.3
SG&A Expense	101.3	121.0	165.2	211.1	241.2	270.7	280.3	273.3	258.5
Operating Profit	23.5	42.8	44.0	40.4	45.0	41.4	19.6	39.9	91.8
Rationalization and Non-recurring Items	–	–	–	–	(18.0)	0.1	(42.8)	(73.8)	(0.4)
Other Income, Net	0.4	1.2	2.2	3.0	3.1	3.8	4.4	2.9	3.1
EBIT	23.9	44.0	46.2	43.4	30.1	45.3	(18.8)	(31.0)	94.5
Interest Expense, Net	(5.6)	(5.9)	(9.7)	(5.1)	(0.3)	10.9	15.6	16.0	14.3
Pre-Tax Earnings	29.5	49.9	55.9	48.5	30.4	34.4	(34.4)	(47.0)	80.2
Income Taxes	13.7	22.3	21.5	21.0	19.3	20.0	11.4	(6.4)	32.2
Accounting Change	–	–	–	–	–	–	–	2.5	–
Net Income	15.8	27.6	34.4	27.5	11.1	14.4	(45.8)	(38.1)	48.0

Source: Lincoln Electric.
Note: Distribution expenses were included in SG&A in the years 1994 and prior and the data was not available to facilitate reclasses to cost of sales.

he had designed. In 1907, John's brother James joined the company as a senior manager out of Ohio State University and over the years introduced a series of innovative human resource policies and management practices. Starting in 1909, the company diversified into the production of welding equipment, and by 1922 welding equipment and welding consumable products had become the company's main business.

The company hit $1 billion in sales for the first time in 1995, its centennial year, and that same year the company's shares began trading on Nasdaq. Between 1995 and 2005, the company rose from being the leading U.S. manufacturer of welding products to the leading global manufacturer in its industry. In 2004, John M. Stropki was named chairman, president, and chief executive officer, becoming only the seventh chairman in the company's then 109-year history. In 2005 the company's operating income was $153.5 million and net income was $122 million on sales of $1.6 billion. The company was the world's largest

designer and manufacturer of arc welding and cutting products, manufacturing a full line of arc welding equipment, consumable welding products, and other welding and cutting products. Because of its technological innovation and product and application support, the company was able to earn a price premium for many of its products. In addition, the company's human resource and incentive system had led to a history of industry-leading productivity advances. The company's 20-year record of performance is described in **Exhibit 4,** and the organizational chart is presented in **Exhibit 5.**

Human   Resources   and   Incentive   System
The Lincoln brothers believed that capitalism could actually lead to a classless society if companies would simply provide the right incentives for individuals to fulfill their potential and richly reward those individuals based on their performance. James F. Lincoln was known to begin each company meeting by saying, "Fellow

1995	1996	1997	1998	1999	2000	2001	2002	2003	2004	2005
1,032.4	1,109.1	1,159.1	1,186.7	1,086.2	1,058.6	978.9	994.1	1,040.6	1,333.7	1,601.2
689.4	742.7	777.6	789.7	714.4	703.5	671.6	694.1	759.9	971.3	1,164.3
343.0	366.4	381.5	397.0	371.8	355.1	307.3	300.0	280.7	362.4	436.9
228.7	243.2	243.2	249.6	223.8	216.2	189.1	198.0	210.7	252.1	283.4
114.3	123.2	138.3	147.4	148.0	138.9	118.2	102.0	70.0	110.3	153.5
(6.3)	(2.5)	(3.5)	–	(32.0)	(13.4)	2.0	(10.5)	(1.7)	(6.9)	(2.3)
2.2	2.1	0.8	1.2	2.3	2.9	0.2	2.3	5.8	7.5	6.6
110.2	122.8	135.6	148.6	118.3	128.4	120.4	93.8	74.1	110.9	157.8
10.6	4.9	0.4	1.6	4.1	6.7	4.4	5.9	4.9	3.1	3.9
99.6	117.9	135.2	147.0	114.2	121.7	116.0	87.9	69.2	107.8	153.9
38.1	43.6	49.8	53.3	40.3	43.6	32.4	21.0	14.7	27.2	31.6
–	–	–	–	–	–	–	(37.6)	–	–	–
61.5	74.3	85.4	93.7	73.9	78.1	83.6	29.3	54.5	80.6	122.3

Exhibit 5   Organization Chart

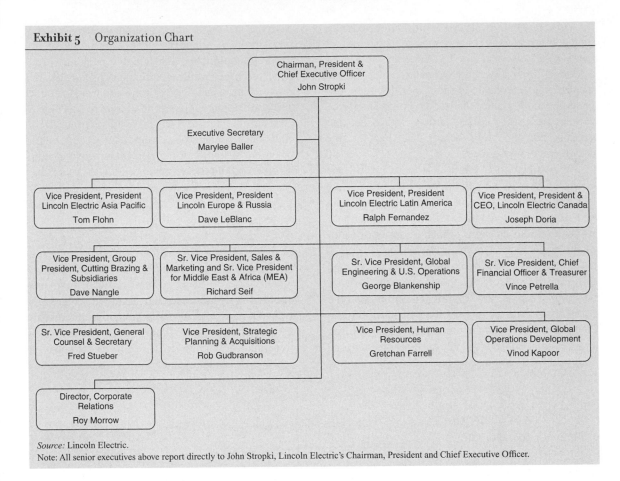

Source: Lincoln Electric.

Note: All senior executives above report directly to John Stropki, Lincoln Electric's Chairman, President and Chief Executive Officer.

Workers."[3] Starting in 1907 and under James F. Lincoln's management, Lincoln was one of the first companies to introduce a number of human resource innovations, several of which would eventually become standard practice across U.S. manufacturing industries. These innovations included the use of employee stock ownership, incentive bonuses determined by merit ratings, the creation of an Employee Advisory Board (which had met bimonthly since 1914), an employee suggestion system, piecework pay, annuities for retired employees, and group life insurance.[4] Since 1958 for the U.S. operation, the company had a no-layoff

policy, and a large share of company profits were shared with workers through annual bonuses (fully 32% of income before interest, taxes, and bonus, in 2005). During industry downturns all employees, including senior managers, shared the pain through reduced discretionary bonuses. As a result of the company's emphasis on incentive pay-for-performance, some 60% of labor costs were variable.

The company encouraged a highly entrepreneurial environment in its manufacturing plants. Lincoln workers managed themselves, with only one foreman in Cleveland for approximately every 68 employees.[5] There were tens of thousands of piecework tasks at

[3]Virginia P. Dawson, *Lincoln Electric: A History* (Cleveland: Lincoln Electric Company, 1999), p. 3.

[4]Dawson, Lincoln Electric: A History.

[5]Data were provided by Lincoln Electric to the casewriter in November 2006.

Exhibit 6   Gross Bonus Trends at Lincoln Electric in the United States

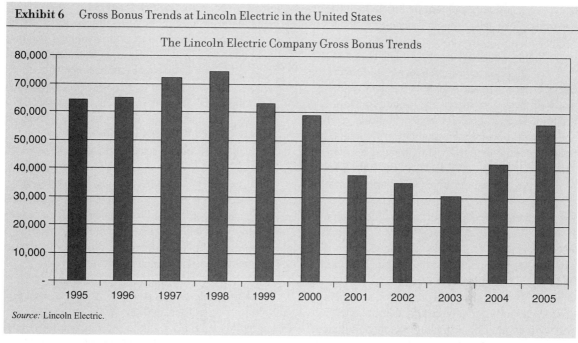

Source: Lincoln Electric.

Lincoln, and hence individual factory employees were given a great deal of autonomy both in solving problems and reporting their own piecework wages. Lincoln production employees had no paid sick days or holidays, and accepted overtime to meet spikes in demand. Factory workers were paid for what they produced and defective work had to be corrected on an employee's own time. Furthermore, whereas the piecework encouraged productivity, a large amount of the employee's annual compensation came from the annual discretionary bonuses. In 1997, for example, the company paid $74 million in bonuses to 3,259 employees (for an average bonus of $23,000; for succeeding years, see **Exhibit 6**).[6] The company determined annual bonuses based on a merit rating, which was based in equal parts on quality, adaptability/flexibility, productivity, dependability/teamwork, and environmental health and safety. Lincoln's incentive system required a high degree of trust between employees and senior management,

as workers needed to believe that they would benefit from suggestions they made on a weekly and even daily basis to improve productivity. Trust was something that the company had to build up over many decades, and the no-layoff policy laid a significant foundation for that culture of trust.

Technology Development   Award-winning engineers were responsible for Lincoln Electric's technological leadership in welding, and the company spent approximately 2% of sales on research and development (R&D). With outstanding R&D productivity, the company led its industry in new market introductions and quality performance. More than 50% of Lincoln Electric's equipment sales in 2005 were generated by welding machines introduced in the previous five years. The company held many valuable patents, primarily in arc welding. Lincoln Electric took pride in its technological focus and believed that its product focus had led it to become known as "The Welding Experts," in contrast to its leading competitors who chose to diversify their resources far away from welding. In 1996 the company approved a multimillion-dollar expansion of

[6]Dawson, *Lincoln Electric: A History*, p. 149. Also, more recent data were supplied by Lincoln Electric to the casewriter.

its research and development facilities. In 2001, the $20 million David C. Lincoln Technology Center was completed, ensuring Lincoln Electric's leadership position in product development. The company had the most aggressive, comprehensive, and successful R&D program in the welding industry. Although many of these activities were located in Cleveland, Lincoln Electric in 2004 began building regional engineering development centers in Shanghai and Poland in addition to its existing training and demonstration centers in Australia, Canada, Italy, Mexico Netherlands, Singapore, and Spain. During the 1990s, the company invested extensively in automated welding products together with its Japanese supplier FANUC Robotics.

Product Mix   Lincoln was one of only a few worldwide broad-line manufacturers of both arc welding equipment and consumable products. The benefits of producing both equipment and consumables were tied to the value of providing welding "solutions" rather than just individual products. Lincoln could solve customers' process problems and improve process productivity with its ability to combine both equipment and consumables development needs into one integrated package. Lincoln's equipment products ranged from $300 units available at Home Depot, Lowes, or Wal-Mart, etc., to automated industrial welding systems costing $250,000, although the majority of equipment products were in the $1,000 to $10,000 range. Many of Lincoln's most advanced equipment products were produced through its supply arrangement with FANUC Robotics. These products combined a robotic arm, a welding power source, and a wire feeder to automatically produce welds using various computer software, welding fixtures and fasteners, and accessories. In 1990, the company expanded its arc welding line by purchasing Harris Calorific, a manufacturer of gas-cutting and gas-welding equipment. Starting in the early 1990s the company began growing sales in the North America retail channel. In 1999 the company completed the divestiture of its motor business. In 2002, the company formed Lincoln Electric Welding, Cutting, Tools and Accessories, Inc., dedicated to

growing the retail channel. In 2003 Lincoln complemented its successful line of retail products with the acquisition of the Century and Marquette welding and battery-charged brands, which had leading positions in the automotive and retail channels. In 2005, the company broadened its metal-joining base when it acquired J.W. Harris Company, a privately held brazing and soldering alloys business based in Mason, Ohio. J.W. Harris was a global leader in the production of brazing and soldering alloys with about $100 million in annual sales. Harris products could be sold to Lincoln's existing set of customers, and vice versa. Also, the introduction of Lincoln's management system and purchasing and logistics capabilities had led to cost savings at the Harris plants. As a result, the acquisition had produced synergies on both the cost and revenue sides by 2006.

Marketing   Lincoln's products were marketed and sold in 86 countries, and one of the company's selling points was that it could offer advice to its customers on how to use its welding equipment without charging them directly for the advice. To the extent possible, the company did receive a product price premium in exchange for the advice it gave, and some Lincoln products also received a higher price premium than others based on the size of the productivity gains they afforded to customers. Lincoln employees applied their skills and knowledge to provide world-class welding training for the company's distributors and customers. The company believed that it had a competitive advantage because of its highly trained technical sales force and the support of its welding research and development staff, which allowed it to assist the consumers of its products in optimizing their welding applications. As part of the sales process, Lincoln employees visited prospective customers, evaluating their welding requirements, and made specific product recommendations together with a return-on-investment projection. Lincoln also employed its technical expertise to present its Guaranteed Cost Reduction Program to end users, through which the company guaranteed that the user would save money in its manufacturing process when it utilized Lincoln's products. This allowed the company to introduce its products to new users and to establish and maintain very close relationships with its consumers. In addition to these sales activities, the company also marketed itself actively as a leading sponsor of the organized motor racing sport industry. At motor racing events like NASCAR, Indy Car, and NHRA, Lincoln used the opportunity to demonstrate its products to local prospects.

Design and Production   As a result of the company's renewed commitment to R&D starting in 1997, Lincoln was able to design an expanded product line and diversify its production across multiple welding technologies. In 1997, over 30 new products, including a new computer-based welding machine and the industry's first digital communications protocol, called ArcLink, were introduced at an international welding show in Essen, Germany. The company, having recovered from the crisis of 1993, also invested heavily in modernization of its Cleveland plant.[7]

Lincoln's Global Strategy

While Lincoln had international operations dating back to the 1940s, its first major international expansion occurred between 1986 and 1992, when the company expanded from five manufacturing plants in the U.S., Canada, Australia, and France, to encompass 22 plants in 15 countries. In 1987 the company expanded its Australian operation by purchasing assets from Air Liquide. Then, the company bought a minority interest in an existing plant and also constructed a new plant in Venezuela. That was followed by a series of acquisitions in Mexico, Brazil, Scotland, Norway, the United Kingdom, the Netherlands, Spain, and Germany. The new acquisitions in Europe and Latin America that had cost $325 million suffered large operating losses, and in 1992, while the U.S. operation continued to be strongly profitable, the losses internationally were so serious that the company faced a stark choice.[8] In order to pay its

U.S. employees their annual bonus, the company had to borrow the money.[9]

There were numerous potential explanations for the difficulties faced after the company's late 1980s-era expansion. Lincoln wanted the new acquisitions to operate in Lincoln USA's image and to be led by managers from Cleveland. The company's international managers were expected to introduce piecework, a bonus system, and an advisory board.[10] As business historian Virginia Dawson noted in a 1999 history of Lincoln Electric, "The inexperience of Lincoln executives with trade unions and lack of knowledge of labor practices and laws in other countries proved major stumbling blocks in the effort to integrate the new acquisitions into Lincoln's distinctive management culture."[11] Many of the local managers and local employees did not believe that these practices were appropriate for their local environment, and as a result, many of the practices were either never implemented or implemented without success. The company was also unlucky in having bought companies in Europe just before a global economic downturn. Anthony Massaro, a 26-year veteran executive at Westinghouse Electric with extensive international experience and a graduate of the Advanced Management Program at Harvard Business School, was recruited to restructure Lincoln's international operations. Massaro closed unprofitable plants in Japan, Venezuela, Germany, and Brazil. He had found that some of the European plants were engaging in duplicative production and actually competing with each other. Massaro rationalized manufacturing so that some plants made consumables while others made welding machinery.[12] The then CEO of the company, Donald Hastings, announced that henceforward the company would learn from its experience and rely more on joint ventures and strategic alliances.[13]

---

[7]Ibid.

[8]Donald F. Hastings, "Lincoln Electric's Harsh Lessons from International Expansion," *Harvard Business Review*, May–June 1999, p.164.

[9]Dawson, Lincoln Electric: A History, p. 138.

[10]Ibid., p. 41.

[11]Ibid., p. 138.

[12]Ibid., pp. 141–142.

[13]Marcus Gleisser, "Lincoln Electric Has Learned Its Lesson and Is Seeking Help in Heading Overseas," *Plain Dealer* (Cleveland, Ohio), June 1, 1996.

Starting in 1996, companywide profitability had returned, and the company renewed its global expansion. In that same year, the company acquired Electronic Welding Systems in Italy and formed a joint venture in Indonesia. Also in 1996, Massaro was promoted to the position of president and chief executive officer. In 1997 the company opened its joint-venture electrode plant in Indonesia. In 1998, the company opened an electrode plant in Shanghai, along with completing acquisitions of Uhrhan & Schwill, a Germany-based designer and installer of pipe welding systems, and Indalco, a Canada-based manufacturer of aluminum wire and rod. In 1998 the company also acquired a 50% interest in ASKaynak, a leading Turkish producer of welding consumables, and opened a distribution center in Johannesburg, South Africa. In 1999 Lincoln acquired a 35% equity position in Taiwan-based Kuang Tai, a leading supplier of welding consumables in Asia. It also completed construction and start-up of a new wire manufacturing facility in Torreón, Mexico. In 2000, Lincoln acquired Italian manufacturer C.I.F.E. Spa, Europe's premier producer of MIG wire, strengthening Lincoln's position as a leader in the European welding consumables business. Also in 2000, production began in Lincoln's new manufacturing facility in Brazil. In 2001 the company expanded its operations in South America with the acquisition of Messer Soldaduras de Venezuela, the country's leading manufacturer of consumable welding products. In 2002, the company acquired Bester S.A., a welding equipment manufacturer based in Poland, driving the company's growth in Eastern Europe. **Exhibit 7** shows the geographic coverage of Lincoln's plants in 2006, and **Exhibit 8** describes how Lincoln senior management viewed their competitive advantage by geographic region. **Exhibit 9** describes Lincoln's subsidiaries according to their operating performance, total sales, and total assets.

In 2004 Massaro retired, and John Stropki, the newly appointed chairman and CEO, continued the company's international expansion with particular emphasis on the China market. In 2004, the company acquired controlling interests in two welding businesses in China, giving Lincoln a leading share in that growing market. Also in 2004, the company started construction of a new welding equipment plant in Shanghai. Adjacent to the plant, Lincoln started building a multistory building that would serve as its regional headquarters, applications, and R&D center, as well as serving as a training, demonstration, and customer service area. Outside China, the company continued its international expansion in 2004 by upgrading its Bester equipment plant in Poland to serve Eastern Europe, another growing and important market for the company; by constructing a new machine manufacturing facility in Mexico; by expanding operations in Brazil, Venezuela, and Australia; and by planning a new welding consumables production facility with its joint venture partner in Turkey. In China, also in 2004, Lincoln obtained a controlling interest in the Shanghai Kuang Tai Metal Industry Co. With increased ownership, all China equipment manufacturing was subsequently incorporated into Lincoln's operations. In addition, Lincoln purchased 70% of Rui Tai Welding and Metal Co., a manufacturer of stick electrodes located in northern China. **Exhibit 10** shows the company's geographic coverage within the country.

Strategic Challenges   The company set a series of ambitious financial goals, but meanwhile growth in its primary market of the United States would be far from sufficient to meet these goals. The company was still dependent on North America for approximately 60% of its sales, and yet other markets for welding products and consumables were growing significantly faster. Long-term company financial targets included sales growth at double the rate of growth in worldwide industrial production, operating margins over 15%, earnings growth of 10% annually, and return on equity exceeding 20%. As a result, as of 2005 the company spent approximately two-thirds of free cash flow for international expansion.[14]

---

[14]Lincoln Electric, personal communication with author on September 5, 2006.

Exhibit 7   Lincoln's Global Presence in 2006

Source: Lincoln Electric.

Exhibit 8   How Lincoln Senior Management Viewed Their Global Advantage in 2006

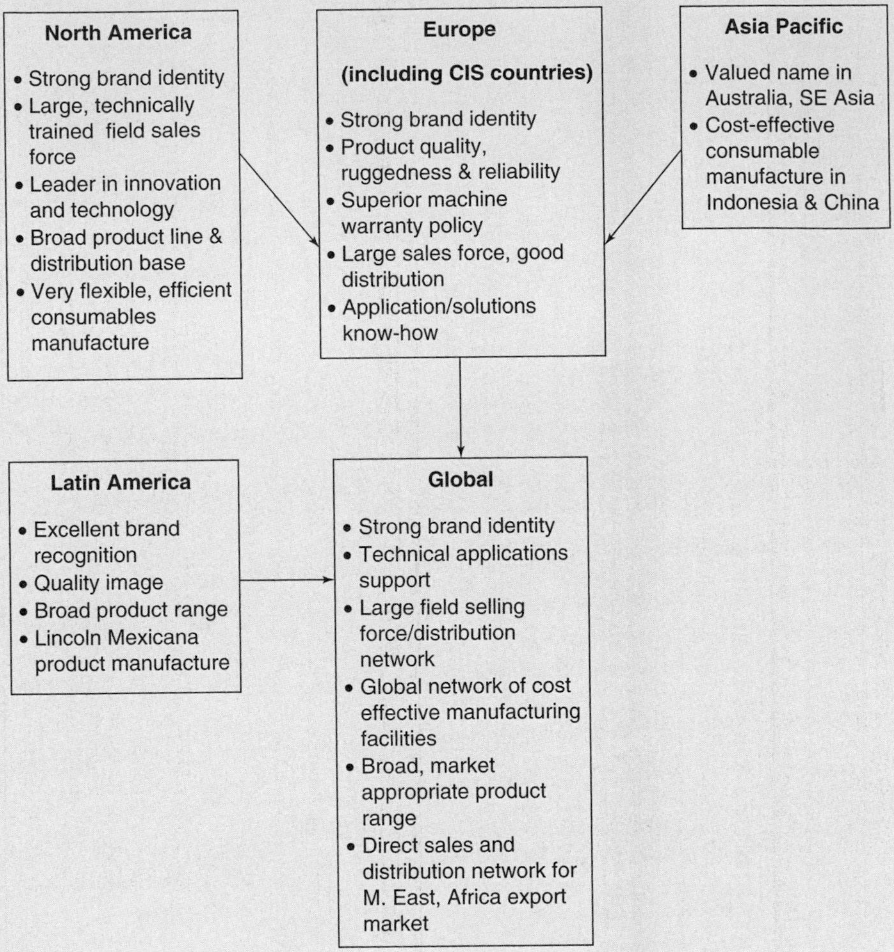

North America

- Strong brand identity
- Large, technically trained field sales force
- Leader in innovation and technology
- Broad product line & distribution base
- Very flexible, efficient consumables manufacture

Europe

(including CIS countries)

- Strong brand identity
- Product quality, ruggedness & reliability
- Superior machine warranty policy
- Large sales force, good distribution
- Application/solutions know-how

Asia Pacific

- Valued name in Australia, SE Asia
- Cost-effective consumable manufacture in Indonesia & China

Latin America

- Excellent brand recognition
- Quality image
- Broad product range
- Lincoln Mexicana product manufacture

Global

- Strong brand identity
- Technical applications support
- Large field selling force/distribution network
- Global network of cost effective manufacturing facilities
- Broad, market appropriate product range
- Direct sales and distribution network for M. East, Africa export market

Source: Lincoln Electric.

Exhibit 9   Lincoln Electric's Regional Performance

Region	Year	ROA	Total Sales (in USD millions)	Total Assets (in USD millions)
U.S.A. and Canada	2005	0.28	1077.5	652.5
Mexico and Latin America	2005	0.16	121.4	83.0
Europe	2005	0.07	426.3	313.3
Asia and Australia	2005	0.05	125.0	98.1

Source: Lincoln Electric.
Note: ROA is defined as Operating Income/Total Assets.

Exhibit 10   Lincoln's Plants in China

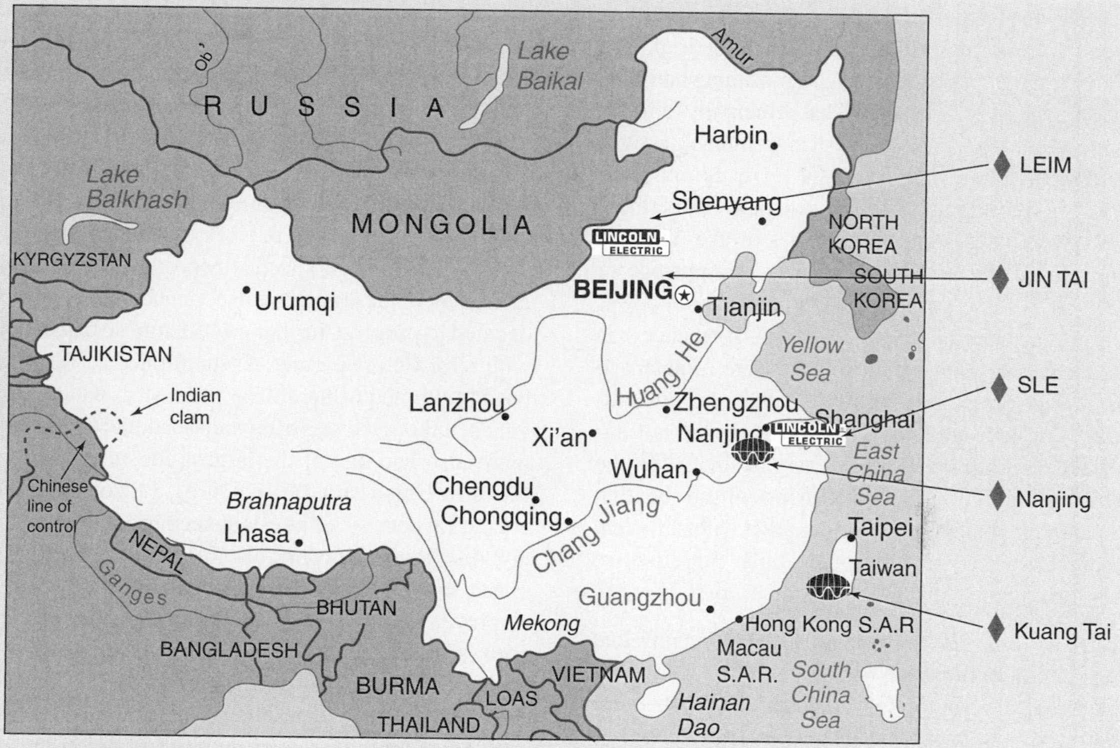

Source: Lincoln Electric.

Lessons from Prior Experience in Asia   Lincoln Electric saw Japan, South Korea, and China as advanced versions of what the Indian welding market was likely to become. Therefore the company wondered which lessons could be gleaned from the company's mixed record of success in these three countries. In Japan, the market for welding had closely tracked the overall explosive development of the manufacturing sector from the 1960s to the 1980s. The country started out producing low-end consumables for domestic production, but as the market grew domestic producers began focusing domestic production on advanced, automated welding equipment products. Low-end consumables were subsequently imported from first South Korea and then China. The Japanese welding market had reached a steady state in which the market demanded the latest high-technology welding products with exceptional pre-sales and post-sales support on the one hand, while also requiring high-quality commodity consumables at competitive prices. South Korea was moving toward that same industry steady-state outcome, albeit at a pace that was twice as fast as in Japan. In China, the country had gone from being a producer of only low-end consumables to embracing the most advanced welding technology. This had occurred within a span of just 5–10 years.

Japan   Lincoln's distribution in Japan was very limited. The company did not have any market access at the commodity end of the market, and the company had limited in-country demonstration or after-sales support capability, which was critical in Japan for high-tech sales. There was also no Lincoln distribution channel, brand recognition, or sales force to sell commodity products that might be imported from China or Taiwan. The Lincoln welding consumables business in Japan consisted principally of niche products sold to a small group of customers. Lincoln's welding machine requirements were complicated by the power supply situation in Japan, where there were two voltages and frequencies in use. The one that caused the problem was the common use of 200 volt 3-phase power. While some Lincoln power sources ran adequately on this, the performance was impaired and Japanese customers were reluctant to pay a price premium for a product that was not optimized for their application. Yet Lincoln did not undertake a program to optimize machines for the Japanese market. The conclusion might be that Lincoln did not enter the Japan market with sufficient resources early enough to establish an effective presence against strong local competitors.

South Korea   In South Korea, the company had no production presence but had used the same reliable local distributor for 27 years. The distributor had good countrywide coverage and was effective in gaining access to most of the business that Lincoln could reasonably expect. Most of the challenge had been that Korean companies were reluctant to invest in high-end welding equipment, but that was changing as Hyundai Heavy Industries and others began to themselves move into high-end shipbuilding and thus demand the latest welding technology. Now that high-end demand was increasing, Lincoln needed to meet the challenge of providing prompt product delivery and complete technical support without any local production presence. Lincoln was still shipping its high-end machines to Korea from Cleveland and faced long lead times to ship the products. As the company developed its machine production line in China, it planned to ship product from China to Korea and other Asian markets.

China   Lincoln had a sales presence in China for several decades, but beginning in 1997 Lincoln was able to establish a viable manufacturing platform.

The company started by creating the Lincoln Electric Shanghai Welding Company in a government-created free trade zone. Establishing the Shanghai operation, however, proved difficult. The company found it difficult to find competent local managers, difficult to deal with the local government authorities, difficult to establish distribution channels, and difficult to make the operation profitable (due to a combination of challenges in day-to-day manufacturing management and the lack of a strong distribution channel for its domestically produced products). As a result of these negative experiences, the company decided to progress further on its Chinese expansion with a Taiwanese partner. As mentioned earlier, this began with acquiring a 35% interest in Kuang Tai, which, although it was a Taiwan-headquartered company, also had one of the largest consumables factories in China (Jin Tai Welding). Lincoln selected Kuang Tai because of its established production plant and distribution network, its ability to locate experienced, bilingual operations managers, its reliability, its proven ability to deal effectively with an extensive Chinese bureaucracy, and the company's concern with the complexities and uncertainties of alternatively partnering with a state-owned enterprise. Over time Lincoln increased its minority position in this consumables factory to 46%, and the company also purchased a controlling interest in two other consumables plants. Efforts to expand this manufacturing platform continued, which included the opening of the Shanghai machine plant in 2005, but the main effort was subsequently focused on developing stronger distribution and marketing, a local R&D capability, a broad logistics network, and local management and technical staffing.

As a result of these efforts, Lincoln had achieved many of its goals to establish a significant presence in China but now saw its future growth restricted due to the partnership structure. The partner was very competent, but the two sides did not always agree on how to grow the business (volume vs. profits). The decision-making process was time-consuming for an operation that Lincoln did not control. Hence, all subsequent major investment in China was done through majority controlled operations. Yet Lincoln senior management acknowledged that they could not have gotten to their current market presence without the joint venture experience. Also, in its majority owned operations the company had continued to battle its way through difficulties in finding, retaining, and affording talented local general managers. The company found that the cost of talented local general managers was equivalent to what the company paid in the U.S. and that there was frequent turnover in the Chinese market. The company also continued to find it challenging to attract and retain the local talent needed to build capabilities in supply chain logistics, IT, quality assurance, product development, and purchasing and sourcing. In 2006 the company had an organization in China in which the two top managers, and six out of 14 senior managers, were expatriates. Lincoln Electric had set up or acquired 16 operations in 11 countries over the previous nine years, but of all those operations, China had proven to be the most challenging. Yet among these challenges, the company was not overly concerned about the loss of its intellectual property. Lincoln Electric had heretofore chosen not to produce its most technologically advanced products in China, although it reserved the option to do so in future years.

Opportunity in India   Since the growth of the welding industry closely tracked the development of a country's entire economy, India had become an attractive market over the previous 15 years. Since 1991 India had enjoyed real average annual growth in GDP of almost 6%, making it one of the faster-growing countries in the world. To put the importance of the Indian market in further perspective, its 2005 market of US$415 million compared to US$601 million for all the countries of Latin America combined and US$312 million for all countries of East Europe, the other two world regions with still-developing economies and above-average welding market growth rates (~ 4% CAG).[15] India's growth reached over 7.5% in 2005, and a

2003 study by Goldman Sachs projected that over the next 50 years India would become the fastest-growing of the world's major economies. In a 2005 interview with the *Pipeline and Gas Journal*, Stropki noted that "India is currently rebuilding its infrastructure and therefore will need thousands of miles of new oil and gas pipelines."[16]

India's welding market was also the third-largest in Asia by 2006, with $500 million in annual industry sales expected by year end.[17] Industry growth was even higher than the country's growth rate because of India's recent focus on construction and infrastructure projects. One of the interesting features of the Indian market was that only approximately 56% of welding consumable sales were taken up by large firms that developed their own designs and technology, whereas the other approximately 44% of welding consumables were sold by over 300 small firms that immediately could try to imitate any new design on the market and try to sell it at a sharp discount.[18]

Significant large competitors who already had a strong presence in the Indian market included Ador Welding Ltd., a company controlled and managed by the local Advani family. As described in **Exhibit 11,** Ador enjoyed over $50 million in sales in 2005 with a 15% operating margin, and a portion of its shares traded on the local stock exchange. In July 2006, a research analyst at Karvy Stock Broking Limited estimated that Ador's revenues would grow at a cost-adjusted annual rate of 20% over the next two years and that Ador would continue to enjoy a return on capital employed at over 40%. The company had shifted some production to Silvassa, a government-created tax-free zone, and by concentrating production at a smaller number of facilities Ador had realized both economies of scale as well as tax savings. In July 2006 the company's publicly

---

[15]Data on market size were supplied by Lincoln Electric to the casewriter in March and September 2006.

[16]Jeff Share, "CEO sees inevitable move to automatic welding," *Pipeline and Gas Journal*, June 1, 2005.

[17]Lincoln Electric, personal communication with author on September 24, 2006.

[18]Estimates on the size of the organized and unorganized Indian welding sector come from Lincoln Electric and were sent to the author in April 2006.

Exhibit 11   Ador Welding Limited

Audited Financial Results for ADOR Welding Limited

(Units: Rupees in Crore)

	Financial Year ended 31st March	
	2006	2005
Net Sales/Income from operations	**276.14**	**223.99**
Less: Excise Duty	34.54	27.15
Net Sales/Income from operations (Net of Excise Duty)	241.60	196.84
Total Expenditure		
(Increase)/Decrease in Stock in Trade	−2.88	2.30
Consumption of Raw Material & Packing Material	131.18	104.43
Staff Cost	22.98	18.52
Other Expenditure	44.79	43.12
Interest & Finance Charges	−0.11	0.38
Depreciation	6.29	6.51
Additional Depreciation		11.09
Profit Before Tax	**48.36**	**28.93**
Provision for Taxation	7.55	6.05
Deferred Tax Impact	−0.29	−5.05
Fringe Benefit Tax	0.90	
Profit After Tax	**40.20**	**27.93**
Prior Period Adjustments (Including Excess/Short Provision of Taxes)	−0.16	−0.80
Net Profit	**40.04**	**27.13**
Basic and diluted EPS excluding exceptional items for the period, for the year to date and for the previous year (not annualized)	29.45	19.95
Basic and diluted EPS excluding exceptional items for the period, for the year to date and for the previous year (not annualized)	25.20	13.17
Aggregate of non-promoter share holding		
Number of shares	5,995,933	5,829,683
Percentage of shareholding	44.09%	42.87%
Segment Revenue (Net of Excise Duty)		
Consumables	180.07	153.99
Equipment & Project Engineering	61.53	42.85
Net Sales/Income from Operations	**241.60**	**196.84**
Segment Profit before Interest and Tax		
Consumables	37.96	28.09
Equipment & Project Engineering	10.94	5.11
Total	**48.90**	**33.20**
Less:		
Interest & Finance Charges	−0.11	0.38
Other Unallocable expenses net of Unallocable Income	0.65	3.89
Total Profit Before Tax	**48.36**	**28.93**
Capital Employed		
Consumables	63.95	33.65
Equipment & Project Engineering	13.62	10.52
Unallocable Corporate Assets net off Unallocable Corporate Liabilities	25.38	42.00
Total Capital Employed	**102.95**	**86.17**

Source: Adapted from Ador Welding Limited company website.

traded shares were valued at 10.9x FY07 estimated net earnings per share, and EBITDA per share was predicted by the same local analyst to grow at a CAGR of 29% and net earnings per share to grow at a CAGR of 23% over the next two years. Ador had annual sales of 241.6 crore (large values of India's currency, the rupee, are counted in terms of crore, with one crore the same as 10,000,000 rupees). The company had produced 17,217 MT of consumable welding products in FY06, and Ador had previously constructed plant lines that could produce far more than that should the market continue to grow.[19]Ador had in FY06 paid a dividend of 15 rupees, equal to a 4% yield on the stock.[20]

As described in **Exhibit 12,** the other large company was ESAB India, which was controlled by Lincoln's multinational competitor ESAB and which enjoyed over $50 million in sales in 2005. ESAB entered the market in 1988 with the acquisition of Philips' Indian welding plant for 6x operating earnings at 60 million rupees (otherwise denominated as 6 Indian crore). Through a series of acquisitions, ESAB India built up its market share but had enjoyed little profitability. In fact, the company only attained its admirable 18% operating margin in 2004 after a series of one-time write-offs to clean up the balance sheet, the introduction of current technology, the introduction of strict internal controls, staff changes, and the reorganization and expansion of distribution channels. Prior to 2005, ESAB India had invested in India entirely through acquisitions to the amount of 40 Indian crore.[21] In August 2005, ESAB India began construction of its first greenfield manufacturing plant in India for an announced cost of 20 Indian crore (the same as 200 million Indian rupees, which

amounted at that time to US$4.6 million). ESAB's announced investment of 20 crore, which included the cost of procuring technology from the parent company, would enable ESAB India to complete a 50,000 square foot facility in eight months.[22] The third and remaining large competitor in India was EWAC Alloys Ltd., a 50–50 joint venture between German welding firm Messer and L&T of India. That joint venture enjoyed $30 million in revenues in 2005.

After those three large competitors, the remaining incumbent companies were relatively small and included D & H Sécheron, a private Indian company; Indo Matsushita, a subsidiary of Japan's Matsushita; and Anand Arc, another privately held Indian company. Anand Arc manufactured a full range of welding consumables and claimed that it produced the highest-quality electrodes in India.[23] From its plants in Mumbai and Pulghar, its product range included electrodes for welding all types of metals encountered in the Indian welding industry. In addition to Anand Arc, D&H Welding was another local company with $3.5 million in sales in 2005.[24] GEE Ltd. and MIG Weld were two even smaller local companies controlled by consortia of investment firms.

In regards to India's labor market institutions, the country was generally friendly to the use of incentive pay-for-performance, although there were a few notable regulations in place. Most importantly, the company was free to implement both piecework and a discretionary bonus without getting approval from a union, a government, or any other third party, and without incurring any future obligation. The remaining restrictions were for the most part

[19]All estimates on Ador Welding's future growth and performance in this paragraph come from the following local analyst report: Vivek Kumar, "Ador Welding (Rs360)," Karvy Stock Broking Limited, July 19, 2006. The analyst sent a copy of the report by request in September 2006.
[20]All estimates on Ador Welding's future performance in this paragraph come from the following local analyst report: Vivek Kumar, "Ador Welding (Rs360)," Karvy Stock Broking Limited, July 19, 2006. The analyst sent a copy of the report by request in September 2006.
[21]"ESAB to Set Up Welding Equipment Plant Near Chennai," *Business Line (The Hindu)*, July 30, 2005.

[22]"Esab's New Plant to Start Operations by April '06; ESAB India Has Begun to Build a Plant at Irungatukottai . . .", *Business Standard* (India), August 1, 2005. The US dollar amount is calculated by multiplying the 20 crore cost of the plant by 10,000,000 to get the number of rupees, in this case 200,000,000 rupees. That 200,000,000 rupee amount is then divided by the exchange rate on August 1, 2005, 43.515 rupees to one U.S. dollar, to get USD$4.6 million.
[23]Company website, accessed from http://www.anandarc.com/flash/profile.html on August 27, 2006.
[24]Securities and Exchange Board of India website, accessed from http://sebiedifar.nic.in/ on September 11, 2006.

Exhibit 12   ESAB India Limited

Audited Financial Results for ESAB INDIA LIMITED

	(Units: Rupees in Millions)	
	Consolidated and Audited for the year ended 31 December	
	2005	**2004**
Gross Sales	2716.0	2138.4
Less Excise Duty	334.4	256.8
Net Sales	2381.6	1881.6
Other Income	53.8	39.6
Profit on sale of land/leasehold rights	45.3	4.2
Total Income	**2480.7**	**1925.4**
Increase in Stock-in-trade	−55.2	−17.6
Consumption of Raw & Packing Materials	1173.0	957.0
Purchases – Finished Goods	213.7	98.4
Staff Cost	160.6	181.1
Other Expenditure	357.6	314.3
Total Expenditure	**1849.7**	**1533.2**
Profit before Interest and Depreciation	**631.0**	**392.2**
Interest	5.0	7.5
Depreciation	44.6	53.4
Profit before Tax	**581.4**	**331.3**
Taxation	−184.7	−127.5
Profit after Taxation	**396.7**	**203.8**
Minority Interest	0.5	
Profit after Minority Interest	**396.7**	**204.3**
Basic and Diluted Earnings Per Share (Rs.)	25.78	13.27
Aggregate of non-promoter shareholding Number of shares	9,649,820	9,649,820
Percentage of holding (to total shareholding)	62.7	62.7
Segment Revenue (Net)		
Consumables	1829.9	1499.6
Equipment	551.7	382.0
Total	**2381.6**	**1881.6**
Segment Profit		
Consumables	483.0	381.4
Equipment	93.8	40.6
Total	**576.8**	**422.0**
Less:		
Interest	5.0	7.5
Other unallocated expenditure net of unallocated income	−9.6	83.2
Total Profit Before Tax	**581.4**	**331.3**
Capital Employed		
Consumables	428.5	411.1
Equipment	122.7	56.3

Source: Adapted from ESAB India company website.

not heavily constraining. Piecework could be implemented, but in most cases pay had to meet a minimum wage level.[25] The minimum wage varied by state and in a few states there was still no minimum wage, though more and more states had been implementing minimum wage levels in recent years. Pieceworkers were entitled to the same number of days of paid annual leave as their salaried counterparts, and annual leave pay was calculated based on average earnings over the preceding month. Discretionary bonuses could be paid, but there was a requirement that they could be paid only in addition to a required statutory bonus.[26] The statutory bonus was required for all workers earning up to 3,500 rupees per month, and could range from a minimum of 8.33% to a maximum of 20% of each worker's annual salary (the exact percent depended on the firm's performance for the year). The base on which the bonus was calculated was capped at 2,500 rupees per month; that is, any employee earning between 2,501 and 3,500 rupees per month would receive a bonus calculated on a base of 2,500 rupees per month.[27] The average industrial worker's salary was estimated to be just under 4,000 rupees per month in 2005 (approximately $88 at the December 2005 exchange rate).[28] However, in August 2006, Indian Prime Minister Manmohan Singh had promised to raise the legislated base on which a discretionary bonus had to be calculated, noting "I agree that current ceilings were set more than a decade ago. We will soon take a favorable decision on it."[29]

Lincoln could enter India by acquisition, by joint venture, or by building a new plant on its own. If the company were to enter by acquisition, it was unclear what type of valuation to apply to any of the Indian incumbent companies. In other markets, Lincoln would go forward with an acquisition only if it met the following criteria: the acquisition was accretive immediately under the new FASB goodwill rule; the investment had a minimum internal rate of return, based upon total investment, of an initial 10%, increasing to a minimum of 18% over the first 3–4 years (with synergy credits); the acquisition price was less than 8x EBITDA; the resulting companywide balance sheet would continue to justify the corporate-targeted credit rating; all liabilities were recognized appropriately on the balance sheet; and full financial and legal due diligence could be conducted before a Lincoln commitment. In India in 2006, the market was booming and any significant welding acquisition would likely require paying an acquisition premium greater than Lincoln Electric had been used to paying in the past. Other factors also making an acquisition strategy difficult included the fact that one of the targets was already owned by a Lincoln Electric competitor and other local targets had a combination of family control and remaining dispersed ownership structures. Alternatively, if the company were to enter by joint venture, the question was: How could Lincoln ensure its ability to make key business decisions? If the company were to build its own plant, the question was: Would the cost of starting from scratch be more than sufficiently compensated by the total control the company would enjoy?

[25]India Minimum Wage Act 1948 and related amending acts through 1961. Sourced on July 29, 2008 at http://indiacode.nic.in/fullact1.asp?tfnm=194811.

[26]India Payment of Bonus Act (1965) and related amending acts through 1995. Sourced on July 29, 2008 at http://labour.nic.in/act/acts/pba.doc.

[27]Ibid.

[28]Daily wage sourced on August 14, 2008 at URL http://labourbureau.nic.in/ASI_Data_2004_05.htm (item 8b), and multiplied by an estimated 22 workdays per month to arrive at a monthly average. The exchange rate for December 31, 2005 was accessed on August 14, 2008 from http://www.oanda.com/convert/fxhistory.

[29]*Business Standard*, "Bonus Ceiling for Workers Increased," October 2, 2007.

Case 1-2   Jollibee Foods Corporation (A): International Expansion

Christopher A. Bartlett and Jamie O'Connell

Protected by his office air conditioner from Manila's humid August air, in mid-1997, Manolo P. ("Noli") Tingzon pondered an analysis of demographic trends in California. As the new head of Jollibee's International Division, he wondered if a Philippine hamburger chain could appeal to mainstream American consumers or whether the chain's proposed US operations could succeed by focusing on recent immigrants and Philippine expatriates. On the other side of the Pacific, a possible store opening in the Kowloon district of Hong Kong raised other issues for Tingzon. While Jollibee was established in the region, local managers were urging the company to adjust its menu, change its operations, and refocus its marketing on ethnic Chinese customers. Finally, he wondered whether entering the nearly virgin fast food territory of Papua New Guinea would position Jollibee to dominate an emerging market—or simply stretch his recently-slimmed division's resources too far.

With only a few weeks of experience in his new company, Noli Tingzon knew that he would have to weigh these decisions carefully. Not only would they shape the direction of Jollibee's future internalization strategy, they would also help him establish his own authority and credibility within the organization.

Company History

Started in 1975 as an ice cream parlor owned and run by the Chinese-Filipino Tan family, Jollibee had diversified into sandwiches after company President Tony

▌ Professor Christopher A. Bartlett and Research Associate Jamie O'Connell prepared this case. HBS cases are developed solely as the basis for class discussion. Cases are not intended to serve as endorsements, sources of primary data, or illustrations of effective or ineffective management.
▌ Harvard Business School Case No 9-399-007, Copyright 1998 President and Fellows of Harvard College. All rights reserved.
This case was prepared by C. Bartlett. HBS Cases are developed solely for class discussion and do not necessarily illustrate either effective or ineffective handling of administrative situation.

Tan Caktiong (better known as TTC) realized that events triggered by the 1977 oil crisis would double the price of ice cream. The Tans' hamburger, made to a home-style Philippine recipe developed by Tony's chef father, quickly became a customer favorite. A year later, with five stores in metropolitan Manila, the family incorporated as Jollibee Foods Corporation.

The company's name came from TTC's vision of employees working happily and efficiently, like bees in a hive. Reflecting a pervasive courtesy in the company, everyone addressed each other by first names prefaced by the honorific "Sir" or "Ma'am," whether addressing a superior or subordinate. Friendliness pervaded the organization and become one of the "Five Fs" that summed up Jollibee's philosophy. The others were flavorful food, a fun atmosphere, flexibility in catering to customer needs, and a focus on families (children flocked to the company's bee mascot whenever it appeared in public). Key to Jollibee's ability to offer all of these to customers at an affordable price was a well developed operations management capability. A senior manager explained:

> It is not easy to deliver quality food and service consistently and efficiently. Behind all that fun and friendly environment that the customer experiences is a well oiled machine that keeps close tabs on our day-to-day operations. It's one of our key success factors.

Jollibee expanded quickly throughout the Philippines, financing all growth internally until 1993. (**Exhibit 1** shows growth in sales and outlets.) Tan family members occupied several key positions particularly in the vital operations functions, but brought in professional managers to supplement their expertise. "The heads of marketing and finance have always been outsiders," TTC noted. (**Exhibit 2** shows a 1997 organization chart.) Many franchisees were also members or friends of the Tan family.

Exhibit 1   Jollibee Philippines Growth, 1975–1997

Year	Total Sales (millions of pesos)	Total Stores at End of Year	Company-Owned Stores	Franchises
1975	NA	2	2	0
1980	NA	7	4	3
1985	174	28	10	18
1990	1,229	65	12	54
1991	1,744	99	21	80
1992	2,644	112	25	89
1993	3,386	124	30	96
1994	4,044	148	44	106
1995	5,118	166	55	113
1996	6,588	205	84	124
1997 (projected)	7,778	223	96	134

NA = Not available

In 1993, Jollibee went public and in an initial public offering raised 216 million pesos (approximately US $8 million). The Tan family, however, retained the majority ownership and clearly controlled Jollibee. Although the acquisition of Greenwich Pizza Corporation in 1994 and the formation of a joint venture with Deli France in 1995 diversified the company's fast food offerings, in 1996 the chain of Jollibee stores still generated about 85% of the parent company's revenues. (**Exhibits 3** and **4** present Jollibee's consolidated financial statements from 1992 through 1996.)

McDonald's: Going Burger to Burger   The company's first serious challenge arose in 1981, when McDonald's entered the Philippines. Although Jollibee already had 11 stores, many saw McDonald's as a juggernaut and urged TTC to concentrate on building a strong second-place position in the market. A special meeting of senior management concluded that although McDonald's had more money and highly developed operating systems, Jollibee had one major asset: Philippine consumers preferred the taste of Jollibee's hamburger by a wide margin. The group decided to go head-to-head with McDonald's. "Maybe we were very young, but we felt we could do anything," TTC recalled. "We felt no fear."

McDonald's moved briskly at first, opening six restaurants within two years and spending large sums on advertising. Per store sales quickly surpassed Jollibee's and, by 1983, McDonald's had grabbed a 27% share of the fast food market, within striking range of Jollibee's 32%. The impressive performance of the Big Mac, McDonald's largest and best-known sandwich, led Jollibee to respond with a large hamburger of its own, called the Champ. Jollibee executives bet that the Champ's one wide hamburger patty, rather than the Big Mac's smaller two, would appeal more to Filipinos' large appetites. Market research indicated that Filipinos still preferred Jollibee burgers' spicy taste to McDonald's plain beef patty, so the Champ's promotions focused on its taste, as well as its size.

But the Champ's intended knockout punch was eclipsed by larger events. In August 1983, political opposition leader Benigno Aquino was assassinated as he returned from exile. The economic and political crisis that followed led most foreign investors, including McDonald's, to slow their investment in the Philippines. Riding a wave of national pride, Jollibee pressed ahead, broadening its core menu with taste-tested offerings of chicken, spaghetti and a unique peach-mango dessert pie, all developed to local consumer tastes. By 1984, McDonald's foreign brand appeal was fading.

In 1986, dictator Ferdinand Marcos fled the Philippines in the face of mass demonstrations of

Exhibit 2 Jollibee Corporation Organization Chart, 1997 (members of Tan family shaded)

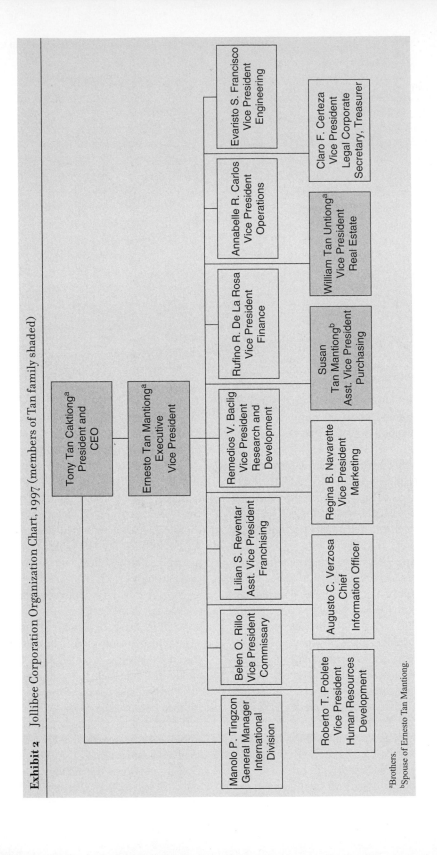

aBrothers.
bSpouse of Ernesto Tan Mantiong.

Exhibit 3   Jollibee Foods Corporation Consolidated Balance Sheets (in Philippine pesos)

	Years Ended December 31				
	1996	**1995**	**1994**	**1993**	**1992**
Assets					
Current assets					
Cash and cash equivalents	480,822,919	355,577,847	474,480,298	327,298,749	116,716,643
Accounts receivable:					
Trade	579,089,680	206,045,303	135,663,597	107,680,327	86,885,668
Advances and others	105,836,646	70,731,546	66,224,534	35,838,295	15,091,648
Inventories	323,019,198	201,239,667	183,154,582	135,263,988	116,828,086
Prepaid expenses and other current assets	223,680,221	132,077,935	88,995,824	41,462,780	66,028,987
Total current assets	1,712,448,664	965,672,298	948,518,835	647,544,139	401,551,032
Investments and advances	283,758,590	274,878,713	132,277,028	67,000,362	60,780,936
Property and equipment	2,177,944,193	1,181,184,783	753,876,765	568,904,831	478,857,474
Refundable deposits and other assets—net	363,648,234	224,052,247	91,575,543	92,035,464	72,310,079
Total assets	4,537,799,681	2,645,788,041	1,926,248,171	1,375,484,796	1,013,499,521
Liabilities and Stockholders' Equity					
Current liabilities:					
Bank loans	771,690,724				
Accounts payable and accrued expenses	1,274,801,219	715,474,384	497,238,433	323,029,967	297,029,436
Income tax payable	58,803,916	28,103,867	17,205,603	23,206,109	19,851,315
Notes payable					133,000,000
Current portion of long-term debt	6,707,027	7,524,098			22,034,635
Dividends payable	16,810,812				
Total current liabilities	2,128,813,698	751,102,349	514,444,036	346,236,076	471,915,386
Long-term debt	28,936,769	33,725,902			
Minority interest	45,204,131	1,479,723	1,331,529		21,127,827
Stockholders' equity					
Capital stock—par value	880,781,250	704,625,000	563,315,000	372,000,000	66,000,000
Additional paid-in capital	190,503,244	190,503,244	190,503,244	190,503,244	
Retained earnings	1,263,560,589	964,351,823	656,654,362	466,745,476	454,456,308
Total stockholders' equity	2,334,845,083	1,859,480,067	1,410,472,606	1,029,248,720	520,456,308
Total liabilities	4,537,799,681	2,645,788,041	1,926,248,171	1,375,484,796	1,013,499,521
Average exchange rate during year: pesos per US$	26.22	25.71	26.42	27.12	25.51

Exhibit 4 Jollibee Foods Corporation Consolidated Statements of Income and Retained Earnings (in Philippine pesos)

	1996	1995	1994	1993	1992
			Years Ended December 31		
Systemwide Sales (incl. franchisees)	8,577,067,000	6,894,670,000	5,277,640,000	4,102,270,000	NA
Company sales	6,393,092,135	4,403,272,755	3,277,383,084	2,446,866,690	2,074,153,386
Royalties and franchise fees	511,510,191	448,200,271	328,824,566	255,325,825	221,884,104
	6,904,602,326	4,851,473,026	3,606,207,650	2,702,192,515	2,296,037,490
Cost and Expenses					
Cost of sales	4,180,809,230	2,858,056,701	2,133,240,206	1,663,600,632	1,469,449,458
Operating expenses	1,943,536,384	1,403,151,840	1,013,999,640	674,288,268	545,749,275
Operating income	780,256,712	590,264,485	458,967,804	364,303,615	280,838,757
Interest and other income—net	44,670,811	102,134,296	83,342,805	32,716,223	(13,599,219)
Minority share in net earnings of a subsidiary		—	499,770		
Provision for income tax	219,900,353	168,589,520	138,001,953	104,230,670	66,172,056
Income before minority interest and cumulative effect of accounting change	605,027,170	523,809,261	403,808,886	292,789,168	201,067,482
Minority interest	2,829,654	137,694	—	—	—
Cumulative effect of accounting change		13,733,644			
Net income	602,197,516	537,405,211	403,808,886	292,789,168	201,067,482
Earnings per share	0.68	0.61	0.81	0.59	0.58
Average exchange rate (pesos per $US)	26.22	25.71	26.42	27.12	25.51

38

"people power" led by Aquino's widow, Corazon. After she took office as president, optimism returned to the country, encouraging foreign companies to reinvest. As the local McDonald's franchisee once again moved to expand, however, its management found that Jollibee now had 31 stores and was clearly the dominant presence in the market.

Industry Background

In the 1960s, fast food industry pioneers, such as Ray Kroc of McDonald's and Colonel Sanders of Kentucky Fried Chicken, had developed a value proposition that became the standard for the industry in the United States and abroad. Major fast food outlets in the United States, which provided a model for the rest of the world, aimed to serve time-constrained customers by providing good-quality food in a clean dining environment and at a low price.

Managing a Store   At the store level, profitability in the fast food business depended on high customer traffic and tight operations management. Opening an outlet required large investments in equipment and store fittings, and keeping it open imposed high fixed costs for rent, utilities, and labor. This meant attracting large numbers of customers ("traffic") and, when possible, increasing the size of the average order (or "ticket"). The need for high volume put a premium on convenience and made store location critical. In choosing a site, attention had to be paid not only to the potential of a city or neighborhood but also to the traffic patterns and competition on particular streets or even blocks.

Yet even an excellent location could not make a store viable in the absence of good operations management, the critical ingredient in reducing waste, ensuring quality service and increasing staff productivity. Store managers were the key to motivating and controlling crew members responsible for taking orders, preparing food, and keeping the restaurant clean. Efficient use of their time—preparing raw materials and ingredients in advance, for example— not only enabled faster service, but could also reduce the number of crew members needed.

Managing a Chain   The high capital investment required to open new stores led to the growth of franchising which enabled chains to stake out new territory by rapidly acquiring market share and building brand recognition in an area. Such expansion created the critical mass needed to achieve economies of scale in both advertising and purchasing.

Fast food executives generally believed that chain-wide consistency and reliability was a key driver of success. Customers patronized chains because they knew, after eating at one restaurant in a chain, what they could expect at any other restaurant. This not only required standardization of the menu, raw material quality, and food preparation, but also the assurance of uniform standards of cleanliness and service. Particularly among the U.S. chains that dominated the industry, there also was agreement that uniformity of image also differentiated the chain from competitors: beyond selling hamburger or chicken, they believed they were selling an image of American pop culture. Consequently, most major fast food chains pushed their international subsidiaries to maintain or impose standardized menus, recipes, advertising themes, and store designs.

Moving Offshore: 1986–1997

Jollibee's success in the Philippines brought opportunities in other Asian countries. Foreign businesspeople, some of them friends of the Tan family, heard about the chain's success against McDonald's and began approaching TTC for franchise rights in their countries. While most of his family and other executives were caught up in the thriving Philippine business, TTC was curious to see how Jollibee would fare abroad.

Early Forays: Early Lessons

Singapore   Jollibee's first venture abroad began in 1985, when a friend of a Philippine franchisee persuaded TTC to let him open and manage Jollibee stores in Singapore. The franchise was owned by a partnership consisting of Jollibee, the local manager, and five Philippine-Chinese investors, each with a one-seventh stake. Soon after the first store opened, however, relations between Jollibee and the local manager began to deteriorate. When corporate inspectors visited to check quality, cleanliness, and efficiency in operations, the franchisee would not let them into his offices to verify the local records. In 1986, Jollibee revoked the franchise agreement and shut down the Singapore store. "When we were closing down the store, we found that all the local company funds were gone, but some suppliers had not been paid," said TTC. "We had no hard evidence that something was wrong, but we had lost each other's trust."

Taiwan   Soon after the closure in Singapore, Jollibee formed a 50/50 joint venture with a Tan family friend in Taiwan. Although sales boomed immediately after opening, low pedestrian traffic by the site eventually led to disappointing revenues. Over time, conflict arose over day-to-day management issues between the Jollibee operations staff assigned to maintain local oversight and the Taiwanese partner. "Because the business demands excellent operations, we felt we had to back our experienced Jollibee operations guy, but the partner was saying, 'I'm your partner, I've put in equity. Who do you trust?'" When the property market in Taiwan took off and store rent increased dramatically, Jollibee decided to dissolve the joint venture and pulled out of Taiwan in 1988.

Brunei   Meanwhile, another joint venture opened in August 1987 in the small sultanate of Brunei, located on the northern side of the island of Borneo. (**Exhibit 5** shows the locations of Jollibee International stores as of mid-1997.) The CEO of Shoemart, one of the Philippines' largest department stores, proposed that Jollibee form a joint-venture with a Shoemart partner in Brunei. By the end of 1993, with four successful stores in Brunei, TTC identified a key difference in the Brunei entry strategy: "In Singapore and Taiwan, the local partners ran the operation, and resented our operating control. In Brunei, the local investor was a silent partner. We sent managers from the Philippines to run the operations and the local partner supported us."

Indonesia   An opportunity to enter southeast Asia's largest market came through a family friend. In 1989, Jollibee opened its first store, in Jakarta. Initially, the operation struggled, facing competition from street vendors and cheap local fast food chains. When conflict between the local partners and the manager they had hired paralyzed the operation, in late 1994, Jollibee dissolved the partnership and sold the operation to a new franchisee. Nevertheless, the company viewed the market as promising.

TTC summed up the lessons Jollibee had learned from its first international ventures:

> McDonald's succeeded everywhere because they were very good at selecting the right partners. They can get 100 candidates and choose the best—we don't have the name to generate that choice yet.
>
> Another key factor in this business is location. If you're an unknown brand entering a new country or city, you have trouble getting access to prime locations. McDonald's name gets it the best sites. People were telling us not to go international until we had solved these two issues: location and partner.

Building an Organization   In 1993, TTC decided that Jollibee's international operations required greater structure and more resources. Because most of his management team was more interested in the fast-growing domestic side of the business, in January 1994, he decided to hire an experienced outsider as Vice President for International Operations. He selected Tony Kitchner, a native of Australia, who had spent 14 years in Pizza Hut's Asia-Pacific regional office in Hong Kong. Reporting directly to TTC, Kitchner asked for the resources and autonomy to create an International Division.

Kitchner felt that his new division needed to be separate from Jollibee's Philippine side, with a different identity and capabilities. He agreed with TTC that attracting partners with good connections in their markets should be a priority, but worried that Jollibee's simple image and basic management approach would hamper these efforts. To project an image of a world-class company, he remodeled his division's offices on the seventh floor of Jollibee's Manila headquarters and instituted the company's first dress code, requiring his managers to wear ties. As one manager explained, "We had to look and act like a multinational, not like a local chain. You can't have someone in a short-sleeved open-neck shirt asking a wealthy businessman to invest millions."

Exhibit 5 Locations of Jollibee International Division Stores, mid-1997
(locations with Jollibee outlets are underlined)

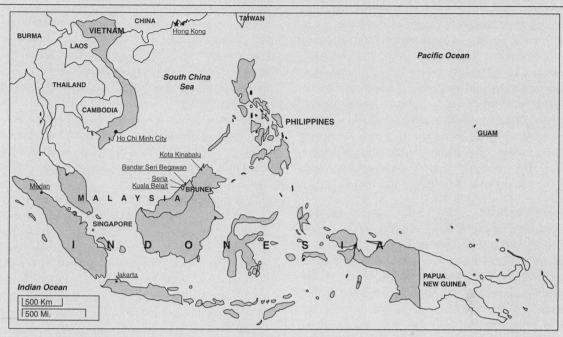

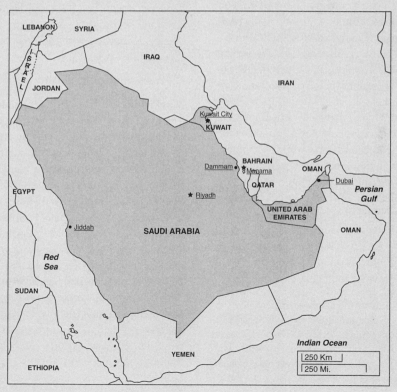

Within weeks of his arrival, Kitchner began recruiting experienced internationalists from inside and outside Jollibee. To his inherited three-person staff, he quickly added seven more professionals, including new managers of marketing, finance, and quality control and product development that he brought in from outside Jollibee. The addition of two secretaries rounded out his staff. He claimed that greater internal recruiting had been constrained by two factors—Philippine management's resistance to having their staff "poached," and employees' lack of interest in joining this upstart division.

Strategic Thrust   While endeavoring to improve the performance of existing stores in Indonesia and Brunei, Kitchner decided to increase the pace of international expansion with the objective of making Jollibee one of the world's top ten fast food brands by 2000. Kitchner's strategy rested on two main themes formulated during a planning session in the fall of 1994—"targeting expats" and "planting the flag."

The Division's new chief saw the hundreds of thousands of expatriate Filipinos working in the Middle East, Hong Kong, Guam, and other Asian territories as a latent market for Jollibee and as a good initial base to support entry. Looking for a new market to test this concept, he focused on the concentrations of Filipino guest-workers in the Middle East. After opening stores in Dubai, Kuwait, and Dammam, however, he found that this market was limited on the lower end by restrictions on poorer workers' freedom of movement, and on the upper end by wealthier expatriates' preference for hotel dining, where they could consume alcohol. Not all overseas Filipinos were potential customers, it seemed.

The other strategic criterion for choosing markets rested on Kitchner's belief in first-mover advantages in the fast food industry. Jay Visco, International's Marketing manager, explained:

> We saw that in Brunei, where we were the pioneers in fast food, we were able to set the pace and standards. Now, we have six stores there, while McDonald's has only one and KFC has three. . . . That was a key learning: even if your foreign counterparts come in later, you already have set the pace and are at top of the heap.

The International Division therefore began to "plant the Jollibee flag" in countries where competitors had little or no presence. The expectation was that by expanding the number of stores, the franchise could build brand awareness which in turn would positively impact sales. One problem with this approach proved to be its circularity: only after achieving a certain level of sales could most franchisees afford the advertising and promotion needed to build brand awareness. The other challenge was that rapid expansion led to resource constraints—especially in the availability of International Division staff to support multiple simultaneous startups.

Nonetheless, Kitchner expanded rapidly. Due to Jollibee's success in the Philippines and the Tan family's network of contacts, he found he could choose from many franchising inquiries from various countries. Some were far from Jollibee's home base—like the subsequently abandoned plan to enter Romania ("our gateway to Europe" according to one manager). In an enormous burst of energy, between November 1994 and December 1996, the company entered 8 new national markets and opened 18 new stores. The flag was being planted. (See **Exhibit 6.**)

Operational Management

Market entry   Once Jollibee had decided to enter a new market, Tony Kitchner negotiated the franchise agreement, often with an investment by the parent company, to create a partnership with the franchisee. At that point he handed responsibility for the opening to one of the division's Franchise Services Managers (FSM). These were the key contacts between the company and its franchisees, and Kitchner was rapidly building a substantial support group in Manila to provide them with the resources and expertise they needed to start up and manage an offshore franchise. (See **Exhibit 7.**)

About a month before the opening, the FSM hired a project manager, typically a native of the new market who normally would go on to manage the first store. The FSM and project manager made most of the important decisions during the startup process, with the franchisees' level of involvement varying

Exhibit 6   Jollibee International Store Openings

Location	Date Opened	
Bandar Seri Begawan, *Brunei*	August 1987	
Bandar Seri Begawan, Brunei (second store)	June 1989	
Seria, Brunei	August 1992	
Jakarta, *Indonesia*	August 1992	
Jakarta, Indonesia (second store)	March 1993	
Bandar Seri Begawan, Brunei (third store)	November 1993	International Division created
Kuala Belait, Brunei	November 1994	
Dubai, *United Arab Emirates*	April 1995	
Kuwait City, *Kuwait*	December 1995	
Dammam, *Saudi Arabia*	December 1995	
Guam	December 1995	
Jiddah, Saudi Arabia	January 1996	
Bahrain	January 1996	
Kota Kinabalu, *Malaysia*	February 1996	
Dubai (second store)	June 1996	
Riyadh, Saudi Arabia	July 1996	
Kuwait City, Kuwait (second store)	August 1996	
Kuwait City, Kuwait (third store)	August 1996	
Jiddah, Saudi Arabia (second store)	August 1996	
Hong Kong	September 1996	
Bandar Seri Begawan, Brunei (fourth store)	October 1996	
Ho Chi Minh City, *Vietnam*	October 1996	
Medan, Indonesia	December 1996	
Hong Kong (second store)	December 1996	
Dammam, Saudi Arabia	April 1997	
Hong Kong (third store)	June 1997	
Jakarta, Indonesia (third store)	July 1997	
Jakarta, Indonesia (fourth store)	September 1997	

Italics represent new market entry.

from country to country. However, one responsibility in which a franchisee was deeply involved was the key first step of selecting and securing the site of the first store, often with advice from International Division staff, who visited the country several times to direct market research. (Sometimes the franchisee had been chosen partly for access to particularly good sites.) Once the franchisee had negotiated the lease or purchase, the project manager began recruiting local store managers.

The FSM was responsible for engaging local architects to plan the store. The kitchen followed a standard Jollibee design that ensured proper production flow, but Kitchner encouraged FSMs to adapt the counter and dining areas to the demands of the space and the preferences of the franchisee. A design manager in the International Division provided support.

During the planning phase, the project manager worked with International Division finance staff to develop a budget for raw materials, labor, and other major items in the operation's cost structure. He or she also identified local suppliers, and—once International Division quality assurance staff had

Exhibit 7 International Division Organization Chart, Late 1996 (pre-restructuring)

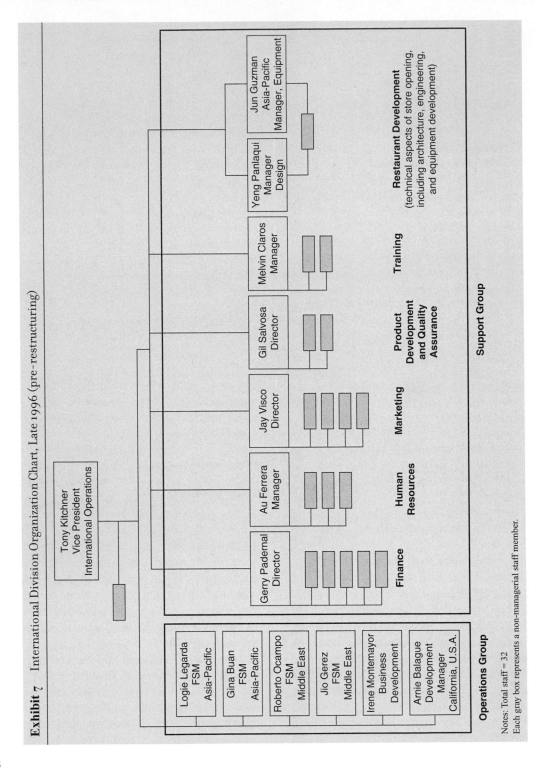

Tony Kitchner
Vice President
International Operations

Operations Group

Logie Legarda
FSM
Asia-Pacific

Gina Buan
FSM
Asia-Pacific

Roberto Ocampo
FSM
Middle East

Jio Gerez
FSM
Middle East

Irene Montemayor
Business
Development

Arnie Balague
Development
Manager
California, U.S.A.

Gerry Padernal
Director

Au Ferrera
Manager

Jay Visco
Director

Gil Salvosa
Director

Melvin Claros
Manager

Yeng Panlaqui
Manager
Design

Jun Guzman
Asia-Pacific
Manager, Equipment

Finance

Human Resources

Marketing

Product Development and Quality Assurance

Training

Restaurant Development
(technical aspects of store opening, including architecture, engineering, and equipment development)

Support Group

Notes: Total staff = 32
Each gray box represents a non-managerial staff member.

accredited their standards—negotiated prices. (Some raw materials and paper goods were sourced centrally and distributed to franchisees throughout Asia.)

Once architectural and engineering plans were approved, construction began. As it often did in other offshore activities, the International Division staff had to develop skills very different from those of their Jollibee colleagues working in the Philippines. For example, high rents in Hong Kong forced them to learn how to manage highly compacted construction schedules: construction there could take one-third to one-half the time required for similar work in the Philippines.

Under FSM leadership, the International Division staff prepared marketing plans for the opening and first year's operation. They included positioning and communications strategies and were based on their advance consumer surveys, aggregate market data, and analysis of major competitors. Division staff also trained the local marketing manager and the local store manager and assistant managers who typically spent three months in Philippine stores. (Where appropriate local managers had not been found, the store managers were sometimes drawn from Jollibee's Philippine operations.) Just before opening, the project manager hired crew members, and International Division trainers from Manila instructed them for two weeks on cooking, serving customers, and maintaining the store. (See **Exhibit 8** for a typical franchise's organization.)

Oversight and Continuing Support   After a store opened, the FSM remained its key contact with Jollibee, monitoring financial and operational performance and working to support and develop the store manager. For approximately two months after opening, FSMs required stores in their jurisdictions to fax them every day their figures for sales by product, customer traffic, and average ticket. As operations stabilized and the store manager started to see patterns in sales and operational needs, FSMs allowed stores to report the same data weekly and provide a monthly summary.

FSMs used this information not only to project and track royalty income for corporate purposes,

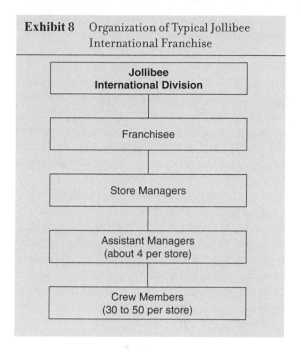

Exhibit 8   Organization of Typical Jollibee International Franchise

but also to identify ways they could support the local franchisee. When the data suggested problems, the FSM would contact the store manager, highlight the issue, and ask for an appropriate plan of action. For example, if FSM Gina Buan saw a decline in sales for two consecutive weeks, she demanded specific plans within 24 hours of her call. If managers could not come up with solutions themselves, she would coach them to help them generate answers. "My aim," she remarked with a smile, "is to turn them into clones of me—or at least teach them my expertise."

In addition to the required sales reports, many stores voluntarily reported on their costs, because they found their FSM's analysis so helpful. This open partnership fit with TTC's view of franchise relations. "We get data from franchisees more to help us provide consulting assistance than for control," he said. Ernesto Tan, TTC's brother, explained that although Jollibee's royalty was a percentage of franchisees' sales, and local operations were focused more on profits, both interests were similar: "We want sales to grow, so that our royalty grows.

But this will not happen if stores are not profitable, because our franchisees will not push to expand."

As well as support, however, the International Division was also concerned with control—especially in quality. Unannounced on-site inspections every quarter were Jollibee's primary tool. Over two days, the FSM evaluated every aspect of operations in detail, including product quality and preparation (taste, temperature, freshness, availability, and appearance), cleanliness, restaurant appearance, service speed, and friendliness. The manual for intensive checks was several inches thick. All international staff had been trained in Jollibee's quality standards and conducted less detailed "quick checks" whenever they traveled. Based on a 15-page questionnaire, a quick check took roughly two hours to complete and covered all of the areas that intensive ones did, although with less rigor and detail. Each store received an average of two quick checks per quarter.

In addition to FSMs' own rich industry experiences—Gina Buan, for example, had managed stores, districts, and countries for Jollibee and another chain—these field managers engaged the expertise of International Division functional staff. While they tried to shift responsibility gradually to the franchisee, division support staff often bore much of the responsibility long after startup. For example, the marketing staff tried to limit their franchise support role to creating initial marketing plans for new openings and reviewing new store plans. However, often they were drawn into the planning of more routine campaigns for particular stores, work they felt should be handled by the franchisee and store managers.

International vs. Domestic Practice   As operations grew, Kitchner and his staff discovered that international expansion was not quite as simple as the metaphor of "planting flags" might suggest. It sometimes felt more like struggling up an unconquered, hostile mountain. After numerous market entry battles, the international team decided that a number of elements of Jollibee's Philippine business model needed to be modified overseas. For example,

the company's experience in Indonesia led Visco to criticize the transplantation of Jollibee's "mass-based positioning":

> When Jollibee arrived in Indonesia, they assumed that the market would be similar to the Philippines. But the Indonesian masses are not willing to spend as much on fast food as the Philippine working and lower-middle class consumers, and there were lots of cheap alternatives available. We decided that we needed to reposition ourselves to target a more up-market clientele.

Kitchner and Visco also felt that Jollibee needed to present itself as "world class," not "local" or "regional." In particular, they disliked the Philippine store design—a "trellis" theme with a garden motif—which had been transferred unchanged as Jollibee exported internationally. Working with an outside architect, a five-person panel from the International Division developed three new store decors, with better lighting and higher quality furniture. After Kitchner got TTC's approval, the Division remodeled the Indonesian stores and used the designs for all subsequent openings.

International also redesigned the Jollibee logo. While retaining the bee mascot, it changed the red background to orange and added the slogan, "great burgers, great chicken." Visco pointed out that the orange background differentiated the chain's logo from those of other major brands, such as KFC, Coca-Cola, and Marlboro, which all had red-and-white logos. The slogan was added to link the Jollibee name and logo with its products in people's minds. Visco also noted that, unlike Wendy's Old Fashioned Hamburgers, Kentucky Fried Chicken, and Pizza Hut, Jollibee did not incorporate its product in its name and market tests had found that consumers outside the Philippines guessed the logo signified a toy chain or candy store.

Kitchner and his staff made numerous other changes to Jollibee's Philippine business operating model. For example, rather than preparing new advertising materials for each new promotion as they did in the Philippines, the international marketing group created a library of promotional photographs of each food product that could be assembled, in-house, into collages illustrating new promotions (e.g., a discounted price for buying a burger, fries, and soda). And purchasing changed from styrofoam to paper packaging to appeal to foreign consumers' greater environmental consciousness.

Customizing for Local Tastes While such changes provoked grumbling from many in the large domestic business who saw the upstart international group as newcomers fiddling with proven concepts, nothing triggered more controversy than the experiments with menu items. Arguing that the "flexibility" aspect of Jollibee's "Five Fs" corporate creed stood for a willingness to accommodate differences in customer tastes, managers in the International Division believed that menus should be adjusted to local preferences.

The practice had started in 1992 when a manager was dispatched from the Philippines to respond to the Indonesian franchisee's request to create a fast food version of the local favorite *nasi lema*, a mixture of rice and coconut milk. Building on this precedent, Kitchner's team created an international menu item they called the Jollimeal. This was typically a rice-based meal with a topping that could vary by country—in Hong Kong, for example, the rice was covered with hot and sour chicken, while in Vietnam it was chicken curry. Although it accounted for only 5% of international sales, Kitchner saw Jollimeals as an important way to "localize" the Jollibee image.

But the International Division expanded beyond the Jollimeal concept. On a trip to Dubai, in response to the local franchisee's request to create a salad for the menu, product development manager Gil Salvosa spent a night chopping vegetables in his hotel room to create a standard recipe. That same trip, he acquired a recipe for chicken masala from the franchisee's cook, later adapting it to fast food production methods for the Dubai store. The International Division also added idiosyncratic items to menus, such as dried fish, a Malaysian favorite. Since other menu items were seldom removed, these additions generally increased the size of menus abroad.

Although increased menu diversity almost always came at the cost of some operating efficiency (and, by implication, complicated the task of store level operating control), Kitchner was convinced that such concessions to local tastes were necessary. In Guam, for example, to accommodate extra-large local appetites, division staff added a fried egg and two strips of bacon to the Champ's standard large beef patty. And franchisees in the Middle East asked the Division's R&D staff to come up with a spicier version of Jollibee's fried chicken. Although Kentucky Fried Chicken (KFC) was captivating customers with their spicy recipe, R&D staff on the Philippine side objected strenuously. As a compromise, International developed a spicy sauce that customers could add to the standard Jollibee chicken.

Overall, the International Division's modification of menus and products caused considerable tension with the Philippine side of Jollibee. While there was no controversy about reformulating hamburgers for Muslim countries to eliminate traces of pork, for example, adding new products or changing existing ones led to major arguments. As a result, International received little cooperation from the larger Philippine research and development staff and customization remained a source of disagreement and friction.

Strained International-Domestic Relations As the International Division expanded, its relations with the Philippine-based operations seemed to deteriorate. Tensions over menu modifications reflected more serious issues that had surfaced soon after Kitchner began building his international group. Philippine staff saw International as newcomers who, despite their lack of experience in Jollibee, "discarded practices built over 16 years." On the other side, International Division staff reported that they found the Philippine organization bureaucratic and slow-moving. They felt stymied by requirements to follow certain procedures and go through proper channels to obtain assistance.

The two parts of Jollibee continued to operate largely independently, but strained relations gradually eroded any sense of cooperation and reduced already limited exchanges to a minimum. Some International Division staff felt that the Philippine side, which controlled most of Jollibee's resources, should do more to help their efforts to improve and adapt existing products and practices. Visco recalled that when he wanted assistance designing new packaging, the Philippine marketing manager took the attitude that international could fend for itself. Similarly, Salvosa wanted more cooperation on product development from Philippine R&D, but was frustrated by the lengthy discussions and approvals that seemed to be required.

However, the domestic side viewed things differently. Executive Vice President Ernesto Tan, who was in charge of Jollibee in the Philippines, recalled:

> The strains came from several things. It started when International tried to recruit people directly from the Philippine side, without consulting with their superiors. There also was some jealousy on a personal level because the people recruited were immediately promoted to the next level, with better pay and benefits.
>
> The international people also seemed to develop a superiority complex. They wanted to do everything differently, so that if their stores did well, they could take all the credit. At one point, they proposed running a store in the Philippines as a training facility, but we thought they also wanted to show us that they could do it better than us. We saw them as lavish spenders while we paid very close attention to costs. Our people were saying, "We are earning the money, and they are spending it!" There was essentially no communication to work out these problems. So we spoke to TTC, because Kitchner reported to him.

Matters grew worse throughout 1996. One of the first signs of serious trouble came during a project to redesign the Jollibee logo, which TTC initiated in mid-1995. Triggered by International's modification of the old logo, the redesign project committee had representatives from across the company. Having overseen International's redesign, Kitchner was included. During the committee's deliberations, some domestic managers felt that the International vice-president's strong opinions were obstructive, and early in 1996 Kitchner stopped attending the meetings.

During this time, TTC was growing increasingly concerned about the International Division's continuing struggles. Around November 1996, he decided that he could no longer support Kitchner's strategy of rapid expansion due to the financial problems it was creating. Many of the International stores were losing money, but the cost of supporting these widespread unprofitable activities was increasing. Despite the fact that even unprofitable stores generated franchise fees calculated as a percentage of sales, TTC was uncomfortable:

> Kitchner wanted to put up lots of stores, maximizing revenue for Jollibee. Initially, I had supported this approach, thinking we could learn from an experienced outsider, but I came to believe that was not viable in the long term. We preferred to go slower, making sure that each store was profitable so that it would generate money for the franchisee, as well as for us. In general, we believe that whoever we do business with— suppliers and especially franchisees—should make money. This creates a good, long-term relationship.

In February 1997, Kitchner left Jollibee to return to Australia. A restructuring supervised directly by TTC shrank the International Division's staff from 32 to 14, merging the finance, MIS and human resources functions with their bigger Philippine counterparts. (See **Exhibit 9.**) Jay Visco became interim head of International while TTC searched for a new Division leader.

A New International Era: 1997

In the wake of Kitchner's departure, TTC consulted intensively with Jollibee's suppliers and other contacts in fast food in the Philippines regarding a replacement. The name that kept recurring was Manolo P. ("Noli") Tingzon, one of the industry's most experienced managers. Although based in the Philippines his entire career, Tingzon had spent much of this time helping foreign chains crack the Philippine market. In 1981 he joined McDonald's as a management trainee and spent the next 10 years in frustrating combat with Jollibee. After a brief experience with a food packaging company, in 1994 he took on the challenge to launch Texas Chicken,

Exhibit 9   International Division Organization Chart, March 1997 (post-restructuring)

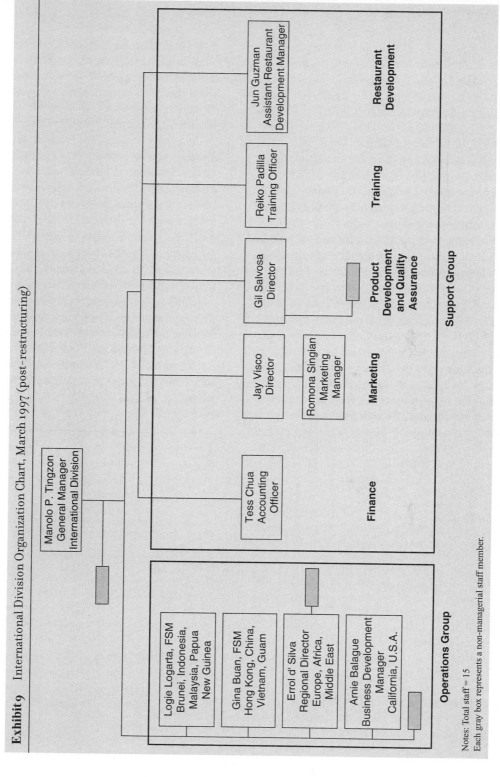

Manolo P. Tingzon
General Manager
International Division

Operations Group

Logie Logarta, FSM
Brunei, Indonesia,
Malaysia, Papua
New Guinea

Gina Buan, FSM
Hong Kong, China,
Vietnam, Guam

Errol d' Silva
Regional Director
Europe, Africa,
Middle East

Arnie Balague
Business Development
Manager
California, U.S.A.

Support Group

Tess Chua
Accounting
Officer

Finance

Jay Visco
Director

Romona Singian
Marketing
Manager

Marketing

Gil Salvosa
Director

**Product
Development
and Quality
Assurance**

Reiko Padilla
Training Officer

Training

Jun Guzman
Assistant Restaurant
Development Manager

**Restaurant
Development**

Notes: Total staff = 15
Each gray box represents a non-managerial staff member.

49

another U.S. fast food chain, in its Philippines entry. When TTC contacted him in late 1996, he was intrigued by the opportunity offered by his old nemesis and joined the company in July 1997 as general manager, International Division.

A Fresh Look at Strategy   Upon his arrival, Tingzon reviewed International's current and historical performance. (See **Exhibit 10.**) He concluded that because of the scale economies of fast food franchising, an "acceptable" return on investment in international operations would require 60 Jollibee restaurants abroad with annual sales of US$800,000 each, the approximate store level sales at McDonald's smaller Asian outlets. Feeling that Jollibee's international expansion had sometimes been driven less by business considerations than by a pride in developing overseas operations, Tingzon thought that a fresh examination of existing international strategies might reveal opportunities for improvement. As he consulted colleagues at Jollibee, however, he heard differing opinions.

Many of his own staff felt that the rapid expansion of the "plant-the-flag" approach had served Jollibee well and should be continued. For example, Visco argued that establishing a presence in each market before competitors conferred important first-mover advantages in setting customer expectations, influencing tastes and building brand. He and others felt that Jollibee's success in the Philippines and Brunei illustrated this point especially well.

Others, particularly on Jollibee's domestic side, felt the flag-planting strategy was ill-conceived, leading the company into what they saw as rash market choices such as the Middle East, where outlets continued to have difficulty attracting either expatriates or locals. For example, Ernesto Tan advised Tingzon to "focus on expanding share in a few countries while making sure each store does well." He urged Tingzon to consolidate and build on existing Jollibee markets that had either high profit potential, such as Hong Kong, or relatively mild competition, such as Malaysia and Indonesia.

With respect to the strategy of initially focusing on Filipino expatriates in new markets, Tingzon appreciated that this approach had eased Jollibee's entry into Guam and Hong Kong, but wondered whether it might trap the chain. "Might we risk boxing ourselves into a Filipino niche that prevents us from growing enough to support operations in each country?" he asked. Again opinion was divided between those favoring the expatriate-led strategy and those who felt it was time for Jollibee to shake its Philippine identity and target the mainstream market wherever it went.

Exhibit 10   International Store Sales by Country: 1996 (in U.S. dollars at contemporary exchange rates)

		1996	
		Sales	**Number of Stores**
Bahrain		262,361	1
Brunei		2,439,538	6
Guam		1,771,202	1
Hong Kong		1,142,240	2
Indonesia		854,259	3
Kuwait		864,531	3
Malaysia		391,328	1
Saudi Arabia		976,748	4
United Arab Emirates		487,438	2
Vietnam		112,578	1
Total	US$	9,302,223	24

Strategy in Action: Three Decisions   Although he eventually wanted to resolve these issues at the level of policy, Tingzon faced three immediate growth opportunities that he knew would shape the emergence of the future strategy.

Papua New Guinea: Raising the Standard   In early 1996, at the recommendation of Quality Assurance Manager Gil Salvosa, a local New Guinea entrepreneur in the poultry business approached Tony Kitchner about a Jollibee franchise. He described a country of five million people served by only one poorly managed, 3-store fast-food chain, that had recently broken ties with its Australian chicken restaurant franchise. "Port Moresby does not have a single decent place to eat," he told Kitchner. He believed Jollibee could raise the quality of service and food enough to take much of the Australian chain's market share while discouraging further entrants.

Although the original plan had been to open just one store in the foreseeable future—in the capital, Port Moresby—Tingzon was certain that the franchisee could only cover the costs of developing the market if he put in at least three or four stores soon after. But he was uncertain whether Papua New Guinea could support the 20 stores that he saw as the target critical mass for new markets. (For comparison, in the Philippines, approximately 1,200 fast food outlets competed for the business of 75 million people. GNP per capita in both countries was almost at US$2,500.)

When Tingzon explained his concerns, the would-be franchisee's response was that he would negotiate with a major petroleum retailer and try to open stores in five of their service stations around the country. Furthermore, he emphasized that he was willing to build more stores if necessary and would put up all the capital so that Jollibee would risk no equity in the venture.

Hong Kong: Expanding the Base   Also on Tingzon's plate was a proposal to expand to a fourth store in Hong Kong. The franchise, owned by Jollibee in partnership with local businessmen and managed by Tommy King, TTC's brother-in-law, opened its first store in September 1996 to instant, overwhelming success. Located near a major transit hub in the Central district, it became a gathering place for Filipino expatriates, primarily domestic workers. However, appealing to the locals had proven more difficult. While volume was high on weekends, when the Filipinos came to Central to socialize, it fell off during the week, when business was primarily from local office workers.

Although two more stores in Central had attracted many Filipinos, they both relied extensively on Chinese customers and generated sales of only about one-third of the first outlet. One problem was that, despite strenuous efforts, Jollibee had been unable to hire many local Chinese as crew members. According to one manager, Chinese customers who did not speak English well were worried that they would be embarrassed if they were not understood by the predominantly Philippine and Nepalese counter staff. Another problem was that in a city dominated by McDonald's, Jollibee's brand recognition among locals was weak. Working with Henry Shih, the subfranchisee who owned the second store, Jollibee staff were trying to help launch a thematic advertising campaign, but due to the Hong Kong operation's small size, the franchise could not inject sufficient funds.

Shih also blamed rigidity over menu offerings for Jollibee's difficulties appealing to Chinese customers. In early 1997, his Chinese managers had suggested serving tea the Hong Kong way—using tea dust (powdered tea leaves) rather than tea bags and adding evaporated milk. More than six months later, he had still not received a go-ahead. His proposal to develop a less-fatty recipe for Chicken Joy, one of Jollibee's core menu items, had met more direct resistance. "The Chinese say that if you eat lots of deep-fried food you become hot inside and will develop health problems," said Shih who believed that the domestic side had pressured the International Division to reject any experimentation with this "core" menu item.

Meanwhile, staffing problems were worsening. The four locally-recruited Chinese managers clashed with the five Filipinos imported from Tommy King's Philippine franchise, with the Chinese calling the Filipinos' discipline lax and their style arrogant, while the Filipinos saw the Chinese managers as uncommitted. By August 1997, all of the Chinese managers had resigned, leaving Jollibee with only Filipinos in store-level management positions. Shih was afraid this would further undermine Jollibee's ability to hire local crews, as Chinese preferred to work for Chinese.

Partly due to staff turnover, store managers were focused on dealing with day-to-day operations issues such as uneven product quality and had little time to design even short-term marketing strategies. King's focus on his Philippine stores slowed decision-making. And while Gina Buan, the FSM, had visited Hong Kong more often than any other markets she supervised (including for an extraordinary month-long stay), she had been unable to resolve the management problems. In June, King appointed Shih General Manager to oversee the entire Hong Kong venture.

In this context, Shih and King proposed to open a fourth store. The site in the Kowloon district was one of the busiest in Hong Kong, located at one of just two intersections of the subway and the rail line that was the only public transport from the New Territories, where much of the city's workforce resided. However, the area saw far fewer Filipinos than Central and the store would have to depend on locals. Acknowledging that the fourth store would test Jollibee's ability to appeal to Hong Kong people, Shih argued that the menu would have to be customized more radically. However, Tingzon wondered whether expansion was even viable at this time, given the Hong Kong venture's managerial problems. Even if he were to approve the store, he wondered if he should support the menu variations that might complicate quality control. On the other hand, expansion into such a busy site might enhance Jollibee's visibility and brand recognition among locals, helping increase business even without changing the menu. It was another tough call.

California: Supporting the Settlers   Soon after signing his contract, Tingzon had learned of a year-old plan to open one Jollibee store per quarter in California starting in the first quarter of 1998.

Supporting TTC's long-held belief that Jollibee could win enormous prestige and publicity by gaining a foothold in the birthplace of fast food, Kitchner had drawn up plans with a group of Manila-based businessmen as 40% partners in the venture. Once the company stores were established, they hoped to franchise in California and beyond in 1999.

Much of the confidence for this bold expansion plan came from Jollibee's success in Guam, a territory of the US. Although they initially targeted the 25% of the population of Filipino extraction, management discovered that their menu appealed to other groups of Americans based there. They also found they could adapt the labor-intensive Philippine operating methods by developing different equipment and cooking processes more in keeping with a high labor cost environment. In the words of one International Division veteran, "In Guam, we learned how to do business in the United States. After succeeding there, we felt we were ready for the mainland."

The plan called for the first store to be located in Daly City, a community with a large Filipino population but relatively low concentration of fast-food competitors in the San Francisco area. (With more than a million immigrants from the Philippines living in California, most relatively affluent, this state had one of the highest concentrations of Filipino expatriates in the world.) The menu would be transplanted from the Philippines without changes. After initially targeting Filipinos, the plan was to branch out geographically to the San Francisco and San Diego regions, and demographically to appeal to other Asian-American and, eventually, Hispanic-American consumers. The hope was that Jollibee would then expand to all consumers throughout the U.S.

Like the expansion strategies in PNG and Hong Kong, this project had momentum behind it, including visible support from Filipino-Americans, strong interest of local investors, and, not least, TTC's great interest in succeeding in McDonald's backyard. Yet Tingzon realized that he would be the one held accountable for its final success and wanted to bring an objective outsider's perspective to this plan before it became accepted wisdom. Could Jollibee hope to succeed in the world's most competitive fast-food market? Could they provide the necessary support and control to operations located 12 hours by plane and eight time zones away? And was the Filipino-to-Asian-to-Hispanic-to-mainstream entry strategy viable or did it risk boxing them into an economically unviable niche?

Looking Forward   Noli Tingzon had only been in his job a few weeks, but already it was clear that his predecessor's plan to open 1000 Jollibee stores

abroad before the turn of the century was a pipe dream. "It took McDonald's 20 years for its international operations to count for more than 50% of total sales," he said. "I'll be happy if I can do it in 10." But even this was an ambitious goal. And the decisions he made on the three entry options would have a significant impact on the strategic direction his international division took and on the organizational capabilities it needed to get there.

Case 1-3   Acer, Inc: Taiwan's Rampaging Dragon

Christopher A. Bartlett and Anthony St. George

With a sense of real excitement, Stan Shih, CEO of Acer, Inc., boarded a plane for San Francisco in early February 1995. The founder of the Taiwanese personal computer (PC) company was on his way to see the Aspire, a new home PC being developed by Acer America Corporation (AAC), Acer's North American subsidiary. Although Shih had heard that a young American team was working on a truly innovative product, featuring a unique design, voice recognition, ease-of-use, and cutting-edge multimedia capabilities, he knew little of the project until Ronald Chwang, President of AAC, had invited him to the upcoming product presentation. From Chwang's description, Shih thought that Aspire could have the potential to become a blockbuster product worldwide. But he was equally excited that

this was the first Acer product conceived, designed, and championed by a sales-and-marketing oriented regional business unit (RBU) rather than one of Acer's production-and-engineering focused strategic business units (SBUs) in Taiwan.

Somewhere in mid-flight, however, Shih's characteristic enthusiasm was tempered by his equally well-known pragmatism. Recently, AAC had been one of the company's more problematic overseas units, and had been losing money for five years. Was this the group on whom he should pin his hopes for Acer's next important growth initiative? Could such a radical new product succeed in the highly competitive American PC market? And if so, did this unit—one of the company's sales-and-marketing-oriented RBUs—have the resources and capabilities to lead the development of this important new product, and, perhaps, even its global rollout?

▌ Professor Christopher A. Bartlett and Research Associate Anthony St. George prepared this case as the basis for class discussion rather than to illustrate either effective or ineffective handling of an administrative situation. Some historical information was drawn from Robert H. Chen, "Made in Taiwan: The Story of Acer Computers," Linking Publishing Co., Taiwan, 1996, and Stan Shih, "Me-too is Not My Style," Acer Foundation, Taiwan, 1996. We would like to thank Eugene Hwang and Professor Robert H. Hayes for their help and advice.
▌ Harvard Business School Case No 9-399-010, Copyright 1998 President and Fellows of Harvard College. All rights reserved. *This case was prepared by C. Bartlett. HBS Cases are developed solely for class discussion and do not necessarily illustrate either effective or ineffective handling of administrative situation.*

▌ Birth of the Company

Originally known as Multitech, the company was founded in Taiwan in 1976 by Shih, his wife, and three friends. From the beginning, Shih served as CEO and Chairman, his wife as company accountant. With $25,000 of capital and 11 employees, Multitech's grand mission was "to promote the application of the emerging microprocessor technology." It

Exhibit 1   Selected Financials: Sales, Net Income, and Headcount, 1976–1994

	1976	1977	1978	1979	1980	1981	1982	1983	1984
Sales ($M)	0.003	0.311	0.80	0.77	3.83	7.08	18.1	28.3	51.6
Net income ($M)	N/A	N/A	N/A	N/A	N/A	N/A	N/A	1.4	0.4
Employees	11	12	18	46	104	175	306	592	1,130

grew by grasping every opportunity available—providing engineering and product design advice to local companies, importing electronic components, offering technological training courses, and publishing trade journals. "We will sell anything except our wives," joked Shih. Little did the founders realize that they were laying the foundations for one of Taiwan's great entrepreneurial success stories. (See **Exhibit 1.**)

Laying the Foundations   Because Multitech was capital constrained, the new CEO instituted a strong norm of frugality. Acting on what he described as "a poor man's philosophy," he leased just enough space for current needs (leading to 28 office relocations over the next 20 years) and, in the early years, encouraged employees to supplement their income by "moonlighting" at second jobs. Yet while Multitech paid modest salaries, it offered key employees equity, often giving them substantial ownership positions in subsidiary companies.

Frugality was one of many business principles Shih had learned while growing up in his mother's tiny store. He told employees that high-tech products, like his mother's duck eggs, had to be priced with a low margin to ensure turnover. He preached the importance of receiving cash payment quickly and avoiding the use of debt. But above all, he told them that customers came first, employees second, and shareholders third, a principle later referred to as "Acer 1-2-3."

Shih's early experience biased him against the patriarch-dominated, family-run company model that was common in Taiwan. "It tends to generate opinions which are neither balanced nor objective," he said. He delegated substantial decision-making responsibility to his employees to harness "the natural entrepreneurial spirit of the Taiwanese." With his informal manner, bias for delegation, and "hands-off" style, Shih trusted employees to act in the best interests of the firm. "We don't believe in control in the normal sense. . . . We rely on people and build our business around them," he said. It was an approach many saw as the polar opposite of the classic Chinese entrepreneur's tight personal control. As a result, the young company soon developed a reputation as a very attractive place for bright young engineers.

Shih's philosophy was reflected in his commitment to employee education and his belief that he could create a company where employees would constantly be challenged to "think and learn." In the early years, superiors were referred to as "shifu," a title usually reserved for teachers and masters of the martial arts. The development of strong teaching relationships between manager and subordinate was encouraged by making the cultivation and grooming of one's staff a primary criterion for promotion. The slogan, "Tutors conceal nothing from their pupils" emphasized the open nature of the relationship and reminded managers of their responsibility.

This created a close-knit culture, where coworkers treated each other like family, and the norm was to do whatever was necessary for the greater good of the company. But it was a very demanding "family," and as the patriarch, Stan Shih worked hard to combat complacency—what he called "the big rice bowl" sense of entitlement—by creating a constant sense of crisis and showering subordinates with ideas and challenges for their examination and follow-up. As long as the managers took responsibility for their actions—acted as responsible older sons or daughters—they had the freedom to make decisions in the intense, chaotic, yet laissez-faire organization. Besides his constant flow of new ideas, Shih's

1985	1986	1987	1988	1989	1990	1991	1992	1993	1994
94.8	165.3	331.2	530.9	688.9	949.5	985.2	1,259.8	1,883	3,220
5.1	3.9	15.3	26.5	5.8	(0.7)	(26.0)	(2.8)	85.6	205
1,632	2,188	3,639	5,072	5,540	5,711	5,216	5,352	7,200	5,825

guidance came mainly in the form of the slogans, stories, and concepts he constantly communicated.

This philosophy of delegation extended to organizational units, which, to the extent possible, Shih forced to operate as independent entities and to compete with outside companies. Extending the model externally, Shih began experimenting with joint ventures as a way of expanding sales. The first such arrangement was struck with a couple of entrepreneurs in central and southern Taiwan. While capturing the partners' knowledge of those regional markets, this approach allowed Multitech to expand its sales without the risk of hiring more people or raising more capital.

Early successes through employee ownership, delegated accountability, management frugality, and joint ventures led to what Shih called a "commoner's culture." This reflected his belief that the way to succeed against wealthy multinationals— "the nobility"—was to join forces with other "commoners"—mass-market customers, local distributors, owner-employees, small investors and supplier-partners, for example. The "poor man's" values supported this culture and guided early expansion. As early as 1978, Shih targeted smaller neighboring markets that were of lesser interest to the global giants. At first, response to Multitech's promotional letters was poor since few foreign distributors believed that a Taiwanese company could supply quality hi-tech products. Through persistence, however, Multitech established partnerships with dealers and distributors in Indonesia, Malaysia, Singapore, and Thailand. Shih described this early expansion strategy:

It is like the strategy in the Japanese game *Go*—one plays from the corner, because you need fewer

resources to occupy the corner. Without the kind of resources that Japanese and American companies had, we started in smaller markets. That gives us the advantage because these smaller markets are becoming bigger and bigger and the combination of many small markets is not small.

Expansion abroad—primarily through Asia, Middle East and Latin America—was greatly helped by a growing number of new products. In 1981, Multitech introduced its first mainstream commercial product, the "Microprofessor" computer. Following the success of this inexpensive, simple computer (little more than an elaborate scientific calculator), Shih and his colleagues began to recognize the enormous potential of the developing PC market. In 1983, Multitech began to manufacture IBM-compatible PCs— primarily as an original equipment manufacturer (OEM) for major brands but also under its own Multitech brand. In 1984 sales reached $51 million, representing a sevenfold increase on revenues three years earlier.

By 1986, the company felt it was ready to stake a claim in Europe, establishing a marketing office in Dusseldorf and a warehouse in Amsterdam. Multitech also supplemented the commission-based purchasing unit it had previously opened in the United States with a fully-fledged sales office.

Birth of the Dragon Dream   By the mid-1980s, Multitech's sales were doubling each year and confidence was high. As the company approached its tenth anniversary, Shih announced a plan for the next ten years that he described as "Dragon Dreams." With expected 1986 revenues of $150 million, employees and outsiders alike gasped at his projected sales of $5 billion by 1996. Critics soon began quoting the old Chinese aphorism, "To allay your hunger, draw a picture of a big cake." But Shih saw huge potential in overseas expansion. After only a few years of international experience, the company's overseas sales already accounted for half the total. In several Asian countries Multitech was already a major player: in Singapore, for example, it had a 25% market share by 1986. To build on this Asian base and the new offices in Europe and the United States, Shih created the slogan, "The Rampaging Dragon Goes International." To implement the initiative, he emphasized the need to identify potential overseas acquisitions, set up offshore companies, and seek foreign partners and distributors.

When the number of Acer employees exceeded 2000 during the tenth year anniversary, Shih held a "Renewal of Company Culture Seminar" at which he invited his board and vice presidents to identify and evaluate the philosophies that had guided Multitech in its first ten years. Middle-level managers were then asked to participate in the process, reviewing, debating, and eventually voting on the key principles that would carry the company forward. The outcome was a statement of four values that captured the essence of their shared beliefs: an assumption that human nature is essentially good; a commitment to maintaining a fundamental pragmatism and accountability in all business affairs; a belief in placing the customer first; and a norm of pooling effort and sharing knowledge. (A decade later, these principles could still be found on office walls worldwide.)

Finally, the anniversary year was capped by another major achievement: Acer became the second company in the world to develop and launch a 32-bit PC, even beating IBM to market. Not only did the product win Taiwan's Outstanding Product Design Award—Acer's fifth such award in seven years—it also attracted the attention of such major overseas high-tech companies as Unisys, ICL and ITT, who began negotiations for OEM supply, and even technology licensing agreements.

Rebirth as Acer: Going Public   Unfortunately, Multitech's growing visibility also led to a major problem. A U.S. company with the registered name "Multitech" informed its Taiwanese namesake that they were infringing its trademark. After ten years of building a corporate reputation and brand identity, Shih conceded he had to start over. He chose the name "Acer" because its Latin root meant "sharp" or "clever," because "Ace" implied first or highest value in cards—but mostly because it would be first in alphabetical listings. Despite advice to focus on the profitable OEM business and avoid the huge costs of creating a new global brand, Shih was determined to make Acer a globally recognized name.

Beyond branding, the success of the 32-bit PC convinced Shih that Acer would also have to maintain its rapid design, development and manufacturing capability as a continuing source of competitive advantage. Together with the planned aggressive international expansion, these new strategic imperatives—to build a brand and maintain its technological edge—created investment needs that exceeded Acer's internal financing capability. When officials from Taiwan's Securities and Exchange Commission approached Shih about a public offering, he agreed to study the possibility although he knew that many Taiwanese were suspicious of private companies that went public.

A program that allowed any employee with one year of company service to purchase shares had already diluted the Shihs' original 50% equity to about 35%, but in 1987 they felt it may be time to go further. (Shih had long preached that it was "better to lose control but make money" and that "real control came through ensuring common interest.") An internal committee asked to study the issue of going public concluded that the company would not only raise needed funds for expansion but also would provide a market for employee-owned shares. In 1988, Acer negotiated a complex multi-tiered financing involving investments by companies (such as Prudential, Chase Manhattan, China Development Corporation, and Sumitomo), additional sales to employees and, finally, a public offering. In total, Acer raised NT $2.2 billion (US $88 million). Issued at NT $27.5, the stock opened trading at NT $47 and soon rose to well over NT $100. After the

IPO, Acer employees held about 65% of the equity including the Shihs' share, which had fallen to less than 25%.

The Professionalization of Acer

While the public offering had taken care of Acer's capital shortage, Shih worried about the company's acute shortage of management caused by its rapid growth. In early 1985, when the number of employees first exceeded 1,000, he began to look outside for new recruits "to take charge and stir things up with new ideas." Over the next few years, he brought in about a dozen top-level executives and 100 middle managers. To many of the self-styled "ground troops" (the old-timers), these "paratroopers" were intruders who didn't understand Acer's culture or values but were attracted by the soaring stock. For the first time, Acer experienced significant turnover.

Paratroopers and Price Pressures Because internally-grown managers lacked international experience, one of the key tasks assigned to the "paratroopers" was to implement the company's ambitious offshore expansion plans. In late 1987, Acer acquired Counterpoint, the U.S.-based manufacturer of low-end minicomputers—a business with significantly higher margins than PCs. To support this new business entry, Acer then acquired and expanded the operations of Service Intelligence, a computer service and support organization. Subsequently, a dramatic decline in the market for minicomputers led to Acer's first new product for this segment, the Concer, being a dismal disappointment. Worse still, the substantial infrastructure installed to support it began generating huge losses.

Meanwhile, the competitive dynamics in the PC market were changing. In the closing years of the 1980s, Packard Bell made department and discount stores into major computer retailers, while Dell established its direct sales model. Both moves led to dramatic PC price reductions, and Acer's historic gross margin of about 35% began eroding rapidly, eventually dropping ten percentage points. Yet despite these problems, spirits were high in Acer,

and in mid-1989 the company shipped its one millionth PC. Flush with new capital, the company purchased properties and companies within Taiwan worth $150 million. However, Acer's drift from its "commoner's culture" worried Shih, who felt he needed help to restore discipline to the "rampaging dragon." The ambition to grow had to be reconciled with the reality of Acer's financial situation.

Enter Leonard Liu Projected 1989 results indicated that the overextended company was in a tailspin. Earnings per share were expected to fall from NT $5 to NT $1.42. The share price, which had been as high as NT $150, fell to under NT $20. (See **Exhibit 2**.) Concerned by the growing problems, Shih decided to bring in an experienced top-level executive. After more than a year of courting, in late 1989, he signed Leonard Liu, Taiwan-born, U.S.-based, senior IBM executive with a reputation for a no-nonsense professional management style. In an announcement that caught many by surprise, Shih stepped down as president of the Acer Group, handing over that day-to-day management role to Liu. In addition, Liu was named CEO and Chairman of AAC, the company's North American subsidiary.

Given Shih's desire to generate $5 billion in sales by 1996, Liu began to focus on opportunities in the networking market in the United States. Despite the continuing problems at Counterpoint and Service Intelligence, he agreed with those who argued that Acer could exploit this market by building on its position in high-end products, particularly in the advanced markets of the United States and Europe. In particular, Liu became interested in the highly regarded multi-user minicomputer specialist, Altos. Founded in 1977, this Silicon Valley networking company had 700 employees, worldwide distribution in 60 countries, and projected sales of $170 million for 1990. Although it had generated losses of $3 million and $5 million in the previous two years, Liu felt that Altos's $30 million in cash reserves and $20 million in real estate made it an attractive acquisition. In August 1990, Acer paid $94 million to acquire the respected Altos brand, its

Exhibit 2   Acer Share Price History, November 1988–January 1995

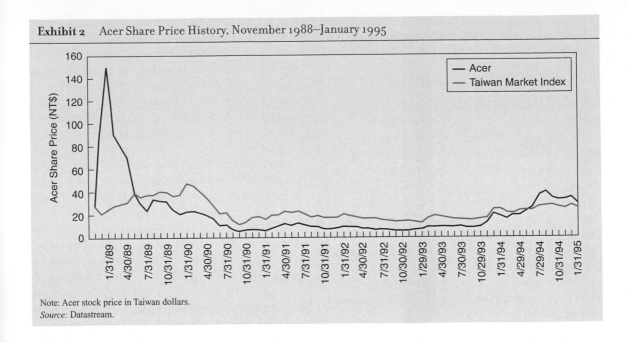

Note: Acer stock price in Taiwan dollars.
Source: Datastream.

technology and its distribution network.[1] Almost immediately, however, powerful new PCs began to offer an alternative means of multi-user networking, and, as if to remind management of the eclipse of Counterpoint's minicomputers, within a year of its purchase, Altos was losing $20 million. Through the 1990s, AAC's losses increased.

In addition to this strategic thrust, Liu also began working on Acer's established organization and management approaches. For example, under Shih's leadership, while managers had been given considerable independence to oversee their business units, they had not been given profit and loss responsibility. Furthermore, because of the family-style relationship that existed among long-time company members, inter-company transfers were often priced to do friends a favor and ensure that a

buyer did not "lose face" on a transaction. Even outsourced products were often bought at prices negotiated to make long-term suppliers look good. With no accountability for the profits of their business units, managers had little incentive to ensure quality or price, and would let the group absorb the loss. As one Acer observer noted, the company was "frugal and hard-working, but with little organizational structure or procedure-based administration."

As Shih had hoped, Liu brought to Acer some of IBM's professional management structures, practices and systems. To increase accountability at Acer, the new president reduced management layers, established standards for intra-company communications, and introduced productivity and performance evaluations. Most significantly, he introduced the Regional Business Unit/ Strategic Business Unit (RBU/ SBU) organization. Acer's long-established product divisions became SBUs responsible for the design, development, and production of PC components and system products, including OEM product sales. Simultaneously, the company's major overseas subsidiaries and marketing companies became RBUs responsible for developing distribution channels,

---

[1]Because this was a much larger deal than either Counterpoint (acquired for $1 million plus a stock swap) or Service Intelligence (a $500,000 transaction), Shih suggested the deal be structured as a joint venture to maintain the Altos managers' stake in the business. However, Liu insisted on an outright acquisition to ensure control, and Shih deferred to his new president's judgment.

providing support for dealers, distributor networks, and customers, and working to establish JVs in neighboring markets. All SBUs and RBUs had full profit responsibility. "The pressure definitely increased. I was eating fourteen rice boxes a week," said one RBU head, referring to the practice of ordering in food to allow meetings to continue through lunch and dinner.

By 1992, in addition to the four core SBUs, five RBUs had been established: Acer Sertek covering China and Taiwan; Acer Europe headquartered in the Netherlands; Acer America (AAC) responsible for North America; and Acer Computer International (ACI), headquartered in Singapore and responsible for Asia, Africa, and Latin America. (See **Exhibits 3a** and **3b**.) One of the immediate effects of the new structures and systems was to highlight the considerable losses being generated by AAC, for which Liu was directly responsible. While no longer formally engaged in operations, Shih was urging the free-spending Altos management to adopt the more frugal Acer norms, and even began

preaching his "duck egg" pricing theory. But demand was dropping precipitously and Liu decided stronger measures were required. He implemented tight controls and began layoffs.

Meanwhile, the company's overall profitability was plummeting. (See **Exhibits 4** and **5.**) A year earlier, Shih had introduced an austerity campaign that had focused on turning lights off, using both sides of paper, and traveling economy class. By 1990, however, Liu felt sterner measures were called for, particularly to deal with a payroll that had ballooned to 5,700 employees. Under an initiative dubbed Metamorphosis, managers were asked to rank employee performance, identifying the top 15% and lowest 30%. In January 1991, 300 of the Taiwan-based "thirty percenters" were terminated—Acer's first major layoffs.

The cumulative effect of declining profits, layoffs, more "paratroopers," and particularly the new iron-fisted management style challenged Acer's traditional culture. In contrast to Shih's supportive, family-oriented approach, Liu's "by-the-numbers"

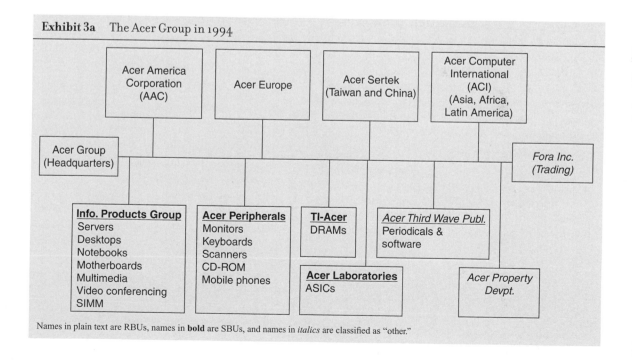

Exhibit 3a   The Acer Group in 1994

Names in plain text are RBUs, names in **bold** are SBUs, and names in *italics* are classified as "other."

Exhibit 3b   Acer's Geographical Distribution in 1994

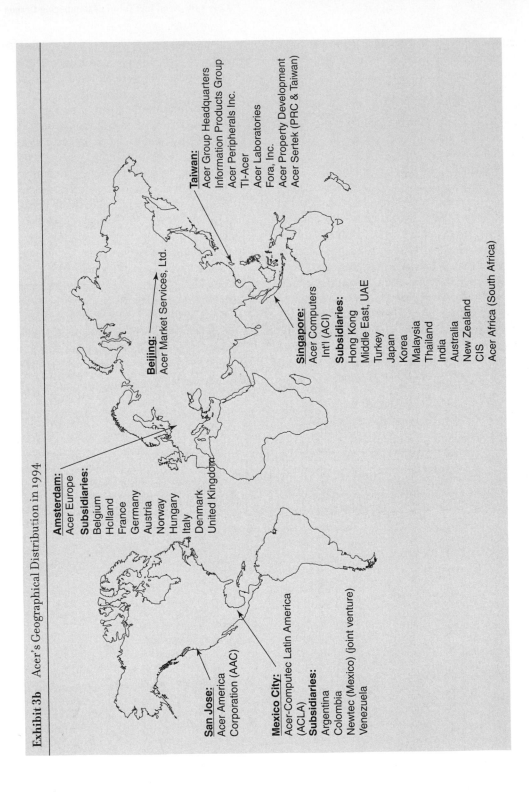

San Jose:
Acer America
Corporation (AAC)

Mexico City:
Acer-Computec Latin America
(ACLA)
Subsidiaries:
Argentina
Colombia
Newtec (Mexico) (joint venture)
Venezuela

Amsterdam:
Acer Europe
Subsidiaries:
Belgium
Holland
France
Germany
Austria
Norway
Hungary
Italy
Denmark
United Kingdom

Beijing:
Acer Market Services, Ltd.

Taiwan:
Acer Group Headquarters
Information Products Group
Acer Peripherals Inc.
TI-Acer
Acer Laboratories
Fora, Inc.
Acer Property Development
Acer Sertek (PRC & Taiwan)

Singapore:
Acer Computers
Int'l (ACI)
Subsidiaries:
Hong Kong
Middle East, UAE
Turkey
Japan
Korea
Malaysia
Thailand
India
Australia
New Zealand
CIS
Acer Africa (South Africa)

Exhibit 4 Acer Combination Income Statement, 1988–1994

Income Statement ($ millions)	1988	1989	1990	1991	1992	1993	1994
TURNOVER	530.9	688.9	949.5	985.2	1,260	1,883	3,220
Cost of sales	(389.4)	(532.7)	(716.7)	(737.7)	(1,000)	(1,498)	(2,615)
GROSS PROFIT	141.6	156.3	232.8	247.5	260	385	605
SG&A expenses	(88.2)	(118.2)	(192.2)	(217.2)	(217)	(237)	(316)
R&D and other expenses	(17.9)	(25.4)	(47.7)	(42.3)	(38)	(48)	(59)
OPERATING PROFIT/(LOSS)	35.6	12.7	(7.1)	(12.0)	5	100	230
Non-operating profit/(loss)	(8)	(6.3)	(1.5)	(15)	(4)	(11)	(19)
PROFIT BEFORE TAX	27.6	6.4	(8.6)	(27.0)	1	89	212
Tax	(1.2)	(1)	(1.2)	1	(3)	(3)	(7)
PROFIT (LOSS) AFTER TAX	26.4	5.4	(9.8)	(26.0)	(3)	86	205
Sales by Region (%)							
North America	na	31	31	31	38	44	39
Europe	na	32	28	28	22	23	17
Rest of world	na	37	41	41	40	33	44
Combination Revenue by Product (%)							
Portables	na	na	3.2	2.9	7.9	18 }	60%
Desktops and motherboards	na	na	60.9	56.3	54.9	47 }	
Minicomputers	na	na	13.9	11.3	6.6		
Peripherals and other	na	na	22	29.5	30.6	35	40%
Combination Revenue by Business (%)							
Brand	na	53	47	na	58	68	56%
OEM	na	34	22	na	18	32	36%
Trading	na	13	31	na	24	na	7%

Source: Company Annual Reports Year ending December 31.

Exhibit 5   Consolidated Balance Sheet, 1988–1994

Acer Group Balance Sheet ($ millions)	1988	1989	1990	1991	1992	1993	1994
Current Assets	277.30	448.80	579.50	600.90	700.20	925.00	1355.00
Fixed Assets							
Land, Plant, and Equipment (after depreciation)	53.10	126.90	191.10	161.50	179.60	590.00	645.00
Deferred charges and other assets	11.50	22.90	60.90	239.50	212.30	69.00	82.00
Total Assets	341.90	598.60	831.50	1001.90	1092.10	1584.00	2082.00
Total Current Liabilities	189.40	248.60	464.60	505.80	504.20	752.00	1067.00
Long-Term Liabilities	11.20	16.60	43.70	168.50	214.30	342.00	312.00
Total Liabilities	200.60	265.20	508.40	674.30	718.50	1094.00	1379.00
Stockholders Equity and Minority Interest (including new capital infusions)	141.30	333.40	323.10	327.60	373.60	490.00	703.00

Source: Company documents.

management model proved grating. There was also growing resentment of his tendency to spend lavishly on top accounting and law firms and hire people who stayed at first-class hotels, all of which seemed out of step with Acer's "commoner's culture." Soon, his credibility as a highly respected world-class executive was eroding and Acer managers began questioning his judgement and implementing his directives half-heartedly.

In January 1992, when Shih realized that Acer's 1991 results would be disastrous, he offered his resignation. The board unanimously rejected the offer, suggesting instead that he resume his old role as CEO. In May 1992, Leonard Liu resigned.

Rebuilding the Base

Shih had long regarded mistakes and their resulting losses as "tuition" for Acer employees' growth— the price paid for a system based on delegation. He saw the losses generated in the early 1990s as part of his personal learning, considering it an investment rather than a waste. ("To make Acer an organization that can think and learn," he said, "we must continue to pay tuition as long as mistakes are unintentional and long-term profits exceed the cost of the education.") As he reclaimed the CEO role, Shih saw the need to fundamentally rethink Acer's management philosophy, the organizational model that reflected it, and even the underlying basic business concept.

"Global Brand, Local Touch" Philosophy   At Acer's 1992 International Distributors Meeting in Cancun, Mexico, Shih articulated a commitment to linking the company more closely to its national markets, describing his vision as "Global Brand, Local Touch." Under this vision, he wanted Acer to evolve from a Taiwanese company with offshore sales to a truly global organization with deeply-planted local roots.

Building on the company's long tradition of taking minority positions in expansionary ventures, Shih began to offer established Acer distributors equity partnerships in the RBU they served. Four months after the Cancun meeting, Acer acquired a 19% interest in Computec, its Mexican distributor. Because of its role in building Acer into Mexico's leading PC brand, Shih invited Computec to form a joint venture company responsible for all Latin America. The result was Acer Computec Latin America (ACLA), a company subsequently floated on the Mexican stock exchange. Similarly, Acer Computers International (ACI), the company responsible for sales in Southeast Asia planned an initial public offering in Singapore in mid-1995. And in Taiwan, Shih was even considering taking some of Acer's core SBUs public.

As these events unfolded, Shih began to articulate an objective of "21 in 21," a vision of the Acer Group as a federation of 21 public companies, each with significant local ownership, by the 21st century. It was what he described as "the fourth way," a strategy of globalization radically different from the control-based European, American or Japanese models, relying instead on mutual interest and voluntary cooperation of a network of interdependent companies.

Client Server Organization Model   To reinforce the more networked approach of this new management philosophy, in 1993, Shih unveiled his client-server organization model. Using the metaphor of the network computer, he described the role of the Taiwan headquarters as a "server" that used its resources (finance, people, intellectual property) to support "client" business units, which controlled key operating activities. Under this concept of a company as a network, business units could leverage their own ideas or initiatives directly through other RBUs or SBUs without having to go through the corporate center which was there to help and mediate, not dictate or control. Shih believed that this model would allow Acer to develop speed and flexibility as competitive weapons.

While the concept was intriguing, it was a long way from Acer's operating reality. Despite the long-established philosophy of decentralization and the introduction of independent profit-responsible business units in 1992, even the largest RBUs were still viewed as little more than the sales and distribution arms of the Taiwan-based SBUs. To operationalize the client server concept, Shih began to emphasize several key principles. "Every man is lord of his

castle," became his battle cry to confirm the independence of SBU and RBU heads. Thus, when two SBUs—Acer Peripherals (API) and Information Products (IPG)—both decided to produce CD-ROM drives, Shih did not intervene to provide a top-down decision, opting instead to let the market decide. The result was that both units succeeded, eventually supplying CD-ROMs to almost 70% of PCs made in Taiwan, by far the world's leading source of OEM and branded PCs.

In another initiative, Shih began urging that at least half of all Acer products and components be sold outside the Group, hoping to ensure internal sources were competitive. Then, introducing the principle, "If it doesn't hurt, help," he spread a doctrine that favored internal suppliers. However, under the "lord of the castle" principle, if an RBU decided to improve its bottom line by sourcing externally, it could do so. But it was equally clear that the affected SBU could then find an alternative distributor for its output in that RBU's region. In practice, this mutual deterrence—referred to as the "nuclear option"—was recognized as a strategy of last resort that was rarely exercised. Despite Shih's communication of these new operating principles, the roles and relationships between SBU and RBUs remained in flux over several years as managers worked to understand the full implications of the client server model on their day-to-day responsibilities.

The Fast Food Business Concept   But the biggest challenges Shih faced on his return were strategic. Even during the two and a half years he had stepped back to allow Liu to lead Acer, competition in the PC business had escalated significantly, with the product cycle shortening to 6 to 9 months and prices dropping. As if to highlight this new reality, in May 1992, the month Liu left, Compaq announced a 30% across-the-board price reduction on its PCs. Industry expectations were for a major shakeout of marginal players. Given Acer's financial plight, some insiders urged the chairman to focus on OEM sales only, while others suggested a retreat from the difficult U.S. market. But Shih believed that crisis was a normal condition in business and that persistence usually paid off. His immediate priority was to halve Acer's five months of inventory—two months being inventory "in transit."

Under Shih's stimulus, various parts of the organization began to create new back-to-basics initiatives. For example, the System PC unit developed the "ChipUp" concept. This patented technology allowed a motherboard to accept different types of CPU chips—various versions of Intel's 386 and 486 chips, for example—drastically reducing inventory of both chips and motherboards. Another unit, Home Office Automation, developed the "2-3-1 System" to reduce the new product introduction process to two months for development, three months for selling and one month for phase-out. And about the same time, a cross-unit initiative to support the launch of Acer's home PC, Acros, developed a screwless assembly process, allowing an entire computer to be assembled by snapping together components, motherboard, power source, etc.[2] Integrating all these initiatives and several others, a team of engineers developed Uniload, a production concept that configured components in a standard parts palette for easy unpacking, assembly, and testing, facilitating the transfer of final assembly to RBU operations abroad. The underlying objective was to increase flexibility and responsiveness by moving more assembly offshore.

Uniload's ability to assemble products close to the customer led the CEO to articulate what he termed his "fast-food" business model. Under this approach, small, expensive components with fast-changing technology that represented 50%–80% of total cost (e.g., motherboards, CPUs, hard disc drives) were airshipped "hot and fresh" from SBU sources in Taiwan to RBUs in key markets, while less-volatile items (e.g., casings, monitors, power supplies) were shipped by sea. Savings in logistics, inventories and import duties on assembled products easily offset higher local labor assembly cost, which typically represented less than 1% of product cost.

As Shih began promoting his fast-food business concept, he met with some internal opposition, particularly from SBUs concerned that giving up systems assembly would mean losing power and control. To convince them that they could increase competitiveness more by focusing on component development, he created a presentation on the value added elements in the PC industry. "Assembly means you are making money from manual labor," he said. "In components and marketing you add value with your brains." To illustrate the point, Shih developed a disintegrated value added chart that was soon dubbed "Stan's Smiling Curve." (See **Exhibit 6.**)

The Turnaround   Describing his role as "to provide innovative stimulus, to recognize the new strategy which first emerges in vague ideas, then to communicate it, form consensus, and agree on action," Shih traveled constantly for two years, taking his message to the organization. Through 1993, the impact of the changes began to appear. Most dramatically, the fast-food business concept (supported by Liu's systems) caused inventory turnover to double by late 1993, reducing carrying costs, while lowering the obsolescence risk. In early 1994, the Group reported a return to profit after three years of losses.

▮ Acer America and the Aspire

After Liu's resignation in April 1992, Shih named Ronald Chwang to head AAC. With a Ph.D. in Electrical Engineering, Chwang joined Acer in 1986 in technical development. After overseeing the start-up of Acer's peripherals business, in 1991 he was given the responsibility for integrating the newly acquired Altos into AAC as president of the Acer/Altos Business Unit.

Because AAC had been losing money since 1987, Chwang's first actions as CEO focused on stemming further losses. As part of that effort, he embraced the dramatic changes being initiated in Taiwan, making AAC's Palo Alto plant the first test assembly site of the Uniload system. Under the new system, manufacture and delivery time was cut from 80 days to 45 days, reducing inventory levels by almost 45%. To support its Uniload site, AAC

▮ [2]To promote the innovative idea, Shih sponsored internal contests to see who could assemble a computer the fastest. Although his personal best time was more than a minute, experts accomplished the task in 30 seconds.

Exhibit 6   Stan Shih's PC Industry Conceptualization

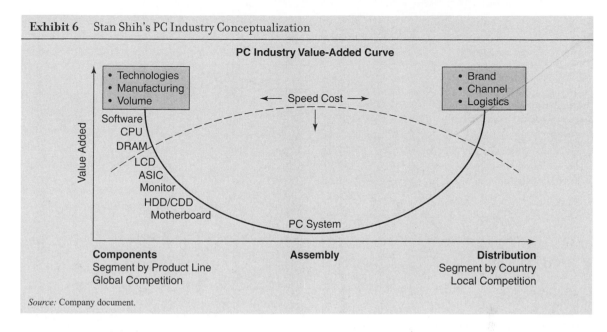

Source: Company document.

established a department of approximately 20 engineers, primarily to manage component testing, but also to adapt software design to local market needs. By 1994, AAC was breaking even. (See **Exhibit 7.**)

Birth of Aspire   Despite these improvements, AAC and other RBUs still felt that Acer's Taiwan-based SBUs were too distant to develop product configurations that would appeal to diverse consumer and competitive situations around the globe. What might sell well in Southeast Asia could be a year out-of-date in the United States, for example. However, the emerging "global brand, local touch" philosophy and the client server organization model supporting it gave them hope that they could change the situation.

In January 1994, Mike Culver was promoted to become AAC's Director of Product Management, a role that gave him responsibility for the product development mandate he felt RBUs could assume under the new client-server model. The 29-year-old engineer and recent MBA graduate had joined Acer America just 2½ years earlier as AAC's product manager for notebook computers. Recently, however, he had become aware of new opportunities in home computing.

Several factors caught Culver's attention. First, data showed an increasing trend to working at home—from 26 million people in 1993 to a projected 29 million in 1994. In addition, there was a rapidly growing interest in the Internet. And finally, developments in audio, telecom, video, and computing technologies were leading to industry rumblings of a new kind of multimedia home PC. Indeed, rumor had it that competitors like Hewlett Packard were already racing to develop new multimedia systems. Sharing this vision, Culver believed the time was right to create "the first Wintel-based PC that could compete with Apple in design, ease-of-use, and multimedia capabilities."

In October of 1994, Culver commissioned a series of focus groups to explore the emerging opportunity. In one of the groups, a consumer made a comment that had a profound impact on him. She said she wanted a computer that wouldn't remind her of work. At that moment, Culver decided that Acer's new home PC would incorporate radically new design aesthetics to differentiate it from the standard putty-colored, boxy PCs that sat in offices throughout the world.

By November, Culver was convinced of the potential for an innovative multimedia consumer PC,

Exhibit 7   AAC Selected Financials (1990–1994)

AAC Results ($millions)	1990	1991	1992	1993	1994
Revenue	161	235	304	434	858
Cost of Sales	133	190	283	399	764
Selling and marketing	27	61	25	23	55
General administration	20	16	17	19	20
Research and development	5	8	6	4	4
Operating profit/(loss)	(24)	(40)	(26)	(11)	15
Non-operating profit/(loss)	(1)	(7)	(3)	(5)	(3)
Profit/(loss) before tax	(25)	(47)	(29)	(16)	12
Tax	1	(2)	0	0	1
Net income/(loss)	(26)	(45)	(29)	(16)	11
Current assets	155	153	123	144	242
Fixed assets (net)	39	43	28	25	25
Other assets (net)	37	37	31	19	11
TOTAL Assets	231	233	182	188	278
Current liabilities	155	169	154	136	218
Long-term debt	17	15	18	58	47
Stockholder equity (including additional capita)	58	50	10	(6)	12
Total Liabilities	231	233	182	188	278

Source: Company documents.
Note: Totals may not add due to rounding.

and began assembling a project team to develop the concept. While the team believed the Acer Group probably had the engineering capability to develop the product's new technical features, they were equally sure they would have to go outside to get the kind of innovative design they envisioned. After an exhaustive review, the team selected Frog Design, a leading Silicon Valley design firm that had a reputation for "thinking outside of the box." Up to this point, Culver had been using internal resources and operating within his normal budget. The selection of Frog Design, however, meant that he had to go to Chwang for additional support. "The approval was incredibly informal," related Culver, "it literally took place in one 20 minute discussion in the hallway in late November. I told Ronald we would need $200,000 for outside consulting to create the cosmetic prototype." Chwang agreed on the spot, and the design process began.

In 1994, Acer was in ninth place in the U.S. market, with 2.4% market share, largely from sales of the Acros, Acer's initial PC product, which was an adaptation of its commercial product, the Acer Power. (See **Exhibit 8** for 1994 market shares.) Culver and Chwang were convinced they could not only substantially improve Acer's U.S. share, but also create a product with potential to take a larger share of the global multimedia desktop market estimated at 10.4 million units and growing at more than 20% annually, primarily in Europe and Asia.

Working jointly with designers from Frog Design, the project team talked to consumers, visited computer retail stores and held discussions to brainstorm the new product's form. After almost two months, Frog Design developed six foam models of possible designs. In January 1995, the Acer team chose a striking and sleek profile that bore little resemblance to the traditional PC. Market research also indicated that customers wanted a choice of colors, so the team decided that the newly named Aspire PC would be offered in charcoal grey and emerald green. (See **Exhibit 9.**)

Exhibit 8	Top Ten PC Manufacturers in the United States and Worldwide in 1994	
Company	U.S. Market Share	Worldwide Market Share
Compaq	12.6%	9.8%
Apple	11.5%	8.1%
Packard Bell	11.4%	5.1%
IBM	9.0%	8.5%
Gateway 2000	5.2%	2.3%
Dell	4.2%	2.6%
AST	3.9%	2.7%
Toshiba	3.6%	2.4%
Acer	2.4%	2.6%
Hewlett-Packard	2.4%	2.5%

Source: Los Angeles Times, January 31, 1996.

Exhibit 9   First-Generation Aspire Prototype Design

Meanwhile, the team had been working with AAC software engineers and a development group in Taiwan to incorporate the new multimedia capabilities into the computer. One significant introduction was voice-recognition software that enabled users to open, close, and save documents by voice commands. However, such enhancements also required new hardware design: to accommodate the voice-recognition feature, for example, a microphone had to be built in, and to properly exploit the machine's enhanced audio capabilities, speakers had to be integrated into the monitor. The multimedia concept also required the integration of CD-ROM capabilities, and a built-in modem and answering machine incorporating fax and telephone capabilities. This type of configuration was a radical innovation for Acer, requiring significant design and tooling changes.

In early 1995 the price differential between upper-tier PCs (IBM, for example) and lower-end products (represented by Packard Bell) was about 20%. Culver's team felt the Aspire could be positioned between these two segments offering a high quality innovative product at a less-than-premium price. They felt they could gain a strong foothold by offering a product range priced from $1,199 for the basic product to $2,999 for the highest-end system with monitor. With a September launch, they budgeted US sales of $570 million and profits of $17 million for 1995. A global rollout would be even more attractive with an expectation of breakeven within the first few months.

Stan Shih's Decisions

On his way to San Jose in February 1995, Stan Shih pondered the significance of the Aspire project. Clearly, it represented the client-server system at work: this could become the first product designed and developed by an RBU, in response to a locally sensed market opportunity. Beyond that, he had the feeling it might have the potential to become Acer's first global blockbuster product.

Despite its promise, however, Shih wanted to listen to the views of the project's critics. Some pointed out that AAC had just begun to generate profits in the first quarter of 1994, largely on the basis of its solid OEM sales, which accounted for almost 50% of revenues. Given its delicate profit position, they argued that AAC should not be staking its future on the extremely expensive and highly competitive branded consumer products business. Established competitors were likely to launch their own multimedia home PCs—perhaps even before Acer. Building a new brand in this crowded, competitive market was extremely difficult as proven by many failed attempts, including the costly failure of Taiwan-based Mitac, launched as a branded PC in the early 1990s.

Even among those who saw potential in the product, there were several who expressed concern about the project's implementation. With all the company's engineering and production expertise located in Taiwan, these critics argued that the task of coordinating the development and delivery of such an innovative new product was just too risky to leave to an inexperienced group in an RBU with limited development resources. If the project were to be approved, they suggested it be transferred back to the SBUs in Taiwan for implementation.

Finally, some wondered whether Acer's client-server organization model and "local touch" management would support Aspire becoming a viable global product. With the growing independence of the RBUs worldwide, they were concerned that each one would want to redesign the product and marketing strategy for its local market, thereby negating any potential scale economies.

As his plane touched down in San Francisco, Shih tried to resolve his feelings of excitement and concern. Should he support the Aspire project, change it, or put it on hold? And what implications would his decisions have for the new corporate model he had been building?

Case 1-4   Research in Motion: Managing Explosive Growth

Rod White and Paul W. Beamish

In early January 2008, David Yach, chief technology officer for software at Research In Motion (RIM), had just come back from Christmas break.

Ivey

Richard Ivey School of Business
The University of Western Ontario

Daina Mazutis wrote this case under the supervision of Professors Rod White and Paul W. Beamish solely to provide material for class discussion. The authors do not intend to illustrate either effective or ineffective handling of a managerial situation. The authors may have disguised certain names and other identifying information to protect confidentiality.

Ivey Management Services prohibits any form of reproduction, storage or transmittal without its written permission. This material is not covered under authorization from any reproduction rights organization. To order copies or request permission to reproduce materials, contact Ivey Publishing, Ivey Management Services, c/o Richard Ivey School of Business, The University of Western Ontario, London, Ontario, Canada, N6A 3K7; phone (519) 661-3208, fax (519) 661-3882, email cases@ivey.uwo.ca

Returning to his desk in Waterloo, Ontario, relaxed and refreshed, he noted that his executive assistant had placed the preliminary holiday sales figures for BlackBerry on top of his in-box with a note that read "Meeting with Mike tomorrow." Knowing 2007 had been an extraordinarily good year, with the number of BlackBerry units sold doubling, Dave was curious: Why did Mike Lazaridis, RIM's visionary founder and co-chief executive officer, want a meeting? A sticky note on page three flagged the issue. Mike wanted to discuss Dave's research and development (R&D) plans—even though R&D spending was up $124 million from the prior year, it had dropped significantly as a percentage of sales. In an industry driven by engineering innovations and evaluated on technological advances, this was an issue.

R&D was the core of the BlackBerry's success—but success, Dave knew, could be a double-edged sword. Although RIM's engineers were continually delivering award-winning products, explosive growth and increased competition were creating pressures on his team to develop new solutions to keep up with changes in the global smartphone marketplace. With 2007 revenue up 98 per cent from the previous year, his team of approximately 1,400 software engineers should also have doubled—but both talent and space were getting increasingly scarce. The current model of "organic" growth was not keeping pace and his engineers were feeling the strain. As the day progressed, Dave considered how he should manage this expansion on top of meeting existing commitments, thinking "How do you change the engine, while you're speeding along at 200 kilometres per hour?" As his BlackBerry notified him of dozens of other urgent messages, he wondered how to present his growth and implementation plan to Mike the next morning.

RIM: Research in Motion Ltd.

RIM was a world leader in the mobile communications market. Founded in 1984 by 23-year-old University of Waterloo student Mike Lazaridis, RIM designed, manufactured and marketed the very popular line of BlackBerry products that had recently reached 14 million subscribers worldwide and had just over $6 billion in revenue (see **Exhibits 1** and **2**). In early 2008, RIM was one of Canada's largest companies with a market capitalization of $69.4 billion.[1]

The BlackBerry wireless platform and line of handhelds could integrate e-mail, phone, Instant Messaging (IM), Short Message Service (SMS), internet, music, camera, video, radio, organizer, Global Positioning System (GPS) and a variety of other applications in one wireless solution that was dubbed "always on, always connected." These features, especially the immediate pushed message delivery, in addition to the BlackBerry's small size, long battery life, and ease of use, made the product extremely popular with busy executives who valued the safe and secure delivery of corporate mail and seamless extension of other enterprise and internet services.

In particular, organizations that relied on sensitive information, such as the U.S. government and large financial institutions, were early and loyal adopters of BlackBerry and RIM's largest customers. RIM's enterprise e-mail servers, which were attached to the customer's e-mail and IM servers behind company firewalls, encrypted and redirected e-mail and other data before forwarding the information to end consumers through wireless service providers (see **Exhibit 3**). Having been the first to market with a "push" e-mail architecture and a value proposition built on security, RIM had more than 100,000 enterprise customers and an estimated 42 per cent market share of converged devices, and significantly higher market share of data-only devices, in North America.[2]

RIM generated revenue through the "complete BlackBerry wireless solution" which included wireless devices, software and services. Revenues, however, were heavily skewed to handheld sales (73 per cent), followed by service (18 per cent), software (6 per cent) and other revenues (3 per cent). In handhelds, RIM had recently introduced the award-winning BlackBerry Pearl and BlackBerry Curve, which were a significant design departure from previous models and for the first time targeted both consumer and business professionals (see **Exhibit 4**). RIM had accumulated a wide range of product design and innovation awards, including recognition from Computerworld as one of the Top 10 Products of the Past 40 Years.[3] Analysts and technophiles eagerly awaited the next-generation BlackBerry series expected for release in 2008.

---

[1]D. George-Cosh, "Analysts cheer RIM results, hike targets," *Financial Post*, April 4, 2008, http://www.nationalpost.com/scripts/story.html?id=420318; accessed April 22, 2008.

[2]Of converged device shipments (smartphones and wireless handhelds). Canalys Smart Mobile Device Analysis service, Press Release, February 5, 2008, http://www.canalys.com/pr/2008/r2008021.htm, accessed April 2, 2008.

[3]http://www.rim.com/newsroom/news/awards/index.shtml

Exhibit 1   Blackberry Subscriber Account Base (in Millions)

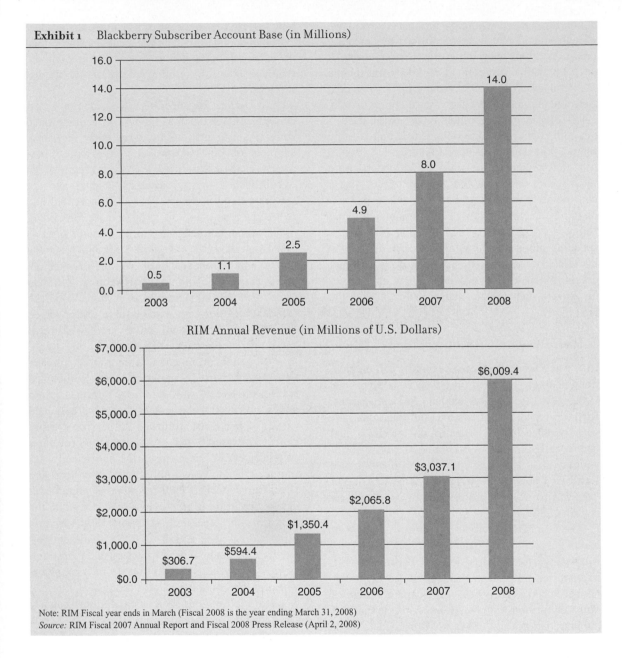

Note: RIM Fiscal year ends in March (Fiscal 2008 is the year ending March 31, 2008)
Source: RIM Fiscal 2007 Annual Report and Fiscal 2008 Press Release (April 2, 2008)

Although originally built for busy professionals, BlackBerry had made considerable headway in the consumer market and had become something of a social phenomenon. Celebrity sightings put the BlackBerry in the hands of Madonna and Paris Hilton among others. The term "crackberry," used to describe the addictive or obsessive use of the BlackBerry, was added to Webster's New Millennium dictionary. Just six months after launching Facebook for BlackBerry, downloads of the

Exhibit 2 Consolidated Statement of Operations

Research In Motion Limited Incorporated under the Laws of Ontario
(United States dollars, in thousands except per share data)

	For the year ended				
	Mar. 1, 2008	Mar. 3, 2007	Mar. 4, 2006	Feb. 26, 2005	Feb. 28, 2004
	(Projected)				
Revenue	$6,009,395	$3,037,103	$2,065,845	$1,350,447	$594,616
Cost of sales	2,928,814	1,379,301	925,598	636,310	323,365
Gross margin	3,080,581	1,657,802	1,140,247	714,137	271,251
Gross margin %	51.30%	54.60%	55.20%	52.88%	45.62%
Expenses					
Research and development	359,828	236,173	158,887	102,665	62,638
Selling, marketing & admin.	881,482	537,922	314,317	193,838	108,492
Amortization	108,112	76,879	49,951	35,941	27,911
Litigation			201,791	352,628	35,187
	1,349,422	850,974	724,946	685,072	234,228
Income from operations	1,731,159	806,828	415,301	29,065	37,023
Investment income	79,361	52,117	66,218	37,107	10,606
Income before income taxes	1,810,520	858,945	481,519	66,172	47,629
Provision for income taxes					
Current	587,845	123,553	14,515	1,425	
Deferred	−71,192	103,820	92,348	(140,865)	
	516,653	227,373	106,863	(139,440)	−4,200
Net Income	$1,293,867	$631,572	$374,656	$205,612	51,829
Earnings per share					
Basic	$2.31	$1.14	$1.98	$1.10	$0.33
Diluted	$2.26	$1.10	$1.91	$1.04	$0.31

Source: Company Annual Reports; Fiscal 2008 form; Press Release, April 2, 2008, Research in Motion reports Fourth Quarter and Year-End Results for Fiscal 2008, http://www.rim.com/news/press/2008/pr-02_04_2008-01.shtml

popular social networking software application had topped one million, indicating that younger consumers were gravitating towards the popular handhelds.[4] RIM also actively sought partnerships with software developers to bring popular games such as Guitar Hero III to the BlackBerry mobile platform,[5] suggesting a more aggressive move to the consumer, or at least prosumer,[6] smartphone space.

Wireless carriers, such as Rogers in Canada and Verizon in the United States, were RIM's primary direct customers. These carriers bundled BlackBerry handhelds and software with airtime and sold the complete solution to end users. In 2007, RIM had over 270 carrier partnerships in more than

[4]AFX International Focus, "RIM: Facebook for BlackBerry downloads top 1M," April 1, 2008, http://global.factiva.com, accessed April 1, 2008.
[5]Business Wire, "Guitar Hero III Mobile will rock your BlackBerry Smartphone," April 1, 2008, http://global.factiva.com, accessed April 1, 2008.

[6]Prosumer refers to "professional consumers," customers that use their mobile devices for both business and personal communications.

Exhibit 3   Blackberry Enterprise Solution Architecture

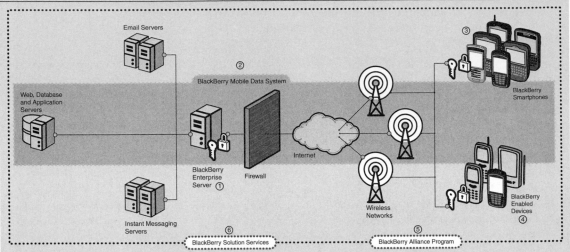

1. **BlackBerry® Enterprise Server:** Robust software that acts as the centralized link between wireless devices, wireless networks and enterprise applications. The server integrates with enterprise messaging and collaboration systems to provide mobile users with access to email, enterprise instant messaging and personal information management tools. All data between applications and BlackBerry® smartphones flows centrally through the server.

2. **BlackBerry® Mobile Data System (BlackBerry MDS):** An optimized framework for creating, deploying and managing applications for the BlackBerry Enterprise Solution. It provides essential components that enable applications beyond email to be deployed to mobile users, including developer tools, administrative services and BlackBerry® Device Software. It also uses the same proven BlackBerry push delivery model and advanced security features used for BlackBerry email.

3. **BlackBerry Smartphones:** Integrated wireless voice and data devices that are optimized to work with the BlackBerry Enterprise Solution. They provide push-based access to email and data from enterprise applications and systems in addition to web, MMS, SMS and organizer applications.

4. **BlackBerry® Connect™ Devices:** Devices available from leading manufacturers that feature BlackBerry push delivery technology and connect to the BlackBerry Enterprise Server.

5. **BlackBerry® Alliance Program:** A large community of independent software vendors, system integrators and solution providers that offer applications, services and solutions for the BlackBerry Enterprise Solution. It is designed to help organizations make the most of the BlackBerry Enterprise Solution when mobilizing their enterprises.

6. **BlackBerry Solution Services:** A group of services that include: BlackBerry® Technical Support Services, BlackBerry® Training, RIM® Professional Services and the Corporate Development Program. These tools and programs are designed to help organizations deploy, manage and extend their wireless solution.

Source: http://na.blackberry.com/eng/ataglance/solutions/architecture.jsp

Exhibit 4   The Evolution of the Blackberry Product Line (Select Models)

RIM Inter@ctive Pager 850

RIM 957

BlackBerry 6200

BlackBerry 8820

BlackBerry Pearl 8110

BlackBerry Curve 8330

Source: http://www.rim.com/newsroom/media/gallery/index.shtml and *Fortune*, "BlackBerry: Evolution of an icon," Jon Fortt, Sept. 21, 2007, accessed April 7, 2008: http://bigtech.blogs.fortune.cnn.com/blackberry-evolution-of-an-icon-photos-610/

110 countries around the world. Through the Black-Berry Connect licensing program other leading device manufacturers such as Motorola, Nokia, Samsung and Sony Ericsson could also equip their handsets with BlackBerry functionality, including push technology to automatically deliver e-mail and other data. Expanding the global reach of Black-Berry solutions was therefore a fundamental part of RIM's strategy. In 2007, 57.9 per cent of RIM's revenues were derived from the United States,

Exhibit 5   Mobile Telephone Users Worldwide (in Millions)

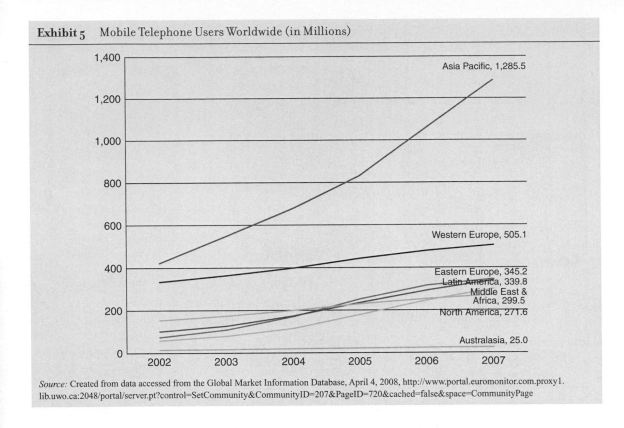

Source: Created from data accessed from the Global Market Information Database, April 4, 2008, http://www.portal.euromonitor.com.proxy1.lib.uwo.ca:2048/portal/server.pt?control=SetCommunity&CommunityID=207&PageID=720&cached=false&space=CommunityPage

7.3 per cent from Canada and the remaining 34.8 per cent from other countries. To date, RIM had offices in North America, Europe and Asia Pacific, however, it had only three wholly owned subsidiaries—two in Delaware and one in England.

The Wireless Communications Market and Smartphones

Mobile wireless communication involved the transmission of signals using radio frequencies between wireless networks and mobile access devices. Although RIM was one of the first to market with two-way messaging, recent technological developments had encouraged numerous handheld and handset vendors to go beyond traditional "telephony" and release new "converged"[7] devices including smart phones, Personal Digital Assistants (PDA), phone/PDA hybrids, converged voice and data devices and other

end-to-end integrated wireless solutions. A shift in the telecommunication industry was moving demand beyond just cellphones to smartphones—complete communications tools that marry all the functions of mobile phones with fully integrated e-mail, browser and organizer applications. In 2007, key competitors to RIM's BlackBerry line-up included the Palm Treo 700 and 750, Sony Ericsson P900 Series, the Nokia E62, Motorola Q and the Apple iPhone.

The number of wireless subscriber connections worldwide had reached three billion by the end of 2007. China led with over 524 million subscribers, followed by the United States at 254 million and India with 237 million (see **Exhibit 5**). Year over

‖ [7]"Converged" refers to the convergence of the digital wireless communication industry (cellular telephony) and information technology industries, signaled by the arrival of 2G networks which merged voice and data transmissions.

year growth in the United States, however, was only 9.5 per cent, with an already high market penetration rate (87 per cent). In contrast, China's growth was 18.3 per cent with only 39 per cent penetration. In sheer numbers, India was experiencing the fastest growth rate with a 60 per cent increase and room to grow with 21 per cent market penetration. To put that into context, in late 2007 there were almost 300,000 new wireless network subscribers in India every day.[8]

Since the launch of Apple's iPhone in June 2007, competition in the smartphone segment of the mobile telecommunications industry had intensified. The iPhone "set a new standard for usability."[9] In 2007, smartphones represented only 10 per cent of the global mobile phone market in units. However, this segment was projected to reach over 30 per cent market share within five years.[10] In the U.S. the number of smartphone users had doubled in 2007 to about 14.6 million[11] while global shipments of smartphones rose by 53 per cent worldwide hitting 118 million in 2007.[12] Some analysts saw the opportunity for smart phones as "immense," predicting that during 2008 and 2009, 500 million smart devices would be sold globally and cumulative global shipments would pass the one billion mark by 2012.[13]

Worldwide demand for wireless handhelds had been fueled by several global trends, including the commercial availability of high-speed wireless networks, the emergence of mobile access to corporate intranets, and the broad acceptance of e-mail and text messaging as reliable, secure and indispensable means of communication. Coupled with the growth of instant messaging as both a business and personal communications tool, the demand for wireless handhelds and smartphones was robust.

Competing Platforms

Symbian, a proprietary Operating System (OS) designed for mobile devices and jointly owned by Nokia, Ericsson, Sony Ericsson, Panasonic, Siemens AG and Samsung, held an estimated 65 per cent worldwide share of the converged devices, shipping 77.3 million smartphones in 2007 (up 50 per cent from 2006).[14] This was significantly ahead of Microsoft's Windows Mobile OS (12 per cent) and RIM's BlackBerry OS (11 per cent). However, in North America, RIM led with 42 per cent of shipments, ahead of Apple (27 per cent), Microsoft (21 per cent) and Palm (less than nine per cent and shrinking).[15]

However, RIM could not afford to rest on its laurels. In the North American market place, Apple had recently announced that it would be actively pursuing the business segment. Conceding that push-email and calendar integration were key to securing enterprise users, Apple licensed ActiveSync Direct Push, a Microsoft technology. Apple hoped to entice corporate users to adopt the iPhone as their converged device of choice.[16] Similarly, Microsoft, which had struggled to gain widespread acceptance for its Windows Mobile OS, had recently revamped its marketing efforts and announced an end-to-end solution for enterprise customers as well as desktop-grade web browsing for Windows Mobile enabled phones.[17] Even Google had entered

[8]GSMA 20 year factsheet, http://www.gsmworld.com/documents/20_year_factsheet.pdf, accessed April 5, 2008.

[9]P. Svensson, "Microsoft Upgrades Windows Mobile," Associated Press Newswire, April 1, 2008, http://global.factiva.com, accessed April 1, 2008.

[10]Esmerk Finish News, "Global: Survey: Nokia has best innovation strategy," March 25, 2008, http://global.factiva.com, accessed April 1, 2008.

[11]N. Gohring, "Smartphones on the rise? Thank the iPhone, panel says," *Washington Post,* March 31, 2008, http://www.washingtonpost.com/wp-dyn/content/article/2008/03/31/AR2008033102392.html, accessed online April 1, 2008.

[12]Canalys Smart Mobile Device Analysis service, Press Release, February 5, 2008, http://www.canalys.com/pr/2008/r2008021.htm, accessed April 2, 2008.

[13]Chris Ambrosio, Strategy Analytics, January 2008 and Pete Cunningham, Canalys, as quoted on www.symbian.com, accessed April 3, 2008.

[14]www.symbian.com, accessed April 3, 2008.

[15]Canalys Smart Mobile Device Analysis service, Press Release, February 5, 2008, http://www.canalys.com/pr/2008/r2008021.htm, accessed April 2, 2008.

[16]A. Hesseldahl, "How the iPhone is suiting up for work," *Business Week,* March 6, 2008, www.businessweek.com, accessed March 21, 2008.

[17]"Microsoft unveils smartphone advancements to improve ability to work and play with one phone," April 1, 2008, Press Release; and "Microsoft announces enterprise-class mobile solution," April 1, 2008, Press Release, www.microsoft.com/prespass/press/2008/apr08.

the fray with Android, an open and free mobile platform which included an OS, middleware and key applications. Rivalry, it seemed, was intensifying.

In early 2008, an analyst commented about the increasing competition in the converged device (smartphone and wireless handheld) segment:

> Apple's innovation in its mobile phone user interface has prompted a lot of design activity among competitors. We saw the beginnings of that in 2007, but we will see a lot more in 2008 as other smart phone vendors try to catch up and then get back in front. Experience shows that a vendor with only one smart phone design, no matter how good that design is, will soon struggle. A broad, continually refreshed portfolio is needed to retain and grow share in this dynamic market. This race is a marathon, but you pretty much have to sprint every lap.[18]

Another analyst observed:

> The good news for RIM? There still aren't many trusted alternatives for business-class mobile e-mail. This company could be one of the world's biggest handset manufacturers one day. It's hard for me to believe there won't be e-mail on every phone in the world. RIM is going to be a major force in this market.[19]

Given the rapid advances in the mobile communications industry, no technological platform had become the industry standard. In light of the dynamic market situation, RIM needed to ensure that its investment in R&D kept up with the pace of change in the industry.

R&D at RIM

R&D and engineering were the heart and soul of RIM. In March 2007, RIM employed just over 2,100 people with different R&D areas of expertise: radio frequency engineering, hardware and software design, audio and display improvement, antenna design, circuit board design, power management, industrial design, and manufacturing engineering, among others. R&D efforts focused on improving the functionality, security and performance of the BlackBerry solution, as well as developing new devices for current and emerging network technologies and market segments. The ratio of software to hardware developers was approximately 2:1 and about 40 per cent of the software engineers were involved in core design work while another 40 per cent were engaged in testing and documentation (the remaining 20 per cent were in management, and support functions like documentation and project management).

R&D had increased significantly both in terms of the total number of employees as well as the geographic scope of its operations. Since 2000, the R&D group had grown more than tenfold, from 200 to 2,100 people and expanded to two more locations in Canada (Ottawa and Mississauga), several in the United States (Dallas, Chicago, Atlanta, Seattle and Palo Alto) and one in England. Waterloo was still the principal location—home to a vibrant and collaborative culture of young and talented engineers.

RIM's cryptographic and software source code played a key role in the success of the company, delivering the safe and secure voice and data transmission on which the BlackBerry reputation was built. Chris Wormald, vice-president of strategic alliances, who was responsible for acquisitions, licensing and partnerships described the challenge as follows:

> At the end of the day, our source code is really among our few enduring technical assets. We have gone through extraordinary measures to protect it. Extraordinary is probably still too shallow of a word. We don't give anyone any access under any circumstances. RIM was founded on a principle of "we can do it better ourselves"—it is a philosophy that is embedded in our DNA. This vertical integration of technology makes geographic expansion and outsourcing of software development very difficult.

Intellectual property rights were thus diligently guarded through a combination of patent, copyright

---

[18]Canalys Smart Mobile Device Analysis service, Press Release, February 5, 2008, http://www.canalys.com/pr/2008/r2008021.htm, accessed April 2, 2008.

[19]Ken Dulaney of Gartner, as quoted in A. Hesseldahl, "RIM: Growth rules the day," February 22, 2008, www.businessweek.com

Exhibit 6   Competitive R&D Spend (Select Competitors)

In Millions (US$)				
Nokia	Dec. 31/04	Dec. 31/05	Dec. 31/06	Dec. 31/07
Revenue	$46,606	$54,022	$64,971	$80,672
R&D	$5,784	$6,020	$6,157	$8,229
	12.41%	11.14%	9.48%	10.20%
Microsoft	June 30/03	June 30/04	June 30/05	June 30/06	June 30/07
Revenue	$32,187	$36,835	$39,788	$44,282	$51,122
R&D	$6,595	$7,735	$6,097	$6,584	$7,121
	20.49%	21.00%	15.32%	14.87%	13.93%
Motorola	Dec. 31/03	Dec. 31/04	Dec. 31/05	Dec. 31/06	Dec. 31/07
Revenue	$23,155	$29,663	$35,310	$42,847	$36,622
R&D	$2,979	$3,316	$3,600	$4,106	$4,429
	12.87%	11.18%	10.20%	9.58%	12.09%
Apple	Sept. 27/03	Sept. 25/04	Sept. 24/05	Sept. 30/06	Sept. 29/07
Revenue	$6,207	$8,279	$13,931	$19,315	$24,006
R&D	$471	$491	$535	$712	$782
	7.59%	5.93%	3.84%	3.69%	3.26%
RIM	Feb. 28/04	Feb. 26/05	Mar. 4/06	Mar. 3/07	Proj. Mar./08
Revenue	$595	$1,350	$2,066	$3,037	$6,009
R&D	$63	$103	$159	$236	$360
	10.59%	7.63%	7.70%	7.77%	5.99%
Palm	May 31/03	May 31/04	May 31/05	May 31/06	May 31/07
Revenue	$838	$950	$1,270	$1,578	$1,561
R&D	$70	$69	$90	$136	$191
	8.35%	7.26%	7.09%	8.62%	12.24%

Note: Nokia 2007 includes Nokia Siemens.
Source: Company Annual Reports.

and contractual agreements. It was also strategically managed through a geography strategy that divided core platform development from product and technology development, with most of the core work (on the chip sets, software source code, product design) still occurring in Waterloo. However, the exponential growth in sales, competition and industry changes was placing tremendous pressures on the R&D teams at the Canadian headquarters.

Similar to other players in the telecommunications industry (see **Exhibit 6**), it was RIM's policy to maintain its R&D spending as a consistent percentage of total sales. Investment analysts often looked to this number to gauge the sustainability of revenue growth. R&D expenses were seen as a proxy for new product or service development and therefore used as a key indicator of future revenue potential. Human capital represented the bulk of R&D dollars and the organizational development team in charge of hiring at RIM was working overtime to try and keep up with the growing demand for the qualified engineers needed to deliver on both customer and investor expectations.

Exhibit 7   Employee Growth at RIM

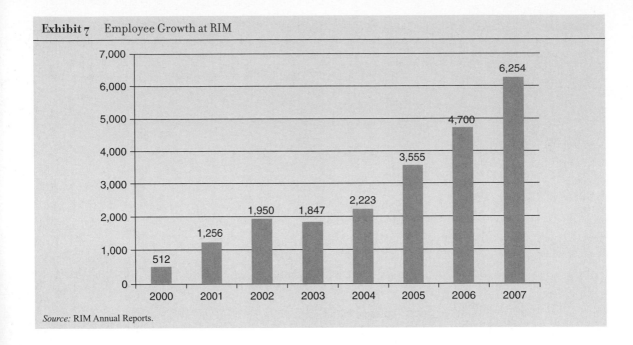

Source: RIM Annual Reports.

Organizational Development for R&D at RIM

The 2,100 R&D employees made up about 35 per cent of RIM's 6,254 employees.[20] Total headcount had also been growing in double digits over the last five years (see **Exhibit 7**). However, if investment analysts were correct and sales grew by almost 70 per cent again in 2008,[21] the large numbers involved could hinder RIM's ability to rely on its historic growth strategy: sourcing from the local talent pool, through employee referrals and new graduate recruitment, and making selective acquisitions of small technology companies. It needed to find upwards of 1,400 new software developers just to maintain the status quo in R&D. And not only did they have to find large numbers of talented individuals, they also had to figure out where they would be located and how to integrate them into RIM's culture.

The culture at RIM headquarters was seen as one of its differentiators and was a key factor in RIM's low employee turnover rate. In fact, the company had recently been recognized as one of "Canada's 10 Most Admired Corporate Cultures."[22] In describing the way things worked in the software development group at RIM, Dayna Perry, director of organizational development for R&D, commented:

> What we have here is flexibility, adaptability and the ability to work collaboratively and collegially. We haven't had a lot of process or the kind of bureaucracy that you may see in other larger organizations. . . . It is what has allowed us to be very responsive to market opportunities. It is sort of the "magic" or the "secret sauce" of how things just work and we get things done.

[20]The remaining groups included 836 in sales, marketing and business development; 1,098 in customer care and technical support; 1,158 in manufacturing; and 1,002 in administration, which included information technology, BlackBerry network operations and service development, finance, legal, facilities and corporate administration.

[21]http://finance.yahoo.com/q/ae?s=RIMM.

[22]Canada's 10 Most Admired Corporate Cultures for 2006, www.waterstonehc.com, accessed on April 5, 2008.

A software developer leading a team working on BlackBerry's many multi-lingual devices agreed, saying:

> RIM, in comparison to some of its competitors, is a nice and dynamic environment . . . RIM is a place engineers like to work. Some of our competitors treat their engineers as something unimportant. They don't participate in decisions. They are interchangeable. There is a very very strong bureaucracy . . . it's crazy. RIM is very different.

Maintaining its unique culture was a priority for RIM. Remaining centered in Waterloo nurtured this ability. But it was becoming clear that growing mostly in Waterloo was going to become increasingly difficult. Not only did RIM already employ most of the best developers in the area, it already attracted the best and brightest of the nearby University of Waterloo's engineering and computer science graduates. About 300 students came on board every semester through the company's coveted co-op program and many were asked to remain with RIM after graduation. In fact, the talent at the University of Waterloo was so widely recognized that even Bill Gates made frequent visits to the university to court the best students[23] and Google had recently opened facilities there, acknowledging that "Waterloo is an incredible pool of talent"[24] and that it was ready to start hiring the best and the brightest "as quickly as possible."[25]

Attracting outside talent to Waterloo was difficult given the competitive nature of the global software development industry. Most of the big players in the smartphone space were also ramping up. For example, Sony Ericsson had posted 230 design and engineering jobs in Sweden, China and the United States. Nokia was looking for 375 R&D employees in Finland, the United States, India and Germany, among other development sites. In California's Silicon Valley, Apple and Google had scooped up many of the top mobile browser developers in a technology cluster famous for its exaggerated employee benefits and unbeatable climate. Motorola could be the exception to the rule, having announced layoffs of engineers. Although Waterloo, Ontario had recently been named ICF's "Intelligent Community of the Year," the city of 115,000 people[26] might not be perceived by some candidates to be as attractive as other high tech centers which were more cosmopolitan, for example: Silicon Valley, or previous winners of the ICF, Taipei (2006), Mitaka (2005) or Glasgow (2004).[27]

Compounding the problem was a shortage of physical space at RIM's Waterloo campus that was a running joke around headquarters. Even company founder Mike Lazaridis had to laugh about it—responding to a reporter's question about his most embarrassing moment, Lazaridis replied: "Scraping my Aston Martin in RIM's driveway. I was leaving a space and a car came from nowhere. The scratches have been fixed, but not the too-busy parking lot. It's a hazard of a growing company."[28]

On top of it all, RIM was looking to hire a very particular mix of engineers. Although new graduates were essential, to be ahead of the game a good proportion of the incoming employees was going to have to be senior hires. RIM needed people who could fit with the culture and hit the ground running. Dayna noted: "We just don't have the luxury of time to grow all our own talent. We do that in parallel and do a lot of internal promotion, but that is an investment you make in the future, it is not going to help you solve your problem today." And it wasn't just a question of the number of engineers.

---

[23]D. Friend, "Microsoft hunting IT grads," *London Free Press,* March 22, 2008.

[24]"Google expands Waterloo base," http://atuw.ca/feature-google-expands-waterloo-base/, accessed April 11, 2008.

[25]A. Petroff, "A Recruiter's Waterloo?" http://www.financialpost.com/trading_desk/technology/story.html?id=389305, accessed April 11, 2008.

[26]The greater Kitchener-Waterloo area had approximately 450,000 inhabitants.

[27]Intelligent Community Forum, 2007 Intelligent Community of the Year Awards, Press release May 18, 2007, http://www.intelligentcommunity.org/displaycommon.cfm?an=1&subarticlenbr=221, accessed April 5, 2008.

[28]J. Shillingford, "A life run by BlackBerry," *Financial Times,* March 19, 2008, http://global.factiva.com, accessed on April 1, 2008.

In software, breakthrough innovations often came from small teams led by a visionary. Many at RIM believed that "software is as much about art as it is about engineering." And in the dynamic wireless communications market, exceptional software developers were scarce.

Managing Explosive Growth

The approach to growth used by RIM in the past would not deliver the scale and scope of R&D resources required to maintain its technical superiority. RIM had several options.

Do What We Do Now, Only More of It   RIM had been very successful in its local recruiting strategy as well as nation-wide campus recruitment drives. It relied heavily on the personal and professional networks of existing employees as an ear-on-the-ground approach to finding new talent. One option was to expand co-op programs to other universities as well as increase the frequency and intensity of its new graduate recruitment efforts. Microsoft's intern program, for example, included subsidized housing and transportation (car rental or bike purchase plan), paid travel to Redmond, health club memberships and even subsidized housecleaning![29]

Likewise, RIM could follow Microsoft's lead and form a global scouting group dedicated to finding the best talent worldwide and bringing them into RIM. Canada ranked as one of the best countries in the world to live in terms of life expectancy, literacy, education and other standards of living.[30] These and other benefits could attract young developers particularly from emerging markets. As well, the stronger dollar made Canada more attractive.

Similar to other players in the industry (e.g., Apple, Motorola, Sony Ericsson, Nokia), RIM posted many of its job openings online and potential employees searched and applied for the positions best suited for their skills and interests. However, with over 800 worldwide job postings, finding the right job was often a daunting task. RIM also had no formal way to manage qualified candidates that may have simply applied to the wrong team and hence good leads were potentially lost. Some competitors allowed candidates to build an open application (similar to Monster or Workopolis) that could then be viewed by anyone in the organization looking for talent. Revamping the careers website and being more creative in the way in which they structured recruiting was being considered.

Some competitors had also formalized hiring and the onboarding processes of computer scientists by hiring in "waves." Rather than posting individual job openings, Symbian, for example, solicited resumes once a year, which were then reviewed, and successful candidates invited to the London, U.K.-based head office to attend one of nine Assessment Days. If the attendees passed a series of tests and interviews, they were then inducted into the company during a formal "bootcamp" training session that lasted five weeks.[31] Symbian had also set up extensive collaborations with 44 universities in 17 countries including China, Russia and India as well as Ethiopia, Kuwait, Lebanon, Thailand and the United States. Dubbed The Symbian Academy, this network allowed partners and licensees to post jobs for Symbian Academy students and for professors to collaborate on the research and development of innovative applications such as pollution monitors on GPS-enabled Symbian smartphones.[32] Although RIM enjoyed an excellent relationship with the University of Waterloo, it did not currently have a recruiting strategy of this scope.

Grow and Expand Existing Geographies   RIM had established R&D operations beyond Waterloo, in Ottawa, Mississauga, Dallas and Chicago over the last five years. It was also expanding the number of product and technology development facilities in locations such as Fort Lauderdale by recruiting through general job fairs. This strategy, however, had to be balanced with a number of trade-offs. First, RIM wanted to ensure that its geographic

[29]http://www.microsoft.com/college/ip_overview.mspx.

[30]United Nations Human Development Index 2007/2008.

[31]http://www.symbian.com/about/careers/graduate%20program/index.html, accessed April 3, 2008.

[32]www.symbian.com, accessed April 3, 2008.

expansion was not haphazard, but rather strategically executed. Second, the cost of talent in various locations had to be considered. Software engineers in Palo Alto, for example, commanded much higher wages than in Waterloo and the competition there was even more intense, with high turnover costs incurred when employees were wooed away by the many other high tech companies in the area.

There was also some internal resistance to expanding R&D to locations outside of Waterloo. Although there was a growing realization that RIM could no longer continue to grow locally, one senior executive commented:

> There are people here, even leaders and senior people, who have said: "What? Products being built elsewhere? No! We can't do that! Then we won't have any control!" So some of it is a cultural shift and a mind shift for the people that have been here and it is hard for them to let go and to be part of a really big company. And RIM is getting to be a big company now. And for some people, from an organizational culture perspective, it just doesn't resonate well with them.

This sentiment was not uncommon among software-centric organizations. Despite some geographic expansion, Microsoft, for example, had recently recommitted to its Redmond, Washington campus, spending over $1 billion on new and upgraded facilities there with room to house an additional 12,000 employees.[33] Google was also strongly committed to maintaining its Mountain View, California headquarters, with only a few satellite offices. Its unique company culture, built on attracting and keeping the best talent in a young and fun environment was part of Google's incredible success story, and helped it achieve the status of the number one company to work for according to Fortune Magazine.[34] Other large software companies such as Oracle and

Apple also kept their software developers in one location to foster innovation. In some ways, RIM was already more geographically distributed than many larger software organizations.

Although establishing a geographic expansion plan posed difficulties, RIM had nevertheless laid out several criteria for selecting new locations for product and technology development sites. First, the area had to already have a pool of talent that housed a mature skill set; the city or region had to have an existing base of software or hardware companies, thus ensuring that a critical mass of highly skilled employees was available. RIM's strategic expansion into Ottawa, for example, was influenced by the availability of talented software engineers in the area in the wake of Nortel's massive layoffs.[35] Lastly, the city or region had to have universities with strong technical programs. This allowed RIM to expand on its successful co-op programs and graduate recruitment initiatives. Once a satellite development site was set up, however, there was still the issue of how to transfer RIM's young and dynamic corporate culture to these locations.

Increase Acquisitions   RIM had success in bringing people on board through acquisition. Several years earlier, RIM had acquired Slangsoft, a high tech start-up in Israel that was developing code which allowed for the ability to display and input Chinese characters—key to tailoring BlackBerry for Asian and other foreign markets. As part of the acquisition, RIM worked with Immigration Canada to relocate 11 of the engineers to Waterloo, 10 of whom were still with RIM more than six years later. Growth by acquisition was a common practice in the high tech and telecommunications sectors. Google had made its initial move to Waterloo in 2006, for example, through the acquisition of a small wireless software company, subsequently discontinuing the company's web browser product,

---

[33]B. Romano, "Microsoft campus expands, transforms, inside out," *The Seattle Times,* November 23, 2007, http://seattletimes.nwsource.com/cgi-bin/PrintStory.pl?document_id=2004007121&zsection_id=2003750725&slug=microsoft11&date=20071111, accessed April 22, 2008.

[34]http://money.cnn.com/magazines/fortune/bestcompanies/2007/snapshots/1.html, accessed April 22, 2008.

[35]Estimated at over 15,000 total jobs in the last eight years; B. Hill, "Nortel to keep Ottawa as main R&D centre," April 4, 2008, *The Montreal Gazette,* http://www.canada.com/montrealgazette/news/business/story.html?id=24aa8d53-154a-4d88-aa9d-593ce9794e10, accessed April 11, 2008.

making it a purchase of talent and intellectual property.[36] Other companies had also made strategic acquisitions of technology. In 2002, Apple, for example, purchased EMagic, a small German company whose software was then used in the development of the popular Mac program Garage Band.[37] In larger and more public acquisitions, Nokia and Motorola had both recently acquired software companies in the hopes of gaining faster access to the growing smartphone market. In 2006, Nokia purchased Intellisync Corporation, a wireless messaging and mobile-software developer for $430 million, creating Nokia's "business mobility solutions" group.[38] Also in 2006, Motorola purchased Good Technology for a rumored $500 million and released Good 5.0, allowing for secure access to corporate intranets so enterprise users could download, edit and send documents remotely.[39]

Given the depressed economic climate in the United States in early 2008, many smaller firms and technology start-ups were struggling financially as were some larger competitors. There were persistent rumors that Palm, for example, was in severe financial trouble.[40] Further, growth by acquisition could also allow for the tactical expansion in other strategic markets.

The European mobile telecommunications market, in particular, was highly "nationalistic," with end users favoring home grown companies over foreign solutions. Establishing a presence there through acquisition could buy RIM goodwill and serve as a portal to this lucrative market. The economic downturn in the United States and recent competitor plant closures in Europe presented RIM with the potential for opportunistic acquisitions, either of technology or of software engineering talent.

Go Global   In early 2008, most of the R&D was still done in Waterloo, with some core work also being done in Ottawa and product and technology sites throughout the United States and in the United Kingdom. RIM was exploring a broader global expansion. It already had customer service operations in Singapore and sales and marketing representative offices in France, Germany, Italy, Spain, China, Australia, Hong Kong and Japan. Yet it had stopped short of establishing core research and development sites outside of Canada. Nonetheless, despite a strong desire to keep R&D close to home, RIM estimated that of all the new hires in 2008, likely half would have to be outside of Canada. In addition to the United States, it was looking to Europe, the Middle East and Africa (EMEA) and Eastern Europe. The same selection criteria of a mature skill set and strong technological universities applied to choosing R&D sites outside North America.

Some of RIM's key competitors had a long history of global expansion of their R&D activities. Symbian, for example, opened an R&D center in Beijing in August 2007, already having three others in the United Kingdom and India.[41] Motorola, had been present in China since 1993 when it established its first R&D center there as part of its Global Software Group (GSG). It had since set up R&D activities in Beijing, Tianjin, Shanghai, Nanjing, Chengdu and Hangzhou, investing an estimated US$800 million and employing more than 3,000 R&D staff in China. In 2007, Motorola added R&D sites in Vietnam and South Korea[42] and announced it would open an additional R&D complex in Wangjing, China, with another 3,000 employees.[43]

▌[36]M. Evans, "Waterloo gets Googled," January 6, 2006, http://www.financialpost.com/story.html?id=c4f6f084-d72f-43ea-8a82-affe38df3830&k=58579, accessed April 11, 2008.

▌[37]A. Hesseldahl, "What to do with Apple's cash," *Business Week,* March 1, 2007, http://www.businessweek.com/technology/content/mar2007/tc20070301_402290.htm, accessed April 11, 2008.

▌[38]TelecomWeb News Digest, "Nokia completes Intellisync purchase," February 10, 2006, http://global.factiva.com, accessed April 11, 2008.

▌[39]RCR Wireless News, "Motorola set to leverage Good in competitive e-mail market," June 25, 2007, http://global.factiva.com, accessed April 11, 2008.

▌[40]S. Weinberg, "Palm acquisition not considered threat to RIM," Dow Jones Newswire, http://global.factiva.com, accessed April 11, 2008.

▌[41]Business Monitor International, Asia Pacific Telecommunications Insight, April 2008, Issue 24.

▌[42]Business Monitor International, Asia Pacific Telecommunications Insight, January 2008, Issue 21.

▌[43]Press Release, "Twenty years' commitment ensures a more successful future," November 8, 2007, http://www.motorola.com/media center/news/detail.jsp?globalObjectId=8923_8852_23&page=archive.

China in particular was beginning to gain world-wide recognition as a center for innovation. The number of patent applications was doubling every two years and the R&D to GDP ratio had also doubled in the last decade. In addition to Motorola, Nokia had set up a number of research bases in China.[44] In 2005, Nokia had five R&D units there, employing more than 600 people; an estimated 40 per cent of its global Mobile Phones Business Group handsets were designed and developed in the Beijing Product Creation Center.[45] The company had also recently announced a long-term joint research program with Tsinghua University in Beijing that would see 20 Nokia researchers working alongside 30 professors and associates and up to 50 students.[46] Globally, Nokia Research Centers (NRC) described its R&D strategy as:

> NRC has a two-fold approach to achieving its mandate of leading Nokia into the future. The work for core technology breakthroughs supporting Nokia's existing businesses takes place in the Core Technology Centers, the CTCs. More visionary, exploratory systems research that goes well beyond any current business model is conducted at the many System Research Centers, the SRCs.[47]

Nokia's core technology centers were in Finland, with the SRCs in China, Germany, the United Kingdom, United States, Finland and Japan. The company employed 112,262 people, of which 30,415, or 27 per cent, were in R&D.[48] The Motorola Global Software Group (GSG) was more decentralized. In addition to China it had R&D centers in Australia, Singapore, Mexico, Argentina, the United Kingdom, Poland, Russia, Italy, Canada and India, among others and employed approximately 27,000 R&D employees worldwide.

The Motorola GSG in India had nearly 3,500 engineers and was responsible for designing 40 per cent of the software used in Motorola phones worldwide, including the MOTORAZR and MOTOQ. However, Motorola was not noted for having world-class smartphone software. The GSG structure was speculated to have contributed to Motorola's inability to deliver a successful follow-up product to the RAZR as well as to have precipitated the company's recent financial downturn.[49]

Nonetheless, partnering with major research institutes to source top talent appeared to be a fairly common strategy. Motorola India collaborated with six of the seven Indian Institutes of Technology (IIT), as well as the Indian Institute of Science (IISC) and the Indian Institute of Information Technology (IIIT).[50] Other technology firms were also partnering with emerging market governmental and educational institutions to secure a foothold in future markets. Cisco Systems, for example, a leading manufacturer of network equipment, had recently announced a US$16 billion expansion plan into China, including investments in manufacturing, venture capital and education. Working with China's Ministry of Education, Cisco had established 200 "Networking Academies" in 70 cities in China and had trained more than 90,000 students.[51]

These types of collaborations and international research consortiums, however, raised not only logistical but also legal issues. Source code loss, software piracy and product imitations were more common in developing countries where IP protection laws (or enforcement) lagged the United States or Canada, leading to both explicit and tacit knowledge "leakage." For example, despite its strong commitment to China, Nokia was recently forced to file suit against two Beijing firms for manufacturing and selling mobile phones that were a direct copy of

[44]Business Monitor International, Asia Pacific Telecommunications Insight, November 2007, Issue 19.
[45]Press Release, May 21, 2004, "Nokia Expands R&D in China," http://press.nokia.com/PR/200405/946603_5.html.
[46]Press Release, May 28, 2007, "Nokia and Tsinghua University announce new research framework," http://www.nokia.com/A4136001?newsid=1129236.
[47]http://research.nokia.com/centers/index.html.
[48]Nokia annual report 2007.

[49]"What's on Motorola's agenda?" *Business Week,* January 9, 2008, http://www.businessweek.com/innovate/content/jan2008/id2008014_304911_page_2.htm, accessed April 16, 2008.
[50]Motorola 2007 10-K and http://www.motorola.com/mot/doc/6/6294_MotDoc.pdf
[51]Business Monitor International, Asia Pacific Telecommunications Insight, January 2008, Issue 21.

its proprietary and legally protected industrial designs.[52] Other large high tech companies such as Cisco and Microsoft had also suffered source code breaches. In late 2006, China Unicom, the state-run telecommunications company, had launched its own wireless e-mail service which it boldly named the Redberry, announcing that their Redberry brand not only continued the already familiar "BlackBerry" image and name, it also fully reflected the symbolic meaning of China Unicom's new red corporate logo.[53] For much of East Asia, reverse engineering and copying foreign products were important sources of learning, helping to transition these markets from imitators of technology to innovators and competitive threats.[54]

Wormald described the difficulties with emerging market dynamics as follows:

> I was just talking to a Fortune 500 CEO the other day who is closing up shop in India. This company had a 45 per cent employee turnover rate. They just walk down the street and go work for his competitor and he was tired of his source code just walking out the door.

For RIM, going global was therefore problematic on a number of fronts, most notably because the BlackBerry source code had to be protected. In addition, expanding to emerging markets was also complicated by restrictions regarding cryptographic software. Most governments, including those of Canada and the United States, along with Russia and China, regulated the import and export of encryption products due to national security issues. Encryption was seen as a "dual-use technology" which could have both commercial and military value and was thus carefully monitored. The U.S. government would not purchase any product that had not passed the "Federal Information Processing Standard" (FIPS) certification tests. This would preclude any product that had encrypted data in China because "if you encrypt data in China, you have to provide the Chinese government with the ability to access the keys."[55]

India had also recently notified RIM that it planned to eavesdrop on BlackBerry users, claiming that terrorists may be hiding behind the encrypted messages to avoid detection.[56]

Even if these hurdles could be overcome, going global also brought with it additional challenges of organizational design, communication, and integration between head office and other geographically dispersed locations. Some competitors had chosen to expand globally by product line, while others had outsourced less sensitive functions such as testing and documentation. Eastern European countries such as Poland and Hungary, for example, were emerging as strong contenders for quality assurance testing. The lower cost of labor in developing and transitional economies, however, was showing signs of inflationary pressures in some locales and any planned savings might be somewhat offset by the increased monitoring, coordination and integration costs. Furthermore, RIM was not set up to manage a multi-country research consortium and the mindset in Waterloo was still very much such that core engineers needed to be seen to be perceived as valuable. On the other hand, the potential could not be ignored. In China, where the penetration rate was only 38 per cent, the Symbian OS system used in Nokia, Samsung, Sony Ericsson and LG smartphones enjoyed a 68.7 per cent share, and iPhone sales had reached 400,000 "unlocked" units.[57] In India, where the penetration rate stood at 21 per cent, Virgin Mobile had recently struck a brand franchise agreement with Tata Teleservices,

[52]Shanghai Daily, "Nokia files suit over alleged copy of model," June 29, 2006, http://global.factiva.com, accessed April 16, 2008.

[53]Hesseldahl, A. "BlackBerry vs. Redberry in China," September 25, 2006, *Business Week* http://www.businessweek.com/technology/content/apr2006/tc20060413_266291.htm?chan=search, accessed April 16, 2008.

[54]United Nations World Investment Report 2005, Transnational Corporations and the Internationalization of R&D, New York and Geneva, 2005, p. 165.

[55]E. Messmer, "Encryption Restrictions" and "Federal encryption purchasing requirements," *Network World,* March 15, 2004, http://www.networkworld.com/careers/2004/0315man.html?page=1; accessed April 22, 2008.

[56]N. Lakshman, "India wants to eavesdrop on BlackBerrys," *Business Week,* April 1, 2008, http://global.factiva.com, accessed April 7, 2008.

[57]Business Monitor International, Asia Pacific Telecommunications Insight, April 2008, Issue 24.

announcing plans to gain at least 50 million young subscribers to its mobile services, generating estimated revenues of US$350 billion.[58] The sheer number of potential new users was overwhelming.

Conclusion

Looking at the holiday sales numbers and the projected growth for 2008, Yach took a minute to think about the path he was on. He knew that first quarter revenue projections alone were estimated at $2.2 billion to $2.3 billion and that RIM was expecting to add another 2.2 million BlackBerry subscribers by the end of May 2008.[59] At that rate, analysts projected that 2008 would bring at least another 70 per cent growth in sales.[60] Furthermore, Mike Lazaridis had recently said in an interview:

> If you really want to build something sustainable and innovative you have to invest in R&D. If you build the right culture and invest in the right facilities and you encourage and motivate and inspire both young and seasoned people and put them all in the right environment—then it really performs for you. It's what I call sustainable innovation. And it's very different from the idea that you come up with something

and then maximize value by reducing its costs. But building a sustainable innovation cycle requires an enormous investment in R&D. You have to understand all the technologies involved.[61]

Yach knew that his software developers were key to RIM's continued success; he was committed to delivering on the expectations for continued and sustainable growth in 2008 and beyond. Although he wanted to keep growing organically, sourcing talent locally and bringing his engineers into the cultural fold of RIM in Waterloo, he suspected this era was ending. In light of the unprecedented and exponential growth of the last year, coupled with the increasing competition and untapped global opportunities, he needed a plan.

Leaving the office after a hectic and frenetic first day back, Yach thought to himself—"How can I plan for this growth when it is just one of 10 burning issues on my agenda? We can't take a time-out to decide how to execute the growth." Grabbing the sales numbers to prepare for tomorrow's meeting, Yach knew he had the evening to consider the way ahead. The vacation was definitely over.

---

[58]Business Monitor International, Asia Pacific Telecommunications Insight, April 2008, Issue 24.

[59]Press Release, April 2, 2008: http://www.rim.com/news/press/2008/pr-02_04_2008-01.shtml.

[60]http://finance.yahoo.com/q/ae?s=RIMM

[61]A. Hesseldahl, "BlackBerry: Innovation Behind the Icon," *Business Week,* April 4, 2008, http://www.businessweek.com/innovate/content/apr2008/id2008044_416784.htm?chan=search, accessed April 6, 2008.

Reading 1-1   The Tortuous Evolution of the Multinational Corporation

Howard V. Perlmutter

Four senior executives of the world's largest firms with extensive holdings outside the home country speak:

Company A: "We are a multinational firm. We distribute our products in about 100 countries. We manufacture in over 17 countries and do research and development in three countries. We look at all new investment projects—both domestic and overseas—using exactly the same criteria."

Company B: "We are a multinational firm. Only 1% of the personnel in our affiliate companies are non-nationals. Most of these are U.S. executives on temporary assignments. In all major markets, the affiliate's managing director is of the local nationality."

Company C: "We are a multinational firm. Our product division executives have worldwide profit responsibility. As our organizational chart shows, the United States is just one region on a par with Europe, Latin America, Africa, etc., in each product division."

Company D (non-American): "We are a multinational firm. We have at least 18 nationalities represented at our headquarters. Most senior executives speak at least two languages. About 30% of our staff at headquarters are foreigners."

While a claim to multinationality based on their years of experience and the significant proportion of sales generated overseas is justified in each of these four companies, a more penetrating analysis changes the image.

The executive from Company A tells us that most of the key posts in Company A's subsidiaries are held by home-country nationals. Whenever replacements for these men are sought, it is the practice, if not the policy, to "look next to you at the head office" and "pick someone (usually a home-country national) you know and trust."

The executive from Company B does not hide the fact that there are very few non-Americans in the key posts at headquarters. The few who are there are "so Americanized" that their foreign nationality literally has no meaning. His explanation for this paucity of non-Americans seems reasonable enough: "You can't find good foreigners who are willing to live in the United States, where our headquarters is located. American executives are more mobile. In addition, Americans have the drive and initiative we like. In fact, the European nationals would prefer to report to an American rather than to some other European."

The executive from Company C goes on to explain that the worldwide product division concept is rather difficult to implement. The senior executives in charge of these divisions have little overseas experience. They have been promoted from domestic posts and tend to view foreign consumer needs "as really basically the same as ours." Also, product division executives tend to focus on the domestic market because the domestic market is larger and generates more revenue than the fragmented European markets. The rewards are for global performance, but the strategy is to focus on domestic. His colleagues say "one pays attention to what one understands—and our senior executives simply do not understand what happens overseas and really do not trust foreign executives in key positions here or overseas."

▌ Trained as an engineer and a psychologist, Howard V. Perlmutter spent eight years at M.I.T.'s Center for International Studies and five years at the Institut pour l'Etude des Methodes de Direction de l'Enterprise (IMEDE) in Lausanne, Switzerland. His main interests are in the theory and practice of institution building, particularly the international corporation. He has recently been appointed Director for Research and Development of Worldwide Institutions in association with the Management Science Center at the University of Pennsylvania, as well as a member of the faculty at the Wharton School.
▌ Used with permission of Howard V. Perlmutter.

The executive from the European Company D begins by explaining that since the voting shareholders must by law come from the home country, the home country's interest must be given careful consideration. In the final analysis he insists: "We are proud of our nationality; we shouldn't be ashamed of it." He cites examples of the previous reluctance of headquarters to use home-country ideas overseas, to their detriment, especially in their U.S. subsidiary. "Our country produces good executives, who tend to stay with us a long time. It is harder to keep executives from the United States."

A Rose by Any Other Name . . .

Why quibble about how multinational a firm is? To these executives, apparently being multinational is prestigious. They know that multinational firms tend to be regarded as more progressive, dynamic, geared to the future than provincial companies which avoid foreign frontiers and their attendant risks and opportunities.

It is natural that these senior executives would want to justify the multinationality of their enterprise, even if they use different yard sticks: ownership criteria, organizational structure, nationality of senior executives, percent of investment overseas, etc.

Two hypotheses seem to be forming in the minds of executives from international firms that make the extent of their firm's multinationality of real interest. The first hypothesis is that the degree of multinationality of an enterprise is positively related to the firm's long-term viability. The "multinational" category makes sense for executives if it means a quality of decision making which leads to survival, growth and profitability in our evolving world economy.

The second hypothesis stems from the proposition that the multinational corporation is a new kind of institution—a new type of industrial social architecture particularly suitable for the latter third of the twentieth century. This type of institution could make a valuable contribution to world order and conceivably exercise a constructive impact on the nation-state. Some executives want to understand how to create an institution whose presence is considered legitimate and valuable in each nation-state. They

want to prove that the greater the degree of multinationality of a firm, the greater its total constructive impact will be on host and home nation-states as well as other institutions. Since multinational firms may produce a significant proportion of the world's GNP, both hypotheses justify a more precise analysis of the varieties and degrees of multinationality.[1] However, the confirming evidence is limited.

State of Mind

Part of the difficulty in defining the degree of multinationality comes from the variety of parameters along which a firm doing business overseas can be described. The examples from the four companies argue that (1) no single criterion of multinationality such as ownership or the number of nationals overseas is sufficient, and that (2) external and quantifiable measures such as the percentage of investment overseas or the distribution of equity by nationality are useful but not enough. The more one penetrates into the living reality of an international firm, the more one finds it is necessary to give serious weight to the way executives think about doing business around the world. The orientation toward "foreign people, ideas, resources," in headquarters and subsidiaries, and in host and home environments, becomes crucial in estimating the multinationality of a firm. To be sure, such external indices as the proportion of nationals in different countries holding equity and the number of foreign nationals who have reached top positions, including president, are good indices of multinationality. But one can still behave with a home-country orientation despite foreign shareholders, and one can have a few home-country nationals overseas but still pick those local executives who are home-country oriented or who are provincial and chauvinistic. The attitudes men hold are clearly more relevant than their passports.

Three primary attitudes among international executives toward building a multinational enterprise are identifiable. These attitudes can be inferred from

[1]H. V Perlmutter, "Super-Giant Firms in the Future," *Wharton Quarterly*, Winter 1968.

Table 1   Three Types of Headquarters Orientation toward Subsidiaries in an International Enterprise

Organization Design	Ethnocentric	Polycentric	Geocentric
Complexity of organization	Complex in home country, simple in subsidiaries	Varied and independent	Increasingly complex and interdependent
Authority; decision making	High in headquarters	Relatively low in headquarters	Aim for a collaborative approach between headquarters and subsidiaries
Evaluation and control	Home standards applied for persons and performance	Determined locally	Find standards which are universal and local
Rewards and punishments; incentives	High in headquarters, low in subsidiaries	Wide variation; can be high or low rewards for subsidiary performance	International and local executives rewarded for reaching local and worldwide objectives
Communication; information flow	High volume to subsidiaries; orders, commands, advice	Little to and from headquarters; little between subsidiaries	Both ways and between subsidiaries; heads of subsidiaries part of management team
Identification	Nationality of owner	Nationality of host country	Truly international company but identifying with national interests
Perpetuation (recruiting, staffing, development)	Recruit and develop people of home country for key positions everywhere in the world	Develop people of local nationality for key positions in their own country	Develop best people everywhere in the world for key positions everywhere in the world

the assumptions upon which key product, functional and geographical decisions were made.

These states of mind or attitudes may be described as ethnocentric (or home-country oriented), polycentric (or host-country oriented) and geocentric (or world-oriented).[2] While they never appear in pure form, they are clearly distinguishable. There is some degree of ethnocentricity, polycentricity or geocentricity in all firms, but management's analysis does not usually correlate with public pronouncements about the firm's multinationality.

[2]H. V. Perlmutter, "Three Conceptions of a World Enterprise," *Revue Economique et Sociale*, May 1965.

Home-Country Attitudes

The ethnocentric attitude can be found in companies of any nationality with extensive overseas holdings. The attitude, revealed in executive actions and experienced by foreign subsidiary managers, is: "We, the home nationals of X company, are superior to, more trustworthy and more reliable than any foreigners in headquarters or subsidiaries. We will be willing to build facilities in your country if you acknowledge our inherent superiority and accept our methods and conditions for doing the job."

Of course, such attitudes are never so crudely expressed but they often determine how a certain type of "multinational" firm is designed. Table 1 illustrates how ethnocentric attitudes are expressed in determining the managerial process at home and overseas. For example, the ethnocentric executive is more apt to say: "Let us manufacture the simple products overseas. Those foreign nationals are not yet ready or reliable. We should manufacture the complex products in our country and keep the secrets among our trusted home-country nationals."

In a firm where ethnocentric attitudes prevailed the performance criteria for men and products are "home-made." "We have found that a salesman should make 12 calls per day in Hoboken, New Jersey (the headquarters location), and therefore we apply these criteria everywhere in the world. The salesman in Brazzaville is naturally lazy, unmotivated. He shows little drive because he makes only two calls per day (despite the Congolese salesman's explanation that it takes time to reach customers by boat)."

Ethnocentric attitudes are revealed in the communication process where "advice," "counsel," and directives flow from headquarters to the subsidiary in a steady stream, bearing this message: "This works at home; therefore, it must work in your country."

Executives in both headquarters and affiliates express the national identity of the firm by associating the company with the nationality of the headquarters: this is "a Swedish company," "a Swiss company," "an American company," depending on the location of headquarters. "You have to accept the fact that the only way to reach a senior post in our firm," an English executive in a U.S. firm said, "is to take out an American passport."

Crucial to the ethnocentric concept is the current policy that men of the home nationality are recruited and trained for key positions everywhere in the world. Foreigners feel like "second-class" citizens.

There is no international firm today whose executives will say that ethnocentrism is absent in their company. In the firms whose multinational investment began a decade ago, one is more likely to hear, "We are still in a transitional stage from our ethnocentric era. The traces are still around! But we are making progress."

▉ Host-Country Orientation

Polycentric firms are those which by experience or by the inclination of a top executive (usually one of the founders), begin with the assumption that host-country cultures are different and that foreigners are difficult to understand. Local people know what is best for them, and the part of the firm which is located in the host country should be as "local in identity" as possible. The senior executives at headquarters believe that their multinational enterprise can be held together by good financial controls. A polycentric firm, literally, is a loosely connected group with quasi-independent subsidiaries as centers—more akin to a confederation.

European multinational firms tend to follow this pattern, using a top local executive who is strong and trustworthy, of the "right" family and who has an intimate understanding of the workings of the host government. This policy seems to have worked until the advent of the Common Market.

Executives in the headquarters of such a company are apt to say: "Let the Romans do it their way. We really don't understand what is going on there, but we have to have confidence in them. As long as they earn a profit, we want to remain in the background." They assume that since people are different in each country, standards for performance, incentives and training methods must be different. Local environmental factors are given greater weight (see Table 1).

Many executives mistakenly equate polycentrism with multinationalism. This is evidenced in the legalistic definition of a multinational enterprise as a cluster of corporations of diverse nationality joined together by ties of common ownership. It is no accident that many senior executives in headquarters take pride in the absence of non-nationals in their subsidiaries, especially people from the head office. The implication is clearly that each subsidiary is a distinct national entity, since it is incorporated in a different sovereign state. Lonely senior executives in the subsidiaries of polycentric companies complain that: "The home office never tells us anything."

Polycentrism is not the ultimate form of multinationalism. It is a landmark on a highway.

Polycentrism is encouraged by local marketing managers who contend that: "Headquarters will never understand us, our people, our consumer needs, our laws, our distribution, etc. . . . ."

Headquarters takes pride in the fact that few outsiders know that the firm is foreign-owned. "We want to be a good local company. How many Americans know that Shell and Lever Brothers are foreign-owned?"

But the polycentric personnel policy is also revealed in the fact that no local manager can seriously aspire to a senior position at headquarters. "You know the French are so provincial; it is better to keep them in France. Uproot them and you are in trouble," a senior executive says to justify the paucity of non-Americans at headquarters.

One consequence (and perhaps cause) of polycentrism is a virulent ethnocentrism among the country managers.

A World-Oriented Concept

The third attitude which is beginning to emerge at an accelerating rate is geocentrism. Senior executives with this orientation do not equate superiority with nationality. Within legal and political limits, they seek the best men, regardless of nationality, to solve the company's problems anywhere in the world. The senior executives attempt to build an organization in which the subsidiary is not only a good citizen of the host nation, but is a leading exporter from this nation in the international community and contributes such benefits as (1) an increasing supply of hard currency, (2) new skills and (3) a knowledge of advanced technology. Geocentrism is summed up in a Unilever board chairman's statement of objectives: "We want to Unileverize our Indians and Indianize our Unileverans."

The ultimate goal of geocentrism is a worldwide approach in both headquarters and subsidiaries. The firm's subsidiaries are thus neither satellites nor independent city states, but parts of a whole whose focus is on worldwide objectives as well as local objectives, each part making its unique contribution with its unique competence. Geocentrism is expressed by function, product and geography. The question asked in headquarters and the subsidiaries is: "Where in the world shall we raise money, build our plant conduct R&D, get and launch new ideas to serve our present and future customers?"

This conception of geocentrism involves a collaborative effort between subsidiaries and headquarters to establish universal standards and permissible local variations, to make key allocational decisions on new products, new plants, new laboratories. The international management team includes the affiliate heads.

Subsidiary managers must ask: "Where in the world can I get the help to serve my customers best in this country?" "Where in the world can I export products developed in this country—products which meet worldwide standards as opposed to purely local standards?"

Geocentrism, furthermore, requires a reward system for subsidiary managers which motivates them to work for worldwide objectives, not just to defend country objectives. In firms where geocentrism prevails, it is not uncommon to hear a subsidiary manager say, "While I am paid to defend our interests in this country and to get the best resources for this affiliate, I must still ask myself the question 'Where in the world (instead of where in my country) should we build this plant?'" This approach is still rare today.

In contrast to the ethnocentric and polycentric patterns, communication is encouraged among subsidiaries in geocentric-oriented firms. "It is your duty to help us solve problems anywhere in the world," one chief executive continually reminds the heads of his company's affiliates. (See Table 1.)

The geocentric firm identifies with local company needs. "We aim not to be just a good local company, but the best local company in terms of the quality of management and the worldwide (not local) standards we establish in domestic and export production." "If we were only as good as local companies, we would deserve to be nationalized."

The geocentric personnel policy is based on the belief that we should bring in the best man in the world regardless of his nationality. His passport should not be the criterion for promotion.

The EPG Profile

Executives can draw their firm's profile in ethnocentric (E), polycentric (P) and geocentric (G) dimensions. They are called EPG profiles. The degree of ethnocentrism, polycentrism and geocentrism by product, function and geography can be established. Typically R&D often turns out to be more geocentric (truth is universal, perhaps) and less ethnocentric than finance. Financial managers are likely to see their decisions as ethnocentric. The marketing function is more polycentric, particularly in the advanced economies and in the larger affiliate markets.

The tendency toward ethnocentrism in relations with subsidiaries in the developing countries is marked. Polycentric attitudes develop in consumer goods divisions, and ethnocentrism appears to be greater in industrial product divisions. The agreement is almost unanimous in both U.S.- and European-based international firms that their companies are at various stages on a route toward geocentrism but none has reached this state of affairs. Their executives would agree, however, that:

1. A description of their firms as multinational obscures more than it illuminates the state of affairs;
2. The EPG mix, once defined, is a more precise way to describe the point they have reached;
3. The present profile is not static but a landmark along a difficult road to genuine geocentrism;
4. There are forces both to change and to maintain the present attitudinal "mix," some of which are under their control.

Forces Toward and Against

What are the forces that determine the EPG mix of a firm? "You must think of the struggle toward functioning as a worldwide firm as just a beginning—a few steps forward and a step backward," a chief executive puts it. "It is a painful process, and every firm is different."

Executives of some of the world's largest multinational firms have been able to identify a series of external and internal factors that contribute to or hinder the growth of geocentric attitudes and decisions. Table 2 summarizes the factors most frequently mentioned by over 500 executives from at least 17 countries and 20 firms.

From the external environmental side the growing world markets, the increase in availability of managerial and technological know-how in different countries, global competition and international customers' advances in telecommunications, regional political and economic communities are positive factors, as is the host country's desire to increase its balance-of-payments surplus through the location of export-oriented subsidiaries of international firms within its borders.

In different firms, senior executives see in various degrees these positive factors toward geocentrism: top management's increasing desire to use human and material resources optimally, the observed lowering of morale after decades of ethnocentric practices, the evidence of waste and duplication under polycentric thinking, the increased awareness and respect for good men of other than the home nationality, and, most importantly, top management's own commitment to building a geocentric firm as evidenced in policies, practices and procedures.

The obstacles toward geocentrism from the environment stem largely from the rising political and economic nationalism in the world today, the suspicions of political leaders of the aims and increasing power of the multinational firm. On the internal side, the obstacles cited most frequently in U.S.-based multinational firms were management's inexperience in overseas markets, mutual distrust between home-country people and foreign executives, the resistance to participation by foreigners in the power structure at headquarters, the increasing difficulty of getting good men overseas to move, nationalistic tendencies in staff, and linguistic and other communication difficulties of a cultural nature.

Any given firm is seen as moving toward geocentrism at a rate determined by its capacities to build on the positive internal factors over which it has control and to change the negative internal factors which are controllable. In some firms the geocentric goal is openly discussed among executives of different nationalities and from different subsidiaries

Table 2   International Executives' View of Forces and Obstacles toward Geocentrism in Their Firms

Forces toward Geocentrism		Obstacles toward Geocentrism	
Environmental	**Intra-Organizational**	**Environmental**	**Intra-Organizational**
1. Technological and managerial know-how increasing in availability in different countries	1. Desire to use human versus material resources optimally	1. Economic nationalism in host and home countries	1. Management inexperience in overseas markets
2. International customers	2. Observed lowering of morale in affiliates of an ethnocentric company	2. Political nationalism in host and home countries	2. Nation-centered reward and punishment structure
3. Local customers' demand for best product at fair price	3. Evidence of waste and duplication in polycentrism	3. Military secrecy associated with research in home country	3. Mutual distrust between home-country people and foreign executives
4. Host country's desire to increase balance of payments	4. Increasing awareness and respect for good people of other than home nationality	4. Distrust of big international firms by host-country political leaders	4. Resistance to letting foreigners into the power structure
5. Growing world markets	5. Risk diversification in having a worldwide production and distribution system	5. Lack of international monetary system	5. Anticipated costs and risks of geocentrism
6. Global competition among international firms for scarce human and material resources	6. Need for recruitment of good people on a worldwide basis	6. Growing differences between the rich and poor countries	6. Nationalistic tendencies in staff
7. Major advances in integration of international transport and telecommunications	7. Need for worldwide information system	7. Host-country belief that home countries get disproportionate benefits of international firms' profits	7. Increasing immobility of staff
8. Regional supranational economic and political communities	8. Worldwide appeal products	8. Home-country political leaders' attempts to control firm's policy	8. Linguistic problems and different cultural backgrounds
	9. Senior management's long-term commitment to geocentrism as related to survival and growth		9. Centralization tendencies in headquarters

as well as headquarters. There is a consequent improvement in the climate of trust and acceptance of each other's views.

Programs are instituted to assure greater experience in foreign markets, task forces of executives are upgraded, and international careers for executives of all nationalities are being designed.

But the seriousness of the obstacles cannot be underestimated. A world of rising nationalism is hardly a precondition for geocentrism; and overcoming distrust of foreigners even within one's own firm is not accomplished in a short span of time. The route to pervasive geocentric thinking is long and tortuous.

▌ Costs, Risks, Payoffs

What conclusions will executives from multinational firms draw from the balance sheet of advantages and disadvantages of maintaining one's present state of ethnocentrism, polycentrism or geocentrism? Not too surprisingly, the costs and risks of ethnocentrism are seen to out-balance the payoffs in the long run. The costs of ethnocentrism are ineffective planning because of a lack of good feedback, the departure of the best men in the subsidiaries, fewer innovations, and an inability to build a high calibre local organization. The risks are political and social repercussions and a less flexible response to local changes.

The payoffs of ethnocentrism are real enough in the short term, they say. Organization is simpler. There is a higher rate of communication of know-how from headquarters to new markets. There is more control over appointments to senior posts in subsidiaries.

Polycentrism's costs are waste due to duplication, to decisions to make products for local use but which could be universal, and to inefficient use of home-country experience. The risks include an excessive regard for local traditions and local growth at the expense of global growth. The main advantages are an intense exploitation of local markets, better sales since local management is often better informed, more local initiative for new products,

more host-government support, and good local managers with high morale.

Geocentrism's costs are largely related to communication and travel expenses, educational costs at all levels, time spent in decision making because consensus seeking among more people is required and an international headquarters bureaucracy. Risks include those due to too wide a distribution of power, personnel problems and those of reentry of international executives. The payoffs are a more powerful total company throughout, a better quality of products and service, worldwide utilization of best resources, improvement of local company management, a greater sense of commitment to worldwide objectives, and last, but not least, more profit.

Jacques Maisonrouge, the French-born president of IBM World Trade, understands the geocentric concept and its benefits. He wrote recently:

> The first step to a geocentric organization is when a corporation, faced with the choice of whether to grow and expand or decline, realizes the need to mobilize its resources on a world scale. It will sooner or later have to face the issue that the home country does not have a monopoly of either men or ideas. . . .
>
> I strongly believe that the future belongs to geocentric companies. . . . What is of fundamental importance is the attitude of the company's top management. If it is dedicated to "geocentrism," good international management will be possible. If not, the best men of different nations will soon understand that they do not belong to the "race des seigneurs" and will leave the business.[3]

Geocentrism is not inevitable in any given firm. Some companies have experienced a "regression" to ethnocentrism after trying a long period of polycentrism, of letting subsidiaries do it "their way." The local directors built little empires and did not train successors from their own country. Headquarters had to send home-country nationals to take over. A period of home-country thinking took over.

There appears to be evidence of a need for evolutionary movement from ethnocentrism to

[3]Jacques Maisonrouge, "The Education of International Managers," *Quarterly Journal of AIESEC International,* February 1967.

polycentrism to geocentrism. The polycentric stage is likened to an adolescent protest period during which subsidiary managers gain their confidence as equals by fighting headquarters and proving "their manhood," after a long period of being under headquarters' ethnocentric thumb.

"It is hard to move from a period of headquarters domination to a worldwide management team quickly. A period of letting affiliates make mistakes may be necessary," said one executive.

Window Dressing

In the rush toward appearing geocentric, many U.S. firms have found it necessary to emphasize progress by appointing one or two non-nationals to senior posts—even on occasion to headquarters. The foreigner is often effectively counteracted by the number of nationals around him, and his influence is really small. Tokenism does have some positive effects, but it does not mean geocentrism has arrived.

Window dressing is also a temptation. Here an attempt is made to demonstrate influence by appointing a number of incompetent "foreigners" to key positions. The results are not impressive for either the individuals or the company.

Too often what is called "the multinational view" is really a screen for ethnocentrism. Foreign affiliate managers must, in order to succeed, take on the traits and behavior of the ruling nationality. In short, in a U.S.-owned firm the foreigner must "Americanize"—not only in attitude but in dress and speech—in order to be accepted.

Tokenism and window dressing are transitional episodes where aspirations toward multinationalism outstrip present attitudes and resources. The fault does not lie only with the enterprise. The human demands of ethnocentrism are great.

A Geocentric Man—?

The geocentric enterprise depends on having an adequate supply of men who are geocentrically oriented. It would be a mistake to underestimate the human stresses which a geocentric career creates. Moving where the company needs an executive involves major adjustments for families, wives and children. The sacrifices are often great and, for some families, outweigh the rewards forthcoming—at least in personal terms. Many executives find it difficult to learn new languages and overcome their cultural superiority complexes, national pride and discomfort with foreigners. Furthermore, international careers can be hazardous when ethnocentrism prevails at headquarters. "It is easy to get lost in the world of the subsidiaries and to be 'out of sight, out of mind' when promotions come up at headquarters," as one executive expressed it following a visit to headquarters after five years overseas. To his disappointment, he knew few senior executives. And fewer knew him!

The economic rewards, the challenge of new countries, the personal and professional development that comes from working in a variety of countries and cultures are surely incentives, but companies have not solved by any means the human costs of international mobility to executives and their families.

A firm's multinationality may be judged by the pervasiveness with which executives think geocentrically—by function, marketing, finance, production, R&D, etc., by product division and by country. The takeoff to geocentrism may begin with executives in one function, say marketing, seeking to find a truly worldwide product line. Only when this worldwide attitude extends throughout the firm, in headquarters and subsidiaries, can executives feel that it is becoming genuinely geocentric.

But no single yardstick, such as the number of foreign nationals in key positions, is sufficient to establish a firm's multinationality. The multinational firm's route to geocentrism is still long because political and economic nationalism is on the rise, and, more importantly, since within the firm ethnocentrism and polycentrism are not easy to overcome. Building trust between persons of different nationality is a central obstacle. Indeed, if we are to judge men, as Paul Weiss put it, "by the kind of world they are trying to build," the senior executives engaged in building the geocentric enterprise could well be the most important social architects of the last third of the twentieth century. For the institution they are trying to erect promises a greater universal sharing of wealth and a consequent control of the explosive centrifugal tendencies of our evolving world community.

The geocentric enterprise offers an institutional and supranational framework which could conceivably make war less likely, on the assumption that bombing customers, suppliers and employees is in nobody's interest. The difficulty of the task is thus matched by its worthwhileness. A clearer image of the features of genuine geocentricity is thus indispensable both as a guideline and as an inviting prospect.

Reading 1-2   Distance Still Matters: The Hard Reality of Global Expansion

Pankaj Ghemawat

When it was launched in 1991, Star TV looked like a surefire winner. The plan was straightforward: The company would deliver television programming to a media-starved Asian audience. It would target the top 5% of Asia's socioeconomic pyramid, a newly rich elite who could not only afford the services, but who also represented an attractive advertising market. Since English was the second language for most of the target consumers, Star would be able to use readily available and fairly cheap English-language programming rather than having to invest heavily in creating new local programs. And by using satellites to beam programs into people's homes, it would sidestep the constraints of geographic distance that had hitherto kept traditional broadcasters out of Asia. Media mogul Rupert Murdoch was so taken with this plan—especially with the appeal of leveraging his Twentieth Century Fox film library across the Asian market—that his company, News Corporation, bought out Star's founders for $825 million between 1993 and 1995.

❚ Pankaj Ghemawat is the Jaime and Josefina Chua Tiampo Professor of Business Administration at Harvard Business School in Boston. His article "The Dubious Logic of Global Megamergers," coauthored by Fariborz Ghadar, was published in the JulyAugust 2000 issue of *HBR*.

The results have not been quite what Murdoch expected. In its fiscal year ending June 30, 1999, Star reportedly lost $141 million, pretax, on revenues of $111 million. Losses in fiscal years 1996 through 1999 came to about $500 million all told, not including losses on joint ventures such as Phoenix TV in China. Star is not expected to turn in a positive operating profit until 2002.

Star has been a high-profile disaster, but similar stories are played out all the time as companies pursue global expansion. Why? Because, like Star, they routinely overestimate the attractiveness of foreign markets. They become so dazzled by the sheer size of untapped markets that they lose sight of the vast difficulties of pioneering new, often very different territories. The problem is rooted in the very analytic tools that managers rely on in making judgments about international investments, tools that consistently underestimate the costs of doing business internationally. The most prominent of these is country portfolio analysis (CPA), the hoary but still widely used technique for deciding where a company should compete. By focusing on national GDP, levels of consumer wealth, and people's propensity to consume, CPA places all the emphasis on potential sales. It ignores the costs and risks of doing business in a new market.

Most of those costs and risks result from barriers created by distance. By distance, I don't mean only geographic separation, though that is important.

Distance also has cultural, administrative or political, and economic dimensions that can make foreign markets considerably more or less attractive. Just how much difference does distance make? A recent study by economists Jeffrey Frankel and Andrew Rose estimates the impact of various factors on a country's trade flows. Traditional economic factors, such as the country's wealth and size (GDP), still matter; a 1% increase in either of those measures creates, on average, a .7% to .8% increase in trade. But other factors related to distance, it turns out, matter even more. The amount of trade that takes place between countries 5,000 miles apart is only 20% of the amount that would be predicted to take place if the same countries were 1,000 miles apart. Cultural and administrative distance produces even larger effects. A company is likely to trade ten times as much with a country that is a former colony, for instance, than with a country to which it has no such ties. A common currency increases trade by 340%. Common membership in a regional trading bloc increases trade by 330%. And so on. (For a summary of Frankel and Rose's findings, see the exhibit "Measuring the Impact of Distance.")

Much has been made of the death of distance in recent years. It's been argued that information technologies and, in particular, global communications are shrinking the world, turning it into a small and relatively homogeneous place. But when it comes to business, that's not only an incorrect assumption, it's a dangerous one. Distance still matters, and companies must explicitly and thoroughly account for it when they make decisions about global expansion. Traditional country portfolio analysis needs to be tempered by a clear-eyed evaluation of the many dimensions of distance and their probable impact on opportunities in foreign markets.

The Four Dimensions of Distance

Distance between two countries can manifest itself along four basic dimensions: cultural, administrative, geographic, and economic. The types of distance influence different businesses in different ways. Geographic distance, for instance, affects the costs of transportation and communications, so it is

of particular importance to companies that deal with heavy or bulky products, or whose operations require a high degree of coordination among highly dispersed people or activities. Cultural distance, by contrast, affects consumers' product preferences. It is a crucial consideration for any consumer goods or media company, but it is much less important for a cement or steel business.

Each of these dimensions of distance encompasses many different factors, some of which are readily apparent; others are quite subtle. (See the exhibit "The CAGE Distance Framework" for an overview of the factors and the ways in which they affect particular industries.) In this article, I will review the four principal dimensions of distance, starting with the two overlooked the most—cultural distance and administrative distance.

Cultural Distance   A country's cultural attributes determine how people interact with one another and with companies and institutions. Differences in religious beliefs, race, social norms, and language are all capable of creating distance between two countries. Indeed, they can have a huge impact on trade: All other things being equal, trade between countries that share a language, for example, will be three times greater than between countries without a common language.

Some cultural attributes, like language, are easily perceived and understood. Others are much more subtle. Social norms, the deeply rooted system of unspoken principles that guide individuals in their everyday choices and interactions, are often nearly invisible, even to the people who abide by them. Take, for instance, the long-standing tolerance of the Chinese for copyright infringement. As William Alford points out in his book *To Steal a Book Is an Elegant Offense* (Stanford University Press, 1995), many people ascribe this social norm to China's recent communist past. More likely, Alford argues, it flows from a precept of Confucius that encourages replication of the results of past intellectual endeavors: "I transmit rather than create; I believe in and love the Ancients." Indeed, copyright infringement was a problem for Western publishers well before communism. Back in the 1920s, for example, Merriam Webster, about to introduce a bilingual dictionary in China, found that the Commercial Press in Shanghai had already begun to distribute its own version of the new dictionary. The U.S. publisher took the press to a Chinese court, which imposed a small fine for using the Merriam Webster seal but did nothing to halt publication. As the film and music industries well know, little has changed. Yet this social norm still confounds many Westerners.

Most often, cultural attributes create distance by influencing the choices that consumers make between substitute products because of their preferences for specific features. Color tastes, for example, are closely linked to cultural prejudices. The word "red" in Russian also means beautiful. Consumer durable industries are particularly sensitive to differences in consumer taste at this level. The Japanese, for example, prefer automobiles and household appliances to be small, reflecting a social norm common in countries where space is highly valued.

Sometimes products can touch a deeper nerve, triggering associations related to the consumer's identity as a member of a particular community. In these cases, cultural distance affects entire categories of products. The food industry is particularly sensitive to religious attributes. Hindus, for example, do not eat beef because it is expressly forbidden by their religion. Products that elicit a strong response of this kind are usually quite easy to identify, though some countries will provide a few surprises. In Japan, rice, which Americans treat as a commodity, carries an enormous amount of cultural baggage.

Ignoring cultural distance was one of Star TV's biggest mistakes. By supposing that Asian viewers would be happy with English-language programming, the company assumed that the TV business

---

Measuring the Impact of Distance

Economists often rely on the so-called gravity theory of trade flows, which says there is a positive relationship between economic size and trade and a negative relationship between distance and trade. Models based on this theory explain up to two-thirds of the observed variations in trade flows between pairs of countries. Using such a model, economists Jeffrey Frankel and Andrew Rose[1] have predicted how much certain distance variables will affect trade.

Distance Attribute	Change in International Trade (%)
Income level: GDP per capita (1% increase)	+0.7
Economic size: GDP (1% increase)	+0.8
Physical distance (1% increase)	−1.1
Physical size (1% increase)*	−0.2
Access to ocean*	+50
Common border	+80
Common language	+200
Common regional trading bloc	+330
Colony–colonizer relationship	+900
Common colonizer	+190
Common polity	+300
Common currency	+340

[1] Jeffrey Frankel and Andrew Rose, "An Estimate of the Effects of Currency Unions on Growth," unpublished working paper, May 2000.
*Estimated effects exclude the last four variables in the table.

was insensitive to culture. Managers either dismissed or were unaware of evidence from Europe that mass audiences in countries large enough to support the development of local content generally prefer local TV programming. If they had taken cultural distance into account, China and India could have been predicted to require significant investments in localization. TV is hardly cement.

Administrative or Political Distance   Historical and political associations shared by countries greatly affect trade between them. Colony-colonizer links between countries, for example, boost trade by 900%, which is perhaps not too surprising given Britain's continuing ties with its former colonies in the commonwealth, France's with the franc zone of West Africa, and Spain's with Latin America. Preferential trading arrangements, common currency, and political union can also increase trade by more than 300% each. The integration of the European Union is probably the leading example of deliberate efforts to diminish administrative and political distance among trading partners. (Needless to say, ties must be friendly to have a positive influence on trade. Although India and Pakistan share a colonial history—not to mention a border and linguistic ties—their mutual hostility means that trade between them is virtually nil.)

Countries can also create administrative and political distance through unilateral measures. Indeed, policies of individual governments pose the most common barriers to cross-border competition. In some cases, the difficulties arise in a company's home country. For companies from the United States, for instance, domestic prohibitions on bribery and the prescription of health, safety, and environmental policies have a dampening effect on their international businesses.

More commonly, though, it is the target country's government that raises barriers to foreign competition: tariffs, trade quotas, restrictions on foreign direct investment, and preferences for domestic competitors in the form of subsidies and favoritism in regulation and procurement. Such measures are expressly intended to protect domestic industries,

and they are most likely to be implemented if a domestic industry meets one or more of the following criteria:

- *It is a large employer.* Industries that represent large voting blocs often receive state support in the form of subsidies and import protection. Europe's farmers are a case in point.
- *It is seen as a national champion.* Reflecting a kind of patriotism, some industries or companies serve as symbols of a country's modernity and competitiveness. Thus the showdown between Boeing and Airbus in capturing the large passenger-jet market has caused feelings on both sides of the Atlantic to run high and could even spark a broader trade war. Also, the more that a government has invested in the industry, the more protective it is likely to be, and the harder it will be for an outsider to gain a beachhead.
- *It is vital to national security.* Governments will intervene to protect industries that are deemed vital to national security—especially in high tech sectors such as telecommunications and aerospace. The FBI, for instance, delayed Deutsche Telekom's acquisition of Voicestream for reasons of national security.
- *It produces staples.* Governments will also take measures to prevent foreign companies from dominating markets for goods essential to their citizens' everyday lives. Food staples, fuel, and electricity are obvious examples.
- *It produces an "entitlement" good or service.* Some industries, notably the health care sector, produce goods or services that people believe they are entitled to as a basic human right. In these industries, governments are prone to intervene to set quality standards and control pricing.
- *It exploits natural resources.* A country's physical assets are often seen as part of a national heritage. Foreign companies can easily be considered robbers. Nationalization, therefore, is a constant threat to international oil and mining multinationals.
- *It involves high sunk-cost commitments.* Industries that require large, geography-specific sunk

The CAGE Distance Framework

The cultural, administrative, geographic, and economic (CAGE) distance framework helps managers identify and assess the impact of distance on various industries. The upper portion of the table lists the key attributes underlying the four dimensions of distance. The lower portion shows how they affect different products and industries.

Cultural Distance	Administrative Distance	Geographic Distance	Economic Distance
Attributes Creating Distance			
Different languages Different ethnicities; lack of connective ethnic or social networks Different religions Different social norms	Absence of colonial ties Absence of shared monetary or political association Political hostility Government policies Institutional weakness	Physical remoteness Lack of a common border Lack of sea or river access Size of country Weak transportation or communication links Differences in climates	Differences in consumer incomes Differences in costs and quality of: • natural resources • financial resources • human resources • infrastructure • intermediate inputs • information or knowledge
Industries or Products Affected by Distance			
Products have high linguistic content (TV) Products affect cultural or national identity of consumers (foods) Product features vary in terms of: • size (cars) • standards (electrical appliances) • packaging Products carry country-specific quality associations (wines)	Government involvement is high in industries that are: • producers of staple goods (electricity) • producers of other "entitlements" (drugs) • large employers (farming) • large suppliers to government (mass transportation) • national champions (aerospace) • vital to national security (telecommunications) • exploiters of natural resources (oil, mining) • subject to high sunk costs (infrastructure)	Products have a low value-to-weight or bulk ratio (cement) Products are fragile or perishable (glass, fruit) Communications and connectivity are important (financial services) Local supervision and operational requirements are high (many services)	Nature of demand varies with income level (cars) Economies of standardization or scale are important (mobile phones) Labor and other factor cost differences are salient (garments) Distribution or business systems are different (insurance) Companies need to be responsive and agile (home appliances)

How Far Away Is China, Really?

As Star TV discovered, China is a particularly tough nut to crack. In a recent survey of nearly 100 multinationals, 54% admitted that their total business performance in China had been "worse than planned," compared with just 25% reporting "better than planned." Why was the failure rate so high? The survey provides the predictable answer: 62% of respondents reported that they had overestimated market potential for their products or services.

A quick analysis of the country along the dimensions of distance might have spared those companies much disappointment. Culturally, China is a long way away from nearly everywhere. First, the many dialects of the Chinese language are notoriously difficult for foreigners to learn, and the local population's foreign-language skills are limited. Second, the well-developed Chinese business culture based on personal connections, often summarized in the term *guanxi*, creates barriers to economic interchange with Westerners who focus on transactions rather than relationships. It can even be argued that Chinese consumers are "home-biased"; market research indicates much less preference for foreign brands over domestic ones than seems to be true in India, for example. In fact, greater China plays a disproportionate role in China's economic relations with the rest of the world.

Administrative barriers are probably even more important. A survey of members of the American Chamber of Commerce in China flagged market-access restrictions, high taxes, and customs duties as the biggest barriers to profitability in China. The level of state involvement in the economy continues to be high, with severe economic strains imposed by loss-making state-owned enterprises and technically insolvent state-owned banks. Corruption, too, is a fairly significant problem. In 2000, Transparency International ranked the country 63rd out of 90, with a rating of one indicating the least perceived corruption. Considerations such as these led Standard & Poor's to assign China a political-risk ranking of five in 2000, with six being the worst possible score.

So, yes, China is a big market, but that is far from the whole story. Distance matters, too, and along many dimensions.

---

investments—in the shape, say, of oil refineries or aluminum smelting plants or railway lines—are highly vulnerable to interference from local governments. Irreversibility expands the scope for holdups once the investment has been made.

Finally, a target country's weak institutional infrastructure can serve to dampen cross-border economic activity. Companies typically shy away from doing business in countries known for corruption or social conflict. Indeed, some research suggests that these conditions depress trade and investment far more than any explicit administrative policy or restriction. But when a country's institutional infrastructure is strong—for instance, if it has a well-functioning legal system—it is much more attractive to outsiders.

Ignoring administrative and political sensitivities was Star TV's other big mistake. Foreign ownership of broadcasting businesses—even in an open society like the United States—is always politically loaded because of television's power to influence people. Yet shortly after acquiring the company, Rupert Murdoch declared on record that satellite television was "an unambiguous threat to totalitarian regimes everywhere" because it permitted people to bypass government-controlled news sources. Not surprisingly, the Chinese government enacted a ban on the reception of foreign satellite TV services soon thereafter. News Corporation has begun to mend fences with the Chinese authorities, but it has yet to score any major breakthroughs in a country that accounts for nearly 60% of Star TV's potential customers. Murdoch of all people should have foreseen this outcome, given his experience in the United States, where he was required to become a citizen in order buy the television companies that now form the core of the Fox network.

Geographic Distance   In general, the farther you are from a country, the harder it will be to conduct business in that country. But geographic distance is not simply a matter of how far away the country is in miles or kilometers. Other attributes that must be considered include the physical size of the country, average within-country distances to borders, access to waterways and the ocean, and topography. Man-made geographic attributes also must be taken into account—most notably, a country's transportation and communications infrastructures.

Obviously, geographic attributes influence the costs of transportation. Products with low value-to-weight or bulk ratios, such as steel and cement, incur particularly high costs as geographic distance increases. Likewise, costs for transporting fragile or perishable products become significant across large distances.

Beyond physical products, intangible goods and services are affected by geographic distance as well. One recent study indicates that cross-border equity flows between two countries fall off significantly as the geographic distance between them rises. This phenomenon clearly cannot be explained by transportation costs—capital, after all, is not a physical good. Instead, the level of information infrastructure (crudely measured by telephone traffic and the number of branches of multinational banks) accounts for much of the effect of physical distance on cross-border equity flows.

Interestingly, companies that find geography a barrier to trade are often expected to switch to direct investment in local plant and equipment as an alternative way to access target markets. But current research suggests that this approach may be flawed: Geographic distance has a dampening effect, overall, on investment flows as well as on trade flows. In short, it is important to keep both information networks and transportation infrastructures

in mind when assessing the geographic influences on cross-border economic activity.

Economic Distance   The wealth or income of consumers is the most important economic attribute that creates distance between countries, and it has a marked effect on the levels of trade and the types of partners a country trades with. Rich countries, research suggests, engage in relatively more cross-border economic activity relative to their economic size than do their poorer cousins. Most of this activity is with other rich countries, as the positive correlation between per capita GDP and trade flows implies. But poor countries also trade more with rich countries than with other poor ones.

Of course, these patterns mask variations in the effects of economic disparities—in the cost and quality of financial, human, and other resources. Companies that rely on economies of experience, scale, and standardization should focus more on countries that have similar economic profiles. That's because they have to replicate their existing business model to exploit their competitive advantage, which is hard to pull off in a country where customer incomes—not to mention the cost and quality of resources—are very different. Wal-Mart in India, for instance, would be a very different business from Wal-Mart in the United States. But Wal-Mart in Canada is virtually a carbon copy.

In other industries, however, competitive advantage comes from economic arbitrage—the exploitation of cost and price differentials between markets. Companies in industries whose major cost components vary widely across countries—like the garment and footwear industries, where labor costs are important—are particularly likely to target countries with different economic profiles for investment or trade.

Whether they expand abroad for purposes of replication or arbitrage, all companies find that major disparities in supply chains and distribution channels are a significant barrier to business. A recent study concluded that margins on distribution within the United States—the costs of domestic transportation, wholesaling, and retailing—play a bigger role, on average, in erecting barriers to imports into the

Industry Sensitivity to Distance

The various types of distance affect different industries in different ways. To estimate industry sensitivity to distance, Rajiv Mallick, a research associate at Harvard Business School, and I regressed trade between every possible pair of countries in the world in each of 70 industries (according to their SIC designations) on each dimension of distance.

The results confirm the importance of distinguishing between the various components of distance in assessing foreign market opportunities. Electricity, for instance, is highly sensitive to administrative and geographic factors but not at all to cultural factors. The following table lists some of the industries that are more and less sensitive to distance.

CULTURAL DISTANCE Linguistic Ties	ADMINISTRATIVE DISTANCE Preferential Trading Agreements	GEOGRAPHIC DISTANCE Physical Remoteness	ECONOMIC DISTANCE Wealth Differences
More Sensitive			
Meat and meat preparations	Gold, nonmonetary	Electricity current	*(Economic distance decreases trade)*
Cereals and cereal preparations	Electricity current	Gas, natural and manufactured	Nonferrous metals
Miscellaneous edible products and preparations	Coffee, tea, cocoa, spices	Paper, paperboard	Manufactured fertilizers
Tobacco and tobacco products	Textile fibers	Live animals	Meat and meat preparations
Office machines and automatic data-processing equipment	Sugar, sugar preparations, and honey	Sugar, sugar preparations, and honey	Iron and steel
			Pulp and waste paper
Less Sensitive			
Photographic apparatuses, optical goods, watches	Gas, natural and manufactured	Pulp and waste paper	*(Economic distance increases trade)*
Road vehicles	Travel goods, handbags	Photographic apparatuses, optical goods, watches	Coffee, tea, cocoa, spices
Cork and wood	Footwear	Telecommunications and sound-recording apparatuses	Animal oils and fats
Metalworking machinery	Sanitary, plumbing, heating, and lighting fixtures	Coffee, tea, cocoa, spices	Office machines and automatic data-processing equipment
Electricity current	Furniture and furniture parts	Gold, nonmonetary	Power-generating machinery and equipment
			Photographic apparatuses, optical goods, watches

More Sensitive ◄─────────────────────────────► Less Sensitive

United States than do international transportation costs and tariffs combined.

More broadly, cross-country complexity and change place a premium on responsiveness and agility, making it hard for cross-border competitors, particularly replicators, to match the performance of locally focused ones because of the added operational complexity. In the home appliance business, for instance, companies like Maytag that concentrate on a limited number of geographies produce far better returns for investors than companies like Electrolux and Whirlpool, whose geographic spread has come at the expense of simplicity and profitability.

A Case Study in Distance

Taking the four dimensions of distance into account can dramatically change a company's assessment of the relative attractiveness of foreign markets. One

company that has wrestled with global expansion is Tricon Restaurants International (TRI), the international operating arm of Tricon, which manages the Pizza Hut, Taco Bell, and KFC fast-food chains, and which was spun off from Pepsico in 1997.

When Tricon became an independent company, TRI's operations were far-flung, with restaurants in 27 countries. But the profitability of its markets varied greatly: Two-thirds of revenues and an even higher proportion of profits came from just seven markets. Furthermore, TRI's limited operating cash flow and Tricon's debt service obligations left TRI with less than one-tenth as much money as archrival McDonald's International to invest outside the United States. As a result, in 1998, TRI's president, Pete Bassi, decided to rationalize its global operations by focusing its equity investments in a limited number of markets.

Exhibit 1a   Country Portfolio Analysis (a flawed approach)

Here's how country portfolio analysis (CPA) works. A company's actual and potential markets are plotted on a simple grid, with a measure of per capita income on one axis and some measure of product performance, often penetration rates, on the other. The location of the market on the grid reflects the attractiveness of the market in terms of individual consumer wealth and propensity to consume. The size of the bubble represents the total size of the market in terms of GDP or the absolute consumption of the product or service in question. The bubbles provide a rough estimate of how large the relative revenue opportunities are. This CPA map compares a number of non–U.S. markets for fast-food restaurants.

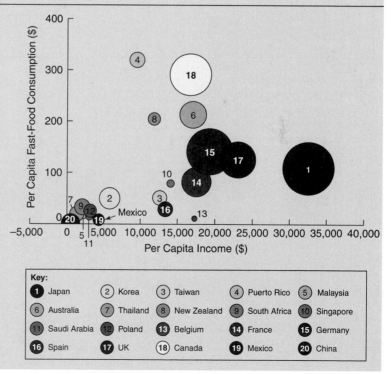

Key:
1 Japan   2 Korea   3 Taiwan   4 Puerto Rico   5 Malaysia
6 Australia   7 Thailand   8 New Zealand   9 South Africa   10 Singapore
11 Saudi Arabia   12 Poland   13 Belgium   14 France   15 Germany
16 Spain   17 UK   18 Canada   19 Mexico   20 China

But which markets? The exhibit "Country Portfolio Analysis: A Flawed Approach" provides a portfolio analysis of international markets for the fast-food restaurant business, based on data used by TRI for its strategy discussions. The analysis suggests that the company's top markets in terms of size of opportunity would be the larger bubbles to the center and right of the chart.

Applying the effects of distance, however, changes the map dramatically. Consider the Mexican market. Using the CPA method, Mexico, with a total fast-food consumption of $700 million, is a relatively small market, ranking 16th of 20. When combined with estimates of individual consumer wealth and per capita consumption, this ranking would imply that TRI should dispose of its investments there. But the exhibit "Country Portfolio Analysis: Adjusted for Distance" tells a different story. When the fast-food consumption numbers for each country are adjusted

for their geographic distance from Dallas, TRI's home base, Mexico's consumption decreases less than any other country's, as you might expect, given Mexico's proximity to Dallas. Based on just this readjustment, Mexico leaps to sixth place in terms of market opportunity.

Further adjusting the numbers for a common land border and for membership in a trade agreement with the United States pushes Mexico's ranking all the way up to second, after Canada. Not all the adjustments are positive: adjusting for a common language—not a characteristic of Mexico—pushes Mexico into a tie for second place with the United Kingdom. Additional adjustments could also be made, but the overall message is plain. Once distance is taken into account, the size of the market opportunity in Mexico looks very different. If TRI had used the CPA approach and neglected distance, the company's planners might well have

Exhibit 1b   Country Portfolio Analysis (adjusted for distance)

Taking distance into account dramatically changes estimates of market opportunities. In this chart, each of the fast-food markets has been adjusted for a number of distance attributes, based on the estimates by Frankel and Rose. The relative sizes of the bubbles are now very different. For example, Mexico, which was less than one-tenth the size of the largest international markets, Japan and Germany, ends up as the second largest opportunity. Clearly, the CPA approach paints an incomplete picture, unless it is adjusted for distance.

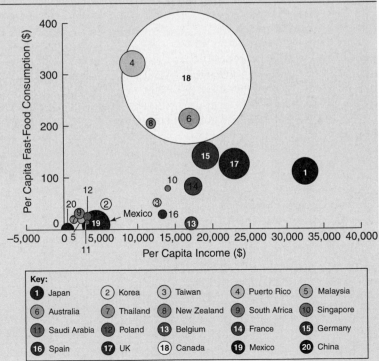

Key:
1 Japan   2 Korea   3 Taiwan   4 Puerto Rico   5 Malaysia
6 Australia   7 Thailand   8 New Zealand   9 South Africa   10 Singapore
11 Saudi Arabia   12 Poland   13 Belgium   14 France   15 Germany
16 Spain   17 UK   18 Canada   19 Mexico   20 China

ended up abandoning a core market. Instead, they concluded, in Bassi's words, that "Mexico is one of TRI's top two or three priorities."

Factoring in the industry effects of distance is only a first step. A full analysis should consider how a company's own characteristics operate to increase or reduce distance from foreign markets. Companies with a large cadre of cosmopolitan managers, for instance, will be less affected by cultural differences than companies whose managers are all from the home country. In TRI's case, consideration of company-specific features made Mexico even more attractive. The company already owned more than four-fifths of its Mexican outlets and had a 38% share of the local market, well ahead of McDonald's.

Consideration of the interaction of company-specific features and distance is beyond the scope of this article. But whether the analysis is at the industry or company level, the message is the same: Managers must always be conscious of distance—in all its dimensions. The CAGE distance framework is intended to help managers meet that challenge. While it is necessarily subjective, it represents an important complement to the tools used by most companies seeking to build or rationalize their country market portfolios. Technology may indeed be making the world a smaller place, but it is not eliminating the very real—and often very high—costs of distance.

Reading 1-3   When You Shouldn't Go Global

Marcus Alexander and Harry Korine

Even as companies are being told that the future lies in globalization, some are severely punished for their international moves. A simple test can help you decide what makes strategic sense for your organization.

Economic globalization is viewed by some as the best hope for world stability, by others as the greatest threat. But almost everyone accepts that businesses of all types must embrace it. Even smaller enterprises—urged on by the financial markets, by investment bankers and consultants, by the media, and by the moves they see rivals making—feel the strategic imperative to go global in one form or another. Although the current financial crisis is

▌ Marcus Alexander is an adjunct professor of strategic and international management at London Business School, a director of the Ashridge Strategic Management Centre in London, and a coauthor, with Andrew Campbell, of "What's Wrong with Strategy?" (HBR November–December 1997).
▌ Harry Korine (hkorine@london.edu) is a teaching fellow in strategic and international management at London Business School and a senior research fellow at IFGE in Lyon, France. He is a coauthor, with Pierre-Yves Gomez, of *The Leap to Globalization* (Jossey-Bass, 2002) and *Entrepreneurs and Democracy* (Cambridge University Press, 2008). Both authors have worked with some of the companies mentioned in this article.
▌ Reprinted by permission of Harvard Business Review. From When You Shouldn't Go Global by Marcus Alexander and Harry Korine .December 2008. Copyright © 2008 by the Harvard Business School Publishing Corporation; all rights reserved.

putting a damper on such activity, the pressure on companies to globalize is likely to persist.

With this sense of inevitability, it's easy to forget the serious mistakes some companies have made because of their global strategies. Dutch financial-services firm ABN Amro, for example, acquired banks in numerous countries but wasn't able to achieve the integration needed to generate value with its international network. AES, a U.S.-based energy firm that operates 124 generation plants in 29 countries on five continents, has in recent years struggled to show that it is worth more than the sum of its individual geographic units. Daimler-Benz merged with Chrysler in 1998 in order to create a *Welt AG*—a world corporation—but never attained the power over markets and suppliers that this global position was supposed to deliver.

And these days, companies can't always chalk their mistakes up to experience and move on. Industry rivals and activist share owners are increasingly forcing firms to undo their international investments—

despite, in many cases, early endorsement by analysts and the market—and even to fire the senior management teams that made them. ABN Amro was dismembered last year by the Royal Bank of Scotland, Fortis, and Banco Santander, largely along geographic lines. AES's share price has tumbled since investors' initial enthusiasm for its globalization strategy, and some investment advisers are calling for the firm to be split into three or more parts. The architect of the Daimler-Chrysler deal, CEO Jürgen Schrempp, finally yielded to share-owner pressure and resigned, freeing up his successor to sell Chrysler to the private-equity giant Cerberus in 2007.

Indeed, we believe that businesses with ill-considered globalization strategies are poised to become the next targets for breakup or corporate overhaul by activist share owners, just as companies with poorly thought-out business diversification strategies were targets in the past. Today's activists include private-equity firms, hedge funds, and traditional pension funds, and they wield influence through a variety of means, from vocal use of the platform offered by a minority stake to all-out takeover and sell-off.

All right, even the best executive teams are going to make mistakes in a business environment as complex as today's. And no one would deny that the forces driving globalization are powerful and that the business benefits of becoming a global player can be tremendous. What concerns us is that so many companies seem to share unquestioned assumptions about the need to go global and are lulled by apparent safety in numbers as they move toward potential disaster. We highlight in this article several industries where this mind-set has been prevalent and a number of companies that have paid a high price for adopting it.

Avoiding Ill-Fated Strategies

Businesses have had international ambitions at least since the founding of the British East India and Hudson's Bay companies in the seventeenth century. Truly global corporations began appearing early in the last century, and their number has grown—with both successes and failures along the way—ever since.

But the accelerated removal of political and regulatory barriers to cross-border trading and investment over the past 15 years, along with the advent of technology that enables companies to conduct business around the world 24 hours a day, has made a global presence a generally accepted requisite in many industries. From the late 1990s onward, with a brief pause during the 2001–2003 bear market, we have witnessed a head-over-heels rush by companies to globalize: Foreign direct investments are at record levels, cross-border partnerships and acquisitions are burgeoning, worldwide sourcing continues to increase, and the pursuit of customers in emerging economies grows ever more heated.

Although such moves have benefited—or at least not irreparably damaged—many companies, we're beginning to see fallout. Sometimes firms have failed because their global strategies were deeply misguided, other times because execution was more difficult than anticipated.

We think that many failures could have been prevented—and would be avoided in the future—if companies seriously addressed three seemingly simple questions.

1. Are there potential benefits for our company? Just because a move makes sense for a rival or for companies in other industries doesn't mean it makes sense for your own company or industry. The race to globalize sometimes leads people to overestimate the size of the prize.

UK-based roof tile maker Redland, for example, expanded aggressively around the world beginning in the 1970s with the aim of leveraging its technical know-how beyond its home market. The problem: It often sought opportunities in countries, such as the United States and Japan, where local building practices provided very little demand for concrete roof tiles. Although the company was fully able to transfer the relevant technology, there was no value in doing so in such markets.

2. Do we have the necessary management skills? Even if potential benefits do exist for your company, you may not be in a position to realize them. The theoretical advantages of globalizing—economies of scale, for example—are devilishly difficult to achieve in practice, and companies often lack the management key needed to unlock the coffer holding the prize.

By the late 1990s, industrial conglomerate BTR had developed a presence in many countries. However, each business unit was run as a largely autonomous entity, with stringent profit accountability and little encouragement to work with others. This approach made sense in a fragmented world, but as BTR's customers globalized, they came to expect coordinated supply and support across borders. Although the opportunity was clear and BTR seemed well positioned to seize it, the company found it impossible to implement an approach so alien to its traditions. Even after a change of CEO and other senior staffers, the company culture blocked attempts at global integration, and the 1999 merger with Siebe was seen by many analysts as an admission that BTR simply could not make the changes needed.

3. Will the costs outweigh the benefits? Even if you are able to realize the benefits of a global move, unanticipated collateral damage to your business may make the endeavor counterproductive. Too often, companies fail to see that the full costs of going global may dwarf even a sizable prize—for example, when an effort to harmonize the practices of national business units drives away customers or distracts national management teams from the needs of their markets.

The increased complexity of managing international operations is also a threat. TCL, a Chinese maker of electronics and home appliances, has expanded rapidly into the United States and Europe through a series of acquisitions and joint ventures. As a result of deals in the past few years with Thomson and Alcatel, TCL has found itself with four R&D headquarters, 18 R&D centers, 20 manufacturing bases, and sales organizations in 45 countries. The cost of managing this infrastructure has outweighed the benefits of increased scale and resulted in large losses for both joint ventures.

Globalization's Siren Song

Companies neglect to ask themselves these seemingly obvious questions because of their complacent assumptions about the virtues of going global—assumptions that are reinforced by seductive messages from, among other places, the stock market. Although the siren song of globalization has lured companies of all kinds into this risky strategic space, recently the call has been particularly insidious in certain industry contexts, three of which we describe here. (For a description of how a management imperative such as "Become more global" can rapidly spread, see the sidebar "The Susceptibility to Managerial Fads.")

Deregulated Industries Many businesses in formerly state-owned industries, such as telecommunications, postal services, and utilities, have responded to deregulation with aggressive global moves. Faced with limited growth opportunities and often increasing competition in their home markets, companies have accepted that geographic expansion is the best way to exercise their new strategic freedom. These companies, the argument goes, can apply existing competencies—providing voice and data communication, delivering letters and parcels, distributing electricity and water, even dealing with the deregulation process itself—in new markets. They will enjoy significant savings by sharing resources across their international operations while "sticking to their knitting." The latter point—the importance of focusing on what they know how to do—is a key part of the argument, since unrelated diversification, itself once a widely touted strategy, has been largely discredited.

This apparently sound logic has turned out in many cases to be oversold by investment bankers or to be just plain flimsy. Companies frequently pay far too much to enter foreign markets. Furthermore, many of the deregulated industries are "glocal"—that is, customer expectations, operating environments, and management practices for what seem to be globally standard services can vary greatly

The Susceptibility to Managerial Fads

The belief that companies must become more global is the latest in a long line of widely held and generally unquestioned assumptions that can undermine the rational behavior of companies or entire industries.

The management trends—you might even call them fads—that grow out of these assumptions can be dangerous because they often lead to sloppy thinking. For example, the label used to describe a trend may get stretched far beyond its original meaning. "Reengineering" has come to mean nearly any corporate reorganization; "related diversification" is used today to justify acquisitions within categories, such as "communications media" and "financial services," that are so broad as to be almost meaningless. More troubling, the stampede by companies to join peers in mindlessly embracing such trends can cloud managers' judgment about what is worthwhile and achievable in their particular case.

The pathology of management fads has an underlying dynamic that is worth exploring:

Company X, with talented people at the helm, pioneers a new management approach. The firm does well, and others take notice. Maybe one or two experiment with similar innovations. Then stock market analysts and journalists spot the new approach. They view it as part of a broader pattern, and someone comes up with a clever-sounding label. The word "paradigm" may even get tossed around. As the phenomenon gains visibility—often in publications like this one—academics develop "frameworks" to help companies understand it. Their codification, intended simply to explain the phenomenon, further validates it. (Consultants also develop frameworks, though usually with the aim of selling the trend as a product.)

Over time, people use the now-familiar label more and more loosely. They group all manner of activities under the heading. Despite its ambiguity, there is a growing sense that activities under the rubric are worthwhile. Investment bankers cite the concept as a reason for companies to make acquisitions or other moves, and in the enthusiasm of deal making everyone glosses over the difficulties of integration and implementation. Financial markets sometimes reward companies just for announcing that they have adopted the new approach.

Sadly, the original insight, not to mention an appreciation of the context that gave rise to it, soon gets lost as companies scramble to become part of the trend. Before long, they are copying all sorts of elements and manifestations that are at best tangential and often irrelevant to the sought-after benefit. By the time a few books have come out on the topic, managers are embarrassed if they can't point to examples within their own organizations.

As the herd piles in, smart managers are already scanning the horizon for a new idea that will give them a competitive advantage. But others continue to give little thought to whether the trend has played out—or was never likely to benefit a company in their situation. There is always a lag before misapplications of the concept start to affect companies' numbers. Even when they do, many corporate managers, with stacks of statements and presentations extolling the virtues of the approach, are reluctant to abandon it. The stubborn ones carry on regardless of mounting costs—thereby setting the stage for activist share owners to step in and force a change.

This discouraging scenario doesn't unfold because the original concept was wrong. (Globalizing isn't necessarily bad; not globalizing isn't necessarily good.) It plays out because embracing a trend often precludes careful examination of the pros and cons of the specific choices made by a single company in a particular context.

depending on location. Water distribution, for instance, may not in fact be the same industry in the regulatory settings of two different countries. In addition, cross-border economies, if they exist at all, may be hard to achieve. It is difficult, for example, to optimize electricity flows over uncoordinated grids.

Faced with such challenges, a number of companies have struggled with or reversed their global moves. Kelda, a UK water utility, sold its U.S. business six years after acquiring it because differences in pricing, environmental regulations, and distribution proved so great that the business could be run only on a stand-alone basis.

Partly because of national differences in customer behavior, Deutsche Telekom has ended up running its U.S. unit, T-Mobile USA, as a completely independent business that could be sold off at any time. Rival telecom operator Vodafone has been forced by dissatisfied share owners to unload its Japanese subsidiary, J-Phone.

Deutsche Post, in assembling an international network of mail, express, and logistics services, overpaid significantly for the U.S. express-delivery services DHL and Airborne. Germany's former state-owned monopoly has also had great difficulty integrating DHL's entrepreneurial management culture with its own. Some analysts value the sum of Deutsche Post's separate businesses as 25% greater than the market value of the company—an assessment that is likely to increase pressure to spin off some of those businesses.

Service Industries Companies in traditionally national and fragmented service industries, such as retailing, consumer banking, and insurance, have viewed globalization as a way to realize scale economies and to generate growth beyond home markets themselves facing an incursion of foreign competition. In some cases, globalization seems to make sense because customers and suppliers are also becoming more global.

As in deregulated industries, however, the "global" customer may be more national than anticipated. And obtaining scale economies across borders requires management skills and experience that many companies lack. For example, serving a customer that is truly global in a consistent way from multiple national offices is no easy task.

Service businesses seeking to capture the benefits of a globalization strategy must, like firms in deregulated industries, pay attention to a mix of global and local factors. Purchasing can benefit from careful coordination across borders, but marketing and sales may suffer from too much standardization. Certain services travel much better than others that seem remarkably similar. In shoe retailing, for instance, offerings targeted at the wealthy or the young are far more global than those aimed at the middle market, which remains doggedly local.

In service businesses, many of the implementation challenges of a global strategy involve the coordination of people or processes. Wal-Mart, for instance, has struggled to get its partner firms and employees abroad to adopt its work routines. ABN Amro's global empire was dismantled by predators because the international business was a collection of mostly unrelated operations in countries ranging from Brazil to Monaco. The company achieved few economies of scale: In marketing, for example, it didn't enjoy the efficiencies resulting from a single global brand, because local banks mostly kept their original names. Furthermore, its attempts at sharing information systems, management processes, and other bits of infrastructure were repeatedly delayed and then implemented haphazardly, creating few savings.

The outcomes of some other service companies' global strategies have not been so dire—but they have still fallen short of expectations. Starbucks has pursued international growth at a breakneck pace, even though margins abroad have been only about half those of the company's U.S. operations. Axa, the global French insurance group, has enjoyed satisfactory financial performance from its many units around the world but has so far been unable to reduce its global cost base or convincingly roll out innovations, such as its U.S. variable-annuity program, internationally. Thus, although the globalization strategy hasn't destroyed value, it also hasn't added as much as originally envisioned.

Manufacturing Industries   Over the past decade, companies in manufacturing industries, such as automobiles and communications equipment, have viewed rapid cross-border consolidation as necessary for survival. Global mergers and partnerships seem to be the only way for companies to obtain the size needed to compete against consolidating rivals, to reduce their reliance on home markets, and to gain manufacturing economies of scale.

These benefits, though arguably easier to achieve than those sought by service companies (because local differences seem less problematic), are often outweighed by operational and organizational challenges. The complexities of integrating organizations and operations can cause costly delays or failures. And companies haven't had the luxury of much time to realize the benefits of integration. Counting on the benefits of size and scale to drop quickly to the bottom line, many manufacturers have become particularly vulnerable to economic slowdowns, which constrain their ability to pay for expansion and consolidation before an increasing debt-to-equity ratio forces their executive teams to cede control to financiers or new management.

The merger of Daimler-Benz and Chrysler is a poster child for this problem: The German and U.S. automakers were different in almost every respect, from company cultures to purchasing practices, and they were never able to attain such benefits as the promised billions of dollars in savings from common supply management.

Taiwanese consumer electronics company BenQ's acquisition of Siemens's mobile-device business followed a similar story line, including incompatibility of cultures and processes, as well as difficulties in integrating R&D activities. In a haunting echo of the scramble by Daimler-Benz and Chrysler to merge, BenQ didn't visit Siemens workshops and production lines before inking the deal, relying only on due diligence documents. Although BenQ continues to be active in mobile equipment, its German unit was declared bankrupt in 2007.

In both of these cases—and in numerous others—the strategic logic for globalization was tenuous, and the skills needed to implement a globalization strategy effectively were in short supply.

A Continuing Danger   We aren't saying that all globalization strategies are flawed. Telefónica, Spain's former telephone monopoly, has successfully expanded throughout much of the Spanish-speaking world. The past five years have seen General Electric's Commercial Finance business move rapidly and effectively into dozens of non-U.S. markets. Renault's pathbreaking alliance with Nissan has to this point proved beneficial for the French and Japanese automakers.

But focusing on such success stories only reinforces the conventional wisdom that a globalization strategy is a blanket requirement for doing business—which in turn leads many companies to insufficiently scrutinize their proposed global initiatives. (For a discussion of one of the gravest cases of failed globalization, see the sidebar "Royal Ahold's Downfall.")

We expect this trend to continue, as firms in various industries recklessly pursue global strategies. Take the emerging renewable-energy industry—companies developing technologies for biofuel, solar energy, and wind energy. We have talked with executives who, racing to establish a global position in this booming field, are planning rapid expansion over the next few years in Africa, Asia, and Latin America—and completely underestimating the management challenges involved. Many will, after initial applause from the financial markets, find their hastily conceived strategies challenged after the fact by activists.

We also anticipate that problems will recur in industries that earlier rushed to adopt globalization strategies, with activist share owners ready to pounce on companies as evidence of poor management

Royal Ahold's Downfall

Dutch supermarket operator Royal Ahold is best known in recent years for an accounting scandal that led to the resignation of its CEO and its CFO in 2003. The financial irregularities must be seen in light of the company's ambitious, and ultimately unsuccessful, globalization strategy.

Royal Ahold began its international expansion in the 1970s and accelerated it in the 1990s, eventually acquiring businesses throughout Europe, Asia, Latin America, and the United States, to become the fourth-largest retailer in the world. But the benefits of owning this network of stores were hard to realize or didn't exist in the first place.

Global economies of scale are one of the main rationales for international expansion. However, such economies, difficult to attain in many businesses, are particularly elusive in food retailing. Purchasing economies can be achieved only with items furnished by global suppliers to all markets—and these typically represent at most 20% of all supermarket items, because of cultural differences and the frequent need to source fresh food locally. Even apparently "international" products, such as hummus, must be adapted to different countries' distinct tastes.

Additionally, realizing synergies across a far-flung network requires common information systems and management processes, and Ahold made little effort to integrate its acquired businesses into the existing organization. Different information systems thus continued to coexist across the company, sometimes even within the same country.

Ironically, the lack of integrated systems and processes needed to secure global benefits helped conceal the company's financial irregularities. And the failure to attain those benefits undoubtedly put pressure on top managers to produce favorable—if false—financial results. When the new executive team finally introduced common management processes in the wake of the scandal, those processes did little to improve such activities as common purchasing across markets. As recently as last year, key suppliers were charging Ahold different prices in different countries.

Ahold's 2007 sale of most of its U.S. operations to private equity firms highlighted the nearly complete abandonment, under pressure from dissatisfied minority share owners, of its once ambitious globalization strategy. The dissidents were concerned not about the usual over-diversification of business types—after all, Royal Ahold remained focused on retailing—but about the over-diversification of geographic locations. (Tests for suitable business diversification are discussed in "Corporate Strategy: The Quest for Parenting Advantage," by Andrew Campbell, Michael Goold, and Marcus Alexander, in the March–April 1995 issue of HBR.) With the focus on governance at Ahold, the underlying story of failed globalization did not receive adequate attention until activist share owners jumped on it.

●

choices surfaces. Activist share owners have already taken significant positions in some companies mentioned in this article. Other target companies, perhaps not quite ripe for direct intervention—and temporarily shielded from attack by the current credit crisis and turbulent equity markets—are nonetheless being discussed in the boardrooms of rivals and by the investment committees of pension funds and private equity firms.

Ironically, some predators, having spotted the weaknesses of other companies' global strategies, may be poised to fall into the same trap. For example, the Royal Bank of Scotland is known for its highly successful 2000 acquisition of

NatWest, a much larger UK rival, and for the subsequent overhaul of its target's culture. But RBS may find it difficult to achieve similar results with the disparate banking assets—spread across more than 50 countries—that it acquired from ABN Amro. And though the recent government bailouts of RBS and Fortis aren't a direct result of the firms' international strategies, the acquisition of ABN Amro assets stretched their balance sheets and made the companies more vulnerable to the financial crisis.

We also worry that activist share owners and private equity firms may reproduce flawed globalization strategies in their own portfolios. The largest of these players are now more diversified, both in type of business and in international footprint, than many of the giant conglomerates of 30 years ago that were subsequently broken up and sold off. Indeed, as you look out on a landscape littered with the remains of dismembered companies weakened by failed globalization strategies, you have to wonder: Could today's predators be tomorrow's prey?

CHAPTER 2

Understanding the International Context:
Responding to Conflicting Environmental Forces

■ ■ ■ ■ ■ ■ ■ ■ ■ ■ ■ ■ ■ ■ ■ ■

In this chapter, we shift our focus from the internal forces that drive companies to expand to the larger, external, international environment in which they must operate. In particular, we focus on three sets of macro forces that drive, constrain, and shape the industries in which entities compete globally. First, we examine the pressures—mostly economic—that drive companies in many industries to integrate and coordinate their activities across national boundaries to capture scale economies or other sources of competitive advantage. Second, we explore the forces—often social and political—that shape other industries and examine how they can drive MNEs to disaggregate their operations and activities to respond to national, regional, and local needs and demands. Third, we examine how, in an information-based, knowledge-intensive economy, players in a growing number of industries must adapt to opportunities or threats wherever they occur in the world by developing innovative responses and initiatives that they diffuse rapidly and globally to capture a knowledge-based competitive advantage.

Recent changes in the international business environment have revolutionized the task facing MNE managers. Important shifts in political, social, economic, and technological forces have combined to create management challenges for today's MNEs that differ fundamentally from those facing companies just a couple of decades ago. Yet despite intense study by academics, consultants, and practicing managers, both the nature of the various external forces and their strategic and organizational implications are still widely disputed.

When Professor Theodore Levitt's classic *Harvard Business Review* article, "The Globalization of Markets," was first published, his ideas provoked widespread debate. In Levitt's view, technological, social, and economic trends were combining to create a unified world marketplace that was driving companies to develop globally standardized products that would enable them to capture global economies. His critics, however, claimed that Levitt presented only one side of the story. They suggested that, like many managers, he had become so focused on the forces for globalization that he was blind to their limitations and equally powerful countervailing forces.

The ensuing debate helped better define the diverse, changeable, and often contradictory forces that reshaped so many industries. In this chapter, we summarize a few of the most powerful of these environmental forces and suggest how they have collectively led to a new and complex set of challenges that require managers of MNEs to respond to three simultaneous yet often conflicting sets of external demands: cross-market integration, national responsiveness, and worldwide learning.

▣ Forces for Global Integration and Coordination

The phenomenon of globalization in certain industries, as described by Levitt, was not a sudden or discontinuous development. It was simply the latest round of change brought about by economic, technological, and competitive factors that, 100 years earlier, had transformed the structures of many industries from regional to national in scope. Economies of scale, economies of scope, and national differences in the availability and cost of productive resources were the three principal economic forces that drove this process of structural transformation of businesses, of which globalization was the latest stage.[1] The impact of these forces on MNE strategy had been facilitated by the increasingly liberal trading environment of the 1980s, 1990s, and 2000s. We now examine these forces of change in more detail.

Forces of Change: Scale, Scope, Factor Costs, and Free Trade

The Industrial Revolution created pressures for much larger plants that could capture the benefits of the *economies of scale* offered by the new technologies it spawned. Cheap and abundant energy combined with good transportation networks and new production technologies and began to restructure capital-intensive industries. For the first time, companies combined intermediate processes into single plants and developed large-batch or continuous-process technologies to achieve low-cost volume production.

However, in many industries, such as fine chemicals, automobiles, airframes, electronics, and oil refining, production at scale-economy volumes often exceeded the sales levels that individual companies could achieve in all but the largest nations, which pushed them to seek markets abroad. Even in industries in which the largest companies could retain a large enough share of their domestic markets to achieve scale economies without exports, those on the next rung were forced to seek markets outside their home countries if they were to remain competitive. In less capital-intensive industries, even companies that were largely unaffected by scale economies were transformed by the opportunities for *economies of scope* that were opened by more efficient, worldwide communication and transportation networks.

One classic example of how such economies could be exploited internationally was provided by trading companies that handle consumer goods. By exporting the products of many companies, they achieved a greater volume and lower per unit cost than any narrow-line manufacturer could in marketing and distributing its own products abroad.

In many industries, there were opportunities for economies of both scale and scope. Consumer electronics companies such as Matsushita, for example, derived scale advantages from their standardized TV, VCR, and DVD plants and scope advantages through

---

▣ [1]For a more detailed analysis of these environmental forces, see Alfred D. Chandler Jr., "The Evolution of the Modern Global Corporation," in *Competition in Global Industries,* ed. Michael Porter (Boston: Harvard Business School Press, 1986), pp. 405–48. For those interested in an even more detailed exposition, Chandler's book, *Scale and Scope* (Cambridge, MA: Harvard University Press, 1990) will prove compelling reading.

their marketing and sales networks that offered service, repair, and credit for a broad range of consumer electronics.

With changes in technology and markets came the requirement for access to new resources at the best possible prices, making differences in *factor costs* a powerful driver of globalization. Often no home-country sources could supply companies wishing to expand into new industry segments. European petroleum companies, for example, explored the Middle East because they had limited domestic crude oil sources. Others went overseas in search of bauxite from which to produce aluminum, rubber to produce tires for a growing automobile industry, or tea to be consumed by an expanding middle class.

Less capital-intensive industries such as textiles, apparel, and shoes turned to international markets as a source of cheap labor. The increased costs of transportation and logistics management were more than offset by much lower production costs. However, many companies found that, once educated, the cheap labor rapidly became expensive. Indeed, the typical life cycle of a country as a source of cheap labor for an industry is now only about 5 years. Therefore, companies chased cheap labor from southern Europe to Central America to the Far East and later to Eastern Europe.

Whereas the economics of scale and scope and the differences in factor costs between countries provided the underlying motivation for global coordination, the *liberalization of world trade* agreements facilitated much of the broad transition that has occurred in the past half-century. Beginning with the formation of the General Agreement on Tariffs and Trade (GATT) in 1945 and moving through various rounds of trade talks, the creation of regional free trade agreements such as the European Union (EU) and North American Free Trade Agreement (NAFTA), and the formation of the World Trade Organization (WTO), the dominant trend has been toward the reduction of barriers to international trade. The result is that the international trading environment of the 21st century is probably less restricted than ever before, which has enabled MNEs to realize most of the potential economic benefits that arise from global coordination.

The Expanding Spiral of Globalization

During the 1970s and 1980s, these forces began to globalize the structure and competitive characteristics of a variety of industries. In some, the change was driven by a major technological innovation that forced a fundamental realignment of industry economics. The impact of transistors and integrated circuits on the design and production of radios, televisions, and other consumer electronics represents a classic example of how new technologies drive the minimum efficient scale of production beyond the demand of most single markets. More recently, advances in semiconductor technology led to the boom in the PC industry, and innovations in wireless technology have led to the creation of the mobile phone industry. Advances in both of these technologies, combined with industry convergence, have resulted in the smart phone.

Many other industries lack strong external forces for change but transformed themselves through internal restructuring efforts, such as rationalizing their product lines, standardizing parts design, and specializing manufacturing operations. This trend led to a further wave of globalization, with companies in industries as diverse as automobiles, office equipment, industrial bearings, construction equipment, and machine tools all seeking to gain competitive advantages by capturing scale economies that extended beyond national markets.

Even some companies in classically local rather than global businesses have begun to examine the opportunities for capturing economies beyond their national borders. Rather than responding to the enduring differences in consumer tastes and market structures across European countries, many large, branded packaged goods companies such as Procter & Gamble and Unilever have transformed traditionally national businesses like soap and detergent manufacturing. By standardizing product formulations, rationalizing package sizes, and printing multilingual labels, they have been able to restructure and specialize their nationally dominated plant configurations and achieve substantial scale economies, which gives them significant advantages over purely local competitors.

Even labor-intensive local industries, such as office cleaning and catering, are not immune to the forces of globalization. For example, ISS, the Danish cleaning services company, has built a successful international business by transferring practices and know-how across countries and offering consistent, high-quality service to its international customers. Sodexo, a French company, has adopted a similar approach in the catering and food services industry and become highly successful on an international basis.

In market terms also, the spread of global forces expanded from businesses in which the global standardization of products was relatively easy (e.g., watches, cameras) to others in which consumers' preferences and habits only slowly converged (e.g., automobiles, appliances). Again, major external discontinuities often facilitate the change process, as in the case of the 2005 global oil price increases, which triggered a worldwide demand for smaller, more fuel-efficient or alternative-energy cars.

Even in markets in which national tastes or behaviors vary widely, globalizing forces can be activated if one or more competitors in a business choose to initiate and influence changes in consumer preference. Food tastes and eating habits were long thought to be the most culture-bound of all consumer behaviors. Yet, as companies like McDonald's, Coca-Cola, and Starbucks have shown, in Eastern and Western countries alike, even these culturally linked preferences can be changed.

Global Competitors as Change Agents

As the forces driving companies to coordinate their worldwide operations spread from industries in which such changes were triggered by some external structural discontinuity to those in which managers had to create the opportunity themselves, there emerged a new globalization force that spread rapidly across many businesses. It was a competitive strategy that some called *global chess* and that could be played only by companies that managed their worldwide operations as interdependent units that implemented a coordinated global strategy. Unlike the traditional multinational strategic approach, which was based on the assumption that each national market was unique and independent of the others, these global competitive games assumed that a company's competitive position in all markets was linked by financial and strategic interdependence.

Regardless of consumer tastes or manufacturing scale economies, it was suggested that corporations with worldwide operations had great advantages over national companies, in that they could use funds generated in one market to subsidize their position in another.

Whereas the classic exponents of this strategy were the Japanese companies that used the profit sanctuary of a protected home market to subsidize their loss-making expansions abroad in the 1980s, many others soon learned to play "global chess." For example, British Airways rose to become one of the most profitable airlines in the world because its dominant position at Heathrow Airport enabled it to make large profits on its long-haul routes (particularly the trans-Atlantic route) and essentially subsidize its lower margin U.K. and European business. In turn, it could fend off new entrants in Europe by pushing its prices down there while not putting its most profitable routes at risk. And existing competitors such as British Midland suffered because they lacked access to the lucrative Heathrow–U.S. routes.

Although few challenged the existence or growing influence of these diverse globalizing forces that were transforming the nature of competition worldwide, some questioned the unidimensionality of their influence and the universality of their strategic implications. They took issue, for example, with Levitt's suggestions that "the world's needs and desires have been irrevocably homogenized," that "no one is exempt and nothing can stop the process," and that "the commonality of preference leads inescapably to the standardization of products, manufacturing, and the institution of trade and commerce." Critics argued that, though these might indeed be long-term trends in many industries, there were important short- and medium-term impediments and countertrends that had to be taken into account if companies were to operate successfully in an international economy that jolts along—*perhaps* eventually toward Levitt's "global village."

Forces for Local Differentiation and Responsiveness

There are many different stories of multinational companies making major blunders in transferring their successful products or ideas from their home countries to foreign markets. General Motors is reported to have faced difficulties in selling the popular Chevrolet Nova in Mexico, where the product name sounded like "no va," meaning "does not go" in Spanish.[2] Similarly, when managers began investigating why the advertising campaign built around the highly successful "come alive with Pepsi" theme was not having the expected impact in Thailand, they discovered that the Thai copy translation read more like "come out of the grave with Pepsi." Although these and other such cases have been widely cited, they represent the most extreme and often simple-minded examples of an important strategic task facing managers of all MNEs: how to sense, respond to, and even exploit the differences in the environments of the many different countries in which their company operates.

National environments differ on many dimensions. For example, there are clear differences in the per capita gross national product or the industry-specific technological capabilities of Japan, Australia, Brazil, and Poland. They also differ in terms of political systems, government regulations, social norms, and the cultural values of their people. It is these differences that force managers to be sensitive and responsive to national, social, economic, and political characteristics of the host countries in which they operate.

---

[2]For this and many other such examples of international marketing problems, see David A. Ricks, *Blunders in International Business,* 4th ed. (Cornwall: Blackwell Publishing, 2006).

Far from being overshadowed by the forces of globalization, the impact of these localizing forces have been felt with increasing intensity and urgency throughout recent decades. First, in the early 1990s, many Japanese companies that had so successfully ridden the wave of globalization began to feel the strong need to become much more sensitive to host-country economic and political forces. This shift led to a wave of investment abroad, as Japanese companies sought to become closer to their export markets and more responsive to host governments.

Second, as the 1990s progressed, many North American and European companies also realized that they had pushed the logic of globalization too far and that a reconnection with the local environments in which they were doing business was necessary. For example, in March 2000, Coca-Cola's incoming CEO, Douglas Daft, explained his company's shift in policy in the *Financial Times*: "As the 1990s were drawing to a close, the world had changed course, and Coca-Cola had not." Said Daft, "We were operating as a big, slow, insulated, sometimes even insensitive 'global' company; and we were doing it in an era when nimbleness, speed, transparency and local sensitivity had become absolutely essential."

Similarly Nokia realized that its standard mobile phones were not capturing the needs of the rural India customer market. A series of seemingly small product adaptions allowed it to access this rapidly growing base, one estimated at 55 million subscribers by 2004.

Cultural Differences

A large body of academic research provides strong evidence that nationality plays an important and enduring role in shaping the assumptions, beliefs, and values of individuals. Perhaps the most celebrated work describing and categorizing these differences in the orientations and values of people in different countries is Geert Hofstede's study that describes national cultural differences along four key dimensions: power distance, uncertainty avoidance, individualism, and "masculinity."[3] The study demonstrates how distinct cultural differences across countries result in wide variations in social norms and individual behavior (e.g., the Japanese respect for elders, the culturally embedded American response to time pressure) and are reflected in the effectiveness of different organizational forms (e.g., the widespread French difficulty with the dual-reporting relationships of a matrix organization) and management systems (e.g., the Swedes' egalitarian culture leads them to prefer flatter organizations and smaller wage differentials).

However, cultural differences are also reflected in nationally differentiated consumption patterns, including the way people dress or the foods they prefer. Take the example of tea as a beverage consumed around the globe. The British drink their tea as a light brew further diluted with milk, whereas Americans consume it primarily as a summer drink served over ice, and Saudi Arabians drink theirs as a thick, hot, heavily sweetened brew.

---

[3]For a more detailed exposition, see Hofstede's book *Culture's Consequences,* 2nd ed. (Beverly Hills, CA: Sage Publications, 2001). A brief overview of the four different aspects of national culture are presented in the reading "Culture and Organization" at the end of this chapter. For managerial implications of such differences in national culture, see also Nancy J. Adler and A. Gundersen, *International Dimensions of Organizational Behavior,* 5th ed. (Mason, OH: Thomson South-Western, 2008), and Fons Trompenaars and Charles Hampden-Turner, *Riding the Waves of Culture* (London: Nicholas Brealey Publishing, 1997).

To succeed in a world of such diversity, companies often must modify their quest for global efficiency through standardization and find ways to respond to the needs and opportunities created by cultural differences. HSBC has gone so far as to define itself as "The world's local bank," for its ability to understand such cultural differences.

Government Demands

Inasmuch as cultural differences among countries have been an important localizing force, the diverse demands and expectations of home and host governments have perhaps been the most severe constraint to the global strategies of many MNEs. Traditionally, the interactions between companies and host governments have had many attributes of classic love–hate relationships.

The "love" of the equation was built on the benefits each could bring to the other. To the host government, the MNE represented an important source of funds, technology, and expertise that could help further national priorities, such as regional development, employment, import substitution, and export promotion. To the MNE, the host government represented the key to local market or resource access, which provided new opportunities for profit, growth, and improvement of its competitive position.

The "hate" side of the relationship—more often emerging as frustration rather than outright antagonism—arose from the differences in the motivations and objectives of the two partners.

To be effective global competitors, MNEs sought three important operating objectives: unrestricted access to resources and markets throughout the world; the freedom to integrate manufacturing and other operations across national boundaries; and the unimpeded right to coordinate and control all aspects of the company on a worldwide basis. The host government, in contrast, sought to develop an economy that could survive and prosper in a competitive international environment. At times, this objective led to the designation of another company—perhaps a "national champion"—as its standard bearer in the specific industry, bringing it into direct conflict with the MNE. This conflict is particularly visible in the international airline business, in which flag-carrying companies such as Air France or Malaysia Airlines compete only after receiving substantial government subsidies. But it also has been a thorny issue among their biggest suppliers, with Boeing complaining to the WTO that Airbus is violating free trade agreements through the support it receives from various European governments.

Even when the host government does not have such a national champion and is willing to permit and even support an MNE's operations within its boundaries, it usually does so only at a price. Although both parties might be partners in the search for global competitiveness, the MNE typically tried to achieve that objective within its global system, whereas the host government strove to capture it within its national boundaries, thereby leading to conflict and mutual resentment.

The potential for conflict between the host government and the MNE arose not only from economic but also from social, political, and cultural issues. MNE operations often cause social disruption in the host country through rural exodus, rising consumerism, rejection of indigenous values, or a breakdown of traditional community structures.

Similarly, even without the maliciousness of MNEs that, in previous decades, blatantly tried to manipulate host government structures or policies (e.g., ITT's attempt to overthrow the Allende government in Chile), MNEs can still represent a political threat because of their size, power, and influence, particularly in developing economies.

Because of these differences in objectives and motivations, MNE–host government relationships are often seen as a zero-sum game in which the outcome depends on the balance between the government's power (arising from its control over local market access and competition among different MNEs for that access) and the MNE's power (arising from its financial, technological, and managerial resources and the competition among national governments for those resources).

If, in the 1960s, the multinational companies had been able to hold "sovereignty at bay," as one respected international researcher concluded,[4] by the 1980s, the balance had tipped in the other direction. In an effort to stem the flood of imports, many countries began bending or sidestepping trade agreements signed in previous years. By the early 1980s, even the U.S. government, traditionally one of the strongest advocates of free trade, began to negotiate a series of orderly marketing agreements and voluntary restraints on Japanese exports, while threats of sanctions were debated with increasing emotion in legislative chambers around the globe. And countries became more sophisticated in the demands they placed on inward-investing MNEs. Rather than allowing superficial investment in so-called "screwdriver plants" that provided only limited, low-skill employment, governments began to specify the levels of local content, technology transfer, and a variety of other conditions, from reexport commitment to plant location requirements.

In the 1990s, however, the power of national governments was once again on the wane. The success of countries such as Ireland and Singapore in driving their economic development through foreign investment led many other countries—both developed and developing—to launch aggressive inward investment policies of their own.

This increased demand for investment allowed MNEs to play countries off one another and, in many cases, to extract a high price from the host country. For example, according to *The Economist,* the incentives paid by Alabama to Mercedes for its 1993 auto plant cost the state $167,000 per direct employee.

In the first years of the new millennium, the once-troublesome issue of MNE–country bargaining power evolved into a relatively efficient market system for inward investment, at least in the developed world. However, the developing world was a rather different story, with MNEs continuing to be embroiled in political disputes, such as the 1995 hanging of environmental activist Ken Saro-Wiwa by the Nigerian government because of his opposition to Shell's exploitation of his people's land. In addition, MNEs have regularly attracted the brunt of criticism from so-called antiglobalization protestors during WTO meetings. The antiglobalization movement includes a diverse mix of groups with different agendas but that are united in their concern that the increasing liberalization of trade through the WTO is being pursued for the benefit of MNEs and at the expense of people and companies in less developed parts of the world.

Although this movement does not have a coherent set of policy proposals of its own, it provides a salutary reminder to policymakers and the executives managing MNEs that

[4]Raymond Vernon, *Sovereignty at Bay* (New York: Basic Books, 1971).

the globalization of business remains a contentious issue. The rewards are not spread evenly, and for many people in many parts of the world, the process of globalization makes things worse before it makes them better. The movement has forced MNEs to re-think their more contentious policies and encouraged them to articulate the benefits they bring to less developed countries. For example, the oil majors Shell and BP now actively promote polices for sustainable development—including research into renewable sources of energy and investments in the local communities in which they operate around the world.

Growing Pressures for Localization

Although there is no doubt that the increasing frequency of world travel and the ease with which communication linkages occur across the globe have done a great deal to reduce the effects of national consumer differences, it would be naïve to believe that worldwide tastes, habits, and preferences have become anywhere near homogenous. One need only look at the breakfast buffet items within any major hotel in Beijing. These hotels need to appeal to large groups of consumers from within China, from North America, from Europe, from Japan, and elsewhere. So separate breakfast stations will variously provide steamed breads and noodles, bacon and eggs, cold cuts and cheese, and miso soup.

Even though many companies have succeeded in appealing to—and accelerating—convergence worldwide, even the trend toward standardized products that are designed to appeal to a lowest common denominator of consumer demand has a flip side. In industry after industry, a large group of consumers has emerged to reject the homogenized product design and performance of standardized global products.

By reasserting traditional preferences for more differentiated products, they have created openings—often very profitable ones—for companies willing to respond to, and even expand, the need for products and services that are more responsive to those needs.

When Office Depot issues a request of its vendors for refrigerators that could be locked for improved security in offices and dormitories, Haier was willing to create such a customized product.[5] The fact that such an innovation originated in a firm from China also underscores how localization solutions may appear from previously unlikely locales. Increasingly, it is MNEs from emerging markets that seem best equipped to compete in other emerging markets.

Other consumer and market trends are emerging to counterbalance the forces of global standardization of products. In an increasing number of markets, from telecommunications to office equipment to consumer electronics, consumers are not so much buying individual products as selecting systems. With advances in wireless and internet technology, for example, the television set is becoming part of a home entertainment and information system, connected to a DVD player, music system, home computer, gaming system, and online databank and information network. This transformation is

---

[5]For further detail, see Peter J. Williamson and Ming Zeng, *Dragons at Your Door: How Chinese Cost Innovation is Disrupting Global Competition* (Boston: Harvard Business School Press, 2007).

forcing companies to adapt their standard hardware-oriented products to more flexible and locally differentiated systems that consist of hardware plus software services. In such an environment, the competitive edge lies less with the company that has the most scale-efficient global production capability and more with the one that is sensitive and responsive to local requirements and able to develop the software and services to meet those demands.

In addition to such barriers, other important impediments exist. Although the benefits of scale economies obviously must outweigh the additional costs of supplying markets from a central point, companies often ignore that those costs consist of more than just freight charges. In particular, the administrative costs of coordination and scheduling worldwide demand through global-scale plants usually is quite significant and must be taken into account. For some products, lead times are so short or market service requirements so high that these scale economies may well be offset by other costs.

More significantly, developments in computer-aided design and manufacturing, robotics, and other advanced production technologies have made the concept of flexible manufacturing a viable reality. Companies that previously had to produce tens or hundreds of thousands of standardized printed circuit boards (PCBs) in a central, global-scale plant now can achieve the minimum efficient scale in smaller, distributed, national plants closer to their customers. Flexible manufacturing technologies mean there is little difference in unit costs between making 1,000 or 100,000 PCBs. When linked to the consumer's growing disenchantment with homogenized global products, this technology appears to offer multinational companies an important tool that will enable them to respond to localized consumer preferences and national political constraints without compromising their economic efficiency.

Forces for Worldwide Innovation and Learning

The trends we have described have created an extremely difficult competitive environment in many industries, and only those firms that have been able to adapt to the often conflicting forces for global coordination and national differentiation have been able to survive and prosper. But on top of these forces, another set of competitive demands has been growing rapidly around the need for fast, globally coordinated innovation. Indeed, in the emerging competitive game, victory often goes to the company that can most effectively harness its access to worldwide information and expertise to develop and diffuse innovative products and processes on a worldwide basis.

The trends driving this shift in the competitive game in many ways derive from the globalizing and localizing forces we described previously. The increasing cost of R&D, coupled with shortening life cycles of new technologies and the products they spawn, have combined to reinforce the need for companies to seek global volume to amortize their heavy investments as quickly as possible. At the same time, even the most advanced technology has diffused rapidly around the globe, particularly during the past few decades. In part, this trend has been a response to the demands, pressures, and coaxing of host governments as they bargain for increasing levels of national production and high levels of local content in the leading-edge products being sold in their markets. But the high cost of product and process development has also encouraged companies to transfer new technologies voluntarily, with licensing becoming an important source of funding, cross-licensing a means to fill technology gaps for many MNEs, and joint development programs and strategic alliances a strategy for rapidly building global competitive advantage.

When coupled with converging consumer preferences worldwide, this diffusion of technology has had an important effect on both the pace and locus of innovation. No longer can U.S.-based companies assume that their domestic environment provides them with the most sophisticated consumer needs and the most advanced technological capabilities, and thus the most innovative environment in the world. Today, the newest consumer trend or market need might emerge in Australia or Italy, and the latest technologies to respond to these new needs may be located in Japan or Sweden. Innovations are springing up worldwide, and companies are recognizing that they can gain competitive advantage by sensing needs in one country, responding with capabilities located in a second, and diffusing the resulting innovation to markets around the globe.

A related trend is the increasing importance of global standards in such industries as computer software, telecommunications, consumer electronics, and even consumer goods. The winners in the battle for a new standard—from software platforms to razor blade cartridges—can build and defend dominant competitive positions that can endure worldwide for decades. First-mover advantages have increased substantially and provided strong incentives for companies to focus attention not only on the internal task of rapidly creating and diffusing innovations within their own worldwide operations, but also on the external task of establishing the new product as an industry standard. This issue is so vital for MNEs today that we will return to examine it in greater detail in Chapter 5.

Responding to the Diverse Forces Simultaneously

Trying to distill key environmental demands in large and complex industries is a hazardous venture but, at the risk of oversimplification, we can make the case that until the late 1980s, most worldwide industries presented relatively unidimensional environmental requirements. Though it led to the development of industries with very different characteristics—those we distinguish as global, multinational, and international industries—more recently, this differentiation has been eroding with important consequences for companies' strategies.

Global, Multinational, and International Industries

In some businesses, the economic forces of globalization were historically strong and dominated other environmental demands. For example, in the consumer electronics industry, the invention of the transistor led to decades of inexorable expansion in the benefits of scale economies: Successive rounds of technological change, such as the introduction of integrated circuits and microprocessors, led to a huge increase in the minimum efficient scale of operations for TV sets. In an environment of falling transportation costs, low tariffs, and increasing homogenization of national markets, these-huge-scale economics dominated the strategic tasks for managers of consumer electronics companies in the closing decades of the last century.

Such industries, in which the economic forces of globalization are dominant, we designate as *global industries*. In these businesses, success typically belongs to companies that adopt the classic *global strategies* of capitalizing on highly centralized, scale-intensive manufacturing and R&D operations and leveraging them through worldwide exports of standardized global products.

In other businesses, the localizing forces of national, cultural, social, and political differences dominate the development of industry characteristics. In laundry detergents, for example, R&D and manufacturing costs were relatively small parts of a company's total expenses, and all but the smallest markets could justify an investment in a detergent tower and benefit from its scale economies. At the same time, sharp differences in laundry practices, perfume preferences, phosphate legislation, distribution channels, and other such attributes of different national markets led to significant benefits from differentiating products and strategies on a country-by-country basis.

This differentiation is typical of what we call *multinational industries*—worldwide businesses in which the dominance of national differences in cultural, social, and political environments allow multiple national industry structures to flourish. Success in such businesses typically belongs to companies that follow *multinational strategies* of building strong and resourceful national subsidiaries that are sensitive to local market needs and opportunities and allow them to manage their local businesses by developing or adapting products and strategies to respond to the powerful localizing forces.

Finally, in some other industries, technological forces are central, and the need for companies to develop and diffuse innovations is the dominant source of competitive advantage. For example, the most critical task for manufacturers of telecommunications switching equipment has been the ability to develop and harness new technologies and exploit them worldwide. In these *international industries,* it is the ability to innovate and appropriate the benefits of those innovations in multiple national markets that differentiates the winners from the losers.

In such industries, the key to success lies in a company's ability to exploit technological forces by creating new products and to leverage the international life cycles of the product by effectively transferring technologies to overseas units. We describe this as an *international strategy*—the ability to effectively manage the creation of new products and processes in one's home market and sequentially diffuse those innovations to foreign affiliates.

Transition to Transnationality

Our portrayal of the traditional demands in some major worldwide industries is clearly oversimplified. Different tasks in the value-added chains of different businesses are subject to different levels of economic, political, cultural, and technological forces. We have described what can be called the *center of gravity* of these activities—the environmental forces that have the most significant impact on industry's strategic task demands.

By the closing years of the 20th century however, these external demands were undergoing some important changes. In many industries, the earlier dominance of a single set of environmental forces was replaced by much more complex environmental demand, in which each of the different sets of forces was becoming strong simultaneously. For example, new economies of scale and scope and intensifying competition among a few competitors were enhancing the economic forces toward increased global integration in many multinational and international industries. In the detergent business, product standardization has become more feasible because the growing penetration and standardization of washing machines has narrowed the differences in washing practices across countries. Particularly in regional markets such as Europe or South America, companies have leveraged this potential for product standardization by developing regional brands, uniform multilingual packaging, and common advertising themes, all of which have led to additional economies.

Similarly, localizing forces are growing in strength in global industries such as consumer electronics. Although the strengths of the economic forces of scale and scope have continued to increase, host government pressures and renewed customer demand for differentiated products are forcing companies with global strategies to reverse their earlier strategies, which were based on exporting standard products. To protect their competitive positions, they have begun to emphasize the local design and production of differentiated product ranges in different countries and for different international segments.

Finally, in the emerging competitive battle among a few large firms with comparable capabilities in global-scale efficiency and nationally responsive strategies, the ability to innovate and exploit the resulting developments globally is becoming more and more important for building durable comparative advantage, even in industries in which global economic forces or local political and cultural influences had previously been dominant. In the highly competitive mobile phone business, for example, all surviving major competitors must have captured the minimum scale efficiency to play on the global field, as well as the requisite government relationships and consumer understanding to respond to market differences. Today, competition in this industry consists primarily of a company's ability to develop innovative new products—perhaps in response to a consumer trend in Japan, a government requirement in Germany, or a technological development in the United States—and then diffuse it rapidly around the world.

In the emerging international environment, therefore, there are fewer and fewer examples of pure global, textbook multinational, or classic international industries. Instead, more and more businesses are driven by *simultaneous* demands for global efficiency, national responsiveness, and worldwide innovation. These are the characteristics of what we call a *transnational industry*. In such industries, companies find it increasingly difficult to defend a competitive position on the basis of only one dominant capability. They need to develop their ability to respond effectively to all the diverse and conflicting forces at one and the same time to manage efficiency, responsiveness, and innovation without trading off any one for the other.

The emergence of the transnational industry has not only made the needs for efficiency, responsiveness, and innovation simultaneous, it has also made the tasks required to achieve each of these capabilities more demanding and complex. Rather than achieve world-scale economies through centralized and standardized production, companies must instead build global efficiency through a worldwide infrastructure of distributed but specialized assets and capabilities that exploit comparative advantages, scale economies, and scope economies simultaneously. In most industries, a few global competitors now compete head-to-head in almost all major markets.

To succeed in such an environment, companies must understand the logic of global chess: Build and defend profit sanctuaries that are impenetrable to competitors; leverage existing strengths to build new advantages through cross-subsidizing weaker products and market positions; make high-risk, preemptive investments that raise the stakes and force out rivals with weaker stomachs and purse strings; and form alliances and coalitions to isolate and outflank competitors. These and other similar maneuvers must now be combined with world-scale economies to develop and maintain global competitive efficiency.

Similarly, responsiveness through differentiated and tailor-made local-for-local products and strategies in each host environment is neither necessary nor feasible anymore. National customers no longer demand differentiation; they demand sensitivity to their needs, along with the level of cost and quality standards for global products to which they have become accustomed. At the same time, host governments' desire to build their national competitiveness dominates economic policy in many countries, and MNEs are frequently viewed as key instruments in the implementation of national competitive strategies. Changes in regulations, tastes, exchange rates, and related factors have become less predictable and more frequent. In such an environment, more responsiveness has become inadequate. The flexibility to change product designs, sourcing patterns, and pricing policies continuously to remain responsive to continually changing national environments has become essential for survival.

Finally, exploiting centrally developed products and technologies is no longer enough. MNEs must build the capability to learn from the many environments to which they are exposed and to appropriate the benefits of such learning throughout their global operations. Although some products and processes must still be developed centrally for worldwide use and others must be created locally in each environment to meet purely local demands, MNEs must increasingly use their access to multiple centers of technologies and familiarity with diverse customer preferences in different countries to create truly transnational innovations. Similarly, environmental and competitive information acquired in different parts of the world must be collated and interpreted to become a part of the company's shared knowledge base and provide input to future strategies.

Concluding Comments: The Strategic and Organizational Challenge

The increasing complexity of forces in the global environment and the need to respond simultaneously to their diverse and often conflicting demands have created some major challenges for many multinational companies. The classic global companies, such as many highly successful Japanese and Korean companies whose competitive advantage is rooted in a highly efficient and centralized system, have been forced to respond more effectively to the demands for national responsiveness and worldwide innovation. The traditional multinational companies—many of them European—have the advantage of national responsiveness but face the challenge of exploiting global-scale economic and technological forces more effectively. And U.S. companies, with their more international approach to leveraging home country innovations abroad, struggle to build more understanding of the cultural and political forces and respond to national differences more effectively while simultaneously enhancing global-scale efficiency through improved scale economies.

Yet despite these efficiencies, vineyards became smaller, not larger. Over many centuries, small agricultural holdings were continually fragmented as land was parceled out by kings, taken in wars, or broken up through inheritance. During the French Revolution, many large estates were seized, divided, and sold at auction. And after 1815, the Napoleonic inheritance code prescribed how land had to be passed on to all rightful heirs. By the mid-19th century, the average holding in France was 5.5 ha. and was still being subdivided. (In Italy, similar events left the average vineyard at 0.8 ha.)

While the largest estates made their own wine, most small farmers sold their grapes to the local wine maker or *vintner*. With payment based on weight, there was little incentive to pursue quality by reducing yield. Some small growers formed cooperatives, hoping to participate in wine making's downstream profit, but grape growing and wine making remained highly fragmented.

Distribution and Marketing   Traditionally, wine was sold in bulk to merchant traders—*négociants* in France—who often blended and bottled the product before distributing it. But poor roads and complex toll and tax systems made cross-border shipping extremely expensive. In the early 19th century, for example, a shipment of wine from Strasbourg to the Dutch border had to pass through 31 toll stations.[2] And since wine did not travel well, much of it spoiled on the long journeys. As a result, only the most sophisticated *négociants* could handle exports, and only the rich could afford the imported luxury.

Late 18th century innovations such as mass production of glass bottles, the use of cork stoppers, and the development of pasteurization revolutionized the industry. With greater wine stability and longevity, distribution to distant markets and bottle aging of good vintages became the norm. Increased vine plantings and expanded production followed, and a global market for wine was born.

Regulation and Classification   As the industry developed, it became increasingly important to the cultural and economic life of the producing countries. By the mid-18th century in France, grape growing supported 1.5 million families and an equal number in wine-related businesses. Eventually, it accounted for one-sixth of France's total trading revenue, and was the country's second-largest export.

The industry's growing cultural and economic importance attracted political attention, and with it, laws and regulations to control almost every aspect of wine making. For example, Germany's 1644 wine classification scheme prescribed 65 classes of quality, with rules for everything from ripeness required for harvesting to minimum sugar content. (Even in 1971, a law was passed in Germany requiring a government panel to taste each vineyard's annual vintage and assign it a quality level.[3]) Similar regulations prescribing wine-making practices also existed in France and Italy.

Rather than resisting such government classifications and controls, producers often supported and even augmented them as a way of differentiating their products and raising entry barriers. For example, the current French classification system was created by a Bordeaux committee prior to the 1855 Exposition in Paris. To help consumers identify their finest wines, they classified about 500 vineyards into five levels of quality, from *premier cru* (first growth) to *cinquième cru* (fifth growth).

Because it helped consumers sort through the complexity of a highly fragmented market, this marketing tool soon gained wide recognition, leading the government to codify and expand it in the *Appellation d'Origin Controllée* (AOC) laws of 1935. These laws also defined regional boundaries and set detailed and quite rigid standards for vineyards and wine makers.[4] Eventually, more than 300 AOC designations were authorized, from the well-known (Saint Emilion or Beaujolais) to the obscure (Fitou or St. Péray). (A similar classification

---

[2]Robinson, p. 308.

[3]Ibid., p. 312.

[4]Dewey Markham, *1855: A History of the Bordeaux Classification* (New York: Wiley, 1998), p. 177.

scheme was later introduced in Italy defining 213 *Denominazione di Origne Controllate* (or DOC) regions, each with regulations prescribing area, allowed grape varieties, yields, required growing practices, acceptable alcohol content, label design, etc.[5])

Later, other wine regions of France were given official recognition with the classification of *Vins Delimités de Qualite Superieure* (VDQS), but these were usually regarded as of lower rank than AOC wines. Below VDQS were *Vins de Pays*, or country wine—inexpensive but very drinkable wines for French tables, and increasingly, for export. These categories were quite rigid with almost no movement across them. This was due to a belief that quality was linked to *terroir*, the almost mystical combination of soil, aspect, microclimate, rainfall, and cultivation that the French passionately believed gave the wine from each region—and indeed, each vineyard—its unique character.

But *terroir* could not guarantee consistent quality. As an agricultural product, wine was always subject to the vagaries of weather and disease. In the last quarter of the 19th century, a deadly New World insect, phylloxera, devastated the French vine stock. From a production level of 500 million liters in 1876, output dropped to just 2 million liters in 1885. But a solution was found in an unexpected quarter: French vines were grafted onto phylloxera-resistant vine roots native to the United States and imported from the upstart Californian wine industry. It was the first time many in the Old World acknowledged the existence of a New World wine industry. It would not be the last.

Stirrings in the New World

Although insignificant in both size and reputation compared with the well-established industry in traditional wine-producing countries, vineyards and wine makers had been set up in many New World countries since the 18th century. In the United States, for example, Thomas Jefferson, an enthusiastic oenologist, became a leading voice for establishing

vineyards in Virginia. And in Australia, vines were brought over along with the first fleet carrying convicts and settlers in 1788. Nascent wine industries were also developing at this time in Argentina, Chile, and South Africa, usually under the influence of immigrants from the Old World wine countries.

Opening New Markets   While climate and soil allowed grape growing to flourish in the New World, the consumption of wine in these countries varied widely. It became part of the national cultures in Argentina and Chile, where per capita annual consumption reached about 80 liters in Argentina and 50 liters in Chile in the 1960s. While such rates were well behind France and Italy, both of which boasted per capita consumption of 110–120 liters in this era, they were comparable with those of Spain.

Other New World cultures did not embrace the new industry as quickly. In Australia, the hot climate and a dominant British heritage made beer the alcoholic beverage of preference, with wine being consumed mostly by Old World immigrants. The U.S. market was more complex. In keeping with the country's central role in the rum trade, one segment of the population followed a tradition of drinking hard liquor. But another group reflected the country's Puritan heritage and espoused temperance or abstinence. (As recently as 1994, a Gallup survey found that 45% of U.S. respondents did not drink at all, and 21% favored a renewal of prohibition.) As a result, in the pre-World War II era, wine was largely made by and sold to European immigrant communities.

In the postwar era, however, demand for wine increased rapidly in the United States, Australia, and other New World producers. In the United States, for example, consumption grew from a post-prohibition per capita level of 1 liter per annum to 9 liters by 2006. In Australia the rate of increase was even more rapid, from less than 2 liters in 1960 to 24 liters by 2006. This growth in consumption was coupled with a growing demand for higher quality wines, resulting in a boom in domestic demand that proved a boost for the young New World wine industry.

[5]Robinson, p. 235.

Challenging Production Norms   On the back of the postwar economic boom, New World wine producers developed in an industry environment different from their European counterparts. First, suitable land was widely available and less expensive, allowing the growth of much more extensive vineyards. As a result, in 2006, the average vineyard holding in the United States was 213 hectares and in Australia 167 hectares, compared to an Italian average of 1.3 hectares, and 7.4 hectares in France.[6]

Unconstrained by tradition, New World producers also began to experiment with grape growing and wine making technology. In Australia, controlled drip irrigation allowed expansion into marginal land and reduced vintage variability. (In contrast, irrigation was strictly forbidden in France under AOC regulations.) The larger vineyards also allowed the use of specialized equipment such as mechanical harvesters and mechanical pruners which greatly reduced labor costs.

Innovation also extended into viniculture where New World producers pursued techniques such as night harvesting to maximize grape sugars, while innovative trellis systems permitted vines to be planted at twice the traditional density. Other experiments with fertilizers and pruning methods increased yield and improved grape flavor. These innovations, when coupled with typically sunny climates, freed New World farmers from many of the stresses of their counterparts in regions like Bordeaux where the rainy maritime climate made late autumn harvests risky, and held wine producers hostage to wide year-to-year vintage variations.

New World wine companies also broke many wine making traditions. Large estates usually had on-site labs to provide analysis helpful in making growing and harvest decisions. In the 1990s, some experimented with a reverse osmosis technology to concentrate the juice (or *must*), ensuring a deeper-colored, richer-tasting wine. (Ironically, the technique was developed in France, but most French producers deplored it as "removing the poetry of wine." Needless to say, it was a forbidden practice under AOC regulations.) New World wine makers also developed processes that allowed fermentation and aging to occur in huge, computer-controlled, stainless steel tanks rather than in traditional oak barrels. To provide oak flavor, some added oak chips while aging their popular priced wines—another practice strictly forbidden in most traditional-producing countries.

The economic impact of these and other innovations became clear in a comparison of the costs of production in the Langedoc region of France with the Riverina district in Australia, both big producers of popular priced wines. The French cost per tonne of €238 was 74% higher than the Australian cost of €137.[7] And South American grape costs were even lower, driving down the price of popular premium wine in Europe to €2 a bottle, while the French vins de pays was priced above €3. (**Exhibit 1** shows the cost composition of a bottle of French wine.)

Reinventing the Marketing Model   Beyond their experiments in growing and wine making, New World

Exhibit 1   Consumer Price Breakdown: French Popular Wines

Cost Structure	EUR/litre	EUR/bottle
Juice	0.50	
Wine making	0.06	
Bulk wine (total)	0.56 =	0.42
Bottling packaging		0.35
Local taxes		0.08
Logistics storage		0.10
Margins/overhead		0.10
Wholesale price		1.05
Excise duties[a]		0.45
Retail and wholesale margins		1.14
If VAT		0.05
Consumer price in EUR		3.14

[a]Example from the Netherlands.
Source: Changing Competitiveness in the Wine Industry, Rabobank Market Study, 2006, p. 16.

[6]Heijbrock, Arend "Changing Competitiveness in the Wine Industry," Rabobank Research Publication, 2007, p. 5.

[7]Heijbrock, p. 16.

producers also innovated in packaging and marketing. While the European targeted the huge basic wine market by selling the popular liter bottle of *vin de table*, the Australians developed the innovative "wine-in-a-box" package. Employing a collapsible plastic bag in a compact cardboard box with a dispensing spigot, the box's shape and weight not only saved shipping costs, it also made storage in the consumer's refrigerator more convenient. More recently, Australian producers began replacing cork stoppers with screw caps, even on premium wines. The logic was based not just on economics, but also on the fact that many wines, particularly the delicate whites, were susceptible to spoiling if corks were deficient.

From their earliest experiences in the marketplace, New World producers learned the value of differentiating their products and making them more appealing to palates unaccustomed to wine. Several early products developed for unsophisticated palates were wildly successful—Ripple in the United States and Barossa Pearl in Australia, for example—but were dismissed by connoisseurs as evidence of the New

World's inferior wine making skills. Yet these experiments provided valuable lessons in branding and marketing—skills that were rare in this industry prior to the 1970s.

With wine showing the potential for mass appeal, in 1977 Coca-Cola acquired Taylor California Cellars. Other experienced consumer marketers such as Nestlé, Pillsbury, and Seagram followed, and conventional wisdom was that their sophisticated marketing techniques would finally crack the last major largely unbranded consumer product. But the challenge proved more difficult than expected, and within a decade the outsiders had sold out. Yet their influence endured in the consumer focused attitudes and the sophisticated marketing skills they left behind.

The other major change driven by New World companies occurred in distribution. Historically, fragmented producers and tight government regulations had created a long, multilevel value chain, with service providers in many of the links lacking either the scale or the expertise to operate efficiently. (See **Exhibit 2** for a representation.) In contrast, the

Exhibit 2   Wine Industry Value Chain

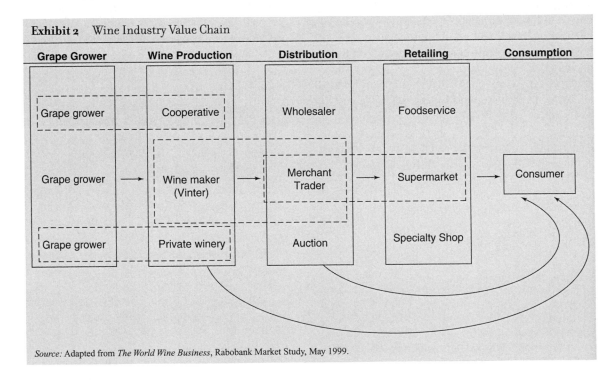

Source: Adapted from *The World Wine Business*, Rabobank Market Study, May 1999.

large New World wine companies typically controlled the full value chain, extracting margins at every level and retaining bargaining power with increasingly concentrated retailers. And because their name was on the final product, they controlled quality at every step.

To traditionalists, the New World's breaks with established grape-growing and wine-making ways were sacrilege. They argued that in the drive for efficiency and consistency, and in the desire to cater to less sophisticated palates, New World producers had lost the character that came with more variable vintages made in traditional ways. And they were shocked that many of these "engineered products" were sold using appellation names—Chablis, Burgundy, Champagne, and so on. In response, the European Community (EC) passed regulations making such practices illegal. New World wine makers gradually adjusted by identifying their wines by the grape variety used, and eventually consumers recognized and developed preferences defined by the varietal name—cabernet sauvignon versus merlot, or chardonnay versus sauvignon blanc, for example. Indeed, many seemed to find this easier to understand than trying to penetrate the many complex regional designations that each of the traditional wine-producing countries had promoted.

The Judgment of Paris   On May 24, 1976, in a publicity-seeking activity linked to America's Bicentenary, a British wine merchant set up a blind-tasting panel to rate top wines from France and California. Despite the enormous "home field advantage" of an event held in Paris with a judging panel of nine French wine critics, the American entries took top honors in both the red and white competitions. When French producers complained that the so-called "The Judgment of Paris" was rigged, a new judging was held two years later. Again, Californian wines triumphed.[8]

The event was a watershed in the industry. The publicity raised awareness that the New World produced quality wines, to the great shock of those

[8]Gideon Rachman, "The Globe in a Glass," *The Economist*, December 18, 1999, p. 91.

who dismissed their innovative approaches. It was also a wake-up call to traditional producers, many of whom began taking their new challengers seriously for the first time. Finally, it gave confidence to New World producers that they could compete in global markets. In short, it was the bell for the opening round in a fight for export sales.

Maturing Markets, Changing Demand

"The Judgment of Paris" signaled the start of many disruptive changes in the wine industry during the last quarter of the 20th century. More immediately alarming for most traditional producers was a pattern of declining demand that saw a 20% drop in worldwide consumption from 1970 to 1990, and a subsequent flattening of demand. When combined with radical changes in consumer tastes, consolidation in the distribution channels, and shifts in government support, these trends presented industry participants with an important new set of opportunities and threats.

Changing Global Demand Patterns   The most dramatic decline in demand occurred in the highest-consumption countries, France and Italy. In the mid-1960s, per capita annual consumption in both countries was around 110 to 120 liters; by 2005 it was about 50 litres. Key causes of the decline were a younger generation's different drinking preferences, an older generation's concern about health issues, and stricter drunk-driving penalties. Simultaneously, steep declines occurred in other major wine drinking cultures—Spain dropped from 60 liters to 35, Argentina from 80 to 30, and Chile from 50 to 15. (See **Exhibit 3.**)

During the same period, demand was growing in many wine-importing countries, although not fast enough to offset losses in Old World wine countries. From 1966 to 2005, per capita annual consumption in the United Kingdom rose from 3 to 20 liters, in Belgium from 10 to 26 liters, and in Canada from 3 to 10 liters. Even more promising was the more recent growth of new markets, particularly in Asia where consumption in China, Japan, Taiwan, South Korea, and Thailand grew at double digit annual rates through

Exhibit 3   Wine Consumption Per Capita, Selected Countries, 1966–2006

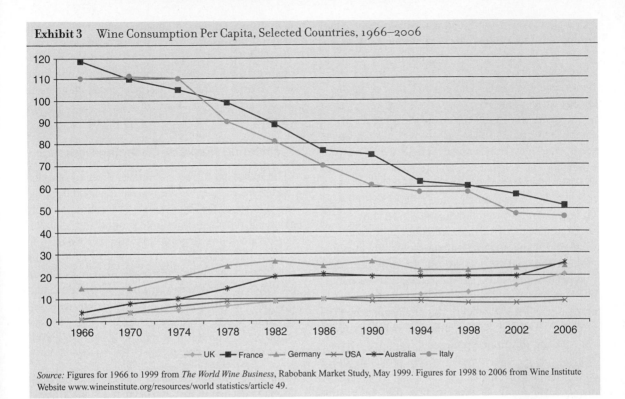

Source: Figures for 1966 to 1999 from *The World Wine Business*, Rabobank Market Study, May 1999. Figures for 1998 to 2006 from Wine Institute Website www.wineinstitute.org/resources/world statistics/article 49.

the 1990s. In fact, by 2005, China had emerged as the world's fifth wine consuming nation—ahead of Spain, Argentina, and the U.K. (**Exhibits 4 and 5** lists the world's major consuming and producing nations.) It was this shift in market demand that escalated the competition for export sales into a global wine war. (See **Exhibit 6** for import and export data.)

Shift to Quality, Rise of Fashion   Partially offsetting the overall volume decline was a growing demand for higher-quality wines. While the basic segment (less than $5 a bottle) still accounted for half the world market in volume, the premium ($5 to $7) and the super-premium ($7 to $14) now represented 40% of the total—and more than 50% of the market in younger markets such as the United States and Australia. (**Exhibit 7** shows one version of price segmentation as defined by a leading industry analyst.)

The trend was worldwide. Even in Old World wine countries where total demand was in decline,

consumption of premium wine kept rising. Despite government subsidies, per capita consumption of basic wine in the EU fell from 31 liters in 1985 to 18 liters in 2005, while demand for quality wine increased from 10 liters to 15 liters. In that same 20 year period, jug wine sales in the United States declined from 800 million to 600 million liters, while consumption of premium wines increased from 150 million to 600 million liters.

With the shift to quality, a greater fashion element began to influence demand. The decline in importance of working families' daily consumption of locally produced table wine was offset by upscale urban consumers who chose bottles on the basis of grape variety, vintage, source—and increasingly fashion. The 1980s' emphasis on lighter foods led to an increase in demand for white wines, making white wine spritzers (wine with soda water) a fashionable drink in the United States market. By the late 1980s, white wine represented over 75% of U.S. sales.

Exhibit 4   World Wine Production: By Country

WORLD GRAPE PRODUCTION BY COUNTRY AVERAGE 1996–2000
ACTUAL 2002–2004
ESTIMATED 2005 & 2006
AND PERCENT CHANGE 2006 VS AVERAGE 1996–2000
U.S. TONS (000)[1]

COUNTRY[2]	96-00	2002	2003	2004	2005	2006	% CHANGE 2006/96-00
WORLD TOTAL	65,648	67,755	69,081	73,490	72,271	71,089	8.29%
ITALY	9,914	8,150	8,249	9,581	8,700	8,700	(12.25%)
FRANCE	8,295	7,544	6,952	8,314	7,600	7,700	(7.17%)
SPAIN	6,127	6,481	7,998	8,037	7,500	7,500	22.41%
UNITED STATES[3]	6,513	7,339	6,573	6,240	7,814	6,417	(1.47%)
CHINA	2,704	4,938	5,705	6,099	6,100	6,100	125.61%
TURKEY	3,968	3,858	3,968	3,858	3,900	3,900	(1.72%)
IRAN	2,484	2,981	3,086	3,086	3,100	3,100	24.82%
ARGENTINA	2,456	2,474	2,537	2,922	2,700	2,700	9.94%
AUSTRALIA	1,261	1,933	1,650	2,221	2,300	2,400	90.37%
CHILE	1,827	2,064	2,386	2,149	2,200	2,200	20.42%
SOUTH AFRICA	1,597	1,654	1,809	1,916	1,790	1,790	12.07%
INDIA	1,057	1,334	1,268	1,323	1,300	1,300	23.03%
GERMANY	1,515	1,453	1,233	1,235	1,300	1,300	(14.21%)
GREECE	1,353	1,213	1,268	1,323	1,300	1,300	(3.92%)
EGYPT	1,070	1,217	1,217	1,406	1,280	1,280	19.61%
BRAZIL	939	1,235	1,163	1,414	1,200	1,200	27.77%
ROMANIA	1,299	1,179	1,162	1,169	1,170	1,170	(9.93%)
PORTUGAL	1,000	1,211	1,042	1,134	1,130	1,130	13.03%
MOLDOVA	576	707	732	661	700	700	21.63%
HUNGARY	757	633	665	698	670	670	(11.45%)

Source: Trade Data and Analysis, The World Wine Institute, 2006.

This all changed following the 1991 publication of a medical report identifying red-wine as a partial explanation of the "French paradox"—low rates of heart disease in a population well-known for its love of rich food. Featured on the U.S. television show *60 Minutes*, the report soon led to an increase in demand, with red wine's market share growing from 27% in 1991 to 43% five years later.

Even within this broad trend of red versus white preference, the demand for different grape varieties also moved with fashion. During the white wine boom, chardonnay was the grape of choice, but by the late 1990s, Pinot Gris and Sauvignon Blanc were emerging white wine fashion favorites. In red wine, a love affair with Cabernet Sauvignon was followed by a mini-boom for Merlot, which in turn was succeeded by a demand spike for Pinot Noir.

Such swings in fashion posed a problem for growers. Although vines had a productive life of 60 to 70 years, they typically took 3 to 4 years to produce their first harvest, 5 to 7 years to reach full productive capacity, and 35 years to produce top

Exhibit 5   World Wine Consumption: By Country

WORLD WINE CONSUMPTION CATEGORY A[1] 2002–2006 AND % CHANGE 2006/2002 HECTOLITERS (000)

COUNTRY [2]	2002	2003	2004	2005	2006	% Change 2006/2002
CATEGORY A TOTAL	**226,179**	**231,547**	**234,064**	**236,991**	**241,553**	**6,80%**
FRANCE	34,820.00	33,340.00	33,141.00	33,000.00	32,800.00	(5.80%)
ITALY	27,709.00	29,343.00	28,300.00	27,600.00	27,300.00	(1.48%)
UNITED STATES[3]	23,650.00	24,363.00	25,114.00	26,180.00	26,883.00	13.67%
GERMANY	20,272.00	20,150.00	19,593.00	19,437.00	19,850.00	(2.08%)
CHINA	11,469.88	11,586.02	13,286.00	15,000.00	16,000.00	39.50%
SPAIN	13,960.00	13,798.00	13,898.00	13,735.00	13,735.00	(1.61%)
UNITED KINGDOM	9,916.00	10,622.00	10,729.00	12,000.00	11,700.00	17.99%
RUSSIA	6,404.00	8,682.00	10,159.00	11,200.00	11,200.00	74.89%
ARGENTINA	11,988.00	12,338.00	11,113.00	11,113.00	10,972.00	(8.48%)
ROMANIA	4,964.00	5,049.70	5,800.00	2,379.00	5,600.00	12.81%
PORTUGAL	4,650.00	5,290.00	4,828.00	4,820.00	4,700.00	1.08%
AUSTRALIA	4,007.00	4,196.00	4,361.00	4,523.00	4,600.00	14.80%
CANADA	2,883.58	3,440.00	3,607.00	4,000.00	4,200.00	45.65%
BRAZIL	3,178.00	3,077.00	3,177.00	3,710.00	3,553.00	11.80%
SOUTH AFRICA	3,884.00	3,487.00	3,509.00	3,450.00	3,519.00	(9.40%)
NETHERLANDS	3,330.00	3,563.00	3,340.00	3,474.00	3,350.00	0.60%
GREECE	2,420.10	2,450.00	3,275.00	3,480.00	3,350.00	38.42%
HUNGARY	3,454.00	3,120.00	3,080.00	3,200.00	3,200.00	(7.35%)
CHILE	2,297.00	2,552.00	2,547.00	2,740.00	2,850.00	24.07%
BELGIUM	2,724.00	2,614.00	2,741.00	2,813.00	2,775.00	1.87%

Source: Trade and Data Analysis, The World Wine Institute, 2006.

quality grapes. But New World wine regions had the capacity and the regulatory freedom to plant new varieties in new vineyards and could respond. For example, in the 1990s, the California acreage planted with chardonnay increased 36%, and merlot plantings increased 31%.

As these various demand trends continued, the rankings of the world's top wine companies underwent radical change. Despite their relative newness and the comparative smallness of their home markets, New World companies took nine slots in a list of the world's top 15 wine companies, a list previously dominated by Old World companies. (See **Exhibit 8** for the listing.)

Increasing Distribution Power   Because marketing had typically been handled by their *négociants*, most Old World producers were still isolated from such fast-changing consumer tastes and market trends—particularly when they occurred in distant export markets. Equally problematic was their lack of understanding of the rapidly concentrating retail channels. In contrast, because most large New World wine companies controlled their distribution chain from the vineyard to the retailer, they were able to sense changes in consumer preferences and respond to shifts in distribution channels.

Furthermore, the New World companies were able to capture even more economic advantage by

Exhibit 6   Consumption, Production, Export, and Import Figures for Selected Old World and New World Wine Producing and Consuming Countries, 2001

	Consumption		Production	Exports	Imports		
	Liters Per Capita	Total hls 000s	Total hls (000s)	Total hls (000s)	Total hls (000s)	Value ($Millions)	$/Litre
France	52	34,200	45,400	15,180	5,370	789	1.40
Italy	46	28,150	45,900	18,480	1,750	474	2.70
Argentina	31	12,200	15,050	3,260	140	NA	1.30
Spain	27	14,260	34,700	15,280	200	NA	3.20
Germany	26	20,380	10,500	3,450	14,240	2,710	1.90
Australia	28	5,960	14,304	7,980	340	NA	4.70
United Kingdom	22	12,760	—	—	12,910	5,090	3.90
United States	9	25,125	20,000	4,240	8,450	4,624	5.40

Source: Rabobank *World Wine Map*, 2008.

Note: In several European countries, production does not equal consumption (plus exports minus imports) due to excess production being subject to government purchase.

Exhibit 7   Quality Segments in the Wine Industry (Rabobank's Categories)

	Icon	Ultra Premium	Super Premium	Premium	Basic
Price range (approx)	More than $50	$20–$50	$10–$20	$5–$10	Less than $5
Consumer profile	Connoisseur	Wine lover	Experimenting consumer	Experimenting consumer	Price-focused consumer
Purchase driver	Image, style	Quality, image	Brand, quality	Price, brand	Price
Retail outlets	Winery, boutique, food service	Specialty shop, food service	Better supermarket, specialty shop	Supermarket	Supermarket, discounter
Market trend	Little growth	Little growth	Growing	Growing	Decreasing
Competition	Limited, "closed" segment	Gradually increasing	Increasing, based on brand and quality/price ratio	Fierce, based on brand, price	Based on price
Volume market share	1%	5%	10%	34%	50%
Availability	Scarce	Scarce	Sufficient, year round	Large quantities, year round	Surplus

Source: Adapted by casewriters from *The World Wine Business*, Market Study, May 1999.

reducing handling stages, holding less inventory, and capturing the intermediaries' markup. Even the transportation economics that once favored European suppliers' proximity to the huge United Kingdom market changed. As trucking costs rose, container-ship rates fell, making the cost of shipping wine from Australia to the U.K. about the same as trucking it from the south of France.

Size also gave New World companies bargaining power in the sophisticated negotiations that a

Exhibit 8   Top 15 World Wine Companies: 2007/08

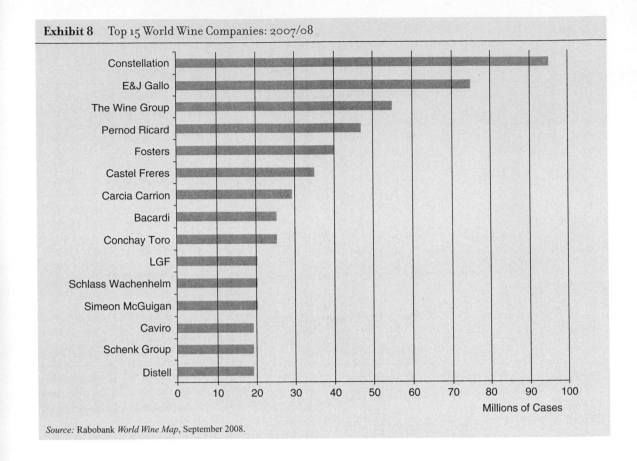

Source: Rabobank *World Wine Map*, September 2008.

concentrated retail sector now demanded. For example, following the huge wine surpluses flooding the market in the early 2000s, Australian producers used their cost advantage to drive prices lower. But equally important in the battle for volume sales was their ability to respond to retailers' need for a consistent supply of strong brands at a good price/quality ratio.[9] In the face of this head-on competitive challenge, the French tried to defend their position through frequent promotions.[10] But they were hampered by their lack of consumer knowledge and marketing skills.

The Old World suppliers' problems became clear from their dealings with Tesco, the world's largest wine retailer with wine sales of £1.5 billion in 2007. To maximize sales, Tesco emphasized that it wanted to work with creative suppliers. "Don't just bring the deals, bring me innovation," said Dan Jago, Tesco's Wine, Beer, and Spirits division head. "If you want your prices to rise, you have to persuade customers why they should pay more."[11]

While a handful of icon brands prospered at the top of the market based on image and quality, the fragmentation of Old World vineyards forced most to compete at the low end on price. When some chose to take on the New World brands under the

[9]Rachman, p. 99.

[10]Annemiek Geene, Arend Heijbroek, Anne Lagerwerf, and Rafi Wazir, "The World Wine Business," Market Study, May 1999, available from Rabobank International.

[11]Anonymous, "The World's Largest Wine Retailer," *Meininger's Wine Business International,* June 2007, pp. 42–45.

umbrella of the AOC's reputation, it soon became clear that they lacked the skills or resources to succeed in the last growth middle market. Tesco's Jago complained that despite its once strong reputation, the Bordeaux "brand" was losing sway with younger consumers. "Heaven knows I've tried to help them, but our consumers have such infinite choice that they don't need to make [Bordeaux] part of it."[12]

Ascendancy in of Brand Power   For years, the wine industry appeared ripe for branding. The extreme fragmentation of the European industry (Bordeaux alone had 20,000 producers) meant that few had the volume to support a branding strategy. Historically, only the handful of Old World producers whose wines achieved icon status—Lafite, Veuve Cliquot, and Chateau d'Yquem, for example—were recognized brands. But these appealed to the elite, who represented only a tiny fraction of the global market.

In providing the consumer confidence that branding offers, government-supported classifications such as France's AOC had been only partially successful. Their value was weakened not only by their complexity (in 2009 there were 327 designated AOC regions), but also by the erosion of consumers' confidence in the classification scheme as an assurance of quality.[13] For example, Burgundy's most famous vineyard, Chambertin, had its 32 acres divided among 23 proprietors. While most produced the high-quality wine that had earned its *grand cru* status, others rode on that reputation to sell—at $150 a bottle—legitimately labeled Chambertin that wine critic Robert Parker described as "thin, watery, and a complete rip-off."[14]

As interest in wine extended beyond educated connoisseurs, new consumers in the fast-growing premium wine segment were faced with hundreds of options and often insufficient knowledge to make an informed—or even a comfortable—choice. Government classification schemes required them to have an understanding of the intricacies of region, vintage, and vineyard reputation, and even if they found a wine they liked, chances were that by their next purchase, that producer was not stocked or the new vintage was less appealing. Unsurprisingly, survey data in the early 1990s showed that 65% of shoppers had no idea what they would choose when they entered a wine store.

Yet even in 2009, despite many attempts, no brand had been able to capture as much as 1% of the global wine market, in contrast to soft drinks, beer, and liquor, where global brands were dominant. Although European producers and their importing agents had successfully launched several mass appeal brands in the 1960s and 1970s (e.g., Blue Nun, Mateus, Liebfraumilch), a decade later New World producers had made branding a routine part of wine marketing. For example, by sourcing grapes from multiple vineyards and regions, Australian wine maker Penfolds built trust in its products by ensuring the vintage-to-vintage consistency that branding demanded. It then leveraged its trusted brand name by creating a hierarchy of Penfolds wines that allowed consumers to move up each step from $9 to $185 wines as their tastes—and their budgets—developed. (See **Exhibit 9.**)

New World producers who built their marketing expertise in their home markets during the 1960s and 1970s, learned how to respond to consumer preferences for the simpler, more fruit-driven wines that were easy to appreciate. They then took those wines and the marketing and branding skills they had developed at home into the export markets. By 2007, New World companies claimed 14 of the world's top 20 wine brands. (See **Exhibit 10.**)

The Government Solution   The radical shifts in demand proved extremely challenging to Old World producers. First, there was often no new land

---

[12]Ibid.

[13]The same problem plagued wines from Italy, where DOC regulations were so often violated that the government eventually introduced a DOCG classification in 1980 (the G stood for *guarantita*) to restore consumer confidence in notable wine regions. And in Germany, government standards were so diluted that, even in mediocre years, over 75% of wine produced was labeled *Qualitatswein* (quality wine), while less than 5% earned the more modest *Tatelwein* (table wine) designation.

[14]Robert M. Parker, Jr., *Parker Wine Buyer's Guide*, 5th Edition (New York: Fireside Press, 1999), p. 276.

Exhibit 9   Penfolds Red Wine U.S. Brand Structure, 2009

Label	Varietal Type	Years Before Release	Price Segment	Suggested U.S. Retail Price per Bottle ($US)
Rawson's Retreat	Varietal range[a]	1	Premium	$8.99
Koonunga Hill	Varietal range[a]	1–2	Premium	$10.99
Thomas Hyland	Varietal range[a]	1–2	Premium	$14.99
Bin 138	Shiraz Mourvedre Grenache	2	Super Premium	$19.00
Bin 128	Shiraz	3	Super Premium	$24.00
Bin 28	Shiraz	3	Super Premium	$24.00
Bin 389	Cabernet Shiraz	3	Super Premium	$26.00
Bin 407	Cabernet Sauvignon	3	Super Premium	$26.00
St. Henri	Shiraz	5	Ultra Premium	$39.00
Magill Estate	Shiraz	4	Ultra Premium	$50.00
RWT	Shiraz	4	Ultra Premium	$69.00
Bin 707	Cabernet Sauvignon	4	Ultra Premium	$80.00
Grange	Shiraz	6	Icon	$185.00

Source: Southcorp Wines, the Americas.
[a]Typical red varietal range included of these brands Merlot, Shiraz Cabernet, and Cabernet Sauvignon. (These brands also offer a range of white wines.)

Exhibit 10   Top 20 Wine Brands 2004–2008

Brand	Company	Source Country	Million Cases 2007
Franzia	Wine Group	US	
Martini	Bacardii	Italy	
Carlo Rossi	Gallo	US	
Conchay Toro	Conchay Toro	Chile	
Gallo	Gallo	US	
Yellowtail	Casella	Australia	
Tavernello	Caviro	Italy	
Beringer	Fosters	US	
Sutter Home	Trinchero	US	
Jacobs Creek	Pernod Richard	Australia	
Almaden	Constellation	US	
Livingstone Cellars	Gallo	US	
Woodbridge	Constellation	US	
Hardy's	Constellation	Australia	
Chenet	Grands Chais de France	France	
Frelxenet	Frelxenet	Spain	
Riunite	Riunite	Italy	
Peter Vella	Gallo	US	
Lindemans	Fosters	Australia	
Rotkappchen	Rotkappchen	Germany	

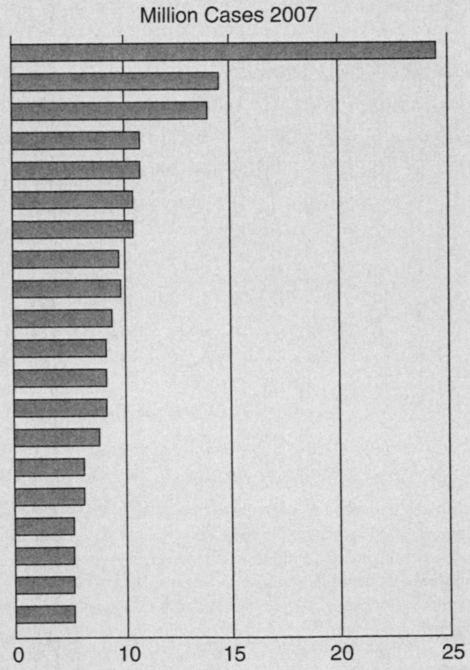

Source: Rabobank *World Wine Map*, September 2008.

available to plant, particularly in controlled AOC regions. Equally restrictive were the regulations prescribing permitted grape varieties and winemaking techniques that greatly limited their flexibility. So, for example, when fashion switched away from sweeter white wines, the German wine industry which was constrained by tight regulations on sugar content, watched its exports drop from over 3 million hectoliters in 1992 to under 2 million just five years later.

But the biggest problem was that declining demand at home and a loss of share in export markets had caused a structural wine surplus—popularly called the European wine lake. The EU's initial response was to pay farmers to uproot their vineyards, leading to 500,000 hectares (13% of production) being uprooted between 1988 and 1996. A parallel "crisis distillation program" provided for the EU to purchase surplus wine for distillation into industrial alcohol. An average of 26 million hectoliters (15% of total production) was distilled annually in the decade since 1999. In a 2006 reform proposal, the EU aimed to uproot a further 200,000 hectares—equal to the size of the U.S. wine industry—and gradually phase out crisis distillation.

Critics contended that despite their intent to move towards more market-driven policies, the EU regulators were still dealing with challenges from the supply-side perspective of the grape growers. Little was being done to address marketing support, wine style, the freedom and willingness to innovate, or the business models Old World wine companies were pursuing so successfully.

But New World wine companies were also facing challenges. Problems of global oversupply were made worse by emerging signs of saturation in several major export markets. For example, after 2003, Australia's wine export value to its major U.K. market was growing at less than half the rate of volume sales. And by 2005, its U.K. export volume increase slowed to only 1.6% while its average price in that market declined by 4.4%. There was also some evidence that New World wines were developing image problems born of their willingness to lower prices aggressively in an era of excess supply. The

challenge now was to remake their image and move out of the highly competitive low price segment.

The Battle for the US Market

Squeezed by chronic oversupply in producer countries and declining demand in mature markets, the Old and New World were again locked in a competitive battle for export markets which in 2008 accounted for 33% of global demand. Nowhere was the battle more intense than in the United States, which one industry analyst called "perhaps the most attractive market in the world." [15]

The US Market   It was easy to see why the U.S. was so attractive. In Germany, the world's largest wine importer, 65% of the market was accounted for by basic wine that sold for less than €2 a bottle. As the second largest importer, the U.K. offered a more attractive market (the €3–5 segment accounted for 57% of sales), but it was showing signs of saturation. But as third-place importer, the United States market had grown faster than any other major wine market—from $11 billion in 1993 to $30 billion in 2007. Better yet, the rate of increase in value was four times the volume growth. This reflected the fact that wine that sold for more than €5 ($7) accounted for 48% of the market, and this segment was growing at 15% p.a.—three times the rate of lower price segments.

Still, the U.S. wine market had long been one of the most difficult for imports to crack due to its distance from most producing countries, its state-by-state regulatory strictures, and particularly its complex three-tier distribution system that forced all sales to pass through state-licensed wholesalers. Not only did these wholesalers add cost, they also exercised great power. (The largest of them, Southern Wine and Spirits, had twice the sales of Consolation Brands, the world's largest wine company.) But all this changed when a 2005 Supreme Court ruling allowed interstate wine shipments, triggering a series of state and federal regulation challenges

---

[15]Stephen Rannekiev, "The Future of the California Wine Industry," F&A Research Advisory, Rabobank Industry Note, August 2007, p.1.

that began to open up the U.S. distribution system. Finally, the largest entry barrier for imports began to erode.

One of the key drivers of U.S. market growth was due to Generation Y (born after 1977) embracing wine much more than Generation X, and almost as much as the Baby Boomers. These new consumers were not only price-sensitive, but also very Internet savvy, and consequently were well educated about their purchases. As they came of drinking age, research showed that they chose imported wines more than earlier generations, a cause for concern for in the U.S. industry.

Not surprisingly, in the first decade of the millennium, the U.S. became a major battleground in the fight for exports. Despite the fact that it had a successful domestic industry, wine imports into the U.S. increased by 185% between 1995 and 2006, by which time they claimed a record 31% market share. Soon, the champions of the Old World and New World were battling head-to-head—the Americans defending their home market against the three countries that accounted for 77% of imports by value: Italy, France, and Australia. It had become a microcosm of the global wine wars.

The American Defense   Some industry critics suggested that because American producers had long focused on their large, high priced domestic market, they had fallen behind the prevailing global price/quality ratio, not only at the low end, but even at the higher price points. One wake-up call was an analysis comparing the prices of all 2004 vintage Cabernet Sauvignon wines that achieved a Robert Parker Wine Enthusiast rating of 90. The average price for the Californian wines was $55, while the price for similarly rated wines from Australia was $20.[16]

Having become a high cost producer, the U.S. industry recognized that it needed to respond to the new competitive challenges. One of the greatest problems was that its land costs were extremely high. In 2008, an average acre of land in Napa cost $150,000, more than 10 times the price of an average Australian vineyard, and 20 times the cost in Chile. Furthermore, there was virtually no land available for expansion in Napa or other premium wine areas. And labor costs were being squeezed as control over illegal immigration increased. The cost of pruning an acre in Napa in 2008 was $350, similar to the cost in France, but much higher than in highly mechanized Australia ($120 an acre), or in low labor cost Chile ($75 an acre).

Because of their high cost, vineyards in North Coast locations such as Napa and Sonoma targeted the super-premium and ultra-premium segments at $12 a bottle and above. Meanwhile, the Central Valley which produced 70% of California's wine volume was focused on the basic segment typified by Gallo's Carlo Rossi brand. And as market oversupply grew in 2002 and beyond, surplus wine purchased on the spot market created the Charles Shaw brand, nicknamed "Two Buck Chuck" for its $1.99 price. Soon it was selling 5 million cases a year.

This bifurcated focus led to the middle segment of the market ($5–$8 a bottle) being underserved. Into that gap stepped Yellow-Tail, an Australian import with a trendy label, and the full-bodied fruity wine the U.S. market preferred. Soon it was selling 10 million cases a year worldwide. With little ability to respond quickly from domestic sources, U.S. wineries began looking to an unexpected source—imported wine from low-cost producing countries, a development we will describe below.

Europe's Renewed Advance   As EU agricultural policy changes shifted the focus from reducing oversupply to subsidizing marketing and promotion, European wines began growing their market share in the U.S. Finally, after years of beating a retreat to New World competitors, the major EU wine exporting countries could boast that they captured 99% of the 2006 dollar volume increase in imported wine sales into the U.S.

With the Australians charging into the popular premium segment, French wines extended their penetration into the super premium segment. While ranked number three in imports by volume, France

---

[16]Ibid, p.5.

beat all other countries in terms of import value. Its price per bottle, at 77% above the average of all imports, reflected its strong position in the luxury segment including champagne. In contrast, the growth in Italian imports was occurring mostly in the popular priced range that was their historic strength. Promoting well-known brands such as Riunite, Cavit and Bolla, they increased their 2006 volume by 2 billion cases, thereby retaining their position as the number one importer by volume.

But ironically, the success of the European imports was also helped by U.S. domestic producers. As they became more global in scope, many U.S. wine companies began divesting vineyards and expanding their marketing role. Foreign wine suppliers benefited from this shift in two ways. First, when domestic companies took advantage of a law that permitted up to 25% foreign wine in products that could still be labeled as American, the imports became the source of the less expensive bulk wine required for blending. Foreign suppliers also benefited when domestic companies broadened their line by importing and marketing country specific wines. Gallo became particularly adept at this strategy, and successfully launched brands such as Bella Sera and Ecco Domani with wines sourced in Italy, and Red Bicyclette, its brand of imported French wine. In essence, the American companies filled the gap in marketing capability and distribution expertise that had previously been a barrier to entry for many European imports.

Australia's New Challenge   For more than a decade, Australia's wine producers had become accustomed to success. In 1996, the industry's "Strategy 2025" plan had detailed a "total commitment to innovation and style" as its means of becoming "the world's most influential and profitable supplier of branded wines by 2025." Ten years later, grape production had more than doubled and exports of had grown by 530% to 782 million liters in 2006, making Australia the world's number four wine exporter. In fact, most of Strategy 2025's goals had been achieved by 2006, almost 20 years ahead of schedule.

But celebrations were dampened by the recognition that in the mid-2000s, exports to the U.K., its largest market, were stagnating and average price was eroding. Fortunately, the U.S. market was growing rapidly, and by 2007 represented 31% of Australia's wine export market value, compared to 33% for the U.K. But with an average price per liter of $4.46 for Australian imports into the U.S., it represented a much more attractive market than the U.K. where the average had slipped to $3.35.

But Australian wine was also facing price and image problems in the U.S. market. Challenged by overproduction since 2000, its bumper crops of 2004, 2005, and 2006 had led Australian producers to aggressively reduce prices in all export markets. While this led to a boom in export sales, it also established an image of Australian wines as "cheap and cheerful." The image was typified by Yellow Tail, the phenomenally successful brand that sold 8.1 million cases into the U.S. in 2007, accounting for 36% of all Australian imports to the country.

Being trapped by this image was particularly problematic as costs started to rise. Serious droughts in Australia led to major cost increases for water at the same time as global energy prices were soaring. Together, these factors caused an increase in production cost of almost $200 at tonne, and forced Australian producers to recognize that regardless of their greater efficiency, Argentina and Chile were lower cost producers. For example, while Australia could land its bulk table wine in the U.S. at $0.80 a liter, Argentina's price was $0.36 a liter.

Like other countries, the Argentineans and Chileans had learned from Australia's success, and had copied its successful strategy to develop their own accessible wines marketed under consistent brands. For example, Concha y Toro was the world's fourth largest wine brand, ahead of Gallo and Yellow Tail, for example. And even where emerging New World producers had not developed the necessary marketing skills, a growing number of global wine companies could offset that shortcoming. For example, in 2007, the top selling new wine in the U.S. was the popular premium South African brand Sebeka—sourced, bottled, branded, and marketed by Gallo. In short, Australia's competitive position in the U.S. was being seriously challenged.

Behind the Battle Lines: Strategy in France and Australia

Buoyed by a decade of success, yet also concerned by the recent weakening of the average price recorded by Australian export wines, the Australian Wine and Brandy Corporation, the government's wine export body, linked up with the industry-led Winemakers Federation of Australia to develop a new strategy supporting the continued growth of the industry. Under the title "Directions to 2025," the document detailed how the industry would implement the second stage of the landmark "Strategy 2025" which had emphasized volume growth to 2002, value growth to 2015, and achieving global preeminence for Australian wine by 2025.

On a broad platform of Wine Australia, "Directions to 2025" planned to support four sub-brands, each targeting a separate consumer group. "Brand Champions" would cover accessible premium brand wines and promote ease of enjoyment; "Generation Next" would emphasize innovation which was important to younger consumers who associated wine with social occasions not grape attributes; "Regional Heroes" would develop an association between Australian regions and wine varieties or styles; and "Landmark Australia" would support Australia's high profile aspirational wines and provide an umbrella of world-class reputation. (**Exhibit 11** shows a map off brand attributes.)

But a 2008 crush of 32% more than the previous year led many to believe that the recent drought-related production declines were over. Within the industry, there were concerns that as supply increased, producers would abandon the long-term strategy and return to their earlier discounting practices, particularly for popular brands that could generate the volume to remove excess supply. Australian wine making icon Wolf Blass despaired at what he called "a wrongheaded approach." He felt that Australian wine could not compete long-term in a low-cost battle, and argued that the export business should focus on full-bodied, quality wines that would raise its image. That would be a real challenge in an industry that was forecasting a 7% oversupply of fruit by 2013.

Meanwhile, in France, the industry and the government were responding differently to the global surplus. In 2005, the grower-led Comite d'Action Viticole (CAV) launched its campaign of violence against imports, blocking highways and overturning the trucks of foreign wine. In a subsequent meeting with the prime minister, a delegation of winemakers extracted his commitment to support a national strategy "to help French wine recover lost markets." The plan, funded to €90 million, offered direct support to wineries in financial difficulty, and promised funds to relaunch French wines into the world market. Furthermore, a new national wine committee would work on simplifying the complex classification systems, perhaps moving towards larger, simpler regional appellations such as Bordeaux or Burgundy. Finally, the prime minister directed his agriculture minister to go to Brussels and argue for more funds to distill surplus wine into industrial alcohol.

But the EU was moving in a different direction. In 2007, it announced plans to use its annual €1.3 billion wine budget more effectively. It would be ending the €500 million annual buyback of unsold wine, redirecting those funds to new incentives encouraging farmers to uproot vines on 200,000 hectares of vineyards, and providing €120 million a year for a marketing campaign. The plans were extremely unpopular with farmers, and when the EU plan passed in spite of their objections, the protests escalated. In France, the CAV claimed responsibility for explosions at supermarkets selling imported wines, particularly in the high productivity Languedoc-Roussillon wine region in the south of France. Then, five balaclava-clad men appeared on French television threatening more violence unless wine prices increased.

Most in the industry felt such actions were unhelpful, and undermined their marketing efforts. They urged winemakers to get behind the new promotion campaign for "South of France" wines that was supported with €20 million from government and industry coffers. In an unusual display

Exhibit 11 Wine Australia's Market Segment

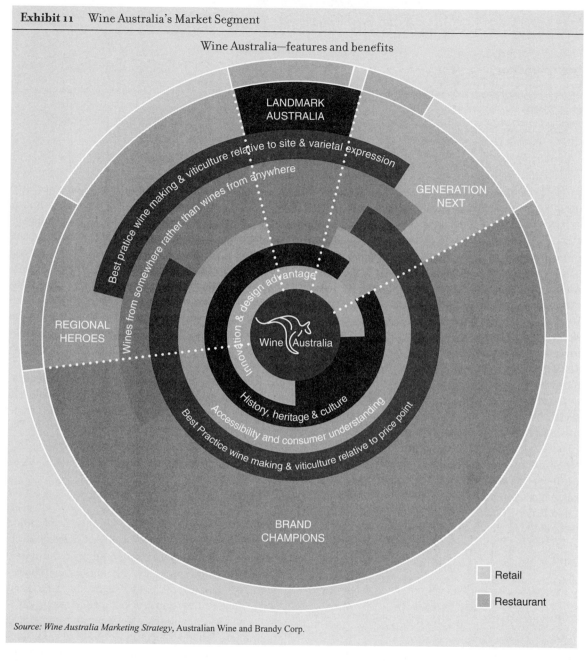

Wine Australia—features and benefits

Source: Wine Australia Marketing Strategy, Australian Wine and Brandy Corp.

of unity, producers from various AOC, VDQS, and Vin de Pays regions had agreed to launch products under this common banner. While some felt it was the only chance they had to compete against strongly branded New World wines, others worried that the "South of France" brand was too generic, and hid the richness of the area's diverse sources of wine. But in the battle for export markets, everyone agreed that something had to be done.

Case 2-2   The Globalization of CEMEX

Pankaj Ghemawat

Geographic diversification enables us to operate in multiple regions with different business cycles. For the long term, we are trying to ensure that no one market accounts for more than one-third of our business. Yet we do not diversify simply to balance cyclic downturns and upswings. We do not see volatility as an occasional, random element added to the cost of doing business in an interconnected global marketplace. We plan for volatility. We prepare for it. We have learned how to profit from it.

—Lorenzo Zambrano, CEO of CEMEX[1]

In 1990, Cementos Mexicanos was a Mexican cement company that faced trade sanctions in its major export market, the United States. By the end of 1999, CEMEX operated cement plants in 15 countries, owned production or distribution facilities in a total of 30, and traded cement in more than 60. Non-Mexican operations accounted for nearly 60% of assets, slightly over 50% of revenues and 40% of EBITDA (earnings before interest, taxes, depreciation, and amortization) that year. CEMEX's sales revenues had increased from less than $1 billion in 1989 to nearly $5 billion in 1999, and it had become the third largest cement company in the world in terms of capacity, as well as the largest international trader. Growth had been achieved without compromising profitability: in the late 1990s, its ratio of EBITDA to sales ranged between 30% and 40%— ten to fifteen percentage points higher than its leading global competitors. In addition, the company was celebrated as one of the few multinationals from Latin America, and as a model user of information technology in an otherwise low-tech setting.

CEMEX executives sometimes characterized the company's international operations as a "ring of grey gold," comprising commitments to high-growth markets, mostly developing and mostly falling in a band that circled the globe north of the Equator. By the end of the 1990s, the addition of countries such as Indonesia and Egypt to the ring had prompted discussions about the scope and speed of CEMEX's international expansion. So had the hostile bid, in early 2000, by Lafarge, the second-largest cement competitor worldwide in cement for Blue Circle, the sixth largest. Hector Medina, CEMEX's Executive Vice President of Planning and Finance, likened the takeover struggle to "ripples in an agitated environment" that could have significant implications for the other cement majors.

This case begins with a brief overview of the cement industry and international competition within it. It then describes the globalization of CEMEX and how it was managed.

The Cement Industry

Cement had been used since antiquity as a binding agent that hardened when mixed with water. It was first made in its modern form in England during the early part of the 19th century. The production process, which remained broadly unchanged, involved burning a blend of limestone (or other calcareous rocks) and smaller quantities of materials containing aluminum, silicon, and iron in a kiln at high temperatures to yield marble-sized pellets of "clinker." Clinker was then ground with gypsum and other minerals to yield cement, a fine gray powder. The mixture of cement, aggregates, and water that hardened into a rocklike mass after hydration was

▌ Professor Pankaj Ghemawat and Research Associate Jamie L. Matthews prepared this case drawing, in part, on a course paper by Pau Cortes, Heriberto Diarte and Enrique A. Garcia. HBS cases are developed solely as the basis for class discussion. Cases are not intended to serve as endorsements, sources of primary data, or illustrations of effective or ineffective management.

▌ Harvard Business School Case No 9-701-017, Copyright 2000 President and Fellows of Harvard College. All rights reserved.
This case was prepared by P. Ghemawat. *HBS Cases are developed solely for class discussion and do not necessarily illustrate either effective or ineffective handling of administrative situation.*

▌ [1]CEMEX 1998 annual report, p. 4.

Exhibit 1   How CEMEX Makes Cement

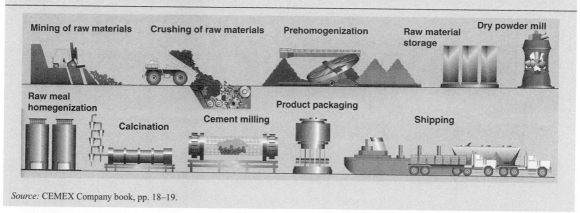

Source: CEMEX Company book, pp. 18–19.

known as concrete. Concrete could be mixed "on site" where it was to be used, or it could be obtained in "ready-mix" form from a central drum at the plant or a ready-mix truck.

Supply   Since limestone, clay and the other raw materials required were abundant in many regions of the world, cement could usually be produced locally. Cement companies often owned raw material quarries and located their production facilities close by to minimize materials handling. The production technology was continuous process, consisted of a number of stages (see **Exhibit 1**) and was marked by high capital- and energy-intensity. It was also considered relatively mature: no major innovations had been recorded in the last 20 years. The minimum efficient scale (MES) for a cement plant approximated 1 million tons of capacity per year. New capacity cost about $120–$180 per ton, depending on local factors such as the cost of land, environmental legislation, and the need for ancillary equipment and infrastructure, including investment in quarries and kilns. A cement plant's assets were largely dedicated to the production of cement and might last for decades. Operating costs typically ranged from $20–$50 per ton, with labor accounting for well under $10 per ton.[2] Transportation costs, in contrast, could account for as much as one-third of total delivered costs.

High transportation costs in relation to production costs meant that there was only a limited distance within which a plant could deliver cement at competitive prices. Road transportation was the most expensive, and limited the effective distribution radius to 150–300 miles.[3] Waterborne transportation was the most economical and, as a result of innovations since the mid-1950s, had led to a substantial expansion of MES.[4] New systems of loading and unloading barges were introduced and specialized ships for carrying cement were developed. As a result, cement producers began to establish much larger plants that shipped cement to distribution terminals in distant markets as well as serving local ones. Still, a host of other costs had to be layered on top of the costs of ocean freight for long-distance trade to take place (see **Exhibit 2**). In the late 1990s, international seaborne traffic in cement and clinker averaged about 50 million tons per year. It was believed that about 10 million tons of this traffic was carried by small vessels on short coastal or estuarial voyages, and about 40 million tons by oceangoing vessels.[5]

Demand   Cross-country comparisons indicated that the long-run demand for cement was directly

[2]Merrill Lynch, Ownership Changes in Asian Cement, December 3, 1999, p. 117.

[3]ING Barings, *European Cement Review*, February 2000, p. 24.

[4]Hervé Dumez and Alain Jeunemaître, *Understanding and Regulating the Market at a Time of Globalization: The Case of the Cement Industry*, p. 113.

[5]Drewry Shipping Consultants, *Cement Shipping: Opportunities in a Complex and Volatile Market*, January 1998.

Exhibit 2   Cost Structure of Asian Exports to the United States

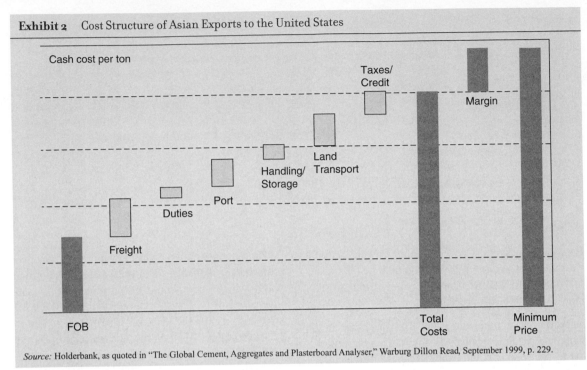

Source: Holderbank, as quoted in "The Global Cement, Aggregates and Plasterboard Analyser," Warburg Dillon Read, September 1999, p. 229.

related to GDP, with per capita consumption increasing up to the $20,000-plus per capita income mark and then declining very gradually. Numerous other local attributes affected cement demand as well. Rainfall had a negative effect since it made cement-based construction more difficult and increased the likelihood of using substitutes such as wood or steel instead. Population density had a positive effect, as higher density led to taller buildings and more complex infrastructure. Demand also tended to be higher in areas with a warm climate and lower under extremes of heat or cold. Demand generally decreased with a long coastline, since more sea transport meant fewer roads, and increased with the share of governmental expenditures in GDP. CEMEX forecast total world demand to grow at slightly under 4% per annum through 2010. Demand growth was expected to be highest in the developing Asian economies, Central America, the Caribbean, and Sub-Saharan Africa, where it would approach or exceed 5%, and lowest in Western Europe and North America, where it would be closer to 1%.

In the short run, cement demand varied directly with GDP and, even more reliably, with construction expenditure/investment. As a result, construction plans could be used to develop short-run forecasts for cement demand. However, the cyclicality of the construction sector made medium-run forecasts somewhat dicey. Bulk sales were very sensitive to GDP growth, interest rates, and other macroeconomic factors that affected the formal construction market. Retail sales to individual consumers for home construction and the like, which were important in developing countries, were discovered to be less cyclical and also offered opportunities for some branding, as described below.

Competition   Cyclicality on the demand side combined with capital-intensity, durability, and specialization on the supply side to meant that overcapacity in the cement industry could be ruinous in its effects. Cement firms tried to cushion their interactions under conditions of overcapacity by relying on "basing point" pricing systems, other leadership strategies, and even direct restraints on competition.

The basing point system had been common in the United States until the end of World War II, and in Europe until much more recently. Under this system, the leading firm set a base price, and the other firms calculated their prices by taking the base price and increasing it by the cost of transportation from the leading firm's plant to the delivery point. This offered a transparent price structure in the absence of hidden discounts, and let the biggest players sell throughout the entire market, while smaller producers ended up selling in relatively small areas around their plants.

Other devices that cement firms relied on to mitigate competition included attempts to collude and to secure protection from imports. There had even been explicit cartels in the industry. Well-documented examples included one in southern Germany during

the 1980s and another in Switzerland during the early 1990s. Governmental support was instrumental in erecting trade barriers to curb foreign competitors as well. The antidumping duties imposed in the late 1980s by the United States on cement imports from Mexico are an example that will be discussed in some detail later on.

International Competitors

By 1999, six major international competitors had emerged in cement: Holderbank, Lafarge, CEMEX, Heidelberger, Italcementi, and Blue Circle. Given their geographic diversification, these competitors tended to be outperformed in any given year by competitors focused on local markets that happened to be "booming" (see **Exhibit 3**), but they had achieved significantly greater stability in their

Exhibit 3 1999 EBITDA Margin

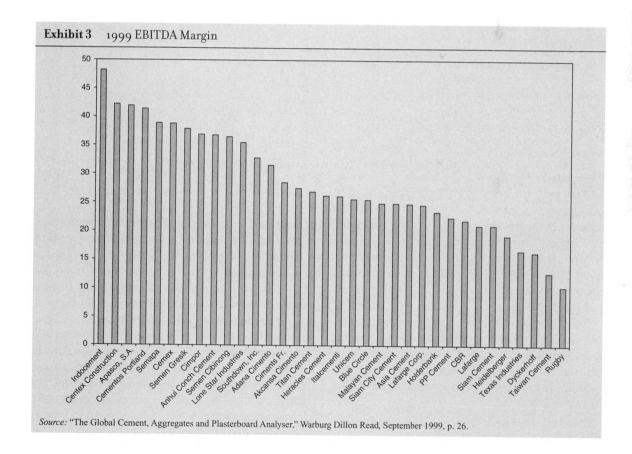

Source: "The Global Cement, Aggregates and Plasterboard Analyser," Warburg Dillon Read, September 1999, p. 26.

Exhibit 4   Selected Data on Global Competitors (December 1999)

Company	Holder-bank	Lafarge	CEMEX	Heidel-berger	Ital-cementi	Blue Circle
Accounting Data						
Sales (US$ m)	7,618	10,552	4,828	6,404	3,414	3,604
Cement volume (m tons)	74.6	64.3	39.1	46.0	37.8	NA
EBIT (US$ m)	1,066	1,766	1,436	645	511	466
EBITDA (US$ m)	1,785	2,446	1,791	1,195	838	684
CAPEX (US$ m)	784	1,144	262	540	310	295
Free Cash Flow (US$ m)	144	511	862	487	200	(294)
Net debt (US$ m)	4,767	5,422	4,794	2,957	1,731	538
Net debt/EBITDA	.7	2.2	2.7	2.5	2.1	0.8
Total debt to capitalization	54.1%	46.5%	44.1%	51.3%	43.0%	31.0%
Interest coverage	4.6	6.6	3.6	4.8	6.8	5.7
Stock Market Data[a] (to Dec. '99)						
Market value (US$ m)	11,122	12,132	7,203	4,209	2,488	4,707
Profitability of stock US$[b] (12 mth)	16%	22%	114%	3%	9%	12%
TEV[c] (US$ m)	17,015	19,157	12,500	7,373	5,050	5,593
TEV adjusted/ton (US$)[d]	160	130	172	86	90	93
Capacity Data						
Footprint[e] (m tons)	140	107	85	71	55	45
Degree of control of footprint	72%	79%	77%	75%	98%	97%
Controlled capacity (m tons)	101	85	65	53	54	44
Number of Countries	53	38	15	33	14	14

[a]End-of-period exchange rate used for calculations.
[b]For Holderbank, class B stock; for CEMEX, New CPO.
[c]TEV defined as total enterprise value (debt plus equity).
[d]Excluding non-cement assets for Lafarge (35%), Heidelberger (10%) and Blue Circle (25%).
[e]Footprint defined as total capacity in which a given company has a significant stake.
Sources: Annual Reports; Datastream; JP Morgan; CEMEX

returns. In aggregate, the six majors controlled 500 million tons of capacity, representing slightly over one-quarter of the world total, or over one-third of the total excluding China. The six-firm concentration ratio had been only 12% in 1988, with Votorantim of Brazil edging out CEMEX for the sixth spot.[6]

In 1999, each of the six major international competitors still had clearly identifiable national origins and controlled a significant share of its home market. But each had also come to operate production facilities in anywhere between a dozen and several

dozen countries around the world. **Exhibit 4** supplies financial data on the six majors, and **Exhibit 5** summarizes their capacity shares in a number of major markets.

Although some of the majors, such as Holderbank, had operated in several countries for decades, internationalization, particularly in an interregional sense, did not begin until the 1970s. This was when European players began to penetrate the United States. During the 1960s and 1970s, the U.S. cement industry had fallen into a crisis as profitability dropped with the collapse in prices, and domestic firms responded by lowering investment in cement and diversifying into other lines of business. This

[6]Podolny, Joel, John Roberts, Joon Han, and Andrea Hodge, 1999, "CEMEX, S.A. de C.V.: Global Competition in a Local Business," Stanford, CA: Stanford University. ECCH #IB17.

Exhibit 5   Capacity Shares of the Big 6 in Selected Markets

Country	Holderbank	Lafarge	CEMEX	Heidelberger	Italcementi	Blue Circle
Japan	0.0%	0.0%	0.0%	0.0%	0.0%	0.0%
Korea	0.0%	12.0%	0.0%	0.0%	0.0%	0.0%
Taiwan	0.0%	0.0%	0.0%	0.0%	0.0%	0.0%
Indonesia	0.0%	2.6%	43.7%	0.0%	0.0%	0.0%
Malaysia	0.0%	6.6%	0.0%	3.9%	0.0%	46.4%
Philippines	37.5%	20.5%	22.0%	0.0%	0.0%	16.7%
Thailand	25.3%	0.0%	0.0%	0.0%	13.2%	0.0%
India	1.4%	0.3%	0.0%	0.0%	0.0%	0.0%
South Africa	36.3%	25.8%	0.0%	0.0%	0.0%	0.0%
Egypt	5.4%	5.0%	16.9%	0.0%	0.0%	3.3%
Greece	0.0%	0.0%	0.0%	0.0%	5.5%	58.9%
Poland	0.0%	21.2%	0.0%	22.4%	0.0%	0.0%
Turkey	0.0%	8.3%	0.0%	17.3%	9.2%	0.0%
France	12.6%	33.9%	0.0%	26.8%	26.4%	0.0%
Germany	6.6%	7.0%	0.0%	25.3%	0.0%	0.0%
Italy	6.2%	5.0%	0.0%	0.0%	36.9%	0.0%
Portugal	0.0%	0.0%	0.0%	0.0%	0.0%	0.0%
Spain	9.9%	19.3%	26.5%	0.0%	6.6%	0.0%
UK	0.0%	0.0%	0.0%	23.8%	0.0%	50.3%
Canada	19.1%	32.9%	0.0%	20.4%	11.2%	13.8%
US	13.5%	8.3%	1.8%	11.2%	4.6%	6.2%
Argentina	37.6%	11.2%	0.0%	0.0%	0.0%	0.0%
Brazil	10.0%	13.4%	0.0%	0.0%	0.0%	0.0%
Mexico	19.2%	4.3%	64.6%	0.0%	0.0%	0.0%
Venezuela	24.5%	23.6%	40.6%	0.0%	0.0%	0.0%

Source: CEMEX

resulted in shortages in some regional markets and provided an opening for European cement firms that had remained strong and were looking to expand. By 2000, European groups controlled 65% of the U.S. market.

Cross-border investment in the United States had been concentrated in certain periods—most recently, 1985–1988 and 1991–1993—instead of trickling in more continuously. Such waves were characteristic of cross-border investment in other regions as well, given the cement majors' emphasis on buying existing capacity rather than adding new capacity to enter new markets (see **Exhibit 6**). Obviously, acquisitions were most attractive to them when the market values of target companies were less than their underlying

Exhibit 6   Waves of Acquisitions

Period	Region	Period	Region
1985–1988	U.S./ Canada	1995–1997	Latin America
1987–1990	Latin America	1996–1998	E. Europe
1989–1991	Mediter- ranean	1998 onwards	SE. Asia
1991–1993	U.S.	1999 onwards	W. Europe
1990–1994	E. Europe		

Source: Adapted by casewriters from ING Barings, *European Cement Review,* February 2000.

Exhibit 7   Market Statistics and Valuations for Selected Countries[a]

Country	Ex-plant Price per Ton (US$)	Cash Cost per Ton (US$)	EBITDA per Ton (US$)	Risk Free Rate (%)	Equity Risk Premium (%)	Market Gearing (%)	WACC (%)
Japan	48	38	10	1.8	5.0	50.0	4.8
Korea	50	33	17	8.5	8.0	20.0	15.1
Taiwan	58	37	21	5.7	8.0	25.0	12.0
Indonesia	41	23	18	12.0	8.0	50.0	16.5
Malaysia	41	28	13	8.0	8.0	25.0	14.3
Philippines	49	34	15	14.0	8.0	50.0	18.5
Thailand	48	26	22	10.0	8.0	40.0	15.2
India	52	38	14	9.5	8.0	40.0	19.0
S. Africa	55	37	18	15.0	6.0	15.0	20.3
Egypt	53	33	20	10.0	8.0	0.0	18.0
Greece	58	30	28	6.4	6.0	20.0	11.4
Poland	38	28	10	9.5	6.0	20.0	14.5
Turkey	40	26	14	10.3	8.0	0.0	18.3
France	78	49	29	4.7	4.0	30.0	7.8
Germany	72	51	21	4.6	4.0	25.0	7.9
Italy	55	38	17	4.8	4.0	25.0	8.1
Portugal	66	40	26	4.8	5.0	10.0	9.4
Spain	64	40	24	4.8	5.0	10.0	9.4
UK	74	51	23	5.4	4.0	10.0	9.1
Argentina	62	40	22	12.0	8.0	40.0	17.2
Brazil	59	39	20	13.0	8.0	40.0	18.2
Mexico	96	40	56	12.0	8.0	50.0	16.5
Venezuela	95	35	60	15.0	8.0	20.0	21.6
Canada	67	42	25	5.5	4.0	0.0	9.5
US	69	48	21	5.7	4.0	0.0	9.7

Source: Adapted by casewriters from ING Barings, *European Cement Review,* February 2000, p. 29.
[a]Franchise value represents the theoretical value of one ton of capacity (assuming all sales are made domestically). The first step in its derivation is to obtain the capital value of cash flow generated in perpetuity by one ton of production. This is calculated by taking EBITDA per ton ($) and dividing by the weighted average cost of capital. The second step is to find the ratio of domestic demand to domestic supply. Dividing the value of one ton of

values—a condition more likely to be fulfilled at the bottom of the local economic cycle rather than the top. The underlying values of acquired franchises could be assessed by estimating their average profitability, capacity utilization, weighted average cost of capital and, probably most problematically, expected long-run growth rates. See **Exhibit 7** for an attempt by an investment bank to perform such calculations at the country level. In practice, of course, such country-level analyses had to be supplemented with target-specific considerations such as the target's

cost position and market share, and the kind of base it afforded for further cost-reduction and expansion.

Starting in 1997 and particularly after the summer of 1998, the largest and most concentrated wave of cross-border investment ever began in South East Asia. The international players had their eye on the market for many years, but had been unable to justify the entry premium—some companies in the region had been valued at up to $300 per ton of capacity on an enterprise value basis! The Asian crisis that began in 1997 changed the

Value/Ton of Demand (US$)	Domestic Demand (m tons)	Domestic Capacity (m tons)	Value/Ton of Capacity (no growth) (US$)	Trend Growth (%)	Value/Ton of Capacity (trended) (US$)
208	72.8	97.0	156	0.1	160
113	47.6	62.1	86	5.0	129
176	20.5	24.5	147	3.0	196
109	18.1	45.3	44	7.5	80
90	8.2	17.5	42	7.8	93
81	12.5	20.4	50	8.0	88
145	25.6	58.0	64	8.0	135
74	80.8	85.0	70	7.5	116
89	8.8	12.0	65	0.9	68
111	24.7	23.0	119	5.9	178
246	8.5	15.0	139	1.5	161
69	13.8	16.3	58	5.0	89
77	36.4	61.0	46	6.5	71
372	19.1	28.1	253	−1.5	211
268	37.0	51.0	194	1.0	221
211	35.0	52.5	141	−0.3	136
277	10.0	9.6	289	0.0	289
255	31.0	39.3	201	2.7	283
253	12.8	14.4	225	−0.2	219
128	8.2	9.5	110	3.0	134
110	40.1	45.8	96	5.0	133
339	25.7	44.0	198	2.5	233
278	4.5	8.6	145	-0.5	142
263	8.6	15.2	148	0.5	157
216	107.1	97.3	238	1.0	266

production by the ratio calculated in the second step gives the value of one ton of capacity. (The idea is that if domestic demand exceeds available supply then the value of owning capacity is greater than the value suggested by current EBITDA alone). The final step is to adjust franchise value for growth in domestic demand, trend growth, which is defined as the average of rolling averages for the previous 5, 10 and 20 years and is therefore less vulnerable to short-run fluctuations in growth rates.

situation dramatically and gave the majors the opportunity they were waiting for. The six majors' Asian cement deals through fall 1999 are summarized in **Exhibit 8.** They quickly increased their share of capacity in Asia, excluding China, from less than 20% to about 60%.

Of the leading international competitors in cement, two, Holderbank and Lafarge, were larger than CEMEX. Holderbank had cement operations on five continents and in more than 50 countries, making it the most global as well as the largest

international competitor. Its globalization strategy could be traced back to the early 1920s when the company (formed in 1912) first moved out of Switzerland and into neighboring France, Belgium, and the Netherlands. The company's 1999 sales were $7,618 million and its EBIT was $1,066 million. Cement accounted for 68% of 1999 sales and concrete and aggregates for 24%.

Lafarge was ranked second in the global cement market and also had strong positions in other building such as plaster, aggregates, concrete, and gypsum.

Exhibit 8   Cement Majors' Asian Deals after the Asian Crisis

	Country	Date	Stake %	Price (US$ m)	Capacity (m tons)	Value/Ton (US$)	Source
Holderbank							
Union Cement	Philippines	Jul-98	40%	210	5.8	146	A
Alsons Cement	Philippines	Jan-99	25%	22	2.5	130	B
Tengara Cement	Malaysia	Jun-98	70%	28	1.1	42	A
Siam City Cement	Thailand	Aug-98	25%	153	12.3	95	A
Huaxin Cement	China	Jan-99	23%	20	1.4	61	A
Total				**433**	**23.1**	**107**	
Lafarge							
Republic Cement	Philippines	Feb-98	14%	25	1.6	119	A
Continental Cement and South East Asia Cement	Philippines	Oct-98	100% 64%	460	4.6	132	C
Haifa Cement	Korea	Jul-99	33%	100	7.4	68	A
Andalas	Indonesia	n/a	16%	10	1.2		D
Tisco	India	1999	100%	127	0.3	107	A
Total[a]				**712**	**13.9**	**109**	
CEMEX							
Rizal and Solid Cement	Philippines	Dec-97, Nov-98	70%	219	2.8	166	C
Apo Cement	Philippines	Jan-99	100%	400	3.0	164	A
Semen Gresik	Indonesia	mid-98	14%	115	20.1	55	A
Semen Gresik	Indonesia	Nov-98	8%	49	20.1	56	A
Semen Gresik	Indonesia	1999	4%	28	20.1	58	A
Total				**811**	**25.9**	**109**	
Italcementi							
Jalaprathan Cement	Thailand	Oct-98	55%	26	1.6	58	A
Asia Cement	Thailand	Jul-99	53%	180	4.8	131	A
Total				**206**	**6.4**	**112**	
Blue Circle							
Iligan Cement Corp	Philippines	Jul-99	95%	53	0.5	109	C
Kedah Cement	Malaysia	Oct-98	65%	185	3.5	164	A
APMC	Malaysia	Dec-98	50%	309	4.7	157	A
Inflow from Minorities in Malaysian rights	Malaysia	Dec-98	65%	−118			D
Republic Cement	Philippines	1998	54%	90	1.6	138	C
Fortune Cement	Philippines	Jul-98	20%	35	1.9	114	A
Fortune Cement	Philippines	Jan-99	31%	86	1.9	147	A
Zeus Holdings	Philippines	Jul-98	73%	31	0.4	204	A
Total[b]				**671**	**12.6**	**153**	

Sources: Adapted by casewriters from: A) CEMEX; B) SDC database, Cembureau, *World Cement Directory 1996*, p. 322; C) Warburg Dillon Read, Global Equity Research, *The Global Cement, Aggregates and Plasterboard Analyser*, September 1999, p. 230; D) Merrill Lynch, *Asian Cement*, December 1999, p. 5.

[a]Excludes Andalas. Also, value/ton includes a weighting of 94% for Continental/SEACem to reflect breakdown of capacity between the companies.

[b]Includes inflow from minorities in Malaysian rights in total price.

Its 1999 sales were $10,552 million and EBIT was $1,766 million. Cement accounted for 35% of 1999 sales and concrete and aggregates for another 30%. Lafarge was not as focused on emerging markets as some of the other global players. In February 2000, it mounted a hostile bid, valued at nearly $5.5 billion, for Britain's Blue Circle, the sixth-largest cement competitor. Motives for the deal included achieving a certain size in order to remain visible and attractive to investors, expanding cashflow and, relatedly, geographic presence and, probably, dislodging Holderbank from the top spot in the global cement industry. However, by May, Lafarge had managed to attract only 44% of Blue Circle's shares with its aggressively priced offer.

■ CEMEX

By the year 2000, CEMEX had become the third largest cement company in the world with approximately 65 million tons of capacity (see **Exhibit 9** for historical financial data). CEMEX traced its origins back to 1906 when the Cementos Hidalgo cement plant was opened, with a capacity of less than 5,000 tons per year, in northern Mexico, near Monterrey. In 1931, it was merged with Cementos Portland Monterrey, founded by Lorenzo Zambrano, to form Cementos Mexicanos, later renamed CEMEX. Over the next half-century, the company expanded its capacity to about 15 million tons, and was well on its way to becoming Mexico's market leader by the early 1980s.

In 1985, Lorenzo Zambrano, scion of the Zambrano family that still controlled CEMEX and a grandson as well as namesake of the company's founder, took over as CEO. In his first few years at the helm, CEMEX continued to grow by constructing additional cement capacity. It also began to diversify horizontally into areas such as petrochemicals, mining, and tourism in order to reduce the risks related to its dependence on a highly cyclical core business. However, it wasn't long before Zambrano decided to refocus the company on cement and cement-related businesses. Based partly on the work of the Boston Consulting Group, he had concluded

that geographic diversification within the cement business was preferable to horizontal diversification outside it. All the non-core assets were eventually divested and CEMEX switched to a strategy of growth through acquisitions.

This strategy focused, in the first instance, on Mexico. As Mexico began to open up in the late 1980s, large firms such as Holderbank and Lafarge viewed it as a possible market to expand their operations. Faced with this threat, CEMEX decided to unify its Mexican operations. In 1987, CEMEX acquired Cementos Anahuac, giving the company access to Mexico's central market and bolstering its export capabilities with the addition of two plants and four million tons of capacity. Two years later, the acquisition of Cementos Tolteca, Mexico's second-largest cement producer with seven new plants and 6.6 million tons of capacity, made CEMEX Mexico's largest producer. These mergers, which cost CEMEX nearly $1 billion, secured its position in Mexico and gave it the size and financial resources to begin the process of geographic expansion.

When the 1994/1995 peso crisis struck, CEMEX had just finished a plan for revamping its Mexican operations. In December 1994, after a year of political instability that included the assassination of a presidential candidate, Mexico's foreign reserves dropped to about $5 billion, down from nearly $30 billion in March. Incoming President Zedillo warned his citizens to prepare for tough times. CEMEX quickly reworked its planned Mexican revamp and compressed it from 18 months to 3 months. Despite the recession that followed, it managed to maintain margins at reasonable levels. One reason was that many Mexicans did not have credit, so the self-construction part of the market was affected to only a limited extent, even though demand from the formal sector went down by 50%.[7] Another was that the company had already begun to expand into foreign markets. At the start of the year 2000, CEMEX was the leader in the

---

■ [7]Interview with Hector Medina, Executive Vice President—Planning and Finance.

Exhibit 9 CEMEX Financials (millions of US dollars, except share and per share amounts)

Income Statement	1988	1989	1990	1991	1992	1993	1994	1995	1996	1997	1998	1999
Net Sales	612	988	1,305	1,706	2,194	2,897	2,101	2,564	3,365	3,788	4,315	4,828
Cost of Sales	428	772	928	1,064	1,371	1,747	1,212	1,564	2,041	2,322	2,495	2,690
Gross Profit	184	215	377	642	823	1,150	889	1,000	1,325	1,467	1,820	2,138
Operating Expenses	61	120	178	221	286	444	325	388	522	572	642	702
Operating Income	123	95	199	420	537	706	564	612	802	895	1,178	1,436
Comprehensive Financing (Cost)	2	52	(5)	124	179	25	(16)	567	529	159	(132)	(29)
Other Income (Expenses) Net	70	4	(42)	(47)	(89)	(101)	(133)	(162)	(171)	(138)	(152)	(296)
Income Before Taxes & Others	195	151	152	498	628	630	415	1,017	1,160	916	893	1,111
Minority Interest	26	25	30	60	70	97	45	109	119	107	39	56
Majority Net Income	167	121	148	442	545	522	376	759	977	761	803	973
Earnings per Share	0.15	0.11	0.13	0.40	0.52	0.49	0.35	0.59	0.75	0.59	0.64	0.77
Dividends per Share	0.01	0.01	0.02	0.06	0.07	0.09	0.06	0.07	0.0	0.12	0.14	0.17
Shares Outstanding (millions)	1,114	1,114	1,114	1,114	1,056	1,056	1,077	1,286	1,303	1,268	1,258	1,366
ROE	14.2	9.5	10.6	24.1	18.7	16.2	13.3	26.4	29.3	21.7	20.7	18.8
Balance Sheet												
Cash and Temporary Investments	189	186	145	202	384	326	484	355	409	380	407	326
Net Working Capital	140	226	236	286	562	595	528	567	611	588	638	699
Property, Plant, & Equipment, Net	1,117	2,037	2,357	2,614	4,124	4,407	4,093	4,939	5,743	6,006	6,142	6,922
Total Assets	1,710	2,940	3,438	3,848	7,457	8,018	7,894	8,370	9,942	10,231	10,460	11,864
Short-Term Debt	69	360	261	144	884	684	648	870	815	657	1,106	1,030
Long-Term Debt	142	792	1,043	1,267	2,436	2,866	3,116	3,034	3,954	3,961	3,136	3,341
Total Liabilities	355	1,354	1,566	1,607	3,897	4,022	4,291	4,603	5,605	5,535	5,321	5,430
Minority Interest	182	306	474	408	649	771	771	889	1,000	1,181	1,251	1,253
Stockholders' Equity, excluding Minority Interest	1,173	1,280	1,398	1,833	2,911	3,225	2,832	2878	3,337	3,515	3,887	5,182
Total Stockholders' Equity	1,355	1,586	1,872	2,242	3,560	3,996	3,603	3767	4,337	4,696	5,138	6,435
Book Value per Share	1.05	1.15	1.25	1.65	2.76	3.05	2.63	2.24	2.57	2.74	3.08	3.79
Other Financial Data												
Operating Margin (%)	20.2	9.6	15.3	24.6	24.5	24.4	26.9	23.9	23.8	23.6	27.3	29.8
EBITDA Margin (%)	28.6	17.9	24.8	33.2	31.9	31.6	34.2	31.8	32.3	31.5	34.4	37.1
EBITDA	175	177	324	567	700	914	719	815	1,087	1,193	1,485	1,791

Source: CEMEX

Exhibit 10 Timeline of CEMEX's International Expansion

Year	Event
1985	GATT signed; CEMEX began to concentrate on cement and divests other business lines
1987	Acquired Cementos Anáhuac in Mexico
1989	Acquired Cementos Tolteca; became Mexico's largest producer and one of ten largest worldwide
1992	Acquired Valenciana and Sanson in Spain; became world's fifth largest cement producer
1993–1994	Acquired 0.7 mt of capacity in Jamaica, 0.4 mt in Barbados, and 0.7 mt in Trinidad & Tobago
1994	Acquired Vencemos in Venezuela, Cemento Bayano in Panama, and the Balcones plant in Texas
1995	Acquired Cementos Nacionales in the Dominican Republic
1996	Acquired a majority stake in Colombia's Cementos Diamante and Industrias e Inversiones Samper; became world's third largest cement company
1997	Acquired 30% stake in Rizal Cement Company in the Philippines
1998–1999	Acquired a 20% interest in PT Semen Gresik in Indonesia; acquired an additional 40% of Rizal, and 99.9% of APO Cement Corp, also in the Philippines
1999	Acquired Assiut in Egypt, a 12% stake in Bio Bio in Chile, and Cemento del Pacifico in Costa Rica
2000	Announced availability of $1.175 billion for global acquisitions during the course of the year (36% more than 1999 spending)

Source: CEMEX

Mexican market, with an installed capacity of 28 million tons, or about 60% of the country's total. Apasco, which Holderbank had acquired and invested heavily in expanding in the early 1990s, was the second largest player, with another 9 million tons of capacity. Analysts did not expect further increases in CEMEX's share of the Mexican market.

International Expansion After having secured its leadership in Mexico, CEMEX began to look for opportunities beyond Mexico's borders. Internationalization began with exports, principally to the United States. By 2000, CEMEX was the largest international cement trader in the world, with projected trading volumes of 13 million tons of cement and clinker that year, 60% of which was expected to be third-party product.[8] International trade offered opportunities to arbitrage price differentials across national boundaries and to divert low-priced imports away from one's own markets. It also expanded the range of options available to

deal with threats from particular competitors and let CEMEX study local markets and their structure at minimal cost before deciding whether to make more of a commitment to them by acquiring capacity locally.

After the imposition of trade sanctions by the United States, foreign direct investment had become a much more important component of CEMEX's internationalization strategy than pure trade. CEMEX's foreign investments focused on acquiring existing capacity rather than building "greenfield" plants. Its major international moves are summarized in **Exhibit 10** and described in more detail in the rest of this section.

The United States CEMEX had begun to export to the U.S. market in the early 1970s. In the late 1980s, it established distribution facilities in the southern United States in order to expand this effort. However, the U.S. economy and the construction industry in particular were experiencing a downturn. As a result, eight U.S. producers banded together to file an antidumping petition claiming that they were being harmed by low-cost Mexican

[8]Interview with Jose L. Saenz de Miera, President of Europe-Asia Region.

imports and demanding protection. After finding that cement prices were higher in Mexico than in the southern United States and inferring that Mexican producers were dumping cement in the U.S. market at artificially low prices, the U.S. International Trade Commission (ITC) imposed a 58% countervailing duty on CEMEX's exports from Mexico to the United States. The duty was reduced to 31% after CEMEX started limiting exports to U.S. states where prices were relatively high.[9] The company tried to fight these actions before the relevant U.S. bodies, but this proved very difficult. Medina recalled that at one point, CEMEX was simultaneously being investigated by the ITC for artificially lowering prices and by the U.S. Federal Trade Commission for purchasing a distribution terminal with the intent of artificially raising them! A ruling by the General Agreement on Tariffs and Trade (GATT) in 1992 sided with Mexico in this dispute, but the United States refused to give way. As of early 2000, the countervailing duty was still in place, although there were also reports that the United States was finally moving closer to repealing it.

After the countervailing duty was imposed, CEMEX had acquired a 1 million ton cement plant in Texas to reinforce its ready-mix and distribution facilities in the southern United States. Zambrano sometimes referred to this constellation of facilities as a firewall protecting the Mexican market from incursions from the United States. In addition, CEMEX's coastal terminals in the United States continued to import cement into the United States, from third parties as well as from the company's other plants. Thus, CEMEX credited imports of Chinese cement to the west coast of the United States for doubling the profits of its activities in the United States during 1999, to the point where they accounted for 12% of CEMEX's total sales and 7% of its EBITDA.

Spain   In 1991, CEMEX built distribution terminals in Spain to trade cement that was produced in Mexico, and also to study the European market. In July 1992, it spent about $1.8 billion to acquire what ended up being 68% of the stock and 94% of the voting rights in two large Spanish cement companies, Valenciana and Sanson, with a total of nearly 12 million tons of capacity. These acquisitions yielded a market-leading 28% share in one of Europe's largest cement markets, which then happened to be in the throes of a major boom. The acquisitions also lowered dependence on the Mexican market, gave CEMEX significant capacity in a major market for Holderbank and Lafarge, and raised its international profile. But shareholders generally took a dim view of the deals: CEMEX's American Depositary Receipts, issued just a year earlier (another first for a Latin American company), tumbled by about one-third around the dates at which the acquisitions were announced. And immediately afterwards, the Spanish economy plunged into its deepest recession in 30 years, with the Spanish peseta having to be devalued three times during late 1992 and 1993. These developments added to the urgency of orchestrating major turnarounds at the two Spanish companies.

It was in this context that CEMEX began to develop and codify its post-merger integration process. Every aspect of the Spanish acquisitions was reviewed, from procurement policies to the location of the mines to the use of automation. Processes were streamlined, as was the workforce (by 25%) and investments in information technology were stepped up. Simultaneously, CEMEX moved quickly to harmonize and integrate the systems for its Spanish operations with its Mexican ones. The post-merger integration process reportedly took a little more than a year, or less than one-half the amount of time originally budgeted, and was followed by major improvements in operating margins, from 7% at the time of the acquisitions to about 20% by 1994 and an average of 25% for the second half of the 1990s. The Spanish operations turned out to be critical in helping CEMEX weather the Mexican peso crisis of 1994/1995.

---

[9]David P. Baron, "Integrated Strategy: Market and Nonmarket Components," *California Management Review*, vol. 37, no. 2 (Winter 1995), pp. 51–52.

In 1998, CEMEX sold its cement plant in Sevilla for $260 million. The Sevilla plant, which had accounted for about 10% of CEMEX's capacity in Spain, was relatively old, and had high production costs. CEMEX remained the largest competitor in the Spanish market after the sale. It used the proceeds to invest in capacity in South East Asia, particularly Indonesia. According to its annual report for 1998, "We effectively exchanged one million metric tons of production capacity in Spain for the equivalent of approximately 4 million metric tons in Southeast Asia, a higher long-term growth market." In 1999, Spain accounted for 16% of CEMEX's revenues and 15% of EBITDA.

Latin America CEMEX's next major international move was entry into Venezuela, which initiated a broader series of engagements in Latin America, mostly around the Caribbean Basin. Venezuela had been wracked by macroeconomic instability since the late 1980s, depressing demand for cement and forcing large losses on the industry. In April 1994, CEMEX paid $360 million for a 61% stake in industry leader Vencemos, which operated about 4 million tons of capacity, or about 40% of the Venezuelan total. Virtually all remaining Venezuelan capacity ended up in the hands of Holderbank and Lafarge. As in Spain, CEMEX moved quickly to integrate and improve the efficiency of its Venezuelan operations. Vencemos' operating margin improved from 9% in the third quarter of 1994 to 41% a year later,[10] and stood at 34% in 1998.[11] Although the Venezuelan economy had continued to disappoint, Vencemos was able to keep capacity utilization high even when domestic demand was low because it was located near a major port facility. This permitted it to export surplus production to places such as the Caribbean islands and the southern United States. In 1998, Venezuela accounted for 12% of CEMEX's revenues and 13% of EBITDA. Earnings were down in 1999, however.

In mid-1996, CEMEX acquired a 54% interest—subsequently increased—in Cementos Diamante, Colombia's second-largest cement producer, for $400 million, and a 94% interest in Inversiones Samper, the third-largest producer, for $300 million. The acquisitions gave CEMEX 3.5 million tons of capacity, or a bit less than one-third of the Colombian total, behind industry leader Sindicato Antioqueño—a loose confederation of small cement producers—with a share of about 50%. Weak demand topped off by a price war caused CEMEX's operating margins in Colombia to decline from more than 20% at the beginning of 1998 to 3% by late in the year. Margins began to recover, however, during 1999.[12] That year, Colombia accounted for 3–4% of CEMEX's revenues and EBITDA.

Next, CEMEX entered Chile, paying $34 million for an 12% stake in Cementos Bio-Bio, Chile's third-largest competitor. The largest producer in Chile was Cement Polpaico, a subsidiary of Holderbank, and the second-largest was one of Blue Circle's subsidiaries. Compared to them, Bio-Bio was relatively focused on the northern and southern parts of Chile rather than on its populous middle. Elsewhere in Latin America, CEMEX acquired controlling stakes in the largest producers in Panama, the Dominican Republic, and Costa Rica.[13]

Other Regions Between late 1997 and early 1999, CEMEX invested in Filipino cement producers Rizal (a 70% interest in 2.3 million tons of capacity for $218 million) and APO (a 100% interest in 2.0 million tons of capacity for $400 million). Both Rizal and APO were close to ports and therefore had export as well as domestic potential. The Philippines itself had been a Spanish colony in the 19th century, and was one of the first East Asian economies to experience macroeconomic pressures in the second half of the 1990s. Less than 20% of Filipino cement capacity had been controlled by foreign firms in early 1997, when there had been

---

[10]"Global Invasion," *International Cement Review*, Jan. 2000, p. 35.
[11]Company fact book.
[12]*International Cement Review*, January 2000, pp. 35–36.
[13]Ibid., p. 36.

nearly 20 producers and a supply shortage as the result of a decade in which demand had grown at about 10% per year.[14] But the Filipino market just as large capacity additions by domestic competitors were coming on line. This gave international competitors their opening. CEMEX ended up controlling about 22% of Filipino cement capacity, well behind Holderbank but slightly ahead of Lafarge and Blue Circle. In 1999, the Philippines accounted for 2.5% of CEMEX's revenues and approximately one-half that percentage of its EBITDA.

Indonesia was the other Southeast Asian market in which CEMEX had established a presence: in September 1998, it paid $115 million for a 14% stake in Semen Gresik, Indonesia's largest cement company with 17 million tons of capacity, and considered by many to be its most efficient. Originally, 35% of the company was supposed to have been sold (out of a total of 65% held by the Indonesian government), but public protests reduced the number of shares offered. By 2000, CEMEX had increased its stake to 25% by spending another $77 million, but continued to have the Indonesian state as a major partner. The political and economic environment in Indonesia remained fluid, and further negotiations to buy out more of the government's stake were complicated by weakened institutions and the turnover of officials as well as by continued public opposition. In addition, excess capacity of almost 20 million tons—the largest such amount in the region—needed to be restructured. Still, the Indonesian market had significant long-run potential, not least because its population numbered 220 million (three times that of the Philippines). As the dollar value of the Indonesian rupiah collapsed, the dollar price of cement in the local market had decreased from about $65 per ton in early 1997 to less than $20 per ton in 1998, before starting to recover in 1999. As part of its investment in Semen Gresik, CEMEX had also entered into export commitments, which it intended to fulfill in part by setting up a grinding mill in Bangladesh to receive and process shipments of clinker from Indonesia.

In November 1999, CEMEX acquired a 77% stake in Assiut Cement Company, the largest cement producer in Egypt with about 4 million tons in capacity, for a total of about $370 million. In May 2000, CEMEX announced plans to invest in expanding Assiut's capacity to 5 million tons, and to add 1.5 million tons of capacity in a new Egyptian facility. These plans catered to the Egyptian government's interest in increasing domestic production of cement to help meet demand that had been growing at an average annual rate of 11% since 1995. But the Egyptian market remained fragmented—Assiut accounted for only 17% of it—and the Egyptian regulatory context cumbersome.

The Future   In May 2000, CEMEX announced that it had accumulated $1.175 billion to spend on global acquisitions. China was an obvious target because of the size of its market, variously pegged at about half a billion tons by official estimates and closer to half that according to independent analysts.[15] However, approximately 75% of Chinese production took place in small, technologically obsolete kilns owned by local authorities and not run on a commercial basis. Even after discounting opportunities in China, the bulk of the capacity that might be consolidated by the six major international competitors was located in emerging markets, particularly in Asia and Africa/the Middle East (see **Exhibit 11**). CEMEX was thought likely to enter India, where it thought the restructuring process was farther advanced, before China. Indian demand amounted to about 100 million tons, or more than three times Mexico's, and was served by 28 competitors, the eight largest of which combined to account for two-thirds of total demand. Holderbank and Lafarge already had a degree of presence there. In Latin America, CEMEX had its eye on Brazil, although it was unwilling to pay prices for acquisitions that, at $250 or more per ton, exceeded its capacity valuations. In May 2000, the company announced that it was negotiating with the Portuguese government over a 10% stake in Cimentos de

---

[14]*International Cement Review*, January 2000, p. 37.

[15]ING Barings, *European Cement Review*, February 2000, p. 40.

Exhibit 11   Capacity Consolidation Potential (millions of tons)

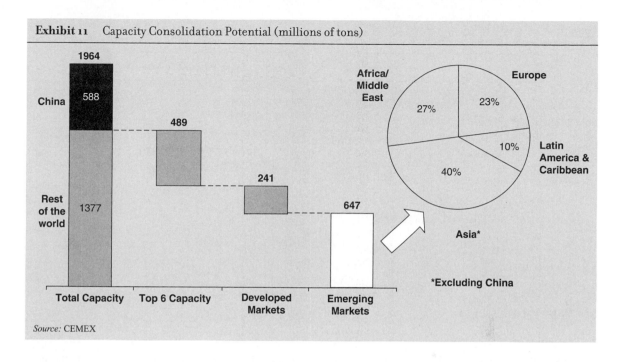

Source: CEMEX

Portugal (Cimpor), that country's largest cement maker. Such a deal might permit consolidation of operations around the Mediterranean as well as giving CEMEX access to Brazil and some African markets. Holderbank and Lafarge were reportedly also interested.

The Expansion Process   As CEMEX moved to more distant markets, the various stages in the expansion process—opportunity identification, due diligence, and post-merger integration—became more formalized and greater attempts were made to standardize them, reflecting past experiences.

Opportunity Identification   While the logic of expanding to the U.S., Spain, and, in particular, Latin America, had been relatively obvious, CEMEX had had to develop better tools for screening opportunities as it ventured farther afield. CEMEX looked at several factors in deciding whether to invest in other countries. A country had to have a large population and high population growth as well as a relatively low level of current consumption. In addition, CEMEX wanted to lead

the market or at least control 25% of it. These considerations tended to favor opportunities in emerging countries. Quantitative factors were assigned a 65% weight in country analysis, and qualitative factors, such as political risk, a weight of 35%. The analysis was complicated by the fact that CEMEX looked at countries in a regional context rather than as independent markets and was particularly interested in the Caribbean Basin, South East Asia, and the Mediterranean. According to CFO Rodrigo Treviño, "We now have a very balanced and well-diversified portfolio and we can afford to be more selective."[16]

If detailed market analysis was the top-down component of the process for identifying opportunities, the process of identifying target companies constituted its bottom-up component. CEMEX's conceptual framework for looking at targets is summarized in **Exhibit 12.** CEMEX pursued controlling stakes—often as close to 100% as possible—in

[16]Tim Duffy, "CEMEX's CFO: Still Eying International Markets for Diversification," *Dow Jones International News*, March 7, 2000.

Exhibit 12   Framework for Acquisition Analyses

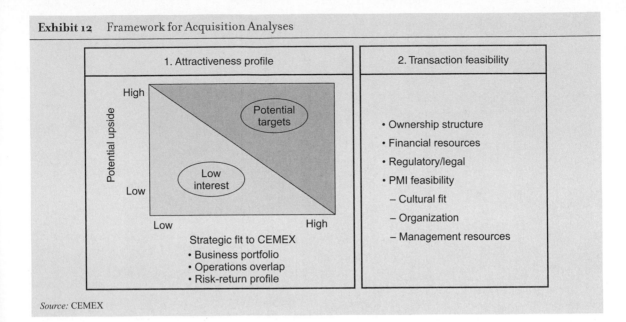

Source: CEMEX

the companies that it bought into, in order to maximize flexibility. When identifying a possible acquisition target, CEMEX also examined the potential for restructuring both the target company and the market as a whole. Restructuring the target company meant increasing its efficiency and optimizing capacity utilization. Restructuring the market might involve reductions in the number of players or volume of imports, moves toward rational pricing, fragmentation of distribution channels, product differentiation and other attempts to get closer to the customer. Speed in both respects was very important to improving target valuations.

Due Diligence   After a target was identified, a process of due diligence was performed whereby it was assessed in depth by a team of people. In 1999, about 20 processes of due diligence were undertaken, resulting in three acquisitions. The due diligence process typically lasted one to two weeks and involved about ten people per team, half of whom usually had prior experience with the process. Once a team was formed, it was briefed on the target company and given a standardized methodology to

follow in assessing it. Negotiations with the government usually continued through the due diligence process, and meetings with local competitors and industry associations were often held as well to allay any concerns about the acquisition. The final output from the due diligence process was a standardized report, to be presented to the Executive Vice President of Planning and Finance, Hector Medina, that was critical in pricing deals. Only rarely, however, would CEMEX bid prices that exceeded top-down estimates of the value of capacity in particular markets (as illustrated in **Exhibit 7**).

Especially in Southeast Asia, CEMEX had recently found itself looking at the same targets as other international cement companies. CEMEX believed that its due diligence process was more specific and systematic. To cite just one example, the human resources component of its process looked at the age, education, and average years of service of the target's employees, and at labor union affiliations, government involvement, and relationship to the community in order to estimate the optimal number of employees and recommend strategies for moving towards those targets. Other issues related to human resources, such as training programs and organizational restructuring, were also covered. Such thoroughness was thought to reduce the possibility of unpleasant surprises down the road, and to speed up the post-merger integration process if an acquisition was, in fact, undertaken. The process methodology was revised every six months to reflect recent experiences.

Post-Merger Integration (PMI) Process   Once the decision to proceed with an acquisition was made, CEMEX formed a PMI team. The purpose was to improve the efficiency of the newly obtained operation and adapt it to CEMEX's standards and culture. PMI teams had become more diverse and multinational over time. The PMI process took anywhere from six months to a year, during which team members kept their original positions and salaries, returning home one week in every six. At the beginning of the process, the team was briefed on the country and methodology, and attended cultural awareness and teambuilding workshops. The process itself had a monthly cadence: the regional director visited every month, the country president of the new operation reported to headquarters in Monterrey every month in the same format as the other CEMEX country presidents, and CEO Zambrano, the regional directors and all the country presidents met every month in Monterrey or, occasionally, New York or Madrid.

The PMI process involved integration at three levels: the improvement of the situation at the plant acquired, the sharing or replication of basic management principles, and the harmonization of cultural beliefs. CEMEX tried to send in a PMI team as soon after an acquisition as possible and, while there were differences in terms of how quickly and to what extent the team tried to take charge, regarded itself as moving much more quickly in this respect than its leading international competitors. Integration almost always involved substantial manpower reductions, most of which were concentrated within the first six months. But the PMI team also tried to discover whom to retain or promote to managerial positions. It was possible for as many as half the members of a PMI team to stay on as expatriates after the process

was over. CEMEX also viewed the PMI process as a vehicle for continuous improvement in existing operations. Thus, every two or three years, a PMI process was performed on CEMEX's Mexican operations, which were looked at as if they had just been acquired.

Management   As CEMEX expanded internationally, other broad aspects of its management changed as well. Geographic diversification had reduced earnings volatility: thus, over 1994–1997, the standard deviation of quarterly cash flow margins averaged 7.1% for CEMEX as a whole, compared to 9.5% for Mexico, 12% for Spain, 22% for the U.S., and 30% for Venezuela. Financing, nevertheless loomed large as an issue because of the asset-intensity of the international acquisition strategy, which included not only paying for equity but also the assumption of significant debt and incurral of large investments in modernization—up to 50% of purchase prices in some cases. While high costs of capital had always been a major issue for Mexican companies, the situation was exacerbated by the peso crisis, which simultaneously raised domestic interest rates and restricted the extent to which Mexican cashflows could be used to finance foreign direct investment (because of the 70% devaluation of the peso against the U.S. dollar). CEMEX responded by folding the ownership of its non-Mexican assets into its Spanish operations and financing new acquisitions through the latter. This was several hundred basis points cheaper for CEMEX, partly because Spain had an investment-grade sovereign rating, and partly because all interest expenses were tax-deductible in Spain (compared to just real interest expenses in Mexico). Consolidating its bank debt through the Spanish operations in 1996 was estimated to have saved CEMEX about $100 million per year in interest costs, and to have better matched dollar-linked assets and its principally dollar-denominated debt.[17]

⬛ [17]CEMEX 1997 Annual Report, and *International Cement Review*, December 1999, p. 40.

CEMEX's net debt amounted to $4.8 billion at the end of 1999, leaving it relatively close to the 55% limit on debt-to-total-capital that was specified in bank covenants. The company had managed, however, to satisfy the cap on leverage and the floor on interest coverage that it had set for itself more than one year ahead of schedule, and further strengthening of capital structure had been promised. CEMEX had also tried to broaden its sources of capital. In 1998, it sold its plant in Sevilla, as described above. In early 1999, it partnered with AIG, the insurance company, and the private equity arm of the Government of Singapore Investment Corporation, among others, to set up a fund of up to $1.2 billion to invest in some of the cement assets it was acquiring in Asia. In September 1999, CEMEX listed and started to trade on the New York Stock Exchange. And while no new shares were offered in conjunction with that listing, the company issued $500 million of warrants later on in the year.

CEMEX also continued to distinguish itself by the intent of its emphasis on emerging markets, even though some of its competitors had moved in the same direction. The company calculated that the weighted average growth rate in cement demand in the countries in which it was present was close to 4%, compared to 3% for Holderbank and Lafarge and 2% for the three other international majors. CEMEX also thought that its emerging market business should command higher price-earnings ratios in cement than business in advanced markets—the reverse of the situation that prevailed. According to CEO Lorenzo Zambrano, "They assign us the ratios of developing-country companies, even though we have very little volatility and our risk is limited due to our geographical diversification."[18]

Despite the increasing number of countries in which CEMEX participated, Mexico continued to play a critical role in its strategy as a lab for developing, testing, and refining new ideas about how to compete in emerging markets. Thus, in addition to reinforcing CEMEX's skills at handling macroeconomic fluctuations, the peso crisis had led to the discovery of a distinct customer segment involving informal construction that demanded bagged cement through retail channels, exhibited less cyclicality than the formal construction sector, and was apparently ubiquitous in emerging markets. Such demand lent itself to branding and promotion, which CEMEX first worked out in Mexico, before rolling out marketing campaigns to other countries. Another example was provided by the idea of using global positioning satellites to link dispatchers, truckers, and customers in a system that could track deliveries and guarantee them to within 20 minutes, rather than the usual three-hours-plus. This idea originated with visits to Federal Express in Memphis and an emergency call center in Houston and required the assistance of consultants from the U.S. in using complexity theory to model cement delivery logistics. The innovation was, once again, first implemented in Mexico, aided by imaginative advertising comparing the speeds of cement and pizza delivery. Customer willingness-to-pay went up while fuel, maintenance, and payroll costs came down.

CEMEX's organizational arrangements also differed in important ways from its competitors'. One key difference was that country-level managers at CEMEX reported directly to regional directors whereas competitors often had an extra layer of area managers between regional and country managers. CEMEX plants were organized into 7–9 departments, each with its own vice president. Every month, the vice presidents reported to the country president and the regional manager during the latter's visit. The reports covered all aspects of the plants and used a standardized format. In addition, the country presidents, regional directors, CEO Zambrano, and his executive committee all met every month as well. Other global competitors might hold such meetings as infrequently as once a quarter and tended to be more decentralized in their decision-making. CEMEX had recently reorganized from a structure with a Mexican division and an international one to a structure with three regional divisions: North America, South America and the Caribbean, and Europe and Asia. Also, while it resisted setting up full-fledged regional offices, it had made some recent attempts to coordinate more formally across different countries within a region. For

[18]James F. Smith, "Making Cement a Household Word," *Los Angeles Times*, January 16, 2000, p. C1.

example, it had consolidated the administrative and financial functions for six countries in the South American and Caribbean region in Venezuela.

At the apex of this structure sat CEMEX's CEO, Lorenzo Zambrano. Zambrano had begun working at CEMEX during the summers in the early 1960s while he was a teenager attending nearby ITESM (Monterrey Tech), and had returned to the company after earning his MBA from Stanford University in 1968. Lorenzo Zambrano favored a very hands-on approach to running CEMEX, often checking kiln statistics and sales data on a daily basis. He was a bachelor who devoted the vast majority of his time to the company, and encouraged his subordinates to do the same. He also got personally involved in sending and receiving e-mail and using Lotus Notes, which was still unusual among local CEOs.

Zambrano's personal commitment to information technology mirrored CEMEX's early and consistent use of IT. When Zambrano took over as CEO in the mid-1980s, heavy investments in IT in Mexico seemed to be overruled by the country's weak telecom infrastructure. Zambrano was convinced, however, that the importance of using IT to increase productivity would become more apparent as the Mexican economy opened up, and that the optimal private response to the disabilities of Mexico's public infrastructure was to invest more rather than less in this area. In 1987, CEMEX created a satellite system to link the Mexican plants it had begun to acquire. In 1988, the company transferred internal voice and data communications to its own private network. The Spanish acquisitions were also connected immediately to each other as well as to the Mexican operations. In 1992, the company founded Cemtec, which was supposed to complement the company's IT department by performing the functions of software development and hardware installation, and which was eventually spun off. In 1987, CEMEX spent about 0.25% of its sales on IT; by 1999, this figure had increased to about 1%. CEMEX's competitors were considered slower at capitalizing on the possibilities afforded by IT, although they were moving in the same direction.

CEMEX's use of IT had transformed the way the company worked in numerous ways. The 20-minute site delivery guarantee, already described, was a very visible example that led to the company's being canonized as a master of "digital business design."[19] The company was also connected via the Internet to distributors and suppliers. More recently, it had announced plans to launch a Latin American e-business development accelerator and, in alliance with B2B specialist Ariba and three large Latin American companies (Alfa of Mexico, and Bradespar and Votorantim of Brazil), a neutral business-to-business integrated supplier exchange, Latinexus, that was supposed to become the leading e-procurement marketplace in Latin America. Within CEMEX, IT made an enormous amount of information became available to Zambrano and his top management. Sales figures were reported daily, broken out by product and geography. On the production side, various operating metrics were available kiln by kiln. Even emissions data were included. And information flowed sideways as well as upwards: country managers could view data from other countries, and kiln managers were able to look at other kilns.

CEMEX provided its employees with a number of IT training programs and had also been aggressive in using new technology to overhaul its training function. A private satellite TV channel was acquired for this purpose, and CEMEX developed a virtual MBA program in collaboration with Monterrey Tech that combined satellite TV, the Internet, and the university's network of campuses to deliver courses to executive (part-time) MBA students. Recruitment was greatly aided by the company's public profile and included not only the graduates of Mexico's top educational institutions, but also Mexican graduates of top foreign business schools and alumni of other leading firms. Thus, while the Boston Consulting Group had long been CEMEX's principal strategy consultant, more than one of the professionals in the company's strategic planning function was a McKinsey alumnus. Overall, many regarded CEMEX as having shifted over time from an engineering-driven approach to one more dependent on economics.

[19]Adrian J. Slywotzky and David J. Morrison, with Ted Moser, Kevin A. Mundt, and James A. Quella, *Profit Patterns: 30 Ways to Anticipate and Profit from Strategic Forces Reshaping Your Business*, New York: Times Business/Random House, April 1999.

Outlook   While CEMEX faced a number of issues in 2000, perhaps the most important one concerned how far its competitive advantage could travel. CEMEX's entry into Indonesia and Egypt, in particular, stirred some concerns about the difficulties of working across language barriers and the challenges of adapting to different cultures—such as incorporating prayer-breaks into continuous process operations in Muslim countries. Others, however, were more optimistic, pointing out that CEMEX already used English as its semiofficial language, arguing that cement itself was a language of sorts, and noting that the company had its own strong culture that could serve as a binder. And everybody recognized that while Lafarge's hostile bid for Blue Circle appeared to have failed, consolidation at a new level—of international competitors rather than by them—might be the next big dynamic in the cement industry.

Case 2-3   Mattel and the Toy Recalls (A)[1]

Hari Bapuji and Paul Beamish

It's sad to say that the most safe product coming out of China these days is fireworks.

—Jay Leno, U.S. Talk Show Host

Jay Leno aptly reflected the mood of U.S. consumers during the summer of 2007. Many Chinese-made goods such as pet food, toothpaste, seafood, and tires had been recalled in recent weeks. These recalls began to severely erode the confidence of U.S. consumers in Chinese-made goods. On July 30, 2007, the senior executive team of Mattel under the leadership of Bob Eckert, CEO received reports that the surface paint on the Sarge Cars made in China contained lead in excess of U.S. federal regulations.[2] It was certainly not good news for Mattel, which was about to recall 967,000 Chinese-made children's character toys such as Dora, Elmo, and Big Bird, because of excess lead in the paint. Not surprisingly, the decision ahead was not only about whether to recall the Sarge Cars and other toys that might be unsafe, but also how to deal with the recall situation.

▌ Proffessors Hari Bapuji and Paul Beamish wrote this case solely to provide material for class discussion. The authors do not intend to illustrate either effective or ineffective handling of a managerial situation. The authors may have disguised certain names and other identifying information to protect confidentiality.

Ivey Management Services prohibits any form of reproduction, storage or transmittal without its written permission. This material is not covered under authorization from any reproduction rights organization. To order copies or request permission to reproduce materials, contact Ivey Publishing, Ivey Management Services, c/o Richard Ivey School of Business, The University of Western Ontario, London, Ontario, Canada, N6A 3K7; phone (519) 661-3208, fax (519) 661-3882, email cases@ivey.uwo.ca

▌[1]This case has been written on the basis of published sources. Consequently, the interpretations and perspectives presented are not necessarily those of Mattel and other organizations represented in this case or any of their employees.

Toy Industry—Overview

The global toy market was estimated to be a $71 billion business in 2007—an increase of about six per cent over the previous year.[3] About 36 per cent

▌[2]Mattel, Inc.'s communication (dated September 5, 2007) to the Subcommittee on Commerce, Trade and Consumer Protection.
▌[3]Source: International Council of Toy Industries and NPD.

Exhibit 1   Key Financial Data of Toy Majors (All figures in thousands of U.S. dollars, except number of employees)

	Mattel		Hasbro		RC2		JAAKS Pacific	
	2006	2005	2006	2005	2006	2005	2006	2005
Sales	5650156	5179016	3151481	3087627	518829	504445	765386	661536
Net Profits	592927	417019	230055	212075	34094	53130	72375	63493
Total Assets	4955884	4372313	3096905	3301143	614640	629736	881894	753955
Debt/Liabilities	940390	807395	494917	528389	22438	82647	98000	98000
Stockholder Equity	2432974	2101733	1537890	1723476	451926	398951	609288	524651
R & D Expenses	173514	182015	171358	150586	N.A.	N.A.	N.A.	N.A.
Marketing/Advertising and Promotion	650975	629115	368996	366371	N.A.	N.A.	N.A.	N.A.
Number of employees (worldwide)	32000	N.A.	5800	N.A.	821	842	N.A.	N.A.
Property, Plant & Equipment	536749	547104	181726	164045	38991	47039	16883	12695
Capital Expenditure	314784	82191	83604	120671	8319	6643	121914	9467

Source: Company Annual Reports

of the global market was concentrated in North America (about $24 billion), but annual sales in this region were growing at a slower pace—about one per cent. European markets accounted for about 30 per cent of the global toy sales and were growing at about five per cent each year. In contrast, the markets in Asia grew at 12 per cent in 2006, and were expected to grow by 25 per cent in 2007.[4] A large part of this growth was expected to occur in China and India, whose burgeoning middle-classes were thriving on the double-digit economic growth in their countries.

The toy industry in the United States had a large number of players. About 880 companies operated in the dolls, toys, and games manufacturing industry in 2002. This figure was about 10 per cent less than the 1,019 companies that operated in 1997. Approximately 70 per cent of the toy companies employed less than 20 persons.[5] The industry was dominated by a few key players such as Mattel, Hasbro, RC2, JAAKS Pacific, Marvel, and Lego. The industry

leaders were Mattel and Hasbro, whose combined sales in 2006 were about US$8.7 billion. The sales of many other major players were under a billion dollars. **Exhibit 1** contains key financial data of some major U.S. toy makers.

Big retailers like Wal-Mart and Target had become major players in the U.S. toy market. They not only sold the products of other toy companies such as Mattel, Hasbro, and Lego, but also sourced toys directly from China. These toys were often sold under their own brand names. For example, Wal-Mart sold toys under its Kid-Connection brand while Target sold toys under its PlayWonder brand.[6] It was estimated that Wal-Mart accounted for about 25 per cent of the toy sales in the United States.[7] As a result of the entry of big-box retailers in the toy industry, specialty toy retailers such as Toys'R'Us had steadily lost market share.[8] The top five retailers sold

[6]Doug Desjardins. Target to leapfrog over Toys 'R' Us into no. 2 spot. *Retailing Today.* 2006. 45(7):36.

[7]Allan Drury. Concerns about China-made toys hurt holiday sales. *The Journal News,* January, 2008.

[8]Kelly Nolan. Toys 'R' Us not playing games with success. *Retailing Today.* Sep 10, 2007. Vol. 46, Iss. 13; p. 24.

[4]Ibid.
[5]Source: U.S. Census Bureau.

about 60 per cent of all the toys sold in the United States.[9]

Toy markets in the United States were categorized into multiple segments such as Action Figures & Accessories, Arts & Crafts, Building Sets, Dolls, Games/Puzzles, Infant/Preschool Toys, Youth Electronics, Outdoor & Sports Toys, and Plush Vehicles. Of these, the infant/preschool toy segment was the largest, followed by outdoor and sport toys, and dolls. These segments had largely remained stagnant over the years. As a result of kids getting old younger (KGOY), the only segment with noticeable growth was youth electronics. By contrast, video games which were outside the traditional toy industry had been experiencing remarkable growth. For segment-wise sales of toys in the United States, see **Exhibit 2.**

While the major markets for toys existed in the United States and Europe, production was concentrated in Asia, primarily China. About 60 per cent of the toys sold in the world were made in China. More than 10,500 toy makers operated in China.[10]

Exhibit 2   U.S. Toy Sales by Product Category (All figures in billion USD)

Product Category	2006	2005
Action Figures & Accessories	1.3	1.4
Arts & Crafts	2.6	2.5
Building Sets	0.67	0.68
Dolls	2.7	2.7
Games/Puzzles	2.4	2.5
Infant/Preschool	3.2	3.2
Youth Electronics	1.1	0.91
Outdoor & Sports Toys	2.9	2.9
Plush	1.3	1.4
Vehicles	2.1	2.0
All Other Toys	2.0	2.1
Total (Traditional Toy Industry)	**22.3**	**22.2**
Total Video Games	**12.5**	**10.5**

Source: Toy Industry Association/NPD Group.

These companies typically had contacts with large Western toy companies. The toy companies in China formed a complex web of supply chains, with contractors themselves sub-contracting production of components, and often, entire products to various companies.

Toy Production in China

Over the years, U.S. toy companies shifted their production overseas and focused their domestic operations on product design, marketing, research and development, and other high-value activities. As a result, employment in the domestic toy industry declined from 42,300 workers in 1993, to 17,400 workers in 2005, while toy imports increased.[11] Approximately 10 per cent of the demand for toys in the U.S. market was met by domestic production, while the rest was met through imports, primarily from China (see **Exhibit 3**).[12]

Chinese toy imports accounted for a full 86 per cent of toy imports to the United States in 2006, up dramatically from 41 per cent in 1992. The rise of China came at the expense of other toy exporting countries, whose combined share of toy imports to the United States plummeted from 59 per cent to 14 per cent during the same period. For instance, Japan remained a strong exporter of toys to the United States until a substantial drop around 2001. Despite its proximity to the United States, Mexico had not been able to sustain the up-tick it experienced in 2002. Further, Taiwan and Hong Kong toy exports had both been in decline for over a decade.

China's rising share of U.S. toy imports, and more generally China's position in the global toy industry, can be attributed to the lower cost business environment in China. China had attracted tremendous foreign direct investment and outsourcing of manufacturing operations. While analysts have often pointed to the phenomenal economic growth in China, they have also noted the resultant pressure

[9]Lazich, Robert S. *Market Share Reporter.* Farmington Hills, MI: Gale Group, 2004.

[10]David Barboza. "China Bars Two Companies From Exporting Toys." *New York Times*. Aug. 10, 2007.

[11]Toy industry outlook 2006 http://www.ita.doc.gov/td/ocg/outlook06_toys.pdf

[12]Ibid.

Exhibit 3   U.S. Toy Imports–Total Vs. China (1989–2006)

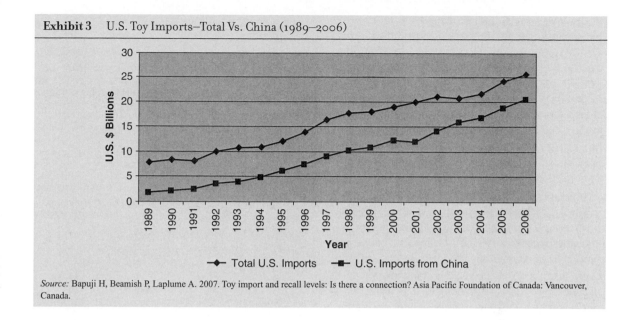

Source: Bapuji H, Beamish P, Laplume A. 2007. Toy import and recall levels: Is there a connection? Asia Pacific Foundation of Canada: Vancouver, Canada.

on the physical, technical, and human resource infrastructures.[13] These pressures, some analysts argue, have resulted in the Chinese manufacturers compromising on the product safety.

According to American regulators, tainted pet food imported from China was responsible for deaths of, or injuries to, about 4,000 cats and dogs. As a result, regulators initiated the biggest pet food recall in U.S. history. This was followed by worldwide recalls of Chinese toothpaste laced with antifreeze called diethylene glycol, which was found to be responsible for nearly 200 deaths in Haiti and Panama. Shortly thereafter, Chinese-made tires were linked to two deaths in an accident in the United States and recalled. The tires lacked a safety feature that prevented tire treads from splitting and falling apart.[14] The spate of recalls of Chinese-made goods began to erode consumer confidence in products made in China.

Toy Safety

The safety of consumer goods in the United States is managed by four federal agencies: (i) the Food and Drug Administration (FDA) has jurisdiction over foods, drugs and cosmetics, (ii) the Department of Transportation oversees the safety of cars, trucks, motorcycles, and their accessories such as tires and car seats, (iii) the Department of Treasury has jurisdiction over alcohol, tobacco and firearms, and (iv) the U.S. Consumer Product Safety Commission (CPSC) has jurisdiction over about 15,000 types of consumer products, from microwave ovens to cribs to lawn mowers.[15]

The safety of toys and other children's products falls within the jurisdiction of CPSC, which was created in 1972 by Congress in the Consumer Product Safety Act to "protect the public against unreasonable risks of injuries and deaths associated with consumer products." In 2007, the CPSC had an operating budget of $66 million and a staff of 393 full-time equivalent employees. Its strategic goals

[13]Paul Beamish. "The High Cost of Cheap Chinese Labor." *Harvard Business Review.* June: 23, 2006.
[14]David Barboza. "China Steps up its Safety Efforts." *New York Times,* July 7, 2007.

[15]Source: CPSC.

for the year were to reduce deaths and injuries by fire hazards, carbon monoxide poisoning hazard, and hazards from children's products.[16] According to CPSC, 22 toy-related deaths and an estimated 220,500 toy-related injuries occurred in 2006.[17] Based on its analysis, CPSC identified the Top Five Hidden Home Hazards. These hazards were listed on the CPSC website to make consumers aware of the hazards and avoid injuries due to those. In 2007, CPSC listed the following as the top hazards: magnets, recalled products, tip-overs, windows and covering, pool and spa drains.

The CPSC collects information about product safety issues from sources such as hospitals, doctors, newspaper reports, industry reports, consumer complaints, investigations conducted by its staff, and reports from companies. When a company becomes aware of hazards associated with the products it sold, it is required by law to immediately inform the CPSC. Based on the information it received, CPSC worked in coordination with the companies involved to recall the hazardous products from the market. **Exhibit 4** presents the number of toy recalls made by CPSC since 1988. Not surprisingly, the majority of recalls in recent years involved toys made in China. See **Exhibit 5** for a list of the toys recalled in the United States since the beginning of 2007. All the toys recalled, with one exception, were made in China. Seven of the recalls were a result of excess lead in the surface paint of the toys.

Lead in children's products poses a serious hazard because exposure to lead can affect almost every organ and system in the human body. Children exposed to high levels of lead can suffer from damage such as IQ deficits, attention deficit hyperactivity disorder, motor skills, and reaction time. Considering the damages that lead can cause to humans, particularly children, the U.S. government limited the permissible amount of lead in products. Under the Consumer Safety Product Act 1972, lead in products accessible to children should not be greater than

[16]CPSC. Performance and accountability report. 2007. http://www.cpsc.gov/cpscpub/pubs/reports/2007par.pdf
[17]CPSC. Toy related deaths and injuries. 2006. http://www.cpsc.gov/library/toymemo06.pdf

Exhibit 4   Toy Recalls by CPSC (1988–2006)

Year	Total Number of Toy Recalls	Recalls of Toys Made in China	
		Number	Percentage
1988	32	2	6
1989	54	5	9
1990	34	6	18
1991	36	14	39
1992	25	10	40
1993	19	5	26
1994	31	19	61
1995	25	11	44
1996	22	9	41
1997	26	9	35
1998	30	12	40
1999	23	4	17
2000	37	20	54
2001	43	21	49
2002	34	16	47
2003	35	20	57
2004	30	22	73
2005	35	29	83
2006	41	33	80

Source: Bapuji H., Laplume A. 2008. Toy Recalls and China: One Year Later. Asia Pacific Foundation of Canada: Vancouver, Canada.

600 parts per million (ppm). The standards for permissible lead in other products vary depending on the usage and amount of lead in the product that is accessible.

Although lead use is banned or restricted in many developed countries, the same is not true for developing countries. In developed countries, the only source of lead exposure to children is from paint. In contrast, lead exposure in developing countries occurs due to lead gasoline, ceramics, mining, batteries, and even medication and cosmetics. Manufacturers use paint with a high percentage of lead because it is highly resistant to corrosion, extremely malleable, and has poor electrical conductivity. In addition, paint with higher lead is heavy and bright, making the products such as jewelry more appealing to consumers.

Exhibit 5   Toy Recalls in the United States (January 2007–July 24, 2007)

1. Risk of Explosion and Hearing Damage Prompts Recall of Remote Control Airplanes (July 24)
2. New Easy-Bake Oven Recall Following Partial Finger Amputation; Consumers Urged to Return Toy Ovens (July 19)
3. AAFES Expands Recall of "Soldier Bear" Toy Sets Due to Lead Poisoning Hazard (July 18)—Made in Hong Kong
4. Serious Intestinal Injury Prompts Kipp Brothers Recall of Mag Stix Magnetic Building Sets (July 5)
5. Infantino Recalls Children's Toy Castles Due to Choking Hazard (July 3)
6. Target Recalls Toy Barbeque Grills Due to Laceration Hazard (June 28)
7. RC2 Corp. Recalls Various Thomas & Friends™ Wooden Railway Toys Due to Lead Poisoning Hazard (June 13)
8. Gemmy Industries Corp. Recalls Flashing Eyeball Toys Due to Chemical Hazard (June 7)
9. Toy Drums Recalled by The Boyds Collection Ltd. Due to Lead Poisoning Hazard (May 30)
10. AAFES Recalls "Soldier Bear" Toy Sets Due to Lead Poisoning Hazard (May 23)—Made in Hong Kong
11. Tri-Star International Recalls Children's Toys Due to Choking Hazard (May 23)
12. Bookspan Recalls Discovery Bunny Books Due to Choking Hazard (May 17)
13. Bookspan Recalls Clip-on Baby Books Due to Choking Hazard (May 17)
14. Small World Toys Recalls Children's Take-Apart Townhouse Toys; Detached Magnets Pose Aspiration and Intestinal Hazards (May 3)
15. Battat Inc. Recalls Parents® Magazine Toy Cell Phones for Choking Hazard (May 3)
16. Graco Children's Products Recalls to Replace Soft Blocks Towers on Activity Centers Due to Choking Hazard (May 2)
17. Target Recalls Anima Bamboo Collection Games Due to Lead Poisoning Hazard (May 2)
18. Magnetix Magnetic Building Set Recall Expanded (April 19)
19. Small World Toys Recalls Children's Wooden Sound Puzzles with Knobs for Choking Hazard (April 11)
20. Target Recalls Activity Cart Toys Due to Choking Hazard (April 4)
21. OKK Trading Recalls Baby Dolls Due to Choking Hazard (April 4)
22. Regent Products Corp. Recalls Stuffed Ball Toys Due to Lead Hazard (March 28)
23. Estes-Cox Radio Control Airplanes with Lithium Polymer Batteries Recalled for Fire Hazard (March 27)
24. Toys "R" Us Recalls "Elite Operations" Toy Sets Due to Lead and Laceration Hazards (March 13)
25. Sportcraft Recalls Inflatable Bounce Houses Due to Impact Injury Hazard (February 27)
26. Jazwares Inc. Recalls Link-N-Lite™ Magnetic Puzzles, Ingested Magnets Pose Aspiration and Intestinal Hazards (February 15)
27. Fisher-Price Recalls "Laugh and Learn" Bunny Toys Due to Choking Hazard (February 15)
28. Battery Packs for Toy Vehicles Recalled by JAKKS Pacific Due to Fire Hazard (February 13)
29. Easy-Bake Ovens Recalled for Repair Due to Entrapment and Burn Hazards (February 6)
30. Geometix International LLC Recalls MagneBlocks™ Toys, Ingested Magnets Pose Aspiration and Intestinal Hazards (January 18)
31. Target Recalls Baby Rattles and Ornaments for Choking Hazard (January 18)

Source: CPSC

While excess lead in toys and other children's products is an issue of concern, CPSC has identified another major hazard associated with small magnets in toys. Due to the availability of powerful rare-earth magnets at cheap prices, the manufacturers began to use them in many toys such as building blocks and jewelry. On some of these products, the magnets came loose. If a child swallowed more than one magnet, they could attach to each other and cause intestinal perforations and blockage, which can be fatal. In April 2006, CPSC and Rose Art Industries recalled 3.8 million Magnetix magnetic building sets following the death of a 20-month-old boy after he swallowed magnets that twisted his small intestine and created a blockage. In addition, several other children required surgery and intensive care to remove the magnets they swallowed.[18]

Following the recall of Magnetix building sets, Rose Art Industries redesigned its building sets to cover the magnets and reinforced these with resins so that the magnets could not be detached from the building set. Further, they changed the age suitability of their product to six years or older and provided new warnings about the dangers associated with ingesting magnets.[19] The recall of Magnetix was followed by another five recalls of toys that contained small magnets that detached. One of those recalls involved 2.4 million Polly Pocket play sets (an additional 2 million sets were sold worldwide), which was prompted by 170 reports of magnets coming loose and three children who swallowed the magnets requiring surgical care.[20] The Polly Pocket play sets, recalled on November 21, 2006, were made by Mattel and sold between May 2003 and September 2006.

Mattel—The No.1 Toy Maker in the World

With a vision to provide "the world's premier toy brands—today and tomorrow," Mattel "designs, manufactures, and markets a broad variety of toy products worldwide through sales to its customers and directly to consumers."[21] Mattel's position as a leader in the global toy industry was so formidable that Mattel's international business division with gross sales of $2.7 billion in 2006 would be the industry's third largest company, if it was a separate company, and Mattel's U.S. business with $3.4 billion would still be No.1.[22]

Mattel was an industry leader not only by its sales, but also through its pioneering efforts to be a good corporate citizen. In 1996, Mattel initiated its Global Manufacturing Principles, which aimed to ensure responsible management practices used in Mattel's factories as well as by its vendors. Mattel's factories were audited by the International Center for Corporate Accountability, an independent body, and its results were made publicly available by Mattel. Mattel engaged in philanthropic activities through Mattel Children's Foundation in 37 countries. It was named one of the top 100 Best Corporate Citizens by CRO Magazine in 2006. More saliently, Mattel's corporate governance received the highest global rating of 10 by Governance Metrics International (GMI), which placed the company among the top one per cent of more than 3,400 global companies.

The journey of Mattel, however, began modestly in 1944, when Harold Matson and Elliot Handler began to make toys out of a converted garage in California. They named the company Mattel, using letters from their last and first names. Matson sold his share to Elliot Handler and his wife, Ruth Handler, who incorporated the company in 1948. Mattel's first products were picture frames and doll house furniture.[23] Their first big product was a mass-produced, and thus, inexpensive music box, which established Mattel firmly in the toy business. The introduction of Barbie in 1959, and Ken two years later, propelled company growth. The products introduced later such as Hot Wheels went further to establish Mattel's position as an industry leader. Mattel went public in 1960.

Mattel's products were organized in three different business groups: (i) Mattel Girls & Boys Brands that includes brands like Barbie dolls and accessories, Polly Pocket, Hot Wheels, Matchbox, Batman, CARS, and Superman. (ii) Fisher-Price Brands consisting of brands such as Fisher-Price, Little People, Sesame Street, Dora the Explorer, Go-Diego-Go!, Winnie the Pooh, and Power Wheels. (iii) American Girl Brands, with brands such as Just Like You and Bitty Baby. In the United States alone, the sales of these three groups in 2006

[18]http://www.cpsc.gov/cpscpub/prerel/prhtml06/06127.html
[19]U.S. PIRG Education Fund. Trouble in Toyland. 21st Annual Toy Safety Survey.
[20]http://www.cpsc.gov/cpscpub/prerel/prhtml07/07039.html
[21]Mattel Annual Report, 2006, p.3.
[22]Letter to Shareholders by Bob Eckert, Mattel CEO, *Mattel Annual Report,* 2006.

[23]J. Amerman. *The story of Mattel, Inc.: Fifty years of innovation.* 1995.

were: Mattel Girls & Boys Brands—$1.57 billion, Fisher-Price Brands—$1.47 billion, and American Girl Brands—$0.44 billion.

About 45 percent of Mattel's sales were accounted for by three major buyers: Wal-Mart, Toys'R'Us, and Target. In addition to its principal competitors, such as Hasbro and RC2, Mattel also competed with a large number of smaller companies that made toys, video games, and consumer electronics, and published children's books.

In the 1990s, Mattel made a number of significant acquisitions, including Fisher-Price (1993, leader in preschool segment), Kransco (1994, made battery-powered ride-on vehicles), Tyco (1997, made Tickle Me Elmo and Matchbox cars), Pleasant Company (1998, mail-order firm that made American Girl-brand books, dolls, and clothing), and Bluebird Toys (1998, made toys such as Polly Pocket and The Tiny Disney Collection). Mattel's acquisition of The Learning Company, a leading educational software maker, in 1999 at a cost of $3.6 billion proved to be troublesome. The company lost money and was later sold. Mattel also made a hostile bid to acquire Hasbro, the second largest toy company. This bid, made in 1996, failed to materialize.

The toy industry is different from other industries on two major counts. First, toy sales are seasonal. Most sales occurred during the third and last quarter of the year, which coincide with the traditional holiday period. Second, there is a lot of uncertainty around new product success. It was difficult, almost impossible, to predict whether a particular toy would be liked by children. Not surprisingly, many companies in the toy industry made millions with one successful toy and also went bankrupt with one big failure.

Over a long period, Mattel had managed the peculiarities of the toy industries well with a number of innovative and often revolutionary ideas. Traditionally, the retailers promoted toys during the holiday season and toy manufacturers had little, if any, role to play. In 1955, Mattel tied-up with ABC Television and sponsored a 15-minute segment of Walt Disney's Mickey Mouse Club for one full year. At that time, Mattel's revenues were only $5 million, but it paid $500,000 for the sponsorship. The

sponsorship quickly established a continuous connection for Mattel with the kids and gave it an opportunity to influence the buying habits of its consumers. Not surprisingly, this move changed the nature of marketing in the toy industry. Also, for Mattel, it paved the way for further partnerships with entertainment companies to produce character toys.

Mattel entered into licensing agreements to make toys based on the characters owned by companies such as Disney, Warner Brothers, Viacom (Nickelodeon), Origin Products, and Sesame Workshop. These agreements gave the company access to characters such as Winnie the Pooh, Disney Princesses, CARS, Dora the Explorer, Go-Diego-Go!, Sponge Bob SquarePants, Polly Pocket, Batman, Superman, and Elmo. In 2005, Mattel partnered with Scholastic Entertainment to produce educational learning systems.

Not only did Mattel license characters, but also licensed some of its core brands to other non-toy companies to design and develop an array of products sporting the core brand names. These deals included Barbie eyewear for little girls (with REM Eyewear), Hot Wheels apparel and accessories (with Innovo Group), Barbie video games (with Activision), and CD Players, learning laptops, and MP3 players. Recently, Mattel was trying to reduce its reliance on its big customers such as Wal-Mart, Target, and Toys'R'Us through internet and catalogue sales.[24]

Traditionally, toy companies relied on point-of-sale (POS) data to forecast demand for toys. With its Hot Wheels brand, Mattel realized that variety was the key driver of the sales and introduced a rolling mix strategy. This strategy involved changing the physical 72-car assortment mix by seven to eight per cent every two weeks. This changed the nature of its practices and instead of relying on POS data, Mattel only needed to design the varieties and supply an assortment pack to the retailer.[25]

Mattel designed and developed toys in the corporate headquarters. In 2006, Mattel spent

---

[24]Hoover Company Report on Mattel.

[25]Eric Johnson and Tom Clock. *Mattel, Inc: Vendor Operations in Asia.* Tuck School of Business at Dartmouth. 2002.

US$174 million on in-house product design and development. In contrast, the company spent US$261 million on royalties and US$651 million on advertising. Mattel manufactured products in its own factories as well as through third-party manufacturers. Also, it marketed the products purchased from unrelated companies that designed, developed, and manufactured those products.

Offshoring the Toy Production   Mattel's principal manufacturing facilities were located in China, Indonesia, Thailand, Malaysia, and Mexico. It closed its last toy factory in the U.S., originally part of its Fisher-Price divisions, in 2002.[26] Mattel produced its core brands such as Barbie and Hot Wheels in company-owned facilities, but used third-party manufacturers to produce its non-core brands. It used third-party manufacturers in a number of countries, including the United States, Mexico, Brazil, India, New Zealand, and Australia. This manufacturing mix minimized Mattel's risk and gave it focus and flexibility. The core brands were a staple business, while the non-core brands tended to be those products that were expected to have a short market life. The non-core brands were typically associated with popular movie characters and had a life of one year.[27]

The development of new toys was done at Mattel's corporate headquarters. Outsourcing for the manufacturing of non-core brand toys followed a strict multi-step process. The design teams created a bid package containing the new product's blueprint and engineering specifications. It often contained a physical model. After the selection of a vendor, the company established the vendor's production infrastructure. At this point, Mattel assumed responsibility for the cost of tooling. The vendor then produced 50 units as "First Shots" to verify if any tool modifications were required. This was followed by one or more "Engineering Pilot," depending on the toy's complexity, and the "Final Engineering Pilot." After this, a "Production Pilot" of 1,000 units was run using the entire assembly line to run the product. Finally, the "Production Start" phase began only when the new toy met design compliance.[28]

Mattel and its vendors manufactured about 800 million products each year. Approximately half of the toys Mattel sold were made in its own plants, a higher proportion than other large toy makers. Also, Mattel made a larger percentage of its toys outside China than other large toy companies. Mattel's manufacturing and offshoring strategy was developed over a period of five decades. The company made its first Barbie doll in Asia in 1959. Since then, Mattel managed the risks of offshored operations by employing a mix of company-owned and vendor-owned manufacturing facilities all over Asia.

In China alone, Mattel had contracts with approximately 37 principal vendors who made toys for the company.[29] The principal vendors further used smaller companies for the full or partial production of toys. As a result, the supply chains in China were long and complex. According to some estimates, about 3,000 Chinese companies made Mattel products.[30] However, Mattel had direct contact only with the principal vendors.

A Recall Underway

In June 2007, a French direct importer of Mattel's products, Auchan, performed pre-shipment tests with the help of Intertek, an independent laboratory. These tests revealed that Mattel's toys, made by a vendor Lee Der Industrial Company, contained lead above permissible limits. Intertek sent the test results, on June 8, 2007, to Mattel employees in China. Consequently, Mattel employees contacted Lee Der instructing it to correct the problem and provide another sample for testing. Another test by Intertek on June 29, for Auchan, on the same toy produced by Lee Der had passed the test.

---

[26]Louis Story, "After stumbling, Mattel cracks down in China." *New York Times*. August 29, 2007.

[27]Company annual reports and chat excerpts of Mattel India CEO on CNN-IBN.

[28]Op. cit. Johnson and Clock. 2002.

[29]Testimony of Robert Eckert, CEO, Mattel, to the Sub-committee on Commerce, Trade, and Consumer Protection of the Committee on Energy and Commerce. September 19, 2007.

[30]David Barboza, "Scandal and Suicide in China: A Dark Side of Toys." *New York Times*. August 23, 2007.

On June 27, 2007, Mattel's call center in the United States received a report from a consumer, who informed them that a home test kit found excessive lead in Mattel's toys. These were also manufactured by Lee Der. Following this, Mattel tested five samples of Lee Der toys and found on July 6 that three of them contained excess lead. As the testing was underway, Auchan informed Mattel on July 3 about lead violations in another toy made by Lee Der. As soon as the test results were out, Mattel employees in China notified Lee Der and stopped accepting products made by Lee Der. Further tests on the toy samples collected from Lee Der were conducted on July 9 in Mattel's own laboratories, which revealed that nine of the 23 samples of Lee Der toys contained excess lead in surface paint.

Mattel's employees in China notified the senior management team at corporate headquarters on July 12 about the issues with Lee Der products. Following this, Mattel management ordered an immediate suspension of all shipments of products made by Lee Der. Further investigations by Mattel revealed that the nonconforming lead levels were because of a yellow pigment in paint used on portions of toys manufactured by Lee Der.[31]

Lee Der Industrial Company was located in Foshan City of Guangdong Province, where thousands of small toy factories existed. The company was founded by two Chinese entrepreneurs, Cheng Shuhung and Xie Yuguang. Mattel first used Lee Der for making a small batch of educational toys in 1993. By July 2007, Lee Der employed approximately 2,500 people and made toys almost exclusively for Mattel. With annual sales of about $25 million, Lee Der was about to open a new $5 million plant.[32]

Lee Der had purchased its paint from Dongxing New Energy Co. since 2003. The owner of Dongxing was a good friend of Cheng Shu-hung. In April 2007, Dongxing ran out of yellow pigment and sourced about 330 pounds of it for $1,250 from Dongguan Zhongxin Toner Powder Factory. Then, Dongxing supplied the paint to Lee Der, which used it in Mattel's toys. Initial reports suggested that Dongguan Zhongxin Toner Powder Factory was fake and that its owners were not traceable.[33]

An essential component of Mattel's contracts with its vendors is that the products made by vendors comply with applicable safety standards. Mattel had systems which required the vendors to either purchase paint from a list of eight certified vendors in China or test for compliance each batch of the paint purchased from a non-certified vendor. Mattel also conducted audits of certified paint suppliers and vendors to ensure that Mattel's requirements were being followed. The frequency of audits depended on Mattel's prior experience with the suppliers and vendors.

Following its investigations, Mattel filed an initial report with the CPSC on July 20 and followed it up with another on July 26, indicating that it would like to issue a recall of all the products manufactured by Lee Der between April 19, 2007 (the date when Lee Der took delivery of the lead-tainted paint from its supplier), and July 6, 2007, the date when Mattel stopped accepting products from Lee Der.[34] Work on this recall was underway and Mattel and the CPSC were scheduled to announce the recall on August 2, 2007. See **Exhibit 6** for the press release announcing the recall, expected to be issued by the CPSC. Mattel had already informed big retailers such as Wal-Mart and Toys'R'Us of the impending recall. The retailers pulled the toys off their shelves and flagged the cash registers so that customers could not buy the toys from the stores.[35]

[31]Mattel's response to the information request from the Sub-committee on Commerce, Trade, and Consumer Protection of the Committee on Energy and Commerce. September 5, 2007.
[32]http://www.ckgsb.edu.cn:8080/article/600/3051.aspx

[33]Ibid.
[34]Testimony of Robert Eckert, CEO, Mattel, to the Sub-committee on Commerce, Trade, and Consumer Protection of the Committee on Energy and Commerce. September 19, 2007.
[35]http://www.reuters.com/article/domesticNews/idUSN0230401920070802

Exhibit 6   Recall Notice of Mattel's Character Toys for Lead Paint Violations

U.S. Consumer Product Safety Commission

Office of Information and Public Affairs
FOR IMMEDIATE RELEASE
August 2, 2007
Release #07-257

Washington, DC 20207
Firm's Recall Hotline: (800) 916-4498
CPSC Recall Hotline: (800) 638-2772
CPSC Media Contact: (301) 504-7908

Fisher-Price Recalls Licensed Character Toys Due To Lead Poisoning Hazard

WASHINGTON, D.C. - The U.S. Consumer Product Safety Commission, in cooperation with the firms named
below, today announced a voluntary recall of the following consumer product. Consumers should stop using
recalled products immediately unless otherwise instructed.

Name of Product: Sesame Street, Dora the Explorer, and other children's toys
Units: About 967,000
Importer: Fisher-Price Inc., of East Aurora, N.Y.
Hazard: Surface paints on the toys could contain excessive levels of lead. Lead is toxic if ingested by young
children and can cause adverse health effects.
Incidents/Injuries: None reported.
Description: The recalled involves various figures and toys that were manufactured between April 19, 2007 and
July 6, 2007 and were sold alone or as part of sets. The model names and product numbers for the recalled toys,
which are all marked with "Fisher-Price," are listed below. The toys may have a date code between 109-7LF and
187-7LF marked on the product or packaging.
Sold at: Retail stores nationwide from May 2007 through August 2007 for between $5 and $40.
Manufactured in: China
Remedy: Consumers should immediately take the recalled toys away from children and contact Fisher-Price.
Consumers will need to return the product and will receive a voucher for a replacement toy of the consumer's
choice (up to the value of the returned product).
Consumer Contact: For additional information contact Fisher-Price at (800) 916-4498 anytime or visit the firm's
Web site at www.service.mattel.com
Product List: A list of about 50 different toys. The case authors excluded this list in the interest of space.

Source: CPSC

Another Instance of Lead and Further Reports of Loose Magnets

While Mattel was preparing to announce its recall, on July 30, 2007, it found that paint on Sarge cars contained excess lead. The Sarge cars were made for Mattel by Early Light Industrial Company, Ltd. of Hong Kong, which made them in its manufacturing facility located in Pinghu, China.[36] Early Light had supplied toys to Mattel for 20 years.[37] Only further investigation would be able to clarify where

exactly in the supply chain the problem originated and why. Initial reports indicated that approximately 250,000 Sarge cars made between May 2007 and August 2007 may have been affected with lead paint.

After the November 2006 recall of eight different Polly Pocket play sets made in China for the problem of magnets coming loose, Mattel reinforced the magnets by locking them in the toys rather than gluing them. Nonetheless, in recent months Mattel had received a few hundred reports of magnets coming loose from a number of play sets sold before November 2006. The play sets affected with magnet problems were: (i) fifty additional models of Polly Pocket play sets (about five million of these play

[36]Ibid.
[37]Op. cit. Louis Story. 2007.

sets were sold between March 2003 and November 2006), (ii) Batman and One Piece action figures (about 350,000 toys sold between June 2006 and June 2007), (iii) Barbie and Tanner play sets (about 683,000 toys sold between May 2006–July, 2007), and (iv) Doggie Day Care play sets (about one million sold between July 2004 and July 2007).

Recalls are a nightmare to companies for several reasons. First, the recalls pose major logistics challenges as the company needs to establish a set-up to handle the recalls. Second, the company has to deal with regulators who tend to push the company to ensure that not only a recall is issued, but the products in consumers' hands are actually returned to the company. Third, recalls are often viewed as an admission of guilt and open the company to consumer litigations. Finally, recalls damage the reputation of the company and result in increased costs, lost sales, and stock price erosion.

Mattel and Fisher Price were not new to recalls. In their long history, they had recalled products in the past (see **Exhibit 7**). Nevertheless, the current situation seemed entirely new, complex, and challenging. It was not clear if and which products needed to be recalled. As importantly, how could the company minimize the negative consequences which are germane to any product recall? Finally, how could the company ensure such recalls did not recur?

Exhibit 7   Product Recalls in Mattel-Fisher Price History (Up to July 2007)

Mattel Recalls

1. Serious Injuries Prompt Recall of Mattel's Polly Pocket Magnetic Play Sets (November 21, 2006)
2. Children's Jewelry Sold at American Girl Stores Recalled for Lead Poisoning Hazard (March 30, 2006)
3. Mattel, Inc. Recall of Batman Batmobile Toy Vehicle (April 14, 2004)
4. Fisher-Price Intelli-Table Toy Recall (March 29, 2001)
5. Barbie Sunglasses Recalled by IMT Accessories (February 21, 2001)
6. Cabbage Patch Kids Snacktime Dolls Refund (January 6, 1997)
7. Disney Play 'N Pop Activity Toy Recalled by Arcotoys (February 23, 1995)
8. Mattel Voluntarily Recalls Disney Poppin' Sounds Pull Train (November 18, 1991)
9. Battlestar Galactica Space Toys Replaced by Mattel (January 11, 1979)

Fisher-Price Recalls

10. Fisher-Price Rainforest Infant Swings Recalled Due to Entrapment Hazard (May 30, 2007)
11. Fisher-Price Recalls "Laugh and Learn" Bunny Toys Due to Choking Hazard (February 15, 2007)
12. Fisher-Price Recalls Infant Musical Toy Chair Posing Strangulation Hazard (January 18, 2006)
13. Fisher-Price Recall of Scooters and Mini Bikes (June 14, 2005)
14. Fisher-Price Recall of Push Toys (May 10, 2005)
15. Fisher-Price Recall of Pogo Sticks (May 10, 2005)
16. Scooters and Mini Bikes Recalled by Fisher-Price (November 13, 2003)
17. Crib Mobile Toys Recalled by Fisher-Price (June 19, 2003)
18. Little People® Animal Sounds Farms Recalled by Fisher-Price (April 23, 2003)
19. Fisher-Price Recall for In-Home Repair of Infant Swings (April 10, 2002)
20. Fisher-Price Portable Bassinet Recall (July 31, 2001)
21. Basketball Sets Recalled by Fisher-Price (May 10, 2001)
22. Fisher-Price Intelli-Table Toy Recall (March 29, 2001)
23. McDonald's "Scooter Bug" Happy Meal Toy Recall (March 5, 2001)
24. Children's Riding Vehicles Recalled by Fisher-Price (August 31, 2000)
25. Swings and Toys Recalled by Fisher-Price (August 23, 2000)
26. Baby Jumper Seats & Construction Toys Recalled by Fisher-Price (July 21, 2000)

(continued)

(*continued*)

27. Swings & Domes Recalled by Fisher-Price (April 7, 2000)
28. Toy Basketball Nets Recalled by Little Tikes, Today's Kids & Fisher-Price (December 22, 1998)
29. Power Wheels Ride-On Battery-Powered Vehicles Recall to Repair (October 22, 1998)
30. Infant Toys Recalled by Fisher-Price (March 2, 1998)
31. Toy Police Cars Recalled by Fisher-Price (May 19, 1997; Revised October 29, 2002)
32. Baseball Training Toy Recall/Repair by Fisher-Price (July 7, 1995; Revised October 29, 2002)
33. Fisher-Price Recalls Kiddicraft Racing Rover Car (August 17, 1993; Revised October 29, 2002)
34. Fisher-Price Recalls Snuggle Light Doll (August 12, 1993; Revised October 29, 2002)
    Fun Bus Safety Modification Program by Fisher-Price (March 15, 1990; Revised October 29, 2002)
35. "Pop-Up Playhouse" Modification by Fisher-Price (July 27, 1988; Revised October 29, 2002)
36. Strollers Repair by Fisher-Price (November 24, 1987; Revised October 29, 2002)
37. Crib Toy Safety Alert issued by Fisher-Price (October 10, 1984; Revised October 29, 2002)
38. "Splash & Stack Bluebird" Toys Recalled by Fisher-Price (July 26, 1984; Revised December 2, 2005)

Source: CPSC

Reading 2-1   Culture and Organization

Susan Schneider and Jean-Louis Barsoux

Intuitively, people have always assumed that bureaucratic structures and patterns of action differ in the different countries of the Western world and even more markedly between East and West. Practitioners know it and never fail to take it into account. But contemporary social scientists . . . have not been concerned with such comparisons.

—Michel Crozier[1]

Just how does culture influence organization structure and process? To what extent do organizational structures and processes have an inherent logic which overrides cultural considerations? Given the nature of today's business demands, do we find convergence in the ways of organizing? To what extent will popular techniques such as team management and empowerment be adopted across cultures? With what speed and with what possible (re) interpretation? What cultural dimensions need to be recognized which may facilitate or hinder organizational change efforts?

In this chapter, we present the evidence for national differences and consider the cultural reasons for these differences. Examining the degree to which organizations have centralized power, specialized jobs and roles, and formalized rules and procedures, we find distinct patterns of organizing which prevail despite pressures for convergence. This raises concerns regarding the transferability of organizational forms across borders and questions the logic of universal "best practices."

Different Schools, Different Cultures

While many managers are ready to accept that national culture may influence the way people relate to each other, or the "soft stuff," they are less convinced that it can really affect the nuts and bolts of organization: structure, systems, and processes.

Schneider, Susan C., Barsoux, Jean-Louis, *Managing Across Cultures*, 2nd Edition, © 2002. Adapted by permission of Pearson Education, Inc., Upper Saddle River, NJ.

[1]Crozier, M. (1964) *The Bureaucratic Phenomenon*, Chicago: University of Chicago Press, p. 210.

The culture-free argument is that structure is determined by *organizational* features such as size and technology. For example, the famous Aston studies,[2] conducted in the late 1960s in the United Kingdom and widely replicated, point to size as the most important factor influencing structure: larger firms tend to have greater division of labor (specialized) and more formal policies and procedures (formalized) although not necessarily more centralized. Furthermore, the nature of technology, such as mass production, is considered to favor a more centralized and formal (mechanistic) rather than decentralized and informal (organic) approach.[3]

Other management scholars argue that the *societal* context, for example culture, creates differences in structure in different countries.[4] In effect, the "structuralists" argue that structure creates culture, while the "culturalists" argue that culture creates structure. The debate continues, with each side arming up with more sophisticated weapons: measurements and methodologies.

Taking an historical perspective, theories about how best to organize—Max Weber's (German) bureaucracy, Henri Fayol's (French) administrative model, and Frederick Taylor's (American) scientific management—all reflect societal concerns of the times as well as the cultural backgrounds of the individuals.[5] Today, their legacies can be seen in the German emphasis on structure and competence, the French emphasis on social systems, roles and relationships (unity of command), and the American emphasis on the task system or machine model of organization, most recently popularized in the form of reengineering.

Indeed, many of the techniques of modern management—performance management, participative management, team approach, and job enrichment all have their roots firmly embedded in a particular historical and societal context. Furthermore, these approaches reflect different cultural assumptions regarding, for example, human nature and the importance of task and relationships. While the scientific management approach focused on how best to accomplish the task, the human relations approach focused on how best to establish relationships with employees. The human resources approach assumed that workers were self-motivated, while earlier schools assumed that workers needed to be motivated by more or less benevolent management.

These models of management have diffused across countries at different rates and in different ways. For example, mass-production techniques promoted by scientific management were quickly adopted in Germany, while practices associated with the human relations school transferred more readily to Spain.[6] For this reason the historical and societal context needs to be considered to understand the adoption and diffusion of different forms of organization across countries. While some theorists focus on the *institutional arrangements,*[7] such as the nature of markets, the educational system, or the relationships between business and government, to explain these differences, we focus here, more specifically, on the cultural reasons.

[2]Pugh, D. S., Hickson, D. J., Hinings, C. R., and Turner, C. (1969) "The context of organization structure," *Administrative Science Quarterly*, 14, 91–114; Miller, G. A. (1987) "Meta-analysis and the culture-free hypothesis," *Organization Studies*, 8(4), 309–25; Hickson, D. J. and McMillan, I. (eds) (1981) *Organization and Nation: The Aston Programme IV*, Farnborough: Gower.

[3]Burns, T. and Stalker, G. M. (1961) *The Management of Innovation*, London: Tavistock.

[4]Child, J. (1981) "Culture, contingency and capitalism in the crossnational study of organizations" in L. L. Cummings and B. M. Staw (eds) *Research in Organizational Behavior*, Vol 3, 303–56, Greenwich, CT: JAI Press; Scott, W. R. (1987) "The adolescence of institutional theory," *Administrative Science Quarterly*, 32, 493–511; Lincoln, J. R., Hanada, M. and McBride, K. (1986) "Organizational structures in Japanese and US manufacturing," *Administrative Science Quarterly*, 31, 338–64.

[5]Weber, M. (1947) *The Theory of Social and Economic Organization*, New York: Free Press; Fayol, H. (1949) *General Industrial Management*, London: Pitman; Taylor, F. (1947, first published 1912) *Scientific Management*, New York: Harper & Row.

[6]Kogut, B. (1991) "Country capabilities and the permeability of borders," *Strategic Management Journal*, 12, 33–47; Kogut, B. and Parkinson, D. (1993) "The diffusion of American organizing principles to Europe" in B. Kogut (ed.) *Country Competitiveness: Technology and the Organizing of Work*, Ch. 10, New York: Oxford University Press, 179–202; Guillen, M. (1994) "The age of eclecticism: Current organizational trends and the evolution of managerial models," *Sloan Management Review*, Fall, 75–86.

[7]Westney, D. E. (1987) *Imitation and Innovation*, Cambridge, MA: Harvard University Press.

This does not mean that institutional factors are irrelevant. In effect, it is quite difficult to separate out the influence of institutions from culture as they have both evolved together over time and are thus intricately linked. For example, the strong role of the state and the cultural emphasis on power and hierarchy often go hand in hand, as in the case of France. Or in the words of the French *roi soleil* Louis XIV, *L'état, c'est moi* ("The state is me"). Our argument (the culturalist perspective) is that different forms of organization emerge which reflect underlying cultural dimensions.

Hofstede's Findings   One of the most important studies which attempted to establish the impact of culture differences on management was conducted by Geert Hofstede, first in the late 1960s, and continuing through the next three decades.[8] The original study, now considered a classic, was based on an employee opinion survey involving 116,000 IBM employees in 40 different countries. From the results of this survey,

which asked people for their preferences in terms of management style and work environment, Hofstede identified four "value" dimensions on which countries differed: power distance, uncertainty avoidance, individualism/collectivism, and masculinity/femininity.

Power distance indicates the extent to which a society accepts the unequal distribution of power in institutions and organizations. **Uncertainty avoidance** refers to a society's discomfort with uncertainty, preferring predictability and stability. **Individualism/collectivism** reflects the extent to which people prefer to take care of themselves and their immediate families, remaining emotionally independent from groups, organizations, and other collectivities. And the **masculinity/femininity** dimension reveals the bias towards either "masculine" values of assertiveness, competitiveness, and materialism, or towards "feminine" values of nurturing, and the quality of life and relationships. Country rankings on each dimension are provided in Table 1.

▌[8]Hofstede, G. (1980) *Cultures Consequences*, Beverly Hills, CA: Sage; Hofstede, G. (1991) *Cultures and Organizations: Software of the Mind*, London: McGraw-Hill.

Table 1   Hofstede's Rankings

Country	Power Distance		Individualism		Masculinity		Uncertainty Avoidance	
	Index	Rank	Index	Rank	Index	Rank	Index	Rank
Argentina	49	35–6	46	22–3	56	20–1	86	10–15
Australia	36	41	90	2	61	16	51	37
Austria	11	53	55	18	79	2	70	24–5
Belgium	65	20	75	8	54	22	94	5–6
Brazil	69	14	38	26–7	49	27	76	21–2
Canada	39	39	80	4–5	52	24	48	41–2
Chile	63	24–5	23	38	28	46	86	10–15
Colombia	67	17	13	49	64	11–12	80	20
Costa Rica	35	42–4	15	46	21	48–9	86	10–15
Denmark	18	51	74	9	16	50	23	51
Equador	78	8–9	8	52	63	13–14	67	28
Finland	33	46	63	17	26	47	59	31–2

Country	Power Distance		Individualism		Masculinity		Uncertainty Avoidance	
	Index	Rank	Index	Rank	Index	Rank	Index	Rank
France	68	15–16	71	10–11	43	35–6	86	10–15
Germany (F.R.)	35	42–4	67	15	66	9–10	65	29
Great Britain	35	42–4	89	3	66	9–10	35	47–8
Greece	60	27–8	35	30	57	18–19	112	1
Guatemala	95	2–3	6	53	37	43	101	3
Hong Kong	68	15–16	25	37	57	18–19	29	49–50
Indonesia	78	8–9	14	47–8	46	30–1	48	41–2
India	77	10–11	48	21	56	20–1	40	45
Iran	58	19–20	41	24	43	35–6	59	31–2
Ireland	28	49	70	12	68	7–8	35	47–8
Israel	13	52	54	19	47	29	81	19
Italy	50	34	76	7	70	4–5	75	23
Jamaica	45	37	39	25	68	7–8	13	52
Japan	54	33	46	22–3	95	1	92	7
Korea (S)	60	27–8	187	43	39	41	85	16–17
Malaysia	104	1	26	36	50	25–6	36	46
Mexico	81	5–6	30	32	69	6	82	18
Netherlands	38	40	80	4–5	14	51	53	35
Norway	31	47–8	69	13	8	52	50	38
New Zealand	22	50	79	6	58	17	49	39–40
Pakistan	55	32	14	47–8	50	25–6	70	24–5
Panama	95	2–3	11	51	44	34	86	10–15
Peru	64	21–3	16	45	42	37–8	87	9
Philippines	94	4	32	31	64	11–12	44	44
Portugal	63	24–5	27	33–5	31	45	104	2
South Africa	49	36–7	65	16	63	13–14	49	39–40
Salvador	66	18–19	19	42	40	40	94	5–6
Singapore	74	13	20	39–41	48	28	8	53
Spain	57	31	51	20	42	37–8	86	10–15
Sweden	31	47–8	71	10–11	5	52	29	49–50
Switzerland	34	45	68	14	70	4–5	58	33
Taiwan	58	29–30	17	44	45	32–3	69	26
Thailand	64	21–3	20	39–41	34	44	64	30
Turkey	66	18–19	37	28	45	31–3	85	16–17
Uruguay	61	26	36	29	38	42	100	4
United States	40	38	91	1	62	15	46	43
Venezuela	81	5–6	12	50	73	3	76	21–2
Yugoslavia	76	12	27	33–5	21	48–9	88	8
Regions:								
East Africa	64	21–3	27	33–5	41	39	52	36
West Africa	77	10–11	20	39–41	46	30–1	54	34
Arab countries	80	7	38	26–7	53	23	68	27

Rank numbers: 1—Highest, 53—Lowest.
Source: Geert Hofstede, *Cultures and Organizations* (New York: McGraw-Hill, 1991).

Although some concern has been voiced that the country differences found by Hofstede were not representative due to the single company sample and that the data he originally collected is over thirty years old, further research supports these dimensions and the preferences for different profiles of organization. Efforts to replicate the factors found in 1994 version of Hofstede's survey proved difficult, however significant differences were found among countries and in most cases similar rankings.[9]

Given the differences in value orientations, Hofstede questioned whether American theories could be applied abroad and discussed the consequences of cultural differences in terms of motivation, leadership, and organization.[10] He argued, for example, that organizations in countries with high power distance would tend to have more levels of hierarchy (vertical differentiation), a higher proportion of supervisory personnel (narrow span of control), and more centralized decision-making. Status and power would serve as motivators, and leaders would be revered or obeyed as authorities.

In countries with high uncertainty avoidance, organizations would tend to have more formalization evident in greater amount of written rules and procedures. Also there would be greater specialization evident in the importance attached to technical competence in the role of staff and in defining jobs and functions. Managers would avoid taking risks and would be motivated by stability and security. The role of leadership would be more one of planning, organizing, coordinating, and controlling.

In countries with a high collectivist orientation, there would be a preference for group as opposed to individual decision-making. Consensus and cooperation would be more valued than individual initiative and effort. Motivation derives from a sense of belonging, and rewards are based on being part of the group (loyalty and tenure). The role of leadership in such cultures is to facilitate team effort and integration, to foster a supportive atmosphere, and to create the necessary context or group culture.

In countries ranked high on masculinity, the management style is likely to be more concerned with task accomplishment than nurturing social relationships. Motivation will be based on the acquisition of money and things rather than quality of life. In such cultures, the role of leadership is to ensure bottom-line profits in order to satisfy shareholders, and to set demanding targets. In more feminine cultures, the role of the leader would be to safeguard employee well-being, and to demonstrate concern for social responsibility.

Having ranked countries on each dimension, Hofstede then positioned them along two dimensions at a time, creating a series of cultural maps. He found country clusters—Anglo, Nordic, Latin, and Asian similar to those found in prior research.[11]

One such cultural map, as shown in Figure 1 (see also Table 2), is particularly relevant to structure in that it simultaneously considers power distance (acceptance of hierarchy) and uncertainty avoidance (the desire for formalized rules and procedures). Countries which ranked high both on power distance and uncertainty avoidance would be expected to be more "mechanistic"[12] or what is commonly known as bureaucratic. In this corner we find the Latin countries.

In the opposite quadrant, countries which rank low both on power distance and uncertainty avoidance are expected to be more "organic"[13]—less hierarchic, more decentralized, having less formalized rules and procedures. Here we find the Nordic countries clustered and to a lesser extent, the Anglo countries.

In societies where power distance is low but uncertainty avoidance is high, we expect to find

[9]Spector, P.E., Cooper, C.L., and Sparks, K. (2001) "An international study of the psychometric properties of the Hofstede values survey module 1994: A comparison of individual and country/province level results," *Applied Psychology: An International Review*, 30 (2), 269–81.

[10]Hofstede, G. (1980) "Motivation, leadership, and organization: Do American theories apply abroad?" *Organizational Dynamics*, Summer, 42–63.

[11]Ronen, S. and Shenekar, O. (1985) "Clustering countries on attitudinal dimensions: A review and synthesis," *Academy of Management Review*, 10(3), 435–54.

[12]Burns and Stalker, *Op. cit.*

[13]*Ibid.*

Figure 1   Hofstede's Maps

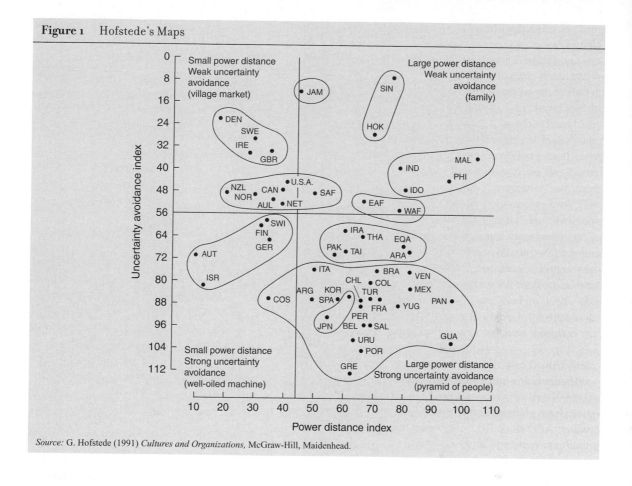

Source: G. Hofstede (1991) *Cultures and Organizations,* McGraw-Hill, Maidenhead.

organizations where hierarchy is downplayed, decisions are decentralized, but where rules and regulations are more formal, and task roles and responsibilities are more clearly defined. Thus there is no need for a boss, as the organization runs by routines. This is characteristic of the Germanic cluster.

In societies where power distance is high but uncertainty avoidance is low, organizations resemble families or tribes. Here, "the boss is the boss", and the organization may be described as paternalistic. Subordinates do not have clearly defined task roles and responsibilities (formalization), but instead social roles. Here we find the Asian countries where business enterprise is often characterized by centralized power and personalized relationships.

Emerging Cultural Profiles: Converging Evidence
These differences in structural preferences also emerged in a study conducted by Stevens[14] at INSEAD. When presented with an organizational problem, a conflict between two department heads within a company, MBA students from Britain, France, and Germany proposed markedly different solutions. The majority of French students referred the problem to the next level up, the president. The Germans argued that the major problem was a lack of structure; the expertise, roles, and responsibilities of the two conflicting department heads had

[14]Stevens, O.J., cited in Hofstede, G. (1991) *Cultures and Organizations,* London: McGraw-Hill, 140–2.

Table 2   Abbreviations for the Countries and Regions Studied

Abbreviation	Country or Region	Abbreviation	Country or Region
ARA	Arabic-speaking countries (Egypt, Iraq, Kuwait, Lebanon, Libya, Saudi Arabia, United Arab Emirates)	ITA	Italy
		JAM	Jamaica
		JPN	Japan
		KOR	South Korea
ARG	Argentina	MAL	Malaysia
AUL	Australia	MEX	Mexico
AUT	Austria	NET	Netherlands
BEL	Belgium	NOR	Norway
BRA	Brazil	NZL	New Zealand
CAN	Canada	PAK	Pakistan
CHL	Chile	PAN	Panama
COL	Colombia	PER	Peru
COS	Costa Rica	PHI	Philippines
DEN	Denmark	POR	Portugal
EAF	East Africa (Ethiopia, Kenya, Tanzania, Zambia)	SAF	South Africa
		SAL	Salvador
EQA	Equador	SIN	Singapore
FIN	Finland	SPA	Spain
FRA	France	SWE	Sweden
GBR	Great Britain	SWI	Switzerland
GER	Germany F.R.	TAI	Taiwan
GRE	Greece	THA	Thailand
GUA	Guatemala	TUR	Turkey
HOK	Hong Kong	URU	Uruguay
IDO	Indonesia	USA	United States
IND	India	VEN	Venezuela
IRA	Iran	WAF	West Africa (Ghana, Nigeria, Sierra Leone)
IRE	Ireland (Republic of)		
ISR	Israel	YUG	Yugoslavia

Source: G. Hofstede (1991) *Cultures and Organizations,* McGraw-Hill, Maidenhead.

never been clearly defined. Their suggested solution involved establishing procedures for better coordination. The British saw it as an interpersonal communication problem between the two department heads which could be solved by sending them for interpersonal skills training, preferably together.

On the basis of these findings, Stevens described the "implicit model" of the organization held by each culture. For the French, the organization represents a "pyramid of people" (formalized and centralized). For the Germans, the organization is like a "well-oiled machine" (formalized but not centralized), in which management intervention is limited to exceptional cases because the rules resolve problems. And for the British, it was more like a "village market" (neither formalized nor centralized) in which neither the hierarchy nor the rules, but rather the demands of the situation determine structure.

Going beyond questionnaires by observing the actual behavior of managers and company practices, further research reveals such cultural profiles as shown in Figure 2. Indeed, in studies comparing firms

Figure 2   Emerging Cultural Profiles

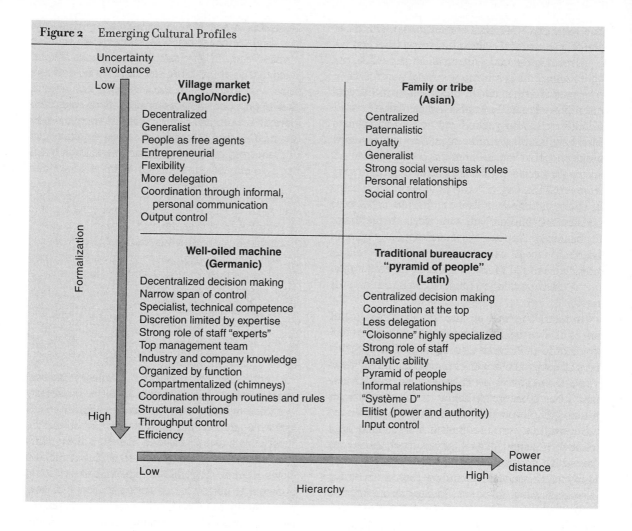

in France, Germany, and the United Kingdom,[15] French firms were found to be more centralized and formalized with less delegation when compared with either German or British firms. The role of the PDG (French CEO) was to provide coordination at the top and to make key decisions, which demands a high level of analytical and conceptual ability that

---

[15]Brossard, A. and Maurice, M. (1976) "Is there a universal model of organization structure?" *International Studies of Management and Organizations*, 6, 11–45; Horovitz, J. (1980) *Top Management Control in Europe*, London: Macmillan; Stewart, R., Barsoux, J. L., Kieser, A., Ganter, D. and Walgenbach, P. (1994) *Managing in Britain and Germany*, London: Macmillan.

need not be industry or company specific. The staff function plays an important role in providing analytic expertise. These capabilities are developed in the elite *grandes écoles* of engineering and administration.

The research findings confirmed the image of German firms as "well-oiled machines" as they were more likely to be decentralized, specialized, and formalized. In fact, German managers were more likely to cite structure as a key success factor, having a logic of its own, apart from people. German firms were more likely to be organized by function (sometimes to the extent that they are referred to as "chimney" organizations) with coordination achieved through routines and procedures.

Although German organizations tended to be flatter and to have a broader span of control when compared with the French, middle managers had less discretion than their British counterparts as they were limited to their specific technical competence. The premium placed on competence was expressed in the concern to find competent people to perform specialized tasks, the strong role of staff to provide technical expertise, and expectations that top management not only has specific technical competence, but also in-depth company knowledge. Furthermore, top management typically consists of a managing board, *Vorstand,* which integrates the specialized knowledge of the various top managers (rather than in the head of a lone individual as in the case of France, Britain, or the United States).

In contrast to the well-oiled machine model with its greater concern for efficiency, the "village market" model reflects a greater concern for flexibility. Indeed, structure in British firms was found to be far more flexible, more decentralized and less formalized, when compared with the French and German firms. Organized by divisions, there is greater decentralization and delegation in the company and the role of central staff is far less important. Here, the burden of coordinating functions was placed on individual managers requiring a constant need for persuasion and negotiation to achieve cooperation.[16]

British managers, compared with Germans, were more ready to adapt the structure to the people working in it. Changes in personnel were often used as opportunities to reshuffle the jobs and responsibilities in order to accommodate available talent, and to create opportunities for personal development (free agents). Top management's role was to identify market opportunities and convince others to pursue them, underlining the importance of taking a more strategic view and of being able to communicate it persuasively.[17]

Studies in Asia have also found companies to fit the "family model," being more hierarchic and less formalized, with the exception of Japan. When compared with the Japanese, Hong Kong Chinese firms were less likely to have written manuals and Hong Kong Chinese bosses were also found to be more autocratic and paternalistic.[18] Another study of thirty-nine multinational commercial banks from fourteen different countries operating in Hong Kong found the Hong Kong banks to have the greatest number of hierarchical levels (eleven); the banks from Singapore, the Philippines, and India were also among those most centralized.[19]

A recent study of Chinese entrepreneurs found the Confucian tradition of patriarchal authority to be remarkably persistent. Being part of the family is seen as a way of achieving security. Social roles are clearly spelled out in line with Confucian precepts, which designate the responsibilities for the roles of father, son, brothers, and so on. Control is exerted through authority, which is not questioned. In 70 percent of the entrepreneurial firms studied, even large ones, the structure of Chinese organizations was found to resemble a hub with spokes around a powerful founder, or a management structure with only two layers.[20]

Recent studies of Russian managers using Hofstede's framework found them to be autocratic and political (reflecting high power distance), while expected to take care of their subordinates (low masculinity). Managers tend to seek security and to be risk averse (high uncertainty avoidance). While performance appraisal is still seen to be highly

[18]Redding, S.G. and Pugh, D.S. (1986) "The formal and the informal: Japanese and Chinese organization structures" in S. Clegg, D. Dunphy, and S.G. Redding (eds) *The Enterprise and Management in East Asia,* Hong Kong: Center of Asian Studies, University of Hong Kong, 153–68; Vertinsky, I., Tse, D.K.,Wehrung, D.A. and Lee, K. (1990) "Organization design and management norms: A comparative study of managers' perceptions in the People's Republic of China, Hong Kong and Canada," *Journal of Management,* 16(4), 853–67.

[19]Wong, G.Y.Y. and Birnbaum-More, P.H. (1994) "Culture, context and structure: A test on Hong Kong banks," *Organization Studies,* 15(l), 99–23.

[20]Kao, J. (1993) "The world wide web of Chinese business," *Harvard Business Review,* March–April, 24–35.

[16]Stewart et al., Op. cit.

[17]Ibid.

political, motivation is however becoming more calculative based on growing individualism.[21]

What begins to emerge from these various research studies is a converging and coherent picture of different management structures when comparing countries within Europe, as well as when comparing countries in Europe, the United States, and Asia. The primary cultural determinants appear to be those related to relationships between people in terms of power and status and relationship with nature, for example how uncertainty is managed and how control is exercised.

These underlying cultural assumptions are expressed in beliefs (and their subsequent importance, or value) regarding the need for hierarchy, for formal rules and procedures, specialized jobs and functions. These beliefs and values, in turn, are observable in behavior and artifacts, such as deference to the boss, the presence of executive parking and dining facilities ("perks"), and the existence of written policies and procedures, specific job descriptions, or manuals outlining standard operating procedures.

The research findings in the above-mentioned studies were based on observations as well as questionnaires and interviews of managers and companies in different countries. The same, of course, can be done comparing companies in different industries or within the same industry, and managers in different functions providing corresponding models of industry, corporate and/or functional cultures. From these findings, management scholars interpret underlying meaning.

The Meaning of Organizations: Task versus Social System

André Laurent argues that the country differences in structure described above reflect different conceptions (or understandings) of what is an organization.[22] These different conceptions were discovered in surveys which asked managers to agree or disagree

with statements regarding beliefs about organization and management. A sample of the questions is shown in Table 3.

The results of this survey are very much in line with the discussion above in that they show similar cultural differences regarding power and uncertainty in views of organizations as systems of hierarchy, authority, politics, and role formalization. What would these different views of organization actually look like, were we to observe managers at work and even to question them? What arguments would managers from different countries put forth to support their responses?

Having a view of organizations as **hierarchical systems** would make it difficult, for example, to tolerate having to report to two bosses, as required in a matrix organization, and it would make it difficult to accept bypassing or going over or around the boss. The boss would also be expected to have precise answers to most of the questions that subordinates have about their work. Asian and Latin managers argue that this is necessary in order for bosses to be respected, or to have power and authority. And if the most efficient way to get things done is to bypass the hierarchical line they would consider that there was something wrong with the hierarchy.

Scandinavian and Anglo managers, on the other hand, argue that it is perfectly normal to go directly to anyone in the organization in order to accomplish the task. It would seem intolerable, for example, to have to go through one's own boss, who would contact his or her counterpart in a neighboring department before making contact with someone in that other department.

Furthermore, they argue that it is impossible to have precise answers, since the world is far too complex and ambiguous, and even if you could provide precise answers, this would not develop the capability of your subordinates to solve problems. Thus a Swedish boss with a French subordinate can anticipate some problems: the French subordinate is likely to think that the boss, not knowing the answers, is incompetent, while the Swedish boss may think that the French subordinate does not know what to do and is therefore incompetent.

[21]Elenkov, D.S. (1998) "Can American management concepts work in Russia?" *Academy of Management Review*, 40(4), 133–56.

[22]Laurent, A. (1983) "The cultural diversity of western conception of management," *International Studies of Management and Organization*, 13(1–2), 75–96.

Table 3   Management Questionnaire

A = Strongly agree
B = Tend to agree
C = Neither agree, nor disagree
D = Tend to disagree
E = Strongly disagree

	A	B	C	D	E
1. When the respective roles of the members of a department become complex, detailed job descriptions are a useful way of clarifying.	A	B	C	D	E
2. In order to have efficient work relationships, it is often necessary to bypass the hierarchical line.	A	B	C	D	E
8. An organizational structure in which certain subordinates have two direct bosses should be avoided at all costs.	A	B	C	D	E
13. The more complex a department's activities, the more important it is for each individual's functions to be well-defined.	A	B	C	D	E
14. The main reason for having a hierarchical structure is so that everyone knows who has authority over whom.	A	B	C	D	E
19. Most organizations would be better off if conflict could be eliminated forever.	A	B	C	D	E
24. It is important for a manager to have at hand precise answers to most of the questions that his/her subordinates may raise about their work.	A	B	C	D	E
33. Most managers have a clear notion of what we call an organizational structure.	A	B	C	D	E
38. Most managers would achieve better results if their roles were less precisely defined.	A	B	C	D	E
40. Through their professional activity, managers play an important role in society.	A	B	C	D	E
43. The manager of tomorrow will be, primarily, a negotiator.	A	B	C	D	E
49. Most managers seem to be more motivated by obtaining power than by achieving objectives.	A	B	C	D	E
52. Today there seems to be an authority crisis in organizations.	A	B	C	D	E

Source: André Laurent. Reproduced by permission.

Those who view the organization as a **political system** consider managers to play an important political role in society, and to negotiate within the organization. Thus obtaining power is seen as more important than achieving specific objectives. Here again, Latin European managers are more likely to adhere to this view than their Nordic and Anglo counterparts.

In France, for example, executives have often played important roles in the French administration before assuming top positions in companies.

Furthermore, Latin managers are acutely aware that it is necessary to have power in order to get things done in the organization. Nordic and Anglo managers, however, tend to downplay the importance of power and therefore reject the need for political maneuvering.

When organizations are viewed as systems of **role formalization,** managers prefer detailed job descriptions, and well-defined roles and functions. These serve to clarify complex situations and tasks. Otherwise it is difficult to know who is responsible for what and to hold people accountable. In addition they argue that lack of clear job descriptions or role definitions creates overlap and inefficiency. Nordic and Anglo managers, on the other hand, argue that the world is too complex to be able to clearly define roles and functions. Furthermore they say that detailed descriptions interfere with maintaining flexibility and achieving coordination.

From his research, Laurent concluded that underlying these arguments managers had different conceptions of organization: one which focused on the task, called **instrumental,** and one which focused on relationships, called **social.** For Latin European managers, organizations are considered as **social systems,** or systems of relationships, where personal networks and social positioning are important. The organization achieves its goals through relationships and how they are managed (as prescribed by Fayol). Roles and relationships are defined formally (by the hierarchy) and informally, based on authority, power, and status which are seen as attributes of the person, not the task or function. Personal loyalty and deference to the boss are expected.

However, getting things done means working around the system—using informal, personal networks to circumvent the hierarchy as well as the rules and regulations—what the French call, *Système D.* According to sociologist Michel Crozier, it is this informal system that gives the French "bureaucratic model" its flexibility.[23] Organizations are thus considered to be necessarily political in nature. When asked to diagnose organizational problems, French social scientists and consultants typically start by analyzing the power relationships and power games (*les enjeux*).[24]

In contrast, for Anglo-Saxon, and northern European managers, the organization is a system of tasks where it is important to know what has to be done, rather than who has power and authority to do so (as in the socio/political view). This instrumental or functionalist view of organizations (very much

in keeping with Taylor's scientific management) focuses on what is to be achieved and whether objectives are met (achievement orientation). Structure is defined by activities—what has to be done—and the hierarchy exists only to assign responsibility. It follows that authority is defined by function and is limited, specific to the job not the person.

Here, coordination and control are impersonal, decentralized, and reside in the structure and systems. Rules and regulations are applied universally. If the rules and regulations are dysfunctional, then they are changed rather than circumvented or broken. Management consultants are called in to figure out the best way to devise strategy, design structure, classify jobs and set salary scales, and develop concrete programs such as "total quality" or "performance management."

These findings can be further corroborated by asking managers to describe the approach to management in their countries, or "how we see us," . . . For example, many of the research results discussed above place Scandinavian managers at one end of a continuum, with Latin and Asian managers at the other. Jan Selmer,[25] a Swedish management professor, proposed the following profile of "Viking Management." Compare this with the self-descriptions of Brazilian[26] and Indonesian managers in Table 4.

According to self-reports, clear differences and similarities emerge in terms of the nature of relationships (hierarchy) and the relationship with nature (uncertainty and control). For example, in keeping with the findings discussed above, Viking Management is characterized as decentralized (less hierarchy) when compared with the Brazilian and Indonesian views, which emphasize status and power or respect for elders.

On the other hand, in each case there is a strong emphasis on the importance of relationships: family and friends, avoiding conflict, being tolerant, seeking consensus, and "keeping everyone happy." For the

[23]Crozier, M. (1964) *The Bureaucratic Phenomenon,* Chicago: University of Chicago Press.
[24]Crozier, M. and Friedberg, E. (1977) *L'Acteur et le système: Les contraintes de l'action collective,* Paris: Seuil.

[25]Selmer, J. (1988) Presentation, International Conference on Personnel and Human Resource Management Conference, Singapore.
[26]Amado, G. and Brasil, H.V. (1991) "Organizational behaviors and cultural context: The Brazilian 'Jeitiñho,'" *International Studies of Management and Organization,* 21(3), 38–61.

Table 4   As We See Us . . .

Viking Management

Decentralized decision making
Organization structure is often ambiguous
Perceived by others to be indecisive
Goal formulation, long-range objectives, and per-
    formance evaluation criteria are vague and implicit
Informal channels of communication
Coordinate by values not rules (normative versus
    coercive)
Case-by-case approach versus standard procedures
Consensus-oriented
Avoid conflict
Informal relationships between foreign subsidiaries
    and headquarters (mother–daughter relationships)

Brazilian Management

Hierarchy and authority; status and power are
    important
Centralized decision making
Personal relationships are more important than the task
Rules and regulations are for enemies
Flexible and adaptable (too much?) *Jeitiñho*
Anything is possible
Short-term oriented—immediatism
Avoid conflict—seen as win/lose
Rely on magic—low control over environment
Decisions based on intuition and feeling

Indonesian Management

Respect for hierarchy and elders
Family-oriented
Group- versus individual-oriented
Friendly and helpful, hospitable
Tolerant
Decisions based on compromise—"keep everyone
    happy"
Importance of religion—Islam
Five principles
Bhinneka Tunggal lka (unity through diversity)

Swedes, this corresponds to their "mother-daughter" relationships between headquarters and subsidiaries, and their keen concern for social well-being and quality of relationships, reflected in their number one ranking on Hofstede's femininity dimension.

In all three self-descriptions there is less emphasis placed on formalization. In Swedish companies, organization structures and decision processes are often experienced as vague and ambiguous. Uncertainty is managed though "values and not rules," and communication is informal. For the Indonesians, higher order principles (The Five Principles) provide guidance not organizational ones. Furthermore, as the perceived control over nature is low, they are more likely to "go with the flow." Brazilian managers, faced with great uncertainty in the day-to-day business environment over which they feel they have little control, say that they have developed a finely tuned sense of intuition, having learned to trust their "gut" feel. For the Brazilians, the notion of *Jeitiñho* is similar to that of the French *Système D,* going around the system in order to get things done. This assures flexibility and adaptability such that anything is possible (although perhaps too much so as Brazilian managers themselves acknowledge).

Now imagine a Brazil–Sweden–Indonesia joint venture. This raises the possibility that three firms would have to resolve their differences on several fronts while using their similarities to create a shared sense of purpose. In particular, there would probably be a clash between the cultural assumptions underlying Swedish management—little concern with power and status and high perceived control over the environment—with those of Brazilian and Indonesian management—more emphasis on power and authority and less perceived control.

This would probably cause the biggest headaches for the Swedes when it came to efforts to delegate decision-making and to encourage individual responsibility and accountability. For the Indonesian and Brazilian managers, the frustration would come from confusion as to "who is the boss?" and "why isn't he/she making decisions?," and "how can I be held responsible when I have no control over what happens?" In decision-making, the Brazilians would find the Indonesians and Swedes interminably slow, seeking consensus or democratic compromise, while they in turn would see the Brazilians as impetuous, and too individualistic. On the other hand, the similarity in importance placed on relationships, on informal communication, and on avoiding conflict can help to work through these difficulties together, on a personal basis.

Although there are variations within countries, due to industry and corporate culture, as well as individual styles of key managers, the above research findings and self-descriptions point to different cultural profiles of organization. The underlying assumptions can be interpreted to reveal the nature of relationships, as seen in the importance of hierarchy, and control over nature, as seen in the need for formal or social rules and procedures. The underlying cultural meaning of the organization can then be interpreted as systems of tasks versus systems of relationships. These cultural profiles provide a starting point to explore different structural preferences and to begin to anticipate potential problems when transferring practices from one country to another or in forming joint ventures and strategic alliances.

On a less serious note, these differences have been caricatured in the organizational charts shown in Figure 3. Using these caricatures can provoke discussion of structural differences across countries in a humorous mode while allowing us to discover the grain of truth within and to imagine how our own organization chart might seem to others. Constructing cultural profiles enables us to appreciate the impact of culture on management as multidimensional. It would therefore be a mistake to base a prediction regarding structure or process on a single cultural dimension.

In addition, managers need to recognize that the relationships between cultural dimensions and structure are not simple cause–effect links, but instead, are multi-determined. Similar approaches may exist for different cultural reasons, and different approaches may exist for the same reason. Thus formalized rules and procedures or participative management approaches may have a different *raison d'être* on different sides of the national border.

Transferability of Best Practice? Alternative Approaches

By pulling together the various experiences of managers and more systematic research studies, we have demonstrated how culture affects organization structure and process. We have proposed different profiles or models of organizing which evolve from different underlying cultural assumptions. This raises questions about what is considered to be "universal wisdom" and the transferability of "best practice." For the most part, arguments for transferability are in line with convergence notions which claim universality; "Management is management and best practice can be transferred anywhere." This was the rationale behind the 1980s rush to copy Japanese management practice and more recent rash of American-style restructuring and re-engineering.

Those that question transferability point to differences in the cultural or national (institutional) context. The culturalists question the effectiveness with which Japanese quality circles, say, can be transferred to individualist countries, such as the United States and France. The institutionalists stress the nature of ownership, and the role of government, and of labor unions in promoting such practices.

The transfer of best practice nevertheless assumes, to some extent, universality. For example, matrix structures were heralded in the 1970s as a means of combining the benefits of product, geographic, and functional structures. In theory, decentralized decision-making, overlapping roles and responsibilities, and multiple information channels were all supposed to enable the organization to capture and analyze external complexity, to overcome internal parochialism, and to enhance response time and flexibility.[27]

While matrix management may have promised more than it could deliver, Laurent found deep resistance to matrix structures among both French and German managers, but for different reasons.[28] For the French, matrix structures violated the principle of "unity of command" and clear hierarchical reporting relationships. The idea of having two bosses was undesirable, as it created divided loyalties and caused unwelcome conflict. On the other hand, German managers resisted matrix structures, as

[27]Davis, S. and Lawrence, P. R. (1977) *Matrix,* Reading, MA: Addison-Wesley.
[28]Laurent, A. (1981) "Matrix organization and Latin cultures," *International Studies of Management and Organization,* 10(4), 101–14.

Figure 3   The Organization Chart

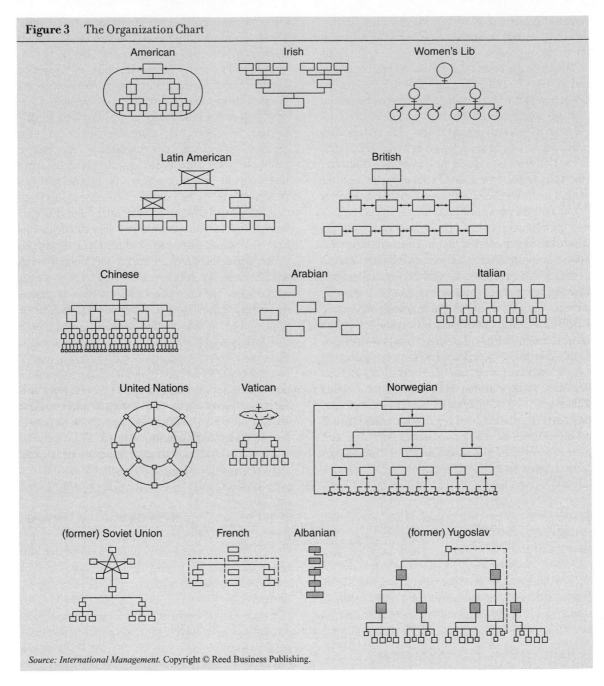

they frustrated the need for clear-cut structure, information channels, roles and responsibilities. Again, the principles underlying matrix management ran counter to the German need to reduce uncertainty.

Thus cultural differences often undermine the best intentions and the assumed rationality of best practices. Different logics of organization exist in different countries, which can be equally effective, if not more so, given different societal contexts. In fact, there seems to be little doubt that some contexts are more favorable to the success of certain management practices, and it need not always be the country where that practice originated. Japanese quality-control methods originally came from the American gurus, Demming and Juran. Quality circles were the Japanese value-added.

Effectively transferring management structures and processes relies on the ability to recognize their inherent assumptions and to compare them with the cultural assumptions of the potential host country recipient. Countries also differ in their readiness to adopt or adapt foreign models, or to manifest a NIH (not invented here) syndrome. Throughout their history, the Japanese have borrowed models from China and then Europe. Other countries, such as Germany, may be more resistant to importing alien management practices. In developing countries, the eagerness to adopt foreign models is tempered by the desire to develop their own models which are more culturally appropriate.

For example, managers in Eastern Europe may reject "team" approaches looking for strong leadership and a sense of clear direction in an effort to break with the more collective approach of the past.[29] Despite the prevailing wisdom that organizations need to be less hierarchical and more flexible, some managers argue that faced with competitive threats and conditions of economic decline or instability, greater centralization and stronger controls are needed.

Indeed, companies in Hong Kong, Japan, and Singapore, where the hierarchy remains firmly in place, have performed well in industries, such as banking, which are facing turbulent environments. Here, other value orientations, not readily apparent in Western business, may be at work. For example, when trying to replicate Hofstede's original study in China, another dimension was discovered— "Confucian dynamism," thrift, persistence and a long-term perspective. This added dimension was considered to account for the competitiveness of the "Five Asian Dragons": China, Hong Kong, Taiwan, Japan, and South Korea.[30]

Consider this testimony regarding the entrepreneurial, family model characteristic of the overseas Chinese business community which has been quite successful whether transplanted to Malaysia or Canada.

> . . . The Confucian tradition of hard work, thrift and respect for one's social network may provide continuity with the right twist for today's fast-changing markets. And the central strategic question for all current multinationals—be they Chinese, Japanese or Western—is how to gather and integrate power through many small units. The evolution of a worldwide web of relatively small Chinese businesses, bound by undeniable strong cultural links, offers a working model for the future.[31]

Whatever the model of the future, be it team management or network organizations, we need to consider how culture may facilitate or hinder their diffusion. Will the more collective culture of Russia facilitate the team approach, while the greater relationship orientation of Chinese culture facilitates creating networks? Could it be that the greater emphasis on the task and the individual, which prevails in the performance management approach, will actually hinder American firms in their attempts to become more team- and network-oriented?

Given recent trends in the United States and Europe towards participative management and empowerment, the role of the leadership is changing. Rather than the more authoritarian notion of being the "boss," the role model is that of the "coach." Rather than directing and controlling, the new role calls for facilitating and developing. Notions of empowerment and the leader as coach, however, may not readily transfer.

Take, for example, two items from the Management Questionnaire designed by Laurent regarding the role of the boss (hierarchy) and of power as shown in Figure 4. Comparing the responses of managers

[29]Cyr, D. J. and Schneider, S. C. (1996) "Implications for learning: human resources management in east-west joint ventures," *Organization Studies*, 17(2), 207–226.

[30]Hofstede, G. and Bond, M. H. (1988) "The Confucius connection: From cultural roots to economic growth," *Organizational Dynamics*, 16, 4–21; see also Hofstede, G. (1991) *Cultures and Organizations: Software of the Mind*, London: McGraw-Hill.

[31]Kao, *Op. cit.*, p. 36.

Figure 4   Convergence?

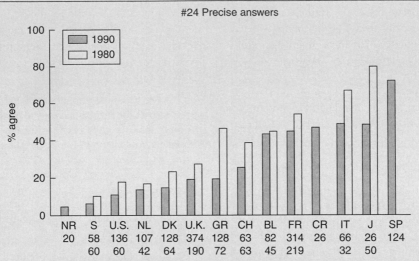

It is important for a manager to have at hand precise answers to most of the questions his/her subordinates may raise about their work.

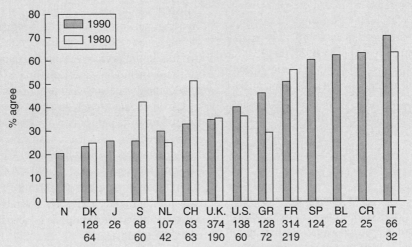

Most managers seem to be more motivated by obtaining power than by achieving objectives.

Source: Reproduced by permission of A. Laurent.

attending training seminars from 1990 to 1994 with the results reported in 1980, we find some signs of convergence. According to self-reports, managers are becoming less authoritarian and more concerned with achieving objectives than obtaining power. Nevertheless, while country differences may have eroded, the different country rankings remain in place.

Even in countries which supposedly do not put much stock in hierarchy, such as The Netherlands and the United Kingdom, this new leadership behavior may be difficult to achieve. Therefore, what will that mean for countries in Asia where the hierarchy is still revered? What would the Asian version of empowerment look like? Perhaps there are different means of achieving this end. In the case of Japanese firms, the hierarchy is clearly, albeit implicitly, present. Nevertheless, there are apparently high levels of participation.

And as hierarchies collapse and as cooperation between units becomes more of a necessity, there is a greater need for negotiation and persuasion. Managers will increasingly have to elicit the cooperation of people over whom they have no formal authority. In fact this may demand a more political view of organizations to which Latin firms may be more attuned.

These are the challenges facing many companies as they remodel their corporate structures. They must not lose sight of the impact of national culture in their search for a model of organization that can respond best to the demands of the rapidly changing business context, and the pressures for internationalization. They must also recognize that the "best models" are not necessarily "home grown," but that other ways of organizing may be equally, if not more, effective. And as local managers in these regions gain experience and knowledge, they become less willing to adopt models imposed by head offices from other countries. Thus searching for 'best practices' wherever they may be located becomes an increasing strategic imperative.

Reading 2-2   Clusters and the New Economics of Competition

Michael E. Porter

Paradoxically, the enduring competitive advantages in a global economy lie increasingly in local things-knowledge, relationships, and motivation that distant rivals cannot match.

Now that companies can source capital, goods, information, and technology from around the world, often with the click of a mouse, much of the conventional wisdom about how companies and nations compete needs to be overhauled. In theory, more open global markets and faster transportation and communication should diminish the role of location in competition. After all, anything that can be efficiently sourced from a distance through global markets and corporate networks is available to any company and therefore is essentially nullified as a source of competitive advantage.

But if location matters less, why, then, is it true that the odds of finding a world-class mutual-fund company in Boston are much higher than in most any other place? Why could the same be said of textile-related companies in North Carolina and South Carolina, of high-performance auto companies in southern Germany, or of fashion shoe companies in northern Italy?

Michael E. Porter is the C. Roland Christensen Professor of Business Administration at the Harvard Business School in Boston, Massachusetts. Further discussion of clusters can be found in two new essays—"Clusters and Competition" and "Competing Across Locations"—in his new collection titled *On Competition* (Harvard Business School Press, 1998).

Today's economic map of the world is dominated by what I call *clusters:* critical masses—in one place—of unusual competitive success in particular fields. Clusters are a striking feature of virtually every national, regional, state, and even metropolitan economy, especially in more economically advanced nations. Silicon Valley and Hollywood may be the world's best-known clusters. Clusters are not unique, however; they are highly typical—and therein lies a paradox: the enduring competitive advantages in a global economy lie increasingly in local things—knowledge, relationships, motivation—that distant rivals cannot match.

Although location remains fundamental to competition, its role today differs vastly from a generation ago. In an era when competition was driven heavily by input costs, locations with some important endowment—a natural harbor, for example, or a supply of cheap labor—often enjoyed a *comparative advantage* that was both competitively decisive and persistent over time.

Competition in today's economy is far more dynamic. Companies can mitigate many input-cost disadvantages through global sourcing, rendering the old notion of comparative advantage less relevant. Instead, competitive advantage rests on making more productive use of inputs, which requires continual innovation.

Untangling the paradox of location in a global economy reveals a number of key insights about how companies continually create competitive advantage. What happens *inside* companies is important, but clusters reveal that the immediate business environment *outside* companies plays a vital role as well. This role of locations has been long overlooked, despite striking evidence that innovation and competitive success in so many fields are geographically concentrated—whether it's entertainment in Hollywood, finance on Wall Street, or consumer electronics in Japan.

Clusters affect competitiveness within countries as well as across national borders. Therefore, they lead to new agendas for all business executives—not just those who compete globally. More broadly, clusters represent a new way of thinking about location, challenging much of the conventional wisdom about how companies should be configured, how institutions such as universities can contribute to competitive success, and how governments can promote economic development and prosperity.

What Is a Cluster?

Clusters are geographic concentrations of interconnected companies and institutions in a particular field. Clusters encompass an array of linked industries and other entities important to competition. They include, for example, suppliers of specialized inputs such as components, machinery, and services, and providers of specialized infrastructure. Clusters also often extend downstream to channels and customers and laterally to manufacturers of complementary products and to companies in industries related by skills, technologies, or common inputs. Finally, many clusters include governmental and other institutions—such as universities, standards-setting agencies, think tanks, vocational training providers, and trade associations—that provide specialized training, education, information, research, and technical support.

The California wine cluster is a good example. It includes 680 commercial wineries as well as several thousand independent wine grape growers. (See the exhibit "Anatomy of the California Wine Cluster.") An extensive complement of industries supporting both wine making and grape growing exists, including suppliers of grape stock, irrigation and harvesting equipment, barrels, and labels; specialized public relations and advertising firms; and numerous wine publications aimed at consumer and trade audiences. A host of local institutions is involved with wine, such as the world-renowned viticulture and enology program at the University of California at Davis, the Wine Institute, and special committees of the California senate and assembly. The cluster also enjoys weaker linkages to other California clusters in agriculture, food and restaurants, and wine-country tourism.

Consider also the Italian leather fashion cluster, which contains well-known shoe companies such as Ferragamo and Gucci as well as a host of specialized

Figure 1   Anatomy of the California Wine Cluster

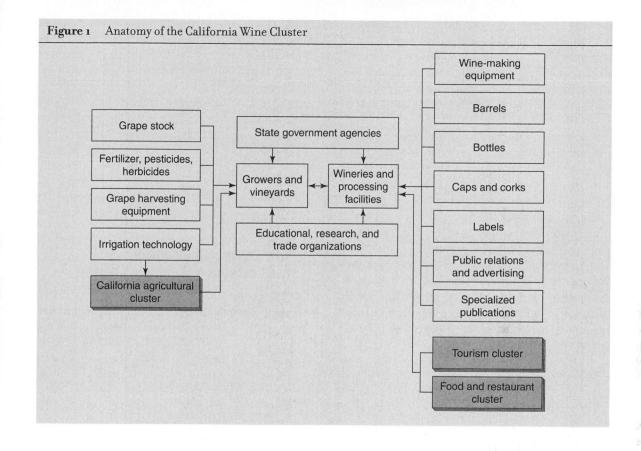

suppliers of footwear components, machinery, molds, design services, and tanned leather. (See the exhibit "Mapping the Italian Leather Fashion Cluster.") It also consists of several chains of related industries, including those producing different types of leather goods (linked by common inputs and technologies) and different types of footwear (linked by overlapping channels and technologies). These industries employ common marketing media and compete with similar images in similar customer segments. A related Italian cluster in textile fashion, including clothing, scarves, and accessories, produces complementary products that often employ common channels. The extraordinary strength of the Italian leather fashion cluster can be attributed, at least in part, to the multiple linkages and synergies that participating Italian businesses enjoy.

A cluster's boundaries are defined by the linkages and complementarities across industries and institutions that are most important to competition. Although clusters often fit within political boundaries, they may cross state or even national borders. In the United States, for example, a pharmaceuticals cluster straddles New Jersey and Pennsylvania near Philadelphia. Similarly, a chemicals cluster in Germany crosses over into German-speaking Switzerland.

Clusters rarely conform to standard industrial classification systems, which fail to capture many important actors and relationships in competition. Thus significant clusters may be obscured or even go unrecognized. In Massachusetts, for example, more than 400 companies, representing at least 39,000 high-paying jobs, are involved in medical devices in some way. The cluster long remained all but invisible, however, buried within larger and overlapping industry categories such as electronic equipment and plastic products. Executives in the medical devices cluster have only recently come together to work on issues that will benefit them all.

Clusters promote both competition and cooperation. Rivals compete intensely to win and retain customers. Without vigorous competition, a cluster will fail. Yet there is also cooperation, much of it vertical, involving companies in related industries and local institutions. Competition can coexist with cooperation because they occur on different dimensions and among different players.

Clusters represent a kind of new spatial organizational form in between arm's-length markets on the one hand and hierarchies, or vertical integration, on the other. A cluster, then, is an alternative way of organizing the value chain. Compared with market transactions among dispersed and random buyers and sellers, the proximity of companies and institutions in one location—and the repeated exchanges among them—fosters better coordination and trust. Thus clusters mitigate the problems inherent in arm's-length relationships without imposing the inflexibilities of vertical integration or the management challenges of creating and maintaining formal linkages such as networks, alliances, and partnerships. A cluster of independent and informally linked companies and institutions represents a robust organizational form that offers advantages in efficiency, effectiveness, and flexibility.

Why Clusters Are Critical to Competition

Modern competition depends on productivity, not on access to inputs or the scale of individual enterprises. Productivity rests on *how* companies compete, not

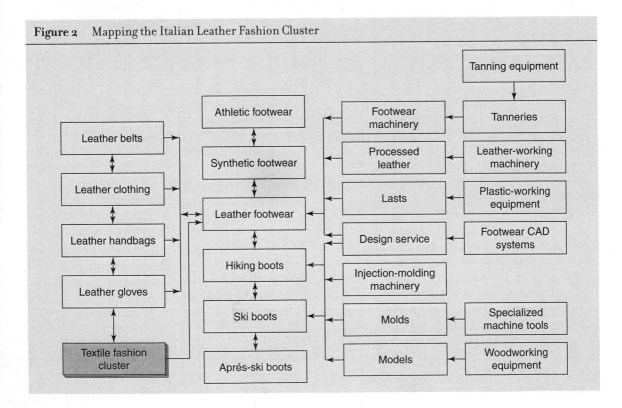

Figure 2   Mapping the Italian Leather Fashion Cluster

on the particular fields they compete in. Companies can be highly productive in any industry—shoes, agriculture, or semiconductors—if they employ sophisticated methods, use advanced technology, and offer unique products and services. All industries can employ advanced technology; all industries can be knowledge intensive.

The sophistication with which companies compete in a particular location, however, is strongly influenced by the quality of the local business environment.[1] Companies cannot employ advanced logistical techniques, for example, without a high-quality transportation infrastructure. Nor can companies effectively compete on sophisticated service without well-educated employees. Businesses cannot operate efficiently under onerous regulatory red tape or under a court system that fails to resolve disputes quickly and fairly. Some aspects of the business environment, such as the legal system, for example, or corporate tax rates, affect all industries. In advanced economies, however, the more decisive aspects of the business environment are often cluster specific; these constitute some of the most important microeconomic foundations for competition.

Clusters affect competition in three broad ways: first, by increasing the productivity of companies based in the area; second, by driving the direction and pace of innovation, which underpins future productivity growth; and third, by stimulating the formation of new businesses, which expands and strengthens the cluster itself. A cluster allows each member to benefit *as if* it had greater scale or *as if* it had joined with others formally—without requiring it to sacrifice its flexibility.

Clusters and Productivity   Being part of a cluster allows companies to operate more productively in sourcing inputs; accessing information, technology, and needed institutions; coordinating with related companies; and measuring and motivating improvement.

Better Access to Employees and Suppliers Companies in vibrant clusters can tap into an existing pool of specialized and experienced employees, thereby lowering their search and transaction costs in recruiting. Because a cluster signals opportunity and reduces the risk of relocation for employees, it can also be easier to attract talented people from other locations, a decisive advantage in some industries.

A well-developed cluster also provides an efficient means of obtaining other important inputs. Such a cluster offers a deep and specialized supplier base. Sourcing locally instead of from distant suppliers lowers transaction costs. It minimizes the need for inventory, eliminates importing costs and delays, and—because local reputation is important—lowers the risk that suppliers will overprice or renege on commitments. Proximity improves communications and makes it easier for suppliers to provide ancillary or support services such as installation and debugging. Other things being equal, then, local outsourcing is a better solution than distant outsourcing, especially for advanced and specialized inputs involving embedded technology, information, and service content.

Formal alliances with distant suppliers can mitigate some of the disadvantages of distant outsourcing. But all formal alliances involve their own complex bargaining and governance problems and can inhibit a company's flexibility. The close, informal relationships possible among companies in a cluster are often a superior arrangement.

In many cases, clusters are also a better alternative to vertical integration. Compared with in-house units, outside specialists are often more cost effective and responsive, not only in component production but also in services such as training. Although extensive vertical integration may have once been the norm, a fast-changing environment can render vertical integration inefficient, ineffective, and inflexible.

---

[1] I first made this argument in *The Competitive Advantage of Nations* (New York: Free Press, 1990). I modeled the effect of the local business environment on competition in terms of four interrelated influences, graphically depicted in a diamond: factor conditions (the cost and quality of inputs); demand conditions (the sophistication of local customers); the context for firm strategy and rivalry (the nature and intensity of local competition); and related and supporting industries (the local extent and sophistication of suppliers and related industries). Diamond theory stresses how these elements combine to produce a dynamic, stimulating, and intensely competitive business environment.

A cluster is the manifestation of the diamond at work. Proximity—the colocation of companies, customers, and suppliers—amplifies all of the pressures to innovate and upgrade.

Even when some inputs are best sourced from a distance, clusters offer advantages. Suppliers trying to penetrate a large, concentrated market will price more aggressively, knowing that as they do so they can realize efficiencies in marketing and in service.

Working against a cluster's advantages in assembling resources is the possibility that competition will render them more expensive and scarce. But companies do have the alternative of outsourcing many inputs from other locations, which tends to limit potential cost penalties. More important, clusters increase not only the demand for specialized inputs but also their supply.

Access to Specialized Information   Extensive market, technical, and competitive information accumulates within a cluster, and members have preferred access to it. In addition, personal relationships and community ties foster trust and facilitate the flow of information. These conditions make information more transferable.

Complementarities   A host of linkages among cluster members results in a whole greater than the sum of its parts. In a typical tourism cluster, for example, the quality of a visitor's experience depends not only on the appeal of the primary attraction but also on the quality and efficiency of complementary businesses such as hotels, restaurants, shopping outlets, and transportation facilities. Because members of the cluster are mutually dependent, good performance by one can boost the success of the others.

Complementarities come in many forms. The most obvious is when products complement one another in meeting customers' needs, as the tourism example illustrates. Another form is the coordination of activities across companies to optimize their collective productivity. In wood products, for instance, the efficiency of sawmills depends on a reliable supply of high-quality timber and the ability to put all the timber to use—in furniture (highest quality), pallets and boxes (lower quality), or wood chips (lowest quality). In the early 1990s, Portuguese sawmills suffered from poor timber quality because local landowners did not invest in timber management. Hence most timber was processed for use in pallets and boxes, a lower-value use that limited the price paid to landowners. Substantial improvement in productivity was possible, but only if several parts of the cluster changed simultaneously. Logging operations, for example, had to modify cutting and sorting procedures, while sawmills had to develop the capacity to process wood in more sophisticated ways. Coordination to develop standard wood classifications and measures was an important enabling step. Geographically dispersed companies are less likely to recognize and capture such linkages.

Other complementarities arise in marketing. A cluster frequently enhances the reputation of a location in a particular field, making it more likely that buyers will turn to a vendor based there. Italy's strong reputation for fashion and design, for example, benefits companies involved in leather goods, footwear, apparel, and accessories. Beyond reputation, cluster members often profit from a variety of joint marketing mechanisms, such as company referrals, trade fairs, trade magazines, and marketing delegations.

Finally, complementarities can make buying from a cluster more attractive for customers. Visiting buyers can see many vendors in a single trip. They also may perceive their buying risk to be lower because one location provides alternative suppliers. That allows them to multisource or to switch vendors if the need arises. Hong Kong thrives as a source of fashion apparel in part for this reason.

Access to Institutions and Public Goods   Investments made by government or other public institutions—such as public spending for specialized infrastructure or educational programs—can enhance a company's productivity. The ability to recruit employees trained at local programs, for example, lowers the cost of internal training. Other quasi-public goods, such as the cluster's information and technology pools and its reputation, arise as natural by-products of competition.

It is not just governments that create public goods that enhance productivity in the private sector. Investments by companies—in training programs, infrastructure, quality centers, testing laboratories,

Figure 3 Mapping Selected U.S. Clusters

Here are just some of the clusters in the United States. A few—Hollywood's entertainment cluster and High Point, North Carolina's household-furniture cluster—are well known. Others are less familiar, such as golf equipment in Carlsbad, California, and optics in Phoenix, Arizona. A relatively small number of clusters usually account for a major share of the economy within a geographic area as well as for an overwhelming share of its economic activity that is "exported" to other locations. *Exporting clusters*—those that export products or make investments to compete outside the local area—are the primary source of an area's economic growth and prosperity over the long run. The demand for local industries is inherently limited by the size of the local market, but exporting clusters can grow far beyond that limit.

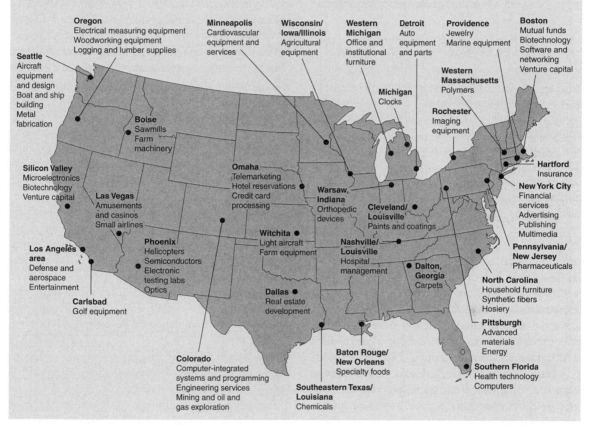

and so on—also contribute to increased productivity. Such private investments are often made collectively because cluster participants recognize the potential for collective benefits.

Better Motivation and Measurement Local rivalry is highly motivating. Peer pressure amplifies competitive pressure within a cluster, even among noncompeting or indirectly competing companies.

Pride and the desire to look good in the local community spur executives to attempt to outdo one another.

Clusters also often make it easier to measure and compare performances because local rivals share general circumstances—for example, labor costs and local market access—and they perform similar activities. Companies within clusters typically have intimate knowledge of their suppliers' costs. Managers are able to compare costs and employees' performance with other local companies. Additionally, financial institutions can accumulate knowledge about the cluster that can be used to monitor performance.

Clusters and Innovation   In addition to enhancing productivity, clusters play a vital role in a company's ongoing ability to innovate. Some of the same characteristics that enhance current productivity have an even more dramatic effect on innovation and productivity growth.

Because sophisticated buyers are often part of a cluster, companies inside clusters usually have a better window on the market than isolated competitors do. Computer companies based in Silicon Valley and Austin, Texas, for example, plug into customer needs and trends with a speed difficult to match by companies located elsewhere. The ongoing relationships with other entities within the cluster also help companies to learn early about evolving technology, component and machinery availability, service and marketing concepts, and so on. Such learning is facilitated by the ease of making site visits and frequent face-to-face contact.

Clusters do more than make opportunities for innovation more visible. They also provide the capacity and the flexibility to act rapidly. A company within a cluster often can source what it needs to implement innovations more quickly. Local suppliers and partners can and do get closely involved in the innovation process, thus ensuring a better match with customers' requirements.

Companies within a cluster can experiment at lower cost and can delay large commitments until they are more assured that a given innovation will pan out. In contrast, a company relying on distant suppliers faces greater challenges in every activity it coordinates with other organizations—in contracting, for example, or securing delivery or obtaining associated technical and service support. Innovation can be even harder in vertically integrated companies, especially in those that face difficult trade-offs if the innovation erodes the value of in-house assets or if current products or processes must be maintained while new ones are developed.

Reinforcing the other advantages for innovation is the sheer pressure—competitive pressure, peer pressure, constant comparison—that occurs in a cluster. Executives vie with one another to set their companies apart. For all these reasons, clusters can remain centers of innovation for decades.

Clusters and New Business Formation   It is not surprising, then, that many new companies grow up within an existing cluster rather than at isolated locations. New suppliers, for example, proliferate within a cluster because a concentrated customer base lowers their risks and makes it easier for them to spot market opportunities. Moreover, because developed clusters comprise related industries that normally draw on common or very similar inputs, suppliers enjoy expanded opportunities.

Clusters are conducive to new business formation for a variety of reasons. Individuals working within a cluster can more easily perceive gaps in products or services around which they can build businesses. Beyond that, barriers to entry are lower than elsewhere. Needed assets, skills, inputs, and staff are often readily available at the cluster location, waiting to be assembled into a new enterprise. Local financial institutions and investors, already familiar with the cluster, may require a lower risk premium on capital. In addition, the cluster often presents a significant local market, and an entrepreneur may benefit from established relationships. All of these factors reduce the perceived risks of entry—and of exit, should the enterprise fail.

The formation of new businesses within a cluster is part of a positive feedback loop. An expanded cluster amplifies all the benefits I have described—it increases the collective pool of competitive resources, which benefits all the cluster's members. The net result is that companies in the cluster advance relative to rivals at other locations.

Birth, Evolution, and Decline

A cluster's roots can often be traced to historical circumstances. In Massachusetts, for example, several clusters had their beginnings in research done at MIT or Harvard. The Dutch transportation cluster owes much to Holland's central location within Europe, an extensive network of waterways, the efficiency of the port of Rotterdam, and the skills accumulated by the Dutch through Holland's long maritime history.

Clusters may also arise from unusual, sophisticated, or stringent local demand. Israel's cluster in irrigation equipment and other advanced agricultural technologies reflects that nation's strong desire for self-sufficiency in food together with a scarcity of water and hot, arid growing conditions. The environmental cluster in Finland emerged as a result of pollution problems created by local process industries such as metals, forestry, chemicals, and energy.

Prior existence of supplier industries, related industries, or even entire related clusters provides yet another seed for new clusters. The golf equipment cluster near San Diego, for example, has its roots in southern California's aerospace cluster. That cluster created a pool of suppliers for castings and advanced materials as well as engineers with the requisite experience in those technologies.

New clusters may also arise from one or two innovative companies that stimulate the growth of many others. Medtronic played this role in helping to create the Minneapolis medical-device cluster. Similarly, MCI and America Online have been hubs for growing new businesses in the telecommunications cluster in the Washington, D.C., metropolitan area.

Sometimes a chance event creates some advantageous factor that, in turn, fosters cluster development—although chance rarely provides the sole explanation for a cluster's success in a location. The telemarketing cluster in Omaha, Nebraska, for example, owes much to the decision by the United States Air Force to locate the Strategic Air Command (SAC) there. Charged with a key role in the country's nuclear deterrence strategy, SAC was the site of the first installation of fiber-optic telecommunications cables in the United States. The local Bell operating company (now U.S. West) developed unusual capabilities through its dealings with such a demanding customer. The extraordinary telecommunications capability and infrastructure that consequently developed in Omaha, coupled with

less unique attributes such as its central-time-zone location and easily understandable local accent, provided the underpinnings of the area's telemarketing cluster.

Once a cluster begins to form, a self-reinforcing cycle promotes its growth, especially when local institutions are supportive and local competition is vigorous. As the cluster expands, so does its influence with government and with public and private institutions.

A growing cluster signals opportunity, and its success stories help attract the best talent. Entrepreneurs take notice, and individuals with ideas or relevant skills migrate in from other locations. Specialized suppliers emerge; information accumulates; local institutions develop specialized training, research, and infrastructure; and the cluster's strength and visibility grow. Eventually, the cluster broadens to encompass related industries. Numerous case studies suggest that clusters require a decade or more to develop depth and real competitive advantage.[2]

Cluster development is often particularly vibrant at the intersection of clusters, where insights, skills, and technologies from various fields merge, sparking innovation and new businesses. An example from Germany illustrates this point. The country has distinct clusters in both home appliances and household furniture, each based on different technologies and inputs. At the intersection of the two, though, is a cluster of built-in kitchens and appliances, an area in which Germany commands a higher share of world exports than in either appliances or furniture.

Clusters continually evolve as new companies and industries emerge or decline and as local institutions develop and change. They can maintain vibrancy as competitive locations for centuries; most successful clusters prosper for decades at least. However, they can and do lose their competitive edge due to both

---

[2] Selected case studies are described in "Clusters and Competition" in my book *On Competition* (Boston: Harvard Business School Press, 1998), which also includes citations of the published output of a number of cluster initiatives. Readers can also find a full treatment of the intellectual roots of cluster thinking, along with an extensive bibliography.

external and internal forces. Technological discontinuities are perhaps the most significant of the external threats because they can neutralize many advantages simultaneously. A cluster's assets—market information, employees' skills, scientific and technical expertise, and supplier bases—may all become irrelevant. New England's loss of market share in golf equipment is a good example. The New England cluster was based on steel shafts, steel irons, and wooden-headed woods. When companies in California began making golf clubs with advanced materials, East Coast producers had difficulty competing. A number of them were acquired or went out of business.

A shift in buyers' needs, creating a divergence between local needs and needs elsewhere, constitutes another external threat. U.S. companies in a variety of clusters, for example, suffered when energy efficiency grew in importance in most parts of the world while the United States maintained low energy prices. Lacking both pressure to improve and insight into customer needs, U.S. companies were slow to innovate, and they lost ground to European and Japanese competitors.

Clusters are at least as vulnerable to internal rigidities as they are to external threats. Overconsolidation, mutual understandings, cartels, and other restraints to competition undermine local rivalry. Regulatory inflexibility or the introduction of restrictive union rules slows productivity improvement. The quality of institutions such as schools and universities can stagnate.

Groupthink among cluster participants—Detroit's attachment to gas-guzzling autos in the 1970s is one example—can be another powerful form of rigidity. If companies in a cluster are too inward looking, the whole cluster suffers from a collective inertia, making it harder for individual companies to embrace new ideas, much less perceive the need for radical innovation.

Such rigidities tend to arise when government suspends or intervenes in competition or when companies persist in old behaviors and relationships that no longer contribute to competitive advantage. Increases in the cost of doing business begin to outrun the ability to upgrade. Rigidities of this nature

currently work against a variety of clusters in Switzerland and Germany.

As long as rivalry remains sufficiently vigorous, companies can partially compensate for some decline in the cluster's competitiveness by outsourcing to distant suppliers or moving part or all of production elsewhere to offset local wages that rise ahead of productivity. German companies in the 1990s, for example, have been doing just that. Technology can be licensed or sourced from other locations, and product development can be moved. Over time, however, a location will decline if it fails to build capabilities in major new technologies or needed supporting firms and institutions.

Implications for Companies

In the new economics of competition, what matters most is not inputs and scale, but productivity—and that is true in all industries. The term *high tech,* normally used to refer to fields such as information technology and biotechnology, has distorted thinking about competition, creating the misconception that only a handful of businesses compete in sophisticated ways.

In fact, there is no such thing as a low-tech industry. There are only low-tech companies—that is, companies that fail to use world-class technology and practices to enhance productivity and innovation. A vibrant cluster can help any company in any industry compete in the most sophisticated ways, using the most advanced, relevant skills and technologies.

Thus executives must extend their thinking beyond what goes on inside their own organizations and within their own industries. Strategy must also address what goes on outside. Extensive vertical integration may once have been appropriate, but companies today must forge close linkages with buyers, suppliers, and other institutions.

Specifically, understanding clusters adds the following four issues to the strategic agenda.

1. Choosing locations. Globalization and the ease of transportation and communication have led many companies to move some or all of their operations

Clusters, Geography, and Economic Development

Poor countries lack well-developed clusters; they compete in the world market with cheap labor and natural resources. To move beyond this stage, the development of well-functioning clusters is essential. Clusters become an especially controlling factor for countries moving from a middle-income to an advanced economy. Even in high-wage economies, however, the need for cluster upgrading is constant. The wealthier the economy, the more it will require innovation to support rising wages and to replace jobs eliminated by improvements in efficiency and the migration of standard production to low-cost areas.

Promoting cluster formation in developing economies means starting at the most basic level. Policymakers must first address the foundations: improving education and skill levels, building capacity in technology, opening access to capital markets, and improving institutions. Over time, additional investment in more cluster-specific assets is necessary.

Government policies in developing economies often unwittingly work against cluster formation. Restrictions on industrial location and subsidies to invest in distressed areas, for example, can disperse companies artificially. Protecting local companies from competition leads to excessive vertical integration and blunted pressure for innovation, retarding cluster development.

In the early stages of economic development, countries should expand internal trade among cities and states and trade with neighboring countries as important stepping stones to building the skills to compete globally. Such trade greatly enhances cluster development. Instead, attention is typically riveted on the large, advanced markets, an orientation that has often been reinforced by protectionist policies restricting trade with nearby markets. However, the kinds of goods developing countries can trade with advanced economies are limited to commodities and to activities sensitive to labor costs.

While it is essential that clusters form, *where* they form also matters. In developing economies, a large proportion of economic activity tends to concentrate around capital cities such as Bangkok and Bogotá. That is usually because outlying areas lack infrastructure, institutions, and suppliers. It may also reflect an intrusive role by the central government in controlling competition, leading companies to locate near the seat of power and the agencies whose approval they require to do business.

This pattern of economic geography inflicts high costs on productivity. Congestion, bottlenecks, and inflexibility lead to high administrative costs and major inefficiencies, not to mention a diminished quality of life. Companies cannot easily move out from the center, however, because neither infrastructure nor rudimentary clusters exist in the smaller cities and towns. (The building of a tourism cluster in developing economies can be a positive force in improving the outlying infrastructure and in dispersing economic activity.)

Even in advanced economies, however, economic activity may be geographically concentrated. Japan offers a particularly striking case, with nearly 50% of total manufacturing shipments located around Tokyo and Osaka. This is due less to inadequacies in infrastructure in outlying areas than to a powerful and intrusive central government, with its centralizing bias in policies and institutions. The Japanese case vividly illustrates the major inefficiencies and productivity costs resulting from such a pattern of economic geography, even for advanced nations. It is a major policy issue facing Japan.

An economic geography characterized by specialization and dispersion—that is, a number of metropolitan areas, each specializing in an array of clusters—appears to be a far more productive industrial organization than one based on one or two huge, diversified cities. In nations such as Germany, Italy, Switzerland, and the United States, this kind of internal specialization and trade—and internal competition among locations—fuels productivity growth and hones the ability of companies to compete effectively in the global arena.

Figure 4   Mapping Portugal's Clusters

In a middle-income economy like Portugal, exporting clusters tend to be more natural-resource labor intensive.

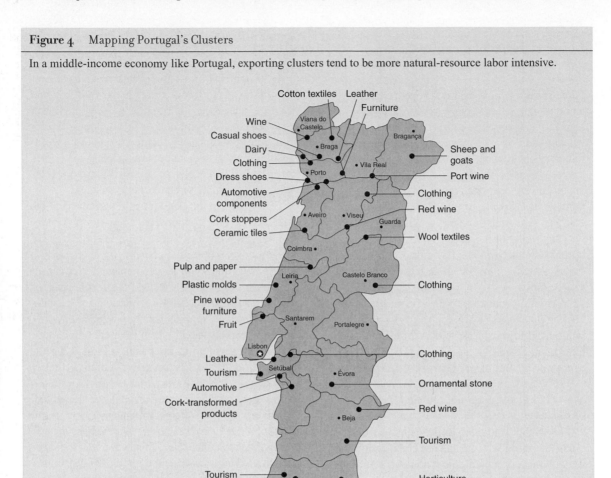

to locations with low wages, taxes, and utility costs. What we know about clusters suggests, first, that some of those cost advantages may well turn out to be illusory. Locations with those advantages often lack efficient infrastructure, sophisticated suppliers, and other cluster benefits that can more than offset any savings from lower input costs. Savings in wages, utilities, and taxes may be highly visible and easy to measure up front, but productivity penalties remain hidden and unanticipated.

More important to ongoing competitiveness is the role of location in innovation. Yes, companies

have to spread activities globally to source inputs and gain access to markets. Failure to do so will lead to a competitive *disadvantage*. And for stable, labor-intensive activities such as assembly and software translation, low factor costs are often decisive in driving locational choices.

For a company's "home base" for each product line, however, clusters are critical. Home base activities—strategy development, core product and process R&D, a critical mass of the most sophisticated production or service provision—create and renew the company's product, processes, and services.

Therefore locational decisions must be based on both total systems costs and innovation potential, not on input costs alone. Cluster thinking suggests that every product line needs a home base, and the most vibrant cluster will offer the best location. Within the United States, for example, Hewlett-Packard has chosen cluster locations for the home bases of its major product lines: California, where almost all of the world's leading personal computer and workstation businesses are located, is home to personal computers and workstations; Massachusetts, which has an extraordinary concentration of world-renowned research hospitals and leading medical instrument companies, is home to medical instruments.

As global competition nullifies traditional comparative advantages and exposes companies to the best rivals from around the world, a growing number of multinationals are shifting their home bases to more vibrant clusters—often using acquisitions as a means of establishing themselves as insiders in a new location. Nestlé, for example, after acquiring Rowntree Mackintosh, relocated its confectionary business to York, England, where Rowntree was originally based, because a vibrant food cluster thrives there. England, with its sweet-toothed consumers, sophisticated retailers, advanced advertising agencies, and highly competitive media companies, constitutes a more dynamic environment for competing in mass-market candy than Switzerland did. Similarly, Nestlé has moved its headquarters for bottled water to France, the most competitive location in that industry. Northern Telecom has relocated its home base for central office switching from Canada to the United States—drawn by the vibrancy of the U.S. telecommunications-equipment cluster.

Cluster thinking also suggests that it is better to move groups of linked activities to the same place than to spread them across numerous locations. Colocating R&D, component fabrication, assembly, marketing, customer support, and even related businesses can facilitate internal efficiencies in sourcing and in sharing technology and information. Grouping activities into campuses also allows companies to extend deeper roots into local clusters, improving their ability to capture potential benefits.

2. Engaging locally. The social glue that binds clusters together also facilitates access to important resources and information. Tapping into the competitively valuable assets within a cluster requires personal relationships, face-to-face contact, a sense of common interest, and "insider" status. The mere colocation of companies, suppliers, and institutions creates the *potential* for economic value; it does not necessarily ensure its realization.

To maximize the benefits of cluster involvement, companies must participate actively and establish a significant local presence. They must have a substantial local investment even if the parent company is headquartered elsewhere. And they must foster ongoing relationships with government bodies and local institutions such as utilities, schools, and research groups.

Companies have much to gain by engaging beyond their narrow confines as single entities. Yet managers tend to be wary, at least initially. They fear that a growing cluster will attract competition, drive up costs, or cause them to lose valued employees to rivals or spin-offs. As their understanding of the cluster concept grows, however, managers realize that many participants in the cluster do not compete directly and that the offsetting benefits, such as a greater supply of better trained people, for example, can outweigh any increase in competition.

3. Upgrading the cluster. Because the health of the local business environment is important to the health of the company, upgrading the cluster should be part of management's agenda. Companies upgrade their clusters in a variety of ways.

Consider Genzyme. Massachusetts is home to a vibrant biotechnology cluster, which draws on the region's strong universities, medical centers, and venture capital firms. Once Genzyme reached the stage in its development when it needed a manufacturing facility, CEO Henri Termeer initially considered the pharmaceuticals cluster in the New Jersey and Philadelphia area because it had what Massachusetts lacked: established expertise in drug manufacturing. Upon further reflection, however, Termeer decided to influence the process of creating a manufacturing capability in Genzyme's home base, reasoning that if his plans were successful, the company could become more competitive.

Thus Genzyme deliberately chose to work with contractors committed to the Boston area, bypassing the many specialized engineering firms located near Philadelphia. In addition, it undertook a number of initiatives, with the help of city and state government, to improve the labor force, such as offering scholarships and internships to local youth. More broadly, Genzyme has worked to build critical mass for its cluster. Termeer believes that Genzyme's success is linked to the cluster's—and that all members will benefit from a strong base of supporting functions and institutions.

4. Working collectively. The way clusters operate suggests a new agenda of collective action in the private sector. Investing in public goods is normally seen as a function of government, yet cluster thinking clearly demonstrates how companies benefit from local assets and institutions.

In the past, collective action in the private sector has focused on seeking government subsidies and special favors that often distort competition. But executives' long-term interests would be better served by working to promote a higher plane of competition. They can begin by rethinking the role of trade associations, which often do little more than lobby government, compile some statistics, and host social functions. The associations are missing an important opportunity.

Trade associations can provide a forum for the exchange of ideas and a focal point for collective action in overcoming obstacles to productivity and growth. Associations can take the lead in such activities as establishing university-based testing facilities and training or research programs; collecting cluster-related information; offering forums on common managerial problems; investigating solutions to environmental issues; organizing trade fairs and delegations; and managing purchasing consortia.

For clusters consisting of many small and mid-size companies—such as tourism, apparel, and agriculture—the need is particularly great for collective bodies to assume scale-sensitive functions.

In the Netherlands, for instance, grower cooperatives built the specialized auction and handling facilities that constitute one of the Dutch flower cluster's greatest competitive advantages. The Dutch Flower Council and the Association of Dutch Flower Growers Research Groups, in which most growers participate, have taken on other functions as well, such as applied research and marketing.

Most existing trade associations are too narrow; they represent industries, not clusters. In addition, because their role is defined as lobbying the federal government, their scope is national rather than local. National associations, however, are rarely sufficient to address the local issues that are most important to cluster productivity.

By revealing how business and government together create the conditions that promote growth, clusters offer a constructive way to change the nature of the dialogue between the public and private sectors. With a better understanding of what fosters true competitiveness, executives can start asking government for the right things. The example of MassMEDIC, an association formed in 1996 by the Massachusetts medical-devices cluster, illustrates this point. It recently worked successfully with the U.S. Food and Drug Administration to streamline the approval process for medical devices. Such a step clearly benefits cluster members and enhances competition at the same time.

What's Wrong with Industrial Policy

Productivity, not exports or natural resources, determines the prosperity of any state or nation. Recognizing this, governments should strive to create an environment that supports rising productivity. Sound macroeconomic policy is necessary but not sufficient. The microeconomic foundations for competition will ultimately determine productivity and competitiveness.

Governments—both national and local—have new roles to play. They must ensure the supply of high-quality inputs such as educated citizens and physical infrastructure. They must set the rules of competition—by protecting intellectual property and enforcing antitrust laws, for example—so that productivity and innovation will govern success in the economy. Finally, governments should promote cluster formation and upgrading and the buildup of public or quasi-public goods that have a significant impact on many linked businesses.

This sort of role for government is a far cry from industrial policy. In industrial policy, governments target "desirable" industries and intervene—through subsidies or restrictions on investments by foreign companies, for example—to favor local companies. In contrast, the aim of cluster policy is to reinforce the development of *all* clusters. This means that a traditional cluster such as agriculture should not be abandoned; it should be upgraded. Governments should not choose among clusters, because each one offers opportunities to improve productivity and support rising wages. Every cluster not only contributes directly to national productivity but also affects the productivity of *other* clusters. Not all clusters will succeed, of course, but market forces—not government decisions—should determine the outcomes.

Government, working with the private sector, should reinforce and build on existing and emerging clusters rather than attempt to create entirely new ones. Successful new industries and clusters often grow out of established ones. Businesses involving advanced technology succeed not in a vacuum but where there is already a base of related activities in the field. In fact, most clusters form independently of government action—and sometimes in spite of it. They form where a foundation of locational advantages exists. To justify cluster development efforts, some seeds of a cluster should have already passed a market test.

Cluster development initiatives should embrace the pursuit of competitive advantage and specialization rather than simply imitate successful clusters in other locations. This requires building on local sources of uniqueness. Finding areas of specialization normally proves more effective than head-on competition with well-established rival locations.

New Public-Private Responsibilities

Economic geography in an era of global competition, then, poses a paradox. In a global economy—which boasts rapid transportation, high-speed communication, and accessible markets—one would expect location to diminish in importance. But the opposite is true. The enduring competitive advantages in a global economy are often heavily local, arising from concentrations of highly specialized skills and knowledge, institutions, rivals, related businesses, and sophisticated customers. Geographic, cultural, and institutional proximity leads to special access, closer relationships, better information, powerful incentives, and other advantages in productivity and innovation that are difficult to tap from a distance. The more the world economy becomes complex, knowledge based, and dynamic, the more this is true.

Leaders of businesses, government, and institutions all have a stake—and a role to play—in the new economics of competition. Clusters reveal the mutual dependence and collective responsibility of all these entities for creating the conditions for productive competition. This task will require fresh thinking on the part of leaders and the willingness to abandon the traditional categories that drive our thinking about who does what in the economy. The lines between public and private investment blur. Companies, no less than governments and universities, have a stake in education. Universities have a stake in the competitiveness of local businesses. By revealing the process by which wealth is actually created in an economy, clusters open new public-private avenues for constructive action.

Developing Transnational Strategies:
Building Layers of Competitive Advantage

In this chapter, we discuss how the numerous conflicting demands and pressures described in the first two chapters shape the strategic choices that MNEs must make. In this complex situation, an MNE determines strategy by balancing the motivations for its own international expansion with the economic imperatives of its industry structure and competitive dynamics, the social and cultural forces of the markets it has entered worldwide, and the political demands of its home- and host-country governments. To frame this complex analysis, in this chapter, we examine how MNEs balance strategic means and ends to build the three required dimensional capabilities: global-scale efficiency and competitiveness, multinational flexibility and responsiveness, and worldwide innovation and learning. After defining each of the dominant historic strategic approaches—what we term classic multinational, international, and global strategies—we explore the emerging transnational strategic model that most MNEs must adopt today. Finally, we describe not only how companies can develop this approach themselves but also how they can defend against transnational competitors.

The strategies of MNEs at the start of the 21st century were shaped by the turbulent international environment that redefined global competition in the closing decades of the 20th century. It was during that turmoil that a number of different perspectives and prescriptions emerged about how companies could create strategic advantage in their worldwide businesses.

Consider, for example, three of the most influential articles on global strategy published during the 1980s—the decade in which many new trends first emerged.[1] Each is reasonable and intuitively appealing. What soon becomes clear, however, is that their prescriptions are very different and often contradictory, a reality that highlights not only the complexity of the strategic challenge that faced managers in large, worldwide companies but also the confusion of advice being offered to them.

- In one of the most provocative articles of that era, Theodore Levitt argued that effective global strategy was not a bag of many tricks but the successful practice of just

[1]See Theodeore Levitt, "The Globalization of Markets" *Harvard Business Review* 61, no. 3 (1983), pp. 92–102; T. Hout, M. E. Porter, and E. Rudden, "How Global Companies Win Out," *Harvard Business Review* 60, no. 5 (1982), pp. 98–109; G. Hamel and C. K. Prahalad, "Do You Really Have a Global Strategy?" *Harvard Business Review* 63, no. 4 (1985), pp. 139–49.

one: product standardization. According to him, the core of a global strategy lay in developing a standardized product to be produced and sold the same way throughout the world.

- In contrast, an article by Michael Porter and his colleagues suggested that effective global strategy required the approach not of a hedgehog, who knows only one trick, but that of a fox, who knows many. These "tricks" include exploiting economies of scale through global volume, taking preemptive positions through quick and large investments, and managing interdependently to achieve synergies across different activities.
- Gary Hamel and C. K. Prahalad's prescription for a global strategy contradicted Levitt's even more sharply. Instead of a single standardized product, they recommended a broad product portfolio, with many product varieties, so that investments in technologies and distribution channels could be shared. Cross-subsidization across products and markets and the development of a strong worldwide distribution system were at the center of these authors' view of how to succeed in the game of global chess.

As we described in the preceding chapter, what was becoming increasingly clear during the next two decades was that to achieve sustainable competitive advantage, MNEs needed to develop layers of competitive advantage—global-scale efficiency, multinational flexibility, and the ability to develop innovations and leverage knowledge on a worldwide basis. Though each of the different prescriptions focuses on one or another of these different strategic objectives, the challenge for most companies today is to achieve all of them simultaneously.

Worldwide Competitive Advantage: Goals and Means

To develop worldwide advantage, a company must achieve three strategic objectives: It must build global-scale efficiency in its existing activities, it must develop multinational flexibility to manage diverse country-specific risks and opportunities, and it must create the ability to learn from its international exposure and opportunities and exploit that learning on a worldwide basis. Competitive advantage is developed by taking strategic actions that optimize a company's achievement of these different and, at times, conflicting goals.

In developing each of these capabilities, the MNE can utilize three very different tools and approaches, which we described briefly in Chapter 1 as the main forces motivating companies to internationalize. It can leverage the scale economies that are potentially available in its different worldwide activities, it can exploit the differences in sourcing and market opportunities among the many countries in which it operates, and it can capitalize on the diversity of its activities and operations to create synergies or develop economies of scope.

The MNE's strategic challenge, therefore, is to exploit all three sources of global competitive advantage—scale economies, national differences, and scope economies—to optimize global efficiencies, multinational flexibility, and worldwide learning. Thus, the key to worldwide competitive advantage lies in managing the interactions between the different goals and the different means.

▮ The Goals: Efficiency, Flexibility, and Learning

Let us now consider each of these strategic goals in a little more detail.

Global Efficiency

Viewing an MNE as an input–output system, we can think of its overall efficiency as the ratio of the value of its outputs to the value of its inputs. In this simplified view of the firm, its efficiency could be enhanced by increasing the value of outputs (i.e., securing higher revenues), lowering the value of its inputs (i.e., lowering costs), or doing both. This is a simple point but one that is often overlooked:

• Efficiency improvement is not just cost reduction but also revenue enhancement.

To help understand the concept of global efficiency, we use the global integration—national responsiveness framework first developed by C. K. Prahalad (see Figure 3-1).[2] The vertical axis represents the potential benefits from the global integration of activities—benefits that largely translate into lower costs through scale and scope economies. The horizontal axis represents the benefits of national responsiveness—those that result from the country-by-country differentiation of product, strategies, and activities. These benefits essentially translate into better revenues from more effective differentiation in response to national differences in tastes, industry structures, distribution systems, and government regulations.

As Figure 3-1 illustrates, the framework can be used to understand differences in the benefits of integration and responsiveness at the aggregate level of industries, as well as to identify and describe differences in the strategic approaches of companies competing in the same industry. Also as the figure indicates, industry characteristics alone do not determine company strategies. In automobiles, for example, Fiat historically pursued a classical multinational strategy, helping establish national auto industries through its joint venture partnerships and host government support in Spain, Yugoslavia, Poland,

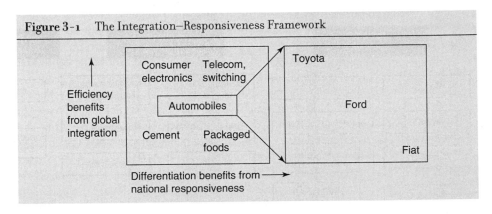

Figure 3-1   The Integration–Responsiveness Framework

▮ [2]For a detailed exposition of this framework, see C. K. Prahalad and Yves Doz, *The Multinational Mission* (New York: The Free Press, 1987).

and many other countries with state-sponsored auto industries. Toyota, by contrast, succeeded originally by developing products and manufacturing them in centralized, globally scaled facilities in Japan. This sort of strategic choice to focus on the objective of global efficiency (rather than local responsiveness) creates vulnerabilities and challenges as well as clear benefits.

Multinational Flexibility

A worldwide company faces an operating environment characterized by diversity and volatility. Some opportunities and risks generated by this environment are endemic to all firms; others, however, are unique to companies operating across national borders. A key element of worldwide competitiveness, therefore, is multinational flexibility—the ability of a company to manage the risks and exploit the opportunities that arise from the diversity and volatility of the global environment.[3]

Although there are many sources of diversity and volatility, it is worth highlighting four that we regard as particularly important. First, there are *macroeconomic risks* that are completely outside the control of the MNE, such as changes in prices, wages, or exchange rates caused by wars, natural calamities, or recessions. Second, there are *political risks* that arise from policy actions of national governments, such as managed changes in exchange rates or interest rate adjustments. Third, there are *competitive risks* arising from the uncertainties of competitors' responses to the MNE's own strategies. Fourth, there are *resource risks*, such as the availability of raw materials, capital, or managerial talent. In all four categories, the common characteristic of the various types of risks is they vary across countries and change over time. This variance makes flexibility the key strategic management requirement, because diversity and volatility create attendant opportunities that must be considered jointly.

In general, multinational flexibility requires management to scan its broad environment to detect changes and discontinuities and then respond to the new situation in the context of the worldwide business. MNEs following this approach exploit their exposure to diverse and dynamic environments to develop strategies—and structures—in more general and more flexible terms so as to be robust to different international environmental scenarios. For example, having a network of affiliated subsidiaries which emphasize global exports rather than individual local markets provides a flexibility to shift production when a particular national market faces an economic crisis.

Worldwide Learning

Most existing theories of the MNE view it as an instrument to extract additional revenues from internalized capabilities. The assumption is that the firm goes abroad to make more profits by exploiting its technology, brand name, or management capabilities in different countries around the world. And most traditional theory assumes that the key competencies reside at the MNE's center.

---

[3]This issue of multinational flexibility is discussed more fully in Bruce Kogut, "Designing Global Strategies: Profiting from Operating Flexibility," *Sloan Management Review*, Fall 1985, pp. 27–38.

Although the search for additional profits or the desire to protect existing revenues may explain why MNEs come to exist, it does not provide a complete explanation of why some of them continue to grow and flourish. As we suggested in Chapter 1, an alternative view may well be that a key asset of the multinational is the diversity of environments in which it operates. This diversity exposes the MNE to multiple stimuli, allows it to develop diverse capabilities, and provides it with broader learning opportunities than are available to a purely domestic firm. Furthermore, its initial stock of knowledge provides the MNE with strength that allows it to create organizational diversity in the first place. In Chapter 5, we engage in a detailed discussion of the approaches that MNEs use to deliver on the objective of worldwide learning.

◾ The Means: National Differences, Scale, and Scope Economies

There are three fundamental tools for building worldwide competitive advantage: exploiting differences in sourcing and market potential across countries, exploiting economies of scope, and exploiting economies of scale. In this section, we explore each of them in more depth.

National Differences

In the absence of efficient markets, the fact that different nations have different factor endowments (e.g., an abundance of labor, land, materials) leads to intercountry differences in factor costs. Because different activities of the firm, such as R&D, production, or marketing, use various factors to different degrees, a firm can gain cost advantages by configuring its value chain so that each activity is located in the country that has the least cost for its most intensively used factor. For example, R&D facilities may be placed in the United Kingdom because of the available supply of high-quality, yet modestly paid, scientists; manufacturing of labor-intensive components may be undertaken in Taiwan to capitalize on the lower cost, efficient labor force; and software development could concentrate in India, where skilled software engineers are paid a fraction of Western salaries. General Electric's "Global Product Concept" was set up to concentrate manufacturing wherever it could be implemented in the most cost-effective way (while still retaining quality).

National differences may also exist in output markets. As we have discussed, customer tastes and preferences may differ in different countries, as may distribution systems, government regulations applicable to the pertinent product markets, or the effectiveness of different promotion strategies. A firm can obtain higher prices for its output by tailoring its offerings to fit the unique requirements in each national market.

Scale Economies

Microeconomic theory provides a strong basis for evaluating the effect of scale on cost reduction, and the use of scale as a competitive tool is common in industries ranging from roller bearings to semiconductors. Whereas scale, by itself, is a static concept, there may be dynamic benefits of scale through what has been variously described as the experience or learning effect. The higher volume that helps a firm exploit scale benefits

Table 3-1   Scope Economies in Product and Market Diversification

	Sources of Scope Economies	
	Product Diversification	**Market Diversification**
Shared physical assets	Factory automation with flexibility to produce multiple products (Ford)	Global brand name (Nokia)
Shared external relations	Using common distribution channels for multiple products (Samsung)	Servicing multinational customers worldwide (Citibank)
Shared learning	Shared R&D in computer and communications business (NEC)	Pooling knowledge developed in different markets (Procter & Gamble)

also allows it to accumulate learning, which leads to progressive cost reduction as the firm moves down its learning curve. So though emerging Korean electronics firms were able to match the scale of experienced Japanese competitors, they were initially unable to compensate for the innumerable process-related efficiencies the Japanese had learned after decades of operating their global-scale plants.

Scope Economies

The concept of scope economies is based on the notion that certain economies arise from the fact that the cost of the joint production (or development or distribution) of two or more products can be less than the cost of producing them separately.[4] Such cost reductions may take place for many reasons—for example, resources such as information or technologies, once acquired for use in producing one item, are available without cost for production of other items.

The strategic importance of scope economies arises from a diversified firm's ability to share investments and costs across the same or different value chains—a source of economies that competitors without such internal and external diversity cannot match. Such sharing can take place across segments, products, or markets and may involve the joint use of different kinds of assets (see Table 3-1).

Implicit with each of these tools is the ability to develop an organizational infrastructure which supports it. As we discuss in later chapters, the organizational ability to leverage a global network and value chain will differentiate the winners and losers.

Mapping Ends and Means: Building Blocks for Worldwide Advantage

Table 3-2 shows a mapping of the different goals and means for achieving worldwide competitiveness. Each goals–means intersection suggests some of the factors that may enhance a company's strategic position. Although the factors are only illustrative, it may be useful to study them carefully and compare them against the proposals of the

[4]For a detailed exposition of scope economies, see W. J. Baumol, J. C. Panzer, and R. D. Willig, *Contestable Markets and the Theory of Industry Structure* (New York: Harcourt Brace Jovanovich, 1982).

Table 3-2 Worldwide Advantage: Goals and Means

	Sources of Competitive Advantage		
Strategic Objectives	**National Differences**	**Scale Economies**	**Scope Economies**
Achieving efficiency in current operations	Benefiting from differences in factor costs—wages and cost of capital	Expanding and exploiting potential scale economies in each activity	Sharing of investments and costs across markets and businesses
Managing risks through multinational flexibility	Managing different kinds of risks arising from market- or policy-induced changes in comparative advantages of different countries	Balancing scale with strategic and operational flexibility	Portfolio diversification of risks and creation of options and side bets
Innovation, learning, and adaptation	Learning from societal differences in organizational and managerial processes and systems	Benefiting from experience—cost reduction and innovation	Shared learning across organizational components in different products, markets, or businesses

different articles mentioned at the beginning of the chapter. It will become apparent that each author focuses on a specific subset of factors—essentially, some different goals–means combinations—and the differences among their prescriptions can be understood in terms of the differences in the particular aspect of worldwide competitive advantage on which they focus.

International, Multinational, Global, and Transnational Strategies

In Chapter 2, we described how environmental forces in different industries shaped alternative approaches to managing worldwide operations that we described as international, multinational, global, and transnational. We now elaborate on the distinctions among these different approaches, as well as their respective strengths and vulnerabilities in terms of the different goals–means combinations we have just described.

International Strategy

Companies adopting this broad approach focus on creating and exploiting innovations on a worldwide basis, using all the different means to achieve this end. MNEs headquartered in large and technologically advanced countries often adopted this strategic approach but limited it primarily to exploiting home-country innovations to develop their competitive positions abroad. The international product cycle theory we described in Chapter 1 encompasses both the strategic motivation and competitive posture of these companies: At least initially, their internationalization process relied heavily on transferring new products, processes, or strategies developed in the home country to less advanced overseas markets.

This approach was common among U.S.-based MNEs such as Kraft, Pfizer, Procter & Gamble, and General Electric. Although these companies built considerable strengths out of their ability to create and leverage innovations, many suffered from deficiencies of both efficiency and flexibility because they did not develop either the centralized and high-scale operations of companies adopting global strategies or the very high degree of local responsiveness that multinational companies could muster through their autonomous, self-sufficient, and entrepreneurial local operations.

Multinational Strategy

The multinational strategic approach focuses primarily on one means (national differences) to achieve most of its strategic objectives. Companies adopting this approach tend to focus on the revenue side, usually by differentiating their products and services in response to national differences in customer preferences, industry characteristics, and government regulations. This approach leads most multinational companies to depend on local-for-local innovations, a process requiring the subsidiary to not only identify local needs but also use its own local resources to respond to those needs. Carrying out most activities within each country on a local-for-local basis also allows those adopting a multinational strategy to match costs and revenues on a currency-by-currency basis.

Historically, many European companies such as Unilever, ICI, Philips, and Nestlé followed this strategic model. In these companies, assets and resources historically were widely dispersed, allowing overseas subsidiaries to carry out a wide range of activities from development and production to sales and services. Their self-sufficiency was typically accompanied by considerable local autonomy. But, though such independent national units were unusually flexible and responsive to their local environments, they inevitably suffered problems of inefficiencies and an inability to exploit the knowledge and competencies of other national units.

Global Strategy

Companies adopting the classic global strategic approach, as we have defined it, depend primarily on developing global efficiency. They use all the different means to achieve the best cost and quality positions for their products.

This means has been the classic approach of many Japanese companies such as Toyota, Canon, Komatsu, and Matsushita. As these and other similar companies have found, however, such efficiency comes with some compromises of both flexibility and learning. For example, concentrating manufacturing to capture global scale may also result in a high level of intercountry product shipments that can raise risks of policy intervention, particularly by host governments in major importer countries. Similarly, companies that centralize R&D for efficiency reasons often find they are constrained in their ability to capture new developments in countries outside their home markets or to leverage innovations created by foreign subsidiaries in the rest of their worldwide operations. Finally, the concentration (most often through centralization) of activities like R&D and manufacturing to achieve a global scale exposes such companies to high sourcing risks, particularly in exchange rate exposure.

The descriptions we have presented to this point regarding multinational versus global strategies have been described in their pure forms. In practice of course many firms do adopt a regional strategy, focusing much of their international expansion on the home region, plus perhaps one or two other regions.

Transnational Strategy

Beneath each of these three traditional strategic approaches lie some implicit assumptions about how best to build worldwide competitive advantage. The global company assumes that the best-cost position is the key source of competitiveness; the multinational company sees differentiation as the primary way to enhance performance; and the international company expects to use innovations to reduce costs, enhance revenues, or both. Companies adopting the transnational strategy recognize that each of these traditional approaches is partial, that each has its own merits but none represents the whole truth.

To achieve worldwide competitive advantage, costs and revenues have to be managed simultaneously, both efficiency and innovation are important, and innovations can arise in many different parts of the organization. Therefore, instead of focusing on any subpart of the set of issues shown in Table 3-2, the transnational company focuses on exploiting each and every goals–means combination to develop layers of competitive advantage by exploiting efficiency, flexibility, and learning simultaneously.

To achieve this ambitious strategic approach, however, the transnational company must develop a very different configuration of assets and capabilities than is typical of traditional multinational, international, and global company structures. The global company tends to concentrate all its resources—either in its home country or in low-cost overseas locations—to exploit the scale economies available in each activity. The multinational company typically disperses its resources among its different national operations to be able to respond to local needs. And the international company tends to centralize those resources that are key to developing innovations but decentralize others to allow its innovations to be adapted worldwide.

The transnational, however, must develop a more sophisticated and differentiated configuration of assets and capabilities. It first decides which key resources and capabilities are best centralized within the home-country operation, not only to realize scale economies but also to protect certain core competencies and provide the necessary supervision of corporate management. Basic research, for example, is often viewed as such a capability, with core technologies kept at home for reasons of strategic security as well as competence concentration. For different reasons, the global account team or international management development responsibility may be located centrally to facilitate top-management control over these key corporate resources.

Certain other resources may be concentrated but not necessarily at home—a configuration that might be termed "excentralization" rather then decentralization. World-scale production plants for labor-intensive products may be built in a low-wage country such as Mexico or Malaysia. The advanced state of a particular technology may demand concentration of relevant R&D resources and activities in Japan, Germany, or the United

States. Such flexible specialization—or excentralization—complements the benefits of scale economies with the flexibility of accessing low input costs or scarce resources and the responsiveness of accommodating national political interests. This approach can also apply to specific functional activities. For example, Sony relocated its treasury operations to London to improve its access to financial markets.

Some other resources may best be decentralized on a regional or local basis, because either potential economies of scale are small or there is a need to create flexibility by avoiding exclusive dependence on a single facility. Local or regional facilities may not only afford protection against exchange rate shifts, strikes, natural disasters, and other disruptions but also reduce logistical and coordination costs. An important side benefit provided by such facilities is the impact they can have in building the motivation and capability of national subsidiaries, an impact that can easily make small efficiency sacrifices worthwhile.

Table 3-3 summarizes the differences in the asset configurations that support the different strategic approaches of the various MNE models. We explore these strategy–organizational linkages in more detail in Chapter 4.

Worldwide Competitive Advantage: The Strategic Tasks

In the final part of this chapter, we look at how a company can respond to the strategic challenges we have described. The task will clearly be very different depending on the company's international posture and history. Companies that are among the major worldwide players in their businesses must focus on defending their dominance while also building new sources of advantage. For companies that are smaller but aspire to worldwide competitiveness, the task is one of building the resources and capabilities needed to challenge the entrenched leaders. For companies that are focused on their national markets and lack either the resources or the motivation for international expansion, the challenge is to protect their domestic positions from others that have the advantage of being MNEs.

Table 3-3 Strategic Orientation and Configuration of Assets and Capabilities in International, Multinational, Global, and Transnational Companies

	International	Multinational	Global	Transnational
Strategic orientation	Exploiting parent-company knowledge and capabilities through worldwide diffusion and adaptation	Building flexibility to respond to national differences through strong, resourceful, and entrepreneurial national operations	Building cost advantages through centralized, global-scale operations	Developing global efficiency, flexibility, and worldwide learning capability simultaneously
Configuration of assets and capabilities	Sources of core competencies centralized, others decentralized	Decentralized and nationally self-sufficient	Centralized and globally scaled	Dispersed, interdependent, and specialized

Defending Worldwide Dominance

Over the past decade or so, the shifting external forces we have described have resulted in severe difficulties—even for those MNEs that had enjoyed strong historical positions in their businesses worldwide.

Typically, most of these companies pursued traditional multinational, international, or global strategies, and their past successes were built on the fit between their specific strategic capability and the dominant environmental force in their industries. In multinational industries such as branded packaged products in which forces for national responsiveness were dominant, companies such as Unilever developed strong worldwide positions by adopting multinational strategies. In contrast, in global industries like consumer electronics or semiconductor chips, companies such as Matsushita or Hitachi built leadership positions by adopting global strategies.

In the emerging competitive environment, however, these companies could no longer rely on their historic ability to exploit global efficiency, multinational flexibility, or worldwide learning. As an increasing number of industries developed what we have termed transnational characteristics, companies faced the need to master all three strategic capabilities simultaneously.

The challenge for the leading companies was to protect and enhance the particular strength they had while simultaneously building the other capabilities.

For many MNEs, the initial response to this new strategic challenge was to try to restructure the configuration of their assets and activities to develop the capabilities they lacked. For example, global companies with highly centralized resources sought to develop flexibility by dispersing resources among their national subsidiaries; multinational companies, in contrast, tried to emulate their global competitors by centralizing R&D, manufacturing, and other scale-intensive activities. In essence, these companies tried to find a new "fit" configuration through drastic restructuring of their existing configuration.

Such a zero-based search for the ideal configuration not only led to external problems, such as conflict with host governments over issues like plant closures, but also resulted in a great deal of trauma inside the company's own organization. The greatest problem with such an approach, however, was that it tended to erode the particular competency the company already had without effectively adding the new strengths it sought.

The complex balancing act of protecting existing advantages while building new ones required companies to follow two fairly simple principles. First, they had to concentrate at least as much on defending and reinforcing their existing assets and capabilities as on developing new ones. Their approach tended to be one of building on—and eventually modifying—their existing infrastructure instead of radical restructuring. To the extent possible, they relied on modernizing existing facilities rather than dismantling the old and creating new ones.

Second, most successful adaptors looked for ways to compensate for their deficiency or approximate a competitor's source of advantage, rather than trying to imitate its asset structure or task configuration. In searching for efficiency, multinational companies with a decentralized and dispersed resource structure found it easier to develop efficiency by adopting new flexible manufacturing technologies in some of their existing plants and upgrading others to become global sources rather than to close those plants and shift production to lower-cost countries to match the structure of competitive global companies.

Similarly, successful global companies found it more effective to develop responsiveness and flexibility by creating internal linkages between their national sales subsidiaries and their centralized development or manufacturing units rather than trying to mimic multinational companies by dispersing their resources to each country operation and, in the process, undermining their core strength of efficiency.

Challenging the Global Leader

Over the past two decades, a number of companies have managed to evolve from relatively small national players to major worldwide competitors, challenging the dominance of traditional leaders in their businesses. Dell in the computer industry, Magna in auto parts, Electrolux in the domestic appliances business, and CEMEX in the cement industry are some examples of companies that have evolved from relative obscurity to global visibility within relatively short periods of time.

The actual processes adopted to manage such dramatic transformations vary widely from company to company. Electrolux, for example, grew almost exclusively through acquisitions, whereas Dell built capabilities largely through internal development, and Magna and CEMEX used a mix of greenfield investments and acquisitions. Similarly, whereas Dell built its growth on the basis of cost advantages and logistics capabilities, it expanded internationally because of its direct-sales business model and its ability to react quickly to changes in customer demand. Despite wide differences in their specific approaches, however, most of these new champions appear to have followed a similar step-by-step approach to building their competitive positions.

Each developed an initial toehold in the market by focusing on a narrow niche—often one specific product within one specific market—and developing a strong competitive position within that niche. That competitive position was built on multiple sources of competitive advantage rather than on a single strategic capability.

Next, they expanded their toehold to a foothold by limited and carefully selected expansion along both product and geographic dimensions and by extending the step-by-step improvement of both cost and quality to this expanded portfolio. Such expansion was typically focused on products and markets that were not of central importance to the established leaders in the business. By staying outside the range of the leaders' peripheral vision, the challenger could remain relatively invisible, thereby building up its strength and infrastructure without incurring direct retaliation from competitors with far greater resources. For example, emerging companies often focused initially on relatively low-margin products such as small-screen televisions or subcompact cars.

While developing their own product portfolio, technological capabilities, geographic scope, and marketing expertise, challengers were often able to build up manufacturing volume and its resulting cost efficiencies by becoming original equipment manufacturer suppliers to their larger competitors. Although this supply allowed the larger competitor to benefit from the challenger's cost advantages, it also developed the supplying company's understanding of customer needs and marketing strategies in the advanced markets served by the leading companies.

Once these building blocks for worldwide advantage were in place, the challenger typically moved rapidly to convert its low-profile foothold into a strong permanent position in the worldwide business. Dramatic scaling up of production facilities—increasing VCR capacity 30-fold in eight years as Matsushita did, or expanding computer production 20-fold in seven years as Acer did a decade later—typically preceded a wave of new product introductions and expansion into the key markets through multiple channels and their own brand names.

Protecting Domestic Niches

For reasons of resources or other constraints, some national companies may not be able to aspire to such worldwide expansion, though they are not insulated from the impact of global competition. Their major challenge is to protect their domestic niches from worldwide players with superior resources and multiple sources of competitive advantage.[5] This concern is particularly an issue in developing markets such as India and China, where local companies face much larger, more aggressive, and deeper-pocketed competitors.

There are three broad alternative courses of action that can be pursued by such national competitors. The first approach is to defend against the competitor's global advantage. Just as MNE managers can act to facilitate the globalization of industry structure, so their counterparts in national companies can use their influence in the opposite direction. An astute manager of a national company might be able to foil the attempts of a global competitor by taking action to influence industry structure or market conditions to the national company's advantage. These actions might involve influencing consumer preference to demand a more locally adapted or service-intensive product; it could imply tying up key distribution channels; or it might mean preempting local sources of critical supplies. Many companies trying to enter the Japanese market claim to have faced this type of defensive strategy by local firms.

A second strategic option would be to offset the competitor's global advantage. The simplest way to do this is to lobby for government assistance in the form of tariff protections. However, in an era of declining tariffs, this is increasingly unsuccessful. A more ambitious approach is to gain government sponsorship to develop equivalent global capabilities through funding of R&D, subsidizing exports, and financing capital investments. As a "national champion," the company would theoretically be able to compete globally. However, in reality, it is very unusual for such a company to prosper. Airbus Industrie, which now shares the global market for large commercial airplanes with Boeing, is one of the few exceptions—rising from the ashes of other attempts by European governments to sponsor a viable computer company in the 1970s and then to promote a European electronics industry a decade later.

The third alternative is to approximate the competitors' global advantages by linking up in some form of alliance or coalition with a viable global company. Numerous such linkages have been formed with the purpose of sharing the risks and costs of operating in a high-risk global environment. By pooling or exchanging market access, technology,

---

[5]For a detailed discussion of such strategies, see N. Dawar and T. Frost, "Competing with Giants: Survival Strategies for Local Companies Competing in Emerging Markets," *Harvard Business Review* 77, no. 2 (1999), pp. 119–30.

and production capability, smaller competitors can gain some measure of defense against global giants. For example, Siemens, ICL, and other small computer companies entered into agreements and joint projects with Fujitsu to enable them to maintain viability against the dominant transnational competitor, IBM. Similarly, the Indian telecom company Bharti has established a variety of inbound alliances with foreign firms such as Nortel Networks and Transcend Technologies to create a winning strategy for the Indian market.

Concluding Comments

Although these three strategic responses obviously do not cover every possible scenario, they highlight two important points from this chapter. First, the MNE faces a complex set of options in terms of the strategic levers it can pull to achieve competitive advantage, and the framework in Table 3-2 helps make sense of those options by separating out means and ends. Second, the competitive intensity in most industries is such that a company cannot just afford to plough its own furrow. Rather, it is necessary to gain competitive parity on all relevant dimensions (efficiency, flexibility, learning) while also achieving differentiation on one. To be sure, the ability to achieve multiple competitive objectives at the same time is far from straightforward, and as a result, we see many MNEs experimenting with new ways of organizing their worldwide activities. And this organization will be the core issue we will address in the next chapter.

Chapter 3 Readings

- In Reading 3-1, "Managing Differences: The Central Challenge of Global Strategy," Ghemawat introduces a framework to help managers think through their options. The three broad strategies available are: aggregation—achieving economies of scale by standardizing regional or global operations; adaptation—boosting market share by customizing processes and offerings to meet local markets' unique needs; and arbitrage—exploiting difference, by such activities as offshoring certain processes to countries with cheaper labor. Each strategy is considered against seven questions.

- In Reading 3-2, "How Local Companies Keep Multinationals at Bay," Bhattacharya and Michael explain the challenges for MNEs of competing with formidable local firms in emerging markets. They outline a six-part strategy used by these firms to fend off foreign MNEs (create customized products or services; develop business models to overcome key obstacles; deploy the latest technologies; take advantage of low-cost labor, and train staff in-house; scale up quickly; invest in talent to sustain rapid growth).

- In Reading 3-3, "Regional Strategies for Global Leadership," Ghemawat argues how regionally focused strategies, when used with local and global initiatives, can increase performance. He outlines five types of regional strategy (home base, portfolio, hub, platform, and mandate) and how they can be switched/combined as their businesses evolve.

As all three readings in this chapter demonstrate, there are a multitude of ways for MNEs to build competitive advantage. The appropriateness of each will evolve over time, yet the constant in a dynamic competitive environment is the need for the MNE to build, layer by layer, its capabilities.

Case 3-1   Marketing the "$100 Laptop" (A)

John A. Quelch and Carin-Isabel Knoop

In 2002, Professor Nicholas Negroponte, successful venture capitalist, author, and cofounder and chairman emeritus of the Massachusetts Institute of Technology (MIT) Media Lab,[1] announced his intention to build a personal computer so cheap as to make it possible to provide Internet- and multimedia-capable machines to millions of children in developing countries.[2] The concept—later referred to as the "$100 Laptop"[3]—was launched at the Media Lab in 2003 before being spun into a separate nonprofit association, One Laptop Per Child (OLPC), founded by Negroponte in January 2005.[4] The news made global headlines that conveyed a mixture of admiration and derision. OLPC's critics said Negroponte's $100 laptop could not be built.[5] Technology executives argued that such an extreme drop in price was impossible.[6] Intel Chairman Craig Barrett dismissed it as a "$100 gadget."[7]

Yet in 2005 Negroponte unveiled a working prototype of a $100 Laptop at the UN World Summit on the Information Society (see **Exhibit 1** for photos). The machine, which used freely available, open source Linux software as its operating system (OS), was the instant hit of the show.[8] Although aimed at primary school children (aged 6 to 12), other age groups could use it too. "People get it quickly, they sleep on it, and very often they wake up the next morning saying, 'Oh my god, this is a really big change,'" said Negroponte. "The appeal was obviously the price, and people realize that you can do one laptop per child. When it sinks in, they realize that you would not propose 'one pencil per classroom.'"[9]

In the two and a half years since the UN summit, technology companies including AMD (Advanced

▌ Professor John A. Quelch and Carin-Isabel Knoop, Executive Director, Global Research Group, prepared this case. This case was developed from published sources. The authors are grateful for the assistance of Global Research Group Research Associate Reed Martin. HBS cases are developed solely as the basis for class discussion. Cases are not intended to serve as endorsements, sources of primary data, or illustrations of effective or ineffective management.

▌ Harvard Business School Case No 9-508-024, Copyright 2007 President and Fellows of Harvard College. All rights reserved. *This case was prepared by J. Quelch. HBS Cases are developed solely for class discussion and do not necessarily illustrate either effective or ineffective handling of administrative situation.*

▌ [1]The MIT Media Lab was a $30 million research center dedicated to advancing multimedia design and implementation.
▌ [2]Stephen Leahy, "Laptops For Kids With No Power," *WIRED*, June 6, 2005, www.wired.com, accessed January 10, 2007.
▌ [3]Douglas McGray, "The Laptop Crusade," *WIRED*, August 2006, www.wired.com, accessed January 10, 2007.
▌ [4]James Surowiecki, "Philanthropy's New Prototype," *Technology Review*, November 13, 2006, www.technologyreview.com/Biztech/17722/, accessed January 10, 2007.
▌ [5]McGray.

Exhibit 1   Early $100 Laptop Prototype

Source: OLPC, http://www.laptop.org/download.en_US.html, accessed June 23, 2007.

▌ [6]Kathrin Hille, "The race for the $100 laptop," *Financial Times*, April 9, 2007.
▌ [7]Jonathan Fildes, "$100 laptop production begins," BBC News, http://news.bbc.co.uk/2/hi/technology/6908946.stm, accessed July 30, 2007.
▌ [8]Kevin Poulsen, "Negroponte: Laptop for Every Kid," *WIRED*, November 17, 2005, www.wired.com, accessed January 10, 2007.
▌ [9]Poulsen.

Micro Devices), Google, Red Hat, and News Corp., had given at least $29 million to fund the project[10] (including $16.5 million in 2006)[11] and had pledged additional monies and technical expertise for the future.[12] OLPC had worked hard to sell its concept to the world's education ministries. Negroponte had set a self-imposed minimum of five million laptop orders before production could commence.[13] In 2006, OLPC had received purchase orders (but no deposits) for six million laptops (at $175 a piece) from education ministries in China, Brazil, and other countries. Making the sale had not been easy, even though OLPC machines cost less than half the normal price of an entry-level computer, and weighed half as much with double the operating battery time as comparable laptops.[14] Quick production had also been assured: Quanta, a large Taiwanese laptop maker, was ready to produce a million laptops per month by the end of 2007, an impressive number given that global laptop production was only 5 million units per month.[15] Finally, OLPC intended to offer local schools around the world a $100 server filled with 200 gigabytes of educational material that students could access remotely.[16] Participating governments could purchase solar, foot-pump, or pull-string chargers for the laptop.

Nevertheless, as of mid-2007, commitments had yet to be finalized.[17] "It's a big check to write," Negroponte conceded. "Nations are being asked to invest in the laptop one million at a time. That's $175 million for the machines alone, at current pricing, plus money for distribution and Internet provision—the actual price tag could be closer to $200 million to $250 million."[18] Only when the project scaled up,

however, would the price drop, possibly to $100 per unit in 2009 and $50 per unit in the next decade.

In the meantime, the computer industry was changing. New entrants and incumbents such as Intel had launched very low-cost machines for individual sale. Intel, an early and vocal critic of OLPC, had launched its $285 Classmate PC in May 2006. In 2007 Dell launched a desktop computer in China at a retail price of $336, which was 60% lower than its previously cheapest offering.[19] Further, major computer makers had begun to target the "next billion," a swath of poorer consumers whose access to PCs had so far been precluded by high prices and poor access to electricity. The OLPC had proven that PCs could be made significantly cheaper with an open source OS, a cheaper liquid crystal display, and by omitting the hard drive. Given the evolving competitive landscape, however, observers wondered if the time had come for the OLPC to rethink its strategy and mission.

▌ Computers in the Classroom[20]

The Idea   In 1999, Negroponte had seen the power of laptops firsthand at a rural village school that he and his wife established in Cambodia. There, children used rugged Panasonic "Toughbook" laptops equipped with Wi-Fi Internet capability via a satellite link.[21] "A village that had no books suddenly had access to Google," recalled Negroponte. "It changed their lives in several ways, improving self-esteem and empowerment and fulfilling the passion for learning."[22] The laptops made school more popular and drew appreciation from parents as well, since, in a village with no electricity, the laptop became the brightest light source in the house. "Talk about a metaphor and a reality simultaneously," Negroponte reflected, "It just illuminated that household."[23]

---

[10]"Low-Cost Laptop Could Transform Learning," January 3, 2007, *AFX Asia*, via Factiva, accessed January 8, 2007.

[11]Steve Stecklow, "A little laptop with big ambitions," *The Wall Street Journal*, November 24, 2007, via Factiva, July 10, 2008.

[12]Leahy.

[13]McGray.

[14]"A computer in every pot," *Economist*, July 27, 2007.

[15]Ethan Zuckerman, "An Update on OLPC from Dr. Negroponte," *Worldchanging*, June 1, 2007, http://www. worldchanging.com/archives/006798.html, accessed June 28, 2007.

[16]McGray.

[17]Leahy.

[18]Zuckerman.

[19]Hille.

[20]This section draws on Douglas MacMillan, "A Laptop at Every Desk," *BusinessWeek*, September 20, 2006, via Factiva, accessed January 20, 2007.

[21]Leahy.

[22]Leahy.

[23]Lesley Stahl, "What if Every Child Had a Laptop," *60 Minutes on the Web*, May 20, 2007, http://www.cbsnews.com/stories/2007/05/20/60minutes/main2830058.shtml, accessed August 10, 2007.

Exhibit 2   The "PC Adoption Pyramid" and Worldwide PC Adoption, 2003–2015

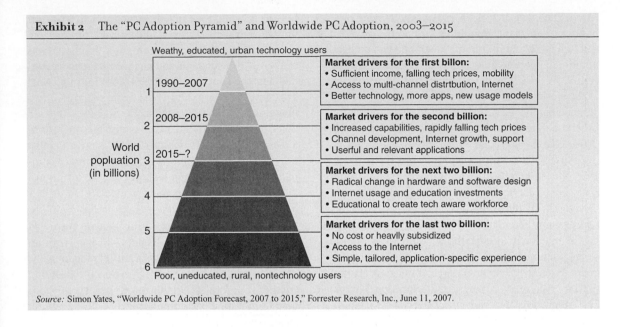

Source: Simon Yates, "Worldwide PC Adoption Forecast, 2007 to 2015," Forrester Research, Inc., June 11, 2007.

That visit prompted the idea of designing a basic laptop model that would link people in developing countries to the world.

At the time, most computers were used in the developed world. By 2003 there were about 496 million PCs in use in the largest 67 countries in the world, with 178 million in the U.S. followed by Japan (45 million), Germany (27 million), and the U.K. (22 million). By the end of 2006, the total number of PCs in use had risen to more than 755 million. While experts estimated that PC usage worldwide would exceed 1 billion in 2008 and double by 2015, the bulk of the growth was expected to come from countries such as Brazil, Russia, India, and China (BRIC), accounting for the more than 800 million new PCs by 2015, and other emerging economies as incomes rose and telecom infrastructures improved.[24] (See **Exhibits 2** and **3** for worldwide forecasts.)

Critics charged that Negroponte's concept would require high-speed fiber-optic T1 lines to run through the center of villages struggling with basic necessities.[25] Negroponte's lead designer, Yves Behar, believed these critics imagined the entire developing world as a string of famine-stricken villages in Africa.[26] "This was the typical ignorance of the West," Behar said. "There are different conditions in different places, and there are a lot of places where kids are not starving, where kids want to learn more than anything else."[27] Supporters of the $100 Laptop initiative seconded this observation, warning against the erroneous assumption that technology was something that only wealthy nations could afford, or that poorer nations were better off concentrating on more basic challenges, such as improving health and providing clean water.[28] The United Nations 2006 Millennium Development Goals report estimated that 1.9 billion children were under the age of 18 (compared with 206 million in the developed world) and that 22% of them lived in households that subsisted on $1 per day or less. One in three of these children lacked access to

[24]Simon Yates, "Worldwide PC Adoption Forecast, 2007 to 2015," Forrester Research, Inc., June 11, 2007.

[25]McGray.

[26]McGray.

[27]McGray.

[28]Surowiecki.

Exhibit 3   Forecasts for PC Adoption in Select Regions (2003–2015)

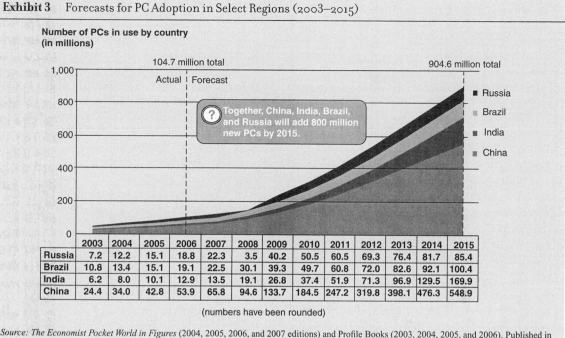

Number of PCs in use by country (in millions)

	2003	2004	2005	2006	2007	2008	2009	2010	2011	2012	2013	2014	2015
Russia	7.2	12.2	15.1	18.8	22.3	3.5	40.2	50.5	60.5	69.3	76.4	81.7	85.4
Brazil	10.8	13.4	15.1	19.1	22.5	30.1	39.3	49.7	60.8	72.0	82.6	92.1	100.4
India	6.2	8.0	10.1	12.9	13.5	19.1	26.8	37.4	51.9	71.3	96.9	129.5	169.9
China	24.4	34.0	42.8	53.9	65.8	94.6	133.7	184.5	247.2	319.8	398.1	476.3	548.9

(numbers have been rounded)

Source: The Economist Pocket World in Figures (2004, 2005, 2006, and 2007 editions) and Profile Books (2003, 2004, 2005, and 2006). Published in Simon Yates, "Worldwide PC Adoption Forecast, 2007 to 2015," Forrester Research, Inc., June 11, 2007.

adequate shelter, one in five had no access to safe drinking water, and one in seven had no access to health services. Although Negroponte saw notebook computers as an educational tool that might eventually alleviate world poverty, critics maintained that achieving such a goal would require far more than inexpensive computers.[29]

The U.S. Experience   The idea that technology could serve as a catalyst for education was not new. "One-to-one" school programs that provided each student with a computer had initially garnered support in 1991 in Australia, where several schools purchased enough PCs to match enrollment.[30] In the U.S. in September 2002, the state of Maine's Department of Education launched The Maine Learning Technology Initiative, a program designed to give every seventh- and eighth-grade public school

child and teacher an Apple iBook laptop. The program was built on the principle that educational transformation occurred through the use of technology by students and teachers on a one-to-one basis.[31] Michigan, New Hampshire, Pennsylvania, and New Mexico instituted laptop programs similar to Maine's, and several other school boards across the U.S. were considering their own laptop initiatives.[32]

In 2006, about 13 million computers served 49.5 million students attending public schools in the U.S.[33] Some companies sought to take technological integration in the classroom even further. In 2006 Dell experimented with a program it called "Intelligent Classrooms," which delivered to schools a $40,000 package of technologies including wireless Internet and electronic whiteboards built around a

[29]Leahy.
[30]MacMillan.

[31]Maine Learning Technology Initiative, "About MLTI," Maine Learning Technology Initiative website, http://www.maine .gov/mlti/about/index.htm, accessed June 18, 2007.
[32]Leahy.
[33]MacMillan.

Exhibit 3　APAC[a] PC Adoption, 2003–2015 (continued)

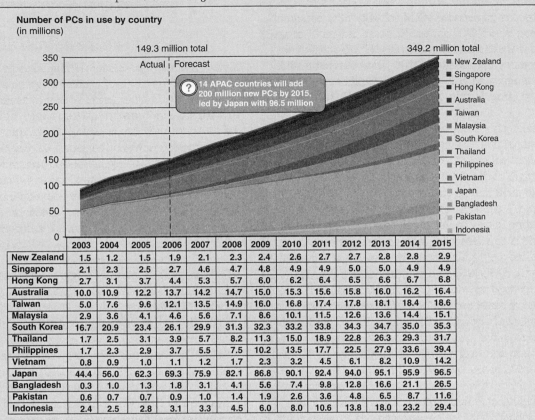

Number of PCs in use by country
(in millions)

149.3 million total

349.2 million total

Actual | Forecast

14 APAC countries will add 200 million new PCs by 2015, led by Japan with 96.5 million

Legend: New Zealand, Singapore, Hong Kong, Australia, Taiwan, Malaysia, South Korea, Thailand, Philippines, Vietnam, Japan, Bangladesh, Pakistan, Indonesia

	2003	2004	2005	2006	2007	2008	2009	2010	2011	2012	2013	2014	2015
New Zealand	1.5	1.2	1.5	1.9	2.1	2.3	2.4	2.6	2.7	2.7	2.8	2.8	2.9
Singapore	2.1	2.3	2.5	2.7	4.6	4.7	4.8	4.9	4.9	5.0	5.0	4.9	4.9
Hong Kong	2.7	3.1	3.7	4.4	5.3	5.7	6.0	6.2	6.4	6.5	6.6	6.7	6.8
Australia	10.0	10.9	12.2	13.7	14.2	14.7	15.0	15.3	15.6	15.8	16.0	16.2	16.4
Taiwan	5.0	7.6	9.6	12.1	13.5	14.9	16.0	16.8	17.4	17.8	18.1	18.4	18.6
Malaysia	2.9	3.6	4.1	4.6	5.6	7.1	8.6	10.1	11.5	12.6	13.6	14.4	15.1
South Korea	16.7	20.9	23.4	26.1	29.9	31.3	32.3	33.2	33.8	34.3	34.7	35.0	35.3
Thailand	1.7	2.5	3.1	3.9	5.7	8.2	11.3	15.0	18.9	22.8	26.3	29.3	31.7
Philippines	1.7	2.3	2.9	3.7	5.5	7.5	10.2	13.5	17.7	22.5	27.9	33.6	39.4
Vietnam	0.8	0.9	1.0	1.1	1.2	1.7	2.3	3.2	4.5	6.1	8.2	10.9	14.2
Japan	44.4	56.0	62.3	69.3	75.9	82.1	86.8	90.1	92.4	94.0	95.1	95.9	96.5
Bangladesh	0.3	1.0	1.3	1.8	3.1	4.1	5.6	7.4	9.8	12.8	16.6	21.1	26.5
Pakistan	0.6	0.7	0.7	0.9	1.0	1.4	1.9	2.6	3.6	4.8	6.5	8.7	11.6
Indonesia	2.4	2.5	2.8	3.1	3.3	4.5	6.0	8.0	10.6	13.8	18.0	23.2	29.4

Source: The Economist Pocket World in Figures (2004, 2005, 2006, and 2007 editions) and Profile Books (2003, 2004, 2005, and 2006). Published in Simon Yates, "Worldwide PC Adoption Forecast, 2007 to 2015," Forrester Research, Inc., June 11, 2007.
[a]Asian Pacific.

specific subject, such as math, science, or English.[34] However, studies showed that laptops boosted student test scores only when teachers were trained to use the machines in their teaching plans.[35] "We've been working now with computers and education for 30 years," Negroponte explained, "with computers in developing countries for 20 years, and trying to make low-cost machines for 10 years. This was not a sudden turn down the road. What put us over the edge was that it [became] possible to do it."[36]

[34]MacMillan.
[35]"Laptops: Easy Fix For Global Education?" *The Christian Science Monitor*, January 5, 2007, via Factiva, accessed February 5, 2007.
[36]Poulsen.

Making It Possible

Design Challenges From the onset, the $100 Laptop's parameters of low-cost, lightweight, and modern seemed contradictory, since lightweight, ultra-thin laptops were typically more expensive and harder to manufacture than heavier and bulkier models. For example, the Toshiba Protégé 2000, three-quarters of an inch thick and 3.25 pounds, was priced at $2,199 in an era when most standard laptops cost $600 to $1,200. The more powerful and compact Sony Vaio PC UX Premium Series VGN-UX390N weighed 1.2 pounds but cost $2,500.

Negroponte and his team set up a website to provide extensive details on the laptop's

Exhibit 3   Eastern European PC Adoption, 2003–2015 (continued)

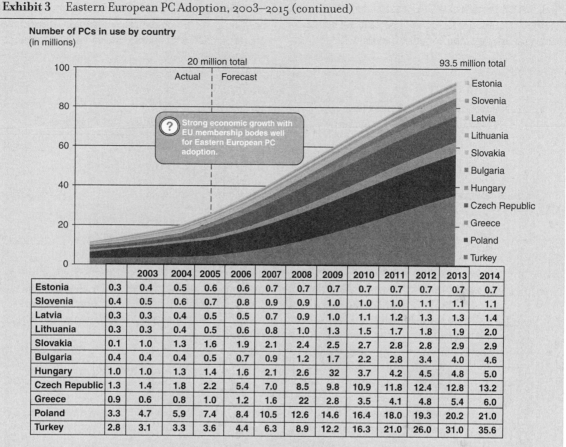

Number of PCs in use by country
(in millions)

	2003	2004	2005	2006	2007	2008	2009	2010	2011	2012	2013	2014
Estonia	0.3	0.4	0.5	0.6	0.6	0.7	0.7	0.7	0.7	0.7	0.7	0.7
Slovenia	0.4	0.5	0.6	0.7	0.8	0.9	0.9	1.0	1.0	1.1	1.1	1.1
Latvia	0.3	0.3	0.4	0.5	0.5	0.7	0.9	1.0	1.1	1.2	1.3	1.3	1.4
Lithuania	0.3	0.3	0.4	0.5	0.6	0.8	1.0	1.3	1.5	1.7	1.8	1.9	2.0
Slovakia	0.1	1.0	1.3	1.6	1.9	2.1	2.4	2.5	2.7	2.8	2.8	2.9	2.9
Bulgaria	0.4	0.4	0.4	0.5	0.7	0.9	1.2	1.7	2.2	2.8	3.4	4.0	4.6
Hungary	1.0	1.0	1.3	1.4	1.6	2.1	2.6	32	3.7	4.2	4.5	4.8	5.0
Czech Republic	1.3	1.4	1.8	2.2	5.4	7.0	8.5	9.8	10.9	11.8	12.4	12.8	13.2
Greece	0.9	0.6	0.8	1.0	1.2	1.6	22	2.8	3.5	4.1	4.8	5.4	6.0
Poland	3.3	4.7	5.9	7.4	8.4	10.5	12.6	14.6	16.4	18.0	19.3	20.2	21.0
Turkey	2.8	3.1	3.3	3.6	4.4	6.3	8.9	12.2	16.3	21.0	26.0	31.0	35.6

Source: The Economist Pocket World in Figures (2004, 2005, 2006, and 2007 editions) and Profile Books (2003, 2004, 2005, and 2006). Published in Simon Yates, "Worldwide PC Adoption Forecast, 2007 to 2015," Forrester Research, Inc., June 11, 2007.

specifications and goals and to report on the latest developments. The website became a home for breakthrough ideas as well as searing skepticism. MIT media lab staffers, suppliers, and volunteers managed the site. "There would be no way to launch and ramp in any way other than open and viral," Negroponte explained. "A command and control model, the way one runs an army, is not well suited for new ideas."[37] The challenge was significant.

Major design contributions came from Hawaii but also from Argentina, Brazil, China, Italy, Israel, and Taiwan. The key user interface was designed in Milan. Key parts of the operating system were developed in Brazil. "It is breaking all the rules of designing something," remarked OLPC's chief technology officer, Mary Lou Jepsen, a former director of technology development at Intel's Display Division. "And it's working better and faster than anything I've ever worked on."[38]

[37]Jonathan Fahey, "The Soul of the New Laptop," *Forbes*, May 7, 2007.

[38]Fahey.

Exhibit 3   Middle East and African PC Adoption, 2003–2015 (continued)

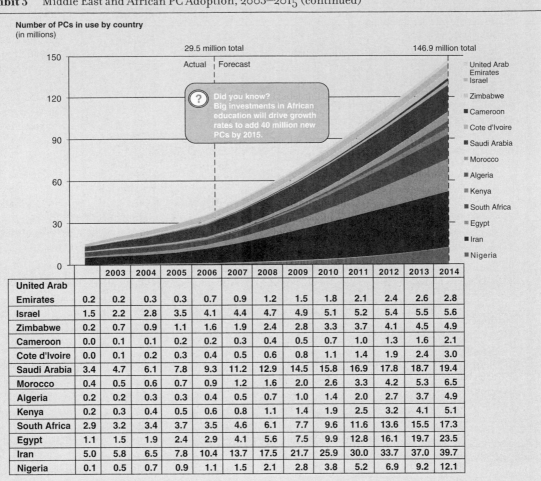

Number of PCs in use by country (in millions)

United Arab	2003	2004	2005	2006	2007	2008	2009	2010	2011	2012	2013	2014
Emirates	0.2	0.2	0.3	0.3	0.7	0.9	1.2	1.5	1.8	2.1	2.4	2.6	2.8
Israel	1.5	2.2	2.8	3.5	4.1	4.4	4.7	4.9	5.1	5.2	5.4	5.5	5.6
Zimbabwe	0.2	0.7	0.9	1.1	1.6	1.9	2.4	2.8	3.3	3.7	4.1	4.5	4.9
Cameroon	0.0	0.1	0.1	0.2	0.2	0.3	0.4	0.5	0.7	1.0	1.3	1.6	2.1
Cote d'Ivoire	0.0	0.1	0.2	0.3	0.4	0.5	0.6	0.8	1.1	1.4	1.9	2.4	3.0
Saudi Arabia	3.4	4.7	6.1	7.8	9.3	11.2	12.9	14.5	15.8	16.9	17.8	18.7	19.4
Morocco	0.4	0.5	0.6	0.7	0.9	1.2	1.6	2.0	2.6	3.3	4.2	5.3	6.5
Algeria	0.2	0.2	0.3	0.3	0.4	0.5	0.7	1.0	1.4	2.0	2.7	3.7	4.9
Kenya	0.2	0.3	0.4	0.5	0.6	0.8	1.1	1.4	1.9	2.5	3.2	4.1	5.1
South Africa	2.9	3.2	3.4	3.7	3.5	4.6	6.1	7.7	9.6	11.6	13.6	15.5	17.3
Egypt	1.1	1.5	1.9	2.4	2.9	4.1	5.6	7.5	9.9	12.8	16.1	19.7	23.5
Iran	5.0	5.8	6.5	7.8	10.4	13.7	17.5	21.7	25.9	30.0	33.7	37.0	39.7
Nigeria	0.1	0.5	0.7	0.9	1.1	1.5	2.1	2.8	3.8	5.2	6.9	9.2	12.1

Source: The Economist Pocket World in Figures (2004, 2005, 2006, and 2007 editions) and Profile Books (2003, 2004, 2005, and 2006). Published in Simon Yates, "Worldwide PC Adoption Forecast, 2007 to 2015," Forrester Research, Inc., June 11, 2007.

Given the fact that most of the children using $100 Laptops would not have ready access to electricity, power generation presented a major design hurdle. The MIT team explored both solar and windup mechanisms and had hoped to rely on a so-called "parasitic power," or the ability to power the laptop simply by typing on the keys.[39] Ultimately they settled on the hand-crank. Although Behar's team planned to put the crank directly onto the machine, engineers soon realized that cranking the handle shook the machine and put stress on the hardware.[40]

The early OLPC computers were made of green and white plastic with seven-inch screens that swiveled like tablet PCs. Power was provided by rotating the computer's electricity-generating crank,

[39]Leahy.

[40]McGray.

resulting in 40 minutes of power for each minute of turning. Built-in Wi-Fi connectivity allowed the $100 Laptops to create their own mini-network, letting users collaborate with each other on screen or communicate via voice through each laptop's microphone and speaker system.[41] Indeed, a couple of wireless antennas rising up from the screen's sides gave the laptop two to three times the normal Wi-Fi range, making each laptop a router as well as its own communication device. Children could create a mini-network of machines up to 10 miles apart without satellites or cellular towers.[42] Each laptop became part of a "wireless mesh" which relayed the broadband signal from laptop to laptop and enabled out-of-range machines to connect to the Internet.[43]

The original working prototype of the $100 Laptop was faulted for trying to look like something for business but colored for kids. "Too many parts were flapping around, too many open places," Behar recalled. "It wasn't realistic. It should have been compact and sealed, like a suitcase. And it should really look and feel different."[44] "It's sort of a cheap plastic look right now which is only because of the prototype nature," Negroponte told journalists at the time. "Future models will be more rugged and have a tougher outer shell."[45] In the end, the computer fit in a tiny white plastic briefcase that could resist a rainstorm. Its keyboard had a waterproof rubber coating and the case was sealed to keep dust out. Folded down, the laptop's Wi-Fi antennas locked the case and sealed off its ports. To make it even more rugged, the design team avoided any rotating parts.

Because the effort to create the $100 Laptop was followed closely in the consumer electronics press, every design misstep was reported, leading to an uncommonly public R&D period in which the OLPC's diverse and demanding client base could participate.[46]

Negroponte relayed feedback from governments around the world, trading e-mails about the design with Behar.[47] "The Brazilians wanted a bigger display, and we did that," Negroponte recalled. "The Thais wanted a taller touch tablet, big enough so kids could write on it in tall Thai script—and we did that."[48]

A key to building the PC cheaply was its innovative, low-power LCD screen, a Jepsen invention that also included a built-in camera.[49] She also found a way to cut each screen's manufacturing cost to $40 while reducing its power consumption by more than 80%, two advances that allowed OLPC to win over many initial skeptics.[50] To save power, the laptop's liquid-crystal display (the component that consumed the most power) could be flipped from backlit color to self-reflecting monochrome to save electricity but also make the screen more visible in direct sunlight. The choice of the computer's processor, the AMD Geode, was also driven by the need to economize on power consumption. It ran at 433 megahertz, compared with the 2–3 gigahertz of conventional laptops. Furthermore, using less power meant generating less heat, obviating the need for a power-consuming cooling fan. Finally, the laptop had a 1 gigabyte flash drive and USB 2.0 ports to which additional storage could be attached, and it had built-in speakers.[51]

Breaking the Wintel Paradigm   Through OLPC, Negroponte hoped to cast off the "Wintel" paradigm of Intel-based processors running Microsoft's Windows software, and in so doing, to reinvent the PC with a simpler and more intuitive user interface for children.[52] The OLPC machines were potentially the first computers that many children would ever experience. This was liberating to Negroponte's design team, since their end users would not be prejudiced about what PCs should be like, enabling them to

[41]Poulsen.

[42]McGray.

[43]"A computer in every pot," *The Economist*, July 27, 2007.

[44]McGray.

[45]"Negroponte OLPC and Intel," *Exclusivo Domino Digital TV*, November 29, 2006, http://www.youtube.com/watch?v= HK90TnOQE0E, accessed January 21, 2007.

[46]McGray.

[47]McGray.

[48]McGray.

[49]"$150 Laptop To Offer Unusual Interface," *AFX Asia*, January 1, 2007, via Factiva, accessed January 8, 2007.

[50]Markoff.

[51]"Low-Cost Laptop Could Transform Learning," January 3, 2007, *AFX Asia*, via Factiva, accessed January 8, 2007.

[52]"$150 Laptop To Offer Unusual Interface," *AFX Asia*, January 1, 2007, via Factiva, accessed January 8, 2007.

employ a stripped-down, simplified interface, colorful and accessible.[53] "Seventy-five percent of your laptop is used just to support the OS and the obesity of the software in it," said Negroponte. "It's like a fat person using their energy to move their weight. I am not picking on Microsoft any more than Adobe or *any* piece of software. It's *outrageous*. People keep adding features and features and features and [in the end], these features cost us."[54]

While some critics believed that an alternative interface would underscore the digital divide between developed and developing nations, and that a facility with Microsoft Office was a requirement of many standardized jobs, Negroponte specifically sought to shield children from the limitations of Microsoft's suite of software.[55] "One of the saddest but most common conditions in elementary school computer labs, when they exist in the developing world, is where children are being trained to use Word, Excel and PowerPoint," Negroponte said. "I consider that criminal, because children should be making things, communicating, exploring, sharing, not running office automation tools!"[56] "We do not focus on computer literacy," the OLPC website explained, "as that is a by-product of the fluency children will gain through use of the laptop for learning."[57] Negroponte explained further: "Giving the kids a programming environment of any sort, whether it's a tool like Squeak or Scratch or Logo to write programs in a childish way—and I mean that in the most generous sense of the word, that is, playing with and building things—is one of the best ways to learn. Particularly to learn about thinking and algorithms and problem solving and so forth."[58]

As a result of Negroponte's vision, the $100 Laptops would come equipped with a completely new OS, organized around a "journal," instead of a legacy paradigm that focused on storage folders. The OS, dubbed "XO" (which evoked the acronym for Operating System (OS) but was also a symbol for kisses (X) and hugs (O) in the U.S.) would automatically generate a log of every file or document created by each user on the laptop.[59] Students could then review their journals to see their work and retrieve files created or altered during each session.[60] In contrast, the folders system used by Windows forced users to remember where they stored their information rather than what they did with it.[61] Initially, students turning on XO-based computers would be greeted by a basic home screen with a stick-figure icon at the center, surrounded by a white ring.[62] (Its creators bristled at the suggestion that the XO operating system made the $100 Laptop a toy.) The $100 Laptop would run a range of programs, including a Web browser, a word processor, and an RSS reader that delivered Internet blog updates.[63]

Red Hat, the world's largest Linux distributor, had provided an extremely compact version of its Fedora operating system, called Sugar, that used only 130 megabytes of the XO's flash memory (Windows XP required 1.65 gigabytes). Sugar organized everything on a user's computer around what had been used recently. Alternatively, it could group applications and files in terms of who was connected on the wireless mesh, providing an array of collaborative tools.[64]

Production   One of Behar's first decisions was to position all of the computer's components behind the display, instead of putting them beneath the keyboard as in most traditional laptops such as Lenovo's ThinkPad. This configuration allowed the device to be folded into a flat "e-book" mode; it also cut

[53]"Low-Cost Laptop Could Transform Learning," January 3, 2007, *AFX Asia*, via Factiva, accessed January 8, 2007.

[54]"$100 Laptop . . . Billion-Dollar Idea," video, eSNTV, accessible from Dennis Pierce, "Educators Salute $100 laptop's architect," *eSchool News Online*, July 7, 2006, http://www.eschoolnews.com/news/showStory.cfm?ArticleID=6425, accessed February 15, 2007. Also available at http://www.youtube.com/watch?v=UvpP3Farb2g.

[55]"Low-Cost Laptop Could Transform Learning," January 3, 2007, *AFX Asia*, via Factiva, accessed January 8, 2007.

[56]Ibid.

[57]For more details, see http://wiki.laptop.org/go/One_Laptop_per_Child, accessed June 14, 2007.

[58]Poulsen.

[59]"$150 Laptop To Offer Unusual Interface," *AFX Asia*, January 1, 2007, via Factiva, accessed January 8, 2007.

[60]Ibid.

[61]Ibid.

[62]Ibid.

[63]Ibid.

[64]"A computer in every pot," *Economist*, July 27, 2007.

production costs and simplified the wiring, but made the machine somewhat top-heavy.[65]

While more established technology firms had well-established supply chains and manufacturing operations around the world, OLPC was starting from scratch. To build the machines, OLPC turned to OEMs. "The process of building the computers, however, was complex. It doesn't just go from zero to one million units overnight," Negroponte underlined.[66] The final design brought together more than 800 parts from multiple suppliers.[67] "The manufacturers were the toughest audience," recalled Jepsen.[68]

Ultimately, the machines would be made by Quanta Computer Inc., the Taiwanese manufacturer that in 2006 made roughly a third of the world's laptops.[69] In 2005, Quanta manufactured 18.4 million laptops for brands such as Dell, Hewlett-Packard, Lenovo Group and Acer.[70] The $100 Laptop project was a risky venture for Quanta since it would not make its normal unit margin, given that each machine would have to be designed to withstand heavy use and to interface in the language of the country of destination.[71] Quanta expected to test the prototypes by dropping them from various heights, exposing them to extreme heat and humidity, soiling them, and pounding on keyboards.[72] For example, while typical laptops were only tested to 35°C (95°F) or 40°C (104°F), unacceptable for children using laptops in hot climates (as well as direct sunlight and without air conditioning), the OLPC computer was tested to sustain 52°C (125°F) during the day.[73] Furthermore, OLPC continually innovated. In March 2007, OLPC began testing Lithium Iron Phosphate battery (LiPeFo4) technology. The battery was praised

for being less toxic and more cost-effective.[74] OLPC's partners made plans to build a factory specifically to produce the LiPeFo4 batteries.

Selling the Concept

In OLPC's early stages, the "$100 Laptop" label was a misnomer; Negroponte had predicted an initial cost closer to $150 per machine, although he expected the price to fall as more units were produced.[75] By November 2006, Negroponte said the $100 Laptop's manufacturing cost was below $150 and that it would fall below $100 by the end of 2008.[76] Negroponte believed that even the poorest country could afford "about $200 per year per child." OLPC had estimated that a connected, unlimited Internet-access $100 laptop would cost about $30 to own and run per year. "That has got to be the very best investment you can make," he believed. "Period."[77]

Furthermore, "each school year you should have something new that lowers the price," Negroponte noted.[78] Based on a $10 per unit margin for OLPC, only 20 full-time OLPC employees,[79] and Negroponte's own target of 100 million laptop sales, the $100 Laptop initiative was often referred to as Negroponte's "billion-dollar idea."[80] "Getting to $100 is not magic," Negroponte explained in 2006, continuing:

> 50% of the cost of your laptop is sales, marketing, distribution, and profit, and that's not unique to laptops. That's true for cellphones . . . PDAs, almost all consumer electronics. And in fact, in the case of laptops, depending on which one you have, it could be as high as 60%. We have none of those . . . When it pops out

[65]McGray.

[66]Poulsen.

[67]Fildes.

[68]Poulsen.

[69]Surowiecki.

[70]Jason Dean, "The Laptop Trail," *The Wall Street Journal*, June 9, 2005, via Factiva, accessed September 8, 2008.

[71]Dean.

[72]"One Laptop Per Child Hits Milestone," *Wireless News*, November 26, 2006, via Factiva, accessed January 23, 2007.

[73]For more details, see http://wiki.laptop.org/go/News, accessed June 14, 2007.

[74]Eric Lai, "OLPC eyes experimental battery for $100 laptop," *Computer World Hardware*, March 29, 2007, http://wiki.laptop.org/images/0/0a/OLPC_eyes_experimental_battery_for_%24100_laptop.pdf, accessed June 6, 2007.

[75]Surowiecki.

[76]John Markoff, "U.S. Group Reaches Deal to Provide Laptops to All Libyan Schoolchildren," *The New York Times*, October 11, 2006, via Factiva, accessed September 8, 2008.

[77]Surowiecki.

[78]"Negroponte OLPC and Intel," *Exclusivo Domino Digital TV*, November 29, 2006, http://www.youtube.com/watch?v=HK90TnOQE0E, accessed January 21, 2007.

[79]Stecklow.

[80]MacMillan.

of the box, it's not going to be $100, it's going to be $138, $137, $142, who knows? The important thing is, the price floats. . . . It's like a spot market for laptops. And the reason the price floats is [because of] currency changes, memory cost float, nickel [pricing]. Our batteries are nickel-metal hydride [and we need] 100 million batteries . . . The price of nickel went up 20% between April and May [of 2006.] So clearly, those things float the price [but] we will guarantee that it [the price per unit] will keep going down. Our target is to hit $100 by the end of 2008 and to hit $50 by 2010. So that's actually more important—it's the slope, not the out-of-the-gate price. And what we promise *not* to do is to keep adding features. We're going to keep the features constant and watch the [production] price go down.[81]

However, convincing the developing country governments that acquiring OLPC machines was indeed "the very best investment" they could ever make had proven challenging. "Governments are hard [to negotiate with]," Negroponte explained, "large governments are harder, [and] ministries of education are harder still."[82] The process required lobbying relevant officials in nations with large and fickle bureaucracies.[83] Governments or donors were expected to buy individual laptops for children to own, as well as the associated server equipment to be kept in schools. There had been some false starts. India's government, for example, had originally expressed interest in the $100 Laptop but later backed out, opting instead to put its resources toward traditional methods of education.[84]

Despite the challenges, some observers believed that selling products to larger, institutional clients could be easier for a nonprofit organization such as OLPC whose motives might not be questioned.[85] "Bringing the idea to national leaders had been easy, partly because I know some of them, or they know me," explained Negroponte. "It's almost easier for me to get in the door than Michael Dell, or Steve Jobs, or Bill Gates, even though they're more famous, richer or more important. It's easier for me to get in because I'm not selling something."[86]

Technology and Emerging Markets

Despite best intentions and innovative technology, the success of the $100 Laptop was far from guaranteed, as demonstrated by the checkered history of technology introductions to emerging markets.[87] With cell phones, for example, despite rapid subscriber growth, pricing had long remained a concern, and was seen by some as the biggest obstacle to broader adoption. Investcom, which ran cell phone networks in Africa and the Middle East, estimated that the number of users would double in those markets if the cheapest handset were priced at $30 instead of $60.[88] Lower handset prices would build subscriptions in developing regions, where prohibitively high hardware costs were blamed for low adoption rates in areas where network coverage was available.[89]

In early 2006, as part of a program to facilitate economic growth in developing nations, the GSM Association (GSMA), a lobbying group made up of hundreds of wireless service providers who sought to make GSM the world's dominant mobile phone standard, sponsored a bid to develop a handset that would wholesale below $40, including follow-up shipments of sub-$30 handsets, with the ultimate goal of attracting 100 million new users.[90] Motorola won the contract.[91] Even though the handsets' low

[81]"$100 Laptop . . . Billion-Dollar Idea," video, eSNTV, available from Dennis Pierce, "Educators Salute $100 laptop's architect," *eSchool News Online*, July 7, 2006.

[82]Surowiecki.

[83]Surowiecki.

[84]"Encore Set To Bag Brazilian Laptop Order," *Economic Times*, December 19, 2006, via Factiva, accessed January 15, 2007.

[85]Surowiecki.

[86]Kevin Poulsen, "Negroponte: Laptop for Every Kid," *WIRED*, November 17, 2005, at www.wired.com, accessed January 10, 2007.

[87]"Laptops: Easy Fix For Global Education?" *The Christian Science Monitor*, January 5, 2007, via Factiva, accessed February 5, 2007.

[88]"Calling An End To Poverty," *Economist*, July 9, 2005, via Factiva, accessed on January 18, 2007.

[89]For more details, see Susmita Dasgupta, Somic Lall and David Wheeler, "Policy Reform, Economic Growth and the Digital Divide," *Oxford Development Studies*, Volume 33 (Routledge: June, 2005).

[90]Kevin Fitchard, "Cheaper by the Globalization," *Telephony*, November 6, 2006, via Factiva, accessed January 21, 2007.

[91]Mike Slocombe, "'Ultra-Low Cost' Mobile Handsets Announced by GSM Association," *Digital-Lifestyles*, February 15, 2005, at www .http://digital-lifestyles.info/2005/02/15/ultra-low-cost-mobile-handsets-announced-by-gsm-association/, accessed February 13, 2007.

cost, made possible by economies of scale, would not be cross-subsidized by high-margin handsets or by any "corporate social responsibility" program, Motorola expected to earn a small margin on each handset sold. Motorola planned to use its factories in mainland China to produce the six million low-cost phones in half a year. By January 2007, Motorola had shipped six million sub-$40 handsets, as well as an additional six million sub-$30 handsets, to mobile telephone operators in emerging markets including India, Pakistan, Bangladesh, Indonesia, Philippines, Malaysia, Thailand, Turkey, South Africa, Nigeria, Egypt, Algeria, Russia, and Ukraine.[92] In the early stages of the rollout, executives acknowledged that the low pricing in emerging markets had been necessary to build market share.[93] "The pricing that we did in those [high-growth] markets was to maintain our share position," said a Motorola executive. "It was a brutal market from a pricing perspective."[94] These moves eventually took a toll on Motorola's earnings.

Importantly, however, low pricing and simpler products were not a guarantee of market success. Because people in poor countries spent a far larger fraction of their income to buy even the cheapest handsets, a Nokia manager explained, phones were a status symbol, so brand and appearance mattered.[95] Intended beneficiaries had been known to reject cheaper phones, viewing them as inferior and substandard. "We assume that the poor will not accept technology," explained University of Michigan Professor and author of *The Fortune at the Bottom of the Pyramid*, C. K. Prahalad.

"The truth is they will accept technology in some ways even more easily than we will, because they have not been socialized to anything else. They accept technology rapidly, as long as that technology is useful. We have a very long forgetting curve. They don't. They have only a learning curve."[96]

Regardless of the challenges, Nokia management believed that by 2008, there would be more than three billion people (half the world's population) using mobile communications, and that almost all growth, even in the next three years, would stem from emerging markets.[97] The company had teamed up with the Grameen Foundation of Bangladesh to develop less expensive cell phones to be used in Africa that were durable, dust-resistant, and had flashlights, a useful added feature for regions without electricity.[98]

Some philanthropists and technologists, including Microsoft cofounder Bill Gates and chief research and strategy officer Craig Mundie, argued that developing countries and their benefactors should be leveraging existing communications infrastructure such as mobile telephony to accelerate learning and modernization efforts, instead of deploying PCs. They agreed with scholars who argued that emerging markets were likely to be wireless-centric, rather than PC-centric.[99] For this reason, Gates advocated distributing Internet-enabled cell phones to children and parents rather than trying to assemble Wi-Fi-enabled mesh networks with donated or subsidized laptops. "The phone itself is going to be the low-cost computer," said the chairman of handset chip-maker Qualcomm.[100] Many saw developing nations such as India and Uganda "leap-frogging" past standard technologies, such as land-line phones, for cell phones. In most emerging markets, mobile phone use had increased more rapidly than Internet use, but both technologies were on the uptake worldwide.[101]

---

[92]"One of Four Handsets Shipped in 2011 Will Cost Less Than $20, Says ABI Research," *Business Wire*, January 22, 2007, via Factiva, accessed February 16, 2007.

[93]"Motorola to cut 3,500 jobs," *AFX Asia*, January 21, 2007, via Factiva, accessed February 16, 2007.

[94] "Motorola Inc. Analyst Meeting—Final," *Voxant FD Wire*, January 19, 2007, via Factiva, accessed February 16, 2007.

[95] "Calling an end to poverty," *Economist*, July 9, 2005, via Factiva, accessed February 13, 2007.

[96]Surowiecki.

[97]Ibid.

[98]Tavia Grant, "World's Poorest Nations New Frontier For Cellphone Giants," *The Globe and Mail*, November 14, 2006, via Factiva, accessed January 21, 2007.

[99]"Calling an end to poverty," *The Economist*, July 9, 2005, via Factiva, accessed January 18, 2007.

[100]Bruce Einhorn, "Intel Inside the Third World," *BusinessWeek*, July 9 and 16, 2007.

[101]World Bank World Development Indicators database, 2007.

The idea of a multifunctional phone had gained traction among a handful of hardware developers. For example, in June 2006, the Israeli technology firm Fourier introduced the Wi-Fi-capable Nova5000, a touch-screen PDA equipped with the handheld version of Microsoft's operating system, Windows CE, and a number of basic computing applications often found in more expensive "smartphones" such as the Blackberry Pearl or the Palm Treo.[102] In July 2006, Microsoft's Mundie unveiled a prototype of a Microsoft phone, called FonePlus, that would eventually allow users to read e-mail, run stripped down versions of Microsoft applications, and surf the Web, in addition to its regular functions. Microsoft also intended to connect the phone to a TV and keyboard to form a stripped-down Web computer.[103]

"Suggesting that cell phones are an alternative to laptops is like saying we can use postage stamps to read textbooks," Negroponte retorted. "Books have a purposeful size based on how the eye works and the ability to [simultaneously read and browse]. It was not by chance that atlases are bigger than timetables."[104] While connecting a Web-enabled cell phone to a TV and keyboard could yield what amounted to a rudimentary Web computer, as Gates had suggested, few families in developing nations owned televisions, nor did many remote villages or rural classrooms have electricity to power TVs. Televisions also lacked the laptop's inherent benefit of mobility.[105]

Competing Options

In May 2006 Intel launched its own cheaper laptop (the Classmate PC) targeting developing nations as part of its "World Ahead" program. The day after announcing plans to invest $1 billion in education and training as part of its program, Intel underlined its commitment to closing the technology gap between rich and poor nations with a device that used flash memory instead of a hard drive and ran Microsoft Windows XP. "No one wants to cross the

digital divide using yesterday's technology," suggested Intel president and CEO Paul Otellini, in a thinly veiled swipe at OLPC.[106] The $285 model cost more than OLPC's price tag of $175 per laptop, but the Classmate PC offered enhanced capabilities and the ability to run stripped-down versions of Linux or Windows XP. Intel hoped to reduce the price below $200 once mass production began.[107]

Negroponte took Intel's entry into the fray in stride: "Intel copied [us]," he said.[108] "When Intel made their laptop, that was a wonderful thing for children because if there's more than one opportunity, that's good. . . . The difference is that Intel's approach is much more teacher-centric [while] ours is much more child-centric, and that is a philosophical difference, not a technological difference."[109] At the 2007 World Economic Forum, Intel's [Craig] Barrett argued that Intel's efforts to train teachers to use PCs was a more helpful approach than the wholesale supply of laptops to children and the concurrent expectation that they would intuit their functionality and use.[110] OLPC had been criticized for discounting the value of teacher training and curriculum development using the devices.[111]

Another competitor was India-based Encore Software, whose "Mobilis" PC had attracted the interest of both the Indian government and Brazil's education ministry.[112] Mobilis ran on Linux, was easy to use, and featured regional Indian languages like Hindi, Kannada, and Marathi.[113] In 2006, Encore Software provided 40 evaluation units to the Brazilian government for inspection, expecting feedback

[102]MacMillan.
[103]Surowiecki.
[104]Surowiecki.
[105]Surowiecki.

[106]Tom Krazit, "Intel Builds $400 Laptop For School Desks Worldwide," *CNET News.com*, May 3, 2006, via Factiva, accessed January 21, 2007.
[107]"Which laptop per child?" Guardian Unlimited on the Web, May 31, 2007, http://technology.guardian.co.uk/weekly/story/0,,2091248,00. html, accessed June 17, 2007.
[108]"Negroponte OLPC and Intel," *Exclusivo Domino Digital TV*, November 29, 2006, http://www.youtube.com/watch?v=HK90TnOQE0E, accessed January 21, 2007.
[109]Ibid.
[110]Markoff.
[111]Markoff.
[112]"Encore Set To Bag Brazilian Laptop Order," *Economic Times*, December 19, 2006, via Factiva, accessed January 15, 2007.
[113]Ibid.

and possibly an initial order by February 2007.[114] Finally, AMD was also developing its own low-cost laptop, the "Personal Internet Communicator," a de facto fourth competitor to OLPC's product.[115] AMD had boldly announced that it could bring half of the world's population online by 2015 with the device.[116]

After Gates questioned whether the $100 Laptop concept was "just taking what we do in the rich world" and assuming it was something good for developing nations,[117] Negroponte responded, "Bill Gates has come out against it. . . . Intel keeps slamming it. . . . [W]hen people like that don't like it, you must be doing something right."[118]

Educating the Poor[119]

As the debate raged about alternative products and visions, education problems in the developing world persisted despite a broad consensus among international organizations, ministries of education, and grassroots organizations that improving education would alleviate hardship in developing nations. Common challenges shared by countries in the developing world were a lack of teachers, classrooms, and textbooks.[120] For example, in the Mwanza district of Malawi, there were only six qualified teachers in four classrooms teaching 772 students.[121] By some estimates, sub-Saharan Africa needed to recruit at least 1.6 million more teachers to provide universal primary education by 2015, with a ratio of 40 pupils to one teacher.[122]

Since 1990, the World Bank had spent $12 billion on primary education in developing countries.[123] In addition, UNESCO reported that participation in primary education had increased by 27% in sub-Saharan Africa between 1999 and 2004; however, the report added that net enrollment ratios remained low, at 65% in 2004.[124] To boost literacy and increase classroom attendance, some countries abolished school fees and saw a consequent surge in school enrollments. For example, in 2003, primary school enrollment in Kenya grew from 5.9 million to 7.2 million, and a similar boost in attendance was recorded in the primary schools of Uganda and Tanzania.[125] Waiving school fees helped more poor students gain access to education, but whether they stayed in school and benefited from the programs depended on other factors, such as health, nutrition, family support, good textbooks, and qualified teaching staff.[126]

The education crisis in the developing world was even worse among women. UNICEF estimated that, on average, only 43% of eligible girls in the developing world attended secondary schools.[127] Young girls were often forced to either drop out of school or not go to school at all because of their parents' inability to care for them.[128] In rural Malawi, many young girls never completed primary school since families placed a greater emphasis on working in the fields, caring for the elderly, and marriage than education.[129] Teenage pregnancy, high birth rates, and scarcity of contraception in most developing nations also affected the ability of young women to attend school. By some

[114]Ibid.

[115]Tom Krazit, "Intel Builds $400 Laptop For School Desks Worldwide," *CNET News.com*, May 3, 2006, via Factiva, accessed January 21, 2007.

[116]Hille.

[117]Markoff.

[118]"Transcript of Negroponte's Presentation," One Laptop Per Child page, July 7, 2006, https://www.newman.ac.uk/Students_Websites/ ~j.e.england/olpct2.htm, accessed June 17, 2007.

[119]This section draws from Kevin Clarke, "Troubled Waters," *U.S. Catholic*, February 1, 2007, via Factiva, accessed February 4, 2007.

[120]Rachel Maser, "Lessons from Malawi: Obstacles to Education Abound in Rural Malawi," *Edmonton Journal*, February 3, 2007, via Factiva, accessed February 5, 2007.

[121]Ibid.

[122]"Early Childhood Education Missing: UNESCO," *Xinhua News Agency*, November 26, 2006, via Factiva, accessed February 4, 2007.

[123]Kristi Heim, "Gates donates $40 million to improve education in poor countries," *Seattle Times*, December 18, 2006, via Factiva, accessed February 5, 2007.

[124]"Early Childhood Education Missing: UNESCO," *Xinhua News Agency*, November 26, 2006, via Factiva, accessed February 4, 2007.

[125]Andrew Mitchell, "We Must Do More To Help Street Children," *Birmingham Post*, December 20, 2006, via Factiva, accessed February 5, 2007.

[126]Kristi Heim, "Gates donates $40 million to improve education in poor countries."

[127]"Study: Children Caught In Vicious Circle of Sexism," *Mail and Guardian*, December 14, 2006, via Factiva, accessed February 5, 2007.

[128]Abubakr-Sadiq Braimah, "Child Sex Market in Ghana," *All Africa*, January 21, 2007, via Factiva, accessed February 5, 2007.

[129]Ibid.

estimates only 14% of women in Uganda, for example, used modern methods of contraception, and 33% of the population completely lacked access to methods of birth control.[130]

Furthermore, in many parts of Africa, young boys and girls under the age of 18 were forced to fight in regional conflicts.[131] As many as 300,000 children worldwide were used not only as fighters, but as messengers, spies, porters, and in some cases, servants and concubines.[132] Drug use, combined with severe urban poverty, a rising cost of living, few job opportunities, and no laws for compulsory education all contributed to the growing ranks of so-called street children around the world.[133]

In Nigeria, large numbers of children did not attend school or were forced to drop out for reasons related to inaccessibility.[134] In Malawi, food scarcity and unemployment were seen as barriers to education. During the "hungry season" from December to April, many families had only one meal each day in the late afternoon, meaning children would often have to walk to school, attend class for five hours, and then walk home on an empty stomach.[135] Millions of children of both genders in developing nations spent the bulk of each day searching for food and drinking water, often foraging for recyclable materials in garbage dumps. Poor health associated with water and sanitation deficits undermined productivity and economic growth.[136] Poor living conditions were frequently exacerbated by lack of running water, electricity, limited medical care, and local violence.[137]

Rethinking the Concept?

In June 2007, an OLPC spokeswoman reported that "OLPC [was] in talks with Argentina, Brazil, Uruguay, Peru, Nigeria, Thailand, Pakistan, Russia, Rwanda and many other countries—but nothing definite just yet."[138] The Inter-American Development Bank was supposedly considering purchasing Negroponte's laptops for multiple Central American countries.[139] (See **Exhibit 4** for a status of OLPC negotiations around the world, **Exhibit 5** for main OLPC milestones, and **Exhibit 6** for the latest OLPC specifications.) In the prior month, OLPC had donated 160 laptops to a public elementary school in Uruguay, making the small town of Villa Cardal the first Latin American recipient of the computers. While the laptops were donated by OLPC, Uruguay has budgeted $15 million for the project. The arrival of the computers invigorated this small community of only 1,300 residents. Students would use the laptops in class, since the machines were loaded with electronic versions of their school books and encyclopedias. But the learning and experience extended beyond the classroom. Because the laptops were owned by each child, they could be taken home and shared with family and friends.

While Negroponte acknowledged the challenge that confronted poorer governments in justifying the expenditure of large portions of their education budgets on laptops,[140] he was not willing to venture into production until he had firm commitments from governments outside the U.S. to buy at least five million of his machines.[141] By late May 2007, with Brazil reportedly planning to order Classmate PCs instead of OLPC laptops, Negroponte described Intel's push as "predatory."[142] "The world is a big

[130]Glenna Gordon, "No Option But Abortion," *All Africa*, November 21, 2006, via Factiva, accessed February 4, 2007.

[131]Genevieve Swart, "Africa's Children Brought to Life, Brutally," *The Sun Herald*, April 30, 2006, via Factiva, accessed February 5, 2007.

[132]Ibid.

[133]Waheed Khan, "Pakistan Street Kids Plagued by Glue Sniffing," *Reuters*, January 8, 2007, via Factiva, accessed February 5, 2007.

[134]Aisha Lemu, "Education Should Be Priority of All Muslim Women," *All Africa*, January 21, 2007, via Factiva, accessed February 5, 2007.

[135]Rachel Maser, "Lessons from Malawi: Obstacles to Education Abound in Rural Malawi," *Edmonton Journal*, February 3, 2007, via Factiva, accessed February 5, 2007.

[136]Kevin Clarke, "Troubled Waters," *U.S. Catholic*, February 1, 2007, via Factiva, accessed February 4, 2007.

[137]Martin Miller, "Trading the good life for a life of doing good," *Los Angeles Times*, July 27, 2005, via Factiva, accessed February 4, 2007.

[138]"Laptops projects for poor states draws big competition," Agence-France Presse on the Web, May 28, 2007, http://www.afp .com/english/home/, accessed June 19, 2007.

[139]"Low-Cost Laptop Could Transform Learning," January 3, 2007, *AFX Asia*, via Factiva, accessed January 8, 2007.

[140]Surowiecki.

[141]Surowiecki.

[142]"Which laptop per child?" Guardian Unlimited on the Web, May 31, 2007, http://technology.guardian.co.uk/weekly/story/0,,2091248,00 .html, accessed June 17, 2007.

Exhibit 4   Status of OLPC Negotiations in Selected Countries, June 2007

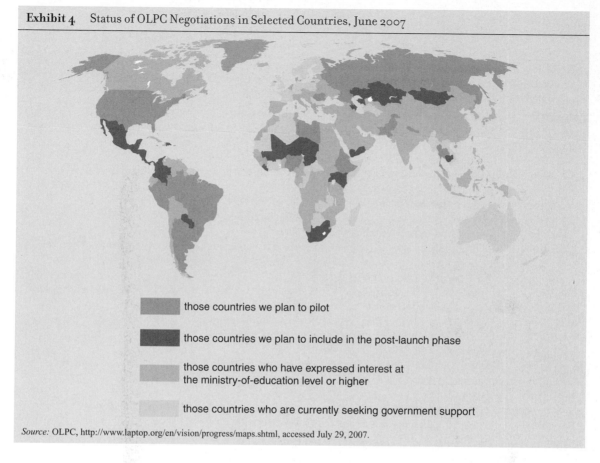

those countries we plan to pilot

those countries we plan to include in the post-launch phase

those countries who have expressed interest at
the ministry-of-education level or higher

those countries who are currently seeking government support

Source: OLPC, http://www.laptop.org/en/vision/progress/maps.shtml, accessed July 29, 2007.

place and there's room for lots of these," retorted an Intel manager.[143] Meanwhile, other countries such as Nigeria, Pakistan, and Thailand were also weighing their options, since every week seemed to bring announcements of low-cost machines.

Indeed, since the announcement of the $100 Laptop, the category had been transformed by falling prices and surging demand. Prices for basic notebook machines fell from $2,000 in 2005 to less than $800 in early 2007.[144] In 2006 global notebook sales grew by 26%, and desktop sales grew by only 2%. Analysts estimated that by 2011, portable PCs would outsell desktops. Further, resale values for relatively brand new machines were low.[145] Meanwhile, desktop prices continued to drop, with HP introducing in June 2007 the rp5700 Business Desktop PC, which was 95% manufactured from recyclable components, priced at $648.[146] In June 2007, Taiwan-based Asus announced its plans to manufacture cheap notebooks for sale to developing as well as developed

[143]Tom Bawden, "Intel targets developing world with basic laptop for children," *The Times on the Web*, June 6, 2007, http://business .timesonline.co.uk/tol/business/industry_sectors/technology/article 1890168.ece, accessed June 19, 2007.

[144]Angus Kidman, "Notebooks sweeping the desktop," *The Australian*, April 10, 2007, via Factiva, accessed June 6, 2007.

[145]Ibid.

[146]Geoff Duncan, "HP's New PC So Green, It's Gold," *Digital Trends News*, June 5, 2007, http://news.digitaltrends.com/news/ story/13190/hps_new_pc_so_green_its_gold, accessed June 6, 2007.

Exhibit 5   OLPC Milestones, January 2005–May 2007

Date	Event
May 2007	Autonomous mesh operates during suspend; First B3 machines are built and deployed; Peru announces it will participate in OLPC.
Apr. 2007	First school server deployed.
Mar. 2007	First mesh network deployed.
Feb. 2007	B2-test machines become available and are shipped to developers and the launch countries.
Jan. 2007	Rwanda announced its participation in the project.
Dec. 2006	Uruguay announced its participation in the project.
Nov. 2006	First B1 machines are built; IDB and OLPC formalize an agreement regarding Latin American and Caribbean education.
Oct. 2006	B-test boards become available; Libya announces plans for one laptop for every child.
Sep. 2006	UI designs presented; integrated software build released; SES-Astra joins OLPC.
Aug. 2006	Working prototype of the dual-mode display.
Jun. 2006	500 developer boards are shipped worldwide; WiFi operational; Csound demonstrated over the mesh network.
	First video with working prototype.
May 2006	eBay joins OLPC; display specs set; A-test boards become available; $100 Server is announced.
Apr. 2006	Pre-A test board boots; Squid and FreePlay present first human-power systems.
Mar. 2006	Yves Behar and FuseProject are selected as industry designers.
Feb. 2006	Marvell joins OLPC and continues to partner on network hardware.
Jan. 2006	World Economic Forum, Switzerland.
	UNDP and OLPC Sign Partnership Agreement.
Dec. 2005	Quanta Computer Inc. to manufacture Laptop.
Nov. 2005	WSIS, Tunisia.
	Prototype unveiled by UN Secretary-General Kofi Annan; Nortel joins OLPC.
Aug. 2005	Design Continuum starts design of first laptop.
Jul. 2005	Formal signing of original members of OLPC.
Mar. 2005	Brightstar and Red Hat come on board.
Jan. 2005	Laptop initiative officially announced at World Economic Forum, Davos, Switzerland; AMD, News Corp. and Google agree to join OLPC.

Source: OLPC, http://wiki.laptop.org/go/milestones, accessed September 5, 2008.

nations.[147] The chairman explained that the $189 laptop, measuring 120 × 100 × 30 mm and weighing only 900 grams, would be the lowest-cost and easiest machine to use. This machine, called EeePC, would use a custom-written Linux operating system, but unlike OLPC, would offer a conventional Windows interface. Asus attributed the low estimated price to its design choices, primarily a flash-based 2GB hard disk.[148] These new alternatives meant that purchasing computing power for education was

[147]Asus was a Taiwan-based technology company that manufactured motherboards, graphics cards, optical drives, PDAs, notebook computers, networking products, mobile phones, computer cases, computer components, and computer cooling systems. The company's motherboards were in one-third of all desktop PCs sold in 2006. ASUSTek Computer Inc., "About ASUS." ASUSTek Computer Inc. website, http://usa.asus.com/aboutasus.aspx?show=1, accessed June 19, 2007.

[148]Doug Mohney, "Foleo, UMPC and OLPC all killed off in one week," *The Inquirer*, June 6, 2007; and Clive Webster, "Asus stuns Compux with 100 laptop," PCPro, June 6, 2007, http://www.pcpro.co.uk/news/114773/computex-2007-asus-stuns-computex-with-100-laptop.html June 6, 2007.

Exhibit 6   Photos and Specifications of OLPC Laptop, June 2007

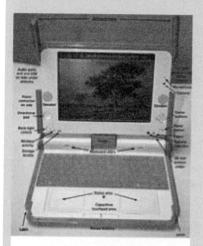

Physical Dimensions

Prototype-A Motherboard

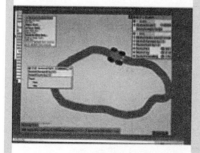

eToys

Physical dimensions:
- Dimensions: 242 mm × 228 mm × 32 mm (approximate—subject to change)
- Weight: Less than 1.5 KG (target only—subject to change)
- Configuration: Convertible laptop with pivoting, reversible display; dirt-and moisture-resistant system enclosure

Core electronics:
- AMD Geode LX-700 @ 0.8w (data sheet)
- CPU clock speed: 433 Mhz
- Compatibility: Athlon instruction set (including MMX and 3DNow! Enhanced) with additional Geode-specific instructions (X86/X87-compatible)
- North Bridge: PCI and Memory Interface integrated with Geode CPU
- Chipset: AMD CS5536 South Bridge (datasheet)
- Graphics controller: Integrated with Geode CPU; unified memory architecture
- Embedded controller (for production), ENE KB3700
- DRAM memory: w56 MiB dynamic RAM
- Data rate: Dual—DDR333—166 Mhz
- Open Firmware bootloader; 1024KB SPI-interface flash ROM
- Mass storage: 1024 MiB SLC NAND flash, high-speed flash controller
- Drives: No rotating media

Display:
- Liquid-crystal display: 7.5" Dual-mode TFT display
- Viewing area: 152.4 mm × 114.3 mm
- Resolution: 1200 (H) × 900 (V) resolution (200 DPI)
- Mono display: High-resolution, quincunx-sampled, transmissive color mode
- Special "DCON" chip, that enables deswizzling and anti-aliasing in color mode, while enabling the display to remain live with the processor suspended.

Integrated peripherals:
- Keyboard: 70+ keys, 1.2 mm stroke; sealed rubber-membrane key-switch assembly
- Keyboard layout details
- Keyboard layout pictures—international, Thai, Arabic, Spanish, Portuguese, West Africa, Urdu, French
- Cursor-control keys: five-key cursor-control pad; four directional keys plus Enter
- Touchpad: Dual capacitance/resistive touchpad; supports written-input mode
- Audio: Analog Devices AD1888, AC97-compatible audio codec; stereo, with dual internal speakers; monophonic, with internal microphone and using the Analog Devices SSM2211 for audio amplification

(continued)

Exhibit 6   Photos and Specifications of OLPC Laptop, June 2007 (continued)

Keyboard Detail

Connectors

Battery

- Wireless: Marvell Libertas 88W8388+88W8015, 802.11b/g compatible; dual adjustable, rotating coaxial antennas; supports diversity reception
- Status indicators: Power, battery, WiFi; visible lid open or closed
- Video camera: 640 × 480 resolution, 30FPS

External connectors:
- Power: 2-pin DC-input, 10 to 20 V usable, −50 to 39 V safe, one-time fuse for excessive input
- Line output: Standard 3.5 mm 3-pin switched stereo audio jack
- Microphone: Standard 3.5 mm 2-pin switched mono microphone jack; selectable sensor-input mode
- Expansion: 3 Type-A USB-2.0 connectors; MMC/SD Card slot
- Maximum power: 1 A (total)

Battery:
- Pack type: 4 or 5 Cells, 6V series configuration
- Fully-enclosed "hard" case; user removable
- Capacity: 22.8 Watt-hours
- Cell type: NiMH (or LiFeP)
- Pack protection: Integrated pack-type identification
- Integrated thermal sensor
- Integrated polyfuse current limiter
- Cycle life: Minimum 2,000 charge/discharge cycles (to 50% capacity of new, IIRC).
- Power Management will be critical.

BIOS/loader
- Open Firmware is used as the bootloader.

Environmental specifications:
- Temperature: somewhere in between typical laptop requirements and Mil spec; exact values have not been settled.
- Humidity: Similar attitude to temperature. When closed, the unit should seal well enough that children walking to and from school need not fear rainstorms or dust.
- Altitude: −15 m to 3048 m (operating), −15 m to 12192 m (non-operating)
- Shock: 125 g, 2 ms, half-sine (operating) 200 g, 2 ms, half-sine (non-operating)
- Random vibration: 0.75 g zero-to-peak, 10 Hz to 500 Hz, 0.25 oct/min sweep rate (operating); 1.5 g zero-to-peak, 10 Hz to 500 Hz, 0.5 oct/min sweep rate (nonoperating)
- 2 mm plastic walls (1.3 mm is typical for most systems).

Regulatory requirements:
- The usual US and EU EMI/EMC requirements will be met.
- The laptop and all OLPC-supplied accessories will be fully UL and is ROoHS compliant.

Source: OLPC, http://www.laptop.org/en/laptop/hardware/specs.shtml, accessed August 1, 2007.

becoming more accessible not only to individuals in developing countries, but also to governments and aid organizations involved in the sector.

Meanwhile, Intel's Classmate PC had been rolling off Chinese assembly lines since March 2007, at a plant owned by a Taiwanese manufacturer. Intel had trials under way in over 10 nations, with 25 planned by late 2007. Intel planned to have over one million machines manufactured before the end of 2007. In many countries, Intel bundled its Classmate laptops with education software and teacher-training support.[149] Intel had also recently launched trials in California and Oregon and was said to be considering a slightly more powerful Classmate PC for sale in the developed world in 2008.[150]

Observers noted that, as a marginal player in the cellular market, and faced with sluggish worldwide PC growth, Intel had to find a way to sell to the next class of yet-unwired billion consumers. This foray into education was seen as a potential Trojan horse. Instead of trying to reinvent the PC, an Intel manager explained, "we have chosen to ride the existing technology curve and drive down the cost." Its purchasing clout, especially with Asia suppliers, allowed it to purchase components at close to cost,

and Intel had moved its Classmate PC model from concept to commercial production in less than 18 months. In early June, Intel announced that it was working with another Taiwanese firm to make another laptop based on the Classmate model, priced at $200.[151] Negroponte remained critical. "[OLPC] is an education project," he explained, "not a laptop project."[152] "[Intel] look(s) at it as a market. But primary education in the developing world is not a market, it's a human right. And I don't think Intel is in the human rights business."[153] "We don't compete with Intel," he added. "They tell me all the time they are very interested in the next billion users and I say, 'I'm interested in the last billion users.' These are very complementary projects. They really go together."[154]

However, in the meantime, some U.S. school systems had started dropping laptops. "After seven years, there was literally no evidence it had any impact on student achievement," said the president of a school board that had been an early laptop-in-the-classroom adopter. "The teachers were telling us that where there's a one-on-one relationship between the student and the laptop, the box gets in the way. It is a distraction to the educational process."[155]

---

[149]Bruce Einhorn, "Intel Inside the Third World," *BusinessWeek*, July 9 and 16, 2007.
[150]Einhorn.

[151]Ibid.
[152]Fildes.
[153]Einhorn.
[154]Ibid.
[155]Winnie Hu, "Seeing no progress, some schools drop laptops," *New York Times*, May 4, 2007.

Case 3-2   The Global Branding of Stella Artois

Paul W. Beamish and Anthony Goerzen

In April 2000, Paul Cooke, chief marketing officer of Interbrew, the world's fourth largest brewer, contemplated the further development of their premium product, Stella Artois, as the company's flagship brand in key markets around the world. Although the long-range plan for 2000–2002 had been approved, there still remained some important strategic issues to resolve.

A Brief History of Interbrew

Interbrew traced its origins back to 1366 to a brewery called Den Hoorn, located in Leuven, a town just outside of Brussels. In 1717, when it was purchased by its master brewer, Sebastiaan Artois, the brewery changed its name to Artois.

The firm's expansion began when Artois acquired a major interest in the Leffe Brewery in Belgium in 1954, the Dommelsch Brewery in the Netherlands in 1968, and the Brassiere du Nord in France in 1970. In 1987, when Artois and another Belgian brewery called Piedboeuf came together, the merged company was named Interbrew. The new company soon acquired other Belgian specialty beer brewers, building up the Interbrew brand portfolio with the

IVEY

Richard Ivey School of Business
The University of Western Ontario

purchase of the Hoegaarden brewery in 1989 and the Belle-Vue Brewery in 1990.

Interbrew then entered into a phase of rapid growth. The company acquired breweries in Hungary in 1991, in Croatia and Romania in 1994, and in three plants in Bulgaria in 1995. Again in 1995, Interbrew completed an unexpected major acquisition by purchasing Labatt, a large Canadian brewer also with international interests. Labatt had operations in the United States, for example, with the Latrobe brewery, home of the Rolling Rock brand. Labatt also held a substantial minority stake in the second largest Mexican brewer, Femsa Cervesa, which produced Dos Equis, Sol, and Tecate brands. Following this major acquisition, Interbrew went on, in 1996, to buy a brewery in the Ukraine and engaged in a joint venture in the Dominican Republic. Subsequently, breweries were added in China in 1997, Montenegro and Russia in 1998, and another brewery in Bulgaria and one in Korea in 1999.

Thus, through acquisition expenditures of US$2.5 billion in the previous four years, Interbrew had transformed itself from a simple Belgian brewery into one of the largest beer companies in the world. By 1999, the company had become a brewer on a truly global scale that now derived more that 90 per cent of its volume from markets outside Belgium. It remained a privately held company, headquartered in Belgium, with subsidiaries and joint ventures in 23 countries across four continents.

The International Market for Beer

In the 1990s, the world beer market was growing at an annual rate of one to two per cent. In 1998, beer consumption reached a total of 1.3 billion hectolitres (hls). There were, however, great regional differences in both market size and growth rates. Most industry analysts split the world market for beer between growth and mature markets. The mature markets were generally considered to be North America,

Exhibit 1   The World Beer Market in 1998

Region	% of Global Consumption	Growth Index ('98 Vs 92)	Per Capita Consumption
Americas	35.1%	112.6	57
Europe	32.8%	97.7	54
Asia Pacific	27.2%	146.2	11
Africa	4.6%	107.7	8
Middle East/Central Asia	0.4%	116.0	2

Source: Canadean Ltd.

Western Europe and Australasia. The growth markets included Latin America, Asia, Central and Eastern Europe including Russia. Although some felt that Africa had considerable potential, despite its low per capita beer consumption, the continent was not considered a viable market by many brewers because of its political and economic instability (see **Exhibit 1**).

Mature Markets   The North American beer market was virtually stagnant, although annual beer consumption per person was already at a sizeable 83 litres per capita (lpc). The Western European market had also reached maturity with consumption of 79 lpc. Some analysts believed that this consumption level was under considerable pressure, forecasting a decline to near 75 lpc over the medium term. Australia and New Zealand were also considered mature markets, with consumption at 93 lpc and 84 lpc, respectively. In fact, volumes in both markets, New Zealand in particular, had declined through the 1990s following tight social policies on alcohol consumption and the emergence of a wine culture.

Growth Markets   Given that average consumption in Eastern Europe was only 29 lpc, the region appeared to offer great potential. This consumption figure, however, was heavily influenced by Russia's very low level, and the future for the large Russian market was unclear. Further, some markets, such as the Czech Republic that consumed the most beer per person in the world at 163 lpc, appeared to have already reached maturity. Central and South America, on the other hand, were showing healthy growth

and, with consumption at an average of 43 lpc, there was believed to be considerable upside. The most exciting growth rates, however, were in Asia. Despite the fact that the market in this region had grown by more than 30 per cent since 1995, consumption levels were still comparatively low. In China, the region's largest market, consumption was only 16 lpc and 20 to 25 lpc in Hong Kong and Taiwan. Although the 1997 Asian financial crisis did not immediately affect beer consumption (although company profits from the region were hit by currency translation), demand in some key markets, such as Indonesia, was reduced and in others growth slowed. The situation, however, was expected to improve upon economic recovery in the medium term.

Beer Industry Structure

The world beer industry was relatively fragmented with the top four players accounting for only 22 per cent of global volume—a relatively low figure as compared to 78 per cent in the soft drinks industry, 60 per cent in tobacco and 44 per cent in spirits. This suggested great opportunities for consolidation, a process that had already begun two decades prior. Many analysts, including those at Interbrew, expected that this process would probably accelerate in the future. The driver behind industry rationalization was the need to achieve economies of scale in production, advertising and distribution. It was widely recognized that the best profit margins were attained either by those with a commanding position in the market or those with a niche position. However, there were several factors that mitigated the trend towards rapid concentration of the brewing industry.

One factor that slowed the process of consolidation was that the ratio of fixed versus variable costs of beer production was relatively high. Essentially, this meant that there was a limited cost savings potential that could be achieved by bringing more operations under a common administration. Real cost savings could be generated by purchasing and then rationalizing operations through shifting production to more efficient (usually more modern) facilities. This approach, however, required large initial capital outlays. As a result, in some markets with "unstable" economies, it was desirable to spread out capital expenditures over a longer period of time to ensure appropriate profitability in the early stages. A second factor that may have had a dampening effect on the trend towards industry consolidation was that local tastes differed. In some cases, beer brands had hundreds of years of heritage behind them and had become such an integral part of everyday life that consumers were often fiercely loyal to their local brew. This appeared to be a fact in many markets around the world.

Interbrew's Global Position

Through Interbrew's acquisitions in the 1990s, the company had expanded rapidly. During this period, the company's total volumes had increased more than fourfold. These figures translated to total beer production of 57.5 million hls in 1998 (when including the volume of all affiliates), as compared to just 14.7 million hls in 1992. Volume growth had propelled the company into the number four position among the world's brewers.

Faced with a mature and dominant position in the declining Belgian domestic market, the company decided to focus on consolidating and developing key markets, namely Belgium, the Netherlands, France and North America, and expansion through acquisition in Central Europe, Asia and South America. Subsequently, Interbrew reduced its dependence on the Belgian market from 44 per cent in 1992 to less that 10 per cent by 1998 (total volumes

including Mexico). Concurrently, a significant milestone for the company was achieved by 1999 when more than 50 per cent of its total volume was produced in growth markets (including Mexico). Interbrew had shifted its volume so that the Americas accounted for 61 per cent of its total volume, Europe added 35 per cent, and Asia Pacific the remaining four per cent.

Taken together, the top 10 markets for beer accounted for 86 per cent of Interbrew's total volume in 1998 (see **Exhibit 2**). The Mexican beer market alone accounted for 37 per cent of total volume in 1998. Canada, Belgium, the United States and the United Kingdom were the next most important markets. However, smaller, growing markets such as Hungary, Croatia, Bulgaria, and Romania had begun to increase in importance.

Adding to its existing breweries in Belgium, France and the Netherlands, Interbrew's expansion strategy in the 1990s had resulted in acquisitions in Bosnia-Herzegovina, Bulgaria, Canada, China, Croatia, Hungary, Korea, Montenegro, Romania, Russia, the Ukraine, the United States, in a joint venture in South Korea, and in minority equity positions in Mexico and Luxembourg. Through these breweries, in addition to those that were covered by licensing

Exhibit 2   Interbrew's 1998 Share of the World's Top 10 Markets

Rank	Country	Volume (000 HL)	Market Share
1	USA	3,768	1.6%
2	China	526	0.3%
3	Germany	—	—
4	Brazil	—	—
5	Japan	—	—
6	UK	3,335	5.5%
7	Mexico	21,269	45.0%
8	Spain	—	—
9	South Africa	—	—
10	France	1,915	8.4%
Total		30,813	3.6%

Source: Canadean Ltd.

agreements in Australia, Italy, Sweden and the United Kingdom, Interbrew sold its beers in over 80 countries.

Interbrew's Corporate Structure

Following the acquisition of Labatt in 1995, Interbrew's corporate structure was divided into two geographic zones: the Americas and Europe/Asia/Africa. This structure was in place until September 1999 when Interbrew shifted to a fully integrated structure to consolidate its holdings in the face of industry globalization. Hugo Powell, formerly head of the Americas division, was appointed to the position of chief executive officer (CEO). The former head of the Europe/Africa/Asia division assumed the role of chief operating officer, but subsequently resigned and was not replaced, leaving Interbrew with a more conventional structure, with the five regional heads and the various corporate functional managers reporting directly to the CEO.

Recent Performance

1998 had been a good year for Interbrew in terms of volume in both mature and growth markets. Overall, sales volumes increased by 11.1 per cent as most of the company's international and local brands maintained or gained market share. In terms of the compounded annual growth rate, Interbrew outperformed all of its major competitors by a wide margin. While Interbrew's 1998 net sales were up 29 per cent, the best performing competitor achieved an increase of only 16 per cent. Of Interbrew's increased sales, 67 per cent was related to the new affiliates in China, Montenegro and Korea. The balance was the result of organic growth. Considerable volume increases were achieved also in Romania (72 per cent), Bulgaria (28 per cent), Croatia (13 per cent), and the United States (14 per cent). While volumes in Western Europe were flat, duty-free sales grew strongly. In the U.S. market, strong progress was made by Interbrew's Canadian and Mexican brands, and Latrobe's Rolling Rock was successfully relaunched. In Canada, performance was strong, fuelled by a two per cent increase in domestic consumption. Labatt's

sales of Budweiser (produced under license from Anheuser Busch) also continued to grow rapidly.

Given that the premium and specialty beer markets were growing quickly, particularly those within the large, mature markets, Interbrew began to shift its product mix to take advantage of this trend and the superior margins it offered. A notable brand success was Stella Artois, for which total global sales volumes were up by 19.7 per cent. That growth came from sales generated by Whitbread in the United Kingdom, from exports, and from sales in Central Europe where Stella Artois volumes took off. The strong growth of Stella Artois was also notable in that it was sold in the premium lager segment. In Europe, Asia Pacific and Africa, Interbrew's premium and specialty beers, which generated a bigger margin, increased as a proportion of total sales from 31 per cent in 1997 to 33 per cent in 1998. This product mix shift was particularly important since intense competition in most markets inhibited real price increases.

Success was also achieved in the United States specialty beer segment where total volume had been growing at nine per cent annually in the 1990s. In 1998, Interbrew's share of this growing market segment had risen even faster as Labatt USA realized increased sales of 16 per cent. The other continuing development was the growth of the light beer segment, which had become over 40 per cent of the total sales. Sales of Labatt's Blue Light, for example, had increased and Labatt Blue had become the number three imported beer in the United States, with volumes up 18 per cent. Latrobe's Rolling Rock brand grew by four per cent, the first increase in four years. Interbrew's Mexican brands, Dos Equis, Tecate and Sol, were also up by 19 per cent.

Following solid volume growth in profitable market segments, good global results were realized in key financial areas. Net profit, having grown for each of the previous six consecutive years, was 7.7 billion Belgian francs (BEF) in 1998, up 43.7 per cent from the previous year. Operating profit also rose 7.9 per cent over 1997, from 14.3 to 15.4 BEF; in both the Europe/Asia/Africa region and the Americas, operating profit was up by 8.5 per cent and 4.9 per cent respectively. Further, Interbrew's EBIT margin was up 58.1 per cent as compared to the best performing competitor's figure of 17.0 per cent. However, having made several large investments in Korea and Russia, and exercising an option to increase its share of Femsa Cerveza in Mexico from 22 per cent to 30 per cent, Interbrew's debt-equity ratio increased from 1.04 to 1.35. As a result, interest payments rose accordingly.

Interbrew also enjoyed good results in volume sales in many of its markets in 1999. Although Canadian sales remained largely unchanged over 1998, Labatt USA experienced strong growth in 1999, with volumes up by 10 per cent. There was a positive evolution in Western European volumes as well, as overall sales were up by 6.5 per cent overall in Belgium, France and the Netherlands. Central European markets also grew with Hungary showing an increase of 9.6 per cent, Croatia up by 5.5 per cent, Romania by 18.9 per cent, Montenegro by 29 per cent, and Bulgaria with a rise of 3.6 per cent in terms of volume. Sales positions were also satisfactory in the Russian and Ukrainian markets. Further, while South Korean sales volume remained unchanged, volumes in China were 10 per cent higher, although this figure was still short of expectations.

Interbrew Corporate Strategy

The three facets of Interbrew's corporate strategy, i.e., brands, markets and operations, were considered the "sides of the Interbrew triangle." Each of these aspects of corporate strategy was considered to be equally important in order to achieve the fundamental objective of increasing shareholder value. With a corporate focus entirely on beer, the underlying objectives of the company were to consolidate its positions in mature markets and improve margins through higher volumes of premium and specialty brands. Further, the company's emphasis on growth was driven by the belief that beer industry rationalization still had some way to go and that the majority of the world's major markets would each end up with just two or three major players.

Operations Strategy Cross fertilization of best practices between sites was a central component of Interbrew's operations strategy. In the company's two main markets, Belgium and Canada, each brewery monitored its performance on 10 different dimensions against its peers. As a result, the gap between the best and the worst of Interbrew's operations had narrowed decisively since 1995. Employees continuously put forward propositions to improve processes. The program had resulted in significantly lower production costs, suggesting to Interbrew management that most improvements had more to do with employee motivation than with pure technical performance. In addition, capacity utilization and strategic sourcing had been identified as two areas of major opportunity.

Capacity Utilization Given that brewing was a capital-intensive business, capacity utilization had a major influence on profitability. Since declining consumption in mature markets had generated excess capacity, several of Interbrew's old breweries and processing facilities were scheduled to be shut down. In contrast, in several growth markets such as Romania, Bulgaria, Croatia and Montenegro, the opposite problem existed, so facilities in other locations were used more fully until local capacities were increased.

Strategic Sourcing Interbrew had begun to rationalize its supply base as well. By selecting a smaller number of its best suppliers and working more closely with them, Interbrew believed that innovative changes resulted, saving both parties considerable sums every year. For most of the major commodities, the company had gone to single suppliers and was planning to extend this approach to all operations worldwide.

Market Strategy The underlying objectives of Interbrew's market strategy were to increase volume and to lessen its dependence on Belgium and Canada, its two traditional markets. Interbrew dichotomized its market strategy into the mature and growth market segments, although investments were considered wherever opportunities to generate sustainable profits existed. One of the key elements of Interbrew's market strategy was to establish and manage strong market platforms. It was believed that a brand strength was directly related to a competitive and dedicated market platform (i.e., sales and distribution, wholesaler networks, etc.) to support the brand. Further, Interbrew allowed individual country teams to manage their own affairs and many felt that the speed of success in many markets was related to this decentralized approach.

Mature markets   Interbrew's goals in its mature markets were to continue to build market share and to improve margins through greater efficiencies in production, distribution and marketing. At the same time, the company intended to exploit the growing trend in these markets towards premium and specialty products of which Interbrew already possessed an unrivalled portfolio. The key markets in which this strategy was being actively pursued were the United States, Canada, the United Kingdom, France, the Netherlands and Belgium.

Growth Markets   Based on the belief that the world's beer markets would undergo further consolidation, Interbrew's market strategy was to build significant positions in markets that had long-term volume growth potential. This goal led to a clear focus on Central and Eastern Europe and Asia, South Korea and China in particular. In China, for example, Interbrew had just completed an acquisition of a second brewery in Nanjing. The Yali brand was thereby added to the corporate portfolio and, together with its Jingling brand, Interbrew became the market leader in Nanjing, a city of six million people.

In Korea, Interbrew entered into a 50:50 joint venture with the Doosan Chaebol to operate the Oriental Brewery, producing the OB Lager and Cafri pilsener brands. With this move, Interbrew took the number two position in the Korean beer market with a 36 per cent share and sales of 5.1 million hls. The venture with Doosan was followed in December 1999 by the purchase of the Jinro Coors brewery. This added 2.5 million hls and increased Interbrew's market share to 50 per cent of total Korean volume. Thus, the Interbrew portfolio in Korea consisted of

two mainstream pilsener brands, OB Lager and Cass, the two local premium brands, Cafri and Red Rock, and Budweiser, an international premium brand.

In Russia, Interbrew expanded its presence by taking a majority stake in the Rosar Brewery in Omsk, adding the BAG Bier and Sibirskaya Korona brands. Rosar was the leading brewer in Siberia with a 25 per cent regional market share, and held the number four position in Russia. New initiatives were also undertaken in Central Europe with acquisitions of a brewery in Montenegro and the Pleven brewery in Bulgaria, as well as the introduction of Interbrew products into the Yugoslavian market. Finally, although Interbrew had just increased its already significant investment in Mexico's second largest brewer from 22 per cent to 30 per cent, Latin America remained a region of great interest.

Brand Strategy   A central piece of Interbrew's traditional brand strategy had been to add to its portfolio of brands through acquisition of existing brewers, principally in growth markets. Since its goal was to have the number one or two brand in every market segment in which it operated, Interbrew concentrated on purchasing and developing strong local brands. As it moved into new territories, the company's first priority was to upgrade product quality and to improve the positioning of the acquired local core lager brands. In mature markets, it drew on the strength of the established brands such as Jupiler, Belgium's leading lager brand, Labatt Blue, the famous Canadian brand, and Dommelsch, an important brand in the Netherlands. In growth markets, Interbrew supported brands like Borsodi Sor in Hungary, Kamenitza in Bulgaria, Ozujsko in Croatia, Bergenbier in Romania, Jingling in China, and OB Lager in Korea. In addition, new products were launched such as Taller, a premium brand in the Ukraine, and Boomerang, an alternative malt-based drink in Canada.

A second facet of the company's brand strategy was to identify certain brands, typically specialty products, and to develop them on a regional basis across a group of markets. At the forefront of this strategy were the Abbaye de Leffe and Hoegaarden brands and, to a lesser extent, Belle-Vue. In fact, both Hoegaarden and Leffe achieved a leading position as the number one white beer and abbey beer in France and Holland. The Loburg premium pilsener brand also strengthened its position when it was relaunched in France. Further, in Canada, Interbrew created a dedicated organization for specialty beers called the Oland Specialty Beer Company. In its first year of operation, the brands marketed by Oland increased its volumes by over 40 per cent. More specifically, sales of the Alexander Keith's brand doubled and the negative volume trend of the John Labatt Classic brand was reversed. The underlying message promoted by Oland was the richness, mystique and heritage of beer.

To support the regional growth of specialty beers, Interbrew established a new type of café. The Belgian Beer Café, owned and run by independent operators, created an authentic Belgian atmosphere where customers sampled Interbrew's Belgian specialty beers. By 1999, Belgian Beer Cafés were open in the many of Interbrew's key markets, including top selling outlets in New York, Auckland, Zagreb and Budapest, to name a few. The business concept was that these cafés were to serve as an ambassador of the Belgian beer culture in foreign countries. They were intended to serve as vehicles to showcase Interbrew's specialty brands, benefiting from the international appeal of European styles and fashions. Although these cafés represented strong marketing tools for brand positioning, the key factors that led to the success of this concept were tied very closely to the individual establishments and the personnel running them. The bar staff, for example, had to be trained to serve the beer in the right branded glass, at the right temperature, and with a nice foamy head. It was anticipated that the concept of the specialty café would be used to support the brand development efforts of Interbrew's Belgian beers in all of its important markets.

The third facet of Interbrew's brand strategy was to identify a key corporate brand and to develop it as a global product. While the market segment for a global brand was currently relatively small, with the bulk of the beer demand still in local brands, the demand for international brands was expected to grow, as many consumers became increasingly attracted to the sophistication of premium and super-premium beers.

The Evolution of Interbrew's Global Brand Strategy

Until 1997, Interbrew's brand development strategy for international markets was largely laissez faire. Brands were introduced to new markets through licensing, export and local production when opportunities were uncovered. Stella Artois, Interbrew's most broadly available and oldest brand, received an important new thrust when it was launched through local production in three of the company's subsidiaries in Central Europe in 1997. This approach was consistent with the company's overall goals of building a complete portfolio in high growth potential markets.

By 1998, however, the executive management committee perceived the need to identify a brand from its wide portfolio to systematically develop into the company's global brand. Although the market for global brands was still small, there were some growing successes (e.g., Heineken, Corona, Fosters and Budweiser) and Interbrew believed that there were several basic global trends that would improve the viability of this class of product over the next couple of decades. First, while many consumers were seeking more variety, others were seeking lower prices. It appeared that the number of affluent and poor consumer segments would increase at the expense of the middle income segments. The upshot of this socioeconomic trend was that eventually all markets would likely evolve in such a way that demand for both premium and economy-priced beers would increase, squeezing the mainstream beers in the middle. A second trend was the internationalization of the beer business. As consumers travelled around the world, consuming global media (e.g., CNN, Eurosport, MTV, international magazines, etc.), global media were expected to become more effective for building brands. A global strategy could, therefore, lead to synergies in global advertising and sponsoring. In addition, the needs of consumers in many markets were expected to converge. As a result of these various factors, Interbrew believed that there would be an increasing interest in authentic, international brands in a growing number of countries. Interbrew had a wide portfolio of national brands that it could set on the international stage. The two most obvious candidates were Labatt Blue and Stella Artois.

The Labatt range of brands included Labatt Blue, Labatt Blue Light and Labatt Ice. To date, however, the exposure of these brands outside of North America had been extremely limited and they were not yet budding global brands. Of the total Labatt Blue volume in 1998, 85 per cent was derived from the Canadian domestic and U.S. markets, with the balance sold in the United Kingdom. The Labatt brands had been introduced to both France and Belgium, and production had been licensed in Italy, but these volumes were minimal. The only real export growth market for Labatt Blue appeared to be the United States, where the brand's volume in 1998 was some 23 per cent higher than in 1995, behind only Corona and Heineken in the imported brand segment. The Labatt Ice brand was also sold in a limited number of markets and, after the appeal of this Labatt innovation had peaked, its total volume had declined by more than 25 per cent since 1996. Total Labatt Ice volume worldwide was just

450,000 hls in 1998, of which 43 per cent was sold in Canada, 33 per cent in the United States, and 21 per cent in the United Kingdom.

Stella Artois as Interbrew's International Flagship Brand

The other potential brand that Interbrew could develop on a global scale was Stella Artois, a brand that could trace its roots back to 1366. The modern version of Stella Artois was launched in 1920 as a Christmas beer and had become a strong market leader in its home market of Belgium through the 1970s. By the 1990s, however, Stella's market position began to suffer from an image as a somewhat old-fashioned beer, and the brand began to experience persistent volume decline. Problems in the domestic market, however, appeared to be shared by a number of other prominent international brands. In fact, seven of the top 10 international brands had experienced declining sales in their home markets between 1995 and 1999 (see **Exhibit 3**).

Stella Artois had achieved great success in the United Kingdom through its licensee, Whitbread, where Stella Artois became the leading premium lager beer. Indeed, the United Kingdom was the largest market for Stella Artois, accounting for 49 per cent of total brand volume in 1998. Stella Artois volume in the U.K. market reached

Exhibit 3   Domestic Sales History of Major International Brands (million hectolitre)

	1995	1996	1997	1998
Budweiser (incl. Bud Light until '98)	69.48	71.10	72.43	40.00
Bud Light	n/a	n/a	n/a	30.00
Heineken	3.87	3.78	3.85	3.78
Beck's	1.68	1.71	1.72	1.78
Carlsberg	1.47	1.39	1.31	1.22
Stella Artois	1.08	1.00	0.96	0.92
Foster's	1.48	1.11	1.40	1.43
Kronenbourg	5.65	5.53	5.35	5.60
Amstel	2.30	2.23	2.21	2.18
Corona	12.89	14.09	14.80	15.18

2.8 million hls in 1998, a 7.6 per cent share of the lager market, and came close to 3.5 million hls in 1999, a 25 per cent increase over the previous year. By this time, over 32,000 outlets sold Stella Artois on draught.

Apart from the United Kingdom, the key markets for Stella Artois were France and Belgium, which together accounted for a further 31 per cent of total brand volume (see **Exhibit 4**). With these three markets accounting for 81 per cent of total Stella Artois volume in 1999, few other areas represented a significant volume base (see **Exhibit 5**). Beyond the top three markets, the largest market for Stella Artois was Italy, where the brand was produced under license by Heineken. Stella Artois volume in Italy had, however, declined slightly to 166,000 hls in 1998. Licensing agreements were also in place in Sweden and Australia, but volume was small.

Stella Artois was also produced in Interbrew's own breweries in Hungary, Croatia and Romania, with very pleasing 1998 volumes of 84,000 hls, 120,000 hls, and 60,000 hls, respectively. After only three years, the market share of Stella Artois in Croatia, for example, had reached four per cent—a significant result, given that the brand was a premium-priced product. In all Central European markets, Stella Artois was priced at a premium; in Hungary, however, that premium was lower than in Croatia and Romania where, on an index comparing Stella's

Exhibit 5	Stella Artois Sales Volume Summary (ooo hectolitre)		
	1997	**1998**	**1999**
Production:			
Belgium	965	921	902
France	1,028	1,110	1,074
Hungary	59	84	117
Croatia	54	120	133
Romania	17	60	112
Bulgaria	—	—	3
Bosnia-Herzegovina	—	—	2
Montenegro	—	—	0
Total Production	**2,123**	**2,295**	**2,343**
License Brewing:			
Italy	162	166	172
Australia	6	11	22
New Zealand	7	11	22
Sweden	29	27	24
Greece	7	7	10
UK	2,139	2,815	3,377
Total Licensed	**2,350**	**3,037**	**3,627**
Export:			
USA	—	—	7
Canada	—	—	5
Other Countries	92	49	202
Duty Free	245	389	507
Total Export	**337**	**438**	**721**
Overall Total	**4,810**	**5,770**	**6,691**

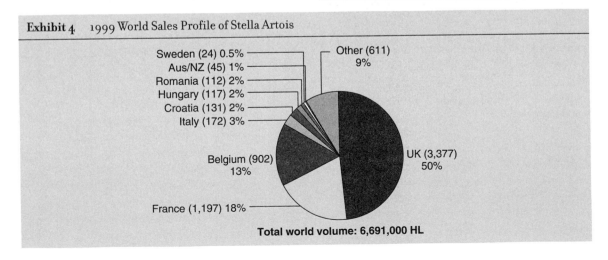

Exhibit 4   1999 World Sales Profile of Stella Artois

Sweden (24) 0.5%
Aus/NZ (45) 1%
Romania (112) 2%
Hungary (117) 2%
Croatia (131) 2%
Italy (172) 3%
Other (611) 9%
Belgium (902) 13%
France (1,197) 18%
UK (3,377) 50%

Total world volume: 6,691,000 HL

price to that of core lagers, the indices by country were 140, 260 and 175 respectively.

Promising first results were also attained in Australia and New Zealand. Particularly in New Zealand, through a "seeding" approach, Interbrew and their local partner, Lion Nathan, had realized great success in the Belgian Beer Café in Auckland where the brands were showcased. After only two years of support, Stella Artois volume was up to 20,000 hls, and growing at 70 per cent annually, out of a total premium segment of 400,000 hls. Interbrew's market development plan limited distribution to top outlets in key metropolitan centres and priced Stella Artois significantly above competitors (e.g., 10 per cent over Heineken and 20 per cent over Steinlager, the leading domestic premium lager brand).

The evolution of the brand looked very positive as world volumes for Stella Artois continued to grow. In fact, Stella Artois volume had increased from 3.4 million hls in 1992 to a total of 6.7 million hls in 1999, a rise of 97 per cent. Ironically, the only market where the brand continued its steady decline was in its home base of Belgium. Analysts suggested a variety of reasons to explain this anomaly, including inconsistent sales and marketing support, particularly as the organization began to favor the rising Jupiler brand.

Overall, given Interbrew's large number of local brands, especially those in Mexico with very high volumes, total Stella Artois volume accounted for only 10 per cent of total Interbrew volume in 1999 (14 per cent if Femsa volumes are excluded). Interbrew's strategy of nurturing a wide portfolio of strong brands was very different as compared to some of its major competitors. For example, Anheuser-Busch, the world's largest brewer, focused its international strategy almost exclusively on the development of the Budweiser brand. Similarly, Heineken sought to centre its international business on the Heineken brand and, to a lesser extent, on Amstel. While the strategies of Anheuser-Busch and Heineken focused primarily on one brand, there were also great differences in the way these two brands were being managed. For example, Budweiser, the world's largest brand by volume, had the overwhelming bulk of its volume in its home U.S. market (see Exhibit 6). Sales of the Heineken brand, on the other hand, were widely distributed across markets around the world

Exhibit 6   Top 10 Brewers by International Sales

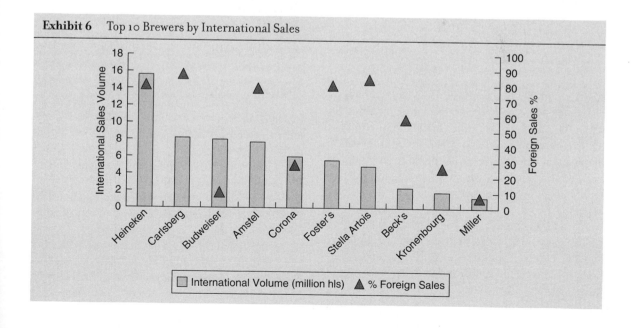

Legend: ☐ International Volume (million hls)   ▲ % Foreign Sales

Exhibit 7   1998 Heineken World Sales Profile

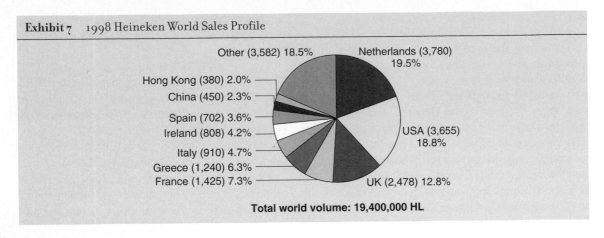

Other (3,582) 18.5%
Netherlands (3,780) 19.5%
Hong Kong (380) 2.0%
China (450) 2.3%
Spain (702) 3.6%
Ireland (808) 4.2%
Italy (910) 4.7%
Greece (1,240) 6.3%
France (1,425) 7.3%
USA (3,655) 18.8%
UK (2,478) 12.8%

Total world volume: 19,400,000 HL

Exhibit 8   1998 Foster's World Sales Profile

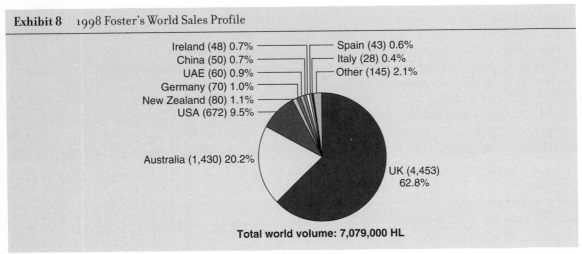

Ireland (48) 0.7%
China (50) 0.7%
UAE (60) 0.9%
Germany (70) 1.0%
New Zealand (80) 1.1%
USA (672) 9.5%
Spain (43) 0.6%
Italy (28) 0.4%
Other (145) 2.1%
Australia (1,430) 20.2%
UK (4,453) 62.8%

Total world volume: 7,079,000 HL

(see Exhibit 7). In this sense, Heineken's strategy was much more comparable to that of Interbrew's plans for Stella Artois. Other brands that were directly comparable to Stella Artois, in terms of total volume and importance of the brand to the overall sales of the company, were Carlsberg and Foster's with annual sales volumes in 1998 of 9.4 million hls and 7.1 million hls, respectively. While Foster's was successful in many international markets, there was a heavy focus on sales in the United Kingdom and the United States (see Exhibit 8). Carlsberg sales volume profile was different in that sales were more widely distributed across international markets (see Exhibit 9).

Stella's Global Launch

In 1998, Interbrew's executive management committee settled on Stella Artois, positioned as the premium European lager, as the company's global flagship brand. In fact, the Interbrew management felt that stock analysts would be favorably disposed to Interbrew having an acknowledged global brand with the potential for a higher corporate valuation and price earnings (P/E) multiple.

As the global campaign got under way, it became clear that the organization needed time to adapt to centralized co-ordination and control of Stella Artois brand marketing. This was, perhaps, not unexpected

Exhibit 9   1998 Carlsberg World Sales Profile

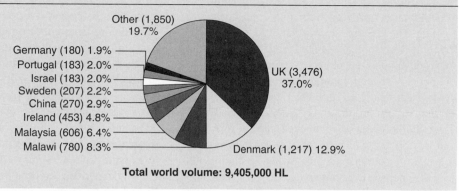

Other (1,850) 19.7%

Germany (180) 1.9%
Portugal (183) 2.0%
Israel (183) 2.0%
Sweden (207) 2.2%
China (270) 2.9%
Ireland (453) 4.8%
Malaysia (606) 6.4%
Malawi (780) 8.3%

UK (3,476) 37.0%

Denmark (1,217) 12.9%

Total world volume: 9,405,000 HL

Exhibit 10   Global Positioning Statement

Brand Positioning

To males, between 21 to 45 years of age, that are premium lager drinkers, Stella Artois is a European premium lager beer, differentially positioned toward the product.

Stella Artois offers a modern, sophisticated, yet accessible drinking experience with an emphasis on the very high quality of the beer supported by the noble tradition of European brewing.

The accent is on the emotional consequence of benefit: a positive feeling of self-esteem and sophistication.

Character, Tone of Voice

Sophistication
Authenticity, tradition, yet touch of modernity
Timelessness
Premium quality
Special, yet accessible
Mysticism
European

given that Interbrew had until recently operated on a regional basis; the new centralized Stella brand management approach had been in place only since September 1998. In addition, there were often difficulties in convincing all parties to become part of a new global approach, particularly the international advertising campaign that was the backbone of the global plan for Stella Artois. Belgium, for example, continued with a specific local advertising program that positioned Stella as a mainstream lager in its home market, and in the United Kingdom, Whitbread maintained its "reassuringly expensive" advertising slogan that had already proved to be so successful. For other less-established markets, a

global advertising framework was created that included a television concept and a series of print and outdoor executions. This base advertising plan was rolled out in 1999 in 15 markets, including the United States, Canada, Italy, Hungary, Croatia, Bulgaria, Romania, New Zealand and France (with a slightly changed format) after research suggested that the campaign had the ability to cross borders. The objective of this campaign was to position Stella Artois as a sophisticated European lager. It was intended that Stella Artois should be perceived as a beer with an important brewing tradition and heritage but, at the same time, also as a contemporary beer (see Exhibit 10).

In 1998, an accelerated plan was devised to introduce Stella Artois to two key markets within the United States, utilizing both local and corporate funding. The U.S. market was believed to be key for the future development of the brand since it was the most developed specialty market in the world (12 per cent specialty market share, growing 10 per cent plus annually through the 1990s), and because of the strong influence on international trends. Thus, Stella Artois was launched in New York City and Boston and was well received by the demanding U.S. consumer and pub owner. Within 1999, over 200 pubs in Manhattan and 80 bars in Boston had begun to sell Stella Artois on tap. To support the heightened efforts to establish Stella Artois in these competitive urban markets, Interbrew's corporate marketing department added several million dollars to Labatt USA's budget for Stella Artois in 2000, with commitments to continue this additional funding in subsequent years.

Current Thinking

Good progress had been made since 1998 when Stella Artois was established as Interbrew's global brand. However, management had revised its expectations for P/E leverage from having a global brand. The reality was that Interbrew would be rewarded only through cash benefits from operational leverage of a global brand. There would be no "free lunch" simply for being perceived as having a global brand. In addition, in an era of tight fiscal management, it was an ongoing challenge to maintain the funding levels required by the ambitious development plans for Stella Artois. As a result, in early 2000 the prevailing view at Interbrew began to shift, converging on a different long-range approach towards global branding. The emerging perspective emphasized a more balanced brand development program, focusing on the highest leverage opportunities.

The experience of other brewers that had established global brands offered an opportunity for Interbrew to learn from their successes and failures. Carlsberg and Heineken, for example, were two comparable global brands that were valued quite differently by the stock market. Both sold over 80 per cent of their total volumes outside their domestic market, and yet Heineken stock achieved a P/E ratio of 32.4 in 1999 versus Carlsberg's figure of only 17.1. According to industry analysts, the driving force behind this difference was that Heineken maintained a superior market distribution in terms of growth and margin (see Exhibit 11). The key lesson from examining these global brands appeared to be that great discipline must be applied to focus resources in the right places.

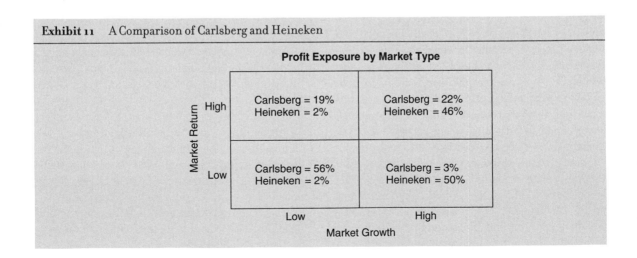

Exhibit 11   A Comparison of Carlsberg and Heineken

Profit Exposure by Market Type

		Low Market Growth	High Market Growth
Market Return	High	Carlsberg = 19% Heineken = 2%	Carlsberg = 22% Heineken = 46%
	Low	Carlsberg = 56% Heineken = 2%	Carlsberg = 3% Heineken = 50%

In line with this thinking, a long range marketing plan began to take shape that made use of a series of strategic filters to yield a focused set of attractive opportunities. The first filter that any potential market had to pass through was its long-term volume potential for Stella Artois. This volume had to trace back to a large and/or growing market, the current or potential sizeable premium lager segment (at least five per cent of the total market), and the possibility for Stella Artois to penetrate the top three brands. The second screen was the potential to achieve attractive margins after an initial starting period of approximately three years. The third filter was whether or not a committed local partner was available to provide the right quality of distribution and to co-invest in the brand. The final screen was the determination that success in the chosen focus markets should increase leverage in other local and regional markets. For example, the size and stature of Stella Artois in the United Kingdom was a significant factor in the easy sell-in of Stella Artois into New York in 1999.

Once filtered through these strategic market development screens, the global branding plans for Stella Artois began to take a different shape. Rather than focus on national markets, plans emerged with an emphasis on about 20 cities, some of which Interbrew was already present in (e.g., London, Brussels, New York, etc.). This approach suggested that the next moves should be in such potential markets as Moscow, Los Angeles and Hong Kong. Some existing cities would receive focused efforts only when distribution partner issues had been successfully resolved to solidify the bases for sustained long term growth. The major cities that fit these criteria provided the right concentration of affluent consumers, who would be attracted to Stella's positioning, thus providing scale for marketing and sales, investment leverage, as well as getting the attention and support of motivated wholesalers and initial retail customers. These venues would thereby become highly visible success stories that would be leveragable in the company's ongoing market development plans.

Thus, the evolving global branding development plan required careful planning on a city-by-city basis. Among the demands of this new approach were that marketing efforts and the funding to support them would have to be both centrally stewarded and locally tailored to reflect the unique local environments. A corporate marketing group was, therefore, established and was charged with the responsibility to identify top priority markets, develop core positioning and guidelines for local execution, assemble broadly based marketing programs (e.g., TV, print advertising, global sponsorships, beer.com content, etc.), and allocate resources to achieve the accelerated growth objectives in these targeted cities. To ensure an integrated development effort the company brought all pivotal resources together, under the leadership of a global brand development director. In addition to the brand management team, the group included regional sales managers who were responsible for licensed partner management, a customer services group, a Belgian beer café manager, and cruise business management group. Another significant challenge that faced the corporate marketing group was to ensure that all necessary groups were supportive of the new approach. This was a simpler undertaking among those business units that were wholly owned subsidiaries; it was a more delicate issue in the case of licensees and joint ventures. A key element of managing brands through a global organizational structure was that the head office team had to effectively build partnerships with local managers to ensure their commitment.

Fortunately, much of the initial effort to establish Stella Artois as a global brand had been done on a city-by-city basis and, as such, there was ample opportunity for Interbrew to learn from these experiences as the new global plan evolved. In the late 1990s, for example, Stella Artois was introduced to various Central European cities (e.g., Budapest, Zagreb, Bucharest and Sofia). In each of these cities, Interbrew's marketing efforts were launched when the targeted premium market was at an early stage of development. Further, distribution and promotion was strictly controlled (e.g., product quality, glassware, etc.) and the development initiatives were delivered in a concentrated manner (e.g., a media "blitz" in Budapest). In addition, results indicated that the presence of a Belgian Beer Café accelerated Interbrew's market development plans in these new areas. These early successes suggested that brand success could be derived from the careful and concentrated targeting of young adults living in urban centres, with subsequent pull from outlying areas following key city success.

The key lessons of these efforts in Central Europe proved to be very valuable in guiding the market development plan in New York City. In this key North American city, the rollout of Stella Artois was perceived by the analysts as "one of the most promising introductions in New York over the last 20 years" and had generated great wholesaler support and excitement. Among the tactics used to achieve this early success was selective distribution with targeted point of sale materials support. In addition, a selective media campaign was undertaken that included only prestigious outdoor advertising (e.g., a Times Square poster run through the Millennium celebrations). Similarly, the sponsoring strategy focused only on high-end celebrity events, Belgian food events, exclusive parties, fashion shows, etc. Finally, the price of Stella Artois was targeted at levels above Heineken, to reinforce its gold standard positioning. This concerted and consistent market push created an impact that resulted in the "easiest new brand sell" in years, according to wholesalers. The success of this launch also built brand and corporate credibility, paving the way to introductions in other U.S. cities as well as "opening the eyes" of other customers and distribution partners around the world.

To pursue this new global development plan over the next three years, a revised marketing budget was required. Given that the corporate marketing department was responsible for both the development of core programs as well as the selective support of local markets, the budget had to cover both of these key elements. To achieve these ends, total spending was expected to more than double over the next three years.

While great progress had been made on the global branding of Stella Artois, Cooke still ruminated on a variety of important interrelated issues. Among these issues was the situation of Stella Artois in Belgium—would it be possible to win in the "global game" without renewed growth in the home market? What specific aspirations should Interbrew set for Belgium over the next three years? Further, what expectations should Interbrew have of its global brand market development (e.g., volumes, profit levels, number of markets and cities, etc.)? How should global success be measured? With respect to Interbrew's promotional efforts, how likely would it be that a single global ad campaign could be successful for Stella Artois? Was there a particular sponsorship or promotion idea that could be singled out for global leverage? And what role should the Internet play in developing Stella Artois as a true global brand?

Case 3-3   GE's Imagination Breakthroughs: The Evo Project

Christopher A. Bartlett, Brian J. Hall, and Nicole S. Bennett

As he prepared for the December 2006 meeting with GE's CEO Jeff Immelt, Pierre Comte faced some difficult decisions. Only eight months into his job as chief marketing officer (CMO) of GE's Transportation business, Comte would be presenting Transportation's recommendations on some of the most visible growth initiatives in its locomotive business— projects that had been designated "Imagination Breakthroughs." IBs, as they were called within GE, were new projects with the potential to generate $100 million in new business within two to three years, and were a key part of Immelt's organic growth strategy. At the IB Review, Immelt expected to hear how Transportation was progressing with each of its locomotive IBs and what plans they had for their future.

Within GE Transportation, however, the future of several IBs had been a source of considerable debate, with none more sensitive than the Hybrid locomotive. Launched two years earlier in the belief that it could become a disruptive technology that could redefine the industry, the Hybrid had struggled to develop cost-effective performance, and some of its key sponsors were beginning to wonder if resources should continue to be committed to it. The ongoing debate had resurfaced in November at a growth review meeting in Erie, Pennsylvania, where Transportation's CEO John Dineen asked Comte and Brett BeGole, head of Transportation's Locomotive P&L unit, to describe how they planned to update Immelt on the Hybrid IB. BeGole, an experienced and effective business leader, explained that problems with the cost and performance of batteries had made the project's future highly uncertain. Feeling it was sapping resources from more profitable growth opportunities, he wondered whether it should be sidelined until the technology was further developed.

Comte was uncomfortable with that proposition. He felt that the Hybrid represented a real opportunity for GE to lead fundamental market change, and that sidelining the project could cause it to lose the resources and attention it needed at this critical stage of its development. He also worried about Immelt's reaction, especially since the Hybrid was one of his favorite IB projects. But while he knew that the IB process was designed to encourage risk-taking, Comte also realized that at the end of the day, it had to be commercially viable. In GE, the bottom line always mattered.

As Dineen listened to his direct reports, he understood the source of their differences. BeGole was responsible for the profitability and growth of the Locomotive P&L unit, and would be held accountable for its bottom-line results. But Comte, with his mandate to develop market knowledge and competitive intelligence, had been asked to challenge and stretch the existing organization. Indeed, Dineen recalled telling his new CMO, "Pierre, your job is to make marketing 'the point of thespear'; to take us to places we don't want to go." Now, after listening to the debate, Dineen wondered what Transportation's position on the Hybrid should be in its upcoming IB Review with Immelt.

Immelt Takes Charge: New Demands, New Responses[a]

On Friday, September 7, 2001, 43-year-old Jeff Immelt became GE's ninth CEO in its 109-year history. Four days later, two planes crashed into the World Trade Center towers. In the turmoil that followed, an already fragile post-Internet bubble stock market dropped further, and the subsequent downturn in the economy resulted in a drop in confidence that spread rapidly around the globe.

Despite his many efforts to tighten operations while continuing to grow the business, the new CEO did not have an easy initiation as he tried to deal with the resulting economic downturn, the post-Enron suspicions of large corporations, and the growing global political instability. In 2002, after promising that earnings would grow by double digits, Immelt had to report a modest 7% increase in GE's profits on revenues that were up only 5% on the 2001 sales, which had declined 3% from the prior year. (See **Exhibit 1** for GE financials, 1996–2006.) By the end of 2002, GE's stock was trading at $24, down 39% from a year earlier and 60% from its all-time high of $60 in August 2000. With considerable understatement, Immelt said, "This was not a great year to be a rookie CEO."[1]

Driving Growth: The Strategic Priority Beyond this immediate market pressure, Immelt was acutely aware that he stood in the very long shadow cast by his predecessor, Jack Welch, under whose leadership GE had generated a total return to shareholders of 23% per annum for 20 years, representing an astonishing $380 billion increase in shareholder wealth over his two decades as CEO. Much of the company's

stock price premium was due to the fact that Welch had built GE into a disciplined, efficient machine that delivered on its promise of consistent growth in sales and earnings. The results were achieved in part through effective operations management that drove a 4% per annum organic growth rate (much of it productivity driven), but primarily through a continuous stream of timely acquisitions and clever deal making. This two-pronged approach had resulted in double-digit revenue and profit increases through most of the 1990s.

But Immelt knew that he could not hope to replicate such a performance by simply continuing the same strategy. The environment in the new millennium had changed too much. The new CEO wanted to use GE's size and diversity as sources of strength and to drive growth by investing in places and in ways that others could not easily follow. He began to articulate a strategy that would rely on technology leadership, commercial excellence, and global expansion to build new business bases that would capitalize on what he described as "unstoppable trends."

Beginning in 2002, he challenged his business leaders to identify these new "growth platforms" with the potential to generate $1 billion in operating profit within the next few years. In response, several opportunities emerged, and the company soon began engaging in new fields such as oil and gas technology, securities and sensors, water technology, Hispanic broadcasting, and consumer finance, all of which were growing at a 15% annual rate. "The growth platforms we have identified are in markets that have above average growth rates and can uniquely benefit from GE's capabilities," said Immelt. "Growth is *the* initiative, *the* core competency that we are building in GE."[2]

Building New Capabilities: Investing in Technology and Marketing

To reposition GE's portfolio to leverage growth, Immelt's team lost little time in acquiring companies such as Telemundo to build a base in Hispanic

[a]This section summarizes "GE's Growth Strategy: The Immelt Initiative," Harvard Business School Case No. 306-087.

[1]GE 2002 Annual Report, p. 5.

[2]GE 2003 Annual Report, p. 9.

Exhibit 1 GE Financial Performance, 1992–2006 ($ millions)

	2006	2005	2004	2003	2002	2001	2000	1995
General Electric Company & Consolidated Affiliates								
Revenues	163,391	147,956	134,291	113,421	132,226	125,913	129,853	70,028
Earnings from continuing operations	20,666	18,631	16,601	15,589	15,133	14,128	12,735	6,573
Loss from discontinued operations	163	(1,922)	559	2,057	(616)	(444)	0	
Net earnings	20,829	16,711	17,160	14,091	14,629	13,684	12,735	6,573
Dividends declared	10,675	9,647	8,594	7,759	7,266	6,555	5,647	2,838
Earned on average shareowner's equity	19.5%	17.8%	17.9%	20%	25.2%	27.1%	27.5%	23.5%
Per share:								
Net earnings	1.99	1.76	1.59	1.4	1.46	1.41	3.87	3.90
Net earnings—diluted	1.99	1.76	1.59	1.4	1.52	1.37	3.81	
Dividends declared	1.03	0.91	0.82	0.77	0.73	0.66	1.71	1.69
Stock price range[a]	38.49–32.06	37.34–32.67	37.75–28.88	32.43–21.30	41.84–21.40	52.90–28.25	60.5–41.66	73.13–49.88
Total assets of continuing operations	697,239	673,321	750,617	647,834	575,018	495,023	437,006	228,035
Long-term borrowings	260,804	212,281	207,871	170,309	138,570	79,806	82,132	51,027
Shares outstanding—average (in thousands)	10,359,320	10,569,805	10,399,629	10,018,587	9,947,113	9,932,245	3,299,037	1,683,812
Employees at year-end:								
United States	155,000	161,000	165,000	155,000	161,000	158,000	168,000	150,000
Other countries	165,000	155,000	142,000	150,000	154,000	152,000	145,000	72,000
Total employees	319,000	316,000	307,000	305,000	315,000	310,000	313,000	222,000

Source: Compiled from GE annual reports, various years.
[a]Stock price adjusted for stock split in 2000.

broadcasting, Interlogix in security systems, BetzDearborn in water-processing services, and Enron Wind in renewable energy. After completing $35 billion worth of acquisitions in 2001 and 2002, GE completed the biggest acquisition year in its history in 2003, including two megadeals: $14 billion for media giant Vivendi Universal Entertainment (VUE), and $10 billion for UK-based Amersham, a leader in biosciences.

But Immelt also recognized that he would have to make equally significant internal investments to ensure that his strategy of technology-driven, commercially-oriented global expansion could build on this new growth platform. Within his first six months, he had committed $100 million to up-grade GE's major R&D facility at Niskayuna in upstate New York. Then, in 2002, he authorized a new Global Research Center (GRC) in Shanghai, and in 2003 agreed to build another GRC in Munich, investments involving another $100 million. And despite the slowing economy, he upped the R&D budget 14% to $359 million in 2003. When asked about the increase in spending during such a diffi-cult time for the company, he said, "Organic growth is the driver. Acquisitions are secondary to that. I can't see us go out and pay a start-up $100 million for technology that, if we had just spent $2 million a year for 10 years, we could have done a better job at it. I hate that, I just hate that."[3]

Rather than concentrating primarily on short-term product development as it had in the past, the GRCs' agenda become more oriented toward the long term. R&D also became more focused, with more than 1,000 projects slashed to just 100. Furthermore, the research group identified five very long-term technology areas for special attention, in fields as diverse as nanotechnology, advanced propulsion, and biotechnology. It was a longer-term R&D focus than GE had seen for many years.

The other core competency Immelt wanted to use to drive organic growth was marketing. As an ex-salesman, he had always focused on the customer

[3]Robert Buderi, "GE Finds Its Inner Edison," *Technology Review,* October, 2003, pp. 46–50.

and felt that an unintended by-product of Welch's obsession with operating efficiency and cost-cutting had been the development of a culture that was too internally focused. He wanted the organization to turn its attention to the marketplace and to bring in a more commercially oriented perspective to its decisions.

In one of Immelt's first appointments, Beth Com-stock was named GE's chief marketing officer, a position Welch had abolished decades earlier. (See **Exhibit 2** for the GE's corporate organization chart.) Immelt also redeployed most of GE's large acquisition-oriented corporate business develop-ment staff into marketing roles, and asked each of GE's businesses to appoint a VP-level marketing head to develop that capability in the business. Because of the shortage of internal talent, many of these marketing leaders had to be recruited from outside, an uncommon practice at GE.

To provide a forum for these new leaders to monitor and drive the change Immelt wanted, in 2003 he formed a Commercial Council made up of 20 respected commercial leaders drawn from a di-verse range of GE businesses. Not all members were corporate officers, or even among the top 600 in GE's Senior Executive Band, but all shared the distinction of being personally selected by the CEO for their innovative thinking. Meeting monthly by phone and quarterly in person, the group used this forum to discuss mega-trends, to identify broad strategies for international growth, and to diffuse best marketing practices rapidly throughout GE. To underline its importance, Immelt chaired the council.

Realigning Personal Competencies: Developing "Growth Leaders"   The investment in new capa-bilities had an immediate impact on GE's manage-ment profile. Within Immelt's first two years, the company recruited over 5000 engineers, and among the 175 corporate officers, the number of engineers grew from seven to 21. The same dramatic change was occurring in sales and marketing, and in 2003, the company began a process to increase GE's under-resourced marketing staff by 2000 over the next two years. To help integrate this influx of senior-level

Exhibit 2   GE Corporate Structure

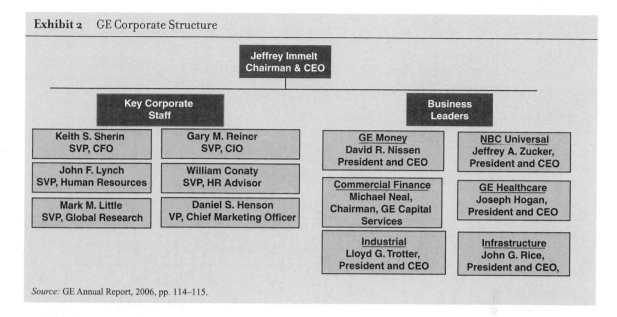

Source: GE Annual Report, 2006, pp. 114–115.

marketers into GE's culture and systems, the Experienced Commercial Leadership Program was created.

As big a task as it was, recruiting top talent into these growth-driving functions was less of a concern to the CEO than the challenge of developing new capabilities in his current management team. While strong in operations and finance, some lacked the skills Immelt felt they would need to succeed in the more entrepreneurial, risk-taking environment he wanted to create. To help define the leadership behaviors that would be required to drive organic growth, the human resources staff researched the competency profiles at 15 large, fast-growth global companies such as Toyota, P&G, and Dell. They concluded that five leadership traits would be key to driving organic growth in GE:

- An external focus
- An ability to think clearly
- Imagination and courage
- Inclusiveness and connection with people
- In-depth expertise

Soon, all courses at GE's Crotonville education center focused on developing these characteristics,

and Immelt made it clear that unless managers had these traits or were developing them, they would not be likely to succeed at GE regardless of their past track record. And to underline his commitment to supporting a new generation of "growth leaders," he began making changes to some of GE's well-established norms and practices. For example, to develop leaders with more in-depth market and technological knowledge and domain expertise, Immelt decided to slow the job rotations that had long been central to management development at GE; to build new technological and marketing capabilities rapidly, he accepted the need to recruit from the outside; and to encourage individuals to take risks, and even to fail, Immelt adjusted the evaluation and reward processes that previously had been tied to flawless execution of short-term budget objectives.

Embedding Growth in Processes and Metrics   In classic GE form, all elements of the new organic growth initiative were soon being reinforced in metrics, systems, and processes to ensure that the new objectives received the disciplined follow-up that characterized GE's management style. It was this cycle of tightly linked and mutually supportive systems and processes and that were the backbone of

Exhibit 3   GE's Operating System

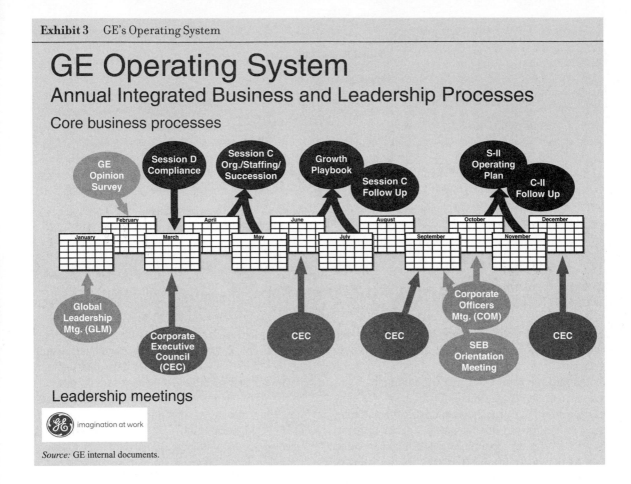

GE Operating System
Annual Integrated Business and Leadership Processes
Core business processes

Leadership meetings

GE imagination at work

Source: GE internal documents.

the company's Operating System that supported GE's reputation for clear strategy and a disciplined implementation.

At the heart of the Operating System were three core processes that had framed management reviews over many decades—Session C, Session I, and Session II. (See **Exhibit 3** for a graphic representation.) Each was now harnessed to drive the growth agenda. For example, the Session C organization, staffing, and succession reviews each May became a powerful tool to reinforce the recruitment, promotion, and deployment of technological and marketing talent, as well as the development of a new generation of "growth leaders" willing to take risks to build new businesses. Next, in July, Session I (GE's strategy

review process that Immelt renamed the Growth Playbook) required each business to drill down on how market trends and customer needs provided opportunities for them to grow their business organically. And in November's Session II, discussions of the operating budget (driven in the GE model by stretch targets rather than line item expense reviews) made sure that each business's commitments to invest in and deliver on growth projects were not cut back in order to meet short-term performance objectives.

Further, the metrics used in the implementation of each of these systems were also changed to reflect the new growth objectives. For example, individual development reviews and performance evaluations leading up to Session C now evaluated managers against the new growth traits. In the first year, only corporate officers were evaluated; the following year, the metrics were extended to the 600 in the Senior Executive Band; and by year three, the top 7000 executives were getting feedback and development support around the required growth traits. New metrics in the Session I/Growth Playbook review required managers to develop and defend strategies to achieve Immelt's objective organic growth rate of 5% above GDP growth by doubling GE's organic growth from 4% to 8% annually. And in Session II, a new Net Promoter Score was added to hold managers accountable for a demanding measure of customer loyalty and repurchase.

Imagination Breakthroughs: Engine of Organic Growth   By the end of 2003, Immelt told investors that he had now completed the big investments needed to re-position the company's business platforms for the future. But results were still disappointing, and with both income and revenue barely above the levels of 2000, some observers were beginning to question whether the GE's greatest growth was behind it. Immelt rejected that notion, and saw no reason for GE to slow down as long as it was able to change its approach and emphasize organic growth. "In the late 1990s, we became business traders not business growers," he said. "Today, organic growth is absolutely the biggest task in every one of our companies."[4]

Having spent his first two years repositioning the business portfolio and investing in new organizational capabilities, Immelt now wanted to drive the pursuit of organic growth much deeper into the company. In September 2003, he convened a meeting of marketing directors from each of GE's businesses and challenged to develop by November five proposals for new growth businesses—"Imagination Breakthroughs" he called them, or IBs as they quickly became known. "We have to put growth on steroids," he said. "I want game changers. Take a big swing."[5]

[4]Jeffrey R. Immelt, "Growth As a Process," *Harvard Business Review,* June 2006, p. 64.
[5]Erick Schonfeld, "GE Sees the Light," *Business 2.0,* July 2004, Vol. 5, Iss. 6, pp. 80–86.

Over the next two months, the marketing leaders engaged management of all of GE's businesses to respond to Immelt's challenge. In November, they presented 50 IB proposals to the CEO and a small group of corporate marketing staff who now became the IB Review Committee. Of this initial portfolio, the CEO green-lighted 35, which the businesses were then expected to fund, adapt, and pursue. And Immelt indicated that he intended to monitor progress—personally and closely.

GE Transportation's First IB: The Evo Story

In September 2003, in response to Immelt's request, GE Transportation identified its five potential IBs. Perhaps the most exciting was the Evolution Locomotive, a product already on the shelf as a planned new product introduction, but struggling to get support due to challenges in both its technical development and its market acceptance. The designation of this project as an IB turned a corporate spotlight on its funding and put a supercharger on its commercialization.

Origins of the Evolution Locomotive   GE began serving the North American rail market in 1918, and through numerous cycles over the better part of the next century, the company steadily built a good business selling to North America's six large rail companies. By the mid-1990s, with revenues approaching $2 billion, GE had built a dominant market share, and its AC4400 long-haul locomotive was recognized as the most successful engine on the market. But it was a mature and conservative industry, and an unlikely place to jumpstart an initiative that called for cutting-edge technology, innovation, and risk taking.

In a rare innovative move in the industry, in 1995 GE introduced its much anticipated "super-loco," the AC 6000. Touted as the most powerful locomotive on the market, its size and hauling capability were impressive. But within a year of its launch, North American customers were reporting that most of the AC6000's new capabilities were unnecessary or uneconomical. This unfortunate misreading of market needs led to only 207 units of the 6000 being sold over the next five years compared with more than 3,000 classic AC4400 locomotives in the same period.[6] Worse, many of those that were sold either failed to deliver on their promised cost-benefit performance or had reliability problems. The AC6000 locomotive was eventually discontinued and became a black eye on GE's otherwise strong record in the industry.

Meanwhile, in December 1997, Environmental Protection Agency (EPA) upset the predictable rail market by announcing strict emissions requirements for all new locomotives to be put in service after January 1, 2005. The regulations posed serious engineering challenges and a major commercial risk for locomotive manufacturers whose safest response was to modify existing models to meet the new standards. While most companies chose to follow this conservative strategy, GE engineers committed to a riskier and more expensive approach of designing a completely new platform able to meet future emissions standards while also keeping fuel costs down.

Over the following three years, engineers in Erie and at the Global Research Center in Niskayuna worked to redefine the paradigm of locomotive design by eliminating the traditional tradeoff between fuel efficiency and emissions. The result was the Evolution Locomotive (quickly dubbed the Evo) which used a revolutionary engine combined with a patented cooling system to achieve 3% to 5% fuel savings while generating 40% less emissions than the previous generation. It also incorporated a locomotive control system enhancement that managed the speed and throttle settings to minimize fuel consumption and/or emissions, taking into account train composition, terrain, track conditions, train dynamics, and weather, without negatively impacting the train's arrival time.

Although this radical new engine represented a clear technical advancement, the decision to take it from design to production was a gamble. Because locomotives delivered before January 1, 2005 were exempt from the new regulations, some predicted that there would be a spike in demand for old models in 2004, leaving little market for the Evo in 2005. Indeed, the sales force reported that most customers were wary about making early commitments to meet the new requirements. But the believers on the GE team argued that the Evo could deliver real savings in fuel and labor, areas in which costs were mounting rapidly in the industry. In a major bet, in 2002 GE committed to building its Evolution locomotive. (See **Exhibit 4** for a photo and basic specifications for the Evo.)

Evo Becomes an IB   The earlier AC6000 product failure coupled with the looming change in environmental regulations in the industry put the locomotive business leaders in Erie under intense pressure to prove to the CEO that they could grow their mature business organically. When Immelt announced his quest for $100 million Imagination Breakthroughs, it was clear that the Evo would be a "make or break" project. Despite the continuing uncertainty around its market potential, the Evo became the centerpiece of Transportation's presentation in its first IB Review with Immelt. The CEO was immediately taken by the project's potential and told the sponsoring managers that he would be monitoring progress in regular review meetings that he planned to conduct monthly with those responsible for IBs.

True to his word, Immelt conducted reviews of several businesses' IBs every month. This meant that every six months or so, those directly responsible for Evo—the P&L leader, the technology leader, and/or the marketing leader—met with him to describe progress and outline next steps for their project. As the team soon learned, PowerPoint presentations were strictly prohibited in these meetings. To encourage an atmosphere of discussion and debate, presenters were allowed no more than one page of documentation for each IB. Although the meetings were small and informal, the managers were not

---

[6]"US loco market still a two-horse race," *Railway Gazette International*, July 1, 2006.

Exhibit 4   Evolution Locomotive Product Specifications

Evolution Series Technology Bears Close Inspection, by Accounting as Well as Engineering.

Overcoming obstacles with technological innovation is meaningless if that technology isn't economically viable for everyday use. That's why every component in an Evolution Series locomotive is proven to meet the demands of those who operate them as well as those who pay for them.

Nowhere is this more evident than with the GEVO-12 engine. The heart of the Evolution Series locomotives, the 45-degree, 12-cylinder, 4-stroke, turbocharged GEVO-12 engine produces the same 4,400 HP as its 16-cylinder predecessor. And it does it with greater fuel efficiency, lower emissions, and extended overhaul intervals. Enhanced cooling and higher-strength materials dramatically improve reliability and allow for future increases in power and efficiency.

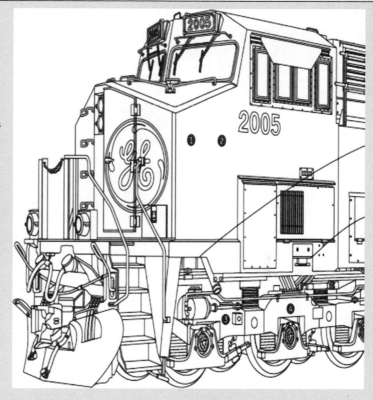

 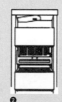

❶ Smart Displays
Several add-on black boxes are eliminated with a new computer display combination, enhancing both reliability and operator ergonomics.

❷ Enhanced Microprocessor Controls
Upgraded components and software improve wheel slip/slide control and reliability while providing more comprehensive and simplified diagnostics. Open architecture enables easier integration of software and third-party devices.

❸ "HiAd" Trucks
Low weight transfer, and improved microprocessor wheel slip/slide system, and a single inverter per motor, combine to optimize adhesion under all rail conditions. Design simplicity and 10-year overhaul intervals significantly reduce maintenance costs.

❹ Low-Slip, High-Performance AC Traction Motors
Get a full 166,000 lbs. (AC) of continuous tractive effort and up to 198,000 lbs. (AC) starting tractive effort from a 6-axle locomotive. Integral pinion design eliminates slippage, extending pinion life to 2 million miles. Million-mile motor overhaul intervals further reduce maintenance costs.

❺ Superior Dynamic Braking
Evolution Series locomotives feature up to 117,000 lbs. (AC) of braking effort, utilizing the proven grids and blowers from our current production AC 4400 & Dash 9. Braking grids are also completely isolated for greater reliability and simplified maintenance.

❻ Air-Cooled Inverters
No coolant. No environmental concerns. A single air-cooled inverter per traction motor provides individual axle control that. improves wheel slip/slide, increases mission reliability, maximizes tractive effort, and improves transmission efficiency.

Exhibit 4   Evolution Locomotive Product Specifications (continued)

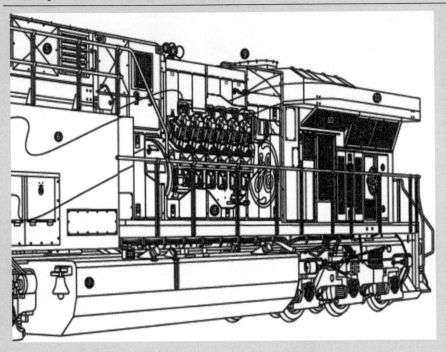

High-Impact Fuel Tank
This tank exceeds AAR
S-5506 with thickened,
reinforced walls and baffles
for even greater puncture
resistance.

Isolation Mounts
Smoother. Quieter.
New isolation
mounts on the en-
gine and alternator
significantly
improve operator
environment with
reduced cab noise
and vibration.

Emissions
"Environmentally compati-
ble" is more than a buzzword
for Evolution Series locomotives. Advanced electronic
fuel injection, air-to-air cooling, adaptive controls, and
GEVO-12 engine technology
combine to reduce emissions
by over 40 percent.

Air-To-Air Intercooler
Manifold Air Temperature
(MAT) is greatly reduced
with the new hybrid cool-
ing system and air-to-air
intercooler. The lower
MAT enables emissions
compliance while
simultaneously improving
fuel efficiency.

Split Cooling
The proven Split Cooling
radiator system reduces
engine-air-inlet tempera-
tures and cools the
engine oil for increased
reliability and longer
engine-bearing life.

Source: Evolution Locomotive brochure, GE TRansportation website: http://www.getransportation.com/na/en/evolution.html.

Exhibit 5   IB Review Preparation: Sample Questions

The following are a few of the questions given to IB teams to help them prepare for reviews:

Market Opportunity
- Can you start with the answer: Where would you like to be and why?
- How does this fit in your strategy?
- What does it take to be good at this?
- How does technology play a role here? Does it give us an advantage?

Competition
- Is anyone else doing this? Who is best at this?
- How we placed vis-à-vis the competition?
- How many others have tried this? Have they succeeded or failed?
- Do our competitors make money at this?

Pricing
- How much would we make on this product?
- How much would the customer pay for this product?
- How do we price it correctly?
- Why aren't we charging a higher price?

Resources
- Where do we have in-house expertise?
- Are you working with any other GE business on this?
- How do we use GE Financial Services as a weapon?
- What resources do we need to hit the growth target? A doubling/tripling of resources?

Go to Market
- What is standing in our way in order to execute this well?
- Is there a way to tap into global suppliers to fill the global pipeline?
- What is the value proposition? How would you differentiate?
- How will you build capability?

Source: GE internal documents.

---

necessarily relaxed. They knew that questioning would be intense, and were advised to be prepared to discuss a range of sample questions. (See **Exhibit 5** for a preparatory list.) So meeting the CEO (supported by just a few of his corporate marketing staff), created some nervous tension. As one manager reflected, "Do you really want to be the only business that shows no imagination or, compared to other business's IBs being presented, has no breakthrough?"

Managers came to IB Review meetings armed with extensive market information, the result of a rigorous analytical process called CECOR that was being rolled out by the corporate marketing group to help business-level marketing teams systematize analysis to support the IB process.[b] (See **Exhibit 6** for an outline of the CECOR process and tools.) Because of Immelt's understanding of the issues and his direct, in-depth questioning, some began calling the IB Review meetings the "Committee of One."

---

[b]CECOR stood for Calibrate, Explore, Create, Organize, and Realize, an analytical process that the corporate marketing group had developed. It was supported by a portfolio of tools borrowed from a variety of sources including the consulting groups Bain and McKinsey, which had proved helpful in doing market segmentation, customer analysis, competitive analysis, etc.

Exhibit 6   CECOR Tool Kit

CECOR Framework
Identifying questions to ask and tools to apply

C CALIBRATE	E EXPLORE	C CREATE	O ORGANIZE	R REALIZE
➤ What industry are you in? ➤ Who are the customers and what do they need?	➤ What are our potential avenues of growth? ➤ Which ones will you target?	➤ What are our best ideas? ➤ What is the customer value?	➤ Is the go-to-market plan aligned with the value proposition? ➤ Are you prepared to implement?	➤ Will you meet your revenue and income plans? ➤ How will you measure customer and GE impact?

Tools

• Five Forces • Market Maps • Profit Pools • Value Chain	• Customer Experience Grid • Segmentation • Competitive Assessment • Targeting	• Capability Assessment • Ideation Sessions • Positioning	• Conjoint Analysis • Value Proposition • Value Based Pricing • Branding	• Go-to-Market Plan • Continuous Feedback (VoC) • Impact Metrics

CECOR's fit in GE's operating rigor

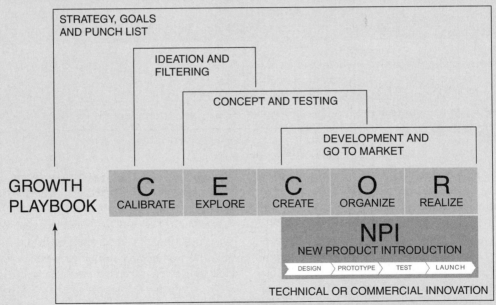

STRATEGY, GOALS AND PUNCH LIST

IDEATION AND FILTERING

CONCEPT AND TESTING

DEVELOPMENT AND GO TO MARKET

GROWTH PLAYBOOK

C CALIBRATE	E EXPLORE	C CREATE	O ORGANIZE	R REALIZE

NPI
NEW PRODUCT INTRODUCTION

DESIGN ❯ PROTOTYPE ❯ TEST ❯ LAUNCH ❯

TECHNICAL OR COMMERCIAL INNOVATION

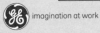

Source: GE internal documents.

In the glare of the IB spotlight, the Evo product management and sales team found themselves under increased pressure to perform. But discussions with customers revealed that GE was still "paying for sins of the past," as one salesman put it, and the team concluded that it would not be able to sell the Evo's value proposition from a piece of paper and a set of specifications. After the failure of the AC6000, customers wanted solid evidence of the benefits being promised.

In a leap of faith, GE Transportation took the financial risk of committing $100 million to build 50 Evo units, which they then planned to lease to customers for a nominal fee. The locomotives were to be carried on GE's books, but would be operated by customers and used on their North American lines. The goal was to log five million miles before the 2005 launch, thereby regaining customers' trust by proving the engine's reliability and the value of the technological advancements.

Preparing to Launch: The Agony . . .   In early 2004, vague concerns about Evo began turning to panic. A year into the leasing plan, the sales team did not have a single firm order. Sales reps were getting positive feedback about performance of the leased Evos, but customers were still reluctant to make the capital expenditure. Transportation's November SII Budget Review for Evo had been grim: worst-case scenarios projected sales of only 30 or 50 locomotives out of a total 2005 capacity of 600 Evos. It was a performance that would result in significant losses. While some felt that GE might have to offer the Evo at an attractive initial price to attract sales, Immelt challenged that assumption. At IB Review meetings, he was pushing the team in the opposite direction, urging them to focus on how to price the soon-to-be-launched product to capture its full value.

Because the Evo offered significant economic savings to the railroads over its lifecycle, Immelt asked why it could not be sold at a premium over the previous model. Discussion about the impact of rising energy costs in the IB Review meetings spilled over into detailed market and product analysis in

Growth Playbook sessions. These meetings with Immelt were very different from the Session I strategy reviews over which Welch had presided. Where Welch had been cost and efficiency-driven, Immelt was focused on the market value of technological advancements like the Evo. "In a deflationary world, you could get margin by working productivity," Immelt said. "Now you need marketing to get a price." [7]

As a result of these discussions, the IB team refined Evo's value story to focus on its lifecycle costs, and decided to reflect the Evo's significant performance improvements in a 10% price premium. Knowing that this decision would cause anxiety within the sales ranks, Dave Tucker, Transportation's VP of Global Sales, turned the annual January sales meeting in Coco Beach, Florida into a call to arms for the Evo. Despite having a single firm order, in the opening session he announced that by June the sales team needed to sell out the factory—and at a significant price premium over the previous model. "It scared the hell out of the sales force," Tucker recalled. "Frankly, we had never had a step-function increase in pricing like that."

Tucker challenged his sales force to come up with the means to implement the plan. In addition to worries about the expected customer reaction, some expressed concerns about the likely response of a key competitor who had not made the same upfront investment. But the marketing group's analysis suggested that rising oil prices, increased rail traffic, and tightening emission standards could make customers more open to Evo's benefits. After several days of joint discussions with marketing and product management, the sales force hit the streets committed to booking orders at the new price.

Implementing the Launch: . . . The Ecstasy   Over the following months, the sales team went back to its customers, emphasizing value to convince them that Evo was worth its price premium. As if responding to a cue, oil prices continued to rise—from $32 a barrel in January 2004, to $40 by

[7] Jeffrey R. Immelt, "Growth As a Process," *Harvard Business Review,* June 2006, p. 64.

June, and $50 by October. At the same time, driven by surging Chinese imports entering the U.S. on the West Coast, transcontinental rail traffic was booming. And state regulatory bodies' demands were making emissions an industry-wide concern. The marketing analyses had proved correct: customers were ready for the Evo.

By the launch date on January 1, 2005, not only was Evo's entire 2005 production sold out, product was on backorder through much of 2006. Despite earlier concerns about a risk of a temporary drop in market share, industry experts estimated that GE maintained or increased its 70% share through the launch and outsold its competition by three to one in the U.S. market during 2005.[8] By mid-2006, there was a backlog of 1500 locomotives, representing two years of production capacity. The early success of the Evo continued into 2007, with all-time highs in deliveries surpassing records set just one year earlier. The Evo had become a poster-child IB success story.

▌ Managing the IB Lifecycle: Raising the Evo Babies

When John Dineen became CEO of GE Transportation in the summer of 2005, Evo was well on its way to being one of the outstanding IB successes. But Dineen made it clear that he wanted to drive even more growth from this old-line, mature portfolio of businesses. To emphasize that objective, he reinforced Immelt's annual corporate Growth Playbook process by creating a Growth Council, to which he invited his entire management team to engage in a monthly review of growth initiatives in each of Transportation's businesses. His objective was to build a growth agenda into the pulse of the business and make it part of the ongoing management discussion.

Birth of an Evo Baby: The Global Modular Locomotive   Acknowledging   that   the   slow-growth domestic markets already dominated by GE

were unlikely to be the major source of new business, Dineen emphasized the opportunities for international expansion. Responding to that challenge, Tim Schweikert, general manager of the Locomotive P&L unit, began to explore with his team the challenge of breaking into the global locomotive market. They soon identified the hurdles they would have to clear in order to sell internationally. First, because railway gauge width, weight limits, and clearance requirements varied widely by country, the team decided that there could be no standardized "global locomotive." Furthermore, the number of locomotives called for in most international tenders (as few as 10 or 15) made the huge upfront investment in engineering a major cost barrier. And finally, because governments were typically the operators of railways, the selling process usually involved complex political negotiations.

Recognizing all of these constraints, Schweikert and his team developed a product concept that it termed the Global Modular Locomotive (GML), a design developed around a set of standard components that could be built to different national requirements using a Lego-like construction approach. With great excitement, they took their idea to Dineen's monthly Growth Council where it was endorsed as a candidate for Immelt's IB Review. Presenting their ideas in this forum in September 2005, the locomotive team preempted Immelt's opening question by identifying GML's three value-creating objectives: to reduce the response time in international tender processing, to reduce the amount spent on nonrecurring engineering, and to reduce the time between the order and the sale. After further probing questions, Immelt congratulated them and approved GML as an IB.

To help Schweikert implement the new IB project, Dineen assigned Gokhan Bayhan to the role of marketing leader for the Locomotive P&L unit. The move was part of a larger strategy of transferring recognized talent into the fledgling business marketing roles. "We took some of our best people from our commercial and engineering organization and put them into these roles," said Dineen. "As soon as you start doing that, the rest of the organization

---

▌ [8]From GE press documents. "Ecomagination: The Hybrid Locomotive," www.ge.com.

realizes it's important. Initially, we had to draft people and assure them that the move was going to be good for their careers. But it was hard. Every bone in their body was telling them not to do it because there was no track record." (See **Exhibit 7** for GE Transportation's organization chart.)

Because Bayhan had earlier worked on a locomotive modernization contract that GE had won to overhaul and rebuild 400 locomotives for the state-owned railway in Kazakhstan, he decided this was a perfect place to explore GML's potential. Soon, he and the sales team were talking to government contacts about the new concept and about the opportunity for GE to help them expand and modernize their railway system to meet the needs of Kazakhstan's fast-growing China trade.

The disciplined process of analyzing the market opportunities and customer needs was part of the marketing group's responsibility. But because this analysis was a new element in the existing process of bringing a product to market, gaining acceptance was not always easy, as Bayhan explained:

> The relationships between product management, sales, and engineering were well established, so a lot of marketing team members had difficulty breaking into that process, and taking on a role that didn't exist before. It was hardest for those from the outside, and they were the majority. It helped that I'd been in the organization in various product management and finance roles because it allowed me to use my access and credibility to contribute a marketing point of view. But lots of others had a hard time with it.

Meanwhile, as sales, engineering, and marketing worked together to test and approve the GML concept, a major boost to the effort occurred in December 2005 when the company announced that it had received an order for 300 GML locomotives from the Chinese railway. In October, Schweikert, who had been close to the Chinese negotiations, was transferred from his position in Erie to become head of GE transportation in China, not only to oversee this important contract, but to use it to expand GE's penetration into this huge market.

Making Marketing Mainstream   As the role and impact of the marketing function grew within Transportation, Dineen accelerated his efforts to find a head of marketing who could not only accelerate existing marketing efforts, but could also provide the function with greater access and influence at the most senior levels of discussion in the company. Finally, in early 2006, he found the person he felt could fill the role. Pierre Comte became chief marketing officer of GE Transportation in May 2006. Surprisingly, although he had a strong commercial background built up through an international career, he did not come from a traditional marketing background. Most recently he had run the rail signaling business at a major European transportation company. But to Dineen, he seemed an ideal fit—someone with relevant industry expertise, good frontline experience, and a strong enough personality to deal credibly with his P&L leaders, and understand their pressures and constraints.

In his first meeting with his new CMO, Dineen told Comte to "create a crisis around growth." But Comte realized he would first have to convince his bottom-line-driven peers that he could help them:

> When you run a $2 billion Locomotive P&L that's doing great, you don't have a pressing need to reinvent yourself and your business. The role of the marketing group is to push the P&L leaders to revisit their portfolios. But they won't listen to chart makers or theoreticians. So I spent three months telling them, "I'm like you, I'm a business guy; I've lived in Asia and Europe. I've run a P&L with a couple of thousand people reporting to me. I know that the last thing you want is another headquarters guy giving you more work to do. I'm not going to do that. I'm here to help you make your P&Ls bigger, stronger."

Under Comte, the new marketing team began to take a more active role in the business, a role that became more and more evident as the Evo offshoot businesses started to grow. The contributions that Gokhan Bayhan made to the redefinition of GML provided a classic example.

The Baby Grows into a Family   In April 2006, as members of the locomotive management team sat

Exhibit 7 GE Transportation Organizational Chart

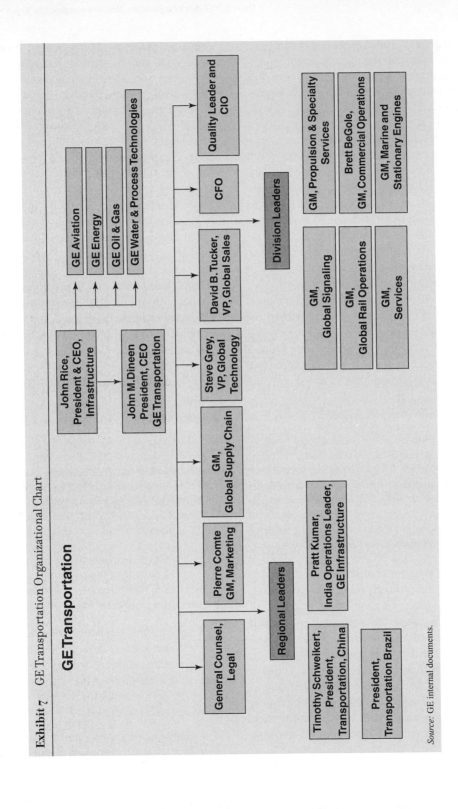

GE Transportation

John Rice, President & CEO, Infrastructure

- GE Aviation
- GE Energy
- GE Oil & Gas
- GE Water & Process Technologies

John M. Dineen, President, CEO GE Transportation

General Counsel, Legal

Pierre Comte GM, Marketing

GM, Global Supply Chain

Steve Grey, VP, Global Technology

David B. Tucker, VP, Global Sales

CFO

Quality Leader and CIO

Regional Leaders

Pratt Kumar, India Operations Leader, GE Infrastructure

Timothy Schweikert, President, Transportation, China

President, Transportation Brazil

Division Leaders

GM, Global Signaling

GM, Global Rail Operations

GM, Services

GM, Propulsion & Specialty Services

Brett BeGole, GM, Commercial Operations

GM, Marine and Stationary Engines

Source: GE internal documents.

down to prepare for their presentation to Immelt at Transportation's Growth Playbook/Session I review in June, some of the initial ideas behind the GML concept were beginning to seem questionable. Doubts were being expressed by people from project management, marketing, and engineering about whether the GML's Lego design would work in practice. To resolve the concerns, Brett BeGole, Schweikert's replacement as global operations general manager for the Locomotive P&L unit, commissioned a "Tiger Team" of six people from engineering, product management, and marketing and gave them two weeks to recommend what changes, if any, should be made to the GML concept.

Much of the team's work was based on a rigorous analysis of a rich set of data on customers, competitors, and market trends that Gokhan Bayhan had assembled. Using CECOR tools including a customer needs analysis, a competitive response analysis, and a market segmentation map, Bayhan presented Steve Gray, his engineering counterpart on the Tiger Team, a rich picture of the critical technical and quality elements that customers were demanding.

After an intense two weeks of analysis, the team came to the conclusion that the GML concept was too complex and too expensive to serve the market efficiently. Instead, they proposed that GML's modular approach be replaced by a platform concept that defined five different families of locomotives, which together would serve 85% to 90% of the global market demand. Three of the five platforms to be developed were based on the Evo engine, while the two other family members would use another engine still under development.

The Tiger Team's recommendations were presented at Transportation's Growth Council in May, where Dineen backed their recommendation by committing to invest in the development engineering required for the Global Locomotive Families (GLF) ahead of any orders being received. It was a major change in practice for the business. With strong analysis and data to support the team's proposal and a clear commitment to invest in it, the new GLF concept was quickly accepted and supported in July's

Growth Playbook /Session I review with Immelt and became one of Transportation's official IBs.

The concept was soon validated when, in September of 2006, the Kazakhstan Railway placed an order for 310 locomotives; soon after, GE received an additional large order from a mining company in Australia; and before year's end it won a tender for 40 more locomotives in Egypt. Bayhan described it as the industry's "perfect storm":

> The big driver was what we call the "China Effect." Our analysis showed how increased trade with China is driving a big surge in demand for all forms of transportation. Around the world, GDP is growing, industrialization is happening, and the China Effect is spreading to other countries. And we were right there when it happened with a good understanding of the customers' needs and the newest technology to meet them. So we were able to respond to the perfect storm with a great product, the right commercial strategy, and perfect market timing.

Like the China order nine months earlier, the big Kazakhstan order came with a condition that after building the first 10 locomotives in Erie, GE would commit to transferring the assembly operation to Kazakhstan in the second half of 2008. The facility would assemble kits shipped from Erie and would become the regional source for locomotives sold to other countries in the CIS (the Commonwealth of Independent States, consisting of 11 former Soviet Republics in Eurasia). It was part of GE's "In Country, For Country" international strategy, and a matter of great pride for the country's prime minister, who proudly announced that Kazakhstan had locomotives with the same technology as the U.S. models.

The Morphing Continues: The New Regional Strategy   As the locomotive contract negotiations were being finalized, they provided a convenient market entrée to other parts of GE's transportation business. In particular, the sales and marketing people from the Services and Signaling P&Ls began using the Locomotive team's contacts to introduce their own products and services. For example, Transportation's Service P&L planned to link any new locomotive sales with a service contract to renew and refurbish worn components locally rather than replacing them with imported new parts. Not only could they promise to save the customer money, they could offer to transfer technology and bring employment to the country.

As initiatives such as this became the norm in markets where locomotive contracts had been signed, the management team of the Locomotive P&L began to explore whether an integrated regional approach to growth might be a more effective business model than the product-based Global Families approach. It was an approach that Comte believed had great value. As he grew the Transportation marketing staff from 14 people to 32, he began moving a significant number of them out of Erie and into the field where they could be closer to the customer. As part of a new geographic-based capability, he

deployed seven Regional Marketing Strategists, each of whom built his own local capabilities to support Transportation's regional general managers. (See **Exhibit 8** for Transportation's marketing organization.)

In December 2006, when the message came down that the Commercial Council would like to see businesses submitting more IB proposals for new emerging countries, it gave support to the growing notion that there was a need to reconfigure the global locomotive IB project once again. One proposal was to morph the major thrust of the GLF project into three integrated regional IBs—one for China, one for Russia/CIS, and one for India—each responsible for driving growth by developing its market for an integrated package of GE locomotives, signals, services, etc. It was an intriguing idea with the potential to roll out to other regions, but would mark

Exhibit 8   Comte's Marketing Organization

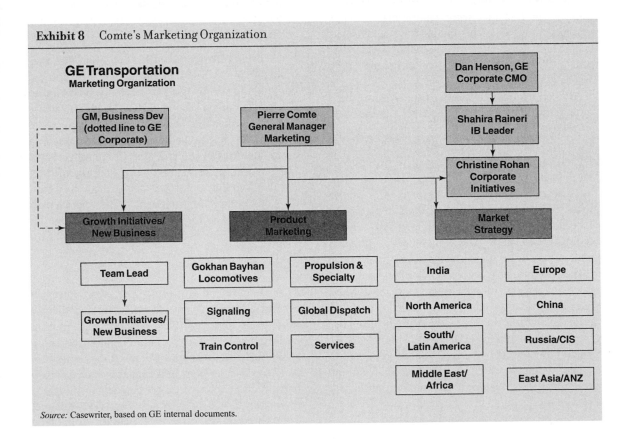

Source: Casewriter, based on GE internal documents.

the third iteration of this IB in its young, less than 18 month life. Some were concerned that it might seem like project churning.

The Hybrid Engine Dilemma: To Be or Not to Be?

At the same December IB Review, the Transportation business was also scheduled to present its latest plans for the Hybrid Locomotive IB. As the entire management team understood, almost three years earlier the Hybrid had captured Immelt's attention as a perfect candidate to fit into the company's just-announced Ecomagination program committed to environmentally responsive innovation. Indeed, it had been the CEO's suggestion to elevate the research on the Hybrid engine and to give it IB status. As he had publicly stated, the Hybrid Locomotive represented "the right solution for the customer, for the market, for the environment, and for GE."

The plans for the Hybrid were centered on a diesel-electric engine that would capture the energy generated during braking and store it in a series of sophisticated batteries. That stored energy could then be used on demand, reducing fuel consumption by as much as 15% and emissions by as much as 50% compared with freight locomotives already in service.[8] But as the concept was translated into a product, it became clear that the battery technology at the core of its design was not able to achieve the proposed customer benefits or provide them at a cost that would make the project economical. As a result, three years into the program, there was no clear evidence that the Hybrid IB would be able to meet any of its original stated objectives—to add value to the customer, to provide returns to GE, and to allow access to new markets. This led some to suggest that the Hybrid should join of the lapsed IBs that had been declared "worthwhile experiments that did not work out."

At Transportation's monthly Growth Council preparing for Immelt's December IB Review, Dineen, BeGole, and Comte explored the options. BeGole argued that with all the opportunities

available in other product-line extensions and geographic expansions, the opportunity cost of the Hybrid project was very high. Specifically, he explained that because of his limited finances and engineering resources (particularly the latter), committing to this option would mean postponing the rollout of some of the promising new international regional platforms for Evo.

On the other hand, as Compte reminded the team, the long-term trend away from fossil fuels and toward alternative energy meant that eventually GE would have to develop hybrid technology. Knowing Immelt's commitment to the Hybrid project, Compte asked whether the team had done enough to understand how customer value could be created in different segments, to explore alternative technological solutions, or to pursue other sources of funding. On the last point, he explained that while his marketing organization had located some potential government funding for hybrid development, they had not applied for funds since this was not GE's normal approach to project financing. In response to questioning, however, Compte acknowledge that even with such additional funds, investing in the Hybrid would mean diverting resources from other growth prospects that seemed more immediately promising.

As Dineen summarized the discussions, he posed three alternative scenarios that could be presented at the December IB Review:

- The first option would be to explain that while the project as currently defined appeared to have very limited to short- to medium-term commercial viability, the business would commit to it as an IB and continue to explore alternative ways to make it successful.
- The second approach would be to acknowledge the Hybrid's long-term potential, but suggest that it be placed on hold as an IB, perhaps by transferring primary responsibility to the Global Research Center to work on the battery technology in collaboration with various GE businesses—including Transportation—that had an interest in its development.

---

[8]From GE press documents. "Ecomagination: The Hybrid Locomotive," www.ge.com.

- The final alternative would be to recommend that the company acknowledge the fact that after three years of hard work on Hybrid, neither the technology development nor the market acceptance of the concept had indicated that it could be a viable commercial proposition in the foreseeable future, and therefore that it be dropped as an IB.

As the management team talked through these options, they tried to balance the best interest of the business with what Immelt was likely to believe was in the best interests of the company. With

83 IBs now approved, and 35 already launched and generating more than $2 billion in additional revenues, the CEO and felt that the process of generating organic growth was established. But that did not mean that he was becoming less involved. He personally tracked every IB, and focused even more intently on those that had caught his attention—like the Hybrid Locomotive. But in true GE fashion, he also held each business responsible for its current performance. As Transportation's management team realized, determining the Hybrid's future was a tough and vital decision that it must now make.

Reading 3-1   Managing Differences: The Central Challenge of Global Strategy

Pankaj Ghemawat

With the globalization of production as well as markets, you need to evaluate your international strategy. Here's a framework to help you think through your options.

When it comes to global strategy, most business leaders and academics make two assumptions: first, that the central challenge is to strike the right balance between economies of scale and responsiveness to local conditions, and second, that the more emphasis companies place on scale economies in their worldwide operations, the more global their strategies will be.

▌**Pankaj Ghemawat** is the Anselmo Rubiralta Professor of Global Strategy at IESE Business School in Barcelona, Spain, and the Jaime and Josefina Chua Tiampo Professor of Business Administration at Harvard Business School in Boston. He is the author of "Regional Strategies for Global Leadership" (HBR December 2005) and the forthcoming book *Redefining Global Strategy: Crossing Borders in a World Where Differences Still Matter,* which will be published in September 2007 by Harvard Business School Press. For a supplemental list of publications on globalization and strategy, go to www.hbr.org and click on the link to this article.
▌Reprinted by permission of Harvard Business Review. From Managing Differences: The Central Challenge of Global Strategy by P. Ghemawat. Copyright © 2007 by the Harvard Business School Publishing Corporation; all rights reserved.

These assumptions are problematic. The main-goal of any global strategy must be to manage the large differences that arise at borders, whether those borders are defined geographically or otherwise. (Strategies of standardization and those of local responsiveness are both conceivably valid responses to that challenge—both, in other words, are global strategies.) Moreover, assuming that the principal tension in global strategy is between scale economies and local responsiveness encourages companies to ignore another functional response to the challenge of cross-border integration: arbitrage. Some companies are finding large opportunities for value creation in exploiting, rather than simply adjusting to or overcoming, the differences they encounter at the borders of their various markets. As a result, we increasingly see value chains spanning multiple countries. IBM's

CEO, Sam Palmisano, noted in a recent *Foreign Affairs* article that an estimated 60,000 manufacturing plants were built by foreign firms in China alone between 2000 and 2003. And trade in IT-enabled services—with India accounting for more than half of IT and business-process offshoring in 2005—is finally starting to have a measurable effect on international trade in services overall.

In this article, I present a new framework for approaching global integration that gets around the problems outlined above. I call it the AAA Triangle. The three A's stand for the three distinct types of global strategy. *Adaptation* seeks to boost revenues and market share by maximizing a firm's local relevance. One extreme example is simply creating local units in each national market that do a pretty good job of carrying out all the steps in the supply chain; many companies use this strategy as they start expanding beyond their home markets. *Aggregation* attempts to deliver economies of scale by creating regional or sometimes global operations; it involves standardizing the product or service offering and grouping together the development and production processes. *Arbitrage* is the exploitation of differences between national or regional markets, often by locating separate parts of the supply chain in different places—for instance, call centers in India, factories in China, and retail shops in Western Europe.

Because most border-crossing enterprises will draw from all three A's to some extent, the framework can be used to develop a summary scorecard indicating how well the company is globalizing. However, because of the significant tensions within and among the approaches, it's not enough to tick off the boxes corresponding to all three. Strategic choice requires some degree of prioritization—and the framework can help with that as well.

Understanding the AAA Triangle

Underlying the AAA Triangle is the premise that companies growing their businesses outside the home market must choose one or more of three basic

strategic options: adaptation, aggregation, and arbitrage. These types of strategy differ in a number of important ways, as summarized in the exhibit "What Are Your Globalization Options?"

The three A's are associated with different organizational types. If a company is emphasizing adaptation, it probably has a country-centered organization. If aggregation is the primary objective, cross-border groupings of various sorts—global business units or product divisions, regional structures, global accounts, and so on—make sense. An emphasis on arbitrage is often best pursued by a vertical, or functional, organization that pays explicit attention to the balancing of supply and demand within and across organizational boundaries. Clearly, not all three modes of organizing can take precedence in one organization at the same time. And although some approaches to corporate organization (such as the matrix) can combine elements of more than one pure mode, they carry costs in terms of managerial complexity.

Most companies will emphasize different A's at different points in their evolution as global enterprises, and some will run through all three. IBM is a case in point. (This characterization of IBM and those of the firms that follow are informed by interviews with the CEOs and other executives.) For most of its history, IBM pursued an adaptation strategy, serving overseas markets by setting up a mini-IBM in each target country. Every one of these companies performed a largely complete set of activities (apart from R&D and resource allocation) and adapted to local differences as necessary. In the 1980s and 1990s, dissatisfaction with the extent to which country-by-country adaptation curtailed opportunities to gain international scale economies led to the overlay of a regional structure on the mini-IBMs. IBM aggregated the countries into regions in order to improve coordination and thus generate more scale economies at the regional and global levels. More recently, however, IBM has also begun to exploit differences across countries. The most visible signs of this new emphasis on arbitrage (not a term the company's leadership uses) are IBM's efforts to exploit wage differentials by increasing the number of employees in India from 9,000 in 2004 to 43,000 by mid-2006 and by planning for massive additional growth. Most of these employees are in IBM Global Services, the part of the company that is growing fastest but has the lowest margins—which they are supposed to help improve, presumably by reducing costs rather than raising prices.

Procter & Gamble started out like IBM, with mini-P&Gs that tried to fit into local markets, but it has evolved differently. The company's global business units now sell through market development organizations that are aggregated up to the regional level. CEO A.G. Lafley explains that while P&G remains willing to adapt to important markets, it ultimately aims to beat competitors—country-centered multinationals as well as local companies—through aggregation. He also makes it clear that arbitrage is important to P&G (mostly through outsourcing) but takes a backseat to both adaptation and aggregation: "If it touches the customer, we don't outsource it." One obvious reason is that the scope for labor arbitrage in the fast-moving consumer goods industry may be increasing but is still much less substantial overall than in, say, IT services. As these examples show, industries vary in terms of the headroom they offer for each of the three A strategies.

Even within the same industry, firms can differ sharply in their global strategic profiles. For a paired example that takes us beyond behemoths from advanced countries, consider two of the leading IT services companies that develop software in India: Tata Consultancy Services, or TCS, and Cognizant Technology Solutions. TCS, the largest such firm, started exporting software services from India more than 30 years ago and has long stressed arbitrage. Over the past four years, though, I have closely watched and even been involved in its development of a network delivery model to aggregate within and across regions. Cognizant, the fourth largest, also started out with arbitrage and still considers that to be its main strategy but has begun to invest more heavily in adaptation to achieve local presence in the U.S. market in particular. (Although the company

is headquartered in the United States, most of its software development centers and employees are in India.)

The AAA Triangle allows managers to see which of the three strategies—or which combination—is likely to afford the most leverage for their companies or in their industries overall. Expense items from businesses' income statements provide rough-and-ready proxies for the importance of each of the three A's. Companies that do a lot of advertising will need to adapt to the local market. Those that do a lot of R&D may want to aggregate to improve economies of scale, since many R&D outlays are fixed costs. For firms whose operations are labor intensive, arbitrage will be of particular concern because labor costs vary greatly from country to country. By calculating these three types of expenses as percentages of sales, a company can get a picture of how intensely it is pursuing each course. Those that score in the top decile of companies along any of the three dimensions—advertising intensity, R&D intensity, or labor intensity—should be on alert. (See the exhibit "The AAA Triangle" for more detail on the framework.)

How do the companies I've already mentioned look when their expenditures are mapped on the AAA Triangle? At Procter & Gamble, businesses tend to cluster in the top quartile for advertising intensity, indicating the appropriateness of an adaptation strategy. TCS, Cognizant, and IBM Global Services are distinguished by their labor intensity, indicating arbitrage potential. But IBM Systems ranks significantly higher in R&D intensity than in labor intensity and, by implication, has greater potential for aggregation than for arbitrage.

From A to AA

Although many companies will (and should) follow a strategy that involves the focused pursuit of just one of the three A's, some leading-edge companies—IBM, P&G, TCS, and Cognizant among them—are attempting to perform two A's particularly well. Success in "AA strategies" takes two forms. In some cases, a company wins because it actually beats

What Are Your Globalization Options?

When managers first hear about the broad strategies (adaptation, aggregation, and arbitrage) that make up the AAA Triangle framework for globalization, their most common response by far is "Let's do all three." But it's not that simple. A close look at the three strategies reveals the differences—and tensions—among them. Business leaders must figure out which elements will meet their companies' needs and prioritize accordingly.

	ADAPTATION	AGGREGATION	ARBITRAGE
Competitive Advantage Why should we globalize at all?	To achieve local relevance through national focus while exploiting some economies of scale	To achieve scale and scope economies through international standardization	To achieve absolute economies through international specialization
Configuration Where should we locate operations overseas?	Mainly in foreign countries that are similar to the home base, to limit the effects of cultural, administrative, geographic, and economic distance		In a more diverse set of countries, to exploit some elements of distance
Coordination How should we connect international operations?	By country, with emphasis on achieving local presence within borders	By business, region, or customer, with emphasis on horizontal relationships for cross-border economies of scale	By function, with emphasis on vertical relationships, even a cross organizational boundaries
Controls What types of extremes should we watch for?	Excessive variety or complexity	Excessive standardization, with emphasis on scale	Narrowing spreads
Change Blockers Whom should we watch out for internally?	Entrenched country chiefs	All-powerful unit, regional, or account heads	Heads of key functions
Corporate Diplomacy How should we approach corporate diplomacy?	Address issues of concern, but proceed with discretion, given the emphasis on cultivating local presence	Avoid the appearance of homogenization or hegemonism (especially for U.S. companies); be sensitive to any backlash	Address the exploitation or displacement of suppliers, channels, or intermediaries, which are potentially most prone to political disruption
Corporate Strategy What strategic levers do we have?	Scope selection Variation Decentralization Partitioning Modularization Flexibility Partnership Recombination Innovation	Regions and other country groupings Product or business Function Platform Competence Client industry	Cultural (country-of-origin effects) Administrative (taxes, regulations, security) Geographic (distance, climate differences) Economic (differences in prices, resources, knowledge)

The AAA Triangle

The AAA Triangle serves as a kind of strategy map for managers. The percentage of sales spent on advertising indicates how important adaptation is likely to be for the company; the percentage spent on R&D is a proxy for the importance of aggregation; and the percentage spent on labor helps gauge the importance of arbitrage. Managers should pay attention to any scores above the median because, most likely, those are areas that merit strategic focus. Scores above the 90th percentile may be perilous to ignore.

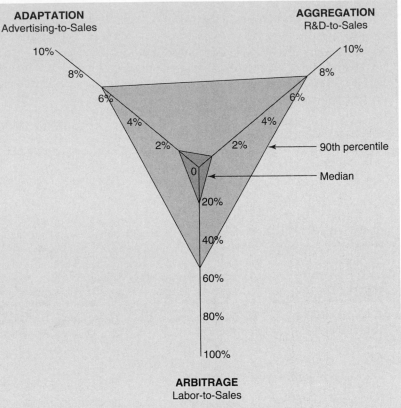

Median and top-decile scores are based on U.S. manufacturing data from Compustat's Global Vantage database and the U.S. Census Bureau. Since the ratios of advertising and R&D to sales rarely exceed 10%, those are given a maximum value of 10% in the chart.

competitors along both dimensions at once. More commonly, however, a company wins because it manages the tensions between two A's better than its competitors do.

The pursuit of AA strategies requires considerable organizational and material innovation. Companies must do more than just allocate resources and monitor national operations from headquarters. They need to deploy a broad array of integrative devices, ranging from the hard (for instance, structures and systems) to the soft (for instance, style and socialization). Let's look at some examples.

Adaptation and Aggregation   As I noted above, Procter & Gamble started out with an adaptation strategy. Halting attempts at aggregation across

Europe, in particular, led to a drawn-out, function-by-function installation of a matrix structure throughout the 1980s, but the matrix proved unwieldy. So in 1999, the new CEO, Durk Jager, announced the reorganization mentioned earlier, whereby global business units (GBUs) retained ultimate profit responsibility but were complemented by geographic market development organizations (MDOs) that actually ran the sales force (shared across GBUs) and went to market.

The result? All hell broke loose in multiple areas, including at the key GBU/MDO interfaces. Jager departed after less than a year. Under his successor, Lafley, P&G has enjoyed much more success, with an approach that strikes more of a balance between adaptation and aggregation and allows room for differences across general business units and markets. Thus, its pharmaceuticals division, with distinct distribution channels, has been left out of the MDO structure; in emerging markets, where market development challenges loom large, profit responsibility continues to be vested with country managers. Also important are the company's decision grids, which are devised after months of negotiation. These define protocols for how different decisions are to be made, and by whom—the general business units or the market development organizations—while still generally reserving responsibility for profits (and the right to make decisions not covered by the grids) for the GBUs. Common IT systems help with integration as well. This structure is animated by an elaborate cycle of reviews at multiple levels.

Such structures and systems are supplemented with other, softer tools, which promote mutual understanding and collaboration. Thus, the GBUs' regional headquarters are often collocated with the headquarters of regional MDOs. Promotion to the director level or beyond generally requires experience on both the GBU and the MDO sides of the house. The implied crisscrossing of career paths reinforces the message that people within the two realms are equal citizens. As another safeguard against the MDOs' feeling marginalized by a lack of profit responsibility, P&G created a structure—initially anchored by the vice chairman of global operations, Robert McDonald—to focus on their perspectives and concerns.

Aggregation and Arbitrage   In contrast to Procter & Gamble, TCS is targeting a balance between aggregation and arbitrage. To obtain the benefits of aggregation without losing its traditional arbitrage-based competitive advantage, it has placed great emphasis on its global network delivery model, which aims to build a coherent delivery structure that consists of three kinds of software development centers:

- The global centers serve large customers and have breadth and depth of skill, very high scales, and mature coding and quality control processes. These centers are located in India, but some are under development in China, where TCS was the first Indian software firm to set up shop.

- The regional centers (such as those in Uruguay, Brazil, and Hungary) have medium scales, select capabilities, and an emphasis on addressing language and cultural challenges. These centers offer some arbitrage economies, although not yet as sizable as those created by the global centers in India.

- The nearshore centers (such as those in Boston and Phoenix) have small scales and focus on building customer comfort through proximity.

In addition to helping improve TCS's economics in a number of ways, a coherent global delivery structure also seems to hold potential for significant international revenue gains. For example, in September 2005, TCS announced the signing of a five-year, multinational contract with the Dutch bank ABN AMRO that's expected to generate more than 200 million. IBM won a much bigger deal from ABN AMRO, but TCS's deal did represent the largest such contract ever for an Indian software firm and is regarded by the company's management as a breakthrough in its attempts to compete with IBM Global Services and Accenture. According to CEO S. Ramadorai, TCS managed to beat out its Indian competitors, including one that was already established at ABN AMRO, largely because it was the only Indian vendor positioned to deploy several hundred professionals to meet the application development and maintenance needs of ABN AMRO's Brazilian operations.

Arbitrage and Adaptation   Cognizant has taken another approach and emphasized arbitrage and adaptation by investing heavily in a local presence in its key market, the United States, to the point where it can pass itself off as either Indian or U.S.-based, depending on the occasion.

Cognizant began life in 1994 as a captive of Dun & Bradstreet, with a more balanced distribution of power than purely Indian firms have. When Cognizant spun off from D&B a couple of years later,

Cognizant's AA Strategy

Cognizant is experimenting with changes in staffing, delivery, and marketing in its pursuit of a strategy that emphasizes both adaptation and arbitrage.

STAFFING	DELIVERY	MARKETING
• Relatively stringent recruiting process • More MBAs and consultants • More non-Indians • Training programs in India for acculturation	• Two global leads—one in the U.S., one in India—for each project • All proposals done jointly (between India and the U.S.) • More proximity to customers • On-site kickoff teams • Intensive travel, use of technology	• Joint Indian—U.S. positioning • Use of U.S. nationals in key marketing positions • Very senior relationship managers • Focus on selling to a small number of large customers

founder Kumar Mahadeva dealt with customers in the United States, while Lakshmi Narayanan (then COO, now vice chairman) oversaw delivery out of India. The company soon set up a two-in-a-box structure, in which there were always two global leads for each project—one in India and one in the United States—who were held jointly accountable and were compensated in the same way. Francisco D'Souza, Cognizant's CEO, recalls that it took two years to implement this structure and even longer to change mind-sets—at a time when there were fewer than 600 employees (compared with more than 24,000 now). As the exhibit "Cognizant's AA Strategy" shows, two-in-a-box is just one element, albeit an important one, of a broad, cross-functional effort to get past what management sees as the key integration challenge in global offshoring: poor coordination between delivery and marketing that leads to "tossing stuff over the wall."

Not all of the innovations that enable AA strategies are structural. At the heart of IBM's recent arbitrage initiatives (which have been added to the company's aggregation strategy) is a sophisticated matching algorithm that can dynamically optimize people's assignments across all of IBM's locations—a critical capability because of the speed with which "hot" and "cold" skills can change. Krisha Nathan, the director of IBM's Zurich Research Lab, describes some of the reasons why such a people delivery model involves much more rocket science than, for example, a parts delivery model. First, a person's services usually can't be stored. Second, a person's functionality can't be summarized in the same standardized way as a part's, with a serial number and a description of technical characteristics. Third, in allocating people to teams, attention must be paid to personality and chemistry, which can make the team either more or less than the sum of its parts; not so with machines. Fourth, for that reason and others (employee development, for instance), assignment durations and sequencing are additionally constrained. Nathan describes the resultant assignment patterns as "75% global and 25% local." While this may be more aspirational than actual, it is clear that to the extent such matching devices are being used more effectively for arbitrage, they represent a massive power shift in a company that has hitherto eschewed arbitrage.

The Elusive Trifecta

There are serious constraints on the ability of any one organization to use all three A's simultaneously with great effectiveness. First, the complexity of doing so collides with limited managerial bandwidth. Second, many people think an organization should have only one culture, and that can get in the way of hitting multiple strategic targets. Third, capable competitors can force a company to choose which dimension it is going to try to beat them on. Finally, external relationships may have a focusing effect as well. For instance, several private-label manufacturers whose businesses were built around arbitrage have run into trouble because of their efforts to aggregate as well as arbitrage by building up their own brands in their customers' markets.

To even contemplate a AAA strategy, a company must be operating in an environment in which the tensions among adaptation, aggregation, and arbitrage are weak or can be overridden by large scale economies or structural advantages, or in which competitors are otherwise constrained.

Consider GE Healthcare (GEH). The diagnostic-imaging industry has been growing rapidly and has concentrated globally in the hands of three large firms, which together command an estimated 75% of revenues in the business worldwide: GEH, with 30%; Siemens Medical Solutions (SMS), with 25%; and Philips Medical Systems (PMS), with 20%.[1] This high degree of concentration is probably related to the fact that the industry ranks in the 90th percentile in terms of R&D intensity. R&D expenditures are greater than 10% of sales for the "big three" competitors and even higher for smaller rivals, many of whom face profit squeezes. All of this suggests that the aggregation-related challenge of building global scale has proven particularly important in the industry in recent years.

GEH, the largest of the three firms, has also consistently been the most profitable. This reflects its success at aggregation, as indicated by the following:

Economies of Scale   GEH has higher total R&D spending than SMS or PMS, greater total sales, and a larger service force (constituting half of GEH's

total employee head count)—but its R&D-to-sales ratio is lower, its other expense ratios are comparable, and it has fewer major production sites.

Acquisition Capabilities   Through experience, GEH has become more efficient at acquiring. It made nearly 100 acquisitions under Jeffrey Immelt (before he became GE's CEO); since then, it has continued to do a lot of acquiring, including the $9.5 billion Amersham deal in 2004, which moved the company beyond metal boxes and into medicine.

Economies of Scope   The company strives, through Amersham, to integrate its biochemistry skills with its traditional base of physics and engineering skills; it finances equipment purchases through GE Capital.

GEH has even more clearly outpaced its competitors through arbitrage. Under Immelt, but especially more recently, it has moved to become a global product company by migrating rapidly to low-cost production bases. Moves have been facilitated by a "pitcher-catcher" concept originally developed elsewhere in GE: A "pitching team" at the existing site works closely with a "catching team" at the new site until the latter's performance is at least as strong as the former's. By 2005, GEH was reportedly more than halfway to its goals of purchasing 50% of its materials directly from low-cost countries and locating 60% of its manufacturing in such countries.

In terms of adaptation, GEH has invested heavily in country-focused marketing organizations, coupling such investments relatively loosely with the integrated development-and-manufacturing back end, with objectives that one executive characterizes as being "more German than the Germans." It also boosts customer appeal with its emphasis on providing services as well as equipment—for example, by training radiologists and providing consulting advice on post-image processing. Such customer intimacy obviously has to be tailored by country. And recently, GEH has cautiously engaged in some "in China, for China" manufacture of stripped-down, cheaper equipment aimed at increasing penetration there.

GEH has managed to use the three A's to the extent that it has partly by separating the three

---

[1]Figures are for 2005. Otherwise, the account is largely based on Tarun Khanna and Elizabeth A. Raabe, "General Electric Healthcare, 2006" (HBS case no. 9-706-478); D. Quinn Mills and Julian Kurz, "Siemens Medical Solutions: Strategic Turnaround" (HBS case no. 9-703-494); and Pankaj Ghemawat, "Philips Medical Systems in 2005" (HBS case no. 9-706-488).

AAA Competitive Map for Diagnostic Imaging

Philips Medical Systems, the smallest of the big three diagnostic-imaging firms, historically emphasized adaptation but has recently placed some focus on aggregation. Siemens Medical Solutions emphasizes aggregation and uses some arbitrage. The most successful of the three, GE Healthcare, beats each of its rivals on two out of the three A's.

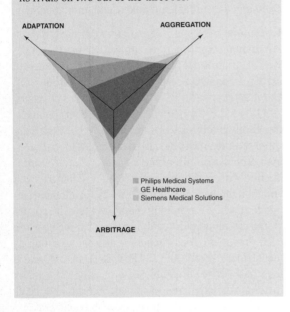

ADAPTATION

AGGREGATION

■ Philips Medical Systems
  GE Healthcare
■ Siemens Medical Solutions

ARBITRAGE

and, paradoxically, by downplaying the pursuit of one of them: adaptation. This is one example of how companies can get around the problem of limited managerial bandwidth. Others range from outsourcing to the use of more market or market-like mechanisms, such as internal markets. GEH's success has also depended on competitors' weaknesses. In addition to facing a variety of size-related and other structural disadvantages relative to GEH, SMS and particularly PMS have been slow in some respects—for instance, in shifting production to low-cost countries. For all these reasons, the temptation to treat the GEH example as an open invitation for everyone to pursue all three A's should be stubbornly resisted.

Besides, the jury is still out on GEH. Adapting to the exceptional requirements of potentially large but low-income markets such as China and India while trying to integrate globally is likely to be an ongoing tension for the company. What's more, GEH isn't clearly ahead on all performance dimensions: SMS has focused more on core imaging, where it is seen as the technological leader.

Developing a AAA Strategy

Let's now consider how a company might use the AAA Triangle to put together a globally competitive strategy. The example I'll use here will be PMS, the smallest of the big three diagnostic-imaging firms.

At a corporate level, Philips had long followed a highly decentralized strategy that concentrated significant power in the hands of country managers and emphasized adaptation. Under pressure from more aggregation-oriented Japanese competitors in areas such as consumer electronics, efforts began in the 1970s to transfer more power to and aggregate more around global product divisions. These were blocked by country chiefs until 1996, when the new CEO abolished the geographic leg of the geography-product matrix. It is sometimes suggested that Philips's traditional focus on adaptation has persisted and remains a source of competitive advantage. While that's true about the parent company, it isn't the case for PMS. Any adaptation advantage for PMS is limited by SMS's technological edge and GEH's service-quality edge. These can be seen as global attributes of the two competitors' offerings, but they also create customer lock-in at the local level.

More generally, any adaptation advantage at PMS is more than offset by its aggregation disadvantages. PMS's absolute R&D expenditures are one-third lower than those of GEH and one-quarter lower than those of SMS, and PMS is a much larger part of a much smaller corporation than its rivals are. (Philips's total acquisition war chest at the corporate level was recently reported to be not much larger than the amount that GEH put down for the Amersham acquisition alone.) In addition, PMS was stitched together out of six separate companies in a series of acquisitions made over three years to improve the original and aging X-ray technology. It is somewhat surprising that this attempt has worked as well as it has in a corporation without much acquisition experience to fall back on—but there have also clearly been negative aftereffects. Most dramatically, PMS paid more than €700 million in 2004 related to past acquisition attempts—one consummated, another considered—nearly wiping out its reported earnings for that year, although profitability did recover nicely in 2005.

PMS's preoccupation (until recently) with connecting its disparate parts is also somewhat to blame for the company's lack of progress on the arbitrage front. PMS has trailed not only its rivals but also other Philips divisions in moving manufacturing to low-cost areas, particularly China. Although Philips claims to be the largest Western multinational in China, PMS did not start a manufacturing joint venture there until September 2004, with the first output for the Chinese market becoming available in 2005 and the first supplies for export in 2006. Overall, PMS's sourcing levels from low-cost countries in 2005 were comparable to levels GEH achieved back in 2001, and they lagged SMS's as well.

Insights on positioning relative to the three A's can be pulled together into a single map, as shown in the exhibit "AAA Competitive Map for Diagnostic Imaging." Assessments along these lines, while always approximate, call attention to where competitors are actually located in strategy space; they also help companies visualize trade-offs across different A's. Both factors are important in thinking through where and where not to focus the organization's efforts.

How might this representation be used to articulate an action agenda for PMS? The two most obvious strategy alternatives for PMS are AA strategies: adaptation-aggregation and adaptation-arbitrage.

Adaptation-aggregation comes closest to the strategy currently in place. However, it is unlikely to solve the aggregation-related challenges facing PMS, so it had better offer some meaningful extras in terms of local responsiveness. PMS could also give up on the idea of creating a competitive advantage and simply be content with achieving average industry profitability, which is high: The big three diagnostic-imaging companies (which also account for another profitable global triopoly, in light bulbs) are described as "gentlemanly" in setting prices. Either way, imitation of bigger rivals' large-scale moves into entirely new areas seems likely to magnify, rather than minimize, this source of disadvantage. PMS does appear to be exercising some discipline in this regard, preferring to engage in joint ventures and other relatively small-scale moves rather than any Amersham-sized acquisitions.

The adaptation-arbitrage alternative would aim not just at producing in low-cost locations but also at radically reengineering and simplifying the product to slash costs for large emerging markets in China, India, and so forth. However, this option does not fit with Philips's heritage, which is not one of competing through low costs. And PMS has less room to follow a strategy of this sort because of GEH's "in China, for China" product, which is supposed to cut costs by 50%. PMS, in contrast, is talking of cost reductions of 20% for its first line of Chinese offerings.

If PMS found neither of these alternatives appealing—and frankly, neither seems likely to lead to a competitive advantage for the company— it could try to change the game entirely. Although PMS seems stuck with structural disadvantages in core diagnostic imaging compared with GEH and SMS, it could look for related fields in which its adaptation profile might have more advantages and fewer disadvantages. In terms of the AAA Triangle, this would be best thought of as a lateral shift to a new area of business, where the organization would have more of a competitive advantage. PMS does seem to be attempting something along these lines— albeit slowly—with its recent emphasis on medical devices for people to use at home. As former Philips CFO Jan Hommen puts it, the company has an advantage here over both Siemens and GE: "With our consumer electronics and domestic appliances businesses, we have gained a lot of experience and knowledge." The flip side, though, is that PMS starts competing with large companies such as Johnson & Johnson. PMS's first product of this sort—launched in the United States and retailing for around $1,500—is a home-use defibrillator. Note also that the resources emphasized in this strategy—that is, brand and distribution—operate at the local (national) level. So the new strategy can be seen as focusing on adaptation in a new market.

What do these strategic considerations imply for integration at PMS? The company needs to continue streamlining operations and speed up attempts at arbitrage, possibly considering tools such as the pitcher-catcher concept. It needs to think about geographic variation, probably at the regional level, given the variation in industry attractiveness as well as PMS's average market share across regions. Finally, it needs to enable its at-home devices business to tap Philips's consumer electronics division for resources and capabilities. This last item is especially important because, in light of its track record thus far, PMS will have to make some early wins if it is to generate any excitement around a relaunch.

▌ Broader Lessons

The danger in discussions about integration is that they can float off into the realm of the ethereal. That's why I went into specifics about the integration challenges facing PMS—and it's why it seems like a good idea to wrap this article up by recapitulating the general points outlined.

Focus on one or two of the A's   While it is possible to make progress on all three A's—especially for a firm that is coming from behind—companies (or, often more to the point, businesses or divisions) usually have to focus on one or at most two A's in trying to build competitive advantage. Can your organization agree on what they are? It may have to shift its focus across the A's as the company's needs change. IBM is just one example of a general shift toward arbitrage. But the examples of IBM, P&G, and, in particular, PMS illustrate how long such shifts can take—and the importance,

therefore, of looking ahead when deciding what to focus on.

Make sure the new elements of a strategy are a good fit organizationally   While this isn't a fixed rule, if your strategy does embody non-trivially new elements, you should pay particular attention to how well they work with other things the organization is doing. IBM has grown its staff in India much faster than other international competitors (such as Accenture) that have begun to emphasize India-based arbitrage. But quickly molding this workforce into an efficient organization with high delivery standards and a sense of connection to the parent company is a critical challenge: Failure in this regard might even be fatal to the arbitrage initiative.

Employ Multiple Integration Mechanisms   Pursuit of more than one of the A's requires creativity and breadth in thinking about integration mechanisms. Given the stakes, these factors can't be left to chance. In addition to IBM's algorithm for matching people to opportunities, the company has demonstrated creativity in devising "deal hubs" to aggregate across its hardware, software, and services businesses. It has also reconsidered its previous assumption that global functional headquarters should be centralized (recently, IBM relocated its procurement office from Somers, New York, to Shenzhen, China). Of course, such creativity must be reinforced by organizational structures, systems, incentives, and norms conducive to integration, as at P&G. Also essential to making such integration work is an adequate supply of leaders and succession candidates of the right stripe.

Think About Externalizing Integration   Not all the integration that is required to add value across borders needs to occur within a single organization. IBM and other firms illustrate that some externalization is a key part of most ambitious global strategies. It takes a diversity of forms: joint ventures in advanced semiconductor research, development, and manufacturing; links to and support of Linux and other efforts at open innovation; (some) outsourcing of hardware to contract manufacturers and services to business partners; IBM's relationship with Lenovo in personal computers; customer relationships governed by memoranda of understanding rather than detailed contracts. Reflecting this increased range of possibilities, reported levels of international joint ventures are running only one-quarter as high as they were in the mid-1990s, even though more companies are externalizing operations. Externalization offers advantages not just for outsourcing non-core services but also for obtaining ideas from the outside for core areas: for instance, Procter & Gamble's connect-and-develop program, IBM's innovation jams, and TCS's investments in involving customers in quality measurement and improvement.

Know When Not to Integrate   Some integration is always a good idea, but that is not to say that more integration is always better. First of all, very tightly coupled systems are not particularly flexible. Second, domain selection—in other words, knowing what not to do as well as what to do—is usually considered an essential part of strategy. Third, even when many diverse activities are housed within one organization, keeping them apart may be a better overall approach than forcing them together in, say, the bear hug of a matrix structure. As Lafley explains, the reason P&G is able to

pursue arbitrage up to a point as well as adaptation and aggregation is that the company has deliberately separated these functions into three kinds of subunits (global business units, market development organizations, and global business shared services) and imposed a structure that minimizes points of contact and, thereby, friction.

•   •   •

For most of the past 25 years, the rhetoric of globalization has been concentrated on markets. Only recently has the spotlight turned to production, as firms have become aware of the arbitrage opportunities available through off-shoring. This phenomenon appears to have outpaced strategic thinking about it. Many academic writings remain focused on the globalization (or nonglobalization) of markets. And only a tiny fraction of the many companies that engage in offshoring appear to think about it strategically: Only 1% of the respondents to a recent survey conducted by Arie Lewin at Duke University say that their company has a corporatewide strategy in this regard. The AAA framework provides a basis for considering global strategies that encompasses all three effective responses to the large differences that arise at national borders. Clearer thinking about the full range of strategy options should broaden the perceived opportunities, sharpen strategic choices, and enhance global performance.

Reading 3-2   How Local Companies Keep Multinationals at Bay

Arindam K. Bhattacharya and David C. Michael

To win in the world's fastest-growing markets, transnational giants have to compete with increasingly sophisticated homegrown champions. It isn't easy.

Since the late 1970s, governments on every continent have allowed the winds of global competition to blow through their economies. As policy makers have lowered tariff barriers and permitted foreign investments, multinational companies have rushed into those countries. U.S., European, and Japanese giants, it initially appeared, would quickly overrun local rivals and grab the market for almost every product or service. After all, they possessed state-of-the-art technologies and products, enormous financial resources, powerful brands, and the world's best management talent and systems. Poor nations such as Brazil, China, India, and Mexico, often under pressure from developed countries, let in transnational companies, but they did so slowly, almost reluctantly. They were convinced that global Goliaths would wipe out local enterprises in one fell swoop.

That hasn't happened, according to our research. Over the past three years, we have been studying companies in 10 rapidly developing economies: Brazil, China, India, Indonesia, Malaysia, Mexico, Poland, Russia, Slovakia, and Thailand. In those countries, smart domestic enterprises are more than holding their own in the face of foreign competition. They have staved off challenges from multinational corporations in their core businesses, have become market leaders or are catching up with them, and have often seized new opportunities before foreign players could. Many of them dominate the market today not because of protectionist

economic policies, but because of their strategies and execution. When we drew up a list of 50 homegrown champions, we found that 21 had revenues exceeding US$1 billion in 2006 and that the entire group's sales had risen by about 50% between 2005 and 2006 (see the exhibit "Fifty Homegrown Champions"). The skeptics should have remembered that David slew Goliath—not the other way around.

Consider a few local companies that have fended off foreign competition during the past five years or more:

- In Brazil, Grupo Positivo has a larger share of the PC market than either Dell or Hewlett-Packard, and Totvs is the enterprise resource planning (ERP) software leader in the small- and midsize-company market, ahead of the world's largest business software provider, SAP.

- In China, daily use of the search engine Baidu exceeds that of Google China by fourfold; QQ, from instant-message leader Tencent, is ahead of MSN Messenger; and online travel service Ctrip has held off Travelsky, Expedia's eLong.com, and Travelocity's Zuji.com.

- In India, Bharti Airtel has taken on Hutchison Telecom, which sold its Indian operations to Vodafone in 2007, and emerged as the leader in the cellular telephone market.

- In Mexico, Grupo Elektra, which has created one of the country's biggest retail networks, has taken the battle to Wal-Mart.

- In Russia, Wimm-Bill-Dann Foods is the biggest producer of dairy products, ahead of Danone and Coca-Cola.

The local companies' success doesn't augur well for the developed world's corporations, many of

▌ Arindam K. Bhattacharya (bhattacharya.arindam@bcg.com) is a Delhi-based partner and managing director, and David C. Michael (michael.david@bcg.com) is a Beijing-based senior partner and managing director, of the Boston Consulting Group.

which are seeking growth and profits in emerging markets. Two-thirds of respondents to a survey of transnational corporations we conducted in 2006 said they planned to expand their commitments to developing economies over the next five years. That isn't surprising. According to the Economist Intelligence Unit, rapidly developing economies will account for 45% of world GDP and 60% of annual GDP growth by 2010. At the same time, several Western and Japanese corporations have been unable to enter or have retreated from emerging markets. For instance, Yahoo and eBay have pulled out of China, and NEC and Panasonic have withdrawn from the Chinese market for cellular handsets. Other corporations have found it tough to fly down from the premium perches they constructed for themselves, and they no longer appear irresistible to consumers or unbeatable by local companies.

Why don't the strategies of the biggest and brightest corporations work well in developing countries? Part of the problem is that many transnational enterprises mistakenly believe that emerging markets are years behind developed nations' and that the former's markets will eventually look like the latter's. Multinational corporations assume it's merely a matter of time before their existing business models and value propositions start delivering results in developing countries. These misconceptions are deadly—for several reasons.

Developing economies neither are behind developed ones nor show signs of converging with them. The emerging markets are different, behind in some ways and advanced in others. For instance, China's telecommunications infrastructure is newer and better than that in most parts of the United States. At the same time, roughly 300 million Chinese live on less than $1 a day, according to the World Bank. In India, an educated elite who command international wages flourish in a nation with high rates of illiteracy. In Russia, abundant venture capital coexists with murky property rights and intimidating bureaucratic barriers. These disparities aren't likely to disappear soon, and they're creating unique markets.

The obstacles and opportunities that characterize emerging markets render useless most cookie-cutter strategies. A simple example: In India, lack of reliable internet access renders online customer service useless. However, wireless telecommunication networks and widespread use of mobile telephones allow companies to help customers, even in rural areas, through text messages and handset-based internet portals. Only companies that are unfazed by such contradictions are likely to succeed.

Western companies often forget that entrepreneurship has recently exploded in most developing countries because of internal reforms. Governments have slashed red tape, and capital is cheaper than ever—and those changes are stoking competition. Emerging markets have become so volatile that multinational companies can't tackle them with strategies they developed decades ago and have since refined in mature home markets.

Multinational companies should, we believe, borrow a page, or more, from the local champions' playbook. When we analyzed how 50 companies have become winners, we found six common strands—and they aren't all about low-cost structures. One, unlike global companies, local leaders are not constrained by existing products or by preconceived notions about customer needs. They customize products and services to meet different consumer requirements, and they initially go after economies of scope. Two, their business models overcome roadblocks and yield competitive advantages in the process. Three, they turn globalization to their advantage, deploying the latest technologies by developing or buying them. Four, many of the homegrown champions find innovative ways to benefit from low-cost labor pools and to overcome shortages of skilled talent. Five, they go national as soon as possible to prevent regional rivals from challenging them. Finally, the domestic dynamos possess management skills and talent that multinational companies often underestimate.

In the following pages, we explore each of these factors in detail. No single element may seem groundbreaking, but the homegrown champions cleverly weave at least four of them—sometimes all six, as we show—into a tight strategy in order to gain competitive advantage. We also discuss three multinational companies that have followed the six-part path and have tasted success in emerging markets.

A Six-Part Strategy for Success

Many types of local companies have been successful in developing countries. Some are part of old conglomerates owned by business families or tycoons; others are young start-ups spawned by a postreforms generation of entrepreneurs. All the companies we studied face stiff competition from domestic peers or government-owned enterprises. Most of them also face foreign competition at home, even though countries and markets vary in their degree of openness. These domestic private-sector enterprises have outperformed competitors by following several strategies.

Create Customized Products or Services   The homegrown champions possess a deep understanding of the consumers in their countries. They know people's preferences by region or even city, by income level, by age group, and by gender. These companies also grasp the structures of the raw-materials, components, and finished-goods markets in which they operate. They are therefore able to provide consumers with a low level of customization inexpensively. These local leaders develop offerings tailored to several niche markets and learn to create a large variety of products or services cost-effectively. For example, Goodbaby, the leader in the Chinese market for baby-related products such as strollers, sells as many as 1,600 items in 16 categories. Customization becomes the basis on which companies like Goodbaby differentiate themselves from and get a leg up on multinational rivals.

Some companies develop sophisticated user-generated customization technologies. In China, consumers favor instant messaging on PCs and text messaging on cellular telephones over e-mail. Despite the presence of U.S. heavyweights—such as Microsoft (which launched a Chinese version of MSN Messenger three years ago), Yahoo, and recently MySpace—Shenzhen-based Tencent is the

leader in the Chinese market. Its free messenger, QQ, had a market share of 70% to 80% in 2006, compared with 15% for MSN Messenger, according to Shanghai-based iResearch. QQ's cute penguin mascot and ultrasimple interface endear it to China's internet users, 70% of whom are younger than 30. In addition to the free chat program and chat rooms, QQ offers games, virtual pets, and ringtone downloads.

The U.S. players have tried to capitalize on users' desire to form cybercommunities, but Tencent has taken a different route: It taps into the Chinese craving for freedom of expression. QQ offers digital avatars that users can personalize online, from the clothes they wear to the virtual cars they drive. People can choose from a dizzying array of virtual outfits and accessories, each costing just RMB 1 or 2. The Chinese love the idea of customizing their online messengers, and in less than a decade QQ has become the market leader. "QQ" has even become a verb, and the phrase "QQ me" has been used in pop songs. Since its founding in 1998, Tencent has made steady progress: It had 220 million active users (caveat: many Chinese have more than one online identity) and US$375 million in revenues in 2006—and counting.

Other local winners' customization techniques are simple. The companies package products innovatively to make them affordable. In India's $500 million hair care market, the well-entrenched multinational incumbent Hindustan Unilever, which has operated there since 1933, and challengers such as America's Procter & Gamble and France's L'Oréal have been slugging it out in the cities for decades. While Hindustan Unilever and P&G are the leaders with 36% and 27% of the market in 2006, respectively, according to Datamonitor, CavinKare, a local company, is giving them a run for their money with its market share of 16%. The Chennai-based start-up, established in 1983, packs shampoo in sachets—an idea its founder borrowed from his father, who pioneered the use of these pouches, and his brothers, who first launched shampoo sachets in 1979.

CavinKare's single-use plastic sachets are convenient to use and easy to store, and they minimize

Fifty Homegrown Champions

Using a largely qualitative approach, we identified successful domestic companies in 10 emerging economies. We chose enterprises that generate almost all their revenues from their home markets and that have been (or are close to being) leaders in their main businesses. Below is a list of 50 companies that we studied in depth; it is neither a ranking nor an exhaustive catalog of homegrown winners.

Company	2006 Net Revenues (in US$ millions)	2006 Net Revenue Growth (% change from 2005)	Domestic Market Position	Main Foreign Rivals in Local Market
BRAZIL				
B2W	728	63%	largest online retailer	fnac.com
Casas Bahia	5,024	not available	biggest consumer electronics and furniture retailer	Carrefour, Wal-Mart
Cosan	1,083	30%	largest manufacturer and seller of ethanol and sugar	Bunge, Cargill
Gol Linhas Aéreas Inteligentes	1,661	42%	second-biggest and fastest-growing airline	none on domestic routes
Grupo Positivo	507	89%	leader in PCs and notebooks	Dell, Hewlett-Packard, Lenovo
O Boticário	1,321	4%	one of the largest cosmetics brands	Avon, Revlon
Totvs	164	21%	leading ERP-solutions provider for medium and small companies	SAP
TV Globo	2,732	12%	number one television network	none
Votorantim Finanças	533	−9%	third-largest automobile finance company	Citibank, Grupo Santander, HSBC
CHINA				
Baidu	104	163%	China's most-used internet search engine	Google China
China Merchants Bank	3,081	29%	one of the top 10 banks	local banks with foreign partners
China Vanke	2,103	70%	largest property developer	joint ventures with foreign partners
Ctrip	97	49%	biggest provider of hotel and flight bookings	eLong.com (Expedia), Zuji.com (Travelocity)
Focus Media	206	213%	largest outdoor advertising company	Clear Channel, JCDecaux
Goldwind Science and Technology	190	209%	biggest maker and seller of wind-power equipment	GE, Vestas

(continued)

Company	2006 Net Revenues (in US$ millions)	2006 Net Revenue Growth (% change from 2005)	Domestic Market Position	Main Foreign Rivals in Local Market
Gome Electrical Appliances	3,064	38%	largest home-appliances retail chain	Best Buy, Carrefour, Wal-Mart
Goodbaby	327	14%	largest seller of baby products	Chicco, Maclaren
New Oriental Education & Technology	129	36%	leader in language education	Wall Street Institute
Shanda	205	−13%	leader in online games	Electronic Arts, Nintendo, Sony
SIM Technology Group	440	26%	largest handset-design house	Bellwave, Compal
Tencent	347	96%	leader in instant messaging	MSN, MySpace
WuXi PharmaTech	68	107%	biotech and pharmaceuticals contract R&D leader	Covance
XinAo Group	1,081	40%	largest gas utility	Hong Kong and China Gas Company
Xinyi Glass	249	40%	one of the biggest glassmakers	Pilkington
INDIA				
Apollo Hospitals	215	23%	largest private hospital chain	joint ventures with foreign partners
Bharti Airtel	4,162	59%	biggest private-sector telecom services provider	Hutchison Telecom
CavinKare	129	0.5%	third-largest shampoo maker	L'Oréal, P&G, Unilever
Gujarat Cooperative Milk Marketing Federation	961	13%	leader in dairy products with its Amul brand	Cadbury, Nestlé, Unilever
ICICI Bank	5,308	63%	biggest private-sector bank	Citibank, HSBC, Standard Chartered
The Indian Hotels Company	347	42%	one of the two biggest domestic hotel chains	none
ITC	2,856	26%	leader in ready-to-cook and other foods	Danone, PepsiCo, Unilever
NIIT	179	76%	largest IT education and training firm	Lionbridge
SKS Microfinance	7	169%	one of the fastest-growing microfinance groups	none
Subhiksha	180	140%	largest no-frills supermarket chain	none
Titan Industries	480	44%	largest watch manufacturer and retailer	Citizen, Swatch

Company	2006 Net Revenues (in US$ millions)	2006 Net Revenue Growth (% change from 2005)	Domestic Market Position	Main Foreign Rivals in Local Market
INDONESIA				
Astra International	6,106	−10%	biggest car maker (with six foreign partners)	Honda, Mitsubishi, Suzuki
MALAYSIA				
Air Asia	230	28%	one of Asia's fastest-growing low-cost airlines	Singapore Airlines
MEXICO				
Controladora Milano	258 (est.)	not available	leading retail apparel chain	Wal-Mart
Corporación Interamericana de Entretenimiento	944	14%	leading live-entertainment company	none
Desarrolladora Homex	1,190	46%	largest low-income-housing developer	none
Farmacia Guadalajara	1,066	13%	second-largest retail pharmaceutical chain	Wal-Mart
Grupo Elektra	3,270	10%	leading retail network	Wal-Mart
Sigma Alimentos	1,836	7%	top producer of refrigerated and frozen foods	Danone, Kraft, Nestlé
POLAND				
Atlas Group	282	5%	biggest construction chemicals and glues manufacturer	Henkel
Maspex Wadowice	634	11%	leader in instant foods, pasta, and fruit juices	Barilla, Cappy
RUSSIA				
Euroset	4,620	79%	largest mobile telecommunications retailer	none
MegaFon	3,733	56%	second-biggest cellular services operator	none
Wimm-Bill-Dann Foods	1,762	26%	leader in dairy products and among the top three in fruit juices	Coca-Cola, Danone
SLOVAKIA				
SkyEurope Airlines	198	41%	country's biggest airline	easyJet, Ryanair
THAILAND				
Siam Cement Group	6,625	18%	largest maker of building materials, cement, chemicals, and paper	Lafarge

Note: For commercial banks, the figures correspond to operating income. For Indian companies, data are for the fiscal year ending March 31, 2007. Most currency conversions were calculated using the average interbank exchange rate from January 1, 2005, through December 31, 2006.

product waste because people are not tempted to use more than what they need for one wash. The packaging size makes shampoo affordable for many Indians who don't earn enough money to spend on big bottles and who regard the product as an expensive indulgence. CavinKare went after lower-income city dwellers and rural consumers for the first time. For years, it found the going tough; the company had to demonstrate how shampoo cleans hair better than soap and used trade-ins and discounts to get people to try it. Once CavinKare tasted success, Hindustan Unilever and P&G started to package shampoo in sachets as well. Price matters, though, and CavinKare's relatively cheap Chik brand has allowed the company to become the largest local shampoo player in India.

Develop Business Models to Overcome Key Obstacles   Multinational corporations often complain about insurmountable problems— structural issues such as a lack of distribution channels, or infrastructural hurdles like limited telecommunications bandwidth—that prevent them from doing business in their usual way. Smart local companies are adept at identifying the key challenges that their markets pose and, from the get-go, at designing strategies to overcome or sidestep those obstacles. Sure, multinational enterprises later copy the same tactics, but by then the local ones have sharpened their first-mover advantage.

For instance, the global leaders in video games, such as Microsoft, Nintendo, and Sony, haven't made much headway in China because of software piracy. Does that mean China doesn't have much of a market for games? Of course not. Chinese companies such as Shanda, which entered the industry in 2001, have developed a thriving game business by developing massively multiplayer online role-playing games (MMORPGs) instead. These products are impossible to pirate since they are live experiences created by technologies that link many players over the internet. China's youth, eager for entertainment options, have warmed to the idea. China's MMORPG industry, which generated revenues of about $600 million in 2005, has been growing at 40% a year since 2003, according to iResearch. Belatedly in 2007, Electronic Arts acquired a 15% equity stake in one of Shanda's competitors, for $167 million.

It's tough to make money on the internet in China because of consumer concerns about online theft and the lack of a credit card culture. Shanda has tackled the online-payment problem by taking transactions off-line. China's gamers purchase prepaid cards from local merchants. When they scratch the film off the card, they get a number that entitles them to a fixed amount of game-playing time online. Shanda keeps adapting its business model. Sensing that Chinese gamers are becoming less willing to pay to play, it now offers free access to old games. It makes money, as Tencent does, by selling virtual merchandise such as weapons and equipment. The company is also moving into mobile gaming, which is set to take off. Later this year, Shanda will launch mobile versions of its popular *World of Legend* and *Magical Land* role-playing games on customized Motorola handsets.

Innovative strategies sometimes create new businesses in addition to giving local champions an edge. In Mexico, Grupo Elektra wanted to be a successful retailer, but it created a banking business along the way. The company realized early that to make money, it had to sell big-ticket items such as washing machines and refrigerators. Many middle- and low-income Mexicans could buy consumer durables only by taking loans or paying in installments. They couldn't get credit easily because Mexico's commercial banks didn't consider them creditworthy or know how to evaluate their repayment potential. Grupo Elektra started offering consumer financing and, effectively, selling products on installment plans. Once the company offered credit, its business took off. In 1987 Grupo Elektra operated 59 stores; today it runs more than 1,600, making it one of the largest retailers in Mexico. Imitation is a form of followership: Wal-Mart, which is Mexico's largest retailer by sales, obtained a banking license in November 2006 to offer financial services in all its 997 Mexican stores.

In 2002, Grupo Elektra, which still sells about 60% of its goods on credit, set up a full-fledged bank, Banco Azteca, with branches inside Elektra stores. The bank's business, measured by assets under management, has had a compound annual growth rate of 133% for the past five years. Given that most customers have no credit histories, the bank has developed a novel credit-appraisal system. A corps of 4,000 loan officers uses motorcycles to visit prospective borrowers' homes. These officers on wheels assess whether each applicant's standard of living matches the claimed income level and conduct an on-the-spot credit assessment. Collectively, the corps clears as many as 13,000 new loans a day. This unique system has worked so far: Banco Azteca's repayment rate in 2006 was 90%.

Deploy the Latest Technologies   Contrary to popular perceptions, local winners' products and services often incorporate the latest technologies, as the cases of Shanda and Tencent show. New technologies keep operating costs low and enable companies to deliver good-quality products and services. That helps them outperform competitors that believe they can satisfy local consumers with older technologies.

Unburdened by past investments or old processes, younger companies in particular invest in the state of the art to lower costs and offer customers novel features. For example, Brazil's Gol Linhas Aéreas Inteligentes, South America's first low-cost airline, has shaken up the market since it started flying with five aircraft in January 2001. Gol's share of the domestic market, based on revenue passenger-kilometers, grew from 5% in 2001 to 37% in 2006, according to Brazil's civil aviation authority, Agência Nacional de Aviação Civil (ANAC). The world's second-most profitable airline after Ireland's Ryanair, Gol can attribute its success partly to its single-aircraft type of fleet—a model Southwest Airlines pioneered—and to investments in the latest models. In 2007, Gol operated 97 single-class Boeing 737 aircraft, and it had placed orders with Boeing for 64 new 737-800 aircraft that would join the fleet between 2008 and 2010. By buying an aircraft

model with a capacity approximately 30% higher than that of its predecessor, Gol will be able to use its landing slots more effectively.

The planes in Gol's fleet were, on average, less than eight years old in December 2006, making it one of the youngest in South America. A young fleet requires less maintenance, so Gol manages quick aircraft turnarounds and operates more flights per day with each plane. In 2006, Gol's aircraft utilization rate (the time between a plane's departure from the gate and arrival at its destination) was 14.2 block hours a day—the highest in South America, according to ANAC—and the airline boasted the lowest cost per available-seat-kilometer. Gol has also reduced costs by using the latest technology in other operational areas. It was the first Brazilian airline to issue e-tickets and promote internet-based sales; in 2006, it sold 82% of its tickets on its website. Customers can check in on the internet or, if they don't have Web access, there are kiosks and attendants with wireless-enabled pocket PCs to process check-ins. Gol's call centers employ the latest automated voice recognition software to handle high call volumes with a limited staff.

New technologies can help old companies get a second wind after economic liberalization. Gujarat Cooperative Milk Marketing Federation (GCMMF), India's largest dairy company, manufactures and markets a range of dairy products under the brand name Amul. Despite the fierce competition that has come with the opening up of India's dairy industry to big business, the enterprise has managed to stay ahead, in part because it has invested in the latest technologies. For instance, it can collect and process 6.5 million liters of fresh milk every day from close to 13,000 villages in the western state of Gujarat. Farmers bring their milk to collection centers, each located roughly five to 10 kilometers away from a village, twice a day. Thanks to a new milk collection system, GCMMF's field staff can weigh the milk, measure the fat content, and pay the farmer—in less than five minutes. That contrasts with the old system whereby employees took samples and performed fat-content tests days later at a central facility. Not only did farmers have to wait for a week to receive payment, but the lack of transparency led to complaints about fraud.

GCMMF employs satellite communication technologies to collect and track transaction data. A customized ERP system coordinates all the back-office functions and analyzes data in real time to forecast imbalances between the demand for milk products and milk supplies. Its technological infrastructure permits the cooperative to make 10 million error-free payments every day, totaling US$4.3 million (170 million rupees) in cash, and to coordinate large numbers of trucks and processing plants with military precision. That efficiency has enabled GCMMF to penetrate India's urban and rural markets deeply.

Take Advantage of Low-cost Labor, and Train Staff In-house   Many local champions have at their core a business model that taps a pool of low-cost labor instead of relying on automation. Consider, for instance, Focus Media, which has become China's largest outdoor advertising firm. It has placed LCD displays that it engineered in-house in more than 130,000 locations in 90 cities to create a national advertising platform. The company's screens are in office buildings, apartment blocks, retail stores, shopping malls, restaurants, hospitals, drugstores, beauty salons, health clubs, golf courses, hotels, airports, and airport transit buses.

Focus Media uses a decidedly low-tech solution to refresh and service all those LCD screens: a veritable army of employees who move from building to building on bicycles and replace, whenever necessary, the DVDs and flashcards that play the advertisements. Focus Media could link the LCD screens electronically—as any blue-blooded transnational company would—but it does not. Using people keeps the company's operating costs low while enabling it to offer clients a great deal of flexibility. For a small premium, Focus Media will allow a client to flash ads on office buildings nationwide on the week of a major product launch; or target only outdoor plaza locations on one weekend in one city; or use a mix of online, in-cinema, and shopping-center advertisements the day before Chinese

New Year. Were Focus Media to use an automated system, the Chinese government could deem it a network-based broadcaster and regulate it as a media company, which might curtail its growth. Focus Media's bicycle-based solution fits well within an otherwise high-tech business.

At the other end of the labor spectrum, skilled talent is hard to find and difficult to retain in emerging markets. Successful companies such as Grupo Elektra, Gol, China Merchants Bank, and India's ITC invest heavily in in-house training. India's Apollo Hospitals, another case in point, has developed a good reputation by recruiting some of the country's best doctors and nurses. The quality of its services is a key differentiator, allowing the chain to charge patients 10 times what they would pay in a public hospital. Although the company employs 4,000 specialists and 3,000 medical officers at 41 facilities, it needs more people to staff new hospitals and to offer additional services. Recognizing that India's medical education infrastructure is growing slowly, Apollo Hospitals established a foundation in 1998 to finance new teaching institutes, including one that offers a postgraduate degree in hospital management and a nursing school. That's not all. In 2000, Apollo Hospitals and a leading Indian technology training company, NIIT, set up a joint venture to offer online medical classes. Medvarsity Online offers postgraduate courses in family medicine, emergency medicine, and health insurance. Apollo Hospitals has also introduced programs to train physiotherapists, medical technicians, and laboratory technicians. It provides nurses with medical training as well as communication and customer-service skills. Without all these investments in training, Apollo Hospitals would not have been able to sustain its growth.

Scale Up Quickly   In many emerging markets, when a new business opportunity becomes apparent, several companies crop up to capitalize on it. The size of countries like China, India, and Brazil—particularly the large number of provinces and cities—allows regional players to flourish. However, only companies that operate nationwide can reap the benefits of scale. Many homegrown champions go after scale economies after generating economies of scope.

Expansion often entails mergers and acquisitions. Focus Media, for instance, faced many rivals scattered across China's cities when it started out in 2003. It pursued an aggressive acquisition-led strategy, which soon gave it the nationwide reach to attract advertisers and diminish the competitiveness of regional rivals. By scaling up quickly, Focus Media vaulted past two global leaders in China's outdoor-advertising industry: America's Clear Channel Communications and France's JC-Decaux. In 2006, Clear Channel was less than half of Focus Media's size in terms of revenue, even though it had set up shop in China back in 1998. JCDecaux, which entered the country by acquiring two companies in 2005, doesn't report its China revenues. However, it operates in only 20 cities, compared with Focus Media's presence in 90. While Clear Channel and JCDecaux have made a few acquisitions in the past decade, Focus Media struck five deals between January 2006 and February 2007 in order to cement its leadership.

Some local champions create regional entities to speed up organic growth. For example, Goodbaby has set up 35 companies, each operating in a Chinese province or a city, to strike local distribution agreements and to open new points of presence quickly. That has spawned one of the most extensive marketing and sales networks in the country: 1,600 stand-alone stores or department-store counters and 300 distributors. By 2010, the company plans to have opened 500 more locations. In addition, Goodbaby opened the first in a series of flagship stores two years ago. These sites offer a few foreign brands, Goodbaby's own products, and access to professionals who dispense parenting advice. By overcoming the distribution challenges of the Chinese market quickly, Goodbaby has laid the foundation for success.

Invest in Talent to Sustain Rapid Growth In market after market in emerging economies, invading multinational corporations encounter domestic rivals with the entrepreneurial zeal and the knack to keep growing quickly for a long time. They discover, to their shock, that there are great local managers in these countries. In fact, most transnational giants underestimate the management depth and capability of rivals that have the additional advantage of not needing to negotiate with headquarters in a distant First World city.

Many companies face the risk of meltdown when they grow at double-digit rates for years. There are no silver bullets to prevent that altogether, but smart organizations minimize senior management turnover and institutionalize management systems to tackle the complexities of rapid growth. Consider Russia's Wimm-Bill-Dann Foods (WBD), which five entrepreneurs founded in 1992 with borrowed funds. They leased a production line at the partially idle Lianozovsky Dairy Plant near Moscow to make fruit juices and decided to make a foray into the dairy industry. Since the short shelf life of dairy products limits their distribution to a radius of 400 kilometers, WBD had to manufacture products close to consumers. Between 1995 and 2003, the company acquired 19 dairy companies and created a national distribution system by appointing 100 distributors. However, by 2003, multinational companies such as Danone and Coca-Cola also built strong sales and distribution systems and capitalized on the growth of local retailers to storm the Russian market. Soon, Danone's dairy products and Coca-Cola's fruit juices were selling faster than WBD's products.

The founders of WBD realized that they needed to adopt a new approach in order to retain the company's leadership position. In April 2006, they hired a new CEO, who had worked with Coca-Cola in Europe for 20 years. To allow him a free hand, the founders moved into new roles as members of a supervisory board. They helped create a more powerful corporate center and a new company mission. Led by the new CEO, WBD focused on reducing costs; improving quality; and investing in its people, including executives. To ensure high quality at a reasonable cost, the company drew up detailed specifications for all of its products and raw materials, improved forecasting and demand planning, reengineered processes to eliminate bureaucracy, simplified its legal structure, and invested in information technology. WBD adopted a number of human resource management practices including a key performance indicator system, semi-annual performance reviews, and individual development plans for the top 500 employees. It also linked salaries with performance and offered stock options to top managers for the first time. Finally, WBD brought in seasoned managers, many from multinational companies, even as it sought to maintain the culture of a Russian company. Partly as a result, WBD had around 34% of the Russian market for packaged dairy products in 2006, according to ACNielsen—more than double Danone's 16% share—and was one of the top three players in fruit juices, with an 18% share.

Like WBD, many national champions have used the appeal of ballooning equity valuations and the prospect of rapid career advancement to attract talent from multinational companies. Gone are the days when executives regarded working for a foreign corporation as something special; now they believe it is just as rewarding to work for a homegrown giant. Several executives have left multinational companies or jobs abroad to join local leaders. In China, for instance, Focus Media CFO Mingdong Wu used to work for Merrill Lynch; Ctrip chairman Jianzhang Liang is a veteran of Oracle, and CFO Jie Sun used to work for KPMG; and Shanda president Jun Tang previously headed Microsoft's China business, and CFO Yong Zhang came from PricewaterhouseCoopers.

How One Local Winner Wove Its Strategy

Many companies pursue one or the other of the success strategies just described. What distinguishes winners is their ability to pursue several, or often all, of them simultaneously and to execute them well. Ctrip, China's largest travel consolidator and online travel agent, has been able to do just that. Founded in 1999, the start-up recognized at the outset that online travel services such as Travelocity, Orbitz, and Expedia wouldn't do well in China with the business models they use so effectively in the United States. At the time, China didn't have a

national ticketing system, such as Sabre, and it still lacks a secure online-payment system. Most of the country's hotels don't belong to a global or national chain, and most local airlines and consumers prefer paper tickets to electronic tickets. Ctrip therefore decided to focus on both off-line and online sales.

Chinese consumers prefer to deal with travel agents, so Ctrip has set up a call center where more than 3,000 representatives can serve 100,000 customers a day. To break into the corporate travel services market, where personal relationships dominate, Ctrip has cleverly developed a loyalty program for executive assistants. Although 70% of Ctrip's revenues still come from off-line sales, it has invested in a sophisticated, automated voice-response system so that it can offer 24/7 booking to consumers. The company has also developed a booking infrastructure that links its online and call center operations to a central database. A large team of researchers constantly updates the database while technical experts integrate it with the systems of Ctrip's airline and hotel partners that are slowly computerizing their operations. The database has yielded the company a formidable advantage since most rivals lack a similar system. In a classic move to use low-cost labor, Ctrip collects payments and provides delivery of paper tickets through couriers who get around China's cities on bicycles and scooters.

It's tough to operate in China's travel market, which comprises hundreds of cities in dozens of provinces, because of regulatory and licensing barriers. Setting up shop in each city requires a license from the local government, which usually owns a competing travel company. There's also the challenge of organizing sales teams and delivery services in many cities. Over the past 10 years, Ctrip has patiently overcome these hurdles and built a national travel business with 5,600 hotel partners and alliances with all of China's leading airlines. Recognizing that Ctrip is a widely dispersed organization, senior executives have created a companywide management culture, the Ctrip Way, and they emphasize the use of common business processes across the company. Ctrip has even established Six Sigma standards for customer-service operations and expects employees to meet them. Furthermore, the company has a strong management team with its cofounders still at the helm. Not surprisingly, Ctrip has beaten back several foreign competitors, such as Expedia's eLong.com and Travelocity's Zuji.com as well as Travelsky, the online portal launched by Chinese state-owned airlines and foreign investors such as Sabre in 2001. At the time, many believed that Travelsky would be the winner in China since it had government backing and priority access to airline tickets. However, it hasn't caught up with Ctrip, at least not yet.

Beating the Locals at Their Own Game

If multinational companies are to succeed on local champions' home turf, they have to fight on two fronts. First, they must emulate some of the local companies' strategies, as we said earlier. Second, they must develop other strategies that local companies cannot easily copy. That's tough but not impossible, as is clear from the recent experiences in China of three multinational companies, each from a different continent and industry.

Kentucky-based Yum Brands, which owns restaurant chains such as KFC, Pizza Hut, and Taco Bell, is thriving in China. The company has adapted in many ways in order to break into the Chinese market. It has customized menus to local tastes and has launched dozens of new items each year. It has also tailored store formats to consumers' behavior, and as preferences change, it modifies those formats. For example, Yum recently introduced drive-throughs to cater to China's growing car-driving population. Its marketing emphasizes educational content, not just food, so its restaurants appeal to parents' priorities. The company positions stores as fun places; for instance, a KFC outlet in China averages two birthday parties a day. In addition, Yum has grown faster than McDonald's. In 2002, KFC outlets in China numbered 766, compared with 538 for McDonald's; by November 2007, the gap had widened to about 2,000 KFC restaurants (in 420 Chinese cities and towns) versus about 800 McDonald's locations.

The company is also expanding Pizza Hut, which has nearly 300 restaurants in China, and its local chain, East Dawning, which serves Chinese food. In fact, Yum opens an average of one new restaurant every day in China.

Yum uses its global expertise to differentiate itself from local players. A network of 16 distribution and two processing centers supports its expansion. To ensure consistent deliveries of quality raw materials, the company has adopted tough supplier-selection policies. Yum also uses its global reputation and resources to influence the Chinese government's policies regarding food safety and supply chain regulations. By doing so, it protects its local reputation, builds government support, and influences industry structure. The result is a combination not easily found in China: a family of quick-service restaurant brands that serve good-quality food in clean environments with local appeal. Yum's strategy is working: Its China business accounted for 20% of its global profits in 2006.

Yum may have set the pace, but Finland's Nokia came from behind to win in China. Five years ago, Nokia trailed Motorola in the Chinese market. It also faced stiff competition from local players such as TCL and Ningbo Bird, whose basic cellular telephones targeted midtier cities and midmarket and low-end customers. In the early 2000s, the local companies moved fast, opening retail outlets and distribution capabilities across China. Surprisingly, Nokia countered equally quickly by investing in a national sales and distribution network. It used a sophisticated IT platform, which provides near real-time information on sales volumes and competitor pricing, as well as an army of 3,000 instore promoters to push products. Nokia also focused on areas where its Chinese rivals were hard-pressed to match its efforts. For instance, it accelerated product development and launched a stream of innovative cellular telephones. The company rapidly ramped up production of these products to high volumes and leveraged its bargaining power to keep costs competitive. Partly because of these factors, Nokia has become the market leader in China today.

The experience of South Korea's Hyundai shows that even late entrants can succeed in crowded emerging markets. The automaker's share rose from zero in 2002, when it entered China, to 7% in 2006; cumulative sales topped the 500,000 mark just 40 months after launch. Hyundai identified a consumer need that other automakers had overlooked, because it sent teams who spent months learning what Chinese consumers want. The company noticed that foreign players held the top end of the market and local players the bottom end, but no company offered a good-quality car at an affordable price. Understanding that China's new middle class wanted such a car, Hyundai refined the Sonata and Elantra models for that market.

Hyundai was determined to bring its expertise and experience to China. China's laws require foreign automakers to enter into joint ventures with domestic firms. These arrangements often result in local enterprises' taking control. Hyundai retained operational control of its joint venture but created a healthy working relationship with its partner, Beijing Automotive Industry Holding Corporation (BAIC). For instance, it insisted that South Korean employees who worked in China learn Chinese. Hyundai minimized its up-front investment by using BAIC's functional but labor-intensive production line. It has kept costs down by forcing its South Korean suppliers to set up operations in China. Buoyed by its success in China's fiercely competitive market, Hyundai is building a $1 billion manufacturing plant in Beijing, which will start operations in April 2008 and will double the company's production capacity to 600,000 units a year.

• • •

Globalization is clearly a double-edged sword. The advantages of being a transnational corporation in emerging markets have declined dramatically in recent times. Smart local companies have used the benefits of globalization to close gaps in technology, capital, and talent with their rivals from the developed. Although the average local competitor is weak, transnational corporations would do well to rethink their strategies. After all, it often takes only one strong homegrown champion to shut a multinational out of an emerging market.

Reading 3-3   Regional Strategies for Global Leadership

Pankaj Ghemawat

It's often a mistake to set out to create a worldwide strategy. Better results come from strong regional strategies, brought together into a global whole.

Let's assume that your firm has a significant international presence. In that case, it probably has something called a "global strategy," which almost certainly represents an extraordinary investment of

▌ Pankaj Ghemawat is the Jaime and Josefina Chua Tiampo Professor of Business Administration at Harvard Business School in Boston. He is the author of "The Forgotten Strategy" (HBR November 2003).
▌ Reprinted by permission of Harvard Business Review. From Regional Strategies for Global Leadership by P. Ghemawat. Copyright © 2007 by the Harvard Business School Publishing Corporation; all rights reserved.

time, money, and energy. You and your colleagues may have adopted it with great fanfare. But, quite possibly, it has proven less than satisfactory as a road map to cross-border competition.

Disappointment with strategies that operate at a global level may explain why companies that do perform well internationally apply a regionally oriented strategy in addition to—or even instead of—a global one. Put differently, global as well as regional companies need to think through strategy at the regional level.

Jeffrey Immelt, CEO of GE, claims that regional teams are the key to his company's globalization initiatives, and he has moved to graft a network of regional headquarters onto GE's otherwise lean product-division structure. John Menzer, president and CEO of Wal-Mart International, tells employees that global leverage is about playing 3-d chess—at the global, regional, and local levels. Toyota may have gone furthest in exploiting the power of regionalized thinking. As Vice Chairman Fujio Cho says, "We intend to continue moving forward with globalization . . . by further enhancing the localization and independence of our operations in each region."

The leaders of these successful companies seem to have grasped two important truths about the global economy. First, geographic and other distinctions haven't been submerged by the rising tide of globalization; in fact, such distinctions are arguably increasing in importance. Second, regionally focused strategies are not just a halfway house between local (country-focused) and global strategies but a discrete family of strategies that, used in conjunction with local and global initiatives, can significantly boost a company's performance.

In the following article, I'll describe the various regional strategies successful companies have employed, showing how they have switched among the strategies and combined them as their markets and businesses have evolved. I'll begin, though, by looking more closely at the economic reasons why regions are often a critical unit of analysis for cross-border strategies.

The Reality of Regions

The most common pitch for taking regions seriously is that the emergence of regional blocs has stalled the process of globalization. Implicit in this view is a tendency to see regionalization as an alternative to further cross-border economic integration.

In fact, a close look at the country-level numbers suggests that increasing cross-border integration has been accompanied by high or rising levels of regionalization. In other words, regions are not an impediment to but an enabler of cross-border integration. As the exhibit "Trade: Regional or Global?" shows, the surge of trade in the second half of the twentieth century was driven more by activity within regions than across regions. The numbers also cast doubt on the idea (held implicitly by advocates of pure global strategies) that economic vitality is promoted more by cross-regional trade. It turns out that regions whose internal trade flows are the lowest relative to trade flows with other regions—Africa, the Middle East, and some of the Eastern European transition economies—are also the poorest economic performers.

Country-level numbers also suggest that foreign direct investment (FDI) is quite regionalized, which is even more surprising than the regionalization of trade. Data from the United Nations Conference on Trade and Development show that for the two dozen countries that account for nearly 90% of the world's outward FDI stock, the median share of intraregional FDI in total FDI was 52% in 2002, the most recent year for which data are available.

The extent and persistence of regionalization in economic activity reflect the continuing importance not only of geographic proximity but also of cultural, administrative, and, to some extent, economic proximity.[1] These four factors are interrelated: Countries that are relatively close to one another are also likely to share commonalities along the other dimensions. What's more, those similarities have intensified in the past few decades through free trade agreements, regional trade preferences and tax treaties, and even currency unification, with NAFTA and the European Union supplying the two most obvious examples. Ironically, some differences between countries within a region can combine with the similarities to expand the region's overall economic activity. For instance, we see U.S. firms in many industries nearshoring production facilities to Mexico,

---

[1]For a systematic way to think about cultural, administrative, geographic, and economic distance, see the CAGE framework described in my article "Distance Still Matters: The Hard Reality of Global Expansion" (HBR September 2001).

thereby arbitraging across economic differences between the two countries while retaining the advantages of geographic proximity and administrative and political similarities, which more distant countries, such as China, do not enjoy.

Evidence from companies' international sales also points to considerable regionalization. According to data analyzed by Susan Feinberg at Rutgers Business School, among U.S. companies operating in only one foreign country, there is a 60% chance that the country is Canada. Even the largest multinational corporations exhibit a significant regional bias. A study published by Alan Rugman and Alain Verbeke in the *Journal of International Business Studies* shows that around 88% of the world's biggest multinationals derive at least 50% of their sales—the weighted average is 80%—from their home regions. Just 2% (a total of nine companies) derive 20% or more of their sales from each of the triad of North America, Europe, and Asia.

Zooming in on large companies with relatively broad regional footprints—roughly akin to the top 12% of the previous sample—we find that even here competitive interactions are often regionally focused. Take the case of the aluminum-smelting industry. As we see in the exhibit "Industry: Regional or Global?" in the last ten years the industry has experienced some increase in concentration as measured by the Herfindahl index (a standard measure of industry concentration; the higher the index, the larger the market shares of the largest firms). But that increase in concentration reverses less than one-half of the decline of the previous 20 years, or about one-tenth of the decline experienced since 1950. In contrast, concentration in North America has doubled in the last ten years after holding more or less steady for the previous 20 years. Similar patterns appear in a range of other industries: personal computers, beer, and cement, to name just three. In other words, regions are often the level at which global oligopolists try to build up powerhouse positions.

Let's now take a closer look at the menu of regional strategies from which your company can choose.

The Regional Strategy Menu

Broadly speaking, regional strategies can be classified into five types, each with distinct strengths and weaknesses. I have ordered the strategies according to their relative complexity, starting with the simplest, but that does not mean companies necessarily progress through the strategies as they evolve. Whereas some companies may indeed adopt the strategies in the order in which I present them, others may find themselves abandoning more-advanced strategies in favor of simpler ones—good business is about striving to maximize value, not complexity. And capable companies will often use elements of several strategies simultaneously.

The Home Base Strategy   Except for the very few companies that are virtually born global, such as Indian software services firms, companies generally start their international expansion by serving nearby foreign markets from their home base, locating all their R&D and, usually, manufacturing in their country of origin. The home base is also where the bulk of the *Fortune* Global 500 still focuses. Even companies that have since moved on to more complex regional strategies nonetheless rely on a home base strategy—at the regional level—for long periods. Thus, for decades, Toyota's international sales came exclusively from direct exports. And some companies that move on eventually return to a home base strategy: GE did so in home appliances, as did Bayer in pharmaceuticals.

For other companies, however, a focus on the home region is a matter of neither default nor devolution but, instead, the desired long-term strategy. Take the case of Zara, the Spanish fashion company. In a cycle that takes between two and four weeks, Zara designs and makes items near its manufacturing and logistics hub in northwestern Spain and trucks those goods to Western European markets. This rapid response lets the company produce what is selling during a fashion season instead of committing to merchandise before the season starts. The enhanced customer appeal and reduced incidence of markdowns have so far more than offset

Trade: Regional or Global?

In many parts of the world, intraregional trade increased steadily as a percentage of a region's total trade in the second half of the twentieth century. For example, in 1958 some 35% of trade in Asia and Oceania took place between countries in that geographic region.

In 2000, the proportion was more than 50%. Globally, the proportion of trade within regions rose from about 47% to 55% between 1958 and 2000. The only significant decline has been in Eastern Europe, but that is explained by the collapse of communism. In general, the numbers indicate that increasing economic integration through international trade has been accompanied by increasing rather than decreasing regionalization.

Intraregional Trade as a Percentage of Total Trade

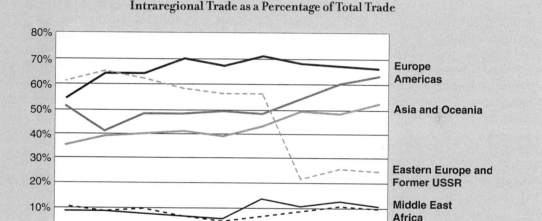

Source: United Nations, *International Trade Statistics Yearbooks,* 1958 to 2000.

the extra costs of producing in Europe instead of Asia.

As Zara illustrates, home base strategies work well when the economics of concentration outweigh the economics of dispersion. Fashion-sensitive items do not travel easily from the Spanish hub to other regions, because the costs of expedited air shipments compromise the company's low-price positioning. More generally, the presence of any factor that collapses distance *within* the local region (such as regional grids in energy) will encourage companies to favor a single-region, home base strategy.

For some companies, the "region" that can be served from the home base is actually the globe. Operating in the highly globalized memory chip

business, the Korean giant Samsung has one of the most balanced worldwide sales distributions of any major business, but it considers the colocation of most R&D and production at one site in South Korea to be a key competitive advantage. Transport costs are so low relative to product value that geographic concentration—which permits rapid interactions and iteration across R&D and production—dominates geographic dispersion even at the global level.

But cases like Samsung are rare. Typically, doing business from the home base effectively limits a company to its local region. As a result, the biggest threats to companies pursuing a home base strategy are running out of room to grow or failing to hedge risk adequately. Growth within Europe will soon be an issue for Zara. And risk has already emerged as a major concern: As of this writing, the sharp decline of the dollar against the euro has inflated Zara's costs of production relative to competitors that rely more on dollar-denominated imports from Asia.

The Portfolio Strategy   This strategy involves setting up or acquiring operations outside the home region that report directly to the home base. It is usually the first strategy adopted by companies seeking to establish a presence outside the markets they can serve from home. The advantages of this approach include faster growth in nonhome regions, significant home positions that generate large amounts of cash, and the opportunity to average out economic shocks and cycles across regions.

A good example of a successful portfolio strategy is provided by Toyota's initial investments in the United States, which seemed tied together by little more than the desire to build up a manufacturing presence in the company's most important overseas market. What prevented this approach from destroying value was Toyota's distinct competitive advantage: the celebrated Toyota Production System (TPS), which was developed and still works best at home in Japan but could be applied to factories in the United States.

Although the portfolio strategy is conceptually simple, it takes time to implement, especially if a company tries to expand organically. It took Toyota more than a decade to establish itself in North America—a process that began with a joint venture with General Motors in the early 1980s. For an automaker lacking an advantage like TPS, the organic buildup of a significant presence in a new region could take far longer. Of course, companies may

---

Industry: Regional or Global?

In many "global" industries, competition is playing out at a regional level. The chart below measures concentration in the aluminum-smelting industry as a summary measure of the distribution of market shares within it. The metric used is the Herfindahl index, which measures the degree to which the industry is fragmented (lots of small to medium-sized companies splitting most of the business) or concentrated (a few players controlling most of the business). The higher the index, the larger the market shares of the largest companies. As the chart shows, the level of global competition was relatively flat from 1975 to 2000, while concentration in North America over the same period increased dramatically.

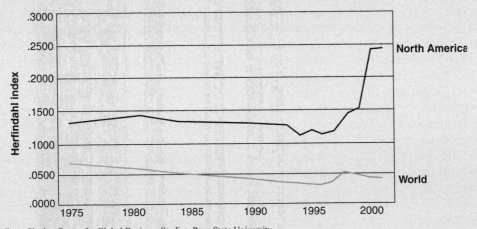

Concentration in the Aluminium-Smelting Industry

Source: Fariborz Ghadar, Center for Global Business Studies, Penn State University.

build a regional portfolio more quickly through acquisitions, but even that can take a decade or more. When Jack Welch began GE's globalization initiative in the second half of the 1980s, he targeted expansion in Europe, giving a trusted confidant, Nani Beccalli, wide latitude for deal making. Thanks to Beccalli's acquisitions, GE built up a strong presence in Europe, but the process of assembling the regional portfolio lasted until the early 2000s.

Companies that adopt a portfolio strategy often struggle to deal with rivals in nonhome regions. That's largely because portfolio strategies offer limited scope for letting regional—as opposed to local or global—considerations influence what happens on the ground at the local level. Indeed, this was precisely the experience of GE, whose European businesses reported to the global headquarters in the United States, run by purported "global leaders"— many of whom were Americans who had never lived or worked abroad. Meanwhile, most of GE's toughest competitors in its nonfinancial businesses were European companies that knew their increasingly regionalized home turf and were prepared to compete aggressively there. During a talk at Harvard Business School in 2002, Immelt described the results: "I think we stink in Europe today."

The Hub Strategy Companies seeking to add value at the regional level frequently begin by adopting this strategy. Originally articulated by McKinsey consultant Kenichi Ohmae, a hub strategy involves building regional bases, or hubs, that provide a variety of shared resources and services to local (country) operations. The logic is that such resources may be hard for any one country to justify, but economies of scale or other factors may make them practical from a cross-country perspective.

Hub strategies often involve transforming a foreign operation into a stand-alone unit. In the early 1990s, for instance, Toyota began producing a limited number of locally exclusive models in its principal foreign plants—previously a taboo— thereby signaling the company's intention to build complete organizations in each of its regions. These plants thus started to serve as regionally distinct hubs, each with its own platform, whose products were designed for sale within the region.

In its purest form, a hub strategy is simply a multiregional version of the home base strategy. For example, if Zara were to add a second hub in, say, Asia by establishing an operation in China to serve the entire Asian market, it would shift from being home based to being a multiregional hubber. Therefore, some of the same conditions that favor a home base strategy also favor hubs. It should also be noted that multiple hubs can be very independent of one another; the more regions differ in their requirements, the weaker the rationale for hubs to share resources and policies.

A regional headquarters can be seen as a minimalist version of a hub strategy. After the European Commission blocked GE's merger with Honeywell, GE felt the need to dedicate more corporate infrastructure and resources to Europe, partly to attract, develop, and retain the best European employees and partly to acquire a more European face for political reasons. In 2001, therefore, GE switched from a portfolio to a hub strategy by establishing a regional HQ structure in Europe— complete with a CEO for GE Europe. The company followed up in 2003 by establishing a parallel organization in Asia.

The impact of the typical regional HQ is limited, however, by its focus on support functions and its weak links to operating activities. For example, the regional presidents within Wal-Mart International perform a communication-and-monitoring role, but otherwise their influence on strategy and resource allocation seems to be mainly personal. In any event, a regional HQ is seldom a sufficient basis for a regional strategy, even though it may be a necessary part of one. (See the sidebar "A Regional HQ Is Not Enough.")

The challenge in executing a hub strategy is achieving the right balance between customization and standardization. Companies too responsive to interregional variation risk adding too much cost or sacrificing too many opportunities to share costs across regions. As a result, they may find themselves vulnerable to attacks from companies taking a more standardized approach. On the other hand, companies that try to standardize across regional hubs—and in so doing overestimate the degree of commonality from region to region—are vulnerable to competition from local players. Thus we see Dell, whose product is relatively standard across its regional operations, forced to modify its plans in China to respond to local companies competing aggressively on cost by producing less-sophisticated, lower quality products.

The Platform Strategy Hubs, as we've seen, spread fixed costs across countries within a region. Interregional platforms go a step further by spreading fixed costs across regions. They tend to be particularly important for back-end activities that can deliver economies of scale and scope. Most major automakers, for example, are trying to reduce the number of basic platforms they offer worldwide in order to achieve greater economies of scale in design, engineering, administration, procurement, and operations. It is in this spirit that Toyota has been reducing the number of its platforms from 11 to six and has invested in global car brands such as the Camry and the Corolla.

It's important to realize that the idea behind platforming is *not* to reduce the amount of product variety on offer but to deliver variety more cost-effectively by allowing customization atop common platforms explicitly engineered for adaptability. Ideally, therefore, platform strategies are almost invisible to a company's customers. Platforming runs into difficulties when managers take standardization too far.

Let's look again at the automobile industry. Sir Nick Scheele, outgoing COO of Ford, points out, "The single biggest barrier to globalization [in the automobile industry] . . . is the relatively cheap cost of motor fuel in the United States. There is a tremendous disparity between the United States and . . . the rest of the world, and it creates an accompanying disparity in . . . the most fundamental of vehicle characteristics: size and power." This reality is precisely what Ford ignored with its Ford 2000 program. Described by one analyst as the biggest business merger in history, Ford 2000 sought to combine Ford's regional operations—principally North America and Europe—into one global operation. This attempt to reduce duplication across the two regions sparked enormous internal turmoil and largely destroyed Ford's European organization. Regional product development capabilities were sacrificed, and unappealingly compromised products were pushed into an unreceptive marketplace. The result: nearly $3 billion in losses in Europe through 2000 and a fall in regional market share from 12% to 9%.

The Mandate Strategy This cousin of the platform strategy focuses on economies of *specialization* as well as scale. Companies that adopt this strategy award certain regions broad mandates to

---

A Regional HQ Is Not Enough

Many companies with explicitly global ambitions have reacted to the regionalization of the world economy by establishing a set of regional headquarters. This kind of organizational response has, in fact, also been the focus of most of the management literature on regions. Michael Enright, for example, has described some interesting patterns in recent articles in the *Management International Review* on the functions performed by regional management centers. But to focus on regional HQs or any other organizational structure as *the* primary object of interest is a little like focusing on the briefcase rather than its contents. Without a clear sense of how a regional structure is supposed to add value, it is impossible to specify what the structure should try to achieve. A company with no regional HQs may still use regions as the building blocks of its overall strategy, and a company with many regional HQs may still not have a clearly articulated regional strategy. In other words, having regional headquarters doesn't mean that you actually have a regional strategy.

supply particular products or perform particular roles for the whole organization. For example, Toyota's Innovative International Multi-purpose Vehicle (IMV) project funnels common engines and manual transmissions for pickup trucks, SUVs, and minivans from Asian plants to four assembly hubs there and in Latin America and Africa, and then on to almost all the major markets around the world except the United States, where such vehicles are larger. Similarly, Whirlpool is sourcing most of its small kitchen appliances from India, and a host of global companies are in the process of broadening the mandates of their production operations in China.

As with platforms, the scope for mandates generally increases with the degree of product standardization around the world, even though the mandate strategy involves focused resource deployments at the regional and local levels. But interregional mandates can be set up in some businesses that afford little room for conventional platforms. For instance, global firms in consulting, engineering, financial services, and other service industries often feature centers of excellence that are recognized as repositories of particular knowledge and skills, and are charged with making that knowledge available to the rest of the firm. Such centers are often concentrated in a single location, around an individual or a small group of people, and therefore have geographic mandates that are much broader than their geographic footprints.

There are of course several risks associated with assigning broad geographic mandates to particular locations. First, such mandates can allow local, national, or regional interests to unduly influence,

The Toyota Way

This exhibit is an almost exact reproduction of a slide presented to Toyota investors at an informational event in New York City in September 2004. The only change I have made is to label the slide to highlight how the various elements identified in the Toyota strategy correspond to the five strategies described in this article. Toyota's "global network," which combines all the other approaches, can be considered a sixth strategy.

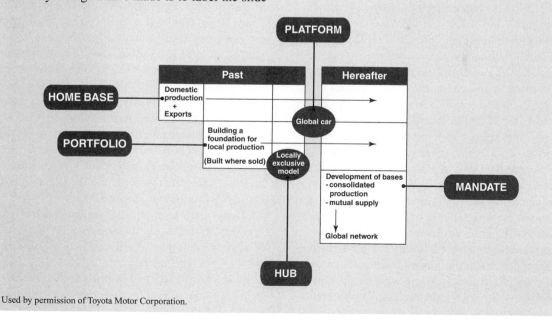

Used by permission of Toyota Motor Corporation.

or even hijack, a firm's overall strategy: More than one professional service firm can be cited in this context. Second, broad mandates cannot handle variations in local, national, or regional conditions, which is why the near-global mandate for Toyota's Asian pickup engine and transmission plants excludes the United States. And finally, carrying the degree of specialization to extremes can create inflexibility. A company that produces everything based on global mandates would be affected worldwide by a disruption at a single location.

The reader will have noticed that Toyota figures as an illustration in all the foregoing descriptions. Indeed, this is because Toyota provides perhaps the most compelling and complete example of how the effective application of regional strategies can produce a global powerhouse. The success is apparent: Toyota surpassed Ford as the world's second-largest automaker in 2004 and is poised to overtake General Motors in the next two to three years. The exhibit "The Toyota Way" reproduces a slide that the company uses to summarize the evolution of its strategy. It shows both that Toyota looks at strategy through a regional lens and that it has, in fact, progressed through all the strategies I've just described.

What is also interesting about Toyota is that new modes of value creation at the regional level have supplemented old ones instead of replacing them. Although Toyota has moved beyond a Japanese manufacturing base (the home base strategy), exports from Japanese manufacturing facilities to the rest of the world continue to account for more than one-quarter of the company's volume and a significantly larger share of its profits. In regions other than the two in which it has strong positions—East and Southeast Asia and North America—Toyota is still following a portfolio approach. In terms of regional hubs, the promotion of a production and procurement specialist to succeed Fujio Cho as president signals an increased commitment to transplanting the Toyota Production System from Japan to the newer production hubs at a time when overseas production is being ramped up rapidly. But even as its hubs gain strength, Toyota continues to reduce the number of its major production platforms and pursue additional specialization through interregional mandates. The IMV project described earlier plays a critical role in all three respects.

The picture that emerges is not one of Toyota progressing through the various regional strategies one at a time but of a company trying to cover all the bases. One can even argue that the application of all five regional strategies itself represents a new form of strategy—the "global network" in Toyota's slide—in which various regional operations interact with one another and the corporate center in multiple ways and at multiple levels.

Of course, Toyota's ability to employ a complex mix of regional strategies to create value is inseparable from the company's basic competitive advantage: TPS's ability to produce high-quality, reliable cars at low cost. Without this fundamental advantage, some of Toyota's coordination attempts would drown in a sea of red ink.

Defining Your Regions

As companies think through the risks and opportunities of various regional strategies, they also need to clarify what they mean by the word "region." I have so far avoided a definition, although most of my examples imply a continental perspective. My goal is not to be elusive but to avoid restricting the strategies to a particular geographic scale. Particularly with large countries, the logic of the strategies can apply to intranational as well as international regions. Oil companies, for example, consider the market for gasoline in the United States to consist of five distinct regions. Other large markets where transport costs are relatively high in relation to product value, such as cement in Brazil or beer in China, can be similarly broken down.

The general point is that one can interpret the regional strategies at different geographic levels. Assessing the level—global, continental, subcontinental, national, intranational, or local—at which scale is most tightly tied to profitability is often a helpful guide to determining what constitutes a region. Put differently, the world economy is made up of many overlapping geographic layers—from local to global—and the idea is to focus not on one layer but on many. Doing so fosters flexibility by helping companies adapt ideas about regional strategies to different geographic levels of analysis.

In addition to reconsidering what might constitute a geographic region, one can imagine being even more creative and redefining distance—and regions—according to nongeographic dimensions: cultural, administrative and political, and economic. Aggregation along nongeographic dimensions will sometimes still imply a focus on geographically contiguous regions. Toyota, for instance, groups countries by existing and expected free trade areas. At other times, however, such definitions will yield regions that aren't geographically compact. After making its first foreign investments in Spain, for example, the Mexican cement company Cemex grew through the rest of the 1990s by aggregating along the economic dimension—that is, by expanding into markets that were emerging, like its Mexican home base. This strategy created the so-called ring of gray gold: developing markets that mostly fell in a band circling the globe just north of the equator, forming a geographically contiguous but dispersed region.

At times, the parts of a region aren't even contiguous. Spain, for example, can be thought of as "closer" to Latin America than to Europe because of long-standing colony-colonizer links. Between 1997 and 2001, 44% of a surge in FDI from Spain was directed at Latin America—about ten times Latin America's share of world FDI. Europe's much larger regional economy was pushed into second place as a destination for Spanish capital.

Finally, it's important to remember that the definition of "region" often changes in response to market conditions and, indeed, to a company's own strategic decisions. By serving the U.S. market from Japan, Toyota in its early days implicitly considered that market to be on the periphery of its own region. The North American West Coast was easy to access by sea, the United States was open to helping the Japanese economy get off the ground, and the company's business there was dwarfed by its domestic business. But as Toyota's U.S. sales grew, political

Is a Regional Strategy Right for Your Company?

Take a couple of minutes to complete this short questionnaire. First, circle one option for each of the following eight categories. Then complete the scoring. Give yourself -1 for each "a" response, 0 for each "b" response, and 1 for each "c" response, and then add up the numbers. A positive score may indicate a significant need for strategy at the regional level. The higher the score, the greater is your need.

Of course, this kind of questionnaire is no substitute for analyzing your company's situation—and regionalization options—in detail. But if the results prompt you to look at your regional strategy more carefully, the exercise will have been useful.

COMPANY FOOTPRINT

Number of countries with significant operations	SCORE
a. **1–5**	
b. **6–15**	
c. **>15**	_____

Percentage of sales from the home region	
a. **>80%**	
b. **50%–80%**	
c. **<50%**	_____

COMPANY STRATEGY

Objective for interregional dispersion	
a. **Decrease**	
b. **Maintain**	
c. **Increase**	_____

Number of bases of aggregation (or grouping) to be pursued	
a. **1**	
b. **2**	
c. **>2**	_____

(continued)

COUNTRY LINKS

Percentage of trade that is intraregional
a. <50%
b. 50%–70%
c. >70%   _____

Percentage of FDI that is intraregional
a. >40%
b. 40%–60%
c. >60%   _____

COMPETITIVE CONSIDERATIONS

Differences in profitability across regions
a. Small
b. Short-term
c. Long-term   _____

Key competitors' strategies
a. Deregionalizing
b. Unchanged
c. Regionalizing   _____

TOTAL SCORE   _____

SCORING:
−1 for each (a) response
0 for each (b) response
1 for each (c) response

pressures increased the political and administrative distance between the two countries, and it became apparent that Toyota needed to look at the United States as part of its own self-contained region.

Leading-edge companies are starting to grapple with these definitional issues. For example, firms in sectors as diverse as construction materials, forest products, telecommunications equipment, and pharmaceuticals have invested significantly in modern mapping technology, using such innovations as enhanced clustering techniques, better measures for analyzing networks, and expanded data on bilateral, multilateral, and unilateral country attributes to visualize new definitions of regions. At the very least, this sort of mapping sparks creativity.

Facing the Organizational Challenge

Regional strategies, as I've noted, can take a long time to implement. One deep-seated reason for this is that an organization's existing structures may be out of alignment with—or even inimical to—a superimposed regional strategy. The question then becomes how best to mesh such strategies with a firm's existing structures, especially when the established organizational players command most of the power.

For some pointers, consider Royal Philips Electronics, which has been a border-crossing enterprise for virtually all of its 114-year history. Philips's saga not only points to alignment challenges but also reminds us that regionalization is rarely a triumphal march from the home base to interregional platforms or mandates.

Starting in the 1930s, Philips evolved into a federal system of largely autonomous national organizations presided over by a cadre of 1,500 elite expatriate managers who championed the country-oriented approach. But as competition emerged in the 1960s and 1970s from Japanese companies that were more centralized and had fewer, larger plants, this highly localized structure became expensive to maintain. Philips responded by installing a matrix organization—with countries and product divisions as its two legs—and spent roughly two decades trying, without much success, to rebalance the matrix away from the countries and toward the product divisions. Finally, in 1997, CEO Cor Boonstra abolished the geographic dimension of the matrix as a way of forcing the organization to align itself around global product divisions.

Given this long and sometimes painful history, it would be unrealistic for today's champions of regional strategies within Philips to expect to overthrow the product division structure. Would-be regionalists have to work within it. Jan Oosterveld, who served as CEO of Asia Pacific from 2003 to 2004—a position created after Philips announced the combination of two Asia Pacific subregions into one—saw that his first task was to facilitate the sharing of resources and knowledge across product divisions within the region. Ultimately, however, he aimed to help develop an Asia Pacific strategy for the company. So although the new Asian regional structure has initially focused on coordinating governmental relations, key account management, branding, joint purchasing, and IT, HR, and other support functions, Oosterveld and others can imagine a day when much more power might be vested in regional headquarters in, say, New York, Shanghai, and Amsterdam than at the corporate level. They also recognize, however, that achieving that kind of regional strategy could take many years.

The obvious implication is that strategic initiatives can be pursued at the regional level only if some decision rights are reallocated—whether from the local or global levels, or from the other repositories of power within the organization (in Philips's case, product divisions). And just as obviously, no one likes to give up power. Leadership from the top, aimed at promoting a "one-company" mentality, is often the only way forward. One of Oosterveld's conditions for taking the job at Philips was that the board of directors hold regional conclaves twice a year to show its commitment to the regional initiative. Such conclaves might be mainly symbolic, but symbolism can go a long way.

Philips has approached regional strategy flexibly, putting in place a wide variety of arrangements that take into account not only the company's existing structure but also competitive realities, region by region. In North America, for example, Philips's principal objective continues to be to rebuild its positions and achieve satisfactory levels of performance in the all-important U.S. market. Its activities there are organized entirely around the global product divisions, which, because of the size of the market and Philips's stake in it, are thought to be capable of achieving the requisite geographic focus.

In Europe, where Philips is better established, the company has rethought the role and status of the large operations in the home country of the Netherlands within the broader regional structure. In April 2002, when Philips announced plans to set up a regional superstructure in Asia Pacific, it also folded the Netherlands into an expanded region comprising Europe, the Middle East, and Africa. The point is that irregular or asymmetric structures (in which some regions seem to be much larger than others) are often preferable to an aesthetically pleasing (and in some respects simpler) symmetry of the sort implicitly evoked by much of the discussion up to this point. Even Toyota seems to be focusing separately on China while its other markets are grouped into multicountry regions.

• • •

If your company has a significant international presence, it already has a regional strategy—even if that strategy has been arrived at by default. But given the variety of regional strategies, and the fact that no one approach is best or most evolved, there is no substitute for figuring out which ways of coordinating within or across regions make sense for your company. As we have seen, however, embracing regional strategies calls for flexibility, creativity, and hard-nosed analysis of the changing business context—all of which take time and effort.

In a highly regionalized world, the right regional strategy (or strategies) can create more value than purely global or purely local ones can. But even so, the regional approaches I have been exploring may not make sense for your company. In that case, here is what you can take away from this article: Regions represent just one way of aggregating across borders to achieve greater efficiencies than would be achievable with a country-by-country approach. Other bases of cross-border aggregation that companies have implemented include products (the global product divisions at Philips), channels (Cisco, which uses channels and partners as its primary basis), customer types or global accounts (many IT services firms), functions (most major oil companies), and technologies (ABB recently, before and after trying some of the bases that are listed above and others that aren't). Each of these bases of aggregation offers, as regions do, multiple possibilities for crafting strategies intermediate to the local and global levels by grouping things. In a world that is neither truly local nor truly global, such strategies can deliver a powerful competitive advantage.

Developing a Transnational Organization:
Managing Integration, Responsiveness, and Flexibility

Having discussed how MNEs are responding to the forces requiring them to develop strategies that optimize the balance among global efficiency, national responsiveness, and worldwide innovation and learning, we now focus our attention on the kind of organizations they must build to manage these often conflicting strategic tasks. In this chapter, we begin by suggesting that this balance requires that MNEs not only understand their present and future strategic task demands but also their historic organizational capabilities—something we call a company's "administrative heritage." As they respond to the need to develop transnational strategies, companies must build transnational organizations that reflect their need for multidimensional and flexible capabilities. In the final section of the chapter, we suggest that this involves more than a search for an ideal structural solution, and explore the attributes of such transnational organizations using a biological analogy. After describing the transnational's structure (anatomy), its processes, (physiology), and its culture (psychology), we examine the processes necessary to build such organizational capabilities.

In the preceding chapters, we described how changes in the international operating environment have forced MNEs to optimize global efficiency, national responsiveness, and worldwide learning simultaneously. Implementing such a complex, three-pronged strategic objective would be difficult under any circumstances, but the very act of "going international" multiplies a company's organizational complexity.

Most companies find it difficult enough to balance product divisions or business units with corporate staff functions. The thought of adding geographically oriented management and maintaining a three-way balance of organizational perspectives and capabilities among products, functions, and regions is intimidating. The difficulty is further increased because the resolution of tensions among the three different management groups must be accomplished by an organization whose operating units are divided by distance and time and whose key members are separated by barriers of culture and language.

Beyond Structural Fit

Because the choice of a basic organizational structure has such a powerful influence on the management process in an MNE, historically much of the attention of managers and researchers alike was focused on trying to find which formal structure provided the right "fit" in various conditions. The most widely recognized early study on this issue was

Figure 4-1 Stopford and Wells's International Structural Stages Model

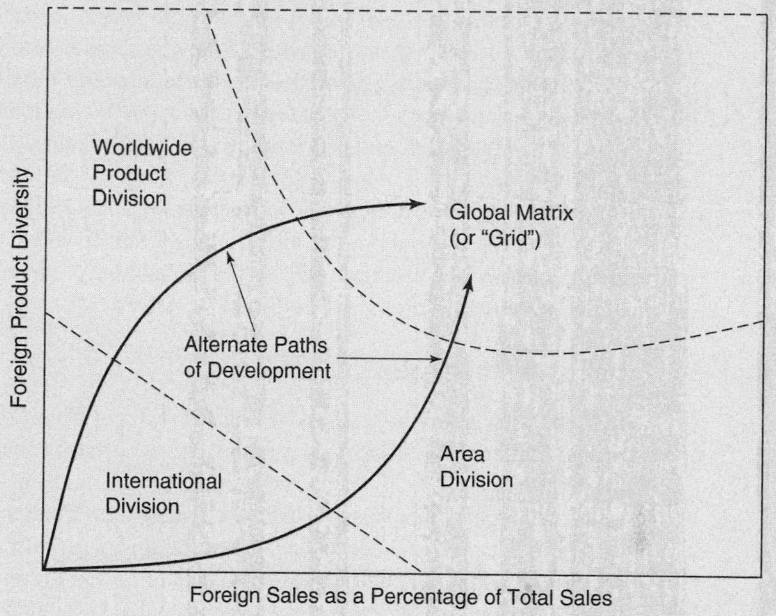

Source: Adapted from John M. Stopford and Louis T. Wells, *Strategy and Structure of the Multinational Enterprise* (New York: Basic Books, 1972).

John Stopford's research on the 187 largest U.S.-based MNEs.[1] His work resulted in a "stages model" of international organization structure that defined two variables to capture the strategic and administrative complexity most companies faced as they expanded abroad: the number of products sold internationally ("foreign product diversity" in Figure 4-1) and the importance of international sales to the company ("foreign sales as a percentage of total sales"). Plotting the structural changes in his sample of 187 companies, he found that worldwide corporations typically adopt different organizational structures at different stages of international expansion.

According to this model, worldwide companies typically managed their international operations through an international division at the early stage of foreign expansion. Subsequently, those companies that expanded their sales abroad without significantly increasing their foreign product diversity typically adopted an area structure (e.g., European region, Asia–Pacific region). Other companies that expanded by increasing their foreign product diversity tended to adopt a worldwide product division structure (e.g., chemicals division, plastics division). Finally, when both foreign sales and foreign product diversity were high, companies resorted to a global matrix in which a French chemicals manager might report to both the European regional head and the global chemicals division president at corporate headquarters.

[1]Stopford's research is described in John M. Stopford and Louis T. Wells, *Managing the Multinational Enterprise* (New York: Basic Books, 1972).

Although these ideas were presented as a descriptive rather than a prescriptive model, and despite the fact that the global matrix was a new font used by relatively few companies, consultants and managers soon began to apply the model prescriptively. For many companies, it seemed that structure followed fashion more than strategy. And in the process, the debate was often reduced to generalized discussions of the comparative value of product- versus geography-based structures on the one hand or to simplistic choices between "centralization" and "decentralization" on the other.

Confronted with increasing complexity, diversity, and change in the 1980s, managers in many worldwide companies looked for ways to restructure. Conventional wisdom provided a ready solution: the global matrix. But for most companies, the results were disappointing. The promised land of the global matrix turned out to be an organizational quagmire from which they were forced to retreat.

Failure of the Matrix

In theory, the solution should have worked. Having frontline managers report simultaneously to different organizational groups (e.g., the French chemicals manager in the preceding example) should have enabled companies to maintain a balance among centralized efficiency, local responsiveness, and worldwide knowledge transfer. The multiple channels of communication and control promised the ability to nurture diverse management perspectives, and the ability to shift the balance of power within the matrix theoretically gave it great flexibility. The reality turned out to be otherwise however, and the history of companies that built formal global matrix structures was an unhappy one.

Dow Chemical, a pioneer of the global matrix organization, eventually returned to a more conventional structure with clear lines of responsibility given to geographic managers. Citibank, once a textbook example of the global matrix, also discarded this mode of dual reporting relationships after a few years of highly publicized experimentation. So too did scores of other companies that tried to manage their worldwide activities through a structure that often seemed to result in complex and rather bureaucratic processes and relationships.

Most encountered the same problems. The matrix amplified the differences in perspectives and interests by forcing all issues through the dual chains of command so that even a minor difference could become the subject of heated disagreement and debate.

Dual reporting led to conflict and confusion on many levels: The proliferation of channels created informational logjams, conflicts could be resolved only by escalating the problem, and overlapping responsibilities resulted in turf battles and a loss of accountability. Separated by barriers of distance, time, language, and culture, managers found it virtually impossible to clarify the confusion and resolve the conflicts. As a result, in company after company, the initial appeal of the global matrix structure quickly faded into a recognition that a different solution was required.

Building Organizational Capability

The basic problem underlying a company's search for a structural fit was that it focused on only one organizational variable—formal structure—and this single tool proved unequal to the job of capturing the complexity of the strategic tasks facing most MNEs.

First, as we indicated previously, this focus on making choices between product- versus geographically based structures often forced managers to ignore the environmental forces' multiple conflicting demands. Second, structure defined a static set of roles, responsibilities, and relationships in a task environment that was dynamic and rapidly evolving. Third, restructuring efforts often proved harmful, as organizations were bludgeoned into a major realignment of roles, responsibilities, and relationships by overnight changes in structure. In an increasing number of companies, managers now recognize that formal structure is a powerful but blunt instrument of strategic change. Structural fit is becoming both less relevant and harder to achieve. To develop its vital multidimensional and flexible capabilities, a company must reorient managers' thinking and reshape the core decision-making systems. In doing so, the company's entire management process—including its administrative systems, communication channels, decision-making forums, and interpersonal relationships—becomes the means for managing such change.

As a first step in exploring some of the more subtle and sophisticated tools, we examine how *administrative heritage*—a company's history and its embedded management culture—influences its organization and its ability and willingness to change. It is a concept to which we have already alluded in previous chapters when we acknowledged how an MNE's management mentality and strategic posture may have been shaped by different motivations for international expansion, different historical and cultural factors, and different external industry forces.

Administrative Heritage

Whereas industry analysis can reveal a company's strategic challenges and market opportunities, its ability to fulfill that promise will be greatly influenced—sometimes facilitated, sometimes constrained—by its existing internal world: its asset configuration and resource distribution, its historical definition of management responsibilities, and its ingrained organizational norms, for example. Clearly, a company's organization is shaped not only by current external task demands but also by past internal management biases. In particular, each company is influenced by the path by which it developed—its organizational history—and the values, norms, and practices of its management—its management culture. Collectively, these factors constitute what we call a company's administrative heritage.

Administrative heritage can be, at the same time, one of the company's greatest assets—the underlying source of its core competencies—and a significant liability, because it resists change and thereby prevents realignment. As managers in many companies have learned, whereas strategic plans can be scrapped and redrawn overnight, there is no such thing as a zero-based organization. Companies are, to a significant extent, captives of their past, and any organizational transformation has to focus at least as much on where the company is coming from—its administrative heritage—as on where it wants to go.

The importance of a company's administrative heritage can be illustrated by contrasting the development of a typical European MNE whose major international expansion occurred in the decades of the 1920s and 1930s, a typical American MNE that expanded abroad in the 1950s and 1960s, and a typical Japanese company that made its main overseas thrust in the 1970s and 1980s. Even if these companies were in the same industry, their different heritages would lead them to adopt some very different strategic and organizational models.

Decentralized Federation

Expanding abroad in a period of rising tariffs and discriminatory legislation, the typical European company was forced to build local production facilities to compete effectively with local competitors. With their own local plants, national subsidiaries of MNEs were able to modify products and marketing approaches to meet widely differing local market needs. The increasing independence of these self-sufficient national units was reinforced by the communication barriers that existed in that era, limiting headquarters' ability to intervene in the management of the company's spreading worldwide operations.

The emerging configuration of distributed assets and delegated responsibility fit well with the ingrained management norms and practices in many European companies. European companies, particularly those from the United Kingdom, the Netherlands, and France, developed an internal culture that emphasized personal relationships (an "old boys' network") rather than formal structures, and financial controls more than operational controls. This management style tended to reinforce these companies' willingness to delegate more operating independence and strategic freedom to their foreign subsidiaries. Highly autonomous national companies were often managed more as a portfolio of offshore investments than a single international business.

The resulting organization pattern was a loose federation of independent national subsidiaries, each focused primarily on its local market. As a result, many of these companies adopted what we have described in previous chapters as the *multinational strategy* and managed it through a *decentralized federation* organization model, as represented in Figure 4-2(a).

Coordinated Federation

American companies, many of which enjoyed their fastest international expansion in the 1950s and 1960s, developed in very different circumstances. Their strength lay in the new technologies and management processes they had developed through being located in the United States—the world's largest, richest, and most technologically advanced market. After World War II, their foreign expansion focused primarily on leveraging this strength, giving rise to the international product cycle theory referred to in Chapter 1.

Reinforcing this strategy was a professional managerial culture in most U.S.-based companies that contrasted with the "old boys' network" that typified the European companies' processes. The U.S. management approach was built on a willingness to delegate responsibility while retaining overall control through sophisticated management systems and specialist corporate staffs. Foreign subsidiaries were often free to adapt products or strategies to reflect market differences, but their dependence on the parent company for new products, processes, and ideas dictated a great deal more coordination and control by headquarters than did the decentralized federation organization. This relationship was facilitated by the existence of formal systems and controls in the headquarters–subsidiary link.

The main handicap such companies faced was that parent-company management often adopted a parochial and even superior attitude toward international operations, perhaps because of the assumption that new ideas and developments all came from the parent.

Figure 4-2 Organizational Configuration Models

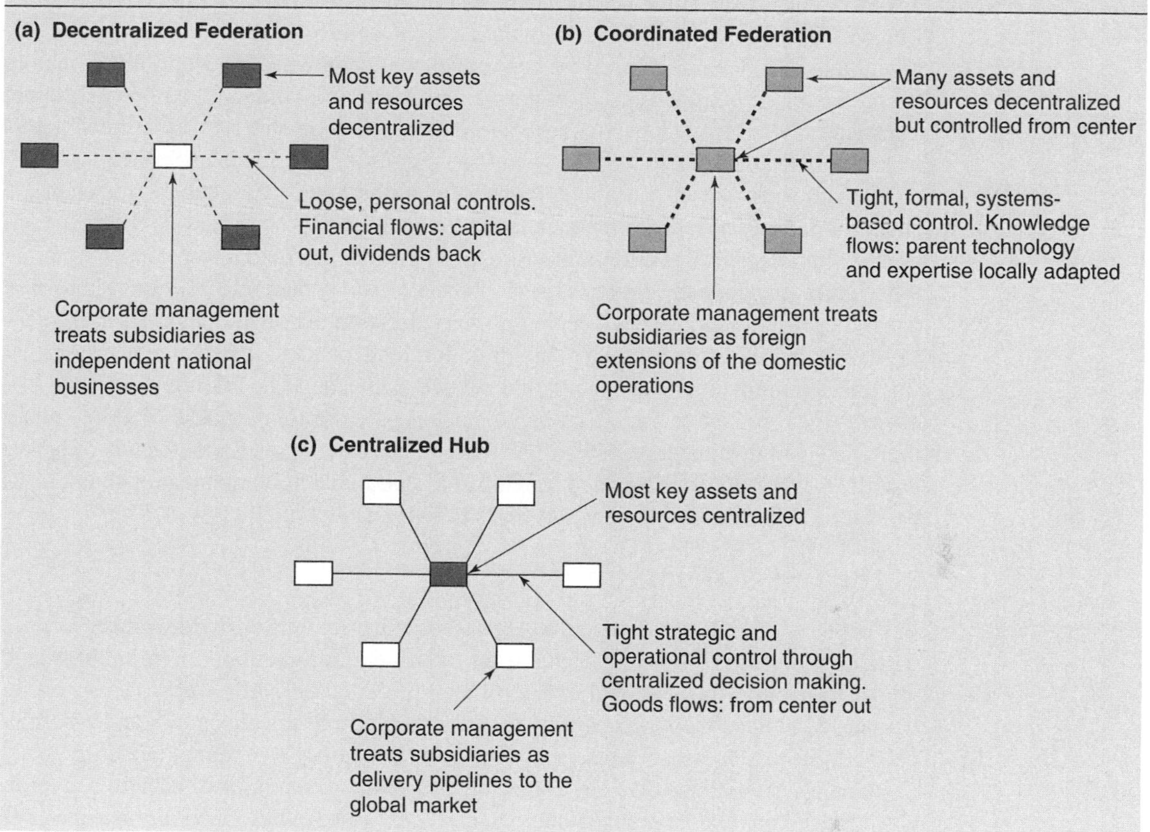

(a) Decentralized Federation

Most key assets and resources decentralized

Loose, personal controls. Financial flows: capital out, dividends back

Corporate management treats subsidiaries as independent national businesses

(b) Coordinated Federation

Many assets and resources decentralized but controlled from center

Tight, formal, systems-based control. Knowledge flows: parent technology and expertise locally adapted

Corporate management treats subsidiaries as foreign extensions of the domestic operations

(c) Centralized Hub

Most key assets and resources centralized

Tight strategic and operational control through centralized decision making. Goods flows: from center out

Corporate management treats subsidiaries as delivery pipelines to the global market

Despite corporate management's increased understanding of its overseas markets, it often seemed to view foreign operations as appendages whose principal purpose was to leverage the capabilities and resources developed in the home market.

Nonetheless, the approach was highly successful in the postwar decades, and many U.S.-based companies adopted what we have described as the *international strategy* and a *coordinated federation* organizational model shown in Figure 4-2(b).

Centralized Hub

In contrast, the typical Japanese company, making its main international thrust in the 1970s and 1980s, faced a greatly altered external environment and operated with very different internal norms and values. With limited prior overseas exposure, it chose not to match the well-established local marketing capabilities and facilities of its European and U.S. competitors. (Indeed, well-established Japanese trading companies often provided it an easier means of entering foreign markets by exporting.) However, the rapid postwar growth of the Japanese economy gave it new, efficient, scale-intensive plants, and it was expanding into a global environment of declining trade barriers.

Together, these factors gave it the incentive to develop a competitive advantage at the upstream end of the value-added chain. Its competitive strategy emphasized cost advantages and quality assurance, demanding tight control over product development, procurement, and manufacturing. When forced, these companies moved some assembly operations offshore, but kept all major value-adding and strategic activities at home. This centrally controlled, export-based internationalization strategy represented a perfect fit with the external environment and companies' competitive capabilities.

Such an approach also fit the cultural background and organizational values in the emerging Japanese MNE. At the foundation of the internal processes were the strong national cultural norms that emphasized group behavior and valued interpersonal harmony reflected in management practices such as *nemawashi* (consensus building) and *ringi* (shared decision making). By keeping primary decision making and control at the center, the Japanese company could retain its culturally dependent management system that was so communications intensive and people dependent. In addition, international growth that kept key operations at home made it possible for Japanese MNEs to retain their system of lifetime employment. As a result, these companies adopted what we have described as a global strategy and developed a centralized hub organizational model, as we show in Figure 4-2(c), to support this strategic orientation.

The Transnational Challenge

In Chapters 2 and 3, we advanced the hypothesis that many worldwide industries were transformed in the 1980s and 1990s from traditional multinational, international, and global forms into transnational forms. Instead of demanding efficiency or responsiveness or learning as the key capability for success, these businesses now require participating firms to achieve all three capabilities simultaneously to remain competitive.

Table 4-1 summarizes the key characteristics of the decentralized federation, coordinated federation, and centralized hub organizations we have described in this chapter as

Table 4-1   Organizational Characteristics of Decentralized Federation, Coordinated Federation, and Centralized Hub Organizations

	Decentralized Federation	**Coordinated Federation**	**Centralized Hub**
Strategic approach	Multinational	International	Global
Key strategic capability	National responsiveness	Worldwide transfer of home country innovations	Global-scale efficiency
Configuration of assets and capabilities	Decentralized and nationally self-sufficient	Sources of core competencies centralized, others decentralized	Centralized and globally scaled
Role of overseas operations	Sensing and exploiting local opportunities	Adapting and leveraging parent-company competencies	Implementing parent company strategies
Development and diffusion of knowledge	Knowledge developed and retained within each unit	Knowledge developed at the center and transferred to overseas units	Knowledge developed and retained at the center

the supporting forms for companies pursuing multinational, international, and global strategies. A review of these characteristics immediately reveals the problems each of the three archetypal company models might face in responding to the transnational challenge.

With its resources and capabilities consolidated at the center, the global company achieves efficiency primarily by exploiting potential scale economies in all its activities. But its national subsidiaries' lack of resources and responsibilities may undermine their motivation and ability to respond to local market needs, whereas the central groups often lack adequate understanding of market needs and production realities outside their home market. These are problems that a global organization cannot overcome without jeopardizing its trump card of global efficiency.

The classic multinational company suffers from other limitations. Although its dispersed resources and decentralized decision making allow its national subsidiaries to respond to local needs, the fragmentation of activities leads to inefficiency. Learning also suffers, because knowledge is not consolidated and does not flow among the various parts of the company. As a result, local innovations often represent little more than the efforts of subsidiary management to protect its turf and autonomy or reinventions of the wheel caused by blocked communication or the not-invented-here (NIH) syndrome.

In contrast, the international company is better able to leverage the knowledge and capabilities of the parent company (but is still not very good at learning from its foreign operations). However, its resource configuration and operating systems make it less efficient than the global company and less responsive than the multinational company.

The Transnational Organization

There are three important organizational characteristics that distinguish the transnational organization from its multinational, international, or global counterparts: It develops and legitimizes multiple diverse internal perspectives, its physical assets and management capabilities are distributed internationally but are interdependent, and it has a robust and flexible internal integrative process. In this section, we describe and illustrate each of these characteristics.

Multidimensional Perspectives

Managing in an environment in which strategic forces are both diverse and changeable, the transnational company must create the ability to sense and analyze the numerous and often conflicting opportunities, pressures, and demands it faces worldwide. Strong *national subsidiary management* is needed to sense and represent the changing needs of local consumers and the increasing pressures from host governments; capable *global business management* is required to track the strategy of global competitors and provide the coordination necessary to respond appropriately; and influential *worldwide functional management* is needed to concentrate corporate knowledge, information, and expertise and facilitate their transfer among organizational units.

Unfortunately, in many companies, power is concentrated with the management group that has historically represented the company's most critical strategic tasks—often with the cost that other groups representing other needs are allowed to atrophy. For example, in *multinational* companies, key decisions were usually dominated by the country management group because it made the most critical contribution to achieving national responsiveness. In *global* companies, managers in worldwide product divisions were typically the most influential, because strong business management played the key role in the company's efforts to seek global efficiency. And in *international* companies, functional management groups often came to assume this position of dominance because of their roles in building, accumulating, and transferring the company's skills, knowledge, and capabilities.

In *transnational* companies, however, biases in the decision-making process are consciously reduced by building up the capability, credibility, and influence of the less powerful management groups while protecting the morale and expertise of the dominant group. The objective is to build a multidimensional organization in which all three management groups have a seat at the table. Some of the cases in this book focus explicitly on this issue of developing and maintaining such a balanced and multidimensional organization.

Distributed, Interdependent Capabilities

Having developed multidimensional management perspectives, the transnational organization must be able to make choices among the diverse opportunities and demands it faces and respond in a timely and effective manner to those that are deemed strategically important. When a company's decision-making process and organizational capabilities are concentrated at the center—as they are in the global organization's centralized hub configuration—it is often difficult to respond appropriately to diverse worldwide demands. Being distant from frontline opportunities and threats, the central group's ability to act in an effective and timely manner is constrained by its reliance on complex and intensive international communications. In contrast, multinational organizations, with their response capabilities spread throughout the decentralized federation of independent operations, suffer from duplication of effort, inefficiency of operations, and barriers to international learning.

In transnational organizations, management breaks away from the restricted view that assumes it must centralize the activities for which a global scale or expertise is important. Instead, management ensures that viable national units achieve global scale by specializing their activities and giving them the responsibility of becoming the company's world source for a given product or expertise. And by securing the cooperation and involvement of the individuals in the relevant national units, they tap into important technological advances and market developments wherever they are occurring around the globe.

One major consequence of such a distribution of specialized assets and responsibilities is that the interdependence of worldwide units automatically increases. Simple structural configurations like the decentralized federation, the coordinated federation, and the centralized hub are inadequate for the task facing the transnational corporation; what is needed is a structure we term the "integrated network" (see Figure 4-3).

In the integrated network configuration, management regards each of the worldwide units as a source of ideas, skills, capabilities, and knowledge that can be harnessed for the benefit of the total organization. Efficient local plants may be converted into regional or global production centers; innovative national or regional development labs may be designated the company's "centers of excellence" for a particular product or process

Figure 4-3 Integrated Network Model

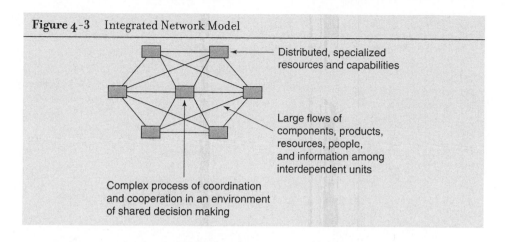

Distributed, specialized resources and capabilities

Large flows of components, products, resources, people, and information among interdependent units

Complex process of coordination and cooperation in an environment of shared decision making

development; and creative subsidiary marketing groups may be given a lead role in developing worldwide marketing strategies for certain products or businesses.

Flexible Integrative Process

Finally, the transnational organization requires a management process that can resolve the diversity of interests and integrate the dispersed assets and resources. In doing so, it cannot be bound by a symmetrical organizational process that defines the task in such simplistic terms as, "Should responsibilities be centralized or decentralized?" It is clear that the benefits to be gained from central control of worldwide research or manufacturing activities may be much more important than those related to the global coordination of the sales and service functions. We have also seen how the pattern of functional coordination varies by business and by geographic area (e.g., aircraft engine companies need central control of more decisions than multinational food packagers; operations in developing countries may need more support from the center than those in advanced countries). Furthermore, all coordination needs to be able to change over time.

Thus, management must be able to differentiate its operating relationships and change its decision-making roles by function, across businesses, among geographic units, and over time. In turn, the management process must be able to change from product to product, from country to country, and even from decision to decision. Elaborating on the integration–responsiveness framework we developed in Chapter 3, we illustrate such a distribution of roles and responsibilities in Figure 4-4.

This distribution requires the development of rather sophisticated and subtle decision-making machinery based on three different but interdependent management processes. The first is a focused and constrained escalation process that allows top management to intervene directly in key decision content (e.g., major resource allocation commitments)—a subtle and carefully managed form of *centralization*. The second is a process in which management structures individual roles and administrative systems to influence specific decisions (typically, repetitive or routine activities like setting transfer prices) through

Figure 4-4   Integration and Differentiation Needs at Unilever

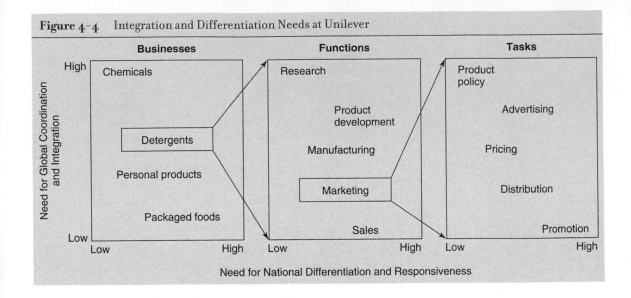

formalization. The third is a self-regulatory capability in which top management's role is to establish a broad culture and set of relationships that provide a supportive organizational context for delegated decisions—a sophisticated management process driven by *socialization.*

Anatomy, Physiology, and Psychology of the Transnational

The kind of organization we have described as a transnational clearly represents something quite different from its predecessors—the multinational, international, and global organizations. Building such an organization requires much more than choosing between a product or a geographic organization structure; managing it implies much more than centralizing or decentralizing decisions. By viewing the organizational challenge as one of creating and managing a decision process that responds to the company's critical task demands, the MNE manager is forced to adopt a very different approach from someone who defines the problem as one of discovering and installing the ideal structure.

If the classic structural stages model no longer provides a helpful description of international organization development, we need a different way to conceptualize the more complex array of tools and processes discussed in our previous descriptions of transnational organizations. The simple but useful framework adopted here describes the organization in terms of a human physiological model. To be effective, change in an organization's anatomy (the formal structure of its assets, resources, and responsibilities) must be complemented by adaptations to its physiology (the organization's systems and decision processes) and its psychology (the organization's culture and management mentality).

We will now describe the different tools and processes used to build and manage the transnational using this physiological model.

Structuring the Organizational Anatomy

As we have noted, the traditional approach to MNE organization problems tended to be defined in macrostructural terms that focused on simple but rather superficial choices, such as the classic "product versus area" structural debate. Developing a transnational organization, however, requires management to pay equal attention to designing and developing a supporting structure that both supplements and counterbalances the embedded power of the dominant line managers.

Having carefully defined the structure and responsibilities of all management groups—geographic, functional, and product—the next challenge is to ensure that particularly those without line authority have appropriate access to and influence in the management process. Microstructural tools such as cross-unit teams, task forces, or committees can create supplemental decision-making forums that allow nonline managers to assume responsibility and obtain authority in a way that is not possible in the formal line organization.

Where task forces and special assignment committees were once considered ad hoc, quick-fix devices, companies building transnational organizations use them as legitimate, ongoing structural tools through which top management can fine-tune or rebalance the basic structure. To stretch our anatomical analogy, if the formal line structure is the organization's backbone, the nonline structure is its rib cage, and these microstructural tools are the muscle and cartilage that give the organizational skeleton its flexibility.

Building the Organizational Physiology

One of the key roles of management is to develop the communication channels through which the organization's decision-making process operates. By adapting the various administrative systems, communication channels, and informal relationships, management can shape—and even control—the volume, content, and direction of information flows. It is this flow of information—the lifeblood of all management processes—that defines the organizational physiology.

Many researchers have shown the strong link between the complexity and uncertainty of the tasks to be performed and the need for information. In the integrated network configuration, task complexity and uncertainty are very high. Operating an interdependent system in such a setting requires large volumes of complex information to be gathered, exchanged, and processed. In the complex integrated network that frames a transnational organization, formal systems alone cannot support the huge information processing needs, and companies are forced to look beyond their traditional tools and conventional systems.

For years, managers have recognized that a great deal of information exchange and even decision making—perhaps the majority—occurs through the organization's innumerable informal channels and relationships. Yet this part of the management process has often been dismissed as either unimportant ("office gossip" or "rumor mill") or unmanageable ("disruptive cliques" or "unholy alliances"). In the management of transnational organizations, such biases need to be reexamined. Because organizational units are widely separated and information is scarce, not only is it more important for managers of international operations to exert some control and influence over informal systems, it is also more feasible for them to do so.

Getting started is often remarkably easy, requiring managers to do little more than use their daily involvement in the ongoing management processes to shape the nature and quality of communications patterns and relationships. The easiest place to start is to recognize, legitimize, and reinforce existing informal relationships that contribute to the corporate objective; and changes can be made by adjusting the frequency and agenda of management trips and corporate meetings (a good way to focus and diffuse information), the pattern of committee assignments (an effective way of building relationships and shaping decisions), and the track of people's career development (a powerful way to reinforce and reward flexibility and collaboration).

Developing the Organizational Psychology

In addition to an anatomy and a physiology, each organization also has a psychology— a set of explicit or implicit corporate values and shared beliefs—that greatly influences the way it operates. Particularly when employees come from a variety of different national backgrounds, management cannot assume that all will share common values and relate to common norms. Furthermore, in an operating environment in which managers are separated by distance and time barriers, shared management understanding is often a much more powerful tool than formal structures and systems for coordinating diverse activities.

Of the numerous tools and techniques that can affect an organization's psychology, our review of transnational organizations has highlighted three that are particularly important. First is the need for a clear, shared understanding of the company's mission and objectives. Matsushita's 250-year vision of its role of promoting general welfare in a world society, Nokia's commitment to "Connecting People," and Bill Gates's aspiration to create a world with "a computer on every desk and in every home running on Microsoft software" represent variants of this approach applied at different strategic and operational levels.

The second important tool is the visible behavior and public actions of senior management. Particularly in a transnational organization in which other signals may be diluted or distorted, top management's actions speak louder than words and tend to have a powerful influence on the company's culture. They represent the clearest role model of behavior and a signal of the company's strategic and organizational priorities. When Sony Corporation founder and CEO Akio Morita relocated to New York for several years to build the company's U.S. operations personally, he sent a message about Sony's commitment to its overseas businesses that could not have been conveyed as strongly by any other means.

The third and most commonly used set of tools for modifying organizational psychology in the transnational organization is nested in the company's personnel policies, practices, and systems. A company can develop a multidimensional and flexible organization process only if its personnel systems develop and reinforce the appropriate kinds of people. At Eli Lilly, we saw a good example of such an approach. Its recruiting and promotion policies emphasized the importance of good interpersonal skills and flexible, nonparochial personalities; its career path management was used not only to develop skills and knowledge but also to broaden individual perspectives and interpersonal relationships; and its measurement and reward systems were designed to reinforce the thrust of other organization-building efforts.

Although the process of adapting an organization's culture, values, or beliefs is slow and the techniques are subtle, this tool plays a particularly important role in the development of a transnational organization, because change in the organizational anatomy and physiology without complementary modifications to its psychology can lead to severe organizational problems.

Managing the Process of Change

Particularly in the United States, many managers have assumed that organizational change is driven and dominated by changes in the formal structure. One of the most dramatic examples was Westinghouse's reorganization of its operations. Dissatisfied with its worldwide product organization, top management assigned a team of executives to study the company's international organization problems for 90 days. Its proposal that Westinghouse adopt a global matrix was accepted, and the team was then given 3 months to "install the new structure."

The example is far from unusual—literally hundreds of other companies have done something similar. The managers involved seemed to assume that changes in formal roles and reporting relationships would force changes in the organizational relationships and decision processes, which in turn would reshape the way individual managers think and act. This model of the process of organizational change is illustrated in Figure 4-5.

But such an approach loses sight of the real organization behind the boxes and lines on the chart. The boxes that are casually shifted around represent people with abilities, motivations, and interests, not just formal positions with specified roles. The lines that are redrawn are not just formal reporting channels but interpersonal relationships that may have taken years to develop. As a result, forcing changes in the organizational process and management mentality by altering the formal structure can have a high cost. The new relationships defined in the reorganized structure will often take months to establish at the most basic level and a year or more to become truly effective. Developing new individual attitudes and behaviors will take even longer, because many employees will be frustrated, alienated, or simply unequal to the new job requirements.

Figure 4-5   Model I: The Traditional Change Process

Change in formal structure and responsibilities
(Anatomy)
↓
Change in interpersonal relationships and processes
(Physiology)
↓
Change in individual attitudes and mentalities
(Psychology)

Most European and Japanese companies tend to adopt a very different approach that relies more on personnel assignments as an important mechanism of organizational change. Building on the informal relationships that dominated their earlier management processes, European companies often use assignments and transfers to forge interpersonal links, build organizational cohesion, and develop policy consistency. And Japanese companies typically place enormous emphasis on socializing the individual into the organization and shaping his or her attitudes to conform with overall corporate values. Organizational change in these companies is often driven more by intensive education programs than by reconfigurations of the structure or systems.

Although the specific change process and sequence must vary from one company to the next, the overall process adopted in these companies to manage change is very different from the process driven by structural realignment. Indeed, the sequence is often the reverse. The first objective for many European and Japanese companies seeking major change is to influence the understanding and perceptions of key individuals. Then follows a series of changes aimed to modify the communication flows and decision-making processes. Only in a final stage are the changes consolidated and confirmed by structural realignment. This process is represented by the model in Figure 4-6. Of course, these two models of organizational change in worldwide companies are both oversimplifications of the process and overgeneralizations of national difference.

All change processes inevitably involve substantial overlap and interaction in the alterations to organizational autonomy, physiology, and psychology; the two sequences merely reflect differences in the relative emphasis on each set of tools during the process. Furthermore, though the two models reflect historical national biases, those differences seem to be eroding. American, European, and Japanese companies appear to be learning from one another.

Although the more gradual change process is much less organizationally traumatic, in times of crisis—chronic poor performance, a badly misaligned structure, or a major structural change in the environment, for example—radical restructuring may be necessary to achieve rapid and sweeping change. For most organizations, however, dramatic structural change is highly traumatic and can distract managers from their external tasks as they focus on the internal realignment. Fortunately, most change processes can be managed in a more evolutionary manner, focusing first on the modification of individual perspectives and interpersonal relationships before tackling the formal redistribution of responsibilities and power.

Figure 4-6   Model II: The Emerging Change Process

Change in individual attitudes and mentalities
↓
Change in interpersonal relationships and processes
↓
Change in formal structure and responsibilities

The Transnational Organization in Transition

During the past decade or so, political, competitive, and social pressures have reinforced the need for MNEs to create organizations that can sense and respond to complex yet often conflicting demands. Yet, as more and more companies confront the need to build worldwide organizations that are both multidimensional and flexible, the form of the transnational organization they are creating continues to adapt. Among the most widespread transnational organizational trends we have observed in recent years are a disenchantment with formal matrix structures, the redefinition of primary organizational dimensions, and the changing role of functional management in transnationals.

Disenchantment with Formal Matrix Structures

As an increasing number of managers recognized the need to develop the multidimensional organizational capabilities that characterize a transnational organization, the initial reaction of many was to impose the new model through a global matrix structure.

Widespread press coverage of ABB's decade-long global expansion through such an organization encouraged some to believe that this structure was the key to exploiting global scale efficiencies while responding to local market needs. But as many soon discovered, the strategic benefits provided by such a complex organization came at an organizational cost.

Although some companies were able to create the culture and process vital to the success of the matrix structure—in ABB's case, they supported the company's ambitious global expansion for more than a decade—others were much less successful. One such failure was Proctor and Gamble's (P&G) much publicized Organization 2005, which boldly imposed a global product structure over the company's historically successful geographic organization. The global matrix so installed created problems that eventually cost CEO Durk Jager his job.

But despite continuing nervousness about the global matrix structure, most MNEs still recognize the need to create multidimensional and flexible organizations. The big lesson of the 1990s was that such organizations are best built by developing overlaid processes and supportive cultures, not just by formalizing multiple reporting relationships. A.G. Lafley, P&G's new CEO, put it well when he said, "We built this new house, then moved in before the plumbing and wiring were connected. You cannot change organization with structure alone."

Redefinition of Key Organization Dimensions

Historically, the dominant organization dimensions around which most MNEs built their worldwide operations were business or product management on one side and country or regional management on the other. But in the past decade or so, the primary organizational characteristics that defined the transnational corporation began to change, with the global customer dimension becoming increasingly important in many worldwide organizations.

The pressure to create such customer-driven organizations grew gradually during the 1990s. First, as global customers began demanding uniform prices and service levels from their suppliers, MNEs were forced to respond by creating dedicated global account managers who would take responsibility for all sales to customers around the world.

Second, as customers expected increasing levels of value-added services, companies began to shift from "selling products" to "providing solutions." These and similar forces led to the creation of transnational organizations in which front-end, customer-facing units bundled products from back-end, product-driven units. A good example of this was IBM's Global Services Organization, one of the most successful customer-facing organizations, which grew rapidly because of its ability to supply customers with a combination of IBM's products, consulting services, and often an additional package of related, outsourced products and services.

Changing the Functional Management Role

In transnational organizations built around business, geography, and, more recently, the customer, the functional managers responsible for finance, human resources, logistics, and other cross-business and cross-organizational specialties were often relegated to secondary staff roles. However, with the expansion of the information-based, knowledge-intensive service economy, the resources and expertise that resided in these specialized functions became increasingly important sources of competitive advantage. As a result, recent years have seen their roles become increasingly important in many transnational organizations.

Managers of finance, HR, and IT functions gained importance because of their control of the scarce strategic resources that were so critical to capture and leverage on a worldwide basis. With the globalization of financial markets in the global financial crisis of 2008–09, the finance function was often able to play a critically important role in lowering the cost of capital and managing cross-border risk exposure. Just as dramatic has been the role of the HR experts as MNEs tapped into scarce knowledge and expertise outside the home country and leveraged it for global competitive advantage. Similarly, the recent rise of chief knowledge officers reflects the importance that many companies are placing on the organization's ability to capture and leverage valuable information, best practices, or scarce knowledge wherever it exists in the company.

Again, this trend is creating a need for transnational companies to create organizational overlays supplemented by new channels of communication and forums of decision making that enable the MNE to develop and leverage its competitive advantage through its sophisticated organizational capabilities. The form and function of the transnational organization continues to adapt as MNE managers seek new ways to develop and deliver layers of competitive advantage.

Concluding Comments

In this chapter, we have looked at the organizational capabilities that the MNE must build to operate effectively in today's fast changing global business environment. The strategic challenge, as we have described it, requires the MNE to optimize global efficiency, national responsiveness, and worldwide learning simultaneously. To deliver on this complex and conflicting set of demands, a new form of organization is required, which we call the transnational. The transnational is characterized by its legitimization of multidimensional perspectives, its distributed and interdependent capabilities, and its flexible integrative processes. It is a model that is increasingly becoming mainstream.

> ## Chapter 4 Readings
>
> - In Reading 4-1, "Managing Multicultural Teams," by Brett, Behfar, and Kern considers how to overcome the unique challenges that arise when members come from different nations and backgrounds. Four strategies are identified: adaptation, structural intervention, managerial intervention, and exit.
> - In Reading 4-2, "Managing Executive Attention in the Global Company," Birkinshaw, Bouquet, and Ambos consider how "executives can prioritize their time to ensure that they are focusing on the countries and subsidiaries that need the most attention." The two key strategies a subsidiary can use to attract parent company attention are to use its "weight" as a player in an important market, and to exert its "voice," by working through company channels.
> - In Reading 4-3, "Matrix Management: Not a Structure, a Frame of Mind," Bartlett and Ghoshal emphasize the need to focus less on the search for an ideal organization structure, and more on developing the abilities, behavior, and performance of individual managers.
>
> Each of these readings underscore the need to build an organization that balances global integration, national responsiveness, and worldwide learning.

Case 4-1   Philips versus Matsushita: Competing Strategic and Organizational Choices

Christopher A. Bartlett

Throughout their long histories, N.V. Philips (Netherlands) and Matsushita Electric (Japan) had followed very different strategies and emerged with very different organizational capabilities. Philips built its success on a worldwide portfolio of responsive national organizations while Matsushita based its global competitiveness on its centralized, highly efficient operations in Japan.

During the first decade of the 21st century, however, both companies experienced major challenges to their historic competitive positions and organizational models. Implementing yet another round of strategic initiatives and organizational restructurings, the CEOs at both companies were taking their respective organizations in very different directions. At the end of the decade, observers wondered how the changes would affect their long-running competitive battle.

▌ Professor Christopher A. Bartlett prepared the original version of this case, "Philips versus Matsushita: A New Century, A New Round," HBS No. 302-049. This version was prepared by the same author and is a continuation of a series of earlier cases by Professor Bartlett including "Philips versus Matsushita: Preparing for a New Round," HBS No. 399-102, "Philips and Matsushita: A Portrait of Two Evolving Companies," HBS No. 392-156, and "Matsushita Electric Industrial (MEI) in 1987," HBS No. 388-144. HBS cases are developed solely as the basis for class discussion. Cases are not intended to serve as endorsements, sources of primary data, or illustrations of effective or ineffective management.
▌ Harvard Business School Case No 9-910-410, Copyright 2009 President and Fellows of Harvard College. All rights reserved.
This case was prepared by C. Bartlett. HBS Cases are developed solely for class discussion and do not necessarily illustrate either effective or ineffective handling of administrative situation.

Philips: Background

In 1892, Gerard Philips and his father opened a small light-bulb factory in Eindhoven, Holland. When their venture almost failed, they recruited Gerard's brother, Anton, an excellent salesman and manager. By 1900, Philips was the third largest light-bulb producer in Europe.

Technological Competence and Geographic Expansion   While larger electrical products companies were racing to diversify, Philips made only light-bulbs. This one-product focus and Gerard's technological prowess enabled the company to create significant innovations. Company policy was to scrap old plants and use new machines or factories whenever advances were made in new production technology. Anton wrote down assets rapidly and set aside substantial reserves for replacing outdated equipment. Philips also became a leader in industrial research, creating physics and chemistry labs to address production problems as well as more abstract scientific ones. The labs developed a tungsten metal filament bulb that was a great commercial success and gave Philips the financial strength to compete against its giant rivals.

Holland's small size soon forced Philips to look aboard for enough volume to mass produce. In 1899, Anton hired the company's first export manager, and soon the company was selling into such diverse markets as Japan, Australia, Canada, Brazil, and Russia. In 1912, as the electric lamp industry began to show signs of overcapacity, Philips started building sales organizations in the United States, Canada, and France. All other functions remained highly centralized in Eindhoven. In many foreign countries Philips created local joint ventures to gain market acceptance.

In 1919, Philips entered into the Principal Agreement with General Electric, giving each company the use of the other's patents, while simultaneously dividing the world into "three spheres of influence." After this time, Philips began evolving from a highly centralized company, whose sales were conducted through third parties, to a decentralized sales organization with autonomous marketing companies in 14 European countries, China, Brazil, and Australia.

During this period, the company also broadened its product line significantly. In 1918, it began producing electronic vacuum tubes; eight years later its first radios appeared, capturing a 20% world market share within a decade; and during the 1930s, Philips began producing X-ray tubes. The Great Depression brought with it trade barriers and high tariffs, and Philips was forced to build local production facilities to protect its foreign sales of these products.

Philips: Organizational Development

One of the earliest traditions at Philips was a shared but competitive leadership by the commercial and technical functions. Gerard, an engineer, and Anton, a businessman, began a subtle competition where Gerard would try to produce more than Anton could sell and vice versa. Nevertheless, the two agreed that strong research was vital to Philips' survival.

During the late 1930s, in anticipation of the impending war, Philips transferred its overseas assets to two trusts, British Philips and the North American Philips Corporation; it also moved most of its vital research laboratories to Redhill in Surrey, England, and its top management to the United States. Supported by the assets and resources transferred abroad, and isolated from their parent, the individual country organizations became more independent during the war.

Because waves of Allied and German bombing had pummeled most of Philips' industrial plant in the Netherlands, the management board decided to build the postwar organization on the strengths of the national organizations (NOs). Their greatly increased self-sufficiency during the war had allowed most to become adept at responding to country-specific market conditions—a capability that became a valuable asset in the postwar era. For example, when international wrangling precluded any agreement on three competing television transmission standards (PAL, SECAM, and NTSC), each nation decided which to adopt. Furthermore, consumer preferences and economic conditions varied: in some countries, rich, furniture-encased TV sets were the norm; in others, sleek, contemporary models dominated the market. In the United Kingdom, the only way to penetrate the market was to establish a rental business; in richer countries, a major marketing challenge was overcoming elitist prejudice against television. In this environment, the independent NOs had a great advantage in being able to sense and respond to the differences.

Eventually, responsiveness extended beyond adaptive marketing. As NOs built their own technical capabilities, product development often became a function of local market conditions. For example, Philips of Canada created the company's first color TV; Philips of Australia created the first stereo TV; and Philips of the United Kingdom created the first TVs with teletext.

While NOs took major responsibility for financial, legal, and administrative matters, fourteen product divisions (PDs), located in Eindhoven, were formally responsible for development, production, and global distribution. (In reality, the NOs' control of assets and the PDs' distance from the operations often undercut this formal role.) The research function remained independent and, with continued strong funding, set up eight separate laboratories in Europe and the United States.

While the formal corporate-level structure was represented as a type of geographic/product matrix, it was clear that NOs had the real power. They reported directly to the management board, which Philips enlarged from four members to 10 to ensure that top management remained in contact with the highly autonomous NOs. Each NO also regularly sent envoys to Eindhoven to represent its interests. Top management, most of whom had careers that included multiple foreign tours of duty, made frequent overseas visits to the NOs. In 1954, the board established the International Concern Council to formalize regular meetings with the heads of all major NOs.

Within the NOs, management structure mimicked the legendary joint technical and commercial leadership of the two Philips brothers. Most were

led by a technical manager and a commercial manager. In some locations, a finance manager filled out the top management triad that typically reached key decisions collectively. This cross-functional coordination capability was reflected down through the NOs in front-line product teams, product-group-level management teams, and at the senior management committee of the NOs' top commercial, technical, and financial managers.

The overwhelming importance of foreign operations to Philips, the commensurate status of the NOs within the corporate hierarchy, and even the cosmopolitan appeal of many of the offshore subsidiaries' locations encouraged many Philips managers to take extended foreign tours of duty, working in a series of two- or three-year posts. This elite group of expatriate managers identified strongly with each other and with the NOs as a group and had no difficulty representing their strong, country-oriented views to corporate management.

Philips: Attempts at Reorganization

In the late 1960s, the creation of the European Common Market eroded trade barriers and diluted the rationale for independent country subsidiaries. New transistor-based technologies demanded larger production runs than most national plants could justify, and many of Philips' competitors were moving production of electronics to new facilities in low-wage areas in Asia and South America.

Simultaneously, Philips' ability to bring its innovative products to market began to falter, and in the 1960s it watched Japanese competitors capture the mass market for audiocassettes and microwave ovens, two technologies it had invented. A decade later, it had to abandon its V2000 videocassette format—superior technically to Sony's Beta or Matsushita's VHS—when North American Philips decided to outsource a VHS product which it manufactured under license from Matsushita.

Over the next four decades, seven chairmen experimented with reorganizing the company to deal with its growing problems. Yet, in 2009, Philips' financial performance remained poor and its global competitiveness was still in question. (See **Exhibits 1** and **2**.)

Van Reimsdijk and the Yellow Booklet   Concerned about what one magazine described as "continued profitless progress," newly appointed CEO Hendrick van Riemsdijk created an organization

committee to prepare a policy paper on the division of responsibilities between the PDs and the NOs. In 1971, their report, dubbed the "Yellow Booklet," outlined the disadvantages of Philips' matrix organization in 1971: "Without an agreement [defining the relationship between national organizations and product divisions], it is impossible to determine in

Exhibit 1   Philips Group Summary Financial Data, 1970–2008 (Reported in millions of Dutch Guilders (F) to 1996; Euros (€) after 1997

	2008	2000	1990	1980	1970
Net sales	€26,385	€37,862	F55,764	F36,536	F15,070
Income from operations (excluding restructuring)	NA	NA	2,260	1,577	1,280
Income from operations (including restructuring)	551	3,022	−2,389	N/A	N/A
As a percentage of net sales	2.1%	8.0%	−4.3%	4.3%	8.5%
Income after taxes	NA	NA	F−4,447	F532	F446
Net income from normal business operations	(178)	9,577	−4,526	328	435
Stockholders' equity (common)	16,267	15,847	11,165	12,996	6,324
Return on stockholders' equity	−1.0%	60.4%	−30.2%	2.7%	7.3%
Distribution per common share, per value F10 (in guilders)	€0.7	€0.36	F0.0	F1.80	F1.70
Total assets	33,048	38,541	51,595	39,647	19,088
Inventories as a percentage of net sales	12.8%	13.9%	20.7%	32.8%	35.2%
Outstanding trade receivables in month's sales	1.9	1.6	1.6	3.0	2.8
Current ratio	1.2	1.2	1.4	1.7	1.7
Employees at year-end (in thousands)	121	219	273	373	359
Selected data in millions of dollars:					
Sales	$36,868	$35,564	$33,018	$16,993	$4,163
Operating profit	770	2,838	1,247	734	NA
Pretax income	155	9,587	−2,380	364	NA
Net income	(260)	9,078	−2,510	153	120
Total assets	46,169	35,885	30,549	18,440	5,273
Shareholders' equity (common)	22,697	20,238	6,611	6,044	1,747

Note: Exchange rate
Guilder/DoUar   1970   3.62
                 1980   2.15
                 1990   1.68
Euro/Dollar   2000   0.94
                 2008   1.40

Source: Annual reports; Standard & Poors' Compustat®; Moody's Industrial and International Manuals.

Exhibit 2 Philips Group, Sales by Product and Geographic Segment, 1985–2003 (Reported in millions of Dutch Guilders (F) to 1996; Euros (€) after 1997)

	2003		2000		1995		1990		1985	
Net Sales by Product Segment:										
Lighting	€4,634	16%	€5,051	13%	F 8,353	13%	F 7,026	13%	F 7,976	12%
Consumer electronics	9,415	33	14,681	39	22,027	34	25,400	46	16,906	26
Domestic appliances	2,183	7	2,107	6	—	—	—	—	6,664	10
Professional products/Systems	—	—	—	—	11,562	18	13,059	23	17,850	28
Components/Semiconductors	3,984	14%	10,440	28	10,714	17	8,161	15	11,620	18
Software/Services	—	—	—	—	9,425	15	—	—	—	—
Medical systems/Health care	6,138	21	3,030	8	—	—	—	—	—	—
Origin	—	—	716	2	—	—	—	—	—	—
Miscellaneous	4,455	15	1,831	5	2,381	4	2,118	4	3,272	5
Total	28,627	100%	37,862	100%	64,462	100%	F55,764	100%	F 64,266	100%
Operating Income by Sector:										
Lighting	591		668	16%	983	24%	419	18%	F 910	30%
Consumer electronics	254		374	9	167	4	1,499	66	34	1
Domestic appliances	407		287	7	—	—	—	—	397	13
Professional products/Systems	—		—	—	157	4	189	8	1,484	48
Components/Semiconductors	–336		1,915	45	2,233	55	–43	–2	44	1
Software/Services	—		—	—	886	22	—	—	—	—
Medical systems	441		169	4	—	—	—	—	—	—
Origin	–845		1,063	25	—	—	—	—	—	—
Miscellaneous	—		–113	–3	423	10	218	10	200	7
Increase not attributable to a sector	—		–82	–2	(805)	(20)	–22	–1	6	0
Total	513		4,280	100%	4,044	100%	2,260	100%	F 3,074	100%

Notes: Totals may not add due to rounding.
Product sector sales after 1988 are external sales only; therefore, no eliminations are made; sector sales before 1988 include sales to other sectors; therefore, eliminations are made.
Data are not comparable to consolidated financial summary due to restating.
Source: Annual reports.

any given situation which of the two parties is responsible. . . . As operations become increasingly complex, an organizational form of this type will only lower the speed of reaction of an enterprise."

On the basis of this report, van Reimsdijk proposed rebalancing the managerial relationships between PDs and NOs—"tilting the matrix towards the PDs" in his words—to allow Philips to decrease the number of products marketed, build scale by concentrating production, and increase the product flows across NOs. He proposed closing the least efficient local plants and converting the best into International Production Centers (IPCs), each supplying many NOs. In so doing, van Reimsdijk hoped that PD managers would gain control over manufacturing operations. Due to the political and organizational difficulty of closing local plants, however, implementation was slow.

Rodenberg and Dekker: "Tilting the Matrix"

In the late 1970s, van Riemsdijk's successor, Dr. Rodenburg, continued his thrust. Several IPCs were established, but the NOs seemed as powerful and independent as ever. He furthered matrix simplification by replacing the dual commercial and technical leadership with single management at both the corporate and national organizational levels. Yet the power struggles continued.

Upon becoming CEO in 1982, Wisse Dekker outlined a new initiative. Aware of the cost advantage of Philips' Japanese counterparts, he closed inefficient operations—particularly in Europe where 40 of the company's more than 200 plants were shut. He focused on core operations by selling peripheral businesses such welding, energy cables, and furniture making, while simultaneously acquiring an interest in Grundig and Westinghouse's North American lamp activities.

He also continued to "tilt the matrix," giving PDs product management responsibility, but leaving NOs responsible for local profits. And he allowed NOs to input into product planning, but gave global PDs the final decision on long-range direction. Still sales declined and profits stagnated.

Van der Klug's Radical Restructuring

When Cor van der Klugt succeeded Dekker as chairman in 1987, Philips had lost its long-held consumer electronics leadership position to Matsushita, and was one of only two non-Japanese companies in the world's top ten. Its net profit margins of 1% to 2% not only lagged behind General Electric's 9%, but even its highly aggressive Japanese competitors' slim 4%. Van der Klugt set a profit objective of 3% to 4% and made beating the Japanese companies a top priority.

As van der Klugt reviewed Philips' strategy, he designated various businesses as core (those that shared related technologies, had strategic importance, or were technical leaders) and non-core (stand-alone businesses that were not targets for world leadership and could eventually be sold if required). Of the four businesses defined as core, three were strategically linked: components, consumer electronics, and telecommunications and data systems. The fourth, lighting, was regarded as strategically vital because its cash flow funded development. The non-core businesses included domestic appliances and medical systems which van der Klugt spun off into joint ventures with Whirlpool and GE, respectively.

In continuing efforts to strengthen the PDs relative to the NOs, van der Klugt restructured Philips around the four core global divisions rather than the former 14 PDs. This allowed him to trim the management board, appointing the displaced board members to a new policy-making Group Management Committee. Consisting primarily of PD heads and functional chiefs, this body replaced the old NO-dominated International Concern Council. Finally, he sharply reduced the 3,000-strong headquarters staff, reallocating many of them to the PDs.

To link PDs more directly to markets, van der Klugt dispatched many experienced product-line managers to Philips' most competitive markets. For example, management of the digital audio tape and electric-shaver product lines were relocated to Japan, while the medical technology and domestic appliances lines were moved to the United States.

Such moves, along with continued efforts at globalizing product development and production efforts, required that the parent company gain firmer control over NOs, especially the giant North American Philips Corp. (NAPC). Although Philips had obtained a majority equity interest after World War II, it was not always able to make the U.S. company respond to directives from the center, as the V2000 VCR incident showed. To prevent replays of such experiences, in 1987 van der Klugt repurchased publicly owned NAPC shares for $700 million.

Reflecting the growing sentiment among some managers that R&D was not market oriented enough, van der Klugt halved spending on basic research to about 10% of total R&D. To manage what he described as "R&D's tendency to ponder the fundamental laws of nature," he made the R&D budget the direct responsibility of the businesses being supported by the research. This required that each research lab become focused on specific business areas (see **Exhibit 3**).

Finally, van der Klugt continued the effort to build efficient, specialized, multi-market production facilities by closing 75 of the company's 420 remaining plants worldwide. He also eliminated 38,000 of its 344,000 employees—21,000 through divesting businesses, shaking up the myth of lifetime employment at the company. He anticipated that all these restructurings would lead to a financial recovery by 1990. Unanticipated losses for that year, however—more than 4.5 billion Dutch guilders ($2.5 billion)—provoked a class-action law suit by angry American investors, who alleged that positive projections by the company had been misleading. In a surprise move, on May 14,1990, van der Klugt and half of the management board were replaced.

Timmer's "Operation Centurion" The new president, Jan Timmer, had spent most of his 35-year Philips career turning around unprofitable businesses. Under the banner "Operation Centurion," he lost no time in launching an initiative that cut headcount by 68,000 or 22% over the next 18 months, earning Timmer the nickname "The Butcher of Eindhoven." Because European laws required substantial compensation for layoffs—Eindhoven workers received 15 months' pay, for example— the first round of 10,000 layoffs alone cost Philips $700 million. To spread the burden around the globe, Timmer asked his PD managers to negotiate cuts with NO managers. But according to one report, country managers were "digging in their heels to save local jobs." Nonetheless, cuts came—many from overseas operations.

To focus resources further, Timmer sold off various businesses including integrated circuits to Matsushita, minicomputers to Digital, defense electronics to Thomson and the remaining 53% of appliances to Whirlpool. Yet profitability was still

Exhibit 3 Philips Research Labs by Location and Specialty, 1987

Location	Size (staff)	Specialty
Eindhoven, The Netherlands	2,000	Basic research, electronics, manufacturing technology
Redhill, Surrey, England	450	Microelectronics, television, defense
Hamburg, Germany	350	Communications, office equipment, medical imaging
Aachen, W. Germany	250	Fiber optics, X-ray systems
Paris, France	350	Microprocessors, chip materials, design
Brussels	50	Artificial intelligence
Briarcliff Manor, New York	35	Optical systems, television, superconductivity, defense
Sunnyvale, California	150	Integrated circuits

Source: Philips, in *BusinessWeek,* March 21, 1988, p. 156.

well below the modest 4% on sales he promised. In particular, consumer electronics lagged with slow growth in a price-competitive market. The core problem was identified by a 1994 McKinsey study that estimated that value added per hour in Japanese consumer electronic factories was still 68% above that of European plants.

After three years of cost-cutting, in early 1994 Timmer finally presented a new growth strategy to the board. His plan was to expand software, services, and multimedia to become 40% of revenues by 2000. He was betting on Philips' legendary innovative capability to restart the growth engines. He hired Hewlett-Packard's director of research and encouraged him to focus on developing 15 core technologies. The list, which included interactive compact disc (CD-i), digital compact cassettes (DCC), high definition television (HDTV), and multimedia software, was soon dubbed "the president's projects." Over the next few years, Philips invested over $2.5 billion in these technologies. But the earlier divestment of some of the company's truly high-tech businesses and a 37% cut in R&D personnel left it with few who understood the technology of the new priority businesses.

By 1996, it was clear that Philips' analog HDTV technology would not become industry standard, that its DCC gamble had lost out to Sony's Minidisc, and that CD-i was a marketing failure. And while costs in Philips were lower, so too was morale, particularly among middle management. Critics claimed that the company's drive for cost-cutting and standardization had led it to ignore new worldwide market demands for more segmented products and higher consumer service.

Boonstra's Reorganization   When Timmer stepped down in October 1996, the board replaced him with a radical choice for Philips—an outsider whose expertise was in marketing and Asia rather than technology and Europe. Cor Boonstra was a 58-year-old Dutchman whose years as CEO of Sara Lee, the U.S. consumer products firm, had earned him a reputation as a hard-driving marketing genius. Joining Philips in 1994, he headed the Asia

Pacific region and the lighting division before being tapped as CEO.

Unencumbered by tradition, he announced strategic sweeping changes designed to reach his goal of increasing return on net assets from 17% to 24% by 1999. "There are no taboos, no sacred cows," he said. "The bleeders must be turned around, sold, or closed." Within three years, he had sold off 40 of Philips' 120 major businesses—including such well known units as Polygram and Grundig.

Promising to transform a structure he described as "a plate of spaghetti" into "a neat row of asparagus," he then initiated a major worldwide restructuring. "How can we compete with the Koreans?" he asked. "They don't have 350 companies all over the world. Their factory in Ireland covers Europe and their manufacturing facility in Mexico serves North America. We need a more structured and simpler manufacturing and marketing organization to achieve a cost pattern in line with those who do not have our heritage. This is still one of the biggest issues facing Philips."

Within a year, 3,100 jobs were eliminated in North America and 3,000 employees were added in Asia Pacific, emphasizing Boonstra's determination to shift production to low-wage countries and his broader commitment to Asia. And after three years, he had closed 100 of the company's 356 factories worldwide. At the same time, he replaced the company's 21 PDs with 7 divisions, but shifted day-to-day operating responsibility to 100 business units, each responsible for its profits worldwide. It was a move designed to finally eliminate the old PD/NO matrix. Finally, in a move that shocked most employees, he announced that the 100-year-old Eindhoven headquarters would be relocated to Amsterdam with only 400 of the 3000 corporate positions remaining.

By early 1998, he was ready to announce his new strategy. Despite early speculation that he might abandon consumer electronics, he proclaimed it as the center of Philips' future. Betting on the "digital revolution," he planned to focus on established technologies such as cellular phones (through a joint venture with Lucent), digital TV, digital videodisc, and web TV. Furthermore, he committed major resources to marketing, including a 40% increase in advertising to raise awareness and image of the Philips brand and de-emphasize most of the 150 other brands it supported worldwide—from Magnavox TVs to Norelco shavers to Marantz stereos.

While not everything succeeded (the Lucent cell phone JV collapsed after nine months, for example), overall performance improved significantly in the late 1990s. By 2000, Boonstra was able to announce that he had achieved his objective of a 24% return on net assets.

Kleisterlee's Refocusing   By the time the Boonstra stepped down in May 2001, however, a global "tech wreck" recession had begun, resulting in what Fortune described as "a tidal wave of red ink" to greet the new CEO, Gerard Kleisterlee, a 54-year-old career Philips man. With the share price in free fall from $60 in $2001 to $13 in 2002, Kleisterlee faced what he described as "the biggest losses in the history of the company."

Moving quickly, the new CEO began restructuring the company, announcing the outsourcing of Philips mobile phone production to CEC of China, and the production of VCRs to Japan's Funai Electric. But it was not sufficient to prevent a 2001 loss of €2.6 billion compared to a €9.6 billion profit in 2000. So, over the next few years, he continued to outsource production of TVs, CD players, and components, while simultaneously moving the remaining in-house production to low-cost countries like China, Poland, or Mexico. He also sold off several businesses including most components, mobile phones, audio, and even the core semiconductor business. Within four years he had removed more than one in four Philips employees, reducing headcount by 60,000.

The shape of that new portfolio soon became clear. Using funds generated by selling businesses, Kleisterlee began acquiring companies in the high-growth medical and lighting segments, and began referring to Philips as "a lifestyle company" centered on health and well-being. "We came to the conclusion that the thing that holds everything together is not the fact that we made our own components and semiconductors. It's the fact that we have a common mission," he said.

A business once at the center of Philips portfolio now had a new role. "Consumer electronics is a very, very small leftover part in our lifestyle portfolio," he explained. "That business is too big a battle to fight now. We plan to be the Dell of consumer electronics, making less and marketing more. That means that we will be focused on product development, brand, and channel management."

So while Phillips continued to create innovations for its TVs, it focused them on its high-definition plasma and LCD sets with breakthroughs like Pixel Plus 2, a digital technology that refined the incoming signal to produce sharper pictures with more vivid color. But in addition to technological breakthroughs, R&D was also focused on more basic products for developing markets—hand-crank radios, high powered mixers designed for exotic foods, and irons with dust tolerant thermostats.

Phillips approach to marketing was also changing. In the developed world, it slashed the number of retail chains it serviced from 600 to 200, focusing particularly on seven giants like Wal-Mart, Tesco, and Carrefour. But in developing countries, it took a different approach. For example in India, its strategy was to sell its adapted low-end products through 35,000 village stores.

Kleisterlee explained how his adaptive product-market strategy worked: "In India, we have vans with diagnostic and lab equipment, equipped with a satellite video link to a top hospital. Instead of making long trips to a city hospital, people can now get cheaper, more convenient treatment where they live." With 700 million people in rural India, the company felt it had a great opportunity.

By 2008, Kleisterlee was ready to confirm his new focused strategy in the organization structure. Having earlier cut the number of divisions to five (there have been 14 as recently as 1995), in early 2008, he defined just three—healthcare, lighting, and consumer lifestyle. "We have to organize around markets," he said. "We're going to organize from the outside in."

But competition in consumer electronics remained brutal, especially in a growing global recession. In late 2008, Philips licensed Funai to make and market TVs under the Philips name in North America. A few months later, it extended that license to cover other markets as well as products such as DVDs, home theater, Blu-Ray, and other products. "We spent the 1980s and 1990s restructuring and trying to find our way," Kleisterlee said. "My goal is to leave behind a company on a successful part to steady, profitable growth." Some wondered whether he had found that path.

Matsushita: Background

In 1918, 23 year old Konosuke Matsushita (or "KM" as he was affectionately known), invested ¥100 to start production of double-ended sockets in is modest home. The company grew rapidly, expanding into battery-powered lamps, electric irons, and radios. On May 5,1932, Matsushita's 14th anniversary, KM announced to his 162 employees a 250-year corporate plan, broken into 25-year sections, each to be carried out by successive generations. His plan was codified in a company creed and in the "Seven Spirits of Matsushita" (see **Exhibit 4**), which provided the basis of the "cultural and spiritual training" all new employees received on joining the company.

In the post-war boom, Matsushita introduced a flood of new products: TV sets in 1952; transistor radios in 1958; color TVs, dishwashers, and electric ovens in 1960. Capitalizing on its broad line of 5,000 products, the company opened 25,000 domestic retail outlets—40% of appliance stores in Japan in the late 1960s. These not only assured sales volume, but also gave the company direct access to market trends. When post-war growth slowed, however, product line expansion and an excellent distribution system no longer insured growth, and the company looked to export markets.

The Organization's Foundation: Divisional Structure Plagued by ill health, KM began to delegate more than was typical in Japanese companies. In 1933, Matsushita became the first Japanese

---

Exhibit 4   Matsushita Creed and Philosophy (Excerpts)

Creed

Through our industrial activities, we strive to foster progress, to promote the general welfare of society, and to devote ourselves to furthering the development of world culture.

Seven Spirits of Matsushita

Service through Industry
Fairness
Harmony and Cooperation
Struggle for Progress
Courtesy and Humility
Adjustment and Assimilation
Gratitude

KM's Business Philosophy (Selected Quotations)

"The purpose of an enterprise is to contribute to society by supplying goods of high quality at low prices in ample quantity."

"Profit comes in compensation for contribution to society. . . . [It] is a result rather than a goal."

"The responsibility of the manufacturer cannot be relieved until its product is disposed of by the end user."

"Unsuccessful business employs a wrong management. You should not find its causes in bad fortune, unfavorable surroundings, or wrong timing."

"Business appetite has no self-restraining mechanism. . . . When you notice you have gone too far, you must have the courage to come back."

Source: Christopher A. Bartlett, "Matsushita Electric Industrial (MEI) in 1987," HBS No. 388–144 (Boston: Harvard Business School Publishing, 1988) p. 17.

---

company to adopt a divisional structure. In addition to creating a "small business" environment, the structure generated internal competition that spurred each business to drive growth by leveraging its technology to develop new products. But after the innovating division had earned substantial profits on its new product, the "one-product-one-division" policy was to spin it off as a new division to maintain the "hungry spirit."

Management provided each division with funds to establish largely self-sufficient development, production, and marketing capabilities. Corporate treasury operated like a commercial bank, reviewing divisions' loan requests for which it charged slightly higher-than-market interest, and accepting interest-bearing deposits on their excess funds. Divisional profitability was determined after deductions for central services and interest on internal borrowings. Each division paid 60% of earnings to headquarters and financed working capital and fixed asset needs from the retained 40%. Transfer prices were based on the market and settled through the treasury on normal commercial terms. KM expected uniform performance across the company's 36 divisions, and division managers whose operating profits fell below 4% of sales for two successive years were replaced.

While basic technology was developed in a central research laboratory (CRL), product development and engineering occurred in each of the product divisions. Matsushita intentionally underfunded the CRL, forcing it to compete for additional funding from the divisions. Annually, the CRL publicized its major research projects to the product divisions, which then provided funding for CRL to develop technology for marketable applications. Rarely the innovator, Matsushita was usually very fast to market—earning it the nickname "Manishita," or copycat.

Matsushita: Internationalization

Although the establishment of overseas markets was a major thrust of the second 25 years in the 250-year plan, in an overseas trip in 1951 KM had been unable to find any American company willing to collaborate with Matsushita. The best he could do was a technology exchange and licensing agreement with Philips. Nonetheless, the push to internationalize continued.

Expanding Through Color TV   In the 1950s and 1960s, trade liberalization and lower shipping allowed Matsushita to build a healthy export business with its black and white TV sets. In 1953, the company opened its first overseas branch office—the Matsushita Electric Corporation of America (MECA). With neither a distribution network nor a strong brand, the company had to resort to selling through mass merchandisers and discounters under their private brands.

During the 1960s, pressure from national governments in developing countries led Matsushita to open plants Southeast Asia and Central and South America. As manufacturing costs in Japan rose, the company shifted more basic production to these low-wage countries, but almost all high-value components and subassemblies remained in its scale-intensive Japanese plants. By the 1970s, political pressure forced Matsushita to establish assembly operations in the Americas and Europe. In 1972, it opened a plant in Canada; in 1974, it bought Motorola's TV business in the United States; and in 1976, it built a plant in Carcliff, Wales, to supply the European Common Market.

Building Global Leadership Through VCRs
The birth of the videocassette recorder (VCR) propelled Matsushita into first place in the consumer electronics industry during the 1980s. Recognizing the potential mass-market appeal of the professional broadcast VCR first developed in 1956 by Californian company Ampex, Matsushita began developing the technology. It launched its commercial broadcast video recorder in 1964, and two years later, introduced a consumer version.

Subsequently, a battle over VCR format developed. In 1975, Sony introduced the technically superior "Betamax" format, and in 1976, JVC launched a competing "VHS" format. Under pressure from MITI, Japan's industrial planning ministry, Matsushita agreed to give up its own format and adopt the VHS standard. During its 20 years of development, Matsushita's research team lived the VCR product cycle, moving from CRL to the product division's development labs, and eventually to the plants producing VCRs.

Between 1977 and 1985, Matsushita increased VCR capacity 33-fold to 6.8 million units, not only to meet its own needs, but also those of OEM customers like GE, RCA, Philips, and Zenith, who decided to forego self-manufacture and outsource to the low-cost Japanese. Increased volume enabled Matsushita to slash prices 50% within five years of launch. In parallel, the company licensed the VHS format to other manufacturers, including Hitachi, Sharp, Mitsubishi and, eventually, Philips. By the mid-1980s, VCRs accounted for 30% of Matsushita's sales and 45% of its profits.

Changing Systems and Controls   In the mid-1980s, Matsushita's growing number of overseas companies reported to the parent in one of two ways: wholly owned, single-product global plants reported directly to the appropriate product

division, while overseas sales and marketing subsidiaries and overseas companies producing a broad product line for local markets reported to Matsushita Electric Trading Company (METC), a separate legal entity. (See **Exhibit 5** for METC's organization.)

Throughout the 1970s, product divisions maintained strong operating control over their offshore operations. They had plant and equipment designed by the parent company, followed manufacturing procedures dictated by the center, and used materials from Matsushita's domestic plants. By the 1980s, increased local sourcing gradually weakened the divisions' direct control, so instead of controlling inputs, they began to monitor output—quality and productivity levels for example.

Exhibit 5   Organization of METC, 1985

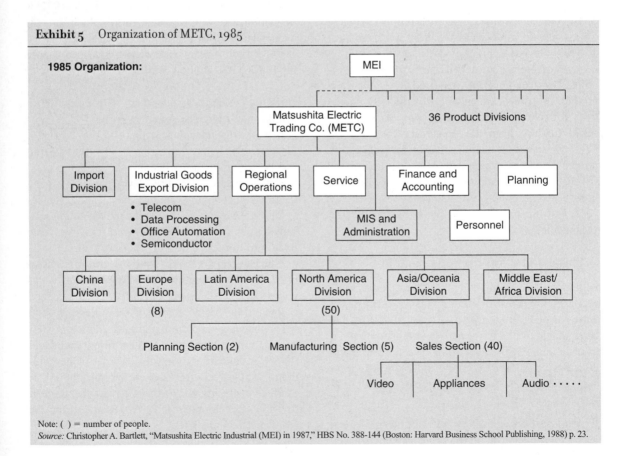

Note: ( ) = number of people.
Source: Christopher A. Bartlett, "Matsushita Electric Industrial (MEI) in 1987," HBS No. 388-144 (Boston: Harvard Business School Publishing, 1988) p. 23.

Headquarters-Subsidiary Relations Although METC and the product divisions set detailed sales and profits targets for their overseas subsidiaries, they told local managers they had autonomy on how to achieve them. But as "Mike" Matsuoko, president of the European source in Cardiff, Wales emphasized, failure forfeited freedom: "Losses show bad health and invite many doctors from Japan who provide advice and support."

In the mid-1980s, Matsushita had over 700 expatriate Japanese managers and technicians on foreign assignment for four to eight years, primarily to play a "vital communication role." Explained one senior executive, "Even if a local manager speaks Japanese, he would not have the long experience that is needed to build relationships and understand our management processes."

Expatriate managers were located throughout foreign subsidiaries, but there were a few positions that were almost always reserved for them. The most visible were subsidiary general managers whose main role was to translate Matsushita philosophy abroad. Expatriate accounting managers were expected to "mercilessly expose the truth" to corporate headquarters; and Japanese technical managers were sent to transfer product and process technologies and provide headquarters with local market information. These expatriates maintained relationships with senior colleagues in their divisions, who acted as career mentors, evaluated performance (with some input from local managers), and provided expatriates with information about parent company developments.

Subsidiary general managers visited Osaka at least two or three times each year—some as often as every month. Corporate managers reciprocated these visits, and on average, major operations hosted a headquarters manager each day of the year. Face-to-face meetings were considered vital: "Figures are important," said one manager, "but the meetings are necessary to develop judgment." Daily faxes and nightly phone calls from headquarters to offshore expatriates were considered vital.

Yamashita's "Operation Localization" Although international sales kept rising, growing host country pressures caused concern about the company's highly centralized operations. In 1982, Matsushita's newly appointed president Toshihiko Yamashita launched "Operation Localization" to boost offshore production from less than 10% of value-added to 25%, or half of overseas sales, by 1990. To support the target, he set out a program of four localizations—personnel, technology, material, and capital.

Over the next few years, Matsushita increased the number of local nationals in key positions. In the United States, for example, American became presidents of three of six local companies, while in Taiwan the majority of division heads were replaced by Chinese managers. In each case, however, local national managers were supported by Japanese advisors who maintained direct links with the parent company. To localize technology and materials, the company developed local subsidiaries' expertise in sourcing equipment locally, modifying designs to local requirements, incorporating local components, and adapting corporate processes and technologies to accommodate the changes. And by the mid-1980s, offshore production subsidiaries were free to buy minor supplies from local vendors, but still had to buy key components from internal sources.

One of the most successful innovations was to give overseas sales subsidiaries more choice over the products they sold. Each year the company held a two-week internal merchandising show and product planning meeting where product divisions exhibited the new lines. Here, foreign subsidiary managers negotiated for changes in product features, quantities, and even prices for products they felt would better meet their local needs. Product division managers, however, could overrule the sales subsidiary if they thought introduction of a particular product was of strategic importance.

President Yamashita's hope was that Operation Localization would help Matsushita's overseas companies develop the innovative capability and entrepreneurial initiatives that he had long admired in the NOs of rival Philips.[1] Yet despite his four localizations, overseas companies continued to act primarily as the implementation arms of Japanese-based product divisions. Unusually for a Japanese CEO, Yamashita publicly expressed his unhappiness with the lack of initiative at the TV plant in Cardiff. Despite the transfer of substantial resources and the delegation of many responsibilities, he felt that the plant remained too dependent on the center.

Tanii's Integration and Expansion   Yamashita's successor, Akio Tanii, expanded on his predecessor's initiatives. In 1986, in an effort to integrate domestic and overseas operations, he brought all foreign subsidiaries under the control of METC, then merged METC into the parent company. Then, to shift operational control nearer to local markets, he relocated major regional headquarters functions from Japan to North America, Europe, and Southeast Asia. Yet still he was frustrated that the overseas subsidiary companies acted as little more than the implementing agents of the Osaka-based product divisions.

Through all these changes, however, Matsushita's worldwide growth continued, generating huge reserves. With $17.5 billion in liquid financial assets at the end of 1989, the company was referred to as the "Matsushita Bank." Frustrated by their inability to develop innovative overseas companies, top management decided to buy them. To obtain a software source for its hardware businesses, in 1991 the company acquired MCA, the U.S. entertainment giant, for $6.1 billion. Within a year, however, Japan's bubble economy had burst, and almost overnight, Tanii had to shift the focus from expansion to cost containment. Despite his best efforts, the problems ran too deep. With 1992 profits less than half their 1991 level, the board took the unusual move of forcing Tanii to resign in February 1993.

---

[1] Past efforts to develop such capabilities abroad had failed. For example, when Matsushita acquired Motorola's TV business in the United States, the U.S. company's highly innovative technology group atrophied as American engineers resigned in response to what they felt to be excessive control from Japan's highly centralized R&D operations.

Morishita 's Challenge and Response   At 56, Yoichi Morishita was the most junior of the company's executive vice presidents when he was tapped as the new president. In a major strategic reversal, he sold 80% of MCI to Seagram, booking a $1.2 billion loss on the transaction. Over the following 18 months, under the slogan "simple, small, speedy and strategic," he then moved 6,000 staff to operating jobs.

Yet the company continued to struggle. Japan's domestic market for consumer electronics collapsed—from $42 billion in 1989 to $21 billion in 1999. And the rise of new competition—from Korea, then China—created a global glut, then a price collapse. With a strong yen making its exports uncompetitive, Matsushita's product divisions shifted production offshore, mostly to low-cost countries like China and Malaysia. By the end of the decade, its 160 factories outside Japan employed 140,000 people—about the same number of employees as in its 133 plants in Japan. Yet management seemed unwilling to close inefficient Japanese plans or lay off staff with the commitment of lifetime employment. Despite Morishita's promises, internal resistance prevented his implementation of much of the promised radical change.

In the closing years of the decade, Morishita began emphasizing the need to develop technology and innovation offshore. Concerned that only 250 of the company's 3,000 R&D scientists and engineers were located outside Japan, he began investing in R&D partnerships and technical exchanges, particularly in emerging fields. For example, an 1998, he signed a joint R&D agreement with the Chinese Academy of Sciences, China's leading research organization. Later that year, he announced the establishment of the Panasonic Digital Concepts Center in California. Its mission was to act as a venture fund and an incubation center for the new ideas and technologies emerging in Silicon Valley. To some it was an indication that Matsushita had given up trying to generate new technology and business initiatives from its own overseas companies.

Nakamura's Transformation   In June 2000, Kunio Nakamura, the 38-year veteran who had headed MEI's North American operations was named president. Operating profits were 2.2% of sales, with consumer electronics generating only 0.4% due to losses in the TV and VCR divisions. Just as Morishita had promised seven years earlier, the new CEO vowed to raise operating margins to 5% in three years.

By December, Nakamura was ready to announce his first three-year plan dubbed "Value Creation 21" or VC 21. Its main objective was to build a "super manufacturing company" on three foundations: a strong technology-based components business, a flexible and responsive manufacturing capability, and customer-oriented, solutions-based businesses. The new CEO emphasized the need to retain Matsushita's fully integrated value chain, justifying it with a "smile curve" which promised high returns in both upstream components and downstream services and solutions to offset lower returns in the highly competitive consumer electronics products in the middle of the value chain.

At the core of VC 21 was a plan to close inefficient scale-driven plants and concentrate production in Manufacturing Centers, facilities transformed from old mass production assembly lines to modern flexible manufacturing cells. The transformation would be implemented first in Japanese mother plants, and then rolled out to the 170 plants it had worldwide.

Furthermore, as part of a plan to replace Matsushita's historic fragmented and compartmentalized structure with a "flat web-based organization", Nakamura separated plants from product divisions which now had to source their products from non-captive and non-exclusive Manufacturing Centers. Sales and marketing was also stripped from the once powerful product divisions, and absorbed in one of two global marketing organizations, one for appliances and the other for consumer electronics. "It was a cultural revolution," said one manager.

But the strong financial performance Nakamura had assumed would support his plan, disappeared with the "tech wreck" recession of 2001, resulting in

Matsushita's first quarterly loss in its history. The CEO and immediately announced five emergency measures to reverse the situation. In one bold move, the company dropped its lifetime employment practice and offered early retirement to 18,000 employees. Over 13,000 accepted, not only reducing costs, but also allowing a new generation of managers to emerge. In total, the domestic workforce was cut by 25,000, and 30 inefficient plants were closed.

Despite these efforts, in March 2002 Matsushita announced an operating loss of ¥199 billion ($1.7 billion), and an even more shocking loss of ¥428 billion ($3.7 billion) including restructuring charges. Calling the situation "an intolerable social evil", Nakamura committed to delivering profit of ¥100 billion the next year. He told his executives that because implementation of his emergency measures had not been satisfactory, he was launching a management improvement initiative. He challenged them to deliver "a V-shaped recovery" driven by V-Products—innovative, customer-focused products launched rapidly into global markets, at competitive prices. He focused 70% of investments on consumer electronics and semiconductors, urging his managers to move past Matsushita's reputation for slow innovation and imitation. "In the digital age, there is no room for imitators," he said.

To eliminate the internal competitiveness he felt that had constrained the turnaround, he grouped all businesses into one of three closely linked domains—Digital Networks (primarily consumer electronics, mobile phones, and telecom), Home Appliances (including lighting and environmental systems), and Components (with semiconductors, batteries, and motors.)

In March 2004, at the end of the three year "VC 21" plan, the company reported a profit of ¥185 billion ($1.9 billion) on sales of ¥7,500 billion ($72 billion). As impressive as the result was, it was still less than half of the promised 5% operating margin. So Nakamura announced a new three-year plan called "Leap Ahead 21" with a 5% objective for 2007 as an interim step on the way to 10% by 2010.

Exhibit 6   Matsushita, Summary Financial Data, 1970–2008[a]

	2008	2000	1995	1990	1985	1980	1975	1970
In billions of yen and percent:								
Sales	¥9,069	¥7,299	¥6,948	¥6,003	¥5,291	¥2,916	¥1,385	¥932
Income before tax	527	219	232	572	723	324	83	147
As % of sales	5.8%	3.0%	3.3%	9.5%	13.7%	11.1%	6.0%	15.8%
Net income	¥282	¥100	¥90	¥236	¥216	¥125	¥32	¥70
As % of sales	3.1%	1.4%	1.3%	3.9%	4.1%	4.3%	2.3%	7.6%
Cash dividends (per share)	¥35.00	¥14.00	¥13.50	¥10.00	¥9.52	¥7.51	¥6.82	¥6.21
Total assets	7,443	7,955	8,202	7,851	5,076	2,479	1,274	735
Stockholders' equity	3,742	3,684	3,255	3,201	2,084	1,092	573	324
Capital investment	503	355	316	355	288	NA	NA	NA
Depreciation	320	343	296	238	227	65	28	23
R&D	554	526	378	346	248	102	51	NA
Employees (units)	305,828	290,448	265,397	198,299	175,828	107,057	82,869	78,924
Overseas employees	170,265	143,773	112,314	59,216	38,380	NA	NA	NA
As % of total employees	56%	50%	42%	30%	22%	NA	NA	NA
Exchange rate (fiscal period end; ¥/$)	100	103	89	159	213	213	303	360
In millions of dollars:								
Sales	$90,949	$68,862	$78,069	$37,753	$24,890	$13,690	$4,572	$2,588
Operating income before depreciation	8,424	4,944	6,250	4,343	3,682	1,606	317	NA
Operating income after depreciation	NA	1,501	2,609	2,847	2,764	1,301	224	NA
Pretax income	4,263	2,224	2,678	3,667	3,396	1,520	273	408
Net income	2,827	941	1,017	1,482	1,214	584	105	195
Total assets	74,648	77,233	92,159	49,379	21,499	11,636	4,206	2,042
Total equity	37,530	35,767	36,575	20,131	10,153	5,129	1,890	900

Source: Annual reports; Standard & Poor's Compustat®; Moody's Industrial and International Manuals.
[a]Data prior to 1987 are for the fiscal year ending November 20; data 1988 and after are for the fiscal year ending March 31.

Ohtsubo's Inheritance   In April 2006, after announcing operating profits of $3.6 billion, Nakamura announced that he would step down as CEO in June. Spontaneously, analysts at the presentation gave him a standing ovation, a unique event in reserved Japan. His successor, Eumio Ohtsubo, previously head the consumer electronics business, embraced Nakamura's commitment to surpass Samsung's 9.4% operating margin by 2010.

Having led effort making Matsushita the world's leading plasma TV maker, Ohtsubo committed to dominating the fast-growing flatscreen market by investing Its $1.3 billion cash balance in focused R&D and more efficient global production. He wanted to build an ability to develop, manufacture, and launch superior new products twice a year, globally. "We will absolutely not be beaten in the flat-panel TV business," he said.

In January 2008, he surprised many when he announced the change in the company's name from Matsushita to Panasonic, reflecting the name of the company's best-known brand. It was part of

Exhibit 7   Matsushita, Sales by Product and Geographic Segment, 1985–2008 (billion yen)

	2008	2000		1995		FY 1990		FY 1985	
By Product Segment:									
Audio, Video, Communications Networks	¥4,319	—	—	—	—	—	—	—	—
Video and Audio Equipment	—	¥1,706	23%	¥1,827	26%	¥2,159	36%	¥2,517	48%
Electronic components	—	—	—	893	13	781	13	573	11
Home appliances and household equipment	1,316	1,306	18	—	—	—	—	—	—
Home appliances	—	—	—	916	13	802	13	763	14
Communication and industrial equipment	—	—	—	1,797	26	1,375	23	849	16
Batteries and kitchen-related equipment	—	—	—	374	4	312	5	217	4
Information and communications equipment	—	2,175	28	—	—	—	—	—	—
Industrial equipment	—	817	11	—	—	—	—	—	—
Components	1,399	1,618	21	—	—	—	—	—	—
Others	123	—	—	530	8	573	10	372	7
Total	¥9,069	¥7,682	100%	¥6,948	100%	¥6,003	100%	¥5,291	100%
By Geographic Segment:									
Domestic	¥6,789	¥3,698	51%	¥3,455	50%	¥3,382	56%	¥2,659	50%
Overseas	5,404	3,601	49	3,493	50	2,621	44	2,632	50
Corporate	(3,120)								

Note: Total may not add due to rounding.
Source: Annual reports.

Ohtsubo's efforts to grow overseas revenues from less than 50% to 60% by 2010. Still, with Panasonic in 78th place on the Interbrand survey of the world brand recognition, he had a way to go.

But any talk about foreign sales growth evaporated when the global financial crisis struck in 2008. In the December quarter, company sales slid 20%, while operating profit plunged 84%. Immediately Ohtsubo initiated a review of the company's 170 overseas plants, vowing to shut down any with operating profit of less than 3%, or declining sales over three years. The review resulted in the closure of 27 plants, and the lay off 15,000 workers. But the global crisis hit hard, and with restructuring charges and write-offs, the company projected a $4.2 billion loss for the full year ending in March 2009. The carefully laid plans for $90 billion in revenues and 10% operating margin by 2010 were vanishing dreams.

Case 4-2   ECCO A/S—Global Value Chain Management

Bo Bernhard Nielsen, Torben Pedersen, and Jacob Pyndt

Despite the summer, the weather was hazy on that day in May 2004 as the airplane took off from Hongqiao International Airport, Shanghai. The plane was likely to encounter some turbulence on its way to Copenhagen Airport in Denmark. The chief operations officer (COO) of the Danish shoe manufacturer ECCO A/S (ECCO), Mikael Thinghuus, did not particularly enjoy bumpy flights, but the rough flight could not overshadow the confidence and optimism he felt after his visit to Xiamen in southeast China. This was his third visit in three months.

During 2003/2004, ECCO spent substantial resources on analyzing where to establish production facilities in China. On this trip, together with Flemming Brønd, the production director in China, Thinghuus had finalized negotiations with Novo Nordisk Engineering (NNE). NNE possessed valuable experience in building factories in China, experience gained through their work for Novozymes and Novo Nordisk. Now everything seemed to be in place. Construction was to begin in August, machines would be installed in January 2005, and the first pair of shoes would be leaving the factory by the end of March 2005 if all went well. The plan was to build five closely connected factories over the next four years with a total capacity of five million pairs of shoes per year, serving both export needs and the Chinese market, which was expected to grow in the future.

Thinghuus felt relieved. He was confident that the massive investments in China would serve as a solid footstep on a fast growing market and provide a unique export platform to the global shoe market. However, he could not rest on his laurels. The massive investment in China was an integrated part of ECCO's continuous attempt to optimize various activities in the value chain. Operating five distinct factories in Portugal, Slovakia, Indonesia, Thailand and shortly in China combined with a declared vision of integrating the global value chain, the task at hand was certainly complicated. Moreover, ECCO had one tannery located in the Netherlands and two located adjacent to shoe production facilities in Indonesia and Thailand. These tanneries enabled ECCO to maintain control of leather processing and ensure the quality of the leather utilized in ECCO's shoe manufacturing.

IVEY

Richard Ivey School of Business
The University of Western Ontario

▌ Professor Bo Bernhard Nielsen, Professor Torben Pedersen and Management Consultant Jacob Pyndt wrote this case solely to provide material for class discussion. The authors do not intend to illustrate either effective or ineffective handling of a managerial situation. The authors may have disguised certain names and other identifying information to protect confidentiality.

Introducing ECCO

It has always been our philosophy that quality is the only thing that endures. That is why we constantly work to create the perfect shoe—so good that you forget you are wearing it. It has to be light and solid, designed on the basis of the newest technology and knowledge about comfort and materials. ECCO have to be the world's best shoes—shoes with internal values.

Karl Toosbuy, founder

With the simple slogan "A perfect fit—a simple idea," Karl Toosbuy founded ECCO in Bredebro, Denmark in 1963. Inspired by the open and harsh landscape of southern Jutland, Toosbuy presented

ECCO as a company with a passion for pleasant walking. Today, after more than 40 years of craftsmanship and dedication to uncompromised quality, ECCO remains extremely committed to comfort, design and a perfectly fitting shoe with the goal of constantly developing shoes that are pleasant to walk in regardless of the weather conditions. The company's vision is to be the "most wanted brand within innovation and comfort footwear—a position that only can be attained by constantly and courageously researching new paths, investing in employees, in our core competencies of product development and production technology."[1]

ECCO aimed at producing the world's most comfortable and modern footwear for work and leisure. Footwear for work, leisure and festive occasions had to be designed and constructed with uncompromising attention to customer comfort. Evidently, trends in the market in terms of fashion and elegance were important, but usability was ECCO's highest design priority. As Søren Steffensen, executive vice-president, stated: "ECCO is not a fashion brand and it never will be. We do not sell shoes where the brand name is the most important and quality is a secondary consideration. Primarily, we sell high-quality shoes and that is where we seek recognition."[2]

Products and Markets   The ECCO group produces various types of shoes including casual and outdoor shoes for men, ladies, and children, as well as semi-sport shoes, for two different seasons— spring/summer and autumn/winter. In 2004, the sales split between the different categories was children 11 per cent, ladies 47 per cent, men 30 per cent, and sport 12 per cent. The sport division produced outdoor, walking, running and golf shoes. ECCO's golf shoes category had experienced particularly significant growth. ECCO's development of golf shoes had started as a joke between Toosbuy and Dieter Kasprzak, chief executive officer (CEO), on the golf course 10 years ago. In 2004, the joke turned into 300,000 pairs sold, sponsorships of international golfers like Thomas Bjørn and Colin Montgomerie, and numerous endorsements in independent tests of golf equipment in the United States. Having tested ECCO's golf shoes, Rankmark, an American company conducting objective tests and analyzes of golf products, stated that "ECCO Golf Footwear was preferred by more than 90 per cent of golfers over their current brands."

In 2004, ECCO exported more than 90 per cent of its production, with the United States, Germany and Japan being the main markets. ECCO's international profile was reflected in the workforce composition. In the same year, ECCO employed 9,657 employees of which 553 were located in Denmark. The company worked constantly on creating new markets, particularly in Asia and Central and Eastern Europe. The North American market—the United States and Canada—was of great importance to ECCO. In 2004, the company's American operations attained 17 per cent growth in sales when compared to 2003. That year, the American operations accounted for DKK 875 million in revenue, roughly 26 per cent of ECCO's total sales.[3] The American subsidiary had streamlined its vendorship, cutting the number from 1,200 in 2002 to 1,000 in 2004, yet the remaining dealers had purchased a higher volume. In addition, ECCO increased its number of partnerships by 18 to 34 in 2004. The American market was lucrative as shoes were selling at high prices. Men's shoes typically cost between US$150 and US$450 and the highly successful golf shoes were sold for between US$200 and US$400. The majority of ECCO's sales in North America went through exclusive department stores, such as Nordstrom's and Dillard's.

Finance and Ownership Structure

During the period from 1999 to 2003, ECCO experienced stagnating productivity and declining operating margins (see **Exhibit 1**). For instance, the operating margin fell from 15 per cent in 2000 to

---

[1] http://www.ecco.com/int/en/aboutus/index.jsp, accessed April 2005.
[2] *Berlingske News Magazine*, March 7, 2004.

[3] *Børsen*, December 22, 2004.

five per cent in 2002. Moreover, company debts increased from DKK 1 billion to DKK 2 billion following investments in expansion and inventories. In response to these negative trends, ECCO launched strategic initiatives to streamline logistics, focus on more modern shoes and facilitate monitoring of the market. 2004 brought signs of improvement as the company achieved earnings of DKK 150 million and lifted its operating margin to eight per cent. The reduction of stock had a particularly notable effect on the 2004 result, further freeing up capital to finance ECCO's ambitious growth plan. The company's goal was to increase revenue to approximately DKK 8 billion to DKK 9 billion by 2013, selling 24 million pairs of shoes per year.

Despite financial constraints in the beginning of the 21st century which could have triggered an Initial public offering (IPO) to raise capital, ownership of the company was kept within the family. Prior to his death, Toosbuy passed on his shares to his daughter Hanni Toosbuy, who was chairman of the supervisory board (see **Exhibit 2**). Commenting on the ownership structure of ECCO, Karl Toosbuy stated:

> I do not believe that an IPO is in the best interest of the company. ECCO is stronger given the family ownership. The family can take higher risks. We are able to allocate. In many cases, we do not have the time to investigate things as profoundly as a listed company ought to do. Yet, we are sure that what we want is the right thing. Then we act instead of waiting.[4]

Organizational Developments Operating on a global scale required employees with international mindsets and good adaptability skills. Since its inception ECCO had given high priority to the continuous education and training of its employees. The company invested aggressively in vocational training, career development, developmental conversations and expatriation. ECCO's establishment of the Education and Conference Centre in 1994, the research centre Futura in 1996, and the ECCO Business Academy in 2001 served as signs of commitment to these issues. According to Karl

Toosbuy, these investments were vital to allowing ECCO to recruit internally for management positions and, thereby, accomplish his strategy announced in 1991. This strategy stated that 80 per cent of the company's leaders should come from inside ECCO. Twice during the 1990s, Toosbuy had stepped down as CEO only to reinstall himself some years later, underpinning the importance of knowing the company inside-out and adapting to ECCO's culture.

Despite the founder's intention of internal recruitment for management positions, on two recent occasions this ambition could not be met. In 2001, ECCO hired Søren Steffensen in the position as sales and marketing director. Coming from a position as retail director in the Danish fashion clothing company, Carli Gry, he had a reputation of knowing every shopping corner in Europe and was an efficient negotiator. In addition, Mikael Thinghuus took over the position of chief operating officer (COO) in 2003, having held positions at IBM and the East Asiatic Company. The third member of the executive committee was Jens Christian Meier, executive vice-president, who had spent most of his career within shoe manufacturing. He actually initiated his career at ECCO, continued at Clarks, and then moved on to Elefanten Shoes as managing director before returning to ECCO. His main responsibilities lay within the fields of logistics, sourcing and handling ECCO's production facilities. When Karl Toosbuy died in June 2004, his son-in-law, Dieter Kasprzak, became CEO. Kasprzak had spent 23 years with ECCO, primarily as the director of design and product development. Whereas Toosbuy was known for his abilities to develop unique production techniques, Kasprzak was a designer by trade and was much more involved in product development and branding. The death of Toosbuy triggered considerations about future development becoming more market oriented. Thinghuus commented: "Evidently, we may learn something from the marketing oriented firms [Nike, Reebok and Adidas]. We should aim at becoming better at telling what we stand for. We cannot expect that

▍[4]*Børsen,* February 20, 1998.

Exhibit 1   ECCO's Financial Highlights 1999 To 2004

ECCO's consolidated financial highlights and key ratios 1999–2004

(DKK million)	1999	2000	2001	2002	2003	2004
Net revenue	2,552	2,836	3,216	3,360	3,169	3,394
Profit before amortization and depreciation	409	560	416	343	370	448
Amortization and	−106	−143	−167	−187	−189	−181
Profit before financials	302	416	249	156	182	267
Net financials	−25	−112	−93	−73	−61	−61
Profit before tax	277	305	156	82	120	206
Group profit	195	216	123	60	71	164
Profit for the year	185	208	115	51	62	151
Key ratios (%)						
Operating margin	11.9	14.7	7.8	4.6	5.7	7.9
Return on assets	11.7	10.6	5	2.8	4.3	7
ROIC	12.7	14.5	8.1	5.3	6.5	9.1
Investment ratio	3.3	2.2	1.5	1.2	1.2	1.2
Return on equity	28.9	25.7	12.4	5.3	6.5	15.2
Solvency ratio	30.9	31.1	31.4	33	34.1	35.1
Liquidity ratio	1.8	1.9	2.1	2	1.9	2
Pairs of shoes sold (millions)	9.160	9.603	10.14	10.65	11.22	12.04
Number of employees (2004)	8,290	8,853	9,087	8,839	9,388	9,657
Sold shoes per employee	**1,104**	**1,084**	**1,116**	**1,205**	**1,195**	**1,247**

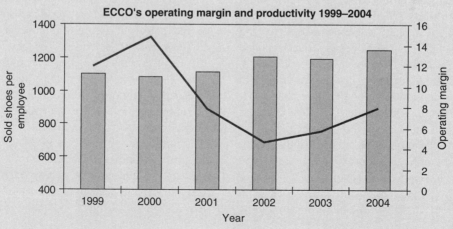

Source: ECCO annual reports 1999–2004.

Exhibit 2   Composition of Management Board as of 2004

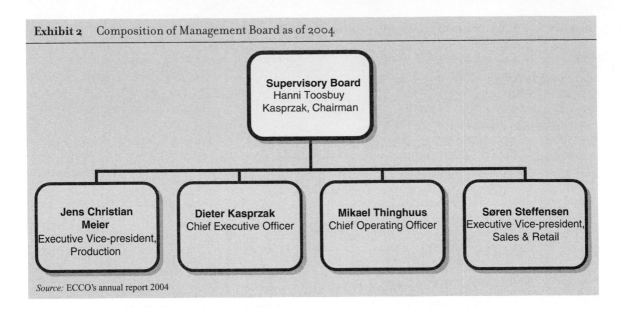

Source: ECCO's annual report 2004

our unique production technology will last an eternity."[5]

ECCO's Global Value Chain

ECCO maintained focus on the entire value chain or from "cow to shoe" as the company liked to put it. ECCO bought raw hides and transformed these into various kinds of leather usable in shoe manufacturing. Leather constituted the main material in shoe uppers which were produced at ECCO's production sites (see **Exhibits 3** and **4**). The company owned several tanneries in the Netherlands, Thailand (opened in 1999) and Indonesia, which supplied leather to ECCO's factories all over the world. ECCO's 2001 acquisition of the largest tannery in the Netherlands, followed by a tannery and leather research centre in 2002, made it possible to access leading expert knowledge about tanning. ECCO's Dutch tannery manufactured around 3,500 rawhides a day, corresponding to approximately one million cows per year. Apart from providing ECCO's factories with "wetblue" (see **Exhibit 3**), the development and research centre's main task was to explore

less polluting tanning methods and experiment with various kinds of leather for the coming generation of ECCO shoes. The centre employed 15 specialists who were also responsible for training employees from Thailand and Indonesia, allowing new technology and improved tannery methods to be disseminated. ECCO was among the five largest producers of leather worldwide. The majority of the rawhides originated from Germany, France, Denmark and Finland. Apart from supplying leather to its shoe factories around the world, it also sold leather to the auto and furniture industries. Explaining ECCO's tanning activities, Toosbuy commented: "To us, it is a matter of the level of ambition. We make high demands on quality and lead times—higher than any of our suppliers have been able to accommodate. In essence, we really do not have an alternative to being self-sufficient."[6]

In addition, the plan was to set up a tannery in conjunction with the factories in China. ECCO's strategy was quite unique, as most of its competitors had phased out in-house production. Companies like Clarks and Timberland had followed Nike's

---

[5]*Berlingske News Magazine,* March 7, 2004.

[6]*Jyllands-Posten,* May 22, 2002.

Exhibit 3 ECCO's Value Chain and Explanation of Tannery Operation

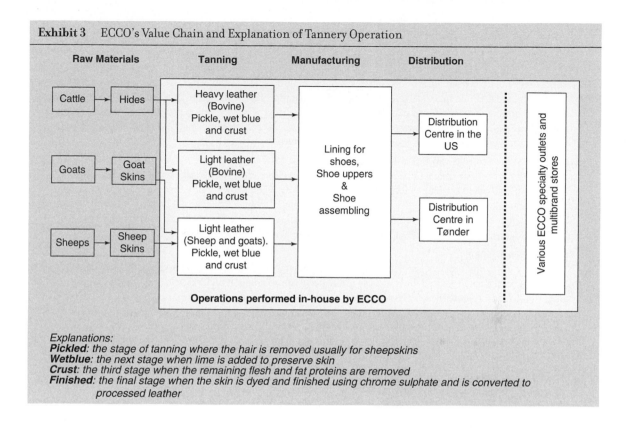

Explanations:
Pickled: the stage of tanning where the hair is removed usually for sheepskins
Wetblue: the next stage when lime is added to preserve skin
Crust: the third stage when the remaining flesh and fat proteins are removed
Finished: the final stage when the skin is dyed and finished using chrome sulphate and is converted to
processed leather

marketing oriented business model by outsourcing the production to a large extent. These companies were described as branded marketers, i.e., manufacturers without factories, who only design and market their goods. While Timberland produced approximately 10 percent of its shoes in-house, Clarks had completely outsourced its production. ECCO, by contrast, produced 80 percent of its shoes in-house. The remaining 20 percent were outsourced as these shoes (for instance, ladies' shoes with thin soles and certain types of sport shoes) contained specific features that would not benefit from ECCO's "direct injected" technology.

ECCO's production process could be divided into five strategic roles or phases: full-scale, benchmarking, ramp-up, prototype and laboratory production. The objectives of full-scale production

were to uphold demand, quality and operational reliability, and still produce high volumes. Benchmarking production, on the other hand, strove to retain knowledge and competencies in terms of opportunities for improvements and production cost structure. ECCO had full-scale production units in Portugal, Indonesia, Thailand, Slovakia and China (in operation from March 2005). A logical consequence of ECCO's control of their value chain was that benchmarking served more to evaluate such aspects as the production unit in Portugal, *vis-à-vis* the plant in Slovakia, than to establish parameters upon which to evaluate external partners. The ramp-up process encompassed the set-up for the production system at large, such as running an assembly system based on new technology. While the newest technology came from Bredebro, Denmark,

Exhibit 4   Converting Skin and Hides into Leather

Steps in leather production

The production of leather from hides and skins involves the treatment of raw materials, i.e., the conversion of the raw hide or skin, a putrecible material, into leather, a stable material. This material is obtained after passing through the different treatment and processing steps described in points 1 to 4. The production processes in a tannery can be divided into four main categories, though the processes employed in each of these categories may change, depending on the raw material used and the final goods that are to be produced.

1. Hides and Skins Storage and Beam-house Operations

Upon delivery, hides and skins can be sorted, trimmed, cured (when the raw material cannot be processed immediately) and stored pending operations in the beam house. The following processes are typically carried out in the beam house of a tannery: soaking, de-haring, liming, fleshing (mechanical scraping off of the excessive organic material) and splitting (mechanically splitting regulates the thickness of hides and skins, splitting them horizontally into a grain layer, and, if the hide is thick enough, a flesh layer).

2. Tannery Operations

Typically the following processes are carried out in the tannery: de-liming, bating, pickling and tanning. Once pickling has been carried out to reduce the pH of the pelt prior to tanning, pickled pelts, i.e., sheepskins can be traded. In the tanning process the collagen fibre is stabilized by the tanning agents so that the hide (the raw material) is no longer susceptible to putrefaction. The two main categories of tanning agents are minerals (trivalent chromium salts) and vegetable (quebracho and mimosa). The tanned hides and skins, once they have been converted to a non-putrescible material called leather, are tradable as intermediate products (wetblue). However, if leather is to be used to manufacture consumer products, it needs further processing and finishing.

3. Post-Tanning Operations

Post-tanning operations generally involve washing out the acids that are still present in the leather following the tanning process. According to the desired leather type to be produced the leather is retanned (to improve the feel and handle of leathers), dyed with water-soluble dyestuffs (to produce even colours over the whole surface of each hide and skin), fat liquored (leathers must be lubricated to achieve product-specific characteristics and to re-establish the fat content lost in the previous procedures) and finally dried. After drying, the leather may be referred to as crust, which is a tradable intermediate product. Operations carried out in the beam house, the tannery, and the post-tanning areas are often referred to as wet processing, as they are performed in processing vessels filled with water to which the necessary chemicals are added to produce the desired reaction. After post-tanning the leather is dried and subsequent operations are referred to as dry processing. Typically, hides and skins are traded in the salted state, or, increasingly, as intermediate products, particularly in the wetblue condition for bovine hides and the pickled condition for ovine skins.

4. Finishing Operations

The art of finishing is to give the leather as thin a finish as possible without harming the known characteristics of leather, such as its look and its ability to breathe. The aim of this process is to treat the upper (grain) surface to give it the desired final look. By grounding (applying a base coat to leather to block pores before applying the true finish coats), coating, seasoning, embossing (to create a raised design upon a leather surface by pressure from a heated engraved plate or roller) and ironing (to pass a heated iron over the grain surface of the leather to smooth it and/or to give it a glossy appearance) the leather will have, as desired by fashion, a shiny or matt, single or multi-coloured, smooth or clearly grained surface. The overall objective of finishing is to enhance the appearance of the leather and to provide the appropriate performance characteristics in terms of colour, gloss, and handling, among others.

Source: A Blueprint for the African Leather Industry—a development, investment and trade guide for the leather industry in Africa, UNIDO 2004, p. 17.

the actual establishment of the production system, including the streamlining of processes and the specific volumes of various kinds of materials, took place in ECCO's foreign production units. The development of new products, prototypes and laboratory production technologies, was carried out at ECCO's production site in Denmark. In particular, ECCO's research centre, Futura in Tønder, Denmark, experimented with new materials, processes and technologies. Over the years ECCO had seen a sharp division of tasks between Denmark and various foreign production sites. Earlier operations in Denmark had encompassed all design, prototype, ramp-up, quality control, branding, marketing and most research and development (R&D) aspects, while ECCO foreign plants performed volume production. For instance, ECCO had split up R&D activities relocating many activities to the production sites, which evidently were more in touch with ECCO's R&D efforts from a practical perspective. The R&D activities conducted at the production sites revolved around support for the production process and optimization of materials.

ECCO's full-scale production process involved both manual labor and capital-intensive machinery. Normally, the uppers were cut by hydraulic presses called clicking machines, although at times hand cutting was used in the manufacture of shoes made of fine leather (see **Exhibit 5**). The upper was then attached to the insole with adhesives, tacks, and staples. Applying advanced machinery, the uppers were then placed in an injection-molding machine where the shoe bottom, including the outsole and heel, was attached to the uppers under very high pressure. Lastly, each pair of shoes went through the finishing process using various operations such as bottom securing and edge trimming which improved the durability and appearance of the shoe. According to ECCO's estimates, each pair of shoes comprised approximately 30 minutes of manual labor.

ECCO's tannery operations revolved around similar phases including prototype, laboratory and ramp-up production of leather, which took place in the Netherlands. The full-scale processing of

leather took place in tanneries in Indonesia and Thailand. ECCO's maintaining ownership of the tannery operations not only reflected the company's commitment to quality but also illustrated a high level of ambition and confidence. ECCO's profound belief that "we cannot get the best quality if we do not do it ourselves," as often stated by Toosbuy, still permeated the company's business philosophy in 2005.

Although design and product development processes were generally conducted by the head office in Bredebro, Denmark, at times the division between the different phases was not clear-cut. For instance, the design and development of shoe uppers happened with the strong involvement of the subsidiary in Indonesia in order to transform the design into high-quality, comfortable shoe uppers. Prior to beginning actual production for the next season, the subsidiary in Indonesia was required to make production samples. ECCO's marketing team would screen the samples to forecast volumes and style of production. Based on the sales forecast headquarters would allocate production orders among its network of subsidiaries and licensees. The production of shoe uppers itself generally involved significant manual work. When the shoe uppers were completed they were shipped by sea to another group's facilities for subsequent processing according to the allocation set by headquarters. Finished shoes were distributed via the group's distribution centre and sales agents.

ECCO's distribution system was also vital to its business. ECCO had two main distribution centres; one in the United States and one in Tønder, Denmark. The latter was expanded in 2001 with four additional warehouses totaling 9,000 square meters, doubling the capacity from one million to two million pairs of shoes. The majority of ECCO's shoe production went through Tønder, however, over the last years only between six and nine per cent of total production was actually sold on the Danish market. The consolidation of distribution in Tønder also involved the closure of ECCO's distribution centre in Brøndby, Denmark and the warehouse in Bredebro, Denmark. The majority of shoe

Exhibit 5   Illustration of Different Components in the Construction of ECCO's Walkathon Shoe

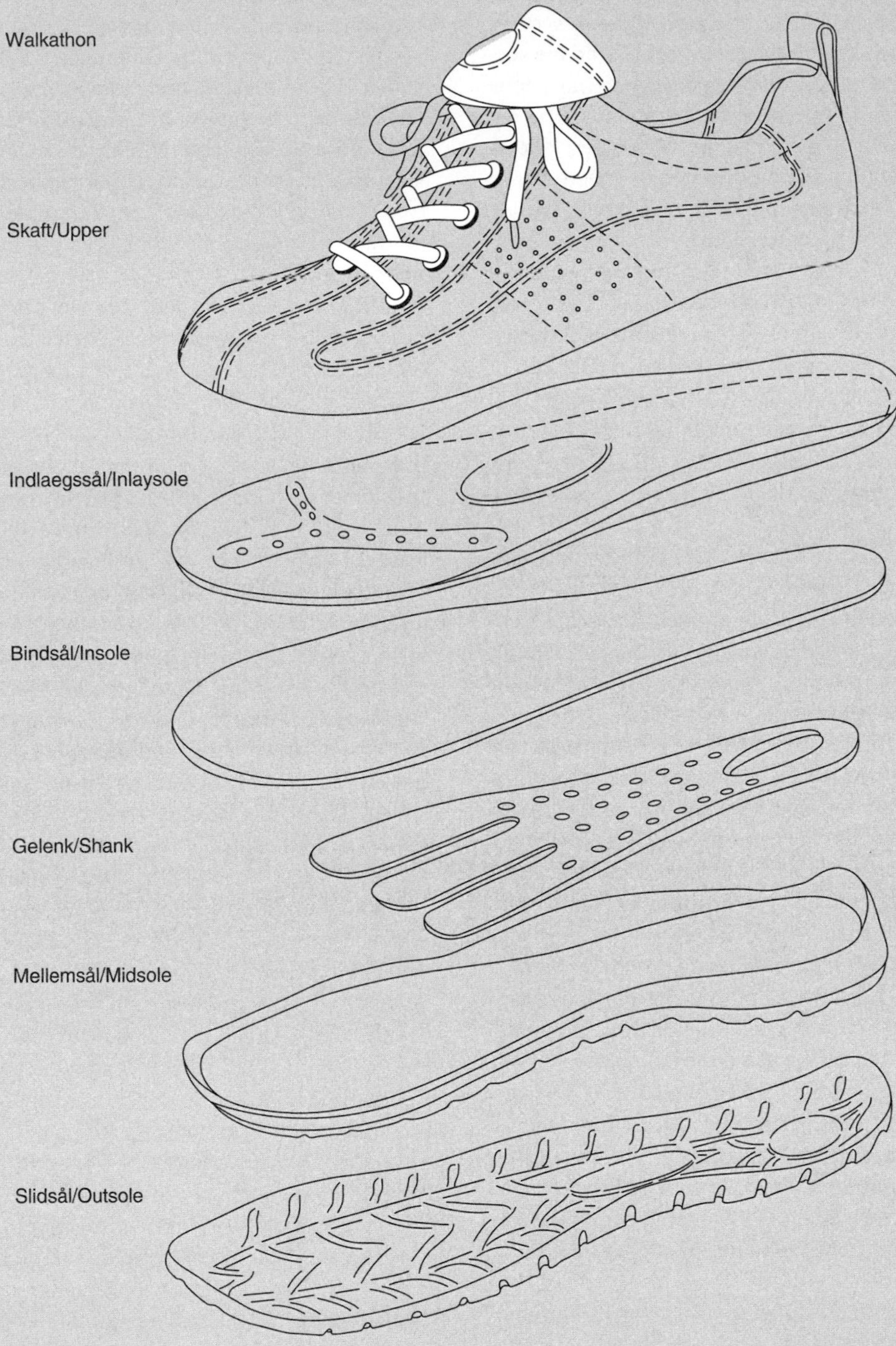

Walkathon

Skaft/Upper

Indlaegssål/Inlaysole

Bindsål/Insole

Gelenk/Shank

Mellemsål/Midsole

Slidsål/Outsole

Source: ECCO internal illustration

shipments arrived through the harbor of Aarhus, Denmark but ECCO also utilized vans for transportation and freight planes in urgent cases. Through the use of a bar code system the distribution centre was able to ship 60,000 pairs of shoes per day by lorry to 25 countries. Shoes for markets outside Europe were shipped by sea.

Recent developments within the shoe business had resulted in retailers ordering a larger proportion of shoes in advance. Retailers typically ordered 75 to 80 per cent of ECCO's production in advance of the season, while 20 to 25 per cent of orders aimed to fill up a retailer's stock. These replenishment orders had to be delivered with only a few days notice.

Production Technology

Since its foundation, ECCO emphasized production technology as a key asset to the company. The founder was, above all, known and recognized for his profound knowledge of inventing and fine-tuning cutting edge production techniques. The core of ECCO's product strategy was shoes based on "direct injection" technology. In simple terms, the shoe uppers were attached to the sole under very high pressure utilizing very capital-intensive machinery. In contrast, both the sewing of uppers and the final finish before shoes left the factory were performed manually. Competitors had tried for a long time to apply the same techniques or to license ECCO's production techniques, however, ECCO performed many small tasks differently throughout the process which improved quality and made it hard to imitate. Of a total production of 12 million pairs of shoes in 2004, 80 per cent were based on the direct injection technology. The remaining pairs, mostly shoes with very thin soles, were outsourced as they would not benefit from ECCO's core technology. Kasprzak's vision was to make individually based shoes fine-tuned to each customer. As he stated: "Our strength is our technology and our ability to produce high-tech products. I believe that we can be the first in the world to produce individual shoes in terms of design and instant fit by applying the newest technology."[7]

As a result of the importance of ECCO's production methods and the fact that production was kept in-house, in 1980 ECCO began cooperating closely with Main Group, an Italian company specialized in injection machine molds and services for footwear. In 2002, Main Group started operations in China and ECCO expected to benefit from cheaper Main Group machines when initiating its production in China in spring 2005.

Internationalization of Production

Following a decade of tremendous growth ECCO's first steps towards globalization occurred through exports and the establishment of upper production in Brazil in 1974. Since then, the main forces driving ECCO's internationalization have been i) establishment of a market presence, and ii) reduction of labor costs and increasing flexibility. ECCO was one of the offshoring pioneers in Danish manufacturing. Over a period of 25 years, ECCO established 26 sales subsidiaries covering the entire world and four international production units. The objective of these establishments, apart from achieving labor cost savings, was to spread risk. Initially, the various production sites were capable of producing the same types of shoes, indicating an insignificant degree of specialization in the production units. However, in recent years ECCO had strived to narrow each unit and capitalize on its core competencies (see **Exhibits 6** and **7**). The early internationalization process affected the composition of employees—by 2004 only 553 worked in Denmark while 9,104 worked outside of Denmark (see **Exhibit 8**). Of these, 8,094 worked in production, while 1,010 worked in sales.

Portugal   ECCO's first relocation of production occurred in 1984 with part of production being moved to Portugal. Although Portugal traditionally

[7]*Berlingske Tidende,* September 5, 2004.

Exhibit 6 ECCO's Production Output Worldwide 2000–2004

	2004	2003	2002	2001	2000
Bredebro, Denmark (1963)					
Activity: Shoe factory. Development and preparation of new articles and prototype testing.					
No. of employees: 124					
- Uppers produced (pairs)	3,805	3,720	4,482	5,281	—
- Shoes produced (pairs)	20,577	38,000	211,413	478,674	800,605
Santa Maria da Feria, Portugal (1984)					
Activity: Shoe factory. Production of uppers and shoes. No. of employees: 720					
- Uppers produced (pairs)	20,737	79,690	241,961	438,299	535,200
- Shoes produced (pairs)	2,649,178	2,442,395	2,590,327	3,769,754	4,150,000
Surabaya, Indonesia (1991)					
Activity: Tannery and shoe factory. Production of wetblue, crust, leather, uppers and shoes.					
No. of employees: 3554					
- Wetblue produced (ft^2)	18,249,560	15,970,001	15,338,582	8,432,162	11,134,743
- Leather produced (ft^2)	15,098,971	14,062,152	12,048,197	15,566,070	15,104,307
- Uppers produced (pairs)	5,326,300	4,664,023	4,063,840	3,968,559	3,750,000
- Shoes produced (pairs)	246,018	29,119	—	—	220,000
Ayudhthaya, Thailand (1993)					
Activity: Tannery and shoe factory. Production of crust, leather, uppers and shoes.					
No. of employees: 2775					
- Leather produced (ft^2)	10,095,425	9,138,590	8,046,037	8,291,589	5,800,000
- Uppers produced (pairs)	3,237,054	2,868,227	2,708,639	2,891,591	3,150,000
- Shoes produced (pairs)	3,910,382	3,319,623	3,264,747	3,102,710	3,200,000
Martin, Slovakia (1998)					
Activity: Shoe factory. Production of uppers and shoes. No. of employees: 824					
- Uppers produced (pairs)	163,297	259,136	792,473	287,694	130,000
- Shoes produced (pairs)	2,771,025	2,265,312	1,974,408	1,657,498	1,500,000
Dongen, The Netherlands (2001)					
Activity: Tannery. Production of wetblue. Leather and development centre. Acquired by ECCO in 2001.					
No. of employees: 79					
- Wetblue produced (ft^2)	19,931,818	26,704,106	30,886,062	23,686,640	

Source: ECCO's environmental report 2004

held a leading position in both the production of uppers and shoe assembly, ECCO then relocated some of these processes to production sites in Thailand and Indonesia in 1993 and 1991, respectively. Few uppers were produced in Portugal and the number of shoes leaving the factory decreased substantially from 2000 to 2004 (see Exhibit 7). In addition, in response to increasing labor costs, ECCO strove to make the Portuguese unit more high-tech, thereby decreasing the number of employees. While the Portuguese unit was more capital intensive, the focus on technology had transformed the plant into ECCO's leading developer within laser-technology.

Exhibit 7   ECCO's Production Output Worldwide 2000–2004

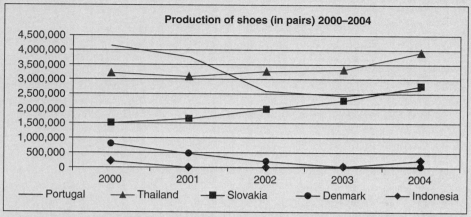

Production of shoes (in pairs) 2000–2004

Legend: Portugal — Thailand ▲ — Slovakia ■ — Denmark ● — Indonesia ◆

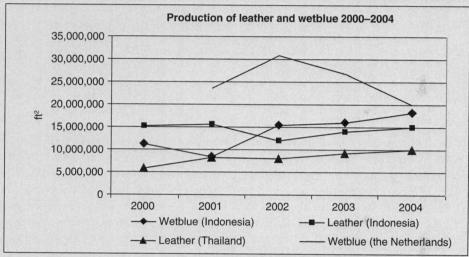

Production of leather and wetblue 2000–2004

ft²

Legend: Wetblue (Indonesia) ◆ — Leather (Indonesia) ■ — Leather (Thailand) ▲ — Wetblue (the Netherlands)

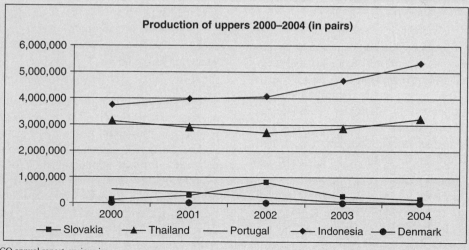

Production of uppers 2000–2004 (in pairs)

Legend: Slovakia ■ — Thailand ▲ — Portugal — Indonesia ◆ — Denmark ●

Source: ECCO annual report, various issues

Exhibit 8   Employee Statistics—Geographical Composition 1980–2004

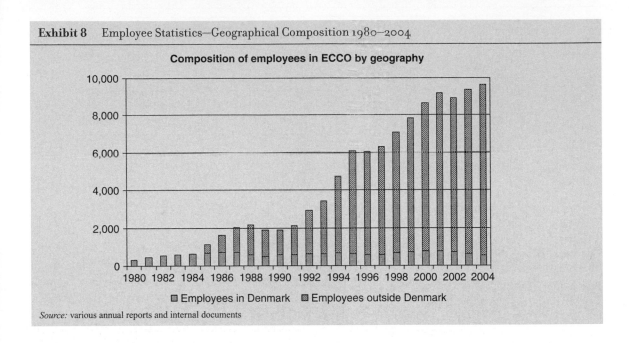

Composition of employees in ECCO by geography

☐ Employees in Denmark   ▨ Employees outside Denmark

Source: various annual reports and internal documents

Indonesia The Indonesian production unit, opened in 1991, specialized in producing shoe uppers for the ECCO group, while the finishing processes, such as attaching shoe uppers to soles, were undertaken in other facilities of the group. The production unit in Indonesia satisfied approximately 40 to 50 per cent of the group's shoe upper demand. In shoe production, the main materials required were rawhides (procured locally as well as imported) that were processed into semi-finished and finished leather. Other materials required for production included reinforcement, yarn and accessories. Apart from the leather, the majority of the materials (70 to 80 per cent) were obtained from European suppliers, in particular granulate and Gore-Tex. Procurement of raw material took eight weeks from the placement of the order until materials were ready to be shipped, and another five weeks for sea shipment.

Thailand ECCO's production facility in Thailand, opened in 1993, encompassed both tannery and assembling facilities. In 2004, the site produced roughly 37 per cent of the uppers, primarily

for shoe assembly in Thailand where 40 per cent of total unit volume was produced. ECCO's production site in Thailand was rather successful in terms of output, employee satisfaction and size. Over the years, the number of employees increased substantially and annual employee turnover was less than seven per cent. Moreover, the Thais had a good eye for small details and were able to deliver first class workmanship. These characteristics led ECCO to concentrate the production of its most complicated shoes in Thailand, including golf shoes and its advanced trekking boots.

Slovakia Opened in 1998, ECCO's production unit in Slovakia primarily assembled shoes and, to a lesser extent, uppers. The plant employed 824 people in 2004 and produced shoes primarily within the men's segment. The underlying rationale for setting up production in Slovakia, apart from lower labor costs, was the country's proximity to promising markets like Russia and Poland. Prior to entering Slovakia, Toosbuy stated: "We need bigger production capacity and quicker deliveries. Our goal is to increase production capacity by 15 per cent per year. One of our challenges associated with production in Asia is the three to four week transportation time."[8] Years later, ECCO's executive production director, Flemming Brønd, added:

> Shoe manufacturing is labor intensive, thus the wage level is of paramount importance. We already had a factory in Portugal yet we were searching for an optimal location for a new plant in Europe as labor costs were raising in Portugal. We have the majority of our uppers flown in from Indonesia and India after which the shoes are assembled. Although we automated the assembly process by using robots, we still needed skilled labor to handle the machines.[9]

Having established production facilities in Slovakia, ECCO set up a production network in close proximity to the company's major markets. This facility also provided some leeway in terms of driving up volume between plants, thereby alleviating the risks of an interruption in production due, for instance, to political unrest in Thailand. Despite ECCO's global production facilities the plant in Bredebro, Denmark still constituted ECCO's primary model in terms of the development of cutting edge production technology.

China ECCO's establishment of production facilities in China was by no means a spontaneous act. Toosbuy had, on various occasions, visited China to assess locations and the timing of entry. China's recent membership of the World Trade Organization (WTO) allowed for 100 per cent foreign ownership of production sites. This, combined with the fact that approximately 50 per cent of the world's shoe production took place in China, made the country too important to ignore. ECCO chose a site in Xiamen just north of the province of Guangdong, which Kasprzak described as "a smaller yet dynamic community where we have been very well received and provided good and competent service from the local authorities." The plan was to build five factories over the next five years, as well as a very advanced

tannery including a beam house to convert rawhides. Total investment including tanneries would amount to approximately DKK 500 million. When realized, the Chinese production site would become ECCO's largest worldwide, delivering some five million pairs of shoes annually. Although mostly targeted for export, one of the factories would serve the Chinese market exclusively. ECCO expected to employ around 3,000 people in China.

Although low labor costs and taxes were considered, access to local manpower was the decisive factor when establishing operations in China. "Taxes are more or less the same in different zones so it did not influence our location decision as such. On the other hand it was important to us that Xiamen could provide local employees who we can train and keep for a longer period of time which is definitely not the case in other places in China."[10]

ECCO had high hopes for sales to the Chinese consumers as well. Over the next three years, the company hoped to double sales to 500,000 pairs. To realize this ambition, a formal sales subsidiary had been formed together with Aibu, ECCO's long-standing partner in China. Over the last eight years their partnership had evolved from one shop to selling approximately 250,000 pairs of shoes targeted at the segment for exclusive shoes. The plan was to strengthen collaborative ties even further through a combination of Aibu's unique market knowledge and position in the Chinese market together with ECCO's strong brand and accumulated experiences with positioning shoes on a global scale. In fact, the experience from other Danish design icons operating in China suggested a network approach to gain the loyalty of the Chinese consumers. However, the approach was not without risks as it involved being complaisant while at the same time keeping critical knowledge close to the chest until formal contracts had been signed. During 2003/2004, ECCO had been plagued by Chinese manufacturers copying the ECCO design. According to Søren Steffensen, executive vice-president of sales, every single case

---

[8]*Berlingske Tidende,* February 2, 1998.
[9]*Jyllands-Posten,* December 12, 2003.

[10]Assistant General Manager, Morten Bay Jensen.

was pursued and handled by a special unit of attorneys at ECCO whose primary task was to protect the company's brand and design.

The Competitive Landscape

Generally, the market for lifestyle casual footwear was highly competitive and subject to changes in consumer preferences. Fierce competition had sparked investments in both cost optimization and new technologies. First, the quest for competitive pricing had driven the search for new ways of producing and assembling in order to lower costs and reduce time to market. Operations were streamlined and formerly manual processes were automated. Second, incumbents invested in new technology, improved customer service, and market knowledge.

Traditionally, the footwear industry had been fragmented yet in recent years the distinction between athletic and lifestyle casual footwear blurred. Financially strong athletic shoe companies, like Nike and Reebok, competed directly with some of ECCO's products. On the other hand, ECCO's expansion into such new segments as golf shoes gave rise to new competitors. In addition, the industry felt increasing pressure from retailers that had established products under private labels. As a consequence of the fuzzy boundaries between different footwear product categories and geographical regions, pinpointing ECCO's competitors was a challenge. However, ECCO itself regarded Geox, Clarks and Timberland as its main competitive threats worldwide (see **Exhibit 9**).

Geox By all measures the Italian shoemaker Geox constituted a competitive threat to ECCO's operations in the casual lifestyle footwear segment. Founded in 1994 by the Italian entrepreneur Mario

---

Exhibit 9   Global Sales of Lifestyle Casual Footwear Brand Sales (In US$ Million) 2002–2003

Rank	Company	2002	2003	% Change
1	Clarks	1,399	1,534	9.6%
		29.2%	29.6%	
2	ECCO	502	590	17.5%
		10.5%	11.4%	
3	Rockport	385	361	6.2%
		8.0%	7.0%	
4	Geox	208	329	58.2%
		4.3%	6.3%	
5	Birkenstock	270	300	11.1%
		5.6%	5.8%	
6	Bass	275	285	3.6%
		5.7%	5.5%	
7	Caterpillar	209	210	0.5%
		4.4%	4.0%	
8	Doc Martens	295	195	−34.0%
		6.2%	3.8%	
	Others	1,252	1,383	
		26.1%	26.7%	
	Total	**$4,795**	**$5,187**	**8.2%**

Note: Timberland is not included in the table. The company offers footwear across different categories including rugged footwear and athletic footwear as well as casual lifestyle footwear.

Moretti Polegato, Geox achieved impressive growth rates, increasing sales from €147.6 million in 2001 to €340.1 million in 2004, corresponding to a compound annual growth rate (CAGR) of 32 per cent. The success of Geox was based on perforated rubber soles in which a special waterproof and breathable membrane was inserted, allowing the vapor from perspiration to leave but still preventing water from entering the shoe—a technology protected by over 30 patents. Geox's headquarters and R&D facilities were located in the centre of a large shoe-making area northwest of Venice—Montebelluna. Geox had its own production facilities in Slovakia and Romania and outsourced to manufacturers in China, Vietnam and Indonesia. The entire production process and logistics were closely monitored in-house from headquarters in Italy.

In terms of distribution, Geox operated with a business model similar to ECCO's. The company's shoes were sold in more than 60 countries through a worldwide distribution network of more than 230 single-brand Geox Shop stores and about 8,000 multibrand points of sale.

Geox had global ambitions. The company still had a strong penetration in the Italian market, which generated approximately 55 per cent of sales. International sales were gaining momentum, however, comprising 45 per cent in 2004, with Germany, France, Iberia (Spain and Portugal) and the United States being the largest markets. Geox increased sales by 250 per cent from 2002 (US$4 million) to 2003 (US$14 million) in the very competitive American market. As a comparison, ECCO grew only 4.5 per cent in this market with sales of US$115 million in 2003 (see **Exhibit 10**). Although extremely successful, Geox planned to enter clothing in order to circumvent sudden shifts in consumer tastes.

Clarks   Clarks, the English shoemaker, was the biggest player within the casual lifestyle footwear segment achieving global sales of US$1,534 million in 2003 (see Exhibit 9). Since its humble beginnings in 1825, Clarks had grown into a global shoemaker producing 35 million pairs and offering a wide

product portfolio under the slogan "from career wear to weekend wear." Clarks' product portfolio included casual, dress casual, boots and sandals. Central to various categories were Clarks' widely used technical features like "active air" (an air-cushioning technology) and "waterproof (impermeable membrane sewn inside the boot), which sought to improve comfort, performance and versatility.

Clarks, like other shoe manufacturers, had vigorously sought lower labor costs in response to fierce competition. The company once had 15 plants across the United Kingdom but by 2005 only one small factory with 37 employees remained in Millom, Cumbria. The most recent closure occurred in early 2005 when the company shifted production to independent factories in Vietnam, Romania and China. According to company spokesman John Keery, this move was vital to ensuring that the business remained financially viable. As he stated: "The cost of manufacturing in the UK has increased over the last 20 years and we have been able to source our shoes cheaper in the Far East."[11] Based on cost considerations, availability of materials and capacity issues within individual countries, Clarks sourced shoes from 12 different manufacturers located primarily in Asia. Clarks kept less than one per cent of its production in-house. By using many independent manufacturers, Clarks was exposed to a variety of technologies, materials and shoemaking techniques and thus could access various types of expertise. However, monitoring material standard and product quality was an enormous task.

Timberland   Founded in Boston in 1918 by Nathan Swartz, Timberland designed, marketed and distributed under the Timberland® and Timberland PRO® brands. Their products included footwear and apparel and accessories products for men, women and children. Having introduced the waterproof boot based on injection-molding technology

---

[11]www.bbc.co.uk/somerset/content/articles/2005/01/10/clarks_feature.shtml , accessed March 2005.

Exhibit 10   U.S. Sales of Lifestyle Casual Footwear Brand Sales (In US$ Million) 2002–2003

Rank	Company	2002	2003	% Change
1	Clarks	339	375	10.6%
		18.8%	21.5%	
2	Rockport	291	266	−8.6%
		16.2%	15.2%	
3	Bass	258	265	2.7%
		14.3%	15.2%	
4	Doc Martens	195	127	−34.9%
		10.8%	7.3%	
5	ECCO	110	115	4.5%
		6.1%	6.6%	
6	Birkenstock	110	80	−27.3%
		6.1%	4.6%	
7	Dansko	62	71	14.5%
		3.4%	4.1%	
8	Mephisto	55	55	0.0%
		3.1%	3.1%	
9	Sperry	49	53	8.2%
		2.7%	3.0%	
10	Josef Seibel	33	35	6.1%
		1.8%	2.0%	
11	Catterpillar	33	30	−9.1%
		1.8%	1.7%	
12	Sebago	20	16	−20.0%
		1.1%	0.9%	
13	Geox	4	14	250.0%
		0.2%	0.8%	
14	Stonefly	10	11	10.0%
		0.6%	0.6%	
15	FinnComfort	10	11	10.0%
		0.6%	0.6%	
	Others	220	224	
		12.2%	12.8%	
	Total	**$1,799**	**$1,748**	**−2.8%**

Source: JP Morgan—Apparel and Footwear Yearbook 2003

in 1973, Timberland's primary strength resided within the outdoor boot category, which competed with ECCO's outdoor and sport product categories. In 1978 and 1979, Timberland added casual and boat shoes to its line to become more than just a boot company. In the eighties, the company strived to be recognized as a lifestyle brand and entered Italy as the first international market. During the 1990s, Timberland introduced kids' footwear and launched the Timberland PRO® series designed for maximum surface contact and targeted at skilled tradesmen and working professionals.

Timberland's 2003 total revenue of US$1.328 million was comprised of footwear (76.7 per cent) and apparel and accessories (23.3 per cent), making Timberland twice the size of ECCO in terms of product sales. Despite the company's late appearance in international markets, international sales comprised 38.5 per cent of total generated revenue—up from 29.5 per cent in 2001. Timberland's products in the United States and internationally were sold through independent retailers, department stores, athletic stores, Timberland specialty stores and factory outlets dedicated exclusively to Timberland products. In Europe, products were sold mostly through franchised retail stores.

In terms of manufacturing, Timberland operated production facilities in Puerto Rico and the Dominican Republic. Contrary to ECCO, which on average produced 80 per cent of its shoes in-house, Timberland manufactured only 10 per cent of total unit volume with the remainder of the footwear production being performed by independent manufactures in China, Vietnam and Thailand. Timberland believed that attaining some internal manufacturing capabilities, such as refined production techniques, planning efficiencies and lead time reduction, might prove beneficial when collaborating with manufactures in Asia. To facilitate this collaboration, Timberland set up a quality management group to develop, review and update the company's quality and production standards in Bangkok, Zhu Hai, Hong Kong and Ho Chi Minh City (Saigon).

In terms of leather supplies, Timberland purchased from an independent web of 60 suppliers who were subject to rigid quality controls. This required substantial resources in order to scrutinize and monitor the supplier network. Analysts argued that Timberland was vulnerable to price increases on raw materials. Gross margins were negatively affected by increases in the cost of leather as selling prices did not increase proportionally. Shoe manufacturers like Timberland found it difficult to pass on the extra cost to the consumer. In order to diminish the effect of increasing prices for leather and other materials, Timberland was forced to closely monitor the market prices and interact closely with suppliers to achieve maximum price stability. By 2003, 10 suppliers provided approximately 80 per cent of Timberland's leather purchases.

As the plane approached Copenhagen Airport, Mikael Thinghuus recalled a management board meeting prior to his visit to China. Several viewpoints concerning ECCO's future strategy had been presented and, while no one discredited ECCO's unique production assets, there was a sentiment that advantages accruing from world-class production technologies could not be sustained forever. "We are not going to exist in 20 years time if we cannot excite and cast a spell over our customers," one member of the committee commented. Another added: "We do not operate marketing budgets of the same magnitude as the big fashion brands. But our shoes are produced with an unconditional commitment to quality and our history is truly unique. We need to be better at telling that story." Thinghuus was pondering:

> "We need to be more concrete about the process towards market orientation. How can we relate better to our customers while at the same time being able to exploit efficiencies from a global value chain? Integrated or not. And what about entering new markets? The recent market expansion in China was just the beginning. Long term outlook seemed favorable. Yet, was it feasible to invest in new markets, increase marketing efforts, and optimize a global value chain—all at the same time?"

Irrespective of the outcome of these thoughts, it was pivotal to consider how strategic initiatives would go hand in hand with ECCO's philosophy of integrating the value chain from cow to shoe.

Case 4-3   World Vision International's AIDS Initiative: Challenging a Global Partnership

Christopher A. Bartlett and Daniel F. Curran

On January 19, 2002, Ken Casey, director of World Vision International's HIV/AIDS Hope Initiative, walked into a safari lodge in South Africa to present the final session of a conference attended by 40 senior staff from 17 countries with the highest prevalence of HIV and AIDS in Africa and nearly 20 senior executives from worldwide support offices. As he stretched his back, he felt a sharp pain from wounds he had received during a vicious attack by a baboon on the hotel's patio the day before the conference began. Badly cut and bruised, Casey had staggered to the conference center where he had been wrapped in towels and rushed to a hospital. It had required 135 stitches and 27 staples to close the wounds.

Determined to proceed with the conference, which he saw as a potential turning point in his year-long struggle to get the Hope Initiative off the ground, Casey had returned the next day. Largely driven by the senior leaders of World Vision International, the initiative was an ambitious attempt to implement common goals and strategies in fundraising, programming, and advocacy across the 48 independent members of the World Vision Partnership. But its future was unclear. Not only did its focus on HIV/AIDS represent a major shift in World Vision's programming, but in many ways, the initiative's top-down implementation challenged the federated organization model the partnership had pursued throughout the 1990s. As he

addressed the conference, Casey worried that if it did not go well, the Hope Initiative might well be dead in the water.

Birth of World Vision International

World Vision International was a $1 billion Christian relief and development partnership linking 48 national members in a global federation. In 2002, the partnership raised over $732 million in cash and nearly $300 million in commodities. (See **Exhibit 1** for representative World Vision Partnership financial data.) Almost 50% of World Vision's funding flowed from private sources, mostly through child sponsorship. Governments and multilateral agencies provided the other 50%.

A Visionary Founder: "Faith in Action"
Founded in the United States in August 1950 by Bob Pierce, a Christian evangelist who was moved by the suffering he witnessed in Korea, World Vision was funded by North American Christians whom Pierce connected to individual Korean orphans through photographs and personal correspondence. This innovative sponsorship program—later widely imitated—helped Pierce translate the massive needs he saw in Asia into personal terms in America. In 1952, the organization's first statement of purpose read: "World Vision is a missionary service organization meeting emergency needs in crisis areas of the world through existing evangelical agencies."

Although Pierce cultivated a small, dedicated staff, he called the shots in his young organization. He challenged his team by telling them, "Cut through the reasons why things can't be done. Don't fail to do something just because you can't do everything."[1] With this entrepreneurial attitude,

▌ Professor Christopher A. Bartlett and Daniel F. Curran, Director—Humanitarian Leadership Program, prepared this case. HBS cases are developed solely as the basis for class discussion. Cases are not intended to serve as endorsements, sources of primary data, or illustrations of effective or ineffective management.
▌ Harvard Business School Case No 9-304-105, Copyright 2004 President and Fellows of Harvard College. All rights reserved.
This case was prepared by C. Bartlett. *HBS Cases are developed solely for class discussion and do not necessarily illustrate either effective or ineffective handling of administrative situation.*

[1]Graeme Irvine, *Best Things in the Worst Times: An Insider's View of World Vision* (Wilsonville, OR: World Vision International, 1996), p. 18.

Exhibit 1   World Vision International FY2002 Financial Data

PARTNERSHIP INCOME FY2002
(Offices receiving $200,000 or more in thousands of U.S. dollars)[a]

National Offices	Contributions	Gifts-in-Kind	Total
Armenia	$ 360		$ 360
Australia	78,543	$ 14,844	93,387
Austria	2,121	543	2,664
Brazil	2,786		2,786
Burundi	205		205
Canada	105,656	38,924	144,580
Chad	339		339
Chile	265		265
Colombia	1,041		1,041
Costa Rica	274		274
Finland	1,407	–	1,407
Germany	34,370	2,987	37,357
Haiti	331		331
Hong Kong	25,885	1,237	27,122
India	1,214		1,214
Indonesia	219		219
Ireland	4,538		4,538
Japan	12,055	2,294	14,349
Korea	20,802	1,282	22,084
Malaysia	918		918
Mexico	1,410		1,410
Myanmar	213		213
Netherlands	3,973	372	4,345
New Zealand	13,459	21	13,480
Philippines	505		505
Sierra Leone	1,287		1,287
Singapore	2,615	–	2,615
South Africa	507		507
Switzerland	12,599	704	13,303
Taiwan	31,221	75	31,296
Tanzania	722		722
Thailand	3,707		3,707
United Kingdom	46,529	1,199	47,728
United States	317,744	235,086	552,830
Zambia	1,030		1,030
Other Offices	1,185		1,185
Total Partnership Income	**$732,035**	**$299,568**	**$1,031,603**

[a] In approximate U.S. dollars. Exact amounts depend on time currency exchange is calculated.

(continued)

Exhibit 1   *(continued)*

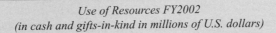

Use of Resources FY2002
(in cash and gifts-in-kind in millions of U.S. dollars)

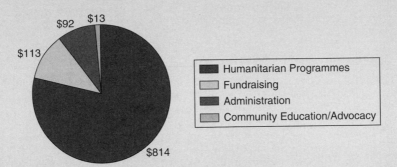

What World Vision's resources accomplish:

Humanitarian Programmes provide for emergency relief in natural and man-made disasters and for development work in food, education, health care, sanitation, income generation and other community needs. Also included are the costs of supporting such programmes in the field.

Fundraising supports humanitarian programmes by soliciting contributions through media and direct marketing appeals. Included are costs of marketing, creative services and publishing materials.

Administration includes donor relations, computer technology, finance, accounting, human resources and managerial oversight.

Community Education/Advocacy promotes awareness of poverty and justice issues through media campaigns, forums, speaking engagements, and public advocacy.

Ministry Support & Programmes by Region FY2002
(in case and gifts-in-kind in millions of U.S. dollars)

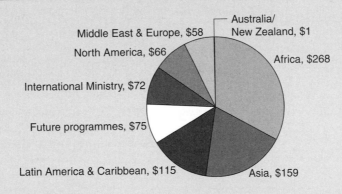

Source: World Vision International 2002 Annual Report.

Pierce soon extended World Vision's work into Hong Kong, Indonesia, Taiwan, India, and Japan.

By the 1960s, World Vision was opening offices in other countries. In 1961, an affiliate office opened in Canada as a separate national entity, and in 1966 a national entity was established in Australia. During this period, it also refined its "child sponsorship" model and, by the mid-1960s, was supporting 15,000 children in Southeast Asia. Responding to church film screenings, radio advertising, and direct-mail appeals, Christians in the United States, Canada, and Australia were promised a loving connection to a poor child in the developing world for a monthly contribution of around $10. Full-time staff and hundreds of volunteers coordinated the delivery of photos and letters between children and sponsors, while more than a dozen marketers created appeals to attract more donors. It was a successful process requiring a great deal of administrative support.

By 1969, World Vision managed $5.1 million in funding of which 80% was delivered to 32,600 children in 388 projects. The remaining 20% supported fund-raising and administrative costs. All funding and most support services flowed through the headquarters offices in Monrovia, California. As the war in Vietnam began absorbing the organization's energy, significant changes in approach occurred. Instead of working through existing orphanages and ministries, World Vision staff opened refugee schools, recruited and trained local teachers, and built houses for the displaced.

A New Leader, A New Approach: The Evolving Mission   Toward the end of the 1960s, however, World Vision began experiencing difficulties. A senior executive described the emerging problems: "Anyone looking at World Vision would see an organization that reflected Bob Pierce himself: action oriented, strongly evangelical, innovative, and progressive. But we had no long-range planning or adequate mechanisms for administration." But Pierce strongly resisted changes that many felt were needed. As money became short, tensions grew between him and his board. Finally, in 1967, Pierce resigned.

Pierce's successor, Stan Mooneyham, was another action-oriented risk taker. With the fall of South Vietnam and Laos and the rise of the Khmer Rouge in Cambodia, World Vision lost contact with much of its program staff in those countries. More importantly, nearly 30,000 sponsors lost contact with their sponsored children. But the four core fund-raising offices—in the United States, Canada, Australia, and New Zealand—found that most of their donors were willing to transfer their assistance to children elsewhere. The organization shifted its focus to Latin America, establishing offices and sponsorship programs in Brazil, Colombia, Ecuador, Guatemala, and Mexico.

At the same time, some in the organization began questioning the sustainability of World Vision's traditional model of selecting and supporting individual children. At a conference in 1971, Gene Daniels, WV director in Indonesia, proposed an alternative model of rural community development. Undeterred by the lukewarm reception his ideas received, for the next two years Daniels quietly experimented with this community development-based approach. As he began to succeed, others voiced an interest. Graeme Irvine, president of World Vision-Australia, supported a shift to longer-term commitments rather than "dump and run" emergency relief. He stated, "Development is not something you do for people. Those who wish to help may walk alongside, but not take over."[2]

Influenced by these voices, in 1972, Mooneyham promised that World Vision would build a Christian Children's Hospital in Phnom Penh. He presented a proposal to the international board but was disappointed to be turned down. Then the presidents of World Vision-Australia and World Vision-New Zealand offered to organize staff and fund the program themselves. Six months later, when World Vision opened the hospital in Phnom Penh, Mooneyham wrote, "The Cambodia medical program was an example of World Vision's emerging international partnership at work. It illustrated our principle of looking for alternative solutions to major problems."[3]

[2]Irvine, p. 71.
[3]Irvine, p. 45.

In 1973, following a series of consultations, the World Vision Board made a commitment to both relief and development in World Vision's mission. But the consensus over becoming a "transform" rather than a "transfer" organization meant significant changes to the structure and governance. "What you are doing in development is according people the dignity of voice and self-determination," stated Irvine. "But a big organization like World Vision has all kinds of baggage—bureaucracy, systems, reports, layers of authority, policies and many committees—that got in the way of development. How would we work as a partnership?"[4]

Moving Toward Partnership: Forming WVI
Until the early 1970s, World Vision's U.S. organization, as the founding country and by far the largest contributor, had made most of the significant programming decisions. Under its guidance, the overall organization had expanded beyond Asia and Latin America into Africa and the Middle East. Typically, each initiative had arisen from special circumstances or through initiatives led by interested groups, churches, or individuals.

Increasingly, however, the presidents of Canada, Australia, and New Zealand—the other key fund-raising (support) offices—wanted to move beyond just providing funds to program-delivery (field) offices. They wanted to participate in policy and strategy decisions. "This was not so much a desire for control as it was a need for accountability to donors," explained a World Vision-NZ executive. In 1973, Mooneyham responded by forming a study committee to recommend a basis for "a true partnership among all national entities: a partnership of both structure and spirit."

Over the next few years, the committee met to define the issues and consider the options. "At the core we saw it not as structure or even as process, but an attitude toward each other that did not view one partner as superior to any other," stated one committee member.[5] Finally, in April 1976, the international board unanimously decided to form a new distinct entity, World Vision International (WVI), as the common program-delivery arm of

World Vision's four main fund-raising support offices—the United States, Canada, New Zealand, and Australia. The directors of each sat on the international board. (World Vision-U.S. maintained the World Vision name and trademark but gave its WVI partners the right to use them.) World Vision national entities in developing countries (the field offices delivering the programs) became members of WVI's council but did not have equal-partner status with the four board members. The council agreed to WVI's mission and, in May 1978, adopted a formal declaration of internationalization.

Building the World Vision Partnership: Defining a Federation

To provide coordinated management of the global field operations funded by the core support offices, WVI's council created a central international office, colocated with the World Vision-U.S. office in Los Angeles. However, rather than functioning as a servant to the four council member organizations, it soon became a separate power base. A WVI manager at the time recalled:

> Mooneyham brought all of the bright and creative folks with him to the international office, and this had two unintended consequences. First, as the program-delivery mechanism became the dominant force in the organization, the value and importance of the fund-raising team left in the WV-U.S. was eroded. Second, because this organization separated its "marketing" and "production" functions, each group developed its own culture.

The separation lasted for almost a decade during which time the national directors of the largest support offices, again feeling frustrated at just delivering the funds they raised to the international office, started to demand more of a say in strategy. Said one senior WVI manager, "Our core competitive advantage—what we did particularly well—was our child sponsorship mechanism. It was the most sustainable form of fund-raising, and we had become one of the best in the world at doing it. But, at that time, we did not recognize it. No wonder they were frustrated."

[4]Irvine, p. 72.

[5]Irvine, p. 136.

Challenging Central Control   When Tom Houston became the new president of WVI in 1984, his attention was drawn to the devastating drought in Ethiopia. The global response from donors was staggering. Under agreements with the U.S. government and UN agencies, WVI's Ethiopia response budget grew from $2.3 million in 1984 to $43.4 million in 1986. To manage the funding, World Vision's staff in Ethiopia grew from 100 to 3,650. In the following year, WVI launched 11 large development projects in six other African nations. Because of the need for coordination, all logistics and program functions were managed from the international office, giving even more power to this fast-growing group.

By 1987, World Vision had survived and grown through a decade of expansion. But there was discontent within the organization, and Houston discovered that the unhappy support-office directors were meeting together informally to share their frustrations. "Tom was abrupt and frank and did not like the notion of a dominant person pushing the little guys around," said one executive. "So he turned our culture upside down." To bring the support-office directors into the inner circle, he asked several of them to sit on the international planning committee, the president's primary consultative group on partnership decisions. In addition, he shook up the management of the international office by requiring that all regional vice presidents come from their regions.

But frustration reached a boiling point in August 1987 when national directors responsible for the work in over 60 countries gathered at a director's conference in Sierra Madre, California. When, as was the norm at these events, executives from the international office began to deliver presentations on strategy and operations, three new regional VPs from Brazil, Nigeria, and Egypt stood together. "If this is a director's conference, why are we working on your agenda?" they asked. The directors of the main support offices joined the "revolt." Recognizing the legitimacy of the challenge, Houston surrendered the agenda. Following the conference, 30 senior executives spent a year studying how to redefine the relationship between field and support offices and the international office.

Creating Area Development Programs   Meanwhile, the 11 large-scale development programs World Vision had launched in 1985 were struggling. Each had a budget of more than $1 million, a time span of more than three years, and a geographic scope greater than a single community. The causes of the problems were diagnosed as unrealistic initial expectations, lack of local management and technical expertise, and a top-down planning and control system.

A study commissioned to propose solutions to these problems recommended a new approach that sought to retain the benefits of scale while engaging more local involvement in community-level transformational development. Through the 1990s a new way to work, referred to as the Area Development Program (ADP), became the dominant means of program delivery for World Vision. In Africa, for example, over 300 ADPs were defined, each aiding 50,000 to 200,000 people. Wilfred Mlay, African regional vice president, explained their operation:

> Each ADP is managed by a coordinator from that country who understands the local language and customs. He or she negotiates an agreement with the community for a 10- to 15-year multisectoral engagement, then they sign a contract promising to work together. . . . Before, communities tended to consider the local projects—a bore hole, a school, a health center—as World Vision projects. If something went wrong, they said, "Come and fix your pump. Come and fix your vehicle." There was no ownership. . . . Now we don't just dig wells and provide clean water; we partner with each ADP area to identify root causes of their problems, then we work with them to provide a long-term program that will address the needs they identify. The strength of the approach is in finding local solutions to local problems.

Engaging Federalism   When Houston resigned as WVI's president in 1988, Irvine, former head of World Vision-Australia, took his place. Upon his appointment, Irvine made a commitment to make WVI "a professional, enlightened, efficient and humane organization [that] will nurture a climate of

Exhibit 2   Extracts from World Vision International's Statement of Core values

WE ARE CHRISTIAN.   We acknowledge one God; Father, Son and Holy Spirit. In Jesus Christ the love, mercy and grace of God are made known to us and all people. . . . We seek to follow him—in his identification with the poor, the powerless, the afflicted, the oppressed, the marginalized; in his special concern for children; in his respect for the dignity bestowed by God on women equally with men; in his challenge to unjust attitudes and systems; in his call to share resources with each other; in his love for all people without discrimination or conditions; in his offer of new life through faith in him . . .

WE ARE COMMITTED TO THE POOR.   We are called to serve the neediest people of the earth; to relieve their suffering and to promote the transformation of their condition of life. . . . We respect the poor as active participants, not passive recipients, in this relationship . . .

WE VALUE PEOPLE.   We regard all people as created and loved by God. We give priority to people before money, structure, systems and other institutional machinery. . . . We celebrate the richness of diversity in human personality, culture and contribution. . . . We practice a participative, open, enabling style in working relationships. We encourage the professional, personal and spiritual development of our staff.

WE ARE STEWARDS.   The resources at our disposal are not our own. They are a sacred trust from God through donors on behalf of the poor. We are faithful to the purpose for which those resources are given and manage them in a manner that brings maximum benefit to the poor. . . . We demand of ourselves high standards of professional competence and accept the need to be accountable through appropriate structures for achieving these standards. We share our experience and knowledge with others where it can assist them.

WE ARE PARTNERS.   We are members of an international World Vision Partnership that transcends legal, structural and cultural boundaries. We accept the obligations of joint participation, shared goals and mutual accountability that true partnership requires. We affirm our inter-dependence and our willingness to yield autonomy as necessary for the common good. We commit ourselves to know, understand and love each other. . . . We maintain a co-operative stance and a spirit of openness towards other humanitarian organizations. We are willing to receive and consider honest opinions from others about our work.

WE ARE RESPONSIVE.   We are responsive to life-threatening emergencies where our involvement is needed and appropriate. We are willing to take intelligent risks and act quickly. We do this from a foundation of experience and sensitivity to what the situation requires. We also recognize that even in the midst of crisis, the destitute have a contribution to make from their experience. . . . We are responsive to new and unusual opportunities. We encourage innovation, creativity and flexibility. We maintain an attitude of learning, reflection and discovery in order to grow in understanding and skill.

OUR COMMITMENT.   We recognize that values cannot be legislated; they must be lived. No document can substitute for the attitudes, decisions and actions that make up the fabric of our life and work. Therefore, we covenant with each other, before God, to do our utmost individually and as corporate entities within the World Vision Partnership to uphold these Core Values, to honor them in our decisions, to express them in our relationships and to act consistently with them wherever World Vision is at work.

Source: World Vision International internal documents.

creativity in which people feel free to contribute."[6] He then launched a process to reexamine the organization's values, mission, and structure, all of which were to be open to challenge and change.

A working group developed a set of core values (see **Exhibit 2**) that was adopted by the board of

World Vision International in 1990. Next, after 24 drafts, in 1992 the board adopted a new mission. Finally, Irvine led the creation of a Covenant of Partnership (see **Exhibit 3**) that was signed by all members of the newly defined World Vision Partnership. "We want to be held together by shared agreements, values, and commitments rather than legal contracts or a controlling center," said Irvine. "The

[6]Irvine, p. 134.

Exhibit 3   Extracts from World Vision's Covenant of Partnership

THE COVENANT (EXTRACTS)

Regarding World Vision as a partnership of interdependent national entities, we, as a properly constituted national World Vision Board (or Advisory Council), do covenant with other World Vision Boards (or Advisory Councils) to:

A. UPHOLD THE FOLLOWING STATEMENTS OF WORLD VISION IDENTITY AND PURPOSE:

    The Statement of Faith

    The Mission Statement

    The Core Values.

B. CONTRIBUTE TO THE ENRICHMENT OF PARTNERSHIP LIFE AND UNITY BY:

    Sharing in strategic decision-making and policy formulation through consultation and mechanisms that offer all members an appropriate voice in Partnership affairs . . .

    Accepting the leadership and organizational structures established by the WVI Council and Board for the operation of the Partnership . . .

    Fostering an open spirit of exchange for ideas, proposals, vision and concern within the Partnership . . .

C. WORK WITHIN THE ACCOUNTABILITY STRUCTURES BY WHICH THE PARTNERSHIP FUNCTIONS, by:

    Affirming the principle of mutual accountability and transparency among all entities . . .

    Accepting Partnership policies and decisions established by WVI Board consultative processes.

    Honoring commitments to adopted budgets to the utmost extent possible . . .

    Executing an agreement with World Vision International to protect the trademark, name and symbols of World Vision worldwide . . .

D. OBSERVE AGREED FINANCIAL PRINCIPLES AND PROCEDURES, especially:

    Using funds raised under the auspices of World Vision exclusively in World Vision approved ministries.

    Keeping overhead and fund-raising expenses to a minimum to ensure a substantial majority of the funds raised are responsibly utilized in ministry among the poor.

    Accepting Financial Planning and Budgeting Principles adopted by the WVI Board.

    Ensuring that funds or commodities accepted from governments or multi-lateral agencies do not compromise World Vision's mission or core values, and that such resources do not become the major ongoing source of support.

E. PRESENT CONSISTENT COMMUNICATIONS MESSAGES, that:

    Reflect our Christian identity in appropriate ways.

    Include words, images, and statistics that are consistent with ministry realities.

    Avoid paternalism and cultural insensitivity.

    Are free from demeaning and degrading images.

    Build openness, confidence, knowledge and trust within the Partnership.

In signing the Covenant, we are mindful of the rich heritage of Christian service represented by World Vision and of the privilege which is ours to join with others of like mind in the work of the Kingdom of God throughout the world. We therefore recognize that consistent failure to honour this Covenant of Partnership may provide cause for review of our status as a member of the Partnership by the Board of World Vision International.

Signed in behalf of (NAME OF NATIONAL ENTITY)

by resolution carried at a meeting of the [Board] (or Advisory Council) on _____

_____

Chair of [Board] (or Advisory Council)

Source: World Vision International internal documents.

Exhibit 4   Key Elements of the WVI Partnership

The World Vision Partnership refers to the entire World Vision family throughout the world. Any expression of the World Vision ministry is in some way connected to the Partnership. The word "Partnership" is used in this document in a broad, informal sense, rather than a legal sense.

World Vision National Entities comprise the membership of the Partnership. The conditions and categories of membership are described in the By-Laws of World Vision International. All function with the guidance and advice of a National Board or Advisory Council.

World Vision International (WVI) is the registered legal entity which, through its Council and Board of Directors, provides the formal international structure for the Partnership.

The WVI Council provides the membership structure for the Partnership. It meets every three years to review the purpose and objectives of World Vision, assess the extent to which they have been accomplished and make recommendations to the WVI Board in relation to policy. All member-entities are represented on the Council.

The WVI Board of Directors is the governing body of World Vision International as outlined in the By-Laws. The membership of the Board is broadly representative of the Partnership and is appointed by a process determined by the Partnership.

The International Office is the functional unit of World Vision International, housing most of the central elements of WVI. It operates under the authority of the WVI Board of Directors.

Source: World Vision International internal documents.

---

covenant is a statement of accountability to each other, setting out the privileges and responsibilities of national member-entities of the World Vision family."

By 1995, with over a million sponsored children in its care—up from 70,000 children 15 years earlier—the World Vision Partnership decided to build its formal organizational architecture on a "federal" model. (See **Exhibit 4**.) Recognizing that that simple decentralization would mean losing economies of scale, the partnership made the goal of the new structure to try to make all partners as self-sufficient as possible but to maintain a strong core of common language, systems, and operations. Bryant Myers, senior vice president of operations, explained the philosophy:

> We wanted to combine the strength of the central organization with centers of expertise and action that existed around the partnership, balancing the contributions and needs of each. That should result in centralizing the things that can be done better and cheaper that way and decentralizing other things that can be managed more effectively on the front lines. . . . We learned that the biggest misreading of federalism is to call it decentralization. The key to federalism is to ensure the right of intervention held by the leader at the center.

Designing the Structure and Governance   Under the resulting federal structure, membership in the WVI Partnership required a commitment to its core documents (mission statement, statement of faith, core values, and Covenant of Partnership), to WVI ministry policies, and to the WVI trademark agreement. Organizationally, the partnership was governed through a set of linked structures (see **Exhibit 5**).

By 2002, there were 48 national partners, each with one vote on the **international council,** the partnership's highest authority. Held once every three years, council meetings were attended by the international board members, the chairs of the national boards or advisory councils, national office directors, and elected delegates from all partner offices. The council reviewed the objectives of World Vision International, assessed the accomplishment of previous goals, and made recommendations to the board in relation to global strategies and policies.

World Vision's **international board** was composed of the international president and 23 directors selected from the governing bodies of WVI's national offices. It oversaw the partnership, meeting twice a year to appoint WVI's senior officers, approve strategic plans and budgets, and set international policy.

Seven **regional forums** were composed of representatives from the national boards or advisory councils of each national office in each region. They shared experiences on regional programs and strategies and nominated representatives to the WVI Board.

Exhibit 5   World Vision International Organizational Structure

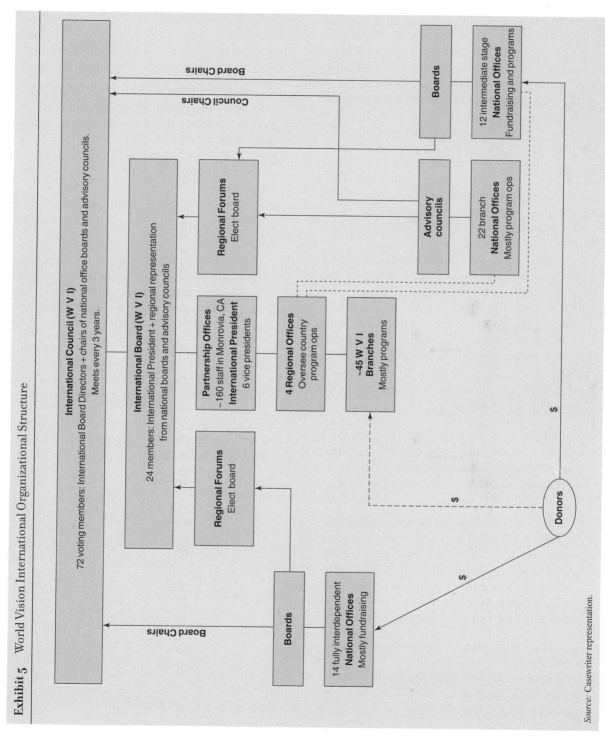

Source: Casewriter representation.

The **partnership office** (previously the international office), located in Monrovia, California, was WVI's executive group. Headed by an international president and four regional and six functional vice presidents, its staff of around 160 supported the day-to-day operations of the partnership. Several other partnership support offices in cities such as Geneva, Los Angeles, and Vienna represented WVI in the international arena through lobbying and advocacy work.

Each of the four **regional offices**—in Costa Rica, Cyprus, Nairobi, and Bangkok—oversaw the program operations of the national offices in its region. These regional offices reported directly to the partnership office.

Most of WVI's 48 **national offices** were either primarily support (fund-raising) offices or field (program-delivery) offices, but a few did both. Each national office had equal direct representation on the international council and also took part in the election of regional representatives to the international board through its regional forum. Local governance and independence from the international office was determined by the national office's stage of development category:

• WVI's 22 **branch** offices were governed by national advisory committees, but WVI maintained legal responsibility and strong management control over their budgetary and personnel decisions through its regional offices.

• The 12 **intermediate-stage** offices were governed by local boards composed of business, church, and social service leaders. They voluntarily agreed to seek approval from WVI for critical management decisions such as appointment or termination of a national director or national board member, budget development, and off-budget expenditures.

• The 14 **fully interdependent** offices were nationally registered nonprofit organizations with their own local boards of directors. Except for certain items specified in the Covenant of Partnership, they did not need WVI approval for decisions. Nonetheless, they were expected voluntarily to coordinate with the partnership office. (Branch and intermediate offices were considered to be in transition toward full interdependence. The process involved peer reviews, WVI consultation, and interaction with the international board.)

By 1996, when Dean Hirsch became the sixth president of WVI, the partnership-based governance model was in place. Hirsch had risen to the top job in WVI following two decades in which he had helped establish World Vision national programs in Rwanda, Zaire, Tanzania, Mali, Ghana, and Malawi then managed major donor marketing for WV-U.S. He described his role in the emerging federated partnership:

> My job is to cast a vision, to make sure that we have alignment between our mission and operations, and to ensure we stay strategic. Because of our dispersed governance, we must operate with trust. The best thing I can do is help to build relationships. So I am the biggest cheerleader in the world . . . but as president of WVI, I also hold a seat on every World Vision board in the world. Either one of my representatives or I attend all meetings. It provides an immediate means of keeping alignment. And I can intervene at any time if one of the partners drifts from our mission or core values.

Fund-raising in the Partnership: World Vision-U.S.

Within the evolving World Vision global partnership, most national entities were adjusting to the more complex structure within which they had to operate. In the United States, for example, the WV-U.S. Board began to look for a new president to strengthen its fund-raising activity. In June 1998, it offered the job to Richard Stearns, an experienced manager who had spent 23 years in strategic and marketing roles in Gillette Company and Parker Brothers Games and as CEO of Lenox, the well-known tableware and gift company. As WV-U.S. president, Stearns was responsible for all WV-U.S. operations, which included fund-raising, advocacy, and international program development, each run by one of the five senior VPs reporting to him.

Revitalizing WV-U.S.: Marketing, Metrics, and Money Over the years, WV-U.S. had remained the largest financial contributor to the partnership, providing almost 50% of global revenues by 1998. "But the organization was missing opportunities and faltering in its operations," said Stearns. "In particular, our appeals had become costly, and we were inefficient. I was given two key goals: increase revenues and lower overhead ratios." (This ratio was the cash income raised divided by the cost of fund-raising. In 1998, it stood at around 3 to 1.)

In 2000, Stearns hired Atul Tandon as senior VP of marketing. Like Stearns, he had come from the corporate sector, serving for over 20 years with Citibank in marketing. In WV-U.S., Tandon saw his primary objectives to be to build the brand and improve customer satisfaction. "I soon realized that I was in a fundamentally different world," he said. "When I asked, 'What is our bottom line? To whom are we accountable?' no one could answer." Furthermore, staff members were unable to describe their outputs and measures. "There were no profit and loss statements, and people were unaware of our spending and the returns we were getting."

Tandon and Stearns reorganized the WV-U.S. office, laying off a number of staff and elevating innovators to senior positions. They replaced the traditional Direct Response Marketing Department with integrated product and channel marketing teams that worked with new communications and creative teams to focus on the key drivers of marketing effectiveness: cost of donor acquisition, costs and methods of donor retention, and long-term donor value. These new teams focused on growth through partnering, brand building, and new channels of recruiting and retaining donors. While the message to donors had to be altered to incorporate the more community development-based model that the ADP concept supported, they were able to do so under the umbrella of a modified $26 monthly child sponsorship program that was still the most effective means of raising funds for WV-U.S. The marketing team also found that while donors were difficult to recruit, if properly cultivated, they were relatively easy to keep.

Tandon expected marketing teams to be research driven in defining what appealed to donors. They were then required to work with three new channel-specific sales teams to design products specifically for church groups, major donors, and Internet sales. Believing strongly in "learning to listen to the customer," Tandon allocated nearly 75% of the $50 million marketing budget to donor recruitment, retention, and communications. With no increases in marketing and communications allocations over a four-year period, Tandon and his team devoted themselves to increasing revenues while holding expenses flat. "We call it widening the jaws," said Tandon.

The results came quickly: double-digit growth every year for four years with an unchanged marketing budget. "Over those four years, we increased our cash income to fund-raising cost ratio from 3 to 1, first, to 3.4 to 1, then to 4.1 to 1, and finally to 5.5 to 1," Tandon reported. Additionally, donor satisfaction increased, as did name awareness in the core target markets—from 49% to 76% over three years. To evaluate WV-U.S.'s efforts more effectively, Stearns introduced a balanced scorecard measurement system. (See **Exhibit 6** for copy of scorecard.) Tandon volunteered to make his marketing group the guinea pig for the new system, explaining:

> We identified specific numbers-driven goals and a few subjective goals. Most revolved around measuring brand strength, brand awareness, and customer satisfaction. Of these, I believe the most important driver is the customer satisfaction number. Ours is measured twice a year by survey, and we have increased satisfaction levels from 84% to 92% over the last three years. We don't have a good benchmark in the nonprofit world, but in the corporate sector, Amazon's customer satisfaction is the highest at 88%. So we are in the right ballpark.

Managing in the Partnership: All in the Family In addition to running the operations at WV-U.S., Stearns sat on the Strategy Working Group (SWG), the key executive decision-making body of the World Vision Partnership. Chaired by WVI's president, Hirsch, the SWG included 16 senior executives from throughout the partnership. Coming from the corporate world, Stearns at first found

Exhibit 6   Balanced Scorecard for WV-U.S. Marketing Department

Marketing & Communications
Level 1 Scorecard

Atul Tandon
Reporting Period: Q4 of FYo3 (Jul, Aug, Sep)

Measure	Actual	Target	Variance (%)	Variance Flag	FYo3-Q1 FYo3 Actuals	FYo3-Q1 FYo2 Actuals	FYo3-Q2 FYo3 Actuals	FYo3-Q2 FYo2 Actuals	FYo3-Q3 FYo3 Actual	FYo3-Q3 FYo2 Actuals	FYo3-Q4 FYo3 Actual	FYo3-Q4 FYo2 Actuals
CHANGE HEARTS												
1 Media Impressions (in millions)	4,515	2,280	98%	●	625	570	2,717	1,880	3,230	2,815	4,515	3,445
INCREASE INVOLVEMENT												
2 Gross Sponsorship Assignments	144,613	182,941	−21%	■	43,139	44,751	82,473	89,921	116,700	129,514	144,613	169,028
3 Matrix Income ($1,000s)	$8,797	$6,950	27%	●	$2,923	$3,514	$4,157	$4,507	$6,612	$6,070	$8,797	$6,795
4 Income ($1,000s)*	$229,007	$230,103	0%	♦	$60,054	$56,487	$114,404	$104,455	$171,997	$155,705	$229,161	$208,553
5 Sponsorship File Size	612,815	625,381	−2%	♦	594,216	555,325	601,842	564,575	610,636	574,131	612,815	581,874
6 Donor Involvement—Avg. Annual Giving	$296	$296	0%	●	$278	$271	$285	$276	$277	$276	$296	$280
INCREASE EFFECTIVENESS												
7 Expenses ($1,000s)*	$52,304	$53,975	3%	●	$14,920	$13,460	$28,912	$25,801	$40,453	$37,477	$52,304	$49,431
8 Sponsor Attrition Rate	16.2%	16.5%	2%	●	17.4%	19.5%	17.0%	18.5%	16.4%	17.7%	16.2%	17.4%
9 Donor Satisfaction	90.8%	N/A	N/A		N/A	N/A	90.3%	88.7%	N/A	N/A	90.8%	89.4%

Variance Thresholds   ● Meets Goal   ♦ <5% Adverse   ■ >5% Adverse

*MAC Yield to Ministry (Revenues less Expenses) was better than previous year by $19.5 million (11.7%) and better than budget by $2.4 million

Metric:

Definition:

CHANGE HEARTS

1 Media Impressions (in millions) — Number of Christian & Secular Media impressions through publication or broadcast story

INCREASE INVOLVEMENT

2 Gross Sponsorship Assignments — Cum total gross sponsorship acquisitions (all channels except RM)

3 Matrix Income ($1,000s) — Income motivated by Marketing & Communications, but booked to other areas – Major Donor + Ethnic Mktg + Corp Partnership

4 Income ($1,000s) — Income generated by Marketing & Communications from all sources

5 Sponsorship File Size — # of Money Sponsorships Ending last period + Acquisitions – Cancels

6a Donor Involvement—Avg. Annual Giving — Rolling 12 mos giving (# donors (cash only for now; GIK to be added later)

INCREASE EFFECTIVENESS

7 Expenses ($1,000s) — YTD Total Marketing & Communications Expenses

8 Sponsor Attrition Rate — # of money sponsorships that have not made a payment in the last 6 months/total money sponsorships 6 months prior

9 Donor Satisfaction — Donor Satisfaction Rating (Sponsorship Only)

Source: World Vision International internal documents.

working at WVI difficult. "I was bewildered by the lack of any real authority structure in the partnership," he said. "I kept wondering who was in charge." He also reflected on the governance structure: "The international board is truly representative. The U.S. appoints two of its 24 members and has a founder's chair. The other 21 are from other nations. Representing 50% of overall revenues, we clearly have financial influence, yet we hold only 12% of the formal political control. This would be unthinkable in the corporate world."

Over time, Stearns recognized that the partnership traded control and efficiency for richness of perspective and strength in local programming and fund-raising: "We are able to make our own decisions and set our own priorities. President Hirsch has no line authority over me. He does not participate in my performance review, and he issues no directives to me or any other CEO. But, through the SWG, we make joint decisions that benefit the global organization and our mission better than if any one of us acted alone."

Program Delivery in the Partnership: The AIDS Hope Initiative

By the late 1990s, the World Vision Partnership was beginning to feel more stable. The ADP concept had made program delivery more effective, the child sponsorship fund-raising model had been refined, and the federal organization framework was helping to integrate the global network of World Vision entities. Yet while World Vision had been struggling to refine its internal operations, the impact of HIV/AIDS was changing the needs of those it served externally. The global pandemic had reached crisis levels in many parts of the world, but nowhere more than in sub-Saharan Africa.

Recognizing the Need: Lessons for a Latecomer
Two months after joining World Vision, Stearns went on a field trip to Uganda. Visiting a household of three boys, aged 11 to 13, who lived alone after being orphaned by AIDS, Stearns learned that an estimated 10 million African children were living in similar circumstances. When he asked what World Vision was doing about it, the answer was, "Very

little." Although he was new to the agency, he felt he had to speak out:

> When I was at Parker Brothers, we failed to realize that games were moving from the parlor table to the video screen. When new competitors came out with fast and interesting computer games, they stole 90% of the market from under our noses. This was what was happening to us with HIV/AIDS. We had developed top-notch skills at rural community organization, water systems, health, childcare, and economic regeneration and responded well to hurricanes, disasters, wars, and other emergencies. But while all of this was exemplary, we were not prepared to face the unprecedented scale of devastation wrought by the AIDS pandemic.

With 58,000 people in Africa dying from AIDS each week—equal to the entire loss of American lives in Vietnam—Stearns felt there was a real chance that decades of progress by the development community would be rolled back. He began to speak more forcefully, telling his colleagues that they were building beautiful sand castles on the beach while an 80-foot-high tidal wave was just offshore. "I kept saying it for over two years, fully mindful that I did not know what specifically I was proposing to do about it," he recounted. He was supported by Bruce Wilkinson, senior vice president of his International Programs Group. But while other members of the partnership listened, Stearns felt that, on their overloaded agenda, it was "just another woe to add to the list."

Then, in July 2000, Wilfred Mlay, African regional vice president, gave a powerful presentation to the SWG. "AIDS is killing our people," he said. "It is devastating our work, our families, our staff. I really need your help." A few months later, when *Time* ran a cover story on the 10 million to 12 million children in Africa estimated to be orphaned by AIDS, Stearns circulated a memo to senior executives of the partnership asking, "Why, as a child-focused organization, are we not addressing the AIDS crisis?"

Mlay's appeal and Stearns's prodding prompted the SWG to appoint Myers, vice president for International Programs Strategy, to study WVI's commitment to the crisis. After speaking with a number of people throughout the partnership, he wrote a draft document suggesting that HIV/AIDS needed to be a priority for World Vision for five reasons: it cared about children, including the 40 million projected to lose one or both parents to HIV/AIDS by 2010; it had over 900,000 sponsored children in the 30 worst-hit countries and nearly 2 million sponsored children at risk worldwide; it was investing almost $200 million a year in the 30 worst-hit countries; its world-wide staff was at risk, and many were personally affected by HIV/AIDS in their own extended families; and as a Christian organization, it had an opportunity to bring its mission to those affected by HIV/AIDS.

Launching the AIDS Hope Initiative   On World AIDS Day in December 2000, Hirsch preempted any formal decision on an HIV/AIDS strategy by announcing that World Vision would launch a $30 million initiative to address the crisis. Believing that the moment was right and that some members were already moving forward, Hirsch pushed the partner-ship into action. Over the following months, Myers prepared a plan entitled "The HIV/AIDS Hope Ini-tiative," outlining the need and identifying the scope of the problem. The plan also categorized a series of programming approaches for high-prevalence coun-tries, medium-prevalence countries, and the rest of World Vision's country programs.

Just before presenting the plan to the SWG at a meeting in Costa Rica in February 2001, Hirsch approached Casey and asked him if he would lead the AIDS initiative. "I was surprised by the re-quest," recalled Casey. "It was an entirely new and different task for me. I had spent six years as a senior line manager in operations for the U.S. orga-nization. Now I would be taking on a key strategic role within WVI's partnership office." For most of his eight years with WV-U.S., Casey had served as senior vice president for fund-raising and pro-grams. But, in 1999, Stearns's reorganization had left him a senior executive without a portfolio. "For about a year, I worked on special projects within the senior management team. They were rewarding, but I was considering moving on," Casey said.

As he thought about it, Casey decided that this new project represented an interesting and worthwhile

challenge. In March 2001, he assumed his new role as director of the HIV/AIDS Hope Initiative. He would report directly to Hirsch but continue to work out of the WV-U.S. office in Seattle.

Assessing the Challenge   Casey returned to Seattle with an approved operating budget of approximately $750,000 but no staff. As he reviewed the existing document, he recognized the difficulty of his task:

> I began working off of the document that Bryant [Myers] had prepared. Although it was good work, it had been devised almost entirely at the headquarters office. Essentially, I was being asked to implement an unprecedented worldwide program effort on perhaps the most controversial issue imaginable that would require new levels of coordination that we had never previously achieved. Yet there was no ownership or buy-in from the regional VPs.

Casey understood that, within the partnership, the four regional VPs (for Africa, Asia, Pacific, and Middle East/Eastern Europe) held a great deal of power over programs and operations due to the fact that all the national directors reported to them. In recent years, however, the national offices had been pushed by the international board to become more independent in their strategies and programs. Casey stated: "In our efforts to devolve autonomy to the national offices, we had worked for 10 years to develop viable governing boards for each one. But we also wanted them to be responsive to WVI's global priorities through their link to the regional VPs. Because national directors were answerable to two masters, this could cause problems."

To build support for the Hope Initiative, Casey began a six-month process of travel and discussion with the regional VPs and national directors. He wanted to make sure that the initiative would remain true to its ideal while also ensuring that the ambitious fund-raising and programmatic objec-tives were realistic from the field's perspective.

Resistance from Donors   Casey knew that funding such a big initiative would be a challenge and hoped to implement a joint marketing effort across the part-nership offices, hopefully reaching out to new donors in the process. He also wanted the marketing effort to be well connected to the programs in the field. But almost from the outset, he encountered resistance from the marketing departments in the major partnership support offices. Stearns remembered:

> Our WV-U.S. marketing people were very skeptical. They told us that any work with HIV/AIDS would never sell with our donors. Our top people in brand building told us that we have a very wholesome child-focused image. People equate us helping children and families in need. They said that if we start talking about AIDS, prostitutes, drug users, long-haul truckers, and sexuality, it would hurt our image.

WV-U.S. commissioned a market survey among evangelical Christians and loyal donors in the United States. "It was devastating news," stated Casey. "We asked them if they would be willing to give to a respectable Christian organization to help children who lost both parents to AIDS. Only 7% said that they would definitely help, while over 50% said probably not or definitely not. Surveys in Canada and Australia found the same thing. It was stark and clear that our donors felt that AIDS sufferers somehow deserved their fate."

Beyond donor reaction, Casey dug deeper to understand the marketing organization's challenge. "Their incentives and targets for the year were based on the efficiency of their appeals," he said. "But by its very nature, this was going to be a costly appeal." Instead of returning a usual 4 or 5:1 ratio of revenues to expenses, the marketers felt that, in the beginning at least, any AIDS appeal would return something closer to 1:1. So when Casey asked the heads of the partnership offices to adjust the targets for HIV/AIDS programs for their marketing teams, the response was mixed. While Stearns convinced his board to remove the HIV/AIDS appeals from the normal cost-ratio calculations for U.S. appeal, Canada, the United Kingdom, and several other key fund-raising countries were less willing to do so.

Resistance from the Field   As he focused on program implications, Casey had Mlay as a natural ally. As regional vice president for Africa, Mlay reported to Hirsch at WVI and was responsible for 25 national country offices with over 8,000 staff (mostly field and program officers, but also technical specialists in areas such as micro-enterprise, health, child protection, and Christian ministry) and a budget of $500 million. To manage his domain, Mlay had divided Africa into three subregions, each headed by a director (based in Johannesburg, Dakar, and Nairobi) responsible for eight or nine countries. "I have structured the African region differently from any of the other regions," he said. "For example, in Asia, all the senior leaders share one office in Bangkok. But because it is difficult to travel and communicate, my senior leadership and technical teams are dispersed. And I want them to be where the action is happening."

Although he managed the African region as he saw fit, Mlay could also use services in the partnership: "I am in charge but have access to resources when needed. For example, we have some sophisticated protocols for emergency operations. If I put out the call for help, we will have a conference call within five hours. And I have access to a global rapid-response team that can allocate $1 million within 72 hours, so I can promise that WV will be present at a crisis within 24 hours."

Mlay worked with the boards and advisory councils in his 26 national offices to implement WVI priorities. But while he held regular meetings with national directors and hosted conferences and forums to determine how to allocate his technical resources, he had only limited ability to determine the strategy of national programs. "The advisory councils and boards help us to connect to the local community and society," he said. "But I have a reserved seat on every board in Africa, so World Vision management and local boards share the governance of our work." Managing the boards was a time-consuming task for Mlay, who sometimes had to act if a board went in a direction that WVI disapproved of: "For example, we discovered that the head of one of our boards had a set of values that conflicted with those of the organization. We intervened and asked him to step down. Most of the board was against us, but we prevailed. There is a fine line between granting autonomy and maintaining standards."

Despite his ability to intervene when necessary, Mlay had long encouraged his national directors to determine their own goals and strategies through the ADP system. Indeed, under the federated partnership structure, they could even have direct contact with any of the support offices to fund their ADP projects. But now that he wanted to push HIV/AIDS programs, he faced resistance. "There is a culture of silence around the issue," he said. "In Tanzania, entire families and villages are being wiped out by AIDS. We have grandmothers caring for 10 and 12 children. The ADPs are strong, but people are ashamed to speak about it. This is especially true of church leaders, who refuse to see this as their problem. Many even talk about AIDS as God's punishment of sinners."

Casey also reflected on the "phenomenon of denial" he encountered. On an early trip to Capetown, he spoke to a taxi driver who told him that his awareness of HIV/AIDS had not changed his lifestyle because it would not get him. "A few minutes later, he was describing how the trucking company for whom his sister worked had just adopted a new HR policy stating that employees could not attend more than three funerals per month," recalled Casey. "It was uncanny how he could hold both thoughts in his head and not make a connection. In the face of such clear evidence, even intelligent people did not want to recognize the crisis."

Casey described the response to his first six months in the field: "Program officers were working flat out on existing projects and we came in telling them that, while those are important, we want you to change your whole focus. In addition, most program officers were skilled in technical sectors such as water, education, and economic development. Few knew about HIV/AIDS work. Their practical response was, 'It's not our expertise. What can we really do about AIDS?'"

Casey hired two teams of HIV/AIDS specialists, one in Uganda and one in Zambia, to create a "Models of Learning" program. He also hired a research associate to work out of the international office (see **Exhibit 7**). Hoping to build an active learning tool for the rest of the field, they prepared

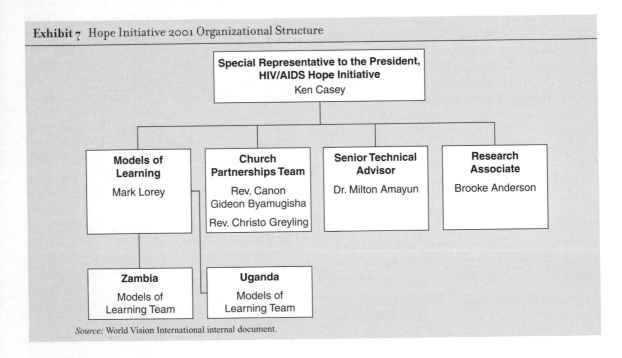

Exhibit 7 Hope Initiative 2001 Organizational Structure

Source: World Vision International internal document.

models of programming that they hoped to make available to others. But early response from a number of national offices was muted. "In the face of the overwhelming need and workload, many felt that this was just the emphasis of the day. Wait it out and it would go away," Casey explained. After all, it was not the first time that field offices had been asked to implement cross-organizational strategies, as Myers recalled:

In the mid-1990s, we embarked on a long and expensive process of rebranding. Many national offices plunged time and resources into the effort but got little value out of it. And a subsequent initiative to move relief activities from the center out into the national offices ran into difficulty trying to mix the cowboy culture of the relief teams with the slower

culture of the development teams on the front lines. Not surprisingly, some national offices are wary of any new top-down initiative—particularly now that they have so much independence.

The South African Conference

In December of 2001, Casey released a first draft of the Hope Initiative matrix (see **Exhibit 8** for a later version), which had been developed over months of dialogue and meetings with key personnel from across the partnership. It laid out the goals, beneficiaries, values, and key design principles for each of the three HIV/AIDS program areas: prevention, care, and advocacy. An accompanying document outlined actions that would

---

Exhibit 8   HIV/AIDS Hope Initiative Program Matrix

Overall Goal	*The overall goal of the HIV/AIDS Hope Initiative is to reduce the global impact of HIV/AIDS through the enhancement and expansion of the World Vision programs and collaborations focused on HIV/AIDS prevention, care and advocacy.*		
	Prevention	**Care**	**Advocacy**
Track Goals	Make a significant contribution to the reduction of national HIV/AIDS prevalence rates	Achieve measurable improvements in the quality of life of children affected by HIV/AIDS	Encourage the adoption of policy and programs that minimize the spread of HIV/AIDS and maximize care for those living with or affected by HIV/AIDS
Target Groups	• Children, aged 5–15 years old • High-risk population groups • Pregnant and lactating mothers	Vulnerable Children (living with, affected by and orphaned by HIV/AIDS, including parents and caregivers of vulnerable children)	Policymakers (local, national, and international)
Values	Bring a Christian response to HIV/AIDS, one that reflects God's unconditional, compassionate love for all people and affirms each individual's dignity and worth.		
Key Program Design Principles	• Clear and measurable impact indicators • Integrated with key agencies and organizations in the country • Multisectoral in approach • Scalable—the ability to impact a large number of people • Empower, engage, and equip the local church as a primary partner, as well as other faith-based organizations • Integrated with WV national office program strategies		

Source: World Vision International internal documents.

seek to meet several goals. First, it would aim to prevent new cases of HIV/AIDS by contributing to the reduction of national incidence rates, especially among children, high-risk groups, and pregnant and lactating mothers. Second, it would aim to provide measurable improvements in the quality of care for children affected by HIV/AIDS, including those orphaned by AIDS, living with HIV-positive parents, and in households fostering AIDS orphans. Finally, it would advocate the adoption of public policy and programs that would minimize the spread of the disease and provide care for those living with or affected by HIV/AIDS.

On January 12, 2002, the real rollout for the Hope Initiative was about to begin at a weeklong high-prevalence country workshop held at a safari lodge in South Africa. Casey's goal was to bring together the national directors, senior program officers, and area development managers from the 17 African countries hardest hit by the crisis. He planned to ask them to tackle the HIV/AIDS problem with the same energy with which they worked to bring communities clean water, education, health care, food security, and economic development. "It was a make-or-break time for the initiative," said Casey. "Without their energy and buy-in, the initiative would only exist on paper."

Reading 4-1   Managing Multicultural Teams

Jeanne Brett, Kristin Behfar, and Mary C. Kern

Teams whose members come from different nations and backgrounds place special demands on managers—especially when a feuding team looks to the boss for help with a conflict.

When a major international software developer needed to produce a new product quickly, the project manager assembled a team of employees from India and the United States. From the start the team members could not agree on a delivery date for the product. The Americans thought the work could be done in two to three weeks; the Indians predicted it would take two to three months. As time went on, the Indian team members proved reluctant to report setbacks in the production process, which the American team members would find out about only when work was due to be passed to them. Such conflicts, of course,

may affect any team, but in this case they arose from cultural differences. As tensions mounted, conflict over delivery dates and feedback became personal, disrupting team members' communication about even mundane issues. The project manager decided he had to intervene—with the result that both the American and the Indian team members came to rely on him for direction regarding minute operational details that the team should have been able to handle itself. The manager became so bogged down by quotidian issues that the project careened hopelessly off even the most pessimistic schedule—and the team never learned to work together effectively.

Multicultural teams often generate frustrating management dilemmas. Cultural differences cancreate substantial obstacles to effective teamwork—but these may be subtle and difficult to recognize until significant damage has already been done. As in the case above, which the manager involved told us about, managers may create more problems than they resolve by intervening.

❚ Jeanne Brett is the DeWitt W. Buchanan, Jr., Distinguished Professor of Dispute Resolution and Organizations and the director of the Dispute Resolution Research Center at Northwestern University's Kellogg School of Management in Evanston, Illinois. Kristin Behfar is an assistant professor at the Paul Merage School of Business at the University of California at Irvine. Mary C. Kern is an assistant professor at the Zicklin School of Business at Baruch College in New York.

The challenge in managing multicultural teams effectively is to recognize underlying cultural causes of conflict, and to intervene in ways that both get the team back on track and empower its members to deal with future challenges themselves.

We interviewed managers and members of multicultural teams from all over the world. These interviews, combined with our deep research on dispute resolution and teamwork, led us to conclude that the wrong kind of managerial intervention may sideline valuable members who should be participating or, worse, create resistance, resulting in poor team performance. We're not talking here about respecting differing national standards for doing business, such as accounting practices. We're referring to day-to-day working problems among team members that can keep multicultural teams from realizing the very gains they were set up to harvest, such as knowledge of different product markets, culturally sensitive customer service, and 24-hour work rotations.

The good news is that cultural challenges are manageable if managers and team members choose the right strategy and avoid imposing single-culture-based approaches on multicultural situations.

The Challenges

People tend to assume that challenges on multicultural teams arise from differing styles of communication. But this is only one of the four categories that, according to our research, can create barriers to a team's ultimate success. These categories are direct versus indirect communication; trouble with accents and fluency; differing attitudes toward hierarchy and authority; and conflicting norms for decision making.

Direct versus indirect communication. Communication in Western cultures is typically direct and explicit. The meaning is on the surface, and a listener doesn't have to know much about the context

or the speaker to interpret it. This is not true in many other cultures, where meaning is embedded in the way the message is presented. For example, Western negotiators get crucial information about the other party's preferences and priorities by asking direct questions, such as "Do you prefer option A or option B?" In cultures that use indirect communication, negotiators may have to infer preferences and priorities from changes—or the lack of them—in the other party's settlement proposal. In cross-cultural negotiations, the non-Westerner can understand the direct communications of the Westerner, but the Westerner has difficulty understanding the indirect communications of the non-Westerner.

An American manager who was leading a project to build an interface for a U.S. and Japanese customer-data system explained the problems her team was having this way: "In Japan, they want to talk and discuss. Then we take a break and they talk within the organization. They want to make sure that there's harmony in the rest of the organization. One of the hardest lessons for me was when I thought they were saying yes but they just meant 'I'm listening to you.'"

The differences between direct and indirect communication can cause serious damage to relationships when team projects run into problems. When the American manager quoted above discovered that several flaws in the system would significantly disrupt company operations, she pointed this out in an e-mail to her American boss and the Japanese team members. Her boss appreciated the direct warnings; her Japanese colleagues were embarrassed, because she had violated their norms for uncovering and discussing problems. Their reaction was to provide her with less access to the people and information she needed to monitor progress. They would probably have responded better if she had pointed out the problems indirectly—for example, by asking them what would happen if a certain part of the system was not functioning properly, even though she knew full well that it was malfunctioning and also what the implications were.

As our research indicates is so often true, communication challenges create barriers to effective teamwork by reducing information sharing, creating interpersonal conflict, or both. In Japan, a typical response to direct confrontation is to isolate the norm violator. This American manager was isolated not just socially but also physically. She told us, "They literally put my office in a storage room, where I had desks stacked from floor to ceiling and I was the only person there. So they totally isolated me, which was a pretty loud signal to me that I was not a part of the inside circle and that they would communicate with me only as needed."

Her direct approach had been intended to solve a problem, and in one sense, it did, because her project was launched problem-free. But her norm violations exacerbated the challenges of working with her Japanese colleagues and limited her ability to uncover any other problems that might have derailed the project later on.

Trouble with accents and fluency. Although the language of international business is English, misunderstandings or deep frustration may occur because of nonnative speakers' accents, lack of fluency, or problems with translation or usage. These may also influence perceptions of status or competence.

For example, a Latin American member of a multicultural consulting team lamented, "Many times I felt that because of the language difference, I didn't have the words to say some things that I was thinking. I noticed that when I went to these interviews with the U.S. guy, he would tend to lead the interviews, which was understandable but also disappointing, because we are at the same level. I had very good questions, but he would take the lead."

When we interviewed an American member of a U.S.-Japanese team that was assessing the potential expansion of a U.S. retail chain into Japan, she described one American teammate this way: "He was not interested in the Japanese consultants' feedback and felt that because they weren't as fluent as he was, they weren't intelligent enough and, therefore, could add no value." The team member described was responsible for assessing one aspect of the feasibility of expansion into Japan. Without input from the Japanese experts, he risked overestimating opportunities and underestimating challenges.

Nonfluent team members may well be the most expert on the team, but their difficulty communicating knowledge makes it hard for the team to recognize and utilize their expertise. If teammates become frustrated or impatient with a lack of fluency, interpersonal conflicts can arise. Nonnative speakers may become less motivated to contribute, or anxious about their performance evaluations and future career prospects. The organization as a whole pays a greater price: Its investment in a multicultural team fails to pay off.

Some teams, we learned, use language differences to resolve (rather than create) tensions. A team of U.S. and Latin American buyers was negotiating with a team from a Korean supplier. The negotiations took place in Korea, but the discussions were conducted in English. Frequently the Koreans would caucus at the table by speaking Korean. The buyers, frustrated, would respond by appearing to caucus in Spanish—though they discussed only inconsequential current events and sports, in case any of the Koreans spoke Spanish. Members of the team who didn't speak Spanish pretended to participate, to the great amusement of their teammates. This approach proved effective: It conveyed to the Koreans in an appropriately indirect way that their caucuses in Korean were frustrating and annoying to the other side. As a result, both teams cut back on sidebar conversations.

Differing attitudes toward hierarchy and authority. A challenge inherent in multicultural teamwork is that by design, teams have a rather flat structure. But team members from some cultures, in which people are treated differently according to their status in an organization, are uncomfortable on flat teams. If they defer to higher-status team members, their behavior will be seen as appropriate when most of the team comes from a hierarchical culture; but they may damage their stature and credibility—and even face humiliation—if most of the team comes from an egalitarian culture.

One manager of Mexican heritage, who was working on a credit and underwriting team for a bank, told us, "In Mexican culture, you're always supposed to be humble. So whether you understand something or not, you're supposed to put it in the form of a question. You have to keep it open-ended, out of respect. I think that actually worked against me, because the Americans thought I really didn't know what I was talking about. So it made me feel like they thought I was wavering on my answer."

When, as a result of differing cultural norms, team members believe they've been treated disrespectfully, the whole project can blow up. In another Korean-U.S. negotiation, the American members of a due diligence team were having difficulty getting information from their Korean counterparts, so they complained directly to higher-level Korean management, nearly wrecking the deal. The higher-level managers were offended because hierarchy is strictly adhered to in Korean organizations and culture. It should have been their own lower-level people, not the U.S. team members, who came to them with a problem. And the Korean team members were mortified that their bosses had been involved before they themselves could brief them. The crisis was resolved only when high-level U.S. managers made a trip to Korea, conveying appropriate respect for their Korean counterparts.

Conflicting norms for decision making. Cultures differ enormously when it comes to decision making—particularly, how quickly decisions should be made and how much analysis is required beforehand. Not surprisingly, U.S. managers like to make decisions very quickly and with relatively little analysis by comparison with managers from other countries.

A Brazilian manager at an American company who was negotiating to buy Korean products destined for Latin America told us, "On the first day, we agreed on three points, and on the second day, the U.S.-Spanish side wanted to start with point four. But the Korean side wanted to go back and rediscuss points one through three. My boss almost had an attack."

What U.S. team members learn from an experience like this is that the American way simply cannot be imposed on other cultures. Managers from other cultures may, for example, decline to share information until they understand the full scope of a project. But they have learned that they can't simply ignore the desire of their American counterparts to make decisions quickly. What to do? The best solution seems to be to make minor concessions on process—to learn to adjust to and even respect another approach to decision making. For example, American managers have learned to keep their impatient bosses away from team meetings and give them frequent if brief updates. A comparable lesson for managers from other cultures is to be explicit about what they need—saying, for example, "We have to see the big picture before we talk details."

Four Strategies

The most successful teams and managers we interviewed used four strategies for dealing with these challenges: adaptation (acknowledging cultural gaps openly and working around them), structural intervention (changing the shape of the team), managerial intervention (setting norms early or bringing in a higher-level manager), and exit (removing a team member when other options have failed). There is no one right way to deal with a particular kind of multicultural problem; identifying the type of challenge is only the first step. The more crucial step is assessing the circumstances—or "enabling situational conditions"—under which the team is working. For example, does the project allow any flexibility for change, or do deadlines make that impossible? Are there additional resources available that might be tapped? Is the team permanent or temporary? Does the team's manager have the autonomy to make a decision about changing the team in some way? Once the situational conditions have been analyzed, the team's leader can identify an appropriate response (see the exhibit "Identifying the Right Strategy").

Adaptation.   Some teams find ways to work with or around the challenges they face, adapting practices or attitudes without making changes to the group's membership or assignments. Adaptation works when team members are willing to acknowledge and name their cultural differences and to assume responsibility for figuring out how to live with them. It's often the best possible approach to a problem, because it typically involves less managerial time than other strategies; and because team members participate in solving the problem themselves, they learn from the process. When team members have this mind-set, they can be creative about protecting their own substantive differences while acceding to the processes of others.

An American software engineer located in Ireland who was working with an Israeli account management team from his own company told us how shocked he was by the Israelis' in-your-face style: "There were definitely different ways of approaching issues and discussing them. There is something pretty common to the Israeli culture: They like to argue. I tend to try to collaborate more, and it got very stressful for me until I figured out how to kind of merge the cultures."

The software engineer adapted. He imposed some structure on the Israelis that helped him maintain his own style of being thoroughly prepared; that accommodation enabled him to accept the Israeli style. He also noticed that team members weren't just confronting him; they confronted one another but were able to work together effectively nevertheless. He realized that the confrontation was not personal but cultural.

In another example, an American member of a postmerger consulting team was frustrated by the hierarchy of the French company his team was working with. He felt that a meeting with certain French managers who were not directly involved in the merger "wouldn't deliver any value to me or for purposes of the project," but said that he had come to understand that "it was very important to really involve all the people there" if the integration was ultimately to work.

A U.S. and UK multicultural team tried to use their differing approaches to decision making to reach a higher-quality decision. This approach, called fusion, is getting serious attention from political scientists and from government officials dealing with multicultural populations that want to protect their cultures rather than integrate or assimilate. If the team had relied exclusively on the Americans' "forge ahead" approach, it might not have recognized the pitfalls that lay ahead and might later have had to back up and start over. Meanwhile, the UK members would have been gritting their teeth and saying "We told you things were moving too fast." If the team had used the "Let's think about this" UK approach, it might have wasted a lot of time trying to identify every pitfall, including the most unlikely, while the U.S. members chomped at the bit and muttered about analysis paralysis. The strength of this team was that some of its members were willing to forge ahead and some were willing to work through pitfalls. To accommodate them all, the team did both—moving not quite as fast as the U.S. members would have on their own and not quite as thoroughly as the UK members would have.

Structural intervention.   A structural intervention is a deliberate reorganization or reassignment designed to reduce interpersonal friction or to remove a source of conflict for one or more groups. This approach can be extremely effective when

Identifying the Right Strategy

The most successful teams and managers we interviewed use four strategies for dealing with problems: adaptation (acknowledging cultural gaps openly and working around them), structural intervention (changing the shape of the team), managerial intervention (setting norms early or bringing in a higher-level manager), and exit (removing a team member when other options have failed). Adaptation is the ideal strategy because the team works effectively to solve its own problem with minimal input from management—and, most important, learns from the experience. The guide below can help you identify the right strategy once you have identified both the problem and the "enabling situational conditions" that apply to the team.

REPRESENTATIVE PROBLEMS	ENABLING SITUATIONAL CONDITIONS	STRATEGY	COMPLICATING FACTORS
• Conflict arises from decision-making differences • Misunderstanding or stonewalling arises from communication differences	• Team members can attribute a challenge to culture rather than personality • Higher-level managers are not available or the team would be embarrassed to involve them	**Adaptation**	• Team members must be exceptionally aware • Negotiating a common understanding takes time
• The team is affected by emotional tensions relating to fluency issues or prejudice • Team members are inhibited by perceived status differences among teammates	• The team can be subdivided to mix cultures or expertise • Tasks can be subdivided	**Structural Intervention**	• If team members aren't carefully distributed, subgroups can strengthen preexisting differences • Subgroup solutions have to fit back together
• Violations of hierarchy have resulted in loss of face • An absence of ground rules is causing conflict	• The problem has produced a high level of emotion • The team has reached a stalemate • A higher-level manager is able and willing to intervene	**Managerial Intervention**	• The team becomes overly dependent on the manager • Team members maybe sidelined or resistant
• A team member cannot adjust to the challenge at hand and has become unable to contribute to the project	• The team is permanent rather than temporary • Emotions are beyond the point of intervention • Too much face has been lost	**Exit**	• Talent and training costs are lost

obvious subgroups demarcate the team (for example, headquarters versus national subsidiaries) or if team members are proud, defensive, threatened, or clinging to negative stereotypes of one another.

A member of an investment research team scattered across continental Europe, the UK, and the U.S.

described for us how his manager resolved conflicts stemming from status differences and language tensions among the team's three "tribes." The manager started by having the team meet face-to-face twice a year, not to discuss mundane day-to-day problems (of which there were many) but to identify a set of values that the team would use to direct and evaluate its progress. At the first meeting, he realized that when he started to speak, everyone else "shut down," waiting to hear what he had to say. So he hired a consultant to run future meetings. The consultant didn't represent a hierarchical threat and was therefore able to get lots of participation from team members.

Another structural intervention might be to create smaller working groups of mixed cultures or mixed corporate identities in order to get at information that is not forthcoming from the team as a whole. The manager of the team that was evaluating retail opportunities in Japan used this approach. When she realized that the female Japanese consultants would not participate if the group got large, or if their male superior was present, she broke the team up into smaller groups to try to solve problems. She used this technique repeatedly and made a point of changing the subgroups' membership each time so that team members got to know and respect everyone else on the team.

The subgrouping technique involves risks, however. It buffers people who are not working well together or not participating in the larger group for one reason or another. Sooner or later the team will have to assemble the pieces that the subgroups have come up with, so this approach relies on another structural intervention: Someone must become a mediator in order to see that the various pieces fit together.

Managerial intervention.   When a manager behaves like an arbitrator or a judge, making a final decision without team involvement, neither the manager nor the team gains much insight into why the team has stalemated. But it is possible for team members to use managerial intervention effectively to sort out problems.

When an American refinery-safety expert with significant experience throughout East Asia got stymied during a project in China, she called in her company's higher-level managers in Beijing to talk to the higher-level managers to whom the Chinese refinery's managers reported. Unlike the Western team members who breached etiquette by approaching the superiors of their Korean counterparts, the safety expert made sure to respect hierarchies in both organizations.

"Trying to resolve the issues," she told us, "the local management at the Chinese refinery would end up having conferences with our Beijing office and also with the upper management within the refinery. Eventually they understood that we weren't trying to insult them or their culture or to tell them they were bad in any way. We were trying to help. They eventually understood that there were significant fire and safety issues. But we actually had to go up some levels of management to get those resolved."

Managerial intervention to set norms early in a team's life can really help the team start out with effective processes. In one instance reported to us, a multicultural software development team's lingua franca was English, but some members, though they spoke grammatically correct English, had a very pronounced accent. In setting the ground rules for the team, the manager addressed the challenge directly, telling the members that they had been chosen for their task expertise, not their fluency in English, and that the team was going to have to work around language problems. As the project moved to the customer-services training stage, the manager advised the team members to acknowledge their accents up front. She said they should tell customers, "I realize I have an accent. If you don't understand what I'm saying, just stop me and ask questions."

Exit.   Possibly because many of the teams we studied were project based, we found that leaving the team was an infrequent strategy for managing challenges. In short-term situations, unhappy team members often just waited out the project. When teams were permanent, producing products or services, the exit of one or more members was a strategy of last resort, but it was used—either voluntarily or after a formal request from management. Exit was likely when emotions were running high and too much face had been lost on both sides to salvage the situation.

An American member of a multicultural consulting team described the conflict between two senior consultants, one a Greek woman and the other a Polish man, over how to approach problems: "The woman from Greece would say, 'Here's the way I think we should do it.' It would be something that she was in control of. The guy from Poland would say, 'I think we should actually do it this way instead.' The woman would kind of turn red in the face, upset, and say, 'I just don't think that's the right way of doing it.' It would definitely switch from just professional differences to personal differences.

"The woman from Greece ended up leaving the firm. That was a direct result of probably all the different issues going on between these people. It really just wasn't a good fit. I've found that oftentimes when you're in consulting, you have to adapt to the culture, obviously, but you have to adapt just as much to the style of whoever is leading the project."

· · ·

Though multicultural teams face challenges that are not directly attributable to cultural differences, such differences underlay whatever problem needed to be addressed in many of the teams we studied. Furthermore, while serious in their own right when they have a negative effect on team functioning, cultural challenges may also unmask fundamental managerial problems. Managers who intervene early and set norms; teams and managers who structure social interaction and work to engage everyone on the team; and teams that can see problems as stemming from culture, not personality, approach challenges with good humor and creativity. Managers who have to intervene when the team has reached a stalemate may be able to get the team moving again, but they seldom empower it to help itself the next time a stalemate occurs.

When frustrated team members take some time to think through challenges and possible solutions themselves, it can make a huge difference. Take, for example, this story about a financial-services call center. The members of the call-center team were all fluent Spanish-speakers, but some were North Americans and some were Latin Americans. Team performance, measured by calls answered per hour, was lagging. One Latin American was taking twice as long with her calls as the rest of the team. She was handling callers' questions appropriately, but she was also engaging in chitchat. When her teammates confronted her for being a free rider (they resented having to make up for her low call rate), she immediately acknowledged the problem, admitting that she did not know how to end the call politely—chitchat being normal in her culture. They rallied to help her: Using their technology, they would break into any of her calls that went overtime, excusing themselves to the customer, offering to take over the call, and saying that this employee was urgently needed to help out on a different call. The team's solution worked in the short run, and the employee got better at ending her calls in the long run.

In another case, the Indian manager of a multicultural team coordinating a company-wide IT project found himself frustrated when he and a teammate from Singapore met with two Japanese members of the coordinating team to try to get the Japan section to deliver its part of the project. The Japanese members seemed to be saying yes, but in the Indian manager's view, their follow-through was insufficient. He considered and rejected the idea of going up the hierarchy to the Japanese team members' boss, and decided instead to try to build consensus with the whole Japanese IT team, not just the two members on the coordinating team. He and his Singapore teammate put together an eBusiness road show, took it to Japan, invited the whole IT team to view it at a lunch meeting, and walked through success stories about other parts of the organization that had aligned with the company's larger business priorities. It was rather subtle, he told us, but it worked. The Japanese IT team wanted to be spotlighted in future eBusiness road shows. In the end, the whole team worked well together—and no higher-level manager had to get involved.

Reading 4-2   Managing Executive Attention in the Global Company

Julian Birkinshaw, Cyril Bouquet, and Tina C. Ambos

Many companies today are truly global in reach. Shell Oil has operations in more than 140 countries, Coca-Cola sells its products in more than 200 countries, and Nestlé boasts that it has factories or operations in almost every country in the world. For the executives running these companies, the challenge of keeping abreast of events in markets around the world is mind boggling. Interestingly, the biggest problem is not a lack of information: Executives are deluged with monthly reports and market analyses for every country in which they operate. The problem is having the time and energy to process the information. Indeed, executive attention is a scarce resource, one that needs to be carefully managed.[1]

How should executives prioritize their time to ensure that it is focused on the countries and subsidiaries that need their attention? Which markets should they emphasize, and which can they allow to fall off their radar screen? We have researched executive attention in global companies for the past five years, interviewing 50 executives at 30 corporations. (See "About the Research," p. 40.) Despite the best of intentions and irrespective of the exhortation that companies should "think global, act local," the evidence shows clearly that corporate executives end up prioritizing a handful of markets at the expense of the others. One reason for selective attention is ethnocentric thinking—the tendency to assume that

the home market is most important. Of course, no executive would state this directly, but the evidence of a home-country bias is widespread and undisputed.[2]

Another factor is the so-called "herd mentality," which causes companies to focus on markets that competitors have identified. It is human nature to go "where the action is," and as a result some countries (most recently, China and India) attract a disproportionate amount of executive attention.

Both of these approaches are entirely defensible: They help channel resources to the most important areas of activity, and they seem relatively safe. But they can also be very wrong. Because executive attention is so limited, focusing on the home market or on a hot market will always come at the expense of other opportunities. The resulting mismatch between what's possible and what's needed can be quite damaging: Too much attention can disempower or suffocate subsidiary managers. As one executive noted, managers can become so preoccupied with representing their operations to executives that they don't have enough time to manage the business.

Too little attention can lead to even bigger problems, because it can result in missed opportunities and decisions by talented employees to leave. Consider, for example, the case of Dun & Bradstreet Corp.'s Australian subsidiary, which was ignored by the U.S. head office for years in the belief that Australia was not a "strategic" market. Frustrated by the lack of attention, the subsidiary's CEO persuaded the parent company to sell the business to a local private equity company in 2001; within three years, it had doubled in size and increased earnings tenfold. As a subsidiary company, its access to investment capital had been hamstrung by how corporate executives viewed Australia; as a standalone company, it could invest in whichever opportunities offered a promising investment return.

▌ Julian Birkinshaw is professor of strategic and international management at London Business School and a senior fellow of the Advanced Institute of Management Research. Cyril Bouquet is an assistant professor of strategic management at the Schulich School of Business, York University in Toronto. Tina C. Ambos is a lecturer at the University of Edinburgh and an assistant professor of economics and business administration at Vienna University. Comment on this article or contact the authors through smrfeedback @ mit.edu
▌ Reprinted from Managing Executive Attention in the Global Company by Birkinshaw, Bouquet and Ambos, MIT Sloan Management Review, Summer 2007, vol. 48, no. 4, pp. 39–45, by permission of publisher.

About the Research

Our research study was organized into two parts. In the first part, we conducted about 50 interviews with executives in corporate headquarters and subsidiaries of 30 global companies. The interviews were conducted in Australia, Canada, the United Kingdom, France, Sweden, Switzerland and the United States. We asked headquarters executives about the systems they used for managing attention in their companies and how they allocated their attention among competing claims from subsidiaries. We also asked subsidiary company executives to discuss strategies they used for gaining the attention of executives at the parent companies. In the second part of the study, we developed a questionnaire to ask managers about the "weight" and the "voice" of the subsidiaries, and the amount of attention the subsidiaries actually received. We received completed questionnaires from 283 subsidiary managers in four countries (Australia, Canada, the United Kingdom, and the United States). We also collected secondary data on the same subsidiary companies: how often they were mentioned in the annual report of their parent company, and market share and sales volume in the local country.

Subsidiary Weight and Attention

Our baseline hypothesis was that attention decisions would be based partially on the structural positions that subsidiary units occupy within the corporate system—their "weight." To test this hypothesis, we undertook a series of regression analyses, which showed that attention correlates with such factors as (1) the size of the subsidiary (measured in terms of total sales, employees and number of officers in the top management team); (2) the strategic importance of the local market (whether conceptualized in terms of sales figures or flows of foreign direct investment); and (3) the strength of the subsidiary's operations (an index capturing the extent to which the subsidiary occupies a highly valued role in the global organization).

Subsidiary Voice and Attention

Our second hypothesis was that subsidiaries also had a "voice" of their own that they could use to attract attention. To test this idea, we asked questions about a range of subsidiary-level activities, out of which we created two indexes (one for initiative taking, the other for profile building). Both factors were found to positively correlate with the level of attention granted to the subsidiary, indicating support for our second hypothesis.

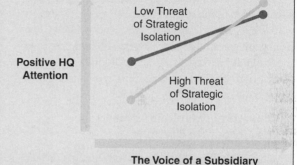

The Voice of a Subsidiary

Note: Attention is the extent to which the parent company recognizes and gives credit to the subsidiary for its contribution to the multinational enterprise as a whole. It is the composite of three factors assessing the relative, supportive and visible aspects of attention, each measured through a variety of indicators.

For a full description of the research and statistical analyses, please refer to C. Bouquet and J. Birkinshaw, "Weight Versus Voice: How Foreign Subsidiaries Gain Attention From Corporate Headquarters," Academy of Management Journal, in press.

Strategic Isolation and Attention

The third hypothesis was that the relationship between subsidiary voice and headquarters attention would be moderated by two specific aspects of the subsidiary's historical situation, which have often contributed to the subsidiary's strategic isolation: geographic distance and a competence anchored in the downstream part of the value chain. Using a series of regression analyses, we found support for this hypothesis. The more subsidiaries are at risk of strategic isolation, the greater the importance of voice in shaping levels of executive attention.

In this article, we examine the nature of executive attention and identify mechanisms by which subsidiary companies draw attention from the top executives of their organizations. Although attention can be harmful as well as helpful, we focus on the positive aspects. In particular, we see executive attention as consisting of three important elements: support, in terms of how headquarters executives interact with and help subsidiary managers achieve their goals; visibility, in terms of the public statements headquarters executives make about how the subsidiary is doing; and relative standing, in terms of the subsidiary's perceived status vis-à-vis other subsidiaries in the organization.

Conceptualized in this way, we address two important questions: How can a subsidiary attract more attention? And what can headquarters executives do to make sure that the right subsidiaries receive the attention they deserve?

Allocating Attention Across the Corporate Portfolio

How do headquarters executives decide which markets to focus on? While ethnocentric bias and herdlike behavior influence executive attention in profound ways, most global companies have nonetheless established reasonably sophisticated mechanisms for directing attention to the markets that need it most. These mechanisms include choices about lines of reporting, which meetings to attend and which individuals to put in positions of influence. Such mechanisms don't just channel executive attention to particular markets or issues. They also provide an important signal within the company about which markets matter most.

Top executives obtain insights about which countries or subsidiaries should receive their attention in two ways: externally, in the form of industry reports, the media and competitor intelligence; and internally, from standard reporting processes and the active lobbying of individuals. From this information, we have identified four distinct markets. (See "Attracting Attention in the Global Company.")

Large global companies often regard countries such as the United States and Japan as "major markets" that attract a high level of attention through both internal and external channels. China and India receive lots of media attention and thus are often seen as "honey pots," but the business opportunities there may not live up to the buzz. In many companies, Canada and Australia receive attention based on relationships; we characterize such markets as "squeaky wheels" because they represent established operations whose achievements are well known to headquarters executives, even if the markets themselves don't justify the emphasis. We call the last group the "forgotten markets" because they have difficulty getting onto the corporate radar screen. Note that our framework says nothing about whether the subsidiary is performing well or badly, only the level of management attention the subsidiary receives. Some squeaky wheels are troubled operations that need to be turned around; others might be rising stars; and some of the forgotten markets, like Dun & Bradstreet (Australia) Pty. Ltd., may actually be hidden gems.

Our framework suggests that a subsidiary can use two very different strategies to attract the attention of executives at the parent company: It can count on its weight as a player in an important market, and it can exert its voice by working through channels within the company. Some subsidiaries focus on one or the other, while others pursue both approaches in parallel. We will explain how these two approaches work.

Attracting Attention With "Weight"

In global organizations, subsidiaries that play pivotal roles in the success of the overall business have no trouble getting attention. China, for example, is a critical market for ABB Ltd., the Switzerland-based engineering group: In 2006, ABB's Chinese subsidiaries contributed $2.9 billion in revenues—approximately 12% of ABB's global business. The previous year, it captured capital funds and investments of $80 million out of $454 million for the whole corporate portfolio. Like other multinational corporations, ABB has high hopes for the Chinese market in the years ahead. But as China prepares for elections in 2008, there is considerable

Attracting Attention in the Global Company

Subsidiary units can be categorized on two dimensions: the amount of attention they gain through external or top-down channels, and the amount of attention they gain through internal or bottom-up channels. Where the subsidiary is located will define the appropriate strategy for gaining additional attention.

Level of Attention
On basis of internal or bottom-up channels

High — **Squeaky Wheels** Internal success stories, problem cases or markets with highly vocal managers — **Major Markets** Markets that represent big opportunities or threats

Low — **Forgotten Markets** Very low visibility at a corporate level — **Honey Pots** Markets that represent big opportunities or threats but limited current activity

Low — **Attention Given to market** — High
On basis of external or top-down channels

uncertainty about how best to maintain a positive climate for investment. ABB executives spend several hours a week on conference calls with their Chinese counterparts to identify and mobilize the necessary corporate resources and to ensure that the company's executives in Zurich are up to speed on major developments in the region. Ulrich Spiesshofer, ABB's head of corporate development, recently noted that "questions related to the activities of our Chinese business get top management preoccupied on a daily basis."[3]

A subsidiary's weight is not simply a function of its size. In many cases, it also reflects the impact it has on the company's global network. Subsidiaries occupying highly valued roles—for example, as centers of competence or as technological hubs—have significant weight as well. Pratt & Whitney Canada Corp., for example, is recognized for its expertise in the small aircraft turbine market. Because of its highly skilled labor force and advanced technologies, many sister subsidiaries look to it for technological advice and support.

Attracting Attention With "Voice"

How does a subsidiary that lacks weight capture the attention of top management? Our research found that subsidiaries without weight often seek other ways to gain visibility in a global company. Many managers rely on two types of proactive efforts: initiative taking and profile building.

Initiative Taking   This approach involves strategically selecting projects or ventures to grow the subsidiary, perhaps by developing new products, penetrating new markets or simply generating new ideas.[4] Such actions can influence the attention of the parent company in very direct ways. For example, when Fred Kindle, the CEO of ABB, visited the managers of the company's Czech subsidiary, he learned that managers there had found an innovative way of networking the company's administrative computers at night (when they were not used) to leverage their built-in processing capacity. This enabled the company to run complex research and development algorithms more quickly and, in turn, gave the Czech subsidiary valuable recognition and corporate support.

Initiative taking can also draw attention from headquarters in ways that are less direct. Individuals behind successful initiatives, for example, can build reputations that open doors to opportunities. For instance, Sara Lee Corp.'s Australian subsidiary became known within the company for its leadership on diversity issues, thus making Angela Laing, the diversity champion, a rising star. She soon became vice president of human resources for the company's worldwide household and body care division, and several others from Sara Lee Australia moved into senior positions elsewhere in the corporation. Nestlé Canada Inc., which developed a new line selling custom batches of frozen foods to food service operators, has leveraged this innovation into increased attention overall. (See "Defining a Value-Added Role for Nestlé Canada.")

Profile Building   Subsidiary managers use a variety of mechanisms to improve their image, credibility and reputation within the global company. If initiative taking occurs in the local context, profile building focuses on the things managers do within the broader corporate network. We found that successful profile builders focused on three types of activities.

They build a stellar track record.   The managers of profile building subsidiaries delivered results above the expectations of the parent company for a number of years. As Mark Masterson, vice president of health care product maker Abbott Laboratories' Pacific, Asia and Africa operations, observed, "Getting attention is about establishing credibility, and it doesn't happen within a short period of time. People need time to evaluate how you run a business. If you demonstrate predictability and results over time, you start to gain more confidence to put more challenging options to the company."[5]

They support corporate objectives.   To the extent that managers pursued their own local priorities, they did not downplay corporate concerns in the least. This may be common sense to seasoned executives, but it can also call for some careful juggling as subsidiary managers attempt to balance local initiatives with commitments to the corporate cause. Many of the subsidiary managers we spoke to described how they "push back" on some corporate requests and how they explain problems to their immediate bosses. "You are stupid if you don't keep some things up your sleeve," one manager explained. "You have to manage expectations, which involves not telling the whole story until you are ready. So I act as a buffer."

They work as internal brokers.   Successful subsidiary managers spend a lot of time building relationships within and beyond their corporate network. Some of this work is to build awareness— letting other parts of the company know what the unit does, how well it does it and what it might be able to contribute in the future. It can also be targeted toward specific projects and take the form of pre-selling ideas and lobbying with key power brokers in the corporate hierarchy. For example, one manager talked about the preselling process: getting all interested parties involved early and "oiling the wheels" so that when the formal proposal is presented it

encounters no resistance. Another manager noted the importance of timing: "If you tell the story too early, you risk getting shot down or building up unreasonable expectations; if you tell it too late and they get mad, you will struggle to get support." It is important to recognize the level of planning required for a successful campaign to build support for new investment and new initiatives.

The Threat of Strategic Isolation

In addition to the strategic approaches subsidiaries used for attracting attention, we found two particular contexts where initiative taking and profile building were especially important: when subsidiaries were located far away from corporate headquarters and when the subsidiary's activities were focused solely on the local market. This finding is not entirely surprising: Remote operations are especially likely to fall off the radar screen of headquarters executives. But for subsidiary managers, it is reassuring to know that there are ways to overcome the "tyranny of distance."

We found that profile building was the more effective approach to capturing attention, either on its own or in combination with initiative taking. One of the dangers of subsidiary managers pursuing initiatives on their own is that unless they have already built a track record with the parent company, the initiatives can be seen as empire building. The initiatives may also compete with the entrepreneurial activities of subsidiaries in other parts of the world for headquarters' attention. Subsidiary managers often seek to mitigate these concerns by approaching initiatives cautiously: focusing on ideas and projects that will add value to the rest of the global company or collaborating with peers in other countries. For example, the CEO of Oracle Corp. Australia Pty. Ltd. sponsored the design of an integrated approach to education, which he believed had the potential to revolutionize methods of learning within the K-12 school system. But pursuing this initiative required substantial funds and did not fit into the existing corporate research and development priorities. By lining up support from his overseas colleagues, the Australian CEO was able to build a critical mass and attract notice from the head office.

Subsidiary managers often argue that their ability to influence their own destiny is undermined by their lack of decision-making power. However, we found that a subsidiary's degree of decision-making autonomy has no meaningful effect on the level of executive attention it receives. Indeed, in many instances subsidiary managers used their limited degrees of freedom to great effect. For example, Yum! Restaurants International's KFC division in Australia has built a reputation as a leading innovator in its global business. One of its most notable breakthroughs involved its drive-through business. For a variety of reasons (some of which had to do with technical problems relating to the drive-through speaker box), customers at many stores had been reluctant to use the drive-through window. With a modest investment, however, Yum Australia redesigned the entire drive-through experience: It expanded the order window, redesigned the menu board and trained employees to assist customers with their menu choices. The result was a dramatic increase in drive-through sales and customer satisfaction and enhanced visibility for Yum Australia within the corporate system, reinforcing its position as a leading global innovator.

Refocusing Executive Attention

What lessons can corporate headquarters executives draw from our research? What sorts of changes should they make to get the most out of their portfolio of subsidiary companies? Our findings suggest four broad approaches.

Create channels for attention. Attention is channelled through a number of formal and informal mechanisms, many of which are designed explicitly to direct executive attention to the biggest or weightiest issues. But if executives want to find ways to amplify the voice of their subsidiaries around the world, they need to give creative thought to the meetings, events and forums they participate in. Some examples of what we observed include:

- Holding performance reviews in the country or region being evaluated. One Australian subsidiary manager had been meeting his European boss in

Bangkok as a way to share the travel time. But once he was able to persuade his boss to travel to Sydney, he noticed a dramatic—and positive—change in his boss's attitude toward the subsidiary.

- Locating board meetings overseas. Companies have found that this often leads to dramatic changes in outlook, providing board members with opportunities to talk directly with distant customers and examine production operations firsthand. Melbourne- and London-based global mining company Rio Tinto, for example, took its entire board to China for a week in 2005. London-based engineering consultancy Arup Group Ltd. holds every other board meeting in an overseas location such as Poland or Brazil.

- Cultivating interpersonal ties. The attention headquarters executives pay to subsidiaries typically stems from past interactions and how well executives know the local people. Accordingly, many companies host forums for the purpose of cultivating ties among different players in the organization. For example, ABB brings its country managers together at least twice a year both to socialize and to share important local insights. In addition, staff from subsidiaries around the world meet with headquarters staff regularly through their involvement in cross-country teams.

- Assigning mentorship responsibilities. At Procter & Gamble Co., country managers are formally linked to a corporate executive, who is expected to keep his antennae out and play a championing role in helping the subsidiary gain access to corporate resources. Ultimately, however, it is up to the subsidiary staff to inform mentors of interesting local developments and to build the case for what they can contribute to the company as a whole.

- Recognizing that regional support for subsidiaries can cut both ways. Regional headquarters can help subsidiaries attract attention, but they can also act as a harmful buffer. IBM Corp., for example, re-evaluated the role of its European headquarters recently, and ended up replacing its Paris headquarters with two new focused headquarters serving North/East Europe and South/West Europe, respectively.

Defining a Value-Added Role for Nestlé Canada

In the years following the North American Free Trade Agreement, Nestlé Canada, like many Canadian subsidiaries, found it increasingly difficult to add value to the company's low-growth lines of business. The reality was that most Canadian markets could be tapped more efficiently from the United States. Nestlé Canada's best hope was to define a distinctive role within the global company. Management came up with the idea of a new line of products: custom batches of restaurant-quality frozen food for food service operators, who would then market to hospitals, hotels and airlines. If successful, it would provide a new revenue stream while positioning Nestlé Canada to test market other new products.

Nestlé Canada has turned into a major success story. In 2006, it employed 3,600 people in 16 facilities across the country, with sales of $2.3 billion, mostly from direct exports to 70 countries worldwide. "Canada has highly sophisticated consumers, and yet [it has] a population base that allows us to experiment without breaking the bank," said Frank Cella, former president and chief executive of Nestlé Canada, who went on to become a senior executive with the corporate parent.[i] "We made a case for allowing us to be an experimental lab, and that has given us a uniqueness that we would not have otherwise. We add value by innovation, by trying new ideas and getting them to market faster. We are so innovative that the worldwide group is sending people [to Canada] to learn about how we do it."

[i] See Business Council on National Issues, "Going For Gold: Winning Corporate Strategies and Their Impact on Canada," working paper released at the CEO Summit 2000, Toronto, April 5, 2000.

Seek out the hidden gems and give them a platform. It is worth paying special attention to subsidiary companies that deliver surprisingly good results in relation to their overall stature. Over and above delivering stellar numbers financially, they may also be sources of new insights or practices. Finding these subsidiaries is partly a matter of opening up the attention channels. But it also may require some extra analysis. Which subsidiaries are attracting more interest internally than their market position might warrant? And which are responsible for the biggest annual jumps in sales and profits?

Groupe Danone, the French food products company, does a good job of giving a platform to its hidden gems. Following a major initiative aimed at increasing the company's top-line growth, Danone recently identified the leading countries in the world for certain activities and designated them as the corporate "champions" that others could learn from. Frucor Beverages Group Ltd., Danone's New Zealand subsidiary, became a center for innovation, and executives from elsewhere in the company have been encouraged to spend time in New Zealand to understand how it has been able to deliver revenue growth of 7% to 10% over the past 10 years in a flat market. Similarly, Indonesia was recognized for its expertise in "affordability."

Measure returns on executive attention. A slightly different challenge is how to assess the value of investments in attention, particularly as they relate to big emerging markets: In essence, this involves understanding how to leverage attention into capability. General Electric Co.'s experience in this area provides useful insights. Like executives of most global companies, GE executives pay huge amounts of attention to growth opportunities in China, India, Russia and markets in the Middle East and Latin America. But they are highly disciplined about how they go about it so that the investment opportunities aren't wasted. Their motto is: "Go big and continuously look back." Indeed, they don't get involved unless they can help the company win mega project proposals in the region—for example, airport expansion programs in China or major water-power programs in India. Less significant opportunities are left for local talent to ponder. Perhaps more importantly, they continually evaluate whether these investments are delivering against their performance expectations, and this analysis becomes a significant input into subsequent investment decisions.[6]

Give subsidiaries a chance to contribute.   Good subsidiary managers are looking for ways to contribute to the company as a whole over and above achieving good results in their own business. One of the roles of headquarters managers is to define the needs. For example, executives at several Australian subsidiaries spoke about how their parent wanted them to develop management talent for the rest of the company. Many were reluctant to give up their most promising managers to careers in Europe or North America. But Roger Eaton, the CEO of Yum Australia, decided to make exporting talent a cornerstone of his strategy. Each year he recommended three senior managers for key assignments outside Australia; as these individuals have excelled in their new assignments, the reputation of the Australian operation has grown. "You can't avoid the Aussies in YUM globally," notes Eaton. "If you look at the top 200 executives in the company, you'd find over 20 Australians!"

MANAGING ATTENTION IN A GLOBAL COMPANY often boils down to specific and apparently small actions: holding a board meeting in a remote city, initiating a forum to discuss emerging market opportunities or asking a division head to groom executives for overseas assignments. However, in an environment where high-level attention is in such short supply, small actions can have enormous consequences. They can furnish opportunities for subsidiaries to showcase their initiatives or gain access to expansion capital. They can trigger important shifts in the parent company's overall growth trajectory.

We are accustomed to thinking of subsidiaries as having fairly fixed roles.[7] But actually, the roles can be fairly fluid, changing to reflect evolving opportunities and new competencies the subsidiary can contribute. Executive attention can facilitate these internal shifts. Attention may not be the ultimate objective, but it is a necessary ingredient for any subsidiary that seeks to play a more pivotal role in the global company.

Acknowledgments

The authors wish to thank the Advanced Institute of Management Research, the Social Sciences and Humanities Research Council of Canada, York University's Institute for Social Research and CEO Forum Group (Australia) for their support.

References

1. Several studies have examined the challenges of managing executive attention. See T. H. Davenport and J. C. Beck, "The Attention Economy: Understanding the New Currency of Business" (Boston: Harvard Business School Press, 2001); C. Bouquet, "Building Global Mindsets: An Attention-Based Perspective" (New York: Palgrave Macmillan, 2005); W. Ocasio, "Towards an Attention-Based View of the Firm," Strategic Management Journal 18, special issue (Dec. 4, 1998): 187–206; and M. T. Hansen and M. R. Haas, "Competing For Attention in Knowledge Markets: Electronic Document Dissemination in a Management Consulting Company," Administrative Science Quarterly 46, no. 1 (March 2001): 1–28.

2. See A. M. Rugman and A. Verbeke, "Subsidiary-Specific Advantages in Multinational Enterprises," Strategic Management Journal 22, no. 3 (January 2001): 237–250.

3. U. Spiesshofer, "Managing the Balance: A Global Player's Perspective On Institutional Change" (keynote address at the 26th Annual Conference of the Strategic Management Society, Vienna, Austria, Oct. 30, 2006).

4. See J. M. Birkinshaw and N. Fry, "Subsidiary Initiative to Develop New Markets," Sloan Management Review 39, no. 3 (spring 1998): 51–61.

5. Interestingly, a poor track record is also conducive to getting attention, but not the type of attention that subsidiary managers feel is most conducive to creating the right set of conditions for the subsidiary to develop in the future. 3M Co., for instance, recently reacted to the disappointing results of its Canadian subsidiary by

almost completely replacing the local management structure. Four out of five VPs were let go; the Canadian CEO who completed our survey was moved to a lesser position in the United States; and a substantial number of middle-level managers ended up being replaced.

6. J. Immelt (untitled presentation at Electrical Products Group conference, Long Boat Keys, Florida, May 24, 2006).
7. See C. A. Bartlett and S. Ghoshal, "Tap Your Subsidiaries For Global Reach," Harvard Business Review 64, no. 6 (November 1986): 87–94.

Reading 4-3   Matrix Management: Not a Structure, a Frame of Mind

Christopher A. Bartlett and Sumantra Ghoshal

Top-level managers in many of today's leading corporations are losing control of their companies. The problem is not that they have misjudged the demands created by an increasingly complex environment and an accelerating rate of environmental change, nor even that they have failed to develop strategies appropriate to the new challenges. The problem is that their companies are organizationally incapable of carrying out the sophisticated strategies they have developed. Over the past 20 years, strategic thinking has far outdistanced organizational capabilities.

All through the 1980s, companies everywhere were redefining their strategies and reconfiguring their operations in response to such developments as

▌ Christopher A. Bartlett is a professor of general management at the Harvard Business School, where he is also chairman of the International Senior Management program. Sumantra Ghoshal is an associate professor who teaches business policy at the European Institute of Business Administration (INSEAD) in Fontainebleau, France. This article is based on their book, *Managing Across Borders: The Transnational Solution* (Harvard Business School Press, 1989).

the globalization of markets, the intensification of competition, the acceleration of product life cycles, and the growing complexity of relationships with suppliers, customers, employees, governments, even competitors. But as companies struggled with these changing environmental realities, many fell into one of two traps—one strategic, one structural.

The strategic trap was to implement simple, static solutions to complex and dynamic problems. The bait was often a consultant's siren song promising to simplify or at least minimize complexity and discontinuity. Despite the new demands of overlapping industry boundaries and greatly altered value-added chains, managers were promised success if they would "stick to their knitting." In a swiftly changing international political economy, they were urged to rein in dispersed overseas operations and focus on the triad markets, and in an increasingly intricate and sophisticated competitive environment, they were encouraged to choose between alternative generic strategies—low cost or differentiation.

Yet the strategic reality for most companies was that both their business and their environment really *were* more complex, while the proposed solutions were often simple, even simplistic. The traditional telephone company that stuck to its knitting was trampled by competitors who redefined their strategies in response to new technologies linking telecommunications, computers, and office equipment into a single integrated system. The packaged-goods company that concentrated on the triad markets quickly discovered that Europe, Japan, and the United States were the epicenters of global competitive activity, with higher risks and slimmer profits than more protected and less competitive markets such as Australia, Turkey, and Brazil. The consumer electronics company that adopted an either-or generic strategy found itself facing competitors able to develop cost and differentiation capabilities at the same time.

In recent years, as more and more managers recognized oversimplification as a strategic trap, they began to accept the need to manage complexity rather than seek to minimize it. This realization, however, led many into an equally threatening organizational trap when they concluded that the best response to increasingly complex strategic requirements was increasingly complex organizational structures.

The obvious organizational solution to strategies that required multiple, simultaneous management capabilities was the matrix structure that became so fashionable in the late 1970s and the early 1980s. Its parallel reporting relationships acknowledged the diverse, conflicting needs of functional, product, and geographic management groups and provided a formal mechanism for resolving them. Its multiple information channels allowed the organization to capture and analyze external complexity. And its overlapping responsibilities were designed to combat parochialism and build flexibility into the company's response to change.

In practice, however, the matrix proved all but unmanageable—especially in an international context. Dual reporting led to conflict and confusion; the proliferation of channels created informational logjams as a proliferation of committees and reports bogged down the organization; and overlapping responsibilities produced turf battles and a loss of accountability. Separated by barriers of distance, language, time, and culture, managers found it virtually impossible to clarify the confusion and resolve the conflicts.

In hindsight, the strategic and structural traps seem simple enough to avoid, so one has to wonder why so many experienced general managers have fallen into them. Much of the answer lies in the way we have traditionally thought about the general manager's role. For decades, we have seen the general manager as chief strategic guru and principal organizational architect. But as the competitive climate grows less stable and less predictable, it is harder for one person alone to succeed in that great visionary role. Similarly, as formal, hierarchical structure gives way to networks of personal relationships that work through informal, horizontal communication channels, the image of top management in an isolated corner office moving boxes and lines on an organization chart becomes increasingly anachronistic.

Paradoxically, as strategies and organizations become more complex and sophisticated, top-level general managers are beginning to replace their historical concentration on the grand issues of strategy and structure with a focus on the details of managing people and processes. The critical strategic requirement is not to devise the most ingenious and well-coordinated plan but to build the most viable and flexible strategic process; the key organizational task is not to design the most elegant structure but to capture individual capabilities and motivate the entire organization to respond cooperatively to a complicated and dynamic environment.

Building an Organization

Although business thinkers have written a great deal about strategic innovation, they have paid far less attention to the accompanying organizational challenges. Yet many companies remain caught in the structural-complexity trap that paralyzes their ability to respond quickly or flexibly to the new strategic imperatives.

For those companies that adopted matrix structures, the problem was not in the way they defined the goal. They correctly recognized the need for a multidimensional organization to respond to growing external complexity. The problem was that they defined their organizational objectives in purely structural terms. Yet the term *formal structure* describes only the organization's basic anatomy. Companies must also concern themselves with organizational physiology—the systems and relationships that allow the lifeblood of information to flow through the organization. They also need to develop a healthy organizational psychology—the shared norms, values, and beliefs that shape the way individual managers think and act.

The companies that fell into the organizational trap assumed that changing their formal structure (anatomy) would force changes in interpersonal relationships and decision processes (physiology), which in turn would reshape the individual attitudes and actions of managers (psychology).

But as many companies have discovered, reconfiguring the formal structure is a blunt and sometimes brutal instrument of change. A new structure creates new and presumably more useful managerial ties, but these can take months and often years to evolve into effective knowledge-generating and decision-making relationships. And because the new job requirements will frustrate, alienate, or simply overwhelm so many managers, changes in individual attitudes and behavior will likely take even longer.

As companies struggle to create organizational capabilities that reflect rather than diminish environmental complexity, good managers gradually stop searching for the ideal structural template to impose on the company from the top down. Instead, they focus on the challenge of building up an appropriate set of employee attitudes and skills and linking them together with carefully developed processes and relationships. In other words, they begin to focus on building the organization rather than simply on installing a new structure.

Indeed, the companies that are most successful at developing multidimensional organizations begin at the far end of the anatomy-physiology-psychology sequence. Their first objective is to alter the organizational psychology—the broad corporate beliefs and norms that shape managers' perceptions and actions. Then, by enriching and clarifying communication and decision processes, companies reinforce these psychological changes with improvements in organizational physiology. Only later do they consolidate and confirm their

progress by realigning organizational anatomy through changes in the formal structure.

No company we know of has discovered a quick or easy way to change its organizational psychology to reshape the understanding, identification, and commitment of its employees. But we found three principal characteristics common to those that managed the task most effectively:

1. They developed and communicated a clear and consistent corporate vision.
2. They effectively managed human resource tools to broaden individual perspectives and to develop identification with corporate goals.
3. They integrated individual thinking and activities into the broad corporate agenda by a process we call co-option.

Building a Shared Vision

Perhaps the main reason managers in large, complex companies cling to parochial attitudes is that their frame of reference is bounded by their specific responsibilities. The surest way to break down such insularity is to develop and communicate a clear sense of corporate purpose that extends into every corner of the company and gives context and meaning to each manager's particular roles and responsibilities. We are not talking about a slogan, however catchy and pointed. We are talking about a company vision, which must be crafted and articulated with clarity, continuity, and consistency. We are talking about clarity of expression that makes company objectives understandable and meaningful; continuity of purpose that underscores their enduring importance; and consistency of application across business units and geographical boundaries that ensures uniformity throughout the organization.

Clarity There are three keys to clarity in a corporate vision: simplicity, relevance, and reinforcement. NEC's integration of computers and communications—C&C—is probably the best single example of how simplicity can make a vision more powerful. Top management has applied the C&C concept so effectively that it describes the company's business focus, defines its distinctive source of competitive advantage over large companies like IBM and AT&T, and summarizes its strategic and organizational imperatives.

The second key, relevance, means linking broad objectives to concrete agendas. When Wisse Dekker became CEO at Philips, his principal strategic concern was the problem of competing with Japan. He stated this challenge in martial terms—the U.S. had abandoned the battlefield; Philips was now Europe's last defense against insurgent Japanese electronics companies. By focusing the company's attention not only on Philips's corporate survival but also on the protection of national and regional interests, Dekker heightened the sense of urgency and commitment in a way that legitimized cost-cutting efforts, drove an extensive rationalization of plant operations, and inspired a new level of sales achievements.

The third key to clarity is top management's continual reinforcement, elaboration, and interpretation of the core vision to keep it from becoming obsolete or abstract. Founder Konosuke Matsushita developed a grand, 250-year vision for his company, but he also managed to give it immediate relevance. He summed up its overall message in the "Seven Spirits of Matsushita," to which he referred constantly in his policy statements. Each January he wove the company's one-year operational objectives into his overarching concept to produce an annual theme that he then captured in a slogan. For all the loftiness of his concept of corporate purpose, he gave his managers immediate, concrete guidance in implementing Matsushita's goals.

Continuity   Despite shifts in leadership and continual adjustments in short-term business priorities, companies must remain committed to the same core set of strategic objectives and organizational values. Without such continuity, unifying vision might as well be expressed in terms of quarterly goals.

It was General Electric's lack of this kind of continuity that led to the erosion of its once formidable position in electrical appliances in many countries. Over a period of 20 years and under successive CEOs, the company's international consumer-product strategy never stayed the same for long. From building locally responsive and self-sufficient "mini-GEs" in each market, the company turned to a policy of developing low-cost offshore sources, which eventually evolved into a de facto strategy of international outsourcing. Finally, following its acquisition of RCA, GE's consumer electronics strategy made another about-face and focused on building centralized scale to defend domestic share. Meanwhile, the product strategy within this shifting business emphasis was itself unstable. The Brazilian subsidiary, for example, built its TV business in the 1960s until it was told to stop; in the early 1970s, it emphasized large appliances until it was denied funding, then it focused on housewares until the parent company sold off that business. In two decades, GE utterly dissipated its dominant franchise in Brazil's electrical products market.

Unilever, by contrast, made an enduring commitment to its Brazilian subsidiary, despite volatile swings in Brazil's business climate. Company chairman Floris Maljers emphasized the importance of looking past the latest political crisis or economic downturn to the long-term business potential. "In those parts of the world," he remarked, "you take your management cues from the way they dance. The samba method of management is two steps forward then one step back." Unilever built—two steps forward and one step back—a profitable $300 million business in a rapidly growing economy with 130 million consumers, while its wallflower competitors never ventured out onto the floor.

Consistency   The third task for top management in communicating strategic purpose is to ensure that everyone in the company shares the same vision. The cost of inconsistency can be horrendous. It always produces confusion and, in extreme cases, can lead to total chaos, with different units of the organization pursuing agendas that are mutually debilitating.

Philips is a good example of a company that, for a time, lost its consistency of corporate purpose. As a legacy of its wartime decision to give some overseas units legal autonomy, management had long experienced difficulty persuading North American Philips (NAP) to play a supportive role in the parent company's global strategies. The problem came to a head with the introduction of Philips's technologically first-rate videocassette recording system, the V2000. Despite considerable pressure from world headquarters in the Netherlands, NAP refused to launch the system, arguing that Sony's Beta system and Matsushita's VHS format were too well established and had cost, feature, and system-support advantages Philips couldn't match. Relying on its legal independence and managerial autonomy, NAP management decided instead to source products from its Japanese competitors and market them under its Magnavox brand name. As a result, Philips was unable to build the efficiency and credibility it needed to challenge Japanese dominance of the VCR business.

Most inconsistencies involve differences between what managers of different operating units see as the company's key objectives. Sometimes, however, different corporate leaders transmit different views of overall priorities and purpose. When this stems from poor communication, it can be fixed. When it's a result of fundamental disagreement, the problem is serious indeed, as illustrated by ITT's problems in developing its strategically vital System 12 switching equipment. Continuing differences between the head of the European organization and the company's chief technology officer over the location and philosophy of the development effort led to confusion and conflict throughout the company. The result was disastrous. ITT had difficulty transferring vital technology across its own unit boundaries and so was irreparably late introducing this key product to a rapidly changing global market. These problems eventually led the company to sell off its core telecommunications business to a competitor.

But formulating and communicating a vision—no matter how clear, enduring, and consistent—cannot succeed unless individual employees under-stand and accept the company's stated goals and objectives. Problems at this level are more often related to receptivity than to communication. The development of

individual understanding and acceptance is a challenge for a company's human resource practices.

Developing Human Resources

While top managers universally recognize their responsibility for developing and allocating a company's scarce assets and resources, their focus on finance and technology often overshadows the task of developing the scarcest resource of all—capable managers. But if there is one key to regaining control of companies that operate in fast-changing environments, it is the ability of top management to turn the perceptions, capabilities, and relationships of individual managers into the building blocks of the organization.

One pervasive problem in companies whose leaders lack this ability—or fail to exercise it—is getting managers to see how their specific responsibilities relate to the broad corporate vision. Growing external complexity and strategic sophistication have accelerated the growth of a cadre of specialists who are physically and organizationally isolated from each other, and the task of dealing with their consequent parochialism should not be delegated to the clerical staff that administers salary structures and benefit programs. Top managers inside and outside the human resource function must be leaders in the recruitment, development, and assignment of the company's vital human talent.

Recruitment and Selection   The first step in successfully managing complexity is to tap the full range of available talent. It is a serious mistake to permit historical imbalances in the nationality or functional background of the management group to constrain hiring or subsequent promotion. In today's global marketplace, domestically oriented recruiting limits a company's ability to capitalize on its worldwide pool of management skill and biases its decision-making processes.

After decades of routinely appointing managers from its domestic operations to key positions in overseas subsidiaries, Procter & Gamble realized that the practice not only worked against sensitivity to local cultures—a lesson driven home by several marketing failures in Japan—but also greatly under-utilized its pool of high-potential non-American managers. (Fortunately, our studies turned up few companies as shortsighted as one that made overseas assignments on the basis of *poor* performance, because foreign markets were assumed to be "not as tough as the domestic environment.")

Not only must companies enlarge the pool of people available for key positions, they must also develop new criteria for choosing those most likely to succeed. Because past success is no longer a sufficient qualification for increasingly subtle, sensitive, and unpredictable senior-level tasks, top management must become involved in a more discriminating selection process. At Matsushita, top management selects candidates for international assignments on the basis of a comprehensive set of personal characteristics, expressed for simplicity in the acronym SMILE: specialty (the needed skill, capability, or knowledge); management ability (particularly motivational ability); international flexibility (willingness to learn and ability to adapt); language facility; and endeavor (vitality, perseverance in the face of difficulty). These attributes are remarkably similar to those targeted by NEC and Philips, where top executives also are involved in the senior-level selection process.

Training and Development   Once the appropriate top-level candidates have been identified, the next challenge is to develop their potential. The most successful development efforts have three aims that take them well beyond the skill-building objectives of classic training programs: to inculcate a common vision and shared values; to broaden management perspectives and capabilities; and to develop contacts and shape management relationships.

To build common vision and values, white-collar employees at Matsushita spend a good part of their first six months in what the company calls "cultural and spiritual training." They study the company credo, the "Seven Spirits of Matsushita," and the philosophy of Konosuke Matsushita. Then they learn how to translate these internalized

lessons into daily behavior and even operational decisions. Culture-building exercises as intensive as Matsushita's are sometimes dismissed as innate Japanese practices that would not work in other societies, but in fact, Philips has a similar entry-level training practice (called "organization cohesion training"), as does Unilever (called, straight-forwardly, "indoctrination").

The second objective—broadening management perspectives—is essentially a matter of teaching people how to manage complexity instead of merely to make room for it. To reverse a long and unwieldy tradition of running its operations with two- and three-headed management teams of separate technical, commercial, and sometimes administrative specialists, Philips asked its training and development group to de-specialize top management trainees. By supplementing its traditional menu of specialist courses and functional programs with more intensive general management training, Philips was able to begin replacing the ubiquitous teams with single business heads who also appreciated and respected specialist points of view.

The final aim—developing contacts and relationships—is much more than an incidental byproduct of good management development, as the comments of a senior personnel manager at Unilever suggest: "By bringing managers from different countries and businesses together at Four Acres [Unilever's international management-training college], we build contacts and create bonds that we could never achieve by other means. The company spends as much on training as it does on R&D not only because of the direct effect it has on upgrading skills and knowledge but also because it plays a central role in indoctrinating managers into a Unilever club where personal relationships and informal contacts are much more powerful than the formal systems and structures."

Career-Path Management   Although recruitment and training are critically important, the most effective companies recognize that the best way to develop new perspectives and thwart parochialism in their managers is through personal experience. By moving selected managers across functions, businesses, and geographic units, a company encourages cross-fertilization of ideas as well as the flexibility and breadth of experience that enable managers to grapple with complexity and come out on top.

Unilever has long been committed to the development of its human resources as a means of attaining durable competitive advantage. As early as the 1930s, the company was recruiting and developing local employees to replace the parent-company managers who had been running most of its overseas subsidiaries. In a practice that came to be known as "-ization," the company committed itself to the Indianization of its Indian company, the Australization of its Australian company, and so on.

Although delighted with the new talent that began working its way up through the organization, management soon realized that by reducing the transfer of parent-company managers abroad, it had diluted the powerful glue that bound diverse organizational groups together and linked dispersed operations. The answer lay in formalizing a second phase of the -ization process. While continuing with Indianization, for example, Unilever added programs aimed at the "Unileverization" of its Indian managers.

In addition to bringing 300 to 400 managers to Four Acres each year, Unilever typically has 100 to 150 of its most promising overseas managers on short- and long-term job assignments at corporate headquarters. This policy not only brings fresh, close-to-the-market perspectives into corporate decision making but also gives the visiting managers a strong sense of Unilever's strategic vision and organizational values. In the words of one of the expatriates in the corporate offices, "The experience initiates you into the Unilever Club and the clear norms, values, and behaviors that distinguish our people—so much so that we really believe we can spot another Unilever manager anywhere in the world."

Furthermore, the company carefully transfers most of these high-potential individuals through a variety of different functional, product, and geographic positions, often rotating every two or three years. Most important, top management tracks about 1,000 of these people—some 5% of Unilever's total management group—who, as they move through the company, forge an informal network of contacts and relationships that is central to Unilever's decision-making and information-exchange processes.

Widening the perspectives and relationships of key managers as Unilever has done is a good way of developing identification with the broader corporate mission. But a broad sense of identity is not enough. To maintain control of its global strategies, Unilever must secure a strong and lasting individual commitment to corporate visions and objectives. In effect, it must co-opt individual energies and ambitions into the service of corporate goals.

Co-Opting Management Efforts

As organizational complexity grows, managers and management groups tend to become so specialized and isolated and to focus so intently on their own immediate operating responsibilities that they are apt to respond parochially to intrusions on their organizational turf, even when the overall corporate interest is at stake. A classic example, described earlier, was the decision by North American Philips's consumer electronics group to reject the parent company's VCR system.

At about the same time, Philips, like many other companies, began experimenting with ways to convert managers' intellectual understanding of the corporate vision—in Philips's case, an almost evangelical determination to defend Western electronics against the Japanese—into a binding personal commitment. Philips concluded that it could co-opt individuals and organizational groups into the broader vision by inviting them to contribute to the corporate agenda and then giving them direct responsibility for implementation.

In the face of intensifying Japanese competition, Philips knew it had to improve coordination in its consumer electronics among its fiercely independent national organizations. In strengthening the central product divisions, however, Philips did not want to deplete the enterprise or commitment of its capable national management teams.

The company met these conflicting needs with two cross-border initiatives. First, it created a top-level World Policy Council for its video business that included key managers from strategic markets—Germany, France, the United Kingdom, the United States, and Japan. Philips knew that its national companies' long history of independence made local managers reluctant to take orders from Dutch headquarters in Eindhoven—often for good reason, because much of the company's best market knowledge and technological expertise resided in its offshore units. Through the council, Philips co-opted their support for company decisions about product policy and manufacturing location.

Second, in a more powerful move, Philips allocated global responsibilities to units that previously had been purely national in focus. Eindhoven gave NAP the leading role in the development of Philips's projection television and asked it to coordinate development and manufacture of all Philips television sets for North America and Asia. The change in the attitude of NAP managers was dramatic.

A senior manager in NAP's consumer electronics business summed up the feelings of U.S. managers: "At last, we are moving out of the dependency relationship with Eindhoven that was so frustrating to us." Co-option had transformed the defensive, territorial attitude of NAP managers into a more collaborative mind-set. They were making important contributions to global corporate strategy instead of looking for ways to subvert it.

In 1987, with much of its TV set production established in Mexico, the president of NAP's consumer electronics group told the press, "It is the commonality of design that makes it possible for us to move production globally. We have splendid cooperation with Philips in Eindhoven." It was a statement no NAP manager would have made a few years earlier, and it perfectly captured how effectively Philips had co-opted previously isolated, even adversarial, managers into the corporate agenda.

◼ The Matrix in the Manager's Mind

Since the end of World War II, corporate strategy has survived several generations of painful transformation and has grown appropriately agile and athletic. Unfortunately, organizational development has not kept pace, and managerial attitudes lag even farther behind. As a result, corporations now commonly design strategies that seem impossible to implement, for the simple reason that no one can effectively implement third-generation strategies through second-generation organizations run by first-generation managers.

Today the most successful companies are those where top executives recognize the need to manage the new environmental and competitive demands by focusing less on the quest for an ideal structure and more on developing the abilities, behavior, and performance of individual managers. Change succeeds only when those assigned to the new transnational and interdependent tasks understand the overall goals and are dedicated to achieving them.

One senior executive put it this way: "The challenge is not so much to build a matrix structure as it is to create a matrix in the minds of our managers." The inbuilt conflict in a matrix structure pulls managers in several directions at once. Developing a matrix of flexible perspectives and relationships within each manager's mind, however, achieves an entirely different result. It lets individuals make the judgments and negotiate the trade-offs that drive the organization toward a shared strategic objective.

Creating Worldwide Innovation and Learning:
Exploiting Cross-Border Knowledge Management

■   ■   ■   ■   ■   ■   ■   ■   ■   ■   ■   ■   ■   ■   ■   ■

In the information-based, knowledge-intensive economy of the 21st century, entities are not competing only in terms of their traditional ability to access new markets and arbitrage factor costs. Today the challenge is to build transnational organizations that can sense an emerging consumer trend in one country, link it to a new technology or capability it has in another, develop a creative new product or service in a third, then diffuse that innovation rapidly around the world. In this chapter, we contrast this transnational innovation process with more traditional "center-for-global" and "local-to-local" approaches that have been the dominant form of cross-border innovation in the past. We then describe the nature of the organizational capabilities that must be developed to make these central, local, and transnational innovations more effective.

In Chapter 3, we described how companies competing in today's global competitive environment are being required to build layers of competitive advantage—the ability to capture global scale efficiencies, local market responsiveness, and worldwide learning capability. As MNEs have found ways to match one another in the more familiar attributes of global scale efficiency and local responsiveness, the leading-edge competitive battles have shifted to companies' ability to link and leverage their worldwide resources and capabilities to develop and diffuse innovation.

Particularly in previous decades, some MNEs regarded their accumulation of knowledge and expertise as an asset they could sell into foreign markets. This was particularly true of the U.S.-based MNEs that followed the "international" strategy we described in Chapter 3. General Sarnoff, the CEO of RCA, decided that licensing the company's leading-edge technology was RCA's most appropriate strategy of international expansion. But by treating the global market just as an opportunity to generate incremental revenue and not as a source of innovation and learning, RCA soon found that after others had learned from everything it had to sell, they quickly overtook it in creating new innovative products more adapted to the global market.

In today's competitive environment, no company can assume that it can accumulate world-class knowledge and expertise by focusing only on its home country environment, or that it can succeed just by tweaking its domestic product line. The ability to develop and rapidly diffuse innovations around the world is vital, and in this challenge, offshore subsidiaries need to take on important new roles. They must act as the sensors of new market trends or technological developments; they must be able to attract scarce talent and expertise; and they must be able to act collectively with other subsidiaries to exploit the resulting new products and initiatives worldwide, regardless of where they originated.

Yet developing this capability to create, leverage, and apply knowledge worldwide is not a simple task for most large MNEs. Although people are innately curious and naturally motivated to learn from one another, most modern corporations are constructed in a way that constrains and sometimes kills this natural human instinct. In this chapter, we focus on one of the most important current challenges facing MNE management: how to develop and diffuse knowledge to support effective worldwide innovation and learning.

Central, Local, and Transnational Innovation

Traditionally, MNEs' innovative capabilities were dominated by one of two classic processes. In what we describe as the *center-for-global* innovation model, the new opportunity was usually sensed in the home country; the centralized resources and capabilities of the parent company were brought in to create the new product or process, usually in the main R&D center; and implementation involved driving the innovation through subsidiaries whose role it was to introduce that innovation to their local market. Pfizer's development of Viagra or Intel's creation of Pentium processors are classic examples of this model.

In contrast, what we call *local-for-local* innovation relies on subsidiary-based knowledge development. Responding to perceived local opportunities, subsidiaries use their own resources and capabilities to create innovative responses that are then implemented in the local market. Unilever's development of a detergent bar in response to the Indian market's need for a product suitable for stream washing is a good illustration of the process, as is Philippines-based Jollibee's strategy of adapting its fast-food products to the local market preferences of each country it entered.

Most MNEs have tried to develop elements of both models of innovation, but the tension that exists between the knowledge management processes supporting each usually means that one dominates. Not surprisingly, the center-for-global innovation tends to dominate in companies we describe as global or international, whereas local-for-local processes fit more easily into the multinational strategic model.

However, in recent years, traditional strategic mentalities have evolved into two new transnational innovation processes. *Locally leveraged* innovation involves ensuring that the special resources and capabilities of each national subsidiary are available not only to that local entity but also to other MNE units worldwide. For example, when U.S.-based electronics retailer Best Buy acquired a share in the 2,000-store network of European mobile phone retailer Carphone Warehouse, it bought more than European market access. Best Buy understood that its overseas operations could also be the source of new ideas and scarce expertise from which it could learn. Recognizing that its retail model was based primarily on its core experience in selling televisions and computers, the company knew that it had a great deal to learn about selling mobile phones in which it had only a small marketshare. By treating its new European operation as the source of that missing expertise, it adapted its approach to incorporate a more intimate store-within-a-store called Best Buy Mobile. Within a year, the company found that lessons from Carphone helped it double its share of the mobile phone sales market in the United States. The approach is now being rolled out worldwide.

Globally linked innovation pools the resources and capabilities of many different units—typically at both the parent company and the subsidiary level—to create and manage an activity jointly. It allows the company to take market intelligence developed in one part of the organization, perhaps link it to specialized expertise located in a second entity and a scarce resource in a third, and then eventually diffuse the new product or proposal worldwide. For example, when P&G wanted to launch an improved liquid laundry detergent, it drew on the diverse technological capabilities it had developed in Europe, Japan, and the United States. Because laundry in Japan is often done in cold water, researchers in that country had developed a more robust surfactant, the ingredient that removes greasy stains. Meanwhile, the Europeans had been working on a liquid detergent with bleach substitutes, water softeners, and enzymes that would work in their high-temperature frontloading washers. These innovations were combined with a new generation of builders developed in the United States to prevent the redisposition of dirt. The result was a global heavy-duty liquid detergent, introduced as Improved Liquid Tide in the United States, Liquid Ariel in Europe, and Liquid Cheer in Japan. Although these processes are becoming more widespread, they have supplemented rather than replaced the traditional center-for-global and local-for-local innovation processes that are so well embedded in many MNEs. In a competitive environment, most companies recognize the need to engage their resources and capabilities in as many ways as they can. The challenge is to build an organization that can simultaneously facilitate all four processes of innovation and learning, which requires that they understand not only the power of each but also their limitations.

Building a portfolio of innovative processes to drive worldwide learning requires that the companies overcome two related but different problems. Not only must they avoid the various pitfalls associated with each process, but also they must find ways to overcome the organizational contradictions among them as they try to manage all the sources of innovation simultaneously.

Making Central Innovations Effective

The key strength on which many Japanese companies built their global leadership positions in a diverse range of businesses, from automobiles to zippers, lay in the effectiveness of their center-for-global innovations. This is not to say that many did not use some other operative modes, but in general, the Japanese became the champion managers of centralized innovation in the 1980s and have remained so. Over time, these companies learned that the greatest risk of center-for-global innovation is market insensitivity and the accompanying resistance of local subsidiary management to what they may view as inappropriate new products and processes. As a result, the most successful developed three important capabilities that are key to managing the center-for-global process: (1) gaining the input of subsidiaries into centralized activities; (2) ensuring that all functional tasks are linked to market needs; and (3) integrating value chain functions such as development, production, and marketing by managing the transfer of responsibilities among them.

Gaining Subsidiary Input: Multiple Linkages

The two most important problems facing a company with highly centralized operations are that those at the center may not understand market needs, and those in the subsidiaries required to implement the central innovation may not be committed to it. These problems are best addressed by building multiple linkages between headquarters and overseas subsidiaries to give not only headquarters managers a better understanding of country-level needs and opportunities but also subsidiary managers greater access to and involvement in centralized decisions and tasks.

Matsushita, for example, does not try to limit the number of linkages between headquarters and subsidiaries or focus them through a single point, as many companies do for the sake of efficiency. Rather, it tries to preserve the different perspectives, priorities, and even prejudices of its diverse groups worldwide and ensure that they have linkages to those in the headquarters who can represent and defend their views.

Responding to National Needs: Market Mechanisms

Like many other companies, Matsushita has created an integrative process to ensure that headquarters managers responsible for R&D, manufacturing, and marketing are not sheltered from the constraints and demands felt by managers on the front lines of the operations. One of the key elements in achieving this difficult organizational task is the company's willingness to use internal "market mechanisms" to direct and regulate central activities.

For example, approximately half of Matsushita's total research budget is allocated to the product divisions. The purpose of the split budget is to create a context in which technologically driven and market-led ideas can compete for attention. Each year, the various research laboratories hold exhibitions to highlight research projects they want to undertake. Specific projects are sponsored by the divisions and allocated to the laboratories or research groups of their choice, along with requisite funds and other resources. And how do the product developers know which projects to support? Each year, they hold the merchandise meetings at which overseas subsidiaries negotiate robust features and prices of the products they would be willing to purchase in the coming year. The internal market connects consumer demand to technological innovation.

Managing Responsibility Transfer: Personnel Flow

In local-for-local innovation processes, cross-functional integration across research, manufacturing, and marketing is facilitated by the smaller size and closer proximity of the units responsible for each stage of activity. Because this is not true when parent company units take the lead role in the development and manufacture of new products and processes, more centralized organizations must build alternative means to integrate different tasks.

At Matsushita, for example, the integrative systems rely heavily on the transfer of people. The career paths of research engineers are structured to ensure that a majority of them spend about 5 to 8 years in the central research laboratories engaged in pure research, then another 5 years in the product divisions in applied research and development, and finally in a direct operational function, such as production or marketing, wherein they take line management positions for the rest of their working lives. More important—and in stark contrast to the approach in most Western companies—each engineer usually makes the transition from one department to the next coincident with the transfer of the major project on which he or she has been working. This parallel advance ensures that specific knowledge about the project moves with the individual.

Another mechanism for cross-functional integration in Matsushita works in the opposite direction. Wherever possible, the company tries to identify the manager who will head the production task for a new product under development and makes that person a full-time member of the research team from the initial stage of the development process. This system not only injects direct production expertise into the development team but also facilitates the transfer of the project after the design is completed.

Making Local Innovations Efficient

If the classic global companies in Japan are the champion managers of central innovation, the archetypal multinational companies from Europe are often masters at managing local innovations. These companies had to deal with the fact that local-for-local innovations often suffer from needless differentiation and "reinvention of the wheel" caused by resource-rich subsidiaries trying to protect their independence and autonomy. Of the many factors that helped them deal with these problems, three abilities proved to be the most significant: to empower local management in national subsidiaries, to establish effective mechanisms for linking these local managers to corporate decision-making processes, and to force tight cross-functional integration within each subsidiary.

Empowering Local Management

Perhaps the most important factor supporting local innovations is the dispersal of the organizational assets and resources and the delegation of authority that occur so easily in decentralized federation companies. Why would companies such as Nestlé or Philips establish a structure in which the country manager is king? Consider the example of Philips. Since it was founded in 1891, Philips has recognized the need to expand its operations beyond its small domestic market, but the successive barriers—poor transport and communication linkages in the early decades of the century, protectionist pressures in the 1930s, and the disruption of World War II—encouraged the company to build national organizations with substantial degrees of autonomy and self-sufficiency. Such dispersed managerial and technological resources, coupled with local autonomy and decentralized control over resources, enabled subsidiary managers to be more effective in managing local development, manufacturing, and other functional tasks.

Linking Local Managers to Corporate Decision-Making Processes

Whereas local resources and autonomy make it feasible for subsidiary managers to be creative and entrepreneurial, linkages to corporate decision-making processes are necessary to make these local-for-local tasks effective for the company as a whole. In many European companies, a cadre of entrepreneurial expatriates plays a key role in developing and maintaining such linkages.

At Philips, many of the best managers spend most of their careers in national operations, working for 3 to 4 years in a series of subsidiaries—jobs that are often much larger and have higher status than those available in the small home-country market of the Netherlands.

Not surprisingly, such a career assignment pattern has an important influence on managerial attitudes and organizational relationships. The expatriate managers tend to identify strongly with the national organization's point of view, and this shared identity creates a strong bond and distinct subculture within the company. In contrast to Philips, Matsushita has been able to generate very little interaction among its expatriate managers, who tend to regard themselves as parent-company executives temporarily on assignment in a foreign company.

Integrating Subsidiary Functions

Finally, the local innovativeness of decentralized federation organizations is enhanced because of the strong cross-functional integration that typically exists within each national operation. Most Philips subsidiaries use integration mechanisms at three organizational levels. For each project, there is what Philips calls an "article team" consisting of relatively junior managers from the commercial and technical functions. It is the responsibility of this team to evolve product policies and prepare annual sales plans and budgets.

At the product level, cross-functional coordination is accomplished through a product group management team of technical and commercial representatives, which meets once a month to review results, suggest corrective actions, and resolve any interfunctional differences. Restraining control and conflict resolution to this level facilitates sensitive and rapid responses to initiatives and ideas generated at the local level.

The highest subsidiary-level coordination forum is the senior management committee (SMC), which consists of the top commercial, technical, and financial managers in the subsidiary. Acting essentially as a local board, the SMC coordinates efforts among the functional groups and ensures that the national operation retains primary responsibility for its own strategies and priorities. Each of these three forums facilitates local initiative by encouraging that issues be resolved without escalation for approval or arbitration.

■ Making Transnational Processes Feasible

In many MNEs, three simplifying assumptions traditionally have blocked the organizational capabilities necessary for managing such transnational operations. The need to reduce organizational and strategic complexity made these assumptions extremely widespread among large MNEs:

• An often implicit assumption that roles of different organizational units are uniform and symmetrical. This assumption leads companies to manage very different businesses, functions, and national operations in essentially the same way.

• An assumption, conscious or unconscious, that headquarters–subsidiary relationships should be based on clear and unambiguous patterns of dependence or independence.

• The assumption that corporate management has a responsibility to exercise decision making and control uniformly.

Companies that are most successful in developing transnational innovations challenge these assumptions. Instead of treating all businesses, functions, and subsidiaries the same way, they systematically differentiate tasks and responsibilities. Instead of seeking organizational clarity by basing relationships on dependence or independence, they build and manage interdependence among the different units of the companies. Instead of considering control their key task, corporate managers search for complex mechanisms to coordinate and co-opt the differentiated and interdependent organizational units into sharing a vision of the company's strategic tasks.

From Symmetry to Differentiation

Like many other companies, Unilever built its international operations with an implicit assumption of organizational symmetry. Managers of diverse local businesses, with products ranging from packaged foods to chemicals and detergents, all reported to strongly independent national subsidiary managers, who in turn reported through regional directors to the board. But as management began to recognize the need to capture potential economies across national boundaries and transfer learning worldwide, product coordination groups were formed at the corporate center, and soon encompassed all businesses.

Eventually, however, there was a recognition that different businesses faced different demands for integration and responsiveness. Whereas standardization, coordination, and integration paid high dividends in the chemical and detergent businesses, for example, important differences in local tastes and national cultures impeded the same degree of coordination in foods.

As Unilever tackled the challenge of managing some businesses in a more globally coordinated manner, it was also confronted with the question of what to coordinate. Historically, most national subsidiaries chose to develop, manufacture, and market products they thought appropriate. Over time, however, decentralization of all functional responsibilities became increasingly difficult to support. For the sake of cost control and competitive effectiveness, Unilever needed to break with tradition and begin centralizing European product development and purchasing, but it was less compelled to pull local sales and promotional responsibilities to the center.

In addition to differentiating the way they managed their various businesses and functions, most companies eventually recognized the importance of differentiating the management of diverse geographic operations. Although various national subsidiaries operated with very different external environments and internal constraints, operations in Sydney, Singapore, and Shanghai often reported through the same channels, were managed by standardized planning and control systems, and worked under a set of common and generalized subsidiary mandates.

Recognizing that such symmetrical treatment could constrain strategic capabilities, many companies made changes. At Unilever, for example, Europe's highly competitive markets and closely linked economies led management gradually to increase the role of European product coordinators until they eventually had direct line responsibility for all operating companies in their businesses. In Latin America, however, national management maintained its historic line management role, and product coordinators acted only as advisers. Unilever has thus moved in sequence from a symmetrical organization managed through a uniformly decentralized federation to a much more differentiated one: differentiating first by product, then by function, and finally by geography.

From Dependence or Independence to Interdependence

As we described in Chapter 4, national subsidiaries in decentralized federation organizations enjoyed considerable independence from the headquarters, whereas those in centralized hub organizations remained strongly dependent on the parent company for resources and capabilities. But the emerging strategic demands make organizational models based on such simple interunit dependence or independence inappropriate.

Independent units risk being picked off one by one by competitors whose coordinated global approach gives them two important strategic advantages: the ability to integrate scale-efficient operations and the opportunity to cross-subsidize the losses from battles in one market with funds generated by profitable operations in others. However, foreign operations that depend totally on a central unit run the risk of being unable to respond effectively to strong national competitors or to sense potentially important local market or technical intelligence.

But it is not easy to change relationships of dependence or independence that have been built over a long history. Most companies found that attempts to improve interunit collaboration by adding layer upon layer of administrative mechanisms to foster greater cooperation were disappointing. Independent units feigned compliance while fiercely protecting their independence, and dependent units discovered that the new cooperative spirit bestowed little more than the right to agree with those on whom they depended.

To create an effective interdependent organization, two requirements must be met. First, the company must develop a configuration of resources that is neither centralized nor decentralized but is both dispersed and specialized. Such a configuration lies at the heart of the transnational company's integrated network mode of operations, as we already discussed in Chapter 4.

Second, it must build interunit integration mechanisms to ensure that task interdependencies lead to the benefits of synergy rather than the paralysis of conflict. Above all else, interunit cooperation requires good interpersonal relations among managers in different units. The experiences of Ericsson, the Swedish telecommunications company, suggest that the movement of people is one of the strongest mechanisms for breaking down local dogmas. Ericsson achieved this with a longstanding policy of transferring large numbers of people back and forth between headquarters and subsidiaries. Whereas its Japanese competitor NEC may transfer a new technology through a few key managers sent on temporary assignment, Ericsson will send a team of 50 or 100 engineers and managers for a year or two; whereas NEC's flow is primarily from headquarters to subsidiary, Ericsson's is a balanced two-way flow in which people come to the parent company to both learn and provide their expertise; and whereas NEC's transfers are predominantly Japanese, Ericsson's multidirectional process involves all nationalities.

However, any organization in which there are shared tasks and joint responsibilities requires additional decision-making and conflict-resolution forums. In Ericsson, the often divergent objectives and interests of the parent company and the local subsidiary are exchanged in the national company's board meetings. Unlike many companies whose local boards are designed solely to satisfy national legal requirements, Ericsson uses its local boards as legitimate forums for communicating objectives, resolving differences, and making decisions.

From Unidimensional Control to Differentiated Coordination

The simplifying assumptions of organizational symmetry and dependence (or independence) allowed the management processes in many companies to be dominated by simple controls—tight operational controls in subsidiaries that depend on the center, or a looser system of administrative or financial controls in decentralized units. When companies began to challenge the assumptions underlying organizational relationships, however, they found they also needed to adapt their management processes. The growing interdependence of organizational units strained the simple control-dominated systems and underlined the need to supplement existing processes with more sophisticated ones.

As organizations simultaneously became more diverse and more interdependent, there was an explosion in the number of issues that had to be linked, reconciled, or integrated. But the costs of coordination are high, in both financial and human terms, and coordinating capabilities are always limited. Most companies, though, tended to concentrate on a primary means of coordination and control—"the company's way of doing things."

In analyzing how managers might develop a coordination system that best fits the needs of various functions and tasks, it is helpful to think about the various flows among the organizational units involved in the execution of each task. Three flows are the lifeblood of any organization but are of particular importance in a transnational company. The first is the flow of goods: the complex interconnections through which companies source their raw materials and other supplies, link the flows of components and subassemblies, and distribute finished goods. The second is the flow of resources, which encompasses not only the allocation of capital and repatriation of dividends but also the transfer of technology and the movement of personnel throughout the system. The third is the flow of valuable information and knowledge—from raw data and analyzed information to accumulated knowledge and embedded expertise—that companies must diffuse throughout the worldwide network of national units.

It can be very difficult to coordinate the flows of *goods* in a complex integrated network of interdependent operations. But in most companies, this coordination process can be managed effectively at lower levels of the organization through clear procedures and strong systems. For example, within its network of manufacturing plants in different countries, Ericsson learned to coordinate product and material flows by standardizing as many procedures as possible and formalizing the logistics control. In other words, the flow of goods is best achieved through the *formalization* of management processes

It is more difficult to coordinate flows of financial, human, and technological *resources*. Allocation of these scarce resources represents the major strategic choices the company makes and must therefore be controlled at the corporate level. We have described the transnational company as an organization of diverse needs and perspectives, many of which conflict and all of which are changing. In such an organization, only managers with an overview of the total situation can make critical decisions about the funding of projects, the sharing of scarce technological resources, and the allocation of organizational skills and capabilities. Managing the flow of resources is a classic example of the need for coordination by *centralization*.

Perhaps the most difficult task is to coordinate the huge flow of strategic information and proprietary *knowledge* required to operate a transnational organization. The diversity and changeability of the flow make it impossible to coordinate through formal systems, and the sheer volume and complexity of the information would overload headquarters if coordination were centralized. The most effective way to ensure that worldwide organizational units analyze their diverse environments appropriately is to sensitize local managers to broader corporate objectives and priorities. That goal is best reached by transferring personnel with the relevant knowledge or creating organizational forums that allow for the free exchange of information and foster interunit learning. In short, the *socialization* process is the classic solution for the coordination of information flows.

Naturally, none of these broad characterizations of the fit between flows and processes is absolute, and companies use a variety of coordinative mechanisms to manage all three flows. Goods flows may be centrally coordinated, for example, for products under allocation, when several plants operate at less than capacity, or if the cost structures or host government demand change. And as information flows become routine, they can be coordinated through formalization if appropriate management information systems have been installed.

Realistically, a one-size-fits-all approach to capturing the benefits of innovation will not work in a large MNE. As Figure 5-1 suggests, the most effective way to exploit the knowledge within an organization depends on the complexity of the technology itself and the understanding of the focal market. In practice, the best way to capture innovation will sometimes be to move people and sometimes to move or exchange the information.

Figure 5-1   Mobilizing Knowledge

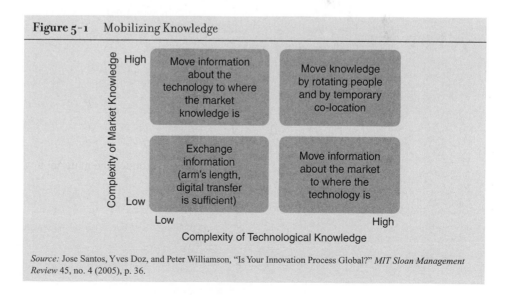

Source: Jose Santos, Yves Doz, and Peter Williamson, "Is Your Innovation Process Global?" *MIT Sloan Management Review* 45, no. 4 (2005), p. 36.

■ Concluding Comments

The approaches to innovation in MNEs have changed considerably. Whereas once MNEs relied on simple models of centralized or localized innovation, the vast majority now find it necessary to build their innovation processes around multiple operating units and geographically disparate sources of knowledge. In this chapter, we identify three generic approaches to innovation, and for each, we identify its typical limitations and the approaches MNEs can use to overcome them. To be clear, there is no one right way of managing the innovation process in an MNE, because each company has its own unique administrative heritage that it cannot and should not disavow. Nonetheless, it is possible to identify certain principles—around the differentiation of roles, interdependence of units, and modes of control—that underpin the development of an effective transnational organization.

Chapter 5 Readings

- In Reading 5-1, "Building Effective R&D Capabilities Abroad," Kuemmerle considers the importance of articulating each foreign R&D site's primary objective, either as a home-base-augmenting laboratory site, or a home-base-exploiting laboratory site. He then discusses the three phases associated with each: the location decision, the ramp-up period, and maximizing lab impact.
- In Reading 5-2, "Connect and Develop: Inside Procter & Gamble's New Model for Innovation," Huston and Sakkab describe the corporate evolution from strict emphasis on an invent-it-ourselves R&D model, to a connect and develop corporate innovation model. In it, the company would now draw upon scientists and engineers outside the company for half their innovations.
- In Reading 5-3, 'Finding, Forming, and Performing: Creating Networks for Discontinuous Innovation', Birkinshaw, Bessant and Delbridge examine how firms can create new networks, with customers, suppliers or other partners, in order to build capacity to implement new technologies, products or business models that represent a dramatic change from the current reality.

All three of these readings underscore the value in exploiting cross-border knowledge management in order to create worldwide innovation and learning for competitive advantage.

Case 5-1   Siemens AG: Global Development Strategy (A)

Stefan Thomke and Ashok Nimgade

It was the spring of 2000, but even under the afternoon shade of the palm trees at the Oberoi hotel in Bangalore, South India, it felt like summer. Horst Eberl sat contemplating the recommendations that he and his subdivisional co-head, Karl-Friedrich Hunke, would be preparing for the Siemens Information and Communications Networks (ICN) management board. Things were neat, tidy, and cool on this grassy side of the hotel. Just outside the main walls however lay the dust, pollution, and confusion of the Indian traffic. And if one took life in one's hands by darting through the traffic, across the street lay Siemens' regional development center in India, scattered among floors rented in three different office buildings. Two back-up power generators, as well as battery backup for all computers, helped ensure a reliable infrastructure for the 600 personnel here.

What vexed Eberl and Hunke was that Deutsche Telekom, Siemens ICN's largest customer, was upset because of slow product delivery on a new telecommunications software product, the so-called NetManager. For a variety of reasons the project had rapidly mushroomed in size and scope beyond what had been initially envisioned. To solve the problem, Eberl, co-head of ICN's largest subdivision,

had to travel some 7000 kilometers to this dusty corner of the world: despite the conveniences of email, telephone, and fax, there was little substitute for face-to-face interaction.

The Germans and Indians regarded each other with mutual respect and camaraderie. The Indians marveled at the meticulousness of the Germans, which had allowed them over four decades to assemble one of the world's finest telecommunications systems. The Germans, in turn, appreciated the diligence and enthusiasm of Indian employees. Yet, both sides did at times find fault with each other. Quite often the Indians appeared more interested in pursuing entrepreneurial jobs rather than in working in one corner of the vast Siemens machine. And to the Indians, the Germans sometimes appeared disloyal by refusing to cancel pre-arranged long vacations at junctions critical to a project.

The Indians' lack of experience with large telecommunications systems had led them to make several wrong assumptions about the current project. Would more personal interaction between the Munich headquarters and Bangalore throughout the project have prevented problems from escalating to this point? Or perhaps, the Indians simply needed more time and project autonomy before graduating to a Center of Competence—the highest distinction of experience and technical competence within the global Siemens R&D network. Solving the current crisis would pave the way for smoother R&D management across national borders in the rapidly changing field of telecommunications equipment. It could also help point out the direction for future growth of the Indian division, by now ICN's third-largest regional development center outside Germany.

▌ Professor Stefan Thomke and Research Associate Ashok Nimgade prepared this case. HBS cases are developed solely as the basis for class discussion. Cases are not intended to serve as endorsements, sources of primary data, or illustrations of effective or ineffective management.
▌ Harvard Business School Case No 9-602-061, Copyright 2001 President and Fellows of Harvard College. All rights reserved.
This case was prepared by S. Thomke. HBS Cases are developed solely for class discussion and do not necessarily illustrate either effective or ineffective handling of administrative situation.

Telecommunications Systems: The Invisible Hand

Telecommunications systems of the turn-of-the-millennium would have evoked far stronger emotions than 167 years ago, when Samuel Morse ushered in the telegraph era of telecommunications with the words "What hath God wrought!" Over the decades, millions of engineering hours and thousands of patents had gone into creating systems that could automatically connect telephone calls via digital "carrier switches." These systems rapidly "routed" a call over a complex network of telephone lines in an optimal manner, while keeping track of each call for billing purposes. Consumers enjoyed low costs thanks to innovations such as digital switching and allowing dozens of conversations to be transmitted simultaneously over a single telephone line. Equally miraculous was the systems' reliability which allowed telephone users to take the presence of a dial tone for granted. Such was hardly the case decades earlier, or even in contemporary third world nations. (See **Exhibit 1** for background on the early history of telecommunications.)

Large telecommunications systems operated smoothly thanks to their installation and maintenance by multinational giants such as Siemens, Lucent, Ericsson, and Alcatel. A telephone system had hundreds if not thousands of different features, most of which were invisible to casual users but not to the large and often national telephone operators that ran these systems around the globe. For decades, providers of these large systems enjoyed a cozy relationship with their traditional customers; relationships that often outlasted the up to 30-year lifespan of a telephony system.

In the mid-1990s, telecommunications had reached a new inflection point. The Internet now allowed for the revolutionary possibility of voice and data transmitted over the same broadband lines using the same protocols. Phone calls or faxes were traditionally handled over telephone lines but could possibly be handled much more cheaply over data lines and lower cost equipment employed for computer networks (see **Exhibit 2** for information on

service transaction cost). Siemens and other major telecommunications companies remained aware that over the next 5–10 years, Internet-based voice transmission could dominate their industry if quality and reliability problems were solved. Already, the upcoming market fielded new terms such as "Voice over Internet Protocol (IP)" and customers could place telephone calls using their personal computers. Many at Siemens feared that the leap from old to new might prove too large for a company that by admission of a U.S. board member himself, people viewed as a "slow-moving dinosaur."[1]

Building an Industrial Giant

In 1847 in Germany, Werner Siemens and J. Halske founded what was to be known as Siemens to manufacture and install telegraphic systems.[2] Early orders came from Germany, Russia, and England, with the company's London branch even helping lay the first deep-sea telegraphic cables connecting England with America as well as India. Over the years, the Siemens family capitalized on several emerging technologies ranging from the telephone to electric power generation to the X-ray tube, laying the foundation for the company's continued presence in these areas and leading *Fortune* magazine to typify Siemens' strategy as "second is best." The company was quick to produce an improved and patented version of Alexander Graham Bell's telephone. In 1909, the company built an automatic telephone exchange to serve Munich's 2500 telephone users.

The independence of Siemens's foreign subsidiaries was reinforced during World War I, when the British nationalized (temporarily) the London branch and Bolsheviks likewise appropriated the St. Petersburg branch. Throughout the twentieth century, however, Siemens continued its international growth, with its presence extending even as far as Mars, through development of space probe technologies for NASA.

---

[1] M. Reardon, "Siemens' Haunted History—As the company shapes its future, it's still forced to confront its past." Data Communications, August 7, 1999.

[2] Much of the early company history draws from "Siemens A. G." Mirabile, L. (Ed.) *International Directory of Company Histories*, V.II, Chicago and London: St. James Press, 1990.

Exhibit 1 History of Telecommunications[a]

Prehistory +	Use of smoke signals, tom-toms, carrier pigeons, runners, horse-back messengers, and many other systems developed independently by many cultures for conveying messages across great distances.
Late 1700s	Visual systems used to convey messages over long distances. Semaphore system developed in France.
1820–1837	Hans Christian Orsted (Denmark) discovers that a wire carrying electric current can deflect a magnetic needle; Michael Faraday (Britain) and others refine science of electromagnetism.
1837	Cooke & Wheatstone (Britain) obtain patents for first telegraph. Samuel Morse, professor of painting and art in New York City, is granted patent on system for communicating information using electromagnets (represented on paper by dots and dashes). His first public transmission from Washington D.C. to Baltimore, "What hath God wrought!" ushers in telegraph era.
1847	Together with business partner Johann Georg Halske, Werner Siemens begins to manufacture pointer telegraphs, a product of his own invention, and lays the foundations for electrical engineering giant Siemens AG.
1876	Alexander Graham Bell patents telephone. Originally intended to supplant telegraphy, the two technologies coexist for decades to come.
1877	First public telephone exchange installed. The first system (New Haven, CT) allows up to 21 callers to contact one another and is manned by human operators who must physically connect the caller's line to the called party's line. Quite rapidly, the system grows to accommodate hundreds of users.
1913	First electromechanical switches installed. By 1974, one of these systems can handle up to 35,000 calls.
1918	"Modulated carrier" technology allows for many different messages to be transmitted simultaneously over a single telephone line. Vacuum tube circuits amplify and regenerate weak signals to allow for more efficient signal transmission.
1947	Transistor invented. Allows for smaller, faster switching devices based on electronic, rather than on electromechanical, components.
1960s	AT&T introduces Electronic Switching System (ESS) that combines numerous new technologies including semiconductors for switching. Allows for up to 65,000 calls per switch
1976	Switching systems developed by AT&T that allow voice data to be digitized into smaller packets of information that can be sent from caller to called party through more flexible, efficient routes. These flexible systems allow for handling 100,000 lines and laid the basis for modern switching systems.
1980	Siemens ICN develops the EWSD digital electronic telephone switch which would become the most reliable and bestselling voice switch in the world.

[a]Much of the timeline information is adapted from: *The New Encyclopaedia Britannica Macromedia*, v. 28, "Telecommunications Systems" 1997, pp. 473–504.

Siemens dominated in areas such as telecommunications, medical technology, data-processing systems, manufacture of heavy electrical equipment, nuclear plants, and railroad equipment. The company had developed a legendary ability to manage large, complex projects and prided itself on quality and durability—its early mobile telephones, for instance, could still function after being hurled across a room at a wall. By 2000, Siemens was one of the top five electronics and electrical engineering

Exhibit 2   Cost per Service Transaction in
Industrialized Countries (estimate)

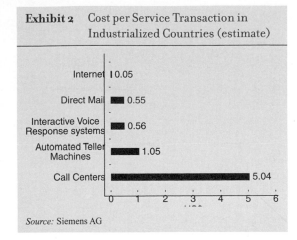

Source: Siemens AG

Exhibit 3   Siemens Statement of Income
(German Marks in millions)

Siemens Worldwide Income (Year Ends Sept. 30)		
Year	**1999**	**1998**
Net Sales	**134,134**	**117,696**
Cost of sales	(96,014)	(85,780)
Gross profit on sales	**38,120**	**31,916**
Research and development expenses	(10,240)	(9,122)
Marketing and selling expenses	(19,120)	(17,672)
General administration expenses	(5,185)	(3,616)
Other operating income	1,618	951
Other operating expenses	(2,570)	(883)
Net income from investment in other companies	544	474
Net Income from financial assets and marketable securities	1,807	1,451
Net interest income (expense) from Operations/ Pension Fund	679	(451)
EBIT from Operations		
Other interest (expense) income	(40)	390
Income from ordinary activities before income taxes	**5,613**	**3,438**
Taxes on income from ordinary activities	(1,965)	(780)
Income before extraordinary items	**3,648**	**2,658**
Extraordinary items after taxes		(1,741)
Net Income	**3,648**	**917**

Source: Siemens AG Annual Report 1999

companies in the world, with annual revenues exceeding 130 billion Euros.[3] It could boast some 464,000 employees scattered across 190 countries, with 57,000 employees dedicated to R&D alone. In 2000, Siemens held some 120,000 patent rights and spent over ten billion Euros on research and development. Its largest group, Information and Communications Networks (ICN), employed 53,000 people, operated in 160 countries and had headquarters that spread over dozens of buildings at two fenced sites in suburban Munich, Germany (see **Exhibits 3 to 5** for financials and corporate structure).

Siemens expanded its markets on the basis of technological competence and close relations with large customers rather than on aggressive marketing. Its conservatism extended even to consumer financing. "Siemens historically has guarded its credit rating," according to Peter Kröbel, a U.S.-based director of international business development. This approach had kept the company from falling prey to traps such as extending credit to unstable Latin American nations as well as aggressive Internet-related acquisitions that had ensnared many of its rivals.

In the 1990s, with a worldwide wave of deregulation affecting various industries including telecommunications, Siemens could no longer rely as heavily on its traditional relationships with large customers.

▌ [3]While the exchange rate between Euro, German mark and U.S. dollar fluctuated, the following rate roughly applied: 2 DM = 1 Euro = 0.90 US$.

With computer and telecommunications industries changing rapidly, productivity gains of as much as ten percent a year were often canceled out by price declines. 1998 marked a crisis point when net income slumped two-thirds from a 1996 peak of $1.36 billion.

Exhibit 4 Siemens Corporate Structure

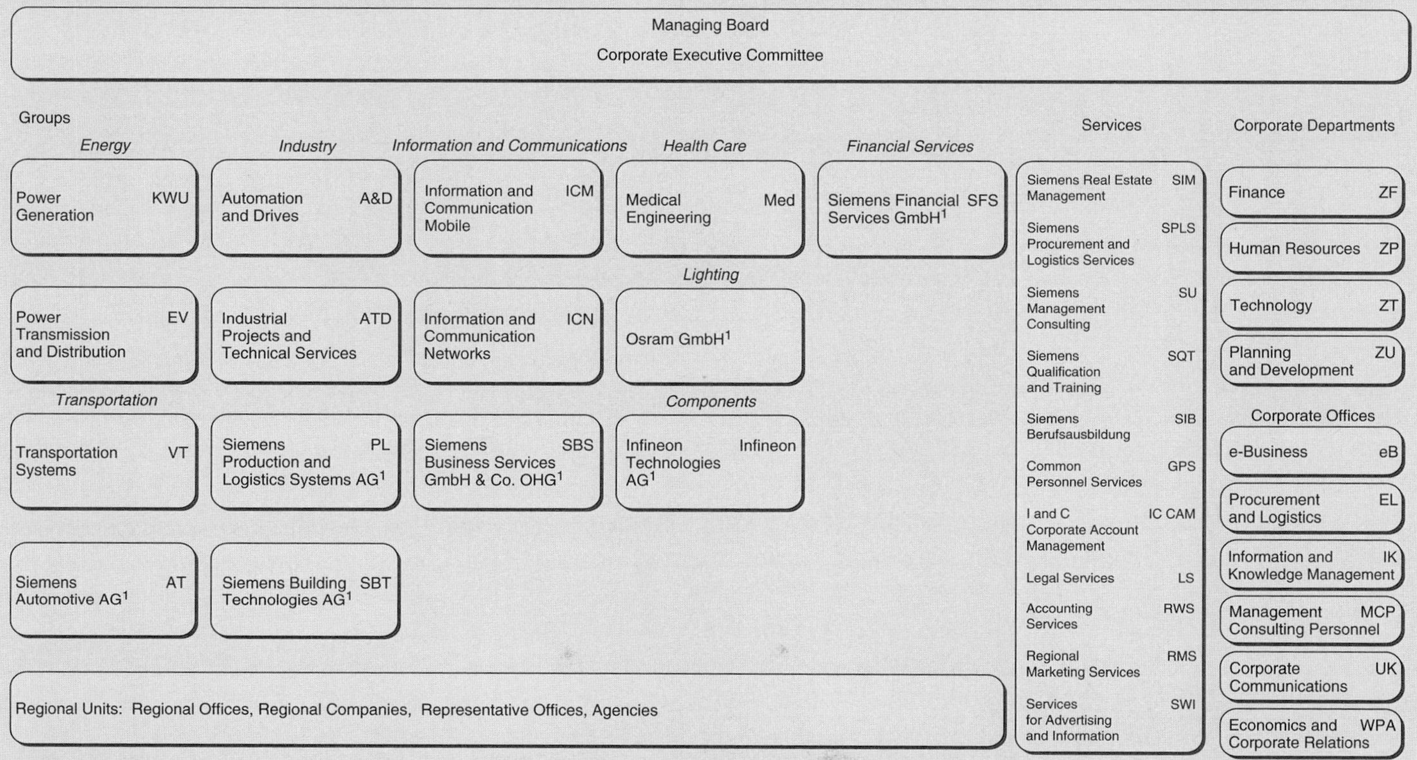

Managing Board
Corporate Executive Committee

Groups

Energy

Power Generation	KWU
Power Transmission and Distribution	EV

Transportation

Transportation Systems	VT
Siemens Automotive AG[1]	AT

Industry

Automation and Drives	A&D
Industrial Projects and Technical Services	ATD
Siemens Production and Logistics Systems AG[1]	PL
Siemens Building Technologies AG[1]	SBT

Information and Communications

Information and Communication Mobile	ICM
Information and Communication Networks	ICN
Siemens Business Services GmbH & Co. OHG[1]	SBS

Health Care

Medical Engineering	Med

Lighting

Osram GmbH[1]	

Components

Infineon Technologies AG[1]	Infineon

Financial Services

Siemens Financial Services GmbH[1]	SFS

Services

Siemens Real Estate Management	SIM
Siemens Procurement and Logistics Services	SPLS
Siemens Management Consulting	SU
Siemens Qualification and Training	SQT
Siemens Berufsausbildung	SIB
Common Personnel Services	GPS
I and C Corporate Account Management	IC CAM
Legal Services	LS
Accounting Services	RWS
Regional Marketing Services	RMS
Services for Advertising and Information	SWI

Corporate Departments

Finance	ZF
Human Resources	ZP
Technology	ZT
Planning and Development	ZU

Corporate Offices

e-Business	eB
Procurement and Logistics	EL
Information and Knowledge Management	IK
Management Consulting Personnel	MCP
Corporate Communications	UK
Economics and Corporate Relations	WPA

Regional Units: Regional Offices, Regional Companies, Representative Offices, Agencies

[1]legally separate Group.
Source: Siemens AG

423

Exhibit 5 Siemens Financials by Segment (German Marks in Millions)

	External Sales		Intersegment Sales		Total Sales		EBIT	
	1999	1998	1999	1998	1999	1998	1999	1998
Operations								
Power Generation (KWU)	15,437	10,566	74	83	15,511	10,649	(261)	(196)
Power Transmission and Distribution (EV)	5,973	6,439	385	510	6,358	6,949	248	191
Automation and Drives (A&D)	11,567	11,368	2,253	2,378	13,820	13,746	1,447	1,385
Industrial Projects and Technical Services (ATD)	5,943	7,923	2,111	2,405	8,054	10,328	279	289
Production and Logistics Systems (PL)	2,136	2,239	375	334	2,511	2,573	150	111
Siemens Building Technologies (SBT)[1]	7,618		716		8,334		319	
Information and Communication Network (ICN)	**23,422**	**23,405**	**607**	**453**	**24,029**	**23,858**	**1,061**	**1,143**
Information and Communication Products (ICP)	16,677	15,179	2,468	2,582	19,145	17,761	956	501
Siemens Business Services (SBS)	4,273	3,852	2,782	2,355	7,055	6,207	8	(258)
Transportation Systems (VT)	5,794	5,029	14	17	5,808	5,046	(122)	(746)
Automotive Systems (AT)	6,380	5,560	9	8	6,389	5,568	310	293
Medical Engineering (Med)	7,887	7,414	93	58	7,980	7,472	660	283
Osram	6,799	6,530	359	28	7,158	6,558	680	643
Infineon (HL)[2]	6,986	5,636	1,275	1,058	8,261	6,694	101	(852)
Passive Components and Electron Tubes (PR)	2,474	2,230	314	353	2,788	2,583	283	327
Electromechanical Components (EC)	1,384	1,325	235	215	1,619	1,540	17	78
Eliminations and other[3]	2,823	2,643	(16,316)	(14,909)	(13,493)	(12,266)	(326)	6
Total	**133,573**	**117,338**			**131,327**	**115,266**	**5,810**	**3,198**

[1]Due to the short time of affiliation with Siemens, only the assets and liabilities of SBT were included in the consolidated financial statements at September 30, 1998.

[2]Comprising substantially all of the former HL activities.

[3]"Other" primarily refers to centrally managed equity investments (such as BSH Bosch and Siemens Hausgeräte GmbH, Munich), liquid assets of operations, corporate items relating to Regional Companies, and corporate headquarters.

Source: Siemens AG Annual Report 1999

Siemens CEO von Pierer acknowledged that "In Germany, competition was like a wind. Now, it's a storm. And it will become a hurricane!"[4]

Industry observers often linked the company's challenges to its geographic location: "Siemens' problems are Germany's problems. Its faults were typical of dozens of German manufacturers: great engineers, iffy marketing. High labor costs and taxes. Overregulation. Complacency after years of government coddling."[5] In response, Siemens shed some of the traditional German consensus-building style in favor of a US-style of management that by CEO von Pierer's own admission was based on the General Electric model. The company officially launched a ten-point plan that called for, among other things: divesting poor-performing units in favor of strengthening remaining businesses with the potential to become world leaders in their field; setting tougher profit targets for managers; tying as much as 60% of managers' pay to performance; trimming the high-cost German workforce and management by as much as a third; reducing overtime pay; adopting U.S. accounting principles; and more aggressively incorporating marketing into its product development processes.

Amid this painful transition, the company betted much of its future on the vast but volatile telecommunications market as firms scrambled to build next-generation mobile networks and upgraded their networks to handle broadband multimedia services. With hundreds of billions of dollars at stake, players in this field faced costly consequences for misreading technology shifts. A conglomerate such as Siemens would have to battle New World telecom stars such as Nokia and Cisco (see **Exhibits 6a** and **6b** for switching equipment competitors and markets). By early 2000, von Pierer's strategic shifts appeared to have reaped dividends. Led in part by the mobile-phone business, its net income doubled in the first quarter of 2000 to $694 million

on sales of $17 billion. A weak Euro had further helped by making its products cheaper overseas. Noticeably, the software component to Siemens' projects had grown to account for almost a fourth of its revenues now.

In the United States, Siemens now became the largest foreign employer, with 73,000 people employed at 700 locations in all 50 states. Thanks to its acquisition of Westinghouse, its products accounted for nearly half the US power generation. In contrast, the ICN division's 10% market share was well below its 25% share of the world's telecommunications systems. As a result, the company sought to bolster its American presence through a series of strategic acquisitions such as Unisphere Networks. Like many very large firms, however, Siemens was still burdened with too many middle managers who resisted changes necessary in a rapidly changing industry.

Siemens Information and Communication Networks (ICN)

Siemens ICN represented a natural outgrowth of Siemens's work in telegraphy and telephony. ICN could offer entire nations turnkey telecommunications switching systems based around its flagship product "EWSD",[6] the best selling and most reliable telecommunications switch in the world. Each EWSD resembled a steel frame the size of a walk-in closet, with hundreds of horizontal slots containing removable modules (see **Exhibit 7**). An EWSD was scaleable to accommodate all switching needs in the range of up to 240,000 telephone lines (or "ports"). Hence, it could cost anywhere between $500,000 and $10 million, with a marginal cost of up to $100 per port.

Although the EWSD did not represent a pioneering effort, it demonstrated the ability of Siemens to be a fast and very successful follower. The technology had started out in the early 1980s as a hybrid analog-digital switching system (which in turn grew out of the EWSA, where the "A" stood for "analog"). In

---

[4] J. Ewing, "Siemens climbs back: the German electronics giant has embraced speed, innovation, and the art of pleasing customers," *Business Week* (International Edition), June 5, 2000.
[5] Ibid.

[6] German acronym of *Elektronisches Wählsystem Digital* (in English: "Electronic Switching System Digital").

Exhibit 6a   Worldwide Voice Switch Equipment Market (1999)—By Supplier

Rank 1999	Supplier	Headquarters	Voice Ports Shipped (in thousands)[a]	
			Worldwide Shipments	% Share
1	Alcatel	France	18,244	18.1%
2	Siemens	Germany	15,135	15.0%
3	Lucent	USA	13,083	13.0%
4	Ericsson	Sweden	10,051	10.0%
5	Nortel	Canada	8,361	8.3%
6	NEC	Japan	6,797	6.7%
7	Fujitsu	Japan	4,559	4.5%
8	Italtel	Italy	778	0.8%
9	Nokia	Finland	383	0.4%
10	Others		23,574	23.3%
			100,965	**100%**

[a]One voice port is equivalent to a single telephone line. Siemens EWSD systems are scalable to roughly 240,000 voice ports, with costs anywhere from $500,000 and $10 million, depending on the number of ports (with a marginal cost of up to $100 per port).
Source: Gartner Dataquest (estimate), Siemens AG

Exhibit 6b   Worldwide Voice Switch Equipment Market (1999)—By Region and Supplier

Supplier	Europe	North America	Latin America	Middle East/Africa	Asia/Pacific
Alcatel	6,969	0	563	2,051	8,661
Siemens	7,319	610	247	2,203	4,756
Lucent	1,049	6,115	434	54	5,431
Ericsson	5,804	57	1,180	256	2,754
Nortel	1,263	4,507	558	627	1,406
NEC	404	731	740	635	4,287
Fujitsu	0	0	11	53	4,495
Italtel	727	0	46	0	5
Nokia	292	0	0	0	91
Others	1,623	13,512	4,911	5,879	73,162
Ports shipped	**25,450**	**12,767**	**4,345**	**5,879**	**52,524**
(in thousands)	(25.2%)	(12.6%)	(4.3%)	(5.8%)	(52.0%)

Source: Gartner Dataquest (estimate), Siemens AG

1981, because of technology breakthroughs by competitors such as AT&T, Siemens piloted its first hybrid switch in faraway South Africa. Despite advances in digital semiconductor technology in the early 1980s, the company hedged its bets by sticking to its hybrid approach, which relied on its decades-old expertise with electromechanical systems.

Then, one Friday afternoon in 1983, in a move highly unusual for Siemens, the head of ICN summoned all 1500 developers for an emergency meeting in the cafeteria, the only place where everyone could fit. He announced: "Stop all your work! As of today, all work on mechanical switches will cease; henceforth we will undertake only work on

Exhibit 7   EWSD Digital Electronic Switching System

- Open EWSD system with flexible hardware and software architecture

- The number of racks depends on the capacity of the system

- EWSD platform can accommodate fixed and mobile communications networks

- Open rack reveals a modular design

- Multiple modules make up EWSD system

- Each module frame consists of assembly rails, side section and guides for modules.

- System capacity can be increased by adding modules to each frame

- EWSD modules are controlled by software such as NetManager (developed in Bangalore)

Source: Siemens AG

digital systems." The announcement sent shockwaves throughout the multinational corporation used to a more gradual, consensus-based approach to technological change.

Altogether, over the next two decades, Siemens ICN invested over 30,000 staff years to create the fully digital EWSD. Its bold move of 1983 was to pay off handsomely. By 2000, ICN equipment controlled almost 300 million telephone lines and routed one in five phone calls worldwide. In its homeland Germany alone, EWSDs controlled almost 50 million telephone lines—representing two-thirds of the German market. Telecommunications systems had to provide a reliability of 99.999% (referred to as the "five nines"), with a downtime of under five minutes per switch per year. Not surprisingly, the "fifth nine" was the hardest to achieve but also mattered the most to its large customers. To achieve this reliability while providing scores of new product features, ICN alone spent 270 million Euros on R&D per year.

EWSD hardware and software development followed a regular release cycle which was a major undertaking, utilizing up to 1,000 staff-years per release, with many subsystems developed from scratch. By the year 2000, ICN was already developing release 15.0 which would be made available to major customers around the world. Later system releases had offered new features such as voice recognition, traffic measurement, voice-mail boxes for end users, caller ID, and automatic dial back for missed calls. As a result of constant improvements, according to director of rapid prototyping Dr. Hermann Granzer, "even after a decade, at a customer's site an EWSD is similar to a brand new car with the new trunk, wheels, windows, and ignition system, and so on."

By 2000, three-fourths of ICN's eleven billion Euro revenues came from hardware and the remainder came from software. Siemens ICN employed about 53,000 people worldwide and was active in 160 countries where it sold telecommunications products with market cycles ranging from over a decade in third world nations such as Indonesia to as short as three months in Germany. Like its top competitors, ICN emphasized good service and maintained close links with its customers. It avoided outsourcing service work on its telecommunications systems to ensure the type of customer commitment that only its staff could provide over the years or decades to come. Its carrier switching (CS) subdivision, headed by Horst Eberl and Karl-Friedrich Hunke, accounted for roughly 25% of ICN's 11 billion Euro revenue and was the largest and most profitable unit (see **Exhibit 8** for ICN's organization).

To its wealthier customers in developed nations, Siemens offered almost yearly EWSD updates and other benefits such as free upgrades, discounts, or even free switches. For customers in developing nations, the most attractive offerings were reliability, durability, and prompt service. For many decades, Siemens even maintained at its Munich headquarters exact replicas of the large systems that it had installed in distant nations in order to expedite problem solving. Most field problems could be solved by customers reading through large product manuals, sometimes with help from local service teams. The harder problems would often have to be referred to any of Siemens's major R&D centers, a more expensive proposition, as it often pulled personnel away from new projects. The entire system of fault management was painstakingly monitored by "FEKAT," a proprietary fault management tool devised and honed by Siemens over the past two decades.

In many ways the traditional German system of work—long, if not lifetime, mutual commitment and loyalty on part of employer and employee—suited a large organization such as Siemens well. Individuals with this mindset would not mind dedicating their entire careers to tasks such as fault analysis monitoring or testing in a small corner of a giant ongoing system such as EWSD. A young employee could expect to work on an initial project lasting 1–2 years while being able to seek advice from a sea of experienced managers. The downside for employers was dealing with circumscribed workweeks and generous vacations. But as one manager himself put it, "Other people may live to work, but we Germans work to live!"

Exhibit 8 Position of Carrier Switching Division (CS) within the Siemens Organization

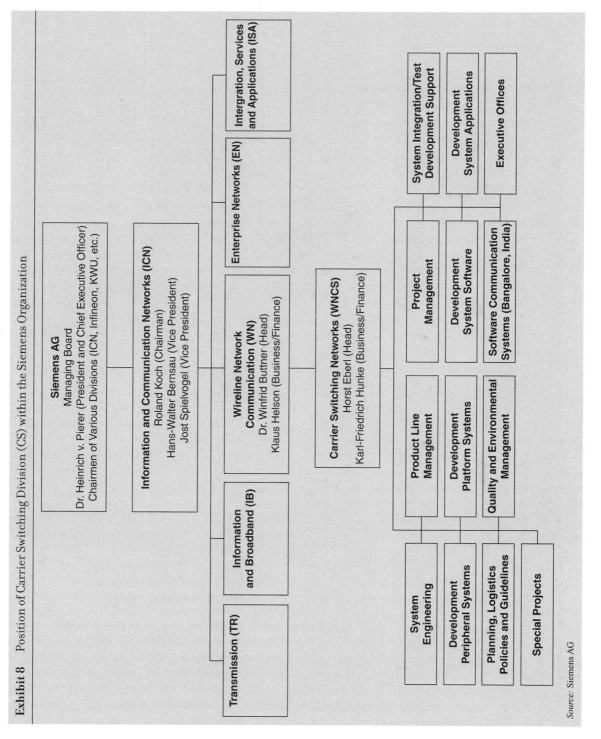

Siemens AG
Managing Board
Dr. Heinrich v. Pierer (President and Chief Executive Officer)
Chairmen of Various Divisions (ICN, Infineon, KWU, etc.)

Information and Communication Networks (ICN)
Roland Koch (Chairman)
Hans-Walter Bernsau (Vice President)
Jost Spielvogel (Vice President)

Enterprise Networks (EN)

Intergration, Services and Applications (ISA)

Transmission (TR)

Information and Broadband (IB)

Wireline Network Communication (WN)
Dr. Winfrid Buttner (Head)
Klaus Helson (Business/Finance)

Carrier Switching Networks (WNCS)
Horst Eberl (Head)
Karl-Friedrich Hunke (Business/Finance)

Product Line Management

Project Management

System Integration/Test Development Support

Development Platform Systems

Development System Software

Development System Applications

Quality and Environmental Management

Software Communication Systems (Bangalore, India)

Executive Offices

System Engineering

Development Peripheral Systems

Planning, Logistics Policies and Guidelines

Special Projects

Source: Siemens AG

429

Exhibit 9   Siemens ICN Regional Development Centers (RDCs) and Manufacturing Sites around the World

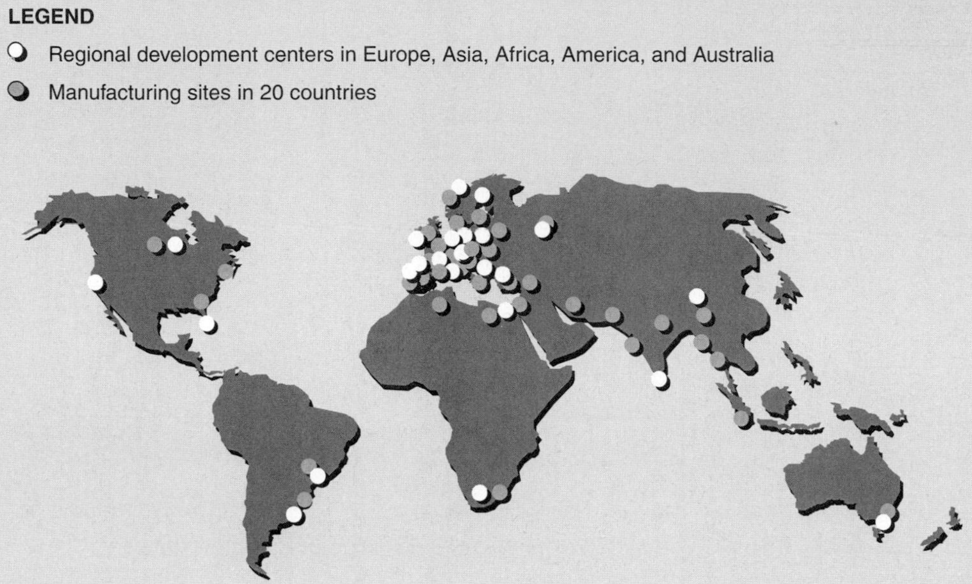

LEGEND

○ Regional development centers in Europe, Asia, Africa, America, and Australia

◐ Manufacturing sites in 20 countries

Source: Siemens AG.

For Siemens ICN, however, gray clouds on the horizon loomed nearer with every year. Despite being a steady cash producer, EWSD faced a zero percent growth rate in the developed world. By the mid-1990s, with the growing importance of the Internet, management realized that EWSD would ultimately die out. The speed with which the Internet would begin to replace traditional data transmission, however, would catch ICN and its competitors by surprise. "We always saw it as a niche market," according to board member Volker Jung.[7] Even industry veteran Horst Eberl admitted that "if transmission of voice over the Internet matches the quality and flexibility of regular telephone, EWSD will die." ICN, however, had no cash-out strategy except to sell as many EWSD units as it could, especially in fast growing developing markets such as China and Brazil. The company could also count on a large installed base that, especially in the developing world, might need servicing for years to come.

To prepare for the future, Siemens ICN launched a new hybrid platform named "SURPASS" which combined traditional EWSD and new broadband technology for data transmission that came in part from acquisitions in the US. Customers would be offered a very reliable and feature rich system solution that met all their data and voice transmission needs and thus resembled ICN's strategy during earlier technology shifts.

Global Product Development and Project Management

Almost from its very inception Siemens viewed itself as a global organization. For two major reasons ICN conducted almost half its R&D efforts at 17 Regional Development Centers (RDCs) scattered across the globe (see **Exhibit 9** for locations). First, because of local labor shortages, ICN could simply not centralize all product development at Munich.

---

[7]W. Boston, "Too Big, Too Slow? Telecoms titans play catch up on the Net(?)," *The Wall Street Journal*, Europe, March 15, 1999.

Second, having regionally-based managers, engineers and technicians facilitated rapid response to local needs such as EWSD customization. A *de facto* partition thus emerged with Munich taking leadership for creating and maintaining new releases of the platform product (baseline projects) and some major RDCs focusing on customization projects and field service (customer projects). Baseline projects were partitioned into subprojects and then placed with regional centers under the project leadership in Munich. Over the years, however, Siemens had followed a strategy of shifting more autonomy to its regional centers to strengthen its global presence. An important consideration for increased autonomy was a center's technical and project management competence. As ICN's Carrier Switching co-head Hunke observed: "In contrast to developing consumer products, telecom system development requires long experience, deep technical skills and the ability to manage complex projects."

Out of a total of 60–70 customization projects per year, about 20 were self-financed by local companies' sales budgets and required no financial support. In such cases, technical managers would start by talking with customers in the early planning stages for new releases. Customers, in turn, gave new product feature "wish-lists," which often magically shrank in size after sales managers returned with a matching price estimate. Some leading customers served as test sites for new system features which gave ICN early feedback on problems.

Great variance existed between different centers: the Greek RDC, for instance, was flush with funds to the point of being able to buy out R&D centers from other companies; at the other extreme, the Hungarian RDC had plateaued in growth to sustain only 15–20 developers. The Indian RDC, though a relative newcomer, had grown to well over 600 people thanks to its access to a talented and inexpensive labor pool for software development. The Florida RDC was quite independent not only because it had been in operation for several decades but also because its responsibility for North American marketing (see **Exhibit 10** for various cost comparisons between ICN's six largest RDCs).

Typically, German managers ran newly formed RDCs, but in later stages local managers gained more control. An ongoing tension was how much independence to provide each center: in general, the more customization an RDC provided for regional customers, the more independent it became. How much direction to provide developers working on

Exhibit 10   Internal Cost Benchmarks of Largest Regional Development Centers (1999)

Regional Development Center (RDC)	Total Development Effort for Siemens ICN-Wireline[a]		Annual Cost of One Developer[b] (Thousand Euros)	Employee Turnover[c] (% of Total Staff)	Coordination Cost[d] (% of Total Effort)
	(Person-Years)	(Thousand Euros)			
Austria	500	50,000	100	4%	8%
USA	200	20,000	150	13%	3%
India	300	8,000	40	35%	15%
Belgium	100	10,000	100	12%	5%
Slovenia	90	5,000	60	5%	6%
Portugal	80	6,000	70	17%	6%

[a]Effort used by ICN only; total size of development center may be significantly larger
[b]Fully-loaded person-year (salary, benefits and overhead)
[c]Annualized turnover (or attrition) of development staff
[d]Travel, meetings, teleconferences, etc. incurred by Munich headquarters in supporting each RDC
Source: Siemens AG

subsystems in different RDCs also proved an ongoing issue. Having Munich specify all parameters of a project upfront decreased regional flexibility but ensured high product quality. In many projects involving a high degree of innovation, however, it was impossible to do so. Nor was this always desirable. As Dr. Jürgen Klunker, a deputy director in the Siemens Carrier Switching group, wryly observed: "a false sense of security can be created from specifying everything!"

Munich headquarters typically coordinated cooperation between RDC's through formal channels, including annual technical conferences at Munich involving representatives from different RDCs, as well as through facilitating informal, often serendipitous encounters between different RDC members at Munich. The biggest challenges in coordinating international efforts occurred because of interdependency of subprojects, delays in assembling crucial employees from differing countries, and international coordination overhead—which could cost as much as 15% of project budgets. The utopian ideal of "development around the clock" by exploiting time zone differences rarely appeared to pan out regardless of which countries were involved. Of course, the potential always existed for cultural or linguistic differences slowing down coordination of work.

Munich coordinated project work through a matrix structure. Generally, individuals worked in different so-called "Centers of Competence" (CoC) groups which were divided along technical lines such as "systems architecture," "systems testing," "peripheral systems," or "core processing." Each CoC controlled budgets and milestones for projects in its technical domain. This structure allowed groups to work on new product releases while simultaneously troubleshooting for products as old as a decade or more.

Some 90 project managers acted as midwives for subprojects, bringing them to fruition in line with milestones. More than 40 of these managers held multiple project responsibilities and twenty were involved with customization projects. Although most engineers or software developers knew their personal responsibilities and their immediate supervisors, they could not always identify exactly who was ultimately in charge. They could rest assured, however, that two or three levels above them conflicts over milestones or technical feasibility would eventually get sorted out.

At its Munich headquarters, ICN emphasized the need for solving problems through finding "common understanding". Every other Monday, CoC heads met with senior project management for up to four hours to focus on critical issues, especially involving larger subprojects. Higher level problems were resolved at a so-called "Development Board" which met biweekly. For projects involving other RDCs, Siemens ICN held meetings—either in Munich or at the RDC—every six weeks with all involved project managers. Unfortunately, decisions were often delayed for weeks because there wasn't enough time to resolve all major issues between CoC heads, project managers and senior executives. Complicating decision-making further was that some regional development centers reported directly to independent Siemens companies located in their respective home countries instead of business divisions such as ICN. In such cases, some conflicts had to be settled at the corporate management board level.

At its American RDC, the company had experimented with the use of strongly defined project teams for each release of a product. Managers claimed to find, however, a decline in quality, increased duplication of efforts, and difficulty in motivating individuals to troubleshoot problems with older product releases. Nonetheless, for critical and time-sensitive projects, ICN was now using two or three "strong" project leaders who were individuals being groomed for upper management.

The motivation for change came from its 14–16 month long market cycles (in the form of new EWSD product releases), which had led to analysts to worry about the company's future. One industry observer noted: "There's not much about Silicon Valley that will be familiar to Continental executives accustomed to gilded traditions of hierarchy, protected markets, and sacrosanct summer vacations."[8]

---

[8]S. Baker, "Technology phone giants on the prowl: Europe's titans are devouring U.S. high-tech Startups," *Business Week* (International Edition), March 22, 1999.

Boca Raton, Florida: An Old RDC in the New World

Amid the stately palm trees and manicured lawns of Southern Florida, stood the second largest overseas outpost, the Boca Raton Regional Development Center (RDC), which was established in 1978. Some 2000 people (including 600 engineers and programmers) operated primarily in warm Boca Raton, with access to three airports, and offered a fairly central location for the Americas and Munich. Technologically, Florida hosted the American space program and had served as birthplace of the IBM personal computer.

Inside the Boca Raton RDC, workers operated in individual cubicles and managerial offices with open doors—a contrast to Munich, where all personnel worked in offices, with junior members sharing office space. Although many of the workers at Boca Raton were foreign-born, they had been to various degrees "Americanized" and acclimated to an informal environment of golf shirts and Docker jeans. With personnel turnover averaging around thirteen percent per year, newcomers could find plenty of experienced employees for help with, what Boca Raton manager Kevin Holwell termed, "bewildering tasks such as figuring out whom in the Siemens Munich telephone book to call."

As with all RDC's, the work of the Florida group centered around the EWSD. Munich engineers would transmit the software for each fresh release of EWSD by high-speed data lines to Florida. The Boca Raton center would then, under project groups as well as Centers of Competence, spend up to a half year customizing the system for the US. To coordinate activities at a senior level, Boca Raton and Munich held joint quarterly meetings with management, alternating between the two locations. Over the years, the center had accumulated the experience and technical skills to manage complex systems projects.

As a large RDC, catering primarily to the vast US market with its unique industry standards, Boca Raton often drifted technologically apart from Munich. Widening this drift was the need to keep pace with fast-moving competitors. Technologists at Boca Raton would on several occasions act first and then inform Munich. Some managers admitted to the existence of the "NIH or 'Not Invented Here' syndrome," which led each side to duplicate certain efforts. As a result, the Boca Raton group had developed, for instance, some of its own fault analysis tools. One Munich manager described the situation thus: "If you ask an engineer in our Indian RDC to test 1, 2, 3, 4 . . . in a keypad, they will test 1, 2, 3, 4, and nothing else; but if you ask an engineer in our American RDC to test 1, 2, 3, 4 . . ., they will test 5, 6, 7, 8 . . .!"

Boca Raton, like other RDCs, also developed specific applications requested by local customers. A prominent example was the "Remote Switching Unit" (RSU), which served as a stripped-down, inexpensive "mini-switch" that could hook up to 5,000 lines in a remote community to one central EWSD via a "trunk" line. By linking several RSU's to one central EWSD a telephone service provider could minimize the length of expensive copper wiring needed. Several of Boca Raton's smaller customers had requested such a system to leverage telephone service coverage of their relatively few EWSDs. Many other Siemens centers such as the Indian RDC were not considered for the RSU project, as they lacked the prerequisite hardware system design capabilities.

Starting June 1997, Boca Raton invested close to 400 person-years on the project. It divided work on the tens of thousands of lines of computer programming into independent subsystems that usually correlated with different areas of technical competence. A project manager kept the entire effort on track which involved coordinated development activities between the U.S., Germany, Austria and Portugal. System developers shuttled across the Atlantic, supplementing their efforts through biweekly video conferences which were viewed as much less effective. To speed up development, all RDCs had access to remote system testing facilities on a mainframe computer in Munich which allowed them to test their components 24 hours per day. Post-mortem analysis showed, however, that over five percent of staff years on the project were spent just traveling. The analysis also indicated that the dream of around the clock development of complex products—taking advantage of the world's time zone differences—had remained just that . . . a dream.

Towards the end of the project, engineers worked 16- to 18-hour days. Intensive bonds developed during these periods between engineers, regardless of national origin, and each side could find much in their counterparts to admire. Many Germans, however, found the non-smoking policies or the lack of public transportation in Florida stifling. For their part, several Americans found it difficult to match Munich beer-drinking abilities. In the Oktoberfest crowds, one American visitor vanished, only to be found, after a tense manhunt, supine in the mud and nodding to a Bavarian band.

Although the RSU project finished with only a few months of delay, Munich and Boca Raton created a "Convergence Group" to stem the divergence between project management styles. As one German manager observed, "we cannot get the Americans in line with our process; they don't analyze things at the beginning of a project the way we do. We want our road maps; they will just proceed and then see what happens. Sometimes a week after starting a subsystem project we would get an e-mail stating 'sorry, we can't do this!'"

Every several weeks, engineers and managers from both sides convened in either Florida or Munich. Both sides agreed to keep work styles on the EWSD base as similar as possible through, for instance, using similar testbeds and common Centers of Competence. With regard to software applications, in the words of Florida manager Keith Hohlin, however, they "agreed to disagree" and followed different development processes.

Bangalore, India: A New RDC in the Old World

After its independence from England in 1947—a hundred years after the founding of Siemens—India developed one of the world's three largest engineering work forces. Under a socialist program, central government planners designated Bangalore in South India as the nation's computational technology center. By 1990, Indian communications engineers had developed a low cost indigenous switching device that could economically link even impoverished rural villages. Over the decades, however, the worldwide high tech explosion would lure away many programmers with substantially higher paying jobs. By the 1990s, up to a fifth of Microsoft software developers in the USA hailed from the Indian subcontinent.

Fears of a one-way "brain drain," however, were mitigated by non-resident Indians investing in their motherland technological firms as well as the burgeoning Indian population's ability to keep churning out talented programmers. Bangalore, with its relatively temperate climate thanks to an elevation of 1000 meters, good educational institutes, and growing cosmopolitanism became known as India's Silicon Valley. It soon hosted leading multinational corporations as well as domestic companies.

Siemens had had a presence in India for decades and enjoyed an excellent reputation. ICN's Bangalore RDC was set up in 1994 at least partly to avail of inexpensive—at 20% of the German labor costs—and readily available English-speaking software specialists. When work at Bangalore started, some German engineers admitted to feeling threatened about losing their jobs to low-cost Indian labor. To escape local corporate taxation, Siemens established the Bangalore center as an "Export Oriented Unit" that would not sell product into the Indian market. Starting with just 20 individuals, including 12 German expatriates, the Bangalore center, eventually grew to over 600 strong to become ICN's fourth largest RDC worldwide.

The Bangalore center featured American-styled offices with employees in individual cubicles and managers in individual offices on the periphery. Siemens maintained an informal, relatively open atmosphere in which young employees could work without the pressures of bureaucracy. Only three layers of management existed here, as compared with seven in Munich. Overall, the Indian programmers, who were organized along the basis of projects, barely noticed organizational or management changes in Munich.

It took three or four months to get an Indian university recruit up to speed on a project, a year to get to full productivity, and up to a two years to gain proficiency in working with Siemens's technology. Because Indian programmers trained on inexpensive personal computers they relied heavily on German guidance for working on large systems. With wages skyrocketing, by 2000, a fresh programmer could earn—in addition to health, housing, and vehicle benefits—about $6000 a year; a considerable amount in India (more than twice that of university professors). Salaries could double in three years based on performance. The average programmer worked 40–45 hours/week, but, with no unions to restrict their activities, would often work longer during crunch times with no overtime benefits.

Young Indians regarded Siemens as one of the best employers to work for in Bangalore. However, with other competitors such as Lucent and Cisco bidding for newly minted software talent, the local job market heated up and Siemens could no longer count on having first pick. Already, by 2000, out of the top 30 most prestigious employers in Bangalore, Siemens had slipped from front-runner status to a middle-ranking.

▨ Early Experiences at Bangalore

The first sizable software project conducted at Bangalore for Munich involved the so-called Advanced Multifunctional Operator Service System" (ADMOSS) project. The purpose of ADMOSS was to allow modern call centers to increase their productivity through capabilities such as facilitating telemarketing, interfacing with non-Siemens equipment, or large conference calls (see **Exhibit 11** for product description). ADMOSS was to field some 500 features, chosen from customer "wish lists" compiled by Munich's marketing group. Because Munich engineers for decades had only programmed larger computers, ICN sought to develop ADMOSS elsewhere. The task ultimately fell upon Bangalore, with its strength in personal computer programming.

Work in India started right after the RDC's founding in 1994 and the project later peaked at 150 software developers. Initially, project management was "top-down," with specifications for various subsystems transmitted from Munich at a high managerial level to Bangalore. Each team of Indian software developers, generally under supervision of a German expatriate or a senior Indian manager, worked from specifications for an entire subsystem. Munich would then test and integrate the work with other subsystems. To complicate matters, specifications were adjusted and fine-tuned throughout the project through a flurry of emails and faxes between Germany and India.

With such a highly complex project, according to senior project managers, "not all specifications were finished by our Munich office since we ourselves were not given enough time!" The first real workshop involving middle and lower level managers and programmers only occurred in late 1995. Up to that point, according to Bangalore-based senior manager, A. Anuradha, "we were groping in the dark."

Like their brethren throughout the world, Indian software developers had faced the frustration of stopping work because of budgetary cuts or because of changing needs of customers. On one occasion work on a billing application was stopped midstream after a half-year's work because of the customer's changing needs. Although this type of work interruption involved only some 15–20 personnel at Bangalore each year, programmers admitted to feeling "demotivated," wondering about how much miscommunication might have been going on several thousand kilometers to the West.

Finally, when all two million lines of the ADMOSS computer code were melded together to attempt to create a seamless, integrated system, many problems surfaced. As it turned out, subsystems were far more interdependent than had been assumed. Since Bangalore developers worked thousands of kilometers away from the Munich test beds, testing of newly integrated system turned out to be a major obstacle. To worsen matters, visa restrictions and bureaucracy on the part of the

Exhibit 11   The Evolution of Call Centers in the Telephone Industry

Siemens transit exchange center

Berlin, Germany, 1906

Modern call center at major
Telecom operator using
ADMOSS call service software
and EWSD telephone
switching system

Examples of ADMOSS (<u>Ad</u>vanced <u>M</u>ultifunctional <u>O</u>perator <u>S</u>ervice
<u>S</u>ystem) Call Center Solution Features:

- Call distribution system and queues (e.g., route call to operator with
  required language skills)
- Switching features (e.g., conference calls of up to 25 participants)
- Booking system (e.g., advance booking of calls between US and India)
- Directory assistance (e.g., number appears as SMS on mobile phone)
- Charging features (e.g., cost information available prior to call)
- Announcements (e.g., position of caller in queue)
- Internet services (e.g., caller contacts operator through Internet link)

Source: Siemens ICN.

German government made it extremely difficult to fly Indians developers to Munich.

For the few Indians who obtained visas, "the first trips were exciting," observed Anuradha. "In fact, there was no substitute for going: this way we could see the full behavior of the system. But with things not working out, we had mixed feelings!" On one occasion, Indians temporarily stationed in Munich were flown to Nuremberg to help solve a customer's problem that, on further investigation, could have been solved by the local service department, had it consulted the basic manuals more carefully. For the Indian team, however, this provided a welcome initial encounter with a Siemens customer.

ADMOSS was finally released to a German customer at the end of 1996—about a year late. "This was with some embarrassment," according to Hans Hauer, VP of software R&D, "because as Germans, we expect delivery on time and with quality!" The system turned out not to be fully stabilized and kept crashing. Other minor problems also emerged. The user interfaces designed by the young Indian programmers were sometimes found to be "flashy and distracting, resembling video game interfaces." "Overall, the customer was upset!" admitted Hauer. Munich immediately standardized user interfaces and also took control of documentation because customers found the Indian-written documents too technical.

ICN managers also found visits to Bangalore more productive with several small meetings. An initial large meeting, in fact, proved a disaster since Indian department heads found it impolite to speak their minds in front of everyone. The groups, however, could never get as small as the Germans would like primarily because of insufficient Indian personnel with large systems experience.

With time, the Indo-German team corrected the system faults and delivered a stable, working system to Munich. ADMOSS ended up highly popular with customers. The Bangalore site remained active with after-sales service, eventually correcting over 90% of ongoing faults. By 2000, a skeletal crew of about 50 programmers in Bangalore and 20 systems

developers in Europe maintained the ADMOSS system and produced yearly updates.

■ East Is East, and West Is West?

The ADMOSS project crystallized several problems in managing the Bangalore division. Primary among the problems was the high turnover rate among Indian programmers in the increasingly heated local job market (see **Exhibit 10**). With competing firms regarding Siemens experience highly, recruiters would entice young software developers with better salary offers. In this environment, annual turnover at the ICN Bangalore center could reach as much as one-third. Making it even harder to retain staff was the eagerness of Indian programmers to openly discuss salaries in the hallways or canteen. This surprised most Germans who had grown up viewing India as supposedly a "non-materialistic" culture. According to German expatriate Richard Bock, "the Bangalore programmers would even ask salary information of the Germans, who would become red in the face."

The career-related impatience of young Indian programmers also caught the Germans by surprise. The fresh recruits at Bangalore were sometimes shocked by the prospect of being on a project for over a year. For many of them, a "dream project" would preferably last less than a half-year long and involve "leading-edge" areas such as mobile communications or Internet protocols (rather than areas such as quality testing or integration).

In every other way, however, the Germans found the Indians polite—almost too polite. Siemens managers observed that the Indians rarely said "no" to any request, even if it turned out beyond their capabilities. Feeling cultural issues might be involved, developer Richard Bock was asked to "decode" the Indian way of communication. Bock's three years in India had tinged his English with a head-turning South Indian accent and taught him that "the cultural awareness materials and role-playing exercises we engaged in at Munich were simplistic and out of date, and did not take into account the wide cultural variation within India. The warnings about

Indian workers not being 'well-motivated,' applied perhaps to factory workers [in a socialist system], and not at all to our Bangalore people."

Bock was soon able to explain that the phrase "there is no problem" meant to Indians that, "we do not see any problems in the *sub-system* on which we have been working." To the Germans, however, it meant, "within the *entire system* there is no problem." A related issue involved the Indians' understanding of fault analysis. To the Indians, the top priority was to solve a fault and not to take an additional four annoying minutes to document each of the hundreds of faults. To the Germans, however, tracking the faults themselves was essential for monitoring the health of systems development and maintenance. It also allowed informing customers about whether a fault was in the 'analysis phase' or in the 'correction phase.'

Bock also found little substitute for face-to-face interaction: "Sometimes you think a point has been settled on the phone, but then three days later you may get a phone call asking, 'why don't we try this other approach?' Programmers in Munich or Vienna will follow customer-defined specifications out of a sense of duty. But in India you have to give the workers a sense of belonging, through early workshops or other means; otherwise, if you ask for a fridge you might get a toaster!"

Few on either side, however, appeared willing to use cultural differences as an excuse for miscommunication, although such clashes were inevitable on occasion—for instance, when one orthodox Indian refused to pick up his official correspondence on astrologically "non-auspicious" occasions. Occasionally, Indians would interpret directness or bluntness on the part of a German as rudeness. Several Indian programmers admitted their frustration when, after learning to say "no," their exercise of this magic word in order to extend a subproject deadline was once met with, "That is not acceptable."

Overall, the Indians felt well-treated by their German employers. The Germans in turn remained relatively pleased by their enthusiastic, hard-working, and talented Bangalore programmers. Expatriates essayed their hand at subcontinental passions including cricket and Indian food. They did receive a bonus "hardship pay," which one expatriate earned after turning beet red from mistakenly swallowing an entire Indian hot pepper (a story the Indians relished in recalling). Expatriate manager Ralph Sussick gamely earned his bonus by spending his first weeks apart from his family in an unlit apartment still under construction. The perks, however, included personal chauffeurs and entry into the highest levels of Indian society. Over the years, one German couple gave birth while in Bangalore, and even a few Indo-German marriages occurred.

Noting a complementarity between the German and Indian approaches to work and life, Indian manager Sai "Charlie" Sreekanth M., stated: "The Germans manage depth well; we manage breadth well. We idolize our 'all-rounder'—the person who does well in sports, debate, and academics. And socially, we're happiest arguing about a great many things in coffeehouse settings!" This contrasted with observations that greatly amused Indians in Munich of certain German employees who with clockwork precision caught exactly the same commuter train everyday.

Managing breadth well implied that the Indians could cover for each other to keep a project rolling even in the midst of vacations, illness, or job resignations on part of any team member. The complementarity between the German and Indian approaches to career, however, allowed Bangalore project manager Santosh Prabhu to observe: "when I was working on a subsystem, I definitely found it simpler to have my Munich counterpart—who had been working on it for well over five years and thus knew it inside-out—make corrections and provide feedback about its eventual performance."

The NetManager Project

The Germans created the world's most reliable telecommunications systems over a period of decades. Even they cannot be expected to produce a new system that is as highly reliable in just two or three years!

—Bangalore Software Developer

By the mid-1990s, personal computers had grown in power and capabilities to the point of controlling access to an entire switching system responsible for routing tens of thousands of calls. At ICN, this realization gave birth to the "EWSD NetManager" project. The user-friendly and graphics-based software product would offer telecom customers a complete range of facilities for performing all operating, administration and maintenance functions on EWSD network nodes and networks (e.g., integration of new telephone subscribers, billing, enable "traffic studies" to understand customer needs, and provide system surveillance). Not surprisingly, NetManager development required a deep understanding of EWSD technology and its 6,000 or so functions.

Creating NetManager would entail, however, programming in desktop computer languages and systems with which Munich product developers lacked experience. ICN over the decades had, after all, developed and refined its own computer language "CHILL" for its large proprietary operating system. It would have taken months to get up to speed with Windows-based systems, let alone learning to deal with quirks of an entirely different system (e.g., memory space problems that necessitated frequent re-booting of computers). Because of budget cuts at Munich, ICN senior managers deliberated over which regional development center should develop the NetManager.

Boca Raton and Bangalore emerged near the top of the pile of contenders. Some argued in favor of Boca Raton because of its greater experience in working on large, complex systems and its knowledge of EWSD systems. Others argued in favor of India because of cost advantages. By now, however, the cost advantages of working in India were rapidly diminishing thanks to roughly 25% annual wage increases for developers in Bangalore. In fact, after factoring in other costs such as information transfer, travel, job-training, and management costs, working in Eastern Europe was now perhaps cheaper than working in India. The NetManager assignment eventually went to Bangalore because of staff availability, familiarity of the Indians with personal computer-based programming, and budgetary restrictions at

Western RDCs. Work at Bangalore commenced in early 1996 with an initial force of 30 programmers. The June 1998 pilot release involved some 300,000 lines of code and proved a hit at the customer test sites. ICN then apprised several important clients including Deutsche Telekom about its forthcoming product.

The world of personal computing and telecommunications, however, had changed rapidly by now. What was envisioned as a simple, isolated, "low-end" product with low reliability gradually transformed into a complex and highly visible product for large customers. Where initially the NetManager was meant to allow one personal computer to control just one element of the system, now it had grown in scope to enabling one PC to control a network using 20 servers and 30 terminals. This implied that the entire project would no longer be shielded from the challenge of managing interdependencies with many other Siemens telecommunications products. It was no wonder that NetManager, by spring 2000, would involve 60% of the Bangalore center's staff.

Thanks to an old "testbed" sent by Munich after lessons learned from the ADMOSS experience, Indian programmers could now test subsystems as they were developed. By November 1999, Bangalore sent its complete NetManager Version 2 to Munich for testing. Typically Munich tested "stability" (or reliability) of new software by installing and launching it on a Friday afternoon and hoping to find no errors in the test log on Monday. NetManager Version 2, however, ran only one hour before crashing to a halt.

A check of the test logs ultimately revealed a staggering 700 faults hidden at various points along some 600,000 lines of computer programming code, with 100 categorized as serious "Level I" faults. Initial trouble-shooting indicated that each fault could not simply be corrected individually, since each correction could create ripple effects across the entire system. The Bangalore RDC quickly boosted its staffing on NetManager and software developers worked seven days a week to solve the crisis. Three Indian developers were sent to Munich for more than one month.

A late-November 1999 workshop in Bangalore involving managers from Munich and India tracked down the root cause of quality problems. As it turned out, the Indian group assumed, as in the case of most desktop computing applications, that the system would be shut off at night, and that it was acceptable for a desktop-based computer system to crash once a week. This assumption was further reinforced by an understanding that operation of the EWSD switch itself would not depend on NetManager. Furthermore, the Indian team underestimated system usage by an entire order of magnitude. "We were ignorant!" admitted an Indian programmer, "we didn't think of asking what loads to test with, but Munich was also at fault for not telling us!"

Some of these erroneous assumptions could ultimately be traced to different work schedules. In the crucial summer months, many Germans went ahead with their several weeks-long pre-booked family vacations—often without leaving contact information—stranding the Indians. During crisis periods, Indian programmers, in contrast, typically took only personal leaves of two or three days, and worked 70–80 hours per week or even more. Balanced against this, however, was the ongoing high attrition rate in Bangalore.

In January 2000, Siemens, with one Bangalore engineer present, went ahead with the planned demonstration of NetManager to Deutsche Telekom. But even the Munich testers did not appear well-prepped for the tests, leaving Bangalore programmers to wonder why it had commenced in the first place. The result proved disastrous: far too many reliability errors cropped up. Deutsche Telekom halted the tests immediately.

In February, post-mortem analysis indicated that the old testbed sent to Bangalore was smaller than those used at present and thus could not detect all design problems. Another three Bangalore programmers went to Munich to help iron out the reliability wrinkles on larger testbeds. One of these was software manager Lalitha J.S., who recounted: "The Munich people were very nice. They did say that 'these problems are causing us commercial consequences,' but they never threatened our group or

said, 'Hey Bangalore, what's up!' The face-to-face interactions helped; otherwise, back home we were sometimes thinking, 'were they making things up?"

Senior management set the deadline of August 2000 for fixing all version 2 faults. The top managers decided that the version 3 release planned for July 2000 should be scrapped and merged into a fully reliable version 4 product, promised to customers for Spring 2001.

Deutsche Telekom Calls

Eberl and Hunke knew that immediate action would be needed. The NetManager Project had clearly mushroomed in size and strategic importance beyond that initially envisioned. Deutsche Telekom, ICN's largest customer was demanding the product but also issued a warning that reliability problems would not be acceptable. As a result, some German executives had already suggested that NetManager development and project management should be moved to Austria, Belgium, or Portugal. In the shorter term, they argued that further delays were inevitable even if the project remained in Bangalore and that decisive action was long overdue. In the longer term, this would also bring the system developers and programmers closer to Siemens's major customers and smooth out coordination problems with India.

But already some 50% of NetManager resources, development and project management were based in Bangalore. Transferring these project activities back to Europe would involve a delay of several weeks during which time Indian and German software developers and managers would have to shuttle back and forth across the Arabian Sea. Relocating the NetManager project might also cast a pall over the Bangalore. Over the years, Indian managers had begun suggesting to change their RDC from a software development outpost for Munich into a center with status equal to that of, say, Boca Raton. As one Indian manager, C. R. Rao, observed: "We would like to climb up the value chain to work with customers, create growth and career opportunities, and start charting our own destiny." Such an evolution would, among other things, require major investments and a significant expansion of system-testing and hardware design capabilities.

As an alternative proposal to relocating core NetManager activities to Europe, some Siemens managers suggested moving major project responsibility and accountability to Munich but leaving all development activities in Bangalore. While travel and coordination cost would increase, this proposal ensured strict project management and quality control while keeping Indian software developers on NetManager. It was unclear, however, if a project of such complexity could be managed by people living thousands of miles away.

In the meantime, the late afternoon pollution thickened as the traffic weaved without slightest regard for lane markings. If Bangalore was to grow into a world stature city, it would need to discipline its pollution and growing traffic.

Exhibit 12	Terminology
ADMOSS	Abbreviation for <u>Ad</u>vanced <u>M</u>ultifunctional <u>O</u>perator <u>S</u>ervice <u>S</u>ystem. Siemens ICN software product used by call centers to manage telephone services such as directory assistance, billing, conference calls, etc. ADMOSS is designed to be used with EWSD voice technology.
Backbone	Part of the communications network which carries the heaviest traffic. The backbone interconnects the devices (switches and edge devices) to which customers are usually connected.
Bandwidth	Bandwidth is the width of a communication channel measured in "bits per second" or bps. High bandwidth implies that more information can be moved through a channel at the same time. Low bandwidth connections (e.g., phone dial-in) are typically fractions of 64 kbps (kilobits per second). High bandwidth connections usually supply several Mbps (megabits per second).
Broadband	Transmission facility providing high bandwidth. Such a facility can carry voice, video, and data channels simultaneously.
EWSD	Abbreviation for *Elektronisches Wählsystem Digital* or Electronic Switching System Digital. EWSD is a voice switch and Siemens ICN's flagship product.
Digital subscriber lines (DSL)	A technology that uses existing copper telephone lines to transmit voice and data at high speeds (up to 8 Mbps).
Integrated services digital network (ISDN)	Switched network allowing for provision of both voice and data services over copper wire (up to 128 kbps).
Internet protocol (IP)	The set of rules that specify how data is cut into packets, routed and addressed for delivery between different Internet nodes.
Packet switching	A way of sending data through a network to another location by subdividing the data into individual units or packets, each with a unique identification and destination address. Data is received by reassembling packets at destination.
Telecom Switch	A device that interconnects traffic (voice or data) from one port to another based on information within traffic (e.g., IP addresses), signaling (e.g., intervoice switch signaling) or predefined routes.
Voice switching	A way of sending and receiving voice through a network of telephone lines and switches. Voice switches reserve resources for the duration of a call which ensures high quality of voice transmission. In contrast, packet switching usually does not reserve similar resources, leading to dropped packets and delays and thus lower voice transmission quality.

Sources: S&P Communications Equipment Industry Survey 2001, Siemens AG, case authors

Case 5-2   P&G Japan: The SK-II Globalization Project

Christopher A. Bartlett

In November 1999, Paolo de Cesare was preparing for a meeting with the Global Leadership Team (GLT) of P&G's Beauty Care Global Business Unit (GBU) to present his analysis of whether SK-II, a prestige skin care line from Japan, should become a global P&G brand. As president of Max Factor Japan, the hub of P&G's fast-growing cosmetics business in Asia, and previous head of its European skin care business, de Cesare had considerable credibility with the GLT. Yet, as he readily acknowledged, there were significant risks in his proposal to expand SK-II into China and Europe.

Chairing the GLT meeting was Alan ("A. G.") Lafley, head of P&G's Beauty Care GBU, to which de Cesare reported. In the end, it was his organization— and his budget—that would support such a global expansion. Although he had been an early champion of SK-II in Japan, Lafley would need strong evidence to support P&G's first-ever proposal to expand a Japanese brand worldwide. After all, SK-II's success had been achieved in a culture where the consumers, distribution channels, and competitors were vastly different from those in most other countries.

Another constraint facing de Cesare was that P&G's global organization was in the midst of the bold but disruptive Organization 2005 restructuring program. As GBUs took over profit responsibility historically held by P&G's country-based organizations, management was still trying to negotiate their new working relationships. In this context, de Cesare, Lafley, and other GLT members struggled

to answer some key questions: Did SK-II have the potential to develop into a major global brand? If so, which markets were the most important to enter now? And how should this be implemented in P&G's newly reorganized global operations?

P&G's Internationalization: Engine of Growth

De Cesare's expansion plans for a Japanese product was just the latest step in a process of internationalization that had begun three-quarters of a century earlier. But it was the creation of the Overseas Division in 1948 that drove three decades of rapid expansion. Growing first in Europe, then Latin America and Asia, by 1980 P&G's operations in 27 overseas countries accounted for over 25% of its $11 billion worldwide sales. (**Exhibit 1** summarizes P&G's international expansion.)

Local Adaptiveness Meets Cross-Market Integration   Throughout its early expansion, the company adhered to a set of principles set down by Walter Lingle, the first vice president of overseas operations. "We must tailor our products to meet consumer demands in each nation," he said. "But we must create local country subsidiaries whose structure, policies, and practices are as exact a replica of the U.S. Procter & Gamble organization as it is possible to create." Under the Lingle principles, the company soon built a portfolio of self-sufficient subsidiaries run by country general managers (GMs) who grew their companies by adapting P&G technology and marketing expertise to their knowledge of their local markets.

Yet, by the 1980s, two problems emerged. First, the cost of running all the local product development labs and manufacturing plants was limiting profits. And second, the ferocious autonomy of national subsidiaries was preventing the global rollout of new products and technology improvements.

▌ Professor Christopher A. Bartlett prepared this case. HBS cases are developed solely as the basis for class discussion. Cases are not intended to serve as endorsements, sources of primary data, or illustrations of effective or ineffective management. Certain data have been disguised, but key relationships have been retained.
▌ Harvard Business School Case No 9-303-003, Copyright 2003 President and Fellows of Harvard College. All rights reserved.
This case was prepared by C. Bartlett. HBS Cases are developed solely for class discussion and do not necessarily illustrate either effective or ineffective handling of administrative situation

Source: Company records.

Year	Markets Entered
1837–1930	United States and Canada
1930–1940	United Kingdom, Philippines
1940–1950	Puerto Rico, Venezuela, Mexico
1950–1960	Switzerland, France, Belgium, Italy, Peru, Saudi Arabia, Morocco
1960–1970	Germany, Greece, Spain, Netherlands, Sweden, Austria, Indonesia, Malaysia, Hong Kong, Singapore, Japan
1970–1980	Ireland
1980–1990	Colombia, Chile, Caribbean, Guatemala, Kenya, Egypt, Thailand, Australia, New Zealand, India, Taiwan, South Korea, Pakistan, Turkey, Brazil, El Salvador
1990–2000	Russia, China, Czech Republic, Hungary, Poland, Slovak Republic, Bulgaria, Belarus, Latvia, Estonia, Romania, Lithuania, Kazakhstan, Yugoslavia, Croatia, Uzbekistan, Ukraine, Slovenia, Nigeria, South Africa, Denmark, Portugal, Norway, Argentina, Yemen, Sri Lanka, Vietnam, Bangladesh, Costa Rica, Turkmenistan

Exhibit 1   P&G's Internationalization Timetable

ing managers to coordinate regionwide product strategy and new product rollouts.

By the mid-1980s, these overlaid coordinating processes were formalized when each of the three European regional vice presidents was also given coordinative responsibility for a product category. While these individuals clearly had organizational influence, profit responsibility remained with the country subsidiary GMs. (See **Exhibit 2** for the 1986 European organization.)

Birth of Global Management   In 1986, P&G's seven divisions in the U.S. organization were broken into 26 product categories, each with its own product development, product supply, and sales and marketing capabilities. Given the parallel development of a European category management structure, it was not a big leap to appoint the first global category executives in 1989. These new roles were given significant responsibility for developing global strategy, managing the technology program, and qualifying expansion markets—but not profit responsibility, which still rested with the country subsidiary GMs.

Then, building on the success of the strong regional organization in Europe, P&G replaced its International Division with four regional entities— for North America, Europe, Latin America, and Asia—each assuming primary responsibility for profitability. (See **Exhibit 3** for P&G's structure in 1990.) A significant boost in the company's overseas growth followed, particularly in opening the untapped markets of Eastern Europe and China.

By the mid-1990s, with operations in over 75 countries, major new expansion opportunities were shrinking and growth was slowing. Furthermore, while global category management had improved cross-market coordination, innovative new products such as two-in-one shampoo and compact detergent were still being developed very slowly– particularly if they originated overseas. And even when they did, they were taking years to roll out worldwide. To many in the organization, the matrix structure seemed an impediment to entrepreneurship and flexibility.

Local GMs often resisted such initiatives due to the negative impact they had on local profits, for which the country subsidiaries were held accountable. As a result, new products could take a decade or more to be introduced worldwide.

Consequently, during the 1980s, P&G's historically "hands-off" regional headquarters became more active. In Europe, for example, Euro Technical Teams were formed to eliminate needless country-by-country product differences, reduce duplicated development efforts, and gain consensus on new-technology diffusion. Subsequently, regionwide coordination spread to purchasing, finance, and even marketing. In particular, the formation of Euro Brand Teams became an effective forum for market-

Exhibit 2 P&G European Organization, 1986

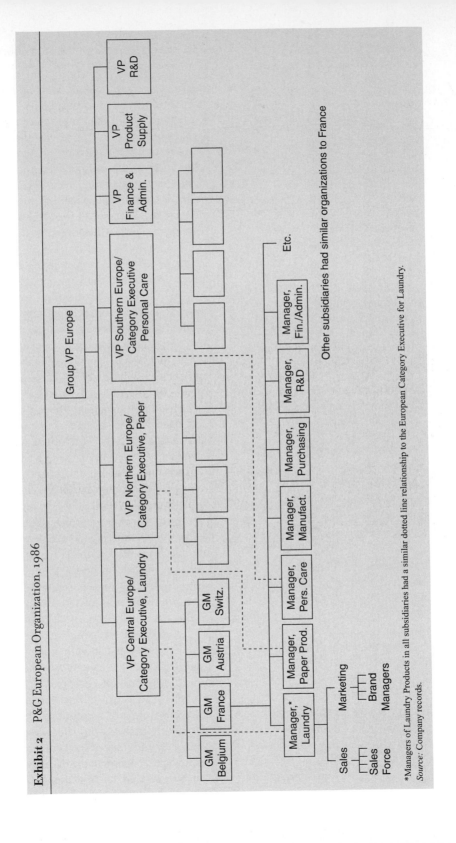

*Managers of Laundry Products in all subsidiaries had a similar dotted line relationship to the European Category Executive for Laundry.

Source: Company records.

Exhibit 3 P&G's Worldwide Organization Structure, 1990

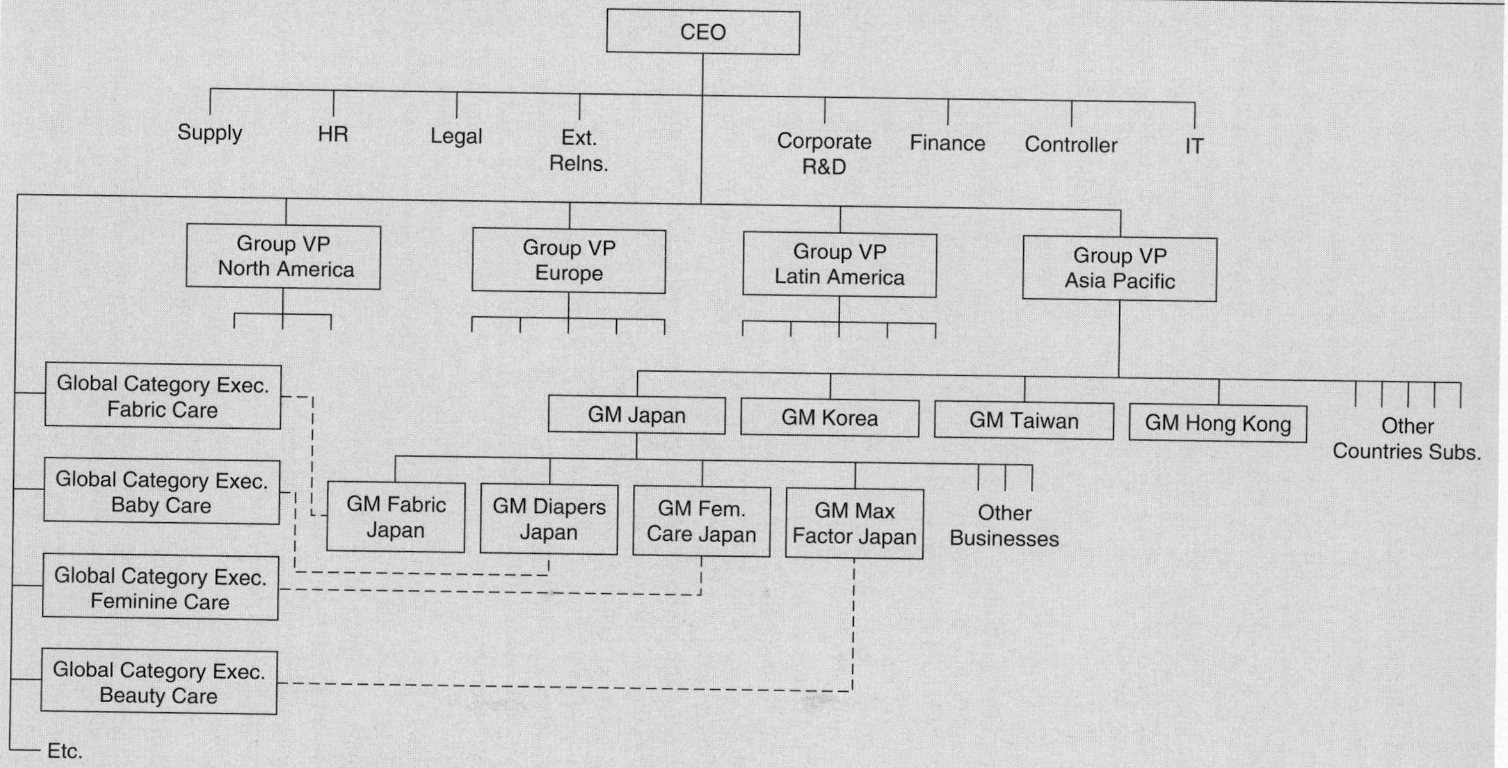

Source: Company records.

P&G Japan: Difficult Childhood, Struggling Adolescence

Up to the mid-1980s, P&G Japan had been a minor contributor to P&G's international growth. Indeed, the start-up had been so difficult that, in 1984, 12 years after entering the Japan market, P&G's board reviewed the accumulated losses of $200 million, the ongoing negative operating margins of 75%, and the eroding sales base—decreasing from 44 billion yen (¥) in 1979 to ¥26 billion in 1984—and wondered if it was time to exit this market. But CEO Ed Artzt convinced the board that Japan was strategically important, that the organization had learned from its mistakes—and that Durk Jager, the energetic new country GM, could turn things around.

The Turnaround   In 1985, as the first step in developing a program he called "Ichidai Hiyaku" ("The Great Flying Leap"), Jager analyzed the causes of P&G's spectacular failure in Japan. One of his key findings was that the company had not recognized the distinctive needs and habits of the very demanding Japanese consumer. (For instance, P&G Japan had built its laundry-detergent business around All Temperature Cheer, a product that ignored the Japanese practice of doing the laundry in tap water, not a range of water temperatures.) Furthermore, he found that the company had not respected the innovative capability of Japanese companies such as Kao and Lion, which turned out to be among the world's toughest competitors. (After creating the market for disposable diapers in Japan, for example, P&G Japan watched Pampers' market share drop from 100% in 1979 to 8% in 1985 as local competitors introduced similar products with major improvements.) And Jager concluded that P&G Japan had not adapted to the complex Japanese distribution system. (For instance, after realizing that its 3,000 wholesalers were providing little promotional support for its products, the company resorted to aggressive discounting that triggered several years of distributor disengagement and competitive price wars.)

Jager argued that without a major in-country product development capability, P&G could never respond to the demanding Japanese consumer and the tough, technology-driven local competitors. Envisioning a technology center that would support product development throughout Asia and even take a worldwide leadership role, he persuaded his superiors to grow P&G's 60-person research and development (R&D) team into an organization that could compete with competitor Kao's 2,000-strong R&D operation.

Over the next four years, radical change in market research, advertising, and distribution resulted in a 270% increase in sales that, in turn, reduced unit production costs by 62%. In 1988, with laundry detergents again profitable and Pampers and Whisper (the Japanese version of P&G's Always feminine napkin) achieving market leadership, Jager began to emphasize expansion. In particular, he promoted more product introductions and a bold expansion into the beauty products category. When P&G implemented its new region-based reorganization in 1990, Jager became the logical candidate to assume the newly created position of group vice president for Asia, a position he held until 1991, when he left to run the huge U.S. business.

The Relapse   In the early 1990s, however, P&G Japan's strong performance began eroding. The problems began when Japan's "bubble economy" burst in 1991. More troubling, however, was the fact that, even within this stagnating market, P&G was losing share. Between 1992 and 1996 its yen sales fell 3% to 4% annually for a cumulative 20% total decline, while in the same period competitor Unicharm's annual growth was 13% and Kao's was 3%.

Even P&G's entry into the new category of beauty care worsened rather than improved the situation. The parent company's 1991 acquisition of Max Factor gave P&G Japan a foothold in the $10 billion Japanese cosmetics market. But in Japan, sales of only $300 million made it a distant number-five competitor, its 3% market share dwarfed by Shiseido's 20% plus. Then, in 1992 P&G's global beauty care category executive announced the global launch of Max Factor Blue, a top-end, self-select color cosmetic line to be sold through general merchandise and drug stores. But in Japan, over 80% of the market was sold by trained beauty counselors in specialty stores or department store cosmetics counters. The new self-select strategy, coupled with a decision to cut costs in the expensive beauty-counselor distribution channel, led to a 15% decline in sales in the Japanese cosmetics business. The previous break-even performance became a negative operating margin of 10% in 1993. Things became even worse the following year, with losses running at $1 million per week.

In 1994, the Japanese beauty care business lost $50 million on sales of less than $300 million. Among the scores of businesses in the 15 countries reporting to him, A. G. Lafley, the newly arrived vice president of the Asian region, quickly zeroed in on Max Factor Japan as a priority problem area. "We first had to clean up the Max Factor Blue mass-market mess then review our basic strategy," he said. Over the next three years, the local organization worked hard to make Max Factor Japan profitable. Its product line was rationalized from 1,400 SKUs (or stock-keeping units) to 500, distribution support was focused on 4,000 sales outlets as opposed to the previous 10,000, and sales and marketing staff was cut from 600 to 150. It was a trying time for Max Factor Japan.

Organization 2005: Blueprint for Global Growth

In 1996 Jager, now promoted to chief operating officer under CEO John Pepper, signaled that he saw the development of new products as the key to P&G's future growth. While supporting Pepper's emphasis on expanding into emerging markets, he voiced concern that the company would "start running out of white space towards the end of the decade." To emphasize the importance of creating new businesses, he became the champion of a Leadership Innovation Team to identify and support major companywide innovations.

When he succeeded Pepper as CEO in January 1999, Jager continued his mission. Citing P&G breakthroughs such as the first synthetic detergent in the 1930s, the introduction of fluoride toothpaste in the 1950s, and the development of the first disposable diaper in the 1960s, he said, "Almost without exception, we've won biggest on the strength of superior product technology. . . . But frankly, we've come

nowhere near exploiting its full potential." Backing this belief, in 1999 he increased the budget for R&D by 12% while cutting marketing expenditures by 9%.

If P&G's growth would now depend on its ability to develop new products and roll them out rapidly worldwide, Jager believed his new strategic thrust had to be implemented through a radically different organization. Since early 1998 he and Pepper had been planning Organization 2005, an initiative he felt represented "the most dramatic change to P&G's structure, processes, and culture in the company's history." Implementing O2005, as it came to be called, he promised would bring 13% to 15% annual earnings growth and would result in $900 million in annual savings starting in 2004. Implementation would be painful, he warned; in the first five years, it called for the closing of 10 plants and the loss of 15,000 jobs—13% of the worldwide workforce. The cost of the restructuring was estimated at $1.9 billion, with $1 billion of that total forecast for 1999 and 2000.

Changing the Culture   During the three months prior to assuming the CEO role, Jager toured company facilities worldwide. He concluded that P&G's sluggish 2% annual volume growth and its loss of global market share was due to a culture he saw as slow, conformist, and risk averse. (See **Exhibit 4** for P&G's financial performance.) In his view, employees were wasting half their time on "non-value-added work" such as memo writing, form filling, or chart preparation, slowing down decisions and making the company vulnerable to more nimble competition. (One observer described P&G's product development model as "ready, aim, aim, aim, aim, fire.") He concluded that any organizational change would have to be built on a cultural revolution.

With "stretch, innovation, and speed" as his watchwords, Jager signaled his intent to shake up norms and practices that had shaped generations of highly disciplined, intensely loyal managers often referred to within the industry as "Proctoids." "Great ideas come from conflict and dissatisfaction with the status quo," he said. "I'd like an organization where there are rebels." To signal the importance of risk taking and speed, Jager gave a green light to the

Exhibit 4 P&G Select Financial Performance Data, 1980–1999

Annual Income Statement ($ millions)	June 1999	June 1998	June 1997	June 1996	June 1995	June 1990	June 1985	June 1980
Sales	38,125	37,154	35,764	35,284	33,434	24,081	13,552	10,772
Cost of Goods Sold	18,615	19,466	18,829	19,404	18,370	14,658	9,099	7,471
Gross Profit	19,510	17,688	16,935	15,880	15,064	9,423	4,453	3,301
Selling, General, and Administrative Expense	10,628	10,035	9,960	9,707	9,632	6,262	3,099	1,977
of which:								
Research and Development Expense	1,726	1,546	1,469	1,399	1,148	693	400	228
Advertising Expense	3,538	3,704	3,466	3,254	3,284	2,059	1,105	621
Depreciation, Depletion, and Amortization	2,148	1,598	1,487	1,358	1,253	859	378	196
Operating Profit	6,734	6,055	5,488	4,815	4,179	2,302	976	1,128
Interest Expense	650	548	457	493	511	395	165	97
Non-Operating Income/Expense	235	201	218	272	409	561	193	51
Special Items	–481	0	0	75	–77	0	0	0
Total Income Taxes	2,075	1,928	1,834	1,623	1,355	914	369	440
Net Income	3,763	3,780	3,415	3,046	2,645	1,554	635	642
Geographic Breakdown: Net Sales								
Americas	58.4%	54.7%	53.8%	52.9%	55.1%			
United States						62.5%	75.4%	80.9%
Europe, Middle East, and Africa	31.9%	35.1%	35.3%	35.2%	32.9%			
International						39.9%	22.3%	22.4%
Asia	9.7%	10.2%	10.9%	11.9%	10.8%			
Corporate					1.2%	–2.1%	2.3%	–3.3%
Number of Employees	110,000	110,000	106,000	103,000	99,200	94,000	62,000	59,000

Abbreviated Balance Sheet ($ millions)	June 1999	June 1998	June 1997	June 1996	June 1995	June 1990	June 1985	June 1980
ASSETS								
Total Current Assets	11,358	10,577	10,786	10,807	10,842	7,644	3,816	3,007
Plant, Property & Equipment, net	12,626	12,180	11,376	11,118	11,026	7,436	5,292	3,237
Other Assets	8,129	8,209	5,382	5,805	6,257	3,407	575	309
TOTAL ASSETS	32,113	30,966	27,544	27,730	28,125	18,487	9,683	6,553
LIABILITIES								
Total Current Liabilities	10,761	9,250	7,798	7,825	8,648	5,417	2,589	1,670
Long-Term Debt	6,231	5,765	4,143	4,670	5,161	3,588	877	835
Deferred Taxes	362	428	559	638	531	1,258	945	445
Other Liabilities	2,701	3,287	2,998	2,875	3,196	706	0	0
TOTAL LIABILITIES	20,055	18,730	15,498	16,008	17,536	10,969	4,411	2,950
TOTAL EQUITY	12,058	12,236	12,046	11,722	10,589	7,518	5,272	3,603
TOTAL LIABILITIES & EQUITY	32,113	30,966	27,544	27,730	28,125	18,487	9,683	6,553

Source: SEC filings, Standard & Poor's Research Insight.

Leadership Innovation Team to implement a global rollout of two radically new products: Dryel, a home dry-cleaning kit; and Swiffer, an electrostatically charged dust mop. Just 18 months after entering their first test market, they were on sale in the United States, Europe, Latin America, and Asia. Jager promised 20 more new products over the next 18 months. "And if you are worried about oversight," he said, "I am the portfolio manager."

Changing the Processes   Reinforcing the new culture were some major changes to P&G's traditional systems and processes. To emphasize the need for greater risk taking, Jager leveraged the performance-based component of compensation so that, for example, the variability of a vice president's annual pay package increased from a traditional range of 20% (10% up or down) to 80% (40% up or down). And to motivate people and align them with the overall success of the company, he extended the reach of the stock option plan from senior management to virtually all employees. Even outsiders were involved, and P&G's advertising agencies soon found their compensation linked to sales increases per dollar spent.

Another major systems shift occurred in the area of budgets. Jager felt that the annual ritual of preparing, negotiating, and revising line item sales and expenses by product and country was enormously time wasting and energy sapping. In future, they would be encouraged to propose ambitious stretch objectives. And going forward, Jager also argued to replace the episodic nature of separate marketing, payroll, and initiative budgets with an integrated business planning process where all budget elements of the operating plan could be reviewed and approved together.

Changing the Structure   In perhaps the most drastic change introduced in O2005, primary profit responsibility shifted from P&G's four regional organizations to seven global business units (GBUs) that would now manage product development, manufacturing, and marketing of their respective categories worldwide. The old regional organizations were reconstituted into seven market development

organizations (MDOs) that assumed responsibility for local implementation of the GBUs' global strategies.[†] And transactional activities such as accounting, human resources, payroll, and much of IT were coordinated through a global business service unit (GBS). (See **Exhibit 5** for a representation of the new structure.)

Beyond their clear responsibility for developing and rolling out new products, the GBUs were also charged with the task of increasing efficiency by standardizing manufacturing processes, simplifying brand portfolios, and coordinating marketing activities. For example, by reducing the company's 12 different diaper-manufacturing processes to one standard production model, Jager believed that P&G could not only reap economies but might also remove a major barrier to rapid new-product rollouts. And by axing some of its 300 brands and evaluating the core group with global potential, he felt the company could exploit its resources more efficiently.

The restructuring also aimed to eliminate bureaucracy and increase accountability. Overall, six management layers were stripped out, reducing the levels between the chairman and the front line from 13 to 7. Furthermore, numerous committee responsibilities were transferred to individuals. For example, the final sign-off on new advertising copy was given to individual executives, not approval boards, cutting the time it took to get out ads from months to days.

New Corporate Priorities Meet Old Japanese Problems

The seeds of Jager's strategic and organizational initiatives began sprouting long before he assumed the CEO role in January 1999. For years, he had been pushing his belief in growth through innovation, urging businesses to invest in new products and technologies. Even the organizational review that resulted in the O2005 blueprint had begun a year before he

---

[†]In an exception to the shift of profit responsibility to the GBUs, the MDOs responsible for developing countries were treated as profit centers.

Exhibit 5   P&G Organization, 1999 (Post O2005 Implementation)

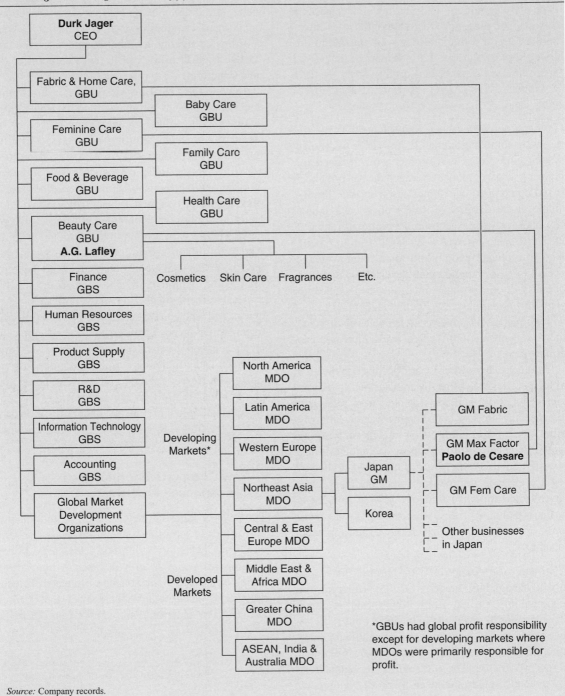

Exhibit 6 Beauty Counselor Work Flow

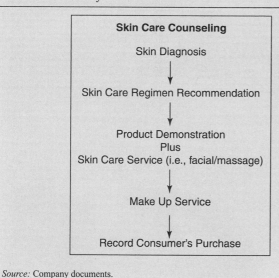
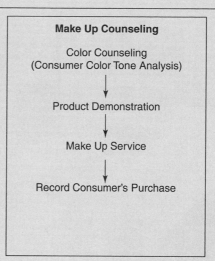

Skin Care Counseling

Skin Diagnosis

↓

Skin Care Regimen Recommendation

↓

Product Demonstration
Plus
Skin Care Service (i.e., facial/massage)

↓

Make Up Service

↓

Record Consumer's Purchase

Make Up Counseling

Color Counseling
(Consumer Color Tone Analysis)

↓

Product Demonstration

↓

Make Up Service

↓

Record Consumer's Purchase

Source: Company documents.

took over. These winds of change blew through all parts of the company, including the long-suffering Japanese company's beauty care business, which was finally emerging from years of problems.

Building the Base: From Mass to Class By 1997 the Japanese cosmetics business had broken even. With guidance and support from Lafley, the vice president for the Asian region, the Japanese team had focused its advertising investment on just two brands—Max Factor Color, and a prestige skin care brand called SK-II.‡ "Poring through the Japanese business, we found this little jewel called SK-II," recalled Lafley. "To those of us familiar with rich Western facial creams and lotions, this clear, unperfumed liquid with a distinctive odor seemed very different. But the discriminating Japanese consumer

loved it, and it became the cornerstone of our new focus on the prestige beauty-counselor segment."

Max Factor Japan began rebuilding its beauty-counselor channels, which involved significant investments in training as well as counter design and installation (see **Exhibits 6** and **7**). And because SK-II was such a high margin item, management launched a bold experiment in TV advertising featuring a well-respected Japanese actress in her late 30s. In three years SK-II's awareness ratings rose from around 20% to over 70%, while sales in the same period more than doubled.

Building on this success, management adapted the ad campaign for Hong Kong and Taiwan, where SK-II had quietly built a loyal following among the many women who took their fashion cues from Tokyo. In both markets, sales rocketed, and by 1997, export sales of $68 million represented about 30% of the brand's total sales. More important, SK-II was now generating significant operating profits. Yet within P&G, this high-end product had little visibility outside Japan. Paolo de Cesare, general manager of P&G's European skin care business in the mid-1990s, felt that, because the company's skin care

---

‡SK-II was an obscure skin care product that had not even been recognized, much less evaluated, in the Max Factor acquisition. Containing Pitera, a secret yeast-based ingredient supposedly developed by a Japanese monk who noticed how the hands of workers in sake breweries kept young looking, SK-II had a small but extremely loyal following. Priced at ¥15,000 ($120) or more per bottle, it clearly was at the top of the skin care range.

Exhibit 7   In-Store SK-II Counter Space

Source: Company documents.

experience came from the highly successful mass-market Olay brand, few outside Japan understood SK-II. "I remember some people saying that SK-II was like Olay for Japan," he recalled. "People outside Japan just didn't know what to make of it."

Responding to the Innovation Push   Meanwhile, Jager had begun his push for more innovation. Given his firmly held belief that Japan's demanding consumers and tough competitors made it an important source of leading-edge ideas, it was not surprising that more innovative ideas and initiatives from Japan began finding their way through the company. For example, an electrostatically charged cleaning cloth developed by a Japanese competitor became the genesis of P&G's global rollout of Swiffer dry

mops; rising Japanese sensitivity to hygiene and sanitation spawned worldwide application in products such as Ariel Pure Clean ("beyond whiteness, it washes away germs"); and dozens of other ideas from Japan—from a waterless car-washing cloth to a disposable stain-removing pad to a washing machine-based dry-cleaning product—were all put into P&G's product development pipeline.

Because Japanese women had by far the highest use of beauty care products in the world, it was natural that the global beauty care category management started to regard Max Factor Japan as a potential source of innovation. One of the first worldwide development projects on which Japan played a key role was Lipfinity, a long-lasting lipstick that was felt to have global potential.

In the mid-1990s, the impressive but short-lived success of long-lasting lipsticks introduced in Japan by Shiseido and Kenebo reinforced P&G's own consumer research, which had long indicated the potential for such a product. Working with R&D labs in Cincinnati and the United Kingdom, several Japanese technologists participated on a global team that developed a new product involving a durable color base and a renewable moisturizing second coat. Recognizing that this two-stage application would result in a more expensive product that involved basic habit changes, the global cosmetics category executive asked Max Factor Japan to be the new brand's global lead market.

Viewing their task as "translating the breakthrough technology invention into a market-sensitive product innovation," the Japanese product management team developed the marketing approach—concept, packaging, positioning, communications strategy, and so on—that led to the new brand, Lipfinity, becoming Japan's best-selling lipstick. The Japanese innovations were then transferred worldwide, as Lipfinity rolled out in Europe and the United States within six months of the Japanese launch.

O2005 Rolls Out   Soon after O2005 was first announced in September 1998, massive management changes began. By the time of its formal implementation in July 1999, half the top 30 managers and a third of the top 300 were new to their jobs. For example, Lafley, who had just returned from Asia to head the North American region, was asked to prepare to hand off that role and take over as head of the Beauty Care GBU. "It was a crazy year," recalled Lafley. "There was so much to build, but beyond the grand design, we were not clear about how it should operate."

In another of the hundreds of O2005 senior management changes, de Cesare, head of P&G's European skin care business, was promoted to vice president and asked to move to Osaka and head up Max Factor Japan. Under the new structure he would report directly to Lafley's Beauty Care GBU and on a dotted-line basis to the head of the MDO for Northeast Asia.

In addition to adjusting to this new complexity where responsibilities and relationships were still being defined, de Cesare found himself in a new global role. As president of Max Factor Japan he became a member of the Beauty Care Global Leadership Team (GLT), a group comprised of the business GMs from three key MDOs, representatives from key functions such as R&D, consumer research, product supply, HR, and finance, and chaired by Lafley as GBU head. These meetings became vital forums for implementing Lafley's charge "to review P&G's huge beauty care portfolio and focus investment on the top brands with the potential to become global assets." The question took on new importance for de Cesare when he was named global franchise leader for SK-II and asked to explore its potential as a global brand.

A New Global Product Development Process
Soon after arriving in Japan, de Cesare discovered that the Japanese Max Factor organization was increasingly involved in new global product development activities following its successful Lipfinity role. This process began under the leadership of the Beauty Care GLT when consumer research identified an unmet consumer need worldwide. A lead research center then developed a technical model of how P&G could respond to the need. Next, the GLT process brought in marketing expertise from lead markets to expand that technology "chassis" to a holistic new-product concept. Finally, contributing technologists and marketers were designated to work on the variations in ingredients or aesthetics necessary to adapt the core technology or product concept to local markets.

This global product development process was set in motion when consumer researchers found that, despite regional differences, there was a worldwide opportunity in facial cleansing. The research showed that, although U.S. women were satisfied with the clean feeling they got using bar soaps, it left their skin tight and dry; in Europe, women applied a cleansing milk with a cotton pad that left their skin moisturized and conditioned but not as clean as they wanted; and in Japan, the habit of using foaming facial cleansers left women satisfied with skin conditioning but not with moisturizing. Globally, however, the unmet need was to achieve soft, moisturized, clean-feeling skin, and herein the GBU saw the product opportunity—and the technological challenge.

A technology team was assembled at an R&D facility in Cincinnati, drawing on the most qualified technologists from its P&G's labs worldwide. For example, because the average Japanese woman spent 4.5 minutes on her face-cleansing regime compared with 1.7 minutes for the typical American woman, Japanese technologists were sought for their refined expertise in the cleansing processes and their particular understanding of how to develop a product with the rich, creamy lather.

Working with a woven substrate technology developed by P&G's paper business, the core technology team found that a 10-micron fiber, when woven into a mesh, was effective in trapping and absorbing dirt and impurities. By impregnating this substrate with a dry-sprayed formula of cleansers and moisturizers activated at different times in the cleansing process, team members felt they could develop a disposable cleansing cloth that would respond to the identified consumer need. After this technology "chassis" had been developed, a technology team in Japan adapted it to allow the cloth to be impregnated with a different cleanser formulation that included the SK-II ingredient, Pitera. (See **Exhibit 8** for an overview of the development process.)

A U.S.-based marketing team took on the task of developing the Olay version. Identifying its consumers' view of a multistep salon facial as the ultimate cleansing experience, this team came up with the concept of a one-step routine that offered the benefits of cleansing, conditioning, and toning— "just like a daily facial." Meanwhile, another team

---

Exhibit 8   Representation of Global Cleansing Cloth Development Program

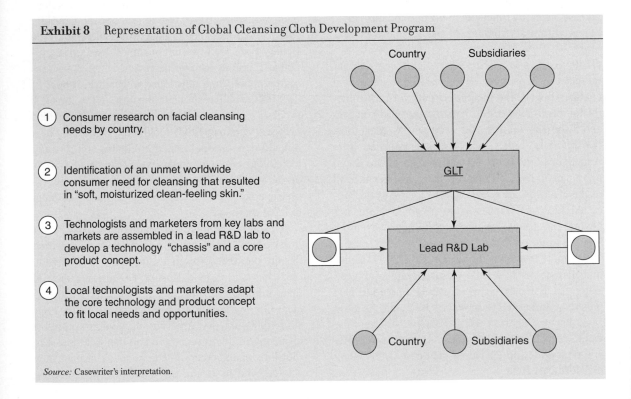

1 Consumer research on facial cleansing needs by country.

2 Identification of an unmet worldwide consumer need for cleansing that resulted in "soft, moisturized clean-feeling skin."

3 Technologists and marketers from key labs and markets are assembled in a lead R&D lab to develop a technology "chassis" and a core product concept.

4 Local technologists and marketers adapt the core technology and product concept to fit local needs and opportunities.

Source: Casewriter's interpretation.

had the same assignment in Japan, which became the lead market for the SK-II version. Because women already had a five- or six-step cleansing routine, the SK-II version was positioned not as a "daily facial" but as a "foaming massage cloth" that built on the ritual experience of increasing skin circulation through a massage while boosting skin clarity due to the microfibers' ability to clean pores and trap dirt. (See **Exhibit 9** for illustration of the Foaming Massage Cloth with other core SK-II products.)

Exhibit 9   Illustration of Part of SK-II Product Line

pitera soak

FACIAL TREATMENT ESSENCE
Skin Balancing Essence

The heart of the SK-II range, the revolutionary **Facial Treatment Essence** is the second point in your Ritual. This unique Pitera-rich product helps boost moisture levels to improve texture and clarity for a more beautiful, glowing complexion.

Women are so passionate about **Facial Treatment Essence** that they describe it as their 'holy' water. It contains the most concentrated amount of Pitera of all our skincare products—around 90% pure SK-II Pitera. It absorbs easily and leaves your skin looking radiant, with a supple, smooth feel.

FOAMING MASSAGE CLOTH
Purifying Cleansing Cloth

These innovative **Foaming Massage Cloths** leave your skin feeling smooth and velvety. A single sheet offers the outstanding effects of a cleanser, facial wash and massage. It gently washes away impurities, excess oil and non-waterproof eye make-up, leaving your skin clean, pure and refreshed.

FACIAL TREATMENT CLEAR LOTION
Clear Purifying Lotion

For a perfectly conditioned and ultra-fresh skin, use the **Facial Treatment Clear Lotion** morning and evening after cleansing your face and neck. The final part of your cleansing process, this Lotion helps remove residual impurities and dead skin cells.

Source: Company brochure.

Because of its premium pricing strategy, the SK-II Foaming Massage Cloth was packaged in a much more elegant dispensing box and was priced at ¥6,000 ($50), compared to $7 for the Olay Facial Cloth in the United States. And Japan assigned several technologists to the task of developing detailed product performance data that Japanese beauty magazines required for the much more scientific product reviews they published compared to their Western counterparts. In the end, each market ended up with a distinct product built on a common technology platform. Marketing expertise was also shared—some Japanese performance analysis and data were also relevant for the Olay version and were used in Europe, for example—allowing the organization to leverage its local learning.

The SK-II Decision: A Global Brand?

After barely six months in Japan, de Cesare recognized that he now had three different roles in the new organization. As president of Max Factor Japan, he was impressed by the turnaround this local company had pulled off and was optimistic about its ability to grow significantly in the large Japanese beauty market. As GLT member on the Beauty Care GBU, he was proud of his organization's contribution to the GBU-sponsored global new-product innovation process and was convinced that Japan could continue to contribute to and learn from P&G's impressive technology base. And now as global franchise leader for SK-II, he was excited by the opportunity to explore whether the brand could break into the $9 billion worldwide prestige skin care market. (See **Exhibit 10** for prestige market data.)

When he arrived in Japan, de Cesare found that SK-II's success in Taiwan and Hong Kong (by 1999, 45% of total SK-II sales) had already encouraged management to begin expansion into three other regional markets—Singapore, Malaysia, and South Korea. But these were relatively small markets, and as he reviewed data on the global skin care and prestige beauty markets, he wondered if the time was right to make a bold entry into one or

Exhibit 10   Global Prestige Market: Size and Geographic Split

Global Prestige Market: 1999 (Fragrances, Cosmetics, Skin) = $15 billion at retail level (of which approximately 60% is skin care)

United States	26%
Canada	2
Asia/Pacific[a]	25
United Kingdom	5
France	5
Germany	5
Rest of Europe	16
Rest of World	16

[a]Japan represented over 80% of the Asia/Pacific total.
Source: Company data.

Exhibit 11   Global Skin Care Market Size: 1999

Skin Care (Main market and prestige)

Region/Country	Retail Sales ($ million)	Two-Year Growth Rate
Western Europe	8,736	7%
France	2,019	7
Germany	1,839	14
United Kingdom	1,052	17
North America	6,059	18
United States	5,603	18
Asia/Pacific	11,220	2
China	1,022	28
Japan	6,869	6
South Korea	1,895	9
Taiwan	532	18
Hong Kong	266	6

Source: Company data.

more major markets. (See **Exhibits 11** and **12** for global skin-care market and consumer data.)

As he reviewed the opportunities, three alternatives presented themselves. First, the beauty care management team for Greater China was interested in expanding on SK-II's success in Taiwan and

Exhibit 12   Skin Care and Cosmetics Habits and Practices: Selected Countries

Product Usage (% Past 7 Days)	United States[a]	Japan[a]	China[b]	United Kingdom[a]
Facial Moisturizer—Lotion	45%	95%	26%	37%
Facial Moisturizer—Cream	25	28	52	45
Facial Cleansers (excluding Family Bar Soap)	51	90	57	41
Foundation	70	85	35	57
Lipstick	84	97	75	85
Mascara	76	27	13	75

[a]Based on broad, representative sample of consumers.
[b]Based on upper-income consumers in Beijing City.
Source: Company data.

Hong Kong by introducing the brand into mainland China. Next, at GLT meetings de Cesare had discussed with the head of beauty care in Europe the possibilities of bringing SK-II into that large Western market. His third possibility—really his first option, he realized—was to build on the brand's success in SK-II's rich and proven home Japanese market.

The Japanese Opportunity Japanese women were among the most sophisticated users of beauty products in the world, and per capita they were the world's leading consumers of these products. Despite its improved performance in recent years, Max Factor Japan claimed less than a 3% share of this $10 billion beauty product market. "It's huge," boasted one local manager. "Larger than the U.S. laundry market."

Although SK-II had sales of more than $150 million in Japan in 1999, de Cesare was also aware that in recent years its home market growth had slowed. This was something the new manager felt he could change by tapping into P&G's extensive technological resources. The successful experience of the foaming massage cloth convinced him that there was a significant opportunity to expand sales by extending the SK-II line beyond its traditional product offerings. For example, he could see an immediate opportunity to move into new segments by adding anti-aging and skin-whitening products to the SK-II range. Although this would take a

considerable amount of time and effort, it would exploit internal capabilities and external brand image. Compared to the new-market entry options, investment would be quite low.

An exciting development that would support this home market thrust emerged when he discovered that his SK-II technology and marketing teams had come together to develop an innovative beauty imaging system (BIS). Using the Japanese technicians' skills in miniaturization and software development, they were working to create a simplified version of scientific equipment used by P&G lab technicians to qualify new skin care products by measuring improvements in skin condition. The plan was to install the modified BIS at SK-II counters and have beauty consultants use it to boost the accuracy and credibility of their skin diagnosis. The project fit perfectly with de Cesare's vision for SK-II to become the brand that solved individual skin care problems. He felt it could build significant loyalty in the analytically inclined Japanese consumer.

With the company's having such a small share of such a rich market, de Cesare felt that a strategy of product innovation and superior in-store service had the potential to accelerate a growth rate that had slowed to 5% per annum over the past three years. Although Shiseido could be expected to put up a good fight, he felt SK-II should double sales in Japan over the next six or seven years. In short, de Cesare was extremely excited about SK-II's potential for growth in its home market. He said: "It's a fabulous opportunity. One loyal SK-II customer in Japan already spends about $1,000 a year on the brand. Even a regular consumer of all P&G's other products—from toothpaste and deodorant to shampoo and detergent—all together spends nowhere near that amount annually."

The Chinese Puzzle   A very different opportunity existed in China, where P&G had been operating only since 1988. Because of the extraordinarily low prices of Chinese laundry products, the company had uncharacteristically led with beauty products when it entered this huge market. Olay was launched in 1989 and, after early problems, eventually became highly successful by adopting a nontraditional marketing strategy. To justify its price premium—its price was 20 to 30 times the price of local skin care products—Shivesh Ram, the entrepreneurial beauty care manager in China, decided to add a service component to Olay's superior product formulation. Borrowing from the Max Factor Japan model, he began selling through counters in the state-owned department stores staffed by beauty counselors. By 1999, Olay had almost 1,000 such counters in China and was a huge success.

As the Chinese market opened to international retailers, department stores from Taiwan, Hong Kong, and Singapore began opening in Beijing and Shanghai. Familiar with Olay as a mass-market brand, they questioned allocating it scarce beauty counter space alongside Estee Lauder, Lancôme, Shiseido, and other premium brands that had already claimed the prime locations critical to success in this business. It was at this point that Ram began exploring the possibility of introducing SK-II, allowing Olay to move more deeply into second-tier department stores, stores in smaller cities, and to "second-floor" cosmetics locations in large stores. "China is widely predicted to become the second-largest market in the world," said Ram. "The prestige beauty segment is growing at 30 to 40% a year, and virtually every major competitor in that space is already here."

Counterbalancing Ram's enthusiastic proposals, de Cesare also heard voices of concern. Beyond the potential impact on a successful Olay market position, some were worried that SK-II would be a distraction to P&G's strategy of becoming a mainstream Chinese company and to its competitive goal of entering 600 Chinese cities ahead of Unilever, Kao, and other global players. They argued that targeting an elite consumer group with a niche product was not in keeping with the objective of reaching the 1.2 billion population with laundry, hair care, oral care, diapers, and other basics. After all, even with SK-II's basic four-step regimen, a three-month supply could cost more than one month's salary for the average woman working in a major Chinese city.

Furthermore, the skeptics wondered if the Chinese consumer was ready for SK-II. Olay had succeeded only by the company's educating its customers to move from a one-step skin care process—washing with bar soap and water—to a three-step cleansing and moisturizing process. SK-II relied on women developing at least a four- to six-step regimen, something the doubters felt was unrealistic. But as Ram and others argued, within the target market, skin care practices were quite developed, and penetration of skin care products was higher than in many developed markets.

Finally, the Chinese market presented numerous other risks, from the widespread existence of counterfeit prestige products to the bureaucracy attached to a one-year import-registration process. But the biggest concern was the likelihood that SK-II would attract import duties of 35% to 40%. This meant that even if P&G squeezed its margin in China, SK-II would have to be priced significantly above the retail level in other markets. Still, the China team calculated that because of the lower cost of beauty consultants, the product could still be profitable. (See **Exhibit 13** for cost estimates.)

Despite the critics, Ram was eager to try, and he responded to their concerns: "There are three Chinas—rural China, low-income urban China, and sophisticated, wealthy China concentrated in Shanghai, Beijing, and Guangzhou. The third group is as big a target consumer group as in many developed markets. If we don't move soon, the

Exhibit 13   Global SK-II Cost Structure (% of net sales)[a]

FY1999/2000	Japan	Taiwan/ Hong Kong	PR China Expected	United Kingdom Expected
Net sales	100%	100%	100%	100%
Cost of products sold	22	26	45	29
Marketing, research, and selling/ administrative expense	67	58	44	63
Operating income	11	16	11	8

[a]Data disguised.
Source: Company estimates.

battle for that elite will be lost to the global beauty care powerhouses that have been here for three years or more."

Ram was strongly supported by his regional beauty care manager and by the Greater China MDO president. Together, they were willing to experiment with a few counters in Shanghai, and if successful, to expand to more counters in other major cities. Over the first three years, they expected to generate $10 million to $15 million in sales, by which time they expected the brand to break even. They estimated the initial investment to build counters, train beauty consultants, and support the introduction would probably mean losses of about 10% of sales over that three-year period.

The European Question   As he explored global opportunities for SK-II, de Cesare's mind kept returning to the European market he knew so well. Unlike China, Europe had a relatively large and sophisticated group of beauty-conscious consumers who already practiced a multistep regimen using various specialized skin care products. What he was unsure of was whether there was a significant group willing to adopt the disciplined six- to eight-step ritual that the most devoted Japanese SK-II users followed.

The bigger challenge, in his view, would be introducing a totally new brand into an already crowded field of high-profile, well-respected competitors including Estee Lauder, Clinique, Lancôme, Chanel, and Dior. While TV advertising had proven highly effective in raising SK-II's awareness and sales in Japan, Taiwan, and Hong Kong, the cost of television—or even print—ads in Europe made such an approach there prohibitive. And without any real brand awareness or heritage, he wondered if SK-II's mystique would transfer to a Western market.

As he thought through these issues, de Cesare spoke with his old boss, Mike Thompson, the head of P&G's beauty business in Europe. Because the Max Faxtor sales force sold primarily to mass-distribution outlets, Thompson did not think it provided SK-II the appropriate access to the European market. However, he explained that the fine-fragrance business was beginning to do quite well. In the United Kingdom, for example, its 25-person sales force was on track in 1999 to book $1 million in after-tax profit on sales of $12 million. Because it sold brands such as Hugo Boss, Giorgio, and Beverly Hills to department stores and Boots, the major pharmacy chain, its sales approach and trade relationship was different from the SK-II model in Japan. Nevertheless, Thompson felt it was a major asset that could be exploited.

Furthermore, Thompson told de Cesare that his wife was a loyal SK-II user and reasoned that since she was a critical judge of products, other women would discover the same benefits in the product she did. He believed that SK-II provided the fine-fragrance business a way to extend its line in the few department stores that dominated U.K. distribution in the prestige business. He thought they would be willing to give SK-II a try. (He was less optimistic about countries such as France and Germany, however, where prestige products were sold through thousands of perfumeries, making it impossible to justify the SK-II consultants who would be vital to the sales model.)

Initial consumer research in the United Kingdom had provided mixed results. But de Cesare felt that while this kind of blind testing could provide useful data on detergents, it was less helpful in this case. The consumers tested the product blind for one week, then were interviewed about their impressions. But because they lacked the beauty counselors' analysis and advice and had not practiced the full skin care regimen, he felt the results did not adequately predict SK-II's potential.

In discussions with Thompson, de Cesare concluded that he could hope to achieve sales of $10 million by the fourth year in the U.K. market. Given the intense competition, he recognized that he would have to absorb losses of $1 million to $2 million annually over that period as the start-up investment.

The Organizational Constraint   While the strategic opportunities were clear, de Cesare also recognized that his decision needed to comply with the organizational reality in which it would be implemented. While GBU head Lafley was an early champion and continuing supporter of SK-II, his boss, Jager, was less committed. Jager was among those in P&G who openly questioned how well some of the products in the beauty care business—particularly some of the acquired brands—fit in the P&G portfolio. While he was comfortable with high-volume products like shampoo, he was more skeptical of the upper end of the line, particularly fine fragrances. In his view, the fashion-linked and promotion-driven sales models of luxury products neither played well to P&G's "stack it high, sell it cheap" marketing skills nor leveraged its superior technologies.

The other organizational reality was that the implementation of O2005 was causing a good deal of organizational disruption and management distraction. This was particularly true in Europe, as Thompson explained:

> We swung the pendulum 180 degrees, from a local to a global focus. Marketing plans and budgets had previously been developed locally, strongly debated with European managers, then rolled up. Now they were developed globally—or at least regionally—by new people who often did not understand the competitive and trade differences across markets. We began to standardize and centralize our policies and practices out of Geneva. Not surprisingly, a lot of our best local managers left the company.

One result of the O2005 change was that country subsidiary GMs now focused more on maximizing sales volume than profits, and this had put the beauty care business under significant budget pressure. Thompson explained the situation in Europe in 1999:

> One thing became clear very quickly: It was a lot easier to sell cases of Ariel [detergent] or Pampers [diapers] than cases of cosmetics, so guess where the sales force effort went? At the same time, the new-product pipeline was resulting in almost a "launch of the month," and with the introduction of new products like Swiffer and Febreze, it was hard for the MDOs to manage all of these corporate priorities. . . . Finally, because cosmetics sales required more time and effort from local sales forces, more local costs were assigned to that business, and that has added to profit pressures.

Framing the Proposal   It was in this context that de Cesare was framing his proposal based on the global potential of SK-II as a brand and his plans to exploit the opportunities he saw. But he knew Lafley's long ties and positive feelings towards SK-II would not be sufficient to convince him. The GBU head was committed to focusing beauty care on the core brands that could be developed as a global franchise, and his questions would likely zero in on whether de Cesare could build SK-II into such a brand.

Case 5-3 McKinsey & Company: Managing Knowledge and Learning

Christopher A. Bartlett

In April 1996, halfway through his first three-year term as managing director of McKinsey & Company, Rajat Gupta was feeling quite proud as he flew out of Bermuda, site of the firm's second annual Practice Olympics. He had just listened to twenty teams outlining innovative new ideas they had developed out of recent project work, and, like his fellow senior partner judges, Gupta had come away impressed by the intelligence and creativity of the firm's next generation of consultants.

But there was another thought that kept coming back to the 47 year old leader of this highly successful $1.8 billion consulting firm (See **Exhibit 1** for a twenty year growth history). If this represented the tip of McKinsey's knowledge and expertise iceberg, how well was the firm doing in developing, capturing, and leveraging this asset in service of its clients worldwide? Although the Practice Olympics was only one of several initiatives he had championed, Gupta wondered if it was enough, particularly in light of his often stated belief that "knowledge is the lifeblood of McKinsey."

▌ The Founders' Legacy†

Founded in 1926 by University of Chicago professor, James ("Mac") McKinsey, the firm of "accounting and engineering advisors" that bore his name grew rapidly. Soon Mac began recruiting experienced executives, and training them in the integrated approach

▌ Professor Christopher A. Bartlett prepared this case as the basis for class discussion rather than to illustrate either effective or ineffective handling of an administrative situation.
▌ Harvard Business School Case No 9-396-357, Copyright 1996 President and Fellows of Harvard College. All rights reserved.
This case was prepared by C. Bartlett. *HBS Cases are developed solely for class discussion and do not necessarily illustrate either effective or ineffective handling of administrative situation.*

he called his General Survey outline. In Saturday morning sessions he would lead consultants through an "undeviating sequence" of analysis—goals, strategy, policies, organization, facilities, procedures, and personnel—while still encouraging them to synthesize data and think for themselves.

In 1932, Mac recruited Marvin Bower, a bright young lawyer with a Harvard MBA, and within two years asked him to become manager of the recently opened New York office. Convinced that he had to upgrade the firm's image in an industry typically regarded as "efficiency experts" or "business doctors," Bower undertook to imbue in his associates the sense of professionalism he had experienced in his time in a law partnership. In a 1937 memo, he outlined his vision for the firm as one focused on issues of importance to top-level management, adhering to the highest standards of integrity, professional ethics, and technical excellence, able to attract and develop young men of outstanding qualifications, and committed to continually raising its stature and influence. Above all, it was to be a firm dedicated to the mission of serving its clients superbly well.

Over the next decade, Bower worked tirelessly to influence his partners and associates to share his vision. As new offices opened, he became a strong advocate of the One Firm policy that required all consultants to be recruited and advanced on a firm-wide basis, clients to be treated as McKinsey & Company responsibilities, and profits to be shared from a firm pool, not an office pool. And through dinner seminars, he began upgrading the size and quality of McKinsey's clients. In the 1945 New Engagement Guide, he articulated a policy that every assignment should bring the firm something more than revenue—experience or prestige, for example.

Exhibit 1   McKinsey & Company: 20 Year Growth Indicators

Year	# Office Locations	# Active Engagements	Number of CSS[a]	Number of MGMs[b]
1975	24	661	529	NA
1980	31	771	744	NA
1985	36	1823	1248	NA
1990	47	2789	2465	348
1991	51	2875	2653	395
1992	55	2917	2875	399
1993	60	3142	3122	422
1994	64	3398	3334	440
1995	69	3559	3817	472

[a]CSS = Client Service Staff (All professional consulting staff).
[b]MGM = Management Group Members (Partners and directors).
Source: Internal McKinsey & Company documents.

Elected Managing Partner in 1950, Bower led his ten partners and 74 associates to initiate a series of major changes that turned McKinsey into an elite consulting firm unable to meet the demand for its services. Each client's problems were seen as unique, but Bower and his colleagues firmly believed that well trained, highly intelligent generalists could quickly grasp the issue, and through disciplined analysis find its solution. The firm's extraordinary domestic growth through the 1950s provided a basis for international expansion that accelerated the rate of growth in the 1960s. Following the opening of the London Office in 1959, offices in Geneva, Amsterdam, Düsseldorf, and Paris followed quickly. By the time Bower stepped down as Managing Director in 1967, McKinsey was a well established and highly respected presence in Europe and North America.

A Decade of Doubt

Although leadership succession was well planned and executed, within a few years, McKinsey's growth engine seemed to stall. The economic turmoil of the oil crisis, the slowing of the divisionalization process that had fueled the European expansion, the growing sophistication of client management, and the appearance of new focused competitors like Boston Consulting Group (BCG) all contributed

to the problem. Almost overnight, McKinsey's enormous reservoir of internal self-confidence and even self-satisfaction began to turn to self-doubt and self-criticism.

Commission on Firm Aims and Goals Concerned that the slowing growth in Europe and the U.S. was more than just a cyclical market downturn, the firm's partners assigned a committee of their most respected peers to study the problem and make recommendations. In April 1971, the Commission on Firm Aims and Goals concluded that the firm has been growing too fast. The authors bluntly reported, "Our preoccupation with the geographic expansion and new practice possibilities has caused us to neglect the development of our technical and professional skills." The report concluded that McKinsey had been too willing to accept routine assignments from marginal clients, that the quality of work done was uneven, and that while its consultants were excellent generalist problem solvers, they often lacked the deep industry knowledge or the substantive specialized expertise that clients were demanding.

One of the Commission's central proposals was that the firm had to recommit itself to the continuous development of its members. This meant that growth would have to be slowed and that the associate to MGM ratio be reduced from 7 to 1 back to 5 or 6 to 1. It further proposed that emphasis be placed on the development of what it termed "T-Shaped" consultants—those who supplemented a broad generalist perspective with an in-depth industry or functional specialty.

Practice Development Initiative   When Ron Daniel was elected Managing Director (MD) in 1976—the fourth to hold the position since Bower had stepped down nine years earlier—McKinsey was still struggling to meet the challenges laid out in the Commission's report. As the head of the New York office since 1970, Daniel had experienced first hand the rising expectations of increasingly sophisticated clients and the aggressive challenges of new competitors like BCG. In contrast to McKinsey's local office-based model of "client relationship" consulting, BCG began competing on the basis of "thought leadership" from a highly concentrated resource base in Boston. Using some simple but powerful tools, such as the experience curve and the growth-share matrix, BCG began to make strong inroads into the strategy consulting market. As McKinsey began losing both clients and recruits to BCG, Daniel became convinced that his firm could no longer succeed pursuing its generalist model.

One of his first moves was to appoint one of the firm's most respected and productive senior partners as McKinsey's first full-time director of training. As an expanded commitment to developing consultants' skills and expertise became the norm, the executive committee began debating the need to formally updating the firm's long-standing mission to reflect the firm's core commitment not only to serving its clients but also to developing its consultants. (**Exhibit 2**.)

But Daniel also believed some structural changes were necessary. Building on an initiative he and his colleagues had already implemented in the New York office, he created industry-based Clientele Sectors in consumer products, banking, industrial goods, insurance, and so on, cutting across the geographic offices that remained the primary organizational entity. He also encouraged more formal development of the firm's functional expertise in areas like strategy, organization and operations where knowl-

Exhibit 2   McKinsey's Mission and Guiding Principles (1996)

McKinsey Mission

To help our clients make positive, lasting, and substantial improvements in their performance and to build a great Firm that is able to attract, develop, excite, and retain exceptional people.

Guiding Principles

Serving Clients

Adhere to professional standards
Follow the top management approach
Assist the client in implementation and capability building
Perform consulting in a cost effective manner

Building the Firm

Operate as one Firm
Maintain a meritocracy
Show a genuine concern for our people
Foster an open and nonhierarchical working atmosphere
Manage the Firm's resources responsibly

Being a Member of the Professional Staff

Demonstrate commitment to client service
Strive continuously for superior quality
Advance the state-of-the-art management
Contribute a spirit of partnership through teamwork and collaboration
Profit from the freedom and assume the responsibility associated with self-governance
Uphold the obligation to dissent

edge and experience were widely diffused and minimally codified. However, many—including Marvin Bower—expressed concern that any move towards a product driven approach could damage McKinsey's distinctive advantage of its local office presence which gave partners strong connections with the business community, allowed teams to work on site with clients and facilitated implementation. It was an approach that they felt contrasted sharply with the "fly in, fly out" model of expert-based consulting that BCG ran from its Boston hub.

Nonetheless, Daniel pressed ahead. Having established industry sectors, the MD next turned his attention to leveraging the firm's functional expertise. He assembled working groups to develop knowledge in two areas that were at the heart of McKinsey's practice—strategy and organization. To head up the first group, he named Fred Gluck, a director in the New York office who had been outspoken in urging the firm to modify its traditional generalist approach. In June 1977, Gluck invited a "Super Group" of younger partners with strategy expertise to a three day meeting to share ideas and develop an agenda for the strategy practice. One described the meeting:

> We had three days of unmitigated chaos. Someone from New York would stand up and present a four-box matrix. A partner from London would present a nine-box matrix. A German would present a 47 box matrix. It was chaos . . . but at the end of the third day some strands of thought were coming together.

At the same time, Daniel asked Bob Waterman who had been working on a Siemens-sponsored study of "excellent companies" and Jim Bennett, a respected senior partner to assemble a group that could articulate the firm's existing knowledge in the organization arena. One of their first recruits was an innovative young Ph.D. in organizational theory named Tom Peters.

Revival and Renewal

By the early 1980s, with growth resuming, a cautious optimism returned to McKinsey for the first time in almost a decade.

Centers of Competence   Recognizing that the activities of the two practice development projects could not just be a one-time effort, in 1980 Daniel asked Gluck to join the central small group that comprised the Firm Office and focus on the knowledge building agenda that had become his passion. Ever since his arrival at the firm from Bell Labs in 1967, Gluck had wanted to bring an equally stimulating intellectual environment to McKinsey. Against

some strong internal resistance, he set out to convert his partners to his strongly held beliefs—that knowledge development had to be a core, not a peripheral firm activity; that it needed to be ongoing and institutionalized, not temporary and project based; and that it had to be the responsibility of everyone, not just a few.

To complement the growing number of Clientele Industry Sectors, he created 15 Centers of Competence (virtual centers, not locations) built around existing areas of management expertise like strategy, organization, marketing, change management, and systems. In a 1982 memo to all partners, he described the role of these centers as two-fold: to help develop consultants and to ensure the continued renewal of the firm's intellectual resources. For each Center, Gluck identified one or two highly motivated, recognized experts in the particular field and named them practice leaders. The expectation was that these leaders would assemble from around the firm, a core group of partners who were active in the practice area and interested in contributing to its development. (See **Exhibit 3** for the 15 Centers and 11 Sectors in 1983.)

Exhibit 3   McKinsey's Emerging Practice Areas: Centers of Competence and Industry Sectors, 1983

Centers of Competence	Clientele Sectors
Building Institutional Skills	Automotive
Business Management Unit	Banking
Change Management	Chemicals
Corporate Leadership	Communications and
Corporate Finance	Information
Diagnostic Scan	Consumer Products
International Management	Electronics
Integrated Logistics	Energy
Manufacturing	Health Care
Marketing	Industrial Goods
Microeconomics	Insurance
Sourcing	Steel
Strategic Management	
Systems	
Technology	

To help build a shared body of knowledge, the leadership of each of the 15 Centers of Competence began to initiate activities primarily involving the core group and, less frequently, the members of the practice network. A partner commented on Gluck's commitment to the centers:

> Unlike industry sectors, the centers of competence did not have a natural, stable client base, and Fred had to work hard to get them going. . . . He basically told the practice leaders, "Spend whatever you can—the cost is almost irrelevant compared to the payoff." There was no attempt to filter or manage the process, and the effect was "to let a thousand flowers bloom."

Gluck also spent a huge amount of time trying to change an internal status hierarchy based largely on the size and importance of one's client base. Arguing that practice development ("snowball making" as it became known internally) was not less "macho" than client development ("snowball throwing"), he tried to convince his colleagues that everyone had to become snowball makers *and* snowball throwers. In endless discussions, he would provoke his colleagues with barbed pronouncements and personal challenges: "Knowing what you're talking about is not necessarily a client service handicap" or "Would you want your brain surgery done by a general practitioner?"

Building a Knowledge Infrastructure As the firm's new emphasis on individual consultant training took hold and the Clientele Sectors and Centers of Competence began to generate new insights, many began to feel the need to capture and leverage the learning. Although big ideas had occasionally been written up as articles for publication in newspapers, magazines or journals like *Harvard Business Review,* there was still a deep-seated suspicion of anything that smacked of packaging ideas or creating proprietary concepts or standard solutions. Such reluctance to document concepts had long constrained the internal transfer of ideas and the vast majority of internally developed knowledge was never captured.

This began to change with the launching of the McKinsey Staff Paper series in 1978, and by the early 1980s the firm was actively encouraging its consultants to publish their key findings. The initiative got a

major boost with the publication in 1982 of two major bestsellers, Peters and Waterman's *In Search of Excellence* and Kenichi Ohmae's *The Mind of the Strategist.* But books, articles, and staff papers required major time investments, and only a small minority of consultants made the effort to write them. Believing that the firm had to lower the barrier to internal knowledge communication, Gluck introduced the idea of Practice Bulletins, two page summaries of important new ideas that identified the experts who could provide more detail. A partner elaborated:

> The Bulletins were essentially internal advertisements for ideas and the people who had developed them. We tried to convince people that they would help build their personal networks and internal reputations. . . . Fred was not at all concerned that the quality was mixed, and had a strong philosophy of letting the internal market sort out what were the really big ideas.

Believing that the firm's organizational infrastructure needed major overhaul, in 1987 Gluck launched a Knowledge Management Project. After five months of study, the team made three recommendations. First, the firm had to make a major commitment to build a common database of knowledge accumulated from client work and developed in the practice areas. Second, to ensure that the data bases were maintained and used, they proposed that each practice area (Clientele Sector and Competence Center) hire a full time practice coordinator who could act as an "intelligent switch" responsible for monitoring the quality of the data and for helping consultants access the relevant information. And finally, they suggested that the firm expand its hiring practices and promotion policies to create a career path for deep functional specialists whose narrow expertise would make them more I-shaped than the normal profile of a T-shaped consultant.

The task of implementing these recommendations fell to a team led by Bill Matassoni, the firm's director of communications and Brook Manville, a newly recruited Yale Ph.D. with experience with electronic publishing. Focusing first on the Firm Practice Information System (FPIS), a computerized data base of client engagements, they installed new systems and procedures to make the data more complete, accurate, and timely so that it could be accessed as a reliable information resource, not just an archival record. More difficult was the task of capturing the knowledge that had accumulated in the practice areas since much of it had not been formalized and none of it had been prioritized or integrated. To create a computer based Practice Development Network (PDNet), Matassoni and Manville put huge energy into begging, cajoling and challenging each practice to develop and submit documents that represented their core knowledge. After months of work, they had collected the 2,000 documents that they believed provided the critical mass to launch PDNet.

At the last minute, Matassoni and his team also developed another information resource that had not been part of the study team's recommendations. They assembled a listing of all firm experts and key document titles by practice area and published it in a small book, compact enough to fit in any consultant's briefcase. The Knowledge Resource Directory (KRD) became the McKinsey Yellow Pages and found immediate and widespread use firmwide. Although the computerized data bases were slow to be widely adopted, the KRD found almost immediate enthusiastic acceptance.

Making the new practice coordinator's position effective proved more challenging. Initially, these roles were seen as little more than glorified librarians. It took several years before the new roles were filled by individuals (often ex-consultants) who were sufficiently respected that they could not only act as consultants to those seeking information about their area of expertise, but also were able to impose the discipline necessary to maintain and build the practice's data bases.

Perhaps the most difficult task was to legitimize the role of a new class of I-shaped consultants—the specialist. The basic concept was that a professional could make a career in McKinsey by emphasizing specialized knowledge development rather than the broad based problem solving skills and client development orientation that were deeply embedded in the firm's value system. While several consultants

with deep technical expertise in specialties like market research, finance or steel making were recruited, most found it hard to assimilate into the mainstream. The firm seemed uncomfortable about how to evaluate, compensate or promote these individuals, and many either became isolated or disaffected. Nonetheless, the partnership continued to support the notion of a specialist promotion track and continued to struggle with how to make it work.

Matassoni reflected on the changes:

> The objective of the infrastructure changes was not so much to create a new McKinsey as to keep the old "one firm" concept functioning as we grew . . . Despite all the talk of computerized data bases, the knowledge management process still relied heavily on personal networks, old practices like cross-office transfers, and strong "One Firm" norms like helping other consultants when they called. And at promotion time, nobody reviewed your PD documents. They looked at how you used your internal networks to have your ideas make an impact on clients.

Managing Success

By the late 1980s, the firm was expanding rapidly again. In 1988, the same year Fred Gluck was elected managing director, new offices were opened in Rome, Helsinki, Sao Paulo, and Minneapolis bringing the total to 41. The growing view amongst the partners, however, was that enhancing McKinsey's reputation as a thought leader was at least as important as attracting new business.

Refining Knowledge Management   After being elected MD, Gluck delegated the practice development role he had played since 1980 to a newly constituted Clientele and Professional Development Committee (CPDC). When Ted Hall took over leadership of this committee in late 1991, he felt there was a need to adjust the firm's knowledge development focus. He commented:

> By the early 1990s, too many people were seeing practice development as the creation of experts and the generation of documents in order to build our reputation. But knowledge is only valuable when it is between the ears of consultants and applied to clients'

problems. Because it is less effectively developed through the disciplined work of a few than through the spontaneous interaction of many, we had to change the more structured "discover-codify-disseminate" model to a looser and more inclusive "engage-explore-apply-share" approach. In other words, we shifted our focus from developing knowledge to building individual and team capability.

Over the years, Gluck's philosophy "to let 1,000 flowers bloom" had resulted in the original group of 11 sectors and 15 centers expanding to become what Hall called "72 islands of activity," (Sectors, Centers, Working Groups, and Special Projects) many of which were perceived as fiefdoms dominated by one or two established experts. In Hall's view, the garden of 1,000 flowers needed weeding, a task requiring a larger group of mostly different gardeners. The CPDC began integrating the diverse groups into seven sectors and seven functional capability groups (See **Exhibit 4**). These sectors and groups were led by teams of five to seven partners (typically younger directors and principals) with the objective of replacing the leader-driven knowledge creation and dissemination process with a "stewardship model" of self-governing practices focused on competence building.

Client Impact   With responsibility for knowledge management delegated to the CPDC, Gluck began to focus on a new theme—client impact. On being elected managing director, he made this a central theme in his early speeches, memos, and his first All Partners Conference. He also created a Client Impact Committee, and asked it to explore the ways in which the firm could ensure that the expertise it was developing created positive measurable results in each client engagement.

One of the most important initiatives of the new committee was to persuade the partners to redefine the firm's key consulting unit from the engagement team (ET) to the client service team (CST). The traditional ET, assembled to deliver a three or four month assignment for a client was a highly efficient and flexible unit, but it tended to focus on the immediate task rather than on the client's long term need. The CST concept was that the firm could add long-term value and increase the effectiveness of individual engagements if it could unite a core of individuals (particularly at the partner level) who were linked across multiple ETs, and commit them to working with the client over an extended period. The impact was to broaden the classic model of a single partner "owning" a client to a group of partners with shared commitment to each client.

In response to concerns within the partnership about a gradual decline in associates' involvement in intellectual capital development, the CPDC began to emphasize the need for CSTs to play a central role in the intellectual life of McKinsey. (See **Exhibit 5** for a CPDC conceptualization.) Believing that the CSTs (by 1993 about 200 firm-wide) represented the real learning laboratories, the CPDC sent memos to the new industry sector and capability group leaders advising them that their practices would be evaluated by their coverage of the firm's CSTs. They also wrote to all consultants emphasizing the importance of the firm's intellectual development and their own professional development, for which they had primary responsibility. Finally, they assembled data on the amount of time consultants were spending on practice and professional development by office, distributing the widely divergent results to partners in offices worldwide.

Developing Multiple Career Paths   Despite (or perhaps because of) all these changes, the specialist consultant model continued to struggle. Over the years, the evaluation criteria for the specialist career path had gradually converged with the mainstream generalist promotion criteria. For example, the specialist's old promotion standard of "world-class expertise" in a particular field had given way to a more pragmatic emphasis on client impact; the notion of a legitimate role as a consultant to teams had evolved to a need for specialists to be "engagement director capable"; and the less pressured evaluation standard of "grow or go" was replaced by the normal associate's more demanding "up or out" requirement, albeit within a slightly more flexible timeframe.

Exhibit 4   Group Framework for Sectors and Centers

Functional Capability Groups	**Clientele Industry Sectors**

Functional Capability Groups

Corporate Governance and Leadership
- Corporate organization
- Corporate management processes
- Corporate strategy development
- Corporate relationship design and management
- Corporate finance
- Post-merger management

Organization (OPP/MOVE)
- Corporate transformation design and leadership
- Energizing approaches
- Organization design and development
- Leadership and teams
- Engaging teams

Information Technology/Systems
- To be determined

Marketing
- Market research
- Sales force management
- Channel management
- Global marketing
- Pricing
- Process and sector support

Operations Effectiveness
- Integrated logistics
- Manufacturing
- Purchasing and supply management

Strategy
- Strategy
- Microeconomics
- Business dynamics
- Business planning processes

Cross Functional Management
- Innovation
- Customer satisfaction
- Product/technology development and commercialization
- Core process redesign

Clientele Industry Sectors

Financial Institutions
- Banking
- Insurance
- Health care payor/provider

Consumer
- Retailing
- Consumer industries
- Media
- Pharmaceuticals

Energy
- Electrical utilities
- Petroleum
- Natural gas
- Other energy

Basic Materials
- Steel
- Pulp and paper
- Chemicals
- Other basic materials

Aerospace, Electronics, and Telecom
- Telecom
- Electronics
- Aerospace

Transportation

Automotive, Assembly, and Machinery
- Automotive
- Assembly

Source: Internal McKinsey & Company document

Exhibit 5   CPDC Proposed Organizational Relationships

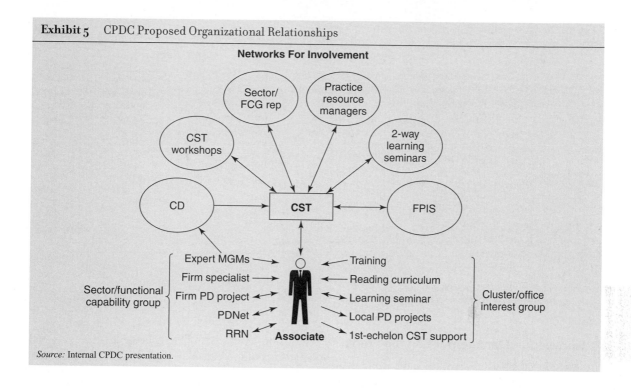

Source: Internal CPDC presentation.

Although these changes had reduced the earlier role dissonance—specialists became more T shaped—it also diluted the original objective. While legitimizing the two client service staff tracks, in late 1992 the Professional Personnel Committee decided to create two career paths for client service support and administrative staff. The first reaffirmed a path to partnership for practice-dedicated specialists who built credibility with clients and CSTs through their specialized knowledge and its expert application. Their skills would have them in high demand as consultants to teams (CDs) rather than as engagement directors (EDs). The second new option was the practice management track designed to provide a career progression for practice coordinators, who had a key role in transferring knowledge and in helping practice leaders manage increasingly complex networks. Valuable administrators could also be promoted on this track. (See **Exhibit 6** for an overview.)

Yet despite the announcement of the new criteria and promotion processes, amongst associates and specialists alike there was still some residual confusion and even skepticism about the viability of the specialist track to partnership. As he dealt with this issue, Gluck kept returning to his long term theme that, "it's all about people," even suggesting people development was the company's primary purpose:

There are two ways to look at McKinsey. The most common way is that we are a client service firm whose primary purpose is to serve the companies seeking our help. That is legitimate. But I believe there is an even more powerful way for us to see ourselves. We should begin to view our primary purpose as building a great institution that becomes an engine for producing highly motivated world class people who in turn will serve our clients extraordinarily well.

Exhibit 6   Alternative Career Path Focus and Criteria

	CSS[1] Paths		CSSA[2] Paths	
Career Paths/Roles	General Consulting	Specialized Consulting	Practice Expertise	Practice Management Administration
Focus	Perform general problem solving and lead implementation Develop client relationships	Apply in-depth practice knowledge to studies Develop client relationships Build external reputation	Leverage practice knowledge across studies Create new knowledge	Codify and transfer knowledge Help administer practice

[1]Client Service Staff
[2]Client Service Support and Administration
Source: Internal McKinsey & Company presentation.

■ Knowledge Management on the Front

To see how McKinsey's evolving knowledge management processes were being felt by those on the firm's front lines, we will follow the activities of three consultants working in three diverse locations and focused on three different agendas.

Jeff Peters and the Sydney Office Assignment
John Stuckey, a director in McKinsey's Sydney office felt great satisfaction at being invited to bid for a financial services growth strategy study for one of Australia's most respected companies. Yet the opportunity also created some challenges. As in most small or medium sized offices, most consultants in Sydney were generalists. Almost all with financial industry expertise had been "conflicted out" of the project due to work they had done for competing financial institutions in Australia.

Stuckey immediately began using his personal network to find how he might tap into McKinsey's worldwide resources for someone who could lead this first engagement for an important new client. After numerous phone calls and some lobbying at a directors' conference he identified Jeff Peters, a Boston-based senior engagement manager and veteran of more than 20 studies for financial institutions. The only problem was that Peters had two ongoing commitments that would make him unavailable for at least the first six weeks of the Australian assignment.

Meanwhile, Stuckey and Ken Gibson, his engagement director on the project, were working with the Sydney office staffing coordinator to identify qualified, available and nonconflicted associates to complete the team. Balancing assignments of over 80 consultants to 25 ongoing teams was a complex process that involved matching the needs of the engagement and the individual consultants' development requirements. A constant flow of consultants across offices helped buffer constraints, and also contributed to the transfer of knowledge. At any one time 15 to 25 Australian consultants were on short- or long-term assignments abroad, while another 10 to 15 consultants from other offices were working in Australia. (Firm-wide, nearly 20% of work was performed by consultants on inter-office loans.)

They identified a three person team to work with Peters. John Peacocke was a New Zealand army engineer with an MBA in finance from Wharton and two years of experience in McKinsey. Although he had served on a four-month study for a retail bank client in Cleveland, since returning to Australia he had worked mostly for oil and gas clients. Patty Akopiantz was a one-year associate who had worked in investment banking before earning an MBA at Harvard. Her primary interest and her developing expertise was in consumer marketing. The business analyst was Jonathan Liew, previously an actuary who was embarking on his first McKinsey assignment.

With Peters' help, Stuckey and Gibson also began assembling a group of internal specialists and experts who could act as consulting directors (CDs) to the team. James Gorman, a personal financial services expert in New York agreed to visit Sydney for a week and to be available for weekly conference calls; Majid Arab, an insurance industry specialist committed to a two-week visit and a similar "on-call" availability; Andrew Doman, a London-based financial industry expert also signed on as a CD. Within the Sydney office, Charles Conn, a leader in the firm's growth strategies practice, agreed to lend his expertise, as did Clem Doherty, a firm leader in the impact of technology.

With Gibson acting more as an engagement manager than an engagement director, the team began scanning the Knowledge Resource Directory, the FPIS and the PDNet for leads. (Firm-wide, the use of PDNet documents had boomed in the eight years since its introduction. By early 1996, there were almost 12,000 documents on PDNet, with over 2,000 being requested each month.) In all, they tracked down 179 relevant PD documents and tapped into the advice and experience of over 60 firm members worldwide. Team member Patty Akopiantz explained:

> Ken was acting as engagement manager, but he was not really an expert in financial services, so we were even more reliant than usual on the internal network. Some of the ideas we got off PDNet were helpful, but the trail of contacts was much more valuable . . . Being on a completely different time zone had great

advantages. If you hit a wall at the end of the day, you could drop messages in a dozen voicemail boxes in Europe and the United States. Because the firm norm is that you respond to requests by colleagues, by morning you would have seven or eight new suggestions, data sources, or leads.

At the end of the first phase, the team convened an internal workshop designed to keep client management informed, involved, and committed to the emerging conclusions. Out of this meeting, the team was focused on seven core beliefs and four viable options that provided its agenda for the next phase of the project. It was at this point that Peters was able to join the team:

> By the time I arrived, most of the hard analysis had been done and they had been able to narrow the focus from the universe to four core options in just over a month. It was very impressive how they had been able to do that with limited team-based expertise and a demanding client. . . . With things going so well, my main priority was to focus the team on the end product. Once we got a clear logical outline, I assigned tasks and got out of the way. Most of my time I spent working on the client relationship . . . It was great learning for John and Patty, and both of them were ready to take on a management role in their next engagements.

In November, the team presented its conclusions to the board, and after some tough questioning and challenging, they accepted the recommendations and began an implementation process. The client's managing director reflected on the outcome:

> We're a tough client, but I would rate their work as very good. Their value added was in their access to knowledge, the intellectual rigor they bring, and their ability to build understanding and consensus among a diverse management group . . . If things don't go ahead now, it's our own fault.

John Stuckey had a little different post-engagement view of the result:

> Overall, I think we did pretty good work, but I was a bit disappointed we didn't come up with a radical breakthrough. . . . We leveraged the firm's knowledge base effectively, but I worry that we rely so much on

our internal expertise. We have to beware of the trap that many large successful companies have fallen into by becoming too introverted, too satisfied with their own view of the world.

Warwick Bray and European Telecoms   After earning his MBA at Melbourne University, Warwick Bray joined McKinsey's Melbourne office in 1989. A computer science major, he had worked as a systems engineer at Hewlett Packard and wanted to leverage his technological experience. For two of his first three years, he worked on engagements related to the impact of deregulation on the Asia-Pacific telecommunications industry. In early 1992, Bray advised his group development leader (his assigned mentor and adviser) that he would be interested in spending a year in London. After several phone discussions the transfer was arranged, and in March the young Australian found himself on his first European team.

From his experience on the Australian telecom projects, Bray had written a PD document, "Negotiating Interconnect" which he presented at the firm's annual worldwide telecom conference. Recognizing this developing "knowledge spike," Michael Patsalos-Fox, telecom practice leader in London, invited Bray to work with him on a study. Soon he was being called in as a deregulation expert to make presentations to various client executives. "In McKinsey you have to earn that right," said Bray. "For me it was immensely satisfying to be recognized as an expert."

Under the leadership of Patsalos-Fox, the telecom practice had grown rapidly in the United Kingdom. With deregulation spreading across the continent in the 1990s, however, he was becoming overwhelmed by the demands for his help. Beginning in the late 1980s, Patsalos-Fox decided to stop acting as the sole repository for and exporter of European telecom information and expertise, and start developing a more interdependent network. To help in this task, he appointed Sulu Soderstrom, a Stanford MBA with a strong technology background, as full-time practice coordinator. Over the next few years she played a key role in creating the administrative glue that bonded together telecom practice groups in offices throughout Europe. Said Patsalos-Fox:

> She wrote proposals, became the expert on information sources, organized European conferences, helped with cross-office staffing, located expertise and supported and participated in our practice development work. Gradually she helped us move from an "export"-based hub and spokes model of information sharing to a true federalist-based network.

In this growth environment and supported by the stronger infrastructure, the practice opportunities exploded during the 1990s. To move the knowledge creation beyond what he described as "incremental synthesis of past experience," Patsalos-Fox launched a series of practice-sponsored studies. Staffed by some of the practice's best consultants, they focused on big topics like "The Industry Structure in 2005," or "The Telephone Company of the Future." But most of the practice's knowledge base was built by the informal initiatives of individual associates who would step back after several engagements and write a paper on their new insights. For example, Bray wrote several well-received PD documents and was enhancing his internal reputation as an expert in deregulation and multimedia. Increasingly he was invited to consult to or even join teams in other parts of Europe. Said Patsalos-Fox:

> He was flying around making presentations and helping teams. Although the internal audience is the toughest, he was getting invited back. When it came time for him to come up for election, the London office nominated him but the strength of his support came from his colleagues in the European telecom network.

In 1996, Patsalos-Fox felt it was time for a new generation of practice leadership. He asked his young Australian protégé and two other partners—one in Brussels, one in Paris—if they would take on a co-leadership role. Bray reflected on two challenges he and his co-leaders faced. The first was to make telecom a really exciting and interesting practice so it could attract the best associates. "That meant taking on the most interesting work, and running our engagements so that people felt they were developing and having fun," he said.

The second key challenge was how to develop the largely informal links among the fast-growing European telecom practices. Despite the excellent job that Soderstrom had done as the practice's repository of knowledge and channel of communication, it was clear that there were limits to her ability to act as the sole "intelligent switch." As a result, the group had initiated a practice-specific intranet link designed to allow members direct access to the practice's knowledge base (PD documents, conference proceedings, CVs, etc.), its members' capabilities (via home pages for each practice member), client base (CST home pages, links to client web sites), and external knowledge resources (MIT's Multimedia Lab, Theseus Institute, etc.). More open yet more focused than existing firm-wide systems like PDNet, the Telecom Intranet was expected to accelerate the "engage-explore-apply-share" knowledge cycle.

There were some, however, who worried that this would be another step away from "one firm" towards compartmentalization, and from focus on building idea-driven personal networks towards creating data-based electronic transactions. In particular, the concern was that functional capability groups would be less able to transfer their knowledge into increasingly strong and self-contained industry-based practices. Warwick Bray recognized the problem, acknowledging that linkages between European telecom and most functional practices "could be better":

> The problem is we rarely feel the need to draw on those groups. For example, I know the firm's pricing practice has world-class expertise in industrial pricing, but we haven't yet learned how to apply it to telecom. We mostly call on the pricing experts within our practice. We probably should reach out more.

Stephen Dull and the Business Marketing Competence Center
After completing his MBA at the University of Michigan in 1983, Stephen Dull spent the next five years in various consumer marketing jobs at Pillsbury. In 1988, he was contacted by an executive search firm that had been retained by McKinsey to recruit potential consultants in consumer marketing. Joining the Atlanta office, Dull soon discovered that there was no structured development program. Like the eight experienced consumer marketing recruits in other offices, he was expected to create his own agenda.

Working on various studies, Dull found his interests shifting from consumer to industrial marketing issues. As he focused on building his own expertise, however, Dull acknowledged that he did not pay enough attention to developing strong client relations. "And around here, serving clients is what really counts," he said. So, in late 1994—a time when he might be discussing his election to principal—he had a long counseling session with his group development leader about his career. The GDL confirmed that he was not well positioned for election, but proposed another option. He suggested that Dull talk to Rob Rosiello, a principal in the New York office who had just launched a business-to-business marketing initiative within the marketing practice. Said Dull:

> Like most new initiatives, "B to B" was struggling to get established without full-time resources, so Rob was pleased to see me. I was enjoying my business marketing work, so the initiative sounded like a great opportunity. . . . Together, we wrote a proposal to make me the firm's first business marketing specialist.

The decision to pursue this strategy was not an easy one for Dull. Like most of his colleagues, he felt that specialists were regarded as second-class citizens—"overhead being supported by real consultants who serve clients," Dull suggested. But his GDL told him that recent directors meetings had reaffirmed the importance of building functional expertise, and some had even suggested that 15%–20% of the firm's partners should be functional experts within the next five to seven years. (As of 1995, over 300 associates were specialists, but only 15 of the 500 partners.) In April 1995, Dull and Rosiello took their proposal to Andrew Parsons and David Court, two leaders of the Marketing practice. The directors suggested a mutual trial of the concept until the end of the year and offered to provide Dull the support to commit full time to developing the B to B initiative.

Dull's first priority was to collect the various concepts, frameworks and case studies that existed within the firm, consolidating and synthesizing them in several PD documents. In the process, he and Rosiello began assembling a core team of interested contributors. Together, they developed an agenda of half a dozen cutting-edge issues in business marketing—segmentation, multi-buyer decision making and marketing partnerships, for example—and launched a number of study initiatives around them. Beyond an expanded series of PD documents, the outcome was an emerging set of core beliefs, and a new framework for business marketing.

The activity also attracted the interest of Mark Leiter, a specialist in the Marketing Science Center of Competence. This center, which had developed largely around a group of a dozen or so specialists, was in many ways a model of what Dull hoped the B to B initiative could become, and having a second committed specialist certainly helped.

In November, another major step to that goal occurred when the B to B initiative was declared a Center of Competence. At that time, the core group decided they would test their colleagues' interest and their own credibility by arranging an internal conference at which they would present their ideas. When over 50 people showed up including partners and directors from four continents, Dull felt that prospects for the center looked good.

Through the cumulative impact of the PD documents, the conference and word of mouth recommendations, by early 1996 Dull and his colleagues were getting more calls than the small center could handle. They were proud when the March listing of PDNet "Best Sellers" listed BtoB documents at numbers 2, 4 and 9 (See **Exhibit 7**). For Dull, the resulting process was enlightening:

> We decided that when we got calls we would swarm all over them and show our colleagues we could really add value for their clients. . . . This may sound strange—even corny—but I now really understand why this is a profession and not a business. If I help a partner serve his client better, he will call me back. It's all about relationships, forming personal bonds, helping each other.

While Dull was pleased with the way the new center was gaining credibility and having impact, he was still very uncertain about his promotion prospects. As he considered his future, he began to give serious thought to writing a book on business to business marketing to enhance his internal credibility and external visibility.

A New MD, A New Focus

In 1994, after six years of leadership in which firm revenue had doubled to an estimated $1.5 billion annually, Fred Gluck stepped down as MD. His successor was 45 year old Rajat Gupta, a 20 year McKinsey veteran committed to continuing the emphasis on knowledge development. After listening to the continuing debates about which knowledge development approach was most effective, Gupta came to the conclusion that the discussions were consuming energy that should have been directed towards the activity itself. "The firm did not have to make a choice," he said. "We had to pursue *all* the options." With that conclusion, Gupta launched a four-pronged attack.

First, he wanted to capitalize on the firm's long term investment in practice development driven by Clientele Industry Sectors and Functional Capability Groups and supported by the knowledge infrastructure of PDNet and FPIS. But he also wanted to create some new channels, forums, and mechanisms for knowledge development and organizational learning.

Then, building on an experiment begun by the German office, Gupta embraced a grass-roots knowledge-development approach called Practice Olympics. Two- to six-person teams from offices around the world were encouraged to develop ideas that grew out of recent client engagements and formalize them for presentation at a regional competition with senior partners and clients as judges. The twenty best regional teams then competed at a firmwide event. Gupta was proud that in its second year, the event had attracted over 150 teams and involved 15% of the associate body.

Next, in late 1995 the new MD initiated six special initiatives—multi-year internal assignments led by senior partners that focused on emerging

Exhibit 7 PDNet "Best-Sellers": March and Year-to-Date, 1996

Number Requested	Title, Author(s), Date, PDNet #	Functional Capability Group/Sector
March 1996		
21	**Developing a Distinctive Consumer Marketing Organization** *Nora Aufreiter, Theresa Austerberry, Steve Carlotti, Mike George, Liz Lempres (1/96, #13240)*	Consumer Industries/ Packaged Goods; Marketing
19	**VIP: Value Improvement Program to Enhance Customer Value in Business to Business Marketing** *Dirk Berensmann, Marc Fischer, Heiner Frankemölle, Lutz-Peter Pape, Wolf-Dieter Voss (10/95, #13340)*	Marketing; Steel
16	**Handbook For Sales Force Effectiveness—1991 Edition** *(5/91, #6670)*	Marketing
15	**Understanding and Influencing Customer Purchase Decisions in Business to Business Markets** *Mark Leiter (3/95, #12525)*	Marketing
15	**Channel Management Handbook** *Christine Bucklin, Stephen DeFalco, John DeVincentis, John Levis (1/95, #11876)*	Marketing
15	**Platforms for Growth in Personal Financial Services (PFS201)** *Christopher Leech, Ronald O'Hanley, Eric Lambrecht, Kristin Morse (11/95, #12995)*	Personal Financial Services
14	**Developing Successful Acquisition Programs to Support Long-Term Growth Strategies** *Steve Coley, Dan Goodwin (11/92, #9150)*	Corporate Finance
14	**Understanding Value-Based Segmentation** *John Forsyth, Linda Middleton (11/95, #11730)*	Consumer Industries/ Packaged Goods; Marketing
14	**The Dual Perspective Customer Map for Business to Business Marketing** *(3/95, #12526)*	Marketing
13	**Growth Strategy—Platforms, Staircases and Franchises** *Charles Conn, Rob McLean, David White (8/94, #11400)*	Strategy
Cumulative Index (January–March)		
54	**Introduction to CRM (Continuous Relationship Marketing)—Leveraging CRM to Build PFS Franchise Value (PFS221)** *Margo Geogiadis, Milt Gillespie, Tim Gokey, Mike Sherman, Marc Singer (11/95, #12999)*	Personal Financial Services
45	**Platforms for Growth in Personal Financial Services (PFS201)** *Christopher Leech, Ronald O'Hanley, Eric Lambrecht, Kristin Morse (11/95, #12995)*	Personal Financial Services
40	**Launching a CRM Effort (PFS222)** *Nick Brown, Margo Georgiadis (10/95, #12940)*	Marketing
38	**Building Value Through Continuous Relationship Marketing (CRM)** *Nick Brown, Mike Wright (10/95, #13126)*	Banking and Securities
36	**Combining Art and Science to Optimize Brand Portfolios** *Richard Benson-Armer, David Court, John Forsyth (10/95, #12916)*	Marketing; Consumer Industries/Packaged Goods
35	**Consumer Payments and the Future of Retail Banks (PA202)** *John Stephenson, Peter Sands (11/95, #13008)*	Payments and Operating Products
34	**CRM (Continuous Relationship Marketing) Case Examples Overview** *Howie Hayes, David Putts (9/95, #12931)*	Marketing
32	**Straightforward Approaches to Building Management Talent** *Parke Boneysteele, Bill Meehan, Kristin Morse, Pete Sidebottom (9/95, #12843)*	Organization
32	**Reconfiguring and Reenergizing Personal Selling Channels (PFS213)** *Patrick Wetzel, Amy Zinsser (11/95, #12997)*	Personal Financial Services
31	**From Traditional Home Banking to On-Line PFS (PFS211)** *Gaurang Desai, Brian Johnson, Kai Lahmann, Gottfried Leibbrandt, Paal Weberg (11/95, #12998)*	Personal Financial Services

Source: Month by Month (McKinsey's internal staff magazine).

issues that were of importance to CEOs. The initiatives tapped both internal and external expertise to develop "state-of-the-art" formulations of each key issue. For example, one focused on the shape and function of the corporation of the future, another on creating and managing strategic growth, and a third on capturing global opportunities. Gupta saw these initiatives as reasserting the importance of the firm's functional knowledge yet providing a means to do longer term, bigger commitment, cross-functional development.

Finally, he planned to expand on the model of the McKinsey Global Institute, a firm-sponsored research center established in 1991 to study implications of changes in the global economy on business. The proposal was to create other pools of dedicated resources protected from daily pressures and client demands, and focused on long term research agendas. A Change Center was established in 1995 and an Operations Center was being planned. Gupta saw these institutes as a way in which McKinsey could recruit more research-oriented people and link more effectively into the academic arena.

Most of these initiatives were new and their impact had not yet been felt within the firm. Yet Gupta was convinced the direction was right:

> We have easily doubled our investment in knowledge over these past couple of years. There are lots more people involved in many more initiatives. If that means we do 5–10% less client work today, we are willing to pay that price to invest in the future. Since Marvin Bower, every leadership group has had a commitment to leave the firm stronger than it found it. It's a fundamental value of McKinsey to invest for the future of the firm.

Future Directions   Against this background, the McKinsey partnership was engaged in spirited debate about the firm's future directions and priorities. The following is a sampling of their opinions:

> I am concerned that our growth may stretch the fabric of the place. We can't keep on disaggregating our units to create niches for everyone because we have exhausted the capability of our integrating mechanisms. I believe our future is in developing around CSTs and integrating across them around common knowledge agendas.

> *Historically, I was a supporter of slower growth, but now I'm convinced we must grow faster. That is the key to creating opportunity and excitement for people, and that generates innovation and drives knowledge development. . . . Technology is vital not only in supporting knowledge transfer, but also in allowing partners to mentor more young associates. We have to be much more aggressive in using it.*

> There is a dark side to technology—what I call technopoly. It can drive out communication and people start believing that e-mailing someone is the same thing as talking to them. If teams stop meeting as often or if practice conferences evolve into discussion forums on Lotus Notes, the technology that has supported our growth may begin to erode our culture based on personal networks.

> *I worry that we are losing our sense of village as we compartmentalize our activities and divide into specialties. And the power of IT has sometimes led to information overload. The risks is that the more we spend searching out the right PD document, the ideal framework, or the best expert, the less time we spend thinking creatively about the problem. I worry that as we increase the science, we might lose the craft of what we do.*

These were among the scores of opinions that Rajat Gupta heard since becoming MD. His job was to sort through them and set a direction that would "leave the firm stronger than he found it."

Reading 5-1   Building Effective R&D Capabilities Abroad

Walter Kuemmerle

An increasing number of companies in technologically intensive industries such as pharmaceuticals and electronics have abandoned the traditional approach to managing research and development and are establishing global R&D networks in a noteworthy new way. For example, Canon is now carrying out R&D activities in 8 dedicated facilities in 5 countries, Motorola in 14 facilities in 7 countries, and Bristol-Myers Squibb in 12 facilities in 6 countries. In the past, most companies—even those with a considerable international presence in terms of sales and manufacturing—carried out the majority of their R&D activity in their home countries. Conventional wisdom held that strategy development and R&D had to be kept in close geographical proximity. Because strategic decisions were made primarily at corporate headquarters, the thinking went, R&D facilities should be close to home.

But such a centralized approach to R&D will no longer suffice—for two reasons. First, as more and more sources of potentially relevant knowledge emerge across the globe, companies must establish a presence at an increasing number of locations to access new knowledge and to absorb new research results from foreign universities and competitors into their own organizations. Second, companies competing around the world must move new products from development to market at an ever more rapid pace. Consequently, companies must build R&D networks that excel at tapping new centers of knowledge and at commercializing products in foreign markets with the speed required to remain competitive. And more and more, superior manufacturers are doing just that. (See the exhibit "Laboratory Sites Abroad in 1995.")

In an ongoing study on corporate strategy and the geographical dispersion of R&D sites, I have been examining the creation of global research networks by 32 U.S., Japanese, and European multinational companies.[1] The most successful companies in my study brought each new site's research productivity up to full speed within a few years and quickly transformed knowledge created there into innovative products. I found that establishing networks of such sites poses a number of new, complex managerial challenges. According to my research, managers of the most successful R&D networks understand the new dynamics of global R&D, link corporate strategy to R&D strategy, pick the appropriate sites, staff them with the right people, supervise the sites during start-up, and integrate the activities of the different foreign sites so that the entire network is a coordinated whole.

Walter Kuemmerle is an assistant professor at the Harvard Business School in Boston, Massachusetts, where he teaches technology and operations management, as well as entrepreneurial finance. His research focuses on the technology strategies of multinational companies, patterns of strategic interaction between small and large companies, and foreign direct investment.

[1]In a systematic effort to analyze the relationship of global strategy and R&D investments in technologically intensive industries, I have been collecting detailed data on all dedicated laboratory sites operated by 32 leading multinational companies. The sample consists of 10 U.S., 12 Japanese, and 10 European companies. Thirteen of the companies are in the pharmaceutical industry, and 19 are in the electronics industry. Data collection includes archival research, a detailed questionnaire, and in-depth interviews with several senior R&D managers in each company. Overall, these companies operate 238 dedicated R&D sites, 156 of them abroad. About 60% of the laboratory sites abroad were established after 1984. I have used this sample, which is the most complete of its kind, as a basis for a number of quantitative and qualitative investigations into global strategy, competitive interaction, and R&D management.

Laboratory Sites Abroad in 1995

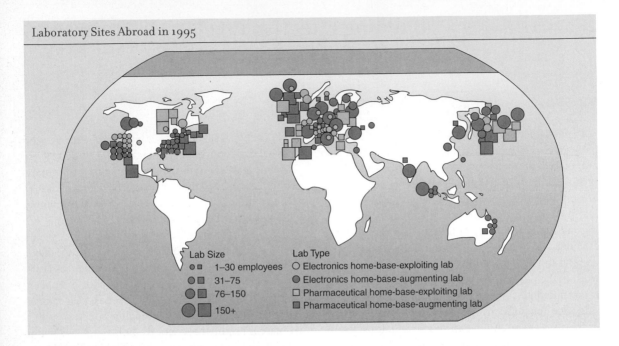

Lab Size
- ● ■ 1–30 employees
- ● ■ 31–75
- ● ■ 76–150
- ● ■ 150+

Lab Type
- ○ Electronics home-base-exploiting lab
- ● Electronics home-base-augmenting lab
- □ Pharmaceutical home-base-exploiting lab
- ■ Pharmaceutical home-base-augmenting lab

Adopting a Global Approach to R&D

Adopting a global approach to R&D requires linking R&D strategy to a company's overall business strategy. And that requires the involvement of managers at the highest levels of a company.

Creating a Technology Steering Committee   The first step in creating a global R&D network is to build a team that will lead the initiative. To establish a global R&D network, the CEOs and top-level managers of a number of successful companies that I studied assembled a small team of senior managers who had both technical expertise and in-depth organizational knowledge. The technology steering committees reported directly to the CEOs of their respective companies. They were generally small—five to eight members—and included managers with outstanding managerial and scientific records and a range of educational backgrounds and managerial responsibilities. The committees I studied included as members a former bench scientist who had transferred into manufacturing and had eventually become the head of manufacturing for the company's most

important category of therapeutic drugs; a head of marketing for memory chips who had worked before in product development in the same electronics company; and an engineer who had started out in product development, had moved to research, and eventually had become the vice president of R&D. Members of these committees were sufficiently senior to be able to mobilize resources at short notice; and they were actively involved in the management and supervision of R&D programs. In many cases, members included the heads of major existing R&D sites.

Categorizing New R&D Sites   In selecting new sites, companies find it helpful first to articulate each site's primary objective. (See the exhibit "Establishing New R&D Sites.") R&D sites have one of two missions. The first type of site—what I call a *home-base-augmenting site*—is established in order to tap knowledge from competitors and universities around the globe; in that type of site, information flows *from* the foreign laboratory *to* the central lab at home. The second type of site—what I call a *home-base-exploiting site*—is established to

Establishing New R&D Sites

Types of R&D Sites	Phase 1 Location Decision	Phase 2 Ramp-Up Period	Phase 3 Maximizing Lab Impact
Home-Base–Augmenting Laboratory Site Objective of establishment: absorbing knowledge from the local scientific community, creating new knowledge, and transferring it *to* the company's central R&D site	–Select a location for its scientific excellence –Promote cooperation between the company's senior scientists and managers	–Choose as first laboratory leader a renowned local scientist with international experience—one who understands the dynamics of R&D at the new location –Ensure enough critical mass	–Ensure the laboratory's active participation in the local scientific community –Exchange researchers with local university laboratories and with the home-base lab
Home-Base–Exploiting Laboratory Site Objective of establishment: commercializing knowledge by transferring it *from* the company's home base to the laboratory site abroad and from there to local manufacturing and marketing	–Select a location for its proximity to the company's existing manufacturing and marketing locations –Involve middle managers from other functional areas in startup decisions	–Choose as first laboratory leader an experienced product-development engineer with a strong companywide reputation, international experience, and knowledge of marketing and manufacturing	–Emphasize smooth relations with the home-base lab –Encourage employees to seek interaction with other corporate units beyond the manufacturing and marketing units that originally sponsored the lab

How Information Flows Between Home-Base and Foreign R&D Sites

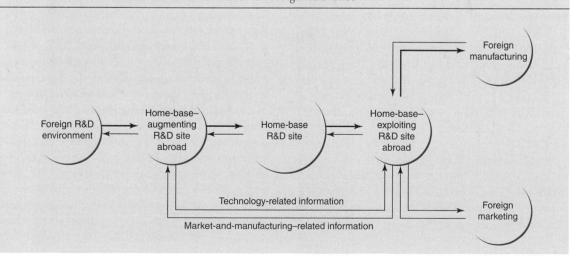

Home-Base–Augmenting and Home-Base–Exploiting Sites: Xerox and Eli Lilly

The particular type of foreign R&D site determines the specific challenges managers will face. Setting up a *home base–augmenting site*—one designed to gather new knowledge for a company—involves certain skills. And launching a *home-base–exploiting site*—one established to help a company efficiently commercialize its R&D in foreign markets   involves others. The cases of Xerox and Eli Lilly present an instructive contrast.

Xerox established a home-base–augmenting laboratory in Grenoble, France. Its objective: to tap new knowledge from the local scientific community and to transfer it back to its home base. Having already established, in 1986, a home-base–augmenting site in Cambridge, England, Xerox realized in 1992 that the research culture in continental Western Europe was sufficiently different and complementary to Great Britain's to justify another site. Moreover, understanding the most advanced research in France or Germany was very difficult from a base in Great Britain because of language and cultural barriers. One senior R&D manager in the United States notes, "We wanted to learn firsthand what was going on in centers of scientific excellence in Europe. Being present at a center of scientific excellence is like reading poetry in the original language."

It was essential that managers from the highest levels of the company be involved in the decision-making process from the start. Senior scientists met with high-level managers and entered into a long series of discussions. Their first decision: to locate the new laboratory at a center of scientific excellence. Xerox also realized that it had to hire a renowned local scientist as the initial laboratory leader. The leader needed to be able to understand the local scientific community, attract junior scientists with high potential, and target the right university institutes and scholars for joint research projects. Finally, Xerox knew that the laboratory would have an impact on the company's economic performance only if it had the critical mass to become an accepted member of the local scientific community. At the same time, it could not become isolated from the larger Xerox culture.

Xerox considered a number of locations and carefully evaluated such aspects as their scientific excellence and relevance, university liaison programs, licensing programs, and university recruiting programs. The company came up with four potential locations: Paris, Grenoble, Barcelona, and Munich. At that point, Xerox also identified potential laboratory leaders. The company chose Grenoble on the basis of its demonstrated scientific excellence and hired as the initial laboratory leader a highly regarded French scientist with good connections to local universities. Xerox designed a facility for 40 researchers and made plans for further expansion. In order to integrate the new laboratory's scientists into the Xerox community, senior R&D management in Palo Alto, California, allocated a considerable part of the initial laboratory budget to travel to other Xerox sites and started a program for the temporary transfer of newly hired researchers from Grenoble to other R&D sites. At the same time, the Grenoble site set out to integrate itself within the local research community.

In 1989, Eli Lilly considered establishing a home-base–exploiting laboratory in East Asia. The company's objective was to commercialize its R&D more effectively in foreign markets. Until then, Eli Lilly had operated one home-base–augmenting laboratory site abroad and some small sites in industrialized countries for clinical testing and drug approval procedures. But in order to exploit Lilly's R&D capabilities and product portfolio, the company needed a dedicated laboratory site in East Asia. The new site would support efforts to manufacture and market pharmaceuticals by adapting products to local needs. To that end, the management team decided that the new laboratory would have to be located close to relevant markets and existing corporate facilities.

It also determined that the initial laboratory leader would have to be an experienced manager from Lilly's home base—a manager with a deep understanding of both the company's local operations and its overall R&D network.

The team considered Singapore as a potential location because of its proximity to a planned Lilly manufacturing site in Malaysia. But ultimately it decided that the new home-base–exploiting laboratory would have the strongest impact on Lilly's sales if it was located in Kōbe, Japan. By establishing a site in the Kōbe-Osaka region—the second-largest regional market in Japan and one that offered educational institutions with high-quality scientists—Lilly would send a signal to the medical community there that the company was committed to the needs of the Japanese market. Kōbe had another advantage. Lilly's corporate headquarters for Japan were located there, and the company was already running some of its drug

approval operations for the Japanese market out of Kōbe. The city therefore was the logical choice.

The team assigned an experienced Lilly researcher and manager to be the initial leader of the new site. Because he knew the company inside and out—from central research and development to international marketing—the team reasoned that he would be able to bring the new laboratory up to speed quickly by drawing on resources from various divisions within Lilly. In order to integrate the new site into the overall company, some researchers from other Lilly R&D sites received temprory transfers of up to two years to Kōbe, and some locally hired researchers were temporarily transferred to other Lilly sites. It took about 30 months to activate fully the Kōbe operation—a relatively short period. Today the site is very productive in transferring knowledge from Lilly's home base to Kōbe and in commercializing that knowledge throughout Japan and Asia.

support manufacturing facilities in foreign countries or to adapt standard products to the demand there; in that type of site, information flows *to* the foreign laboratory *from* the central lab at home. (See the exhibit "How Information Flows Between Home-Base and Foreign R&D Sites.")

The overwhelming majority of the 238 foreign R&D sites I studied fell clearly into one of the two categories. Approximately 45% of all laboratory sites were home-base-augmenting sites, and 55% were home-base-exploiting sites. The two types of sites were of the same average size: about 100 employees. But they differed distinctly in their strategic purpose and leadership style.[2] (See the

[2]My research on global R&D strategies builds on earlier research on the competitiveness of nations and on research on foreign direct investment, including Michael E. Porter, *The Competitive Advantage of Nations* (New York: The Free Press, 1990), and Thomas J. Wesson, "An Alternative Motivation for Foreign Direct Investment" (Ph.D. dissertation, Harvard University, 1993). My research also builds on an existing body of knowledge about the management of multinational companies. See, for example, Christopher A. Bartlett and Sumantra Ghoshal, *Managing Across Borders* (New York: The Free Press, 1989).

insert "Home-Base-Augmenting and Home-Base-Exploiting Sites: Xerox and Eli Lilly.")

Choosing a Location for the Site Home-base-augmenting sites should be located in regional clusters of scientific excellence in order to tap new sources of knowledge. Central to the success of corporate R&D strategy is the ability of senior researchers to recognize and combine scientific advancements from different areas of science and technology. Absorbing the new knowledge can happen in a number of ways: through participation in formal or informal meeting circles that exist within a geographic area containing useful knowledge (a knowledge cluster), through hiring employees from competitors, or through sourcing laboratory equipment and research services from the same suppliers that competitors use.

For example, the Silicon Valley knowledge cluster boasts a large number of informal gatherings of experts as well as more formal ways for high-tech companies to exchange information with adjacent universities, such as industrial liaison programs with Stanford University and the University of California at Berkeley. In the field of communication technology, Siemens, NEC, Matsushita, and Toshiba all operate laboratory sites near Princeton University and Bell Labs (now a part of Lucent Technologies) to take advantage of the expertise located there. For similar reasons, a number of companies in the same industry have established sites in the Kanto area surrounding Tokyo. Texas Instruments operates a facility in Tsukuba Science City, and Hewlett-Packard operates one in Tokyo.

After a company has picked and established its major R&D sites, it might want to branch out. It might selectively set up secondary sites when a leading competitor or a university succeeds in building a critical mass of research expertise in a more narrowly defined area of science and technology outside the primary cluster. In order to benefit from the resulting miniclusters of expertise, companies sometimes establish additional facilities. For that reason, NEC operates a small telecommunications-oriented R&D facility close to a university laboratory in London, and Canon operates an R&D facility in Rennes, France, close to one of France Telecom's major sites.

Home-base-exploiting sites, in contrast, should be located close to large markets and manufacturing facilities in order to commercialize new products rapidly in foreign markets. In the past, companies from industrialized countries located manufacturing facilities abroad primarily to benefit from lower wages or to overcome trade barriers. Over time, however, many of those plants have taken on increasingly complex manufacturing tasks that require having an R&D facility nearby in order to ensure the speedy transfer of technology from research to manufacturing. A silicon-wafer plant, for example, has to interact closely with product development engineers during trial runs of a new generation of microchips. The same is true for the manufacture of disk drives and other complex hardware. For that reason, Hewlett-Packard and Texas Instruments both operate laboratories in Singapore, close to manufacturing facilities.

The more complex and varied a manufacturing process is, the more often manufacturing engineers will have to interact with product development engineers. For example, in the case of one of Toshiba's laptop-computer-manufacturing plants, a new model is introduced to the manufacturing line every two weeks. The introduction has to happen seamlessly, without disturbing the production of existing models on the same line. In order to predict and remedy bugs during initial production runs, development engineers and manufacturing engineers meet several times a week. The proximity of Toshiba's laptop-development laboratory to its manufacturing plant greatly facilitates the interaction.

◼ Establishing a New R&D Facility

Whether establishing a home-base-augmenting or a home-base-exploiting facility, companies must use the same three-stage process: selecting the best laboratory leader, determining the optimal size for the new laboratory site, and keeping close watch over the lab during its start-up period in order to ensure that it is merged into the company's existing global R&D network and contributes sufficiently to the company's product portfolio and its economic performance.

Selecting the Best Site Leader   Identifying the best leader for a new R&D site is one of the most important decisions a company faces in its quest to establish a successful global R&D network. My research shows that the initial leader of an R&D site has a powerful impact not only on the culture of the site but also on its long-term research agenda and performance. The two types of sites require different types of leaders, and each type of leader confronts a particular set of challenges.

The initial leaders of home-base-augmenting sites should be prominent local scientists so that they will be able to fulfill their primary responsibility: to nurture ties between the new site and the local scientific community. If the site does not succeed in becoming part of the local scientific community quickly, it will not be able to generate new knowledge for the company. In addition to hiring a local scientist, there are a variety of other ways to establish local ties. For example, Toshiba used its memory-chip joint venture with Siemens to develop local ties at its new R&D site in Regensburg, Germany. The venture allowed Toshiba to tap into Siemens's dense network of associations with local universities. In addition, it helped Toshiba develop a better understanding of the compensation packages required to hire first-class German engineering graduates. Finally, it let the company gain useful insights into how to establish effective contract-research relationships with government-funded research institutions in Germany.

In contrast, the initial leaders of home-base-exploiting sites should be highly regarded managers from within the company—managers who are intimately familiar with the company's culture and systems. Such leaders will be able to fulfill their primary responsibility: to forge close ties between the new lab's engineers and the foreign community's manufacturing and marketing facilities. Then the transfer of knowledge from the company's home base to the R&D site will have the maximum impact on manufacturing and marketing located near that site. When one U.S. pharmaceutical company established a home-base-exploiting site in Great Britain, executives appointed as the initial site leader a manager who had been with the company for several years. He had started his career as a bench scientist first in exploratory research, then in the development of one of the company's blockbuster drugs. He had worked closely with marketing, and he had spent two years as supervisor of manufacturing quality at one of the company's U.S. manufacturing sites. With such a background, he was able to lead the new site effectively.

However, the best candidates for both home-base-augmenting and home-base-exploiting sites share four qualities: they are at once respected scientists or engineers and skilled managers; they are able to integrate the new site into the company's existing R&D network; they have a comprehensive understanding of technology trends; and they are able to overcome formal barriers when they seek access to new ideas in local universities and scientific communities.

Appointing an outstanding scientist or engineer who has no management experience can be disastrous. In one case, a leading U.S. electronics company decided to establish a home-base-augmenting site in the United Kingdom. The engineer who was appointed as the first site leader was an outstanding researcher but had little management experience outside the company's central laboratory environment. The leader had difficulties marshaling the necessary resources to expand the laboratory beyond its starting size of 14 researchers. Furthermore, he had a tough time mediating between the research laboratory and the company's product development area. Eleven of the 14 researchers had been hired locally and therefore lacked deep ties to the company. They needed a savvy corporate advocate who could understand company politics and could promote their research results within the company. One reason they didn't have such an advocate was that two of the three managers at the company's home base—people who had promoted the establishment of the new R&D lab–had quit about six months after the lab had opened because they disagreed about the company's overall R&D strategy. The third manager had moved to a different department.

In an effort to improve the situation, the company appointed a U.S. engineer as liaison to the U.K. site. He realized that few ideas were flowing from the site to the home base; but he attributed the problem to an inherently slow scientific-discovery process rather than to organizational barriers within the company. After about two years, senior management finally replaced the initial laboratory leader and the U.S. liaison engineer with two managers—one from the United Kingdom and one from the United States. The managers had experience overseeing one of the company's U.S. joint ventures in technology, and they also had good track records as researchers. Finally, under their leadership, the site dramatically increased its impact on the company's product portfolio. In conjunction with the increase in scientific output, the site grew to its projected size of 225 employees and is now highly productive.

In the case of both types of sites, the ideal leader has in-depth knowledge of both the home-base culture and the foreign culture. Consider Sharp's experience. In Japan, fewer corporate scientists have Ph.D.'s than their counterparts in the United Kingdom; instead they have picked up their knowledge and skills on the job. That difference presented a management challenge for Sharp when it established a home-base-augmenting facility in the United Kingdom. In order to cope with that challenge, the company hired a British laboratory leader who had previously worked as a science attaché at the British embassy in Japan. In that position, he had developed a good understanding of the Japanese higher-education system. He was well aware that British and Japanese engineers with different academic degrees might have similar levels of expertise, and, as a result, he could manage them better.

The pioneer who heads a newly established home-base-augmenting or home-base-exploiting site also must have a broad perspective and a deep understanding of technology trends. R&D sites abroad are often particularly good at combining knowledge from different scientific fields into new ideas and products. Because those sites start with a clean slate far from the company's powerful central laboratory, they are less plagued by the "not-invented-here" syndrome. For example, Canon's home-base-augmenting laboratory in the United Kingdom developed an innovative loudspeaker that is now being manufactured in Europe for a worldwide market. Senior researchers at Canon in Japan acknowledge that it would have been much more difficult for a new research team located in Japan to come up with the product. As one Canon manager puts it, "Although the new loudspeaker was partially based on knowledge that existed within Canon already, Canon's research management in Japan was too focused on existing product lines and would probably not have tolerated the pioneering loudspeaker project."

Finally, leaders of new R&D sites need to be aware of the considerable formal barriers they might confront when they seek access to local universities and scientific communities. These barriers are often created by lawmakers who want to protect a nation's intellectual capital. Although foreign companies do indeed absorb local knowledge and transfer it to their home bases—particularly in the case of home-base-augmenting sites—they also create important positive economic effects for the host nation. The laboratory leader of a new R&D site needs to communicate that fact locally in order to reduce existing barriers and prevent the formation of new ones.

Determining the Optimal Size of the New R&D Site My research indicates that the optimal size for a new foreign R&D facility during the start-up phase is usually 30 to 40 employees, and the best size for a site after the ramp-up period is about 235 employees, including support staff. The optimal size of a site depends mainly on a company's track record in international management. Companies that already operate several sites abroad tend to be more successful at establishing larger new sites.

Companies can run into problems if their foreign sites are either too small or too large. If the site is too small, the resulting lack of critical mass produces an environment in which there is little cross-fertilization of ideas among researchers. And a small R&D site generally does not command a sufficient level of respect in the scientific community surrounding the laboratory. As a result, its researchers have a harder time gaining access to informal networks and to scientific meetings that provide opportunities for an exchange of knowledge. In contrast, if the laboratory site is too large, its culture quickly becomes anonymous, researchers become isolated, and the benefits of spreading fixed costs over a larger number of researchers are outweighed by the lack of cross-fertilization of ideas. According to one manager at such a lab, "Once people stopped getting to know one another on an informal basis in the lunchroom of our site, they became afraid of deliberately walking into one another's laboratory rooms to talk about research and to ask questions. Researchers who do not know each other on an informal basis are often hesitant to ask their colleagues for advice: they are afraid to reveal any of their own knowledge gaps. We realized that we had crossed a critical threshold in size. We subsequently scaled back somewhat and made an increased effort to reduce the isolation of individual researchers within the site through communication tools and through rotating researchers among different lab units at the site."

Supervising the Start-Up Period   During the initial growth period of an R&D site, which typically lasts anywhere from one to three years, the culture is formed and the groundwork for the site's future productivity is laid. During that period, senior management in the home country has to be in particularly close contact with the new site. Although it is important that the new laboratory develop its own identity and stake out its fields of expertise, it also has to be closely connected to the company's existing R&D structure. Newly hired scientists must be aware of the resources that exist within the company as a whole, and scientists at home and at other locations must be aware of the opportunities the new site creates for the company as a whole. Particularly during the start-up period, senior R&D managers at the corporate level have to walk a fine line and decide whether to devote the most resources to connecting the new site to the company or to supporting ties between the new site and its local environment.

To integrate a new site into the company as a whole, managers must pay close attention to the site's research agenda and create mechanisms to integrate it into the company's overall strategic goals. Because of the high degree of uncertainty of R&D outcomes, continuous adjustments to research agendas are the rule. What matters most is speed, both in terms of terminating research projects that go nowhere and in terms of pushing projects that bring unexpectedly good results.

The rapid exchange of information is essential to integrating a site into the overall company during the start-up phase. Companies use a number of mechanisms to create a cohesive research community in spite of geographic distance. Hewlett-Packard regularly organizes an in-house science fair at which teams of researchers can present projects and prototypes to one another. Canon has a program that lets researchers from home-base-augmenting sites request a temporary transfer to home-base-exploiting sites. At

Xerox, most sites are linked by a sophisticated information system that allows senior R&D managers to determine within minutes the current state of research projects and the number of researchers working on those projects. But nothing can replace face-to-face contact between active researchers. Maintaining a global R&D network requires personal meetings, and therefore many researchers and R&D managers have to spend time visiting not only other R&D sites but also specialized suppliers and local universities affiliated with those sites.

Failing to establish sufficient ties with the company's existing R&D structure during the start-up phase can hamper the success of a new foreign R&D site. For example, in 1986, a large foreign pharmaceutical company established a biotechnology research site in Boston, Massachusetts. In order to recruit outstanding scientists and maintain a high level of creative output, the company's R&D management decided to give the new laboratory considerable leeway in its research agenda and in determining what to do with the results—although the company did reserve the right of first refusal for the commercialization of the lab's inventions. The new site was staffed exclusively with scientists handpicked by a newly hired laboratory leader. A renowned local biochemist, he had been employed for many years by a major U.S. university, where he had carried out contract research for the company. During the start-up phase, few of the company's veteran scientists were involved in joint research projects with the site's scientists—an arrangement that hindered the transfer of ideas between the new lab and the company's other R&D sites. Although the academic community now recognizes the lab as an important contributor to the field, few of its inventions have been patented by the company, fewer have been targeted for commercialization, and none have reached the commercial stage yet. One senior scientist working in the lab commented that ten years after its creation, the lab had become so much of an "independent animal" that it would take a lot of carefully balanced guidance from the company to instill a stronger sense of commercial orientation without a risk of losing the most creative scientists.

There is no magic formula that senior managers can follow to ensure the success of a foreign R&D site during its start-up phase. Managing an R&D network, particularly in its early stages, is delicate and complex. It requires constant tinkering—evaluation and reevaluation. Senior R&D managers have to decide how much of the research should be initiated by the company and how much by the scientist, determine the appropriate incentive structures and employment contracts, establish policies for the temporary transfer of researchers to the company's other R&D or manufacturing sites, and choose universities from which to hire scientists and engineers.

Flexibility and experimentation during a site's start-up phase can ensure its future productivity. For example, Fujitsu established a software-research laboratory site in San Jose, California, in 1992. The company was seriously thinking of establishing a second site in Boston but eventually reconsidered. Fujitsu realized that the effort that had gone into establishing the San Jose site had been greater than expected. Once the site was up and running, however, its productive output also had been higher than expected. Furthermore, Fujitsu found that its R&D managers had gained an excellent understanding of the R&D community that created advanced software-development tools. Although initially leaning toward establishing a second site, the managers were flexible. They decided to enlarge the existing site because of its better-than-expected performance as well as the limited potential benefits of a second site. The San Jose site has had a major impact on Fujitsu's software development and sales—particularly in Japan but in the United States, too. Similarly, at Alcatel's first foreign R&D site in Germany, senior managers were flexible. After several months, they realized that the travel-and-communications budget would have to be increased substantially beyond initial projections in order to improve the flow of knowledge from the French home base. For instance, in the case of a telephone switchboard project, the actual number of business trips between the two sites was nearly twice as high as originally projected.

Integrating the Global R&D Network

As the number of companies' R&D sites at home and abroad grows, R&D managers will increasingly face the challenging task of coordinating the network. That will require a fundamental shift in the role of senior managers at the central lab. Managers of R&D networks must be global coordinators, not local administrators. More than being managers of people and processes, they must be managers of knowledge. And not all managers that a company has in place will be up to the task.

Consider Matsushita's R&D management. A number of technically competent managers became obsolete at the company once it launched a global approach to R&D. Today managers at Matsushita's central R&D site in Hirakata, Japan, continue to play an important role in the research and development of core processes for manufacturing. But the responsibility of an increasing number of senior managers at the central site is overseeing Matsushita's network of 15 dedicated R&D sites. That responsibility includes setting research agendas, monitoring results, and creating direct ties between sites.

How does the new breed of R&D manager coordinate global knowledge? Look again to Matsushita's central R&D site. First, high-level corporate managers in close cooperation with senior R&D managers develop an overall research agenda and assign different parts of it to individual sites. The process is quite tricky. It requires that the managers in charge have a good understanding of not only the technological capabilities that Matsushita will need to develop in the future but also the stock of technological capabilities already available to it.

Matsushita's central lab organizes two or three yearly off-site meetings devoted to informing R&D scientists and engineers about the entire company's current state of technical knowledge and capabilities. At the same meetings, engineers who have moved from R&D to take over manufacturing and marketing responsibilities inform R&D members about trends in Matsushita's current and potential future markets. Under the guidance of senior project managers, members from R&D, manufacturing, and marketing determine timelines and resource requirements for specific home-base-augmenting and home-base-exploiting projects. One R&D manager notes, "We discuss not only why a specific scientific insight might be interesting for Matsushita but also how we can turn this insight into a product quickly. We usually seek to develop a prototype early. Prototypes are a good basis for a discussion with marketing and manufacturing. Most of our efforts are targeted at delivering the prototype of a slightly better mousetrap early rather than delivering the blueprint of a much better mousetrap late."

To stimulate the exchange of information, R&D managers at Matsushita's central lab create direct links among researchers across different sites. They promote the use of videoconferencing and frequent face-to-face contact to forge those ties. Reducing the instances in which the central lab must act as mediator means that existing knowledge travels more quickly through the company and new ideas percolate more easily. For example, a researcher at a home-base-exploiting site in Singapore can communicate with another researcher at a home-base-exploiting

site in Franklin Park, Illinois, about potential new research projects much more readily now that central R&D fosters informal and formal direct links.

Finally, managers at Matsushita's central lab constantly monitor new regional pockets of knowledge as well as the company's expanding network of manufacturing sites to determine whether the company will need additional R&D locations. With 15 major sites around the world, Matsushita has decided that the number of sites is sufficient at this point. But the company is ever vigilant about surveying the landscape and knows that as the landscape changes, its decision could, too.

As more pockets of knowledge emerge worldwide and competition in foreign markets mounts, the imperative to create global R&D networks will grow all the more pressing. Only those companies that embrace a global approach to R&D will meet the competitive challenges of the new dynamic. And only those managers who embrace their fundamentally new role as global coordinators and managers of knowledge will be able to tap the full potential of their R&D networks.

Reading 5-2   Connect and Develop: Inside Procter & Gamble's New Model for Innovation*

Larry Huston and Nabil Sakkab

Procter & Gamble launched a new line of Pringles potato crisps in 2004 with pictures and words—trivia questions, animal facts, jokes—printed on each crisp. They were an immediate hit. In the old days, it might have taken us two years to bring this

*Larry Huston (huston.la@pg.com) is the vice president for innovation and knowledge and Nabil Sakkab (sakkab.ny@pg.com) is the senior vice president for corporate research and development at Procter & Gamble in Cincinnati.

product to market, and we would have shouldered all of the investment and risk internally. But by applying a fundamentally new approach to innovation, we were able to accelerate Pringles Prints from concept to launch in less than a year and at a fraction of what it would have otherwise cost. Here's how we did it.

Back in 2002, as we were brainstorming about ways to make snacks more novel and fun, someone suggested that we print pop culture images on Pringles. It was a great idea, but how would we do it? One of our researchers thought we should try ink-jetting pictures onto the potato dough, and she used the printer in her office for a test run. (You can imagine her call to our computer help desk.) We quickly realized that every crisp would have to be printed as it came out of frying, when it was still at a high humidity and temperature. And somehow, we'd have to produce sharp images, in multiple colors, even as we printed thousands upon thousands of crisps each minute. Moreover, creating edible dyes that could meet these needs would require tremendous development.

Traditionally, we would have spent the bulk of our investment just on developing a workable process. An internal team would have hooked up with an ink-jet printer company that could devise the process, and then we would have entered into complex negotiations over the rights to use it.

Instead, we created a technology brief that defined the problems we needed to solve, and we circulated it throughout our global networks of individuals and institutions to discover if anyone in the world had a ready-made solution. It was through our European network that we discovered a small bakery in Bologna, Italy, run by a university professor who also manufactured baking equipment. He had invented an ink-jet method for printing edible images on cakes and cookies that we rapidly adapted to solve our problem. This innovation has helped the North America Pringles business achieve double-digit growth over the past two years.

From R&D to C&D

Most companies are still clinging to what we call the invention model, centered on a bricks-and-mortar R&D infrastructure and the idea that their innovation must principally reside within their own four walls. To be sure, these companies are increasingly trying to buttress their laboring R&D departments with acquisitions, alliances, licensing, and selective innovation outsourcing. And they're launching Skunk Works, improving collaboration between marketing and R&D, tightening go-to-market criteria, and strengthening product portfolio management.

But these are incremental changes, bandages on a broken model. Strong words, perhaps, but consider the facts: Most mature companies have to create organic growth of 4% to 6% year in, year out. How are they going to do it? For P&G, that's the equivalent of building a $4 billion business this year alone. Not long ago, when companies were smaller and the world was less competitive, firms could rely on internal R&D to drive that kind of growth. For generations, in fact, P&G created most of its phenomenal growth by innovating from within—building global research facilities and hiring and holding on to the best talent in the world. That worked well when we were a $25 billion company; today, we're an almost $70 billion company.

By 2000, it was clear to us that our invent-it-ourselves model was not capable of sustaining high levels of top-line growth. The explosion of new technologies was putting ever more pressure on our innovation budgets. Our R&D productivity had leveled off, and our innovation success rate—the percentage of new products that met financial objectives—had stagnated at about 35%. Squeezed by nimble competitors, flattening sales, lackluster new launches, and a quarterly earnings miss, we lost more than half our market cap when our stock slid from $118 to $52 a share. Talk about a wake-up call.

The world's innovation landscape had changed, yet we hadn't changed our own innovation model since the late 1980s, when we moved from a centralized approach to a globally networked internal model—what Christopher Bartlett and Sumantra Ghoshal call the transnational model in *Managing Across Borders*.

We discovered that important innovation was increasingly being done at small and midsize entrepreneurial companies. Even individuals were eager to license and sell their intellectual property. University and government labs had become more interested in forming industry partnerships, and they were hungry for ways to monetize their research. The Internet had opened up access to talent markets throughout the world. And a few forward-looking companies like IBM and Eli Lilly were beginning to experiment with the new concept of open innovation, leveraging one another's (even competitors') innovation assets—products, intellectual property, and people.

As was the case for P&G in 2000, R&D productivity at most mature, innovation-based companies today is flat while innovation costs are climbing faster than top-line growth. (Not many CEOs are going to their CTOs and saying, "Here, have some more money for innovation.") Meanwhile, these companies are facing a growth mandate that their existing innovation models can't possibly support. In 2000, realizing that P&G couldn't meet its growth objectives by spending more and more on R&D for less and less payoff, our newly appointed CEO, A.G. Lafley, challenged us to reinvent the company's innovation business model.

We knew that most of P&G's best innovations had come from connecting ideas across internal businesses. And after studying the performance of a small number of products we'd acquired beyond our own labs, we knew that external connections could produce highly profitable innovations, too. Betting that these connections were the key to future growth, Lafley made it our goal to acquire 50% of our innovations outside the company. The strategy wasn't to replace the capabilities of our 7,500 researchers and support staff, but to better leverage them. Half of our new products, Lafley said, would come *from* our own labs, and half would come *through* them.

It was, and still is, a radical idea. As we studied outside sources of innovation, we estimated that for every P&G researcher there were 200 scientists or engineers elsewhere in the world who were just as good—a total of perhaps 1.5 million people whose talents we could potentially use. But tapping into the creative thinking of inventors and others on the outside would require massive operational changes. We needed to move the company's attitude from resistance to innovations "not invented here" to enthusiasm for those "proudly found elsewhere." And we needed to change how we defined, and perceived, our R&D organization—from 7,500 people inside to 7,500 *plus* 1.5 million outside, with a permeable boundary between them.

It was against this backdrop that we created our *connect and develop* innovation model. With a clear sense of consumers' needs, we could identify promising ideas throughout the world and apply our own R&D, manufacturing, marketing, and purchasing capabilities to them to create better and cheaper products, faster.

The model works. Today, more than 35% of our new products in market have elements that originated from outside P&G, up from about 15% in 2000. And 45% of the initiatives in our product development portfolio have key elements that were discovered externally. Through connect and develop—along with improvements in other aspects of innovation related to product cost, design, and marketing—our R&D productivity has increased by nearly 60%. Our innovation success rate has more than doubled, while the cost of innovation has fallen. R&D investment as a percentage of sales is down from 4.8% in 2000 to 3.4% today. And, in the last two years, we've launched more than 100 new products for which some aspect of execution came from outside the company. Five years after the company's stock collapse in 2000, we have doubled our share price and have a portfolio of 22 billion-dollar brands.

According to a recent Conference Board survey of CEOs and board chairs, executives' number one concern is "sustained and steady top-line growth." CEOs understand the importance of innovation to growth, yet how many have overhauled their basic approach to innovation? Until companies realize that the innovation landscape has changed and acknowledge that their current model is unsustainable, most will find that the top-line growth they require will elude them.

Where to Play

When people first hear about connect and develop, they often think it's the same as outsourcing innovation—contracting with outsiders to develop innovations for P&G. But it's not. Outsourcing strategies typically just transfer work to lower-cost providers. Connect and develop, by contrast, is about finding good ideas and bringing them in to enhance and capitalize on internal capabilities.

To do this, we collaborate with organizations and individuals around the world, systematically searching for proven technologies, packages, and products that we can improve, scale up, and market, either on our own or in partnership with other companies. Among the most successful products we've brought to market through connect and develop are Olay Regenerist, Swiffer Dusters, and the Crest SpinBrush.

For connect and develop to work, we realized, it was crucial to know exactly what we were looking for, or where to play. If we'd set out without carefully defined targets, we'd have found loads of ideas but perhaps none that were useful to us. So we established from the start that we would seek ideas that had some degree of success already; we needed to see, at least, working products, prototypes, or technologies, and (for products) evidence of consumer interest. And we would focus on ideas and products that would benefit specifically from the application of P&G technology, marketing, distribution, or other capabilities.

Then we determined the areas in which we would look for these proven ideas. P&G is perhaps best known for its personal hygiene and household-cleaning products—brands like Crest, Charmin, Pampers, Tide, and Downy. Yet we produce more than 300 brands that span, in addition to hygiene and cleaning, snacks and beverages, pet nutrition, prescription drugs, fragrances, cosmetics, and many other categories. And we spend almost $2 billion a year on R&D across 150 science areas, including materials, biotechnology, imaging, nutrition, veterinary medicine, and even robotics.

To focus our idea search, we directed our surveillance to three environments:

Top ten consumer needs   Once a year, we ask our businesses what consumer needs, when addressed, will drive the growth of their brands. This may seem like an obvious question, but in most companies, researchers are working on the problems that they find interesting rather than those that might contribute to brand growth. This inquiry produces a top-ten-needs list for each business and one for the company overall. The company list, for example, includes needs such as "reduce wrinkles, improve skin texture and tone," "improve soil repellency and restoration of hard surfaces," "create softer paper products with lower lint and higher wet strength," and "prevent or minimize the severity and duration of cold symptoms."

These needs lists are then developed into science problems to be solved. The problems are often spelled out in technology briefs, like the one we sent out to find an ink-jet process for Pringles Prints. To take another example, a major laundry need is for products that clean effectively using cold water. So, in our search for relevant innovations, we're looking for chemistry and biotechnology solutions that allow products to work well at low temperatures. Maybe the answer to our cold-water-cleaning problem is in a lab that's studying enzymatic reactions in microbes that thrive under polar ice caps, and we need only to find the lab.

Adjacencies   We also identify adjacencies—that is, new products or concepts that can help us take advantage of existing brand equity. We might, for instance, ask which baby care items—such as wipes and changing pads—are adjacent to our Pampers disposable diapers, and then seek out innovative emerging products or relevant technologies in those categories. By targeting adjacencies in oral care, we've expanded the Crest brand beyond toothpaste to include whitening strips, power toothbrushes, and flosses.

Technology game boards   Finally, in some areas, we use what we call technology game boards to evaluate how technology acquisition moves in one area might affect products in other categories. Conceptually, working with these planning tools is like playing a multilevel game of chess. They help us explore questions such as "Which of our key technologies do we want to strengthen?" "Which technologies do we want to acquire to help us better compete with rivals?" and "Of those that we already own, which do we want to license, sell, or codevelop further?" The answers provide an array of broad targets for our innovation searches and, as important, tell us where we shouldn't be looking.

How to Network

Our global networks are the platform for the activities that, together, constitute the connect-and-develop strategy. But networks themselves don't provide competitive advantage any more than the phone system does. It's how you build and use them that matters.

Within the boundaries defined by our needs lists, adjacency maps, and technology game boards, no source of ideas is off-limits. We tap closed proprietary networks and open networks of individuals and organizations available to any company. Using these networks, we look for ideas in government and private labs, as well as academic and other research institutions; we tap suppliers, retailers, competitors, development and trade partners, VC firms, and individual entrepreneurs.

Here are several core networks that we use to seek out new ideas. This is not an exhaustive list; rather, it is a snapshot of the networking capabilities that we've found most useful.

Proprietary networks   We rely on several proprietary networks developed specifically to facilitate connect-and-develop activities. Here are two of the largest ones.

Technology entrepreneurs   Much of the operation and momentum of connect and develop depends on our network of 70 technology entrepreneurs based around the world. These senior P&G people lead the development of our needs lists, create adjacency maps and technology game boards, and write the technology briefs that define the problems we are trying to solve. They create external connections by, for example, meeting with university and industry researchers and forming supplier networks, and they actively promote these connections to decision makers in P&G's business units.

The technology entrepreneurs combine aggressive mining of the scientific literature, patent databases, and other data sources with physical prospecting for ideas—say, surveying the shelves of a store in Rome or combing product and technology fairs. Although it's effective and necessary to scout for ideas electronically, it's not sufficient. It was a technology entrepreneur who, exploring a local market in Japan, discovered what ultimately became the Mr. Clean Magic Eraser. We surely wouldn't have found it otherwise. (See the exhibit "The Osaka Connection.")

The technology entrepreneurs work out of six connect-and-develop hubs, in China, India, Japan, Western Europe, Latin America, and the United States. Each hub focuses on finding products and technologies that, in a sense, are specialties of its region: The China hub, for example, looks in particular for new high-quality materials and cost innovations (products that exploit China's unique ability to make things at low cost). The India hub seeks out local talent in the sciences to solve problems—in our manufacturing processes, for instance—using tools like computer modeling.

Thus far, our technology entrepreneurs have identified more than 10,000 products, product ideas, and promising technologies. Each of these discoveries has undergone a formal evaluation, as we'll describe further on.

Suppliers   Our top 15 suppliers have an estimated combined R&D staff of 50,000. As we built connect and develop, it didn't take us long to realize that they represented a huge potential source of innovation. So we created a secure IT platform that would allow us to share technology briefs with our suppliers. If we're trying to find ways to make detergent perfume last longer after clothes come out of the dryer, for instance, one of our chemical suppliers may well have the solution. (Suppliers can't see others' responses, of course.) Since creating our supplier network, we've seen a 30% increase in innovation projects jointly staffed with P&G's and suppliers' researchers. In some cases, suppliers' researchers come to work in our labs, and in others, we work in theirs—an example of what we call "cocreation," a type of collaboration that goes well beyond typical joint development.

The Osaka Connection

In the connect-and-develop world, chance favors the prepared mind. When one of P&G's technology entrepreneurs discovered a stain-removing sponge in a market in Osaka, Japan, he sent it to the company for evaluation. The resulting product, the Mr. Clean Magic Eraser, is now in third-generation development and has achieved double its projected revenues.

German chemical company BASF manufactures a melamine resin foam called Basotect for soundproofing and insulation in the construction and automotive industries.

LEC, a Tokyo-based consumer-products company, markets Basotect foam in Japan as a household sponge called Cleenpro.

2001

Discover Japan-based technology entrepreneur with P&G discovers the product in an Osaka grocery store, evaluates its market performance in Japan, and establishes its fit with the P&G home-care product development and marketing criteria.

2002

Evaluate The technology entrepreneur sends samples to R&D product researchers in Cincinnati for performance evaluation and posts a product description and evaluation of market potential on P&G's internal "eureka catalog" network.

Market research confirms enthusiasm for the product. Product is moved into portfolio for development; P&G negotiates purchase of Basotect from BASF and terms for further collaboration.

2003

Launch Basotect is packaged as-is and launched nationally as Mr. Clean Magic Eraser.

Mr. Clean Magic Eraser is launched in Europe.

BASF and P&G researchers collaborate in shared labs to improve Basotect's cleaning properties, durability, and versatility.

2004

Cocreate The first cocreated Basotect product, the Magic Eraser Duo, is launched nationally in the United States.

The cocreated Magic Eraser Wheel & Tire is launched nationally in the United States.

BASF and P&G collaborate on next-generation Magic Eraser products.

We also hold top-to-top meetings with suppliers so our senior leaders can interact with theirs. These meetings, along with our shared-staff arrangements, improve relationships, increase the flow of ideas, and strengthen each company's understanding of the other's capabilities—all of which helps us innovate.

Open networks A complement to our proprietary networks are open networks. The following four are particularly fruitful connect-and-develop resources.

NineSigma P&G helped create NineSigma, one of several firms connecting companies that have science and technology problems with companies, universities, government and private labs, and consultants that can develop solutions. Say you have a technical problem you want to crack—for P&G, as you'll recall, one such problem is cold-temperature washing. NineSigma creates a technology brief that describes the problem, and sends this to its network of thousands of possible solution providers worldwide. Any solver can submit a nonconfidential proposal back to NineSigma, which is transmitted to the contracting company. If the company likes the proposal, NineSigma connects the company and solver, and the project proceeds from there. We've distributed technology briefs to more than 700,000 people through NineSigma and have as a result completed over 100 projects, with 45% of them leading to agreements for further collaboration.

InnoCentive   Founded by Eli Lilly, InnoCentive is similar to NineSigma—but rather than connect companies with contract partners to solve broad problems across many disciplines, InnoCentive brokers solutions to more narrowly defined scientific problems. For example, we might have an industrial chemical reaction that takes five steps to accomplish and want to know if it can be done in three. We'll put the question to InnoCentive's 75,000 contract scientists and see what we get back. We've had problems solved by a graduate student in Spain, a chemist in India, a freelance chemistry consultant in the United States, and an agricultural chemist in Italy. About a third of the problems we've posted through Inno-Centive have been solved.

YourEncore   In 2003, we laid the groundwork for a business called YourEncore. Now operated independently, it connects about 800 high-performing retired scientists and engineers from 150 companies with client businesses. By using YourEncore, companies can bring people with deep experience and new ways of thinking from other organizations and industries into their own.

Through YourEncore, you can contract with a retiree who has relevant experience for a specific, short-term assignment (compensation is based on the person's preretirement salary, adjusted for inflation). For example, we might tap a former Boeing engineer with expertise in virtual aircraft design to apply his or her skills in virtual product prototyping and manufacturing design at P&G, even though our projects have nothing to do with aviation. What makes this model so powerful is that client companies can experiment at low cost and with little risk on cross-disciplinary approaches to problem solving. At any point, we might have 20 retirees from YourEncore working on P&G problems.

Yet2.com   Six years ago, P&G joined a group of *Fortune* 100 companies as an initial investor in Yet2.com, an online marketplace for intellectual property exchange. Unlike NineSigma and InnoCentive, which focus on helping companies find solutions to technology problems, Yet2.com brokers technology transfer both into and out of companies, universities, and government labs. Yet2.com works with clients to write briefs describing the technology that they're seeking or making available for license or purchase, and distributes these briefs throughout a global network of businesses, labs, and institutions. Network members interested in posted briefs contact Yet2.com and request an introduction to the relevant client. Once introduced, the parties negotiate directly with each other. Through Yet2.com, P&G was able to license its low-cost microneedle technology to a company specializing

---

Leading Connect and Develop

The connect-and-develop strategy requires that a senior executive have day-to-day accountability for its vision, operations, and performance. At P&G, the vice president for innovation and knowledge has this responsibility. Connect-and-develop leaders from each of the business units at P&G have dotted-line reporting relationships with the VP. The managers for our virtual R&D networks (such as NineSigma and our supplier network), the technology entrepreneur and hub network, our connect-and-develop legal resources, and our training resources report directly.

The VP oversees the development of networks and new programs, manages a corporate budget, and monitors the productivity of networks and activities. This includes tracking the performance of talent markets like NineSigma and InnoCentive as well as measuring connect-and-develop productivity by region—evaluating, for example, the costs and output (as measured by products in market) of foreign hubs. Productivity measurements for the entire program are reported annually.

in drug delivery. As a result of this relationship, we have ourselves licensed technology that has applications in some of our core businesses.

When to Engage

Once products and ideas are identified by our networks around the world, we need to screen them internally. All the screening methods are driven by a core understanding, pushed down through the entire organization, of what we're looking for. It's beyond the scope of this article to describe all of the processes we use to evaluate ideas from outside. But a look at how we might screen a new product found by a technology entrepreneur illustrates one common approach.

When our technology entrepreneurs are meeting with lab heads, scanning patents, or selecting products off store shelves, they're conducting an initial screening in real time: Which products, technologies, or ideas meet P&G's where-to-play criteria? Let's assume a technology entrepreneur finds a promising product on a store shelf that passes this initial screening. His or her next step will be to log the product into our online "eureka catalog," using a template that helps organize certain facts about the product: What is it? How does it meet our business needs? Are its patents available? What are its current sales? The catalog's descriptions and pictures (which have a kind of Sharper Image feel) are distributed to general managers, brand managers, R&D

teams, and others throughout the company worldwide, according to their interests, for evaluation.

Meanwhile, the technology entrepreneur may actively promote the product to specific managers in relevant lines of business. If an item captures the attention of, say, the director of the baby care business, she will assess its alignment with the goals of the business and subject it to a battery of practical questions—such as whether P&G has the technical infrastructure needed to develop the product —meant to identify any showstopping impediments to development. The director will also gauge the product's business potential. If the item continues to look promising, it may be tested in consumer panels and, if the response is positive, moved into our product development portfolio. Then we'll engage our external business development (EBD) group to contact the product's manufacturer and begin negotiating licensing, collaboration, or other deal structures. (The EBD group is also responsible for licensing P&G's intellectual property to third parties. Often, we find that the most profitable arrangements are ones where we both license to and license from the same company.) At this point, the product found on the outside has entered a development pipeline similar in many ways to that for any product developed in-house.

The process, of course, is more complex and rigorous than this thumbnail sketch suggests. In the end, for every 100 ideas found on the outside, only one ends up in the market.

Words of Warning

Procter & Gamble's development and implementation of connect and develop has unfolded over many years. There have been some hiccups along the way, but largely it has been a methodical process of learning by doing, abandoning what doesn't work and expanding what does. Over five years in, we've identified three core requirements for a successful connect-and-develop strategy.

- Never assume that "ready to go" ideas found outside are truly ready to go. There will always be development work to do, including risky scale-up.

- Don't underestimate the internal resources required. You'll need a full-time, senior executive to run any connect-and-develop initiative.

- Never launch without a mandate from the CEO. Connect and develop cannot succeed if it's cordoned off in R&D. It must be a top-down, companywide strategy.

Push the Culture

No amount of idea hunting on the outside will pay off if, internally, the organization isn't behind the program. Once an idea gets into the development pipeline, it needs R&D, manufacturing, market research, marketing, and other functions pulling for it. But, as you know, until very recently, P&G was deeply centralized and internally focused. For connect and develop to work, we've had to nurture an internal culture change while developing systems for making connections. And that has involved not only opening the company's floodgates to ideas from the outside but actively promoting internal idea exchanges as well.

For any product development program, we tell R&D staff that they should start by finding out whether related work is being done elsewhere in the company; then they should see if an external source—a partner or supplier, for instance—has a solution. Only if those two avenues yield nothing should we consider inventing a solution from scratch. Wherever the solution comes from (inside or out), if the end product succeeds in the marketplace, the rewards for employees involved in its development are the same. In fact, to the extent that employees get recognition for the speed of product development, our reward systems actually favor innovations developed from outside ideas since, like Pringles Prints, these often move more quickly from concept to market.

We have two broad goals for this reward structure. One is to make sure that the best ideas, wherever they come from, rise to the surface. The other is to exert steady pressure on the culture, to continue to shift mind-sets away from resistance to "not invented here." Early on, employees were anxious that connect and develop might eliminate jobs or that P&G would lose capabilities. That stands to reason, since as you increase the ideas coming in from the outside you might expect an equivalent decrease in the need for internal ideas. But with our growth objectives, there is no limit to our need for solid business-building ideas. Connect and develop has not eliminated R&D jobs, and it has actually required the company to develop new skills. There are still pockets within P&G that have not embraced connect and develop, but the trend has been toward accepting the approach, even championing it, as its benefits have accrued and people have seen that it reinforces their own work.

Adapt or Die

We believe that connect and develop will become the dominant innovation model in the twenty-first century. For most companies, as we've argued, the alternative invent-it-ourselves model is a sure path to diminishing returns.

To succeed, connect and develop must be driven by the top leaders in the organization. It is destined to fail if it is seen as solely an R&D strategy or isolated as an experiment in some other corner of the company. As Lafley did at P&G, the CEO of any organization must make it an explicit company strategy and priority to capture a certain amount of innovation externally. In our case, the target is a demanding—even radical—50 percent, but we're well on our way to achieving it.

Don't postpone crafting a connect-and-develop strategy, and don't approach the process incrementally. Companies that fail to adapt to this model won't survive the competition.

Reading 5-3   Finding, Forming, and Performing: Creating Networks for Discontinuous Innovation

Julian Birkinshaw, John Bessant, and Rick Delbridge

Many industries today face a fast pace of technological and market change where the shifts are not just more-of-the-same. Instead, they are characterized by periods of discontinuous change in which the companies that emerge as the new winners often have competencies, backgrounds, and networks of relationships that are very different from the previous incumbents. Lego used to compete head-to-head with Mattel and Hasbro in brick sets and action figures; now it has to come to grips with the latest digital device or online offering from Sony, Nintendo, and Electronic Arts. GSK used to see Merck, Novartis, and Pfizer as its principal competitors; now it is equally worried about the proliferation of new drug compounds from biotechnology companies. While discontinuous changes of this type have occurred throughout history, there is evidence that they are becoming more frequent and more severe.[1] The implication for many firms—and particularly those in fast-moving, high-technology industries—is that they need to increase their capacity for *discontinuous innovation*, i.e., the implementation of new technologies, products, or business models that represent a dramatic departure from the current state of the art in the industry.[2] This article examines how firms create new networks (with customers, suppliers or other partners) as one part of this capacity for discontinuous innovation.

The Challenge of Discontinuous Innovation

Discontinuous innovation can take many forms. It is often driven by the development of an entirely new technology, such as the solid-state white-light-emitting diode technology patented by Nichia Chemical that threatens to make the traditional heated-filament light bulb obsolete;[3] it may be brought about by the emergence of new markets, such as digital

▌ Julian Birkinshaw is Professor of Strategic and International Management at the London Business School and a Senior Fellow of the Advanced Institute of Management Research (UK). (jbirkinshaw@london.edu)

▌ John Bessant is Professor and Chair of Innovation Management at the Tanaka Business School, Imperial College, and a Senior Fellow of the Advanced Institute of Management Research (UK). (j.bessant@imperial.ac.uk)

▌ Rick Delbridge is Professor of Organizational Analysis at Cardiff Business School, Cardiff University, and a Senior Fellow of the Advanced Institute of Management Research (UK). (delbridger@cardiff.ac.uk)

▌ [1] Several authors point to the increasing pace of change driven by: acceleration and globalization in the production of knowledge; internationalization and fragmentation of markets (and their increasing "virtualization" via growth in Internet usage); and increasing political and regulatory uncertainty. See, for example, H. Chesbrough, *Open Innovation: The New Imperative for Creating and Profiting form Technology* (Boston, MA: Harvard Business School Press, 2003); D. Ellis, *Technology and the Future of Health Care: Preparing for the Next 30 Years* (San Francisco, CA: AHA Press/Jossey-Bass, 2000); R. Foster and S. Kaplan. *Creative Destruction.* (Cambridge, MA: Harvard University Press, 2002).

▌ [2] This definition is consistent with but not identical to other definitions in the literature. See, for example, G.S. Lynn, J.G. Morone, and A.S. Paulson, "Marketing and Discontinuous Innovation." *California Management Review*, 38/3 (Spring 1996): 8–36; R.W. Verzyer, "The Roles of Marketing and Industrial Design in Discontinuous New Product Development," *Journal of Product Innovation Management*, 22/1 (January 2005): 22–41.

▌ [3] For more detail on the LED story, see J. Tidd, J. Bessant, and K. Pavitt, "The Dimming of the Light Bulb," in J. Tidd, J.Bessant, and K. Pavitt, eds., *Managing Innovation: Integrating Technological, Market and Organizational Change* (Chichester: John Wiley and Sons, 2005), pp. 25–28; D. Talbot, "LEDs vs. the Lightbulb," *Technology Review* (May 2003), pp. 30–36.

photography or mobile telephony; and it may be triggered by dramatic shifts in the political or economic scenery, such as the deregulation of the national postal services in Europe that is underway at the moment.

Regardless of the initial source of change, the effect of such discontinuities on incumbent firms can be dramatic. Research has shown consistently that new technology or market opportunities are typically developed first by new entrants, and established players either find themselves scrambling to catch up (Lego in digital games, Motorola in mobile infrastructure) or they lose out altogether (Polaroid in digital photography, DEC in the PC industry).[4] There are also cases where incumbent firms have successfully managed the transition of their business models to incorporate discontinuous technological changes (retail banking and the Internet, IBM and the emergence of the IT services industry). Such cases suggest that it is certainly possible for firms to be successful at discontinuous innovation, even if the chances of success are low.[5]

There are three broad sets of reasons why so many firms struggle with discontinuous innovation. First, the fruits of discontinuous innovation are uncertain, hard to make sense of, and typically slow to emerge. The new offering does not emerge perfectly formed like Venus from the sea; instead, it typically comes together in a fragmented and apparently *ad hoc* manner, so many firms give up along the way and fall back on their investments in more incremental but predictable projects. For example, RR Donnelley, the Chicago-based printing company, created a digital printing business in the late 1980s, but it struggled to build a coherent offering for the relevant target markets and the initiative failed.[6]

Second, firms find it difficult to break out of established and hitherto successful routines. Their existing structures and processes are organized around a historically determined set of customers and products, and their reward and incentive systems are geared to maintaining and improving on the established system. Intel, for example, has poured hundreds of millions of dollars into new opportunities beyond its core microprocessor business, but it continues to be completely reliant on that business for its revenues and its profits.[7]

Third, and of most relevance to this article, the forces of inertia extend to the firm's networks and systems of relationships. It is well known that long-term and deep relationships are powerful positive resources for incremental innovation.[8] However, research has also recognized an important corollary: *the ties that bind may become the ties that blind*.[9] In other words, the strength of an existing web of relationships is itself a fundamental obstacle to change. For example, UK retailer Laura Ashley found itself in trouble in the 1980s by staying committed to a shrinking target market of women wanting traditional floral designs as well as to a high-cost workforce in Wales. Apple Computer's well-publicized problems in the mid-1990s were at least partly the result of its refusal to build relationships with new suppliers, distributors, or software partners outside its own inner circle of allies.[10]

The challenge of discontinuous innovation has been recognized for many years, and it has been the

---

[4]See G. Gavetti and M. Tripsas, "Capabilities, Cognition, and Inertia: Evidence from Digital Imaging," *Strategic Management Journal*, 21/10–11 (October/November 2000): 1147–1161.

[5]C. Markides and P. Geroski, *Fast Second: How Smart Companies Bypass Radical Innovation to Enter and Dominate New Markets* (San Francisco, CA: Jossey Bass, 2005).

[6]D.A. Garvin and A. March, "R.R. Donnelley and Sons: The Digital Division," Harvard Business School case 9-396-154, Harvard Business School Publishing, Cambridge, MA, 1996.

[7]R.A. Burgelman, *Strategy is Destiny* (New York, NY: Free Press, 2002).

[8]See J. Dyer and K. Nobeoka, "Creating and Managing a High-Performance Knowledge-Sharing Networks: The Toyota Case," *Strategic Management Journal*, 21/3 (March 2000): 345–367.

[9]See D. Cohen and L. Prusak, *In Good Company: How Social Capital Makes Organizations Work* (Boston, MA: Harvard Business School Press, 2001).

[10]Both the Laura Ashley and Apple examples are taken from D. Sull, *Revival of the Fittest: Why Good Companies Go Bad, and How Great Managers Remake Them* (Cambridge, MA: Harvard Business School Press, 2003).

subject of a considerable amount of academic research. One line of research has focused on the effect that different types of innovation have on industry structure and on the performance of incumbent and entering firms.[11] A second set of studies has attempted to understand emerging customer needs in newly formed markets and the approaches firms can use to address them.[12] A third approach has been to focus on the cognitive barriers managers face in building awareness and making investments in unfamiliar areas and the tactics they can use to overcome these barriers.[13] Finally, a fourth major line of research has focused on understanding the internal mechanisms firms use to manage their innovation activities, including the role of marketing and design, the "probe and learn" process, and the creation of separate venturing units.[14]

Our approach here is to focus on one particular aspect of the problem, namely, how firms create new networks to enable discontinuous innovation. Our research suggests that such networks can be an important source of new insights, competencies, and relationships for the firm as it attempts to make sense of the changes affecting its industry. Unlike the other approaches mentioned above, it has received very limited research attention to date. Many other researchers have examined the roles of networks in building an innovation system, but their focus has typically been on building and maintaining an existing network rather than on the challenge of creating a new set of relationships that might complement or even supplant the existing ones.[15]

The research we report here offers a framework for making sense of the management challenges associated with creating new networks. It is based on detailed case studies of firms in Europe and North America that were seeking out ways of addressing the discontinuous changes underway in their business environments (see Appendix). Clearly, the nature of the changes facing these firms varied enormously, but the common theme facing all of them was a recognition that they had to move beyond their existing, tried-and-tested relationships if they were to succeed in capturing value from the emerging opportunities in their industries. The networks created by these firms took many forms—some involved identifying prospective suppliers of new ideas or technologies, others were prospective customers or governmental institutions that the firm was seeking to better understand (see Table 1).

[11]See W. Abernathy and K.B. Clark, "Innovation: Mapping the Winds of Creative Destruction," *Research Policy*, 14/1 (February 1985): 3–21; P. Anderson and M. Tushman, "Technological Discontinuities and Dominant Designs: A Cyclical Model of Technological Change," *Administrative Science Quarterly*, 35/4 (December 1990): 604–633; J. Utterback, *Mastering the Dynamics of Innovation* (Cambridge, MA: Harvard Business School Press, 1995).

[12]See E. von Hippel, "Lead Users: A Source of Novel Product Concepts," *Management Science*, 32/7 (July 1986): 791–805; C. Herstatt and E. von Hippel, "Developing New Product Concepts via the Lead User Method," *Journal of Product Innovation Management*, 9/3 (September 1992): 213–221; A. Ulnwick, *What Customers Want: Using Outcome-Driven Innovation to Create Breakthrough Products and Services* (New York, NY: McGraw-Hill, 2005); C. Christensen, *The Innovator's Dilemma* (Boston, MA: Harvard Business School Press, 1997); C. Christensen, E. Roth, and S. Anthony, *Seeing What's Next: Using Theories of Innovation to Predict Industry Change* (Cambridge, MA: Harvard Business School Publishing, 2005); R. McGrath and I. MacMillan, *The Entrepreneurial Mindset* (Cambridge, MA: Harvard Business School Press, 2000).

[13]There is a long tradition of research concerned with understanding and capitalizing on emerging business trends. See H. Kahn, *Thinking about the Unthinkable* (New York, NY: Simon & Schuster, 1984); P. Schwarz, *The Art of the Long View: Planning for the Future in an Uncertain World* (New York, NY: Currency Doubleday, 1996). For a recent and broader discussion of these issues, see G. Day and P. Schoemaker, *Peripheral Vision: Detecting Weak Signals that Will Make or Break Your Company* (Boston, MA: Harvard Business School Press, 2005).

[14]See R.A. Burgelman, "Managing the Internal Corporate Venturing Process," *Sloan Management Review*, 25/2 (Winter 1984): 33–48; R. Leifer, G.C. O'Connor, and M. Rice, "Implementing Radical Innovation in Mature Firms: The Role of Hubs," *Academy of Management Executive*, 15/3 (August 2001): 102–113; Lynn, Morone, and Paulson, op. cit.

[15]See A. Hargadon, *How Breakthroughs Happen* (Boston, MA: Harvard Business School Press, 2003). Hargadon builds on important insights from the social network literature, including: M.S. Granovetter, "The Strength of Weak Ties," *American Journal of Sociology*, 78/6 (May 1973): 1360–1380: R. Burt, "Structural Holes: The Social Structure of Competition," in N. Nohria and R. Eccles, eds., *Networks and Organizations: Structure, Form and Action* (Boston, MA: Harvard Business School Press, 1992): 57–91. For a detailed description of Ford's innovation in mass production, see D. A. Hounshell, *From the American System to Mass Production 1800–1932* (Baltimore, MD: Johns Hopkins University Press, 1992).

Table 1   Examples of Networks for Discontinuous Innovation

Idea Networks	A set of relationships with individuals and organizations who the firm can tap into to help solve technical problems or to brainstorm new ideas. For example, P&G's Connect and Develop and Eli Lilly's Innocentive.
Corporate Venturing Networks	Involves building relationships with hundreds of prospective new ventures and other VCs with a view to developing a window on new technologies and making selective investments in promising new ventures. For example, Intel Capital Nokia Ventures.
Lead User Groups	A set of relationships with leading-edge customers who help the firm to experiment with and try out new product ideas. For example, Lego's Mindstorm User Group or the BBC's Backstage.com project.
Cross-Industry Alliances	Creation of relationships with various different actors in a particular industry to achieve something that they cannot achieve on their own. For example, Rio Tinto's work with sustainable development agencies on its Breaking New Ground initiative.
Communities of Practice	Cross-boundary and cross-organizational groupings engaged in experience and idea sharing around shared knowledge fields, particularly at the intersection point where two "knowledge worlds" collide. For example, technical groups/knowledge communities at 3M, Xerox, and HP.
Supplier Networks	Networks of partners with whom firms share their strategic roadmaps and invite ideas and inputs to shaping and delivering on new and alternative visions. For example, Rolls Royce and its strategic supplier program.
Open Invitation Networks	Networks of self-selecting volunteer partners who organize around a specific project or issue. A recent example was the innovative approach to film financing by Thai-American film producer Tao Ruspoli who invited investors to contribute a dollar (or more) and become associate producers of his next film.

Building Networks for Discontinuous Innovation

The challenge facing firms in building new networks can be broken down into two separate activities: identifying the relevant new partners; and learning how to work with them. Once the necessary relationships have been built, they can then be converted into high-performing partnerships. It's like the recipe for effective teamworking (forming, storming, norming, and performing) except that here it is a three-stage process: finding, forming, and performing.

Consider first the finding and forming parts of the process.[16] *Finding* refers essentially to the

breadth of search that is conducted. How easy is it to identify the right individuals or organizations with which you want to interact? Do you already know exactly who they are, or will you need to put considerable effort into locating the right actors? Finding is enabled by the scope and diversity of your operations and by your capacity to move beyond the traditional way of thinking in your industry. It is hindered by a combination of geographical, technological, and institutional barriers (see Table 2).

Forming refers to the attitude of prospective partners towards your firm. How keen are they likely to be to work with you? Do you expect them to work hard to build the relationship themselves, or do you expect them to resist your overtures because of their different perspectives? Forming is enabled by your past experiences with relationship building, the strength of your position within your industry,

[16]This distinction between finding partners vs. forming relationships has some interesting parallels to Jim March's distinction between an organization's imperative to engage in both exploration-oriented and exploitation-oriented activities. See J. March, "Exploration and Exploitation in Organizational Learning," *Organization Science*, 2/1 (February 1991): 71–88.

Table 2   Barriers to New Network Formation

Primary Objective	Type of Barrier	Description
Finding Prospective Partners	Geographical	Discontinuities often emerge in unexpected corners of the world. For example, world leadership in wind power emerged in Denmark, a small country with economic and social reasons to push alternative energy. The result was small scale but scaleable wind turbines—a classic piece of disruptive innovation.[a] Geographical and cultural distance makes complex opportunities more difficult to assess, and as a result they typically get discounted.
	Technological	Discontinuous opportunities often emerge at the intersection of two technological domains: for example the nutraceuticals market emerged by linking advances in the food and pharmaceutical industries. However scientists from different disciplines struggle to communicate effectively, partly because of language differences,[b] and partly because of the different communities in which they work.
	Institutional	Institutional barriers often arise because of the different objectives or origins[c] of two groups, such as those dividing public sector from private sector; and profit-seeking from not-for-profit organizations. For example, one entrepreneur interviewed during the research had no interest in building a company around the novel medical product he had created: he just wanted to generate a fair return on his intellectual property so that he could get back into his research laboratory. When a large firm approached him about commercializing his product, it took a while for them to fully understand his perspective.
Forming Relationships with Prospective Partners	Ideological	Many potential partners do not share the values and norms of the focal firm, which can blind it from seeing the threats or opportunities that might arise at the interfaces between the two world views. For example, McDonalds has experienced a serious backlash as social attitudes to fast foods have shifted from those valuing convenience to growing concerns about childhood obesity and its complications.
	Demographic	Barriers to building effective networks can arise from the different values and needs of different demographic groups. On the customer side, every company has an implicit target market it understands, but opportunities often emerge in new demographic groups they don't understand, such as female customers in the auto industry, or children in mobile phones. On the employee side, the needs of Generations X and Y are very different to those of their parents, and require innovative approaches in the workplace.

Primary Objective	Type of Barrier	Description
	Ethnic	Ethnic barriers arise from the deep-rooted cultural differences between countries or regions of the world. Such differences (for example, in terms of attitudes to time, uncertainty, or gender differences) have been well researched[d] and continue to represent substantial barriers to the formation of new business networks. For example, banks doing business in the Islamic world have to adapt to the demands of Sharia law, which, among other things, forbids usury, i.e., the payment of interest.

[a.] For a detailed discussion of Denmark's success in the wind energy industry, see R. Garud and P. R Karnoe, "Bricolage versus Breakthrough," *Research Policy*, 32/2 (February 2003): 277–301.

[b.] Sometimes even a simple language gap can be a big barrier—and occasionally the misunderstandings can have dramatic effects. The Mars Climate Orbiter, launched in 1998, almost completed its epic voyage to Mars but unexpectedly disappeared from radar screens just 49 seconds before landing. NASA's investigation into the $125m disaster discovered the problem was simply that the JPL controllers were working in metric units whereas engineers at Lockheed Martin had been working in Imperial units.

[c.] It is widely acknowledged in the social networks literature that similar actors are more likely to form close ties. See J.M. McPherson, L. Smith-Lovin, and J.M. Cook "Birds of a Feather: Homophily in Networks," *Annual Review of Sociology*, 27 (August 2001): 415–444.

[d.] For research on differences in national culture, see G. Hofstede, *Culture's Consequences* (Thousand Oaks, CA: Sage Publishing 1980); F. Trompenaars, *Riding the Waves of Culture* (New York, NY: McGraw Hill, 1997).

and an open attitude towards knowledge sharing. It is hindered by a range of barriers that may be ideological, demographic, or ethnic in nature, as well as by more generic concerns about the protection of intellectual property.

Generic Strategies for Building Networks

When these two aspects are set against each other, four separate approaches can be identified. Figure 1 illustrates this simple framework.[17] It is important to note that while this framework captures the static positions a firm might find itself in vis-à-vis one prospective partner network, it also has a dynamic element. For example, it suggests ways in which a firm can develop its competencies and re-evaluate its opportunities to switch from one position in the framework to another, and thereby change its approach.

Creating New Networks in Proximate Areas
The bottom-left part of Figure 1 represents the relatively straightforward challenge of creating new networks with potential partners that are both easy to find and happy to do business with you. Many traditional business relationships sit in this box, and the emphasis in such cases is typically on negotiating the appropriate terms for a commercial relationship, and then on managing the relationship on an ongoing basis. In the present context, however, this box still offers considerable challenges because we are concerned primarily with those networks of relationships that are not "business as usual." So, even though the actors in question may be well known to the firm and are keen to become involved, the decision to invest in relationships with them is likely to have an uncertain and perhaps long-term payoff.

Consider, for example, Lego's decision to develop its next generation Mindstorms product using a network of lead users of the first generation product. The company created a Mindstorms User Panel for this user community. Working for the most part remotely over an 11-month period, these lead users collaborated with Lego to finalize their product for the launch of Mindstorms NXT at the Consumer Electronics Show in Las Vegas in 2005. Lego also

[17]The different strategies for building relationships to potential partners have some parallels to Pfeffer and Salancik's ideas about how a firm reduces its dependency on external actors. See J. Pfeffer and G. Salancik, *The External Control of Organizations: A Resource-Dependence Perspective* (Stanford, CA: Stanford University Press, 1978).

Figure 1   Four Generic Approaches to Network Building

How easy is it to form a relationship with the potential partner?	Reluctant to engage with you	**3.** **Building relationships with unusual partners, e.g., Novo Nordisk, Rio Tinto**	**4.** **Moving into uncharted territory, e.g., BBC, Tempus**
	Keen to engage with you	**1.** **Creating new networks in proximate areas, e.g., Lego, Ericsson**	**2.** **Seeking out new networks in distant areas, e.g., BT, Procter & Gamble**
		Easy to find	Hard to find

How difficult is it to find your potential partners?

decided to outsource the new software for the NXT version (the software for the previous version had been created in-house) as they wanted more intuitive software. Lego's experience after the first Mindstorms product had been that the enthusiastic user community was an asset, despite its hacking into the old software and sharing this information on the web. As described by Lego Senior Vice President Mads Nipper, "We came to understand that this is a great way to make the product more exciting. It's a totally different business paradigm."

By thinking differently, Lego was able to reach out to its lead users in what was—by their standards—a highly unusual collaboration. Mads Nipper and his team guessed correctly that their "lead users" would love to be involved in the development of their next generation product, so it proved to be quite straightforward to set up the appropriate forum in which they could interact. In recognition of the success of this program, Lego stated in January 2006 that it was looking for 100 more citizen developers.

Another example is provided by the Swedish mobile infrastructure company Ericsson, which in

1999 sought to improve the quality of its access to university-based research. Rather than sponsor research studies at arm's-length, as they had done in the past, they designated key individuals to liaise directly with sponsored faculty and to hold quarterly meetings to review progress against their goals. As with the Lego example, this new approach was relatively simple to put in place, but it quickly helped to build personal relationships that facilitated a more effective two-way transfer of knowledge between Ericsson and its university partners.

Taken together, the cases that are located in the lower-left quadrant suggest three key elements to new network building:

- Approach the potential new partners directly; you know who they are, and there is every reason to think they will be receptive to your proposals.
- Structure the relationship carefully to overcome the institutional or demographic differences that separate you; lead users and university professors often have very different world views to profit-making firms, and it takes time to understand what motivates and excites them.

- Build personal relationships at the interfaces with partners to ensure that knowledge transfer occurs; otherwise the potential of the relationships will be squandered.

In sum, creating new networks in proximate areas is relatively straightforward, but it requires a significant investment on the part of the firm to ensure that the knowledge and insights of the partners are internalized.

Seeking Out New Networks in Distant Areas   In the bottom-right corner of the framework, the emphasis is on *finding* new network partners. The barriers here are typically geographical, ethnic, and institutional. The challenge is to locate the appropriate individuals or organizations from among the many thousands of prospective partners. However, once they have been identified, the process of forming commercial relationships with them tends to be relatively straightforward.

The most appropriate strategy in this scenario involves investing in boundary-spanners and scouts who collectively can forge links with potential partners. Boundary-spanners are individuals who understand both worlds and can make the necessary links between them. Scouts are individuals who have or are prepared to build diverse networks into places or sectors that your firm is unfamiliar with.

Consider two examples from the cases we studied. The first is Procter & Gamble's well-known initiative called Connect and Develop.[18] Building on CEO A.G. Lafley's stated objective to source 50% of the company's innovations from outside the boundaries of the company, P&G has built a massive network of "outside contacts" to complement its internal R&D staff of 8,500. This network has several elements: there are teams of technology entrepreneurs in attractive nodes such as China, Japan, and Italy who seek out individuals and companies doing interesting work in the food science arena; there are more than 800 retirees who work part time in making contacts for P&G that might prove useful; and there are web-based systems for connecting to people with interesting skills and ideas.

The second example is BT's four-man scouting operation in Silicon Valley.[19] It was established in 1999 to make venture investments in promising telecom start-ups, but after the dot-com bubble burst it shifted its mission towards identifying partners and technologies that BT was interested in. The small team looks at more than 1000 companies per year and then, based on their deep knowledge of the issues facing the R&D operations back in England, they target the small number of cases where there is a direct match between BT's needs and the Silicon Valley company's technology. While the number of successful partnerships that result from this activity is small—typically 4 or 5 per year—the unit serves an invaluable role in keeping BT abreast of the latest developments in its technology domain. As Jean-Marc Frangos, the head of the unit observed:

> "The most important thing is to have your radar in such a way so the technologies you identify at Silicon Valley are really useful as opposed to 'a nice to have.' Being able to identify the mapping of what you see with the various interests is the challenge here . . . You won't find the cure for your patient if you don't really understand what he suffers from."

These two examples are different in one important respect. P&G's network of scientists is used in a problem-focused way, in that they are asked for their input whenever P&G's internal R&D employees have a problem they cannot solve. BT's California venturing operation, in contrast, is solution-driven, in that it taps into a set of new technologies that may or may not be useful to core R&D activities. However, the point is that both of these networks were difficult to build primarily because of the diversity of potential partners, not because those partners had ideological or demographic differences with P&G or BT.

---

[18]The P&G Connect and Develop program is described by its founders in L. Huston and N. Sakkab, "Connect and Develop," *Harvard Business Review*, 84/3 (March 2006): 58–66. For an academic treatment, see M. Dodgson, D. Gann, and A. Salter, "The Role of Technology in the Shift to Open Innovation: The Case of Procter & Gamble," *R&D Management*, 36/3 (June 2006): 333–346.

[19]This account is drawn from F. Monteiro and D. Sull, "External Innovation at BT," London Business School teaching case.

In sum, the approaches firms used for seeking out new networks in distant areas can be summarized as follows:

- Rather than attempting to do it yourself, new potential partners are best approached through boundary spanners or scouts who specialize in building and maintaining relationships with many people.
- Be prepared to accept redundancy or duplication in the networks that you create; they are designed to be learning opportunities, not contracts for specific services.
- Do not underestimate the difficulty of absorbing the insights gained from these distant networks; give specific individuals direct responsibility for internalizing and applying the knowledge gained from new partners.

Building Relationships with Unusual Partners
The third scenario is where the potential partners are easy to find but potentially reluctant to engage with you (i.e., the top-left quadrant of Figure 1). This might occur for ideological reasons, or because of institutional or demographic barriers between you and your potential partners. Whatever the circumstances, the challenge of building a relationship with such prospective partners is qualitatively very different to the challenge of seeking out new partners in distant areas.

An effective strategy in this situation involves co-opting prospective partners around a shared goal. Given their initial reluctance to engage with you, our research suggests it is necessary to find a way of transcending the real or imagined differences between them and you and to create a specific project or activity that they find attractive.

Consider the Danish pharmaceutical company, Novo Nordisk. As a commercial organization selling insulin and other diabetes-related therapies into the healthcare industry, Novo Nordisk did not find it easy to build deep relationships with specialists, nurses, and health insurers. Institutional and ideological barriers made close engagement difficult. However, faced with long-term changes in the business environment towards greater obesity and rising healthcare costs, Novo Nordisk realized that it needed to start exploring opportunities for discontinuous innovation in its products and offerings. Its "Diabetes 2020" process involved exploring radical alternative scenarios for chronic disease treatment and the roles that a player like Novo-Nordisk could play. As part of the follow-up from this initiative, in 2003 the company helped set up the Oxford Health Alliance, a non-profit collaborative entity which brought together key stakeholders—medical scientists, doctors, patients, and government officials—with views and perspectives that were sometimes quite widely separated. To make it happen, Novo Nordisk made clear that its goal was nothing less than the prevention or cure of diabetes—a goal which if it were achieved would potentially kill off the company's main line of business. As Lars Rebien Sørensen, the CEO of Novo Nordisk, explained:

"In moving from intervention to prevention—that's challenging the business model where the pharmaceuticals industry is deriving its revenues! . . . We believe that we can focus on some major global health issue—mainly diabetes—and at the same time create business opportunities for our company."

By committing itself to the ultimate goal of curing diabetes, Novo Nordisk was able to transcend the barriers that had historically separated it from other stakeholders. The company is now in a strong position to shape the future evolution of the diabetes industry and to build new offerings—for example, around preventative care—ahead of their competitors.

Several other companies in our sample used similar types of approaches. In 2000, mining giant Rio Tinto took the initiative to reach out to NGOs (such as the International Institute for Environment and Development) by sponsoring an industry-wide study of the role of minerals in sustainable development.[20] This was potentially risky for Rio Tinto, but the initiative allowed the company to develop a good dialogue with actors who had traditionally kept their distance from the company.

[20]The work that Rio Tinto initiated was published in a report, "Breaking New Ground: Mining, Minerals and Sustainable Development," in 2002 www.iied.org.mmsd.

At around the same time, oil major BP identified a rather different challenge, namely the emergence of the so-called "Generation Y" whose values in and around work were dramatically different from those of their Baby-Booomer parents. Rather than push them to conform and risk alienating them, BP's executives put in place a project called "Ignite" in which a group of 20- to 30-year-old employees were asked to brainstorm possible changes to the strategy and organization of the company. By giving them *carte blanche* to pursue the project on their own terms, the executives gained the trust of their Generation Y employees, and in the process some useful new insights into the workplace of the future were uncovered.[21]

Taken as a whole, these and other cases suggest a number of specific tactics that can be used to build relationships with unusual partners.

- Focus on the higher-order purpose or issue that transcends your differences; it may be a major concern such as global warming or disease prevention, or it may be a common "enemy" that you are both competing with.[22]
- Be prepared for a lengthy dialogue to take place before the new partners begin to trust you; the process of mutual adjustment often takes years.
- Try to identify cross-over individuals who have switched allegiance from the world of the prospective partner to your world; they can be very useful in proposing the appropriate ways of making the personal connections between the two sides.

Moving into Uncharted Territory   In the final scenario, represented by the top-right box of Figure 1, the potential partners are neither actors you can easily identify nor are they (once you find them) likely to be keen to engage with you. This is moving into

uncharted territory. Of course, the territory may be so hard to navigate that it is not even worth trying, but depending on the nature of the change affecting your industry you may have no choice. For example, many traditional media companies had no choice but to engage with upstart companies and the anti-establishment culture of the Internet when its disruptive potential became apparent.

How do you engage with potential partners in this situation? One approach is gradually to reduce the reluctance of prospective partners by breaking down the institutional or demographic barriers that separate them from you. This essentially pushes the prospective relationship into the bottom-right corner of Figure 1 and allows you to use boundary-spanners and scouts to engage with your prospective partners. For example, consider the case of the BBC, the UK's publicly funded broadcaster. The BBC had a long and illustrious tradition as a producer of broadcast media but in the early 2000s it was trying to deal with the discontinuous challenges of the new digital media environment. How should it deal with this major change in its marketplace? By trying to second-guess a massively complex new world through the efforts of a small R&D group? Or by trying to engage a rich variety of players in those emerging spaces via a series of open source experiments?

Their answer was BBC Backstage, a project that sought to do with new media development what the open source community did with LINUX and other software development. The model was deceptively simple—developers were invited to make free use of various elements of the BBC's site (such as live news feeds, weather, and TV listings) to integrate and shape innovative applications. The strap line was "use our stuff to build your stuff." As soon as the site was launched in May 2005, it attracted the interest of hundreds of software developers and led to some high-potential product ideas. Ben Metcalf, one of the program's founders, summed up the approach:

> "Top line, we are looking to be seen promoting innovation and creativity on the Internet, and if we can be seen to be doing that, we will be very pleased. In terms of projects coming out of it, if we can see a few examples that

---

[21]See L. Gratton and S. Ghoshal, "Improving the Quality of Conversations," *Organizational Dynamics*, 31/3 (Winter 2002): 209–224.

[22]Biggart and Delbridge distinguish between instrumental and value rationality as bases of action in exchange. Substantive rationality is oriented to values where actors are morally or emotionally bound to pursue the substantive goal. See N. W. Biggart and R. Delbridge, "Systems of Exchange," *Academy of Management Review*, 29/1 (January 2004): 28–49.

offered real value to our end users to build something new, we would be happy with that as well. And if someone is doing something really innovative, we would like to invite them into the BBC and see if some of that value can be incorporate into the BBC's core propositions."

As this example suggests, the BBC was able to win over a skeptical group of independent developers by showing that they were progressive in their approach to new media development and open-minded to non-mainstream ideas. There is still, of course, some distance between the parties, but BBC Backstage has succeeded in reducing the size of the gap.

A second approach to moving into uncharted territory is to use a middleman, an agent who can act on your behalf in making the link to prospective partners. Consider the case of Tempus,[23] a large consumer products group, and its international launch strategy for Tambura beer. While most of its products had been marketed through traditional big-budget advertising campaigns, Tambura beer launched in Spain through a low-key, word-of-mouth promotional strategy. Whereas most of Tempus's brands were seen as mass-market offerings, Tambura in Spain had developed a cult-like following among independent-minded people—the sort of consumer who Tempus usually failed to sell to.

Tempus decided to launch Tambura internationally by replicating the Spanish model. They hired two consultants who were very well connected in the trendy world of artists, designers, and musicians, and they asked them to start a word-of-mouth promotional campaign for Tambura. Starting in the UK and the U.S., the consultants used their contacts to identify the "cool" bars, clubs, and galleries in key cities, and then they approached up-and-coming artists and opinion leaders in these places to get them interested in Tambura beer. For example, they would give away free Tambura beer when a particular band was playing in a bar or when an artist was exhibiting their latest art.

At the time of writing, the preliminary results of the Tambura campaign were very positive, in terms of the demand for the product among the communities they had reached. However, there is a long way to go to prove its overall success. From the perspective of this research, Tempus's approach provides useful insight into how to build a network where both the "finding" and the "forming" parts of the process are difficult. Tempus used independent agents as a route into a world they did not understand. As well as generating sales of Tambura beer, Tempus also benefits from the insights and perspectives they gained, through the two consultants, into the needs and desires of a community of potential consumers they previously had little contact with.

In sum, moving into uncharted territory involves a combination of the tactics identified around quadrants two and three. You need to work with specialist network builders (some of whom directly work for you, some of whom are free-agents) and you need to develop a reason for the potential partners to work with you in the first place. If the challenges associated with the other quadrants of the framework were substantial, the challenges here are even larger, and the process of creating the necessary networks is likely to take substantially more time.

Turning New Networks into "Performing" Partners

Consider the broader challenges firms face in turning their new networks into valuable and high-performing partners.[24] Just as with the finding and forming parts of the process, performing requires the firm to overcome a number of specific barriers. These included such things as different attitudes (between partners) towards the protection of intellectual property and differing concepts of equity and trust in commercial relationships, both of which

---

[23]Tempus and Tambura are both disguised names. The project in question was experimental and confidential at the time of writing.

[24]Academic research has addressed this issue in terms of encouraging partners to identify with the network as a whole, creating a stable and equitable context for the network (perhaps through "umbrella contracts" or exchange forums) and a proactive approach to managing the portfolio of network ties. See S. Mouzas, "Negotiating Umbrella Agreements," *Negotiation Journal*, 22/3 (July 2006): 279–301; B.R. Koka, R. Madhavan, and J. E. Prescott, "The Evolution of Interfirm Networks: Environmental Effects on Patterns of Network Change," *Academy of Management Review*, 31/3 (July 2006): 721–737; C. Dhanaraj and A. Parkhe, "Orchestrating Innovation Networks," *Academy of Management Review*, 31/3 (July 2006): 659–669.

typically stemmed from the underlying ethnic, institutional, or ideological differences between partners.

While most of the firms we studied were still in the process of finding and forming their new networks, a few had reached a level of maturity that allowed us to understand the difficulties that arise in creating long-term business value from such activities. We identified four specific sets of challenges and some initial thoughts about how to resolve them:

- *Keeping the network up-to-date and engaged.* Very often these networks are built in anticipation of future needs, rather than to tackle an immediate and pressing problem; and as such they may not have any immediate value to either side. For example, the international network of scientists P&G created as part of its Connect & Develop model is not on the company's payroll and is not required to deliver any ongoing services to the company. However, its *latent* value—its ability to spring into action when requested—is enormous. In such cases, the challenge is one of creating realistic expectations and ensuring that the members in the network are kept up-to-date with developments inside the company. P&G makes extensive use of its web site to celebrate successful partnerships that have emerged through its network. It updates its partners with e-mails, web-briefings, and events; and it makes good use of periodic face-to-face meetings to keep the relationship fresh.

- *Building trust and reciprocity across the network.* Old habits die hard for many large firms, and it is tempting when working with smaller partners to be very selective about what information gets shared and to seek to impose control over them. However, partnerships rely on the precepts of trust and reciprocity to be effective, and increasingly firms are realizing that the more they give away, the more they get back in return. One recent example is IBM's Innovation Jam, a 72-hour web-based discussion forum in which IBM employees *and* suppliers, customers, family members, and others developed a collective point of view about emerging business opportunities in specific domains. IBM emphasized, at the outset, that the output from the Jam

would be a public good. While the company planned to subsequently develop its own proprietary projects around the insights from the Jam, it invited others to do the same. This approach ensured that the Jam was visible and successful—it had 100,000 individual postings, and it resulted in 31 follow-up projects in various parts of IBM.

- *Understanding your own position in the network.* It is tempting for large firms to see themselves as network "orchestrators" who achieve some level of control by virtue of their central position in the network. While this can be beneficial—as it is in P&G's Connect & Develop—it can also be misguided, because the network may become more valuable if it is given the opportunity to develop its own dynamic. For example, when Sun Microsystems created its Java Developer Network in the early 1990s, it initially tried to control the activities of its partners (the independent software companies who were writing Java code). However, it failed to do so and instead decided to create an open-source community, which quickly took off and took on a life of its own. It is an important reminder that business networks, like ecosystems, cannot be controlled by any single player in them.

- *Learning to let go.* The fourth challenge was only apparent in those cases where firms had been successful in building and learning from their new networks and were faced with the prospect of realigning their core activities away from some of their traditional networks. For example, the German group TUI AG has been enjoying increasing growth as a major player in tourism and related transportation services, but this has required them to let go many of the core activities—and the related networks of players—with which the business began. Founded in 1917 as Preussag AG, it was involved in lead mining and smelting and for much of the 20th century concentrated on commodities such as steel and related fields, bringing with it a network of suppliers of related goods and services. Its strategic progress towards a services-dominated business has meant not only finding, forming, and getting new network relationships to perform, but also letting go of sometimes long-established links.

Whereas in 1997 93% of the business was in industrial markets, today 72% comes from tourism and a further 19% from shipping.

Conclusions

The challenge of building networks for managing discontinuous innovation is—by definition—a tricky one. While it is always obvious in retrospect where a new technology or market opportunity has come from, at the time of its emergence the signals are ambiguous and vague. So companies face two distinct challenges. One is about knowing which technology or market domains to start looking in, and this has been written about for many years by others.[25] The other is about finding and forming relationships with specific partners once those domains have been selected, and this is what we have focused on in this article. Companies need to be conversant with the types of obstacles they will encounter in building new networks and the types of approaches that are likely to be successful in overcoming these obstacles in each case. Table 3 summarizes the key insights and recommendations from the research.

Appendix

About the Research   This article is based on the findings from a four-year year research program looking at the ways in which companies approach the challenge of discontinuous innovation. The research was undertaken in two parallel streams. One stream was a series of case studies looking at companies that had responded well or badly to significant changes in their business environment. In total, we interviewed 73 executives in 22 companies, as indicated in the following table. The second stream of work was a series of interactive seminars in which we sought to help companies think through the challenges of discontinuous innovation and put in place new approaches to dealing with these challenges. This second stream of work allowed us to try out some of the ideas in this article and get some feedback on their applicability in a real-world setting. In total, we conducted 15 workshops over a two-year period: nine of these were with single-company groups, the other six were with multi-company groups. Interviews were conducted with a range of managers in the organizations listed below. Their roles ranged from marketing through purchasing to R&D and long-term planning. What they had in common was a responsibility for extending and exploring the selection environment from which the firm drew its innovation trigger signals. Interviews lasted between 1 and 2 hours, and on many occasions we held multiple meetings with the same people to explore and review the emerging themes.

Table 3   Key Insights and Recommendations
• Creating new networks involves two distinct activities: *finding* the right prospective partners and *forming* relationships with those prospective partners. There are substantial barriers to each activity.
• Where the challenges in finding and forming relationships are relatively low, approach potential new partners directly, and structure the relationship to minimize whatever obstacles separate you.
• Where the challenge is mostly around finding new partners, approach them through boundary spanners or scouts who specialize in such activities, and work very hard on building the capability to absorb insights from these partners.
• Where the challenge is mostly around forming new relationships with prospective partners, focus on the higher-order purpose that transcends your ideological differences, and try to identify crossover individuals who can link the two sides.
• Where the challenge involves finding and forming new networks, be prepared to work with specialist and independent network-builders to bridge the gap, and look for ways of gradually breaking down barriers to enable some of the approaches identified above to work.
• Once the new relationships have been formed, there are a number of things to keep in mind to turn them into high-performing networks: continually keep the network fresh and engaged, build trust and reciprocity across the network, understand your own position in the network, and learn when to "let go" of old relationships.

[25]See Christensen, op. cit.; Day and Schoemaker, op. cit.; Hargardon, op. cit.

Firm	Number of Interviews	Job Titles of Interviewees	Which quadrants (in Figure I) does this firm illustrate?			
			Q1	Q2	Q3	Q4
AstraZeneca	2	Director of Market Intelligence, Director R&D Strategy	X	X		
BBC	2	Head of Innovation, New Media Coordinator				X
BMW	3	Head of Innovation Lab, New Projects Manager, External Sourcing Manager		X		
BP	1	VP, Chief Technology Office			X	
BT	7	Chief Technology Officer Group Strategy Director, Innovation Managers (x3), 21 Century Network Manager, Futures Program		X		
Cerulean	3	Managing Director, New Product Development Manager, Purchasing Director	X			
Coloplast	6	CEO, Vice President R&D Ostomy Division, VP R&D UCC Division, Team Leader New Business, Development Group, COF Co-ordinator	X	X		
Diageo	3	Group Innovation Director (past, present), New Venture Manager			X	
Ericsson	3	Group Innovation Directors (x2), Head of Venturing		X		
Grundfos	4	Product Development Director, New Products Manager, Purchasing Manager, Innovation Team Co-ordinator		X		
GSK	3	OTC Innovation Manager, Director of University Linkages, Head of Venturing		X		
IBM	3	VPs Responsible for Innovation Jam (x3)	X			
Lego	3	Engineering Manager, NPD Co-ordinator, Global Sourcing Manager	X			
McDonalds	1	Chief Marketing Officer, UK			X	
Novo Nordisk	6	New Venture Planning Head, Innovation Manager, PDS Director, Stakeholder Relations Coordinator, New Business Development Manager in Novozymes, CEO Northern Europe			X	
Procter & Gamble	3	VP responsible for Connect + Develop, Research Fellow, Technical Centre Innovation Manager		X		
Rio Tinto	5	CEO, Group Head of Innovation, Business Unit Heads (x3)			X	
Shell	3	Innovation Manager, Manager, Global Procurement (Expro)			X	
Siemens	5	Purchasing Manager, Medical R&D Co-ordinator, Telecomms Systems Development Head, New Projects Manager, Marketing Development Head		X		
Unilever	4	R&D Coordinator Manager, European Development Section NPD Manager, Head of Unilever Ventures		X		
UBS	2	Head of Market Strategy & Development; Director of Strategic Planning	X			
Visteon	1	Innovation Director		X		

Engaging in Cross-Border Collaboration:
Managing across Corporate Boundaries

■ ■ ■ ■ ■ ■ ■ ■ ■ ■ ■ ■ ■ ■ ■

In this chapter, we acknowledge that in the international business environment of the 21st century, few companies have all the resources and capabilities they need to develop the kind of multidimensional strategies and adaptive organizational capabilities we have described. Increasingly, they must collaborate with their suppliers, distributors, customers, agents, licensors, joint venture partners, and others to meet the needs of the increasingly complex global environment. This requirement implies that today's MNEs must develop the skills to not only manage assets and resources under their own direct control but also to span their corporate boundaries and capture vital capabilities in the partnerships and alliances that are central to the strategic response capability of so many companies. After exploring the motivation for entering into such partnerships, we examine some of the costs and risks of collaboration before discussing the organizational and managerial skills required to build and manage these boundary-spanning relationships effectively.

Historically, the strategic challenge for a company has been viewed primarily as one of protecting potential profits from erosion through either competition or bargaining. Such erosion of profits could be caused not only by the actions of competitors but also by the bargaining powers of customers, suppliers, and governments. The key challenge facing a company was assumed to be its ability to maintain its independence by maintaining strong control over its activities. Furthermore, this strategic approach emphasized the defensive value of making other entities depend on it by capturing critical resources, building switching costs, and exploiting other vulnerabilities.[1]

This view of strategy subsequently underwent a sea change. The need to pursue multiple sources of competitive advantage simultaneously (see Chapter 3) led to the need for building not only an interdependent and integrated network organization within the company (Chapter 5) but also collaborative relationships externally with other firms, be they competitors, customers, suppliers, or a variety of other institutions.

This important shift in strategic perspective was triggered by a variety of factors, including rising R&D costs, shortened product life cycles, growing barriers to market entry, increasing needs for global-scale economies, and the expanding importance of global standards. Such dramatic changes led managers to recognize that many of the

---

■ [1]For the most influential exposition of this view, see Michael E. Porter, *Competitive Strategy* (New York: Free Press, 1980).

human, financial, and technological resources they required to compete effectively lay beyond their boundaries, and were sometimes—for political or regulatory reasons—not for sale. In response, many shifted their strategic focus away from an all-encompassing obsession with preempting competition to a broader view of building competitive advantage through selective, often simultaneous reliance on both collaboration and competition.

The previously dominant focus on value appropriation that characterized all dealings across a company's organizational boundary changed to the simultaneous consideration of both value creation and value appropriation. Instead of trying to enhance their bargaining power over customers, companies began to build partnerships with them, thereby bolstering the customer's competitive position and, at the same time, leveraging their own competitiveness and innovative capabilities.

However, perhaps the most visible manifestation of this growing role of collaborative strategies appears in the phenomenon often described as strategic alliances: the increasing propensity of MNEs to form cooperative relationships with their competitors. The Renault/Nissan alliance provides a good illustration. As described by Carlo de Benedetti, the ex-chairman of Olivetti and the key instigator of the variety of partnerships that Olivetti developed with companies such as AT&T and Toshiba, "We have entered the age of alliances. . . . In high-tech markets. . . . , we will see a shaking out of the isolated and a shaking in of the allied." Strategic alliances have become central components of most MNE strategies.

Although our analysis of the causes and consequences of such collaborative strategies in this chapter focuses on the phenomenon of strategic alliances among global companies, some of our arguments can be applied to a broader range of cooperative relations, including those with customers, suppliers, and governments. We begin with a discussion of the key motivations for forming strategic alliances.

Why Strategic Alliances?

The term *strategic alliance* currently is widely used to describe a variety of interfirm cooperation agreements, ranging from shared research to formal joint ventures and minority equity participation (see Figure 6-1).

The key challenges surrounding the management of the various types of alliances detailed in Figure 6-1 will vary. In some it may relate to the "fairness" of management or technology payments; in others, it may be related to where the organizational problems typically will arise. Every form of alliance has predictable strengths and weaknesses, because each form is intended for particular circumstances.

Large numbers of firms worldwide, including many industry leaders, are increasingly involved in strategic alliances. Furthermore, several surveys suggest that such partnerships may be distinguished from traditional foreign investment joint ventures in important ways.

Classically, traditional joint ventures were formed between a senior multinational headquartered in an industrialized country and a junior local partner in a less-developed or less-industrialized country. The primary goal that dominated their formation was to gain new market access for existing products. In this classic contractual agreement, the

Figure 6-1   Range of Strategic Alliances

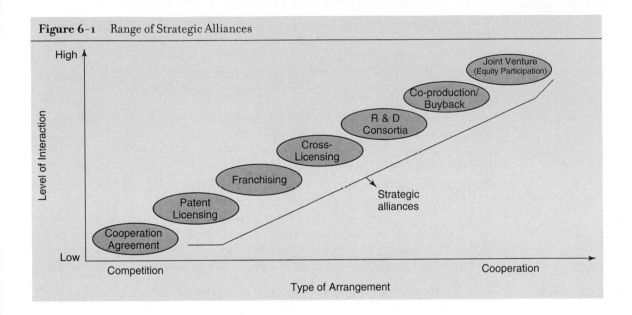

senior partner provided existing products while the junior partner provided the local marketing expertise, the means to overcome any protectionist barriers, and the governmental contacts to deal with national regulations. Both partners benefited: The multinational achieved increased sales volume, and the local firm gained access to new products and often learned important new skills from its partner.

In contrast, the scope and motivations for the modern form of strategic alliances are clearly broadening. There are three trends that are particularly noteworthy. First, present-day strategic alliances are frequently between firms in industrialized countries. Second, the focus is often on the creation of new products and technologies rather than the distribution of existing ones. Third, present-day strategic alliances are often forged for only short durations.

All of these characteristics mean the new forms of strategic alliances considerably expand the strategic importance of cooperation beyond that which existed for classic joint ventures, and today the opportunity for competitive gain and loss through partnering is substantial. In the following sections, we discuss in more detail why this form of business relationship has become so important by focusing on five key motivations that are driving the formation of strategic alliances: technology exchange, global competition, industry convergence, economies of scale, and alliances as an alternative to merger.

Technology Exchange

Technology transfer or R&D collaboration is a major objective of many strategic alliances. The reason that technological exchange is such a strong driver of alliances is simple: As more and more breakthroughs and major innovations are based on interdisciplinary and interindustry advances, the formerly clear boundaries between different industrial sectors and technologies become blurred. As a result, the necessary capabilities and resources are often beyond the scope of a single firm, making it increasingly difficult to compete effectively on the strength of one's own internal R&D efforts. The need to collaborate is further intensified by shorter product life cycles that increase both the time pressure and risk exposures while reducing the potential payback of massive R&D investments.

Not surprisingly, technology-intensive sectors such as telecommunications, information technology, electronics, pharmaceuticals, and specialty chemicals have become the central arenas for major and extensive cooperative agreements. Companies in these industries face an environment of accelerating change, short product life cycles, small market windows, and multiple vertical and lateral dependencies in their value chains. Because interfirm cooperation has provided solutions to many of these strategic challenges, much of the technological development in these industries is being driven by some form of R&D partnership.

Even mainstream industrial MNEs have employed strategic alliances to meet the challenge of coordinating and deploying discrete pools of technological resources without sacrificing R&D and commercialization scale advantages. For example, several advanced material suppliers have teamed up with global automotive companies to transfer their specialized technology across geographic borders, as exemplified by the key role GEC played in transferring the Ford Xenoy bumper technology from Europe and adapting it to the U.S. market.

Global Competition

A widespread perception has emerged that global competitive battles will increasingly be fought between teams of players aligned in strategic partnerships. Robert P. Collin, former head of the U.S. subsidiary of a joint venture between General Electric and Fanuc, the Japanese robot maker, was blunt in his evaluation of the importance of using alliances as a key tool in competitive positioning. "To level out the global playing field," he said, "American companies will have to find partners." In the new game of global networks, successful MNEs from any country of origin may well be those that have chosen the best set of corporate allies.

Particularly in industries in which there is a dominant worldwide market leader, strategic alliances and networks allow coalitions of smaller partners to compete more effectively against a global "common enemy" rather than one another. For example, the Nokia-led Symbian alliance with members including Samsung, LG Electronics, Ericsson, Matsushita, and Vodafone was created as a response to Microsoft's entry into the personal digital assistant (PDA) market. The partners recognized that their only hope of challenging Microsoft's new PDA operating system, Windows CE, was to develop a common standard in mobile phone and PDA operating systems.

Industry Convergence

Many high-technology industries are converging and overlapping in a way that seems destined to create a huge competitive traffic jam. Producers of computers, telecommunications, and components are merging; biological and chip technologies are intersecting; and advanced materials applications are creating greater overlaps in diverse applications from the aerospace to the automotive industry. Again, the preferred solution has been to create cross-industry alliances.

Furthermore, strategic alliances are sometimes the only way to develop the complex and interdisciplinary skills necessary in the time frame required. Alliances become a way of shaping competition by reducing competitive intensity, excluding potential entrants and isolating particular players, and building complex integrated value chains that can act as barriers to those who choose to go it alone.

Nowhere are the implications of this cross-industry convergence and broad-based collaboration clearer than in the case of high-definition television (HDTV). As with many other strategically critical technologies of the future—biotechnology, supercon-ductivity, advanced ceramics, artificial intelligence—HDTV not only dwarfs previous investment requirements but extends beyond the technological capabilities of even the largest and most diversified MNEs. As a result, the development of this important industry segment has been undertaken almost exclusively by country-based, cross-industry alliances of large powerful companies. In Japan, companies allied to develop the range of products necessary for a system offering. At the same time, a European HDTV consortium banded together to develop a competitive system. But in the United States, the legal and cultural barriers that prevented companies from working together in such partnerships threatened to compromise U.S. competitiveness in this major industry.

Economies of Scale and Reduction of Risk

There are several ways strategic alliances and networks allow participating firms to reap the benefits of scale economies or learning—advantages that are particularly interesting to smaller companies trying to match the economic benefits that accrue to the largest MNEs. First, partners can pool their resources and concentrate their activities to raise the scale of activity or the rate of learning within the alliance significantly over those of each firm were it to operate separately. Second, alliances enable partners to share and leverage the specific strengths and capabilities of each of the other participating firms. Third, trading different or complementary resources among companies can result in mutual gains and save each partner the high cost of duplication.

One company activity that is particularly motivated by the risk-sharing opportunities of such partnerships is R&D, where product life cycles are shortening and technological complexity is increasing. At the same time, R&D expenses are being driven sharply higher by personnel and capital costs. Because none of the participating firms bears the full risk and cost of the joint activity, alliances are often seen as an attractive risk-hedging mechanism.

One alliance driven by these motivations is the Renault–Nissan partnership. These two companies came together in 1999, with Renault taking a 36 percent share in Nissan and installing Carlos Ghosn as its chief operating officer. Although Nissan's perilous financial position was evidently a key factor in the decision to bring in a foreign partner, the underlying driver of the alliance was the need—on both sides—for greater economies of scale and scope to achieve competitive parity with General Motors (GM), Ford, and Toyota. The alliance led to a surprisingly fast turnaround of Nissan's fortunes, largely through Ghosn's decisive leadership, and subsequently to a broad set of projects to deliver synergies in product development, manufacturing, and distribution. Although still much smaller than GM or Ford, Renault–Nissan is now believed likely to be one of the long-term surviving players in the global automobile industry. In the first half of fiscal 2008, Nissan sales grew significantly despite overall industry decline in the largest global markets.

Alliance as an Alternative to Merger

There remain industry sectors in which political, regulatory, and legal constraints limit the extent of cross-border mergers and acquisitions. In such cases, companies often create alliances not because they are inherently the most attractive organizational form but because they represent the best available alternative to a merger.

The classic examples of this phenomenon occur in the airline and telecommunications industries. Many countries still preclude foreign ownership in these industries. But a simple analysis of the economics of the industry—in terms of potential economies of scale, concentration of suppliers, opportunities for standardization of services, and competitive dynamics—would highlight the availability of substantial benefits from global integration. So as a means of generating at least some of the benefits of global integration but not breaking the rules against foreign ownership, most major airlines have formed themselves into marketing and code-sharing partnerships, including Star Alliance and OneWorld, and many telecom companies have formed telecommunications alliances.

Alliances of this type often lead to full-scale global integration if restrictions on foreign ownership are lifted. For example, as the telecommunications industry was gradually deregulated during the 1990s, alliances such as Concert and Unisource gave way to the emergence of true multinational players such as Verizon, Vodafone, Telefonica, France Telecom, and Deutsche Telekom.

The Risks and Costs of Collaboration

Because of these different motivations, there was an initial period of euphoria during which partnerships were seen as the panacea for most of MNEs' global strategic problems and opportunities. The euphoria of the 1980s to form relationships was fueled by two fashionable management concepts of the period: triad power[2] and stick to your knitting.[3]

The triad power concept emphasized the need to develop significant positions in the three key markets of the United States, western Europe, and Japan as a prerequisite for competing in global industries. Given the enormous costs and difficulties of accessing any one of these developed and highly competitive markets independently, many companies with unequal legs on their geographic stool regarded alliances as the only feasible way to develop this triadic position.

---

[2]See Kenichi Ohmae, *Triad Power* (New York: Free Press, 1985).

[3]This idea is one of the lessons developed in the highly influential book by Thomas Peters and Robert Waterman, *In Search of Excellence* (New York: Harper & Row, 1982).

The stick-to-your-knitting prescription in essence urged managers to disaggregate the value chain and focus their investments, efforts, and attention on only those tasks in which the company had a significant competitive advantage. Other operations were to be externalized through outsourcing or alliances. The seductive logic of both arguments, coupled with rapidly evolving environmental demands, led to an explosion in the formation of such alliances.

Since then, the experience companies have gathered through such collaborative ventures highlighted some of the costs and risks of such partnerships. Some risks arise from the simultaneous presence of both collaborative and competitive aspects in the relationships. Others arise from the higher levels of strategic and organizational complexity involved in managing cooperative relationships outside the company's own boundaries.

The Risks of Competitive Collaboration

Some strategic alliances—including some of the most visible—involve partners who are fierce competitors outside the specific scope of the cooperative venture. Such relationships create the possibility that the collaborative venture might be used by one or both partners to develop a competitive edge over the other, or at least that the benefits from the partnership will be asymmetrical for the two parties, which might change their relative competitive positions. There are several factors that might cause such asymmetry.

A partnership is often motivated by the desire to join and leverage complementary skills and resources. For example, the two partners may have access to different technologies that could be combined to create new businesses or products. For example, SonyEricsson was created to bring together Sony's world-leading capabilities in consumer electronics and design with Ericsson's advanced technological know-how in mobile phones and strong relationships with mobile operators. Such an arrangement for competency pooling inevitably entails the possibility that, in the course of the partnership, one of the partners will learn and internalize the other's skills while carefully protecting its own, thereby creating the option of discarding the partner and appropriating all the benefits created by the partnership. This possibility becomes particularly salient when the skills and competencies of one partner are tacit and deeply embedded in complex organizational processes (and thereby difficult to learn or emulate), whereas those of the other partner are explicit and embodied in specific individual machines or drawings (and thereby liable to relatively easy observation and emulation).

When General Foods entered into a partnership with Ajinimoto, the Japanese food giant, it agreed to make available its advanced processing technology for products such as freeze-dried coffee. In return, its Japanese partner would contribute its marketing expertise to launch the new products on the Japanese market. After several years, however, the collaboration deteriorated and was eventually dissolved when Ajinomoto had absorbed the technology transfer and management felt it was no longer learning from its American partner. Unfortunately, General Foods had not done such a good job learning about the Japanese market and left the alliance with some bitterness.

Another predatory tactic might involve capturing investment initiative to use the partnership to erode the other's competitive position. In this scenario, the company ensures that it, rather than the partner, makes and keeps control over the critical investments.

Such investments can be in the domain of product development, manufacturing, marketing, or wherever the most strategically vital part of the business value chain is located. Through these tactics, the aggressive company can strip its partner of the necessary infrastructure for competing independently and create one-way dependence in the collaboration that can be exploited at will.

Although they provide lively copy for magazine articles, such Machiavellian intentions and actions remain the exception, and the vast majority of cross-company collaborations are founded and maintained on a basis of mutual trust and shared commitment. Yet even the most carefully constructed strategic alliances can become problematic. Although many provide short-term solutions to some strategic problems, they also serve to hide the deeper and more fundamental deficiencies that cause those problems. The short-term solution takes the pressure off the problem without solving it and makes the company highly vulnerable when the problem finally resurfaces, usually in a more extreme and immediate form.

Furthermore, because such alliances typically involve task sharing, each company almost inevitably trades off some of the benefits of "learning by doing" the tasks that it externalizes to its partner. Thus, even in the best-case scenario of a partnership that fully meets all expectations, the very success of the partnership leads to some benefits for each partner and therefore to some strengthening of a competitor. Behind the success of the alliance, therefore, lies the ever-present possibility that a competitor's newly acquired strength will be used against its alliance partner in some future competitive battle.[4] Consider the example of Shanghai Automotive Industry Corp., one of China's larger state-owned enterprises. In April 2006, it announced that it was going to start producing a car under its own name. Shanghai Automotive had been operating large joint ventures with both Volkswagen and GM for the Chinese market for many years; under Chinese law, foreign companies wishing to produce automobiles in China must have a local partner who owns at least 50 percent of the business. Henceforth, the Volkswagen and GM joint ventures with Shanghai Automotive would be competing with Shanghai Automotive's wholly owned subsidiary. By 2009, SAIC had the largest market share in China.

Finally, there is the risk that collaborating with a competitor might be a precursor to a takeover by one of the firms. In early 2000, General Motors Defense was assessing whether to bid on a multibillion-dollar contract alone or in partnership with a firm that was much larger in this sector, General Dynamics. The company was concerned first with the short-term issue of building firewalls around information flows so that only contract-specific proprietary knowledge would be shared. More fundamentally though, it confronted the question of whether this partnership might lead to eventually being acquired. Although this question legitimately arises in many alliances and joint ventures, it is worth reiterating that in most instances, MNEs are able to resolve the risks and costs of collaboration.

The Cost of Strategic and Organizational Complexity

Cooperation is difficult to attain even in the best of circumstances. One of the strongest forces facilitating such behavior within a single company's internal operations is the

---

[4]These potential risks of competitive collaboration are the focus of Reading 6–2 by Gary Hamel, Yves L. Doz, and C. K. Prahalad, "Collaborate with Your Competitor—and Win," *Harvard Business Review*, January/February 1989.

understanding that the risks and rewards ultimately accrue to the company's own accounts and therefore, either directly or indirectly, to the participants. This basic motivation is diluted in strategic alliances. Furthermore, the scope of most alliances and the environmental uncertainties they inevitably face often prevent a clear understanding of the risks that might be incurred or rewards that might accrue in the course of the partnership's evolution. As a result, cooperation in the context of allocated risks and rewards and divided loyalties inevitably creates additional strategic and organizational complexity that in turn involves additional costs to manage.

International partnerships bring together companies that are often products of different economic, political, social, and cultural systems. Such differences in the administrative heritages of the partner companies, each of which brings its own strategic mentality and managerial practices to the venture, further exacerbate the organizational challenge. For example, tensions between Xerox and Fuji Xerox—a successful but often troubled relationship—were as much an outgrowth of the differences in the business systems in which each was located as of the differences in the corporate culture between the U.S. company and its Japanese joint venture.

Organizational complexity, due to the very broad scope of operations typical of many strategic alliances, also contributes to added difficulties. As we have described, one of the distinguishing characteristics of present-day alliances is that they often cover a broad range of activities. This expansion of scope requires partners not only to manage the many areas of contact within the alliance but also to coordinate the different alliance-related tasks within their own organizations. And the goals, tasks, and management processes for the alliance must be constantly monitored and adapted to changing conditions.

Building and Managing Collaborative Ventures

As we have described in the preceding sections, alliances are neither conventional organizations with fully internalized activities nor well-specified transaction relationships through which externalized activities may be linked by market-based contracts. Instead, they combine elements of both. The participating companies retain their own competitive strategies and performance expectations, as well as their national, ideological, and administrative identities. Yet to obtain the required benefits of a partnership, diverse organizational units in different companies and different countries must effectively and flexibly coordinate their activities.

There are numerous reasons such collaborative ventures inevitably present some significant management challenges: strategic and environmental disparities among the partners, lack of a common experience and perception base, difficulties in interfirm communication, conflicts of interest and priorities, and inevitable personal differences among the individuals who manage the interface. As a result, though it is clear to most managers that strategic alliances can provide great benefits, they also realize that there is a big difference between establishing alliances and making them work.

The challenge can be considered in two parts, reflecting the prealliance tasks of analysis, negotiation, and decision making and the postalliance tasks of coordination, integration, and adaptation.

Building Cooperative Ventures

The quality of the prealliance processes of partner selection and negotiation influence the clarity and reciprocity of mutual expectations from the alliance. There are three aspects of the prealliance process to which managers must pay close attention if the alliance is to have the best possible chance of success: partner selection, escalating commitment, and alliance scope.[5]

Partner Selection: Strategic and Organizational Analysis

The process of analyzing a potential partner's strategic and organizational capabilities is an important yet difficult prealliance task. Several factors impede the quality of the choice-making process.

The most important constraint lies in the availability of information required for an effective evaluation of the potential partner. Effective prealliance analysis needs data about the partner's relevant physical assets (e.g., the condition and productivity of plants and equipment), as well as less tangible assets (e.g., strength of brands, quality of customer relationships, level of technological expertise) and organizational capabilities (e.g., managerial competence, employee loyalty, shared values). The difficulty of obtaining such information in the short time limits in which most alliances are finalized is further complicated by the barriers of cultural and physical distance that MNEs must also overcome.

The pressures of time and distance sometimes result in suboptimal partner selection. As Figure 6-2 suggests, there is no real upside to selecting a partner who is competent but with whom you may not be comfortable working. Nor, however, should partners be selected on the basis of comfort rather than competence.

A key lesson emerging from the experience of most strategic alliances is that changes in each partner's competitive positions and strategic priorities have crucial impacts on the viability of the alliance over time. Even if the strategic trajectories of two companies cross at a particular point of time, creating complementarities and the potential for a partnership, their paths may be so divergent as to make such complementarities too transient for the alliance to have any lasting value. Case 6-3, about Eli Lilly in India, explores whether the Eli Lilly–Ranbaxy joint venture still meets each partner's strategic objectives, 15 years after it was established.

Although it is difficult enough to make a static assessment of a potential partner's strategic and organizational capabilities, it is almost impossible to make an effective prealliance analysis of how those capabilities are likely to evolve over time.

There probably is no solution to this problem, but companies that recognize alliances as a permanent and important part of their future organization have made monitoring their partners an ongoing rather than an ad hoc process. Some have linked such activities to their integrated business intelligence system, which was set up to monitor competitors. By having this group not only analyze competitors' potential strategies but also assess their value as acquisition or alliance candidates, these companies find themselves much better prepared when a specific alliance opportunity arises.

[5]The prealliance process is in many ways similar to a preacquisition process and shares the same needs. See David B. Jemison and Sim B. Sitkin, "Acquisitions: The Process Can Be a Problem," *Harvard Business Review*, no. 2 (1986), pp. 107–14.

Figure 6-2 Partner Selection: Comfort vs. Competence

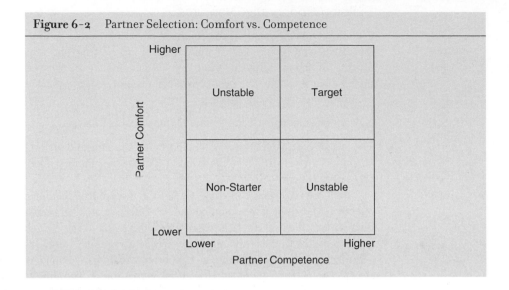

Escalating Commitment: Thrill of the Chase

The very process of alliance planning and negotiations can cause unrealistic expectations and wrong choices. In particular, some managers involved in the process can build up a great deal of personal enthusiasm and expectations in trying to sell the idea of the alliance within their own organization. This escalation process is similar to a process observed in many acquisition decisions where, in one manager's words, "The thrill of the chase blinds pursuers to the consequences of the catch." Because the champions of the idea—those most often caught in a spiral of escalating commitment—may not be the operational managers who are later given responsibility for making the alliance work, major problems arise when the latter are confronted with inevitable pitfalls and less visible problems.

The most effective way to control this escalation process is to ensure that at least the key operating managers likely to be involved in the implementation stage of the alliance are involved in the predecision negotiation process. Their involvement not only ensures greater commitment but also creates continuity between pre- and postalliance actions. But the greatest benefit accrues to the long-term understanding that must develop between the partners. By ensuring that the broader strategic goals that motivate the alliance are related to specific operational details in the negotiation stage, the companies can enhance the clarity and consistency of both the definition and the understanding of the alliance's goals and tasks. The Nora Sakari example in Case 6-1 considers in detail the challenges of negotiating such a venture.

Alliance Scope: Striving for Simplicity and Flexibility

All too often, in an effort to show commitment at the time of the agreement, partners press for broad and all-encompassing corporate partnerships and equity participation or exchange. Yet a key to successful alliance building lies in defining as simple and focused a scope for the partnership as is adequate to get the job done but to retain at the same time the possibility to redefine and broaden the scope if needed. Alliances that are more complex also require more management attention to succeed and tend to be more difficult to manage.

Three factors add to the management complexity of a partnership: complicated cross-holdings of ownership or equity, the need for cross-functional coordination or integration, and breadth in the number and scope of joint activities. Before involving any alliance in such potentially complicated arrangements, management should ask: "Are these conditions absolutely necessary, given our objectives?" If a simple OEM (original equipment manufacturer) arrangement can suffice, it is not only unnecessary to enter into a more committed alliance relationship but also is undesirable because the added complexity will increase the likelihood of problems and difficulties in achieving the objectives of the partnership.

At the same time, it might be useful to provide some flexibility in the terms of the alliance for renegotiating and changing the scope, if and when necessary. Even when a broad-based and multifaceted alliance represents the ultimate goal, many companies have found it preferable to start with a relatively simple and limited partnership whose scope is expanded gradually as both partners develop a better understanding of and greater trust in each other's motives, capabilities, and expectations.

Managing Cooperative Ventures

Although the prealliance analysis and negotiation processes are important, a company's ability to manage an ongoing relationship also tends to be a key determining factor for the success or failure of an alliance. Among the numerous issues that influence a company's ability to manage a cooperative venture, there are three that appear to present the greatest challenges: managing the boundary, managing knowledge flows, and providing strategic directions.

Managing the Boundary: Structuring the Interface

There are many different ways in which the partners can structure the boundary of an alliance and manage the interface between this boundary and their own organizations. At one extreme, an independent legal organization can be created and given complete freedom to manage the alliance tasks. Alternatively, the alliance's operations can be managed by one or both parents with more substantial strategic, operational, or administrative controls. In many cases, however, the creation of such a distinct entity is not necessary, and simpler, less bureaucratic governance mechanisms such as joint committees may be enough to guide and supervise shared tasks. Also, given the potentially enormous breadth in the scope of activities (see Figure 6-3), it may be more practical to start with a limited agreement. It is always easier to gain a partner's agreement to expand than to contract an alliance's terms of reference.

The choice among alternative boundary structures depends largely on the scope of the alliance. When the alliance's tasks are characterized by extensive functional interdependencies, there is a need for a high level of integration in the decision-making process related to those shared tasks. In such circumstances, the creation of a separate entity is

Figure 6-3   Scope of Activity

Narrow	vs.	Wide
Single, geographic market	vs.	Multi-country
Single function	vs.	Complete value chain
Single industry/customer group	vs.	Multi-industry
Modest investment	vs.	Large scale
Existing business	vs.	New business
Limited term	vs.	Forever

often the only effective way to manage such dense interlinkages. In contrast, an alliance between two companies with the objective of marketing each other's existing products in noncompetitive markets may need only a few simple rules that govern marketing parameters and financial arrangements and a single joint committee to review the outcomes periodically.

Managing Knowledge Flows: Integrating the Interface

Irrespective of the specific objectives of any alliance, the very process of collaboration creates flows of information across the boundaries of the participating companies and creates the potential for learning from each other. Managing these knowledge flows involves two kinds of tasks for the participating companies. First, they must ensure full exploitation of the created learning potential. Second, they must prevent the outflow of any information or knowledge they do not wish to share with their alliance partners.

In terms of the first point, the key problem is that the individuals managing the interface may not be the best users of such knowledge. To maximize its learning from a partnership, a company must effectively integrate its interface managers into the rest of its organization. The gatekeepers must have knowledge of and access to the different individuals and management groups within the company that are likely to benefit most from the diverse kinds of information that flow through an alliance boundary. Managers familiar with the difficulties of managing information flows within the company's boundaries will readily realize that such cross-boundary learning is unlikely to occur unless specific mechanisms are in place to make it happen.

The selection of appropriate interface managers is perhaps the single most important factor for facilitating such learning. Interface managers should have at least three key attributes: They must be well versed in the company's internal organizational process; they must have the personal credibility and status necessary to access key managers in different parts of the organization; and they must have a sufficiently broad understanding of the company's business and strategies to be able to recognize useful information and knowledge that might cross their path.

Merely placing the right managers at the interface is not sufficient to ensure effective learning, however. Supportive administrative processes also must be developed to facilitate the systematic transfer of information and monitor the effectiveness of those transfers. Such support is often achieved most effectively through simple systems and mechanisms, such as task forces or periodic review meetings.

While exploiting the alliance's learning potential, however, each company must also manage the interface to prevent unintended flows of information to its partner. It is a delicate balancing task for the gatekeepers to ensure the free flow of information across the organizational boundaries while effectively regulating the flow of people and data to ensure that sensitive or proprietary knowledge is appropriately protected.

Providing Strategic Direction: The Governance Structure

The key to providing leadership and direction, ensuring strategic control, and resolving interorganizational conflicts is an effective governance structure. Unlike acquisitions, alliances are often premised on the equality of both partners, but an obsession to protect such equality can prevent companies from creating an effective governance structure for the partnership. Committees consisting of an equal number of participants from both companies and operating under strict norms of equality are often incapable of providing clear directions or forcing conflict resolution at lower levels. Indeed, many otherwise well-conceived alliances have floundered because of their dependence on such committees for their leadership and control.

To find their way around such problems, partners must negotiate on the basis of "integrative" rather than "distributive" equality. With such an agreement, each committee is structured with clear, single-handed leadership, but each company takes the responsibility for different tasks. However, such delicately balanced arrangements can work only if the partners can agree on specific individuals, delegate the overall responsibility for the alliance to these individuals, and protect their ability to work in the best interests of the alliance itself rather than those of the parents.

Concluding Comments

Perspectives on strategic alliances have oscillated between the extremes of euphoria and disillusionment. Finally, however, there seems to be some recognition that though such partnerships may not represent perfect solutions, they are often the best solution available to a particular company at a particular point in time.

Easy—but Sometimes Not the Best Solution

Perhaps the biggest danger for many companies is to pretend that the "quick and easy" option of a strategic alliance is also the best or only option available. Cooperative arrangements are perhaps too tempting in catch-up situations in which the partnership might provide a façade of recovery that masks serious problems.

Yet, though going it alone may well be the most desirable option for a specific objective or task in the long term, almost no company can afford to meet all of its objectives in this way. When complete independence and self-sufficiency are not possible because of resource scarcity, lack of expertise, or time—or any other such constraint—strategic alliances often become the most realistic option.

Alliances Need Not Be Permanent

Another important factor commonly misunderstood is that the dissolution of a partnership is not synonymous with failure. Many companies appear to have suffered because of their unwillingness or inability to terminate partnership arrangements when changing circumstances made those arrangements inappropriate or because they failed to discuss upfront with their partner whether the alliance should have a sunset clause. All organizations create internal pressures for their own perpetuation, and an alliance is no exception to this enduring reality. One important task for senior managers of the participating companies is to ask periodically why the alliance should not be terminated and then continue with the arrangement only if they find compelling reasons to do so.

Flexibility Is Key

The original agreement for a partnership typically is based on limited information and unrealistic expectations. Experience gained from the actual process of working together provides the opportunity for fine-tuning and often finding better ways to achieve higher levels of joint value creation. In such circumstances, the flexibility to adapt the goals, scope, and management of the alliance to changing conditions is essential. In addition, changing environmental conditions may make original intentions and plans obsolete. Effective partnering requires the ability to monitor such changes and allow the partnership to evolve in response.

An Internal Knowledge Network: Basis for Learning

Learning is one of the main benefits that a company can derive from a partnership, irrespective of whether it represents one of the formal goals. For such learning to occur, however, a company must be receptive to the knowledge and skills available from the partner and have an organization able to diffuse and leverage such learning. In the absence of an internal knowledge network, information obtained from the partner cannot be transferred and applied, regardless of its potential value. Thus, building and managing an integrated network organization, as described in Chapter 4, is an essential prerequisite for not only effective internal processes but also effective management across organizational boundaries.

Chapter 6 Readings

- In Reading 6-1, Beamish discusses "The Design and Management of International Joint Ventures." This is typically the alliance form which requires the greatest level of interaction, cooperation, and investment. This reading focuses on two primary issues: the reasons why companies create international joint ventures, and the requirements for international joint venture success.

- In Reading 6-2, "Collaborate with Your Competitors—and Win," Hamel, Doz, and Prahalad focus on a special type of alliance: those formed with a competitor. Considered risky by many people, the authors demonstrate how companies can use such a collaboration to enhance their competitive strength. Consideration is given to "How to Build Secure Defenses" and the need to "Enhance the Capacity to Learn."

Case 6-1   Nora-Sakari: A Proposed JV in Malaysia (Revised)

R. Azimah Ainuddin and Paul Beamish

On Monday, July 15, 2003 Zainal Hashim, vice-chairman of Nora Holdings Sdn Bhd[1] (Nora), arrived at his office about an hour earlier than usual. As he looked out the window at the city spreading below, he thought about the Friday evening reception which he had hosted at his home in Kuala Lumpur (KL), Malaysia, for a team of negotiators from Sakari Oy[2] (Sakari) of Finland. Nora was a leading supplier of telecommunications (telecom) equipment in Malaysia while Sakari, a Finnish conglomerate, was a leader in the manufacture of cellular phone sets and switching systems. The seven-member team from Sakari was in KL to negotiate with Nora the formation of a joint-venture (JV) between the two telecom companies.

This was the final negotiation which would determine whether a JV agreement would materialize. The negotiation had ended late Friday afternoon, having lasted for five consecutive days. The JV Company, if established, would be set up in Malaysia to manufacture and commission digital switching exchanges to meet the needs of the telecom industry in Malaysia and in neighbouring countries, particularly Indonesia and Thailand. While Nora would benefit from the JV in terms of technology transfer, the venture would pave the way for Sakari to acquire knowledge and gain access to the markets of South-east Asia.

The Nora management was impressed by the Finnish capability in using high technology to enable Finland, a small country of only five million people, to have a fast-growing economy. Most successful Finnish companies were in the high-tech industries. For example, Kone was one of the world's three largest manufacturers of lifts, Vaisala was the world's major supplier of meteorological equipment, and Sakari was one of the leading telecom companies in Europe. It would be an invaluable opportunity for Nora to learn from the Finnish experience and emulate their success for Malaysia.

The opportunity emerged two and half years earlier when Peter Mattsson, president of Sakari's Asian regional office in Singapore, approached Zainal[3] to explore the possibility of forming a cooperative venture between Nora and Sakari. Mattsson said:

> While growth in the mobile telecommunications network is expected to be about 40 percent a year in Asia in the next five years, growth in fixed networks would not be as fast, but the projects are much larger. A typical mobile network project amounts to a maximum of €50 million, but fixed network projects can be estimated in hundreds of millions. In Malaysia and Thailand, such latter projects are currently approaching contract stage. Thus it is imperative that Sakari establish its presence in this region to capture a share in the fixed network market.

[1]Sdn Bhd is an abbreviation for Sendirian Berhad, which means private limited company in Malaysia.

[2]Oy is an abbreviation for Osakeyhtiot, which means private limited company in Finland.

[3]The first name is used because the Malay name does not carry a family name. The first and/or middle names belong to the individual and the last name is his/her father's name.

The large potential for telecom facilities was also evidenced in the low telephone penetration rates for most South-east Asian countries. For example, in 1999, telephone penetration rates (measured by the number of telephone lines per 100 people) for Indonesia, Thailand, Malaysia and the Philippines ranged from three to 20 lines per 100 people compared to the rates in developed countries such as Canada, Finland, Germany, United States and Sweden where the rates exceeded 55 telephone lines per 100 people.

The Telecom Industry in Malaysia

Telekom Malaysia Bhd (TMB), the national telecom company, was given the authority by the Malaysian government to develop the country's telecom infrastructure. With a paid-up capital of RM2.4 billion,[4] it was also given the mandate to provide telecom services that were on par with those available in developed countries.

TMB announced that it would be investing in the digitalization of its networks to pave the way for offering services based on the ISDN (integrated services digitalized network) standard, and investing in international fibre optic cable networks to meet the needs of increased telecom traffic between Malaysia and the rest of the world. TMB would also facilitate the installation of more cellular telephone networks in view of the increased demand for the use of mobile phones among the business community in KL and in major towns.

As the nation's largest telecom company, TMB's operations were regulated through a 20-year licence issued by the Ministry of Energy, Telecommunications and Posts. In line with the government's Vision 2020 program which targeted Malaysia to become a developed nation by the year 2020, there was a strong need for the upgrading of the telecom infrastructure in the rural areas. TMB estimated that it would spend more than RM1 billion each year on the installation of fixed networks, of which 25 percent would be allocated for the expansion of

rural telecom. The objective was to increase the level of telephone penetration rate to over 50 percent by the year 2005.

Although TMB had become a large national telecom company, it lacked the expertise and technology to undertake massive infrastructure projects. In most cases, the local telecom companies would be invited to submit their bids for a particular contract. It was also common for these local companies to form partnerships with large multinational corporations (MNCs), mainly for technological support. For example, Pernas-NEC, a JV company between Pernas Holdings and NEC, was one of the companies that had been successful in securing large telecom contracts from the Malaysian authorities.

Nora's Search for a JV Partner

In October 2002, TMB called for tenders to bid on a five-year project worth RM2 billion for installing digital switching exchanges in various parts of the country. The project also involved replacing analog circuit switches with digital switches. Digital switches enhanced transmission capabilities of telephone lines, increasing capacity to approximately two million bits per second compared to the 9,600 bits per second on analog circuits.

Nora was interested in securing a share of the RM2 billion contract from TMB and more importantly, in acquiring the knowledge in switching technology from its partnership with a telecom MNC. During the initial stages, when Nora first began to consider potential partners in the bid for this contract, telecom MNCs such as Siemens, Alcatel, and Fujitsu seemed appropriate candidates. Nora had previously entered into a five-year technical assistance agreement with Siemens to manufacture telephone handsets.

Nora also had the experience of a long-term working relationship with Japanese partners which would prove valuable should a JV be formed with Fujitsu. Alcatel was another potential partner, but the main concern at Nora was that the technical standards used in the French technology were not compatible with the British standards already

---

[4]RM is Ringgit Malaysia, the Malaysian currency. As at December 31, 2002, US$1 = RM3.80.

adopted in Malaysia. NEC and Ericsson were not considered, as they were already involved with other local competitors and were the current suppliers of digital switching exchanges to TMB. Their five-year contracts were due to expire soon.

Subsequent to Zainal's meeting with Mattsson, he decided to consider Sakari as a serious potential partner. He was briefed about Sakari's SK33, a digital switching system that was based on an open architecture, which enabled the use of standard components, standard software development tools, and standard software languages. Unlike the switching exchanges developed by NEC and Ericsson which required the purchase of components developed by the parent companies, the SK33 used components that were freely available in the open market. The system was also modular, and its software could be upgraded to provide new services and could interface easily with new equipment in the network. This was the most attractive feature of the SK33 as it would lead to the development of new switching systems.

Mattsson had also convinced Zainal and other Nora managers that although Sakari was a relatively small player in fixed networks, these networks were easily adaptable, and could cater to large exchanges in the urban areas as well as small ones for rural needs. Apparently Sakari's smaller size, compared to that of some of the other MNCs, was an added strength because Sakari was prepared to work out customized products according to Nora's needs. Large telecom companies were alleged to be less willing to provide custom-made products. Instead, they tended to offer standard products that, in some aspects, were not consistent with the needs of the customer.

Prior to the July meeting, at least 20 meetings had been held either in KL or in Helsinki to establish relationships between the two companies. It was estimated that each side had invested not less than RM3 million in promoting the relationship. Mattsson and Ilkka Junttila, Sakari's representative in KL, were the key people in bringing the two companies together. (See Exhibits 1 and 2 for brief background information on Malaysia and Finland respectively.)

Nora Holdings Sdn Bhd

The Company Nora was one of the leading companies in the telecom industry in Malaysia. It was established in 1975 with a paid-up capital of RM2 million. Last year, the company recorded a turnover of RM320 million. Nora Holdings consisted of 30 subsidiaries, including two public-listed companies: Multiphone Bhd, and Nora Telecommunications Bhd. Nora had 3,081 employees, of which 513 were categorized as managerial (including 244 engineers) and 2,568 as non-managerial (including 269 engineers and technicians).

The Cable Business Since the inception of the company, Nora had secured two cable-laying projects. For the latter project worth RM500 million, Nora formed a JV with two Japanese companies, Sumitomo Electric Industries Ltd (held 10 percent equity share) and Marubeni Corporation (held five percent equity share). Japanese partners were chosen in view of the availability of a financial package that came together with the technological assistance needed by Nora. Nora also acquired a 63 percent stake in a local cable-laying company, Selangor Cables Sdn Bhd.

The Telephone Business Nora had become a household name in Malaysia as a telephone manufacturer. It started in 1980 when the company obtained a contract to supply telephone sets to the government-owned Telecom authority, TMB, which would distribute the sets to telephone subscribers on a rental basis. The contract, estimated at RM130 million, lasted for 15 years. In 1985 Nora secured licenses from Siemens and Nortel to manufacture telephone handsets and had subsequently developed Nora's own telephone sets—the N300S (single line), N300M (micro-computer controlled), and N300V (hands-free, voice-activated) models.

Upon expiry of the 15-year contract as a supplier of telephone sets to the TMB, Nora suffered a major setback when it lost a RM32 million contract to supply 600,000 N300S single line telephones. The contract was instead given to a Taiwanese manufacturer, Formula Electronics, which quoted a lower

Exhibit 1   Malaysia: Background Information

Malaysia is centrally located in South-east Asia. It consists of Peninsular Malaysia, bordered by Thailand in the north and Singapore in the south, and the states of Sabah and Sarawak on the island of Borneo. Malaysia has a total land area of about 330,000 square kilometres, of which 80 percent is covered with tropical rainforest. Malaysia has an equatorial climate with high humidity and high daily temperatures of about 26 degrees Celsius throughout the year.

In 2000, Malaysia's population was 22 million, of which approximately nine million made up the country's labour force. The population is relatively young, with 42 percent between the ages of 15 and 39 and only seven percent above the age of 55. A Malaysian family has an average of four children and extended families are common. Kuala Lumpur, the capital city of Malaysia, has approximately 1.5 million inhabitants.

The population is multiracial; the largest ethnic group is the Bumiputeras (the Malays and other indigenous groups such as the Ibans in Sarawak and Kadazans in Sabah), followed by the Chinese and Indians. Bahasa Malaysia is the national language but English is widely used in business circles. Other major languages spoken included various Chinese dialects and Tamil.

Islam is the official religion but other religions (mainly Christianity, Buddhism and Hinduism) are widely practised. Official holidays are allocated for the celebration of Eid, Christmas, Chinese New Year and Deepavali. All Malays are Muslims, followers of the Islamic faith.

During the period of British rule, secularism was introduced to the country, which led to the separation of the Islamic religion from daily life. In the late 1970s and 1980s, realizing the negative impact of secularism on the life of the Muslims, several groups of devout Muslims undertook efforts to reverse the process, emphasizing a dynamic and progressive approach to Islam. As a result, changes were introduced to meet the daily needs of Muslims. Islamic banking and insurance facilities were introduced and prayer rooms were provided in government offices, private companies, factories, and even in shopping complexes.

Malaysia is a parliamentary democracy under a constitutional monarchy. The Yang DiPertuan Agung (the king) is the supreme head, and appoints the head of the ruling political party to be the prime minister. In 2000 the Barisan Nasional, a coalition of several political parties representing various ethnic groups, was the ruling political party in Malaysia. Its predominance had contributed not only to the political stability and economic progress of the country in the last two decades, but also to the fast recovery from the 1997 Asian economic crisis.

The recession of the mid 1980s led to structural changes in the Malaysian economy which had been too dependent on primary commodities (rubber, tin, palm oil and timber) and had a very narrow export base. To promote the establishment of export-oriented industries, the government directed resources to the manufacturing sector, introduced generous incentives and relaxed foreign equity restrictions. In the meantime, heavy investments were made to modernize the country's infrastructure. These moves led to rapid economic growth in the late 1980s and early 1990s. The growth had been mostly driven by exports, particularly of electronics.

The Malaysian economy was hard hit by the 1997 Asian economic crisis. However, Malaysia was the fastest country to recover from the crisis after declining IMF assistance. It achieved this by pegging its currency to the USD, restricting outflow of money from the country, banning illegal overseas derivative trading of Malaysian securities and setting up asset management companies to facilitate the orderly recovery of bad loans. The real GDP growth rate in 1999 and 2000 were 5.4% and 8.6%, respectively (Table 1).

Malaysia was heavily affected by the global economic downturn and the slump in the IT sector in 2001 and 2002 due to its export-based economy. GDP in 2001 grew only 0.4% due to an 11% decrease in exports. A US $1.9 billion fiscal stimulus package helped the country ward off the worst of the recession and the GDP growth rate rebounded to 4.2% in 2002 (Table 1). A relatively small foreign debt and adequate foreign exchange reserves make a crisis similar to the 1997 one unlikely. Nevertheless, the economy remains vulnerable to a more protracted slowdown in the US and Japan, top export destinations and key sources of foreign investment.

(continued)

Exhibit 1   (concluded)

Table 1   Malaysian Economic Performance 1999 to 2002

Economic Indicator	1999	2000	2001	2002
GDP per capita (US$)	3,596	3,680	3,678	3,814
Real GDP growth rate	5.4%	8.6%	0.4%	4.2%
Consumer price inflation	2.8%	1.6%	1.4%	1.8%
Unemployment rate	3.0%	3.0%	3.7%	3.5%

Source: IMD. Various years. "The World Competitiveness Report."

In 2002, the manufacturing sector was the leading contributor to the economy, accounting for about 30 percent of gross national product (GDP). Malaysia's major trading partners are United States, Singapore, Japan, China, Taiwan, Hong Kong and Korea.

Source: Ernst & Young International. 1993. "Doing Business in Malaysia." Other online sources.

Exhibit 2   Finland: Background Information

Finland is situated in the north-east of Europe, sharing borders with Sweden, Norway and the former Soviet Union. About 65 percent of its area of 338,000 square kilometres is covered with forest, about 15 percent lakes and about 10 percent arable land. Finland has a temperate climate with four distinct seasons. In Helsinki, the capital city, July is the warmest month with average mid-day temperature of 21 degrees Celsius and January is the coldest month with average mid-day temperature of –3 degrees Celsius.

Finland is one of the most sparsely populated countries in Europe with a 2002 population of 5.2 million, 60 percent of whom lived in the urban areas. Helsinki had a population of about 560,000 in 2002. Finland has a well-educated work force of about 2.3 million. About half of the work force are engaged in providing services, 30 percent in manufacturing and construction, and eight percent in agricultural production. The small size of the population has led to scarce and expensive labour. Thus Finland had to compete by exploiting its lead in high-tech industries.

Finland's official languages are Finnish and Swedish, although only six percent of the population speaks Swedish. English is the most widely spoken foreign language. About 87 percent of the Finns are Lutherans and about one percent Finnish Orthodox.

Finland has been an independent republic since 1917, having previously been ruled by Sweden and Russia. A President is elected to a six-year term, and a 200-member, single-chamber parliament is elected every four years.

In 1991, the country experienced a bad recession triggered by a sudden drop in exports due to the collapse of the Soviet Union. During 1991–1993, the total output suffered a 10% contraction and unemployment rate reached almost 20%. Finnish Markka experienced a steep devaluation in 1991–1992, which gave Finland cost competitiveness in international market.

With this cost competitiveness and the recovery of Western export markets the Finnish economy underwent a rapid revival in 1993, followed by a new period of healthy growth. Since the mid 1990s the Finnish growth has mainly been bolstered by intense growth in telecommunications equipment manufacturing. The Finnish economy peaked in the year 2000 with a real GDP growth rate of 5.6% (Table 2).

Finland was one of the 11 countries that joined the Economic and Monetary Union (EMU) on January 1, 1999. Finland has been experiencing a rapidly increasing integration with Western Europe. Membership in the EMU provide the

(*continued*)

Exhibit 2   (*concluded*)

Table 2   Finnish Economic Performance 1999 to 2002

Economic Indicator	1999	2000	2001	2002
GDP per capita (US$)	24,430	23,430	23,295	25,303
Real GDP growth rate	3.7%	5.6%	0.4%	1.6%
Consumer price inflation	1.2%	3.3%	2.6%	1.6%
Unemployment	10.3%	9.6%	9.1%	9.1%

Source: IMD. various years. "The World Competitiveness Report."

Finnish economy with an array of benefits, such as lower and stable interest rates, elimination of foreign currency risk within the Euro area, reduction of transaction costs of business and travel, and so forth. This provided Finland with a credibility that it lacked before accession and the Finnish economy has become more predictable. This will have a long-term positive effect on many facets of the economy.

Finland's economic structure is based on private ownership and free enterprise. However, the production of alcoholic beverages and spirits is retained as a government monopoly. Finland's major trading partners are Sweden, Germany, the former Soviet Union and United Kingdom.

Finland's standard of living is among the highest in the world. The Finns have small families with one or two children per family. They have comfortable homes in the cities and one in every three families has countryside cottages near a lake where they retreat on weekends. Taxes are high, the social security system is efficient and poverty is virtually non-existent.

Until recently, the stable trading relationship with the former Soviet Union and other Scandinavian countries led to few interactions between the Finns and people in other parts of the world. The Finns are described as rather reserved, obstinate, and serious people. A Finn commented, "We do not engage easily in small talk with strangers. Furthermore, we have a strong love for nature and we have the tendency to be silent as we observe our surroundings. Unfortunately, others tend to view such behaviour as cold and serious." Visitors to Finland are often impressed by the efficient public transport system, the clean and beautiful city of Helsinki with orderly road networks, scenic parks and lakefronts, museums, cathedrals, and churches.

Source: Ernst & Young International. 1993. "Doing Business in Finland." Other online sources.

price of RM37 per handset compared to Nora's RM54. Subsequently, Nora was motivated to move towards the high end feature phone domestic market. The company sold about 3,000 sets of feature phones per month, capturing the high-end segment of the Malaysian market.

Nora had ventured into the export market with its feature phones, but industry observers predicted that Nora still had a long way to go as an exporter. The foreign markets were very competitive and many manufacturers already had well-established brands.

The Payphone Business   Nora's start-up in the payphone business had turned out to be one of the company's most profitable lines of business. Other than the cable-laying contract secured in 1980, Nora had a 15-year contract to install, operate and maintain payphones in the cities and major towns in Malaysia. In 1997, Nora started to manufacture card payphones under a license from GEC Plessey Telecommunications (GPT) of the United Kingdom. The agreement had also permitted Nora to sell the products to the neighbouring countries in South-east Asia as well as to eight other markets approved by GPT.

While the payphone revenues were estimated to be as high as RM60 million a year, a long-term and stable income stream for Nora, profit margins were only about 10 percent because of the high investment and maintenance costs.

Other Businesses Nora was also the sole Malaysian distributor for Nortel's private automatic branch exchange (PABX) and NEC's mobile telephone sets. It was also an Apple computer distributor in Malaysia and Singapore. In addition, Nora was involved in: distributing radio-related equipment; supplying equipment to the broadcasting, meteorological, civil aviation, postal and power authorities; and manufacturing automotive parts (such as the suspension coil, springs, and piston) for the local automobile companies.

The Management When Nora was established, Osman Jaafar, founder and chairman of Nora Holdings, managed the company with his wife, Nora Asyikin Yusof, and seven employees. Osman was known as a conservative businessman who did not like to dabble in acquisitions and mergers to make quick capital gains. He was formerly an electrical engineer who was trained in the United Kingdom and had held several senior positions at the national Telecom Department in Malaysia.

Osman subsequently recruited Zainal Hashim to fill in the position of deputy managing director at Nora. Zainal held a master's degree in microwave communications from a British university and had several years of working experience as a production engineer at Pernas-NEC Sdn Bhd, a manufacturer of transmission equipment. Zainal was later promoted to the position of managing director and six years later, the vice-chairman.

Industry analysts observed that Nora's success was attributed to the complementary roles, trust, and mutual understanding between Osman and Zainal. While Osman "likes to fight for new business opportunities," Zainal preferred a low profile and concentrated on managing Nora's operations.

Industry observers also speculated that Osman, a former civil servant and an entrepreneur, was close to Malaysian politicians, notably the Prime Minister, while Zainal had been a close friend of the Finance Minister. Zainal disagreed with allegations that Nora had succeeded due to its close relationships with Malaysian politicians. However, he acknowledged that such perceptions in the industry had been beneficial to the company.

Osman and Zainal had an obsession for high-tech and made the development of research and development (R&D) skills and resources a priority in the company. About one percent of Nora's earnings was ploughed back into R&D activities. Although this amount was considered small by international standards, Nora planned to increase it gradually to five to six percent over the next two to three years. Zainal said:

> We believe in making improvements in small steps, similar to the Japanese *kaizen* principle. Over time, each small improvement could lead to a major creation. To be able to make improvements, we must learn from others. Thus we would borrow a technology from others, but eventually, we must be able to develop our own to sustain our competitiveness in the industry. As a matter of fact, Sakari's SK33 system was developed based on a technology it obtained from Alcatel.

To further enhance R&D activities at Nora, Nora Research Sdn Bhd (NRSB), a wholly-owned subsidiary, was formed, and its R&D department was absorbed into this new company. NRSB operated as an independent research company undertaking R&D activities for Nora as well as private clients in related fields. The company facilitated R&D activities with other companies as well as government organizations, research institutions, and universities. NRSB, with its staff of 40 technicians/engineers, would charge a fixed fee for basic research and a royalty for its products sold by clients.

Zainal was also active in instilling and promoting Islamic values among the Malay employees at Nora. He explained:

> Islam is a way of life and there is no such thing as Islamic management. The Islamic values, which must be reflected in the daily life of Muslims, would influence their behaviours as employers and employees. Our Malay managers, however, were often influenced by their western counterparts, who tend to stress knowledge and mental capability and often forget the effectiveness of the softer side of management which emphasizes relationships, sincerity and consistency. I believe that one must always be sincere to be able to develop good working relationships.

Sakari Oy

Sakari was established in 1865 as a pulp and paper mill located about 200 kilometres northwest of Helsinki, the capital city of Finland. In the 1960s, Sakari started to expand into the rubber and cable industries when it merged with the Finnish Rubber Works and Finnish Cable Works. In 1973 Sakari's performance was badly affected by the oil crisis, as its businesses were largely energy-intensive.

However, in 1975, the company recovered when Aatos Olkkola took over as Sakari's president. He led Sakari into competitive businesses such as computers, consumer electronics, and cellular phones via a series of acquisitions, mergers and alliances. Companies involved in the acquisitions included: the consumer electronics division of Standard Elektrik Lorenz AG; the data systems division of L.M. Ericsson; Vantala, a Finnish manufacturer of colour televisions; and Luxury, a Swedish state-owned electronics and computer concern.

In 1979, a JV between Sakari and Vantala, Sakari-Vantala, was set up to develop and manufacture mobile telephones. Sakari-Vantala had captured about 14 percent of the world's market share for mobile phones and held a 20 percent market share in Europe for its mobile phone handsets. Outside Europe, a 50-50 JV was formed with Tandy Corporation which, to date, had made significant sales in the United States, Malaysia and Thailand.

Sakari first edged into the telecom market by selling switching systems licensed from France's Alcatel and by developing the software and systems to suit the needs of small Finnish phone companies. Sakari had avoided head-on competition with Siemens and Ericsson by not trying to enter the market for large telephone networks. Instead, Sakari had concentrated on developing dedicated telecom networks for large private users such as utility and railway companies. In Finland, Sakari held 40 percent of the market for digital exchanges. Other competitors included Ericsson (34 percent), Siemens (25 percent), and Alcatel (one percent).

Sakari was also a niche player in the global switching market. Its SK33 switches had sold well in countries such as Sri Lanka, United Arab Emirates, China and the Soviet Union. A derivative of the SK33 main exchange switch called the SK33XT was subsequently developed to be used in base stations for cellular networks and personal paging systems.

Sakari attributed its emphasis on R&D as its key success factor in the telecom industry. Strong in-house R&D in core competence areas enabled the company to develop technology platforms such as its SK33 system that were reliable, flexible, widely compatible and economical. About 17 percent of its annual sales revenue was invested into R&D and product development units in Finland, United Kingdom and France. Sakari's current strategy was to emphasize global operations in production and R&D. It planned to set up R&D centres in leading markets, including South-east Asia.

Sakari was still a small company by international standards (see Exhibit 3 for a list of the world's major telecom equipment suppliers). It lacked a strong marketing capability and had to rely on JVs such as the one with Tandy Corporation to enter the world market, particularly the United States. In its efforts to develop market position quickly, Sakari had to accept lower margins for its products, and often the Sakari name was not revealed on the product. In recent years, Sakari decided to emerge from its hiding place as a manufacturer's manufacturer and began marketing under the Sakari name.

In 1989 Mikko Koskinen took over as president of Sakari. Koskinen announced that telecommunications, computers, and consumer electronics would be maintained as Sakari's core business, and that he would continue Olkkola's efforts in expanding the company overseas. He believed that every European company needed global horizons to be able to meet global competition for future survival. To do so, he envisaged the setting up of alliances of varying duration, each designed for specific purposes. He said, "Sakari has become an interesting partner with which to cooperate on an equal footing in the areas of R&D, manufacturing and marketing."

The recession in Finland which began in 1990 led Sakari's group sales to decline substantially

Exhibit 3   Ten Major Telecommunication Equipment Vendors

Rank	Company	Country	1998 Telecom Equipment Sales (US$ billions)
1	Lucent	USA	26.8
2	Ericsson	Sweden	21.5
3	Alcatel	France	20.9
4	Motorola	USA	20.5
5	Nortel	Canada	17.3
6	Siemens	Germany	16.8
7	Nokia	Finland	14.7
8	NEC	Japan	12.6
9	Cisco	USA	8.4
10	Hughes	USA	5.7

Source: International Telecommunication Union. 1999. Top 20 Telecommunication Equipment Vendors 1998. http://www.itu.int/ITU-D/ict/statistics/at_glance/Top2098.html.

from FIM22 billion[5] in 1990 to FIM15 billion in 1991. The losses were attributed to two main factors: weak demand for Sakari's consumer electronic products, and trade with the Soviet Union which had come to almost a complete standstill. Consequently Sakari began divesting its less profitable companies within the basic industries (metal, rubber, and paper), as well as leaving the troubled European computer market with the sale of its computer subsidiary, Sakari Macro. The company's new strategy was to focus on three main areas: telecom systems and mobile phones in a global framework, consumer electronic products in Europe, and deliveries of cables and related technology. The company's divestment strategy led to a reduction of Sakari's employees from about 41,000 in 1989 to 29,000 in 1991. This series of major strategic moves was accompanied by major leadership succession. In June 1992, Koskinen retired as Sakari's President and was replaced by Visa Ketonen, formerly the President of Sakari Mobile

Phones. Ketonen appointed Ossi Kuusisto as Sakari's vice-president.

After Ketonen took over control, the Finnish economy went through a rapid revival in 1993, followed by a new period of intense growth. Since the mid 1990s the Finnish growth had been bolstered by intense growth in telecommunications equipment manufacturing as a result of exploding global telecommunications market. Sakari capitalized on this opportunity and played a major role in the Finnish telecommunications equipment manufacturing sector.

In 2001, Sakari was Finland's largest publicly-traded industrial company and derived the majority of its total sales from exports and overseas operations. Traditionally, the company's export sales were confined to other Scandinavian countries, Western Europe and the former Soviet Union. However, in recent years, the company made efforts and succeeded in globalizing and diversifying its operations to make the most of its high-tech capabilities. As a result, Sakari emerged as a more influential player in the international market and had gained international brand recognition. One of Sakari's strategies was to form JVs to enter new foreign markets.

---

[5]FIM is Finnish Markka, the Finnish currency until January 1, 1999. Markka coins and notes were not withdrawn from circulation until January 1, 2002, when Finland fully converted to the Euro. As at December 31, 2000, US$1 = FIM6.31, and €1 = FIM5.95.

▓ The Nora-Sakari Negotiation

Nora and Sakari had discussed the potential of forming a JV company in Malaysia for more than two years. Nora engineers were sent to Helsinki to assess the SK33 technology in terms of its compatibility with the Malaysian requirements, while Sakari managers travelled to KL mainly to assess both Nora's capability in manufacturing switching exchanges and the feasibility of gaining access to the Malaysian market.

In January 2003, Nora submitted its bid for TMB's RM2 billion contract to supply digital switching exchanges supporting four million telephone lines. Assuming the Nora-Sakari JV would materialize, Nora based its bid on supplying Sakari's digital switching technology. Nora competed with seven other companies short listed by TMB, all offering their partners' technology— Alcatel, Lucent, Fujitsu, Siemens, Ericsson, NEC, and Samsung. In early May, TMB announced five successful companies in the bid. They were companies using technology from Alcatel, Fujitsu, Ericsson, NEC, and Sakari. Each company was awarded one-fifth share of the RM2 billion contract and would be responsible in delivering 800,000 telephone lines over a period of five years. Industry observers were critical of TMB's decision to select Sakari and Alcatel. Sakari was perceived to be the least capable in supplying the necessary lines to meet TMB's requirements, as it was alleged to be a small company with little international exposure. Alcatel was criticized for having the potential of supplying an obsolete technology.

The May 21 Meeting   Following the successful bid and ignoring the criticisms against Sakari, Nora and Sakari held a major meeting in Helsinki on May 21 to finalize the formation of the JV. Zainal led Nora's five-member negotiation team which comprised Nora's general manager for corporate planning division, an accountant, two engineers, and Marina Mohamed, a lawyer. One of the engineers was Salleh Lindstrom who was of Swedish origin, a Muslim and had worked for Nora for almost 10 years.

Sakari's eight-member team was led by Kuusisto, Sakari's vice-president. His team comprised Junttila, Hussein Ghazi, Aziz Majid, three engineers, and Julia Ruola (a lawyer). Ghazi was Sakari's senior manager who was of Egyptian origin and also a Muslim who had worked for Sakari for more than 20 years while Aziz, a Malay, had been Sakari's manager for more than 12 years.

The meeting went on for several days. The main issue raised at the meeting was Nora's capability in penetrating the South-east Asian market. Other issues included Sakari's concerns over the efficiency of Malaysian workers in the JV in manufacturing the product, maintaining product quality and ensuring prompt deliveries.

Commenting on the series of negotiations with Sakari, Zainal said that this was the most difficult negotiation he had ever experienced. Zainal was Nora's most experienced negotiator and had single-handedly represented Nora in several major negotiations for the past 10 years. In the negotiation with Sakari, Zainal admitted making the mistake of approaching the negotiation applying the approach he often used when negotiating with his counterparts from companies based in North America or the United Kingdom. He said:

> Negotiators from the United States tend to be very open and often state their positions early and definitively. They are highly verbal and usually prepare well-planned presentations. They also often engage in small talk and 'joke around' with us at the end of a negotiation. In contrast, the Sakari negotiators tend to be very serious, reserved and 'cold.' They are also relatively less verbal and do not convey much through their facial expressions. As a result, it was difficult for us to determine whether they are really interested in the deal or not.

Zainal said that the negotiation on May 21 turned out to be particularly difficult when Sakari became interested in bidding a recently-announced tender for a major telecom contract in the United Kingdom. Internal politics within Sakari led to the formation of two opposing "camps." One "camp" held a strong belief that there would be very high growth in the Asia-Pacific region and that the JV company in

Malaysia was seen as a hub to enter these markets. Although the Malaysian government had liberalized its equity ownership restrictions and allowed the formation of wholly-owned subsidiaries, JVs were still an efficient way to enter the Malaysian market for a company that lacked local knowledge. This group was represented mostly by Sakari's managers positioned in Asia and engineers who had made several trips to Malaysia, which usually included visits to Nora's facilities. They also had the support of Sakari's vice-president, Kuusisto, who was involved in most of the meetings with Nora, particularly when Zainal was present. Kuusisto had also made efforts to be present at meetings held in KL. This group also argued that Nora had already obtained the contract in Malaysia whereas the chance of getting the U.K. contract was quite low in view of the intense competition prevailing in that market.

The "camp" not in favour of the Nora-Sakari JV believed that Sakari should focus its resources on entering the United Kingdom, which could be used as a hub to penetrate the European Union (EU) market. There was also the belief that Europe was closer to home, making management easier, and that problems arising from cultural differences would be minimized. This group was also particularly concerned that Nora had the potential of copying Sakari's technology and eventually becoming a strong regional competitor. Also, because the U.K. market was relatively "familiar" and Sakari has local knowledge, Sakari could set up a wholly-owned subsidiary instead of a JV company and consequently, avoid JV-related problems such as joint control, joint profits, and leakage of technology.

Zainal felt that the lack of full support from Sakari's management led to a difficult negotiation when new misgivings arose concerning Nora's capability to deliver its part of the deal. It was apparent that the group in favour of the Nora—Sakari JV was under pressure to further justify its proposal and provide counterarguments against the U.K. proposal. A Sakari manager explained, "We are tempted to pursue both proposals since each has its own strengths, but our current resources are very limited. Thus a choice has to made, and soon."

The July 8 Meeting   Another meeting to negotiate the JV agreement was scheduled for July 8. Sakari's eight-member team arrived in KL on Sunday afternoon of July 7, and was met at the airport by the key Nora managers involved in the negotiation. Kuusisto did not accompany the Sakari team at this meeting.

The negotiation started early Monday morning at Nora's headquarters and continued for the next five days, with each day's meeting ending late in the evening. Members of the Nora team were the same members who had attended the May 21 meeting in Finland, except Zainal, who did not participate. The Sakari team was also represented by the same members in attendance at the previous meeting plus a new member, Solail Pekkarinen, Sakari's senior accountant. Unfortunately, on the third day of the negotiation, the Nora team requested that Sakari ask Pekkarinen to leave the negotiation. He was perceived as extremely arrogant and insensitive to the local culture, which tended to value modesty and diplomacy. Pekkarinen left for Helsinki the following morning.

Although Zainal had decided not to participate actively in the negotiations, he followed the process closely and was briefed by his negotiators regularly. Some of the issues which they complained were difficult to resolve had often led to heated arguments between the two negotiating teams. These included:

1. Equity Ownership   In previous meetings both companies agreed to form the JV company with a paid-up capital of RM5 million. However, they disagreed on the equity share proposed by each side. Sakari proposed an equity split in the JV company of 49 percent for Sakari and 51 percent for Nora. Nora, on the other hand, proposed a 30 percent Sakari and 70 percent Nora split. Nora's proposal was based on the common practice in Malaysia as a result of historical foreign equity regulations set by the Malaysian government that allowed a maximum of 30 percent foreign equity ownership unless the company would export a certain percentage of its products. Though these regulations were liberalized by the Malaysian government effective from July,

1998 and new regulations had replaced the old ones, the 30–70 foreign—Malaysian ownership divide was still commonly observed.

Equity ownership became a major issue as it was associated with control over the JV company. Sakari was concerned about its ability to control the accessibility of its technology to Nora and about decisions concerning the activities of the JV as a whole. The lack of control was perceived by Sakari as an obstacle to protecting its interests. Nora also had similar concerns about its ability to exert control over the JV because it was intended as a key part of Nora's long-term strategy to develop its own digital switching exchanges and related high-tech products.

2. Technology Transfer   Sakari proposed to provide the JV company with the basic structure of the digital switch. The JV company would assemble the switching exchanges at the JV plant and subsequently install the exchanges in designated locations identified by TMB. By offering Nora only the basic structure of the switch, the core of Sakari's switching technology would still be well-protected.

On the other hand, Nora proposed that the basic structure of the switch be developed at the JV company in order to access the root of the switching technology. Based on Sakari's proposal, Nora felt that only the technical aspects in assembling and installing the exchanges would be obtained. This was perceived as another "screw-driver" form of technology transfer while the core of the technology associated with making the switches would still be unknown.

3. Royalty Payment   Closely related to the issue of technology transfer was the payment of a royalty for the technology used in building the switches. Sakari proposed a royalty payment of five percent of the JV gross sales while Nora proposed a payment of two percent of net sales.

Nora considered the royalty rate of five percent too high because it would affect Nora's financial situation as a whole. Financial simulations prepared by Nora's managers indicated that Nora's return on investment would be less than the desired 10 percent if royalty rates exceeded three percent of net sales. This was because Nora had already agreed to make

large additional investments in support of the JV. Nora would invest in a building which would be rented to the JV company to accommodate an office and the switching plant. Nora would also invest in another plant which would supply the JV with surface mounted devices (SMD), one of the major components needed to build the switching exchanges.

An added argument raised by the Nora negotiators in support of a two percent royalty was that Sakari would receive side benefits from the JV's access to Japanese technology used in the manufacture of the SMD components. Apparently the Japanese technology was more advanced than Sakari's present technology.

4. Expatriates' Salaries and Perks   To allay Sakari's concerns over Nora's level of efficiency, Nora suggested that Sakari provide the necessary training for the JV technical employees. Subsequently, Sakari had agreed to provide eight engineering experts for the JV company on two types of contracts, short-term and long-term. Experts employed on a short-term basis would be paid a daily rate of US$1260 plus travel/accommodation. The permanent experts would be paid a monthly salary of US$20,000. Three permanent experts would be attached to the JV company once it was established and the number would gradually be reduced to only one, after two years. Five experts would be available on a short-term basis to provide specific training needs for durations of not more than three months each year.

The Nora negotiation team was appalled at the exorbitant amount proposed by the Sakari negotiators. They were surprised that the Sakari team had not surveyed the industry rates, as the Japanese and other western negotiators would normally have done. Apparently Sakari had not taken into consideration the relatively low cost of living in Malaysia compared to Finland. In 2000, though the average monthly rent for a comfortable, unfurnished three-bedroom apartment was about the same (660 US$) in Helsinki and Kuala Lumpur, the cost of living was considerably lower in KL. The cost of living index (New York = 100) of basket of goods in major cities, excluding housing, for Malaysia was only 83.75, compared to 109.84 for Finland.[6]

In response to Sakari's proposal, Nora negotiators adopted an unusual "take-it or leave-it" stance. They deemed the following proposal reasonable in view of the comparisons made with other JVs which Nora had entered into with other foreign parties:

Permanent experts' monthly salary ranges to be paid by the JV company were as follows:

1. Senior expert (seven to 10 years experience) RM24,300–RM27,900.
2. Expert (four to six years experience) RM22,500–RM25,200.
3. Junior expert (two to three years experience) RM20,700–RM23,400.
4. Any Malaysian income taxes payable would be added to the salaries.
5. A car for personal use.
6. Annual paid vacation of five weeks.
7. Return flight tickets to home country once a year for the whole family of married persons and twice a year for singles according to Sakari's general scheme.
8. Any expenses incurred during official travelling.

Temporary experts are persons invited by the JV company for various technical assistance tasks and would not be granted residence status. They would be paid the following fees:

1. Senior expert RM1,350 per working day
2. Expert RM1,170 per working day
3. The JV company would not reimburse the following:
   • Flight tickets between Finland (or any other country) and Malaysia.
   • Hotel or any other form of accommodation.
   • Local transportation.

In defense of their proposed rates, Sakari's negotiators argued that the rates presented by Nora were too low. Sakari suggested that Nora's negotiators take into consideration the fact that Sakari would have to subsidize the difference between the experts' present salaries and the amount paid by the JV company. A large difference would require that large amounts of subsidy payments be made to the affected employees.

5. Arbitration   Another major issue discussed in the negotiation was related to arbitration. While both parties agreed to an arbitration process in the event of future disputes, they disagreed on the location for dispute resolution. Because Nora would be the majority stakeholder in the JV company, Nora insisted that any arbitration should take place in KL. Sakari, however, insisted on Helsinki, following the norm commonly practised by the company.

At the end of the five-day negotiation, many issues could not be resolved. While Nora could agree on certain matters after consulting Zainal, the Sakari team, representing a large private company, had to refer contentious items to the company board before it could make any decision that went beyond the limits authorized by the board.

The Decision

Zainal sat down at his desk, read through the minutes of the negotiation thoroughly, and was disappointed that an agreement had not yet been reached. He was concerned about the commitment Nora had made to TMB when Nora was awarded the switching contract. Nora would be expected to fulfil the contract soon but had yet to find a partner to provide the switching technology. It was foreseeable that companies such as Siemens, Samsung and Lucent, which had failed in the bid, could still be potential partners. However, Zainal had also not rejected the possibility of a reconciliation with Sakari. He could start by contacting Kuusisto in Helsinki. But should he?

---

[6]IMD & World Economic Forum. 2001. The World Competitiveness Report.

Case 6-2   Mahindra & Mahindra Ltd.—Farm
Equipment Sector: Acquisition of Jiangling
Tractor Company

R. Chandrasekhar and Jean-Louis Schaan

In June 2004, Anjanikumar Choudhari, president, Farm Equipment Sector (FES), Mahindra & Mahindra Ltd. (M&M), India's largest tractor manufacturer, was facing a managerial dilemma. He had been asked to recommend to the company's board whether or not it should pursue the formation of a joint venture (JV) with Jiangling Tractor Co. (JTC), a state-owned tractor maker in China. A formal clearance by the board was necessary before commencing negotiations with the target company for a JV which would be M&M's first foray into China.

Choudhari had earlier spent five years in China, from 1994 to 1999, both as sales director for Unilever China and as vice chairman and managing director of Unilever Shanghai Sales Co. Choudhari was, thus, personally familiar with the dynamics of the Chinese business environment. Although the board would be the final arbiter, Choudhari knew his judgment would be an important input to the decision. He had already reviewed a preliminary plan, prepared by his core team, which addressed two fronts: restructuring JTC

IVEY

Richard Ivey School of Business
The University of Western Ontario

to bring it on the road to profitability and integrating its operations with M&M.

Said Choudhari:

M&M had declared its intention of increasing the sales from international operations from less than five percent to 20 percent of turnover by the year 2009. We also aimed at becoming the world's largest producer, by volume, of tractors by 2009, from being the fifth in the pecking order.

Choudhari had to weigh his recommendation in the light of a few other developments.

*   Three global tractor majors were in India, turning their Indian capacities into export hubs in their international network.
*   M&M was consolidating its greenfield tractor manufacturing project in the United States, set up at two American locations—Texas and Georgia.
*   M&M was planning the launch of marketing operations in Australia as a prelude to setting up an assembly plant in Brisbane.
*   M&M was already in an acquisition mode, particularly in Europe, with some aggressive overtures. The company had bid for Valtra, a Finnish tractor major, which drew media attention, and lost the bid to AGCO Corp, its American competitor, on price.
*   M&M was in talks with Romanian officials for the takeover of a state-owned tractor firm.

The Chinese acquisition, currently under review, was consistent with M&M's long-term vision of securing global leadership. It would help increase the sales volume of M&M and improve its ranking, based on the number of units sold, among global tractor companies (see Exhibit 1).

Exhibit 1   Global Tractor Majors (in alphabetical order)

Company	Year of founding	HQ	Estimated Sales Volume ('000 units)		
			2002	2003	2004
AGCO	1990	Georgia, USA	100	NA	130
Case New Holland	1831	Illinois, USA	134	NA	>140
Deere & Co	1837	Illinois, USA	>115	NA	>120
Kubota Tractor Co.	1890	Osaka, Japan	70	NA	>75
Mahindra & Mahindra	1945	Mumbai, India	60	50	54
Same Deutz-Fahr	1927	Treviglio, Italy	NA	NA	NA

Source: Sales volume figures of M&M are from the 2003–2004 Annual Report, "Summary of Operations", p. 48. It is difficult to get the exact figures for international players operating in different geographies. These are estimates based on available data and may not include sales through franchises and licence agreements.

Note: There is no structured, industry-wide compilation of data for global tractor industry except as done by individual companies. For example, AGCO's sales in 2004 as shown above comprises only its largest selling brand of years, Massey Ferguson. The exhibit however provides a reasonable estimate of the global rankings in 2004.

Company Background

Set up in 1945 to manufacture general-purpose utility vehicles, M&M had diversified into unrelated businesses during the next few decades. By 1990, it was a conglomerate with interests in oil drilling, bearings, time-share resorts and instrumentation, in addition to jeeps and tractors. The company had been organized until then on functional lines. An M&M salesperson would, for example, sell both jeeps and tractors.

The induction of Anand Mahindra, a second-generation entrepreneur, as deputy managing director of M&M in April 1991, marked the beginning of change. One of the growth criteria the Harvard-educated scion laid out for the group was that it would not, over time, remain in a business that did not have a global potential. As a first step towards this focus, the company made a decision to reorganize its activities into strategic business units (SBUs). Over time, the businesses were regrouped, after divestitures, into four independent SBUs within the group. By 2000, there were four SBUs: Automotive, Farm Equipment Services, IT Services, and Trade and Financial Services. Each was headed by a president supported by a corporate centre. Each president was a member of the group management board headed by the managing director (see Exhibit 2). The company had begun lateral recruitment by that time and Choudhari, who had joined M&M in 1999, was among the first few senior managers to come aboard.

In December 2001, when Anand Mahindra was the vice chairman and managing director, the company identified the manufacturing, distribution and sale of farm equipment and utility vehicles as a core business.[1] In 2002, M&M witnessed a second round of refocusing on fundamentals. Entitled Operation Blue Chip, the refocusing was aimed at strengthening domestic operations as a precursor to going global. It replaced performance measures such as market share, sales and profits with two new benchmarks: free cash flow (cash after appropriating for investments and profits) and return on capital employed (ROCE). Free cash flow compelled every SBU to declare a surplus, as a dividend payable to the holding company, at the end of a financial period. ROCE forced each business to utilize capital efficiently.

[1]M&M Annual Report 2001–2002, p. 10.

Exhibit 2   M&M - Segment-Wise Contribution to Turnover

Year ending March (in INR million)	2004	%	2003	%	2002	%
Automotive	44,048	54.9	31,529	50.9	23,124	42.2
Farm Equipment Services	18,619	23.2	15,938	25.7	17,711	32.3
IT Services	7,830	9.8	6,618	10.7	5,590	10.3
Trade & Financial Services	3,040	3.7	2,471	4.0	1,867	3.4
Other business segments	6,670	8.4	5,394	8.7	6,435	11.8
Total Sales	**80,207**	100	**61,950**	100	**54,727**	100

Sources: M&M 2004 Annual Report, p. 124 and 2003 Annual Report, p. 123.

Exhibit 3   Mahindra & Mahindra Consolidated Income Statement

Year ending March (in INR million)	2004	2003	2002
Sales	**80,207**	**61,950**	**54,727**
Less: Excise	9,736	8,076	7,033
Net sales	70,471	53,874	47,694
Less: Operating expenditure			
- Raw materials	38,932	28,406	24,354
- Personnel	7,824	6,269	6,063
- Interest and finance charges	1,643	2,183	1,999
- Depreciation	2,094	2,129	2,153
- Other expenses	14,409	11,402	11,273
Profit before tax	**5,569**	**3,484**	**1,852**

Source: M&M 2003 Annual Reports, p. 99 and 2004 Annual Report, p. 99.

Said Choudhari:

By April 2004, when the new financial year began, the company was ready to move to the next level of growth—becoming a world class organization by driving competitiveness, innovation and market leadership. Improvements in working capital and credit management practices had generated a reserve of INR7 billion.[2] It became a war chest with which to finance global acquisitions.

M&M had achieved a consolidated turnover of INR80.2 billion for the year ending March 2004 and a profit before tax of INR5.6 billion (see Exhibits 3 and 4).

The Farm Equipment Sector

M&M's Farm Equipment Sector (FES) was on a productivity drive well before Operation Blue Chip officially got under way at the company. The drive had been launched in 2000, in anticipation of a downturn in the domestic tractor industry in 2001. Entitled Project Vishwajeet (meaning conqueror of

[2]At the time the case was written, the exchange between the Indian rupee and the U.S. dollar was INR44.50 = US$1.

Exhibit 4 M&M - Consolidated Balance Sheet

Year ending March (in INR million)	2004	2003	2002
SOURCES OF FUNDS			
Shareholder's Funds			
- Capital	1,160	1,160	1,160
- Reserves and Surplus	18,972	16,645	16,431
Minority Interest	2,485	2,369	2,660
Loan Funds	24,954	26,292	24,915
Deferred Income	1,211	979	730
	48,782	**47,445**	**45,896**
APPLICATION OF FUNDS			
Fixed Assets	17,081	18,346	16,699
Capital Work In Progress	635	952	3,876
Intangible Assets	643	—	—
Investments	5,385	4,430	4,184
Net Current Assets	26,301	24,582	22,089
Deferred Tax Liability	(1,485)	(1,397)	(1,101)
Miscellaneous Expenditure	222	532	149
	48,782	**47,445**	**45,896**

Source: M&M 2004 Annual Report, p. 98 and 2003 Annual Report, p. 98.

the world) and conceptualized by McKinsey & Co., this drive was designed to build a platform of cost leadership on which FES could become a global tractor producer by 2005. The more immediate goal was to reduce the break-even point from 54,000 units to 35,000 units by 2003, so that even if the sales volumes fell by 30 per cent, FES would still make a profit. The domestic market for tractors collapsed in 2001, as expected, and M&M was the only company in the Indian tractor industry that made profits that year. FES went on to win the Deming Prize in 2003, making M&M the lone tractor manufacturer in the world to have won the quality award. Said Choudhari:

> FES could become a global leader faster than other businesses at M&M because it was already a leader in the domestic market, the second largest market for tractors in the world at the time. Among its other credentials were low cost location, skilled manpower and existence of robust internal systems and processes.

The Indian Tractor Industry

India was the world's second largest manufacturer of tractors. Most tractor producers initially entered into technical collaboration in the 1970s and 1980s with world renowned companies. On absorption of technology, the country stopped importing tractors for meeting domestic requirements. Indigenous production was sufficient to meet the demand. In the 1990s, India was also able to start exporting tractors to more competitive markets, such as the United States. M&M, which had been leading the domestic market since 1984, was quick to capitalize on this opportunity by setting up an assembly plant at Tomball, Texas in 1994. The product range was in the 20–60 hp segment comprising hobby farmers.

As elsewhere, the Indian tractor industry was categorized on the basis of power delivered by the engine's horsepower (see Exhibit 5). There were 13 players in the Indian tractor industry, including three multinational corporations (MNCs): New

Exhibit 5   Market Composition — India

Segments	Horse power	Market share	Suitability
Small Tractors	21–30	25	Suited for soft soil conditions and preferred in well irrigated northern Indian states
Medium Tractors	31–40	56	Used in southern and western India due to hard soil conditions
Large Tractors	41–50	17	Preferred by rich farmers with larger land holdings, in Punjab and Haryana states.
Large Tractors	>50 Hp	2	Used in turnkey project sites such as building sites for canals and dams

Source: www.krchoksey.com/weekender/16102004, accessed July 31, 2006.

Exhibit 6   India - Market Players

	Company	2004		2003	
		Sales (in units)	Market share	Sales (in units)	Market share
1	Mahindra & Mahindra Ltd	49,576	25.9	47,028	27.3
2	Punjab Tractors Ltd	25,602	13.4	24,275	14.1
3	Escorts	25,550	13.3	21,013	12.2
4	Tractors & Farm Equipment Ltd	24,895	13.0	24,465	14.2
5	Sonalika	20,021	10.4	16,451	9.5
6	Eicher	16,775	8.8	15,821	9.2
7	L & T John Deere	9,526	5.0	5,189	3.0
8	Case New Holland	7,723	4.0	6,316	3.7
9	HMT Ltd	5,563	2.9	6,802	3.9
10	Bajaj Tempo	3,910	2.0	3,594	2.1
11	Gujarat Tractor Co	2,009	1.0	1,247	0.7
12	VST Tillers	517	0.3	333	0.2
	Total	**191,667**	**100.0**	**172,534**	**100.0**

Note: SAME Italy's data is not available as it is not a member of the Tractor Manufacturers Association.
Source: Tractor Manufacturers Association, from M&M company files.

Holland, John Deere and SAME (see Exhibit 6). The latter had all fumbled by entering the wrong segments. SAME had moved into the "vacant" high-horsepower segment with technology-intensive products but quickly withdrew to migrate to the lower end of the market. Consolidation of land holdings in India and a rise in farm income, over time, were expected to add to the margins of MNC players.

There were several growth drivers in the Indian tractor industry. Because of an emphasis by the federal government on increasing the share of agriculture in the gross domestic product (GDP), the flow of farm credit had been rising over the years. Five million new borrowers were expected to be added to the farm sector under the formal banking network by 2007.[3] Agri-businesses (e.g. cotton yarn manufacturers) were entering into alliances with farmers for guaranteed returns on purchase of farm produce. Large-scale irrigation projects were underway in various Indian states, which indicated a potential increase in the supply of farm land. The infrastructure sector was growing, which would likely lead to an increase in the use of tractors in non-farm activities, such as civil construction. Retail finance options were expanding, making it easier for an end-user to buy a tractor. There was a shift in India from sustenance farming to commercial farming, which encouraged productive use of land through mechanization.

Said Choudhari:

> At about 11 tractors per thousand hectares of land, the tractor density in India was lower than the world average of 19 tractors and the U.S. average of 27 tractors. The domestic growth potential was thus considerable.

The Global Tractor Industry

The global export trade in tractors and related parts and accessories was valued at $8.6 billion in 2003 (see Exhibit 7). The world market for branded tractors comprised 500,000 units per annum. North America was the largest tractor market accounting for 27 percent of global tractor sales, followed by India (21.5 per cent), West Europe (21.2 per cent) and China (20 per cent). The growth markets of the future were the United States, India, China, East Europe and South America. There were four major players globally: John Deere, Case New Holland, AGCO and

Kubota. They were all technology leaders producing superior quality products. Their product portfolio went beyond assorted farm equipment (including tractors) to construction, forestry and commercial equipment. M&M itself, for example, was a diversified company in which the tractor business comprised only about 25 percent of consolidated revenues.

M&M Globalization in the Farm Equipment Sector

The Farm Equipment Sector's globalization began in a small way, with exports to the countries of the South Asian Association for Regional Cooperation (SAARC), such as Nepal, Bangladesh and Sri Lanka. Although it had set up a manufacturing plant in the United States as early as in 1994, there was little evidence of a globalization strategy at M&M until the launch of Operation Blue Chip. The drive mandated the strengthening of domestic competitiveness as a precursor to going global. A template for globalization soon began to evolve at FES when the company was planning to establish a second assembly and distribution center in the United States, at Calhoun, Georgia, in 2002. Said Choudhari:

> The template was built around a series of filters. We used the filters to zero down, by a process of elimination, on the particular global market and the particular company within it, that we wanted to do business with. There were three filters to start with: industry filter; product/technology filter; and price/earning filter. By applying these filters, we segmented the total market into three categories: attractive but low volume market; price sensitive but high volume market; and high tech and high hp market. We focused on the first two categories, comprising USA, China, Australia and Africa. The selection of the company for alliance was on the basis of seven filters: product portfolio; product technology; market reach; quality systems and processes; scalability; openness of management; and liabilities [see Exhibit 8]. The template also had an entry mode for exports, greenfield, JV and acquisition [see Exhibit 9].

---

[3]Credit Analysis & Research Ltd (CARE) report "Impact of Union Budget 2006–07," pp. 119–120.

Exhibit 7   Global Tractor Exports—2003

Rank	Country	Exports (in US$ thousands)	% of Global Exports
1	United Kingdom	1,760,854	20.39
2	United States	1,329,487	15.39
3	Germany	1,313,652	15.21
4	Italy	1,132,126	13.11
5	Japan	967,431	11.20
6	Finland	372,089	4.31
7	France	339,898	3.94
8	Russia	297,563	3.45
9	Canada	232,746	2.69
10	Austria	119,130	1.38
11	Belgium	110,342	1.28
12	Mexico	68,213	0.79
13	China	61,840	0.72
14	Sweden	57,891	0.67
15	Brazil	55,080	0.64
16	Czech Republic	53,892	0.62
17	Poland	43,641	0.51
18	Netherlands	36,091	0.42
19	Spain	35,774	0.41
20	Turkey	30,129	0.35
21	South Korea	30,078	0.35
22	Switzerland	22,108	0.26
23	Denmark	21,344	0.25
24	Romania	21,186	0.25
25	Thailand	15,352	0.18
26	India	14,571	0.17
27	Ireland	11,367	0.13
28	Singapore	9,892	0.11
29	Algeria	9,387	0.11
30	South Africa	9,356	0.11
21	Serbia & Montenegro	6,734	0.08
32	Iran	6,699	0.08
33	Bolivia	5,792	0.07
34	Norway	4,078	0.05
35	Malaysia	2,777	0.03
36	Other	27,705	0.32
	Total	**8,636,295**	

Source: M. Philip Parker, "The World Market for Tractors: A 2003 Global Trade Perspective," INSEAD, www.icongrouponline.com, accessed September 6, 2006.

Exhibit 8   Market Entry Strategy

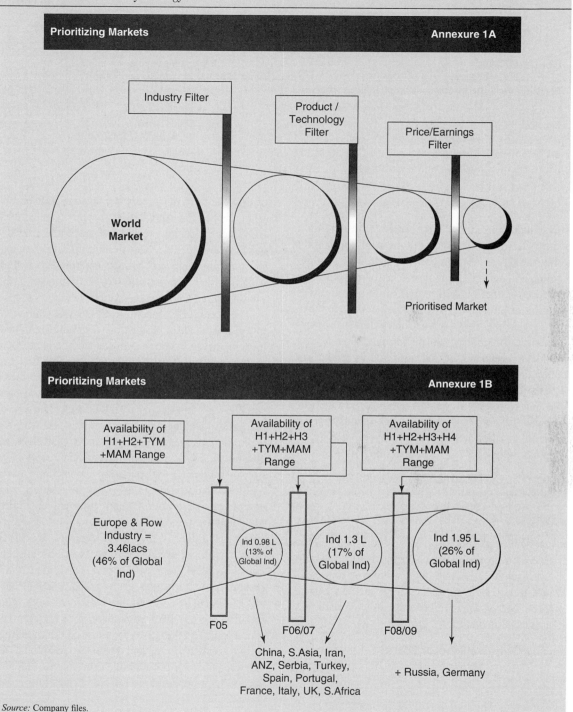

Exhibit 9	Market Entry Mode	
Operations		**Annexure 2**
Multi faceted operations to suit market requirements		
Distributor Model		South Asia, Turkey, E. Europe, SE Asia
Subsidiary / JV		China, USA
Branch Office / direct dealer model		Australia and New Zealand
Satellite Plant + Govt tie up		Africa
Representative office + Distributor model		Eastern Europe

Entry Strategy—China

M&M had started its China initiative by sending a team from India and tractors to test out the market opportunity. The company targeted a single province in central China where large land holdings suited the range of the 25- to 75-hp tractors it was offering. It pitched its prices 20 percent above those of its rivals in China, such as John Deere, to convey the "superior quality and performance" of M&M products. Quickly, the team of Indian managers concluded that the next logical step of establishing a footprint should leverage local advantages (like low costs) so as to compete effectively with low Chinese prices. This meant local manufacturing through an alliance with a local player.
Said Choudhari:

> If you are entering China for the first time it is often quite useful, and some would say prudent, to have a local partner. We looked at the options and concluded that it would be best to have a joint venture where we would have management control.

M&M believed that local manufacturing would also power its global strategy, which, in any case, would not work without factoring in the Chinese market. M&M considered a greenfield plant but dismissed this option.

The Chinese Tractor Market

China had been importing tractors from the USSR in 1950s and 1960s. In 1978, China started making its own tractors. The adoption of the "responsibility system" in China facilitated not only farm ownership but also machinery ownership. By 1994, 71 percent of Chinese farm machinery belonged to individuals, 10 percent to the state and 19 percent to collectives. Farm mechanization created a virtual cycle, improving farm productivity and freeing up rural labor to work in township and village enterprises (TVEs), which were to become a source of much of the wealth among Chinese peasant households.

The average plot size in most parts of China was tiny, and the scale of production was small. Hand-held tractors, driven by a one-cylinder diesel engine, were most suited to China. They were especially used in central and southern China and parts of the northeast for rice cultivation. They were also useful in non-farm activities on Chinese roads. These tractors had a flexible, belt-driven, mechanical power train, allowing the engine to power farm machinery, pumps and electrical generators. Many farmers hitched their tractors to two-ton trailers for transportation and hauling.

Most manufacturers of farm machinery and equipment were state-owned enterprises (SOEs) regulated by the Ministry of Machinery Industry (MMI). Of the 11 industries overseen by MMI, farm machinery was the most profitable because incomes in rural areas were rising, partly due to adjustments in the state's grain procurement prices. All SOEs carried the double burden of high taxation and the provision of pension for a vast staff in retirement. In 1996, there were 88 SOEs manufacturing small tractors, and 16 SOEs accounted for 70 percent of all production.[4] The tractor industry was under a consolidation phase. Privatization was

---

[4] "Farm Mechanization in China," <u>U.S. Embassy Beijing, Environment, Science and Technology Section,</u> June 1996, http://www.usembassy-china.org.cn/sandt/mu4fmmk.htm, accessed July 3, 2006.

encouraged by the government. There were problems such as irregular product quality, lack of industry standards and price wars eroding profitability. Said Choudhari:

> There were four prerequisites for a tractor manufacturer to succeed in China: a good business model facilitating monitoring and control of operating costs, a good dealership network, a good fit for the products with the unique local requirements, and a good brand image.

The Chinese tractor market was tilted in favor of power tillers, which sold more than 1.5 million units per annum. Small belt-driven tractors comprised another significant market at 0.6 million units per annum. The domestic market for higher horsepower tractors was pegged at around 100,000 units. Within it, the 30- to 80-hp range comprised the largest—at 70,000 units—and was growing at six to eight percent per annum. The output and sales of large and medium sized, gear driven tractors were growing rapidly at about 60,000 units per annum (see Exhibit 10). M&M perceived that the small tractor had a significant upside because it was a large market and because the small belt-driven power tillers that had been used in the former communes/cooperative farms were fuel inefficient and highly polluting. The Chinese government wanted to change this.

There was a progressive shift towards higher horsepower tractors in China because of two reasons: farm reforms were enabling consolidation of land holdings leading to improved efficiency, and a robust trend in farm product prices had rendered high-priced tractors affordable to more households. About 8,000 units were being exported to the United States in the 20- to 30-hp range targeted at landscapers, golf course greenskeepers and weekend farmers. The Chinese economy was expected to grow by 13.2 percent during the period 2004 to 2008 with agricultural GDP forecast to grow by 11.1 per cent.

The customers were segmented as follows: 81 percent private farm owners, eight percent state-owned farmers and 11 percent service providers. In the less than 25-hp category, the customer desired a low technology and a low-priced product. The application was for rotation, plowing, shredding and haulage. The 26- to 49-hp segment, characterized by a four-wheel drive and high lug tires, was price-sensitive. The tractors in this segment were used for rice cultivation, rotation, shredding and haulage. The segment for greater than 50-hp tractors incorporated product features such as a cabin, four-wheel drive and pneumatic brakes. These tractors were used for primary tillage, harvesting, haulage and shredding.

Since the banking system in China was underdeveloped, tractors were purchased with cash. Dealers were the main sales channel. They were multi-franchisees and not exclusive. There was no concept of after-sales support in the Chinese tractor market.

Exhibit 10   Major Chinese Tractor Manufacturers

Company	Product category (hp)	Number of dealers	Estimated category share (%)
China No 1 Tractor Engineering & Machinery Group	20–180	117	18
Changdou Dongfeng Automotive Group	20–90	100	7
Futian	20–180	300	23
John Deere Tiantuo	>60	—	—
Jiangling Tractor Company	20–30	42	13
Shanghai New Holland	50–60	—	—

Source: Company files.

But because of its size and the future potential, the Chinese tractor market was, according to Choudhary, like a "honey pot" for global majors. They were seeking a foothold mostly through strategic alliances. John Deere, for example, had a JV with Tianjin Tractor Manufacturing Company, 100 miles from Beijing, to cater to the greater than 60-hp market. It sold its products locally under the brand name JDT instead of as John Deere. Reservations about the quality of Chinese manufacture were common among new tractor entrants. The Chinese tractor manufacturers, numbering about 100 in 2004, were in various stages of disarray, awaiting new managements. They provided a fast track, as opposed to a greenfield route, to commence local manufacture.

Said Choudhari:

> It costs about $11 million for an Indian company to set up a greenfield tractor venture, a non-integrated plant of about 40,000 tractor capacity, in an Indian location. It would cost 50 to 100 percent higher for the same company to set up an overseas plant in China on its own steam. It is prudent to have a local partner who can steer you through. It is particularly prudent when the partner is the government, which not only owns much of the local tractor assets but regulates them.

▌ Acquisition Target: JTC

The M&M team in China short listed eight to 10 prospects, pared it down to three and zeroed on JTC as a potential partner.

History   JTC was part of Jiangling Motor Company Group (JMCG), a state-owned enterprise, in which the U.S. Ford Motor Company had a 30 percent stake. Located in Nanchang, the capital of Jiangxi province, JMCG was manufacturing light trucks, pick-up trucks and mini-buses. It had acquired its tractor assets from Jiangxi Tractor & Truck Co., an ailing unit, whose products had once straddled the 18- to 33-hp range and were sold locally under the Feng Shou brand. After restarting tractor operations in 2000, JMCG built a new tractor factory in Nanchang in 2002. With a production capacity of 10,000 units and 3,000 engines

annually, JTC operated in the 20- to 30-hp range of tractors. It had a distribution network of 42 dealerships (see Exhibit 11).

By 2004, JTC was in trouble again, due to low-capacity utilization, surplus labor and escalating costs. The company's output had fallen to 1,477 units for the year ending July 2003 and was expected to improve, only marginally, for the year ending July 2004. It had a workforce of 710 of which nearly 50 percent was surplus. JTC's contribution to JMCG's turnover of more than $1 billion fell to $3.5 million in 2004. By mid-2004, the production had come to a standstill. JMCG had ambitious plans of expansion and diversification in the mainline automobile business and decided to de-focus on JTC by offloading 80 percent of the tractor affiliate. The government was interested in exiting the tractor business and had conducted significant due diligence about M&M.

Strategy   The company had generated a database of competitors' products, which it was updating regularly. Once the benchmark was identified, it would undertake reverse engineering and develop a product of its own with a supplier partner. It was also partnering with local universities for new technology development.

Of the 710 JTC employees, 210 were technical. All workers had more than three years of experience, adequate skill levels and the ability to study and understand drawings. JTC's top and middle managers had good educational level and training (see Exhibit 12).

With an overall market share of 2.5 percent in the Chinese tractor market (13 percent in the less than 25-hp category in China), JTC was planning to go global. Its first export tractor model, Lenar FS274-1, had sold well in the competitive U.S. market. The main trigger for globalization was the low price realization in the domestic market. JTC was targeting new export markets around the time it appeared on M&M's radar.

Although the Feng Shou brand was popular in China, JTC was not doing well for many reasons. Being an SOE, it had higher overhead costs. Its

Exhibit 11   Jiangling Tractor Co. Income Statement

	Budget 2004	% of sales	As of July 2004	% of sales	2003	% of sales
Volume (Units)						
Domestic	1,940		1,051		1,162	
Export	610		464		315	
Total	**2,550**		**1,515**		**1,477**	
	RMB		RMB		RMB	
Sales Value	**61,290,133**	100.0	**28,863,602**	100.0	**26,408,065**	100.0
Less - Cost of sales	54,542,888	89.0	29,259,429		29,338,207	111.1
- Sales expenses	2,250,000	3.7	931,606	3.2	2,149,195	8.1
- Admn. expenses	27,594,513	46.0	11,693,004	40.5	49,792,484	188.6
- Financial expenses	5,901,928	9.6	4,154,534	14.4	2,820,234	10.7
Operating profit	(28,999,196)	(47.3)	17,174,971	(59.5)	57,692,055	(218.5)
Other income	–	–	780,595	–	(6,007,217)	–
Earnings before tax	**(28,999,196)**	–	**(16,394,376)**	–	**63,699,272**	–

Source: Company files.

Exhibit 12   Jiangling Tractor Co. Organization Structure

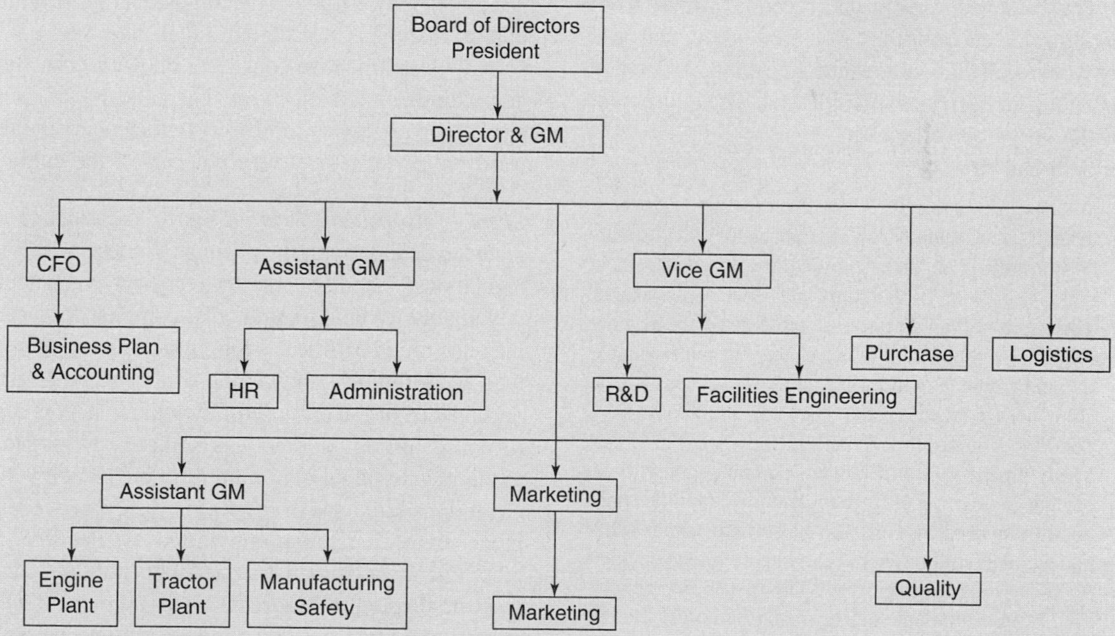

Source: Company files.

product range was limited to low-horsepower tractors. It could not get any cost leverage from suppliers because the overall domestic tractor market was limited to 60,000 in 2003 (although the market had expanded, unexpectedly, by 60 percent in 2004). Besides, customers for the 18-hp tractors preferred the belt-driven category because it cost less the gear-driven category made by JTC. Lower sales, inventory building and higher operating costs had generated working capital constraints at the company. Moreover, the frequent change of ownership of the company had led to the discontinuity of production at the shop floor. There were significant amounts of money outstanding to suppliers who were no longer a priority for JMCG. Dealers were progressively switching to competitors' products. However, in searching for greener pastures, JTC had developed a compact model (FS-254) for the United States where the demand was high. It had thus started focusing on exports. The product was deemed acceptable for the Chinese market but M&M concluded that it would need work to make it an M&M branded tractor.

The tractor company had recently moved from old dilapidated buildings to a new plant that was not very well laid out. With free land, efficiency was not a key driver in plant layout. The equipment was in very good condition.

Said Choudhari:

> We have short-listed JTC as a prospective company. There is good chemistry with management and we are comfortable with their straight forward management style, degree of cooperation and level of assistance. This is important because at the end of the day we might have 80 percent of the shares but our partner is the government, which has given us permission to come here in the first place. The Feng Shou brand has a good recognition in the small tractor market in China. The company's product range is complementary to the current M&M range. Its manufacturing facilities have been influenced by Ford and Isuzu with whom it has had a collaboration. There is an internal focus on quality and a readiness to employ M&M's quality practices. JTC is a government enterprise and willing to give us full control of day to day management. But the two primary reasons why we are interested in JTC are its product portfolio and the focus on quality.

Due Diligence

Having zeroed in on the Chinese market and further refined its target to JTC, the team at Choudhari's office began to examine the potential for a JV. A team at the president's office started conducting due diligence at three levels: financial, cultural and legal.

Financial Considerations   M&M was a typical commercial enterprise, focused on resource productivity. The latter was a concept that was not rooted at JMCG, a state owned enterprise with its own social mandates like safeguarding jobs. The tractor unit was carrying employees, classified as redundant, on its rolls on partial salaries. The concept of work-in-progress and of finished goods inventory seemed to be different. There was a need to understand the accounting and costing structures of JTC and how they might be integrated with those of M&M.

Cultural Considerations   M&M needed to break the barriers of language, food habits and culture in China. M&M management was aware of the necessity of training Chinese officers with M&M values and philosophy. Although the mindset at JTC was that quality mattered, M&M found that there was not a strong commitment to consistent delivery of quality day after day, year after year. The concepts of managerial accountability, profit, cost efficiencies and reward for performance were not part of the culture.

Legal   Considerations   Legal   considerations included dealing with the peculiar Chinese rules and regulations; handling the government valuations, seeking clarity on environmental compliance, securing registration certificates for physical assets, such as land and buildings; and getting a grip on operational dependence of the proposed JV on the JMCG group.

An external agency was enlisted to suggest modalities to be kept in mind (e.g. the launch vehicle and the structure of the JV) in the event of commencement of negotiations with JTC. The agency recommended that an intermediate holding company be formed in Mauritius as a 100 percent subsidiary of M&M. To be called Mahindra Overseas Investment Co. (Mauritius) Ltd., the holding company would have 80 percent stake in a joint venture, to be called Mahindra (China) Tractor Co. Ltd. (MCTCL), in which JMCG would have 20 percent stake. MCTCL would acquire the tractor manufacturing assets from JTC for $10 million: $2 million in payment for JMCG and $8 million to be invested in the unit to nurse it back to health. MCTCL would have a 10-member board comprising eight nominees from M&M and two from JMCG. The managing director would be a nominee from M&M. Said Choudhari:

> As we scanned the company in detail, we saw areas of concern. JTC's product range was limited to 18–33 hp. The company's manufacturing locations were far away from the market locations. Capacity was a constraint, especially in engines. A majority of the dealers was ineffective. JTC's plan to exit from domestic Chinese market to concentrate on exports was detrimental to M&M's strategic intent.

The JV would help M&M gain a foothold in the largest tractor market in the world. It would enable M&M to source low-horsepower tractors for the growing Indian market and to sell Indian-made tractors of higher horsepower in China. The JV could leverage M&M's domestic competencies in not only sourcing tractor components and subsystems but also in manufacturing, product development and marketing services. It could also leverage JTC's competency of rapid product development by way of reverse engineering.

Choudhari's team looked for measures with which to track the success or failure of the proposed JV in the future. They pinned down six measures:

1. Domestic market share in China
2. Cost reduction through sourcing in China
3. Exports to the United States and India
4. Break-even volumes
5. Return on investment (ROI), return on sales (ROS) and revenue growth
6. Revenue from exports from M&M India's product portfolio

The Integration Plan

A time frame of 100 days was set for completion of the integration of the operations of JTC with M&M. A mini business process re-engineering

(BPR) plan was prepared, and a cell was formed to execute and monitor the plan. The transactional processes pertaining to integration were as follows:

- Drafting the asset transfer contract, incorporating protocol for takeover of plant equipment, inventory, land and building.
- Mapping the skill sets of all existing employees; provision of training and development; accommodating expatriate managers; preparing fresh employment contracts for all employees, new and old.
- Finalizing contracts with suppliers and dealers of JTC; identifying their training needs
- Conducting work study and time study of all critical plant activities and aligning them to M&M standards; identifying areas of manpower reduction.
- Improving the existing accounting and costing system; proposing an independent information technology (IT) system.

The team also identified the processes pertaining to the formation of the JV, such as the preparation of JV agreement, securing approval of the company name from Beijing, procuring the business license in Nanchang and acquiring permissions for the board composition. In addition, the team examined grassroots initiatives in three functions: operations (streamlining the manufacturing, sourcing and marketing operations in line with those of M&M); accounts (opening a bank account in Nanchang, tracking the costing and accounting systems of JTC, and setting up an independent IT system for MCTCL); and human resources.

One of the issues the team examined in detail was the people issue. It recommended that all the middle-and top-level managers be retained but that the number of workers be reduced by 50 per cent. The latter move required support from the federal government at Beijing. Those to be retained would be trained, some of them in India for two months. Expatriates from India would fill some of the mid-level managerial positions at various functions. A senior executive from M&M would be a mentor for the expatriate community. Provisions for housing and for the education of the expatriates' children were also to be made. A change management cell was also to be formed, with a mandate to facilitate smooth cultural transition. One of its responsibilities was to ensure that JTC officers learn English and Indian expatriates learn Chinese.

As he reviewed the data before him, once again, Choudhari wondered whether he should recommend

that the board provide a formal clearance and set the stage for his team to commence negotiations with JTC, or whether he should withhold such a recommendation.

▋ The Richard Ivey School of Business gratefully acknowledges the generous support of J. Armand Bombardier Foundation in the development of these learning materials.

Case 6-3   Eli Lilly in India: Rethinking the Joint Venture Strategy

Nikhil Celly, Charles Dhanaraj, and Paul W. Beamish

In August 2001, Dr. Lorenzo Tallarigo, president of Intercontinental Operations, Eli Lilly and Company (Lilly), a leading pharmaceutical firm based in the United States, was getting ready for a meeting in New York, with D. S. Brar, chairman and chief executive officer (CEO) of Ranbaxy Laboratories Limited (Ranbaxy), India. Lilly and Ranbaxy had started a joint venture (JV) in India, Eli Lilly-Ranbaxy

IVEY

Richard Ivey School of Business
The University of Western Ontario

Private Limited (ELR) that was incorporated in March 1993. The JV had steadily grown to a full-fledged organization employing more than 500 people in 2001. However, in recent months Lilly was re-evaluating the directions for the JV, with Ranbaxy signaling an intention to sell its stake. Tallarigo was scheduled to meet with Brar to decide on the next steps.

The Global Pharmaceutical Industry in the 1990s

The pharmaceutical industry had come about through both forward integration from the manufacture of organic chemicals and a backward integration from druggist-supply houses. The industry's rapid growth was aided by increasing worldwide incomes and a universal demand for better health care; however, most of the world market for pharmaceuticals was concentrated in North America, Europe and Japan. Typically, the largest four firms claimed 20 percent of sales, the top 20 firms 50 percent to 60 percent and the 50 largest companies accounted for 65 percent to 75 percent of sales (see Exhibit 1). Drug discovery was an expensive process, with leading firms spending more than 20 percent of their sales on research and development (R&D).

Exhibit 1   World Pharmaceutical Suppliers 1992 and 2001 (US$ millions)

Company	Origin	1992 Sales*	Company	Origin	2001 Sales**
Glaxo	US	8,704	Pfizer	USA	25,500
Merck	UK	8,214	GlaxoSmithKline	UK	24,800
Bristol-Myers Squibb	US	6,313	Merck & Co	USA	21,350
Hoechst	GER	6,042	AstraZeneca	UK	16,480
Ciba-Geigy	SWI	5,192	Bristol-Myers Squibb	USA	15,600
SmithKline Beecham	US	5,100	Aventis	FRA	15,350
Roche	SWI	4,897	Johnson & Johnson	USA	14,900
Sandoz	SWI	4,886	Novartis	SWI	14,500
Bayer	GER	4,670	Pharmacia Corp	USA	11,970
American Home	US	4,589	Eli Lilly	USA	11,540
Pfizer	US	4,558	Wyeth	USA	11,710
Eli Lilly	US	4,537	Roche	SWI	8,530
Johnson & Johnson	US	4,340	Schering-Plough	USA	8,360
Rhone Poulenc Rorer	US	4,096	Abbott Laboratories	USA	8,170
Abbott	US	4,025	Takeda	JAP	7,770
			Sanofi-Synthélabo	FRA	5,700
			Boehringer Ingelheim	GER	5,600
			Bayer	GER	5,040
			Schering AG	GER	3,900
			Akzo Nobel	NTH	3,550

* Market Share Reporter, 1993.
** Pharmaceutical Executive, May 2002.

Developing a drug, from discovery to launch in a major market, took 10 to 12 years and typically cost US$500 million to US$800 million (in 1992). Bulk production of active ingredients was the norm, along with the ability to decentralize manufacturing and packaging to adapt to particular market needs. Marketing was usually equally targeted to physicians and the paying customers. Increasingly, government agencies, such as Medicare, and health management organizations (HMOs) in the United States were gaining influence in the buying processes. In most countries, all activities related to drug research and manufacturing were strictly controlled by government agencies, such as the Food and Drug Administration (FDA) in the United States, the Committee on Proprietary Medicinal Products (CPMP) in Europe, and the Ministry of Health and Welfare (MHW) in Japan.

Patents were the essential means by which a firm protected its proprietary knowledge. The safety provided by the patents allowed firms to price their products appropriately in order to accumulate funds for future research. The basic reason to patent a new drug was to guarantee the exclusive legal right to profit from its innovation for a certain number of years, typically 20 years for a product patent. There was usually a time lag of about eight to 10 years from the time the patent was obtained and the time of regulatory approval to first launch in the United States or Europe. Time lags for emerging markets and in Japan were longer. The "product patent" covered the chemical substance itself, while a "process patent" covered the method of processing or manufacture. Both patents guaranteed the inventor a 20-year monopoly on the innovation, but the process patent offered much less protection, since it was fairly easy to modify a chemical process. It was also very difficult to legally prove that a process patent had been created to manufacture a product identical to that of a competitor. Most countries relied solely on process patents until the mid-1950s, although many countries had since recognized the product patent in law. While companies used the global market to amortize the huge investments required to produce a new drug, they were hesitant to invest in countries where the intellectual property regime was weak.

As health-care costs soared in the 1990s, the pharmaceutical industry in developed countries began coming under increased scrutiny. Although patent protection was strong in developed countries, there were various types of price controls. Prices for the same drugs varied between the United States and Canada by a factor of 1.2 to 2.5.[1] Parallel trade or trade by independent firms taking advantage of such differentials represented a serious threat to pharmaceutical suppliers, especially in Europe. Also, the rise of generics, unbranded drugs of comparable efficacy in treating the disease but available at a fraction of the cost of the branded drugs, were challenging the pricing power of the pharmaceutical companies. Manufacturers of generic drugs had no expense for drug research and development of new compounds and only had limited budgets for popularizing the compound with the medical community. The generic companies made their money by copying what other pharmaceutical companies discovered, developed and created a market for. Health management organizations (HMOs) were growing and consolidating their drug purchases. In the United States, the administration under President Clinton, which took office in 1992, investigated the possibility of a comprehensive health plan, which, among other things, would have allowed an increased use of generics and laid down some form of regulatory pressure on pharmaceutical profits.

The Indian Pharmaceutical Industry in the 1990s

Developing countries, such as India, although large by population, were characterized by low per capita gross domestic product (GDP). Typically, healthcare expenditures accounted for a very small share of GDP, and health insurance was not commonly available. The 1990 figures for per capita annual expenditure on drugs in India were estimated at US$3, compared to US$412 in Japan, US$222 in Germany and US$191 in the United Kingdom.[2] Governments and large corporations extended health coverage, including prescription drug coverage, to their workers.

In the years before and following India's independence in 1947, the country had no indigenous capability to produce pharmaceuticals, and was dependent on imports. The Patent and Designs Act of 1911, an extension of the British colonial rule, enforced adherence to the international patent law, and gave rise to a number of multinational firms' subsidiaries in India, that wanted to import drugs from their respective countries of origin. Post-independence, the first public sector drug company, Hindustan Antibiotics Limited (HAL), was established in 1954, with the help of the World Health Organization, and Indian Drugs and Pharmaceutical Limited (IDPL) was established in 1961 with the help of the then Soviet Union.

The 1970s saw several changes that would dramatically change the intellectual property regime and give rise to the emergence of local manufacturing companies. Two such key changes were the passage of the Patents Act 1970 (effective April 1972) and the Drug Price Control Order (DPCO). The Patents Act in essence abolished the product patents for all pharmaceutical and agricultural products, and permitted process patents for five to seven years. The DPCO instituted price controls, by which a government body stipulated prices for all drugs. Subsequently, this list was revised in 1987 to 142 drugs (which accounted for 72 percent of the turnover of the industry). Indian drug prices were estimated to be five percent to 20 percent of the U.S. prices and among the lowest in the world.[3] The

---

[1]Estimates of industry average wholesale price levels in Europe (with Spanish levels indexed at 100 in 1989) were: Spain 100; Portugal 107; France 113; Italy 118; Belgium 131: United Kingdom 201; The Netherlands 229; West Germany 251. Source: T. Malnight, Globalization of an Ethnocentric Firm: An Evolutionary Perspective, *Strategic Management Journal*, 1995, Vol. 16, p.128.

[2]Organization of Pharmaceutical Producers of India Report.
[3]According to a study from Yale University, Ranitidine (300 tabs/10 pack) was priced at Rs18.53, whereas the U.S. price was 57 times more, and Ciprofloxacin (500 mg/4 pack) was at Rs28.40 in India, whereas the U.S. price was about 15 times more.

DPCO also limited profits pharmaceutical companies could earn to approximately six percent of sales turnover. Also, the post-manufacturing expenses were limited to 100 percent of the production costs. At the World Health Assembly in 1982 Indira Gandhi, then Prime Minister of India, aptly captured the national sentiment on the issue in an often-quoted statement:

> The idea of a better-ordered world is one in which medical discoveries will be free of patents and there will be no profiteering from life and death.

With the institution of both the DPCO and the 1970 Patent Act, drugs became available more cheaply, and local firms were encouraged to make copies of drugs by developing their own processes, leading to bulk drug production. The profitability was sharply reduced for multinational companies, many of which began opting out of the Indian market due to the disadvantages they faced from the local competition. Market share of multinational companies dropped from 80 percent in 1970 to 35 percent in the mid-1990s as those companies exited the market due to the lack of patent protection in India.

In November 1984, there were changes in the government leadership following Gandhi's assassination. The dawn of the 1990s saw India initiating economic reform and embracing globalization. Under the leadership of Dr. Manmohan Singh, then finance minister, the government began the process of liberalization and moving the economy away from import substitution to an export-driven economy. Foreign direct investment was encouraged by increasing the maximum limit of foreign ownership to 51 percent (from 40 per cent) in the drugs and pharmaceutical industry (see Exhibit 2). It was in this environment that Eli Lilly was considering getting involved.

Exhibit 2   India Economy at a Glance

	1992	1994	1996	1998	2000
Gross domestic product (GDP) at current market prices in US$	244	323	386	414	481
Consumer price index (June 1982 = 100) in local currency, period average	77.4	90.7	108.9	132.2	149.3
Recorded official unemployment as a percentage of total labor force	9.7	9.3	9.1	9.2	9.2
Stock of foreign reserves plus gold (national valuation), end-period	8,665	23,054	23,784	29,833	48,200
Foreign direct investment inflow (in US$ millions)[1]	252	974	2,525	2,633	2,319
Total exports	19,563	25,075	33,055	33,052	43,085
Total imports	23,580	26,846	37,376	42,318	49,907

Year	Population*
1991	846
2001	1,027

[1] United Nations Commission on Trade and Development.
[2] 1991, 2001 Census of India.
* In millions.
Source: The Economist Intelligence Unit.

Eli Lilly and Company

Colonel Eli Lilly founded Eli Lilly and Company in 1876. The company would become one of the largest pharmaceutical companies in the United States from the early 1940s until 1985 but it began with just $1,400 and four employees, including Lilly's 14-year-old son. This was accomplished with a company philosophy grounded in a commitment to scientific and managerial excellence. Over the years, Eli Lilly discovered, developed, manufactured and sold a broad line of human health and agricultural products. Research and development was crucial to Lilly's long-term success.

Before 1950, most OUS (a company term for "Outside the United States") activities were export focused. Beginning in the 1950s, Lilly undertook systematic expansion of its OUS activities, setting up several affiliates overseas. In the mid-1980s, under the leadership of then chairman, Dick Wood, Lilly began a significant move toward global markets. A separate division within the company, Eli Lilly International Corporation, with responsibility for worldwide marketing of all its products, took an active role in expanding the OUS operations. By 1992, Lilly's products were manufactured and distributed through 25 countries and sold in more than 130 countries. The company had emerged as a world leader in oral and injectable antibiotics and in supplying insulin and related diabetic care products. In 1992, Lilly International was headed by Sidney Taurel, an MBA from Columbia University, with work experience in South America and Europe, and Gerhard Mayr, an MBA from Stanford, with extensive experience in Europe. Mayr wanted to expand Lilly's operations in Asia, where several countries including India were opening up their markets for foreign investment. Lilly also saw opportunities to use the world for clinical testing, which would enable it to move forward faster, as well as shape opinion with leaders in the medical field around the world; something that would help in Lilly's marketing stage.

Ranbaxy Laboratories

Ranbaxy began in the 1960s as a family business, but with a visionary management grew rapidly to emerge as the leading domestic pharmaceutical firm in India. Under the leadership of Dr. Parvinder Singh, who held a doctoral degree from the University of Michigan, the firm evolved into a serious research-oriented firm. Singh, who joined Ranbaxy to assist his father in 1967, rose to become the joint managing director in 1977, managing director in 1982, and vice-chairman and managing director in 1987. Singh's visionary management, along with the operational leadership provided by Brar, who joined the firm in 1977, was instrumental in turning the family business into a global corporation. In the early 1990s, when almost the entire domestic pharmaceutical industry was opposing a tough patent regime, Ranbaxy was accepting it as given. Singh's argument was unique within the industry in India:

> The global marketplace calls for a single set of rules; you cannot have one for the Indian market and the other for the export market. Tomorrow's global battles will be won by product leaders, not operationally excellent companies. Tomorrow's leaders must be visionaries, whether they belong to the family or not. Our mission at Ranbaxy is to become a research based international pharmaceutical company.[4]

By the early 1990s, Ranbaxy grew to become India's largest manufacturer of bulk drugs[5] and generic drugs, with a domestic market share of 15 percent (see Exhibit 3).

One of Ranbaxy's core competencies was its chemical synthesis capability, but the company had begun to outsource some bulk drugs in limited quantities. The company produced pharmaceuticals in four locations in India. The company's capital costs were typically 50 percent to 75 percent lower than those of comparable U.S. plants and were meant to serve foreign markets in addition to the Indian market. Foreign markets, especially

[4]Quoted in *Times of India,* June 9, 1999.
[5]A bulk drug is an intermediate product that goes into manufacturing of pharmaceutical products.

Exhibit 3   Top 20 Pharmaceutical Companies in India by Sales 1996 to 2000 (Rs billions)

Company	1996*	Company	2000
Glaxo-Wellcome	4.97	Ranbaxy	20.00
Cipla	2.98	Cipla	12.00
Ranbaxy	2.67	Dr. Reddy's Labs	11.30
Hoechts-Roussel	2.60	Glaxo (India)	7.90
Knoll Pharmaceutical	1.76	Lupin Labs	7.80
Pfizer	1.73	Aurobindo Pharma	7.60
Alembic	1.68	Novartis	7.20
Torrent Pharma	1.60	Wockhardt Ltd.	6.80
Lupin Labs	1.56	Sun Pharma	6.70
Zydus-Cadila	1.51	Cadilla Healthcare	5.80
Ambalal Sarabhai	1.38	Nicholas Piramal	5.70
Smithkline Beecham	1.20	Aventis Pharma	5.30
Aristo Pharma	1.17	Alembic Ltd.	4.80
Parke Davis	1.15	Morepen Labs	4.70
Cadila Pharma	1.12	Torrent Pharma	4.40
E. Merck	1.11	IPCA Labs	4.20
Wockhardt	1.08	Knoll Pharma	3.70
John Wyeth	1.04	Orchid Chemicals	3.60
Alkem Laboratories	1.04	E Merck	3.50
Hindustan Ciba Geigy	1.03	Pfizer	3.40

*1996 figures are from ORG, Bombay as reported in Lanjouw, J.O., www.oiprc.ox.ac.uk/EJWP0799.html, NBER working paper No. 6366.
Source: "Report on Pharmaceutical Sector in India," *Scope Magazine,* September 2001, p.14.

those in more developed countries, often had stricter quality control requirements, and such a difference meant that the manufacturing practices required to compete in those markets appeared to be costlier from the perspective of less developed markets. Higher prices in other countries provided the impetus for Ranbaxy to pursue international markets; the company had a presence in 47 markets outside India, mainly through exports handled through an international division. Ranbaxy's R&D efforts began at the end of the 1970s; in 1979, the company still had only 12 scientists. As Ranbaxy entered the international market in the 1980s, R&D was responsible for registering its products in foreign markets, most of which was directed to process R&D; R&D expenditures ranged from two percent to five percent of the annual sales with future targets of seven percent to eight per cent.

The Lilly Ranbaxy JV

Ranbaxy approached Lilly in 1992 to investigate the possibility of supplying certain active ingredients or sourcing of intermediate products to Lilly in order to provide low-cost sources of intermediate pharmaceutical ingredients. Lilly had earlier relationships with manufacturers in India to produce human or animal insulin and then export the products to the Soviet Union using the Russia/India trade route, but those had never developed into on-the-ground relationships within the Indian market. Ranbaxy was the second largest exporter of all products in India and the second largest pharmaceutical company in India after Glaxo (a subsidiary of the U.K.-based firm).

Rajiv Gulati, at that time a general manager of business development and marketing controller at Ranbaxy, who was instrumental in developing the strategy for Ranbaxy, recalled:

In the 1980s, many multinational pharmaceutical companies had a presence in India. Lilly did not. As a result of both the sourcing of intermediate products as well as the fact that Lilly was one of the only players not yet in India, we felt that we could use Ranbaxy's knowledge of the market to get our feet on the ground in India. Ranbaxy would supply certain products to the joint venture from its own portfolio that were currently being manufactured in India and then formulate and finish some of Lilly's products locally. The joint venture would buy the active ingredients and Lilly would have Ranbaxy finish the package and allow the joint venture to sell and distribute those products.

The first meeting was held at Lilly's corporate center in Indianapolis in late 1990. Present were Ranbaxy's senior executives, Dr. Singh, vice-chairman, and D.S. Brar, chief operating officer (COO), and Lilly's senior executives including Gene Step and Richard Wood, the CEO of Lilly. Rickey Pate, a corporate attorney at Eli Lilly who was present at the meeting, recalled:

> It was a very smooth meeting. We had a lot in common. We both believed in high ethical standards, in technology and innovation, as well as in the future of patented products in India. Ranbaxy executives emphasized their desire to be a responsible corporate citizen and expressed their concerns for their employees. It was quite obvious Ranbaxy would be a compatible partner in India.

Lilly decided to form the joint venture in India to focus on marketing of Lilly's drugs there, and a formal JV agreement was signed in November 1992. The newly created JV was to have an authorized capital of Rs200 million (equivalent of US$7.1 million), and an initial subscribed equity capital of Rs84 million (US$3 million), with equal contribution from Lilly and Ranbaxy, leading to an equity ownership of 50 percent each. The board of directors for the JV would comprise six directors, three from each company. A management committee was also created comprising two directors, one from each company, and Lilly retained the right to appoint the CEO who would be responsible for the day-to-day operations. The agreement also provided for transfer of shares, in the event any one of the partners desired to dispose some or its entire share in the company.

In the mid-1990s, Lilly was investigating the possibility of extending its operations to include generics. Following the launch of the Indian JV, Lilly and Ranbaxy, entered into two other agreements related to generics, one in India to focus on manufacturing generics, and the other in the United States to focus on the marketing of generics. However, within less than a year, Lilly made a strategic decision not to enter the generics market and the two parties agreed to terminate the JV agreements related to the generics. Mayr recalled:

> At that time we were looking at the Indian market although we did not have any particular time frame for entry. We particularly liked Ranbaxy, as we saw an alignment of the broad values. Dr. Singh had a clear vision of leading Ranbaxy to become an innovation driven company. And we liked what we saw in them. Of course, for a time we were looking at the generic business and wondering if this was something we should be engaged in. Other companies had separate division for generics and we were evaluating such an idea. However, we had a pilot program in Holland and that taught us what it took to be competitive in generics and decided that business wasn't for us, and so we decided to get out of generics.

The Start-Up   By March 1993, Andrew Mascarenhas, an American citizen of Indian origin, who at the time was the general manager for Lilly's Caribbean basin, based in San Juan, Puerto Rico, was selected to become the managing director of the joint venture. Rajiv Gulati, who at the time spearheaded the business development and marketing efforts at Ranbaxy, was chosen as the director of marketing and sales at the JV. Mascarenhas recalled:

> Lilly saw the joint venture as an investment the company needed to make. At the time India was a country of 800 million people: 200 million to 300 million of them were considered to be within the country's middle class that represented the future of India. The concept of globalization was just taking hold at Lilly.

India, along with China and Russia were seen as markets where Lilly needed to build a greater presence. Some resistance was met due to the recognition that a lot of Lilly's products were already being sold by Indian manufacturers due to the lack of patent protection and intellectual property rights so the question was what products should we put in there that could be competitive. The products that were already being manufactured had sufficient capacity; so it was an issue of trying to leverage the markets in which those products were sold into.

Lilly was a name that most physicians in India did not recognize despite its leadership position in the United States, it did not have any recognition in India. Ranbaxy was the leader within India. When I was informed that the name of the joint venture was to be Lilly Ranbaxy, first thing I did was to make sure that the name of the joint venture was Eli Lilly Ranbaxy and not just Lilly Ranbaxy. The reason for this was based on my earlier experience in India, where "good quality" rightly or wrongly, was associated with foreign imported goods. Eli Lilly Ranbaxy sounded foreign enough!

Early on, Mascarenhas and Gulati worked getting the venture up and running with office space and an employee base. Mascarenhas recalled:

> I got a small space within Ranbaxy's set-up. We had two tables, one for Rajiv and the other for me. We had to start from that infrastructure and move towards building up the organization from scratch. Rajiv was great to work with and we both were able to see eye-to-eye on most issues. Dr. Singh was a strong supporter and the whole of Ranbaxy senior management tried to assist us whenever we asked for help.

The duo immediately hired a financial analyst, and the team grew from there. Early on, they hired a medical director, a sales manager and a human resources manager. The initial team was a good one, but there was enormous pressure and the group worked seven days a week. Ranbaxy's help was used for getting government approvals, licenses, distribution and supplies. Recalled Gulati:

> We used Ranbaxy's name for everything. We were new and it was very difficult for us. We used their

distribution network as we did not have one and Lilly did not want to invest heavily in setting up a distribution network. We paid Ranbaxy for the service. Ranbaxy was very helpful.

By the end of 1993, the venture moved to an independent place, began launching products and employed more than 200 people. Within another year, Mascarenhas had hired a significant sales force and had recruited medical doctors and financial people for the regulatory group with assistance from Lilly's Geneva office. Mascarenhas recalled:

> Our recruiting theme was 'Opportunity of a Lifetime' i.e., joining a new company, and to be part of its very foundation. Many who joined us, especially at senior level, were experienced executives. By entering this new and untested company, they were really taking a huge risk with their careers and the lives of their families.

However, the employee turnover in the Indian pharmaceutical industry was very high. Sandeep Gupta, director of marketing recalled:

> Our biggest problem was our high turnover rate. A sales job in the pharmaceutical industry was not the most sought-after position. Any university graduate could be employed. The pharmaceutical industry in India is very unionized. Ranbaxy's HR practices were designed to work with unionized employees. From the very beginning, we did not want our recruits to join unions. Instead, we chose to show recruits that they had a career in ELR. When they joined us as sales graduates they did not just remain at that level. We took a conscious decision to promote from within the company. The venture began investing in training and used Lilly's training programs. The programs were customized for Indian conditions, but retained Lilly's values (see Exhibit 4).

Within a year, the venture team began gaining the trust and respect of doctors, due to the strong values adhered to by Lilly. Mascarenhas described how the venture fought the Indian stigma:

> Lilly has a code of ethical conduct called the Red Book, and the company did not want to go down the path where it might be associated with unethical behavior. But Lilly felt Ranbaxy knew how to do

---

Exhibit 4 Values at Eli Lilly Ranbaxy Limited

People

"The people who make up this company are its most valuable assets."

- Respect for the individual
  - o Courtesy and politeness at all times
  - o Sensitivity to other people's views
  - o Respect for ALL people regardless of caste, religion, sex or age
- Careers NOT jobs
  - o Emphasis on individual's growth, personal and professional
  - o Broaden experience via cross-functional moves

"The first responsibility of our supervisors is **to build men, then medicines**."

Attitude

"There is very little difference between people. But that difference makes a BIG difference. The little difference is attitude. The BIG difference is … whether it is POSITIVE or NEGATIVE."
"Are we part of the PROBLEM or part of the SOLUTION?"

Team

"None of us is as smart as all of us."

Integrity

- Integrity outside the company
  - a. "We should not do anything or be expected to take any action that we would be ashamed to explain to our family or close friends"
  - b. "The red-faced test"
  - c. "Integrity can be our biggest competitive advantage"
- Integrity inside the company
  - o With one another: openness, honesty

Excellence

- Serving our customers

"In whatever we do, we must ask ourselves: how does this serve my customer better?"

- Continuous improvement

"Nothing is being done today that cannot be done better tomorrow."

- Become the Industry Standard

"In whatever we do, we will do it so well that we become the Industry Standard."

---

things the right way and that they respected their employees, which was a very important attribute. So following Lilly's Red Book values, the group told doctors the truth; both the positive and negative aspects of their drugs. If a salesperson didn't know the answer to something, they didn't lie or make up something; they told the doctor they didn't know. No bribes were given or taken, and it was found that honesty and integrity could actually be a competitive

advantage. Sales people were trained to offer product information to doctors. The group gradually became distinguished by this "strange" behavior.

Recalled Sudhanshu Kamat, controller of finance at ELR:

Lilly from the start treated us as its employees, like all its other affiliates worldwide. We followed the same systems and processes that any Lilly affiliate would worldwide.

Much of the success of the joint venture is attributed to the strong and cohesive working relationship of Mascarenhas and Gulati. Mascarenhas recalled:

> We both wanted the venture to be successful. We both had our identities to the JV, and there was no Ranbaxy versus Lilly politics. From the very start when we had our office at Ranbaxy premises, I was invited to dine with their senior management. Even after moving to our own office, I continued the practice of having lunch at Ranbaxy HQ on a weekly basis. I think it helped a lot to be accessible at all times and to build on the personal relationship.

The two companies had very different business focuses. Ranbaxy was a company driven by the generics business. Lilly, on the other hand, was driven by innovation and discovery.

Mascarenhas focused his effort on communicating Eli Lilly's values to the new joint venture:

> I spent a lot of time communicating Lilly's values to newly hired employees. In the early days, I interviewed our senior applicants personally. I was present in the two-day training sessions that we offered for the new employees, where I shared the values of the company. That was a critical task for me to make sure that the right foundations were laid down for growth.

The first products that came out of the joint venture were human insulin from Lilly and several Ranbaxy products; but the team faced constant challenges in dealing with government regulations on the one hand and financing the affiliate on the other. There were also cash flow constraints.

The ministry of health provided limitations on Lilly's pricing, and even with the margin the Indian government allowed, most of it went to the wholesalers and the pharmacies, pursuant to formulas in the Indian ministry of health. Once those were factored out of the gross margin, achieving profitability was a real challenge, as some of the biggest obstacles faced were duties imposed by the Indian government on imports and other regulatory issues. Considering the weak intellectual property rights regime, Lilly

did not want to launch some of its products, such as its top-seller, Prozac.[6] Gulati recalled:

> We focused only on those therapeutic areas where Lilly had a niche. We did not adopt a localization strategy such as the ones adopted by Pfizer and Glaxo[7] that manufactured locally and sold at local prices. India is a high-volume, low price, low profit market, but it was a conscious decision by us to operate the way we did. We wanted to be in the global price band. So, we did not launch several patented products because generics were selling at 1/60th the price.

Product and marketing strategies had to be adopted to suit the market conditions. ELR's strategy evolved over the years to focus on two groups of products: one was off-patent drugs, where Lilly could add substantial value (e.g. Ceclor), and two, patented drugs, where there existed a significant barrier to entry (e.g. Reopro and Gemzar). ELR marketed Ceclor, a Ranbaxy manufactured product, but attempted to add significant value by providing medical information to the physicians and other unique marketing activities. By the end of 1996, the venture had reached the break-even and was becoming profitable.

The Mid-Term Organizational Changes   Mascarenhas was promoted in 1996 to managing director of Eli Lilly Italy, and Chris Shaw, a British national, who was then managing the operations in Taiwan, was assigned to the JV as the new managing director. Also, Gulati, who was formally a Ranbaxy employee, decided to join Eli Lilly as its employee, and was assigned to Lilly's corporate office in Indianapolis in the Business Development—Infectious Diseases therapeutic division. Chris Shaw recalled:

> When I went to India as a British national, I was not sure what sort of reception I would get, knowing its history. But my family and I were received very warmly. I found a dynamic team with a strong sense of values.

Shaw focused on building systems and processes to bring stability to the fast-growing organization;

---

[6]Used as an antidepressant medication.

[7]An industry study by McKinsey found that Glaxo sold 50 percent of its volume, received three percent of revenues and one percent of profit in India.

his own expertise in operations made a significant contribution during this phase. He hired a senior level manager and created a team to develop standard operating procedures (SOPs) for ensuring smooth operations. The product line also expanded. The JV continued to maintain a 50-50 distribution of products from Lilly and Ranbaxy, although there was no stipulation to maintain such a ratio. The clinical organization in India was received top-ratings in internal audits by Lilly, making it suitable for a wider range of clinical trials. Shaw also streamlined the sales and marketing activities around therapeutic areas to emphasize and enrich the knowledge capabilities of the company's sales force. Seeing the rapid change in the environment in India, ELR, with the support of Mayr, hired the management-consulting firm, McKinsey, to recommend growth options in India. ELR continued its steady performance with an annualized growth rate of about eight percent during the late 1990s.

In 1999, Chris Shaw was assigned to Eli Lilly's Polish subsidiary, and Gulati returned to the ELR as its managing director, following his three-year tenure at Lilly's U.S. operations. Recalled Gulati:

> When I joined as MD in 1999, we were growing at eight percent and had not added any new employees. I hired 150 people over the next two years and went about putting systems and processes in place. When we started in 1993 and during Andrew's time, we were

like a grocery shop. Now we needed to be a company. We had to be a large durable organization and prepare ourselves to go from sales of US$10 million to sales of US$100 million.

ELR created a medical and regulatory unit, which handled the product approval processes with government. Das, the chief financial officer (CFO), commented:

> We worked together with the government on the regulatory part. Actually, we did not take shelter under the Ranbaxy name but built a strong regulatory (medical and corporate affairs) foundation.

By early 2001, the venture was recording an excellent growth rate (see Exhibit 5), surpassing the average growth rate in the Indian pharmaceutical industry. ELR had already become the 46th largest pharmaceutical company in India out of 10,000 companies. Several of the multinational subsidiaries, which were started at the same time as ELR, had either closed down or were in serious trouble. Das summarized the achievements:

> The JV did add some prestige to Ranbaxy's efforts as a global player as the Lilly name had enormous credibility while Lilly gained the toehold in India. In 10 years we did not have any cannibalization of each other's employees, quite a rare event if you compare with the other JVs. This helped us build a unique culture in India.

Exhibit 5   Eli Lilly-Ranbaxy India Financials 1998 to 2001 (Rs'000s)

	1998–1999	1999–2000	2000–2001
Sales	559,766	632,188	876,266
Marketing Expenses	37,302	61,366	96,854
Other Expenses	157,907	180,364	254,822
Profit after Tax	5,898	12,301	11,999
Current Assets	272,635	353,077	466,738
Current Liabilities	239,664	297,140	471,635
Total Assets	303,254	386,832	516,241
No. of Employees	358	419	460
Exchange Rate (Rupees/US$)	42.6	43.5	46.8

Note: Financial year runs from April 1 to March 31.
Source: Company reports.

The New World, 2001

The pharmaceutical industry continued to grow through the 1990s. In 2001, worldwide retail sales were expected to increase 10 percent to about US$350 billion. The United States was expected to remain the largest and fastest growing country among the world's major drug markets over the next three years. There was a consolidation trend in the industry with ongoing mergers and acquisitions reshaping the industry. In 1990, the world's top 10 players accounted for just 28 percent of the market, while in 2000, the number had risen to 45 percent and continued to grow. There was also a trend among leading global pharmaceutical companies to get back to basics and concentrate on core high-margined prescription preparations and divest non-core businesses. In addition, the partnerships between pharmaceutical and biotechnology companies were growing rapidly. There were a number of challenges, such as escalating R&D costs, lengthening development and approval times for new products, growing competition from generics and follow-on products, and rising cost-containment pressures, particularly with the growing clout of managed care organizations.

By 1995, Lilly had moved up to become the 12th leading pharmaceutical supplier in the world, sixth in the U.S. market, 17th in Europe and 77th in Japan. Much of Lilly's sales success through the mid-1990s came from its antidepressant drug, Prozac. But with the wonder drug due to go off patent in 2001, Lilly was aggressively working on a number of high-potential products. By the beginning of 2001, Lilly was doing business in 151 countries, with its international sales playing a significant role in the company's success (see Exhibits 6 and 7). Dr. Lorenzo Tallarigo recalled:

> When I started as the president of the intercontinental operations, I realized that the world was very different in the 2000s from the world of 1990s. Particularly there were phenomenal changes in the markets in India and China. While I firmly believed that the partnership we had with Ranbaxy was really an excellent one, the fact that we were facing such a different market in the 21st century was reason enough to carefully evaluate our strategies in these markets.

Exhibit 6   Lilly Financials 1992 to 2000 (US$ millions)

	1992	1994	1996	1998	2000
Net sales	4,963	5,711	6,998	9,236	10,862
Foreign sales	2,207	2,710	3,587	3,401	3,858
Research and development expenses	731	839	1,190	1,739	2,019
Income from continuing operations before taxes and extraordinary items	1,194	1,699	2,131	2,665	3,859
Net income	709	1,286	1,524	2,097	3,058
Dividends per share*	1.128	1.260	0.694	0.830	1.060
Current assets	3,006	3,962	3,891	5,407	7,943
Current liabilities	2,399	5,670	4,222	4,607	4,961
Property and equipment	4,072	4,412	4,307	4,096	4,177
Total assets	8,673	14,507	14,307	12,596	14,691
Long-term debt	582	2,126	2,517	2,186	2,634
Shareholder equity	4,892	5,356	6,100	4,430	6,047
Number of employees*	24,500	24,900	27,400	29,800	35,700

*Actual value
Source: Company files.

Exhibit 7 Product Segment Information Lilly and Ranbaxy 1996 and 2000

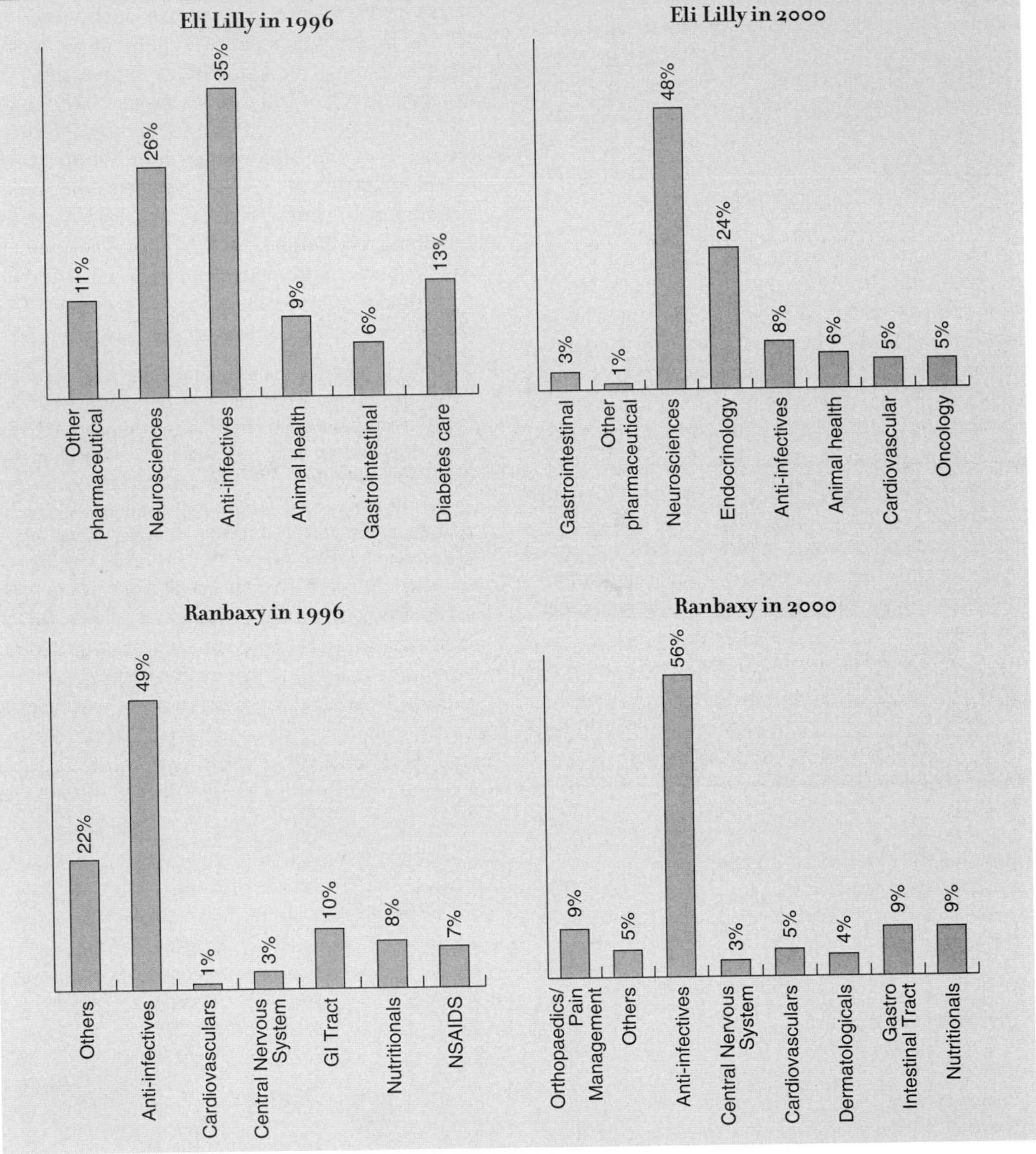

Eli Lilly in 1996

- Other pharmaceutical — 11%
- Neurosciences — 26%
- Anti-infectives — 35%
- Animal health — 9%
- Gastrointestinal — 6%
- Diabetes care — 13%

Eli Lilly in 2000

- Gastrointestinal — 3%
- Other pharmaceutical — 1%
- Neurosciences — 48%
- Endocrinology — 24%
- Anti-infectives — 8%
- Animal health — 6%
- Cardiovascular — 5%
- Oncology — 5%

Ranbaxy in 1996

- Others — 22%
- Anti-infectives — 49%
- Cardiovasculars — 1%
- Central Nervous System — 3%
- GI Tract — 10%
- Nutritionals — 8%
- NSAIDS — 7%

Ranbaxy in 2000

- Orthopaedics/Pain Management — 9%
- Others — 5%
- Anti-infectives — 56%
- Central Nervous System — 3%
- Cardiovasculars — 5%
- Dermatologicals — 4%
- Gastro Intestinal Tract — 9%
- Nutritionals — 9%

Exhibit 8   Ranbaxy Financials 1992 to 2000 (Rs millions)

	1992–93	1994–95	1996–97	1998*	2000
Sales	4,607	7,122	11,482	10,641	17,459
Foreign sales	1,408	3,019	5,224	4,414	8,112
Profit before tax	358	1,304	1,869	1,240	1,945
Profit after tax	353	1,104	1,604	1,170	1,824
Equity dividend	66.50	199.80	379.10	560.10	869.20
Earnings per share (Rs)	16.21	25.59	32.47	13.46	15.74
Net current assets	1,737	5,790	9,335	8,321	8,258
Share capital	217.90	430.50	494.00	1,159.00	1,159.00
Reserves and surplus	1,028	6,000	11,056	12,849	16,448
Book value per share (Rs)	57.16	149.08	233.70	120.90	136.60
No. of employees	4,575	4,703	6,131	5,469	5,784
Exchange rate (US$1 = Rs)	29.00	31.40	35.90	42.60	46.80

*The financial year for Ranbaxy changed from April 1 to March 31 to calendar year in 1998. Also, the company issued a 1:2 bonus issue (see the changes in share capital and book value per share). The 1998 figures are based on nine months April to December 1998.
Source: Company files.

Ranbaxy, too, had witnessed changes through the 1990s. Dr. Singh became the new CEO in 1993 and formulated a new mission for the company: to become a research-based international pharmaceutical company with $1 billion in sales by 2003. This vision saw Ranbaxy developing new drugs through basic research, earmarking 20 percent of the R&D budget for such work. In addition to its joint venture with Lilly, Ranbaxy made three other manufacturing/marketing investments in developed markets: a joint venture with Genpharm in Canada ($1.1 million), and the acquisitions of Ohm Labs in the United States ($13.5 million) and Rima Pharmaceuticals ($8 million) in Ireland. With these deals, Ranbaxy had manufacturing facilities around the globe. While China and Russia were expected to remain key foreign markets, Ranbaxy was looking at the United States and the United Kingdom as its core international markets for the future. In 1999, Dr. Singh handed over the reins of the company to Brar, and later the same year, Ranbaxy lost this visionary leader due to an untimely death. Brar continued Singh's vision to keep Ranbaxy in a

leadership position. However, the vast network of international sales that Ranbaxy had developed created a large financial burden, depressing the company's 2000 results, and was expected to significantly affect its cash flow in 2001 (see Exhibit 8). Vinay Kaul, vice-chairman of Ranbaxy in 2001 and chairman of the board of ELR since 2000, noted:

We have come a long way from where we started. Our role in the present JV is very limited. We had a smooth relationship and we have been of significant help to Lilly to establish a foothold in the market here in India. Also, we have opened up a number of opportunities for them to expand their network. However, we have also grown, and we are a global company with presence in a number of international markets including the United States. We had to really think if this JV is central to our operations, given that we have closed down the other two JV agreements that we had with Lilly on the generics manufacturing. It is common knowledge that whether we continue as a JV or not, we have created a substantial value for Lilly.

There were also significant changes in the Indian business environment. India signed the General

Agreement on Tariffs and Trade (GATT) in April 1994 and became a World Trade Organization (WTO) member in 1995. As per the WTO, from the year 2005, India would grant product patent recognition to all new chemical entities (NCEs), i.e., bulk drugs developed then onward. Also, the Indian government had made the decision to allow 100 percent foreign direct investment into the drugs and pharmaceutical industry in 2001.[8] The Indian pharmaceutical market had grown at an average of 15 percent through the 1990s, but the trends indicated a slowdown in growth, partly due to intense price competition, a shift toward chronic therapies and the entry of large players into the generic market. India was seeing its own internal consolidation of major companies that were trying to bring in synergies through economies of scale. The industry would see more mergers and alliances. And with India's entry into the WTO and its agreement to begin patent protection in 2004– 2005, competition on existing and new products was expected to intensify. Government guidelines were expected to include rationalization of price controls and the encouragement of more research and development. Recalled Gulati:

The change of institutional environment brought a great promise for Lilly. India was emerging into a market that had patent protection and with tremendous potential for adding value in the clinical trials, an important component in the pharmaceutical industry. In Ranbaxy, we had a partner with whom we could work very well, and one which greatly respected Lilly. However, there were considerable signals from both sides, which were forcing us to evaluate the strategy.

Dr. Vinod Mattoo, medical director of ELR commented:

We have been able to achieve penetration in key therapeutic areas of diabetes and oncology. We have created a high caliber, and non-unionized sales force with

world-class sales processes. We have medical infrastructure and expertise to run clinical trials to international standards. We have been able to provide clinical trial data to support global registrations, and an organization in place to maximize returns post-2005.

Evaluating Strategic Options

Considering these several developments, Tallarigo suggested a joint task force comprising senior executives from both companies:

Soon after assuming this role, I visited India in early 2000, and had the pleasure of meeting Dr. Brar and the senior executives. It was clear to me that both Brar and I were in agreement that we needed to think carefully how we approached the future. It was there that I suggested that we create a joint task force to come up with some options that would help us make a final decision.

A task force was set up with two senior executives from Lilly's Asia-Pacific regional office (based in Singapore) and two senior executives from Ranbaxy. The task force did not include senior executives of the ELR so as to not distract the running of the day-to-day operations. Suman Das, the chief financial officer of ELR, was assigned to support the task force with the needed financial data. The task force developed several scenarios and presented different options for the board to consider.

There were rumors within the industry that Ranbaxy expected to divest the JV, and invest the cash in its growing portfolio of generics manufacturing business in international markets. There were also several other Indian companies that offered to buy Ranbaxy's stake in the JV. With India recognizing patent protection in 2005, several Indian pharmaceutical companies were keen to align with multinationals to ensure a pipeline of drugs. Although there were no formal offers from Ranbaxy, the company was expected to price its stakes as high as US$70 million. One of the industry observers in India commented:

I think it is fair for Ranbaxy to expect a reasonable return for its investment in the JV, not only the initial capital, but also so much of its intangibles in the JV.

---

[8]In order to regulate the parallel activities of a foreign company, which had an ongoing joint venture in India, the regulations stipulated that the foreign partner must get a "No objection letter" from its Indian partner, before setting up a wholly owned subsidiary.

Ranbaxy's stock has grown significantly. Given the critical losses that Ranbaxy has had in some of its investments abroad, the revenue from this sale may be a significant boost for Ranbaxy's cash flow this year.

Gerhard Mayr, who in 2001, was the executive vice-president and was responsible for Lilly's demand realization around the world, continued to emphasize the emerging markets in India, China and Eastern Europe. Mayr commented on Ranbaxy:

India is an important market for us and especially after patent protection in 2005. Ranbaxy was a wonderful partner and our relationship with them was outstanding. The other two joint ventures we initiated with them in the generics did not make sense to us once we decided to get out of the generics business. We see India as a good market for Lilly. If a partner is what it takes to succeed, we should go with a partner. If it does not, we should have the flexibility to reconsider.

Tallarigo hoped that Brar would be able to provide a clear direction as to the venture's future. As he prepared for the meeting, he knew the decision was not an easy one, although he felt confident that the JV was in a good shape. While the new regulations allowed Lilly to operate as a wholly owned subsidiary in India, the partnership has been a very positive element in its strategy. Ranbaxy provided manufacturing and logistics support to the JV, and breaking up the partnership would require a significant amount of renegotiations. Also, it was not clear what the financial implications of such a move would be. Although Ranbaxy seemed to favor a sell-out, Tallarigo thought the price expectations might be beyond what Lilly was ready to accept. This meeting with Brar should provide clarity on all these issues.

Reading 6-1   The Design and Management of International Joint Ventures[1]

Paul W. Beamish

An international joint venture is a company that is owned by two or more firms of different nationality. International joint ventures may be formed from a starting (or greenfield) basis or may be the result of several established companies deciding to merge existing divisions. However they are formed, the purpose of most international joint ventures is to allow partners to pool resources and coordinate their efforts to achieve results that neither could obtain acting alone.

A broad range of strategic alliances exists. They vary widely in terms of the level of interaction and type. Most of the comments in this reading focus on equity joint venture—the alliance form usually requiring the greatest level of interaction, cooperation, and investment. While the discussion which follows usually considers a two-party joint venture, it is worth noting that many joint ventures have three or more partners.

Joint ventures have moved from being a way to enter foreign markets of peripheral interest to become a part of the mainstream of corporate activity. Virtually all MNEs are using international joint ventures, many as a key element of their corporate strategies. Merck, for example, has joint ventures with Johnson & Johnson (2007 JV

[1]For more detail, see Paul W. Beamish, *Joint Venturing,* (Charlotte, North Carolina: Information Age Publishing 2008).

sales of $.2 billion), Sanofi Pasteur S.A. (2007 JV sales of $1.4 billion), Merial with Sanofi-Aventis S.A.(2007 JV sales of $2.4 billion), and so forth. Even firms that have traditionally operated independently around the world are increasingly turning to joint ventures.

The popularity and use of international joint ventures and cooperative alliances has remained strong. The rate of joint venture use does not change much from year to year. In general, joint ventures are the mode of choice 25–35 percent of the time by U.S. multinationals and in about 40 percent of foreign subsidiaries formed by Japanese multinationals.

The popularity of alliances has continued despite their reputation for being difficult to manage. Failures exist and are usually widely publicized. Dow Chemical, for example, reportedly lost more than $100 million after a dispute with its Korean joint venture partners caused the firm to sell its 50 percent interest in its Korean venture at a loss, and to sell below cost its nearby wholly owned chemical plant. Also, after Lucent's joint venture in wireless handsets with Philips Electronics ended, Lucent took a $100 million charge at the time on selling its consumer phone equipment business. Similarly, HealthMatics, a joint venture between Glaxo Smith Kline and Physician Computer Network Inc., shut down after losing more than $50 million.

While early surveys suggested that as many as half the companies with international joint ventures were dissatisfied with their ventures' performance, there is reason to believe that some of the earlier concern can now be ameliorated. This is primarily because there is far greater alliance experience and insight to draw from. There is now widespread appreciation that joint ventures are not necessarily transitional organization forms, shorter-lived, or less profitable. For many organizations they are the mode of choice.

There now also exists an Association of Strategic Alliance Professionals (ASAP). It was created to support the professional development of alliance managers and executives to advance the state-of the-art of alliance formation and management and to provide a forum for sharing alliance best practices, resources and opportunities to help companies improve their alliance management capabilities.

Why do managers keep creating new joint ventures? The reasons are presented in the remainder of this reading, as are some guidelines for international joint venture success.

Why Companies Create International Joint Ventures

International joint ventures can be used to achieve one of four basic purposes. As shown in Exhibit 1, these are: to strengthen the firm's existing business, to take the firm's existing products into new markets, to obtain new products that can be sold in the firm's existing markets, and to diversify into a new business.

Companies using joint ventures for each of these purposes will have different concerns and will be looking for partners with different characteristics. Firms wanting to strengthen their existing business, for example, will most likely be looking for partners among their current competitors, while those wanting to enter new geographic markets will be looking for overseas firms in related businesses with good local market knowledge. Although often treated as a single category of business activity, international joint ventures are remarkably diverse, as the following descriptions indicate.

Strengthening the Existing Business International joint ventures are used in a variety of ways by firms wishing to strengthen or protect their existing businesses. Among the most important are joint ventures formed to achieve economies of scale, joint ventures that allow the firm to acquire needed technology and know-how, and ventures that reduce the financial risk of major projects. Joint ventures formed for the latter two reasons may have the added benefit of eliminating a potential competitor from a particular product or market area.

Achieving Economies of Scale Firms often use joint ventures to attempt to match the economies of

Exhibit 1   Motives for International Joint Venture Formation

	Existing Products	New Products
New Markets	To take existing products to foreign markets	To diversify into a new business
Existing Markets	To strengthen the existing business	To bring foreign products to local markets

scale achieved by their larger competitors. Joint ventures have been used to give their parents economies of scale in raw material and component supply, in research and development, and in marketing and distribution. Joint ventures have also been used as a vehicle for carrying out divisional mergers, which yield economies across the full spectrum of business activity.

Very small, entrepreneurial firms are more likely to participate in a network than an equity joint venture in order to strengthen their business through economies of scale. Small firms may form a network to reduce the costs, and increase the potential, of foreign market entry, or to meet some other focused objective. Most of these networks tend to have a relatively low ease of entry and exit and a loose structure and require a limited investment (primarily time, as they might be self-financing through fees). International equity joint ventures by very small firms are unusual because such firms must typically overcome some combination of liabilities of size, newness, foreignness, and relational orientation (often the small firms were initially successful because of their single-minded, do-it-themselves orientation).

Raw Material and Component Supply   In many industries the smaller firms create joint ventures to obtain raw materials or jointly manufacture components. Automakers, for instance, may develop a jointly owned engine plant to supply certain low-volume engines to each company. Producing engines for the parents provides economies of scale, with each company receiving engines at a lower cost than it could obtain if it were to produce them itself.

The managers involved in such ventures are quick to point out that these financial savings do not come without a cost. Design changes in jointly produced engines, for example, tend to be slow because all partners have to agree on them. In fact, one joint venture that produced computer printers fell seriously behind the state of the art in printer design because the parents could not agree on the features they wanted in the jointly designed printer. Because all of the venture's output was sold to the parents, the joint venture personnel had no direct contact with end customers and could not resolve the dispute.

Transfer pricing is another issue that arises in joint ventures that supply their parents. A low transfer price on products shipped from the venture to the parents, for instance, means that whichever parent buys the most product obtains the most benefit. Many higher-volume-taking parents claim that this is fair, as it is their volume that plays an important role in making the joint venture viable. On the other hand, some parents argue for a higher transfer price, which means that the economic benefits are captured in the venture and will flow, most likely via dividends, to the parents in proportion to their share holdings in the venture. As the share holdings generally reflect the original asset contributions to the venture and not the volumes taken out every year, this means that different parents will do well under this arrangement. Clearly, the potential for transfer price disputes is significant.

Research and Development   Shared research and development efforts are increasingly common. The rationale for such programs is that participating firms can save both time and money by collaborating and may, by combining the efforts of the participating companies' scientists, come up with results that would otherwise have been impossible.

The choice facing firms wishing to carry out collaborative research is whether to simply coordinate their efforts and share costs or to actually set up a jointly owned company. Hundreds of multicompany research programs are not joint ventures. Typically, scientists from the participating companies agree on the research objectives and the most likely avenues of exploration to achieve those objectives. If there are, say, four promising ways to attack a particular problem, each of four participating companies would be assigned one route and told to pursue it. Meetings would be held, perhaps quarterly, to share results and approaches taken and when (hopefully) one route proved to be successful, all firms would be fully informed on the new techniques and technology.

The alternative way to carry out collaborative research is to establish a jointly owned company and to provide it with staff, budget, and a physical location. Yet even here, problems may occur. In the United States, the president of a joint research company established by a dozen U.S. computer firms discovered that the participating companies were not sending their best people to the new company. He ended up hiring more than 200 of the firm's 330 scientists from the outside.

A sensitive issue for firms engaging in collaborative research, whether through joint ventures or not, is how far the collaboration should extend. Because the partners are usually competitors, the often expressed ideal is that the joint effort will focus only on "precompetitive" basic research and not, for example, on product development work. This is often a difficult line to draw.

Marketing and Distribution   Many international joint ventures involve shared research, development, and production but stop short of joint marketing. The vehicles which came out of the NUMMI joint venture between Toyota and General Motors in California, which ceased operations in 2010, were clearly branded as GM or Toyota products and were sold competitively through each parent's distribution network. Antitrust plays a role in the decision to keep marketing activities separate, but so does the partners' intrinsic desire to maintain separate brand identities and increase their own market share. These cooperating firms have not forgotten that they are competitors.

There are, nevertheless, some ventures formed for the express purpose of achieving economies in marketing and distribution. Here, each firm is hoping for wider market coverage at a lower cost. The trade-off is a loss of direct control over the sales force, potentially slower decision making, and a possible loss of direct contact with the customer.

Some-what similar in intent are cooperative marketing agreements, which are not joint ventures but agreements by two firms with related product lines to sell one another's products. Here companies end up with a more complete line to sell, without the managerial complications of a joint venture. Sometimes the cooperative marketing agreement can in fact entail joint branding.

Divisional Mergers   Multinational companies with subsidiaries that they have concluded are too small to be economic have sometimes chosen to create a joint venture by combining their "too small" operations with those of a competitor. Fiat and Peugeot, for example, merged their automobile operations in Argentina, where both companies were doing poorly. The new joint venture started life with a market share of 35 percent and a chance for greatly improved economies in design, production, and marketing. Faced with similar pressures, Ford and Volkswagen did the same thing in Brazil, creating a jointly owned company called Auto Latina.

A divisional merger can also allow a firm a graceful exit from a business in which it is no longer interested. Honeywell gave up trying to continue alone in the computer industry when it folded its business into a venture with Machines Bull of France and NEC of Japan. Honeywell held a 40 percent stake in the resulting joint venture.

Acquiring Technology in the Core Business Firms that have wanted to acquire technology in their core business area have traditionally done so through license agreements or by developing the technology themselves. Increasingly, however, companies are turning to joint ventures for this purpose, because developing technology in-house is seen as taking too long, and license agreements, while giving the firm access to patent rights and engineers' ideas, may not provide much in the way of shop floor know-how. The power of a joint venture is that a firm may be able to have its employees working shoulder to shoulder with those of its partner, trying to solve the same problems. For example, the General Motors joint venture with Toyota provided an opportunity for GM to obtain a source of low-cost small cars and to watch firsthand how Toyota managers, who were in operational control of the venture, were able to produce high-quality automobiles at low cost. Some observers even concluded that the opportunity for General Motors to learn new production techniques was potentially more valuable—if absorbed—than the supply of cars coming from the venture.

Reducing Financial Risk Some projects are too big or too risky for firms to tackle alone. This is why oil companies use joint ventures to split the costs of searching for new oil fields, and why the aircraft industry is increasingly using joint ventures and "risk-sharing subcontractors" to put up some of the funds required to develop new aircraft and engines.

Do such joint ventures make sense? For the oil companies the answer is a clear yes. In these ventures, one partner takes a lead role and manages the venture on a day-to-day basis. Management complexity, a major potential drawback of joint ventures, is kept to a minimum. If the venture finds oil, transfer prices are not a problem—the rewards of the venture are easy to divide between the partners. In situations like this, forming a joint venture is an efficient and sensible way of sharing risk.

It is not as obvious that some other industry ventures are a good idea, at least not for industry leaders. Their partners are not entering these ventures simply in the hopes of earning an attractive return on their investment. They are gearing up to produce, sooner or later, their own product. Why would a company be willing to train potential competitors? For many firms, it is the realization that their partner is going to hook up with someone anyway, so better to have a portion of a smaller future pie than none at all, even if it means you may be eventually competing against yourself. This is consistent with the old adage: keep your friends close, and your enemies (here competitors) even closer.

Taking Products to Foreign Markets Firms with domestic products that they believe will be successful in foreign markets face a choice. They can produce the product at home and export it, license the technology to local firms around the world, establish wholly owned subsidiaries in foreign countries, or form joint ventures with local partners. Many firms conclude that exporting is unlikely to lead to significant market penetration, building wholly owned subsidiaries is too slow and requires too many resources, and licensing does not offer an adequate financial return. The result is that an international joint venture, while seldom seen as an ideal choice, is often the most attractive compromise.

Moving into foreign markets entails a degree of risk, and most firms that decide to form a joint venture with a local firm are doing so to reduce the risk associated with their new market entry. Very often, they look for a partner that deals with a related product line and, thus, has a good feel for the local market. As a further risk-reducing measure, the joint venture may begin life as simply a sales and marketing operation, until the product begins to sell well and volumes rise. Then a "screwdriver" assembly plant may be set up to assemble components shipped from the foreign parent. Eventually, the venture may modify or redesign the product to better suit the local market and may establish complete local manufacturing, sourcing raw material and components locally. The objective is to withhold major investment until the market uncertainty is reduced.

Following Customers to Foreign Markets
Another way to reduce the risk of a foreign market entry is to follow firms that are already customers at home. Thus, many Japanese automobile suppliers have followed Honda, Toyota, and Nissan as they set up new plants in North America and Europe. Very often these suppliers, uncertain of their ability to operate in a foreign environment, decide to form a joint venture with a local partner. There are, for example, a great many automobile supplier joint ventures in the United States originally formed between Japanese and American auto suppliers to supply the Japanese "transplant" automobile manufacturers. For the Americans, such ventures provide a way to learn Japanese manufacturing techniques and to tap into a growing market.

Investing in "Markets of the Future"   Some joint ventures are established by firms taking an early position in what they see as emerging markets. These areas offer very large untapped markets, as well as a possible source of low-cost raw materials and labor. The major problems faced by Western firms in penetrating such markets are their unfamiliarity with the local culture, establishing Western attitudes toward quality, and, in some areas, repatriating earnings in hard currency. The solution (sometimes imposed by local government) has often been the creation of joint ventures with local partners who "know the ropes" and can deal with the local bureaucracy.

Bringing Foreign Products to Local Markets
For every firm that uses an international joint venture to take its product to a foreign market, a local company sees the joint venture as an attractive way to bring a foreign product to its existing market. It is, of course, this complementarity of interest that makes the joint venture possible.

Local partners enter joint ventures to get better utilization of existing plants or distribution channels, to protect themselves against threatening new technology, or simply as an impetus for new growth. Typically, the financial rewards that the local partner receives from a venture are different from those accruing to the foreign partner. For example:

- Many foreign partners make a profit shipping finished products and components to their joint ventures. These profits are particularly attractive because they are in hard currency, which may not be true of the venture's profits, and because the foreign partner captures 100 percent of them, not just a share.
- Many foreign partners receive a technology fee, which is a fixed percentage of the sales volume of the joint venture. The local partner may or may not receive a management fee of like amount.
- Foreign partners typically pay a withholding tax on dividends remitted to them from the venture. Local firms do not.

As a result of these differences, the local partner is often far more concerned with the venture's bottom line earnings and dividend payout than the foreign partner. This means the foreign partner is likely to be happier to keep the venture as simply a marketing or assembly operation, as previously described, than to develop it to the point where it buys less imported material.

Although this logic is understandable, such thinking is shortsighted. The best example of the benefits that can come back to a parent from a powerful joint venture is Fuji Xerox, a venture begun in Japan in 1962 between Xerox and Fuji Photo. This is among the best known American–Japanese joint ventures in Japan.

For the first 10 years of its life, Fuji Xerox was strictly a marketing organization. It did its best to sell Xerox copiers in the Japanese market, even though the U.S. company had done nothing to adapt the machine to the Japanese market. For example, to reach the print button on one model, Japanese secretaries had to stand on a box. After 10 years of operation, Fuji Xerox began to manufacture its own machines, and by 1975 it was redesigning U.S. equipment for the Japanese market. Soon thereafter, with the encouragement of Fuji Photo, and in spite of the resistance of Xerox engineers in the United States, the firm began to design its own copier equipment. Its goal was to design and build a copier in half the time and at half the cost of previous machines. When this was accomplished, the firm set its sights on winning the Deming award, a highly coveted Japanese prize for excellence in total quality control. Fuji Xerox won the award in 1980.

It was also in 1980 that Xerox, reeling under the impact of intense competition from Japanese copier companies, finally began to pay attention to the lessons that it could learn from Fuji Xerox. Adopting the Japanese joint venture's manufacturing techniques and quality programs, the parent company fought its way back to health in the mid-1980s. By 1991, Xerox International Partners was established as a joint venture between Fuji Xerox and Xerox Corporation to sell low-end printers in North America and Europe. In 1998, exports to the United States grew substantially with digital color copiers and OEM printer engines. In 2000, Xerox Corporation transferred its China/Hong Kong Operations to Fuji Xerox and Fuji Photo raised its stake in the venture to 75 percent in 2001. By 2007, Fuji Xerox Co. Ltd. employed 42,000 people, had about $11 billion in revenues, was responsible for the design and manufacture of many digital color copiers and printers for Xerox worldwide, and was an active partner in research and development. Both the lessons learned from Fuji Xerox and the contributions they have made to Xerox have inevitably helped Xerox prosper as an independent company.

Using Joint Ventures for Diversification   As the previous examples illustrate, many joint ventures take products that one parent knows well into a market that the other knows well. However, some break new ground and move one or both parents into products and markets that are new to them.

Arrangements to acquire the skills necessary to compete in a new business is a long-term proposition, but one that some firms are willing to undertake. Given the fact that most acquisitions of unrelated businesses do not succeed, and that trying to enter a new business without help is extremely difficult, choosing partners who will help you learn the business may not be a bad strategy if you are already familiar with the partner. However, to enter a new market, with a new product, and a new partner—even when the probability of success for each is 80 percent— leaves one with an overall probability of success of (.8 .8 .8) about 50 percent!

Joint ventures can also be viewed as vehicles for learning. Here the modes of learning go beyond knowledge transfer (i.e., existing know-how) to include transformation and harvesting. In practice, most IJV partners engage in the transfer of existing knowledge, but stop short of knowledge transformation or harvesting. Although many multinational enterprises have very large numbers of international equity joint ventures and alliances, only a small percentage dedicate resources explicitly to learning about the alliance process. Few organizations go to the trouble of inventorying/cataloguing the corporate experience with joint ventures, let alone how the accumulated knowledge might be transferred within or between divisions. This oversight will be increasingly costly for firms, especially as some of the bilateral alliances become part of multilateral networks.

Requirements for International Joint Venture Success

The checklist in Exhibit 2 presents many of the items that a manager should consider when establishing an international joint venture. Each of these is discussed in the following sections.

Exhibit 2   Joint Venture Checklist

---

1. Test the strategic logic.
   - Do you really need a partner? For how long? Does your partner?
   - How big is the payoff for both parties? How likely is success?
   - Is a joint venture the best option?
   - Do congruent performance measures exist?
2. Partnership and fit.
   - Does the partner share your objectives for the venture?
   - Does the partner have the necessary skills and resources? Will you get access to them?
   - Will you be compatible?
   - Can you arrange an "engagement period"?
   - Is there a comfort versus competence trade-off?
3. Shape and design.
   - Define the venture's scope of activity and its strategic freedom vis-à-vis its parents.
   - Lay out each parent's duties and payoffs to create a win-win situation. Ensure that there are comparable contributions over time.
   - Establish the managerial role of each partner.
4. Doing the deal.
   - How much paperwork is enough? Trust versus legal considerations?
   - Agree on an endgame.
5. Making the venture work.
   - Give the venture continuing top management attention.
   - Manage cultural differences.
   - Watch out for inequities.
   - Be flexible.

Testing the Strategic Logic   The decision to enter a joint venture should not be taken lightly. As mentioned earlier, joint ventures require a great deal of management attention, and, in spite of the care and attention they receive, many prove unsatisfactory to their parents.

Firms considering entering a joint venture should satisfy themselves that there is not a simpler way, such as a nonequity alliance, to get what they need. They should also carefully consider the time period for which they are likely to need help. Some joint ventures have been labeled "permanent solutions to temporary problems" by firms that entered a venture to get help on some aspect of their business; then, when they no longer needed the help, they were still stuck with the joint venture.

The same tough questions a firm may ask itself before forming a joint venture need to be asked of its partner(s). How long will the partner(s) need it? Is the added potential payoff high enough to each partner to compensate for the increased coordination/communications costs which go with the formation of a joint venture?

A major issue in the discussion of strategic logic is to determine whether congruent measures of performance exist. As Exhibit 3 suggests, in many joint ventures, incongruity exists. In this example the foreign partner was looking for a joint venture that would generate 20 percent return on sales in a 1–2 year period and require a limited amount of senior management time. The local partner in turn was seeking a JV that would be quickly profitable and be able to justify some high-paying salaried positions (for the local partner and several family members/friends). While each partner's performance objectives seem defensible, this venture would need to resolve several major problem areas in order to succeed. First, each partner did not make explicit all their primary performance objectives. Implicit measures (those below the dotted line in Exhibit 3), are a source of latent disagreement/misunderstanding. Second, the explicit versus implicit measures of each partner were internally inconsistent. The foreign partner wanted high profitability while using little senior management time and old technology. The local partner wanted quick profits but high-paying local salaries.

Congruity is not just an inter-partner issue. From an intra-partner perspective, it is also essential that the internal managers speak and act from a common platform.

Partnership and Fit   Joint ventures are sometimes formed to satisfy complementary needs. But when one partner acquires (learns) another's

Exhibit 3   Measuring JV Performance: The Search for Congruity

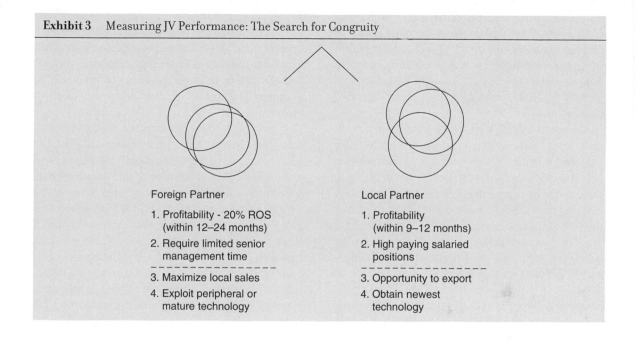

Foreign Partner

1. Profitability - 20% ROS
   (within 12–24 months)
2. Require limited senior
   management time
   - - - - - - - - - - - - - - - -
3. Maximize local sales
4. Exploit peripheral or
   mature technology

Local Partner

1. Profitability
   (within 9–12 months)
2. High paying salaried
   positions
   - - - - - - - - - - - - - - - -
3. Opportunity to export
4. Obtain newest
   technology

capabilities, the joint venture becomes unstable. The acquisition of a partner's capabilities means that the partner is no longer needed. If capabilities are only accessed, the joint venture is more stable. It is not easy, before a venture begins, to determine many of the things a manager would most like to know about a potential partner, like the true extent of its capabilities, what its objectives are in forming the venture, and whether it will be easy to work with. A hasty answer to such questions may lead a firm into a bad relationship or cause it to pass up a good opportunity.

For these reasons, it is often best if companies begin a relationship in a small way, with a simple agreement that is important but not a matter of life and death to either parent. As confidence between the firms grows, the scope of the business activities can broaden.

A good example is provided by Corning Glass, which in 1970 made a major breakthrough in the development of optical fibers that could be used for telecommunication applications, replacing traditional copper wire or coaxial cable. The most likely customers of this fiber outside the United States were the European national telecoms, which were well known to be very nationalistic purchasers. To gain access to these customers, Corning set up development agreements with companies in England, France, Germany, and Italy that were already suppliers to the telecoms. These agreements called for the European firms to develop the technology necessary to combine the fibers into cables, while Corning itself continued to develop the optical fibers. Soon the partners began to import fiber from Corning and cable it locally. Then, when the partners were comfortable with each other and each market was ready, Corning and the partners set up joint ventures to produce optical fiber locally. These ventures worked well.

When assessing issues around partnership and fit, it is useful to consider whether the partner not only shares the same objectives for the venture but also has a similar appetite for risk. In practice this often results in joint ventures having parents of roughly comparable size. It is difficult for parent firms of very different size to establish sustainable joint ventures because of varying resource sets, payback period requirements, and corporate cultures.

Corporate culture similarity—or compatibility—can be a make-or-break issue in many joint ventures. It is not enough to find a partner with the necessary skills; you need to be able to get access to them and to be compatible. Managers are constantly told that they should choose a joint venture partner they trust. As these examples suggest, however, trust between partners is something that can only be developed over time as a result of shared experiences. You can't start with trust.

Shape and Design   In the excitement of setting up a new operation in a foreign country, or getting access to technology provided by an overseas partner, it is important not to lose sight of the basic strategic requirements that must be met if a joint venture is to be successful. The questions that must be addressed are the same when any new business is proposed: Is the market attractive? How strong is the competition? How will the new company compete? Will it have the required resources? And so on.

In addition to these concerns, three others are particularly relevant to joint venture design. One is the question of strategic freedom, which has to do with the relationship between the venture and its parents. How much freedom will the venture be given to do as it wishes with respect to choosing suppliers, a product line, and customers? In the Dow Chemical venture referred to earlier, the dispute between the partners centered on the requirement that the venture buy materials, at what the Koreans believed to be an inflated price, from Dow's new wholly owned Korean plant. Clearly the American and Korean vision of the amount of strategic freedom open to the venture was rather different.

The second issue of importance is that the joint venture be a win-win situation. This means that the payoff to each parent if the venture is successful should be a big one, because this will keep both parents working for the success of the venture when times are tough. If the strategic analysis suggests that the return to either parent over time will be marginal, the venture should be restructured or abandoned.

Finally, it is critical to decide on the management roles that each parent company will play. The venture will be easier to manage if one parent plays a dominant role and has a lot of influence over both the strategic and the day-to-day operations of the venture, or if one parent plays a lead role in the dayto-day operation of the joint venture. More difficult to manage are shared management ventures, in which both parents have a significant input into both strategic decisions and the everyday operations of the venture. A middle ground is split management decision making, where each partner has primary influence over those functional areas where it is most qualified. This is the most common and arguably most effective form.

In some ventures, the partners place too much emphasis on competing with each other about which one will have management control. They lose sight of the fact that the intent of the joint venture is to capture complementary benefits from two partners that will allow the venture (not one of the partners) to compete in the market better than would have been possible by going it alone.

The objective of most joint ventures is superior performance. Thus the fact that dominant-parent ventures are easier to manage than shared-management ventures does not mean they are the appropriate type of venture to establish. Dominant-parent ventures are most likely to be effective when one partner has the knowledge and skill to make the venture a success and the other party is contributing simply money, a trademark, or perhaps a one-time transfer of technology. Such a venture, however, begs the question "What are the unique continuing contributions of the partner?" Shared-management ventures are necessary when the venture needs active consultation between members of each parent company, as when deciding how to modify a product supplied by one parent for the local market that is well known by the other, or to modify a production process designed by one parent to be suitable for a workforce and working conditions well known by the other.

A joint venture is headed for trouble when a parent tries to take a larger role in its management than makes sense. An American company with a joint venture in Japan, for instance, insisted that one of its people be the executive vice president of the venture. This was not reasonable, because the manager had nothing to bring to the management of the venture. He simply served as a constant reminder to the Japanese that the American partner did not trust them. The Americans were pushing for a shared-management venture when it was more logical to allow the Japanese, who certainly had all the necessary skills, to be the dominant or at least the leading firm. The major American contribution to the venture was to allow it to use its world-famous trademarks and brand names.

A second example, also in Japan, involved a French firm. This company was bringing complex technology to the venture that needed to be modified for the Japanese market. It was clear that the French firm required a significant say in the management of the venture. On the other hand, the French had no knowledge of the Japanese market and, thus, the Japanese also needed a significant role in the venture. The logical solution would have been a shared-management venture and equal influence in decisions made at the board level. Unfortunately, both companies wanted to play a dominant role, and the venture collapsed in a decision-making stalemate.

Finally, every joint venture must resolve how much of the JV will be owned by each of the partners. Some firms equate ownership with control, assuming more is always better. Such an assumption would be incorrect. Research has shown that once a foreign firm has about a 40 percent equity stake, there is little difference in the survivability of that subsidiary than if they had had, for example, an 80 percent stake (see Exhibit 4).

Doing the Deal Experienced managers argue that it is the relationship between the partners that is

Exhibit 4   Effect of Foreign Equity Holding on Subsidiary Mortality Risk

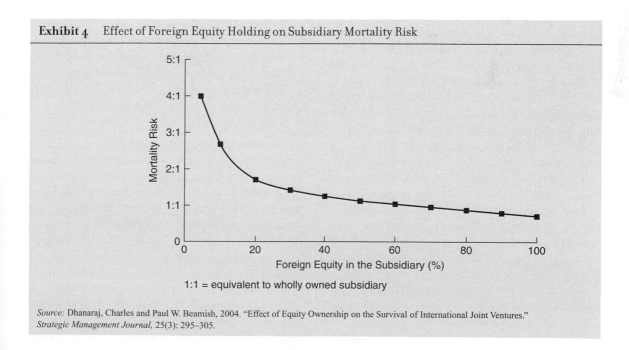

1:1 = equivalent to wholly owned subsidiary

Source: Dhanaraj, Charles and Paul W. Beamish, 2004. "Effect of Equity Ownership on the Survival of International Joint Ventures." *Strategic Management Journal*, 25(3): 295–305.

of key importance in a joint venture, not the legal agreement that binds them together. Nevertheless, most are careful to ensure that they have a good agreement in place—one that they understand and are comfortable with.

Most of the principal elements of a joint venture agreement are straightforward. One item that often goes un-discussed is the termination of the venture.

Although some managers balk at discussing termination during the getting-acquainted period, it is important to work out a method of terminating the venture in the event of a serious disagreement, and to do this at a time when heads are cool and goodwill abounds. The usual technique is to use a shotgun clause, which allows either party to name a price at which it will buy the other's shares in the venture. However, once this provision is activated and the first company has named a price, the second firm has the option of selling at this price or buying the first company's shares at the same price. This ensures that only fair offers are made, at least as long as both parents are large enough to be capable of buying each other out.

Making the Venture Work   Joint ventures need close and continuing attention, particularly in their early months. In addition to establishing a healthy working relationship between the parents and the venture general manager, and appropriate metrics, managers should be on the lookout for the impact that cultural differences may be having on the venture and for the emergence of unforeseen inequities.

International joint ventures, like any type of international activity, require that managers of different national cultures work together. This requires the selection of capable people in key roles. Unless managers have been sensitized to the characteristics of the culture that they are dealing with, this can lead to misunderstandings and serious problems. Many Western managers, for instance, are frustrated by the slow, consensus-oriented decision-making style of the Japanese. Equally, the Japanese find American individualistic decision making to be surprising, as the decisions are made so quickly, but the implementation is often so slow. Firms that are

sophisticated in the use of international joint ventures are well aware of such problems and have taken action to minimize them. Ford, for example, has put more than 1,500 managers through courses to improve their ability to work with Japanese and Korean managers.

It is important to remember that cultural differences do not just arise from differences in nationality. For example:

- Small firms working with large partners are often surprised and dismayed by the fact that it can take months, rather than days, to get approval of a new project. In some cases the cultural differences appear to be greater between small and large firms of the same nationality than, say, between multinationals of different nationality, particularly if the multinationals are in the same industry.

- Firms working with two partners from the same country have been surprised to find how different the companies are in cultural habits. A Japanese automobile firm headquartered in rural Japan may be a very different company from one run from Tokyo.

- Cultural differences between managers working in different functional areas may be greater than those between managers in the same function in different firms. European engineers, for example, discovered when discussing a potential joint venture with an American partner that they had more in common with the American engineers than with the marketing people in their own company.

A very common joint venture problem is that the objectives of the parents, which coincided when the venture was formed, diverge over time. Such divergences can be brought on by changes in the fortunes of the partners. This was the case in the breakup of the General Motors–Daewoo joint venture in Korea. Relations between the partners were already strained due to GM's unwillingness to put further equity into the venture, in spite of a debt to equity ratio of more than 8 to 1, when, faced with rapidly declining market share, the Korean parent decided that the venture should go for growth and maximize market share. In contrast General Motors, itself in a poor financial position at the time, insisted that the emphasis be on current profitability. When Daewoo, without telling General Motors, introduced a concessionary financing program for the joint venture's customers, the relationship was damaged, never to recover.

A final note concerns the unintended inequities that may arise during the life of a venture. Due to an unforeseen circumstance, one parent may be winning from the venture while the other is losing. A venture established in the late 1990s between Indonesian and American parents, for instance, was buying components from the American parent at prices based in dollars. As the rupiah declined in value, the Indonesian partner could afford fewer components in each shipment. The advice of many experienced venture managers is that, in such a situation, a change in the original agreement should be made, so the hardship is shared between the parents. That was done in this case, and the venture is surviving, although it is not as profitable as originally anticipated.

In reviewing any checklist of the things to be considered when forming a joint venture, it is important to recognize that such a list will vary somewhat depending on where the international joint venture is established. The characteristics of joint ventures will vary according to whether they are established in developed versus emerging markets.

Most of the descriptions of the characteristics considered are self-explanatory. Yet, more fine-grained analyses are always possible. For example, the discussion in this reading has generally assumed a traditional equity joint venture, one focused between two firms from two different countries. Yet other types of equity joint ventures exist, including those between firms from two different countries that set up in a third country (i.e., trinational), those formed between subsidiaries of the same MNE (i.e., intrafirm) and those formed with companies of the same nationality but located in a different country (i.e., cross-national domestic joint ventures). Further, many joint ventures have more than two partners. Interestingly, the traditional JVs (at least those formed by Japanese MNEs) tend to simultaneously be more profitable and to have a higher termination rate than the alternative structures available.

Summary

International joint ventures are an increasingly important part of the strategy of many firms. They are, however, sometime difficult to design and manage well, in part because some organizations do not treat them as "true" "joint" ventures (see Exhibit 5). The fact that some ventures are performing below their management's expectations should not be an excuse for firms to avoid such ventures. In many industries, the winners are going to be the companies that most quickly learn to manage international ventures effectively. The losers will be the managers who throw up their hands and say that joint ventures are too difficult, so we had better go it alone.

Exhibit 5   The True Joint Venture versus the Pseudo Joint Venture

	The True Alliance	The Pseudo Alliance
Planned level of parent input and involvement	Continuing	One-time
Distribution of risks/rewards	Roughly even	Uneven
Parent attitude toward the JV	A unique organization with unique needs	One more subsidiary
The formal JV agreement	Flexible guidelines	Frequently referenced rulebook
Performance objectives	Clearly specified and congruent	Partially overlapping/ambiguous

In the future, will we see more or fewer international joint ventures? Certainly the reduction in investment regulations in many countries, coupled with increased international experience by many firms, suggests there may be fewer joint ventures. Yet other countervailing pressures exist. With shortening product life cycles, it is increasingly difficult to go it alone. And with the increase in the number of MNEs from emerging markets, both the supply and demand of potential partners will likely escalate.

Reading 6-2   Collaborate with Your Competitors—and Win

Gary Hamel, Yves L. Doz, and C.K. Prahalad

Collaboration between competitors is in fashion. General Motors and Toyota assemble automobiles, Siemens and Philips develop semiconductors, Canon supplies photocopiers to Kodak, France's Thomson and Japan's JVC manufacture videocassette recorders. But the spread of what we call "competitive collaboration"—joint ventures, outsourcing agreements, product licensings, cooperative research— has triggered unease about the long-term consequences. A strategic alliance can strengthen both companies against outsiders even as it weakens one partner vis-à-vis the other. In particular, alliances between Asian companies and Western rivals seem to work against the Western partner. Cooperation becomes a low-cost route for new competitors to gain technology and market access.[1]

Yet the case for collaboration is stronger than ever. It takes so much money to develop new products and to penetrate new markets that few companies can go it alone in every situation. ICL, the British computer company, could not have developed its current generation of mainframes without Fujitsu. Motorola needs Toshiba's distribution capacity to break into the Japanese semiconductor market. Time is another critical factor. Alliances can provide shortcuts for Western companies racing to improve their production efficiency and quality control.

We have spent more than five years studying the inner workings of 15 strategic alliances and monitoring scores of others. Our research (see the insert "About Our Research") involves cooperative ventures between competitors from the United States and Japan, Europe and Japan, and the United States and Europe. We did not judge the success or failure of each partnership by its longevity— a common mistake when evaluating strategic alliances—but by the shifts in competitive strength on each side. We focused on how companies use competitive collaboration to enhance their internal skills and technologies while they guard against transferring competitive advantages to ambitious partners.

There is no immutable law that strategic alliances *must* be a windfall for Japanese or Korean partners. Many Western companies do give away more than they gain—but that's because they enter partnerships without knowing what it takes to win.

▌ Gary Hamel is lecturer in business policy and management at the London Business School. Yves L. Doz is professor of business strategy at INSEAD, Fontainebleau, France. C.K. Prahalad is professor of corporate strategy and international business at the University of Michigan. The authors often collaborate in research and writing on international business. Professors Prahalad and Doz are the authors of The Multinational Mission (Free Press, 1987).

▌ [1.]For a vigorous warning about the perils of collaboration, see Robert B. Reich and Eric D. Mankin, "Joint Ventures with Japan Give Away Our Future," *HBR* March–April 1986, p. 78.

Companies that benefit most from competitive collaboration adhere to a set of simple but powerful principles.

Collaboration is competition in a different form. Successful companies never forget that their new partners may be out to disarm them. They enter alliances with clear strategic objectives, and they also understand how their partners' objectives will affect their success.

Harmony is not the most important measure of success. Indeed, occasional conflict may be the best evidence of mutually beneficial collaboration. Few alliances remain win-win undertakings forever. A partner may be content even as it unknowingly surrenders core skills.

Cooperation has limits. Companies must defend against competitive compromise. A strategic alliance is a constantly evolving bargain whose real terms go beyond the legal agreement or the aims of top management. What information gets traded is determined day to day, often by engineers and operating managers. Successful companies inform employees at all levels about what skills and technologies are off-limits to the partner and monitor what the partner requests and receives.

Learning from partners is paramount. Successful companies view each alliance as a window on their partners' broad capabilities. They use the alliance to build skills in areas outside the formal agreement and systematically diffuse new knowledge throughout their organizations.

About Our Research

We spent more than five years studying the internal workings of 15 strategic alliances around the world. We sought answers to a series of interrelated questions. What role have strategic alliances and outsourcing agreements played in the global success of Japanese and Korean companies? How do alliances change the competitive balance between partners? Does winning at collaboration mean different things to different companies? What factors determine who gains most from collaboration?

To understand who won and who lost and why, we observed the interactions of the partners firsthand and at multiple levels in each organization. Our sample included four European–U.S. alliances, two intra-European alliances, two European–Japanese alliances, and seven U.S.–Japanese alliances. We gained access to both sides of the partnerships in about half the cases and studied each alliance for an average of three years.

Confidentiality was a paramount concern. Where we did have access to both sides, we often wound up knowing more about who was doing what to whom than either of the partners. To preserve confidentiality, our article disguises many of the alliances that were part of the study.

Why Collaborate?

Using an alliance with a competitor to acquire new technologies or skills is not devious. It reflects the commitment and capacity of each partner to absorb the skills of the other. We found that in every case in which a Japanese company emerged from an alliance stronger than its Western partner, the Japanese company had made a greater effort to learn.

Strategic intent is an essential ingredient in the commitment to learning. The willingness of Asian companies to enter alliances represents a change in competitive tactics, not competitive goals. NEC, for example, has used a series of collaborative ventures to enhance its technology and product competences. NEC is the only company in the world with a leading position in telecommunications, computers, and semiconductors—despite its investing less in R&D (as a percentage of revenues) than competitors like Texas Instruments, Northern Telecom, and L.M. Ericsson. Its string of partnerships, most notably with Honeywell, allowed NEC to leverage its in-house R&D over the last two decades.

Western companies, on the other hand, often enter alliances to avoid investments. They are more interested in reducing the costs and risks of entering new businesses or markets than in acquiring new skills. A senior U.S. manager offered this analysis of his company's venture with a Japanese rival: "We complement each other well—our distribution capability and their manufacturing skill. I see no reason to invest upstream if we can find a secure source of product. This is a comfortable relationship for us."

An executive from this company's Japanese partner offered a different perspective: "When it is necessary to collaborate, I go to my employees and say, 'This is bad, I wish we had these skills ourselves. Collaboration is second best. But I will feel worse if after four years we do not know how to do what our partner knows how to do.' We must digest their skills."

The problem here is not that the U.S. company wants to share investment risk (its Japanese partner does too) but that the U.S. company has no ambition *beyond* avoidance. When the commitment to learning is so one-sided, collaboration invariably leads to competitive compromise.

Many so-called alliances between Western companies and their Asian rivals are little more than sophisticated outsourcing arrangements (see the insert "Competition for Competence"). General Motors buys cars and components from Korea's Daewoo. Siemens buys computers from Fujitsu. Apple buys laser printer engines from Canon. The traffic is almost entirely one way. These OEM deals offer Asian partners a way to capture investment initiative from Western competitors and displace customer-competitors from value-creating activities. In many cases this goal meshes with that of the Western partner: to regain competitiveness quickly and with minimum effort.

Consider the joint venture between Rover, the British automaker, and Honda. Some 25 years ago, Rover's forerunners were world leaders in small car design. Honda had not even entered the automobile business. But in the mid-1970s, after failing to penetrate foreign markets, Rover turned to Honda for

technology and product-development support. Rover has used the alliance to avoid investments to design and build new cars. Honda has cultivated skills in European styling and marketing as well as multinational manufacturing. There is little doubt which company will emerge stronger over the long term.

Troubled laggards like Rover often strike alliances with surging latecomers like Honda. Having fallen behind in a key skills area (in this case, manufacturing small cars), the laggard attempts to compensate for past failures. The latecomer uses the alliance to close a specific skills gap (in this case, learning to build cars for a regional market). But a laggard that forges a partnership for short-term gain may find itself in a dependency spiral: as it contributes fewer and fewer distinctive skills, it must reveal more and more of its internal operations to keep the partner interested. For the weaker company, the issue shifts from "Should we collaborate?" to "With whom should we collaborate?" to "How do we keep our partner interested as we lose the advantages that made us attractive to them in the first place?"

There's a certain paradox here. When both partners are equally intent on internalizing the other's skills, distrust and conflict may spoil the alliance and threaten its very survival. That's one reason joint ventures between Korean and Japanese companies have been few and tempestuous. Neither side wants to "open the kimono." Alliances seem to run most smoothly when one partner is intent on learning and the other is intent on avoidance—in essence, when one partner is willing to grow dependent on the other. But running smoothly is not the point; the point is for a company to emerge from an alliance more competitive than when it entered it.

One partner does not always have to give up more than it gains to ensure the survival of an alliance. There are certain conditions under which mutual gain is possible, at least for a time:

The partners' strategic goals converge while their competitive goals diverge. That is, each partner allows for the other's continued prosperity in the shared business. Philips and Du Pont collaborate to develop and manufacture compact discs, but neither side invades the other's market. There is a clear upstream/downstream division of effort.

The size and market power of both partners is modest compared with industry leaders. This forces each side to accept that mutual dependence may have to continue for many years. Long-term collaboration may be so critical to both partners that neither will risk antagonizing the other by an overtly competitive bid to appropriate skills or competences. Fujitsu's 1 to 5 size disadvantage with IBM means it will be a long time, if ever, before Fujitsu can break away from its foreign partners and go it alone.

Each partner believes it can learn from the other and at the same time limit access to proprietary skills. JVC and Thomson, both of whom make VCRs, know that they are trading skills. But the two companies are looking for very different things. Thomson needs product technology and manufacturing prowess; JVC needs to learn how to succeed in the fragmented European market. Both sides believe there is an equitable chance for gain.

How to Build Secure Defenses

For collaboration to succeed, each partner must contribute something distinctive: basic research, product development skills, manufacturing capacity, access to distribution. The challenge is to share enough skills to create advantage vis-à-vis companies outside the alliance while preventing a wholesale transfer of core skills to the partner. This is a very thin line to walk. Companies must carefully select what skills and technologies they pass to their partners. They must develop safeguards against unintended, informal transfers of information. The goal is to limit the transparency of their operations.

The type of skill a company contributes is an important factor in how easily its partner can internalize the skills. The potential for transfer is greatest when a partner's contribution is easily transported (in engineering drawings, on computer tapes, or in the heads of a few technical experts); easily interpreted (it can be reduced to commonly understood equations or symbols); and easily absorbed (the skill or competence is independent of any particular cultural context).

Western companies face an inherent disadvantage because their skills are generally more vulnerable to transfer. The magnet that attracts so many

---

Competition for Competence

In the article "Do You Really Have a Global Strategy?" (HBR, July–August 1985), Gary Hamel and C. K. Prahalad examined one dimension of the global competitive battle: the race for brand dominance. This is the battle for control of distribution channels and global "share of mind." Another global battle has been much less visible and has received much less management attention. This is the battle for control over key technology-based competences that fuel new business development.

Honda has built a number of businesses, including marine engines, lawn mowers, generators, motorcycles, and cars, around its engine and power train competence. Casio draws on its expertise in semiconductors and digital display in producing calculators, small-screen televisions, musical instruments, and watches. Canon relies on its imaging and microprocessor competences in its camera, copier, and laser printer businesses.

In the short run, the quality and performance of a company's products determine its competitiveness. Over the longer term, however, what counts is the ability to build and enhance core competences—distinctive skills that spawn new generations of products. This is where many managers and commentators fear Western companies are losing. Our research helps explain why some companies may be more likely than others to surrender core skills.

Alliance or Outsourcing?

Enticing Western companies into outsourcing agreements provides several benefits to ambitious OEM partners. Serving as a manufacturing base for a Western partner is a quick route to increased manufacturing share without the risk or expense of building brand share. The Western partners' distribution capability allows Asian suppliers to focus all their resources on building absolute product advantage. Then OEMs can enter markets on their own and convert manufacturing share into brand share.

Serving as a sourcing platform yields more than just volume and process improvements. It also generates low-cost, low-risk market learning. The downstream (usually Western) partner typically provides information on how to tailor products to local markets. So every product design transferred to an OEM partner is also a research report on customer preferences and market needs. The OEM partner can use these insights to read the market accurately when it enters on its own.

A Ratchet Effect

Our research suggests that once a significant sourcing relationship has been established, the buyer becomes less willing and able to reemerge as a manufacturing competitor. Japanese and Korean companies are, with few exceptions, exemplary suppliers. If anything, the "soft option" of outsourcing becomes even softer as OEM suppliers routinely exceed delivery and quality expectations.

Outsourcing often begins a ratchetlike process. Relinquishing manufacturing control and paring back plant investment leads to sacrifices in product design, process technology, and, eventually, R&D budgets. Consequently, the OEM partner captures product-development as well as manufacturing initiative. Ambitious OEM partners are not content with the old formula of "You design it

and we'll make it." The new reality is, "You design it, we'll learn from your designs, make them more manufacturable, and launch our products alongside yours."

Reversing the Verdict

This outcome is not inevitable. Western companies can retain control over their core competences by keeping a few simple principles in mind.

A Competitive Product Is Not the Same Thing as a Competitive Organization   While an Asian OEM partner may provide the former, it seldom provides the latter. In essence, outsourcing is a way of renting someone else's competitiveness rather than developing a long-term solution to competitive decline.

Rethink the Make-Or-Buy Decision   Companies often treat component manufacturing operations as cost centers and transfer their output to assembly units at an arbitrarily set price. This transfer price is an accounting fiction, and it is unlikely to yield as high a return as marketing or distribution investments, which require less research money and capital. But companies seldom consider the competitive consequences of surrendering control over a key value-creating activity.

Watch Out for Deepening Dependence   Surrender results from a series of outsourcing decisions that individually make economic sense but collectively amount to a phased exit from the business. Different managers make outsourcing decisions at different times, unaware of the cumulative impact.

Replenish Core Competencies   Western companies must outsource some activities; the economics are just too compelling. The real issue is whether a company is adding to its stock of technologies and competences as rapidly as it is surrendering them. The question of whether to outsource should always provoke a second question: Where can we outpace our partner and other rivals in building new sources of competitive advantage?

companies to alliances with Asian competitors is their manufacturing excellence—a competence that is less transferable than most. Just-in-time inventory systems and quality circles can be imitated, but this is like pulling a few threads out of an oriental carpet. Manufacturing excellence is a complex web of employee training, integration with suppliers, statistical process controls, employee involvement, value engineering, and design for manufacture. It is difficult to extract such a subtle competence in any way but a piecemeal fashion.

There is an important distinction between technology and competence. A discrete, stand-alone technology (for example, the design of a semiconductor chip) is more easily transferred than a process competence, which is entwined in the social fabric of a company. Asian companies often learn more from their Western partners than vice versa because they contribute difficult-to-unravel strengths, while Western partners contribute easy-to-imitate technology.

So companies must take steps to limit transparency. One approach is to limit the scope of the formal agreement. It might cover a single technology rather than an entire range of technologies; part of a product line rather than the entire line; distribution in a limited number of markets or for a limited period of time. The objective is to circumscribe a partner's opportunities to learn.

Moreover, agreements should establish specific performance requirements. Motorola, for example, takes an incremental, incentive-based approach to technology transfer in its venture with Toshiba. The agreement calls for Motorola to release its microprocessor technology incrementally as Toshiba delivers on its promise to increase Motorola's penetration in the Japanese semiconductor market. The greater Motorola's market share, the greater Toshiba's access to Motorola's technology.

Many of the skills that migrate between companies are not covered in the formal terms of collaboration. Top management puts together strategic alliances and sets the legal parameters for exchange. But what actually gets traded is determined by day-to-day interactions of engineers, marketers, and product developers: who says what to whom, who gets access to what facilities, who sits on what joint committees. The most important deals ("I'll share this with you if you share that with me") may be struck four or five organizational levels below where the deal was signed. Here lurks the greatest risk of unintended transfers of important skills.

Consider one technology-sharing alliance between European and Japanese competitors. The European company valued the partnership as a way to acquire a specific technology. The Japanese company considered it a window on its partner's entire range of competences and interacted with a broad spectrum of its partner's marketing and product-development staff. The company mined each contact for as much information as possible.

For example, every time the European company requested a new feature on a product being sourced from its partner, the Japanese company asked for detailed customer and competitor analyses to justify the request. Over time, it developed a sophisticated picture of the European market that would assist its own entry strategy. The technology acquired by the European partner through the formal agreement had a useful life of three to five years. The competitive insights acquired informally by the Japanese company will probably endure longer.

Limiting unintended transfers at the operating level requires careful attention to the role of gatekeepers, the people who control what information flows to a partner. A gatekeeper can be effective only if there are a limited number of gateways through which a partner can access people and facilities. Fujitsu's many partners all go through a single office, the "collaboration section," to request information and assistance from different divisions. This way the company can monitor and control access to critical skills and technologies.

We studied one partnership between European and U.S. competitors that involved several divisions of each company. While the U.S. company could only access its partner through a single gateway, its partner had unfettered access to all participating divisions. The European company took advantage of its free rein. If one division refused to provide certain information, the European partner made the same request of another division. No single manager in the U.S. company could tell how much information had been transferred or was in a position to piece together patterns in the requests.

Collegiality is a prerequisite for collaborative success. But *too much* collegiality should set off warning bells to senior managers. CEOs or division presidents should expect occasional complaints from their counterparts about the reluctance of lower level employees to share information. That's a sign that the gatekeepers are doing their jobs. And senior management should regularly debrief operating personnel to find out what information the partner is requesting and what requests are being granted.

Limiting unintended transfers ultimately depends on employee loyalty and self-discipline. This was a real issue for many of the Western companies we studied. In their excitement and pride over technical achievements, engineering staffs sometimes shared information that top management considered sensitive. Japanese engineers were less likely to share proprietary information.

There are a host of cultural and professional reasons for the relative openness of Western technicians. Japanese engineers and scientists are more loyal to their company than to their profession. They are less steeped in the open give-and-take of university research since they receive much of their training from employers. They consider themselves team members more than individual scientific contributors. As one Japanese manager noted, "We don't feel any need to reveal what we know. It is not an issue of pride for us. We're glad to sit and listen. If we're patient we usually learn what we want to know."

Controlling unintended transfers may require restricting access to facilities as well as to people. Companies should declare sensitive laboratories and factories off-limits to their partners. Better yet, they might house the collaborative venture in an entirely new facility. IBM is building a special site in Japan where Fujitsu can review its forthcoming mainframe software before deciding whether to license it. IBM will be able to control exactly what Fujitsu sees and what information leaves the facility.

Finally, which country serves as "home" to the alliance affects transparency. If the collaborative team is located near one partner's major facilities, the other partner will have more opportunities to learn—but less control over what information gets traded. When the partner houses, feeds, and looks after engineers and operating managers, there is a danger they will "go native." Expatriate personnel need frequent visits from headquarters as well as regular furloughs home.

Enhance the Capacity to Learn

Whether collaboration leads to competitive surrender or revitalization depends foremost on what employees believe the purpose of the alliance to be. It is self-evident: to learn, one must *want* to learn. Western companies won't realize the full benefits of competitive collaboration until they overcome an arrogance borne of decades of leadership. In short, Western companies must be more receptive.

We asked a senior executive in a Japanese electronics company about the perception that Japanese companies learn more from their foreign partners than vice versa. "Our Western partners approach us with the attitude of teachers," he told us. "We are quite happy with this, because we have the attitude of students."

Learning begins at the top. Senior management must be committed to enhancing their companies' skills as well as to avoiding financial risk. But most learning takes place at the lower levels of an alliance. Operating employees not only represent the front lines in an effective defense but also play a vital role in acquiring knowledge. They must be well briefed on the partner's strengths and weaknesses and understand how acquiring particular skills will bolster their company's competitive position.

This is already standard practice among Asian companies. We accompanied a Japanese development engineer on a tour through a partner's factory. This engineer dutifully took notes on plant layout, the number of production stages, the rate at which the line was running, and the number of employees. He recorded all this despite the fact that he had no manufacturing responsibility in his own company, and that the alliance didn't encompass joint manufacturing. Such dedication greatly enhances learning.

Collaboration doesn't always provide an opportunity to fully internalize a partner's skills. Yet just acquiring new and more precise benchmarks of a partner's performance can be of great value. A new benchmark can provoke a thorough review of internal performance levels and may spur a round of competitive innovation. Asking questions like, "Why do their semiconductor logic designs have fewer errors than ours?" and "Why are they investing in this technology and we're not?" may provide the incentive for a vigorous catch-up program.

Competitive benchmarking is a tradition in most of the Japanese companies we studied. It requires many of the same skills associated with competitor analysis: systematically calibrating performance against external targets; learning to use rough estimates to determine where a competitor (or partner) is better, faster, or cheaper; translating those estimates into new internal targets; and recalibrating to establish the rate of improvement in a competitor's performance. The great advantage of competitive collaboration is that proximity makes benchmarking easier.

Indeed, some analysts argue that one of Toyota's motivations in collaborating with GM in the much-publicized NUMMI venture is to gauge the quality of GM's manufacturing technology. GM's top manufacturing people get a close look at Toyota, but the reverse is true as well. Toyota may be learning whether its giant U.S. competitor is capable of closing the productivity gap with Japan.

Competitive collaboration also provides a way of getting close enough to rivals to predict how they will behave when the alliance unravels or runs its course. How does the partner respond to price changes? How does it measure and reward executives? How does it prepare to launch a new product? By revealing a competitor's management orthodoxies, collaboration can increase the chances of success in future head-to-head battles.

Knowledge acquired from a competitor-partner is only valuable after it is diffused through the organization. Several companies we studied had established internal clearinghouses to collect and disseminate information. The collaborations manager at one Japanese company regularly made the rounds of all employees involved in alliances. He identified what information had been collected by whom and then passed it on to appropriate departments. Another company held regular meetings where employees shared new knowledge and determined who was best positioned to acquire additional information.

Proceed with Care—But Proceed

After World War II, Japanese and Korean companies entered alliances with Western rivals from weak positions. But they worked steadfastly toward independence. In the early 1960s, NEC's computer business was one-quarter the size of Honeywell's, its primary foreign partner. It took only two decades for NEC to grow larger than Honeywell, which eventually sold its computer operations to an alliance between NEC and Group Bull of France. The NEC experience demonstrates that dependence on a foreign partner doesn't automatically condemn a company to also-ran status. Collaboration may sometimes be unavoidable; surrender is not.

Managers are too often obsessed with the ownership structure of an alliance. Whether a company controls 51% or 49% of a joint venture may be much less important than the rate at which each partner learns from the other. Companies that are confident of their ability to learn may even prefer some ambiguity in the alliance's legal structure. Ambiguity creates more potential to acquire skills and technologies. The challenge for Western companies is not to write tighter legal agreements but to become better learners.

Running away from collaboration is no answer. Even the largest Western companies can no longer outspend their global rivals. With leadership in many industries shifting toward the East, companies in the United States and Europe must become good borrowers—much like Asian companies did in the 1960s and 1970s. Competitive renewal depends on building new process capabilities and winning new product and technology battles. Collaboration can be a low-cost strategy for doing both.

Implementing the Strategy:
Building Multidimensional Capabilities

▪ ▪ ▪ ▪ ▪ ▪ ▪ ▪ ▪ ▪ ▪ ▪ ▪ ▪ ▪ ▪ ▪ ▪

> Just as the new transnational strategic imperatives put demands on MNEs' existing organizational capabilities, so have emerging transnational organization models defined new managerial tasks for those operating within them. In this chapter, we examine the changing roles and responsibilities of three typical management groups that find themselves at the table in today's transnational organizations: the global business manager, the worldwide functional manager, and the national subsidiary manager. Although different organizations may define the key roles differently (bringing global account managers or regional executives to the table, for example), the major challenge facing all MNEs is to allocate their many complex strategic tasks and organizational roles among key management groups, then give each of those groups the appropriate legitimacy and influence within the ongoing organization decision-making process. The chapter concludes with a review of the role of top management in integrating these diverse perspectives and engaging them around a common direction.

The MNE in the early 21st century is markedly different from its ancestors. It has been transformed by an environment in which multiple, often conflicting forces accelerate simultaneously. The globalization of markets, the acceleration of product and technology life cycles, the assertion of national governments' demands, and, above all, the intensification of global competition have created an environment of complexity, diversity, and change for most MNEs.

As we have seen, the ability to compete on the basis of a single dominant competitive advantage gave way to a need to develop multiple strategic assets: global-scale efficiency and competitiveness, national responsiveness and flexibility, and worldwide innovation and learning capabilities. In turn, these new strategic task demands put pressure on existing organization structures and management processes. Traditional hierarchical structures, with their emphasis on either-or choices, have evolved toward organizational forms we have described as transnational, characterized by integrated networks of assets and resources, multidimensional management perspectives and capabilities, and flexible coordinative processes.

The managerial implications of all this change are enormous. To succeed in the international operating environment of the present, managers must be able to sense and interpret complex and dynamic environmental changes; they must be able to develop and integrate multiple strategic capabilities; and they must be able to build and manage complicated yet subtle new organizations required to deliver coordinated action on a worldwide basis. Unless those in key management positions are highly skilled and knowledgeable, companies simply cannot respond well to the major new challenges they face.

Yet surprisingly little attention is devoted to the study of the implications of all these changes in the roles and responsibilities of those who manage today's MNEs. Academics, consultants, and even managers themselves focus an enormous amount of time and energy on analyzing the various international environmental forces, on refining the concepts of global strategy, and on understanding the characteristics of effective transnational organizations. But without effective managers in place, sophisticated strategies and organizations will fail. The great risk for most MNEs today is that they are trying to implement third-generation strategies through second-generation organizations with first-generation managers.

In this chapter, we examine the management roles and responsibilities implied by the new challenges facing MNEs—those that take the manager beyond the first-generation assumptions. The tasks differ considerably for those in different parts and different levels of the organization, so rather than generalizing, we focus on the core responsibilities of different key management groups. In this chapter, we examine the roles and tasks of three specific groups in the transnational company: the global business manager, the worldwide functional manager, and the country subsidiary manager. (Recall that in Chapter 4, we suggested that variations often occur in the nature of transnational structures. As a result, other key executives—global account managers, for example—may also have a seat at the table.) To close the chapter, we review the role of top management in integrating these often-competing perspectives and capabilities.

Global Business Management

The challenge of developing global efficiency and competitiveness requires that management capture the various scale and scope economies available to the MNE as well as capitalize on the potential competitive advantages inherent in its worldwide market positioning. These requirements demand a management with the ability to see opportunities and risks across national boundaries and functional specialties, and the skill to coordinate and integrate activities across these barriers to capture the potential benefits. This is the fundamental task of the global business manager.

In implementing this important responsibility, the global business manager will be involved in a variety of diverse activities, whose balance varies considerably depending on the nature of the business and the company's administrative heritage. Nonetheless, there are three core roles and responsibilities that almost always fall to this key manager: He or she will be the global product or business strategist, the architect of worldwide asset and resource configuration, and the coordinator and controller of cross-border transfers.

Global Business Strategist

Because competitive interaction increasingly takes place on a global chessboard, only a manager with a worldwide perspective and responsibility can assess the strategic position and capability in a given business. Therefore, companies must configure their information, planning, and control systems so that they can be consolidated into consistent, integrated global business reports. This recommendation does not imply that the global business manager alone has the perspective and capability to formulate strategic priorities, or that he or she should undertake that vital task unilaterally. Depending on the nature of the business, there will almost certainly be some need to incorporate the perspectives of geographic and functional managers who represent strategic interests that may run counter to the business manager's drive to maximize global efficiency. Equally important, the business strategy must fit within the broader corporate strategy, which should provide a clear vision of what the company wants to be and explicit values pertaining to how it will accomplish its mission.

In the final analysis, however, the responsibility to reconcile different views falls to the global business manager, who needs to prepare an integrated strategy of how the company will compete in his or her particular business. In many companies, the manager's ability to do so is compromised because the position has been created by anointing domestic product division managers with the title of global business manager. Overseas subsidiary managers often feel that these managers are not only insensitive to nondomestic perspectives and interests but also biased toward the domestic organization in making key strategic decisions like product development and capacity plans. In many cases, their concerns are justified.

The preferred career path for the global business strategist is arguably via the country manager route. The challenges facing the manager of a major subsidiary are inevitably multidimensional and can serve as good training ground for future overall business strategists. And in the true transnational company, the global business manager need not be located in the home country, and in many cases, great benefits can accrue to relocating several such management groups abroad.

Even well-established MNEs with a tradition of close control of worldwide business strategy are changing. The head of IBM's $6 billion telecommunications business moved her division headquarters to London. She explained that the rationale was not only to move the command center closer to the booming European market for computer networking but also "[to] give us a different perspective on all our markets." And when General Electric acquired Amersham, the British-based life sciences and diagnostics leader, it not only tapped CEO Sir William Castell to head GE's $15 billion health care business, it relocated the business headquarters to the United Kingdom to better leverage the technology and entrepreneurial management it had acquired with Amersham.

Architect of Asset and Resource Configuration

Closely tied to the challenge of shaping an integrated business strategy is the global business manager's responsibility for overseeing the worldwide distribution of key assets and resources. Again, we do not mean to imply that he or she can make such decisions unilaterally. The input of interested geographic and functional managers must be weighed. It is the global business manager, however, who is normally best placed to initiate and lead the debate on asset configuration, perhaps through a global strategy committee or a world board with membership drawn from key geographic and functional management groups.

In deciding where to locate key plants or develop vital resources, the business manager can never assume a zero base. Indeed, such decisions must be rooted in the company's administrative heritage. In multinational companies like Philips, Unilever, ICI, or Nestlé, many of the key assets and resources that permitted them to expand internationally have long been located in national companies operating as part of a decentralized federation. Any business manager trying to shape such companies' future configurations must build on rather than ignore or destroy the important benefits that such assets and resources represent. And particularly in cases of plant closures, he or she has to demonstrate enormous political dexterity to overcome the inevitable resistance from local stakeholders.

The challenge to the business manager is to shape the future configuration by leveraging existing resources and capabilities and linking them in a configuration that resembles the integrated network form. When GE Medical Systems (GEMS) reconfigured its global structure, it did so by scaling up operations in the most efficient production centers and making them global sources. This led to the designation of plants in Budapest, Shanghai, and Mexico City being designated "Centers of Excellence," while operations in Paris, Tokyo, and Milwaukee were scaled back to become specialized assembly operations. The same process redefined the roles of its development centers, making GEMS a classic model of a distributed yet integrated transnational structure.

Cross-Border Coordinator

The third key role played by most global business managers is that of a cross-border coordinator. Although less overtly strategic than the other two responsibilities, it is nonetheless a vital operating function, because it involves deciding on sourcing patterns and managing cross-border transfer policies and mechanisms.

The task of coordinating flows of materials, components, and finished products becomes extremely complex as companies build transnational structures and capabilities. Rather than producing and shipping all products from a fully integrated central plant (the centralized hub model) or allowing local subsidiaries to develop self-sufficient capabilities (the decentralized federation model), transnational companies specialize their operations worldwide, building on the most capable national operations and capitalizing on locations of strategic importance.

But the resulting integrated network of specialized operations is highly interdependent, as illustrated by the structure that GEMS created to link high labor content component plants in Eastern Europe and China with highly skilled subassembly operations in Germany and Singapore, which in turn supply specialized finished-product plants in the United States, England, France, and Japan. To achieve such interdependence involves both corporate-owned and outsourced supply. Either form requires the resolution of issues ranging from how to divide the task of serving end-users to controlling the quality of the end product to managing the flow of design and production knowledge to subcontractors. And all of this must occur while trying to minimize the likelihood of technology loss if outsourcing is used.

The coordination mechanisms available to the global business manager vary from direct central control over quantities shipped and prices charged to the establishment of rules that essentially create an internal market mechanism to coordinate cross-border activities.

The former means of control is more likely for products of high strategic importance (e.g., Pfizer's control over quantities and pricing of shipments of the active ingredients of Viagra, or Coca-Cola's coordination of the supply of Coke syrup worldwide).

As products become more commoditylike, however, global product managers recognize that internal transfers should reflect the competitive conditions set by the external environment. This recognition has led many to develop internal quasi-markets as the principal means of coordination.

For example, in the consumer electronics giant Matsushita, once the parent company develops prototypes of the following year's models of video cameras, plasma televisions, and so on, global product managers offer them internally to buyers at merchandise meetings that are, in effect, huge internal trade fairs. At these meetings, national sales and marketing directors from Matsushita's sales subsidiaries worldwide enter into direct discussions with the global product managers, negotiating modifications in product design, price, and delivery schedule to meet their local market needs.

■ Worldwide Functional Management

Worldwide functional management refers to those individuals with the specialist responsibility for activities like R&D, manufacturing, and marketing, as well as those responsible for support activities, such as the chief financial officer and the chief information officer. Their job, broadly speaking, is to diffuse innovations and transfer knowledge on a worldwide basis. This vital task is built on knowledge that is highly specialized by function—technological capability, marketing expertise, manufacturing know-how, and so on—and to do it effectively requires that functional managers evolve from the secondary staff roles they often have played and take active roles in transnational management.

The tasks facing functional managers vary widely by specific function (e.g., technology transfer may be more intensive than the transfer of marketing expertise) or by business (companies in transnational industries such as telecommunications usually demand more functional linkages and transfers than do those in multinational industries such as retailing). Nonetheless, we highlight three basic roles and responsibilities that most worldwide functional managers should play: worldwide scanner of specialized information and intelligence, cross-pollinator of "best practices," and champion of transnational innovation.

Worldwide Intelligence Scanner

Most innovations start with some stimulus driving the company to respond to a perceived opportunity or threat. It may be a revolutionary technological breakthrough, an emerging consumer trend, a new competitive challenge, or a pending government regulation. And it may occur anywhere in the world. A typical example occurred when a commercial market for alternative energy began developing in Europe soon after 2001. In particular, strong public support backed by widespread government requirements resulted in explosive growth in the demand for wind power generators. In 2008, 43 percent of new electric generation capacity installed in the European Union was wind power.

Power generation companies with good sensory mechanisms in Europe recognized the significance of these developments early, and began adjusting their consumer communications, technological capabilities, and product line configuration. As these political forces and market demands spread worldwide over the next few years, those companies without the benefit of advance warning systems found themselves trying to respond not only to the growing political and consumer pressures but also to more responsive competitors touting that they had several years' head start in developing alternative energy technologies, products, and strategies.

But awareness alone is not sufficient. Historically, even when strategically important information was sensed in the foreign subsidiaries of classic multinational or global companies, it was rarely transmitted to those who could act on it or was ignored when it did get through. The communication problem was due primarily to the fact that the intelligence was usually of a specialist nature, not always well understood by the geographic- or business-focused generalists who controlled the line organization. To capture and transmit such information across national boundaries required the establishment of functional specialist information channels that linked local technologists, marketers, and production experts with others who understood their needs and shared their perspective.

In transnational companies, functional managers are linked through informal networks that are nurtured and maintained through frequent meetings, visits, and transfers. Through such linkages, these managers develop the contacts and relationships that enable them to transmit information rapidly around the globe. The functional managers at the corporate level become the linchpins in this worldwide intelligence scanning effort and play a vital role as facilitators of communication and repositories of specialist information.

Cross-Pollinator of "Best Practices"

Overseas subsidiaries can be more than sources of strategic intelligence, however. In a truly transnational company, they can also be the source of capabilities, expertise, and innovation that can be transferred to other parts of the organization. Caterpillar's leading-edge flexible manufacturing first emerged in its French and Belgian plants, for example, and much of P&G's liquid detergent technology was developed in its European Technology Center. In both cases, this expertise was transferred to other countries with important global strategic impact.

Such an ability to transfer new ideas and developments requires a considerable amount of management time and attention to break down the not-invented-here (NIH) syndrome that often thrives in international business. In this process, those with worldwide functional responsibilities are ideally placed to play a central cross-pollination role. Not only do they have the specialist knowledge required to identify and evaluate leading-edge practices, they also tend to have a well-developed informal communications network developed with others in their functional area.

Corporate functional managers in particular can play a vital role in this important task. Through informal contacts, formal evaluations, and frequent travel, they can identify where the best practices are being developed and implemented. They are also in a position to arrange cross-unit visits and transfers, host conferences, form task forces, or take other initiatives that will expose others to the new ideas. For example, when the manufacturing of GE's highly successful European developed 2.5 MW wind turbines was being started up in Florida, in preparation for the 2010 launch of this product in the United States, it was a global manufacturing technology group in GE's power generation business that linked the technical expertise that existed in the established European plants in Germany and Spain to the new manufacturing site in Florida.

Champion of Transnational Innovation

The two previously identified roles ideally position the functional manager to play a key role in developing what we call transnational innovations. As described in Chapter 5, these are different from the predominantly local activity that dominated the innovation process in multinational companies or the centrally driven innovation in international and global companies. The first (and simplest) form of transnational innovation is what we call locally leveraged. By scanning their companies' worldwide operations, corporate functional managers can identify local innovations that have applications elsewhere. In Unilever, for example, product and marketing innovation for many of its global brands occurred in national subsidiaries. Snuggle fabric softener was born in Unilever's German company, Timotei herbal shampoo originated in its Scandinavian operations, and Impulse body spray was first introduced by its South African unit. Recognizing the potential that these local innovations had for the wider company, the parent company's marketing and technical groups created the impetus to spread them to other subsidiaries.

The second type of transnational innovation, which we call globally linked, requires functional managers to play a more sophisticated role. This type of innovation fully exploits the company's access to worldwide information and expertise by linking and leveraging intelligence sources with internal centers of excellence, wherever they may be located. For example, the revolutionary design of GE's 2.5 MW wind turbine generator drew on jet engine turbine expertise developed in GE's transportation group in the United States, carbon composite materials technology that came out of its Niskayuna R&D facility, blade design developed in its engineering center in Warsaw, Poland, and software to properly locate the wind towers and feed power into the grid that was written in its Indian R&D facility.

◾ Geographic Subsidiary Management

In many MNEs, a successful tour as a country subsidiary manager is often considered the acid test of general management potential. Indeed, it is often a necessary qualification on the résumé of any candidate for a top management position. Not only does it provide frontline exposure to the realities of today's international business environment, but it also puts the individual in a position where he or she must deal with enormous strategic complexity from an organizational position that is severely constrained. Moreover, the role of "country manager" is, if anything, becoming more difficult as more MNEs move toward structures dominated by global business units and global customers. In such situations, the manager of the country is often held accountable for results but has only limited formal authority over the people and assets within his or her jurisdiction.

We have described the strategic challenge facing the MNE as one that requires resolving the conflicting demands for global efficiency, multinational responsiveness, and worldwide learning. The country manager is at the center of this strategic tension—defending the company's market positions against global competitors, satisfying the demands of the host government, responding to the unique needs of local customers, serving as the "face" of the entire organization at the national level, and leveraging its local resources and capabilities to strengthen the company's competitive position worldwide.

There are many vital tasks the country manager must play. We identify three that capture the complexity of the task and highlight its important linkage role: acting as a bicultural interpreter, becoming the chief advocate and defender of national needs, and the vital frontline responsibility of being the implementer of the company's strategy.

Bicultural Interpreter

The requirement that the country manager become the local expert who understands the needs of the local market, the strategy of competitors, and the demands of the host government is clear. But his or her responsibilities are also much broader. Because managers at headquarters do not understand the environmental and cultural differences in the MNE's diverse foreign markets, the country manager must be able to analyze the information gathered, interpret its implications, and even predict the range of feasible outcomes. This role suggests an ability not only to act as an efficient sensor of the national environment but also to become a cultural interpreter able to communicate the importance of that information to those whose perceptions may be obscured by ethnocentric biases.

There is another aspect to the country manager's role as an information broker that is sometimes ignored. Not only must the individual have a sensitivity to and understanding of the national culture, he or she must also be comfortable in the corporate culture at the MNE. Again, this liaison-style bicultural role implies much more than being an information conduit communicating the corporation's goals, strategies, and values to a group of employees located thousands of miles from the parent company. The country subsidiary manager must also interpret those broad goals and strategies so they become meaningful objectives and priorities at the local level of operation and apply those corporate values and organizational processes in a way that respects local cultural norms.

National Defender and Advocate

As important as the communication role is, it is not sufficient for the country manager to act solely as an intelligent mailbox. Information and analysis conveyed to corporate headquarters must be not only well understood but also acted upon, particularly in MNEs where strong business managers are arguing for a more integrated global approach and corporate functional managers are focusing on cross-border linkages. The country manager's role is to counterbalance these centralizing tendencies and ensure that the needs and opportunities that exist in the local environment are well understood and incorporated into the decision-making process.

As the national organization evolves from its early independence to a more mature role as part of an integrated worldwide network, the country manager's normal drive for national self-sufficiency and personal autonomy must be replaced by a less parochial perspective and a more corporate-oriented identity. This shift does not imply, however, that he or she should stop presenting the local perspective to headquarters management or stop defending national interests. Indeed, the company's ability to become a true transnational depends on having strong advocates of the need to differentiate its operations locally and be responsive to national demands and pressures.

Two distinct but related tasks are implied by this important role. The first requires the country manager to ensure that the overall corporate strategies, policies, and organization processes are appropriate from the national organization's perspective. If the interests of local constituencies are violated or the subsidiary's position might be compromised by the global strategy, it is the country manager's responsibility to become the defender of national needs and perspectives.

In addition to defending national differentiation and responsiveness, the country manager must become an advocate for his or her national organization's role in the corporation's worldwide integrated system, of which it is a part. As MNEs develop a more transnational strategy, national organizations compete not only for corporate resources but also for roles in the global operations. To ensure that each unit's full potential is realized, country managers must be able to identify and represent their particular national organization's key assets and capabilities, as well as the ways in which they can contribute to the MNE as a whole.

It is the country manager's job to mentor local employees and support those individuals in their fight for corporate resources and recognition. In doing so, they build local capability that can be a major corporate asset. As the former head of the Scottish subsidiary of a U.S. computer company observed, "It is my *obligation* to seek out new investment. No one else is going to stand up for these workers at head office. They are doing a great job, and I owe it to them to build up this operation. I get very angry with some of my counterparts in other parts of the country, who just toe the party line. They have followed their orders to the letter, but when I visit their plants I see unfulfilled potential everywhere."

Frontline Implementer of Corporate Strategy

Although the implementation of corporate strategy may seem the most obvious of tasks for the manager of a frontline operating unit, it is by no means the easiest. The first challenge stems from the multiplicity and diversity of constituents whose demands and pressures compete for the country manager's attention. Being a subsidiary company of some distant MNE seems to bestow a special status on many national organizations and subject them to a different and a more intense type of pressure than that put on other local companies. Governments may be suspicious of their motives, unions may distrust their national commitment, and customers may misunderstand their way of operating. Compounding the problem, corporate management often underestimates, or appears to the subsidiary general manager to underestimate, the significance of these demands and pressures.

In addition, the country manager's implementation task is complicated by the corporate expectation that he or she take the broad corporate goals and strategies and translate them into specific actions that are responsive to the needs of the national environment. As we have seen, these global strategies are usually complex and finely balanced, reflecting multiple conflicting demands. Having been developed through subtle internal negotiation, they often leave the country manager with very little room to maneuver.

Pressured from without and constrained from within, the country manager needs keen administrative sense to plot the negotiating range in which he or she can operate. The action decided on must be sensitive enough to respect the limits of the diverse local constituencies, pragmatic enough to achieve the expected corporate outcome, and creative enough to balance the diverse internal and external demands and constraints.

As if this were not enough, the task is made even more difficult by the fact that the country manager does not act solely as the implementer of corporate strategy. As we discussed previously, it is important that he or she also plays a key role in its formulation. Thus, the strategy the country manager is required to implement will often reflect some decisions against which he or she lobbied hard. Once the final decision is taken, however, the country manager must be able to convince his or her national organization to implement it with commitment and enthusiasm.

Top-Level Corporate Management

Nowhere are the challenges facing management more extreme than at the top of an organization that is evolving toward becoming a transnational corporation. Not only do these senior executives have to integrate and provide direction for the diverse management groups we have described, but in doing so, they also first have to break with many of the norms and traditions that historically defined their role.

Historically, as increasingly complex hierarchical structures forced them further and further from the frontlines of their businesses, top management's role became bureaucratized in a rising sea of systems and staff reports. As layers of management slowed decision making, and the corporate headquarters role of coordination and support evolved to one of control and interference, top management's attention was distracted from the external demands of customers and competitive pressures and began to focus internally on an increasingly bureaucratic process.

The transnational organization of today cannot afford to operate this way. Like executives at all levels of the organization, top management must add value, which means liberating rather than constraining the organization below them. For those at the top of a transnational, this means more than just creating a diverse set of business, functional, and geographic management groups and assigning them specific roles and responsibilities. It also means maintaining the organizational legitimacy of each group, balancing and integrating their often divergent influences in the ongoing management process, and maintaining a unifying sense of purpose and direction in the face of often conflicting needs and priorities.

This constant balancing and integrating role is perhaps the most vital aspect of top management's job. It is reflected in the constant tension managers feel between ensuring long-term viability and achieving short-term results, or between providing a clear overall corporate direction and leaving sufficient room for experimentation. This tension is reflected in the three core top management tasks we highlight here. The first, which focuses on the key role of providing long-term direction and purpose, is in some ways counterbalanced by the second, which highlights the need to achieve current results by leveraging performance. The third key task of ensuring continual renewal again focuses on long-term needs but at the same time may require the organization to challenge its current directions and priorities.

Providing Direction and Purpose

In an organization built around the need for multidimensional strategic capabilities and the legitimacy of different management perspectives, diversity and internal tension can create an exciting free market of competing ideas and generate an enormous amount of individual and group motivation. But there is always the risk that these same powerful centrifugal forces could pull the company apart. By creating a common vision of the future and a shared set of values that overarch and subsume managers' more parochial objectives, top management can, in effect, create a corporate lightning rod that captures this otherwise diffuse energy and channels it toward powering a single company engine.

We have identified three characteristics that distinguish an energizing and effective strategic vision from a catchy but ineffective public relations slogan. First, the vision must be clear; simplicity, relevance, and continuous reinforcement are the key to such clarity. NEC's integration of computers and communications—C&C—is a good example of how clarity can make a vision more powerful and effective. Top management in NEC has applied the C&C concept so effectively that it describes the company's business focus, defines its distinctive source of competitive advantage over large companies like IBM and AT&T, and summarizes its strategic and organizational initiatives. Throughout the company, the rich interpretations of C&C are understood and believed.

Second, continuity of a vision can provide direction and purpose. Despite shifts in leadership and continual adjustments in short-term business priorities, top management must remain committed to the company's core set of strategic objectives and organizational values. Without such continuity, the unifying vision takes on the transitory characteristics of the annual budget or quarterly targets—and engenders about as much organizational enthusiasm.

Third, in communicating the vision and strategic direction, it is critical to establish consistency across organizational units—in other words, to ensure that the vision is shared by all. The cost of inconsistency can be horrendous. At a minimum, it can result in confusion and inefficiency; at the extreme, it can lead individuals and organizational units to pursue agendas that are mutually debilitating.

Leveraging Corporate Performance

Although aligning the company's resources, capabilities, and commitments to achieve common long-term objectives is vital, top management must also achieve results in the short term to remain viable among competitors and credible with stakeholders. Top management's role is to provide the controls, support, and coordination to leverage resources and capabilities to their highest level of performance.

In doing so, top managers in transnational companies must abandon old notions of control that are based primarily on responding to below-budget financial results. Effective top managers rely much more on control mechanisms that are personal and proactive. In discussions with their key management groups, they ensure that their particular responsibilities are understood in relation to the overall goal and that strategic and operational priorities are clearly identified and agreed upon. They set demanding standards and use frequent informal visits to discuss operations and identify new problems or opportunities quickly.

When such issues are identified, the old model of top-down interference must be replaced by one driven by corporate-level support. Having created an organization staffed by experts and specialists, top management must resist the temptation to send in the headquarters "experts" to take charge at the first sign of difficulty. Far more effective is an approach of delegating clear responsibilities, backing them with rewards that align those responsibilities with the corporate goals, then supporting each of the management groups with resources, specialized expertise, and other forms of support available from the top levels of the company.

Perhaps the most challenging task for top management as it tries to leverage the overall performance of the corporation is the need to coordinate the activities of an organization deliberately designed around diverse perspectives and responsibilities. As we described in Chapter 4, there are three basic cross-organizational flows that must be carefully managed—goods, resources, and information—and each demands a different means of coordination. Goods flows can normally be routinized and managed through formal systems and procedures. Decisions involving the allocation of scarce resources (e.g., capital allocation, key personnel assignments) are usually centralized because top management wants to be involved directly and personally. And flows of information and knowledge are generated and diffused most effectively through personal contact.

These three flows are the lifeblood of any company, and any organization's ability to make them more efficient and effective depends on top management's ability to develop a rich portfolio of coordinative processes. By balancing the formalization, centralization, and socialization processes, they can exploit the company's synergistic potential and greatly leverage performance.

Ensuring Continual Renewal

Despite their enormous value, either of these first two roles, if pursued to the extreme, can result in a company's long-term demise. A fixation on an outmoded mission can be just as dangerous as a preoccupation with short-term performance. Even together, they can doom a company with its continuing success, especially if successful strategies become elevated to the status of unquestioned wisdom and effective organizational processes become institutionalized as routines. As strategies and processes ossify, management loses its flexibility, and eventually the organization sees its role as protecting its past heritage. Thus, when Jin Zhiguo became the president of China's massive Tsingtao Brewery Co. Ltd., not only did he have competitive challenges, he needed to implement internal reforms. As he noted, "Tsingtao Brewery has been an arrogant company. We must have an open mind and learn from other companies. A strong learning ability will lead to powerful innovations."

It is top management's role to prevent this ossification from occurring, and there are several important ways it can ensure that the organization continues to renew itself rather than just reinventing its past. First, by reducing the internal bureaucracy and constantly orienting the organization to its customers and benchmarking it against its best competitors, top management can ensure an external orientation.

Second, equally important is its role in constantly questioning, challenging, and changing things in a way that forces adaptation and learning. By creating a "dynamic imbalance" among those with different objectives, top management can prevent a myopic strategic posture from developing. (Clearly, this delicate process requires a great deal of top management time if it is not to degenerate into anarchy or corporate politics.)

Third, top management can ensure renewal by defining the corporate mission and values statements so that they provide some stretch and maneuverability for management, and also legitimize new initiatives. More than this, those at the top levels must monitor closely the process of dynamic imbalance they create and strongly support some of the more entrepreneurial experimentation or imaginative challenges to the status quo that emerge from such a situation.

▪ Concluding Comments

In this chapter, we shifted the level of analysis down from the MNE as an organization to the individual manager. Rather than think in terms of the changing nature of the business environment or the conflicting strategic imperatives facing the MNE, we examined the new roles of three groups of managers—those responsible for a global business (e.g., a product SBU or division), a worldwide function (e.g., finance, marketing, or technology), and a geographic territory (e.g., a country or region). We also looked at the new role of top-level corporate management in integrating and providing direction for these three groups. We saw how each role involves many familiar tasks as well as several new ones. Worldwide functional managers, for example, must become thought leaders in their discipline and active cross-pollinators of best practices across countries. And country managers need to develop the capacity to translate political and social trends in their local market into business imperatives for the MNE.

These new roles and responsibilities are hard to put in place because they require managers to rethink many of their traditional assumptions about the nature of their work. This is ultimately the biggest challenge facing the transnational organization—to create a generation of managers that have the requisite skills and the sense of perspective needed to operate in a multibusiness, multifunctional, multinational system.

Chapter 7 Readings

- In Reading 7-1, "Local Memoirs of a Global Manager," Das describes the key lessons he learned as a manager of international brands in an emerging market. Particular emphasis is placed on the need to tap into the roots of diversity.

- In Reading 7-2, "Tap Your Subsidiaries for Global Reach," Bartlett and Ghoshal introduce a simple conceptualization of the important roles for national subsidiaries in overall MNE success. In balancing the strategic importance of the local environment with the competence of the local organization, four roles/responsibilities are possible: strategic leader, contributor, implementor, and black hole.

Both of these readings emphasize the multidimensional capabilities which must be built for effective strategy implementation in the transnational organization.

Case 7-1   ING Insurance Asia/Pacific

Andreas Schotter, Rod White, and Paul Beamish

In June 2003, Jacques Kemp, newly appointed chief executive officer (CEO) of ING Insurance Asia/Pacific (ING A/P) was reviewing the regional operating structure, performance, and growth strategy. After arriving in Asia in July 2002 as regional general manager, Kemp traveled extensively throughout the region, in order to gain many insights into the existing ING A/P organization, the individual business units (countries) and their strategies. He also solicited ideas from major consulting firms on how to further strengthen ING A/P. The company was doing well, but he felt that ING's existing market position, strategy and operations in Asia/Pacific could be enhanced.

Kemp was concerned that ING needed to prepare for the time when the general market growth in Asia slowed and the competitive pressure intensified. He also was determined to make a difference during his tenure as ING's Asia/Pacific chief executive officer and to take the company to the next level.

IVEY

Richard Ivey School of Business
The University of Western Ontario

International Netherlands Group (ING)

ING was a global financial services company of Dutch origin, with more than 150 years of history. The company provided an array of banking, insurance and asset management services in more than 50 countries. With over 120,000 employees, ING served a broad customer base, including individuals, families, small businesses, large corporations, institutions and governments. Based on market capitalization, ING was one of the 20 largest financial institutions globally and ranked in the top 10 in Europe. The company was organized along six major business lines, which included both regions and product groups. While the banking business was divided into wholesale, retail and direct banking with a global management structure, the insurance business was organized into three regional business lines, including the Americas, Europe and Asia/Pacific (see **Exhibit 1**).

Jacques Kemp

Jacques Kemp started his career on the banking side of ING in 1974, in risk management at a local office in the Netherlands, and later moved to the foreign division at the head offices in Amsterdam. He was involved in setting up the ING Los Angeles office in 1982, and from 1984 to 1990, he was general manager in Brazil. In 1990, he returned to Amsterdam to take a general manager position, and one year later, became chairman of ING Bank International. One of his main achievements was the set-up of the emerging market banking network. After the merger and integration with Barings Bank in the mid-1990s, he became a member of the executive committee with responsibility for ING's general banking activities and the international banking network worldwide. In 2000, Kemp became Global Head of e-Business for ING Group, and was responsible for initiating and coordinating ING's strategy on Web-enabling, integrated financial services on a global

Exhibit 1   ING Global Business Lines and Shares

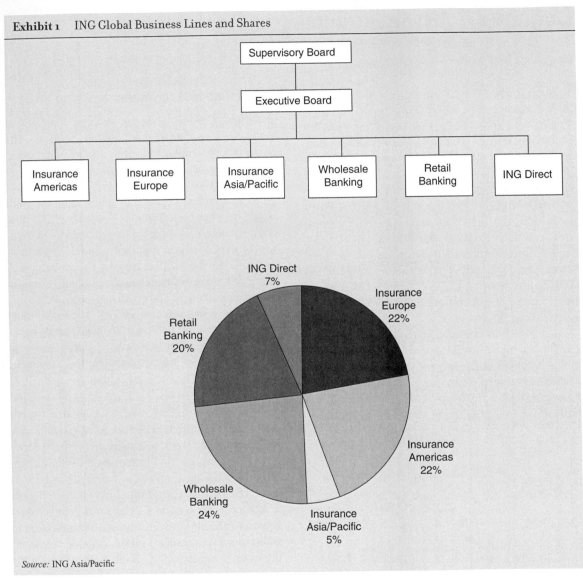

Source: ING Asia/Pacific

basis. He joined the executive committee of ING Insurance Asia/Pacific in July 2002 and became CEO for Asia/Pacific on April 1, 2003.

The Insurance Industry in Asia

The insurance industry in Asia was expected to expand dramatically, driven by rapid economic growth and a general increase in the popularity of insurance products, resulting from rising incomes. Gradual deregulation and the opening up of the Asian insurance markets were making them increasingly accessible to foreign insurers.

The proportion of gross domestic product (GDP) accounted for by life insurance premiums in Asia was relatively high when measured against income levels. The demand for life insurance in Asian markets was greater than in other countries at a comparable stage of development. Japan and South Korea, in fact, displayed the second- and third-highest degrees of insurance penetration in the world.

There were several reasons for the popularity of life insurance in Asia. Life insurance (like every other form of saving) profited from the high rates of saving in Asia. In this respect, insurers in some Asian countries had stolen the march on the banks by intensively marketing whole life policies.[1] Further, in most Asian nations, state or company pensions were modest, and private insurance products filled the gap. Life insurance enjoyed slight tax advantages in most Asian countries. Premium volume in Asia (excluding Japan) was expected to experience real growth of more than 10 percent per year between 2003 and 2008. Global premium volume was expected to increase by about four percent during the same period.

At the end of 2002, approximately 900 insurance companies (about 265 of them foreign) were operating in 12 Asian insurance markets. The size of the companies, their capital assets and the share of the market in foreign hands varied considerably from country to country. Regulations on the part of the supervisory bodies also had highly varying effects on market activities. The liberal regulations of Hong Kong ensured adherence only to minimum capital regulations, while the additional (and in some cases far-reaching) regulations of other countries covered the licensing of companies, products and prices. However, under pressure from the World Trade Organization (WTO), these Asian markets were expected to become more open.

ING in Asia/Pacific

ING Insurance Asia/Pacific was responsible for the life insurance operations and asset/wealth management activities of ING throughout Asia Pacific. ING was the first European company to enter the life insurance markets of Japan, Taiwan and South Korea. By the beginning of 2003, ING was ranked among the top five foreign financial services providers in Asia/Pacific with more than six million clients. The portfolio consisted of large businesses across six mature markets—Australia/New Zealand, Taiwan, Malaysia, Hong Kong, Japan and Korea—some smaller, semi-mature markets, such as the Philippines and Singapore, as well as newly emerging life insurance markets, including China, India, Indonesia and Thailand.

ING Insurance Asia/Pacific's business units offered various types of life insurance, wealth management, retail and institutional asset management products (including annuity, endowment, disability/morbidity insurance, unit linked/universal life, whole life, participating life, group life, accident and health, term life and employee benefits) and services (see Exhibits 2 and 3). In Hong Kong and Malaysia, non-life insurance products (including employees' compensation, medical, motor, fire, marine, personal accident and general liability) were also offered. ING Asia/Pacific's distribution channels included tied or career agents, independent agents, financial planners, bancassurance,[2] telemarketing and e-business channels. In several countries, ING had strategic alliances with local companies to enhance distribution capacity.

In 2002, several regional shared service centers were established to lower operating costs. With 60,000 points of distribution in Asia, ranging from tied agents, independent agents and brokers/dealers to banks, ING's strategy was able to access its clients through the channel of their choice.

ING had leading positions in Australia, Taiwan, Korea and Malaysia, and it was a fast-growing niche player in Japan. In New Zealand, ING managed about 16 percent of all mutual funds, making it the number-three player in terms of assets under management. ING was well positioned in the two largest Asian growth markets, China and India. It had two joint venture operations in life insurance in China and a 44 percent stake in ING Vysya Bank, India's fifth largest private bank, as well as a life insurance joint venture and a mutual funds business.

---

[1] Unlike term insurance which only paid out when the principal died (or was disabled); whole life policies had an insurance component and a savings component.

[2] Bancassurance is a French term referring to the selling of insurance through a bank's established distribution channels.

Exhibit 2 ING Asia/Pacific Insurance Product Offerings

Country	Term	Endowment	Whole Life	Health	Critical Illness	United Linked / Universal Life	Variable Annuity	General Insurance	Group Insurance
Australia	✓	×	×	×	✓	✓	×	✓	✓
China-PALIC[1]	✓	✓	✓	✓	✓	✓	×	×	✓
China-ICLIC[2]	✓	✓	✓	✓	✓	✓	×	×	✓
Hong Kong	✓	✓	✓	✓	✓	✓	×	✓	✓
India	✓	✓	✓	×	✓	×	✓	×	✓
Japan	✓	✓	✓	✓	✓	✓	✓	×	✓
ING Life Korea	✓	×	✓	✓	✓	✓	×	×	✓
KB Life Korea	×	×	×	×	×	✓	×	×	✓
Malaysia	✓	✓	✓	✓	✓	✓	×	✓	×
New Zealand	✓	×	×	✓	✓	✓	✓	✓	✓
Taiwan	✓	✓	✓	✓	✓	×	×	×	✓
Thailand	✓	✓	✓	✓	✓	✓	×	✓	✓
Indonesia	✓	✓	✓	✓	×	×	×	✓	×
Singapore	×	×	×	✓	×	×	×	×	✓
The Philippines	✓	✓	✓	✓	×	×	×	×	✓

Notes:
Group insurance covers all types of products.
Education plans are considered as endowment plans.
Universal Life products are offered in Korea and China.
Hong Kong offers both universal life and unit linked products.
In Taiwan, General insurance only includes travel insurance products.
ING does not currently have insurance operations in Singapore, Indonesia or the Philippines.
Source: ING Asia/Pacific

[1] *50/50 joint venture operations in life insurance with Pacific Antai Life (PALIC) in Shanghai.*
[2] *50/50 joint venture operations in life insurance with Beijing Capital Group in the northern city of Dalian.*
The new joint venture was known as ING Capital Life Insurance Company Ltd (ICLIC).

Source: ING Asia/Pacific.

Business Unit	Product Offerings
Australia	Australian equities and fixed income, Diversified (balanced) funds, International equities & fixed Income, Multi-manager (Optimix), Private equity, Global property securities and Global high dividend
China	Equity funds, Balanced funds and Bond funds
Hong Kong	Asian equities, Hong Kong equities & fixed income, Asian & Emerging Market debt, Proprietary equities and fixed income
India	Equity funds, Balanced funds and Bond funds
Japan	Japanese bonds and equities, International bonds and equities and Balanced funds
Korea	Domestic Korean bonds and equities, Offshore funds and Balanced funds
Malaysia	Proprietary domestic equities & fixed income, Unit-linked insurance investment products, Discretionary investment mandates, Corporate/residential mortgage loans and Domestic real estate
New Zealand	Domestic and International fixed income and equities
Philippines	Balanced funds, Advisory services, Peso fixed income, Domestic equities, Philippines USD bonds, Deposits, Securities and structured product offerings
Singapore	Offshore mutual funds, Singapore $ bond funds, ASEAN equity funds, Institutional discretionary mandates
Taiwan	Domestic Taiwanese equities, fixed income & balanced investments, Localized versions of ING global products, Discretionary account management and Offshore funds of various labels
Thailand	Mutual funds, Property funds, Real estate investment trusts, Private funds and Provident funds
Indonesia	ING Investment Management A/P does not have asset management business in Indonesia

Exhibit 3   Asset Management Product Offerings

Source: ING Asia Pacific.

ING was doing well in Asia Pacific (see Exhibit 4). Although 2002 was marked by continuing declines in global equity markets, the aggregate financial results of ING Asia/Pacific showed robustness against this market volatility. ING Asia/Pacific's regional results exceeded its financial expectations for the year with the businesses in Australia, Japan and Korea delivering the most outstanding results.

The Aetna Integration

By 2003, the integration of Aetna, a major acquisition undertaken during 2000, was accomplished, and rebranding was completed in almost all countries. This challenging integration was the major achievement of Kemp's predecessor.

ING Group acquired the life insurance activities of American-based Aetna International, which at the time had a much stronger position and an insurance organization that was four times larger in Asia than ING. The integration caused the departure of many of Aetna's top managers but there were also examples of non-disruptive transitions, such as the one in Hong Kong, where the local general manager of Aetna embraced the opportunities provided by the merger and led the local joint operation to become the most recognized foreign financial services provider in Hong Kong. Overall, the business remained strong, and ING Asia/Pacific benefited substantially from the Aetna acquisition. The merger helped ING became one of the largest life insurance companies in Asia-Pacific.

To rebalance the portfolio, ING sold its life and non-life operations in the Philippines, Singapore and Indonesia. ING felt these three countries

Exhibit 4. ING Asia/Pacific Financial Overview

Figures in Euro million	2002	2001	Change
Premium Income	7,798	6,497	20%
Annual Premium Equivalent	1,283	1,395	−8%
Underlying Profit before Tax	324	281	15%
Value of New Life Business	280	247	13%
Internal Rate of Return	15.4%	14.9%	3%
Assets under Management (€ billion)	37.3	25.6	46%

Source: ING Asia/Pacific.

would not produce enough "substance" in premiums to allow foreign insurance companies to make decent returns and profits, and the business units in these countries would need huge amounts of resources to manage these markets properly and to meet ING's standards of risk and compliance. Strategically ING decided that it had enough substance and growth potential in the other 12 Asian countries in which it operated while retaining the asset management operations in the Philippines and Singapore.

Regional Structure

ING A/P's activities were organized by business units (countries). The regional office in Hong Kong fulfilled the role as monitoring center. The regional goal was to be a top player in the key markets of Australia, Hong Kong, Japan, Korea, Malaysia and Taiwan, while further developing the major growth markets of China and India. What this goal meant and how it could be achieved was left largely to the local country business units.

Individual business units (countries) had a relatively high level of autonomy. This culture created a very entrepreneurial environment, but also some frictions between the regional office in Hong Kong and the country business units. The functional managers at the regional office had difficulties maintaining common standards across the region. As one regional office manager stated:

> All business units have different ideas, standards and priorities. It is hard to keep track of activities, especially since the business unit managers only report to

the regional managers and not to us, who are supposed to be in charge for the coordination of the operational activities.

The region was divided into four country clusters, each under the nominal supervision of either one of two regional general managers or one of two executive members who then reported to the regional CEO (see Exhibit 5). The regional CEO reported directly to the chairman of the executive committee. The regional office had several regional office professionals reporting to the chief of staff, including actuarial staff, the controller, as well as professionals engaged in the areas of legal issues, compliance issues, information technology (IT), investment product development, human resources (HR), E-business, security and finance. The chief of staff, the executive members and the regional managers were part of the regional management committee. The regional functional department managers did not have direct responsibility for their respective counterparts within each business unit. For example, the IT manager in Thailand reported to the Thailand country manager, not to the regional IT manager. The regional IT manager received information from the country manager by request.

The individual business units varied greatly in terms of their internal organizational characteristics and operating styles. Some business units, like Taiwan, Japan and Hong Kong, were organized along product lines. Other business units were organized as "do it alls," such as Australia, which marketed itself as a total financial solution provider. In each country, the local management followed their own

Exhibit 5 ING Asia/Pacific Organization Chart Prior to April 2003

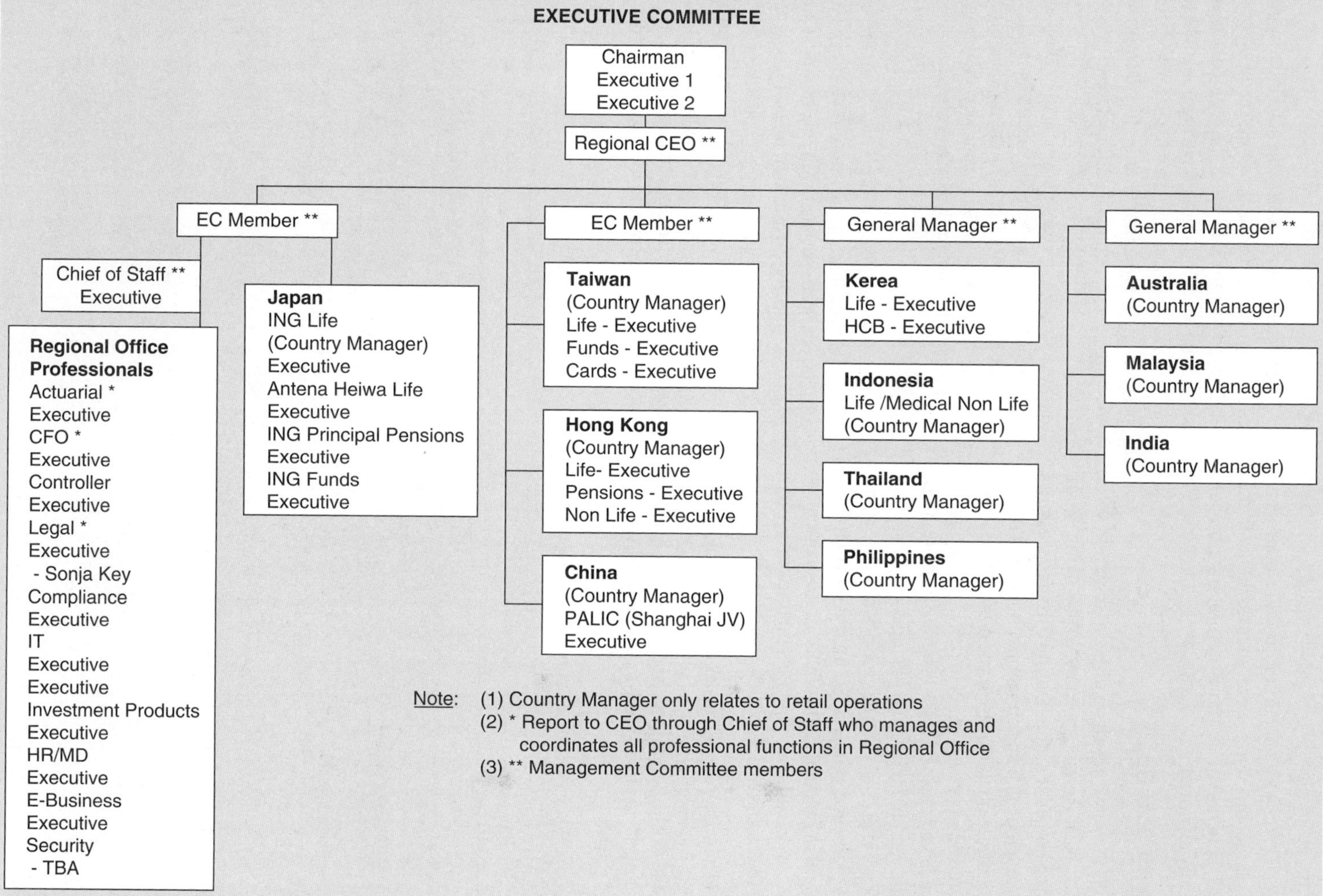

EXECUTIVE COMMITTEE

Chairman
Executive 1
Executive 2

Regional CEO **

Chief of Staff **
Executive

EC Member **

Japan
ING Life
(Country Manager)
Executive
Antena Heiwa Life
Executive
ING Principal Pensions
Executive
ING Funds
Executive

Regional Office Professionals
Actuarial *
Executive
CFO *
Executive
Controller
Executive
Legal *
Executive
- Sonja Key
Compliance
Executive
IT
Executive
Investment Products
Executive
HR/MD
Executive
E-Business
Executive
Security
- TBA

EC Member **

Taiwan
(Country Manager)
Life - Executive
Funds - Executive
Cards - Executive

Hong Kong
(Country Manager)
Life- Executive
Pensions - Executive
Non Life - Executive

China
(Country Manager)
PALIC (Shanghai JV)
Executive

General Manager **

Kerea
Life - Executive
HCB - Executive

Indonesia
Life /Medical Non Life
(Country Manager)

Thailand
(Country Manager)

Philippines
(Country Manager)

General Manager **

Australia
(Country Manager)

Malaysia
(Country Manager)

India
(Country Manager)

Note: (1) Country Manager only relates to retail operations
(2) * Report to CEO through Chief of Staff who manages and
coordinates all professional functions in Regional Office
(3) ** Management Committee members

Source: ING Asia-Pacific.

607

instincts. There was no corporate-wide approach. By and large the units were successful, and the potential benefits of a more common approach were rarely explored.

Kemp's Size-Up

Although the latest results had been solid and ING Insurance Asia/Pacific appeared to be doing well, something bothered Kemp. During off-site meetings, where the senior line and functional managers of the regional office and the local business units discussed, what could be improved to get to better performance, Kemp received clear calls for better coordination between the regional office and the individual business units. The executives asked specifically for more aligned plans and procedures, improved communication, and more delegated authority (see Exhibit 6). There was a clear belief that a detailed roadmap was needed to get things done. Kemp pondered:

> Would it be an operating model, a business model, or a process framework and whatever the name, where can I find it. Could the head office provide me with one; or perhaps I should try to involve consulting firms?

Regional reports were characterized by a multitude of different formats, which made comparisons difficult. Functional heads at the regional office spent several days each month preparing consolidated presentations. Business unit managers defined their own performance benchmarks and agendas for regional meetings. As the chief of staff recalled:

> Sometimes it appears that we speak totally different languages and that nobody understands one another. This is frustrating for us at the regional office and I believe that this is the reason why the business unit managers do not really buy into ideas proposed by the regional office's functional groups.

Kemp sensed the difficulties with the existing level of organizational heterogeneity. Strategic objectives were set according to business unit preferences and they were not formally aligned with regional strategy. Pay for performance was difficult to implement, since results were reported in local formats and not measured against group benchmarks. Local marketing campaigns did not always reflect existing corporate identity standards. In fact,

---

Exhibit 6   Jacques Kemp's Key Issues

Sounds familiar.....?

⇨ Line and functions should be better aligned...

⇨ We should set lear objectives...

⇨ We should pay for performance...

⇨ We need a better operating / business model to execute...

Question: HOW??

Source: ING Asia/Pacific.

many business unit managers did not even know the current corporate standards.

Each country had its own ideas where the best business opportunities could be found, and thought its own market was special. Consequently, it was difficult to identify commonalities across the region. As Kemp recalled from some of the feedback that he received during his initial tour of the region:

> There are no clear mission statements, despite that every country wants to be the leader in something. For example India wants to be the leader in asset management but without presenting a clear plan, outlining how to get there with for example acquisition, organic growth or through partnerships and what this means for the organization, marketing and so on.

Another problem was the ambiguity in terms of the roles of the managers at the regional office. The managers knew their titles but nobody was really clear how the roles tied into the operational structure. During the last couple of months, Kemp heard many times the question: "What is the actual function of the regional office?" This issue caused frustration especially with the functional managers at the regional office who felt disconnected from the operations of the business units.

As Kemp observed:

> Strategic actions are mainly characterized by reactions and less by planning. As the new CEO I have to handle all kinds of strategic plans for the various business units, most are different, inconsistent, incomplete, not aligned with the overall goals of ING, and short of details and specifics. I am therefore wondering what is the "better" way for getting from strategy to execution. I have checked the literature, I checked with consultants and my own study papers and I have not come across any solid and pragmatic operating model or framework for getting close to what I think we need.

The Consultants

Kemp exchanged ideas with several top international consulting firms, including McKinsey & Company, Monitor, and Boston Consulting Group (BCG) about ING Insurance Asia/Pacific's situation. The inputs were initial overviews and not detailed

analyses, but Kemp wanted to get a feeling for the thought processes of these firms and whether it would be worthwhile to engage one of them for follow-on work. Each firm identified different key issues (see Exhibit 7).

McKinsey & Company identified strategic portfolio management and pro-active human resource management as the key areas for improvement. Kemp could see the importance of these issues but he noted the lack of marketing and operational recommendations. For him, the proposal did not get to the day-to-day operational issues. He did not see how a different approach to HR management could solve the operational issues that he had already identified. He believed that ING Insurance Asia/Pacific had a great talent pool and that HR management could not be the only key driver for further improvement.

Monitor Group, on the other side, focused on branding as the key driver for improvements in all areas, including, finance, HR, sales, marketing, manufacturing and operations, distribution and research and development (R&D). Kemp was aware of the importance of branding, which, in fact, was a core strength of ING globally. However, he did not think that branding could or should overwhelm the other key drivers for success.

BCG's proposal focused on building professional capabilities and identified six functional categories in which capabilities should be improved or developed. These categories included strategy and business planning, sales and distribution, products and marketing, finance management, operational processes and infrastructure, and human resources and organization. Kemp liked the approach of BCG but he still noted the lack the important issue of reputation management and compliance. Like the other consulting firms, BCG applied a generic framework to ING. Kemp still thought that the solution was detached from ING Insurance Asia/Pacific's specific operational issues. After all, the company was doing well, so if he started a change process, he needed the full support of his team; and the consultants' proposals, though interesting, did not provide a clear pathway for involving ING Insurance Asia/Pacific's managers.

Exhibit 7   The Consulting Proposals

The Problem:
Consultants Have Their Own Ideas

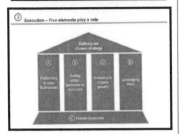

- Focus on business portfolio management
- Human resources seen as fundamental

- Branding is the driving force for all processes

- BCG: 6 functional categories, in which capabilities should be built

Issue:

Vital functions such as marketing and operations are missing!

Issue:

Branding should be considered in most processes, but not as the driver of everything!

Issue:

Reputation management (including Compliance) is still missing!

7

Kemp summarized:

Even if BCG gets the closest, the model lacks completeness and comprehensiveness (specific operational drivers). It is also incomplete in that it does not follow through with clear "objectives and key performance measures." For me it comes to the question how to get from strategy to execution, especially in an aligned way and how to list and connect all the "dots" needed to build (and keep building) a "lasting" and efficient organization. Most models talk about it but do not give me a framework to connect the "dots" with tools like for example pay-for-performance, knowledge-management, intra-firm communication, or planning and auditing.

Another problem for Kemp was the regular disconnect between the functional managers at the regional office and the business unit managers in the countries. He believed this lack of coherence created inefficiencies and potential vulnerability for the entire organization.

Over the years, Kemp had always been interested in the management literature. He met many of the top strategists in industry and academia at conventions and seminars. He particularly liked the idea of "managing managers," which to him was a key gap in the existing management literature. He thought leaders should build organizational capabilities and the internal discipline to help everyone in the organization to excel. He did not want to add complexity, a pitfall he believed many leaders fell into when restructuring organizations. He believed that strategy, and strategic thinking, while important, could only be as good as its implementation.

Kemp had always felt inspired by Alfred Sloan's restructuring success of General Motors in the 1920s and 1930s. When Sloan took over GM, he inherited an amalgamation of independent, entrepreneurial companies assembled by his predecessor, William Durant. Sloan saw that the strategies of the

businesses could be made more coherent and that the entire organization could be more efficient by building systems to manage the managers. At the time, Sloan's approach was revolutionary.

Kemp pondered over the consultant's proposals and his own ideas and he wondered how to create a coherent strategy, which could be executed by the entire organization. He was determined to present his concept at the next executive committee meeting in two weeks' time but he had to decide where to focus (see Exhibit 8).

Exhibit 8   The Problem

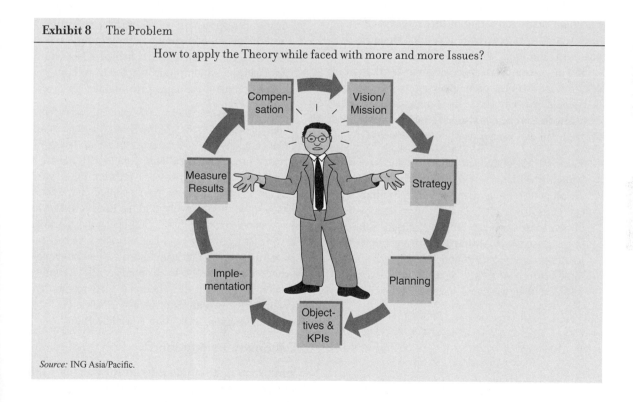

Source: ING Asia/Pacific.

Case 7-2   BRL Hardy: Globalizing an Australian Wine Company

Christopher A. Bartlett

In January 1998, Christopher Carson smiled as he reviewed the Nielsen market survey results that showed Hardy was the top-selling Australian wine brand in Great Britain and held the overall number two position (to Gallo) among all wine brands sold in Britain's off-trade (retailers, excluding hotels and restaurants). As managing director of BRL Hardy Europe, Carson felt proud of this achievement that reflected a 10-fold increase in volume since his first year with Hardy in 1991.

But his mental celebration was short-lived. In front of him were two files, each involving major decisions that would not only shape the future success of the company in Europe but also have major implications for BRL Hardy's overall international strategy:

- The first file contained details of the proposed launch of *D'istinto,* a new line of Italian wines developed in collaboration with a Sicilian winery. Carson and his U.K. team were deeply committed to this project, but several questions had been raised by Australian management. Not least was their concern about *Mapocho,* another joint-venture sourcing agreement Carson had initiated that was now struggling to correct a

disappointing market launch and deteriorating relations with the Chilean sourcing partner.

- The second issue he had to decide concerned two competing proposals for a new entry-level Australian wine. His U.K.-based management had developed considerable commitment to *Kelly's Revenge,* a brand they had created specifically in response to a U.K. market opportunity. But the parent company was promoting *Banrock Station,* a product it had launched successfully in Australia which it now wanted to roll out as a global brand at the same price point.

Watching over these developments was Steve Millar, managing director of the South Australia-based parent company that had experienced a period of extraordinary growth, due in large part to BRL Hardy's successful overseas expansion (**Exhibit 1**). A great believer in decentralized responsibility, he wanted Carson to be deeply involved in the decisions. But he also wanted to ensure that the European unit's actions fit with the company's bold new strategy to become one of the world's first truly global wine companies. Neither did he want to jeopardize BRL Hardy's position in the critically important U.K. market that accounted for two-thirds of its export sales. For both Millar and Carson, these were crucial decisions.

Industry Background[1]

Vines were first introduced into Australia in 1788 by Captain Arthur Phillip, leader of the group of convicts and settlers who comprised the first fleet

Professor Christopher A. Bartlett prepared this case. Some names and data have been disguised. HBS cases are developed solely as the basis for class discussion. Cases are not intended to serve as endorsements, sources of primary data, or illustrations of effective or ineffective management.

Harvard Business School Case No 9-300-018, Copyright 2000 President and Fellows of Harvard College. All rights reserved. *This case was prepared by C. Bartlett. HBS Cases are developed solely for class discussion and do not necessarily illustrate either effective or ineffective handling of administrative situation.*

[1]For a full account, see Christopher A. Bartlett, *Global Wine Wars: New World Challenges Old (A),* HBS No. 303-056 (Boston: Harvard Business School Publishing, 2002) and (*B*), HBS. No. 304-016 (Boston: Harvard Business School Publishing, 2003).

Exhibit 1   BRL Hardy Limited: Summary Group Financial Results—1992–1997 (Aus$millions)

	1992	1993	1994	1995	1996	1997
Sales revenue	151.5	238.3	256.4	287.0	309.0	375.6
Operating profit (before interest, tax)	16.7	26.6	30.2	34.0	39.3	49.2
Net after tax profit	8.8	13.3	15.8	17.4	21.2	28.4
Earnings per share	13.2¢	14.1¢	15.7¢	15.7¢	18.1¢	23.3¢
Total assets	216.8	234.6	280.7	329.0	380.6	455.5
Total liabilities	117.4	127.4	146.6	160.4	194.4	205.8
Shareholders' equity	99.4	107.2	134.1	168.6	186.2	249.7
Debt/equity ratio	70%	57%	57%	53%	58%	41%

Source: Company documents.

of migrants to inhabit the new British colony. A wave of European settlers attracted by the gold rush of the mid-nineteenth century provided a boost to the young industry, both in upgrading the availability of vintner skills and in increasing primary demand for its output. Still, the industry grew slowly, and as late as 1969 annual per capita wine consumption in this beer-drinking country was only 8.2 liters—mostly ports and fortified wines—compared with over 100 liters per person per annum in France and Italy.

In the following 25 years, the Australian wine industry underwent a huge transformation. First, demand for fortified wines declined and vineyards were replanted with table wine varieties. Then, as consumers became more sophisticated, generic bulk wine sales—often sold in the two-liter "bag in a box" developed in Australia—were replaced by bottled varietals such as cabernet sauvignon, chardonnay, and shiraz, the classic grape type increasingly associated with Australia. By the mid-1990s, domestic consumption stood at 18½ liters per capita, eighteenth in the world.

Over this two-century history, more than 1,000 wineries were established in Australia. By 1996, however, the 10 largest accounted for 84 percent of the grape crush and 4 controlled over 75 percent of domestic branded sales. Most of these were public corporations, the largest of which was Southcorp whose brands included Penfolds, Lindeman, and Seppelt. The number two company was BRL

Hardy Ltd. (BRLH), selling under the Hardy, Houghton, Leasingham, and other labels.

During the 1980s and 1990s changes in the global wine industry had a major impact on these emerging Australian companies. A rationalization and consolidation among wine wholesalers and retailers was increasing the power of historically fragmented distribution channels. At the same time, however, large-scale wine suppliers from New World countries such as United States, South America, South Africa, and Australia were exploiting modern viticulture and more scientific wine-making practices to produce more consistent high-quality wine. These developments were occurring in an environment of rapidly growing demand from new consumers in nontraditional markets.

During this period of change, Australian wines began to find large markets abroad, and by 1995 exports accounted for more than 27% of production. But despite its rapid growth, the Australian industry accounted for less than 2% of the world wine production by volume and 2.5% by value. However, because only A$13 billion of the total A$65 billion global wine sales was traded product (80% of wine was consumed in the country of production), the Australian companies' A$450 million in 1995 exports represented 3.5% of the world export market. But in an industry that was becoming increasingly fashion-driven, Australian wine was becoming a "hot trend," and an ambitious industry association saw export potential growing to A$2.5 billion by

Exhibit 2 Australian Wine Export Forecasts—Selected Markets 1996–2025

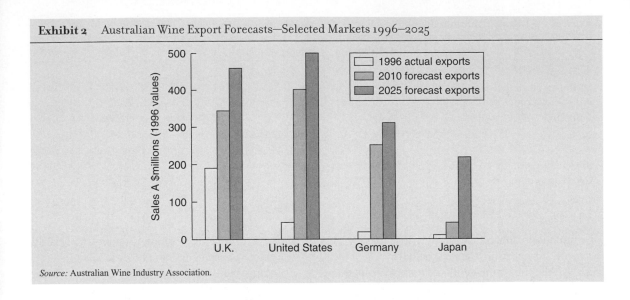

Source: Australian Wine Industry Association.

2025—a 16% share of the projected traded value.[2] Together with an increase in domestic consumption, this translated to A$4.5 billion in Australian wine sales and a doubling of production to 1.7 million tonnes by 2025.

The Australian industry association saw four export markets as key—the United Kingdom, the United States, Germany, and Japan. While the U.K. market would decrease in relative importance (in 1996 it was the world's largest non-producing wine importer and accounted for over 40% of Australian wine exports), over the next 25 years these four markets were expected to continue accounting for 60% of export sales. (See **Exhibit 2**.)

▨ Company Background and History

BRLH's roots could be traced back to 1853 when Thomas Hardy, a 23-year-old English vineyard laborer, acquired land near Adelaide, South Australia, and planted it with vines. In 1857 he produced his first vintage, exporting two hogsheads to England, and by 1882 he had won his first international gold medal at Bordeaux. When Hardy died in 1912, his

company was Australia's largest winemaker, but also one of the most respected.

Shortly after Hardy's death, in the Riverland region northeast of Adelaide, 130 Italian grape growers formed Australia's first cooperative winery in 1916, naming it the Renmano Wine Cooperative. In 1982 Renmano merged with the Riverland's largest winery and distillery, the Berri Cooperative to form Berri Renmano Limited (BRL). By the early 1990s, almost 500 member growers were delivering over 50,000 tonnes of grapes to BRL, giving it the second-largest crush in Australia. This huge-volume grape crush and its bulk-packaging operations led some to refer to BRL disparagingly as "the oil refinery of the wine industry."

Throughout their respective histories, Thomas Hardy & Sons and BRL followed quite different strategies and developed very different organizations. Hardy became known for award-winning quality wines, while the combined cooperatives specialized in fortified, bulk, and value wines—some sold under private labels. And in contrast to Hardy's "polite and traditional" values, BRL's culture was more "aggressive and commercial," according to one observer of both companies.

▌ [2] All forecast values are in 1996 Australian dollars at wholesale prices. At 1996 year-end, the exchange rate was A$1 = US$0.8.

International Roots   Although BRL experienced considerable success when it began selling abroad in the late 1980s (particularly in Scandinavia where it sold 6 million liters of bulk wines per annum), its efforts seemed quite modest when compared with Hardy's long history of exporting much higher-value-added bottled products and the huge additional commitments it was making in that same period. To expand on its U.K. sales base of 12,000 cases per annum, Hardy believed it needed to stop relying on importers, distributors, and agents who carried scores of brands from dozens of vineyards. After a long search, in 1989 it acquired Whiclar and Gordon, a respected U.K.-based wine importer-distributor, including its agency rights for a range of French, Chilean, and South African wines.

This move led management to begin talking about the possibility of buying European wineries that could provide their newly acquired distributors with the critical mass and credibility to give Hardy's wines greater access to Europe. Motivated by the looming 1992 target date for a unified European Community (EC) market, and stimulated by the notion that such alternative sources of supply could cushion the ever-present risk of a poor vintage in one region, Hardy's board felt this was an ideal time to invest. In contrast to the painstaking process of identifying acquisition targets for U.K. distribution, however, the vineyard purchasing decision seemed more opportunistic. In 1990, two Hardy directors visited the wine-growing regions in France and Italy, looking at properties on the market. Passing through southern France, they acquired the century-old Domaine de la Baume, a winery with extensive sources in the Languedoc region and several established domestic and export brands. Six months later, they took over Brolio de Ricasoli, a beautiful castle on a Tuscan hillside that made a well-known Chianti and was reputed to be Italy's oldest winery.

Almost immediately, however, problems surfaced in all three of the European acquisitions and soon they were bleeding the parent company of millions of dollars. Combined with a recession-driven market slowdown at home, these problems plunged Hardy into losses. Meanwhile, BRL was also struggling

and was looking for ways to expand and upgrade its business. When one of Hardy's banks called in a loan and the company was forced to look for a financial partner, BRL was there. Despite its own marginal financial performance, BRL management decided to propose a merger. Said one ex-BRL manager, "We had access to fruit, funds, and disciplined management; they brought marketing expertise, brands, and winemaking know-how. It was a great fit if we could learn to work together." Others, however, were less sanguine. Despite the fact that together the companies accounted for 22% of the Australian wine market and 17% of national wine exports, the dismissive industry view was, "When you put two dogs together, all you get is louder barking." Nonetheless, the companies merged in June 1992 and three months later became a publicly listed company.[3]

New Management, New Strategies

Following the merger, ex-BRL executives assumed the majority of top jobs in BRLH: the newly merged company's deputy-chairman, CEO, operations and technical director, and the international trading director all came from BRL. From the other side, only Hardy's managing director (who became BRLH's business development director) and the Australian sales and marketing manager survived as members of the new top executive team. Steve Millar, formerly BRL's managing director and now CEO of the merged company, explained his early priorities:

> Our first task was to deal with the financial situation. Both companies had performed poorly the previous year, and although we thought our forecasts were conservative, the market was concerned we would not meet the promises made in our IPO [initial public offering]. . . . Then we had to integrate the two organizations. This meant selecting a management team that could both implement the necessary retrenchments and position us for growth. Since the Australian market accounted for the vast bulk of our profit, we initially concentrated our attention at home. . . . Only after getting these two priorities straight could we focus on our new strategy.

---

[3] The Italian Ricasoli operations were explicitly excluded from the merger due to their continued substantial losses and the likelihood they would continue.

The Domestic Turnaround   The strategy that emerged was simple: the company would protect its share of the bulk cask business but concentrate on branded bottle sales for growth. This would require a commitment to quality that would support its brands. The initial management focus would be on the domestic market, first getting merger efficiencies, then implementing the new strategy.

As important as developing a clear strategy, in Millar's mind, was the need to change the company's culture and management style. His sense was that, although there was great potential in the company's middle management, much of it—particularly in the ex-Hardy team—had been held back by being resource constrained and excluded from major decisions. Millar's objective was to create a more decentralized approach, but to hold management accountable. He explained:

> It took time to get the message understood because Hardy management had tended to take a few big swings on high-risk decisions while keeping tight control over the small decisions. I wanted to delegate the small risks—to create a "have a go" mentality. The objective was to have us trying 20 things and getting 80% right rather than doing one or two big things that had to be 100% right.

The prerequisite to delegation, however, was that managers had to be willing to challenge the status quo, accept responsibility for the outcome of decisions that were delegated, and admit when they had made a mistake. David Woods, previously Hardy's national sales manager and now appointed to the same position in the merged company, recalled that the new management style was not easy for everyone to adopt: "Many of us from Hardy felt like outsiders, unsure if we would be allowed into meetings. It became easier after the first year or so when you had shown you could perform. But you definitely had to earn your stripes."

Woods "earned his stripes" by integrating the two sales forces, capturing the economies from the combination, and repositioning the product portfolio in line with the new strategy emphasizing quality branded bottle sales. The results were impressive with both domestic bottle market share and profitability increasing significantly in the first two years of BRLH's operation.

Relaunching International   Meanwhile, Millar had appointed Stephen Davies, an ex-BRL colleague who he regarded as a first-class strategic marketer, as group marketing and export manager for BRLH. A 12-year veteran of BRL, Davies had been responsible for establishing that company's export division in 1985 and had been credited with its successful expansion abroad. While the rest of top management's attention was focused on a major restructuring of the domestic operations, Davies began evaluating the company's international operations. What he found was a dispersed portfolio of marginal-to-weak market positions: a U.K. business selling a small volume of Hardy wines and just breaking even, a rapidly eroding BRL bulk business in Sweden, a weak Hardy-U.S. presence supported by a single representative, and a virtually nonexistent presence in Asia or the rest of Europe.

In Davies's mind, a few clear priorities began to emerge, many of which shadowed the domestic approach. The first priority had to be to clean up the operating problems that were the source of the financial problems. Only then would they focus on building on their strengths, starting with their position in the U.K. market. Making "Quality Wines for the World" the company's marketing slogan, Davies began to build the export strategy on the basis of a strong quality brand image. From the existing broad portfolio of exported products, he initiated a program to rationalize the line and reposition a few key brands in a stepstair hierarchy from simple entry level products to fine wines for connoisseurs. At the mass market price points, for example, he focused the line on *Nottage Hill* and *Stamps* as the Hardy's "fighting brands," while at the top end he targeted the *Eileen Hardy* brand. (See **Exhibit 3** for rationalized export portfolio of brands.)

Exhibit 3   BRL Hardy Domestic versus Export Product Portfolio, 1993

Soft Pack (Cask) Wine

• 2 litre	Benmano and Stanley range
• 3 litre	Berri fortified range
• 4 and 5 litre	Stanley, Berri and Buronga Ridge range
• 10, 15, and 20 litre	Stanley and Berri range

Bottled Table Wine

- Less than $6.00

  Brentwood range
  Brown Bin 60
  Hardy Traditional range
  * Hardy Stamp Series
  Spring Gully range
  * Nottage Hill
  Leasingham Hutt Creek
  McLaren Vale hermitage

- $6.00 to $10.00

  * Houghton White Burgandy
  Hardy Siegersdorf range
  * Leasingham Domaine range
  * Houghton Wildflower Ridge range
  Hardy Bird Series range
  Hardy Tintara range
  Moondah Brook Estate range
  Renmano Chairman's Selection range
  Redman Claret and Cabernet Sanvignon
  Barossa Valley Estate range
  Chais Baumiere range

- $10.00 to $15.00

  * Hardy Collection range
  * Houghton Gold Reserve range
  * Chateau Reynella Stony Hill range

- Over $15.00

  * Eileen Hardy range
  Lauriston range
  E&E Black Pepper Shiraz

Sparkling Wine

- Less than $6.00

  Courier Brut
  Hardy Grand Reserve
  Chateau Reynella Brut

- $6.00 to $10.00
  * Hardy's Sir James Cuvee Brut
- Over $10.00
  Hardy's Classique Cuvee
  Lauriston Methode Champenoise

Fortified Wine

- Less than $6.00

  Brown Bin 60
  Cromwell
  * Tall Ships
  Stanley 2 litre port soft pack (cask)

- $6.00 to $10.00
  Rumpole
  * Old Cave
- Over $10.00
  Lauriston Port & Muscat
  Hardy Show Port
  Vintage Port
  Chateau Reynella Vintage Port

Brandy

  * Hardy Black Bottle
  Berri
  Renmano

All prices are based on the recommended retail price.
* **Rationalized export line** (13 of 48 brands)
Source: Company documents

Exhibit 4   BRL Hardy Europe Ltd.: Key Historical Data (£'000)

		1990	1991	1992	1993	1994
Net sales turnover	In GB £	£10,788	£12,112	£12,434	£15,521	£18,813
	In Australian $	A$22,243	A$24,973	A$29,965	A$33,830	A$37,946
Gross profit (after distribution expense)		£1,173	£1,429	£1,438	£1,595	£1,924
GP %/sales		10.9%	11.8%	11.6%	10.3%	10.2%
Administrative cost		£1,104	£1,261	£1,164	£1,172	£1,308
Admin %/sales		10.2%	10.4%	9.4%	7.6%	7.0%
Profit after tax		−£26	£6	£157	£266	£395
PAT %/sales		−0.2%	0.0%	1.3%	1.7%	2.1%
Average no. of employees		31	27	19	20	22
£ Sales per employee		£348	£449	£654	£776	£855
Stock @ year end		£1,226	£1,043	£605	£897	£1,392
Stock turnover		7.8	10.2	18.2	15.5	12.1
Return on investment		−2.1%	0.5%	11.2%	17.9%	24.5%

Source: Company documents

▌ BRL Hardy in Europe

In the large, developed U.K. market, Davies found a turnaround had already begun under the leadership of Christopher Carson, managing director of Hardy's U.K. company. Carson was an experienced marketing manager with over 20 years in the wine business and particular expertise in Italian wines. He had been hired by Hardy in October 1990 to head the U.K. company's sales and marketing function, including the recently acquired distributor. Within a week of his joining, however, Carson realized that the financial situation in these companies was disastrous. He flew to Australia to tell Hardy's management that they would own a bankrupt U.K. organization unless drastic action was taken. He then proposed a series of cost-cutting steps.

In February 1991, Carson was appointed U.K. managing director and immediately began to implement his cost-cutting plan. Over the next 18 months, he pruned the product line from 870 items to 230 and reduced the headcount from 31 to 18 (including a separation with three of the six executive directors). He also installed strong systems, controls, and policies that put him firmly in charge of key decisions. As these actions were implemented, the 1990 losses became a breakeven operation in 1991, and by the time of the mid-1992 merger, it looked as if the European operations would be profitable again. (For BRLH Europe financials, see **Exhibit 4**.)

Developing the Headquarters Relationship   In his discussions with Davies in late 1992, Carson highlighted the key problems and priorities as he saw them. First was the need to build quickly on the 178,000 cases of Hardy-brand products that had represented less than a quarter of his total volume in 1991 (500,000 of his 700,000 case sales in 1991 were accounted for by a variety of low-margin French wines handled under agency agreements that had come with the purchase of Whiclar and Gordon). At the same time, if the company was going to restore the financial health of its French winemaker, Domaine de la Baume, he felt he would have to build substantially on the 10,000 cases of its product which he had sold in 1991. (He reported 1992 sales were on

			Forecast per BRLH Europe Strategic Plan			
1995	1996	1997	Plan 1998	Plan 1999	Plan 2000	Plan 2001
£27,661	£32,271	£40,100	£53,848	£66,012	£78,814	£91,606
A$57,734	A$69,532	A$82,680	A$111,027	A$136,107	A$162,503	A$188,878
£2,592	£3,202	£4,212	£5,453	£6,488	£7,630	£8,787
9.4%	9.9%	10.5%	10.1%	9.8%	9.7%	9.67%
£1,896	£2,118	£2,717	£3,649	£4,473	£5,340	£6,207
6.9%	6.8%	6.8%	6.8%	6.8%	6.8%	6.8%
£426	£723	£948	£1,087	£1,286	£1,460	£1,644
1.5%	2.2%	2.4%	2.0%	1.9%	1.9%	1.8%
24	28	34	48	62	76	91
£1,153	£1,153	£1,179	£1,122	£1,065	£1,037	£1,007
£1,265	£1,504	£1,500	£2,100	£2,600	£3,300	£3,900
19.8	19.3	23.9	23.0	22.9	21.6	21.2
23.5%	35.7%	39.7%	38.0%	37.8%	36.1%	37.2%

track to double their previous year's volume.) And finally, he wanted to protect an unstable imported Chilean product that had come as a Whiclar and Gordon agency. Carson told Davies of his plans to grow the high potential brand from 20,000 cases in 1991 to a forecast 60,000 cases for 1992.

Davies agreed with Carson's plans, particularly endorsing the focus on the Hardy brands. Yet the relationship was an uneasy one in the post-merger management uncertainties. The BRL-dominated headquarters management supported delegation—but only to those who had "earned their stripes." Within the Hardy-built European company, on the other hand, there were questions about whether their bulk-wine-oriented BRL colleagues understood international marketing. "There was a real tension," said one observer. "A real feeling of us versus them. I think Christopher and Stephen had some difficult conversations." The relationship was delicate enough that Steve Millar decided to have Carson report directly to him on the U.K. company's profit performance but through Davies for marketing and brand strategy. (For BRLH international organization, see **Exhibit 5**.) But Millar did not want the shared reporting relationship to pull him into a role of resolving disputes on operating issues. Instead, he hoped for negotiation:

> Christopher had a good reputation and knew the market well. I assumed he would be a key player and was willing to let him prove it. He and Stephen just clashed, but confrontation can be healthy as long as it is constructive. I just kept urging them to work with together—they could learn a lot from one another.

The biggest disputes seemed to emerge around marketing strategies, particularly branding and labeling issues. Although Hardy exported a dozen brands covering the full price range, its entry-level brands in the United Kingdom were Hardy's *Stamps*, blended red and white wines that then retailed for £2.99 and Hardy's *Nottage Hill*, a single varietal red and white at the £3.69 price point. Together, these two brands accounted for over 80% of Hardy brand sales by value and even more by

Exhibit 5   BRL Hardy's International Organization, 1993

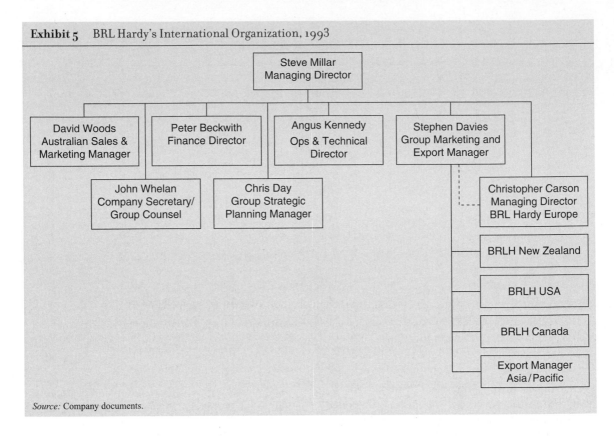

Source: Company documents.

volume. Carson was concerned that the image of these brands had eroded in the United Kingdom, and that he wanted to relabel, reposition, and relaunch them. But it was difficult to convince the home office, and he expressed his frustration:

> Australia controlled all aspects of the brand and they kept me on a pretty tight leash. When I took my message to Reynella [BRLH's corporate office near Adelaide], they didn't want to hear. They expect you to get runs on the board before they give you much freedom. . . . But we were in the U.K. market and they weren't. Finally they agreed, and in 1993 we relabeled and relaunched *Nottage Hill* and repositioned *Stamps*. By 1994 our volume of Hardy's brands quadrupled from 1992 and represented more than half our total sales. (See **Exhibit 6**.)

Davies acknowledged that he yielded on the *Stamps* and *Nottage Hill* decisions, believing "it was better to let people follow a course they believe in—then the implementation will be better." But he

became increasingly concerned about the demand for local control over branding, labeling, and pricing decisions, especially as the company's long-term strategy began to evolve.

The Evolving Strategy   In Reynella, by the mid-1990s, Millar and Davies began to conceive of BRL Hardy not as just a "quality exporter" but as an "international wine company" with worldwide product access backed by the marketing capability and distribution muscle to create global brands. As Millar explained:

> It was an important strategic shift. Most packaged goods businesses are dominated by multinational companies with global brands—like Coke or Kraft. We realized that there were no really established global wine companies and, despite our newness at the game, we had a real chance to be one. . . . I began describing BRL Hardy to our shareholders as a company

Exhibit 6   BRL Hardy Europe Ltd.: Case Summary History

In Std. 9 Liter Cases	1991	1992	1993	1994	1995	1996	1997
Hardy	178,500	194,303	411,084	856,876	1,031,071	1,383,772	1,763,698
Domaine de la Baume	10,000	19,564	49,698	63,540	89,256	155,608	158,587
Chile	20,000	58,848	24,855	76,775	112,954	120,540	50,537
French Agencies (AGW)	497,500	618,878	528,606	545,198	446,445	51,257	{186,180
French Projects					2,162	58,744	
Grand total	706,000	891,593	1,014,243	1,542,389	1,681,888	1,769,921	2,159,002

Source: Company documents

based on three core strengths: our world-class production facilities, our global brands, and our international distribution. Controlling those assets allows us to control our destiny in any major market in the world.

Within the industry, the notion of building global wine brands ran counter to the established wisdom. For example, Jean-Louis Duneu, the head of the Paris office of Lander, a branding consulting firm, recognized the potential of global branding, but was skeptical about its applicability to wine. "The promise of a brand is that it will be the same quality every time," he said. "That means that branded wine probably has to be blended to ensure consistency. The result is never as satisfying." Jonathan Knowles, another corporate identity consultant warned of another potential problem. "Wine lovers look for something they haven't heard of," he claimed. "There's almost an anti-branding mentality. When people who are not in the know get to know the brand name, people in the know no longer want the product."

That view also seemed widespread among traditional wine producers. In the highly fragmented European industry—there were 12,000 producers in Bordeaux alone—only a few top-of-the-market names like Lafite, d'Yquem, and Veuve Clicquot had achieved global recognition, but these held minuscule market shares. Of those that had attempted to build mass market global brands over the years, only a handful—Mateus Rosé, Blue Nun, Mouton Cadet, and Hirondelle, for example— had succeeded. And of these, most had managed to

capture only relatively small volumes and for brief periods of time. After years of trying, Gallo, the world's biggest wine brand, accounted for considerably less than 1% of global wine sales, mostly in its home market.

Nonetheless, Millar and Davies believed that changes in wine-making, the opening of global markets, and the changing consumer profile would all support their objective to become a truly international wine company built on a global branding capability. To implement this strategic shift, Davies felt the Reynella headquarters had to be the "global brand owners." He explained:

> Although we believe in decentralization and want to listen to and support overseas ideas and proposals, we also have to be clear about Reynella's role. Everyone has opinions on label design, but we'll lose control of the brand if we decentralize too much. Our role should be as brand owners deciding issues relating to labeling, pricing, and branding, and overseas should be responsible for sales, distribution, and promotion strategy.

Carson and his U.K. management team had some difficulty with this concept, and disagreements between the two executives continued through the mid-1990s. Carson tried to convince Davies that, unlike the Australian market where branded products accounted for 90% of sales mostly through hotels and bottle shops, the United Kingdom was not yet a branded wine market. Retailers' own labels dominated, particularly in the supermarkets that accounted for more than 50% of retail wine sales. (Indeed, both BRL and Hardy had previously been sources for private labels, but had since discontinued the practice.) Proximity to Continental sources meant that another big segment was claimed by a proliferation of tiny vineyard or village labels with little or no brand recognition, leaving only 12% of sales to recognized proprietary branded wines in 1995. In such a market, Carson argued, it would be hard to support a brand-driven strategy. He elaborated:

> We have to manage a progression from commodity to commodity brand to soft brand to hard brand. And at the early stage of that progression, distribution is key. It's more push than pull, and you need retailers' support to get your product on their shelves. That's why labeling is so important. Women represent 60% of the supermarket wine buyers and the label has to appeal to them.

As the decade rolled on, the debate between Carson and Davies continued. But, as Steve Millar put it, "With 70% growth, we could support the tension."

The 1997 Watershed Decisions

On the basis of the U.K. company's excellent performance, Carson was appointed chief executive of BRL Hardy Europe in 1995. He immediately began putting together some bold plans for the company's continued growth and, over the next couple of years, set in motion some initiatives that were to create a mixture of excitement and apprehension within the organization.

The Outsourcing Ventures   For the first five years following the merger, Carson had focused most of his attention on building sales of the Hardy brand wines. However, he remained acutely aware of the importance of the other non-Australian product lines he had inherited through the Whiclar and Gordon acquisition. Not only did the added volume bring scale economies to his sales and distribution operation, they also provided BRLH Europe with some other important strategic benefits.

As an agricultural product, every region's grape harvest was vulnerable to weather, disease, and other factors affecting the quality and quantity of a vintage. Carson recognized that sourcing from

Exhibit 7   Key Currency Fluctuations Affecting BRLH Europe

	$Aus/£	It Lira/£	Chilean Peso/£	$US/£
12/92	2.197	2239	NA	1.514
12/93	2.213	2516	NA	1.492
12/94	2.013	2546	NA	1.559
12/95	2.080	2455	630.8	1.541
12/96	2.088	2544	703.0	1.664
12/97	2.505	2892	727.1	1.659

Source: Company documents

multiple regions was one way to minimize that risk. Furthermore, he became increasingly aware that major retailers—particularly grocery chains like Sainsburys—were trying to rationalize their suppliers. To simplify wine buying, they wanted to deal with only a few key suppliers who could provide them with a broad line of quality products. And finally, currency fluctuations exposed traded products like wine exports to currency-driven price variations that could substantially affect marketability, particularly for lower-priced products. (See **Exhibit 7.**)

For all these reasons, in 1997 Carson began to devote more of his time and attention to two non-Australian wine sources—a move that seemed to fit with Reynella's new emphasis on becoming "an international wine company." This shift was triggered by the unpleasant revelation in late 1996 that *Caliterra*, a brand he and his sales organization had built into the leading Chilean import in the United Kingdom, would not be renewing its distribution agreement. The supplier, Caliterra Limitade, had signed a joint venture agreement with U.S. winemaker Robert Mondavi.

Determined never again to invest in a brand he did not control, Carson initiated action on two fronts. In early 1997, he negotiated a 50/50 joint venture agreement with Jose Canopa y CIA Limitada under which the Chileans would provide the fruit and the winemaking facility while BRL Hardy would send in one of its winemakers to make several wines that it would sell in Europe under the *Mapocho* brand, using its marketing and distribution capabilities. Despite several mishaps, difficulties, and delays during the negotiations (including a near derailing when Carson's main contact left Canepa), by late 1997 the supply arrangements were in place.

At the same time he was finalizing the Chilean deal, Carson was also exploring alternative European sources, particularly for red wine. In March 1997, he made initial contact with Casa Vinicola Calatrasi, a family-owned winery in Sicily with links to a major grape grower's cooperative. After explaining his interest in developing a line of branded products to be sold through BRLH's distribution channels, he began analyzing product availability, volume forecasts, and prices.

Over the following months, he returned to Sicily a couple more times, meeting with the co-op farmers to explain how branding could give them security of demand and eventually better prices for their fruit. He told them of BRL Hardy's expertise in viticulture, and offered the help of the company's highly regarded technical experts to further enhance the value of their harvest through more productive vineyard techniques and new winemaking methods. Having experienced difficult negotiations with the Chilean joint venture, Carson wanted to avoid similar problems and emphasized that this would work only if it was a true partnership. He wanted the farmers' best fruit and their commitment to make the project work. At his first presentation, 60 farmers showed up. When the word spread, Carson found he had an audience of 135 receptive co-op members at his second presentation. "We all had a very good feeling about the relationship," said Carson. "It felt much more like a partnership than the Chilean JV where they were acting more like suppliers than part owners."

Returning to London, Carson engaged his organization in developing a strategy for the product code-named *Mata Hardy*. While detailed marketing plans were being developed internally, an external consultant began generating over 2,000 possible brand names. As Carson and his sales and marketing staff began narrowing the choices, they engaged a designer to develop labels and packaging that would capture the Mediterranean lifestyle they wanted the brand to reflect.

By July 1997, the marketing plans were developed to the point that Carson was ready to review his proposal with management in Reynella. He described how he wanted to offset projected Australian red wine shortages with alternative sources. Presenting his vision of sourcing from both the northern and southern hemispheres, he outlined his need for a full line to maximize his leverage as a distributor. He then described the broad objective of developing a brand that would respond to the average wine consumer who was interested in wine but not necessarily very knowledgeable about it. The new product was designed to give them the information they needed on appealing, easy-to-read labels with a pronounceable brand name. The objective was to give them a wine they would enjoy and a brand they would trust.

Carson then presented the portfolio of eight new Italian-sourced wines spread across the low and low-middle price points. At the baseline £3.49 price point would be wines made from less well known indigenous Sicilian grapes. At the next level would be blends of indigenous and premium varietals (a Catarrato-Chardonnay white and Nero d'Avola-Sangiovese red, for example) priced at £3.99. At £4.99 he planned to offer pure premium varietals such as Syrah and Sangiovese, while to top out the line he wanted to offer blends of super-varietals such as Cabernet-Merlot at £5.99.

The highlight of the presentation was when Carson unveiled his idea about creating a strong branded product, revealing both the final name choice—*D'istinto,* which translated as "instinctively"—and the boldly distinctive labels and other packaging designs. (See **Exhibit 8.**) (He swore all who saw the branding materials to secrecy since his intention was to reveal the new name and label with great fanfare just before its planned launch in early 1998.) The plan was to give *D'istinto* a unique image built around the Mediterranean lifestyle—passionate, warm, romantic, and relaxed—and to link it strongly to food. Each

Exhibit 8   *D'istinto* Proposed Packaging and Positioning

Capsule Product Position/Brand Image

- Value
- Quality
- Mass appeal
- Mediterranean lifestyle
- Food-friendly
- Relaxed
- Warm
- Romantic

Source: Company documents

bottle would have a small booklet hung on its neck, describing the wine and inviting the buyer to write for free recipes. The intention was to create a database of wine-and-food-loving consumers to whom future promotions could be mailed. "This line can help us build BRLH Europe in size, impact, and reputation," said Carson. "We need to become known as a first-class branding company— a company able to leverage great distribution and strong marketing into recognized consumer brands."

In the meanwhile, however, early signs were that the *Mapocho* project was not going well. For months, Canepa managers had been raising doubts and concerns about the JV. For example, they claimed their costs went up, and wanted to renegotiate the supply price. By the time things got back on track, the Chilean company had made other commitments and the new venture lost its opportunity to get early

access to the pick of the 1997 grape harvest. As a result, first samples of *Mapocho* sent to London by BRL Hardy's winemaker were disappointing. The Chileans thought the problem was due to the winemaker sent from BRL Hardy being unfamiliar with Chilean wine, while he insisted they had not provided him with quality fruit. Early sales were disappointing and forecasts were that the first vintage would sell only 15,000 cases against the 80,000 originally planned. Unless there was a rapid turnaround, the company stood to lose up to £400,000. Despite this poor showing, however, the U.K. sales and marketing group was forecasting 1998 sales of 150,000 cases and the company was about to make a commitment to Canepa for this volume of their new vintage due in February. It was a forecast that made many in the Reynella headquarters very nervous.

As a consequence, while the Australians were impressed by Carson's ambitious ideas for *D'istinto*, many questions and doubts were raised and approval was slow in coming. Some senior management still had bad feelings about the Italian wine business left over from Hardy's earlier ill-fated Italian venture. Even those who had not lived through the Ricasoli losses had concerns about the troublesome ongoing experiment with the Chilean sourcing joint venture. And still others, including Stephen Davies, were concerned that the new Sicilian line could cannibalize Hardy's two fighting brands. *D'istinto* was initially proposed as a product to fill the price points that had been vacated as *Stamps* and *Nottage Hill* had become more expensive. But, as the Australian management pointed out, the extended Sicilian line now clearly overlapped with Hardy's core offerings—not only *Stamps* at £4.49 but even with *Nottage Hill* now selling for £5.49 (see **Exhibit 9**).

Finally, Steve Millar raised a more organizational concern. He was worried about the possibility of Carson losing his focus and about the strength of the European sales organization to carry another brand when it was already struggling with *Mapocho*. In the context of the U.K.'s over-commitment to the *Mapocho* launch, he was

Exhibit 9 U.K. Product Price Point Matrix

Recommended Retail Price Point (£)	Hardy	Leasingham Chateau Reynella	Houghton	Mapocho	D'istinto
27.99	Eileen Hardy Shiraz Thomas Hardy Cab Sauv		Jack Mann Red		
24.99		E&E Black Pepper			
19.99		Classic Clare Shiraz			
12.99	Eileen Hardy Chardonnay	Ebenezer Shiraz Ebenezer Cab Merlot	Crofters Cab Merlot		
11.99		Ch Reynella Shiraz Ch Rey Cab Merlot			
9.99	Coonawarra Cab Sauv	Leasingham Shiraz Leas Cab Malbec			
8.99		Ebenezer Chardonnay Ch Rey Chard Leas Chard	Crofters Chardonnay		
7.99	Pathway Chardonnay	Domain Grenache Leas Chardonnay Leas Semillon	Wildflower Shiraz		
6.99	Bankside Shiraz Nottage Hill Sparkling				
6.49	Bankside Chardonnay				
5.99	Nottage Hill Shiraz Stamps Sparkling		Wildflower Chardonnay Wildflower Chenin Blanc	Merlot	Cabernet Merlot
5.49	Nottage Hill Cab Shiraz				
4.99	Nottage Hill Chardonnay Nottage Hill Reisling Stamp Shiraz Cabernet Stamp Grenche Shiraz			Cab. Sauv. Chardonnay	Syrah Sangiovese
4.49	Stamp Chardonnay Sem Stamp ReislingG/Traminer			Sauv. Blanc	
3.99					Cataratto/Chardonnay Sangiovese/Merlot
3.49					Trebiano/Insolia Nero d'Aviola

Source: Company documents

625

even more concerned when he saw *D'istinto's* projected sales of 160,000 cases in the first year rising to 500,000 by year four. "You will never do those numbers," said Millar. Carson's response was that he thought *D'istinto* had global potential and could eventually reach a million cases. "By the next century, we'll even be exporting Italian wine to Australia!" he said.

Yet despite the lighthearted exchange with his boss, the widely expressed doubts he confronted in the Australian review meeting caused Carson to reflect. The financial investment in the branding, packaging, and launch expenses was relatively small—probably less than £100,000. But in a situation of continued difficulty with *Mapocho* sales, Carson understood that the real financial risk could come later in the form of contract commitments and excess inventory. Furthermore, he knew that the questions Steve Millar had raised about organizational capacity and his own risk of distraction were real. Would *D'istinto* overload human resources already stretched thin by the rapid expansion of the previous five years? And would it prove to be too big a competitor for management time, corporate funding, and eventually consumer sales? The questions were complicated by another decision Carson faced—one relating to the development of a new Australian product to extend the company's existing range of fighting brands.

The Australian Opportunity   As the *Stamps* and *Nottage Hill* brands gradually migrated upward to straddle the £4.49/£4.99/£5.49 price points, Carson believed there was an opening for a new low-end Australian brand to fill in the first rungs on the Hardy's price ladder. Because the price points below £4.49 represented more than 80% of the market, he felt it was an important gap to fill. Being fully occupied with the Chilean and Italian projects, however, he found himself unable to devote the time he wanted to developing a new Australian brand. To Steve Millar, this presented the ideal opportunity to push an agenda he had been urging on Carson for some time—the need to develop the

senior levels of the U.K. organization, particularly on the marketing side. Said Millar:

> Christopher had done an amazing job of building the U.K. But he had driven much of it himself. . . . For a couple of years I'd been telling him, "Get people even better than you *below* you." We'd even sent a few Australians to support him in marketing and help the communication back home. But most of them got chewed up pretty quickly.

Finding himself stretched thin, and recognizing he had to stand back from controlling operations, Carson agreed to take on a new expat Australian marketing manager. The person he chose was Paul Browne, an eight-year company veteran whose career had taken him from public relations to brand management in Australia. Most recently, he had been responsible for export marketing for the United States and Oceania, reporting to the president of BRL Hardy USA. Carson explained his choice:

> I wanted a driver. Someone who could take charge and get things done. As an Australian with an understanding of group level activities, Paul fit our need to fill the weakness in marketing. He roared into the business with great enthusiasm and linked up with our sales director and national accounts manager to understand the local market's needs.

Browne concluded that there was an opportunity for a Hardy's brand positioned at the £3.99 price point, but able to be promoted at £3.49. He felt the market was ready for a fun brand—even slightly quirky—which would appeal to a younger consumer, perhaps a first-time wine drinker who would later trade up to *Stamps* and *Nottage Hill*. The brand he came up with was *Kelly's Revenge*, named for an important character in the history of the Australian wine industry, but also suggestive of Ned Kelly, the infamous Australian bushranger (outlaw) of the early nineteenth century. With backing and support of the U.K. sales management, they pursued the concept, designing a colorful label and preparing a detailed marketing plan. (See **Exhibit 10**.) As excitement and enthusiasm increased, Carson stood back and gave his new product team its head.

Exhibit 10   *Kelly's Revenge:* Label and Product Concept

Proposed Promotion Material/Back Label

It has taken 130 years for Dr. Alexander Kelly to have his revenge. Kelly was the first to recognize the wine growing potential to Australia's McLaren Vale region. His vision, however, was ahead of its time, and his eventual bankruptcy enabled the acquisition of the original Tintara Winery by Thomas Hardy. Hardy's wines eventually established the reputation of the McLaren Vale, winning tremendous praise at the Colonial and Indian Wine Exhibition in 1885. Kelly's descendents have continued to forge Hardy's wine making tradition, and to this day Tintara Cellars are the home of Hardy's Wines, one of Australia's finest and most highly awarded winemakers. This wine is dedicated to the spirit of our pioneers.

Source: Company documents

Meanwhile, in Reynella, BRLH in Australia was developing a major new product targeted at a similar price point. In 1995, the company had acquired Banrock Station, a 1,800-hectare cattle grazing property in South Australia's Riverland district, with the intention of converting a portion of it to viticulture. During the planting and development phase, visitors' universally positive reaction to BRLH's ongoing conservation efforts—planting only 400 hectares while returning the remaining land to its native state including the restoration of natural wetlands—convinced management that the property had brand potential. (See **Exhibit 11.**)

Positioned as an environmentally responsible product with part of its profits allocated to conservation groups, the *Banrock Station* brand was launched in Australia in 1996. The brand's image was reflected in its earth-tone labels and its positioning as an unpretentious, down-to-earth wine was captured by the motto "Good Earth, Fine Wine." Blended *Banrock Station* wines started at A$4.95, but the line extended up to premium varietals at A$7.95. In the United Kingdom, it would be positioned at the same price points as the proposed *Kelly's Revenge*. The product was an immediate success in Australia, and soon thereafter became the largest-selling imported brand in New Zealand.

Convinced of *Banrock Station's* potential as a global brand, Davies and Millar urged BRLH companies in Europe and North America to put their best efforts behind it. Canadian management agreed to launch immediately, while in the United States, the decision was made to withdraw the *Stamps* product, which local management felt was devaluing the Hardy's image, and replace it with *Banrock Station*. But in Europe, where the *Kelly's Revenge* project was in its final development stages, the management team expressed grave doubts about *Banrock Station*. They argued that the label

Exhibit 11   *Banrock Station:* Environmentally Responsible Product Positioning

Proposed Product Promotion Material

Banrock Station's precious soil is treated with respect and in return it nurtures the premium grape varieties that create our value-for-money, easy drinking wines of great character. Situated in the heart of South Australia's Riverland region, directly opposite the historic Cobb & Co. stage coach station, Banrock Station is a 4,500 acre property featuring some of the world's most picturesque scenery. In its midst lie 400 acres of premium sun-soaked vineyard.

Because we understand that good earth is the starting point for most of nature's bounty, we are working with like minded organizations to ensure this natural haven which surrounds the vineyards of Banrock Station is preserved for future generations to appreciate and enjoy. Every sip of Banrock Station fine wine gives a little back to the good earth from whence it came.

Banrock Station: Good Earth, Fine Wine.

Source: Company documents

design was too dull and colorless to stand out on supermarket shelves, and that the product's environmental positioning would have limited appeal to U.K. consumers half a world away.

Steve Millar described the conflict that emerged around the competing concepts:

> I accept it as my mistake. I'd been pushing Christopher to delegate more and trying to get more Australians on

his staff to help build links back to Australia. But Paul Browne became our biggest problem. He just didn't have the skills for the job but he wanted to control everything. Then on top of that he started playing politics to block *Banrock Station*. When we asked him to give the new concept a try, he kept insisting it would never work. We got the feeling he had even organized customers to tell us how bad the label was. Instead of helping communications between Australia and Europe he became a major barrier.

Meanwhile, Browne presented his new *Kelly's Revenge* concept to the Australian management to a very skeptical reception. Davies's reaction was immediate, strong, and negative, seeing it as "kitsch, downmarket, and gimmicky." He and his Reynella-based staff felt they knew more about marketing Australian wines than the European management. In Davies's words, "By decentralizing too much responsibility, we realized we risked losing control of brand issues. We wanted to take back more control as the brand owners."

Steve Millar recalled his reaction to the *Kelly's Revenge* proposal:

> I told them I thought it was terrible, but that it really didn't matter what I thought. I suggested we get the customers' reaction. When we took *Kelly's Revenge* to ASDA, the UK grocery chain, they were not enthralled. So I took that as an opportunity to suggest we give *Banrock Station* a try.

Although Christopher Carson had been backing his new marketing manager to this point, with *Banrock Station* succeeding elsewhere and senior management behind it as a global brand, the issue was becoming very complex. He knew the organization could not support both brands and felt the time had come when he would have to commit to one project or the other. For Steve Millar, the situation was equally complex. Given the U.K.'s strong performance, he wanted to give Carson as much freedom as possible, but also felt responsible for the implementation of the company's global strategy. Running through his mind was how he would respond if Carson and his U.K. organization remained firm in its commitment to *Kelly's Revenge* over *Banrock Station*.

Case 7-3   Silvio Napoli at Schindler India (A)

Perry L. Fagan, Michael Y. Yoshino, and Christopher A. Bartlett

"Monsieur Napoli, si vous vous plantez ici vous êtes fini! Mais si vous réussissez, vous aurez une très bonne carrière." (Translation: "Mr. Napoli, if you fall on your face here you are finished! But if you succeed, you will have a very nice career.") The words echoed off the walls of Silvio Napoli's empty living room and disappeared down the darkened hallway like startled ghosts. The parquet was still wet from the five inches of water that had flooded the first floor of the Napoli home in suburban New Delhi several days before, during one of the sewer system's periodic backups. Standing in the empty room were Napoli and Luc Bonnard, vice chairman, board of directors of Schindler Holdings Ltd., the respected Swiss-based manufacturer of elevators and escalators. It was November 1998, and Bonnard was visiting New Delhi for the first time to review progress on the start-up of the company's Indian subsidiary, which Napoli had been dispatched to run eight months earlier. Things were not going according to plan.

Napoli, a 33-year-old Italian former semiprofessional rugby player, had arrived in March with his pregnant wife and two young children and had quickly set about creating an entirely new organization from scratch. Since March, he had established offices in New Delhi and Mumbai, hired five Indian top managers, and begun to implement the aggressive business plan he had written the previous year while head of corporate planning in Switzerland. The plan called for a $10 million investment and hinged on selling "core, standardized products," with no allowance for customization. To keep costs down and avoid India's high import tariffs, the plan also proposed that all manufacturing and logistics activities be outsourced to local suppliers.

Shortly before Bonnard's visit, however, Napoli was confronted with three challenges to his plan. First, he learned that for the second time in two months, his Indian managers had submitted an order for a nonstandard product—calling for a glass rear wall in one of the supposedly standard elevators. At the same time, his business plan had come under intense cost pressures, first from a large increase in customs duties on imported elevator components, then from an unanticipated rise in transfer prices for the "low-cost" components and materials imported from Schindler's European factories. Finally, as Napoli began accelerating his strategy of developing local sources for elevator components, he found that his requests for parts lists, design specifications, and engineering support were not forthcoming from Schindler's European plants.

As the implementation of his business plan stalled, Napoli wondered what he should do. Eight months in India and he still had not installed a single elevator, while his plan showed first-year sales of 50 units. And now Bonnard was visiting. Should he seek his help, propose a revised plan, or try to sort out the challenges himself? These were the thoughts running through Napoli's head as the vice

Senior Research Associate Perry L. Fagan and Professor Michael Y. Yoshino prepared the original version of this case, "Silvio Napoli at Schindler India (A)," HBS No. 302-053 (Boston: Harvard Business School Publishing, 2002). This version was prepared by Professor Christopher A. Bartlett. HBS cases are developed solely as the basis for class discussion. Cases are not intended to serve as endorsements, sources of primary data, or illustrations of effective or ineffective management.

Harvard Business School Case No 9-303-086, Copyright 2003 President and Fellows of Harvard College. All rights reserved. *This case was prepared by C. Bartlett. HBS Cases are developed solely for class discussion and do not necessarily illustrate either effective or ineffective handling of administrative situation.*

chairman asked him, "So, how are things going so far, Mr. Napoli?"

Schindler's India Explorations

Schindler had a long and rather disjointed history with the Indian market. Although its first elevator in India was installed in 1925, the company did not have a local market presence until it appointed a local distributor in the late 1950s. Almost 40 years later, Schindler decided it was time to take an even bolder step and enter the market through its own wholly owned subsidiary.

The Growing Commitment   Established in 1874 in Switzerland by Robert Schindler, the company began manufacturing elevators in 1889. Almost a century later, the 37-year-old Alfred N. Schindler became the fourth generation of the family to lead the company, in 1987. Over the next decade, he sought to transform the company's culture from that of an engineering-based manufacturing company to one of a customer-oriented service company.

By 1998, Schindler had worldwide revenues of 6.6 billion Swiss francs (US$4 billion) and was widely perceived as a technology leader in elevators. It was also the number one producer of escalators in the world. The company employed over 38,000 people in 97 subsidiaries but did not yet have its own operations in India, a market Alfred Schindler felt had great potential.

Although the first Schindler elevator in India was installed in 1925, it was not until 1958 that the company entered into a long-term distribution agreement with ECE, an Indian company. In 1985, Schindler terminated that agreement and entered into a technical collaboration with Mumbai-based Bharat Bijlee Ltd. (BBL) to manufacture, market, and sell its elevators. After acquiring a 12 percent equity stake in BBL, Schindler supported the local company as it became the number two player in the Indian elevator market, with a 10%–15% share a decade later.

On assuming the role of chairman in 1995, Alfred Schindler decided to take a six-month "sabbatical" during which he wanted to step back and review the long-term strategy of Schindler. As part of that process, he undertook to travel through several markets—China, Japan, and several other Far Eastern markets—that he felt were important to the company's growth. He spent several weeks in India, traveling over 3,000 kilometers in a small Ford rental car. "After his trip Mr. Schindler saw India as a second China," said a manager in Switzerland. "He saw huge growth potential. And once he targets something, he's like a hawk."

With the objective of raising its involvement, Schindler proposed to BBL that a separate joint venture be created solely for the elevator business, with Schindler taking management control. But negotiations proved difficult and eventually collapsed. In late 1996, collaboration with BBL ended, and Schindler began considering options to establish its own operation in India.

Silvio Napoli's Role   Meanwhile, after graduating from the MBA program at Harvard Business School, Silvio Napoli had joined Schindler in September 1994. He accepted a position at the company's headquarters in Ebikon, Switzerland, reporting directly to the CEO as head of corporate planning.

With its 120 years of history, Schindler was a formal Swiss company where the hierarchy was clear, politeness important, and first names rarely used. Napoli's office was on the top floor of the seven-story headquarters building, a floor reserved for the three members of the company's executive committee and the legal counsel. (For profiles of top management, see **Exhibit 1**.) "As soon as I arrived, I was aware that people were very responsive to my requests," said Napoli. "Just by my physical location, I generated fearful respect, and I realized I would have to manage my situation very carefully." A 20-year Schindler veteran recalled his reaction to Napoli's arrival: "He was the assistant to Mr. Schindler, so I knew I'd better be nice to him."

Exhibit 1 Schindler Top Management Profiles

Name:	Alfred N. Schindler	Luc Bonnard	Alfred Spöerri
Position:	Chairman and Chief Executive Officer	Vice Chairman of the Board and Member of the Executive Committee	Member of the Board of Directors Member of the Executive Committee
Date of Birth:	March 21, 1949	October 8, 1946	August 22, 1938
Education:	1976–1978: MBA, Wharton, USA 1974–1976: Certified Public Accountant School, Bern 1969–1974: University of Basel–Law School (lic. jur.), Abschluss:lic.iur.	1971: Diploma in Electrical Engineering at ETH (Technical University), Zurich	
Experience:	Since 1995: Chairman of the Board and Chief Executive Officer 1985–1995: Chairman of the Corporate Executive (CEO) 1984–1985: Member of Corporate Management 1982–1984: Head of Corporate Planning 1978–1979: Deputy Head of Corporate Planning	1996: Vice Chairman 1991–1996: Member of the Executive Committee 1986–1990: COO Elevators and Escalators, Member Corporate Executive Committee 1985–1986: Member, Executive Committee 1983–1985: Group Management Member, North Europe 1973: Management, Schindler, in France	1991–1998: Member, Executive Committee 1997–1998: Chief Financial Officer 1979–1988: Corporate Controller—Treasurer 1975–1979: COO of Mexico 1971–1974: Area Controller, Latin America 1968–1974: Financial Officer of Mexico 1968: Joined Schindler Group

Source: Schindler India.

As head of corporate planning, Napoli was responsible for coordinating the annual strategic review process and undertaking external benchmarking and competitor analysis. But his most visible role was as staff to the corporate executive committee, the Verwaltungsrat Ausschuss (VRA)—which was composed of Alfred Schindler, Luc Bonnard, and Alfred Spöerri, the chief financial officer. As the only nonmember to attend VRA meetings, Napoli was responsible for taking meeting minutes and for following up on action items and special projects defined by the VRA.

The Swatch Project   In 1995, Napoli took on the Swatch Project, a major assignment that grew out of a concern by VRA members that margins on new-product sales were eroding as each competitor strove to expand its installed base of elevators. Since such sales were a vital source of profitable long-term maintenance and service contracts, the project's goal was to develop a standardized elevator at a dramatically lower cost than the existing broad line of more customized products. It was an assignment that involved the young newcomer in sensitive discussions with Schindler's plants in Switzerland, France, and Spain to discuss design, determine costs, and explore sourcing alternatives. Napoli described the process and outcome of the Swatch Project:

> As you might imagine, I was viewed with some suspicion and concern. Here was this young MBA talking about getting costs down or outsourcing core tasks that the plants felt they owned. . . . In the end, we developed the S001, a standard elevator that would not be customized, incorporated processes never before seen in the group, and used many parts sourced from outside suppliers. All of this was unthinkable in the past. We redesigned the entire supply chain and in doing so, halved the industry's standard 20- to 30-week cycle time.

The Indian Entry Project   Meanwhile, as negotiations with BBL broke down in India, the VRA engaged Boston Consulting Group to identify and evaluate alternative local partners with whom Schindler might build its business in India. As the company's point man on the project, Napoli worked with the consultants to narrow the list of 34 potential partners to eight candidates for review by the VRA. As the team pursued the final choices, however, it concluded that there was no ideal partner. But it learned that it was now legally feasible to start up a 100% wholly owned company in India. The VRA then asked Napoli and the head of Schindler's mergers and acquisitions department to explore that option.

Napoli contacted experts in India who helped him expand his understanding of the situation. Through discussions with market experts and studies by local consultants, Napoli spent nine months developing a detailed analysis of the market size, legal environment, and competitive situation in the Indian elevator market. He integrated this into a business plan for Schindler's market entry and submitted it to the VRA. The plan was approved in October. Soon after, Napoli was offered the job of creating the Indian subsidiary. Napoli recalled his reaction:

> I realized that the future manager of the new company would be key to the success of the business plan I had been working on. I was conscious that my early involvement in the project made me a candidate, so when the offer came, I was not surprised. Deep down, I knew I could do it. More surprising was the reaction of my headquarters' colleagues, who thought I was crazy to take such a high-risk career move that involved dragging my family to a developing country.

Bonnard explained the choice of Napoli:

> There are two possible profiles in a country like India. The first is a young guy who knows the company, people, and products; the second is someone who is 55 years old with grown kids looking for a new challenge. . . . Mr. Napoli knew lots of people. He was open to go new ways. We needed someone who could handle different cultures, who was young and flexible. We needed to trust the person we sent, and we trusted him 100%. And we needed a generalist, not a pure specialist. We needed someone who had courage. Finally, I believe that the people who make the business plan should have to realize it. Of course, we also needed to have someone who was willing to go.

In November Napoli and his wife Fabienne, a French-German dual national, made their first trip to India. "We went on a 'look and see' visit, starting in Mumbai," Napoli recounted. "When we arrived in Delhi my wife looked around and said she would be more comfortable living here. After reaching an agreement on the relocation package back in Switzerland, I accepted the job."

Over the next several months, Napoli made three more trips to India to lay the groundwork for the move. In one key move, he engaged the executive search firm Egon Zehnder to identify candidates for his top management team. Although he had to await government approval to start the new company, when he moved to India, he wanted to have key managers in place.

Forming Schindler India

As vice president for South Asia, Napoli was responsible for India and a few nearby export markets in Schindler's elevators and escalators division (see **Exhibit 2**). In March, Napoli relocated to India and began the task of building the company that would implement his business plan.

New Culture, New Challenges   On his first day in the Delhi office, Napoli got stuck in one of BBL's elevators. As he recalled, it proved to be an omen of things to come:

> On our first morning in Delhi, six hours after the family had landed, my two-year-old daughter opened her forehead falling in the hotel room. The deep wound required hospitalization and stitching under total anesthesia. Two weeks later, my wife Fabienne got infectious food poisoning, which required one-week hospitalization, even threatening a miscarriage. The day she came back from hospital, my three-year-old son fell in the hotel bathroom and broke his front tooth. Rushing to an emergency dentist in a hotel car, I really wondered, for the only time in my life, whether I could stand this much longer.

Although Napoli and his family were in New Delhi, where he had opened a marketing and service office, he spent most of a typical week at the company's headquarters in Mumbai. "The first two months were really a hard-fought battle between family relocation and company start-up," he recalled. "Weeks were consumed shuttling between Delhi and Mumbai, hunting for office space, filing government registrations, and completing legal paperwork. On the family front, I had to get them started in a totally different system: housing, schools, doctors, grocery shopping . . . all things which are totally different in India."

In the process, Napoli found he had to adapt his management approach. "For example," he recalled, "all types of characters started to approach me offering their services. They had heard that I was representing a Swiss firm about to invest in India. I soon learned to be careful in deciding who I could trust."

Recruiting the Team   Over the previous couple of months, Egon Zehnder had identified several promising candidates who became the pool from which Napoli recruited for his top positions in the new company. Mehar Karan ("M.K.") Singh, 42, was tapped for the role of managing director, a position that reported to Napoli but was viewed as a stepping stone to heading the subsidiary. (For profiles of key Indian managers, see **Exhibit 3**). "At some point in your career you will report to someone younger than yourself," said Singh. "I decided that Schindler was an exciting opportunity to test this scenario."

Napoli explained the choice of Singh: "Having led construction projects for some of India's largest hotels, M.K. had firsthand experience in building an organization from scratch. But most of all, he had been on our customers' side. He would know how to make a difference in service." In addition, being 10 years older and having grown up in India, Singh brought valuable experience and a different perspective. He was also more sensitive to organizational power and relationships, as Napoli soon recognized:

> The first question M.K. asked me after joining the company was, "Who are your friends inside the company? Who doesn't like you?" I never thought about it

Exhibit 2   Schindler Organization Chart, Elevator and Escalator Division

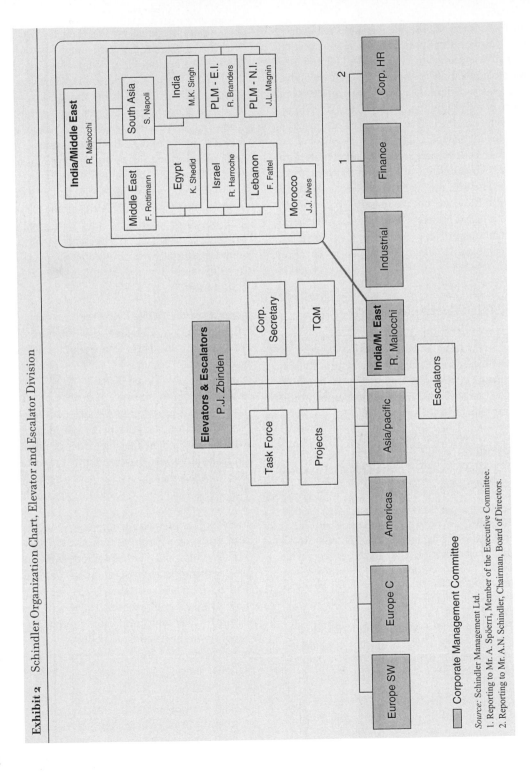

Source: Schindler Management Ltd.
1. Reporting to Mr. A. Spöerri, Member of the Executive Committee.
2. Reporting to Mr. A.N. Schindler, Chairman, Board of Directors.

Exhibit 3   Schindler India: Key Managers' Profiles

Name:	Silvio Napoli	Mehar Karan (M.K.) Singh	T.A.K. Matthews	Ronnie Dante	Jujudhan Jena
Position:	Vice President, Schindler South Asia	Managing Director	Vice President—Field Operations	General Manager—Engineering	Chief Financial Officer
Date of Birth:	August 23, 1965	April 12, 1955	March 12, 1964	November 3, 1959	March 3, 1967
Education:	*1992–1994*: MBA, Harvard University Graduate School of Business Administration, Boston, Massachusetts	*1977*: B.E.—Mechanical Engineering; ranked top of his class in Indian Institute of Technology, Delhi, India	*1986*: B.Sc.—Civil Engineering, University of Dar-E-Salaam, Tanzania	*1977*: HSC, D.G. Ruparel College, Mumbai, India	*1990*: Chartered Accountant, Institute of Chartered Accountancy, India
	1984–1989: Graduate degree in Materials Science Engineering, Swiss Federal Institute of Technology (EPFL), Lausanne, Switzerland; Lausanne University rugby captain (1987)	*1979*: MBA, Indian Institute of Management, Ahmedabad, India (Awarded President of India's Gold Medal)	*1989*: MBA, Birla Institute of Technology, Ranchi, India		
	1983–1984: Ranked among top 20% foreign students admitted to EPFL, one-year compulsory selection program, Swiss Federal Institute of Technology (EPFL), Cours de Mathematiques Special, Lausanne, Switzerland				

Experience:

Since 1998: Vice President, South Asia, Schindler Management Ltd.	*Since 1998:* Managing Director, Schindler India Pvt. Ltd., Mumbai, India	*Since 1998:* Vice President—Field Operations, Schindler India Pvt. Ltd., Mumbai	*Since 1998:* General Manager—Engineering, Schindler India Pvt. Ltd., Mumbai	*Since 1998:* Chief Financial Officer, Schindler India Pvt. Ltd., Mumbai
1994–1997: Vice President, Head of Corporate Planning, Schindler, Switzerland	*1979–1998:* Head of Projects and Development Group, Taj Group of Hotels, India (setting up hotels in India and abroad; joint ventures with state governments, local authorities, and international investors, including the Singapore Airlines, Gulf Co-operation Council Institutional investors. Responsible for financial restructuring of the international operations after the Gulf War, culminating with the successful 1995 GDR offering).	*1998:* Modernization Manager, Otis Elevator Company, Mumbai	*1995–1998:* National Field Engineering Manager, Otis Elevator, Mumbai	*1997–1998:* Financial Controller, Kellogg India Ltd., Mumbai
1991–1992: Technical Market Development Specialist, Dow Europe, Rheinmuenster, Germany		*1989–1998:* Otis Elevator Company, New Delhi • Service & Service Sales Manager • Construction Manager • Assistant Construction Manager • Management Trainee	*1991–1995:* National Field Auditor, Otis Elevator, Mumbai	*1996–1997:* Group Manager, Procter & Gamble India Ltd., Mumbai
1989–1991: Technical Service & Development Engineer, Dow Deutscheland, Rheinmuenster, Germany		*1986–1987:* Civil Engineer, Construction Companies, Tanzania	*1989–1991:* Supervisor, Otis Elevator	*1995–1996:* Treasury Manager, Procter & Gamble India Ltd.
1989–1992: French Semi-Pro Rugby League (Strasbourg)			*1984–1989:* Commissioning of New Products, Otis Elevator, Singapore, Malaysia, and Mumbai	*1990–1995:* Financial Analyst, Procter & Gamble India Ltd.
			1982–1984: Commissioning Engineer, Otis Elevator Company, Gujarat	
			1977–1982: Apprentice, Otis Elevator Company, Maharashtra	

Source: Schindler India

this way. And I said to him: "Listen, you will have to develop a sense of that yourself. As far as I know, probably people are a little bit cautious of me because they know I used to work for the big bosses at headquarters. But we will have to wait and see."

To head field operations (sales, installation, and maintenance) Napoli hired T.A.K. Matthews, 35, who had worked for nine years at Otis India. Matthews recalled: "I had been approached before by elevator people, but after hearing a bit about Schindler's plans, I realized that you don't have a chance to get involved with a start-up every day." For Napoli, Matthews brought the business expertise he needed: "With M.K. and I as generalists, I absolutely needed someone with in-depth elevator experience to complement our management team. T.A.K. came across as a dynamic and ambitious hands-on manager waiting for the chance to exploit his potential."

Next, Napoli hired Ronnie Dante, 39, as his general manager for engineering. Dante had 24 years of experience at Otis. "Even with T.A.K., we missed a real hard-core elevator engineer capable of standing his ground in front of his European counterparts," said Napoli. "Such people are the authentic depositories of an unpublished science, and they are really very hard to find. Honestly, nobody in the group expected us to find and recruit someone like Ronnie. He is truly one of the best."

Hired to head the company's human resources department, Pankaj Sinha, 32, recalled his interview: "Mr. Napoli and Mr. Singh interviewed me together. There was a clarity in terms of what they were thinking that was very impressive." Napoli offered his assessment of Sinha: "Mr. Schindler had convinced me that the company really needed a front-line HR manager who was capable of developing a first-class organization. But I certainly did not want a traditional Indian ivory tower personnel director. Pankaj convinced us to hire him through his sheer commitment to care about our employees."

Finally, he recruited Jujudhan Jena, 33, as his chief financial officer. (See **Exhibit 4** for an organization chart.) Napoli explained his approach to hiring: "You try to see whether the character of the person is compatible with yours, whether you

have a common set of values, which in our case range from high ethical standards, integrity, assiduousness to work, and drive. Mostly we were looking for people with the right attitude and energy, not just for elevator people."

Developing the Relationships   As soon as the senior managers were on board, Napoli began working to develop them into an effective team. He recalled the early meetings with his new hires:

> Because some of them were still finishing up their previous jobs, the first Schindler India staff meetings were held at night, in the Delhi Hotel lounge. I'll never forget working together on our first elevator project offer, late after holding a series of interviews for the first employees who would report to the top team. But most of those "undercover" sessions were dedicated to educating the new team about their new company and building consensus around our business plan. . . . The team was really forged through days of late work, fueled by the common motivation to see our project succeed.

In the team-forming process, the different management styles and personal characteristics of Schindler India's new leaders became clear. Even before he was assigned to India, Napoli was recognized as a "strong-headed and single-minded manager," as one manager at Swiss headquarters described him. "There couldn't have been a better environment to send Silvio than India," said another Swiss colleague. "He wants everything done yesterday. And in India, things don't get done yesterday."

Napoli acknowledged the personal challenge. "To survive in India you have to be half monk and half warrior," he said. "I was certainly more inclined to the warrior side, and when I left Switzerland, Mr. Bonnard told me, 'You will have to work on your monk part.'"

Napoli's Indian staff and colleagues described him as "driving very hard," "impulsive," "impatient," and at times "over-communicative." "Mr. Napoli gets angry when deadlines are not met," added a member of his New Delhi staff. "He's a pretty hard taskmaster." The HR director, Sinha, was more circumspect: "Silvio has a lot of energy. When he

Exhibit 4   Schindler India Organization Chart

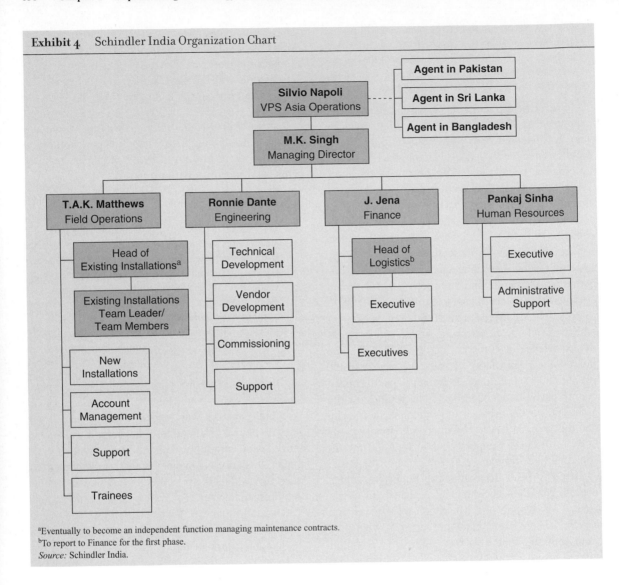

[a]Eventually to become an independent function managing maintenance contracts.
[b]To report to Finance for the first phase.
Source: Schindler India.

focuses on an issue he manages to get everybody else's focus in that direction."

Descriptions of Napoli contrasted sharply with those of Singh, whom one manager saw as "friendly and easygoing." Another described him as "much more patient, but he can also be tough." Jena, the finance director, reflected on his first encounter with the two company leaders: "During the interview Silvio came across banging on the

table, but I don't think that concerned me. Still, I remember wondering during the interview how two guys as different as M.K. and Silvio would fit together in a start-up." Matthews, the field operations manager, added another perspective:

It's true that if you look at Silvio, M.K., and me we are all very different. At first we had sessions where the discussion would get pulled in every direction, but I think in the end, it did bring about a balance . . . I would put it this way. Silvio came to India from Switzerland. But things here are very different: You can't set your watch by the Indian trains. M.K. came from the hotel industry where even if you say "no," it's always made to sound like "yes."

"Silvio was the driver and clearly was the boss," said another Indian executive. "M.K. was great in helping Silvio understand the Indian environment. Having worked in the hotel industry he had a very good network. He had been on the customer side. But he had to learn the elevator business."

Out of this interaction emerged a company culture that employees described as "informal," "open," "responsive," and "proactive." It was also a lean, efficient organization. For example, furniture and office space were rented, and there were only two secretaries in the company—one for the Delhi office and one for Mumbai. "People must do their own administrative work or they won't survive," said Singh.

The India Business Plan

As soon as his team was in place, Napoli worked to gain their commitment to his business plan. At its core were two basic elements: the need to sell a focused line of standard products, and the ability to outsource key manufacturing and logistics functions. This plan had been built on an analysis of the Indian market and competitive environment that Napoli also communicated to his team (see **Exhibits 5** and **6** for data from the plan).

The Indian Elevator Market   Economic liberalization in India in the early 1990s had revived the construction industry, and along with it, the fortunes of the elevator industry. Roughly 50% of demand was for low-tech manual elevators, typically fitted with unsafe manual doors (see Exhibit 5). But a ban on collapsible gate elevators had been approved by the Indian Standards Institute, and, at the urging of the Indian government, individual states were making the ban legally enforceable. This low end of the market was characterized by intense competition among local companies, but was expected to make this market segment more interesting to major international players when the ban was fully implemented.

The middle segment of low- and mid-rise buildings was promising due to India's rapid urbanization which had led to a shortage of space in Mumbai and fast-growing cities such as Bangalore, Pune, and Madras. Concurrently, traditional builders were becoming more sophisticated and

Exhibit 5   Indian Elevator Market, Structure, and Product Segmentation

Indian Market Structure	Segment	Stops	Speeds MPS	Schindler Products
	Manual	2–8	0.5–0.7	NIL
	Low rise	2–15	0.6–1.5	S001
	Mid rise	16–25	1.5	S300P
	High rise	>25	>1.5	S300P

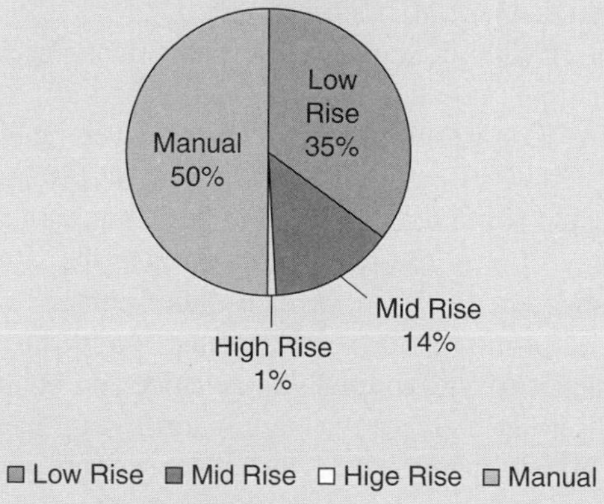

Manual 50% · Low Rise 35% · Mid Rise 14% · High Rise 1%

□ Low Rise   ■ Mid Rise   □ Hige Rise   □ Manual

Source: Schindler India.

professionalized, leading to an emphasis on better services and facilities and on higher quality, safer, and more technologically advanced elevators.

At the top end of the market, there was small but growing demand for top-quality, high-rise office facilities, particularly from multinational companies. Tourism was also expanding, greatly aiding the domestic hotel industry, a major buyer of top-line elevators. The average value per top end elevator was five to six times that of low end installations.

At the end of 1997, the installed base of elevators in India was 40,000, with an estimated 5,600 units sold during the year. Although this installed base was small compared with those of China (140,000 units) and Japan (400,000 units), India's growth potential was significant. The rapidly expanding residential segment accounted for 70% of the Indian market, followed by the commercial segment (office buildings and shopping centers) with a 20% share. The balance was accounted for by hotels (4%) and others (6%). Total revenues for the industry were US$125 million, including service income. For the first half of the decade, the market grew at a compound annual rate of 17% in units and 27% by value, but due to a slump in the real estate market, the unit growth forecast for 1998 was just 5%. It was expected to rise to 8%–12% in subsequent years. Together, Mumbai and New Delhi represented 60% of the total Indian elevator market.

In India, most sales were of single-speed elevators (65%), followed by two-speed (20%), variable frequency (13%), and hydraulic (2%). Sales of single-speed elevators dominated the residential market, while variable frequency was most commonly used in higher-end commercial applications. Although the Indian market was biased toward the simplest products, it was expected to shift gradually toward two-speed or higher technology in the future.

Competition   Napoli's business plan also documented that four major players accounted for more than three-quarters of the Indian market value: Otis (50%), BBL (8.6%), Finland's Kone (8.8%), and ECE (8.4%). Mitsubishi had recently begun importing premium elevators for hotels and commercial developments, and Hyundai Elevators had entered into a joint venture to manufacture high-end elevators in India. At this stage, however, they accounted for only 1% of sales. With the exception of Mitsubishi, all multinational players relied on local manufacturing for the majority of their components. The remaining 23% of the market—mostly the price-sensitive low end—was controlled by 25 regional players characterized by a lack of technical expertise and limited access to funds.

Otis India had an installed base of 26,000 elevators, 16,000 of which were under maintenance contracts. It manufactured its own components, spare parts, and fixtures at an aging plant in Mumbai and a new state-of-the art manufacturing plant near Bangalore. The company staffed 70 service centers, including a national service center in Mumbai, and held an estimated 85% of the high-end hotels and commercial segment. ("You couldn't name any building over 15 floors that did not have an Otis elevator," said ex-Otis employee Matthews. "Otis, Otis, Otis. Any special equipment, it goes Otis. Any fast elevator goes Otis.") Otis was reportedly one of the most profitable industrial companies in India, and its 3,500 employees had an average tenure of 20 years.

The Indian market was highly price sensitive, and most analysts agreed that elevators were becoming commodity products and that price pressures would increase. However, surveys indicated that service was also important in the buying decision, as were the financial terms (**Exhibit 6**).

The elevator life cycle had seven distinct phases: engineering, production, installation, service, repair, modernization, and replacement. Over the 30-year life cycle of an elevator, the first three stages accounted for about one-third of the labor content but only 20% of the profits. In contrast, the latter four accounted for two-thirds of labor content but 80% of profits. As a result, annual maintenance contracts covering routine maintenance and breakdown service were vital. (High-margin spare parts were billed separately.) Service response time varied across segments. Most five-star hotels with multiple installations had a technician on call or on-site; for important commercial buildings and hospitals, the response time was usually within two hours, but many residential and some commercial customers reported an average response time of between six and eight hours.

The Standard Product Strategy   Napoli felt that Schindler could not compete just by matching what others did. It had to find its own unique source of advantage. His analysis of the Indian environment coupled with his work on the Swatch Project led him to conclude that, although it was a radically different approach from that of his key competitors, the most effective way for Schindler to enter this market would be to focus on a narrow product line of simple, standardized elevators.

Exhibit 6   Market Research on Indian Elevator Market, 1996

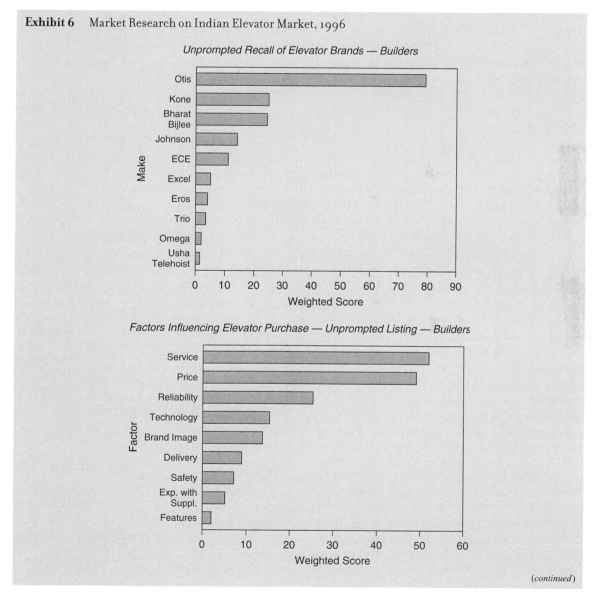

Unprompted Recall of Elevator Brands — Builders

Factors Influencing Elevator Purchase — Unprompted Listing — Builders

(*continued*)

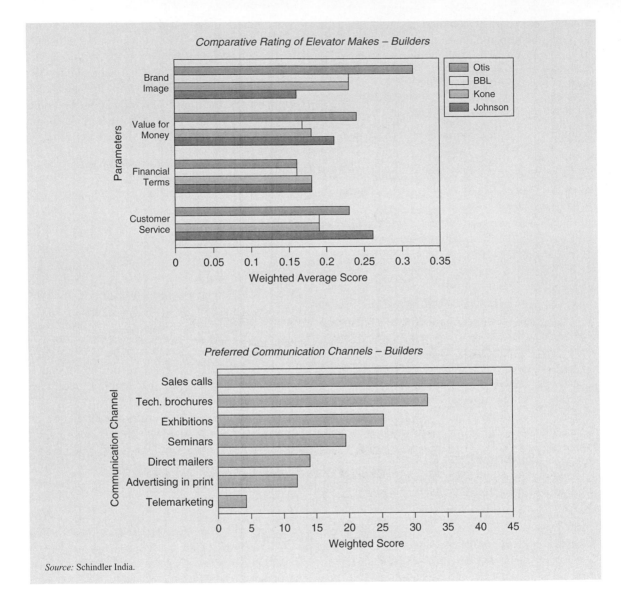

Source: Schindler India.

He proposed building the business around the Schindler 001 (S001)—the product developed in the Swatch Project—and the Schindler 300P (S300P), a more sophisticated model being manufactured in Southeast Asia. The plan was to use the S001 to win share in the low-rise segment as a primary target, then pick up sales opportunistically in the mid-rise segment with the S300P. Both products could be adapted to meet Indian requirements with only minor modifications (e.g., adding a ventilator, a fire rescue controller function, a stop button, and different guide rails). Equally important, as long as the company stuck to the principle of no customization, both products could be priced appropriately for the local market. The plan called for Schindler India to sell 50 units in the first year and to win a

20% share of the target segments in five years. It also projected Schindler India would break even after four years and eventually would generate double-digit margins.

After communicating this strategy to his Indian management team, Napoli was pleased when they came back with an innovative approach to selling the standard line. If the product was standardized, they argued, the sales and service should be differentiated. Singh's experience with hotel construction led him to conclude that projects were more effectively managed when one individual was responsible for designing, planning, contracting, and implementing. Yet, as Matthews knew, the traditional sales structure in the elevator industry had different specialists dedicated to sales, technical, and installation, each of whom handed the project off to the next person. Together, these managers proposed to Napoli that Schindler organize around an account-management concept designed to give the customer a single "hassle-free" point of contact.

The Outsourcing Strategy   India's high import duties had forced most foreign elevator companies to manufacture locally. But again, Napoli chose a different approach. To keep overheads low, his business plan proposed a radical sourcing concept for the S001 that was expected to account for 75% of sales: Schindler India would have no in-house manufacturing, no centralized assembly, and no logistics infrastructure. Instead, the production of most components for the dominant S001 model would be outsourced to approved local suppliers. (The S300P would be wholly imported from Southeast Asia.) Only safety-related components (the safety gear and speed governor, together representing 10% of the value), would be imported from Schindler plants in Europe. In addition, the entire logistics function would be handled by to an internationally reputed logistics service provider. And some basic installation work—part of the on-site assembly of the drive, controller, car, doors, rails, and counterweight—would also be outsourced. However, maintenance contracts resulting from new sales would stay with Schindler.

Inspired by the local automotive industry— Mercedes outsourced most components of its Indian vehicles—Napoli believed he could set up a local manufacturing network that would preserve Schindler's quality reputation. To ensure this, localization of each component would follow the same "product-creation process" criteria used by Schindler worldwide. Furthermore, before the first pre-series batch could be released, it would face an additional hurdle of testing and approval by experts from Schindler's European factories and competence centers.

From Analysis to Action: Implementing the Plan

By June, Napoli's management team members had settled into their roles, and the newly hired sales force was in the field. Almost immediately, however, the young expatriate leader began to experience questions, challenges, and impediments to his carefully prepared business plan.

Business Challenges   From the outset, several of Napoli's new management team had questioned him on the feasibility of his plan. In particular, those from the elevator industry wondered how the company would survive selling only standard elevators. They also worried about the outsourcing strategy, since no other company in the industry worked this way. "Some of the doubts were expressed as questions," said Napoli. "Many more were unspoken. My guess is they thought, 'We'll soon convince this crazy guy from Europe that we have to do something a bit less unusual.'"

In August, Napoli traveled to Italy to be with his wife when she gave birth to their third child. On one of his daily telephone calls to key managers in India, he discovered that the company had accepted an order for an expensive custom glass pod elevator that was to be imported from Europe. "I was at first just surprised, and then pretty angry, since it clearly was a violation of the strategy we had all agreed on," said Napoli. "The project was committed, and it was too late to stop it. But I had a long talk with M.K. and followed it up with an e-mail reminding him and the others of our strategy."

After his return to India, Napoli was delighted when he heard that the company was ready to accept another order for four S001 elevators for a government building in Mumbai. But in later conversations with a field salesman he discovered that there was a good possibility that each of the elevators would be specified with a glass wall. Although the managers insisted that this was really a minor modification to the standard S001 product, Napoli believed that, especially for a new team, installing it would be much more difficult than they expected.

The next challenge to his plan came when price estimates for the proposal was received to Schindler's plants in Europe. (Sources had not yet been qualified for local production.) Napoli was shocked when he saw the transfer prices on the basic S001 elevators at 30% above the costs he had used to prepare his original plans. "When I called to complain, they told me that my calculations had been correct six months ago, but costs had increased, and a new transfer costing system had also been introduced," recalled Napoli.

The impact of the transfer price increase was made worse by the new budget the Indian government had passed during the summer. It included increased import duties on specific "noncore goods" including elevators, whose rates increased from 22% to 56%. Napoli recalled the impact:

> This was devastating to our planned break-even objectives. The first thing I did was to accelerate our plans to outsource the S001 to local suppliers as soon as possible. We immediately started working with the European plants to get design details and production specifications. Unfortunately, the plants were not quick to respond, and we were becoming frustrated at our inability to get their assistance in setting up alternative local sources.

Reflections of a Middle Manager   As darkness enveloped the neighborhood surrounding his townhouse, Napoli sat in his living room reflecting on his job. Outside, the night was filled with the sounds of barking dogs and the piercing whistles of the estate's security patrol. "Each family here has its own security guard," he explained.

"But because guards fall asleep at their posts, our neighborhood association hired a man who patrols the neighborhood blowing his whistle at each guard post and waiting for a whistle in response. But now the whistling has gotten so bad that some families have begun paying this man not to whistle in front of their houses. Incredible, isn't it?"

Thinking back on his eight months in his new job, Napoli described the multiple demands. On one hand, he had to resolve the challenges he faced in India. On the other, he had to maintain contact with the European organization to ensure he received the support he needed. And on top of both these demands was an additional expectation that the company's top management had of this venture. Napoli explained:

> When we were discussing the business plan with Mr. Schindler, he said, "India will be our Formula One racing track." In the auto industry, 90% of all innovations are developed for and tested on Formula One cars and then reproduced on a much larger scale and adapted for the mass market. We are testing things in India—in isolation and on a fast track—that probably could not be done anywhere else in the company. The expectation is that what we prove can be adapted to the rest of the group.

While the viability of the Formula One concept was still unclear, Alfred Schindler commented on Napoli's experience:

> This job requires high energy and courage. It's a battlefield experience. This is the old economy, where you have to get involved in the nitty-gritty. We don't pay the big salaries or give stock options. We offer the pain, surprises, and challenges of implementation. The emotions start when you have to build what you have written. Mr. Napoli is feeling what it means to be in a hostile environment where nothing works as it should.

Napoli reflected, "You know the expression, 'It's lonely at the top?' Well, I'm not at the top, but I feel lonely in the middle. . . . Somehow I have to swim my way through this ocean. Meanwhile, we have yet to install a single elevator and have no maintenance portfolio." At this point, Napoli's reflections were interrupted by the question of visiting vice chairman Luc Bonnard, "So, how are things going so far, Mr. Napoli?"

Reading 7-1   Local Memoirs of a Global Manager

Gurcharan Das

Managing in my homeland taught me to treasure the provincial as well as the universal.

There was a time when I used to believe with Diogenes the Cynic that "I am a citizen of the world," and I used to strut about feeling that a "blade of grass is always a blade of grass, whether in one country or another." Now I feel that each blade of grass has its spot on earth from where it draws its life, its strength; and so is man rooted to the land from where he draws his faith, together with his life.

In India, I was privileged to help build one of the largest businesses in the world for Vicks Vaporub, a hundred-year-old brand sold in 147 countries and now owned by Procter & Gamble. In the process, I learned a number of difficult and valuable lessons about business and about myself. The most important lesson was this: to learn to tap into the roots of diversity in a world where global standardization plays an increasingly useful role.

"Think global and act local," goes the saying, but that's only half a truth. International managers must also think local and then apply their local insights on a global scale.

The fact is that truths in this world are unique, individual, and highly parochial. They say all politics is local. So is all business. But this doesn't keep either from being global. In committing to our work we commit to a here and now, to a particular place and time; but what we learn from acting locally is often universal in nature.

■ Formerly chairman and managing director of Procter & Gamble India, Gurcharan Das is vice president and managing director of worldwide strategic planning for health and beauty care at Procter & Gamble. He is the author of a novel, A Fine Family, (Penguin, 1990) and three plays. He wrote this article while a fellow at the Center for Business and Government at the Kennedy School at Harvard University.

This is how globalization takes place. Globalization does not mean imposing homogeneous solutions in a pluralistic world. It means having a global vision and strategy, but it also means cultivating roots and individual identities. It means nourishing local insights, but it also means reemploying communicable ideas in new geographies around the world.

The more human beings belong to their own time and place, the more they belong to *all* times and places. Today's best global managers know this truth. They nourish each "blade of grass."

Managerial basics are the same everywhere, in the West and in the Third World. There is a popular misconception among managers that you need merely to push a powerful brand name with a standard product, package, and advertising in order to conquer global markets, but actually the key to success is a tremendous amount of local passion for the brand and a feeling of local pride and ownership.

I learned these lessons as a manager of international brands in the Third World and as a native of India struggling against the temptation to stay behind in the West.

▌On Going Home

I was four years old when India became free. Before they left, the British divided us into two countries, India and Pakistan, and on a monsoon day in August 1947 I suddenly became a refugee. I had to flee east for my life because I was a Hindu in predominantly Muslim West Punjab. I survived, but a million others did not, and another 12 million were rendered homeless in one of the great tragedies of our times.

I grew up in a middle-class home in East Punjab as the eldest son of a civil engineer who built canals and dams for the government. Our family budget was always tight: after paying for milk and school fees, there was little left to run the house. My mother told us heroic stories from the *Mahabharata* and encouraged in us the virtues of honesty, thrift, and responsibility to country.

I grew up in the innocence of the Nehru age when we still had strong ideals. We believed in secularism, democracy, socialism, and the U.N.; and we were filled with the excitement of building a nation.

I came to the United States at the age of 12, when the Indian government sent my father to Washington, D.C. on temporary assignment. When my family returned to India a few years later, I won a scholarship to Harvard College and spent four happy years on the banks of the Charles River. My tutor taught me that the sons of Harvard had an obligation to serve, and I knew that I must one day use my education to serve India.

In 1964, in the towering confidence of my 21 years, I returned home. Some of my friends thought I had made a mistake. They said I should have gone on to graduate school and worked for a few years in the West. In fact, I missed the West in the beginning and told myself that I would go back before long; but I soon became absorbed in my new job with Richardson-Vicks in Bombay, and like the man who came to dinner, I stayed on.

From a trainee, I rose to become CEO of the company's Indian subsidiary, with interim assignments at Vicks headquarters in New York and in the Mexican subsidiary. When I became CEO, the Indian company was almost bankrupt, but with the help of a marvelous all-Indian organization, I turned it around in the early 1980s and made it one of the most profitable companies on the Bombay Stock Exchange. In 1985 we were acquired by Procter & Gamble, and so began another exciting chapter in my life. We successfully incorporated the company into P&G without losing a single employee, and we put ourselves on an aggressive growth path, with an entry first into sanitary napkins and then into one of the largest detergent markets in the world.

At three stages in my life, I was tempted to settle in the West. Each time I could have chosen to lead the cosmopolitan life of an expatriate. Each time I chose to return home. The first after college; the second when I was based in the New York office of Vicks, where I met my Nepali wife with her coveted Green Card (which we allowed to lapse); the third when I was in Mexico running our nutritional foods business, when once again I came home to earn a fraction of what I would have earned abroad.

Apart from a lurking wish to appear considerable in the eyes of those I grew up with, I ask myself why I keep returning to India. I have thrice opted for what appeared to be the less rational course in terms of career and money. The only remotely satisfying answer I have found comes from an enigmatic uncle of mine who once said, "You've come back, dear boy, because as a child you listened to the music of your mother's voice. They all say, 'I'll be back in a few years,' but the few years become many, until it is too late and you are lost in a lonely and homeless crowd."

Yet I think of myself as a global manager within the P&G world. I believe my curious life script has helped to create a mind-set that combines the particular with the universal, a mind-set rooted in the local and yet open and nonparochial, a mind-set I find useful in the global management of P&G brands.

On One-Pointed Success

I first arrived on the island of Bombay on a monsoon day after eight years of high school and college in America. That night, 15-foot waves shattered thunderously against the rocks below my window as the rain advanced from the Arabian sea like the disciplined forward phalanx of an army.

The next morning I reported for duty at Richardson-Vicks' Indian headquarters, which turned out to be a rented hole-in-the-wall with a dozen employees. This was a change after the company's swank New York offices in midtown Manhattan, where I had been interviewed. That evening my cousin invited me for dinner. He worked in a big British company with many factories, thousands of employees, and plush multistoried marble offices. I felt ashamed to talk about my job.

"How many factories do you have?" he wanted to know.

"None," I said.

"How many salesmen do you have?" he asked.

"None," I said.

"How many employees?"

"Twelve."

"How big are your offices?"

"A little smaller than your house."

Years later I realized that what embarrassed me that night turned out to be our strength. All twelve of our employees were focused on building our brands without the distraction of factories, sales forces, industrial relations, finance and other staff departments. Our products were made under contract by Boots, an English drug company; they were distributed under contract by an outside distribution house with 100 salesmen spread around the country; our external auditors had arranged for someone to do our accounting; and our lawyers took care of our government work. We were lean, nimble, focused, and very profitable.

All my cousin's talk that night revolved around office politics, and all his advice was about how to get around the office bureaucracy. It was not clear to me how his company made decisions. But he was a smart man, and I sensed that with all his pride in working for a giant organization, he had little respect for its bureaucratic style.

If marketing a consumer product is what gives a company its competitive advantage, then it seems to me it should spend all its time building marketing and product muscle and employ outside suppliers to do everything else. It should spin off as many services as someone else is willing to take on and leave everyone inside the company focused on one thing–creating, retaining, and satisfying consumers.

There is a concept in Yoga called one-pointedness (from the Sanskrit *Ekagrata*). All twelve of us were one-pointedly focused on making Vicks a household name in India, as if we were 12 brand managers. I now teach our younger managers the value of a one-pointed focus on consumer satisfaction, which P&G measures every six months for all of its major brands.

Concentrating on one's core competence thus was one of the first lessons I learned. I learned it because I was face-to-face with the consumer, focused on the particular. Somehow I feel it would have taken me longer to learn this lesson in a glass tower in Manhattan.

As so often in life, however, by the time I could apply the lesson I had learned, we had a thousand people, with factories, sales forces, and many departments that were having a lot of fun fighting over turf. I believe that tomorrow's big companies may well consist of hundreds of small decentralized units, each with a sharp focus on its particular customers and markets.

On the Kettle That Wrote My Paycheck

For months I believed that my salary came from the payroll clerk, so I was especially nice to her. (She was also the boss's secretary.) Then one day I discovered the most important truth of my career–I realized who really paid my salary.

Soon after I joined the company, my boss handed me a bag and a train ticket and sent me "up-country." A man of the old school, he believed that you learned marketing only in the bazaar, so I spent 10 of my first 15 months on the road and saw lots of up-country bazaars.

On the road, I typically would meet our trade customers in the mornings and consumers in the evenings. In the afternoons everyone slept. One evening I knocked on the door of a middle-class home in Surat, a busy trading town 200 miles north of Bombay. The lady of the house reluctantly let me in. I asked her, "What do you use for your family's coughs and colds?" Her eyes lit up, her face became animated. She told me that she had discovered the most wonderful solution. She went into the kitchen and brought back a jar of Vicks Vaporub and a kettle. She then showed me how she poured a spoon of Vaporub into the boiling kettle and inhaled the medicated vapors from the spout.

"If you don't believe me, try it for yourself," she said. "Here, let me boil some water for you."

Before I could reply she had disappeared into the kitchen. Instead of drinking tea that evening we inhaled Vicks Vaporub. As I walked back to my hotel, I felt intoxicated: I had discovered it was she who paid my salary. My job also became clear to me: I must reciprocate her compliment by striving relentlessly to satisfy her needs.

The irony is that all the money a company makes is made *outside* the company (at the point of sale), yet the employees spend their time *inside* the company, usually arguing over turf. Unfortunately, we don't see customers around us when we show up for work in the mornings.

When I became the CEO of the company I made a rule that every employee in every department had to go out every year and meet 20 consumers and 20 retailers or wholesalers in order to qualify for their annual raise. This not only helps to remind us who pays our salaries, we also get a payoff in good ideas to improve our products and services.

The idea of being close to the customer may be obvious in the commercial societies of the West, but it was not so obvious 20 years ago in the protected, bureaucratic Indian environment. As to the lady in Surat, we quickly put her ideas into our advertising. She was the first consumer to show me a global insight in my own backyard.

Of Chairs, Armchairs, and Monsoons

Two years after I joined, I was promoted. I was given Vicks Vaporub to manage, which made me the first brand manager in the company. I noticed we were building volume strongly in the South but having trouble in the North. I asked myself whether I should try to fix the North or capitalize on the momentum in the South. I chose the latter, and it was the right choice. We later discovered that North Indians don't like to rub things on their bodies, yet the more important lesson was that it is usually better to build on your strength than to try and correct a weakness. Listen to and respect the market. Resist the temptation to impose your will on it.

We were doing well in the South partially because South Indians were accustomed to rubbing

on balms for headaches, colds, bodyaches, insect bites, and a host of other minor maladies. We had a big and successful balm competitor, Amrutanjan, who offered relief for all these symptoms. My first impulse was to try to expand the use of Vaporub to other symptoms in order to compete in this larger balm market.

My boss quickly and wisely put a stop to that. In an uncharacteristically loud voice, he explained that Vaporub's unique function was to relieve colds.

"Each object has a function," he said. "A chair's function is to seat a person. A desk is to write on. You don't want to use a chair for writing and a desk for sitting. You never want to mix up functions."

A great part of Vaporub's success in India has been its clear and sharp position in the consumer's mind. It is cold relief in a jar, which a mother rubs tenderly on her child's cold at bedtime. As I thought more about balms, I realized that they were quite the opposite. Adults rub balms on themselves for headaches during the day. Vaporub was succeeding precisely because it was not a balm; it was a rub for colds.

Every brand manager since has had to learn that same lesson. It is of the utmost importance to know who you are and not be led astray by others. Tap into your roots when you are unsure. You cannot be all things to all people.

This did not prevent us from building a successful business with adults, but as my boss used to say, "Adult colds, that is an armchair. But it is still a chair and not a desk."

When I took over the brand we were spending most of our advertising rupees in the winter, a strategy that worked in North America and other countries. However, my monthly volume data stubbornly suggested that we were shipping a lot of Vaporub between July and September, the hot monsoon season. "People must be catching lots of colds in the monsoon," I told my boss, and I got his agreement to bring forward a good chunk of our media to the warm monsoon months. Sure enough, we were rewarded with an immediate gain in sales.

I followed this up by getting our agency to make a cinema commercial (we had no television at that time) showing a child playing in the rain and catching cold. We coined a new ailment, "wet monsoon colds," and soon the summer monsoon season became as important as the winter in terms of sales.

Another factor in our success was the introduction of a small 5-gram tin, which still costs 10 cents and accounts for 40% of our volume. At first it was not successful, so we had to price it so that it was cheaper to buy four 5-gram tins than a 19-gram jar. The trade thought we were crazy. They said henceforth no one would buy the profitable jar; they would trade down to the tin. But that didn't happen. Why? Because we had positioned the tin for the working class. We were right in believing that middle class consumers would stay loyal to the middle-class size.

Moves like these made us hugely successful and placed us first in the Indian market share by far. But instead of celebrating, my boss seemed depressed. He called me into his office, and he asked me how much the market was growing.

"Seven percent," I said.

"Is that good?"

"No," I replied. "But *we* are growing twenty percent, and that's why we're now number one in India."

"I don't give a damn that we are number one in a small pond. That pond has to become a lake, and then an ocean. We have to grow the market. Only then will we become number one in the world."

Thus I acquired another important mind-set: when you are number one, you must not grow complacent. Your job is to grow the market. You always must benchmark yourself against the best in the world, not just against the local competition. In the Third World this is an especially valuable idea, because markets there are so much less competitive.

Being receptive to regional variations, tapping the opportunity that the monsoon offered, introducing a size for the rural and urban poor, and learning to resist complacency and grow the market–all are variations on the theme of local thinking, of tapping into the roots of pluralism and diversity.

On Not Reinventing the Wheel

We could not have succeeded in building the Vicks business in India without the support of the native traders who took our products deep into the hinterland, to every nook and corner of a very large country. Many times we faced the temptation to set up an alternative Western-style distribution network. Fortunately, we never gave in to it. Instead, we chose each time to continue relying on the native system.

Following the practice of British companies in India, we appointed the largest wholesaler in each major town to become our exclusive stock point and direct customer. We called this wholesaler our stockist. Once a month our salesman visited the stockist, and together they went from shop to shop redistributing our products to the retailers and wholesalers of the town. The largest stockist in each state also became our Carrying-and-Forwarding Agent (in other words, our depot) for re-shipping our goods to stockists in smaller towns. Over time, our stockists expanded their functions. They now work exclusively on P&G business under the supervision of our salesmen; they hire local salesmen who provide interim coverage of the market between the visits of our salesmen; they run vans to cover satellite villages and help us penetrate the interior; they conduct local promotions and advertising campaigns; and they are P&G's ambassadors and lifeline in the local community. The stockists perform all these services for a five percent commission, and our receivables are down to six days outstanding.

In our own backyard, we found and adopted an efficient low-cost distribution system perfected by Indian traders over hundreds of years. Thank God we chose to build on it rather than reinvent the wheel.

On Taking Ancient Medicine

We learned our most important lesson about diversity and tapping into roots shortly after I became head of the company in the early 1980s. We found ourselves against a wall. The chemists and pharmacists had united nationwide and decided to target our company and boycott our products in their fight for higher margins from the entire industry. At the same time, productivity at our plant was falling, while wages kept rising. As a result, our profitability had plummeted to two percent of sales.

Beset by a hostile environment, we turned inward. The answer to our problems came as a flash of insight about our roots, for we suddenly realized that Vicks Vaporub and other Vicks products were all-natural, herbal formulas. All their ingredients were found in thousand-year-old Sanskrit texts. What was more, this ancient *Ayurvedic* system of medicine enjoyed the special patronage of the government. If we could change our government registration from Western medicine to Indian medicine, we could expand our distribution to food shops, general stores, and street kiosks and thus reduce dependence on the pharmacists. By making our products more accessible, we would enhance consumer satisfaction and build competitive advantage. What was more, a new registration would also allow us to set up a new plant for Vicks in a tax-advantaged "backward area," where we could raise productivity dramatically by means of improved technology, better work practices, and lower labor costs.

I first tested the waters with our lawyers, who thought our solution to the problem quite wonderful. We then went to the government in Delhi, which was deeply impressed to discover all the elements of Vaporub's formula in the ancient texts. They advised us to check with the local FDA in Bombay. The regulators at the FDA couldn't find a single fault with our case and, to our surprise and delight, promptly gave us a new registration.

Lo and behold, all the obstacles were gone! Our sales force heroically and rapidly expanded the distribution of our products to the nondrug trade, tripling the outlets which carried Vicks to roughly 750,000 stores. Consumers were happy that they could buy our products at every street corner. At the same time we quickly built a new plant near Hyderabad, where productivity was four times what it was in our Bombay plant. Our after-tax profits rose from 2% to 12% of sales, and we became a blue chip on the Bombay Stock Exchange.

Finally, we decided to return the compliment to the Indian system of medicine. We persuaded our headquarters to let us establish an R&D Center to investigate additional all-natural, Ayurvedic therapies for coughs and colds. When I first mooted this idea, my bosses at the head office in the United States practically fell off their chairs. Slowly, however, the idea of all-natural, safe, and effective remedies for a self-limiting ailment sold around the world under the Vicks name grew on them.

We set up labs in Bombay under the leadership of a fine Indian scientist who had studied in the United States. They began by creating a computerized data bank of herbs and formulas from the ancient texts; they invented a "finger-printing" process to standardize herbal raw materials with the help of computers; and they organized clinical trials in Bombay hospitals to confirm the safety and efficacy of the new products. We now have two products being successfully sold in the Indian market–Vicks Vaposyrup, an all-natural cough liquid, and Vicks Hot-sip, a hot drink for coughs and colds. The lab today is part of P&G's global health-care research effort and has 40 scientists and technicians working with state-of-the-art equipment.

Of Local Passions and Golden Ghettos

The story of Vicks in India brings up a mistaken notion about how multinationals build global brands. The popular conception is that you start with a powerful brand name, add standardized product, packaging and advertising, push a button, and bingo–you are on the way to capturing global markets. Marlboro, Coke, Sony Walkman, and Levis are cited as examples of this strategy.

But if it's all so easy, why have so many powerful brands floundered? Without going into the standardization vs. adaptation debate, the Vicks story demonstrates at least one key ingredient for global market success: *the importance of local passion.* If local managers believe a product is theirs, then local consumers will believe it too. Indeed, a survey of Indian consumers a few years ago showed that 70% believed Vicks was an Indian brand.

What is the universal idea behind Vicks Vaporub's success in India? What is it that made it sell? Was it "rubbing it on the child with tender, loving care?" Could that idea be revived in the

United States? Some people argue that the United States has become such a rushed society that mothers no longer have time to use a bedtime rub on their children when they've got a cold. Others feel that Vaporub could make its marketing more meaningful by striking a more contemporary note.

The Vicks story shows that a focus on the particular brings business rewards. But there are also psychic rewards for the manager who invests in the local. Going back to my roots reinvigorated me as a person and brought a certain fullness to my life. Not only was it pleasant to see familiar brown faces on the street, it also was enormously satisfying to be a part of the intense social life of the neighborhood, to experience the joys and sorrows of politics, and to share in the common fate of the nation. But at another level I also began to think of my work as a part of nation building, especially training and developing the next generation of young managers who would run the company and the country. It discharged a debt to my tutor at Harvard and a responsibility that we all have to the future.

Equally, it seems to me, there are powerful though less obvious psychic rewards for an international manager on transfer overseas who chooses to get involved in the local community. When such people approach the new country with an open mind, learn the local language, and make friends with colleagues and neighbors, they gain access to the wealth of a new culture. Not only will they be more effective as managers, they also will live fuller, richer lives.

Unfortunately, my experience in Mexico indicates that many expatriate managers live in "golden ghettos" of ease with little genuine contact with locals other than servants. Is it any surprise that they become isolated and complain of rootlessness and alienation in their new environment? The lesson for global companies is to give each international manager a local "mentor" who will open doors to the community. Ultimately, however, it is the responsibility of individual managers to open their minds, plunge into their local communities, and try to make them their own.

On Global Thinking

It would be wrong to conclude from the Vicks story that managing a global brand is purely a local affair. On the contrary, the winners in the new borderless economy will be the brands and companies that make best use of the richness of experience they get from their geographical diversity. Multinational companies have a natural advantage over local companies because they have talented people solving similar problems for identical brands in different parts of the world, and these brand managers can learn from each other's successes and failures. If a good idea emerges in Egypt, a smart brand manager in Malaysia or Venezuela will at least give it a test.

The Surat lady's teakettle became the basis of a national campaign in India. "One-pointedness" emerged from a hole-in-the-wall in Bombay, but it became the fulcrum on which we built a world-class business over a generation. Advertising for colds during the hot monsoon months seems highly parochial, but it taught us the importance of advertising year round in other places. The stockist system found applicability in Indonesia and China. Even the strange Ayurvedic system of medicine might plausibly be reapplied in the form of efficacious herbal remedies for common ailments in Western countries.

Business truths are invariably local in origin, but they are often expressions of fundamental human needs that are the same worldwide. Local insights with a universal character thus can become quickly global—though only in the hands of flexible, open-minded managers who can translate such ideas into new circumstances with sensitivity and understanding. My admonition to think local is only half the answer. Managers also must remember to think global. The insights we glean from each microcosm are ultimately universal.

Organizational specialists often express a fear that companies will demotivate their local managers by asking them to execute standardized global marketing packages. If they impose these standardized marketing solutions too rigidly, then this fear may be justified. However, this does not happen in successful companies. In fact, the more common disease in a global company is the "not invented here" syndrome, which especially afflicts subsidiaries and managers whose local triumphs have left them arrogant and unwilling to learn from successes in other parts of the world.

We in India were no different. But slowly and painfully we learned that useful lessons can emerge anywhere. For all our efforts to tap into the roots of Indian pluralism, we were dealing with a global brand. The product itself, the positioning, and the packaging were basically the same everywhere. Global brands are not free-for-alls, with each subsidiary doing its own thing. It took us six months, for example, to persuade our marketing people to try a new advertising idea for Vaporub that came from Mexico. It asked the consumer to use Vaporub on three parts of the body to obtain three types of relief. When we finally tried "Three-by-Three" in our advertising, it worked brilliantly.

It is deeply wrong to believe that going global is a one-stop, packaged decision. Local managers can add enormous value as they tap into local roots for insights. But it is equally wrong to neglect the integrity of the brand's core elements. Smart global managers nourish each blade of grass without neglecting the garden as a whole.

On Karma

Although the principles of managing a business in the Third World are the same as in the West, there are still big differences between the two. For me, the greatest of these is the pervasive reality of poverty.

I have lost the towering confidence of my youth, when I believed that socialism could wipe away poverty. The problem of socialism is one of performance, not vision. If it worked, we would all be socialists. Ironically, the legacy of the collectivist bias in Indian thinking has been the perpetuation of poverty. We created an over-regulated private sector and an inefficient public sector. We did not allow the economy to grow and produce the surplus that might have paid for direct poverty programs. We created an exploitative bureaucracy that fed on itself. Today, happily, we are righting the balance by liberalizing the economy, reducing state control, and restoring legitimacy to the market. I am confident that these changes will foster the entrepreneurialism and economic vitality India needs to create prosperity and eliminate the destitution of so many of its people.

Despite the problems, I find managers in India and other poor countries more optimistic than their counterparts in rich nations. The reason is that we believe our children will be better off than our parents were, and this idea is a great source of strength. We see our managerial work as nation building. We are the benign harbingers of technology and modernity. As we learn to manage complex enterprises, we empower people with the confidence they need to become responsible, innovative, and self-reliant.

It seems to come down to commitment. In committing to our work we commit to a here and now, to a particular place and time. The meaning in our lives comes from nourishing a particular blade of grass. It comes from absorbing ourselves so deeply in the microcosm of our work that we forget ourselves, especially our egos. The difference between subject and object disappears. The Sanskrit phrase *nishkama karma* describes this state of utter absorption, in which people act for the sake of the action, not for the sake of the reward from the action. This is also the meaning of happiness.

Reading 7-2   Tap Your Subsidiaries for Global Reach

Christopher A. Bartlett and Sumantra Ghoshal

In 1972, EMI developed the CAT scanner. This technological breakthrough seemed to be the innovation that the U.K.-based company had long sought in order to relieve its heavy dependence on the cyclical music and entertainment business and to strengthen itself in international markets. The medical community hailed the product, and within four years EMI had established a medical electronics business that was generating 20% of the company's worldwide earnings. The scanner enjoyed a dominant market position, a fine reputation, and a strong technological leadership situation.

Nevertheless, by mid-1979 EMI had started losing money in this business, and the company's deteriorating performance eventually forced it to accept a takeover bid from Thorn Electric. Thorn immediately divested the ailing medical electronics business. Ironically, the takeover was announced the same month that Godfrey Hounsfield, the EMI scientist who developed the CAT scanner, was awarded a Nobel Prize for the invention.

How could such a fairy-tale success story turn so quickly into a nightmare? There were many contributing causes, but at the center were a structure and management process that impeded the company's ability to capitalize on its technological assets and its worldwide market position.

The concentration of EMI's technical, financial, and managerial resources in the United Kingdom made it unresponsive to the varied and changing needs of international markets. As worldwide demand built up, delivery lead times for the scanner stretched out more than 12 months. Despite the protests of EMI's U.S. managers that these delays were opening opportunities for competitive entry, headquarters continued to fill orders on the basis of when they were received rather than on how strategically important they were. Corporate management would not allow local sourcing or duplicate manufacturing of the components that were the bottlenecks causing delays.

The centralization of decision making in London also impaired the company's ability to guide strategy to meet the needs of the market. For example, medical practitioners in the United States, the key market for CAT scanners, considered reduction of scan time to be an important objective, while EMI's central research laboratory, influenced by feedback from the domestic market, concentrated on improving image resolution. When General Electric eventually brought out a competitive product with a shorter scan time, customers deserted EMI.

In the final analysis, it was EMI's limited organizational capability that prevented it from capitalizing on its large resource base and its strong global competitive position. The company lacked:

The ability to sense changes in market needs and industry structure occurring away from home.

The resources to analyze data and develop strategic responses to competitive challenges that were emerging worldwide.

The managerial initiative, motivation, and capability in its overseas operations to respond imaginatively to diverse and fast-changing operating environments.

While the demise of its scanner business represents an extreme example, the problems EMI faced are

Christopher A. Bartlett teaches management of international business at the Harvard Business School, where he is an associate professor. Before joining HBS he was a consultant for McKinsey & Company and general manager of the French subsidiary of Baxter Travenol Laboratories. Sumantra Ghoshal is an assistant professor of business policy at the European Institute of Business Administration (INSEAD) in Fontainebleau, France. Before turning to teaching, he held line and staff positions with the Indian Oil Corporation Ltd. and directed domestic and foreign marketing for a large private commercial organization in India.

common. With all the current attention being given to global strategy, companies risk underestimating the organizational challenge of managing their global operations. Indeed, the top management in almost every one of the MNCs we have studied has had an excellent idea of what it needed to do to become more globally competitive; it was less clear on how to organize to achieve its global strategic objectives.

United Nations Model & HQ Syndrome

Our study covered nine core companies in three industries and a dozen secondary companies from a more diverse industrial spectrum. They were selected from three areas of origin—the United States, Europe, and Japan. Despite this diversity, most of these companies had developed their international operations around two common assumptions on how to organize. We dubbed these well-ingrained beliefs the "U.N. model assumption" and the "headquarters hierarchy syndrome."

Although there are wide differences in importance of operations in major markets like Germany, Japan, or the United States, compared with subsidiaries in Argentina, Malaysia, or Nigeria, for example, most multinationals treat their foreign subsidiaries in a remarkably uniform manner. One executive we talked to termed this approach "the U.N. model of multinational management." Thus it is common to see managers express subsidiary roles and responsibilities in the same general terms, apply their planning control systems uniformly systemwide, involve country managers to a like degree in planning, and evaluate them against standardized criteria. The uniform systems and procedures tend to paper over any differences in the informal treatment of subsidiaries.

When national units are operationally self-sufficient and strategically independent, uniform treatment may allow each to develop a plan for dealing with its local environment. As a company reaches for the benefits of global integration, however, there is little need for uniformity and symmetry among units. Yet the growing complexity of the corporate management task heightens the appeal of a simple system.

The second common assumption we observed, the headquarters hierarchy syndrome, grows out of and is reinforced by the U.N. model assumption. The symmetrical organization approach encourages management to envision two roles for the organization, one for headquarters and another for the national subsidiaries. As companies moved to build a consistent global strategy, we saw a strong tendency for headquarters managers to try to coordinate key decisions and control global resources and have the subsidiaries act as implementers and adapters of the global strategy in their localities.

As strategy implementation proceeded, we observed country managers struggling to retain their freedom, flexibility, and effectiveness, while their counterparts at the center worked to maintain their control and legitimacy as administrators of the global strategy. It's not surprising that relationships between the center and the periphery often became strained and even adversarial.

The combined effect of these two assumptions is to severely limit the organizational capability of a company's international operations in three important ways. First, the doctrine of symmetrical treatment results in an overcompensation for the needs of smaller or less crucial markets and a simultaneous underresponsiveness to the needs of strategically important countries. Moreover, by relegating the national subsidiaries to the role of local implementers and adapters of global directives, the head office risks grossly underutilizing the company's worldwide assets and organizational capabilities. And finally, ever-expanding control by headquarters deprives the country managers of outlets for their skills and creative energy. Naturally, they come to feel demotivated and even disenfranchised.

Dispersed Responsibility

The limitations of the symmetrical, hierarchical mode of operation have become increasingly clear to MNC executives, and in many of the companies we surveyed we found managers experimenting with alternative ways of managing their worldwide operations. And as we reviewed these various approaches, we saw a new pattern emerging that suggested a significantly different model of global organization based on some important new assumptions and beliefs. We saw companies experimenting with ways of selectively varying the roles and responsibilities of their national organizations to reflect explicitly the differences in external environments and internal capabilities. We also saw them modifying central administrative systems to legitimize the differences they encountered.

Such is the case with Procter & Gamble's European operations. More than a decade ago, P&G's European subsidiaries were free to adapt the parent company's technology, products, and marketing approaches to their local situation as they saw fit—while being held responsible, of course, for sales and earnings in their respective countries. Many of these subsidiaries had become large and powerful. By the mid-1970s, economic and competitive pressures were squeezing P&G's European profitability. The head office in Cin-cinnati decided that the loose organizational arrangement inhibited product development, curtailed the company's ability to capture Europewide scale economies, and afforded poor protection against competitors' attempts to pick off product lines country by country.

So the company launched what became known as the Pampers experiment—an approach firmly grounded in the classic U.N. and HQ assumptions. It created a position at European headquarters in Brussels to develop a Pampers strategy for the whole continent. By giving this manager responsibility for the Europewide product and marketing strategy, management hoped to be able to eliminate the diversity in brand strategy by coordinating activities across subsidiary boundaries. Within 12 months, the Pampers experiment had failed. It not only ignored local knowledge and underutilized subsidiary strengths but also demotivated the country managers to the point that they felt no responsibility for sales performance of the brand in their areas.

Obviously, a different approach was called for. Instead of assuming that the best solutions were to be found in headquarters, top management decided to find a way to exploit the expertise of the national

units. For most products, P&G had one or two European subsidiaries that had been more creative, committed, and successful than the others. By extending the responsibilities and influence of these organizations, top management reasoned, the company could make the success infectious. All that was needed was a means for promoting intersubsidiary cooperation that could offset the problems caused by the company's dispersed and independent operations. For P&G the key was the creation of "Eurobrand" teams.

For each important brand the company formed a management team that carried the responsibility for development and coordination of marketing strategy for Europe. Each Eurobrand team was headed not by a manager from headquarters but by the general manager and the appropriate brand group from the "lead" subsidiary—a unit selected for its success and creativity with the brand. Supporting them were brand managers from other subsidiaries, functional managers from headquarters, and anyone else involved in strategy for the particular product. Team meetings became forums for the lead-country group to pass on ideas, propose action, and hammer out agreements.

The first Eurobrand team had charge of a new liquid detergent called Vizir. The brand group in the lead country, West Germany, had undertaken product and market testing, settled on the package design and advertising theme, and developed the marketing strategy. The Eurobrand team ratified all these elements, then launched Vizir in six new markets within a year. This was the first time the company had ever introduced a new product in that many markets in so brief a span. It was also the first time the company had got agreement in several subsidiaries on a single product formulation, a uniform advertising theme, a standard packaging line, and a sole manufacturing source. Thereafter, Eurobrand teams proliferated; P&G's way of organizing and directing subsidiary operations had changed fundamentally.

On reflection, company managers feel that there were two main reasons why Eurobrand teams succeeded where the Pampers experiment had failed. First, they captured the knowledge, the expertise, and most important, the commitment of managers closest to the market. Equally significant was the fact that relationships among managers on Eurobrand teams were built on interdependence rather than on independence, as in the old organization, or on dependence, as with the Pampers experiment. Different subsidiaries had the lead role for different brands, and the need for reciprocal cooperation was obvious to everyone.

Other companies have made similar discoveries about new ways to manage their international operations—at NEC and Philips, at L.M. Ericsson and Matsushita, at ITT and Unilever, we observed executives challenging the assumptions behind the traditional head office—subsidiary relationship. The various terms they used—lead-country concept, key-market subsidiary, global-market mandate, center of excellence—all suggested a new model based on a recognition that their organizational task was focused on a single problem: the need to resolve imbalances between market demands and constraints on the one hand and uneven subsidiary capabilities on the other. Top officers understand that the option of a zero-based organization is not open to an established multinational organization. But they seem to have hit on an approach that works.

Black Holes, etc.   The actions these companies have taken suggest an organizational model of differentiated rather than homogeneous subsidiary roles and of dispersed rather than concentrated responsibilities. As we analyzed the nature of the emerging subsidiary roles and responsibilities, we were able to see a pattern in their distribution and identify the criteria used to assign them. The *Exhibit* represents a somewhat oversimplified conceptualization of the criteria and roles, but it is true enough for discussion purposes.

The strategic importance of a specific country unit is strongly influenced by the significance of its national environment to the company's global strategy. A large market is obviously important, and so is a competitor's home market or a market that is particularly sophisticated or technologically advanced. The organizational competence of a particular subsidiary can, of course, be in technology, production, marketing, or any other area.

Strategic Leader   This role can be played by a highly competent national subsidiary located in a strategically important market. In this role, the subsidiary serves as a partner of headquarters in developing and implementing strategy. It must not only be a sensor for detecting signals of change but also a help in analyzing the threats and opportunities and developing appropriate responses.

The part played by the U.K. subsidiary of Philips in building the company's strong leadership position in the teletext-TV business provides an illustration. In the early 1970s, the BBC and ITV (an independent British TV company) simultaneously launched projects to adapt existing transmission capacity to permit broadcast of text and simple diagrams. But teletext, as it was called, required a TV receiver that would accept and decode the modified transmissions. For TV set manufacturers, the market opportunity required a big investment in R&D and production facilities, but commercial possibilities of teletext were highly uncertain, and most producers decided against making the investment. They spurned teletext as a typical British

Exhibit   Roles for national subsidiaries

toy—fancy and not very useful. Who would pay a heavy premium just to read text on a TV screen?

Philips' U.K. subsidiary, however, was convinced that the product had a future and decided to pursue its own plans. Its top officers persuaded Philips' component manufacturing unit to design and produce the integrated-circuit chip for receiving teletext and commissioned their Croydon plant to build the teletext decoder.

In the face of poor market acceptance (the company sold only 1,000 teletext sets in its first year), the U.K. subsidiary did not give up. It lent support to the British government's efforts to promote teletext and make it widely available. Meanwhile, management kept up pressure on the Croydon factory to find ways of reducing costs and improving reception quality—which it did.

In late 1979, teletext took off, and by 1982 half a million sets were being sold annually in the United Kingdom. Today almost three million teletext sets are in use in Britain, and the concept is spreading abroad. Philips has built up a dominant position in markets that have accepted the service. Corporate management has given the U.K. subsidiary formal responsibility to continue to exercise leadership in the development, manufacture, and marketing of teletext on a companywide basis. The Croydon plant is recognized as Philips' center of competence and international sourcing plant for teletext-TV sets.

Contributor   Filling this role is a subsidiary operating in a small or strategically unimportant market but having a distinctive capability. A fine example is the Australian subsidiary of L.M. Ericsson, which played a crucial part in developing its successful AXE digital telecommunications switch. The down-under group gave impetus to the conversion of the system from its initial analog design to the digital form. Later its engineers helped construct several key components of the system.

This subsidiary had built up its superior technological capability when the Australian telephone authority became one of the first in the world to call for bids on electronic telephone switching equipment. The government in Canberra, however,

had insisted on a strong local technical capability as a condition for access to the market. Moreover, heading this unit of the Swedish company was a willful, independent, and entrepreneurial country manager who strengthened the R&D team, even without full support from headquarters.

These various factors resulted in the local subsidiary having a technological capability and an R&D resource base that was much larger than subsidiaries in other markets of similar size or importance. Left to their own devices, management worried that such internal competencies would focus on local tasks and priorities that were unnecessary or even detrimental to the overall global strategy. But if the company inhibited the development activities of the local units, it risked losing these special skills. Under the circumstances, management saw the need to co-opt this valuable subsidiary expertise and channel it toward projects of corporate importance.

Implementer   In the third situation, a national organization in a less strategically important market has just enough competence to maintain its local operation. The market potential is limited, and the corporate resource commitment reflects it. Most national units of most companies are given this role. They might include subsidiaries in the developing countries, in Canada, and in the smaller European countries. Without access to critical information, and having to control scarce resources, these national organizations lack the potential to become contributors to the company's strategic planning. They are deliverers of the company's value added; they have the important task of generating the funds that keep the company going and underwrite its expansion.

The implementers' efficiency is as important as the creativity of the strategic leaders or contributors—and perhaps more so, for it is this group that provides the strategic leverage that affords MNCs their competitive advantage. The implementers produce the opportunity to capture economies of scale and scope that are crucial to most companies' global strategies.

In Procter & Gamble's European introduction of Vizir, the French company played an important contributing role by undertaking a second market test and later modifying the advertising approach. In the other launches during the first year, Austria, Spain, Holland, and Belgium were implementers; they took the defined strategy and made it work in their markets. Resisting any temptation to push for change in the formula, alteration of the package, or adjustment of the advertising theme, these national subsidiaries enabled P&G to extract profitable efficiencies.

The Black Hole   Philips in Japan, Ericsson in the United States, and Matsushita in Germany are black holes. In each of these important markets, strong local presence is essential for maintaining the company's global position. And in each case, the local company hardly makes a dent.

The black hole is not an acceptable strategic position. Unlike the other roles we have described, the objective is not to manage it but to manage one's way out of it. But building a significant local presence in a national environment that is large, sophisticated, and competitive is extremely difficult, expensive, and time consuming.

One common tack has been to create a sensory outpost in the black hole environment so as to exploit the learning potential, even if the local business potential is beyond reach. Many American and European companies have set up small establishments in Japan to monitor technologies, market trends, and competitors. Feedback to headquarters, so the thinking goes, will allow further analysis of the global implications of local developments and will at least help prevent erosion of the company's position in other markets. But this strategy has often been less fruitful than the company had hoped. Look at the case of Philips in Japan.

Although Philips had two manufacturing joint ventures with Matsushita, not until 1956 did it enter Japan by establishing a marketing organization. When Japan was emerging as a significant force in the consumer electronics market in the late 1960s, the company decided it had to get further into that market. After years of unsuccessfully trying to penetrate the captive distribution channels of the principal Japanese manufacturers, headquarters settled for a Japan "window" that would keep it informed of technical developments there. But results were disappointing. The reason, according to a senior manager of Philips in Japan, is that to sense effectively, eyes and ears are not enough. One must get "inside the bloodstream of the business," he said, with constant and direct access to distribution channels, component suppliers, and equipment manufacturers.

Detecting a new development after it has occurred is useless, for there is no time to play catch-up. One needs to know of developments as they emerge, and for that one must be a player, not a spectator. Moreover, being confined to window status, the local company is prevented from playing a strategic role. It is condemned to a permanent existence as a black hole.

So Philips is trying to get into the bloodstream of the Japanese market, moving away from the window concept and into the struggle for market share. The local organization now sees its task as winning market share rather than just monitoring local developments. But it is being very selective and focusing on areas where it has advantages over strong local competition. The Japanese unit started with coffee makers and electric shavers. Philips' acquisition of Marantz, a hi-fi equipment producer, gives it a bid to expand on its strategic base and build the internal capabilities that will enable the Japanese subsidiary to climb out of the black hole.

Another way to manage one's way out of the black hole is to develop a strategic alliance. Such coalitions can involve different levels of cooperation. Ericsson's joint venture with Honeywell in the United States and AT&T's with Philips in Europe are examples of attempts to fill up a black hole by obtaining resources and competence from a strong local organization in exchange for capabilities available elsewhere.

Shaping, Building, Directing   Corporate management faces three big challenges in guiding the dispersion of responsibilities and differentiating subsidiaries' tasks. The first is in setting the strategic direction for the company by identifying its mission and its business objectives. The second is in building the differentiated organization, not only by designing the diverse roles and distributing the assignments but also by giving the managers responsible for filling them the legitimacy and power to do so. The final challenge is in directing the process to ensure that the several roles are coordinated and that the distributed responsibilities are controlled.

Setting the Course   Any company (or any organization, for that matter) needs a strong, unifying sense of direction. But that need is particularly strong in an organization in which tasks are differentiated and responsibilities dispersed. Without it, the decentralized management process will quickly degenerate into strategic anarchy. A visitor to any NEC establishment in the world will see everywhere the company motto "C&C," which stands for computers and communications. This simple pairing of words is much more than a definition of NEC's product markets; top managers have made it the touchstone of a common global strategy. They emphasize it to focus the attention of employees on the key strategy of linking two technologies. And they employ it to help managers think how NEC can compete with larger companies like IBM and AT&T, which are perceived as vulnerable insofar as they lack a balance in the two technologies and markets.

Top management at NEC headquarters in Tokyo strives to inculcate its worldwide organization with an understanding of the C&C strategy and philosophy. It is this strong, shared understanding that permits greater differentiation of managerial processes and the decentralization of tasks.

But in addition to their role of developing and communicating a vision of the corporate mission, the top officers at headquarters also retain overall responsibility for the company's specific business strategies. While not abandoning this role at the heart of the company's strategic process, executives of many multinational companies are co-opting other parts of the organization (and particularly its diverse national organizations) into important business strategy roles, as we have already described. When it gives up its lead role, however, headquarters management always tracks that delegated responsibility.

Building Differentiation   In determining which units should be given the lead, contributor, or follower roles, management must consider the motivational as well as the strategic impact of its decisions. If unfulfilled, the promise offered by the new organization model can be as demotivating as the symmetrical hierarchy, in which all foreign subsidiaries are assigned permanent secondary roles. For most national units, an organization in which lead and contributor roles are concentrated in a few favorite children represents little advance from old situations in which the parent dominated the decision making. In any units continually obliged to implement strategies developed elsewhere, skills atrophy, entrepreneurship dies, and any innovative spark that existed when it enjoyed more independence now sputters.

By dealing out lead or contributing roles to the smaller or less developed units, even if only for one or two strategically less important products, the headquarters group will give them a huge incentive. Although Philips N.V. had many other subsidiaries closer to large markets or with better access to corporate know-how and expertise, headquarters awarded the Taiwan unit the lead role in the small-screen monitor business. This vote of confidence gave the Taiwanese terrific motivation to do well and made them feel like a full contributing partner in the company's worldwide strategy.

But allocating roles isn't enough; the head office has to empower the units to exercise their voices in the organization by ensuring that those with lead positions particularly have access to and influence in the corporate decision-making process. This is not a trivial task, especially if strategic initiative and decision-making powers have long been concentrated at headquarters.

NEC discovered this truth about a decade ago when it was trying to transform itself into a global enterprise. Because NTT, the Japanese telephone authority, was dragging its feet in converting its exchanges to the new digital switching technology, NEC was forced to diverge from its custom of designing equipment mainly for its big domestic customer. The NEAC 61 digital switch was the first outgrowth of the policy shift; it was aimed primarily at the huge, newly deregulated U.S. telephone market.

Managers and engineers in Japan developed the product; the American subsidiary had little input. Although the hardware drew praise from customers, the switch had severe software deficiencies that hampered its penetration of the U.S. market.

Recognizing the need to change its administrative setup, top management committed publicly to becoming "a genuine world enterprise" rather than a Japanese company operating abroad. To permit the U.S. subsidiary a greater voice, headquarters helped it build a local software development capability. This plus the unit's growing knowledge about the Bell operating companies—NEC's target customers—gave the American managers legitimacy and power in Japan.

NEC's next-generation digital switch, the NEAC 61E, evolved quite differently. Exercising their new influence at headquarters, U.S. subsidiary managers took the lead in establishing its features and specifications and played a big part in the design.

Another path to empowerment takes the form of dislodging the decision-making process from the home office. Ericsson combats the headquarters hierarchy syndrome by appointing product and functional managers from headquarters to subsidiary boards. The give-and-take in board meetings is helpful for both subsidiary and parent. Matsushita holds an annual review of each major worldwide function (like manufacturing and human resource management) in the offices of a national subsidiary it considers to be a leading exponent of the particular function. In addition to the symbolic value for employees of the units, the siting obliges officials from Tokyo headquarters to consider issues that the front lines are experiencing and gives local managers the home-court advantage in seeking a voice in decision making.

Often the most effective means of giving strategy access and influence to national units is to create entirely new channels and forums. This approach permits roles, responsibilities, and relationships to be defined and developed with far less constraint than through modification of existing communication patterns or through shifting of responsibility boundaries. Procter & Gamble's Eurobrand teams are a case in point.

Directing the Process   When the roles of operating units are differentiated and responsibility is more dispersed, corporate management must be prepared to deemphasize its direct control over the strategic content but develop an ability to manage the dispersed strategic process. Furthermore, headquarters must adopt a flexible administrative stance that allows it to differentiate the way it manages one subsidiary to the next and from business to business within a single unit, depending on the particular role it plays in each business.

In units with lead roles, headquarters plays an important role in ensuring that the business strategies developed fit the company's overall goals and priorities. But control in the classic sense is often quite loose. Corporate management's chief function is to support those with strategy leadership responsibility by giving them the resources and the freedom needed for the innovative and entrepreneurial role they have been asked to play.

With a unit placed in a contributor role, the head-office task is to redirect local resources to programs outside the unit's control. In so doing, it has to counter the natural hierarchy of loyalties that in most national organizations puts local interests above global ones. In such a situation, headquarters must be careful not to discourage the local managers and technicians so much that they stop contributing or leave in frustration. This has happened to many U.S. companies that have tried to manage their Canadian subsidiaries in a contributor role. Ericsson has solved the problem in its Australian subsidiary by attaching half the R&D team to headquarters, which farms out to these engineers projects that are part of the company's global development program.

The head office maintains tighter control over a subsidiary in an implementer role. Because such a group represents the company's opportunity to capture the benefits of scale and learning from which it gets and sustains its competitive advantage, headquarters stresses economy and efficiency in selling the products. Communication of strategies developed elsewhere and control of routine tasks can be carried out through systems, allowing headquarters to manage these units more efficiently than most others.

As for the black hole unit, the task for top executives is to develop its resources and capabilities to make it more responsive to its environment. Managers of these units depend heavily on headquarters for help and support, creating an urgent need for intensive training and transfer of skills and resources.

Firing the Spark Plugs

Multinational companies often build cumbersome and expensive infrastructures designed to control their widespread operations and to coordinate the diverse and often conflicting demands they make. As the coordination and control task expands, the typical headquarters organization becomes larger and more powerful, while the national subsidiaries are increasingly regarded as pipelines for centrally developed products and strategy.

But an international company enjoys a big advantage over a national one: it is exposed to a wider and more diverse range of environmental stimuli. The broader range of customer preferences, the wider spectrum of competitive behavior, the more serious array of government demands, and the more diverse sources of technological information represent potential triggers of innovation and thus a rich source of learning for the company. To capitalize on this advantage requires an organization that is sensitive to the environment and responsive in absorbing the information it gathers.

So national companies must not be regarded as just pipelines but recognized as sources of information and expertise that can build competitive advantage. The best way to exploit this resource is not through centralized direction and control but through a cooperative effort and co-option of dispersed capabilities. In such a relationship, the entrepreneurial spark plugs in the national units can flourish.

The Future of the Transnational:
An Evolving Global Role

▪ ▪ ▪ ▪ ▪ ▪ ▪ ▪ ▪ ▪ ▪ ▪ ▪ ▪ ▪ ▪

In this final chapter, we address the question of how the role and responsibility of the MNE might evolve in the global political economy in the 21st century. In the closing decades of the last century, the powerful forces of globalization unleashed a period of growth that drove the overseas development and expansion of many MNEs. The same was true for the vast majority of countries in which MNEs operated, as their economic and social infrastructure benefited from the value created through booming cross-border trade and investment.

However, there was another group of countries that remained in the backwash of the powerful development will forces of globalization. While the richest nations argued that the rising tide of globalization would lift all boats, to those in the poorest countries, it appeared to be lifting mainly the luxury yachts. And developed country government-sponsored aid programs designed to narrow the growing gap between rich and poor nations had exhibited little positive impact despite half a century of effort. With almost half the world's population subsisting on less than $2 a day, many began to feel that the MNEs that had benefited so greatly from global economic expansion now had a responsibility to help deal with the unequal distribution of their benefits. It was a point emphasized at demonstrations outside WTO and World Bank meetings in the early years of the new millennium.

In this chapter, after discussing this evolving situation, we describe four different postures that MNEs have adopted in recent decades, ranging from the exploitative and the transactional, to the responsive and the transformational. Although these are presented as descriptive rather than normative categories, in today's global environment there is a clear push to have companies move away from the exploitive end of the spectrum toward the responsive and even transformative end. In a variety of industries, voluntary norms and standards have been set to provide guidance to the way the MNEs might think about their responsibilities abroad; and the United Nations Global Compact also sets a standard of behavior to which companies can aspire as they expand their operations into the 21st century.

For most transnational companies, the dawning of the new millennium offered exciting prospects of continued growth and prosperity. Yet, in the poorest nations on earth, the reputation of large Western MNEs was shaky at best, and in some quarters, it was in complete tatters. Indeed, a series of widely publicized events in the closing years of the

20th century led many to ask what additional constraints and controls needed to be placed on the largely unregulated activities of these companies:

- In Indonesia, Nike's employment of children and others in unhealthy work environments, paying them $1.80 a day to make athletic shoes being sold for a $150 a pair to affluent Western buyers.
- In Europe, Coca-Cola's refusal to take responsibility when consumers of soft drinks produced at its Belgian plant reported getting sick, then finally acknowledging the problem 2 weeks later, but only after 100 people had been hospitalized and five countries had banned the sale of its products.
- In India, Enron's high-profile dispute with a regional government that was trying to cancel a contract for the construction of the Dabhol power station and the supply of power, citing the company's "fraud and misrepresentation" during the original negotiations.
- In South Africa, 39 Western pharmaceutical companies' action in suing the government and President Nelson Mandela to prevent the importation of cheap generic versions of patented AIDS drugs to treat the country's 4.5 million HIV-positive patients.

Each of these situations involved complex, multifaceted issues to which intelligent managers apparently were trying to respond in what they saw as a logical, justifiable manner—conforming to local labor laws and practices at Nike, conducting quality tests and communicating the data at Coke, enforcing legal contract provisions at Enron, and protecting intellectual property rights by the drug companies. Yet in the court of public opinion, their rational, subtle, or legalistic arguments were swamped by an overarching view of Western multinational companies operating out of greed, arrogance, and self-interest. They were seen as the hammer driving home the widening wedge between the "haves" and the "have nots."

The Growing Discontent

Partly as a result of this growing distrust of MNEs, a popular groundswell against globalization began to gather strength during the closing years of the 20th century and has continued into the 21st century. Prior to this movement, in most countries in the developed world—and certainly within the MNEs they had spawned—globalization was viewed as a powerful engine of economic development, spreading the benefits of free market capitalism around the world. Yet far fewer developing countries had seen the benefits of this much discussed tidal wave of trade and investment. Indeed, to some living in these countries, the growing gap between the rich and the poor offered clear evidence that "globalization" was just the latest term for their continued exploitation by MNEs.

As a result, delegates from a number of developing nations agreed to block what they saw as unfair rules being imposed by richer nations at the World Trade Organization (WTO) meeting in Seattle in 1999. Supported by a large number of demonstrators, this conference represented the first high-profile protest against the increasing globalization of the world's economy, which many in the West had seen as being as beneficial as it was inevitable. And the prime targets of the protests were the trade ministers from the

G7countries (as they were then) and the multinational corporations that the demonstrators saw as the main drivers and beneficiaries of globalization.

Their protests were given even more public attention when Seattle police began using pepper spray and tear gas against demonstrators, mobilizing a great deal of public sympathy and support for their cause. In subsequent years, as the protesters continued their actions, their arguments were being buttressed by some powerful allies, including the Nobel Laureate Joseph Stiglitz, a former chairman of the Council of Economic Advisors and chief economist at the World Bank. In his book *Globalization and Its Discontents*, Stiglitz suggests that previous actions of WTO, the International Monetary Fund (IMF), and the World Bank had often damaged developing countries' economies more than they had helped them.[1] Regarding the WTO, he points out that though the First World preaches the benefits of free trade, it still protects and subsidizes agricultural products, textiles, and apparel, precisely the goods exported by Third World countries. Rather than seeing MNEs as creating value in developing countries, he suggests that their effect is often to crowd out local enterprise, then use their monopoly power to raise prices.

The most helpful support of the protesters' arguments was provided by the World Bank's ongoing annual reports of the number of people worldwide living below the poverty threshold.[2] Its data showed that 2.8 billion of the world's 6 billion people were living on less than $2 a day, with more than 40 percent of that number living on less than $1 a day. Despite the great progress made in reducing the number of people in this category in rapidly industrializing countries like India and China, the World Bank reported that the number had increased during the 1990s, the decade of globalization-driven growth for the economies of the developed world and of the profitable expansion of most large MNEs.

The Challenge Facing MNEs

Given the extent of global poverty and the lack of clear significant progress in reducing it, there is a growing view that perhaps it is time to radically rethink an approach that relied so heavily on government-funded aid programs. William Easterly, a former research economist at the World Bank, points out that after $2.3 trillion of aid has flowed from developed countries to developing countries over the past five decades, it is clear that the West's model of development has failed.[3] He argues that, just like the old colonialist model, a large portion of foreign aid takes a paternalistic view, in that it defines both the problems and the solutions and provides for neither accountability nor feedback. As a result, for example, over the past 25 years, $5 billion of internationally funded aid has been spent on a publicly owned steel mill in Nigeria that has yet to produce any steel.

In contrast, the outstanding success stories such as India and China have been achieved by unleashing the power of their market economies rather than through massive aid programs. In what the World Bank has called this "the greatest poverty reduction

---

[1]Joseph E. Stiglitz, *Globalization and Its Discontents* (New York: WW Norton & Company, 2002).
[2]World Bank, *Poverty Reduction and the World Bank* (Washington, DC: World Bank, 1999); World Bank, *Attacking Poverty* (New York, Oxford University Press, 2001).
[3]William Easterly, *White Man's Burden* (New York: Penguin Press, 2006).

program in human history," hundreds of millions of people have moved out of poverty during the past 25 years. In large part, this amazing transformation has been due to the actions of the many MNEs that, following the announcement of China's open-door policy in 1979, 300,000 foreign enterprises have been approved, and by 2008 had invested $870 billion in that rapidly developing country. Included in that total are 490 of the world's top 500 companies, who not only see China providing them access to low-cost labor, but also as a technology source in which they have established 1,160 R&D centers. In addition to helping China, their investments are now having a significant economic impact on these firms which sent almost $300 billion in profits out of China in the period from 1990 to 2007. Such a win–win consequence is due to one undeniable reality: The faster the poor gain wealth, the faster they become customers.

In light of this impressive record, the eyes of many in the international community began to turn toward the MNEs to provide at least a part of the solution to the problems that had proven to be so intractable in so many other countries. But this has required more than just a public relations exercise extolling the benefits of free trade and openness to foreign investment, it has meant understanding what role MNEs might play in dealing with some of the underlying causes of the widespread discontent in the developing world. Clearly, they controlled much of the financial resources, technical and commercial expertise, and managerial talent that would be necessary to bring about lasting change to the lives of people living in the world's most underdeveloped economies. In financial power alone, the World Bank estimated that the flows of foreign direct investment into developing countries in 2002 was about $155 billion, more than four times the amount of foreign aid and development funding flowing into that same group of countries.

Particularly in the past decade or so, there has been a growing sense in the global community that because MNEs controlled such significant resources and power, they should be playing a much larger role in global development. For the MNEs, the immediate challenge has been to decide how to respond to the growing resistance to the forces of globalization that drove their growth and expansion during the previous half-century. Their longer term challenge is to determine whether they are willing to step up and take a leadership role in dealing with the problems that are the underlying causes of the antiglobalization movement.

Responding to Developing World Needs: Four MNE Postures

To understand how MNEs have faced such issues in the past and how they might in the future, we will describe four somewhat archetypical responses along a spectrum of possible action, ranging from an approach we label "exploitive" to one we describe as "transformative." Our observations suggest that most MNEs have clearly moved away from the former model; it is our hope that they are shifting toward the latter.

The Exploitive MNE: Taking Advantage of Disadvantage

As we saw in Chapter 1, because one of the strongest and most enduring motivations for a company to internationalize is its desire to access low-cost factors of production, the ability to locate low-cost labor has long encouraged many MNEs to locate in emerging markets. To anyone operating in these environments, it soon became clear that not only were the wages and hours worked vastly different than those in developed countries but so too were the health and safety of the working conditions, and even the human rights of the workers. The question facing management was how to respond to that situation.

For a subset of the companies that we describe as "exploitive MNEs," the lower the labor rate, the longer the workweek, the fewer the restrictions on working conditions, and the less regulation on workers' rights, the better. These companies believe that cross-country differences in wages, working conditions, legal requirements, and living standards all represent unfettered opportunities to capture competitive advantage.

Such an attitude received its strongest support in the 1970s in the writings and speeches of University of Chicago economist Milton Friedman. Guided by the view that all companies had a responsibility to maximize profits and that shareholders were their only legitimate stakeholder, he argued that "[those who believe that] business has a 'social conscience' and takes seriously its responsibilities for providing employment, eliminating discrimination, avoiding pollution . . . are preaching pure and unadulterated socialism."[4] Such bold, clear absolutes from a Nobel Laureate in Economics provided those desirous of such an approach all the comfort they needed to embrace an exploitive stance. And particularly during the 1960s and 1970s, many did.

One of the most commonly held negative images of MNEs relates to the use of what are often called "sweatshops"—work places characterized by some combination of hot, crowded, poorly ventilated, poorly lit, and unsafe environments, in which the labor force—often including children only 10 or 12 years old—receives less than a "living wage" despite their long hours of work.

Far from being examples of extreme situations from an era long past, sweatshops still exist in many countries today. For example, *The New York Times* reported that a large number of workers from Bangladesh each paid $1,000 to $3,000 in return for the promise of work in Jordanian factories producing garments for Target and Wal-Mart. After they arrived at their new place of work, their passports were confiscated to ensure they did not quit. Not only were they paid less than promised and far less than the country's minimum wage, but they also were forced to work 20-hour days and were hit by supervisors if they complained.[5]

Some MNEs have tried to sidestep the sweatshop issue by outsourcing manufacturing to arm's-length suppliers, but as Nike and many other high-profile companies found, such tactics are no longer effective in insulating the MNE from taking responsibility. As other experiences seem to confirm, the relentless attempt to exploit low-cost labor has great risks attached and often can backfire.[6]

Yet despite the risks, when the pressure from governments, nongovernmental organization (NGO) advocates, and supranational agencies becomes too great, MNEs committed to an exploitive approach will simply close down and move the factory to another

[4]Milton Friedman, "The Social Responsibility of Business Is to Increase Its Profits," *The New York Times Magazine*, September 13, 1970.

[5]Steven Greenhouse and Michael Barbaro, "An Ugly Side of Free Trade: Sweatshops in Jordan," *The New York Times*, May 3, 2006.

[6]See, for example, Paul Beamish, "The High Cost of Cheap Chinese Labor," *Harvard Business Review,* June 2006; Ivey Case # 9B04M033, "Jinjian Garment Factory: Motivating Go-Slow Workers."

city, state, or country. In doing so, they often find another opportunity to exploit the situation. Understanding that because most countries are actively working to develop employment, increase their tax base, and capture spin-off benefits from new investment, the exploitive MNE will not hesitate to play countries against one another, demanding more and more concessions to guarantee their investment.

In countries where corruption and bribery are common, this push for concessions and subsidies from local government officials and regulators has led some exploitive MNEs to illegal activities. Justifying their actions with an attitude of "when in Rome . . .," some firms have been willing to engage in such practices in the name of maximizing profits. For example, in the mid-1970s, the president of United Brands was charged with bribing the president of Honduras to help maintain a banana monopoly. In more extreme cases, when local politicians did not cooperate, some exploitive MNEs even proved they were willing to help remove democratically elected governments. In the early 1970s, the American conglomerate ITT was accused of not only making political payoffs in the United States but also conspiring to work with the CIA to overthrow the democratically elected government of Chile.[7]

Global exploitation can move well beyond the relentless pursuit of low-cost labor and subsidized investment. It has led some companies to seek market expansion regardless of the likely resulting economic, social, or cultural damage. One classic example unfolded in the 1970s, when Nestlé and other infant formula manufacturers became concerned that birth rates in most industrialized countries were flattening and declining. Shifting their attention to what seemed like huge opportunities in the emerging country markets, they began a major marketing push in those countries, employing dozens of sales promoters dressed as nurses to hand out samples of their product.

The product was soon seen as "modern and Western," and as sales increased, the practice of breast feeding declined. But subsequent reports of increases in infant mortality and malnourishment soon had many concerned that the practice was having major negative health consequences. It was discovered that mothers who could not afford to use the formula at the recommended level diluted it to make it last longer. Not only was the baby not receiving the nutrients it needed, but the water being used to mix the formula often was unsanitary, leading to diarrhea, dehydration, and malnutrition. Equally concerning was the fact that the baby was not receiving all the immunities that normally would be transferred from the mother via breast feeding, again making the child less resistant to sickness. A great deal of public outrage followed, with consumers worldwide boycotting Nestlé products. What was immediately clear, not only to Nestlé but also to other MNEs selling into the developing world, was that products intended for developed country markets could have seriously harmful effects if sold into emerging markets without a full appreciation of and responsiveness to the particular country's different cultural, social, and economic situation.

Beyond the direct way it affects the lives of its employees and customers, the MNE also has an impact on the local communities in which it operates. In its single-minded focus on maximizing profit, however, an exploitive MNE accepts no responsibility for the social or environmental consequences of its actions, even when the impact is severe.

[7]Anthony Sampson, *The Sovereign State of ITT* (City: Stein and Day, 1973).

One of the most severe industrial tragedies in history involved a gas leak from a Union Carbide facility in Bhopal, India, in 1984. Thousands of people died, and many others suffered long-term disabilities. Union Carbide was accused of using unproven technology at the plant, conducting insufficient safety checks, and being unprepared for and slow to respond to problems, along with many other negligent acts. But the company claimed that the gas release was caused by employee sabotage and that it had responded as quickly and comprehensively as it could. What is not subject to debate is that Union Carbide paid $470 million to the Indian government in a legal settlement and, with the rest of the chemical industry, "worked to develop and implement its 'Responsible Case' program, designed to prevent any future events through improving community awareness, emergency preparedness and process safety standards."[8]

Particularly during the 1970s, when controversies were raging around the events such as those raised by the United Brands, ITT, and Nestlé cases, many felt that the MNE's ability to operate outside the legal framework of any single government had made it a force that needed to be better regulated and controlled. In short, there were concerns that too many companies were adopting the attitude of exploitive MNEs. Because most supranational organizations and agencies (e.g., ILO, UNCTAD, UNESCO) had been relatively ineffective in influencing or controlling MNE behavior, various global NGOs began to assume the role of monitors and controllers of the actions of exploitive MNEs. As the earlier Nestlé example illustrated, these NGOs exercised their power through their ability to organize protests, boycotts, or political action, targeting the MNE's customers, stock owners, or regulators.

Not surprisingly, exploitive MNEs soon developed adversarial attitudes toward NGOs, and that relationship was reciprocated. Consider the example of the multinational tobacco companies that had been targeting developing country markets for decades as regulatory pressure and consumer education shrank their markets in the West. During the early 1990s, when the former Soviet Union split into several independent countries, the laws previously in place banning tobacco advertising, forbidding smoking in many public places, and requiring health warnings on cigarette packages were no longer binding in the newly created states. According to researchers, "post-transition, the (multinational) tobacco companies exploited confusion over the legality of this Soviet legislation by advertising heavily to establish their brands."[9] Subsequent surveys indicate there has been an increase in youth smoking, particularly among women in cities. All of this is occurring in a part of the world where tobacco is already responsible for twice the number of deaths among men as in the West and with a product that public health professionals view as the greatest single cause of preventable mortality in the developed world.

The response from public health researchers and anti-MNE and antismoking NGOs has been loud and sustained. They have lobbied various newly established governments to reestablish antismoking controls and worked actively to publicize the negative implications of MNE activities in the region. The tobacco MNEs have countered by

---

[8]See www.bhopal.com and www.responsiblecare.org.

[9]A.B. Gilmore and M. McKee, "Tobacco and Transition: An Overview of Industry Investment, Impact, and Influence in the Former Soviet Union," *Tobacco Control* 13 (2004), pp. 136–42.

emphasizing the job creation and increased taxes available to local governments from the investments they have made. The adversarial relationship between the groups continues.

Overall, the picture of the exploitive MNE is not a pretty one. It is an organization that is willing to ignore the welfare of its end consumers and employees, collude with political elites, violate environmental norms, and expose emerging market communities to potential harm. Fortunately, it seems to be a species in rapid decline.

The Transactional MNE: Doing Deals, Respecting Laws

Few companies today operate in the extreme manner of profit maximization in the sole service of the shareholder, as Milton Friedman advocated. For example, whereas he opposed corporations making any charitable donations or acting in response to any social issue, most publicly owned corporations demonstrate at least a little charitable generosity and show at least some sensitivity toward their communities. Because there is little evidence that such actions have been frowned on by shareholders, it is hardly surprising that in the international environment, one finds fewer examples of truly exploitive MNEs today than previously. The minimum expectation of MNE behavior today tends to be based on what we describe as a transactional attitude.

The difference between a transactional attitude and an exploitive one is that the former implies an approach that is both legally compliant and nonoppressive in its emerging market dealings. Yet though the transactional MNE's relationships with its environment remain almost exclusively commercial, unlike its exploitive counterpart, it does not pursue the bottom line at all costs. Indeed, many companies that once were un-caring about or insensitive to the serious problems that their aggressive or indifferent attitudes created have evolved from their exploitive approach (often under pressure from NGOs or regulatory authorities) to adopt a more responsible transactional posture. It is a position that manifests itself in a somewhat different attitude toward each stakeholder.

The transactional MNE's relationship toward its emerging market customers avoids the egregious missteps that the Nestlé experience highlighted. This shift implies having the sensitivity not to promote socially or economically unsuitable products originally developed for consumers with very different needs or markets with very different characteristics. Beyond this appropriate caution, these companies are often willing to make minor product or service adaptations to meet local needs or preferences, but only if there is a high degree of certainty that the change will expand market share, increase profits, or meet some other commercial need.

For example, global fast-food giants such as McDonald's and KFC are often willing to make minor changes to their product offering or service approach on a country-by-country basis, but they seldom stray very far from their standard menu. And though they are generally regarded as good, law-abiding, tax-paying corporate citizens in the countries in which they operate, they have also been accused of cultural insensitivity or worse. For example, many national health services have expressed concern about the increasing health risks for people in developing countries who are persuaded to change their eating habits from the high-fiber natural foods of their local diets to the high-fat refined foods that dominate fast-food menus.

With regard to employee relations, because the transactional MNE respects local labor laws and ILO guidelines, it usually relates to its employees in a much less brutal or oppressive way than the exploitive company. For example, the transactional MNE would not be willing to have its own employees, or those of its subcontractors, work in the sweatshop-like conditions we described in the previous section. Yet, though they conform to labor laws and workplace regulations, these companies would be more likely to maintain pressure on employees and suppliers to capture the value of the lower cost labor that attracted their original investment.

In one widely publicized example, Nike was forced to move some way along this learning curve when it was confronted by well-organized boycotts to protest what several NGOs claimed were well-documented exploitive activities in developing countries. For many years, Nike had either ignored pressure from NGOs about labor practices employed in the manufacture if its shoes or denied that they were its responsibility, arguing that it was the subcontractors, not Nike, that employed the workers. But in the mid-1990s, following relentless NGO pressure in many countries, Nike changed its position. After *Life Magazine* ran a photo of a very young Pakistani boy stitching a Nike soccer ball, the company raised its minimum age for workers from 14 to 16 years for apparel and to 18 years for footwear, both above the ILO minimum of 15; after organized strikes by thousands of workers in Indonesia, Vietnam, and China protesting Nike's subminimum wages, it set a policy of paying the higher of the minimum wage or the industry standard; and after investigations found toxic fumes at 177 times the legal Vietnamese limit, the company agreed to set U.S. standards for occupational health and safety in plants worldwide.

In its attitude toward local communities and the broader society, the transactional MNE does not exhibit the same level of indifference and irresponsibility that characterizes the exploitive MNE. The experiences of Union Carbide in Bhopal, the multinational tobacco companies in the former Soviet Union, ITT in Chile, and United Fruit in Central America have all served as cautionary tales. One of the lessons that transactional-oriented MNEs appear to have learned is that it usually makes economic sense to obey both the letter and the spirit of local and international laws and regulations. Take the example of environmental standards. Historically, any MNE's announcement of plans to establish potentially environmentally sensitive facilities in emerging markets immediately raised the question as to whether it was doing so to take advantage of low environmental standards or lax enforcement. So when the Free Trade Agreement between Canada and the United States was extended to include Mexico, much discussion ensued as to whether that country would become a pollution haven for dirty industries. Twelve years later, careful research has concluded that "no discernable migration of dirty industry has occurred."[10] That the expected migration to Mexico of dirty chemical, metals, or paper plants has not occurred tends to suggest that most MNEs have established at least a law-abiding, nonexploitive attitude toward emerging markets.

At a minimum, the transactional-oriented MNE takes a Hippocratic Oath–style approach to communities. (The ancient Greek physician Hippocrates is credited with the expression "First, do no harm," which forms part of the oath taken by physicians.) Such an attitude, applied to MNEs, increases the likelihood that the worst potential corporate

---

[10]Gustavo Alanis-Ortega, "Is Global Environmental Governance Working?" *The Environmental Forum*, May/June 2006, p. 23.

abuses will be avoided, but that does not mean that transactional MNEs are fully trusted or that their actions are not carefully monitored by regulators or NGOs. And in recent years, it has often been the global NGOs that have taken the more active role in pushing MNEs to take more responsibility for their social, economic, and environmental impact.

Take the case of Nike. Despite the major concessions it made to the NGOs' many demands in the late 1990s, it was clear NGOs would remain interested in the company's practices simply because it is a highly profitable, highly visible industry leader, dealing with 700 factories that collectively employ over half a million people, mostly in emerging markets. But Nike's relationship with the many NGOs with which it sparred in the mid-1990s has slowly changed. Although some remnants of the activist-driven boycotts and protests remain in place, the heat has been greatly reduced. As the company moved to comply with more of the NGOs' demands, their role evolved from active adversary to vigilant watchdog.

Although not enthusiastically embraced by Nike and other MNEs, this relationship between NGOs and transactional companies is based less on confrontation and accusation and more on monitoring and challenging. Yet though the NGOs might agree that "doing no harm" is certainly a positive characteristic, they also challenge companies to consider whether that is a sufficient role for the multinational enterprise of the 21st century.

The Responsive MNE: Making a Difference

In the past, a large number—perhaps a majority—of MNEs might have exhibited behavior that was significantly or even predominantly exploitive or transactional, as we have described those behaviors. In recent years, however, the concept of "sustainability" has gained far more attention within the corporate world. As it has, management's concept of a sustainable strategy has migrated from a passing acknowledgement of the need to develop a responsible corporate environmental policy to a recognition that companies must articulate a philosophy that reflects their long-term viability as key participants in the broader social and economic environment. This perspective requires managers to take a somewhat broader perspective of their constituencies and their roles and responsibilities in the societies in which they operate.

A recent McKinsey survey seems to support the notion that executives around the world are becoming more aware of their larger responsibilities and increasingly convinced that they have a broader role to play. In the survey of 4,238 executives from 116 countries, only 16 percent of respondents saw their own responsibility as being to focus on the maximization of shareholder returns, whereas 84 percent expressed the opinion that high returns to shareholders must be balanced with contributions to a broader good.[11]

The responsive MNE, as we have dubbed it, reflects this view and undertakes to be more than merely a law-abiding entity: It makes a conscious commitment to be a contributing corporate citizen in all the environments in which it operates. In contrast to its exploitive and transactional counterparts, the responsive MNC is more sensitive to the different needs of the stakeholders in developing countries and manifests this behavior

[11]"McKinsey Global Survey of Business Executives: Business and Society," *McKinsey Quarterly,* January 2006, available at http://www.mckinseyquarterly.com/article_page.aspx?ar=1741&L2=39&L3=29.

more proactively in the way in which it deals with its customers, employees, and the community at large.

In his book *The Fortune at the Bottom of the Pyramid*, C. K. Prahalad argues that MNEs have not only a responsibility to contribute to development in the poorest nations of the world (i.e., "Big corporations should solve big problems") but also a huge opportunity to access a largely untapped market of four billion people. By investing in developing markets, creating jobs and wealth, and catering to underserved consumers, Prahalad argues that MNEs have an opportunity to bring millions of consumers into the marketplace from among the two-thirds of the global population that earns less than $2,000 per annum.[12]

Some companies have understood this opportunity for decades, probably none more so than Hindustan Lever. As Unilever's operating company in India for more than a century, this company has long understood that the key to developing scale and driving growth in that densely populated country is to expand its target market well beyond the middle- and upper-class consumers that are the typical focus of most MNEs entering huge developing markets like India. For many decades, Hindustan Lever has aimed at expanding its operations to serve the rural poor by adapting the company's products and technologies to their very different needs and economic means. For example, it developed a way to incorporate Unilever's advanced detergent technology into simple laundry bars, thereby providing superior washing capabilities in the cold-water, hand-washing methods that characterize India's widespread practice of doing laundry in the local stream or village washhouse. At the same time, the company adapted to local economic realities by selling the product as affordable single bars.

Even in sophisticated product markets such as medical diagnostic equipment, there is opportunity for MNEs to adopt a more responsive approach that can bring advanced technology to developing countries. For example, GE Medical Systems has adapted its range of diagnostic products to the simpler needs and more cost-constrained budgets of developing country health care systems. Although the economy model of its CT scanner sells for about one-third of the price of the advanced models in the United States, the market potential for such a product in less developed markets is huge. Already, this low-end product range accounts for approximately 20 percent of the CT scanner market worldwide.

To meet the needs of this large, previously unserved market, GE has gone beyond the adaptation of its current line to create a business it calls its Gold Seal Program. Through this program, the company acquires used x-ray machines and CT scanners, refurbishes them to their original specifications, and then resells them to developing country markets. Although these may not be the latest models with the most up-to-date technological features, they are in high demand, and GE's initiative has earned it a 30 percent share of a $1 billion global market for refurbished diagnostic equipment. Better still, the market is growing at 15 percent per annum.

But the responsive MNE sees its role as more than being an open and receptive commercial participant in developing countries' economies. These companies also feel

---

[12]C.K. Prahalad, *The Fortune at the Bottom of the Pyramid* (Upper Saddle River, NJ: Wharton School Publishing/Pearson, 2005).

the responsibility to be good corporate citizens that have a positive impact on those whose lives they touch. For example, Starbucks has accepted the responsibility to help its farmer suppliers in the face of lower global commodity prices for coffee.

In 2004, it collaborated with Conservation International to create its Coffee and Farmer Equity (CAFE) practices, which set out Starbucks's expectations about its suppliers' labor and environmental practices. In return for their compliance, Starbucks promises those who meet CAFE standards "preferred supplier" status, which involves long-term contracts and a price premium—$1.20 per pound compared with the prevailing 2004 market price of 60 to 70 cents. In 2007, 60 percent of its supply came from farms that followed its CAFE guidelines for environmental and labor practices.

Heineken has gone even further in reaching out to its stakeholders. To help deal with the devastating impact of AIDS in Africa, it provides antiretroviral drug coverage not only to its 6,000 African employees but also their dependents. It is a commitment that costs the company $2 million a year, but it reflects a sense of responsibility that Heineken and a growing number of other employers in Africa feel toward their employees and their families.

Many of the actions of these and other responsive MNEs reflect the aspirational standards of behavior contained in the voluntary Global Compact, signed by more than 5,000 companies from 120 countries in the 10 years following its introduction in 1999 at the World Economic Forum in Davos by Kofi Annan, then secretary general of the United Nations. (See Exhibit 8-1 for a summary of the key principles of the Global Compact.) Although it is a voluntary and self-regulated set of aspirational norms, rather than a legislated and enforceable code, the Global Compact seems to represent a way forward that can encourage MNEs to embrace a more responsive and constructive role in the developing world.

Exhibit 8-1   The Global Compact's 10 Principles

Human Rights
1. Businesses should support and respect the protection of internationally proclaimed human rights; and
2. make sure that they are not complicit in human rights abuses.

Labour Standards
3. Businesses should uphold the freedom of association and the effective recognition of the right to collective bargaining;
4. the elimination of all forms of forced and compulsory labour;
5. the effective abolition of child labour; and
6. the elimination of discrimination in respect of employment and occupation.

Environment
7. Businesses should support a precautionary approach to environmental challenges;
8. undertake initiatives to promote greater environmental responsibility; and
9. encourage the development and diffusion of environmentally friendly technologies

Anti-Corruption
10. Businesses should work against all forms of corruption, including extortion and bribery.

Source: www.unglobalcompact.org/AboutTheGC/TheTenPrinciples/index.html.

The Transformative MNE: Leading Broad Change

In recent years, there has been a growing number of examples of private enterprises not only being sensitive and responsive to the problems and needs of the developing world but also taking the initiative to lead broad-scale efforts to deal with their root causes. Because of the cost and commitment required to take such action, it is hardly surprising that the boldest and most visible of such initiatives have been those taken by private individuals and/or their foundations. George Soros and Bill Gates are perhaps the most visible of these individual entrepreneurs who are using funds generated by their highly successful global companies to attack some of the biggest problems of health, education, and welfare among the world's neediest populations.

Yet despite the commitment required, a growing number of companies is also leading major initiatives to help deal with problems facing the developing world. We describe these as transformative MNEs. Beyond being good corporate citizens, these companies have come to the conclusion that they can and should take a larger role in the less advantaged countries in which they operate by bringing their resources to bear on the massive problems their populations and governments face.

One way they do so is to make significant investments in developing products or services to meet important unfilled needs in poorer nations. And they often do so even if the economics do not support such developments or when other investments offer greater returns. For example, Nokia recognized the need for a lower cost mobile cellular telephone in emerging markets, most of which lack the hard-wired infrastructure necessary to provide landline telephone service to remote communities. After extensive ethnographic research and numerous consumer interviews in China, India, and Nepal, they developed an understanding of how illiterate people manage in their lives without understanding letters and numbers. This understanding led to the development of a software program built around a menu that uses a list of images rather than numbers and letters. At the same time, Nokia's hardware developers were working on designing a phone that would be simple, durable, and appropriate for outdoor use in the tropics. Understanding that it would be one of the most expensive purchases ever made by their potential consumers, the company also specified that the phone should be able to last for many years. The result was a product designed specifically for the needs of the developing world, built with a durable, moisture-resistant casing and a screen that would be legible even in bright sunlight. Most important, Nokia made this product simple enough for anyone to use and available at an extremely low price. Although these design decisions resulted in a product that will take a long time—if ever—to reach break-even, it responded to a social need of less educated, poor people living in remote communities.

Some truly transformative MNEs even go beyond a commercial relationship with consumers and offer their products and services to those who most desperately need them, regardless of their ability to pay. One of the largest and most sustained commitments was made by the pharmaceutical giant Merck in 1987 after it developed a drug to prevent river blindness. Recognizing that few of the more than 18 million sufferers of this debilitating disease—almost all of whom live in the developing world—could afford the treatment, the company decided to make the drug freely available for as long as it was needed to anyone suffering from or at risk of becoming exposed. Over the past

20 years, the program has delivered over 1 billion tablets in 350 million patient treatments. It currently reaches 45 million people and prevents an estimated 40,000 cases of blindness each year.

Transformational MNEs' desire to bring about a positive change also extends to the workplace and the communities in which they operate. They reject the notion of passively complying with local labor laws that do not meet their own higher standard of fairness to employees, and they are willing to challenge established community norms that deny human rights. In doing so, these companies become agents of change, willing to use their influence to bring about improvements in exploitive or unfair situations. For example, where local employment practices are unsafe, unhealthy, or do not provide a living wage, the transformational MNE becomes the new standard that others must eventually match; where social or economic conditions are oppressive or unjust, they become advocates for the disadvantaged, often leading the action to bring about change.

Because they typically challenge deeply embedded practices, developing such transformational responses is often difficult, particularly in the very different social and economic environments governed by very different cultural norms and legal frameworks. As a result, it often requires a long process of learning and adaptation on the company's part.

Another characteristic of the transformational NME is that it moves beyond fulfilling its responsibility to its direct stakeholders and begins to contribute to the broader social and economic needs of the countries in which it operates. For example, Nokia, in partnership with Pearson Publishing, the International Youth Foundation (IYF), and the U.N. Development Program, created a program called BridgeIt that uses mobile technology to deliver digital education materials to schools in remote areas of developing countries. Nokia has also joined with IYF to run an initiative called Make a Connection that has delivered educational development programs aimed at young people, primarily in developing countries. Through training, mentoring, and other means, the program develops a range of life skills, from teamwork to conflict resolution and from self-confidence to active leadership. Since its launch in 2000, Make a Connection has reached almost 240,000 young people in 23 countries.

In many of these activities, the MNEs have found themselves working in partnership with NGOs or supragovernment agencies that can provide expertise in social program delivery that the companies typically lack. In doing so, they have developed a very different relationship with these groups than the adversarial or defensive exchanges that characterize exploitive or transactional MNEs' experiences with NGOs. It is a partnership that appears to leverage the resources and capabilities of both groups and may well prove the engine that can drive the changes that have been so elusive in attempts to accelerate economic and social development in the world's poorest nations.

Conclusion

Over time, there has been an evolution in the roles, responsibilities, and expectations of MNEs operating in host countries around the world. In his seminal books *Sovereignty at Bay* and *Storm over the Multinationals,* both published in the 1970s, Ray Vernon expressed concerns about the "economic hegemony and economic dependence" that often characterized the relationship between MNEs and host country governments in the developing world in that era.[13] And various corrupt or exploitive acts by those companies during this time period created what Vernon described as a sense of "tension and anxiety on the part of many nation-states."

As the anecdotes that open this chapter illustrate, MNEs are still susceptible to charges of insensitivity and irresponsibility. But in the three decades since Vernon's research was published, the widespread concerns once held about MNE domination of host governments have largely subsided. (Indeed, the careful reader will have noted that most of the examples in the "exploitive" section describe activities that occurred in the 1970s.) And though there has been little success in creating the effective supranational global agencies that once were thought vital to reining in the unfettered power of the MNE, the rise of numerous, highly effective, global NGOs has filled the role of the active "watchdog." As the several examples cited in this chapter show, NGOs have become very effective at using their clout with consumers, share owners, and other company stakeholders as a way to bring about change.

But the biggest change has occurred in the evolving attitudes of companies toward their sense of corporate social responsibility and their commitment to a strategy of sustainability. Although a few firms have remained stuck in an exploitive mode with regard to the most vulnerable foreign environments in which they operate, most have adopted, at a minimum, a transactional approach. And with the growing shareholder and social expectations that MNEs should play a more active role, the trend is clearly moving toward responsive and even transformative models.

The social needs in emerging markets are great, and multinational enterprises and their managers have much to contribute. Increasingly, they are feeling both pressure and encouragement to ignore any uncertainty or timidity that could lead to inaction. In addition to transforming the lives of those in emerging markets, their commitment of resources, sensibly and sensitively provided to those at the "bottom of the pyramid," may very well represent one of the most important investments the MNE will ever make.

Chapter 8 Readings

- In Reading 8-1, "Values in Tension: Ethics Away from Home," Donaldson considers the question: When is different just different, and when is different wrong? He suggests that there are three principles which can shape ethical behavior: respect for core human values, respect for local traditions, and a belief that context matters. In addition, five guidelines are provided for developing a global ethical perspective among managers.

- Reading 8-2, "Serving the World's Poor, Profitably," by Prahalad and Hammond, details how multinationals can build businesses aimed at the bottom of the economic pyramid in order to build competitive advantage. They argue that such investments in the world's poorest markets can result in both tangible business benefits and major contributions to poverty reduction.

The roles and responsibilities of the MNE continue to evolve, as these readings suggest. MNEs have much to contribute.

---

[13]Raymond Vernon, *Sovereignty at Bay* (New York: Basic Books, 1971); Raymond Vernon, *Storm over the Multinationals: The Real Issues* (Cambridge: Harvard University Press, 1977).

MNE/Stakeholder Relationships in Emerging Markets: A Typology

Stakeholders

	Economic			Societal	Political/Regulatory	
MNE Responses and Attitudes	**Shareholders**	**Customers**	**Employees/ Suppliers**	**Local Communities**	**Government and Supranational Agencies/ Regulators (e.g., U.N. Agencies)**	**NGOs**
Exploitive *Views differences in wages, working conditions and living standards as exploitable opportunities.*	Adopts classic Milton Friedman view: Its only legitimate role is to maximize returns to shareholders.	Sells existing products and services, even if they have negative social or economic impact.	Exploits existing local wages, working conditions, and suppliers, driving them lower if possible.	Accepts no community responsibility for its social or environmental impact.	Seeks concessions and subsidies, using bargaining power to play national investment boards against each other. If bribery and corruption exist, engages in local practices to win benefits.	An adversary: NGOs actively work to force the MNE to change its behavior through protests, boycotts, political activism, etc.
Transactional *Engages in law-abiding, nonexploitive, commercial interactions.*	Focus on shareholder returns, but believes a pure Friedman approach is inconsistent with the long-term interests of its shareholders.	Treats it as any another market. Makes product adaptations if they are economically viable and can increase market share.	Complies with local labor laws and workplace regulations. Uses cost-efficient local sources, pressuring them on price.	Adopts a Hippocratic Oath approach toward communities: (i.e., "First, do no harm").	Obeys local laws and regulations but uses country differences to gain competitive advantage.	A watchdog: NGO monitors the MNE's actions, urging or pushing it to do more.

Stakeholders

	Economic			Societal	Political/Regulatory	
	Shareholders	**Customers**	**Employees/ Suppliers**	**Local Communities**	**Government and Supranational Agencies/ Regulators (e.g., U.N. Agencies)**	**NGOs**
Responsive *Acts in a way that is sensitive and responsive to the needs of all its immediate stakeholders.*	Feels a responsibility to be a "good corporate citizen" in the environments in which it operates.	Invests in potentially significant product or service developments and/or adaptations to meet local needs.	Committed to caring for its employees and developing their skills. Actively engages local sources, using its buyer power to improve working conditions for employees.	Aims to affect positively those whose lives it touches in communities in which it operates.	Sets its standard of behavior above minimum local legal requirements. Conforms to higher international standards (e.g., set by ILO or UNESCO).	An observer: NGO may be neutral or partially engaged with MNE. Limited mutual trust.
Transformative *Commits to leading initiatives to bring life-enhancing changes to the broader society.*	Persuades investors of the need for companies to be part of the solution by bringing their resources to bear on the root causes of problems.	Believes that by helping move people out of poverty, it will create stability and goodwill and help grow the world's customer base. Develops products or services specifically to meet local needs.	Committed to upgrading the lives of its employees, inside and outside the workplace. Brings work standard–compliant local suppliers into global supply chain networks.	Leads in developing the quality of life in the broad community (e.g., upgrading health, education).	Actively raises local standards (e.g., transferring developed world workplace health and safety standards.) Supports change agenda of international agencies (e.g., WHO, UNESCO).	A partner: NGO works with and supports the MNE working toward the same objectives.

Case 8-1   Hitting the Wall: Nike and International Labor Practices

Debora L. Spar and Jennifer L. Burns

Moore: Twelve year olds working in [Indonesian] factories? That's O.K. with you?
Knight: They're not 12-year-olds working in factories . . . the minimum age is 14.
Moore: How about 14 then? Does that bother you?
Knight: No.

—Phil Knight, Nike CEO, talking to Director Michael Moore in a scene from documentary film *The Big One,* 1997.

Nike is raising the minimum age of footwear factory workers to 18 . . . Nike has zero tolerance for underage workers.[1]

—Phil Knight, 1998

In 1997, Nguyen Thi Thu Phuong died while making sneakers. As she was trimming synthetic soles in a Nike contracting factory, a co-worker's machine broke, spraying metal parts across the factory floor and into Phuong's heart. The 23 year-old Vietnamese woman died instantly.[2]

Although it may have been the most dramatic, Phuong's death was hardly the first misfortune to hit Nike's far-flung manufacturing empire. Indeed, in the 1980s and 1990s, the corporation had been plagued by a series of labor incidents and public relations nightmares: underage workers in Indonesian plants, allegations of coerced overtime in China, dangerous working conditions in Vietnam. For a while, the stories had been largely confined to labor circles and activist publications. By the time of Phuong's death, however, labor conditions at Nike had hit the mainstream. Stories of reported abuse at Nike plants had been carried in publications such as *Time* and *Business Week* and students from major universities such as Duke and Brown had organized boycotts of Nike products. Even Doonesbury had joined the fray, with a series of cartoons that linked the company to underage and exploited Asian workers. Before these attacks, Nike had been widely regarded as one of the world's coolest and most successful companies. Now Nike, the company of Michael Jordan and Tiger Woods; Nike, the sign of the swoosh and athletic prowess, was increasingly becoming known as the company of labor abuse. And its initial response—"We don't make shoes"— was becoming harder and harder to sustain.[3]

Nike, Inc.

Based in Beaverton, Oregon, Nike had been a corporate success story for more than three decades. It was a sneaker company, but one armed with an inimitable attitude, phenomenal growth, and the apparent ability to dictate fashion trends to some of the world's most influential consumers. In the

Research Associate Jennifer L. Burns prepared this case under the supervision of Professor Debora L. Spar. This case was developed from published sources. HBS cases are developed solely as the basis for class discussion. Cases are not intended to serve as endorsements, sources of primary data, or illustrations of effective or ineffective management.
Harvard Business School Case No 9-700-047, Copyright 2000 President and Fellows of Harvard College. All rights reserved.
This case was prepared by D. Spar. HBS Cases are developed solely for class discussion and do not necessarily illustrate either effective or ineffective handling of administrative situation.

[1]"Nike CEO Phil Knight Announces New Labor Initiatives," *PR Newswire,* May 12, 1998.
[2]Tim Larimer, "Sneaker Gulag: Are Asian Workers Really Exploited?" *Time International,* May 11, 1998, p. 30.

[3]The quote is from Martha Benson, Nike's regional spokeswoman in Asia. See Larimer, p. 30.

1970s, Nike had first begun to capture the attention of both trend-setting teenagers and financial observers. Selling a combination of basic footwear and street-smart athleticism, Nike pushed its revenues from a 1972 level of $60,000 to a startling $49 million in just ten years.[4] It went public in 1980 and then astounded Wall Street in the mid-1990s as annual growth stayed resolutely in the double digits and revenues soared to over $9 billion. By 1998, Nike controlled over 40% of the $14.7 billion U.S. athletic footwear market. It was also a growing force in the $64 billion sports apparel market, selling a wide range of sport-inspired gear to consumers around the globe.[5]

What differentiated Nike from its competitors was not so much its shoes as its strategy. Like Reebok and adidas and New Balance, Nike sold a fairly wide range of athletic footwear to a fairly wide range of consumers: men and women, athletes and non-athletes, in markets around the world. Its strategy, though, was path breaking, the product of a relatively simple idea that CEO Phil Knight had first concocted in 1962 while still a student at Stanford Business School. The formula had two main prongs. First, the company would shave costs by outsourcing *all* manufacturing. There would be no in-house production, no dedicated manufacturing lines. Rather all product would be made by independent contracting factories, creating one of the world's first "virtual" corporations—a manufacturing firm with no physical assets. Then, the money saved through outsourcing would be poured into marketing. In particular, Knight focussed from the start on celebrity endorsements, using high-profile athletes to establish an invincible brand identity around the Nike name. While other firms had used celebrity endorsements in the past, Nike took the practice to new heights, emblazoning the Nike logo across athletes such as Michael Jordan and Tiger Woods, and letting their very

celebrity represent the Nike image. "To see name athletes wearing Nike shoes," Knight insisted, "was more convincing than anything we could say about them."[6] With the help of the "swoosh," a distinctive and instantly recognizable logo, Nike became by the 1990s one of the world's best known brands, as well as a global symbol of athleticism and urban cool.

But within this success story lay a central irony that would only become apparent in the late 1990s. While the *marketing* of Nike's products was based on selling a high profile fashion item to affluent Americans who only wished they could "Just Do It" as well as Woods or Jordan, the *manufacture* of these sneakers was based on an arms-length and often uneasy relationship with low-paid, non-American workers. For according to Knight's original plan, not only would Nike outsource, but it would outsource specifically to low cost parts of the world.

Nike signed its first contracts with Japanese manufacturers but eventually shifted its supply base to firms in South Korea and Taiwan, where costs were lower and production reliable. In 1982, 86% of Nike sneakers came from one of these two countries and Nike had established a large network of suppliers in both nations. But as South Korea and Taiwan grew richer, costs rose and Nike began to urge its suppliers to move their operations to new, lower cost regions. Eager to remain in the company's good graces, most manufacturers rapidly complied, moving their relatively inexpensive plants to China or Indonesia. By 1990, these countries had largely replaced South Korea and Taiwan as the core of Nike's global network. Indonesia, in particular, had become a critical location, with six factories that supplied Nike and a booming, enthusiastic footwear industry.[7]

▌ Taking Care of Business

At first, Indonesia seemed an ideal location for Nike. Wages were low, the workforce was docile, and an authoritarian government was yearning for

---

▌ [4]David B. Yoffie, *Nike: A (Condensed),* HBS Case 391-238 (Boston: HBS Press, 1991), p. 1.

▌ [5]Both figures are for retail sales. *Footwear 1999,* (North Palm Beach; Athletic Footwear Association, 1999), introduction; Dana Eisman Cohen and Sabina McBride, *Athletic Footwear Outlook 1999,* (New York: Donaldson, Lufkin & Jenrette, 1998), p. 3.

▌ [6]Yoffie, p. 6.

▌ [7]Philip M. Rosenzweig and Pam Woo, *International Sourcing in Footwear: Nike and Reebok,* HBS Case 394-189 (Boston: HBS Press, 1994), pp. 2–5.

foreign direct investment. There were unions in the country and occasional hints of activism, but the Suharto government clearly was more interested in wooing investors than in acceding to any union demands. So wages stayed low and labor demands were minimal. In 1991, the daily minimum wage in Indonesia's capital city was barely $1, compared to a typical daily wage of $24.40 in South Korea[8] and a U.S. hourly wage in athletic shoe manufacturing of about $8.[9] For firms like Nike, this differential was key: according to a reporter for the *Far Eastern Economic Review,* shoes coming out of China and Indonesia cost roughly 50% less than those sourced from Taiwan and South Korea.[10]

Just as Nike was settling into its Indonesian operations, though, a rare wave of labor unrest swept across the country. Strikes, which had been virtually nonexistent in the 1980s, began to occur with increasing frequency; according to government figures, there were 112 strikes in 1991,[11] a sharp increase from the 19 reported in 1989.[12] A series of polemical articles about foreign companies' labor abuses also appeared in Indonesian newspapers, triggering unprecedented demands from factory workers and empowering a small but potent band of labor organizers.

The source of these strikes and articles was mysterious. Some claimed that the Indonesian government was itself behind the movement, trying to convince an increasingly suspicious international community of the country's commitment to freedom of speech and labor rights. Others saw the hand of outside organizers, who had come to Indonesia solely to unionize its work force and embarrass its foreign investors. And still others saw the outbursts as random eruptions, cracks in the authoritarian veneer

which quickly took on a life of their own. In any case, though, the unrest occurred just around the time of Nike's expansion into Indonesia. In 1991 the Asian-American Free Labor Association (AAFLI, a branch of the AFL-CIO) published a highly critical report on foreign companies in Indonesia. Later that year, a group of Indonesian labor economists at the Institut Teknology Bandung (ITB), issued a similar report, documenting abusive practices in Indonesian factories and tracing them to foreign owners. In the midst of this stream of criticism was a labor organizer with a deep-seated dislike for Nike and a determination to shape its global practices. His name was Jeff Ballinger.

The Role of Jeff Ballinger   A labor activist since high school, Ballinger felt passionately that any company had a significant obligation towards even its lowliest workers. He was particularly concerned about the stubborn gap between wage rates in developed and developing worlds, and about the opportunities this gap created for rich Western companies to exploit low-wage, politically repressed labor pools. In 1988, Ballinger was assigned to run the AAFLI office in Indonesia, and was charged with investigating labor conditions in Indonesian plants and studying minimum wage compliance by overseas American companies. In the course of his research Ballinger interviewed workers at hundreds of factories and documented widespread worker dissatisfaction with labor conditions.

Before long, Nike emerged as a key target. Ballinger believed that Nike's policy of competing on the basis of cost fostered and even encouraged contractors to mistreat their workers in pursuit of unrealistic production quotas. Although Indonesia had worker protection legislation in place, widespread corruption made the laws essentially useless. While the government employed 700 labor inspectors, Ballinger found that out of 17,000 violations reported in 1988, only 12 prosecutions were ever made. Bribery took care of the rest.[13] Nike contractors, in

---

[8]Elliot B. Smith, "K-Swiss in Korea," *California Business,* October 1991, p. 77.

[9]Rosenzweig and Woo, p. 3.

[10]Mark Clifford, "Pain in Pusan," *Far Eastern Economic Review,* November 5, 1992, p. 59.

[11]Suhaini Aznam, "The Toll of Low Wages," *Far Eastern Economic Review,* April 2, 1992, p. 50.

[12]Margot Cohen, "Union of Problems: Government Faces Growing Criticism on Labour Relations," *Far Eastern Economic Review,* August 26, 1993, p. 23.

[13]Interview with casewriter, Cambridge, MA, July 6, 1999.

particular, he believed, were regularly flouting Indonesian labor laws and paying below-subsistence wages that did not enable workers to meet their daily requirements for food and other necessities. And to top matters off, he found Nike's attitude in the face of these labor practices galling: "It was right around the time that the swoosh started appearing on everything and everyone," Ballinger remembered. "Maybe it was the swagger that did it."[14]

What also "did it," though, was Ballinger's own strategic calculation—a carefully crafted policy of "one country-one company." Ballinger knew that his work would be effective only if it was carefully focused. And if his goal was to draw worldwide attention to the exploitation of third-world factory workers by rich U.S. companies, then Nike made a nearly ideal target. The arithmetic was simple. The same marketing and branding power that drove Nike's bottom line could also be used to drive moral outrage against the exploitation of Asian workers. After the publication of his AAFLI report, Ballinger set out to transform Nike's competitive strength into a strategic vulnerability.

For several years he worked at the fringes of the activist world, operating out of his in-laws' basement and publishing his own newsletter on Nike's practices. For the most part, no one really noticed. But then, in the early 1990s Ballinger's arguments coincided with the strikes that swept across Indonesia and the newfound interest of media groups. Suddenly his stories were big news and both the Indonesian government and U.S. firms had begun to pay attention.

Early Changes   The first party to respond to criticism from Ballinger and other activists was the government itself. In January 1992 Indonesia raised the official minimum daily wage from 2100 rupiah to 2500 rupiah (US $1.24). According to outside observers, the new wage still was not nearly enough: it only provided 70% of a worker's required minimal physical need (as determined by the Indonesian government) and was further diluted by the way in which many factories distributed wages and benefits.[15] The increased wage also had no impact on "training wages," which were lower than the minimum wage and often paid long after the training period had expired. Many factories, moreover, either ignored the new wage regulations or successfully petitioned the government for exemption. Still, the government's actions at least demonstrated some willingness to respond. The critics took note of this movement and continued their strikes and media attacks.

Despite the criticism, Nike insisted that labor conditions in its contractors' factories were not—could not—be Nike's concern or its responsibility. And even if labor violations did exist in Nike's contracting factories, stated the company's general manager in Jakarta, "I don't know that I need to know."[16] Nike's company line on the issue was clear and stubborn: without an inhouse manufacturing facility, the company simply could not be held responsible for the actions of independent contractors.

Realizing the severity of the labor issue, though, Nike did ask Dusty Kidd, a newly-hired member of its public relations department, to draft a series of regulations for its contractors. In 1992, these regulations were composed into a Code of Conduct and Memorandum of Understanding and attached to the new contracts sent to Nike contractors. In the Memorandum, Nike addressed seven different aspects of working conditions, including safety standards, environmental regulation and worker insurance. It required its suppliers to certify they were following all applicable rules and regulations and outlined general principles of honesty, respect, and non-discrimination.

Meanwhile, other shoe companies had been facing similar problems. Reebok, a chief competitor of Nike, also sourced heavily from Indonesia and South Korea. Like Nike, it too had been the subject of activist pressure and unflattering media.

---

[14]Ibid.

[15]A factory, for example, could pay a base wage lower than 2500 rupiah, but bring total compensation up to legal levels by the addition of a food allowance and incentive payments (see Aznam, p. 50).

[16]Adam Schwarz, "Running a Business," *Far Eastern Economic Review,* June 20, 1991, p. 16.

But unlike Nike, Reebok had moved aggressively into the human rights arena. In 1988, it created the Reebok Human Rights Award, bestowed each year on youthful contributors to the cause of human rights, and in 1990 it adopted a formal human rights policy.[17] When activists accused the company of violating workers' rights in Indonesia, Reebok responded with a far-reaching set of guidelines, one that spoke the explicit language of human rights, set forth specific standards for the company's contractors and promised to audit these contractors to ensure their compliance.[18] It was a big step for an American manufacturer and considerably farther than Nike had been willing to go.

Into the Spotlight

By 1992, criticism of Nike's labor practices had begun to seep outside of Indonesia. In the August issue of *Harper's* magazine, Ballinger published an annotated pay-stub from an Indonesian factory, making the soon-to-be famous comparison between workers' wages and Michael Jordan's endorsement contract. He noted that at the wage rates shown on the pay stub, it would take an Indonesian worker 44,492 years to make the equivalent of Jordan's endorsement contract.[19] Then the Portland *Oregonian,* Nike's hometown newspaper, ran a series of critical articles during the course of the 1992 Barcelona Olympics. Also at the Olympics, a small band of protestors materialized and handed out leaflets that charged Nike with exploitation of factory workers. The first mainstream coverage of the issue came in July 1993, when CBS interviewed Indonesian workers who revealed that they were paid just 19¢ an hour. Women workers could only leave the company barracks on Sunday, and needed a special letter of permission from management to do so. Nike responded somewhat more forcefully to this next round of allegations, hiring accounting firm Ernst & Young to conduct formal audits of its overseas factories. However, because Ernst & Young was paid by Nike to perform these audits, activists questioned their objectivity from the start. Public criticism of Nike's labor practices continued to mount.

Then suddenly, in 1996, the issue of foreign labor abuse acquired a name and a face: it was Kathie Lee Gifford, a popular daytime talk show host. In April human rights activists revealed that a line of clothing endorsed by Gifford had been manufactured by child labor in Honduras. Rather than denying the connection Gifford instantly rallied to the cause. When she appeared on television, crying and apologetic, a wave of media coverage erupted. Or as Ballinger recalls, "That's when my phone really started ringing."[20] Although Nike was not directly involved in the Gifford scandal, it quickly emerged as a symbol of worker exploitation and a high-profile media scapegoat.

Child labor was the first area of concern. In July, *Life* magazine ran a story about child labor in Pakistan, and published a photo of a 12 year old boy stitching a Nike soccer ball.[21] Then Gifford herself publicly called upon fellow celebrities such as Michael Jordan to investigate the conditions under which their endorsed products were made and to take action if need be. Jordan brushed away suggestions that he was personally responsible for conditions in Nike factories, leaving responsibility to the company itself. When Nike refused to let Reverend Jesse Jackson tour one of its Indonesian factories the media jumped all over the story, noting by contrast that Reebok had recently flown an executive to Indonesia just to give Jackson a tour.

At this point, even some pro-business observers began to jump on the bandwagon. As an editorial in *Business Week* cautioned: "Too few executives understand that the clamor for ethical sourcing isn't going to disappear with the wave of a magic press

---

[17]Rosenzweig and Woo, p. 7.

[18]Ibid., pp. 16–17.

[19]Jeff Ballinger, "The New Free-Trade Heel," *Harper's Magazine,* August 1992, p. 64.

[20]Casewriter interview.

[21]Nike's vigorous protests stopped the magazine from running the photo on its cover. Nike convincingly argued that the photo was staged, because the ball was inflated so that the Nike "swoosh" was clearly visible. In fact, soccer balls are stitched while deflated. However, the company did admit it had inadvertently relied on child labor during its first months of production in Pakistan.

release. They have protested, disingenuously, that conditions at factories run by subcontractors are beyond their control . . . Such attitudes won't wash anymore. As the industry gropes for solutions," the editorial concluded, "Nike will be a key company to watch."[22]

The View From Washington   Before long, the spotlight on the labor issue extended all the way to Washington. Sensing a hot issue, several senators and representatives jumped into the action and began to suggest legislative solutions to the issue of overseas labor abuse. Representative George Miller (D-CA) launched a campaign aimed at retailers that would mandate the use of "No Sweat" labels to guarantee that no exploited or child labor had been employed in the production of a garment. "Parents," he proclaimed, "have a right to know that the toys and clothes they buy for their children are not made by exploited children." To enforce such guarantees, Miller added, "I think Congress is going to have to step in."[23]

On the heels of this public outcry, President Clinton convened a Presidential task force to study the issue, calling on leaders in the apparel and footwear industries to join and help develop acceptable labor standards for foreign factories. Known as the Apparel Industry Partnership (AIP), the coalition, which also included members of the activist, labor, and religious communities, was meant to be a model collaboration between industry and its most outspoken critics, brokered by the U.S. government. Nike was the first company to join.

In order to supplement its hiring of Ernst & Young, in October 1996 Nike also established a Labor Practices Department, headed by former public relations executive Dusty Kidd. In a press release, Knight announced the formation of the new department and praised Nike's recent initiatives regarding fair labor practices, such as participation in Clinton's AIP, membership in the organization

Business for Social Responsibility, and an ongoing dialogue with concerned non-governmental organizations (NGOs). "Every year we continue to raise the bar," said Knight. "First by having Ernst & Young audits, and now with a group of Nike employees whose sole focus will be to help make things better for workers who make Nike products. In labor practices as in sport, we at Nike believe 'There is No Finish Line.'"[24] And indeed he was right, for the anti-Nike campaign was just getting started.

The Hotseat   As far as public relations were concerned, 1997 was even worse for Nike than 1996. Much as Ballinger had anticipated, Nike's giant marketing machine was easily turned against itself and in a climate awash with anti-Nike sentiment, any of Nike's attempts at self promotion became easy targets. In 1997 the company began expanding its chain of giant retail stores, only to find that each newly opened Niketown came with an instant protest rally, complete with shouting spectators, sign waving picketers, and police barricades. Knowing a good story when they saw it, reporters eagerly dragged Nike's celebrity endorsers into the fracas. Michael Jordan was pelted with questions about Nike at press conferences intended to celebrate his athletic performance, and football great Jerry Rice was hounded to the point of visible agitation when he arrived at the grand opening of a new Niketown in San Francisco.[25]

Perhaps one of the clearest indicators that Nike was in trouble came in May 1997, when Doonesbury, the popular comic strip, devoted a full week to Nike's labor issues. In 1,500 newspapers, millions of readers watched as Kim, Mike Doonesbury's wife, returned to Vietnam and found a long-lost cousin laboring in dismal conditions at a Nike factory. The strips traced Kim's growing involvement in the activist movement and the corrupt factory manager's attempts to deceive her about true working conditions in Nike contracting factories. In Doonesbury, Nike had reached an

---

[22]Mark L. Clifford, "Commentary: Keep the Heat on Sweatshops," *Business Week*, December 23, 1996, p. 90.

[23]"Honduran Child Labor Described," *The Boston Globe*, May 30, 1996, p. 13.

[24]"Nike Establishes Labor Practices Department," *PR Newswire*, October 2, 1996.

[25]"Protestors Swipe at the Swoosh, Catch Nike's Jerry Rice Off Guard," *The Portland Oregonian*, Feburary 21, 1997, p. C1.

unfortunate cultural milestone. As one media critic noted: "It's sort of like getting in Jay Leno's monologue. It means your perceived flaws have reached a critical mass, and everyone feels free to pick on you."[26] The appearance of the Doonesbury strips also marked the movement of anti-Nike sentiment from the fringes of American life to the mainstream. Once the pet cause of leftist activists, Nike bashing had become America's newest spectator sport.

Even some of the company's natural friends took a dim view of its actions. The *Wall Street Journal* ran an opinion piece alleging that "Nike Lets Critics Kick it Around." The writer argued that Nike had been "its own worst enemy" and that its public relations efforts had only made the problem worse. According to the writer, had Nike acknowledged its wrongdoing early on and then presented economic facts that showed the true situation of the workers, the crisis would have fizzled.[27] Instead it had simply gathered steam. Even more trouble loomed ahead with the anticipated release of *The Big One,* a documentary film by Michael Moore that was widely expected to be highly critical of Nike's labor practices.

Damage Control

Late in 1996 the company decided to turn to outside sources, hiring Andrew Young, the respected civil rights leader and former mayor of Atlanta, to conduct an independent evaluation of its Code of Conduct. In January 1997, Knight granted Young's newly-formed GoodWorks International firm "blanket authority . . . to go anywhere, see anything, and talk with anybody in the Nike family about this issue."[28]

Shortly thereafter Young went to Asia, visited Nike suppliers and returned to issue a formal report. On the day the report was released, Nike took out full-page advertisements in major newspapers that highlighted one of Young's main conclusions: "It is my sincere belief that Nike is doing a good job . . . But Nike can and should do better."[29] Young did not give Nike carte blanche with regard to labor practices. Indeed, he made a number of recommendations, urging Nike to improve their systems for reporting workers' grievances, to publicize their Code more widely and explain it more clearly, and to implement cultural awareness and language training programs for expatriate managers. Young also stated that third party monitoring of factories was necessary, but agreed that it was not appropriate for Nike's NGO critics to fulfill that function.

Rather than calming Nike's critics, though, Young's report had precisely the opposite effect. Critics were outraged by the report's research methodology and conclusions, and unimpressed by Young's participation. They argued that Young had failed to address the issue of factory wages, which was for many observers the crux of the issue, and had spent only 10 days interviewing workers. During these interviews, moreover, Young had relied on translators provided by Nike, a major lapse in accepted human rights research technique. Finally, critics also noted that the report was filled with photos and used a large, showy typeface, an unusual format for a research report.

From the start, Nike executives had argued in vain that they were the target of an uninformed media campaign, pointing out that although Nike was being vigorously monitored by activists and the media, no one was monitoring the monitors. This point was forcefully made by the publication of a five page *New Republic* article in which writer Stephen Glass blasted the Young report for factual inaccuracies and deception, and summed up: "This was a public relations problem, and the world's largest sneaker company did what it does best: it purchased a celebrity endorsement."[30] Glass's claims were echoed by several other media outlets that also decried Nike's disingenuousness and Young's ineptitude. However, within months a major scandal erupted at the *New Republic* when it was discovered that most

[26]Jeff Manning, "Doonesbury Could Put Legs on Nike Controversy," *The Portland Oregonian*, May 25, 1997, p. D01.

[27]Greg Rushford, "Nike Lets Critics Kick it Around," *The Wall Street Journal,* May 12, 1997, p. A14.

[28]Andrew Young, *Report: The Nike Code of Conduct,* (GoodWorks International, LLC, 1997) p. 27.

[29]Young, p. 59.

[30]Stephen Glass, "The Young and the Feckless," *The New Republic,* September 8, 1997, p. 22.

of Glass's articles were nearly fictional. Apparently, Glass routinely quoted individuals with whom he had never spoken or who did not even exist, and relied upon statistics and information from organizations he invented himself.

The Issue of Wages

In the public debate, the question of labor conditions was largely couched in the language of human rights. It was about child labor, or slave labor, or workers who toiled in unsafe or inhumane environments. Buried beneath these already contentious issues, though, was an even more contentious one: wages. According to many labor activists, workers in the developing world were simply being paid too little—too little to compensate for their efforts, too little compared to the final price of the good they produced, too little, even, to live on. To many business economists, though, such arguments were moot at best and veiled protectionism at worst. Wages, they maintained, were simply set by market forces: by definition, wages could not be too low, and there was nothing firms could or should do to affect wage rates. As the debate over labor conditions evolved, the argument over wages had become progressively more heated.

Initially, Nike sought to defuse the wage issue simply by ignoring it, or by reiterating the argument that this piece of the labor situation was too far beyond their control. In the Young Report, therefore, the issue of wages was explicitly set aside. As Young explained in his introduction: "I was not asked by Nike to address compensation and 'cost of living' issues which some in the human rights and NGO community had hoped would be a part of this report." Then he went on: "Are workers in developing countries paid far less than U.S. workers? Of course they are. Are their standards of living painfully low by U.S. standards? Of course they are. This is a blanket criticism that can be leveled at almost every U.S. company that manufactures abroad . . . But it is not reasonable to argue that any one particular U.S. company should be forced to pay U.S. wages abroad while its direct competitors do not."[31] It was a standard argument,

and one that found strong support even among many pro-labor economists. In the heat of public debate, however, it registered only as self-serving.

The issue of wages emerged again in the spring of 1997, when Nike arranged for students at Dartmouth's Amos Tuck School of Business to conduct a detailed survey on "the suitability of wages and benefits paid to its Vietnamese and Indonesian contract factory workers."[32] Completed in November 1997, the students' *Survey of Vietnamese and Indonesian Domestic Expenditure Levels* was a 45 page written study with approximately 50 pages of attached data. The authors surveyed both workers and residents of the areas in which the factories were located to determine typical spending patterns and the cost of basic necessities.

In Vietnam, the students found that "The factory workers, after incurring essential expenditures, can generate a significant amount of discretionary income."[33] This discretionary income was often used by workers to purchase special items such as bicycles or wedding gifts for family members. In Indonesia, results varied with worker demographics. While 91% of workers reported being able to support themselves individually, only 49% reported being able to also support their dependents. Regardless of demographic status, 82% of workers surveyed in Indonesia either saved wages or contributed each month to their families.[34]

Additionally, the survey found that most workers were not the primary wage earners in their households. Rather, in Vietnam at least, factory wages were generally earned by young men or women and served "to *augment* aggregate household income, with the primary occupation of the household parents being farming or shopkeeping."[35] The same was often true in Indonesia. For instance, in one Indonesian household the students visited, a family of

---

[31]Young, p. 9–11.

[32]Derek Calzini, Shawna Huffman, Jake Odden, Steve Tran, and Jean Tsai, *Nike, Inc: Survey of Vietnamese and Indonesian Domestic Expenditure Levels,* November 3, 1997, Field Study in International Business (Dartmouth, NH: The Amos Tuck School, 1997), p. 5.

[33]Ibid., p. 8.

[34]Ibid., p. 9.

[35]Ibid., p. 31.

six had used one daughter's minimum wage from a Nike factory to purchase luxury items such as leather couches and a king sized bed.[36] While workers in both countries managed to save wages for future expenditure, the authors found that Indonesians typically put their wages in a bank, while Vietnamese workers were more likely to hold their savings in the form of rice or cows.

Economically, data such as these supported the view that companies such as Nike were actually furthering progress in the developing countries, providing jobs and wages to people who formerly had neither. In the public view, however, the social comparison was unavoidable. According to the Tuck study, the average worker in a Vietnamese Nike factory made about $1.67 per day. A pair of Penny Hardaway basketball sneakers retailed at $150. The criticism continued to mount.

In November there was even more bad news. A disgruntled Nike employee leaked excerpts of an internal Ernst & Young report that uncovered serious health and safety issues in a factory outside of Ho Chi Minh City. According to the Ernst & Young report, a majority of workers suffered from a respiratory ailment caused by poor ventilation and exposure to toxic chemicals. The plant did not have proper safety equipment and training, and workers were forced to work 15 more hours than allowed by law. But according to spokesman Vada Manager the problems no longer existed: "This shows our system of monitoring works. We have uncovered these issues clearly before anyone else, and we have moved fairly expeditiously to correct them."[37] Once again, the denial only made the criticism worse.

▮ Hitting the Wall

Fiscal Year 1998   Until the spring of 1997, Nike sneakers were still selling like hotcakes. The company's stock price had hit $76 and futures orders reached a record high. Despite the storm of criticism lobbied against it, Nike seemed invincible.

Just a year later, however, the situation was drastically different. As Knight admitted to stockholders, Nike's fiscal year 1998 "produced considerable pain." In the third quarter 1998, the company was beset by weak demand and retail oversupply, triggered in part by the Asian currency crisis. Earnings fell 69%, the company's first loss in 13 years. In response, Knight announced significant restructuring charges and the layoff of 1,600 workers.[38]

Much the same dynamic that drove labor criticism drove the 1998 downturn: Nike became a victim of its own popularity. Remarked one analyst: "When I was growing up, we used to say that rooting for the Yankees is like rooting for U.S. Steel. Today, rooting for Nike is like rooting for Microsoft."[39] The company asserted that criticism of Nike's labor practices had nothing to do with the downturn. But it was clear that Nike was suffering from a serious image problem. For whatever reasons, Americans were sick of the swoosh. Although Nike billed its shoes as high performance athletic gear, it was well known that 80% of its shoes were sold for fashion purposes. And fashion was a notoriously fickle patron. Competing sneaker manufacturers, particularly adidas, were quick to take advantage of the giant's woes. Adidas' three-stripe logo fast replaced Nike's swoosh among the teen trendsetter crowd; rival brands New Balance and Airwalk tripled their advertising budgets and saw sales surge.

To make matters worse, the anti-Nike headlines had trickled down to the nation's campuses, where a newly invigorated activist movement cast Nike as a symbol of corporate greed and exploitation. With its roots deep in the University of Oregon track team (Knight had been a long distance runner for the school), Nike had long treasured its position as supplier to the top athletic universities. Now, just as young consumers were choosing adidas over Nike at the cash register, campus activists rejected Nike's contracts with their schools and demanded all

---

▮ [36]Ibid., p. 44.
▮ [37]Tunku Varadarajan, "Nike Audit Uncovers Health Hazards at Factory," *The Times of London*, November 10, 1997, p. 52.

▮ [38]Nike Corporation, *Annual Report 1998,* (Nike, Inc.: Beaverton, OR) p. 1, 17–30.
▮ [39]Quoted in Patricia Sellers, "Four Reasons Nike's Not Cool," *Fortune,* March 30, 1998, p. 26.

Exhibit 1 Nike Inc. Financial History, 1989–1999 (in millions of dollars)

Year Ended May 31	1999	1998	1997	1996	1995	1994	1993	1992	1991	1990	1989
Revenues	$8,776.9	$9,553.1	$9,186.5	$6,470.6	$4,760.8	$3,789.7	$3,931.0	$3,405.2	$3,003.6	$2,235.2	$1,710.8
Gross margin	3,283.4	3,487.6	3,683.5	2,563.9	1,895.6	1,488.2	1,544.0	1,316.1	1,153.1	851.1	636.0
Gross margin %	37.4	36.5	40.1	39.6	39.8	39.3	39.3	38.7	38.4	38.1	37.2
Restructuring charge, net	45.1	129.9	—	—	—	—	—	—	—	—	—
Net income	451.4	399.6	795.8	553.2	399.7	298.8	365.0	329.2	287.0	243.0	167.0
Cash flow from operations	961.0	517.5	323.1	339.7	254.9	576.5	265.3	435.8	11.1	127.1	169.4
Price range of common stock											
High	65.500	64.125	76.375	52.063	20.156	18.688	22.563	19.344	13.625	10.375	4.969
Low	31.750	37.750	47.875	19.531	14.063	10.781	13.750	8.781	6.500	4.750	2.891
Cash and equivalents	$198.1	$108.6	$445.4	$262.1	$216.1	$518.8	$291.3	$260.1	$119.8	$90.4	$85.7
Inventories	1,199.3	1,396.6	1,338.6	931.2	629.7	470.0	593.0	471.2	586.6	309.5	222.9
Working capital	1,818.0	1,828.8	1,964.0	1,259.9	938.4	1,208.4	1,165.2	964.3	662.6	561.6	419.6
Total assets	5,247.7	5,397.4	5,361.2	3,951.6	3,142.7	2,373.8	2,186.3	1,871.7	1,707.2	1,093.4	824.2
Long-term debt	386.1	379.4	296.0	9.6	10.6	12.4	15.0	69.5	30.0	25.9	34.1
Shareholders' equity	3,334.6	3,261.6	3,155.9	2,431.4	1,964.7	1,740.9	1,642.8	1,328.5	1,029.6	781.0	558.6
Year-end stock price	60.938	46.000	57.500	50.188	19.719	14.750	18.125	14.500	9.938	9.813	4.750
Market capitalization	17,202.2	13,201.1	16,633.0	14,416.8	5,635.2	4,318.8	5,499.3	4,379.6	2,993.0	2,942.7	1,417.4
Geographic Revenues:											
United States	$5,042.6	$5,460.0	$5,538.2	$3,964.7	$2,997.9	$2,432.7	$2,528.8	$2,270.9	$2,141.5	$1,755.5	$1,362.2
Europe	2,255.8	2,096.1	1,789.8	1,334.3	980.4	927.3	1,085.7	919.8	664.7	334.3	241.4
Asia/Pacific	844.5	1,253.9	1,241.9	735.1	515.6	283.4	178.2	75.7	56.2	29.3	32.0
Americas (exclusive of U.S.)	634.0	743.1	616.6	436.5	266.9	146.3	138.3	138.8	141.2	116.1	75.2
Total revenues	$8,776.9	$9,553.1	$9,186.5	$6,470.6	$4,760.8	$3,789.7	$3,931.0	$3,405.2	$3,003.6	$2,235.2	$1,710.8

All per common share data has been adjusted to reflect the 2-for-1 stock splits paid October 23, 1996, October 30, 1995 and October 5, 1990. The Company's Class B Common Stock is listed on the New York and Pacific Exchanges and traded under the symbol NKE. At May 31, 1999, there were approximately 170,000 shareholders.

Source: Nike, Inc., *Annual Report 1999*

Exhibit 2	Estimated Cost Breakdown of an Average Nike Shoe, 1999
$ 3.37	Labor costs
$ 3.41	Manufacturer's overhead
$14.60	Materials
$ 1.12	Profit to factory
$22.50	Factory price to Nike
$45	Wholesale price
$90	Retail price

Source: Jennifer Lin, "Vietnam Gives Nike a Run for Its Money," *The Philadelphia Enquirer,* March 23, 1998, p. 1.

contracts cease until labor practices were rectified. In late 1997, Nike's $7.2 million endorsement deal with the University of North Carolina sparked protests and controversy on campus; in early 1998 an assistant soccer coach at St. John's University, James Keady, publicly quit his job rather than wear the swoosh. "I don't want to be a billboard for a company that would do these things," said Keady. [40]

Before long, the student protests spread to campuses where Nike had no merchandising contracts. Organized and trained by unions such as UNITE! and the AFL-CIO, previously apathetic college students stormed university buildings to protest sweatshop labor and the exploitation of foreign workers. In 1999, activists took over buildings at Duke, Georgetown, the University of Michigan and the University of Wisconsin, and staged sit-ins at countless other colleges and universities. The protests focused mostly on the conditions under which collegiate logo gear was manufactured. Declared Tom Wheatley, a Wisconsin student and national movement leader: "It really is quite sick. Fourteen-year-old girls are working 100-hour weeks and earning poverty-level wages to make my college T-shirts. That's unconscionable." [41] University administrators heeded the student protests, and many began to consider codes of conduct for contract manufacturers.

[40] William McCall, "Nike's Image Under Attack: Sweatshop Charges Begin to Take a Toll on the Brand's Cachet," *The Buffalo News,* October 23, 1998, p. 5E.

[41] Nancy Cleeland, "Students Give Sweatshop Fight the College Try," *Los Angeles Times,* April 22, 1999, p. C1.

Saving the Swoosh   Nike's fiscal woes did what hundreds of harsh articles had failed to do: they took some of the bravado out of Phil Knight. In a May 1998 speech to the National Press Club, a humbled Knight admitted that "the Nike product has become synonymous with slave wages, forced overtime, and arbitrary abuse." [42] Knight announced a series of sweeping reforms, including raising the minimum age of all sneaker workers to 18 and apparel workers to 16; adopting U.S. OSHA clean air standards in all its factories; expanding its monitoring program; expanding educational programs for workers; and making micro loans available to workers. Although Nike had been formally addressing labor issues since 1992, Knight's confession marked a turning point in Nike's stance towards its critics. For the first time, he and his company appeared ready to shed their defensive stance, admit labor violations did occur in Nike factories, and refashion themselves as leaders in the effort to reform third world working conditions.

Nike's second step was to get more involved with Washington-based reform efforts. In the summer of 1998, President Clinton's initial task force on labor, the Apparel Industry Partnership (AIP), lay deadlocked over the ever-delicate issues of factory monitoring and wages. Although the AIP had a tentative proposal, discussion ground to a halt when the task force's union, religious, and corporate members clashed.

While the AIP proclaimed itself as an exemplar of cooperative solution making, it soon became apparent that its members had very different views. One key concept—"independent monitoring"— was highly contentious. To Nike, the hiring of a separate and unrelated multinational firm like Ernst & Young fulfilled any call for independent monitoring. But activists and other critics alleged that if an independent monitor, such as an accounting firm, was hired by a corporation, it thereby automatically lost autonomy and independence. According to such critics, independent monitoring could only be done by an

[42] John H. Cushman Jr., "Nike to Step Forward on Plant Conditions," *The San-Diego Union-Tribune,* May 13, 1998, p. A1.

Exhibit 3   Prices of Some Popular Running Shoe Styles in New York City, 1996

	Nike Air Max		New Balance 999		Saucony Grid Shadow	
	Men's	Women's	Men's	Women's	Men's	Women's
Foot Locker	$140	$135	$124	$105	$85	$85
Paragon Sports	140	135	135	109	70	70
Sports Authority	140	140	101	101	78	78
Super Runners Shop	140	130	125	110	85	85

Source: "Feet Don't Fail . . .," *The New York Times*, November 3, 1996, Section 13, p. 12.

Exhibit 4   Summary Revenue and Expense Profile of Minimum Wage Workers by Demographic Type
(in Indonesian Rupiah)

	SH	SO	Dorm	MH	MO	Total (weighted)
Number of respondents	67	161	33	21	32	314
Base wages	172,812	172,071	172,197	173,905	172,650	172,424
Total wages	**225,378**	**238,656**	**239,071**	**248,794**	**244,458**	**236,893**
Rent	14,677	40,955	12,121[a]	24,775	56,050	32,838
Food	84,774	95,744	90,455	103,421	128,793	103,020
Transportation	48,984	24,189	7,219	17,471	38,200	28,560
Savings	38,369	41,783	70,303	29,412	49,185	44,154
Contribution to home	22,175	37,594	57,644	25,222	25,089	34,441
Total uses	**208,980**	**240,266**	**237,741**	**200,301**	**297,318**	**243,013**

[a]17 of the 33 respondents were provided free housing by the factory. The remaining 16 paid a subsidized monthly rent of Rp 25,000.
Note: Monthly Wages and Total Uses of wages may not match due to averaging.
Key to demographic type:
SH–Single workers living at home
SO–Single workers living away from home and paying rent
Dorm–Single workers living away from home and living in factory subsidized housing
MH–Married workers living at home
MO–Married workers living away from home
Source: Derek Calzini, Shawna Huffman, Jake Odden, Steve Tran, and Jean Tsai, *Nike, Inc: Survey of Vietnamese and Indonesian Domestic Expenditure Levels,* November 3, 1997, Field Study in International Business (Dartmouth, NH: The Amos Tuck School, 1997), pp. 9–10.

organization that was not on a corporate payroll, such as an NGO or a religious group. The corporations, by contrast, insisted that a combination of internal monitoring and audits by accounting firms was sufficient. Upset at what they saw as corporate intransigence, the task force's union and religious membership abruptly exited the coalition.

The remaining corporate members of the AIP were soon able to cobble together a more definitive agreement, complete with an oversight organization known as the Fair Labor Association (FLA). The FLA was to be a private entity controlled evenly by corporate members and human rights or labor representatives (if they chose to rejoin the coalition). It would support a code of conduct that required its members to pay workers the legal minimum wage or the prevailing local standard, whichever was higher. The minimum age of workers was set at 15, and

Exhibit 5	Typical "Basket" of Basic Food Expenditures for Indonesian workers (in rupiah)	
Rice	800–1,300	per 5 servings
Instant Noodles	300–500	per serving
Eggs	2,800–3,000	per 18 eggs
Tofu	1,500	per 15 servings
Tempe	1,500	per 15 servings
Kancang Pangung	1,500	per 15 servings
Peanuts	2,600	per kilogram
Oil	2,300	per liter
Other "luxury" foods		
Fish	6,000	per kilogram
Chicken	4,500–5,000	per chicken

Source: Derek Calzini, Shawna Huffman, Jake Odden, Steve Tran, and Jean Tsai, *Nike, Inc: Survey of Vietnamese and Indonesian Domestic Expenditure Levels,* November 3, 1997, Field Study in International Business (Dartmouth, NH: The Amos Tuck School, 1997), p. 45.

employees could not be required to work more than 60 hours per week. Companies that joined the Association would be required to comply with these guidelines and to establish internal monitoring systems to enforce them; they would then be audited by certified independent inspectors, such as accounting firms. In the first three years after a company joined, auditors would inspect 30% of a company's factories; later they would inspect 10%. All audits would be confidential.

Nike worked tirelessly to bring other manufacturers into the FLA, but the going was tough. As of August 1999, the only other corporate members were adidas, Liz Claiborne, Reebok, Levi's, L.L. Bean, and Phillips Van Heusen. However, Nike's efforts to foster the FLA hit pay dirt with U.S. colleges and universities. The vocal student anti-sweatshop movement had many administrators scrambling to find a solution, and over 100 colleges and universities

Exhibit 6   Strikes and Lockouts in Indonesia, 1988–1997

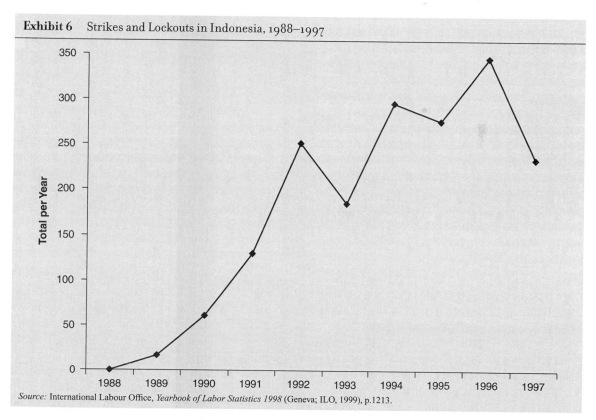

Source: International Labour Office, *Yearbook of Labor Statistics 1998* (Geneva; ILO, 1999), p.1213.

Exhibit 7   Wages and Productivity in Industrialized and Developing Nations (figures in $ per year)

	Average Hours Worked Per Week		Yearly Minimum Wage		Labor Cost Per Worker in Manufacturing		Value Added Per Worker in Manufacturing	
	1980-84	1990-94	1980-84	1990-94	1980-84	1990-94	1980-84	1990-94
North America								
United States	35	34	6,006	8,056[b]	19,103	32,013[b]	47,276	81,353
Canada	32	33	4,974	7,897[b]	17,710	28,346[b]	36,903	60,712
Mexico	—	34	1,002	843	3,772	6,138	17,448	25,991
Europe								
Denmark	—	37	9,170	19,933[b]	16,169	35,615[b]	27,919	49,273
France	39	39	10,815	22,955[b]	16,060	38,900[b]	26,751	61,019[e]
Germany	41	40	a	a	21,846[d]	63,956[b,d]	—	—
Greece	—	41	—	5,246	6,461	15,899[b]	14,561	30,429
Ireland	41[c]	41[c]	—	—	10,190	25,414[b]	26,510	86,036
Netherlands	40	39	9,074	15,170[b]	18,891	39,865[b]	27,491	56,801
Asia								
China (PRC)	—	—	—	—	472	434[d]	3,061	2,885
Hong Kong	48	46	—	—	4,127	13,539[b]	7,886	19,533
India	48	48	—	408	1,035	1,192	2,108	3,118
Indonesia	—	—	—	241	898	1,008	3,807	5,139
Japan	47	46	3,920	8,327[b]	12,306	40,104[b]	34,456	92,582
South Korea	52	48	—	3,903[b]	3,153	15,819[b]	11,617	40,916
Malaysia	—	—	—	a	2,519	3,429	8,454	12,661
Philippines	—	43	—	1,067	1,240	2,459	5,266	9,339
Singapore	—	46	—	—	5,576	21,534[b]	16,442	40,674
Thailand	48	—	—	1,083	2,305	2,705	11,072	19,946

[a]Country has sectoral minimum wage but no minimum wage policy.
[b]Data refer to 1995–1999.
[c]Data refer to hours worked per week in manufacturing.
[d]Data refer to wage per worker in manufacturing.
[e]International Labor Organisation data.
Source: World Bank, *World Development Indicators 1999* (Washington, D.C.; World Bank, 1999), pp.62–64.

eventually signed on. Participants ranged from the large state universities that held Nike contracts to the eight Ivy League schools. The FLA was scheduled to be fully operational by the fall of 2000.

Meanwhile, by 1999 Nike was running extensive training programs for its contractors' factory managers. All managers and supervisors were required to learn the native language of their workers, and received training in cultural differences and acceptable management styles. In addition to 25 employees who would focus solely on corporate responsibility, Nike's 1,000 production employees were explicitly required to devote part of their job to maintaining labor standards. In Vietnam, the company partnered with the National University of Vietnam in a program designed to identify and meet worker needs. It also helped found the Global Alliance, a partnership between the International Youth Foundation, the

Exhibit 8 Indonesia: Wages and Inflation, 1993–97

	1993		1994		1995		1996		1997	
	Minimum	Maximum	Minimum	Maximum	Minimum	Maximum	Minimum	Maximum	Minimum	Maximum
Monthly wages in manufacturing industry (thousands of rupiah)	196	2,920	207	3,112	238	3,453	241	3,453	439	6,050
Minimum wage regional average[a] (thousands of rupiah)		72		94		112		118		130
Annual percent change		17.7		30.8		19.5		5.4		10.2
Consumer price inflation		8.5		9.4		8.0		6.7		57.6
Exchange rates (average Rp:$)		2,161		2,249		2,342		2,909		10,014

Figures are based on periodic surveys of primarily urban-based business establishments and include transportation, meal, and attendance allowances.
[a] Calculated from minimum daily figure for 30 days per month. Increased by 9% to Rp122,000 in 1996 and by 10% to Rp135,000 in 1997.
Source: International Monetary Fund, Economist Intelligence Unit.

Exhibit 9   *Life* magazine photo of Pakistani child worker

Source: Life Magazine, June 1996, p. 39.

Exhibit 10   Doonesbury Cartoons About Nike

Doonesbury

BY GARRY TRUDEAU

KIM? YOU SEEN MY RUNNING SHOES?

YOUR RUNNING SHOES? YOU MEAN THE ONES MADE BY EXHAUSTED WORKERS DURING FORCED OVERTIME?

THE ONES MADE BY THE COMPANY WHOSE NAME HAS BECOME SYNONYMOUS WITH CHRONIC VIOLATIONS OF MINIMUM WAGE LAWS?

I'M NEVER GOING TO SEE MY SHOES AGAIN, AM I?

I HID MINE.

Doonesbury

BY GARRY TRUDEAU

I THINK WHAT MAKES ME MADDEST IS HOW *EASY* IT WOULD BE FOR NIKE TO DO THE RIGHT THING...

DO YOU KNOW IF YOU **DOUBLED** THE SALARIES OF NIKE'S 30,000 EMPLOYEES HERE, THE ANNUAL PAYROLL WOULD BE ABOUT WHAT THE COMPANY PAYS MICHAEL JORDAN?

OH, C'MON, KIM, GET REAL. NIKE CAN'T PAY THEIR VIETNAMESE WORK FORCE WHAT THEY PAY MICHAEL JORDAN.

WHY NOT?

MICHAEL WOULD WANT MORE. HE'S **VERY** COMPETITIVE.

Doonesbury

BY GARRY TRUDEAU

I JUST DON'T GET IT, MIKE— NIKE COULD *EASILY* PAY ITS WORK FORCE LIVING WAGES AND **STILL** MAKE HUMONGOUS PROFITS!

I'M NOT GOING TO LET THIS GO, MIKE! I'M TAKING THIS TO THE TOP! I'M TAKING IT TO THE STOCKHOLDERS! I'M TAKING IT TO THE MEDIA!

WHOEVER THE MANAGER OF THAT PLANT IS, HE'S GOING TO BE IN A **WORLD** OF TROUBLE!

WE HAD ANOTHER HUMAN RIGHTS TOURIST THIS WEEK.

THAT'S NICE. DID YOU CONFIRM MY GOLF DATE?

Exhibit 11   Anti-Nike Activist Materials

Nike, Inc. in Indonesia I

JUST DO IT!

"You know when you need a break. And you know when it's time to take care of yourself, for yourself. Because you know it's never too late to have a life. " (Nike advertisement)

Twelve thousand Indonesian woman work 60 hours a week making Nike shoes. Many earn less than their government's minimum wage of $1.80 a day. Numerous strikes and protests have been broken up by security forces eager to placate foreign capital; labor activists have even been murdered. Factories producing Nike shoes have been cited in the State Department's Human Rights Report to Congress. Asked about local labor practices, Nike VP David Taylor said: "I don't feel bad about it. I don't think we are doing anything wrong."

One percent of Nike's advertising budget would double the wages of the women making the company's shoes and raise them above the poverty line.

Nike, Inc. in Indonesia newsletter: $20 *for six months, teachers free*
Press for Change, Inc. PO Box 230, Bayonne, New Jersey, 07002-9998

Source: Jeff Ballinger; http://www.nikeworkers.org [10/29/99]; http://www.corpwatch.org/nike/ [10/29/99].

MacArthur Foundation, the World Bank, and Mattel, that was dedicated to improving the lives of workers in the developing world.

Although Nike's various concessions and new programs were welcomed as a victory by several human rights groups, other observers argued that Nike still failed to deal with the biggest problem, namely wages.[43] Wrote *New York Times* columnist Bob Herbert: "Mr. Knight is like a three-card monte player. You have to keep a close eye on him at all times. The biggest problem with Nike is that its

[43]John H. Cushman, Jr., "Nike Pledges to End Child Labor and Apply U.S. Rules Abroad," *The New York Times,* May 13, 1998, p. D1.

overseas workers make wretched, below-subsistence wages. It's not the minimum age that needs raising, it's the minimum wage."[44] Similarly, while some labor leaders accepted the FLA as the best compromise possible, others decried it as sham agreement that simply provided cover for U.S. corporations. A main objection of these critics was that the FLA standards included notification of factories that were to be inspected, a move criticized by some as

equivalent to notifying a restaurant when a critic was coming to dine. According to Jeff Ballinger, Nike's original critic, the company's reform record was mixed. Ballinger was confident that Nike had at least removed dangerous chemicals from factories, but otherwise he remained skeptical: "If you present yourself as a fitness company you can't very well go around the globe poisoning people. But on wages, they're still lying through their teeth."[45]

---

[44]Bob Herbert, "Nike Blinks," *The New York Times,* May 21, 1998, p. A33.

[45]Casewriter interview.

Case 8-2   IKEA's Global Sourcing Challenge: Indian Rugs and Child Labor (A)

Christopher A. Bartlett, Vincent Dessain, and Anders Sjöman

In May 1995, Marianne Barner faced a tough decision. After just two years with IKEA, the world's largest furniture retailer, and less than a year into her job as business area manager for carpets, she was faced with the decision of cutting off one of the company's major suppliers of Indian rugs. While such a move would disrupt supply and affect sales,

she found the reasons to do so quite compelling. A German TV station had just broadcast an investigative report naming the supplier as one that used child labor in the production of rugs made for IKEA. What frustrated Barner was that, like all other IKEA suppliers, this large, well-regarded company had recently signed an addendum to its supply contract explicitly forbidding the use of child labor on pain of termination.

Even more difficult than this short-term decision was the long-term action Barner knew IKEA must take on this issue. On one hand, she was being urged to sign up to an industry-wide response to growing concerns about the use of child labor in the Indian carpet industry. A recently formed partnership of manufacturers, importers, retailers, and Indian nongovernmental organizations (NGOs) was proposing to issue and monitor the use of "Rugmark," a label to be put on carpets certifying that they were made

Professor Christopher A. Bartlett, Executive Director of the HBS Europe Research Center Vincent Dessain, and Research Associate Anders Sjöman prepared this case. HBS cases are developed solely as the basis for class discussion. Certain details have been disguised. Cases are not intended to serve as endorsements, sources of primary data, or illustrations of effective or ineffective management.

without child labor. Simultaneously, Barner had been conversing with people at the Swedish Save the Children organization who were urging IKEA to ensure that its response to the situation was "in the best interest of the child"—whatever that might imply. Finally, there were some who wondered if IKEA should not just leave this hornet's nest. Indian rugs accounted for a tiny part of IKEA's turnover, and to these observers, the time, cost, and reputation risk posed by continuing this product line seemed not worth the profit potential.

The Birth and Maturing of a Global Company[1]

To understand IKEA's operations, one had to understand the philosophy and beliefs of its 70-year-old founder, Ingvar Kamprad. Despite stepping down as CEO in 1986, almost a decade later, Kamprad retained the title of honorary chairman and was still very involved in the company's activities. Yet perhaps even more powerful than his ongoing presence were his strongly held values and beliefs, which long ago had been deeply embedded in IKEA's culture.

Kamprad was 17 years old when he started the mail-order company he called IKEA, a name that combined his initials with those of his family farm, Elmtaryd, and parish, Agunnaryd, located in the forests of southern Sweden. Working out of the family kitchen, he sold goods such as fountain pens, cigarette lighters, and binders he purchased from low-priced sources and then advertised in a newsletter to local shopkeepers. When Kamprad matched his competitors by adding furniture to his newsletter in 1948, the immediate success of the new line led him to give up the small items.

In 1951, to reduce product returns, he opened a display store in nearby Älmhult village to allow customers to inspect products before buying. It was an immediate success, with customers traveling seven

hours from the capital Stockholm by train to visit. Based on the store's success, IKEA stopped accepting mail orders. Later Kamprad reflected, "The basis of the modern IKEA concept was created [at this time] and in principle it still applies. First and foremost, we use a catalog to tempt people to visit an exhibition, which today is our store. . . . Then, catalog in hand, customers can see simple interiors for themselves, touch the furniture they want to buy and then write out an order."[2]

As Kamprad developed and refined his furniture retailing business model he became increasingly frustrated with the way a tightly knit cartel of furniture manufacturers controlled the Swedish industry to keep prices high. He began to view the situation not just as a business opportunity but also as an unacceptable social problem that he wanted to correct. Foreshadowing a vision for IKEA that would later be articulated as "creating a better life for the many people," he wrote: "A disproportionately large part of all resources is used to satisfy a small part of the population. . . . IKEA's aim is to change this situation. We shall offer a wide range of home furnishing items of good design and function at prices so low that the majority of people can afford to buy them. . . . We have great ambitions."[3]

The small newsletter soon expanded into a full catalog. The 1953 issue introduced what would become another key IKEA feature: self-assembled furniture. Instead of buying complete pieces of furniture, customers bought them in flat packages and put them together themselves at home. Soon, the "knockdown" concept was fully systemized, saving transport and storage costs. In typical fashion, Kamprad turned the savings into still lower prices for his customers, gaining an even larger following among young postwar householders looking for well-designed but inexpensive furniture. Between 1953 and 1955, the company's sales doubled from SEK 3 million to SEK 6 million.[4]

---

[1]This section draws on company histories detailed in Bertil Torekull, "Leading by Design—The IKEA Story" (New York: Harper Business, 1998), and on the IKEA website, available at http://www.ikea.com/ms/en_GB/about_ikea/splash.html, accessed October 5, 2005.

[2]Ingvar Kamprad, as quoted in Torekull, "Leading by Design—The IKEA Story," p. 25.

[3]Quoted in Christopher A. Bartlett and Ashish Nanda, "Ingvar Kamprad and IKEA," HBS No. 390–132 (Boston: Harvard Business School Publishing, 1990).

[4]Ibid.

Managing Suppliers: Developing Sourcing Principles   As its sales took off in the late 1950s, IKEA's radically new concepts began to encounter stiff opposition from Sweden's large furniture retailers. So threatened were they that when IKEA began exhibiting at trade fairs, they colluded to stop the company from taking orders at the fairs and eventually even from showing its prices. The cartel also pressured manufacturers not to sell to IKEA, and the few that continued to do so often made their deliveries at night in unmarked vans.

Unable to meet demand with such constrained local supply, Kamprad was forced to look abroad for new sources. In 1961, he contracted with several furniture factories in Poland, a country still in the Communist eastern bloc. To assure quality output and reliable delivery, IKEA brought its know-how, taught its processes, and even provided machinery to the new suppliers, revitalizing Poland's furniture industry as it did so. Poland soon became IKEA's largest source and, to Kamprad's delight, at much lower costs—once again allowing him to reduce his prices.

Following its success in Poland, IKEA adopted a general procurement principle that it should not own its means of production but should seek to develop close ties by supporting its suppliers in a long-term relationship.[a] Beyond supply contracts and technology transfer, the relationship led IKEA to make loans to its suppliers at reasonable rates, repayable through future shipments. "Our objective is to develop long-term business partners," explained a senior purchasing manager. "We commit to doing all we can to keep them competitive—as long as they remain equally committed to us. We are in this for the long run."

Although the relationship between IKEA and its suppliers was often described as one of mutual dependency, suppliers also knew that they had to remain competitive to keep their contract. From the outset they understood that if a more cost-effective alternative appeared, IKEA would try to help them respond, but if they could not do so, it would move production.

In its constant quest to lower prices, the company developed an unusual way of identifying new sources. As a veteran IKEA manager explained: "We do not buy products from our suppliers. We buy unused production capacity." It was a philosophy that often led its purchasing managers to seek out seasonal manufacturers with spare off-season capacity. There were many classic examples of how IKEA matched products to supplier capabilities: they had sail makers make seat cushions, window factories produce table frames, and ski manufacturers build chairs in their off-season. The manager added, "We've always worried more about finding the right management at our suppliers than finding high-tech facilities. We will always help good management to develop their capacity."

Growing Retail: Expanding Abroad   Building on the success of his first store, Kamprad self-financed a store in Stockholm in 1965. Recognizing a growing use of automobiles in Sweden, he bucked the practice of having a downtown showroom and opted for a suburban location with ample parking space. When customers drove home with their furniture in flat packed boxes, they assumed two of the costliest parts of traditional furniture retailing—home delivery and assembly.

In 1963, even before the Stockholm store had opened, IKEA had expanded into Oslo, Norway. A decade later, Switzerland became its first non-Scandinavian market, and in 1974 IKEA entered Germany, which soon became its largest market. (See **Exhibit 1** for IKEA's worldwide expansion.) At each new store the same simple Scandinavian-design products were backed up with a catalog and offbeat advertising, presenting the company as "those impossible Swedes with strange ideas." And reflecting the company's conservative values, each new entry was financed by previous successes.[b]

---

[a] This policy was modified after a number of East European suppliers broke their contracts with IKEA after the fall of the Berlin Wall opened new markets for them. IKEA's subsequent supply chain problems and loss of substantial investments led management to develop an internal production company, Swedwood, to ensure delivery stability. However, it was decided that only a limited amount of IKEA's purchases (perhaps 10%) should be sourced from Swedwood.

[b] By 2005, company lore had it that IKEA had only taken one bank loan in its corporate history—which it had paid back as soon as the cash flow allowed.

Exhibit 1   IKEA Stores, Fiscal Year Ending August 1994

a. Historical Store Growth

	1954	1964	1974	1984	1994
Number of Stores	0	2	9	52	114

b. Country's First Store

	First Store (with city)	
Year	**Country**	**City**
1958	Sweden	Älmhult
1963	Norway	Oslo
1969	Denmark	Copenhagen
1973	Switzerland	Zürich
1974	Germany	Munich
1975	Australia	Artamon
1976	Canada	Vancouver
1977	Austria	Vienna
1978	Netherlands	Rotterdam
1978	Singapore	Singapore
1980	Spain	Gran Canaria
1981	Iceland	Reykjavik
1981	France	Paris
1983	Saudi Arabia	Jeddah
1984	Belgium	Brussels
1984	Kuwait	Kuwait City
1985	United States	Philadelphia
1987	United Kingdom	Manchester
1988	Hong Kong	Hong Kong
1989	Italy	Milan
1990	Hungary	Budapest
1991	Poland	Platan
1991	Czech Republic	Prague
1991	United Arab Emirates	Dubai
1992	Slovakia	Bratislava
1994	Taiwan	Taipei

Source: IKEA website, http://franchisor.ikea.com/txtfacts.html, accessed October 15, 2004.

During this expansion, the IKEA concept evolved and became increasingly formalized. (**Exhibit 2** summarizes important events in IKEA's corporate history.) It still built large, suburban stores with knockdown furniture in flat packages the customers brought home to assemble themselves. But as the

Exhibit 2   IKEA History: Selected Events

Year	Event
1943	IKEA is founded. Ingvar Kamprad constructs the company name from his initials (**I**ngvar **K**amprad), his home farm (**E**lmtaryd), and its parish (**A**gunnaryd).
1945	The first IKEA ad appears in press, advertising mail-order products.
1948	Furniture is introduced into the IKEA product range. Products are still only advertised through ads.
1951	The first IKEA catalogue is distributed.
1955	IKEA starts to design its own furniture.
1956	Self-assembly furniture in flat packs is introduced.
1958	The first IKEA store opens in Älmhult, Sweden.
1961	Contract with Polish sources, IKEA's first non-Scandinavian suppliers. First delivery is 20,000 chairs.
1963	The first IKEA store outside Sweden opens in Norway.
1965	IKEA opens in Stockholm, introducing the self-serve concept to furniture retailing.
1965	IKEA stores add a section called the "The Cook Shop," offering quality utensils at low prices.
1973	The first IKEA store outside Scandinavia opens in Spreitenbach, Switzerland.
1974	A plastic chair developed at a supplier that usually makes buckets.
1978	The BILLY bookcase is introduced to the range, becoming an instant top seller.
1980	One of IKEA's best-sellers, the KLIPPAN sofa with removable, washable covers, is introduced.
1980	Introduction of LACK coffee table, made from a strong, light material by an interior door factory.
1985	The first IKEA Group store opens in the U.S.
1985	MOMENT sofa with frame built by a supermarket trolley factory is introduced. Wins a design prize.
1991	IKEA establishes its own industrial group, Swedwood

Source: Adapted from IKEA Facts and Figures, 2003 and 2004 editions and IKEA internal documents.

concept was refined, the company required that each store follow a predetermined design, set up to maximize customers' exposure to the product range. The concept mandated, for instance, that the living room interiors should follow immediately after the entrance. IKEA also serviced customers with features such as a playroom for children, a low-priced restaurant, and a "Sweden Shop" for groceries that had made IKEA Sweden's leading food exporter. At the same time, the range gradually expanded beyond furniture to include a full line of home furnishing products such as textiles, kitchen utensils, flooring, rugs and carpets, lamps, and plants.

The Emerging Culture and Values[5]   As Kamprad's evolving business philosophy was formalized into the IKEA vision statement, "To create a better everyday life for the many people," it became the foundation of the company's strategy of selling affordable, good-quality furniture to mass-market consumers around the world. The cultural norms and values that developed to support the strategy's implementation were also, in many ways, an extension of Kamprad's personal beliefs and style. "The true IKEA spirit," he remarked, "is founded on our enthusiasm, our constant will to renew, on our cost-consciousness, on our willingness to assume responsibility and to help, on our humbleness before the task, and on the simplicity of our behavior." As well as a summary of his aspiration for the company's behavioral norms, it was also a good statement of Kamprad's own personal management style.

Over the years a very distinct organizational culture and management style emerged in IKEA reflecting these values. For example, the company operated very informally as evidenced by the open-plan office landscape, where even the CEO did not have a separate office, and the familiar and personal way all employees addressed one another. But that informality often masked an intensity that derived from the organization's high self-imposed standards. As one senior executive explained, "Because there is no security available behind status or closed doors, this environment actually puts pressure on people to perform."

The IKEA management process also stressed simplicity and attention to detail. "Complicated rules paralyze!" said Kamprad. The company organized "anti-bureaucrat week" every year, requiring all managers to spend time working in a store to reestablish contact with the front line and the consumer. The workpace was such that executives joked that IKEA believed in "management by running around."

Cost consciousness was another strong part of the management culture. "Waste of resources," said Kamprad, "is a mortal sin at IKEA. Expensive solutions are often signs of mediocrity, and an idea without a price tag is never acceptable." Although cost consciousness extended into all aspects of the operation, travel and entertainment expenses were particularly sensitive. "We do not set any price on time," remarked an executive, recalling that he had once phoned Kamprad to get approval to fly first class. He explained that economy class was full and that he had an urgent appointment to keep. "There is no first class in IKEA," Kamprad had replied. "Perhaps you should go by car." The executive completed the 350-mile trip by taxi.

The search for creative solutions was also highly prized with IKEA. Kamprad had written, "Only while sleeping one makes no mistakes. The fear of making mistakes is the root of bureaucracy and the enemy of all evolution." Though planning for the future was encouraged, overanalysis was not. "Exaggerated planning can be fatal," Kamprad advised his executives. "Let simplicity and common sense characterize your planning."

In 1976, Kamprad felt the need to commit to paper the values that had developed in IKEA during the previous decades. His thesis, *Testament of a Furniture Dealer*, became an important means for spreading the IKEA philosophy, particularly during its period of rapid international expansion. (Extracts of the *Testament* are given in **Exhibit 3**.) Specially trained "IKEA ambassadors" were assigned to key positions in all units to spread the company's philosophy and values by educating their subordinates and by acting as role models.

[5]Ibid.

Exhibit 3   "A Furniture Dealer's Testament"—A Summarized Overview

In 1976, Ingvar Kamprad listed nine aspects of IKEA that he believed formed the basis of the IKEA culture together with the vision statement "To create a better everyday life for the many people." These aspects are given to all new employees a pamphlet titled "A Furniture Dealer's Testament." The following table summarizes the major points:

Cornerstone	Summarize Description
1. The Product Range—Our Identity	IKEA sells well-designed, functional home furnishing products at prices so low that as many people as possible can afford them.
2. The IKEA Spirit—A Strong and Living Reality	IKEA is about enthusiasm, renewal, thrift, responsibility, humbleness toward the task and simplicity.
3. Profit Gives Us Resources	IKEA will achieve profit (which Kamprad describes as a "wonderful word") through the lowest prices, good quality, economical development of products, improved purchasing processes and cost savings.
4. Reaching Good Results with Small Means	"Waste is a deadly sin."
5. Simplicity is a Virtue	Complex regulations and exaggerated planning paralyze. IKEA people stay simple in style and habits as well as in their organizational approach.
6. Doing it a Different Way	IKEA is run from a small village in the woods. IKEA asks shirt factories to make seat cushions and window factories to make table frames. IKEA discounts its umbrellas when it rains. IKEA does things differently.
7. Concentration—Important to Our Success	"We can never do everything everywhere, all at the same time." At IKEA, you choose the most important thing to do and finish that before starting a new project.
8. Taking Responsibility—A Privilege	"The fear of making mistakes is the root of bureaucracy." Everyone has the right to make mistakes; in fact, everyone has obligation to make mistakes.
9. Most Things Still Remain to be Done. A Glorious Future!	IKEA is only at the beginning of what it might become. 200 stores is nothing. "We are still a small company at heart."

Source: Adapted by casewriters from IKEA's "A Furniture Dealer's Testament"; Bertil Torekull, "Leading by Design: The IKEA Story" (New York: Harper Business, 1998, p. 112); and interviews.

In 1986, when Kamprad stepped down, Anders Moberg, a company veteran who had once been Kamprad's personal assistant, took over as president and CEO. But Kamprad remained intimately involved as chairman, and his influence extended well beyond the ongoing daily operations: he was the self-appointed guardian of IKEA's deeply embedded culture and values.

Waking up to Environmental and Social Issues

By the mid-1990s, IKEA was the world's largest specialized furniture retailer. Sales for the IKEA Group for the financial year ending August 1994 totaled SEK 35 billion (about $4.5 billion). In the previous year, more than 116 million people had visited one of the 98 IKEA stores in 17 countries, most of them drawn there by the company's product catalog, which was printed yearly in 72 million copies in 34 languages. The privately held company did not report profit levels, but one estimate put its net margin at 8.4% in 1994, yielding a net profit of SEK 2.9 billion (about $375 million).[6]

After decades of seeking new sources, in the mid-1990s IKEA worked with almost 2,300 suppliers in 70 countries, sourcing a range of around 11,200

[6]Estimation in Bo Pettersson, "Han släpper aldrig taget," *Veckans Affärer*, March 1, 2004, pp. 30–48.

Exhibit 4 IKEA in Figures, 1993/1994 (fiscal year ending August 31, 1994)

a. Sales

Country/Region	SEK Billion	Percentage
Germany	10.4	29.70%
Sweden	3.9	11.20%
Austria, France, Italy, Switzerland	7.7	21.90%
Belgium, Netherlands, United Kingdom, Norway	7.3	20.80%
North America (U.S.A and Canada)	4.9	13.90%
Czech Republic, Hungary, Poland, Slovakia	0.5	1.50%
Australia	0.4	1.00%
	35.0	

b. Purchasing

Country/Region	Percentage
Nordic Countries	33.4%
East and Central Europe	14.3%
Rest of Europe	29.6%
Rest of the World	22.7%

Source: IKEA Facts and Figures, 1994.

products. Its relationship with its suppliers was dominated by commercial issues, and its 24 trading service offices in 19 countries primarily monitored production, tested new product ideas, negotiated prices, and checked quality. (See **Exhibit 4** for selected IKEA figures in 1994.) That relationship began to change during the 1980s, however, when environmental problems emerged with some of its products. And it was even more severely challenged in the mid-1990s when accusations of IKEA suppliers using child labor surfaced.

The Environmental Wake-Up: Formaldehyde
In the early 1980s, Danish authorities passed regulations to define limits for formaldehyde emissions permissible in building products. The chemical compound was used as binding glue in materials such as plywood and particleboard and often seeped out as gas. At concentrations above 0.1 mg/kg in air, it could cause watery eyes, headaches, a burning sensation in the throat, and difficulty breathing. With IKEA's profile as a leading local furniture retailer using particleboard in many of its products, it became a prime target for regulators wanting to publicize the new standards. So when tests showed that some IKEA products emitted more formaldehyde than was allowed by legislation, the case was widely publicized and the company was fined. More significantly—and the real lesson for IKEA—was that due to the publicity, its sales dropped 20% in Denmark.

In response to this situation, the company quickly established stringent requirements regarding formaldehyde emissions but soon found that suppliers were failing to meet its standards. The problem was that most of its suppliers bought from subsuppliers, who in turn bought the binding materials from glue manufacturers. Eventually, IKEA decided it would have to work directly with the glue-producing chemical companies and, with the collaboration of companies such as ICI and BASF, soon found ways to reduce the formaldehyde off-gassing in its products.[7]

A decade later, however, the formaldehyde problem returned. In 1992, an investigative team from a large German newspaper and TV company found that IKEA's best-selling bookcase series, Billy, had emissions higher than German legislation allowed. This time, however, the source of the problem was not the glue but the lacquer on the bookshelves. In the wake of headlines describing "deadly poisoned bookshelves," IKEA immediately stopped both the production and sales of Billy bookcases worldwide and corrected the problem before resuming distribution. Not counting the cost of lost sales and production or the damage to goodwill, the Billy incident was estimated to have cost IKEA $6 million to $7 million.[8]

These events prompted IKEA to address broader environmental concerns more directly. Since wood

---

[7]Based on case study by The Natural Step, "Organizational Case Summary: IKEA," available at http://www.naturalstep.org/learn/docs/cs/case_ikea.pdf, accessed October 5, 2005.
[8]Ibid.

was the principal material in about half of all IKEA products, forestry became a natural starting point. Following discussions with both Greenpeace and World Wide Fund for Nature (WWF, formerly World Wildlife Fund) and using standards set by the Forest Stewardship Council, IKEA established a forestry policy stating that IKEA would not accept any timber, veneer, plywood, or layer-glued wood from intact natural forests or from forests with a high conservation value. This meant that IKEA had to be willing to take on the task of tracing all wood used in IKEA products back to its source.[9] To monitor compliance, the company appointed forest managers to carry out random checks of wood suppliers and run projects on responsible forestry around the world.

In addition to forestry, IKEA identified four other areas where environmental criteria were to be applied to its business operations: adapting the product range; working with suppliers; transport and distribution; and ensuring environmentally conscious stores. For instance, in 1992, the company began using chlorine-free recycled paper in its catalogs; it redesigned the best-selling OGLA chair—originally manufactured from beech—so it could be made using waste material from yogurt cup production; and it redefined its packaging principles to eliminate any use of PVC. The company also maintained its partnership with WWF, resulting in numerous projects on global conservation, and funded a global forest watch program to map intact natural forests worldwide. In addition, it engaged in an ongoing dialogue with Greenpeace on forestry.[10]

The Social Wake-Up: Child Labor   In 1994, as IKEA was still working to resolve the formaldehyde problems, a Swedish television documentary showed children in Pakistan working at weaving looms. Among the several Swedish companies mentioned in the film as importers of carpets from Pakistan, IKEA was the only high-profile name on the list. Just two months into her job as business area manager for

carpets, Marianne Barner recalled the shockwaves that the TV program sent through the company:

> The use of child labor was not a high-profile public issue at the time. In fact, the U.N. Convention on the Rights of the Child had only been published in December 1989. So, media attention like this TV program had an important role to play in raising awareness on a topic not well known and understood— including at IKEA. . . . We were caught completely unaware. It was not something we had been paying attention to. For example, I had spent a couple of months in India learning about trading but got no exposure to child labor. Our buyers met suppliers in their city offices and rarely got out to where production took place. . . . Our immediate response to the program was to apologize for our ignorance and acknowledge that we were not in full control of this problem. But we also committed to do something about it.

As part of its response, IKEA sent a legal team to Geneva to seek input and advice from the International Labor Organization (ILO) on how to deal with the problem. They learned that Convention 138, adopted by the ILO in 1973 and ratified by 120 countries, committed ratifying countries to working for the abolition of labor by children under 15 or the age of compulsory schooling in that country. India, Pakistan, and Nepal were not signatories to the convention.[11] Following these discussions with the ILO, IKEA added a clause to all supply contracts—a "black-and-white" clause, as Barner put it—stating simply that if the supplier employed children under legal working age, the contract would be cancelled.

To take the load off field trading managers and to provide some independence to the monitoring process, the company appointed a third-party agent to monitor child labor practices at its suppliers in India and Pakistan. Because this type of external monitoring was very unusual, IKEA had some difficulty locating a reputable and competent company to perform the task. Finally, they appointed a well-known Scandinavian company with extensive

[9]"IKEA—Social and Environmental Responsibility Report 2004," p. 33, available at http://www.ikea-group.ikea.com/corporate/PDF/IKEA_SaER.pdf, accessed October 5, 2005.
[10]Ibid., pp. 19–20.

[11]Ratification statistics available on ILO website, page titled "Convention No. C138 was ratified by 142 countries," available at http://www.ilo.org/ilolex/cgi-lex/ratifce.pl?C138, accessed December 4, 2005.

experience in providing external monitoring of companies' quality assurance programs and gave them the mandate not only to investigate complaints but also to undertake random audits of child labor practices at suppliers' factories.

Early Lessons: A Deeply Embedded Problem
With India being the biggest purchasing source for carpets and rugs, Barner contacted Swedish Save the Children, UNICEF, and the ILO to expand her understanding and to get advice about the issue of child labor, especially in South Asia. She soon found that hard data was often elusive. While estimates of child labor in India varied from the government's 1991 census figure of 11.3 million children under 15 working[12] to Human Rights Watch's estimate of between 60 million and 115 million child laborers,[13] it was clear that a very large number of Indian children as young as five years old worked in agriculture, mining, quarrying, and manufacturing, as well as acting as household servants, street vendors, or beggars. Of this total, an estimated 200,000 were employed in the carpet industry, working on looms in large factories, for small subcontractors, and in homes where whole families worked on looms to earn extra income.[14]

Children could be bonded—essentially placed in servitude—in order to pay off debts incurred by their parents, typically in the range of 1,000 to 10,000 rupees ($30 to $300). But due to the astronomical interest rates and the very low wages offered to children, it could take years to pay off such loans. Indeed, some indentured child laborers eventually passed on the debt to their own children. The Indian government stated that it was committed to the abolition of bonded labor, which had been illegal since the Children (Pledging of Labour) Act passed under British rule in 1933. The practice continued to be widespread, however, and to reinforce the earlier law, the government passed the Bonded Labour System (Abolition) Act in 1976.[15]

But the government took a less absolute stand on unbonded child labor, which it characterized as "a socioeconomic phenomenon arising out of poverty and the lack of development." The Child Labour (Prohibition and Regulation) Act of 1986 prohibited the use of child labor (applying to those under 14) in certain defined "hazardous industries" and regulated children's hours and working conditions in others. But the government felt that the majority of child labor involved "children working alongside and under the supervision of their parents" in agriculture, cottage industries, and service roles. Indeed, the law specifically permitted children to work in craft industries "in order not to outlaw the passage of specialized handicraft skills from generation to generation."[16] Critics charged that even with these laws on the books, exploitive child labor—including bonded labor—was widespread because laws were poorly enforced and prosecution rarely severe.[17]

Action Required: New Issues, New Options

In the fall of 1994, after managing the initial response to the crisis, Barner and her direct manager traveled to India, Nepal, and Pakistan to learn more. Barner recalled the trip: "We felt the need to educate ourselves, so we met with our suppliers. But we also met with unions, politicians, activists, NGOs, U.N. organizations, and carpet export organizations. We even went out on unannounced carpet factory raids with local NGOs; we saw child labor, and we were thrown out of some places."

On the trip, Barner also learned of the formation of the Rugmark Foundation, a recently initiated industry response to the child labor problem in the Indian carpet industry. Triggered by a consumer awareness program started by human rights organizations,

[12]Indian Government Policy Statements, "Child Labor and India," available at http://www.indianembassy.org/policy/Child_Labor/childlabor_2000.htm, accessed October 1, 2005.

[13]Human Rights Watch figures, available at http://www.hrw.org/reports/1996/India3.htm, accessed October 1, 2005.

[14]Country Reports in Human Rights, U.S. State Department, February 2000, available at http://www.state.gov/g/drl/rls/hrrpt/2000/, accessed October 1, 2005.

[15]Indian Government Policy Statements, "Child Labor and India," available at http://www.indianembassy.org/policy/Child_Labor/childlabor_2000.htm, accessed October 1, 2005.

[16]Ibid.

[17]Human Rights Watch data, available at http://www.hrw.org/reports/1996/India3.htm, accessed October 1, 2005.

consumer activists, and trade unions in Germany in the early 1990s, the Indo-German Export Promotion Council had joined up with key Indian carpet manufacturers and exporters and some Indian NGOs to develop a label certifying that the hand-knotted carpets to which it was attached were made without the use of child labor. To implement this idea, the Rugmark Foundation was organized to supervise the use of the label. It expected to begin exporting rugs carrying a unique identifying number in early 1995. As a major purchaser of Indian rugs, IKEA was invited to sign up with Rugmark as a way of dealing with the ongoing potential for child labor problems on products sourced from India.

On her return to Sweden, Barner again met frequently with the Swedish Save the Children's expert on child labor. "The people there had a very forward-looking view on the issue and taught us a lot," said Barner. "Above all, they emphasized the need to ensure you always do what is in the best interests of the child." This was the principle set at the heart of the U.N. Convention on the Rights of the Child (1989), a document with which Barner was now quite familiar. (See **Exhibit 5** for Article 32 from the U.N. Convention on the Rights of the Child.)

The more Barner learned, the more complex the situation became. As a business area manager with full profit-and-loss responsibility for carpets, she knew she had to protect not only her business but also the IKEA brand and image. Yet she viewed her responsibility as broader than this: She felt the company should do something that would make a difference in the lives of the children she had seen. It was a view that was not universally held within IKEA, where many were concerned that a very proactive stand could put the business at a significant cost disadvantage to its competitors.

A New Crisis   Then, in the spring of 1995, a year after IKEA began to address this issue, a well-known German documentary maker notified the company that a film he had made was about to be broadcast on German television showing children working at looms at Rangan Exports, one of IKEA's major suppliers. While refusing to let the company preview the video, the filmmaker produced still shots taken directly from the video. The producer then invited IKEA to send someone to take part in a live discussion during the airing of the program. Said Barner, "Compared to the Swedish program, which documented the use of child labor in Pakistan as a serious report about an important issue without targeting any single company, it was immediately clear that this German-produced program planned to take a confrontational and aggressive approach aimed directly at IKEA and one of its suppliers."

For Barner, the first question was whether to recommend that IKEA participate in the program or decline the invitation. Beyond the immediate public relations issue, she also had to decide how to

---

Exhibit 5   The U.N. Convention on the Rights of the Child: Article 32

1. States Parties recognize the right of the child to be protected from economic exploitation and from performing any work that is likely to be hazardous or to interfere with the child's education, or to be harmful to the child's health or physical, mental, spiritual, moral, or social development.
2. States Parties shall take legislative, administrative, social, and educational measures to ensure the implementation of the present article. To this end, and having regard to the relevant provisions of other international instruments, States Parties shall in particular:

   a.   Provide for a minimum age for admission to employment
   b.   Provide for appropriate regulation of hours and conditions of employment.
   c.   Provide for appropriate or other sanctions to ensure the effective enforcement of the present article.

Source: Excerpt from "Convention on the Rights of the Child," from the website of the Office of the United Nations High Commissioner for Human Rights, available at http://www.unhchr.ch/html/menu3/b/k2crc.htm, accessed October 2005.

deal with Rangan Exports' apparent violation of the contractual commitment it had made not to use child labor. And finally, this crisis raised the issue of whether the overall approach IKEA had been taking to the issue of child labor was appropriate. Should the company continue to try to deal with the issue through its own relationships with its suppliers? Should it step back and allow Rugmark to monitor the use of child labor on its behalf? Or should it recognize that the problem was too deeply embedded in the culture of these countries for it to have any real impact and simply withdraw?

Case 8-3   Killer Coke: The Campaign Against Coca-Cola[1]

David Wesley and Henry W. Lane

. . .the world of Coco-Cola, a world filled with lies, deception, immorality and widespread labour, human rights and environmental violations.

—Ray Rogers, Director, Campaign to Stop Killer Coke[2]

The people who are part of the [Killer Coke] campaign are trying to use the [Coca-Cola] brand to advance a political agenda that has nothing to do with the company.

—Pablo Largacha, Communications Manager for Colombia, The Coca-Cola Company[3]

David Wesley wrote this case under the supervision of Professor Henry W. Lane solely to provide material for class discussion. The authors do not intend to illustrate either effective or ineffective handling of a managerial situation. The authors may have disguised certain names and other identifying information to protect confidentiality.

Ivey Management Services prohibits any form of reproduction, storage or transmittal without its written permission. This material is not covered under authorization from any reproduction rights organization. To order copies or request permission to reproduce materials, contact Ivey Publishing, Ivey Management Services, c/o Richard Ivey School of Business, The University of Western Ontario, London, Ontario, Canada, N6A 3K7; phone (519) 661-3208, fax (519) 661-3882, e-mail cases@iveyouwo.ca.

When Douglas Daft, CEO of Coca-Cola, arrived at the Hotel du Pont in Delaware to address the company's annual shareholders meeting, he was greeted by a crowd of protesters gathered near the hotel entrance. Most were there to denounce Coca-Cola's alleged complicity in the murders of union leaders in Colombia. The issue had garnered considerable media attention, and Daft knew that shareholders were wondering how the company planned to deal with the issue. He now hoped to put their concerns to rest. "Some in organized labor have been working overtime in college campuses to keep allegations about Colombia alive through misinformation and a twisting of the facts," he began.

The charges linking our company to atrocities in Colombia are false and they are outrageous. Now what is happening in Colombia today is a tragedy. And during the past 40 years, 60,000 people have died as victims of terrorism and civil war there. We all know employees, colleagues, and friends, who have been victims of that violence, which we absolutely abhor.

But the Coca-Cola Company has nothing to do with it.

Our bottling partners have been good employers in Colombia for more than 70 years and have good relationships with a number of unions there. We contribute to an improved standard of living for Colombians, and that is why we continue to operate in that country.

Later, when Daft opened the floor to discussion, the first to the podium was Ray Rogers, a 60-year-old activist and director of the Campaign to Stop Killer Coke. "You lied about the situation in Colombia," he declared.

You said that at no time was any union leader ever harmed by paramilitary security forces at any of your plants. Yet Isidro Gil was assassinated—murdered—in one of your bottling plants in Colombia. The next day, those same paramilitary security forces went into the plant and rounded up the workers. Coca-Cola managers in the plant had prepared resignation forms. Those workers were told that if they did not resign by 4 p.m. that day, they too would be murdered like their union officer, Isidro Gil. They all resigned en masse and the wages in that plant went from $380 a month down to $130 a month.

As Rogers continued to cite cases of alleged abuses, Daft interrupted. "Mr. Rogers, could you please finish?"

"I'm not done. I will finish very shortly," replied Rogers. When his microphone was cut off, Rogers raised his voice.

Right now, there are five colleges and universities that have terminated Coca-Cola contracts over the Colombia issue. They have banned Coca-Cola products from all student-owned and operated facilities. Do stockholders know that? That was University College Dublin. Trinity College soon followed. In the United States, Carleton College, Lake Forest College and Bard College . . .

Suddenly Rogers was struck on the back by a security guard, followed by a number of others who forced him to the floor.

Appalled by what had happened, Daft pleaded with the security guards to "be gentle." He then turned to one of his executives and whispered, "We shouldn't have done that."

With Rogers ejected, the meeting was allowed to proceed. Civil rights activist Reverend Jesse Jackson rose to the podium and upbraided Daft for having Rogers silenced.

Mr. Daft and members of the board let me say at the outset that while many disagreed with the first person making a comment, the violent removal was beneath the dignity of this company, it was by the security forces an overreaction and if he had been hurt and if he is hurt, that would be another lawsuit. It was an excessive use of power.

One by one, activist shareholders rose to rebuke Daft, many focusing on the human rights situation in Colombia. When one challenged Daft to "have an objective investigation," Daft rose to the company's defense.

There have been objective evaluations and investigations. In every case, the company was cleared and any allegation was dismissed. The independent investigation has taken place.

The Republic of Colombia: A Brief History

Colombia was established as a colony of Spain in 1525, and remained under Spanish colonial rule until the early 19th century. The peace was broken in 1810 when several regions in the colony declared independence. The resulting civil war lasted 13 years, and ended with independence for most of South America. It also firmly established a culture of internal conflict.

While Spain no longer governed Colombia, the Catholic church continued to exert great influence in political matters. A civil war between liberals, who opposed the influence of the church, and conservatives, who supported it, began in 1840 and lasted until 1903. When the liberal government confiscated all church-owned lands in 1861, a wide-spread guerrilla war erupted.

Between 1863 and 1885, Colombia saw more than 50 armed insurrections and 42 separate constitutions. "The army and the police force were kept small and weak to exclude them from politics, and as a consequence, law enforcement, especially in rural areas of the country, was left in private hands."[4] The war reached its climax between 1899 and 1903, following a collapse in the economy and increasing disparity of wealth under the liberal administration. By 1903, more than 100,000 lives had been lost and Colombia was in ruins.

Growing worldwide demand for coffee, oil and bananas helped Colombia to recover from the war and post strong growth during the next two and a half decades. In the early 1930s, a liberal government confiscated dormant land from mainly conservative land owners. When the conservatives were returned to power in 1946, they quickly seized the opportunity to reclaim their land. Many desired to return to the "glories" of Spanish colonial rule and looked to Spanish president Francisco Franco "as the sole defender of Christian civilization."[5]

La Violencia   In rural areas of the country, liberal-backed guerrilla groups, which were the precursors for modern-day Marxist guerrillas, formed in order to violently defend land that conservative land owners were trying to reclaim. In 1948, they went on a rampage, burning churches in the colonial city of Santa Fe de Bogotá. This deeply offended the religious sentiments of many Colombians and created deep and long-lasting wounds. It also became the basis for the most violent period in Colombia's history, one that saw the loss of some 200,000 lives and became known as *La Violencia* (The Violence). "Toward the end of *La Violencia* a new generation

of young Colombians who had been socialized to think that violence was a normal way of life . . . increasingly took to banditry."[6] In a successful effort to reestablish order, the military seized control of the country in 1953.

The military government offered amnesty to guerrillas who surrendered their weapons. And most did. However, liberal guerrilla groups included a large number of communists who refused to surrender their arms, but instead retreated to isolated areas of the country where they continued to operate with impunity.

The Revolutionary Armed Forces of Colombia
Civilian rule was restored in 1958 after moderate conservatives and liberals, with the support of the military, agreed to unite under a coalition known as the National Front. Meanwhile, communists successfully established their own government in a remote region of the country, known as the "republic" of *Marquetalia*. The government ignored the growing influence of communists until 1964 when, under pressure by conservatives, the Colombian army razed the communist controlled "republic."

Following the attack, the guerrillas reorganized under the banner *Fuerzas Armadas Revolucionarias de Colombia* (FARC). While the group officially came into existence in 1964, it continued to be led by former liberal guerrillas, and therefore "was the continuation of the revolutionary movement that had begun in 1948."[7] As FARC continued to grow, it established itself throughout the country in semi-autonomous fronts.

FARC financed itself through kidnapping ransoms, extortion and protection of the drug trade. Fronts also overran small communities in order to

[4] H. F. Kline, Colombia: Democracy Under Assault, Harper Collins, 1995.
[5] Ibid.

[6] Ibid.
[7] J. P. Osterling, Democracy in Colombia: Clientelist Politics and Guerrilla Warfare, Transaction Publishers, 1989.
[8] Drug Control: U.S. Counternarcotics Efforts in Colombia Face Continuing Challenges, United States General Accounting Office, February 1998.

distribute propaganda and, more importantly, to pillage local banks. Businesses operating in rural areas, including agricultural, oil and mining interests, were required to pay vaccines (monthly payments) which "protected" them from attacks and kidnappings. An additional, albeit less lucrative, source of revenue was highway blockades where guerrillas stopped motorists and buses in order to confiscate jewelry and money.

Over time, fewer recruits joined the organization for ideological reasons, but rather as a means to escape poverty. "FARC's narcotics-related income for 1995 reportedly totaled $647 million."[8] And per capita income for Colombian guerrilla fighters was at least 40 times the national average.[9]

By 1998, FARC's ranks had swelled to approximately 15,000 guerrilla fighters, up from 7,500 in 1992, and effectively controlled about half the country. They were also "better armed, equipped, and trained than the Colombian armed forces."[10] Over a period of 10 years, the war had cost the lives of an estimated 35,000 civilians and reduced the country's GDP by four per cent.[11]

United Self-Defense Forces of Colombia   The United Self-Defense Forces of Colombia (AUC)[12] was formed in April 1997 in an effort to consolidate local and regional paramilitary groups in Colombia. Its mission was to protect local economic, social and political interests from leftist rebels. While FARC and other guerrilla groups were obvious targets, the AUC also targeted trade unions, human rights workers and others suspected of having leftist sympathies. The AUC's paramilitary fighters were funded primarily through the production and sale of illegal narcotics and from businesses that paid the AUC for "protection."

Trade unionists were frequently victims of paramilitary death squads. According to a U.S. State Department report on human rights in Colombia, 1,875 labor activists were killed between 1991 and 2002, and "labor leaders nationwide continued to be attacked by paramilitaries, guerrillas, and narcotics traffickers." Although the Colombian government "operated a protection program for threatened human rights workers, union leaders, journalists, mayors, and several other groups," AUC members acted with relative impunity. Accordingly, only five of the more than 300 labor-related murder cases investigated since 1986 resulted in a conviction.[13]

FARC was also implicated in the murder of unionists, albeit to a lesser extent. In 2002, leftist guerillas were linked to 19 murders of trade unionists, 17 attempted murders, 189 death threats, 26 kidnappings, and 8 disappearances.[14]

The human rights situation noticeably improved following the election of Álvaro Uribe Vélez in 2002. Under his administration, the government began to take a harder line against all armed groups in Colombia, including the AUC. With more than $3 billion in support from the United States under "Plan Colombia," Uribe significantly augmented military capacity. By 2004, homicides, kidnappings and terrorist attacks in Colombia decreased to their lowest levels in almost 20 years, resulting in unprecedented public support for the Colombian president.[15]

Coca-Cola Colombia

Coca-Cola Colombia was a wholly-owned subsidiary of the Coca-Cola Company (see **Exhibits 1** to **3**) with corporate offices in Bogotá. It was responsible for manufacturing and distributing Coke products to its Colombian bottlers. Major decisions concerning production, distribution and

---

[8]Drug Control: U.S. Counternarcotics Efforts in Colombia Face Continuing Challenges, United States General Accounting Office, February 1998.
[9]Colombia: Guerrilla Economics, The Economist, January 13, 1996.
[10]The Suicide of Colombia, Foreign Policy Research Institute, September 7, 1998.
[11]Las FARC lamentan expectativas exageradas, El Nuevo Herald, April 22, 1999.
[12]Autodefensas Unidas de Colombia.

[13]Colombia: Country Reports on Human Rights Practices, U.S. Department of State, Bureau of Democracy, Human Rights, and Labor, March 31, 2003.
[14]Ibid.
[15]Background Note: Colombia, U.S. Department of State, Bureau of Western Hemisphere Affairs, February 2005.

Exhibit 1   The Coca-Cola Company Financial and Operational Performance Highlights

The Coca-Cola Company and Subsidiaries

Year Ended December 31	2006	2005	2004	2003	2002
(In millions except per share data)					
SUMMARY OF OPERATIONS					
Net operating revenues	**$24,088**	$23,104	$21,742	$20,857	$19,394
Cost of goods sold	**8,164**	8,195	7,674	7,776	7,118
Gross profit	**15,924**	14,909	14,068	13,081	12,276
Selling, general and administrative expenses	**9,431**	8,739	7,890	7,287	6,818
Other operating charges	**185**	85	480	573	—
Operating income	**6,308**	6,085	5,698	5,221	5,458
Interest income	**193**	235	157	176	209
Interest expense	**220**	240	196	178	199
Equity income (loss)–net	**102**	680	621	406	384
Other income (loss)–net	**195**	(93)	(82)	(138)	(353)
Gain on issuances of stock by equity investees	—	23	24	8	—
Income before income taxes	**6,578**	6,690	6,222	5,495	5,499
Income taxes	**1,498**	1,818	1,375	1,148	1,523
Net income	**$5,080**	$4,872	$4,847	$4,347	$3,976
Per Share Data					
Cash dividends	**1.24**	1.12	1.00	0.88	0.80
Market price on December 31	**48.25**	40.31	41.64	50.75	43.84
Case Volume (millions)[1]					
Worldwide	**21,400**	20,600	19,800	19,400	18,700
North America	**5,778**	5,768	5,742	5,626	5,516
Africa	**1,284**	1,236	1,188	1,164	1,109
East, South Asia and Pacific Rim	**1,722**	1,854	N/A	N/A	N/A
European Union	**3,424**	3,296	N/A	N/A	N/A
Latin America	**5,564**	5,150	4,950	4,850	4,675
North Asia, Eurasia and Middle East	**3,628**	3,296	N/A	N/A	N/A

[1]Coca-Cola redefined its European and Asian sales regions in 2005; therefore comparative data is unavailable for these regions prior to 2005.
Source: www.thecoca-colacompany.com/investors/

marketing came from the company's U.S. headquarters, while Coca-Cola Colombia was responsible for ensuring that these directives were carried out by the company's bottlers and other contractors.

Bebidas y Alimentos de Urabá (Bebidas) was a small corporation owned by two Florida residents, Richard Kirby and his son, Richard Kielland. Kirby was responsible for overall company strategy, while Kielland, as manager of plant operations,

implemented company policy at the Colombian plants. The company operated one plant in Colombia, in Carepa, Urabá, a town of 42,075 inhabitants, located approximately 200 miles north of Medellín.

Coca-Cola beverages were also produced in 17 plants owned by Panamerican Beverages, a publicly traded corporation headquartered in Miami. In addition to its Colombian plants, Panamerican Beverages was the "anchor bottler" for Coca-Cola

Exhibit 2   Coca-Cola Timeline

Date	Event
1894	Coca-Cola is first produced in a candy store in Vicksburg, Mississippi.
1899	Exclusive bottling rights sold to three Chattanooga, Tennessee lawyers for one dollar.
1904	Coca-Cola becomes the most recognized brand in America.
1905	Cocaine is removed from the Coca-Cola formula.
1920–1939	First international plants were opened in France, Guatemala, Honduras, Mexico, Belgium, Italy and South Africa. By 1939, Coca-Cola had bottling operations in 44 countries.
1940	Coca-Cola Colombia is founded in Medellín. In its first year, Coca-Cola Colombia sells 67,761 cases of soda.
1945	"Coke" becomes a registered trademark of Coca-Cola.
June 1993	Coca-Cola acquires 30% of FEMSA Refrescos S.A de C.V., a Mexican producer of carbonated beverages.
1994–1996	Paramilitary death squads murder five Sinaltrainal union leaders at a Coca-Cola bottling plant in Carepa, Colombia.
February 1996	Coca-Cola FEMSA acquires 100% of Coca-Cola's bottling operations in Argentina.
July 20, 2001	The United Steelworkers and the International Labor Rights Fund bring suit against Coca-Cola and its Colombian bottlers on behalf of Sinaltrainal, a Colombian union.
March 31, 2003	Coca-Cola is dismissed as a defendant in Sinaltrainal v. Coca-Cola Co., United States District Court For The Southern District Of Florida
May 2003	Coca-Cola FEMSA acquires 100% of Panamerican Beverages, Inc. creating the second-largest Coca-Cola bottler in the world, accounting for almost 10% of Coca-Cola's global sales.
December 31, 2003	Coca-Cola ends the year with record net earnings of $4.3 billion on revenues of $21.0 billion.
April 13, 2003	Labor activist Ray Rogers begins "Killer Coke" campaign
2004	Coca-Cola launches cokefacts.org to promote its side of the Colombia controversy. The site receives only 800 visitors a month compared with killercoke.org's 25,000 visitors a month.
July 21, 2005	Interbrand, the world's leading international brand consultancy, ranks Coca-Cola first among the world's leading brands for the fifth consecutive year. It estimates the company's brand value at $67.5 billion.
December 8, 2005	New York University bans Coca-Cola products from its campus.
December 29, 2005	University of Michigan bans Coca-Cola products from its campus.
December 31, 2005	Coca-Cola ends the year with record net earnings of $4.9 billion on revenues of $23.1 billion.

in Brazil, Costa Rica, Guatemala, Mexico, Nicaragua and Venezuela. In 2003, Panamerican Beverages was purchased by Coca-Cola FEMSA, a subsidiary of Coca-Cola U.S.A.[16]

[16]Coca-Cola FEMSA was a joint venture between Mexican brewer Fomento Económico Mexicano, S.A. de C.V. (FEMSA) (46 per cent) and the Coca-Cola Company (40 per cent). The remaining shares were publicly held.

The Case against Coca-Cola and its Colombian Bottlers

Background   Although union members at several Coca-Cola bottling plants were targeted by paramilitaries, Coca-Cola's troubles centered on the events at one particular plant, the Bebidas plant in Carepa, Urabá. According to an Amnesty International

---

Exhibit 3   The Coca-Cola Company Corporate Responsibility Policy

---

Strategic Vision

The health of our business depends on the health of our consumers, their communities and the environment. The people of The Coca-Cola Company work together with our bottling partners, our business partners and members of the communities where we operate – and even our critics – to identify and address existing and emerging social and environmental issues, as well as potential solutions.

With our technical and marketing expertise, our reputation and network of influence, and our global production and distribution system, we have a tremendous opportunity to make a meaningful difference in the more than 200 countries we call home. We believe that the greater our presence, the greater our responsibility.

Corporate Responsibility is an integral part of our mission, values, and actions.[1]

UN Global Compact

In March 2006, The Coca-Cola Company became a signatory to the United Nations (UN) Global Compact, affirming our commitment to the advancement of its 10 universal principles in the areas of human rights, labor, the environment and anti-corruption. Several of our bottling partners are also signatories.

Our 2006 Corporate Responsibility Review is our first communication on progress for the UN Global Compact and provides a cross-referenced index of the UN Global Compact principles.

Human Rights

Principle 1: Businesses should support and respect the protection of international human rights within their sphere of influence; and

Principle 2: make sure that they are not complicit in human rights abuses.

Labor

Principle 3: Businesses should uphold the freedom of association and the effective recognition of the right to collective bargaining;

Principle 4: the elimination of all forms of forced and compulsory labor;

Principle 5: the effective abolition of child labor; and

Principle 6: the elimination of discrimination in respect of employment and occupation.

Environment

Principle 7: Businesses should support a precautionary approach to environmental challenges;

Principle 8: undertake initiatives to promote greater environmental responsibility; and

Principle 9: encourage the development and diffusion of environmentally friendly technologies.

Anti-Corruption

Principle 10: Businesses should work against corruption in all its forms, including extortion and bribery.

---

[1] The company's full Corporate Responsibility guidelines are discussed in its 2006 Corporate Responsibility Review (http://www.thecoca-colacompany.com/ourcompany/pdf/corporate_responsibility_review2006.pdf)

report, Urabá was one of the most violent regions in the country, a place where reprisal killings of civilians by communist guerillas and paramilitaries was common place.

In the mid-1990s, paramilitaries:

> launched major offensives from the northern municipalities of the Urabá region of Antioquia and pushed southwards rooting out and killing those they considered guerrilla collaborators or sympathizers. FARC guerrilla forces, operating in alliance with dissident groups, responded by carrying out a number of massacres of [civilians] they considered to be supporting army or paramilitary forces.
>
> Armed opposition groups have been responsible for forced displacement of communities who have fled their homes as a result of death threats or the deliberate and arbitrary killings of those accused of collaboration with the security or paramilitary forces. Many families have also fled their homes in order to escape forcible recruitment of their children by armed opposition groups.[17]

Torture Victims Protection Act Claim   In 2001, Sinaltrainal and representatives of several slain union leaders brought suit against Coca-Cola and Bebidas under the Alien Tort Claims Act (ATCA) and the Torture Victims Protection Act (TVPA) (see **Exhibit 4**).[18] The petition, filed by lawyers from the International Labor Rights Fund and the United Steel Workers of America, argued that Coca-Cola and Bebidas "contracted with or otherwise directed paramilitary security forces that utilized extreme violence and murdered, tortured, unlawfully detained or otherwise silenced trade union leaders."[19] The suit also named Panamerican Beverages as a defendant for its alleged complicity in the kidnappings and murders of several union members and their relatives at three Panamerican plants in northern Colombia.

The use of ATCA in such cases was not without precedent. According to Michael Ratner, vice-president of the Center for Constitutional Rights,

"courts in the United States pioneered the use of civil remedies to sue human rights violators."

> Litigation under the Alien Tort Claims Act and the Torture Victim Protection Act have resulted in billions of dollars in judgments, and have had an important impact on plaintiffs and human rights both in the United States and internationally. Such cases do not require official approval; they can be brought by individuals who have control over the lawsuits and thus are less subject to political vagaries.
>
> Civil remedies include damage awards for injuries and punitive damages meant to deter future abusive conduct as well as send a message to others that such conduct is unacceptable. In addition to any money that can be collected, these cases are important to the victims and their families. Plaintiffs are allowed to tell their stories to a court, can often confront their abusers, and create an official record of their persecutions. This in turn could lead to a criminal prosecution.[20]

The Murder of Isidro Segundo Gil   The plaintiffs sought compensation specifically for the murder of 27-year-old Isidro Segundo Gil, an employee of the Carepa plant, as well as other murdered union members at the Carepa plant and at three plants owned by Panamerican Beverages.[21]

In 1996, Bebidas hired Ariosto Milan Mosquera to manage the Carepa bottling plant. Mosquera allegedly began threatening to destroy the union. He allowed paramilitaries access to the plant and made a specific agreement with local paramilitary leaders to drive the union out of the Bebidas plant by using threats and violence, if necessary.

On September 27, 1996 Sinaltrainal submitted a letter to both Bebidas and Coca-Cola Colombia accusing Mosquera of working with the paramilitary to destroy the union, and urging Bebidas to protect trade unionists from the paramilitaries who were threatening employees.

---

[17]Return to Hope, Forcibly displaced communities of Urabá and Medio Atrato region, Amnesty International Report 23/023/2000, June 1, 2000.

[18]The Torture Victims Protection Act was enacted in 1992 and added as a provision under the Alien Tort Claims Act.

[19]Coca-Cola Accused, The New York Times, July 29, 2001.

[20]Michael Ratner, "Civil Remedies for Gross Human Rights Violations," PBS.org, February 2, 1999 (www.pbs.org/wnet/justice/law_background_torture.html).

[21]Five of the eight murder cases cited by Coca-Cola opponents took place between 1994 and 1996 at the Carepa plant owned and operated by Bebidas & Alimentos de Urabá.

Exhibit 4 The Alien Tort Claims Act (28 USCS § 1350)

§1350. Alien's action for tort

The district courts shall have original jurisdiction of any civil action by an alien for a tort only, committed in violation of the law of nations or a treaty of the United States.

History:

(June 25, 1948, ch 646, § 1, 62 Stat. 934.)

History; Ancillary Laws and Directives

Prior law and revision:
 Based on title 28, U.S.C., 1940 ed., § 41(17) (Mar. 3, 1911, ch. 231, § 24, P 17, 36 Stat. 1093).
 Words "civil action" were substituted for "suits," in view of Rule 2 of the Federal Rules of Civil Procedure.
 Changes in phraseology were made.

Other provisions:
 Torture Victim Protection Act of 1991. Act March 12, 1992, P.L. 102–256, 106 Stat. 73, provides:

"Section 1. Short title
"This Act may be cited as the 'Torture Victim Protection Act of 1991'.

"Sec. 2. Establishment of civil action
"(a) Liability. An individual who, under actual or apparent authority, or color of law, of any foreign nation—
 "(1) subjects an individual to torture shall, in a civil action, be liable for damages to that individual; or
 "(2) subjects an individual to extrajudicial killing shall, in a civil action, be liable for damages to the individual's legal representative, or to any person who may be a claimant in an action for wrongful death.
"(b) Exhaustion of remedies. A court shall decline to hear a claim under this section if the claimant has not exhausted adequate and available remedies in the place in which the conduct giving rise to the claim occurred.
"(c) Statute of limitations. No action shall be maintained under this section unless it is commenced within 10 years after the cause of action arose.

"Sec. 3. Definitions
"(a) Extrajudicial killing. For the purposes of this Act, the term 'extrajudicial killing' means a deliberated killing not authorized by a previous judgment pronounced by a regularly constituted court affording all the judicial guarantees which are recognized as indispensable by civilized peoples. Such term, however, does not include any such killing that, under international law, is lawfully carried out under the authority of a foreign nation.
"(b) Torture. For the purposes of this Act—
 "(1) the term 'torture' means any act, directed against an individual in the offender's custody or physical control, by which severe pain or suffering (other than pain or suffering arising only from or inherent in, or incidental to, lawful sanctions), whether physical or mental, is intentionally inflicted on that individual for such purposes as obtaining from that individual or a third person information or a confession, punishing that individual for an act that individual or a third person has committed or is suspected of having committed, intimidating or coercing that individual or a third person, or for any reason based on discrimination of any kind; and
 "(2) mental pain or suffering refers to prolonged mental harm caused by or resulting from—
"(A) the intentional infliction or threatened infliction of severe physical pain or suffering;
"(B) the administration or application, or threatened administration or application, of mind altering substances or other procedures calculated to disrupt profoundly the senses or the personality;
"(C) the threat of imminent death; or
"(D) the threat that another individual will imminently be subjected to death, severe physical pain or suffering, or the administration or application of mind altering substances or other procedures calculated to disrupt profoundly the senses or personality."

On the morning of December 5, 1996, two paramilitaries approached Gil as he arrived at work. They said they needed to enter the Bebidas plant. When Gil opened the door, the paramilitaries shot and killed him. Witnesses claimed the murderers were the same paramilitaries who had met with Mosquera at the plant. Two days later, paramilitaries arrived at the Bebidas plant, where they assembled the employees and told them that unless they resigned from the union, they would face the same fate as Gil. The employees then entered Mosquera's office and signed resignation forms that he had prepared. Many union members permanently fled Carepa after the forced resignations and continued to live in hiding (For a more detailed summary of the Carepa events, see Exhibit 5).[22]

Exhibit 5   Court Filing (July 20, 2001) The Events at Bebidas Y Alimentos in Carepa (Abridged)

In April of 1994, paramilitary forces murdered Jose Eleazar Manco David and Luis Enrique Gomez Granado, both of whom were workers at Bebidas y Alimentos and members of Sinaltrainal. The paramilitary forces in Carepa then began to intimidate other Sinaltrainal members as well as the local leadership of Sinaltrainal, telling them, upon threat of physical harm, to resign from the union or to flee Carepa altogether. The management of Bebidas y Alimentos permitted these paramilitary forces to appear within the plant to deliver this message to Union members and leaders. A number of Union members began leaving town as a result. And, in April of 1995, following more death threats, every member of the executive board of the Sinaltrainal local representing the Bebidas y Alimentos workers fled Carepa in fear for their lives.

In June of 1995, the Sinaltrainal local union elected a new executive board to replace the one that had fled. Isidro Gil was elected as a member of this new board as was an individual named Dorlahome Tuborquia. Shortly thereafter, in July of 1995, Bebidas y Alimentos began to hire members of the paramilitaries who had threatened the first Union executive board into fleeing. These members of the paramilitaries were hired both into the sales and production departments.

In September of 1995, Ariosto Milan Mosquera took over as the manager of the Bebidas y Alimentos plant in Carepa. Mosquera proceeded to discharge Dorlahome Tuborquia. Sinaltrainal challenged this discharge through the legal process, and a judge, finding the discharge to be unlawful, ordered Bebidas y Alimentos to rehire Tuborquia. He returned to work at Bebidas y Alimentos in December of 1995. Shortly after the return of Tuborquia, Mosquera announced that he had given an order to the paramilitaries to carry out the task of destroying the union. In keeping with these threats of Mosquera, the paramilitaries began to renew threats against Sinaltrainal members, including Dorlahome Tuborquia. Specifically, the paramilitaries threatened to kill Tuborquia. In response to these threats, Tuborquia fled Carepa and went into hiding. The paramilitaries then seized Tuboquia's home to use for their operations.

Throughout 1996, Sinaltrainal members witnessed Mosquera socializing with members of the paramilitary forces and providing the paramilitaries with Coke products for their parties. Meanwhile, Bebidas y Alimentos and Sinaltrainal began negotiating a new labor agreement. These negotiations included Sinaltrainal's proposals for increased security for threatened trade unionists and a cessation of Mosquera's threats against the union as well as his collusion with the paramilitaries. Defendant Richard Kirby Keilland personally participated in these negotiations on behalf of Bebidas y Alimentos and he flatly refused the union's requests.

In response, Sinaltrainal began a national campaign in August of 1996 to call upon Bebidas y Alimentos, as well as Panamco Colombia and Coca-Cola Colombia, to protect the Sinaltrainal leadership and members in Carepa from

(continued)

---

[22]The account of Gil's murder is summarized from: Sinaltrainal v. Coca-Cola Co., United States District Court For The Southern District Of Florida , 256 F. Supp. 2d 1345; 2003 U.S. Dist. LEXIS 7145; 16 Fla. L. Weekly Fed. D 382, March 28, 2003, Decided, March 31, 2003.

Exhibit 5   Court Filing (July 20, 2001) The Events at Bebidas Y Alimentos
in Carepa (Abridged)   (continued)

what it feared was the imminent threat of attack by the paramilitaries. By letter dated September 27, 1996, national leaders of Sinaltrainal accused Mosquera of working with the paramilitaries to destroy the union, and they urged that Bebidas y Alimentos ensure the security of the workers in the Carepa plant in the face of the paramilitary threats. Copies of this letter were contemporaneously sent to Coca-Cola Colombia as well as Panamco Colombia. In response to this letter, Mosquera told the union to retract its accusations.

On December 5, 1996, at 9:00 in the morning, two paramilitaries approached Isidro Gil, who was then involved in negotiations on behalf of the union with Bebidas y Alimentos, as he stood in the entrance of the Bebidas y Alimentos plant. The paramilitaries stated that they needed to go into the plant to talk to someone inside. Isidro Gil proceeded to open the door and the two paramilitaries then shot him to death inside the plant. That same night, these same paramilitaries went to the local union hall of Sinaltrainal and started a fire.

On December 6, 1996, paramilitaries approached several more members of the local Sinaltrainal executive board. These paramilitaries told the union board members that they killed Isidro Gil and burned the union office and that they would kill the remaining board members if they did not leave town. The paramilitaries also explained that they would have a meeting with the workers at the Bebidas y Alimentos plant the next day to tell them that they would have to resign from the union or face being killed.

On December 7, 1996 at 8:00 a.m., the paramilitaries appeared at the Bebidas y Alimentos plant as threatened. They assembled the workers and told them that Bebidas y Alimentos did not want the union at the plant. The paramilitaries explained that the workers had the option of either resigning from the union or leaving Carepa altogether lest they be killed. The paramilitaries then proceeded to direct the workers into the manager's office to sign resignation forms which were prepared by Defendant Bebidas y Alimentos itself. As a result of the threats of the paramilitaries, workers resigned en masse from Sinaltrainal.

In fear for their life, fourteen Sinaltrainal members, including the remainder of the local Sinaltrainal executive board, fled Carepa after this meeting on December 7, 1996. As a result of the flight of these individuals and the resignation of the other workers from the union, the local Sinaltrainal union in Carepa was destroyed. This union has never returned to Carepa. The Sinaltrainal members who fled Carepa on December 7, 1996 continue to fear for their lives and remain in hiding, moving frequently from house to house. Plaintiff Sinaltrainal, as it does for all such displaced members, helps provide support to these individuals.

After the murder of Isidro Gil, the paramilitaries presented themselves at the Bebidas y Alimentos plant with the medical cards of workers which they had taken from the local union office before they burned it. Bebidas y Alimentos paid the paramilitaries remuneration in the amount owed under these cards. The paramilitaries repaired the union office which they had burned and took it over for the purpose of storing their weapons. On December 26, 1996, the paramilitaries killed another Bebidas y Alimentos worker, José Herrerra. The same paramilitaries later killed the wife of Isidro Gil in 2000, leaving their two children without parents.

In 1997, Peggy Ann Keilland, a close relative of Defendants Richard I. Kirby and Richard Kirby Keilland, took over as the Manager of the Bebidas y Alimentos plant in Carepa. Very shortly after taking over, Ms. Keilland worked with the Chief of the Colombian military in the zone to ensure that the paramilitaries were kept out of the plant. Also in 1997, Defendants Richard I. Kirby and Richard Kirby Keilland asked Defendant Coke if they could sell the Bebidas y Alimentos business along with the Carepa plant. Defendant Coke denied them this request and these Defendants still maintain ownership of the Carepa operations, under the direction and control of Defendants Coke and Coke Colombia.

Coca-Cola's initial response was to deny any wrongdoing. "We adhere to the highest standards of ethical conduct and business practices and we require all of our companies, operating units and suppliers to abide by the laws and regulations in the countries that they do business," a company spokesperson explained.[23]

For nearly two years, both sides presented evidence to back up their cases. In 2003, the court agreed that Mosquera colluded with paramilitaries in an effort to break the union. It further argued,

> Bebidas have not produced any evidence to refute the allegation that Bebidas had ties to Mosquera's decision to hire the paramilitary to impede Sinaltrainal's union activity at Bebidas.[24]

However, while the Bottler's Agreement between Coca-Cola and Bebidas granted Coca-Cola U.S.A. the right to supervise and control the quality, distribution and marketing of its products, including the right to terminate or suspend a bottler's operations for noncompliance with its terms and conditions, it did not give Coca-Cola direct control over plant operations. As such, the court determined that Coca-Cola U.S.A. and Coca-Cola Colombia were not agents that conspired or acted jointly with the paramilitary through Bebidas. As such, the court dismissed Coca-Cola as a defendant because it lacked jurisdiction over Coca-Cola under ATCA.[25]

Bebidas and Panamerican Beverages, on the other hand, could be held liable as "an individual who, under color of law of any foreign nation, subjects another person to torture or extrajudicial killing," thereby overruling the company's defense that a private corporation is not an "individual" in the legal sense, and should not be held liable for acts of torture and killing in foreign countries.

---

[23]"Union Says Coca-Cola in Colombia Uses Thugs," The New York Times, July 26, 2001.
[24]Sinaltrainal v. Coca-Cola Co., United States District Court For The Southern District Of Florida, 256 F. Supp. 2d 1345; 2003 U.S. Dist. LEXIS 7145; 16 Fla. L. Weekly Fed. D 382, March 28, 2003, Decided, March 31, 2003.
[25]After Coca-Cola acquired a stake in Panamerican Beverages in 2003, the plaintiffs moved to have Coca-Cola reinstated as a defendant. The court agreed to consider the motion, but as of 2005 had not made a ruling.

The Anti-Globalization Movement

The incidents at Coca-Cola's bottling plants in Colombia coincided with the rise of the anti-globalization movement, which targeted large multinational corporations as symbols of "the damaging effects of globalization." The movement's goals included labor rights, environmental protection, preservation of indigenous peoples and cultures, food safety and social welfare. It found wide support on college campuses in North America and Europe, as well as from environmental organizations such as Greenpeace. Much of the criticism of globalization focused on alleged exploitation of workers in less-developed countries, such as the use of sweatshops by Nike, the Gap and others.

The Case of Nike: A model for change   Anti-globalization protesters viewed Nike, in particular, as a model for social change brought about through public pressure. In the 1990s, Nike came under scrutiny for alleged human rights violations by its outsourcing contractors in Asia. The company denied any wrongdoing and, to prove its case, hired Goodworks International, an Atlanta-based non-profit organization, to audit its Asian contractors. In early 1997, Goodworks director and former civil rights leader, Andrew Young, led the investigation. After a two-week tour of China, Vietnam and Indonesia, Young returned to the United States to report that Nike was "doing a good job."

> We found Nike to be in the forefront of a global economy. Factories we visited that produce Nike goods were clean, organized, adequately ventilated and well lit.[26]

Young further cited Ernst & Young audits of particular plants.

> I did not find in the audit reports or in my own conversations with workers at these factories or in our other research a pattern of these factories violating national laws, local laws or the [Nike] Code of Conduct as relates to age or working conditions.[27]

---

[26]Andrew Young, and H. Jordan, The Nike Code of Conduct Report, Good Works International, June 27, 1997.
[27]Ibid.

Following Young's report, a widely criticized New York Times article reported "no evidence of widespread or systematic mistreatment of workers."[28] Medea Benjamin of San Francisco-based CorpWatch, who had expected Young to "maintain his credibility as a defender of the poor," was sorely disappointed.

A few months later, a disgruntled Nike employee handed CorpWatch a copy of one of the Ernst & Young audits. In contrast to Young's report, it cited gross human rights violations at company plants in Vietnam. Feeling that it had been misled, the New York Times lambasted Nike. A front page headline read, "Nike Shoe Plant in Vietnam is Called Unsafe for Workers." It continued,

> In an inspection report that was prepared in January for the company's internal use only, Ernst & Young wrote that workers at the factory near Ho Chi Minh City were exposed to carcinogens that exceeded local legal standards by 177 times in parts of the plant and that 77 percent of the employees suffered from respiratory problems. The report also said that employees at the site, which is owned and operated by a Korean subcontractor, were forced to work 65 hours a week, far more than Vietnamese law allows, for $10 a week.[29]

Within months a proliferation of newspaper articles reported similar abuses at factories throughout Asia and Latin America. Almost overnight, anti-globalization organizers mobilized a worldwide movement against Nike that eventually forced the company to rethink its business practices.

Nike created a department to monitor suppliers in less-developed countries. Todd McKean, the company's new Director of Corporate Responsibility Compliance recognized that some Nike factories violated worker rights and that the company had to improve the way it monitored working conditions. "How much do we really know about issues in all of these factories?" he asked.

> Not enough. Every time we look closer, we find another thing wrong. Too much overtime. Wage errors.

Too much heat. Involuntary pregnancy testing. An abusive supervisor. Every time we peel another layer off the onion we find another complex set of issues that our compliance and production people work with factory management to try to resolve.[30]

The company also hired independent agencies, such as the Fair Labor Association, to regularly monitor its 700 contract factories. When audits uncovered abusive practices, Nike required its contractors to implement changes or risk losing their contracts. For CorpWatch, it was a major victory.

> Student organizers demanding that universities doing business with Nike hold the company to higher standards kept Nike's labor practices in the spotlight. Meanwhile, faced with the increasing clout of activist groups, falling stock prices and weak sales, Nike announced major concessions to its critics in May, 1998.[31]

While some continued to criticize Nike's labor practices, most anti-globalization activists focused their efforts elsewhere.

Killer Coke Campaign

Shortly after the U.S. court dismissed Coca-Cola as a defendant in 2003, Ray Rogers mounted the Killer Coke campaign. The organization's website, killercoke.org (see **Exhibit 6**), dubbed Coca-Cola "the New Nike," and urged students to pressure colleges to cancel their Coca-Cola contracts. "Like Nike, Coke will only remedy its practices with significant pressure and the fear of a tarnished image," exclaimed a web article.[32]

Rogers, a long-time activist for labor rights, began his career as a labor organizer for the Amalgamated Clothing Workers of America. In 1978, the New York Times recognized Rogers as the moving force behind a successful campaign against J. P. Stevens, a large textile company, which forced the resignation the chairman of Stevens and the chairman of

[28]"Nike's Asian Factories Pass Young's Muster," The New York Times, June 25, 1997.
[29]"Nike Shoe Plant in Vietnam Is Called Unsafe for Workers," The New York Times, November 8, 1997.

[30]Factory Monitoring Practices, Labor Practices, Nike, 2001.
[31]CorpWatch Takes on Nike, Sweatshops, (www.corpwatch.org) February 17, 2006.
[32]Tremendous Victories on Campus, Campaign to Stop Killer Coke Update, May 20, 2005 (www.killercoke.org/nl0520.htm) February 17, 2006.

Exhibit 6   Killercoke.org Home Page

WHO WE ARE   COKE'S CRIMES   NEWS   SUPPORT US   RESOLUTIONS   NEWSLETTERS
PROTEST PICS   CONTACT US   STUDENT ACTIVISM   REPORTS   UNION ACTIVISM   LINKS

MMMURDER...
IT'S THE REAL THING

Campaign to Stop

We are seeking your help to stop a gruesome cycle of murders,
kidnappings and torture of union leaders and organizers involved
in daily life-and-death struggles at Coca-Cola bottling plants in
Colombia, South America.

KillerCola
TARGET:
COLOMBIAN LABOR
www.killercoke.org

**Please fill out the following information to receive our action alerts and our newsletter!
If you tell us where you live and skills you have, this helps us with organizing.**

E-mail address:

Name/City/State/Country:

Volunteer Interests, Skills, Languages:

Submit

Please help Support the Campaign to Stop Killer Coke pdf — html

CONTRIBUTIONS
secure through Paypal

the New York Life Insurance Co. from each other's board of directors. "The important thing isn't just organizing people into unions," explained Rogers. "It's disorganizing the power structure."[33]

Rogers' early success allowed him to create Corporate Campaign, Inc., a public relations and labor strategy firm. In the 1980s, Corporate Campaign confronted Consolidated Edison Utilities, Hormel Foods, American Airlines, Bank of Boston, Campbell Soup, and International Paper, often winning important victories for labor unions. Tactics included walkouts, consumer boycotts, demonstrations and letter-writing campaigns. "I'd much rather see rich businessmen fight it out in the boardroom," Rogers asserted. "You can't embarrass them. You have to make them deal with real economic or political pressure." [34]

Rogers' strategy often pitted one company against another. For example, he encouraged trade unions to put pressure on financial institutions that managed union funds to withdraw support from companies opposed to union organizing activities. Other times he would target the largest company in an industry hoping that competitors would use it to their advantage.

> You have to create a situation where you're beating on one institution. They're taking heavy losses, and all the other institutions are standing behind them saying, "Whatever you do, don't set a precedent, don't give in." But finally the institution you're putting pressure on is going to say, "Hey, wait a minute. We're losing a lot of business. And where is that business going? It's going to you, our competitors, and to your banks. You're benefiting at our expense. So if you don't want to set a precedent, then don't you set it, but we're getting out of this thing."[35]

Killer Coke was a continuation of Roger's tradition of activism, and it followed many of the same grassroots tactics. Campaign flyers distributed to university students as part of the "Coke Organizing Manual" demanded that Coca-Cola,

- Denounce the violence that is occurring in the name of Coca-Cola in Colombia.
- Respect the fundamental rights to free association and to organize trade unions, as reflected in Colombian law, Article 22 of the International Covenant on Civil & Political Rights, as well as Conventions 87 & 88 of the International Labor Organization.
- Announce publicly in Colombia its intention to participate in an investigation of the violence at its bottling plants.
- Reinforce Coca-Cola's public stance against violence by directing all bottling plants in Colombia to stop dealing with any armed groups that are participating in violence against trade unionists.
- Establish a complaint and reporting process which will allow union members to report violations occurring in Coca-Cola bottling plants to an official of the company who will then investigate and take swift remedial action against these violations.
- Provide compensation to the known victims of violence at Coca-Cola bottling plants.[36]

Serving as a conduit of information, the website sought to foment support on college campuses. Pamphlets, banner templates, web icons, news links, and other resources were provided to help students put pressure on university administrators to suspend contracts with the Coca-Cola Company.

Coke Facts

When the Killer Coke campaign brought Coca-Cola increased notoriety among young consumers, some business analysts began to criticize the company's decision not to investigate the murders in Colombia.[37] Coca-Cola responded by sending high level executives to college campuses to explain its side of the story, and by creating a company-owned website (cokefacts.org) to counter the Killer Coke website (see **Exhibit 7**).[38] Finally, it hired Cal-Safety

---

[33]"Rogers' Tough, Unorthodox Tactics Prevail in Stevens Organizing Fight," The Wall Street Journal, October 21, 2006.

[34]"Labor's Boardroom," Time, June 20, 1988.

[35]"An Interview with Ray Rogers," Working Papers Magazine, January/February 1982.

[36]Coke Organizing Manual, July 8, 2002.

[37]"The Real Story: How did Coca-Cola's management go from first-rate to farcical in six short years?" Fortune, May 31, 2004.

[38]Other company URLs, such as killercoke.com and stopkillercoke.org, redirected visitors to the cokefacts.org site.

Exhibit 7   Cokefacts.org Home Page

CokeFacts.org
Coca-Cola

The Truth About The Coca-Cola Company Around the Globe

English / Español

| THE FACTS | CORPORATE CITIZENSHIP | BACKGROUND | NEWS |

Colombia · India · Around the World

● BREAKING NEWS : ..SE AND INFLAMMATORY" ALLEGATIONS MADE BY TEAMSTERS. Click here to read more...

Colombia: Community Building

Working with Colombians to Create a Stronger Nation

The Coca-Cola Company has been operating in Colombia for more than 70 years. Our bottling partners distribute products to about a half million retailers, including everyone from supermarkets like the internationally owned Carrefour and the Colombian-owned Alkosto supermarkets, as well as the small, family-run bodegas that still control about 40 percent of the retail market in Colombia. As a community partner, our bottlers contribute significant resources – through donations and volunteer hours – to address such issues as hunger relief, education and the environment.

Over the past seven decades, Colombia has experienced internal conflict, which affects trade union activists and other civilians from all walks of life. Despite the volatile environment, The Coca-Cola Company and our bottling partners have maintained operations and worked to provide safe, stable economic opportunities for the people of Colombia.

Read More >>

Colombia: Rebuilding Shattered Lives – One Child at a Time

Reaching Across Continents to Help the Youngest Victims of War

No society can be made whole after decades of strife if the needs of its children are not addressed first. That's why The Coca-Cola Company is proud to be a founding sponsor of Colombianitos, the brainchild of a group of Colombian professionals living in Atlanta, Georgia, striving to rescue a generation of children whose lives have been shattered by Colombia's ongoing conflict. The plight of children in Colombia is acute. More than 6.5 million live in abject poverty, and children represent nearly a third of the victims of Colombia's countless land mines.

But Colombianitos is making a difference. Its land mine program provides prosthetic devices and the physical – and psychological – support required to master them. Additionally, scores of children are touched by other Colombianitos programs, which are helping turn back the tide on the drugs, violence and poverty that are robbing young Colombians of their childhoods. It is of course not possible to erase the past. But by matching resources with a passion for change, it is possible to rewrite the future – one child at a time.

FAST FACTS

Coca-Cola produces nearly 400 brands in more than 200 countries.

❖ LEARN MORE

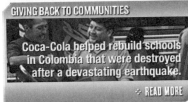

GIVING BACK TO COMMUNITIES

Coca-Cola helped rebuild schools in Colombia that were destroyed after a devastating earthquake.

❖ READ MORE

SPREAD THE WORD

Enter friend's email address here.

❖ SEND

Compliance Corporation to audit its Colombian bottling plants.[39]

In an article on cokefacts.org, Ed Potter, director of Global Labor Relations for Coca-Cola, criticized the anti-Coke campaign. "I would stand our Company's labor relations practices alongside any other company on the planet," he wrote.

> These unjustified attacks do a disservice to the men and women of Coca-Cola; they mislead the public and impede progress for workers' rights worldwide. The Coca-Cola system is one of the most highly unionized multinational corporations in Colombia and throughout the world. Last year, the Company signed a joint statement with the IUF, the international organization for food and beverage unions, confirming that Coca-Cola workers are "allowed to exercise rights to union membership and collective bargaining without pressure or interference."
>
> Two different judicial inquiries in Colombia have found no evidence to support allegations that bottler management there conspired to intimidate or threaten trade unionists. An additional independent assessment conducted by Cal-Safety Compliance Corporation [see Exhibit 8], an international social compliance auditor certified by the Fair Labor Association and Social Accountability 8000, confirmed that workers in Coca-Cola plants in Colombia enjoy freedom of association, collective bargaining rights and an atmosphere free of anti-union intimidation.[40]

According to Pablo Largacha, Communications Manager for Colombia, the problem was one of perception. Foreigners simply didn't understand the political reality that is Colombia. "In general," he explained, "Colombians have a better sense of what is happening."

> We have a better understanding of the political situation and the history of armed conflict. The vast majority believe that these are unfounded accusations. Last year, in

2005, Coca-Cola was ranked in Portafolio magazine as the company with the third best reputation in Colombia, with the best marketing, and as one of the best places to work. Therefore, given the better understanding of the situation, that Coca-Cola is an economic engine driving the advancement of this country, people here have a radically different opinion.[41]

An International Cause CéLèbre

While the company attempted to defend its position, the Killer Coke campaign continued to gain momentum. On December 31, 2005, the University of Michigan joined Rutgers, NYU, and several other U.S. colleges in banning all Coke products from its campus.[42]

The university's board of directors had earlier rejected Coca-Cola's audit of its Colombian bottlers through Cal-Safety Compliance Corporation, calling it "problematic."[43] As a for-profit corporation hired by Coca-Cola to undertake the audit, Cal-Safety did not meet the university's definition of independent. The university essentially agreed with the United Students against Sweatshops, a U.S.-based network of college students working to end sweatshops. It noted Cal-Safety's documented history of giving favorable reports to factories that were later discovered to have been involved in gross human rights violations.[44] The fact that factory audits typically took three hours and involved interviewing employees in offices provided by plant managers was also deemed unacceptable.

Taking its cue from the United Students against Sweatshops, the University of Michigan demanded,

- Unannounced factory visits to deny management the opportunity to hide abuses.

---

[39]Cal Safety Compliance Corporation, a subsidiary of Specialized Technology Resources, Inc., was part of a worldwide organization "dedicated to ensuring the integrity of its clients' products and technologies." Services included compliance, inspection, and quality assurance testing. Specialized Technology Resources Inc. History & Highlights (www.struk.co.uk/comphistory.htm) February 23, 2006.
[40]The Coca-Cola Company Addresses "False And Inflammatory" Allegations Made By Teamsters, Cokefacts.org, February 7, 2006.

[41]Translated from an interview by El Tiempo. Diez universidades de Estados Unidos y Europa vetaron el consumo de Coca-Cola por presuntos nexos con 'paras', El Tiempo (Colombia), January 4, 2006.
[42]"In the fiscal year 2005, the University of Michigan had 13 contracts for selling Coca-Cola products, totaling $1.4 million." Products sold by Coca-Cola included Sprite, Dasani water, Minute Maid juice and PowerAde. U. of Michigan Becomes 10th College to Join Boycott of Coke, The New York Times, December 31, 2005.
[43]"University of Michigan seeks probe of Coke's Colombia operations," Atlanta Journal-Constitution, June 17, 2005.
[44]United Students Against Sweatshops Statement, April 15, 2005 (www.killercoke.org/usascal.htm).

Exhibit 8   Cal-Safety Workplace Assessment Colombia (Overview)[1]

Perhaps most significant about the CSCC auditors' Colombia findings was what they did *not* find based on private interviews with employees.

> It should be noted that in the assessment of our Colombian bottling partners' plants, not one worker was afraid to speak to the CSCC auditors; none asked for a union leader to be present during the interview; and no one showed any sign of concern about responding to very direct questions related to management labor relations during the interview process.

Workers were not afraid to speak to outside auditors.

Employees did not ask to be excluded from interviews or for union representation during the interview process.

Auditors found no cases of improper disciplinary action against workers by plant supervisors and managers.

There were no threats by management discovered nor attempts to attack or intimidate a worker for bein affiliated with a union, or for being a union organizer or for being a union official. Nonunion workers did not indicate that they were pressured to remain non-union and they were not pressured to join a union.

Security guards were not being used to harass, intimidate or threaten workers.

Auditors *did* find union officials of the plant able to operate in these facilities "free from obstruction and discrimination."

CSCC was told of demonstrations by some our bottler's workers, all peaceful, all without reprisals.

Several of these demonstrations even involved employees showing their support for workers laid off at other plants within the Coc-Cola system. Both union and non-union workers felt free to exercise their rights of dissent and unionized workers referenced a number of examples when they freely used the broad range of tools available to them under freedom of association and collective bargaining.

The auditors recorded several complaints about management not adhering to the terms of their collective bargaining agreements. The auditors examined each complaint, and in each instance they found documents indicating that plant managers followed proper procedures in dealing with disagreements with the union over contract terms, without intimidation or harassment on either side; thereby indicating compliance with the terms of collective bargaining agreements and adherence to proper procedures.

In addition, CSCC looked at the entirety of the workplace experience for workers at six facilities, five of which are owned by Panamco Colombia, S.A., a subsidiary of Coca-Cola FEMSA, S.A. de CV., and the sixth by the family-owned company Bebidas & Alimentos de Uraba. Unfortunately, at a few of the plants, shortcomings were found that cannot be ignored. Areas that need attention and improvement have been highlighted in this report and a blueprint for improving plant conditions is provided. Our bottling partners have committed to addressing these findings immediately.

We will work diligently with our bottling partners as they take action to ensure compliance with all laws and regulations that apply to workplace practices and conditions.

[1]Workplace Assessments in Colombia, Conducted by Cal Safety Compliance Corporation for The Coca-Cola Company 2005.

- More extensive interviews of employees in off-site locations. "U.S. Department of Labor investigations take roughly 20 hours to complete," it noted. "Worker Rights Consortium investigations often take hundreds of person hours over a period of months."
- Audits conducted by non-profit organizations with "experience or expertise investigating violations of associational rights overseas."[45]

In its coverage of the Michigan decision, the Financial Times noted that "Coke's public relations offensive [had] so far failed to slow the [Killer Coke] campaign's momentum." Furthermore,

> The value of the Coke brand has been edging down in recent years, following a series of blows to its reputation. Over recent years, the deaths [in Colombia] have become an international cause célèbre for labour rights groups and student activists, who accuse Coke of turning a blind eye to the murders. Anti-Coke campaigns have spread across more than 100 university campuses throughout the U.S., Canada and Europe, including the U.K., where activists are pushing for a nationwide student boycott.[46]

[45]Ibid.

[46]"Coke struggles to defend positive reputation," The Financial Times, January 6, 2006.

Case 8-4   Genzyme's CSR Dilemma: How to Play its HAND

Christopher A. Bartlett, Tarun Khanna, and Prithwiraj Choudhury

On a cold but sunny day in January 2009, as sunlight reflected through the adjustable mirror panels of Genzyme's landmark 'Green' headquarters, Jim Geraghty was reflecting on discussions in a just concluded phone call. Geraghty, Senior Vice President at Genzyme had been instrumental in creating the Humanitarian Assistance for Neglected Diseases (HAND) program. Launched in April 2006, HAND was a cornerstone of Genzyme's corporate social responsibility (CSR) initiatives and its steering committee had just completed a conference call meeting to decide its future priorities.

Two special invitees on the call—Sandeep Sahney, Managing Director of Genzyme India and Rogerio Vivaldi, Senior Vice President and head of the Latin American operations—had been asked to provide information to help the committee decide which HAND initiative to support going forward. Sahney was championing the malaria research project with the Indian partner ICGEB, while Vivaldi was making a strong case for extending the Brazilian research program on Chagas disease with local partner Fiocruz. There were other options on the

Professors Christopher A. Bartlett and Tarun Khanna and Doctoral Candidate Prithwiraj Choudhury prepared this case. HBS cases are developed solely as the basis for class discussion. Cases are not intended to serve as endorsements, sources of primary data, or illustrations of effective or ineffective management.

This case was prepared by C. Bartlett. HBS Cases are developed solely for class discussion and do not necessarily illustrate either effective or ineffective handling of administrative situation.

table, including the idea of starting a HAND tuberculosis project.

When Sahney and Vivaldi left the call, Geraghty focused the committee on the recommendations they would take to Henri Termeer, Genzyme CEO. Which research initiative would have maximum impact? What was the right future model for partnering? And what were the funding and resource needs for scaling up the program?

▮ Laying the Corporate Foundation Stones[1]

From modest beginning in 1981 as a supplier of enzymes, fine chemicals, and re-agents to research labs and pharmaceutical companies, Genzyme had grown to become a leader in biotechnology with revenues of almost $4 billion in 2007 (**Exhibits 1 and 2**). It had done so by identifying with its patients' needs, targeting a focused technology capability, and developing a set of values that clearly defined its role as a corporation within society. From its earliest days, Genzyme had focused on orphaned diseases (those with too small a population of sufferers to attract drug development attention), a strategy reflected in its portfolio of drugs (**Exhibits 3 and 4**).

Nurturing an Early Breakthrough   Two years after creating the company, founder Henry Blair recognized that he needed help in managing his fast-growing startup. In 1983, he hired Henri Termeer, a 36 year old division president at medical products giant Baxter International, bringing him in as Genzyme's president. Recognizing the importance of R&D to build a diversified pipeline of products, Termeer initiated a series of weekend technology strategy discussions involving top management, MIT and Harvard faculty, key investors and a few outside advisors.

One potential opportunity that caught Termeer's eye was an ongoing trial being conducted by Dr. Roscoe Brady of the National Institute of Health (NIH). Brady was conducting research on Gaucher (pronounced GO-shay) disease, and Genzyme had received a contract to supply an enzyme called GCR. Gaucher is an extremely rare and deadly condition caused by the body's inability to manufacture the GCR enzyme. It affected fewer than six of every one million people, of whom only a quarter were thought to be ill enough to require treatment.

Early trials of Brady's treatment were disappointing. Only one of seven patients in the trial showed any response to the therapy, but the intriguing fact was that in this particular case, the symptoms were dramatically reversed. Most within Genzyme were pessimistic about the therapy. In addition to questions about the therapy's efficacy, there were two other major concerns—whether it was safe (the enzyme was extracted from human placentas and there were risks of HIV and Hepatitis C transmission), and whether the investment would earn a significant return.

But Termeer wasn't ready to give up. After learning that the one patient in dramatic recovery was a 4-year old boy from the Washington D.C. area, he visited the boy's family regularly over the next few months and was impressed with the treatment's effectiveness. Eventually, despite the many concerns being expressed, Termeer decided to proceed with the development.

In 1985, soon after Termeer was appointed CEO and had taken the company public, Genzyme made an orphan drug application for the Ceredase® enzyme under the Orphan Drug Act.[2] The company estimated that *if* further trials were successful and *if* the orphan drug status was awarded, it could serve around 2000 patients worldwide, with projected annual sales of $100 million. Finally, in 1991, the U.S. Food and Drug Administration approved Ceredase for marketing in the United States.

▮ [1]This section is adapted from Christopher A. Bartlett and Andrew McLean, "Genzyme's Gaucher Initiative: Global Risk and Responsibility," HBS No. 303-048 (Boston: Harvard Business School Publishing, 2002).

▮ [2]Under the Orphan Drug Act of January 1983, companies doing research on rare diseases affecting fewer than 200,000 people in the United States were awarded tax breaks and marketing exclusivity on that drug for seven years post-approval.

Weathering Political and Regulatory Pressures
Ceredase was launched into a difficult political environment for pharmaceutical and biotech companies. President Clinton's emphasis on health care reform turned the spotlight on high priced thera-

pies, and with Gaucher medication costing $50-100,000 a year per patient, Genzyme was under scrutiny. Termeer's response was to go to Washington and meet with members of Congress and the regulatory authorities. As he recalled later,

Exhibit 1   Key financial indicators at Genzyme

(Dollars in thousands, except for share data)	2003	2004	2005	2006	2007	2008
Revenues	1,574,817	2,201,145	2,734,842	3,187,013	3,813,519	4,605,039
Gross margin	1,143,123	1,599,997	2,082,030	2,433,856	2,856,774	3,414,436
Operating income (loss)	174,012	252,913	600,862	(190,509)	653,865	581,479
Net income (loss)	94,283	86,527	441,489	(16,797)	480,193	421,081
Earnings per share (diluted)	$0.42	$0.37	$1.65	$(0.06)	$1.74	$1.50
Cash and investments	1,227,460	1,079,454	1,089,102	1,285,604	1,460,394	973,691
Working capital	930,951	1,009,231	1,114,976	1,338,062	1,137,904	1,601,852
Total assets	5,004,528	6,069,421	6,878,865	7,191,188	8,314,375	8,671,276
Long term obligations	1,676,091	1,064,867	1,178,975	879,038	217,511	451,000
Stockholder's equity	2,936,412	4,380,156	5,149,867	5,660,711	6,612,937	7,305,993

Source: Genzyme website, http://www.genzyme.com/corp/investors/2008_annualreport.pdf, accessed on 08/12/2009.

Exhibit 2   Stock price movement at Genzyme benchmarked against pharmaceutical index (2003–2008)

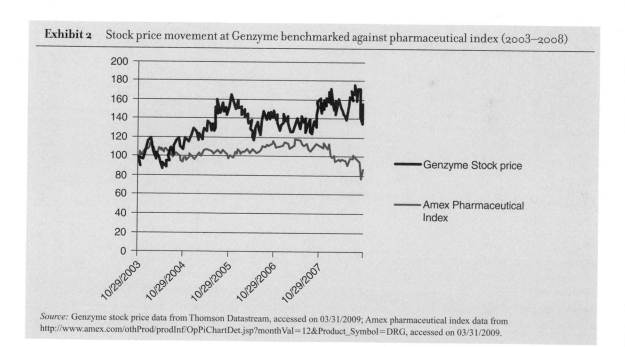

Source: Genzyme stock price data from Thomson Datastream, accessed on 03/31/2009; Amex pharmaceutical index data from http://www.amex.com/othProd/prodInf/OpPiChartDet.jsp?monthVal=12&Product_Symbol=DRG, accessed on 03/31/2009.

Exhibit 3   Product portfolio at Genzyme

Major Current products ranked by sales*

Product Name	Disease/Condition	Is the medication for an 'orphan disease'?	Revenue in 2007
Cerezyme®	Gaucher disease	Yes	$1.13 billion
Renagel®	End-stage renal disease	No	$603 million
Fabrazyme®	Fabry disease	Yes	$424 million
Synvisc®	Osteoarthritis of the knee	No	$242 million

*List not complete

Products in the pipeline

Product Name	Disease/Condition
Mozobil™ (plerixafor)	Stem cell transplant
Alemtuzumab (Campath®)	Multiple sclerosis
Clolar® (clofarabine)	Adult acute myeloid leukemia
Mipomersen	High-risk hypercholesterolemia

Revenue breakdown by product area

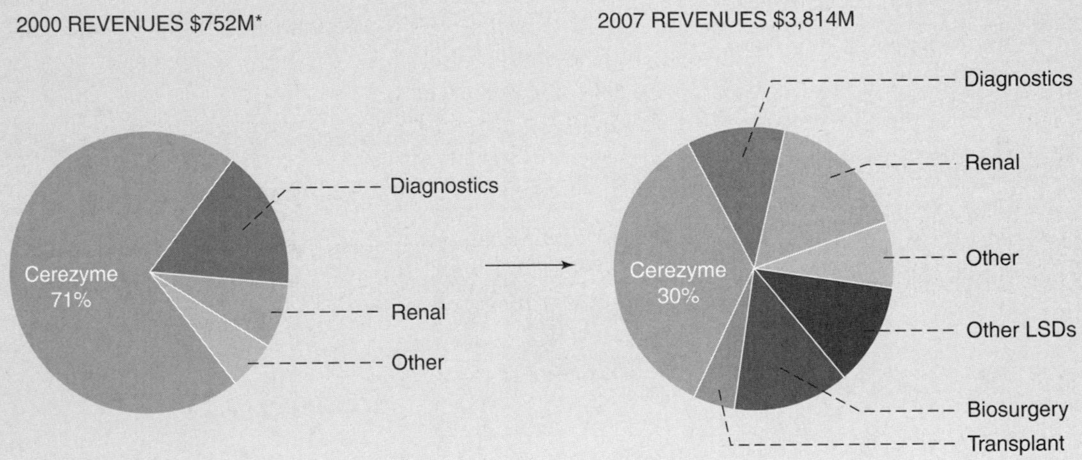

2000 REVENUES $752M*

2007 REVENUES $3,814M

Cerezyme 71%

Diagnostics

Renal

Other

Cerezyme 30%

Diagnostics

Renal

Other

Other LSDs

Biosurgery

Transplant

Source: Genzyme company documents.

"I invited them to visit our operations and offered to open our books so they could see what it cost to develop and produce the product. Our approach was to be completely open and transparent. We were proud of what we had done and had nothing to hide."

After showing his visitors the facilities and giving the Congressional Office of Technology Assessment open access to his books, Termeer explained the company's philosophy: "Since the beginning, I have told this organization that our first responsibility is to treat patients with the

Exhibit 4   Genzyme's existing product portfolio for orphan or neglected diseases*

Neglected/Orphan Disease	Treatment	First approved	Patients on therapy as of January 1, 2008	Approx. annual treatment cost per patient ($)	Percentage of patients who get free treatment
Type 1 Gaucher disease	Cerezyme	1991 (first generation product Ceredase)	5,200	$200,000	10% (through Project Hope)
Fabry disease	Fabrazyme	2001	2,200	$200,000	10%
MPS I	Aldurazyme (with BioMarin Pharmaceutical)	2003	600	$200,000	10%
Pompe disease	Myozyme	2006	900	$300,000	10%

*Note: As the last column of this table indicates, Genzyme sells most of these products commercially. The HAND program is completely separate to these initiatives.
Source: Interviews with Genzyme executives.

disease, not to maximize financial returns." With this objective, even before Ceredase was approved Genzyme created the Ceredase Assistance Program (CAP) to provide free medication to the patients in most need. After a detailed examination, in October 1992 the OTA concluded that while the Orphan Drug Act protection did reduce risks, Genzyme had invested significantly in R&D and production facilities and the company's pretax margin on the drug was within industry norms.

Building a Global Organization   As the Ceredase trials continued, Genzyme began building a new $180 million manufacturing facility. With such a small population of Gaucher sufferers, Termeer realized the company needed to expand into global markets in order to generate volume for the plant. As Genzyme expanded abroad, the CEO insisted that the marketing focus be on the core corporate value of "putting patients first."

Assembling a go-to-market team for an extremely expensive therapy for a rare and seldom diagnosed disease was a daunting task. Sales people would have to educate doctors, pharmacies and hospitals about the disease in a variety of different healthcare environments. Management quickly concluded that the key was to recruit "passionate practical dreamers" as they called them. Termeer tapped his Baxter alumni network to hire senior people to lead Genzyme's entry into Europe, the Middle East, Asia, Canada, and Latin America into the new millennium.

Paralleling its domestic commitment to provide treatment to all Gaucher sufferers, in 1998 the company launched a global version of CAP called the Gaucher Initiative with the objective of delivering treatment to those in less developed countries. To help deliver treatment to these countries, Genzyme teamed up with Project HOPE (Health Opportunities for People Everywhere) as its global NGO partner, deciding to focus first on untreated sufferers in Egypt and China.

In implementing the Gaucher Initiative, the embedded corporate value of putting patients first was translated into a "two price policy" for the drug— full price, or free for patients who could not afford it. An independent six member medical review board was created to review and approve economically challenged patients. Project HOPE would handle the drug's delivery to developing countries, while Genzyme agreed to provide free drugs, pay for the program manager and the secretariat, and provide training, travel and office peripherals for local treatment centers. In 1998 the Gaucher Initiative took on 60 patients worldwide. Three years later, this number was 140.

Shaping a New Industry Image   While Genzyme was developing the Gaucher Initiative, Termeer was becoming increasingly concerned about the failure of the pharmaceutical industry to create sustainable goodwill with NGOs, government agencies, and the public at large, especially in emerging markets. He was astounded in 1999, when 28 big pharmaceutical companies sued the South African government and President Mandela personally for passing a law allowing the import of affordable generic versions of patented AIDS drugs to treat millions of sufferers for the first time. While the companies argued that the law treated them unfairly, NGOs and AIDS activists were up in arms about pitting "commercial interests of the companies against the human rights of the people just trying to stay alive."[1]

Termeer was determined to take a radically different approach at Genzyme. Given the company's patient-focused culture and its sense of corporate social responsibility, he saw an opportunity to seize the initiative by responding to requests he had been receiving from governments in developing countries to invest locally in helping them respond to neglected diseases—diseases that were not attracting drug development attention despite the large number of sufferers. The company was accustomed to working with government health-care agencies worldwide to achieve its goal of obtaining treatment for rare orphaned diseases like Gaucher. Now he felt it might be able to leverage those relationships and offer help in finding solutions for more common neglected diseases.

[1]March 5, 2001 press article; accessed at http://www.thepost.ohiou.edu/ archives3/mar01/030501/ brief4.html website accessed on August 15, 2009.

Beyond Orphan Diseases to Neglected Diseases

In the spring of 2005, as Termeer began testing this idea with his staff, Peter Wirth, Genzyme's corporate counsel, suggested that he talk to his wife Dyann Wirth, Chair of the Department of Immunology and Infectious Diseases at the Harvard School of Public Health. It was the first step in an exploration of neglected diseases where Genzyme's capabilities could be brought to bear.

Malaria   In her conversation with Termeer, Dyann Wirth described the work she was doing on malaria in collaboration with the Broad Institute, a joint venture of Massachusetts Institute of Technology (MIT), Harvard, and the Whitehead Institute. Following that discussion, Termeer asked Geraghty to schedule a follow-up meeting with Wirth and Eric Lander, MIT Professor and Director of the Broad Institute. At that meeting, Termeer and Geraghty learned that an estimated 500 million people were affected by malaria, a number that was expected to increase to 1 billion by 2025.

They also learned that while malaria caused more than 1 million deaths every year, only 0.3% of global health R&D was spent on its drug research. Geraghty explained the potential for Genzyme to contribute: "We had complementary skills to academics like Wirth and Lander who were experts in basic research focused on drug discovery. Genzyme had skills in translating projects from the research stage to a clinical case. Between us we could make a real contribution."

Chagas Disease/ Sleeping Sickness   Another candidate for the emerging idea of developing cures for neglected diseases was brought to light by conversations Geraghty had with a Brazilian researcher he met at a malaria conference, about parasitic illness called Chagas disease, or American trypanosomiasis. That conversation triggered a recollection. In March 2004, Genzyme had bought Ilex Oncology Inc., a biotechnology company focused on the treatment of bladder cancer, solid tumors, and other forms of cancer. But as part of its oncology repertoire, Ilex had on its shelves a drug called eflornithine which had been shown to have an unexpected yet positive effect on African trypanosomiasis, or sleeping sickness.

Sleeping sickness is a parasitic disease in people and animals that is transmitted by the tsetse fly. It is especially prevalent in Sub-Saharan Africa and affects around 50,000 to 70,000 people a year. After it was nearly eradicated in the 20th century, relaxation in control methods led to a resurgence. Although treatments existed, they were highly toxic and resistance was spreading fast. Early research indicated that eflornithine was very effective in treating Stage II sleeping sickness, with the only problem being that its requirement for intravenous treatment four times per day was too difficult to be practical in remote sections of Africa.

Exhibit 5   Comparison of key neglected diseases

	Malaria	Chagas	Sleeping sickness	Tuberculosis
Region affected	In the equatorial areas of the Americas, Asia, and Africa. However, 85–90% of malaria fatalities occur in sub-Saharan Africa	Mexico, Central and South America	36 countries in sub-Saharan Africa	Throughout the developing world; 22 "high burden" countries include India, Pakistan China, Indonesia, Nigeria, Bangladesh
Total people affected every year	250 million cases every year	16–18 million	~500,000	~25 million
Total number of people for whom the disease poses a threat	3.3 billion	100 million	60 million	>4 billion
Number of deaths every year	1 million	50,000	>40,000	1.5–2 million
Spread	Caused by protozoan parasites spread by female Anopheles mosquitoes. Two strains: falciparum (Africa, India, elsewhere) and vivax (mostly in India)	Transmission is mainly through triatomine bugs, which hide during the day, but emerge at night to bight and infect sleeping victims	Infected tsetse fly injects metacyclic trypomastigotes parasite into the skin tissue while bighting the mammalian host.	Spread through the air, when people who have the disease cough, sneeze or spit.

http://www.who.int/mediacentre/factsheets/fs094/ en/index.html, accessed on 03/31/2009 http://www.who.int/features/factfiles/malaria/en/index.html, accessed on 08/12/2009 http://www.who.int/ neglected_diseases/diseases/chagas/en/index.html, accessed on 03/31/2009 http://www.who.int/ mediacentre/factsheets/fs259/en/, accessed on 03/31/2009 http://www.sleepingsickness.org/Background.html, accessed on 08/15/2009.
Source: Data collected from interviews with Genzyme executives and from the following websites

Chagas disease, named after the Brazilian physician Carlos Chagas who first described it in 1909, is caused by a related parasite and is widespread in Latin America. A disease without a vaccine, it is transmitted to humans and other mammals mostly by blood-sucking assassin bugs.

Tuberculosis A third major neglected disease candidate presented itself in 2006 in discussions that followed an approach from the Global Alliance for TB Drug Development, a New York-based non-profit dedicated to the discovery and development of faster acting and more affordable tuberculosis (TB) treatments. Through that contact, Geraghty began to learn about TB, and felt Genzyme may be able to help.

A widespread and highly infectious disease, TB has a footprint across large parts of Africa, China, South Asia and elsewhere and is responsible for among the highest deaths of all neglected diseases (**Exhibit 5**). It infects one third of the world's population, and is spread when those with the disease cough or spit, causing new infections at the rate of one per second. Although most of these cases are latent, about one in ten became full-blown TB. If left untreated, the disease will kill more than half its victims. In 2004, there were almost 15 million active chronic cases of TB, 9 million new cases, and 1.6 million deaths in the year, almost all in developing countries.

Despite these disturbing statistics, TB was still being treated by a combination of four drugs developed in the 1960s. Pharmaceutical companies had done little R&D in recent decades due to the disease's concentration in developing countries which could not afford expensive health care. Drugs were available to less than half of the most infectious cases, and even when they were provided, treatment took six months. The need for constant drug administration and monitoring was beyond the capability of most developing countries, so treatment was often abandoned before it was completed. This had fueled the rise of XDR-TB, a new and highly drug-resistant form of the disease.

Opening a Helping HAND: Forming the Program

With these exploratory discussions in motion, Termeer decided to outline his vision for how Genzyme could contribute to the plight of those suffering from such widespread neglected diseases. The opening of Genzyme's U.K. R&D center in September, 2005 provided him with an opportunity. In his speech dedicating the center, he said: "In the new millennium the challenge will be to find dramatic new ways to serve people suffering from neglected diseases around the world, especially the billions ignored by traditional pharma companies in emerging markets."

Caren Arnstein, VP Corporate Communications at Genzyme recalled listening to the speech: "Henri's speech caught us all a bit by surprise. He was way ahead of us. But what he said was not only uplifting and inspirational, it also showed his deep personal commitment to act. It was as if he was trying to raise the game for all of us. That's how the HAND initiative was born."

Setting Goals and Guidelines After many internal conversations, in February 2006, Termeer formed a Steering Committee of Geraghty, Arnstein, Ted Sybertz, Senior VP Scientific Affairs, and Jeff Klinger, VP Infectious Diseases. In April, the committee formally launched the Humanitarian Assistance for Neglected Diseases (HAND) program. Termeer articulated the thinking behind the program's creation: "Genzyme's customers are mostly government agencies that buy expensive medication for rare diseases like Gaucher. In the long term, these organizations are not comfortable engaging on the basis of cold commerce alone, and neither are we. The HAND initiative is Genzyme's way of giving back."

Technically, any entry on the World Health Organization (WHO) list of Neglected Tropical Diseases could qualify for the HAND program. However, the Steering Committee proposed some simple criteria to guide their choices going ahead (**Exhibit 6**). Projects had to be related to an 'important unmet medical need' where Genzyme had

Exhibit 6	HAND Steering Committee meeting minutes, February 2006 (selected text)

Mission of HAND Program

Neglected diseases such as malaria are enormous public health problems in many areas, killing more than a million people each year, mostly children. There is an urgent need to discover new and effective drugs. Industry has a unique contribution to make by applying drug discovery and preclinical development capabilities to create new solutions. In partnership with others, Genzyme seeks to be a catalyst in advancing the development of novel therapies for neglected diseases.

Objectives

- Partner with others in conducting work that can advance the development of novel therapies for important neglected diseases
- Create a vehicle for Genzyme's global health initiative that has a structure and process for screening, selecting and accounting for scientific projects
- Establish a process for making IP available for use in the field

Project Selection Criteria

- Important unmet medical need, ideally recognized as public health priority
- Medically effective product profile, ideally very inexpensive
- Evidence based scientific rationale, ideally with a well defined pathway and development plan
- Ability to make a significant impact for patients, ideally using unique capabilities
- Credible academic and medical partners, ideally with a well organized framework
- Ability to afford the next phase of development, ideally with long term funding

Source: Interviews with Genzyme executives.

'technological capability', 'credible partners' and the 'ability to afford the next phase of development, ideally with long term funding.'

Geraghty explained the rationale behind the company's strong preference for engaging others in partnerships: "Even if we increased our own investment by two- or three-fold to $6 to 10 million, we would have very little incremental impact. We not only need to leverage our own capabilities, we want to influence others and become an industry role model." He also explained that HAND's objectives were explicitly "beyond narrow commercial interests" and emphasized that Genzyme "would not seek profit from these programs". Indeed, the company committed to make available all intellectual property generated from the HAND program so that partners and governments around the world could benefit.

Building Capability   HAND was going to require significant resources, and the challenge for Genzyme

was to provide it with the technology access it needed without compromising the commercial activities that would fund and support the program. (**Exhibit 7** describes Genzyme's R&D operations.)

Like the Gaucher Initiative, HAND created a lot of excitement among employees. Many at the Waltham R&D center that housed its projects wanted to contribute, and for the first year or so, researchers mostly worked on the program in their free time. A couple of the first to participate described the excitement, "A lot of people wanted to be on this program given its social impact. We were just lucky to be among the first employees assigned to projects."

As the exploration of various neglected diseases and potential partnerships expanded, Genzyme found it had to commit more resources to the program. As Klinger described it, "HAND started to transform itself from being a hip pocket organization to being more formal, almost a shadow organization." From the employees' perspective, this created issues around being recognized for working on HAND. One project member quipped, "I work on a HAND project, but I also report to my regular cost center manager. It's like working 150%. At the end of the day, I am not even sure my manager knows what my contribution to the HAND program has been."

Furthermore, as key researchers' time and energy was diverted to the HAND program, there was push back from cost center managers and project managers. Jim Burns, who managed resources in Waltham, often had to play the role of referee. "The HAND program is the right thing to do and we can add real value in areas like formulation," he said. "But there is a fine balance and we must not overcommit ourselves." Klinger agreed: "Everyone is after scarce technical resources like DMPK (Drug Metabolism and Pharmacokinetics) and medicinal chemistry[3]—commercial project managers as well the HAND program partners. So the question is not just how many resources HAND needs, but what kinds of resources."

HAND in Hand: Engaging Partners

In parallel to engaging its own internal resources in HAND, Genzyme also began exploring various partnerships that seemed to offer the potential for collaborative research in each of the identified neglected disease areas. It was a slow, iterative process that gradually identified a portfolio of potential long-term research collaborators.

The DNDi Experience   In 2006, early in its search for partners, Genzyme initiated discussions with the Drugs for Neglected Diseases initiative. DNDi was a global organization formed in 2003 when five public sector institutions joined forces with leading NGO Médecins sans Frontière and the Special Programme for Research and Training in Tropical Diseases (TDR) sponsored by UNDP, World Bank, and WHO.

Given DNDi's expertise in neglected diseases and its worldwide presence, it appeared to be an ideal partner with which to develop and test novel compounds to treat sleeping sickness. In discussions about this possibility, DNDi seemed glad to involve Genzyme, and even proposed bringing additional partners like the Swiss Tropical Institute into the project to do some testing.

However DNDi was in the midst of a transition and the new team took a different view of how development should proceed. DNDi was also sponsoring research on other promising sleeping sickness drug candidates. Soon, the two organizations started moving in different directions on the project.

The relationship remained cordial and Genzyme continued to use DNDi facilities to test compounds. But while the possibility of future collaboration remained open, by 2008 the two organizations no longer funded projects jointly. For Genzyme, it was an early lesson in how difficult it could be to pursue an objective on a project where partners had different interests.

The Broad/Harvard/MMV Negotiations   Meanwhile the malaria work with Broad and Harvard was moving ahead. The Broad Institute would contribute in the area of medicinal chemistry and cheminformatics[4], the Harvard School of Public Health had expertise in molecular genetics and clinical investigation, and Genzyme would screen its chemical libraries of millions of compounds to check whether any of the compounds were effective in treating the disease targets.

But in this partnership also, differences cropped up–this time over funding. In an initial budget meeting, the partners estimated annual funding needs of about $1.6 million in the first year of the project, increasing to around $6.6 million in year 3. Initially, the Broad Institute explored the possibility that Genzyme act as the sponsor for the work at the Broad. After making it clear that they were not in a

---

[3]Medicinal chemistry is at the intersection of pharmacology and chemistry and involves testing, synthesizing and developing chemical entities suitable for therapeutic use.

[4]Cheminformatics is at the intersection of chemistry and computer science and involves storing and retrieving data related to molecules and compounds.

Exhibit 7   R&D, employee and CSR indicators at Genzyme

Indicator	Value in year 2008
Total number of employees	11,000
Total number of R&D employees[5]	~900
R&D employees at the Waltham center (that housed the HAND projects)	205
Total R&D budget	$750 million
R&D budget for drugs and bio-materials devices division[6]	~$80 million
Average fully loaded cost of 1 R&D FTE	~$300,000
Global product donations (for year 2007)	$110 million
U.S. cash donations (for year 2007)	$14 million

[5]The R&D organization at Genzyme has the following locations: (1)Drug and bio-materials R&D focused on small molecules and bio material devices (based in Waltham MA); (2)Therapeutic proteins division focused on cell and gene therapies (based in Framingham MA); (3)Molecular antibiotics division based in Cambridge U.K. and two smaller centers in Oklahoma and San Antonio. The Waltham center had around 205 scientists and engineers. Framingham had around 600 R&D employees, while Cambridge U.K., Oklahoma and San Antonio had around 50, 12 and 12 R&D employees respectively

[6]Most of the remaining R&D budget at Genzyme is allocated to the 'Therapeutic Proteins' division

Source: Data on total employees, total R&D budget from http://www.genzyme.com/corp/structure/fastfacts.asp, accessed on 08/12/2009. Data on number of R&D employees at Waltham, R&D budget for drugs and bio-materials, cost of FTE and other data from interviews with Genzyme executives.

position to finance the entire program, Genzyme's representatives offered to help raise the money.

The search for both funding and additional capabilities led to the Medicines for Malaria Venture (MMV), a Geneva based nonprofit organization that focused on the public-private partnership model involving academics, NGOs, and pharma companies like Novartis and GSK. With $263 million in funding (much of it from the Gates Foundation), MMV was looking for new partners, and the Broad-Genzyme-Harvard partnership looked very attractive given the credibility of the partners and their complementary skills. Soon, Genzyme and its partners received funding to the tune of $4 million from MMV and began work on five projects focused on malaria.

Looking back, Geraghty saw the early tension with Broad as a blessing in disguise. "It was a pleasant surprise to learn that we also could get funding," he said. "It freed us to contribute our people and technology to the program, without the constraint of funding it 100% ourselves."

The Fiocruz Relationship   In 2006, soon after the HAND program was announced, Latin American general manager Rogerio Vivaldi opened discussions with the Oswald Cruz Institute or Fiocruz, a Brazilian public science organization that was part of the Ministry of Health. It conducted research, produced vaccines, and was involved in public health education. Fiocruz had previously approached Vivaldi with a request for the technology to produce Cerezyme in Brazil. Vivaldi had responded by saying that perhaps the two organizations could create more value by working together on neglected diseases like Chagas.

To explore this possibility, Vivaldi proposed sending Fiocruz scientists to Genzyme's Waltham R&D center to learn how to take new therapies through the drug development process. From Genzyme's point of view, while the visit provided a way to get to know this potential partner, it was not without its challenges. "Our most valuable resource is the time and energy of our scientists and those who manage them," said Geraghty. "Clearly a partnership with an organization like Fiocruz makes more of a demand on that resource than a local partnership but our scientists also learn from it."

The TB Alliance Discussions   As Geraghty continued his discussions with the Global Alliance for TB Drug Development (or the TB Alliance as it was known), he learned that it was a product development partnership that operated like a virtual biotechnology firm. It had significant financial support from the Gates and Rockefeller Foundations as well as several governments worldwide, and used those funds to outsource the development of potential drugs to pharmaceutical companies like Bayer and GlaxoSmithKline. However, unlike traditional product development in those companies, the clear objective of these projects was to create treatments that were both affordable and accessible to the developing world.

As an initial project, the TB Alliance proposed funding a specific research program where Genzyme would take responsibility for screening some existing targets by allocating scientists with DMPK and medicinal chemistry skills to the project. Geraghty indicated that these were scarce resources at Genzyme, but that he would take the proposal to the company for consideration.

Extending the HAND: Exploring New Opportunities

After almost three years, HAND's activities were beginning to coalesce around the malaria and Chagas projects. But as Geraghty and the HAND steering committee began talking about the program's future, they wondered if they had identified the most appropriate neglected diseases, were engaged in the most effective partnerships, and were applying the most appropriate resources to the program. With a review in process, advocates and champions for each of the options quickly arose.

The Chagas Project: A Champion in Brazil   As soon as the HAND program was announced, Rogerio Vivaldi had seen an opportunity to link this initiative to the growth of Genzyme's operations in Brazil. Vivaldi was a doctor who had treated Brazil's first

Gaucher patient in 1991. After Genzyme opened an office in São Paolo in 1997, Vivaldi had painstakingly built up the operations and had elevated Genzyme Brazil into the top tier of pharmaceutical companies of the country, with 100 employees on its rolls.

While Genzyme Brazil was in a startup mode, José Serra, São Paulo's mayor was positioning himself as a Presidential candidate in 2002. National healthcare reform was a priority for Serra, widely credited with boosting the generics industry in Brazil and creating ANVISA (Agência Nacional de Vigilância Sanitária), the Brazilian food and drug regulatory agency. In this context, Vivaldi succeeded in getting Cerezyme (a later version of Ceredase) on the list of exceptional drugs for rare diseases, thereby ensuring direct reimbursement from the federal government. In 2008, $100 million of the $108 million revenues that Genzyme had in Brazil came from federal reimbursements. "Brazil has created a template for emerging markets in Latin America, South Asia and Eastern Europe," said Geraghty. "We were able to convince governments in countries like Chile and Venezuela to follow the example of Brazil and create programs that supported the treatment of Gaucher."

Still, retaining Cerezyme's place on the coveted list wasn't easy. "There were healthcare officials who claimed that they could eradicate tuberculosis in Brazil with the money being a directed into Gaucher," Vivaldi explained. "What really helped us was our commitment to treating poor patients under the Gaucher Initiative and our direct communication with the government." But the list for "exceptional drugs" was coming up for a revision in 2011, and more than 100 drugs had staked their claim to be included, including five from Genzyme. To Vivaldi, the HAND project represented an important means of raising Genzyme's profile ahead of that decision.

Following Geraghty's meeting with a leading Fiocruz scientist, Vivaldi began exploring with his Brazilian partner how the two organizations might work together in other disease areas like malaria and tuberculosis. Within Genzyme, he became an extremely strong and passionate advocate for such extended partnership activity.

On the January 2009 HAND conference call, Vivaldi was very upbeat about the Chagas initiative which he emphasized would be a true give back to Brazil. He also reminded them that several Brazilian Health Ministry officials had involvement with Fiocruz, and that continued success in the project would enhance Genzyme's credibility with Federal Health authorities, a particularly important objective given that the list of federally approved drugs would soon be updated.

The Malaria Initiative: Lobbying in India   On the other side of the world, Sandeep Sahney, Managing Director of Genzyme India was equally excited about HAND. Genzyme had entered India in 2002 when it launched Synvisc, a biotech product indicated for the treatment of osteoarthritis of the knee. In 2007, the company hired Sahney, a local industry veteran, to build the organization.

Compared to its position in Brazil, Genzyme was still in a startup mode in India. Even though the government had no program to reimburse Gaucher patients, Genzyme hoped to generate sales of $30-50 million within five years. But without government reimbursement, most of this growth would have to come from sales of treatments for cancer, osteo-arthritis and renal disease to private practice doctors and for-profit hospitals.

But Sahney also believed that Genzyme had another great untapped opportunity in India—to access world class R&D resources in government and private labs. He felt that the HAND program provided the ideal platform to bring together resources and ideas across various local labs and tap into that knowledge. Supported by Geraghty and Ted Sybertz, Genzyme's VP of Scientific Affairs, Sahney spent much of 2007 and 2008 in discussions with several Indian public science organizations like the Council for Scientific and Industrial Research. "The Indian scientific community has great talent, but its people work in silos," Sahney said. "Genzyme could help break some of the walls."

Given malaria's widespread occurrence in India, Sahney saw HAND providing an opportunity to begin discussions with ICGEB, a Delhi-based organization working on developing a new vaccine for the disease. "ICGEB is funded by the United Nations and the Indian government, and has great skills in vaccines," Sahney reported. "It has been working on malaria vaccines for 15 years and has deep knowledge of local issues like how the disease is spread here."

ICGEB also had new expertise to contribute to the project. Most human malaria is caused by two distinct species—*Plasmodium falciparum* and *Plasmodium vivax*. Though most of the existing malaria research (including the Broad-Harvard initiative) was focused on the former, in India 65% of the disease cases were attributed to the latter. This lesser researched species appeared to cause more virulent disease in recent years, and ICGEB had demonstrated novel ideas around targets and certain plant-based treatment strategies effective for both *vivax* and *falciparum*.

The company decided to explore this potential partnership, and it was agreed that ICGEB, like Fiocruz would get rights to all the intellectual property (IP) that came out of the program in the field of neglected diseases. But early communication problems with the new Indian collaborators underscored how challenging cross-border partnerships could be. Klinger recalled, "On an early videoconference call, I was bringing the discussion to a close by listing the seven initiatives that seemed to interest people. But when I asked for suggestions about how to prioritize them, someone on the Indian side said, 'It's very inefficient to prioritize. Why not do all of them at the same time?' At that point, it was clear that our approaches might be different."

Meanwhile, Genzyme had committed to a partnership with Advinus, an Indian research company with great skills in chemistry, DMPK, and crystallography. But the deal with Advinus was fundamentally different from that with ICGEB: the partner would be paid on an hourly basis for specific assignments, and their services would be used on an "as needed basis" by multiple HAND program teams, including the Broad and Harvard malaria research team.

With time, the ICGEB relationship had overcome some of the initial cultural barriers, and on the conference call, Sahney was passionate about the need to support this emerging partnership. He explained that malaria, especially the *vivax* strain was a real unsolved problem in India and ICGEB had shown great promise by coming up with concrete ideas on molecules that could be tested. He firmly believed that success in this project would position Genzyme as an "Indian" R&D player and build its reputation with the local medical and research communities. Sahney also suggested that the Indian malaria template could be used in other countries like Brazil and parts of Africa.

The TB Option: A Voice in the Center   Meanwhile, at Genzyme's Cambridge headquarters, Jim Geraghty wanted to keep questioning the assumptions and challenging the priorities that shaped HAND's future direction. In that role, one of the issues he had kept alive was the question about whether Genzyme could devote resources and capabilities to helping develop treatments for TB.

A year after Geraghty's initial contact with the TB Alliance in 2006, the CEO with whom he had been having discussions resigned and the relationship stalled. In 2008, at a Gates Foundation meeting, he struck up a conversation with the new CEO, and promptly invited him to visit Genzyme. "We sat down with scientists from both organizations to discuss collaborative possibilities," said Geraghty. "We all learned a lot, but had difficulty finding a way to get started. Beyond our normal worry about being stretched too thin, some of our people expressed concerns that we did not know much about TB. But as I pointed out, we didn't know much about malaria either until the HAND program started."

About this time, Geraghty was also contacted by scientists working on TB at the Harvard School of Public Health (led by outgoing Dean Barry Bloom, a world authority on TB) and at the Broad Institute. The scientists had developed novel assays and had identified novel targets for TB drugs using sophisticated genomic analyses and felt that Genzyme could help move them forward as in the case of malaria. Geraghty offered assistance on project management, but the relationship did not develop. Still, it was a potential resource that might be engaged in the future.

One question the HAND steering committee faced was deciding which neglected diseases offered the most effective use of its scarce resources going forward. By this criterion, TB demanded attention because it was such a massive global healthcare problem. In comparison, the number of people affected by Chagas was relatively small and its impact was focused on Central and South America (**Exhibit 5**). While malaria was more widespread and had higher morbidity and mortality rates, it had recently attracted significant funding and technological resources, particularly due to its priority status within the Gates Foundation. One outcome of this was that in early 2009, Bill Gates announced a potential breakthrough vaccine that could be ready by 2014[5]. Given the large number of global players and the significant resources aimed at malaria's cure, some industry observers had begun questioning whether it could still be classified as a "neglected disease."

In contrast, despite the fact that TB was a worldwide problem with among the highest mortality rates, it received much less global attention. In that context, Geraghty wondered whether Genzyme should restart discussions with TB Alliance, the Harvard School of Public Health and the Broad Institute. "I remain a champion for HAND to consider TB because I think it is good if we keep questioning how we are using our scarce resources," he said. And a project with partners based in New York and Boston could be a lot easier to manage than one linked into Brazil or India.

[5] Page 15 of Gates Foundation annual letter. Accessed from http://www.gatesfoundation.org/annual-letter/Documents/2009-bill-gates-annual-letter.pdf. Website accessed on August 15, 2009.

On One HAND . . .: Weighing the Options

After presenting their cases, the two invited guests dropped off the conference call, leaving the steering committee to review some of the other opportunities and risk factors they would have to take into account in making their recommendations about HAND's future direction and priorities.

END of U.S. Government Inaction   On the positive side, Genzyme and its partners had received good news from Washington where the U.S. Senate had recently adopted the 'Elimination of Neglected Diseases Act' (END) amendment to the Food and Drug Administration Reauthorization Bill[6]. The END Act would award a "treatment priority review voucher" to any company that brought to market a treatment for a neglected disease.

The voucher, which could be used for any new drug coming up for review, would ensure that an FDA priority review could be completed in about 6 months compared to 18 months under a regular review. The twelve months saved could be worth up to $300 million to a pharma or biotech company–perhaps more for a blockbuster drug. Senator Sam Brownback commented: "We are blessed to live in a nation in which diseases like malaria and cholera are not serious threats, but must not forget that one-sixth of the world's population faces death and suffering from easily treatable diseases . . . Private companies have the potential to be major players in the fight against neglected diseases."[7]

The I.P. Risk: The Novartis Experience   Of greater concern to the HAND steering committee were developments involving an ongoing patent dispute between Novartis and the Indian government. After Indian regulatory authorities refused to grant Novartis a patent on its cancer drug Glivec, Novartis had taken legal action challenging India's 2005 law which allowed patents to be refused for drug modifications that could not prove significant increases in the original drug's efficacy. The company contended that this was in violation of WTO rules relating to trade-related intellectual property rights.[8]

The appeal created headlines, causing several NGOs to strongly criticize Novartis' actions. For example, a spokesman for Doctors Without Borders, an organization that relied on India as a source of 84% of its generic AIDS drugs said, "People the world over who rely on India as a source of their medicines may be affected if Novartis gets its way."[9] After pointing out that 99% of patients treated with Glivec in India received it free from Novartis, a company spokesman said, "Our actions in India do not hinder the supply of medicines to poor countries given the international safeguards now in place. We are seeking clarity about India's laws . . . We believe that limiting patents only to new chemical entities does not recognize genuine innovation. Medical progress happens through steps in innovation, also called incremental innovation."[10]

Through its contact with Novartis at MMV, Genzyme had become increasingly aware of the company's commitment to finding cures for neglected diseases. In addition to its involvement in nine MMV projects, it had created its own non-profit Institute for Tropical Diseases in collaboration with the Singapore Economic Development Board. But apparently, these commitments to developing countries' needs had not carried much weight with the Indian government.

As corporate counsel, Peter Wirth was concerned about these developments. Previously a respected partner at a Boston law firm, Wirth was known to ask difficult but insightful questions within Genzyme. "While most of us would be looking at the bright side, Peter would be thinking of the potential

[6]News release dated May 10, 2007. Accessed from http://brownback.senate.gov/pressapp/record.cfm?id=273870. Website accessed on August 15, 2009.

[7]News release dated September 21, 2007. Accessed from http://brownback.senate.gov/public/press/record.cfm?id=283848. Website accessed on August 15, 2009.

[8]http://www.medicalnewstoday.com/articles/61932.php. Website accessed on August 15, 2009.

[9]http://doctorswithoutborders.org/press/release.cfm?id=1870. Website accessed on August 15, 2009.

[10]Novartis release. Accessed from http://www.novartis.com/downloads/ about-novartis/Novartis_position-Glivec_Gleevec_patent_case_india.pdf. Website accessed on August 15, 2009.

risks and pulling us back to reality," said Geraghty. Taking that role, Wirth challenged the HAND committee to think about what implications the Novartis case held for Genzyme—its relationships with India, its intellectual property positions, and even its altruistic motives.

The question led Geraghty to reflect on a recent Gates Foundation discussion about how to stimulate more corporate research involvement in neglected diseases. The two major impediments cited by most companies were the difficulty of making money in neglected diseases and the fear of losing control of their intellectual property. Rightly or wrongly, they believed some developing countries did not have the same respect for IP as in most developed countries.

The Management Challenge: Managing Partnerships and Expectations

Wirth also articulated concerns about "setting the right expectations" with Genzyme's various partners, especially those in developing countries where each party's future hopes and expectations were not always made clear. He recalled that during the Gaucher Initiative, its government and NGO partners had expressed strong concerns when Genzyme eventually applied for partial reimbursement for supplying Cerezyme to patients in Egypt when the local healthcare system could eventually afford it. This had led to tensions and disputes that Wirth did not want to repeat.

In his opinion, Genzyme would have to clearly define upfront where it could help and where it could not. However with the barriers of language, culture, and distance, he saw lots of opportunity for miscommunication. "It will be imperative for us to etch a strong impression in the minds of partners, governments and the public at large of our constraints and limitations," he said.

Geraghty too was concerned about the increasing network of complex partnerships. Although the initial startup challenges with DNDi and Broad had taught him important lessons, over the last couple of years, HAND had added many more partners to its projects. The sleeping sickness team now included Pace University in New York, the Swiss Tropical Institute, and most recently, Fiocruz in Brazil. In addition to Broad and Harvard, the malaria initiative now involved ICGEB and Advinus, with Fiocruz was showing interest. "It takes a lot to manage all these relationships," said Geraghty. "Maintaining the managerial bandwidth to deal with this level of complexity is very challenging."

The Resource Decision: Allocating Funds and Capabilities

HAND had moved far beyond the part-time volunteer staffing of its early days, and by 2009, there were around 10 employees at Waltham working virtually fulltime on its projects. With the fully loaded cost of an employee at around $300,000, this was an annual investment of around $3 million. In addition, Klinger's title was now 'VP Infectious Diseases and Neglected Diseases,' with the latter designation reflecting the amount of time and attention he was now giving to HAND.

Watching this growing activity, Wirth questioned whether Genzyme could sustainably invest the financial and human resources to manage multiple programs and partners. He urged the committee to balance global medical need with the best technology- and partner-fit (**Exhibits 5, 8 and 9** provide data). He also worried that pursuing too many initiatives would lead to less oversight and therefore greater risk.

With all this advice ringing in his ears, Geraghty knew that the time for analysis was over. Now was the time for decisions. Termeer would be expecting the HAND steering committee to provide some clear proposals about which projects to undertake, which partners to engage, and what resources to allocate to them.

Exhibit 8   Malaria–Scientific strategy and skills of partners

Recent scientific breakthroughs

- Sequencing of multiple strains of P. falciparum has provided information on available targets and their diversity
- High density genetic mapping (HapMap) has
  enabled detailed mapping of genes responsible for disease severity and drug resistance
- New drug discovery efforts focused on Protease inhibators

	Novel Target Discovery	Compound Screening	Lead Selection & Optimization	Preclinical Development	Clinical Trials & Approvals
Genzyme	Support role	Lead role: make libraries comprising millions of compounds available for screening to find 'hits' with target	Lead role: design and synthesize hundreds of analogues of 'hits' to improve property of 'hits'	Lead role: confirm potency and safety of drug using animal and lab tests	Support role
Broad & Harvard	Lead role: lead biology research in identifying potential intervention points (targets) for the disease	Lead role: contribute library of 120,000 compounds to screen compounds to screen for anti-plasmodial activity using Kan reactors	Lead role: share medicinal chemistry effort with Genzyme	Lead role: share cheminformatics effort chemin-formatics effort with Genzyme	Support role
MMV	Support role	Support role	Support role	Support role	Lead role: organize testing and animal models
ICGEB	Lead role: target ideas for vivax and falciparum	Support role	Support role	Support role on chemin-formatics	Possible support role

Source: Interviews with Genzyme executives.

Exhibit 9   Chagas—Scientific strategy and skills of partners

Recent scientific breakthroughs

- Two focus areas–(1) Identifying novel biological targets within the parasite that causes Chagas disease; (2) test effectiveness of using monoclonal antibodies to neutralize a protein that contributes to heart damage in Chagas disease
- New drug discovery efforts focused on Megazol Analogs

	Novel Target Discovery	Compound Screening	Lead Selection & Optimization	Preclinical Development	Clinical Trials & Approvals
Genzyme	Support role	Lead role: make libraries comprising million of compounds available for screening to find 'hits' with target. Also test compounds that have been effective in sleeping sickness parasite	Lead role: design and synthesize hundreds of analogues of 'hits' to improve property of 'hits'	Lead role: confirm potency and safety of drug using animal and lab tests	Support role
Fiocruz	Lead role: scientists at Fiocruz have developed metabolic maps of the Trypanosoma cruzi parasite that causes the disease; these maps will be used to explore specific metabolic pathways that may serve as targets for potential drugs	Support role	Support role	Support role	Support role

Source: Interviews with Genzyme executives.

Reading 8-1 Values in Tension: Ethics Away from Home

Thomas Donaldson

When is different just different, and when is different wrong?

When we leave home and cross our nation's boundaries, moral clarity often blurs. Without a backdrop of shared attitudes, and without familiar laws and judicial procedures that define standards of ethical conduct, certainty is elusive. Should a company invest in a foreign country where civil and political rights are violated? Should a company go along with a host country's discriminatory employment practices? If companies in developed countries shift facilities to developing nations that lack strict environmental and health regulations, or if those companies choose to fill management and other top-level positions in a host nation with people from the home country, whose standards should prevail?

Even the best-informed, best-intentioned executives must rethink their assumptions about business practice in foreign settings. What works in a company's home country can fail in a country with different standards of ethical conduct. Such difficulties are unavoidable for businesspeople who live and work abroad.

But how can managers resolve the problems? What are the principles that can help them work through the maze of cultural differences and establish codes of conduct for globally ethical business practice? How can companies answer the toughest question in global business ethics: What happens

▌ Thomas Donaldson is a professor at the Wharton School of the University of Pennsylvania in Philadelphia where he teaches business ethics. He wrote The Ethics of International Business (Oxford University Press, 1989) and is the coauthor, with Thomas W. Dunfee, of Business Ethics as Social Contracts, to be published by the Harvard Business School Press in the fall of 1997.

when a host country's ethical standards seem lower than the home country's?

Competing Answers One answer is as old as philosophical discourse. According to cultural relativism, no culture's ethics are better than any other's; therefore there are no international rights and wrongs. If the people of Indonesia tolerate the bribery of their public officials, so what? Their attitude is no better or worse than that of people in Denmark or Singapore who refuse to offer or accept bribes. Likewise, if Belgians fail to find insider trading morally repugnant, who cares? Not enforcing insider-trading laws is no more or less ethical than enforcing such laws.

The cultural relativist's creed–When in Rome, do as the Romans do–is tempting, especially when failing to do as the locals do means forfeiting business opportunities. The inadequacy of cultural relativism, however, becomes apparent when the practices in question are more damaging than petty bribery or insider trading.

In the late 1980s, some European tanneries and pharmaceutical companies were looking for cheap waste-dumping sites. They approached virtually every country on Africa's west coast from Morocco to the Congo.

Values in Tension

Nigeria agreed to take highly toxic polychlorinated biphenyls. Unprotected local workers, wearing thongs and shorts, unloaded barrels of PCBs and placed them near a residential area. Neither the residents nor the workers knew that the barrels contained toxic waste.

We may denounce governments that permit such abuses, but many countries are unable to police transnational corporations adequately even if they want to. And in many countries, the combination of ineffective enforcement and inadequate regulations leads to behavior by unscrupulous companies that is clearly wrong. A few years ago, for example, a group of investors became interested in restoring the SS *United States*, once a luxurious ocean liner. Before the actual restoration could begin, the ship had to be stripped of its asbestos lining. A bid from a U.S. company, based on U.S. standards for asbestos removal, priced the job at more than $100 million. A company in the Ukranian city of Sevastopol offered to do the work for less than $2 million. In October 1993, the ship was towed to Sevastopol.

A cultural relativist would have no problem with that outcome, but I do. A country has the right to establish its own health and safety regulations, but in the case described above, the standards and the terms of the contract could not possibly have protected workers in Sevastopol from known health risks. Even if the contract met Ukranian standards, ethical businesspeople must object. Cultural relativism is morally blind. There are fundamental values that cross cultures, and companies must uphold them. (For an economic argument against cultural relativism, see the insert "The Culture and Ethics of Software Piracy")

Ethics Away from Home

At the other end of the spectrum from cultural relativism is ethical imperialism, which directs people to do everywhere exactly as they do at home. Again, an understandably appealing approach but one that is clearly inadequate. Consider the large U.S. computer-products company that in 1993 introduced a course on sexual harassment in its Saudi Arabian facility. Under the banner of global consistency, instructors used the same approach to train Saudi Arabian managers that they had used with U.S. managers: the participants were asked to discuss a case in which a manager makes sexually explicit remarks to a new female employee over drinks in a bar. The instructors failed to consider how the exercise would work in a culture with strict conventions governing relationships between men and women. As a result, the training sessions were ludicrous. They baffled and offended the Saudi

participants, and the message to avoid coercion and sexual discrimination was lost.

The theory behind ethical imperialism is absolutism, which is based on three problematic principles. Absolutists believe that there is a single list of truths, that they can be expressed only with one set of concepts, and that they call for exactly the same behavior around the world.

The first claim clashes with many people's belief that different cultural traditions must be respected. In some cultures, loyalty to a community–family, organization, or society–is the foundation of all ethical behavior. The Japanese, for example, define business ethics in terms of loyalty to their companies, their business networks, and their nation. Americans place a higher value on liberty than on loyalty; the U.S. tradition of rights emphasizes equality, fairness, and individual freedom. It is hard to conclude that truth lies on one side or the other, but an absolutist would have us select just one.

The second problem with absolutism is the presumption that people must express moral truth using only one set of concepts. For instance, some absolutists insist that the language of basic rights provide the framework for any discussion of ethics. That means, though, that entire cultural traditions must be ignored. The notion of a right evolved with the rise of democracy in post-Renaissance Europe and the United States, but the term is not found in either Confucian or Buddhist traditions. We all learn ethics in the context of our particular cultures, and the power in the principles is deeply tied to the way in which they are expressed. Internationally accepted lists of moral principles, such as the United Nations' Universal Declaration of Human Rights, draw on many cultural and religious traditions. As philosopher Michael Walzer has noted, "There is no Esperanto of global ethics."

The third problem with absolutism is the belief in a global standard of ethical behavior. Context must shape ethical practice. Very low wages, for example, may be considered unethical in rich, advanced countries, but developing nations may be acting ethically if they encourage investment and improve living standards by accepting low wages.

The Culture and Ethics of Software Piracy

Before jumping on the cultural relativism band-wagon, stop and consider the potential economic consequences of a when-in-Rome attitude toward business ethics. Take a look at the current statistics on software piracy: In the United States, pirated software is estimated to be 35% of the total software market, and industry losses are estimated at $2.3 billion per year. The piracy rate is 57% in Germany and 80% in Italy and Japan; the rates in most Asian countries are estimated to be nearly 100%.

There are similar laws against software piracy in those countries. What, then, accounts for the differences? Although a country's level of economic development plays a large part, culture, including ethical attitudes, may be a more crucial factor. The 1995 annual report of the Software Publishers Association connects software piracy directly to culture and attitude. It describes Italy and Hong Kong as having "'first world' per capita incomes, along with 'third world' rates of piracy." When asked whether one should use software without paying for it, most people, including people in Italy and Hong Kong, say no. But people in some countries regard the practice as *less* unethical than people in other countries do. Confucian culture, for example, stresses that individuals should share what they create with society. That may be, in part, what prompts the Chinese and other Asians to view the concept of intellectual property as a means for the West to monopolize its technological superiority.

What happens if ethical attitudes around the world permit large-scale software piracy? Software companies won't want to invest as much in developing new products, because they cannot expect any return on their investment in certain parts of the world. When ethics fail to support technological creativity, there are consequences that go beyond statistics–jobs are lost and livelihoods jeopardized.

Companies must do more than lobby foreign governments for tougher enforcement of piracy laws. They must cooperate with other companies and with local organizations to help citizens understand the consequences of piracy and to encourage the evolution of a different ethic toward the practice.

Likewise, when people are malnourished or starving, a government may be wise to use more fertilizer in order to improve crop yields, even though that means settling for relatively high levels of thermal water pollution.

When cultures have different standards of ethical behavior–and different ways of handling unethical behavior–a company that takes an absolutist approach may find itself making a disastrous mistake. When a manager at a large U.S. specialty-products company in China caught an employee stealing, she followed the company's practice and turned the employee over to the provincial authorities, who executed him. Managers cannot operate in another culture without being aware of that culture's attitudes toward ethics.

If companies can neither adopt a host country's ethics nor extend the home country's standards, what is the answer? Even the traditional litmus test–What would people think of your actions if they were written up on the front page of the newspaper?–is an unreliable guide, for there is no international consensus on standards of business conduct.

Balancing the Extremes: Three Guiding Principles
Companies must help managers distinguish between practices that are merely different and those that are wrong. For relativists, nothing is sacred and nothing is wrong. For absolutists, many things that are different are wrong. Neither extreme illuminates the real world of business decision making. The answer lies somewhere in between.

When it comes to shaping ethical behavior, companies must be guided by three principles.

- Respect for core human values, which determine the absolute moral threshold for all business activities.
- Respect for local traditions.
- The belief that context matters when deciding what is right and what is wrong.

Consider those principles in action. In Japan, people doing business together often exchange gifts—sometimes expensive ones–in keeping with long-standing Japanese tradition. When U.S. and European companies started doing a lot of business in Japan, many Western business-people thought that the practice of gift giving might be wrong rather than simply different. To them, accepting a gift felt like accepting a bribe. As Western companies have become more familiar with Japanese traditions, however, most have come to tolerate the practice and to set different limits on gift giving in Japan than they do elsewhere.

Respecting differences is a crucial ethical practice. Research shows that management ethics differ among cultures; respecting those differences means recognizing that some cultures have obvious weaknesses–as well as hidden strengths. Managers in Hong Kong, for example, have a higher tolerance for some forms of bribery than their Western counterparts, but they have a much lower tolerance for the failure to acknowledge a subordinate's work. In some parts of the Far East, stealing credit from a subordinate is nearly an unpardonable sin.

People often equate respect for local traditions with cultural relativism. That is incorrect. Some practices are clearly wrong. Union Carbide's tragic experience in Bhopal, India, provides one example. The company's executives seriously underestimated how much on-site management involvement was needed at the Bhopal plant to compensate for the country's poor infrastructure and regulatory capabilities. In the aftermath of the disastrous gas leak, the lesson is clear: companies using sophisticated technology in a developing country must evaluate that country's ability to oversee its safe use. Since the incident at Bhopal, Union Carbide has become a leader in advising companies on using hazardous technologies safely in developing countries.

Some activities are wrong no matter where they take place. But some practices that are unethical in one setting may be acceptable in another. For instance, the chemical EDB, a soil fungicide, is banned for use in the United States. In hot climates, however, it quickly becomes harmless through exposure to intense solar radiation and high soil temperatures. As long as the chemical is monitored, companies may be able to use EDB ethically in certain parts of the world.

Defining the Ethical Threshold: Core Values

Few ethical questions are easy for managers to answer. But there are some hard truths that must guide managers' actions, a set of what I call *core human values*, which define minimum ethical standards for all companies.[1] The right to good health and the right to economic advancement and an improved standard of living are two core human values. Another is what Westerners call the Golden Rule, which is recognizable in every major religious and ethical tradition around the world. In Book 15 of his *Analects*, for instance, Confucius counsels people to maintain reciprocity, or not to do to others what they do not want done to themselves.

Although no single list would satisfy every scholar, I believe it is possible to articulate three core values that incorporate the work of scores of theologians and philosophers around the world. To be broadly relevant, these values must include elements found in both Western and non-Western cultural and religious traditions. Consider the examples of values in the insert "What Do These Values Have in Common?"

[1.] In other writings, Thomas W. Dunfee and I have used the term *hypernorm* instead of *core human value*.

What Do These Values Have in Common?

Non-Western	Western
Kyosei (Japanese): Living and working together for the common good.	Individual liberty
Dharma (Hindu): The fulfillment of inherited duty.	Egalitarianism
Santutthi (Buddhist): The importance of limited desires.	Political participation
Zakat (Muslim): The duty to give alms to the Muslim poor.	Human rights

At first glance, the values expressed in the two lists seem quite different. Nonetheless, in the spirit of what philosopher John Rawls calls *overlapping consensus*, one can see that the seemingly divergent values converge at key points. Despite important differences between Western and non-Western cultural and religious traditions, both express shared attitudes about what it means to be human. First, individuals must not treat others simply as tools; in other words, they must recognize a person's value as a human being. Next, individuals and communities must treat people in ways that respect people's basic rights. Finally, members of a community must work together to support and improve the institutions on which the community depends. I call those three values *respect for human dignity*, *respect for basic rights*, and *good citizenship.*

Those values must be the starting point for all companies as they formulate and evaluate standards of ethical conduct at home and abroad. But they are only a starting point. Companies need much more specific guidelines, and the first step to developing those is to translate the core human values into core values for business. What does it mean, for example, for a company to respect human dignity? How can a company be a good citizen?

I believe that companies can respect human dignity by creating and sustaining a corporate culture in which employees, customers, and suppliers are treated not as means to an end but as people whose intrinsic value must be acknowledged, and by producing safe products and services in a safe workplace. Companies can respect basic rights by acting in ways that support and protect the individual rights of employees, customers, and surrounding communities, and by avoiding relationships that violate human beings' rights to health, education, safety, and an adequate standard of living. And companies can be good citizens by supporting essential social institutions, such as the economic system and the education system, and by working with host governments and other organizations to protect the environment.

The core values establish a moral compass for business practice. They can help companies identify practices that are acceptable and those that are intolerable–even if the practices are compatible with a host country's norms and laws. Dumping pollutants near people's homes and accepting inadequate standards for handling hazardous materials are two examples of actions that violate core values.

Similarly, if employing children prevents them from receiving a basic education, the practice is intolerable. Lying about product specifications in the act of selling may not affect human lives directly, but it too is intolerable because it violates the trust that is needed to sustain a corporate culture in which customers are respected.

Sometimes it is not a company's actions but those of a supplier or customer that pose problems. Take the case of the Tan family, a large supplier for Levi Strauss. The Tans were allegedly forcing 1,200 Chinese and Filipino women to work 74 hours per week in guarded compounds on the Mariana Islands. In 1992, after repeated warnings to the Tans, Levi Strauss broke off business relations with them.

Creating an Ethical Corporate Culture The core values for business that I have enumerated can help companies begin to exercise ethical judgment and think about how to operate ethically in foreign cultures, but they are not specific enough to guide

managers through actual ethical dilemmas. Levi Strauss relied on a written code of conduct when figuring out how to deal with the Tan family. The company's Global Sourcing and Operating Guidelines, formerly called the Business Partner Terms of Engagement, state that Levi Strauss will "seek to identify and utilize business partners who aspire as individuals and in the conduct of all their businesses to a set of ethical standards not incompatible with our own." Whenever intolerable business situations arise, managers should be guided by precise statements that spell out the behavior and operating practices that the company demands.

Ninety percent of all *Fortune* 500 companies have codes of conduct, and 70% have statements of vision and values. In Europe and the Far East, the percent-

ages are lower but are increasing rapidly. Does that mean that most companies have what they need? Hardly. Even though most large U.S. companies have both statements of values and codes of conduct, many might be better off if they didn't. Too many companies don't do anything with the documents; they simply paste them on the wall to impress employees, customers, suppliers, and the public. As a result, the senior managers who drafted the statements lose credibility by proclaiming values and not living up to them. Companies such as Johnson & Johnson, Levi Strauss, Motorola, Texas Instruments, and Lockheed Martin, however, do a great deal to make the words meaningful. Johnson & Johnson, for example, has become well known for its Credo Challenge sessions, in which managers discuss ethics in the context of

their current business problems and are invited to criticize the company's credo and make suggestions for changes. The participants' ideas are passed on to the company's senior managers. Lockheed Martin has created an innovative site on the World Wide Web and on its local network that gives employees, customers, and suppliers access to the company's ethical code and the chance to voice complaints.

Codes of conduct must provide clear direction about ethical behavior when the temptation to behave unethically is strongest. The pronouncement in a code of conduct that bribery is unacceptable is useless unless accompanied by guidelines for gift giving, payments to get goods through customs, and "requests" from intermediaries who are hired to ask for bribes.

Motorola's values are stated very simply as "How we will always act: [with] constant respect for people [and] uncompromising integrity."

The company's code of conduct, however, is explicit about actual business practice. With respect to bribery, for example, the code states that the "funds and assets of Motorola shall not be used, directly or indirectly, for illegal payments of any kind." It is unambiguous about what sort of payment is illegal: "the payment of a bribe to a public official or the kickback of funds to an employee of a customer . . . ." The code goes on to prescribe specific procedures for handling commissions to intermediaries, issuing sales invoices, and disclosing confidential information in a sales transaction–all situations in which employees might have an opportunity to accept or offer bribes.

Codes of conduct must be explicit to be useful, but they must also leave room for a manager to use his or her judgment in situations requiring cultural sensitivity. Host-country employees shouldn't be forced to adopt all home-country values and renounce their own. Again, Motorola's code is exemplary. First, it gives clear direction: "Employees of Motorola will respect the laws, customs, and traditions of each country in which they operate, but will, at the same time, engage in no course of conduct which, even if legal, customary, and accepted in any such country, could be deemed to be in violation of the accepted business ethics of Motorola or the laws of the United States relating to business ethics." After laying down such absolutes, Motorola's code then makes clear when individual judgment will be necessary. For example, employees may sometimes accept certain kinds of small gifts "in rare circumstances, where the refusal to accept a gift" would injure Motorola's "legitimate business interests." Under certain circumstances, such gifts "may be accepted so long as the gift inures to the benefit of Motorola" and not "to the benefit of the Motorola employee."

Striking the appropriate balance between providing clear direction and leaving room for individual judgment makes crafting corporate values statements and ethics codes one of the hardest tasks that executives confront. The words are only a start. A company's leaders need to refer often to their organization's credo and code and must themselves be credible, committed, and consistent. If senior managers act as though ethics don't matter, the rest of the company's employees won't think they do, either.

Conflicts of Development and Conflicts of Tradition   Managers living and working abroad who are not prepared to grapple with moral ambiguity and tension should pack their bags and come home. The view that all business practices can be categorized as either ethical or unethical is too simple. As Einstein is reported to have said, "Things should be as simple as possible–but no simpler."

Many business practices that are considered unethical in one setting may be ethical in another. Such activities are neither black nor white but exist in what Thomas Dunfee and I have called *moral free space.*[2] In this gray zone, there are no tight prescriptions for a company's behavior. Managers must chart their own courses–as long as they do not violate core human values.

Consider the following example. Some successful Indian companies offer employees the opportunity for one of their children to gain a job with the company once the child has completed a certain level in school. The companies honor this commitment even when other applicants are more qualified than an employee's child. The perk is extremely valuable in a country where jobs are hard to find, and it reflects the Indian culture's belief that the West has gone too far in allowing economic opportunities to break up families. Not surprisingly, the perk is among the most cherished by employees, but in most Western countries, it would be branded unacceptable nepotism. In the United States, for example, the ethical principle of equal opportunity holds that jobs should go to the applicants with the best qualifications. If a U.S. company made such promises to its employees, it would violate regulations established by the Equal Employment Opportunity Commission. Given this difference in ethical attitudes, how should U.S. managers react to Indian nepotism? Should they condemn the Indian companies, refusing to accept them as partners or suppliers until they agree to clean up their act?

Despite the obvious tension between nepotism and principles of equal opportunity, I cannot condemn the practice for Indians. In a country, such as India, that emphasizes clan and family relationships and has catastrophic levels of unemployment, the practice must be viewed in moral free space. The decision to allow a special perk for employees

[2]Thomas Donaldson and Thomas W. Dunfee, "Toward a Unified Conception of Business Ethics: Integrative Social Contracts Theory," *Academy of Management Review*, April 1994; and "Integrative Social Contracts Theory: A Communitarian Conception of Economic Ethics," *Economics and Philosophy*, spring 1995.

and their children is not necessarily wrong–at least for members of that country.

How can managers discover the limits of moral free space? That is, how can they learn to distinguish a value in tension with their own from one that is intolerable? Helping managers develop good ethical judgment requires companies to be clear about their core values and codes of conduct. But even the most explicit set of guidelines cannot always provide answers. That is especially true in the thorniest ethical dilemmas, in which the host country's ethical standards not only are different but also seem lower than the home country's. Managers must recognize that when countries have different ethical standards, there are two types of conflict that commonly arise. Each type requires its own line of reasoning.

In the first type of conflict, which I call a *conflict of relative development*, ethical standards conflict because of the countries' different levels of economic development. As mentioned before, developing countries may accept wage rates that seem inhumane to more advanced countries in order to attract investment. As economic conditions in a developing country improve, the incidence of that sort of conflict usually decreases. The second type of conflict is a *conflict of cultural tradition*. For example, Saudi Arabia, unlike most other countries, does not allow women to serve as corporate managers. Instead, women may work in only a few professions, such as education and health care. The prohibition stems from strongly held religious and cultural beliefs; any increase in the country's level of economic development, which is already quite high, is not likely to change the rules.

To resolve a conflict of relative development, a manager must ask the following question: Would the practice be acceptable at home if my country were in a similar stage of economic development? Consider the difference between wage and safety standards in the United States and in Angola, where citizens accept lower standards on both counts. If a U.S. oil company is hiring Angolans to work on an offshore Angolan oil rig, can the company pay them lower wages than it pays U.S. workers in the Gulf of Mexico? Reasonable people have to answer yes if the alternative for Angola is the loss of both the foreign investment and the jobs.

Consider, too, differences in regulatory environments. In the 1980s, the government of India fought hard to be able to import Ciba-Geigy's Entero Vioform, a drug known to be enormously effective in fighting dysentery but one that had been banned in the United States because some users experienced side effects. Although dysentery was not a big problem in the United States, in India, poor public sanitation was contributing to epidemic levels of the disease. Was it unethical to make the drug available in India after it had been banned in the United States? On the contrary, rational people should consider it unethical not to do so. Apply our test: Would the United States, at an earlier stage of development, have used this drug despite its side effects? The answer is clearly yes.

But there are many instances when the answer to similar questions is no. Sometimes a host country's standards are inadequate at any level of economic development. If a country's pollution standards are so low that working on an oil rig would considerably increase a person's risk of developing cancer, foreign oil companies must refuse to do business there. Likewise, if the dangerous side effects of a drug treatment outweigh its benefits, managers should not accept health standards that ignore the risks.

When relative economic conditions do not drive tensions, there is a more objective test for resolving ethical problems. Managers should deem a practice permissible only if they can answer no to both of the following questions: Is it possible to conduct business successfully in the host country without undertaking the practice? and Is the practice a violation of a core human value? Japanese gift giving is a perfect example of a conflict of cultural tradition. Most experienced businesspeople, Japanese and non-Japanese alike, would agree that doing business in Japan would be virtually impossible without adopting the practice. Does gift giving violate a core human value? I cannot identify one that it violates. As a result, gift giving may be permissible for foreign companies in Japan even if it conflicts with ethical attitudes at home. In

The Problem with Bribery

Bribery is widespread and insidious. Managers in transnational companies routinely confront bribery even though most countries have laws against it. The fact is that officials in may developing countries wink at the practice, and the salaries of local bureaucrats are so low that many consider bribes a form of remuneration. The U.S. Foreign Corrupt Practices Act defines allowable limits on petty bribery in the form of routine payments required to move goods through customs. But demands for bribes often exceed those limits, and there is seldom a good solution.

Bribery disrupts distribution channels when goods languish on docks until local handlers are paid off, and it destroys incentives to compete on quality and cost when purchasing decisions are based on who pays what under the table. Refusing to acquiesce is often tantamount to giving business to unscrupulous companies.

I believe that even routine bribery is intolerable. Bribery undermines market efficiency and predictability, thus ultimately denying people their right to a minimal standard of living. Some degree of ethical commitment–some sense that everyone will play by the rules–is necessary for a sound economy. Without an ability to predict outcomes, who would be willing to invest?

There was a U.S. company whose shipping crates were regularly pilfered by handlers on the docks of Rio de Janeiro. The handlers would take about 10% of the contents of the crates, but the company was never sure which 10% it would be. In a partial solution, the company began sending two crates–the first with 90% of the merchandise, the second with 10%. The handlers learned to take the second crate and leave the first untouched. From the company's perspective, at least knowing which goods it would lose was an improvement.

Bribery does more than destroy predictability; it undermines essential social and economic systems. That truth is not lost on businesspeople in countries where the practice is woven into the social fabric. CEOs in India admit that their companies engage constantly in bribery, and they say that they have considerable disgust for the practice. They blame government policies in part, but Indian executives also know that their country's business practices perpetuate corrupt behavior. Anyone walking the streets of Calcutta, where it is clear that even a dramatic redistribution of wealth would still leave most of India's inhabitants in dire poverty, comes face-to-face with the devastating effects of corruption.

---

fact, that conclusion is widely accepted, even by companies such as Texas Instruments and IBM, which are outspoken against bribery.

Does it follow that all nonmonetary gifts are acceptable or that bribes are generally acceptable in countries where they are common? Not at all. (See the insert "The Problem with Bribery.") What makes the routine practice of gift giving acceptable in Japan are the limits in its scope and intention. When gift giving moves outside those limits, it soon collides with core human values. For example, when Carl Kotchian, president of Lockheed in the 1970s,

carried suitcases full of cash to Japanese politicians, he went beyond the norms established by Japanese tradition. That incident galvanized opinion in the United States Congress and helped lead to passage of the Foreign Corrupt Practices Act. Likewise, Roh Tae Woo went beyond the norms established by Korean cultural tradition when he accepted $635.4 million in bribes as president of the Republic of Korea between 1988 and 1993.

Guidelines for Ethical Leadership   Learning to spot intolerable practices and to exercise good judgment when ethical conflicts arise requires practice. Creating a company culture that rewards ethical behavior is essential. The following guidelines for developing a global ethical perspective among managers can help.

Treat corporate values and formal standards of conduct as absolutes Whatever ethical standards a company chooses, it cannot waver on its principles either at home or abroad. Consider what has become part of company lore at Motorola. Around 1950, a senior executive was negotiating with officials of a South American government on a $10 million sale that would have increased the company's annual net profits by nearly 25%. As the negotiations neared completion, however, the executive walked away from the deal because the officials were asking for $1 million for "fees." CEO Robert Galvin not only supported the executive's decision but also made it clear that Motorola would neither accept the sale on any terms nor do business with those government officials again. Retold over the decades, this story demonstrating Galvin's resolve has helped cement a culture of ethics for thousands of employees at Motorola.

Design and implement conditions of engagement for suppliers and customers. Will your company do business with any customer or supplier? What if a customer or supplier uses child labor? What if it has strong links with organized crime? What if it pressures your company to break a host country's laws? Such issues are best not left for spur-of-the-moment decisions. Some companies have realized that. Sears, for instance, has developed a policy of not contracting production to companies that use prison labor or infringe on workers' rights to health and safety. And BankAmerica has specified as a condition for many of its loans to developing countries that environmental standards and human rights must be observed.

Allow foreign business units to help formulate ethical standards and interpret ethical issues. The French pharmaceutical company Rhône-Poulenc Rorer has allowed foreign subsidiaries to augment lists of corporate ethical principles with their own suggestions. Texas Instruments has paid

special attention to issues of international business ethics by creating the Global Business Practices Council, which is made up of managers from countries in which the company operates. With the overarching intent to create a "global ethics strategy, locally deployed," the council's mandate is to provide ethics education and create local processes that will help managers in the company's foreign business units resolve ethical conflicts.

In host countries, support efforts to decrease institutional corruption. Individual managers will not be able to wipe out corruption in a host country, no matter how many bribes they turn down. When a host country's tax system, import and export procedures, and procurement practices favor unethical players, companies must take action.

Many companies have begun to participate in reforming host-country institutions. General Electric, for example, has taken a strong stand in India, using the media to make repeated condemnations of bribery in business and government. General Electric and others have found, however, that a single company usually cannot drive out entrenched corruption. Transparency International, an organization based in Germany, has been effective in helping coalitions of companies, government officials, and others work to reform bribery-ridden bureaucracies in Russia, Bangladesh, and elsewhere.

Exercise moral imagination. Using moral imagination means resolving tensions responsibly and creatively. Coca-Cola, for instance, has consistently turned down requests for bribes from Egyptian officials but has managed to gain political support and public trust by sponsoring a project to plant fruit trees. And take the example of Levi Strauss, which discovered in the early 1990s that two of its suppliers in Bangladesh were employing children under the age of 14–a practice that violated the company's principles but was tolerated in Bangladesh. Forcing the suppliers to fire the children would not have ensured that the children received an education, and it would have caused serious hardship for the families depending on the children's wages. In a creative arrangement, the suppliers agreed to pay the children's regular wages while they attended school and to offer each child a job at age 14. Levi Strauss, in turn, agreed to pay the children's tuition and provide books and uniforms. That arrangement allowed Levi Strauss to uphold its principles and provide long-term benefits to its host country.

Many people think of values as soft; to some they are usually unspoken. A South Seas island society uses the word *mokita*, which means, "the truth that everybody knows but nobody speaks." However difficult they are to articulate, values affect how we all behave. In a global business environment, values in tension are the rule rather than the exception. Without a company's commitment, statements of values and codes of ethics end up as empty platitudes that provide managers with no foundation for behaving ethically. Employees need and deserve more, and responsible members of the global business community can set examples for others to follow. The dark consequences of incidents such as Union Carbide's disaster in Bhopal remind us how high the stakes can be.

Reading 8-2   Serving the World's Poor, Profitably

C.K. Prahalad and Allen Hammond

Improving the lives of the billions of people at the bottom of the economic pyramid is a noble endeavor. It can also be a lucrative one.

CONSIDER THIS BLEAK VISION of the world 15 years from now: The global economy recovers from its current stagnation but growth remains anemic. Deflation continues to threaten, the gap between rich and poor keeps widening, and incidents of economic chaos, governmental collapse, and civil war plague developing regions. Terrorism remains a constant threat, diverting significant public and private resources to security concerns. Opposition to the global market system intensifies. Multinational companies find it difficult to expand, and many become risk averse, slowing investment and pulling back from emerging markets.

Now consider this much brighter scenario: Driven by private investment and widespread entrepreneurial activity, the economies of developing regions grow vigorously, creating jobs and wealth and bringing hundreds of millions of new consumers into the global marketplace every year. China, India, Brazil, and, gradually, South Africa become new engines of global economic growth, promoting prosperity around the world. The resulting decrease in poverty produces a range of social benefits, helping to stabilize many developing regions and reduce civil and cross-border conflicts. The threat of terrorism and war recedes. Multinational companies expand rapidly in an era of intense innovation and competition.

Both of these scenarios are possible. Which one comes to pass will be determined primarily by one factor: the willingness of big, multinational companies to enter and invest in the world's poorest markets. By stimulating commerce and development at the bottom of the economic pyramid, MNCs could radically improve the lives of billions of people and help bring into being a more stable, less dangerous world. Achieving this goal does not require multinationals to spearhead global social development initiatives for charitable purposes. They need only act in their own self-interest, for there are enormous business benefits

C.K. Prahalad is the Harvey C. Fruehauf Professor of Business Administration at the University of Michigan Business School in Ann Arbor and the chairman of Praja, a software company in San Diego. Allen Hammond is the CIO, senior scientist, and director of the Digital Dividend project at the World Resources Institute in Washington, DC.

to be gained by entering developing markets. In fact, many innovative companies– entrepreneurial outfits and large, established enterprises alike–are already serving the world's poor in ways that generate strong revenues, lead to greater operating efficiencies, and uncover new sources of innovation. For these companies–and those that follow their lead–building businesses aimed at the bottom of the pyramid promises to provide important competitive advantages as the twenty-first century unfolds.

Big companies are not going to solve the economic ills of developing countries by themselves, of course. It will also take targeted financial aid from the developed world and improvements in the governance of the developing nations themselves. But it's clear to us that prosperity can come to the poorest regions only through the direct and sustained involvement of multinational companies. And it's equally clear that the multinationals can enhance their own prosperity in the process.

Untapped Potential

Everyone knows that the world's poor are distressingly plentiful. Fully 65% of the world's population earns less than $2,000 each per year–that's 4 billion people. But despite the vastness of this market, it remains largely untapped by multinational companies. The reluctance to invest is easy to understand. Companies assume that people with such low incomes have little to spend on goods and services and that what they do spend goes to basic needs like food and shelter. They also assume that various barriers to commerce–corruption, illiteracy, inadequate infrastructure, currency fluctuations, bureaucratic red tape–make it impossible to do business profitably in these regions.

But such assumptions reflect a narrow and largely outdated view of the developing world. The fact is, many multinationals already successfully do business in developing countries (although most currently focus on selling to the small upper-middle-class segments of these markets), and their experience shows that the barriers to commerce–although real–are much lower than is typically

thought. Moreover, several positive trends in developing countries–from political reform, to a growing openness to investment, to the development of low-cost wireless communication networks–are reducing the barriers further while also providing businesses with greater access to even the poorest city slums and rural areas. Indeed, once the misperceptions are wiped away, the enormous economic potential that lies at the bottom of the pyramid becomes clear.

Take the assumption that the poor have no money. It sounds obvious on the surface, but it's wrong. While individual incomes may be low, the aggregate buying power of poor communities is actually quite large. The average per capita income of villagers in rural Bangladesh, for instance, is less than $200 per year, but as a group they are avid consumers of telecommunications services. Grameen Telecom's village phones,which are owned by a single entrepreneur but used by the entire community, generate an average revenue of roughly $90 a month–and as much as $1,000 a month in some large villages. Customers of these village phones, who pay cash for each use, spend an average of 7% of their income on phone services–a far higher percentage than consumers in traditional markets do.

It's also incorrect to assume that the poor are too concerned with fulfilling their basic needs to "waste" money on nonessential goods. In fact, the poor often do buy "luxury" items. In the Mumbai shantytown of Dharavi, for example, 85% of households own a television set, 75% own a pressure cooker and a mixer, 56% own a gas stove, and 21% have telephones. That's because buying a house in Mumbai, for most people at the bottom of the pyramid, is not a realistic option. Neither is getting access to running water. They accept that reality, and rather than saving for a rainy day, they spend their income on things they can get now that improve the quality of their lives.

Another big misperception about developing markets is that the goods sold there are incredibly cheap and, hence, there's no room for a new competitor to come in and turn a profit. In reality, consumers at the bottom of the pyramid pay much higher prices for most things than middle-class consumers do, which means that there's a real opportunity for companies, particularly big corporations with economies of scale and efficient supply chains, to capture market share by offering higher quality goods at lower prices while maintaining attractive margins. In fact, throughout the developing world, urban slum dwellers pay, for instance, between four and 100 times as much for drinking water as middle- and upper-class families. Food also costs 20% to 30% more in the poorest communities since there is no access to bulk discount stores. On the service side of the economy, local moneylenders charge interest of 10% to 15% *per day*, with annual rates running as high as 2,000%. Even the lucky small-scale entrepreneurs who get loans from nonprofit microfinance institutions pay between 40% and 70% interest per year—rates that are illegal in most developed countries. (For a closer look at how the prices of goods compare in rich and poor areas, see the exhibit "The High-Cost Economy of the Poor.")

It can also be surprisingly cheap to market and deliver products and services to the world's poor. That's because many of them live in cities that are densely populated today and will be even more so in the years to come. Figures from the UN and the World Resources Institute indicate that by 2015, in Africa, 225 cities will each have populations of more than 1 million; in Latin America, another 225; and in Asia, 903. The population of at least 27 cities will reach or exceed 8 million. Collectively, the 1,300 largest cities will account for some 1.5 billion to 2 billion people, roughly half of whom will be bottom-of-the-pyramid (BOP) consumers now served primarily by informal economies. Companies that operate in these areas will have access to millions of potential new customers, who together have billions of dollars to spend. The poor in Rio de Janeiro, for instance, have a total purchasing power of $1.2 billion ($600 per person). Shantytowns in Johannesburg or Mumbai are no different.

The slums of these cities already have distinct ecosystems, with retail shops, small businesses, schools, clinics, and moneylenders. Although there are few reliable estimates of the value of commercial transactions in slums, business activity appears to be thriving. Dharavi–covering an area of just 435 acres–boasts scores of businesses ranging from leather, textiles, plastic recycling, and surgical sutures to gold jewelry, illicit liquor, detergents, and groceries. The scale of the businesses varies from one-person operations to bigger, well-recognized producers of brand-name products. Dharavi generates an estimated $450 million in manufacturing revenues, or about $1 million per acre of land. Established shantytowns in São Paulo, Rio, and Mexico City are equally productive. The seeds of a vibrant commercial sector have been sown.

While the rural poor are naturally harder to reach than the urban poor, they also represent a large untapped opportunity for companies. Indeed, 60% of India's GDP is generated in rural areas. The critical barrier to doing business in rural regions is distribution access, not a lack of buying power. But new information technology and communications infrastructures–especially wireless–promise to become an inexpensive way to establish marketing and distribution channels in these communities.

Conventional wisdom says that people in BOP markets cannot use such advanced technologies, but that's just another misconception. Poor rural women in Bangladesh have had no difficulty using GSM cell phones, despite never before using phones of any type. In Kenya, teenagers from slums are being successfully trained as Web page designers. Poor farmers in El Salvador use telecenters to negotiate the sale of their crops over the Internet. And women in Indian coastal villages have in less than a week learned to use PCs to interpret real-time satellite images showing concentrations of schools of fish in the Arabian Sea so they can direct their husbands to the best fishing areas. Clearly, poor communities are ready to adopt new technologies that improve their economic opportunities or their quality of life. The lesson for multinationals: Don't hesitate to deploy advanced technologies at the bottom of the pyramid while, or even before, deploying them in advanced countries.

A final misperception concerns the highly charged issue of exploitation of the poor by MNCs.

The informal economies that now serve poor communities are full of inefficiencies and exploitive intermediaries. So if a microfinance institution charges 50% annual interest when the alternative is either 1,000% interest or no loan at all, is that exploiting or helping the poor? If a large financial company such as Citigroup were to use its scale to offer microloans at 20%, is that exploiting or helping the poor? The issue is not just cost but also quality—quality in the range and fairness of financial services, quality of food, quality of water. We argue that when MNCs provide basic goods and services that reduce costs to the poor and help improve their standard of living—while generating an acceptable return on investment—the results benefit everyone.

> Markets at the bottom of the economic pyramid are fundamentally new sources of growth for multinationals. And because these markets are in the earliest stages, growth can be extremely rapid.

▮ The Business Case

The business opportunities at the bottom of the pyramid have not gone un-noticed. Over the last five years, we have seen nongovernmental organizations (NGOs), entrepreneurial start-ups, and a handful of forward-thinking multinationals conduct vigorous commercial experiments in poor communities. Their experience is a proof of concept: Businesses can gain three important advantages by serving the poor—a new source of revenue growth, greater efficiency, and access to innovation. Let's look at examples of each.

Top-Line Growth   Growth is an important challenge for every company, but today it is especially critical for very large companies, many of which appear to have nearly saturated their existing markets. That's why BOP markets represent such an opportunity for MNCs: They are fundamentally new sources of growth. And because these markets are in the earliest stages of economic development, growth can be extremely rapid.

Latent demand for low-priced, high-quality goods is enormous. Consider the reaction when Hindustan Lever, the Indian subsidiary of Unilever, recently introduced what was for it a new product category—candy—aimed at the bottom of the pyramid. A high-quality confection made with real sugar and fruit, the candy sells for only about a penny a serving. At such a price, it may seem like a marginal business opportunity, but in just six months it became the fastest-growing category in the company's portfolio. Not only is it profitable, but the company estimates it has the potential to generate revenues of $200 million per year in India and comparable markets in five years. Hindustan Lever has had similar successes in India with low-priced detergent and iodized salt. Beyond generating new sales, the company is establishing its business and its brand in a vast new market.

There is equally strong demand for affordable services. TARAhaat, a start-up focused on rural India, has introduced a range of computer-enabled education services ranging from basic IT training to English proficiency to vocational skills. The products are expected to be the largest single revenue generator for the company and its franchisees over the next several years.[1] Credit and financial services are also in high demand among the poor. Citibank's ATM-based banking experiment in India, called Suvidha, for instance, which requires a minimum deposit of just $25, enlisted 150,000 customers in one year in the city of Bangalore alone.

Small-business services are also popular in BOP markets. Centers run in Uganda by the Women's Information Resource Electronic Service (WIRES) provide female entrepreneurs with information on markets and prices, as well as credit and trade support services, packaged in simple, ready-to-use formats in local languages. The centers are planning to offer other small-business services such as printing, faxing, and copying, along with access to accounting, spreadsheet, and other software. In Bolivia, a start-up has partnered with the Bolivian Association of Ecological Producers Organizations to offer business information and communications services

---

[1] Andrew Lawlor, Caitlin Peterson, and Vivek Sandell, "Catalyzing Rural Development: TARAhaat.com" (World Resources Institute, July 2001).

The World Pyramid

Most companies target consumers at the upper tiers of the economic pyramid, completely overlooking the business potential at its base. But though they may each be earning the equivalent of less than $2,000 a year, the people at the bottom of the pyramid make up a colossal market 4 billion strong–the vast majority of the world's population.

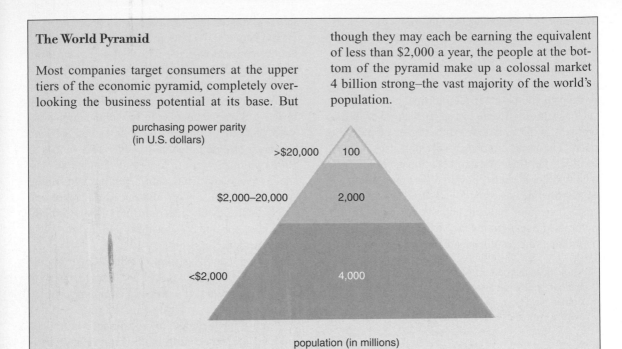

purchasing power parity
(in U.S. dollars)

>$20,000   100

$2,000–20,000   2,000

<$2,000   4,000

population (in millions)

to more than 25,000 small producers of ecoagricultural products.

It's true that some services simply cannot be offered at a low-enough cost to be profitable, at least not with traditional technologies or business models. Most mobile telecommunications providers, for example, cannot yet profitably operate their networks at affordable prices in the developing world. One answer is to find alternative technology. A microfinance organization in Bolivia named PRODEM, for example, uses multilingual smart-card ATMs to substantially reduce its marginal cost per customer. Smart cards store a customer's personal details, account numbers, transaction records, and a fingerprint, allowing cash dispensers to operate without permanent network connections–which is key in remote areas. What's more, the machines offer voice commands in Spanish and several local dialects and are equipped with touch screens so that PRODEM's customer base can be extended to illiterate and semiliterate people.

Another answer is to aggregate demand, making the community–not the individual–the network customer. Gyan-doot, a start-up in the Dhar district of central India, where 60% of the population falls below the poverty level, illustrates the benefits of a shared access model. The company has a network of 39 Internet-enabled kiosks that provide local entrepreneurs with Internet and telecommunications access, as well as with governmental, educational, and other services. Each kiosk serves 25 to 30 surrounding villages; the entire network reaches more than 600 villages and over half a million people.

Networks like these can be useful channels for marketing and distributing many kinds of low-cost products and services. Aptech's Computer Education division, for example, has built its own network of 1,000 learning centers in India to market and distribute Vidya, a computer-training course specially designed for BOP consumers and available in seven Indian languages. Pioneer Hi-Bred, a DuPont company, uses Internet kiosks in Latin

America to deliver agricultural information and to interact with customers. Farmers can report different crop diseases or weather conditions, receive advice over the wire, and order seeds, fertilizers, and pesticides. This network strategy increases both sales and customer loyalty.

Reduced Costs   No less important than top-line growth are cost-saving opportunities. Outsourcing operations to low-cost labor markets has, of course, long been a popular way to contain costs, and it has led to the increasing prominence of China in manufacturing and India in software. Now, thanks to the rapid expansion of high-speed digital networks, companies are realizing even greater savings by locating such labor-intensive service functions as call centers, marketing services, and backoffice transaction processing in developing areas. For example, the nearly 20 companies that use OrphanIT.com's affiliate-marketing services, provided via its telecenters in India and the Philippines, pay one-tenth the going rate for similar services in the United States or Australia. Venture capitalist Vinod Khosla describes the remote-services opportunity this way: "I suspect that by 2010, we will be talking about [remote services] as the fastest-growing part of the world economy, with many trillions of dollars of new markets created." Besides keeping costs down, outsourcing jobs to BOP markets can enhance growth, since job creation ultimately increases local consumers' purchasing power.

But tapping into cheap labor pools is not the only way MNCs can enhance their efficiency by operating in developing regions. The competitive necessity of maintaining a low cost structure in these areas can push companies to discover creative ways to configure their products, finances, and supply chains to enhance productivity. And these discoveries can often be incorporated back into their existing operations in developed markets.

For instance, companies targeting the BOP market are finding that the shared access model, which disaggregates access from ownership, not only widens their customer base but increases asset productivity as well. Poor people, rather than buying

their own computers, Internet connections, cell phones, refrigerators, and even cars, can use such equipment on a pay-per-use basis. Typically, the providers of such services get considerably more revenue per dollar of investment in the underlying assets. One shared Internet line, for example, can serve as many as 50 people, generating more revenue per day than if it were dedicated to a single customer at a flat fee. Shared access creates the opportunity to gain far greater returns from all sorts of infrastructure investments.

In terms of finances, to operate successfully in BOP markets, managers must also rethink their business metrics—specifically, the traditional focus on high gross margins. In developing markets, the profit margin on individual units will always be low. What really counts is capital efficiency—getting the highest possible returns on capital employed (ROCE). Hindustan Lever, for instance, operates a $2.6 billion business portfolio with zero working capital. The key is constant efforts to reduce capital investments by extensively outsourcing manufacturing, streamlining supply chains, actively managing receivables, and paying close attention to distributors' performance. Very low capital needs, focused distribution and technology investments, and very large volumes at low margins lead to very high ROCE businesses, creating great economic value for shareholders. It's a model that can be equally attractive in developed and developing markets.

Streamlining supply chains often involves replacing assets with information. Consider, for example, the experience of ITC, one of India's largest companies. Its agribusiness division has deployed a total of 970 kiosks serving 600,000 farmers who supply it with soy, coffee, shrimp, and wheat from 5,000 villages spread across India. This kiosk program, called e-Choupal, helps increase the farmers' productivity by disseminating the latest information on weather and best practices in farming, and by supporting other services like soil and water testing, thus facilitating the supply of quality inputs to both the farmers and ITC. The kiosks also serve as an e-procurement system, helping farmers earn higher prices by minimizing transaction costs involved in marketing farm produce. The head of ITC's agribusiness reports that the company's procurement costs have fallen since e-Choupal was implemented. And that's despite paying higher prices to its farmers: The program has enabled the company to eliminate multiple transportation, bagging, and handling steps—from farm to local market, from market to broker, from broker to processor— that did not add value in the chain.

Innovation   BOP markets are hotbeds of commercial and technological experimentation. The Swedish wireless company Ericsson, for instance, has developed a small cellular telephone system, called a MiniGSM, that local operators in BOP markets can use to offer cell phone service to a small area at a radically lower cost than conventional equipment entails. Packaged for easy shipment and deployment, it provides stand-alone or networked voice and data communications for up to 5,000 users within a 35-kilometer radius. Capital costs to the operator can be as low as $4 per user, assuming a shared-use model with individual phones operated by local entrepreneurs. The MIT Media Lab, in collaboration with the Indian government, is developing low-cost devices that allow people to use voice commands to communicate—without keyboards—with various Internet sites in multiple languages. These new access devices promise to be far less complex than traditional computers but would perform many of the same basic functions.[2]

As we have seen, connectivity is a big issue for BOP consumers. Companies that can find ways to dramatically lower connection costs, therefore, will have a very strong market position. And that is exactly what the Indian company n-Logue is trying to do. It connects hundreds of franchised village kiosks containing both a computer and a phone with centralized nodes that are, in turn, connected to the national phone network and the Internet. Each node, also a franchise, can serve between 30,000 and 50,000 customers, providing phone, e-mail, Internet services, and relevant local information at affordable prices to villagers in rural India. Capital costs for the n-Logue system are now about $400 per wireless "line" and are projected to decline to $100—at least ten times lower than conventional telecom costs. On a per-customer basis, the cost may amount to as little as $1.[3] This appears to be a powerful model for ending rural isolation and linking untapped rural markets to the global economy.

New wireless technologies are likely to spur further business model innovations and lower costs even more. Ultra-wideband, for example, is currently licensed in the United States only for limited, very low-power applications, in part because it spreads a signal across already-crowded portions of the broadcast spectrum. In many developing countries, however, the spectrum is less congested. In fact, the U.S.-based Dan-din Group is already building an ultra-wideband communications system for the Kingdom of Tonga, whose population of about 100,000 is spread over dozens of islands, making it a test bed for a next-generation technology that could transform the economics of Internet access.

E-commerce systems that run over the phone or the Internet are enormously important in BOP markets because they eliminate the need for layers of intermediaries. Consider how the U.S. start-up Voxiva has changed the way information is shared and business is transacted in Peru. The company partners with Telefónica, the dominant local carrier, to offer automated business applications over the phone. The inexpensive services include voice mail, data entry, and order placement; customers can check account balances, monitor delivery status, and access prerecorded information directories. According to the Boston Consulting Group, the Peruvian Ministry of Health uses Voxiva to disseminate information, take pharmaceutical orders, and link health care workers spread across 6,000 offices and clinics. Microfinance institutions use Voxiva to process loan applications

[2]Michael Best and Colin M. Maclay, "Community Internet Access in Rural Areas: Solving the Economic Sustainability Puzzle," *The Global Information Technology Report 2001–2002: Readiness for the Networked World*, ed., Geoffrey Kirkman (Oxford University Press, 2002), available on-line at http://www.cid.harvard.edu/cr/ gitrr_030202.html.
[3]Joy Howard, Erik Simanis, and Charis Simms, "Sustainable Deployment for Rural Connectivity: The n-Logue Model" (World Resources Institute, July 2001).

The High-Cost Economy of the Poor

When we compare the costs of essentials in Dharavi, a shantytown of more than 1 million people in the heart of Mumbai, India, with those of Warden Road, an upper-class community in a nice Mumbai suburb, a disturbing picture emerges. Clearly, costs could be dramatically reduced if the poor could benefit from the scope, scale, and supply-chain efficiencies of large enterprises, as their middle-class counterparts do. This pattern is common around the world, even in developed countries. For instance, a similar, if less exaggerated, disparity exists between the inner-city poor and the suburban rich in the United States.

Cost	Dharavi	Warden Road	Poverty premium
credit (annual interest)	600%–1,000%	12%–18%	53X
municipal-grade water (per cubic meter)	$1.12	$0.03	37X
phone call (per minute)	$0.04–$0.05	$0.025	1.8X
diarrhea medication	$20	$2	10X
rice (per kilogram)	$0.28	$0.24	1.2X

and communicate with borrowers. Voxiva offers Web-based services,too,but far more of its potential customers in Latin America have access to a phone.

E-commerce companies are not the only ones turning the limitations of BOP markets to strategic advantage. A lack of dependable electric power stimulated the UK-based start-up Free-play Group to introduce hand-cranked radios in South Africa that subsequently became popular with hikers in the United States. Similar breakthroughs are being pioneered in the use of solar-powered devices such as battery chargers and water pumps. In China, where pesticide costs have often limited the use of modern agricultural techniques, there are now 13,000 small farmers–more than in the rest of the world combined–growing cotton that has been genetically engineered to be pest resistant.

Strategies for Serving BOP Markets

Certainly, succeeding in BOP markets requires multinationals to think creatively. The biggest change, though, has to come in the attitudes and practices of executives. Unless CEOs and other business leaders confront their own preconceptions, companies are unlikely to master the challenges of BOP markets. The traditional workforce is so rigidly conditioned to operate in higher-margin markets that, without formal training, it is unlikely to see the vast potential of the BOP market. The most pressing need, then, is education. Perhaps MNCs should create the equivalent of the Peace Corps: Having young managers spend a couple of formative years in BOP markets would open their eyes to the promise and the realities of doing business there.

To date, few multinationals have developed a cadre of people who are comfortable with these markets. Hindustan Lever is one of the exceptions.The company expects executive recruits to spend at least eight weeks in the villages of India to get a gut-level experience of Indian BOP markets. The new executives must become involved in some community project–building a road, cleaning up a water catchment area,teaching in a school, improving a health clinic. The goal is to engage with the local population. To buttress this effort, Hindustan Lever is initiating a massive program for managers at all levels–from the CEO down–to reconnect with their poorest customers. They'll talk with the poor in both rural and urban areas, visit the shops these customers frequent, and ask them about their experience with the company's products and those of its competitors.

In addition to expanding managers' understanding of BOP markets, companies will need to make structural changes. To capitalize on the innovation potential of these markets, for example, they might set up R&D units in developing countries that are specifically focused on local opportunities. When Hewlett-Packard launched its e-Inclusion division, which concentrates on rural markets, it established a branch of its famed HP Labs in India charged with developing products and services explicitly for this market. Hindustan Lever maintains a significant R&D effort in India, as well.

Companies might also create venture groups and internal investment funds aimed at seeding entrepreneurial efforts in BOP markets. Such investments reap direct benefits in terms of business experience and market development. They can also play an indirect but vital role in growing the overall BOP market in sectors that will ultimately benefit the multinational. At least one major U.S. corporation is planning to launch such a fund, and the G8's Digital Opportunity Task Force is proposing a similar one focused on digital ventures.

MNCs should also consider creating a business development task force aimed at these markets. Assembling a diverse group of people from across the corporation and empowering it to function as a skunk works team that ignores conventional dogma will likely lead to greater innovation. Companies that have tried this approach have been surprised by the amount of interest such a task force generates. Many employees want to work on projects that have the potential to make a real difference in improving the lives of the poor. When Hewlett-Packard announced its e-Inclusion division, for example, it was overwhelmed by far more volunteers than it could accommodate.

Making internal changes is important, but so is reaching out to external partners. Joining with businesses that are already established in these markets can be an effective entry strategy, since these companies will naturally understand the market dynamics better. In addition to limiting the risks for each player, partnerships also maximize the existing infrastructure—both physical and social. MNCs seeking partners should look beyond businesses to NGOs and community groups. They are key

sources of knowledge about customers' behavior, and they often experiment the most with new services and new delivery models. In fact, of the social enterprises experimenting with creative uses of digital technology that the Digital Dividend Project Clearinghouse tracked, nearly 80% are NGOs. In Namibia, for instance, an organization called School-Net is providing low-cost, alternative technology solutions—such as solar power and wireless approaches—to schools and community-based groups throughout the country. SchoolNet is currently linking as many as 35 new schools every month.

Entrepreneurs also will be critical partners. According to an analysis by McKinsey & Company, the rapid growth of cable TV in India—there are 50 million connections a decade after introduction—is largely due to small entrepreneurs. These individuals have been building the last mile of the network, typically by putting a satellite dish on their own houses and laying cable to connect their neighbors. A note of caution, however. Entrepreneurs in BOP markets lack access to the advice, technical help, seed funding, and business support services available in the industrial world. So MNCs may need to take on mentoring roles or partner with local business development organizations that can help entrepreneurs create investment and partnering opportunities.

It's worth noting that, contrary to popular opinion, women play a significant role in the economic development of these regions. MNCs, therefore, should pay particular attention to women entrepreneurs. Women are also likely to play the most critical role in product acceptance not only because of their child-care and household management activities but also because of the social capital that they have built up in their communities. Listening to and educating such customers is essential for success.

Regardless of the opportunities, many companies will consider the bottom of the pyramid to be too risky. We've shown how partnerships can limit risk; another option is to enter into consortia. Imagine sharing the costs of building a rural network with the communications company that would operate it, a consumer goods company seeking channels to expand its sales, and a bank that is financing

Sharing Intelligence

What creative new approaches to serving the bottom-of-the-pyramid markets have digital technologies made possible? Which sectors or countries show the most economic activity or the fastest growth? What new business models show promise? What kinds of partnerships–for funding, distribution, public relations–have been most successful?

The Digital Dividend Project Clearinghouse (digitaldividend.org) helps answer those types of questions. The Web site tracks the activities of organizations that use digital tools to provide connectivity and deliver services to underserved populations in developing countries. Currently, it contains information on 700 active projects around the world. Maintained under the auspices of the nonprofit World Resources Institute, the site lets participants in different projects share experiences and swap knowledge with one another. Moreover, the site provides data for trend analyses and other specialized studies that facilitate market analyses, local partnerships, and rapid, low-cost learning.

the construction and wants to make loans to and collect deposits from rural customers.

Investing where powerful synergies exist will also mitigate risk. The Global Digital Opportunity Initiative, a partnership of the Markle Foundation and the UN Development Programme, will help a small number of countries implement a strategy to harness the power of information and communications technologies to increase development. The countries will be chosen in part based on their interest and their willingness to make supportive regulatory and market reforms. To concentrate resources and create reinforcing effects, the initiative will encourage international aid agencies and global companies to assist with implementation.

All of the strategies we've outlined here will be of little use, however, unless the external barriers we've touched on–poor infrastructure, inadequate connectivity, corrupt intermediaries, and the like–are removed. Here's where technology holds the most promise. Information and communications technologies can grant access to otherwise isolated communities, provide marketing and distribution channels, bypass intermediaries, drive down transaction costs, and help aggregate demand and buying power. Smart cards and other emerging technologies are inexpensive ways to give poor customers a secure identity, a transaction or credit history, and even a virtual address–prerequisites for interacting with the formal economy. That's why high-tech companies aren't the only ones that should be interested in closing the global digital divide; encouraging the spread of low-cost digital networks at the bottom of the pyramid is a priority for virtually all companies that want to enter and engage with these markets. Improved connectivity is an important catalyst for more effective markets, which are critical to boosting income levels and accelerating economic growth.

Moreover, global companies stand to gain from the effects of network expansion in these markets. According to Metcalfe's Law, the usefulness of a network equals the square of the number of users. By the same logic, the value and vigor of the economic activity that will be generated when hundreds of thousands of previously isolated rural communities can buy and sell from one another and from urban markets will increase dramatically–to the benefit of all participants.

• • •

Since BOP markets require significant rethinking of managerial practices, it is legitimate for managers to ask: Is it worth the effort?

We think the answer is yes. For one thing, big corporations should solve big problems–and what is a more pressing concern than alleviating the poverty that 4 billion people are currently mired in? It is hard to argue that the wealth of technology and talent within leading multinationals is better allocated to producing incremental variations of existing products than to addressing the real needs–and real opportunities–at the bottom of the pyramid. Moreover, through competition, multinationals are likely to bring to BOP markets a level of accountability for performance and resources that neither international development agencies nor national governments have demonstrated during the last 50 years. Participation by MNCs could set a new standard, as well as a new market-driven paradigm, for addressing poverty.

But ethical concerns aside, we've shown that the potential for expanding the bottom of the market is just too great to ignore. Big companies need to focus on big market opportunities if they want to generate real growth. It is simply good business strategy to be in volved in large, untapped markets that offer new customers, cost-saving opportunities, and access to radical innovation. The business opportunities at the bottom of the pyramid are real, and they are open to any MNC willing to engage and learn.

Index

■ ■ ■ ■ ■ ■ ■ ■ ■ ■ ■ ■ ■ ■ ■ ■ ■ ■

('f' indicates a figure; 'n' indicates a note; 't' indicates a table)

A

AAA Competitive Map for Diagnostic
    Imaging, 286
Abernathy, W., 498n.11
Absolutism, 744–745
Accents, 386
Acer American Corporation (AAC),
    53, 59, 64, 66
Acer Inc. case study, 53–68
Adaptation
    global strategy, 279, 281, 282, 283
    multicultural teams intervention,
        387, 388, 389
Adjacencies, 490
Adler, Nancy J., 118n.3
Administrative distance
    sensitive industries, 102
    trade impact, 96, 98, 99, 100–101
Administrative heritage, 314, 317–320
Advanced Multifunctional Operator
    Service System (ADMOSS),
    435–437, 441
Advocate, 595–596
Aetna, 605–606
Africa, 237–238
Aggregation
    and arbitrage, 283–284
    as global strategy, 279, 281, 282, 282
AIDS, retroviral medication coverage, 673
AIDS Initiative case study, 366–384
Ainuddin, R. Azimah, 525
Air Liquide, 17, 18
Ajinimoto Company, 516
Akopiantz, Patty, 471
Alanis-Ortega, Gustavo, 670n.10
Alcatel, 486
Alexander, Marcus, 105
Alford, William, 96–97
Alien Tort Claim Act (ACTA), 714, 715
Ambos, Tina C., 331, 392
Ambrosio, Chris, 75n.13
Amnesty International, Colombia, 712,
    714, 714n.17
Amos Tuck School of Business, 686
Analects, 746
Anderson, P., 498n.11
Annan, Kofi, 673
Anthony, S., 498n.12
Antiglobalization movement, 120
Anuradha, A., 435, 437
Apparel Industry Partnership (AIP),
    684, 689–690

Appellation d'Origin Controllée
    (AOC), 129
Aquino, Corazon, 35, 39
Arab, Majid, 471
Arbitrage
    and adaptation, 283–284
    as global strategy, 279, 281, 282, 283
Arbitration, 537
ArcLink, 23
Area Development Program (ADP),
    371, 382
Arnstein, Caren, 732
Artois, Sebastiaan, 244
Artzt, Ed, 446
Asia, 185f, 186
Asian-American Free Labor Association
    (AAFLI), 681, 682
Assets/resources configuration architect,
    590–591
Association of Strategic Alliance
    Professions (ASAP), 568
Aston studies, 179
AT&T, 421
Athletic shoes case study, 680, 682–683
Attention decisions
    subsidiary "voice," 393, 395–396
    subsidiary "weight," 393, 394–395
Australia
    BRL Hardy wine company,
        612, 626–628
    McKinsey & Company, 470–472
    wine case study, 130, 132, 143–145
    wine industry, 612–614, 626
Ayurvedic system, 650
Aznam, Suhaini, 681n.11

B

Bahrain, 43
Baidu, 290, 293
Baker, S., 432n.8
Ballinger, Jeff, 681–682, 683, 683n.
    19, 684, 697
Bangalore, Siemens, 434–438, 439,
    440, 441
Banrock Station wine, 612, 627–628
Bapuji, Hari, 166
Barbaro, Michael, 666n.5
Barboza, David, 169n.14, 174n.30
Barner, Marianne, 697–698, 704,
    705, 706–707
Barsoux, Jean-Louis, 178, 185n.15

Bartlett, Christopher A., 34, 53, 128, 259,
    331, 340, 366, 400, 442, 461, 488,
    600, 612, 612n.1, 629, 653, 697,
    698n.3, 725, 726n.1
"Basing point" pricing, 148–149
Bassi, Pete, 103
Bawden, Tom, 239n.143
Bayer, 304
Bayhan, Gokhan, 272, 273, 275
BBC, 505–506
Beamish, Paul W., 5n.5, 9n.13, 11n.15,
    68, 166, 169n.13, 244, 524, 525,
    567, 666n.6
Beauty Care Global Business Unit
    (GBU), 442, 449, 453
Beer
    Stella Artois case study, 244–258
    Tambura, 506
BeGole, Brett, 259, 277
Behar, Yves, 226, 230, 231, 232
Behfar, Kristin, 331, 384
Belgium, 244
Bell, Alexander Graham, 420
Benjamin, Medea, 719
Bennett, Jim, 464
Bennett, Nicole S., 259
Benson, Martha, 679n.3
Berri Renmano Limited (BRL), 614–615
Bessant, John, 418, 496, 496n.3, 497
Best, Michael, 760n.2
"Best Practices," 593–594
Bharat Bijlee Ltd. (BBL), 630, 640, 641
Bharti Airtel, 290, 294
Bhattacharya, Arindam K., 223, 290
Bhide, Amar V., 461
Big One, The, 685
Biggart, N. W., 505n.22
Birkinshaw, Julian, 331, 392,
    418, 496, 497
Birnbaum-More, P. H., 186n.19
Bjørn, Thomas, 349
Black holes, 656, 658, 661
BlackBerry products, 68–74
Blair, Henry, 726
Bloom, Barry, 738
Blue Circle cement, 146, 149, 150, 151, 154
Boca Raton, 433–434, 439
Bock, Richard, 437–438
Bolivian Association of Ecological
    Producers Organizations, 757–758
Bond, M. H., 193n.30
Bonded Labour System (Abolished)
    Act, 705

Bonnard, Luc, 629, 631, 632, 637, 644
Boonstra, Cor, 312, 338
Boston Consulting Group (BCG)
  growth, 462, 463
  and ING Insurance, 609–610
  and Schindler Holdings, 632
Bottom of the pyramid (BOP)
  business strategies, 761–764
  growth potential, 757–759
  innovation, 760–761
  reduced costs, 759–760, 761
  untapped potential, 755–757
Bouquet, Cyril, 331, 392
Bower, Marvin, 461–462
Brady, Roscoe, 726
Braimah, Abubakr-Sadiq,
    237nn.128–129
Branch offices, 375, 376
Brand strategy, 250–251
Brar, D. S., 552, 556, 558, 565
Bray, Warwick, 472, 473
Brazil
  Chagas project, 736–737
  locally successful firms,
    290, 293, 297
  management model, 189, 190, 190t
Brett, Jeanne, 331, 384
Bribery
  MNE's, 667
  Motorola policy, 749–750
  as unacceptable, 752
BridgeIt, 675
British Philips (BP), 332, 505
BRL Hardy case study, 612–628
Broad Institute, 730, 734, 738
Brolio de Ricasoli, 615
Brønd, Flemming, 348, 361
Brossard, A., 185n.15
Brownback, Sam, 739
Browne, Paul, 626, 628
Brunei, 40, 43
"Building Effective R&D Capabilities
    Abroad," 418, 477–487
Burgelman, R. A., 497n.7, 498n.14
Burns, Jennifer L., 679
Burns, Jim, 734
Burns, T., 179n.3, 182n.12
Burt, R., 498n.15
Business ethics
  codes of conduct, 748–750
  common conflicts, 751–752
  corporate culture, 747–750
  corporate values, 753–754
  cultural relativism, 743–745
  ethical imperialism, 744–745
  guiding principles, 745–747
Business for Social Responsibility, 684
Business formation, 202
Business Partner Terms of
    Engagement, 748

C

Cable industry, 527
CAGE Distance Framework, 96, 99, 105
Caktiong, Ton Tan, 34, 36
Cal-Safety Compliance Corporation,
    721, 723, 724
California, 52–53
Caliterra brand, 622
Calof, Jonathan, 9n.13
Calzini, Derek, 686nn.32–35, 687n.36,
    690, 691
Campaign to Stop Killer Coke, 708
Canon, 484
"Carrier switches," 420
Carson, Christopher, 612, 618–624,
    626, 628
Case studies
  Acer Inc, 53–68
  BRL Hardy Wine Company,
    612–628
  CEMEX, 146–166
  ECCO A/S, 348–365
  Eli Lilly in India, 552–567
  GE: Evo Project, 259–278
  Genzyme's CSR Dilemma,
    725–742
  Global Wine War, 128–145
  IKEA, 697–707
  ING Insurance Asia/Pacific,
    601–611
  Jollibee Foods Corporation, 34–53
  Killer Coke, 707–725
  Lincoln Electric, 15–33
  Mahindra & Mahindra/Jiangling
    Tractor Company, 538–552
  Mattel, 166–178
  McKinsey & Company, 461–476
  Nike, 679–697
  Nora-Sakari joint venture,
    520, 525–537
  $100 Laptop, 224–243
  P&G Japan, 442–460
  Philips versus Matsushita, 331–347
  Research in Motion, 68–85
  Siemens AG: 419–441
  Silvio Napoli at Schindler India,
    629–644
  Stella Artois, 244–258
  World Vision International's AIDS
    Initiative, 366–384
Casey, Ken, 366, 380–384
Castell, Sir William, 590
CAT scanners, 653–654
Caves, Richard E., 8n.9
CavinKare, 292, 294, 296
Cavusgil, Tamar, 10n.14
CECOR process/tools, 269, 269n.6,
    270, 275

Cell phones
  Indian company, 74–76, 290
  Nokia, 674
Cella, Frank, 398
Celly, Nikhil, 552
CEMEX case study, 146–166
Center of excellence, 656
Center of gravity, 124
Center-for-global innovation
  effectiveness, 410–411
  model, 409
  term, 408
Centers of Competence (CoC)
  McKinsey & Company, 464–465
  Siemens, 432
"Centers of Excellence," 591
Central research library (CRL), 341
Centralization
  transnational innovation, 417
  transnational organizations, 323
Centralized hub, 319f, 319–320, 320t
Ceredase, 726–730
Chagas, Carlos, 732
Chagas disease, 725, 730–731, 732,
    736–737, 742
Chandler, Alfred D. Jr., 114n.1
Chandrasekhar, R., 538
Change process model, 324, 327f
"Chassis,"453, 454
Chemical cluster, 197
Chesbrough, H., 496n.1
Child, J., 179n.4
Child labor
  IKEA case study, 704–707
  Nike case study, 683
Child Labour (Prohibition and
    Regulation) Act, 705
"Child sponsorship" model, 369
Children
  AIDS orphans, 379
  Pledging of Labour Act, 705
  worldwide demographics, 226–227
Chile, 622–623
"CHILL" operating system, 439
China
  ECCO case study, 361
  JTC acquisition, 538, 546–552
  Lincoln Electric, 28–29
  locally successful firms, 290, 291,
    292–300
  Mattel case study, 166, 168–169,
    174–175
  MNE growth, 301–302
  MNE impact, 665
  organizational chart, 192f
  P&G case study, 457, 458, 459
  penetration difficulties, 100
  technical innovation, 83–85
  tractor market, 546–548
Cho, Fujio, 303

Choudhari, Anjanikumar, 538, 540, 543, 546, 547, 548, 550, 551, 552
Choudhury, Prithwiraj, 725
Christensen, C., 498n.12, 508n.25
Chwang, Ronald, 53, 64–65, 66
Ciba-Geigy, 751
Cinquième cru, 129
Clark, K. B., 498n.11
Clarke, Kevin, 237n.119, 238n.136
Clarks, 362, 363
Cleeland, Nancy, 689n.41
Client Impact Committee, 467
Client Service Team (CST), 467, 469
Clientele and Professional Development Committee (CPDC), 466, 467, 469
Clientele Industry Sectors and Functional Capability Groups, 468, 474
Clientele Sectors, 463, 464, 465, 468
Clifford, Mark, 681n.10, 684n.22
Clinton, William Jefferson, 684
Cluster boundaries, 197
Clusters
    business implications, 204, 206–208
    economic development, 205, 206f
    life cycle, 203
    and productivity, 199–200
    R&D sites, 481–482
    selected U. S., 201f
    terms, 196–198
"Clusters and the New Economics of Competition," 195–209
Coca Cola Colombia, 710–712
    case study, 707–725
    health practices, 663
    responsibility policy, 713
    timeline, 712
Coffee and Farmer Equity (CAFé) practices, 673
Cohen, D., 497n.9
Cohen, Dana Eisman, 680n.5, 681n.12
"Collaborate with Your Competitors—and Win," 517n.4, 524, 580–587
Collaboration
    and competition, 581
    goals, 582–583
    and secure defenses, 583, 585
    value of, 581–583
Collin, Robert P., 513
Colombia
    brief history, 708–710
    and Coca Cola, 707–708, 712–718
Commission on Firm Aims and Goals, 462
Communication, 384–385
Communities of practice, 499t
Comparative advantage, 196
Competence, 585
Competition, clusters, 198–199

Competitive advantage
    AAA Triangle, 281
    MNE motivation, 7
    MNE strategies, 211–216
Competitive benchmarking, 587
Complementarities, 200
Component supply, 569–570
Computer education, 758
Computers
    Acer Inc., 53–68
    adoption pyramid, 226
    $100 Laptop, 224–243
Comstock, Beth, 262
Comte, Pierre, 259, 273, 274, 276, 277
Conflict of cultural tradition, 751
Conflict of relative development, 751
"Confucian dynamism," 193
Conn, Charles, 471
"Connect and Develop: Inside Procter & Gamble's New Model for Innovation," 418, 487–495
Consulting firms, 461–476
Consumer goods
    innovation, 490
    regulatory agencies, 169–172
Consumer Product Safety Act, 169
Convention No. C138, 704, 704n.11
Convention on the Rights of the Child, 706
"Convergence Group," 434
Cook, J. M., 501t
Cooke, Paul, 244
Cooper, C. L., 182n.9
Coordinated federation, 318–319, 319f, 320t
Core human values, 746–747
Corning Glass, 575
Corporate Campaign, Inc., 721
Corporate Responsibility Compliance, 719
Corporate Social Responsibility (CSR), 725
Corporate venturing networks, 499t
Corruption
    business ethics, 753
    global compact, 673
    and MNEs, 667
Cortes, Pau, 146
Cosmetics, 442–460
Cost factors, 5
"Country manager," 594
Country Portfolio Analysis (CPA), 95, 103, 104–105
Court, David, 473
Covenant of Partnership, 372, 373
Credit demand, 757
Cross-border collaboration
    building, 519–521, 520f
    challenges, 518
    costs, 517–518

    management, 521–523, 522t
    motivation, 510–511
    reevaluation, 523–524
    risks, 516–517
    strategic alliances, 511–515, 512f
Cross-border coordinator, 591–592
Cross-industry alliances, 499t
Crozier, Michel, 178, 189nn.23, 24
Ctrip, 293, 300–301
Cultural differences, 118–119
Cultural distance
    industry sensitivity, 102
    trade impact, 96–98, 99
Cultural profiles, 183–187
Cultural relativism, 743, 744, 745
Culture
    organizational charts, 192f
    organizational structure, 179
    value cluster maps, 182, 183f, 184t
    value dimensions, 118, 180t–181t, 180–182
"Culture and Organization," 178–195
Culver, Mike, 65–66, 67
Curran, Daniel F., 366
Cushman, John H., Jr., 689n.42, 696n.43
Customization strategies, 292, 296
Cyr, D. J., 193n.29

D

Daft, Douglas, 118, 707–708
Daniel, Ron, 463–464
Daniels, Gene, 369
Dante, Ronnie, 635–636, 637
Das, Gurcharan, 600, 645–652
Das, Suman, 562, 566
Dasgupta, Susmita, 234n.89
David C. Lincoln Technology Center, 22
David, Jose Eleazar Manco, 716
Davies, Stephen, 616, 618–622, 624, 628
Davis, S., 191n.27
Dawar, Niraj, 222n.5
Dawson, Virginia P., 20nn.3, 4, 21n.6, 23nn.9–12
Day, G., 498n.13, 508n.25
De Cesare, Paolo, 442, 450, 451–452, 453, 456, 457–458, 459, 460
Dean, Jason, 233n.70
Decentralized federation, 318, 319f, 320t
Decision-making, 387
Dekker, Wisse, 336, 403
Delbridge, Rick, 418, 496, 505n.22
Deming Prize, 541
Den Hoorn brewerey, 244
Denominazione di Origine Controllate (DOC) regions, 129–130
Denominazione di Origine Controllate Guarantita (DOCG), 139n.13

Deregulation, 107, 109
"Design and Management of International Joint Ventures, The," 524, 567–580
Dessain, Vincent, 697
Deutsche Telekom, 439, 440
Development model failure, 664
Dhanaraj, Charles, 506n.24
Diarte, Heriberto, 146
Differentiation, 414–415
Digital Divide Project, 762, 763
Dineen, John, 259–260, 272–273, 274, 277
"Direct injection" technology, 357
Direct investment, 2, 303
Discontinuous innovation
    challenge of, 496–498
    insights/recommendations, 508t
    network barriers, 500t–501t
    network building, 499, 501–506, 502f
    performing partners, 506–508
Distance dimensions, 96–103
Distance sensitivity, 102
"Distance Still Matters: The Hard Reality of Global Expansion," 95–105
D'istinto wines, 612, 623–624, 626
Distributed/interdependent capabilities, 322–323, 323f
Distribution, 570
Diversification, 573
"Do You Really Have a Global Strategy," 583–584
Dodgson, M., 503n.18
Doherty, Clem, 471
Doman, Andrew, 471
Domestic companies
    homegrown champions, 293–295
    successful strategies, 291–292, 296–300
Donaldson, Thomas, 676, 743, 744, 750n.2
Dongguan Zhongxin Toner Powder Factory, 175
"Doonesbury," 679, 684–685, 695
Doz, Yves L., 212n.2, 417f, 517n.4, 524, 580
Drug Price Control Order (India), 554–555
Drugs for Neglected Diseases initiative (DNDi), 734, 739
Dubai, 42, 43
Duffy, Tim, 161n.16
Dulaney, Ken, 76n.19
Dull, Stephen, 473–474
Duncan, Geoff, 239n.146
Duneu, Jean-Louis, 621
Dunfee, Thomas W., 746n.1, 750, 750n.2
Dunning, John, 8n.11
Dyer, J., 497n.8
Dysentery, 751

E

Early Light Industrial Company, Ltd., 176
Easterly, William, 664
Eaton, Roger, 399
Eberl, Horst, 419, 428, 429, 430, 440
Eccles, R., 498n.15
ECCO A/S case study, 348–365
ECE, 640, 641
Eckert, Bob, 166, 174n.29, 175n.34
Economic distance
    industries sensitive to, 102
    trade impact, 99, 101, 103
Economic geography, 205, 209
Economic pyramid, 758
Economies of scale
    GEH, 285
    and globalization, 114–115
    joint ventures, 568–569
    local business strategies, 298
Economies of scope
    GEH, 285
    and globalization, 114–115
Education
    BOP market, 761
    developing world, 237–238
Education and Conference Centre, 350
Egon Zehnder, 633
Egypt, 160
Eileen Hardy wine, 616, 625
Einhorn, Bruce, 235n.100, 243nn.149–151, 243nn.153
Electronics
    Jollibee Foods Corporation, 34–53
    Philips versus Matsushita case study, 331–347
Elenkov, D. S., 187n.21
Elevators
    Indian market, 639–643
    Schindler Holdings, 629
Eli Lilly and Company
    case study, 552–567
    home-base-exploiting site, 480–481
    InnoCentive, 493
    open innovation, 488–489
    Ranbaxy joint venture, 519, 552, 556–567
Elimination of Neglected Diseases (END) Act, 739
Ellis, D., 496n.1
EMI, 653–654
Employee Advisory Board, 20
Enright, Michael, 308
Enron, 663
Environment
    global compact, 673
    IKEA, 703–704
Environmental Protection Agency (EPA), 266

EPG profiles, 91
Ericsson
    BOP market, 760
    key-market subsidiary, 657
    management structure, 658, 660–661
    strategic alliance risks, 516
    transnational innovation, 415
ESAB, 17, 31
Escalators, 629
Ethical imperialism, 744–745
Ethnocentric firms, 88t, 88–89, 91
"Eureka catalog," 494
Euro Technical Teams, 443
"Eurobrand" teams, 654–655
Europe
    decentralized federation, 318, 319f
    MNE practices, 663
    organizational change model, 328
    P&G case study, 457, 459–460
European Union (EU), 115
Evans, M., 82n.36
Evo Project case study, 259–278
Evolution locomotive, 267–268
Ewing, J., 425n.4
EWSD, 421, 425–426, 427, 428, 430, 433, 441
Executive attention, 392–400
Exit, 387, 389, 390–391
Expatriate salaries, 536–537
Experienced Commercial Leadership Program, 262–263
Expertise, 408
Exploitative MNE, 665–669, 677
Exporting clusters, 201f
Factor costs, 115

F

Fagan, Perry L., 629
Fahey, Jonathan, 229nn.37, 38
Fair Labor Association (FLA), 690–692, 697, 719
Family/tribe model, 185f
Faraday, Michael, 421
Farm equipment, 538–552
Fayol, Henri, 179n.5
Feinberg, Susan, 304
"FEKAT," 428
"Fellow Workers," 19–20
Fildes, Jonathan, 224n.7, 233n.67, 243n.152
Financial services demand, 757
"Finding, Forming, and Performing: Creating Networks for Discontinuous Innovation," 418, 496–509
"Finger-printing" herbs, 650
Finland
    background information, 529–530, 530t
    Nora-Sakari joint venture, 525–537

Finnish Cable Works, 532
Finnish Rubber Works, 532
Fiocruz, 735–736
Firm Practice Information System
    (FPIS), 465–466
Fitchard, Kevin, 234n.90
"Flat-web-based organization," 345
Flexibility
    MNE strategies, 213, 213n.3
    strategic alliances, 524
Flexible/integrative process,
    323–324, 324f
Fluency, 386
Foaming massage cloth, 456–457
Focus Media, 298,–299, 300
Food industry
    Jollibee Foods Corporation, 34–53
    Tricon Restaurant International
        (TRI), 103–105
Ford, 308
Foreign Corrupt Practices Act, 752
Foreign direct investment (FDI), 2, 303
Forest Stewardship Council, 704
Formaldehyde, 703–704
Formalization
    transnational innovation, 416
    transnational organizations, 323–324
*Fortune at the Bottom of the Pyramid,
    The* (Prahalad), 235, 672
Foster, R., 496n.1
France
    organizational chart, 192f
    organizational model, 183f, 183–185,
        185f, 188
    wine case study, 129–130, 133,
        138–141, 144
Franchise Service Management (FSM),
    42–43, 45–46
Franco, Francisco, 709
Frangos, Marc, 503
Frankel, Jeffrey, 96, 97
"French paradox," 135
Friedman, Milton, 666, 666n.4, 669
Friend, D., 79n.23
Frost, Tony, 222n.5
*Fuerzas Armadas Revolucionarias de
    Colombia* (FARC), 709–710
Fuji Xerox joint ventures, 572–573
Fujitsu, 486
Furniture case study, 697–707

G

Galvin, Robert, 753
Gandhi, Indira, 555
Gann. D., 503n.18
Ganter, D., 185n.15
Garcia, Enrique A., 146

Garud, R., 501t
Garvin, D. A., 497n.6
Gates, Bill
    malaria research, 738
    $100 Laptop, 235, 236, 237
    organizational psychology, 326
    philanthropy, 674
Gaucher disease, 726, 727–730, 736
Gavetti, G., 497n.4
GE
    Evo Project case study, 259–278
    matrix management, 403
    regional strategy, 304
GE Medical Systems (GEMS), 591, 672
Geene, Annemiek, 138n.10
General Agreements on Tariffs and
    Trade (GATT)
    CEMEX decision, 158
    India, 565–566
    trade liberalization, 115
General Electric Healthcare (GEH),
    285–286
General Foods, 516
General Survey outline, 461
"Generation Y," 505
Genzyme Assistance Program, 729
Genzyme case study, 725–742
Geocentric firms, 88, 88t, 90, 91, 92t, 93
Geographic distance
    sensitive industries, 102
    and subsidiaries, 393
    trade impact, 96, 99, 101
George-Cosh, D., 69n.1
Geox, 362–363
Geraghty, Jim, 725, 730, 732, 733,
    735–736, 737, 738, 740
Germany
    organizational model,
        183f, 183–186, 185f
    Siemens case study, 419–441
Geroski, P., 497n.5
Ghazi, Hussein, 534
Ghemawat, Pankaj, 95–105, 146,
    223, 278, 302
Ghosn, Carlos, 514–515
Ghoshal, Sumantra, 331, 400, 488,
    505n.21, 600, 653
Gibson, Ken, 470, 471
Gifford, Kathie Lee, 683
Gil, Isidro Segundo, 708, 714, 716,
    716n.22, 717
Gilmore, A. B., 668n.9
Glass, Stephen, 685n.30, 685–686
Gleisser, Marcus, 23n.13
Global, 11n.16
Global Alliance for TB Drug
    Development, 732, 736
Global business management
    core roles/responsibilities, 589–592
    in transnational organizations, 321

Global business manager, 588
Global Business Practices Council, 753
Global chess strategy, 116–117
Global compact, 662, 673
Global companies/enterprises/industries,
    1n.1, 123–124, 322
Global competition, 513
Global integration-responsiveness
    framework, 212f, 212–213
Global Labor Relations, 723
Global Leadership Team (GLT), P&G,
    442, 453
Global-market mandate, 656, 657–658
Global matrix, 316, 329
Global mentality, 12–13
Global modular locomotive (GML), 272
Global product/business strategist,
    589–590
Global Research Center (GRC), 262, 266
Global Sourcing and Operating
    Guidelines, 748
Global strategies
    AA strategies, 280–281
    AAA Triangle, 279–280
    AAA Triangle strategies, 286–288
    approaches, 217–218, 219t
    broader lessons, 288–289
    global industries, 123–124
    and regional markets, 302–303
"Global village," 117
Global Wine War 2009 case study,
    128–145
Globalization
    challenges, 126–127
    differentiation/responsiveness forces,
        117–121
    environmental forces, 113–115
    ill-fated strategies, 106–107
    innovation/learning forces, 122–123
    integration/coordination forces,
        114–117
    and local identities, 645
    localization pressures, 121–122
    multiforce responses, 123–126
    opposition to, 662, 663–664, 718–719
    siren song, 107, 109–112
Globalization and Its Discontents
    (Stiglitz), 664
"Globalization of Markets,
    The" (Levitt), 113
Globally linked innovation pools, 410
Gluck, Fred, 464–465, 466, 467, 469, 474
Goerzen, Anthony, 5n.5, 244
Gohring, N., 75n.11
Gol Linhas Aéreas Inteligentes (Gol),
    293, 297
Gold Seal Program, 672
"Golden ghettos," 651
Gomez Granado, Luis Enrique, 716
Goodbaby, 292, 294

GoodWorks International, 685, 718
Gordon, Glenna, 238n.130
Gorman, James, 471
Governance
    global differentiation, 119–121
    strategic alliances, 523
Grandes écoles, 185
Granovetter, M. S., 498n.15
Grant, Tavia, 235n.98
Granzer, Hermann, 428
Gratton, L., 505n.21
Gravity theory of trade flows, 97
Greenhouse, Steven, 666n.5
"Growth platforms," 260
Grupo Elektra, 290, 295, 296, 297
Grupo Positivo, 290, 293
Guam, 43, 50
Guillen, M., 179n.6
Gujarat Cooperative Milk Marketing
    Federation (GCMMF), 294, 297–298
Gulati, Rajiv, 557–558, 559, 561,
    562, 566
Gundersen, A., 118n.3
Gupta, Rajat, 461, 474, 476
Gupta, Sandeep, 559

H

Hall, Brian J., 259
Hall, Ted, 466–467
Halske, Johann Georg, 420, 421
Hamel, G., 210n.1
Hamel, Gary, 211, 517n.4, 524, 580, 583
Hammond, Allen, 676, 754
Hampden-Turner, Charles, 118n.3
Handler, Elliot, 172
Handler, Ruth, 172
Hardy, Thomas, 614
Hargadon, A., 498n.15, 508n.25
Harris Calorific, 22
Hashim, Zainal, 525, 527, 531, 534,
    535, 537
Hastings, Donald F., 23, 23n.8
Hauer, Hans, 437
Headquarters hierarchy syndrome,
    654, 660
Heijbroek, Arend, 138n.10
Heim, Kristi, 237n.123
Heineken, 673
Herbal medicine, 650
Herbert, Bob, 696–697
"Herd mentality," 392
Herfindahl index, 304
Herstatt, C., 498n.12
Hesseldahl, A., 75n.16, 76n.19, 82n.37,
    84n.53, 85n.61
Hickson, D. J., 179n.2
Hierarchy

multicultural teams, 386
    organizations, 187
High-definition television (HDTV), 514
Hille, Kathrin, 224n.6, 225n.19, 237n.116
Hindustan Antibiotics Limited
    (HAL), 554
Hindustan Lever
    BOP market, 761
    candy maker, 757
    as responsive MNE, 672
Hinings, C. R., 179n.2
Hirsch, Dean, 376, 377, 379, 380
HIV/AIDS Hope Initiative case study,
    366–384
Hofstede, Geert, 118, 118n.3, 180n.8,
    180–182, 182n.10, 193n.30, 501t
Hohlin, Keith, 434
Holderbank, 149, 150, 151, 153, 154
Holwell, Kevin, 433
Home-base-augmenting site, 478, 479,
    480, 481–482
Home-base-exploiting site, 478, 479,
    480, 481
Home base strategy, 304–305
Home-country bias, 392
Hommen, Jan, 287
Honda, 582
Hong Kong
    business ethics, 746
    Jollibee Foods, 43, 47, 50, 51–52
Hope initiative, 366–384
Horovitz, J., 185n.15
Hounsfield, Godfrey, 653
Hounshell, D. A., 498n.15
Hout, T., 210n.1
"How Local Companies Keep
    Multinationals at Bay," 223, 290–302
Howard, Joy, 760n.3
Hu, Winnie, 243n.155
Hub strategy, 307–308
Huffman, Shawna, 686nn.32–35,
    687n.36, 691
Human rights, 673
Humanitarian Assistance for Neglected
    Diseases (HAND) program,
    725, 732–738
Hunke, Karl-Friedrich, 419, 428,
    429, 431, 440
Huston, Larry, 418, 487, 503n.18
Huston, Tom, 371
Hybrid locomotive, 259
Hyundai, 301–302

I

"Ichidai Hiyaku," 446
Idea networks, 499t
"IKEA ambassadors," 701

IKEA case study, 697–707
Illinois Tool Works (ITW), 17–18
"Imagination Breakthroughs," 259
Immelt, Jeffrey R.
    Evo Project, 259, 260, 262, 264, 265,
        271, 271n.7
    regional strategies, 303, 307
Implementation task, 596–597
"Implicit model," 184
In Search of Excellence, 465
India
    Bhopal gas leak, 668, 670, 746
    economic overview, 555
    economic system, 652
    IKEA case study, 697–707
    Lincoln Electric, 29, 31
    locally successful firms, 290, 294,
        297–298
    malaria initiative, 737–738
    MNE practices, 663
    nepotism, 750
    Novartis patent, 739
    and the pharmaceutical industry,
        554–555, 556–557
    post-colonial division, 645
    Schindler Holdings, 630, 632–633,
        639–643
    Siemens NetManager Project, 439–441
    Siemens RDC, 434–441
    tractor industry, 541–543
Indian Drugs and Pharmaceutical Limited
    (IDPL), 554
Indian Minimum Wage Act 1948,
    33, 33n.25
Individualism, 118, 180, 180t–181t
Indo-German Export Promotion Council,
    705–706
Indonesia
    CEMEX case study, 160
    ECCO case study, 359, 360
    Jollibee Foods case study, 40, 43, 50
    locally successful firms, 295
    management model, 189, 190, 190t
    MNE practices, 663
    Nike case study, 680–682, 686–687,
        691, 693
Industrial policy, 209
Industries
    regional concentrations, 304–305
    sensitivities to distance, 102
Industry convergence, 513–514
Infant formula, 667
Information clusters, 200
ING Insurance case study, 601–611
InnoCentive, innovation networks, 493
Innovation
    clusters, 202
    discontinuous networks, 418, 496–509,
        499t, 502f, 508t
    global market, 408

invention model, 488
    management function, 592–593, 594
Innovative International Multi-purpose
    Vehicle (IMV) Project, 309–310
Innovative process types, 409–410
Institut Teknology Bandung (ITB), 681
Institutional
    arrangements, 179–180
    clusters, 200
Instrumental model, 189
Insurance industry
    in Asia, 602–603
    in Asia/Pacific, 603–608
    ING Insurance, 601–602
"Integrated network," 322, 323f
"Intelligent Classroom," 227–228
Interbrew, 244, 246–251
Interdependent offices, 375, 376
Intermediate-stage offices, 375, 376
International board, 374, 375
International Concern
    Council, 333, 336
International Council, 374, 375
International enterprise
    headquarter orientations,
        88t, 88–89
    term, 1n.1
International Labor Organization (ILO)
    IKEA, 704
    Nike, 670
International Labor Rights Fund, 714
International Production Centers
    (IPC), 336
International strategy
    and coordinated federation
        structure, 319
    in international industries, 124
    types, 216–219, 219t
International Youth Foundation (IYF),
    675, 692, 697
Internationalization
    prerequisites, 7–8, 8nn.9–11, 10f
    process, 9–11
Internet services, 758–759, 760
Interviews, 509
Investment
    BOP market, 762
    direct MNE, 2
    governmental demand, 120
    MNE motivation, 6–7
    risk, 582
Ireland, 192f
Irvine, Graeme, 366n.1, 369, 370, 371
Isenberg, Daniel J., 10n.14
Islam, 531
Italcementi, 149, 150, 151, 154
Italy
    leather cluster, 197, 198f
    organizational chart, 192f
ITT, 667

J

Jaafar, Osman, 531
Jackson, Jesse, 683, 708
Jager, Durk, 282, 329, 446, 447–448,
    449, 450, 460
Japan
    central innovation, 410–412
    centralized hub, 319, 320
    company loyalty, 744
    gift giving tradition, 746, 751–752
    and Lincoln Electric, 27, 28
    organizational change model, 338
    P&G case study, 442, 443, 446–447,
        449, 450, 451–453,
        457–458, 459
    regional strategies, 310
Jefferson, Thomas, 130
Jemison, David B., 519n.5
Jena, Jujudhan, 635–636, 637, 638
Jepsen, Mary Lou, 229, 231
Jensen, Morton Bay, 361n.10
Jiangling Motor Company Group
    (JMCG), 548, 550
Jiangling Tractor Co. (JTC), 538–552
Johanson, Jan, 9n.12
Joint Venture Checklist, 573, 574
Joint ventures
    four basic purposes, 568, 569
    international strategy, 567–568
    requirements for success, 573–579
    true vs. pseudo alliances, 579
Jollibee Foods Corporation case
    study, 34–53
Jordan, Michael, 679, 680, 683
"Judgment of Paris, The," 133
Jung, Volker, 430
Junttila, Ilkka, 527, 534

K

Kahn, H., 498n.13
Kamat, Sudhanshu, 560–561
Kamprad, Ingvar, 698, 698n.2,
    699–702
Kao, J., 186n.20, 193n.31
Kaplan, S., 496n.1
Karavis, Lambros, 5n.5
Karnoe, R., 501t
Kasprzak, Dieter, 349, 350, 357, 361
Kaul, Vinay, 565
Keady, James, 689
Keery, John, 363
Keilland, Peggy Ann, 717
Kelly's Revenge wine, BRL Hardy,
    612, 626, 627, 628
Kemp, Jacques, 601–602, 608–609,
    610–611

Kentucky Fried Chicken (KFC)
    fast food pioneer, 39
    Jollibee Foods case study, 42
    transactional MNE, 669–671
Kern, Mary C., 331, 384
Key-market subsidiary, 656, 657
Khan, Waheed, 238n.133
Khanna, Tarun, 725
Kidd, Dusty, 682, 684
Kidman, Angus, 239nn.144, 145
Kielland, Richard Kirby,
    711, 716, 717
Kieser, A., 185n.15
Killer Coke case study, 719–725
Kindle, Fred, 395
Kitchner, Tony, 40, 42–44, 46–48
Kleisterlee, Gerard, 339
Kline, H. F., 709nn.4–6
Klinger, Jeff, 732–734, 737, 740
Klunker, Jürgen, 432
Knight, Gary A., 10n.14
Knight, Phil, 679, 679n.1, 680, 684,
    685, 687, 688
Knoop, Carin-Isabel, 224
Knowledge
    as international asset, 408
    strategic flows, 522, 523
    transfer function, 592
    and transnational innovation,
        417f, 417–418
Knowledge Management
    Program, 465
Knowledge Resource Directory
    (KRD), 466
Kobelco, 17, 18
Kogut, Bruce, 179n.6, 213n.3
Koka, B. R., 506n.24
Kone elevators, 640, 641
Korine, Harry, 105
Koskinen, Mikko, 532–533
Kotchian, Carl, 752
Krazit, Tom, 236n.106, 237n.115
Kröbel, Peter, 422
Kroc, Ray, 39
Kuemmerle, Walter, 418, 477
Kuusisto, 534, 535
Kuwait, 42, 43

L

Labor (Labour)
    exploitive MNE's, 663, 665–666
    local business strategies, 298
    Nike case study, 679, 681–686
    standards, 673
Labor laws, 670
Labor unions, 710
Lafarge, 149, 150, 153, 154, 155, 158

Lafley, Alan (A. G.)
  AAA Triangle, 280
  adaptation and aggregation, 283
  innovation, 489, 495, 503
  matrix structure, 329
  P&G case study, 442, 447, 451, 453, 460
Lagerwerf, Anne, 138n.10
Lai, Eric, 233n.74
Laing, Angela, 395
Lakshman, N., 84n.56
Lalitha, J, S., 440
Lall, Somic, 234n.89
Lander, Eric, 730
Lane, Christopher, 5n.5
Lane, Henry W., 707
Largacha, Pablo, 707, 723
Larimer, Tim, 679n.2
Latin America
  CEMEX case study, 159, 161
  organizational chart, 192f
Laurent, André, 187, 187n.22, 189,
    191n.28, 193
La Violencia, 709
Lawlor, Andrew, 757n.1
Lawrence, P. R., 191n.27
Lazaridis, Mike, 68, 69, 79, 85
Lead user groups, 499t, 502
Lead-country concept, 656–657
Leadership, 482–484
Leahy, Stephen, 224n.2, 225n.12,
    227nn.29, 32, 230n.39 Learning
  collaborative alliances, 581, 583,
    586–587
  strategic alliances, 524
Leather
  Italian cluster, 196–197, 198f
  production steps, 354
Lee Der Industrial Company, 175
Lee, K., 186n.18
Leifer, R., 498n.14
Leiter, Mark, 474
Lemu, Aisha, 238n.134
Leno, Jay, 166
Levi Strauss, 747–748, 753–754
Levitt, Theodore
  global strategies, 12, 12n.17,
    210n.1, 210–211
  globalization article, 113, 114, 117
Lewis, David, 2n.2
Liang, Jianzhang, 300
Liew, Jonathan, 471
Lilly, Eli, 556
Lincoln, John C., 18–19, 20
Lincoln Electric case study, 15–33
Lindstrom, Salleh, 534
Lingle, Walter, 443
Lipstick, 452–453
Liu, Leonard, 57–58, 59–60, 62, 64
"Local Memoirs of a Global Manager,"
  600, 645–652

Local-to-local innovation
  efficiency, 412–413
  model, 409
  personnel flow, 411–412
  term, 408
Localization
  clusters, 207
  global pressures, 121–122
Locally leverage innovation model, 409
Location
  clusters, 207
  global economy, 195–196
Lockheed Martin, 749
Lu, Jane, 11n.15
Lundan, Sarianna M., 8n.11
Lynn, G. S., 496n.2, 498n.14

M

MacArthur Foundation, 696
Maclay, Colin M., 760n.2
MacMillan, Douglas, 225n.20, 227nn.30,
    33, 233n.80, 236n.102
MacMillan, I., 498n.12
Macroeconomic risks, 213
Madhavan, R., 506n.24
Mahindra & Mahindra case study,
    538–552
Mahindra, Anand, 539
Maine Learning Technology Initiative,
    227, 227n.31
Maisonrouge, Jacques, 93, 93n.3
Majid, Aziz, 534
Make a Connection, 675
Malaria research, 725, 730, 731, 734–735,
    737–738, 741
Malaysia
  background information, 528, 529t
  Jollibee Foods case study, 43, 50
  locally successful firms, 295
  Nora-Sakari joint venture, 525–537
Maljers, Floris, 403
Mallick, Rajiv, 102
Management
  active MNE, 2, 3
  best practices, 191–193
  BOP market, 761
  geographic subsidiary, 594–597
  global business, 589–592
  headquarters hierarchy syndrome, 654
  local business strategies, 299–300
  modern practices, 179
  multicultural teams, 387, 389, 390
  new global environment, 588–589
  R&D networks, 486
  strategic alliances, 511, 521–523, 522f
  subsidiary initiatives, 395–396
  three challenges, 658–659

  top-level role/responsibilities, 597–600
  transnational organizations, 321,
    323–324, 329–330
  trends/fads, 108
  U.N. model assumption, 654
  worldwide function, 592–594
Management questionnaire, 188t, 193,
    194f, 195
Manager, Vada, 687
Managers
  career-path management, 405–406
  corporate vision, 404
  matrix minds, 407
  organization conceptions, 189
  recruitment and selection, 404–405
  training/development, 405–406
"Managing Differences: The Central
    Challenge of Global Strategy,"
    223, 278–289
"Managing Executive Attention in the
    Global Company," 331, 392–400
"Managing managers," 610
"Managing Multicultural Teams,"
    331, 384–391
Mandate strategies, 310
Mandela, Nelson, 663, 730
Mankin, Eric D., 580n.1
Manning, Jeff, 685n.26
Manufacturing industries, 110
Manville, Brook, 465
Mapocho wines, 612, 622–623, 624, 626
Mapping, 215–216, 216t
March, A., 497n.6
March, Jim, 499n.16
Marcos, Ferdinand, 35
Market imperfection theory, 8n.9
"Market mechanisms," 411
Marketing, 570
Markets, 4–5
"Markets of the future," 572
Markides, C., 497n.5
Markoff, John, 231n.50, 233n.76,
    236nn.110–111, 237n.117
Marquetalia, 709
Mascarenhas, Andrew, 558–560, 561
Masculinity, 118, 180, 180t–181t
Maser, Rachel, 237n.120, 238n.135
Massachusetts Institute of Technology
    (MIT) Media Lab, 224, 224n.1
Massaro, Anthony, 23, 24
Masterson, Mark, 396
Mata Hardy wine, 623
Matassoni, Bill, 465–466
Matrix management, 191–192
"Matrix Management: Not a Structure, a
    Frame of Mind," 331, 400–407
Matrix structures, 316, 329
Matson, Harold, 172
Matsushita, Konosuke, 340–341,
    403, 405

Matsushita Electric
  central innovation, 411
  case study, 331, 333, 340–347
  internal transfers, 592
  management structure, 568, 660
  personnel flow, 411–412
  R&D sites, 486–487
Matsushita Electric Corporation of
    America (MECA), 341
Matsushita Electric Trading Company
    (METC), 342, 344
Mattel case study, 166–178
Matthews, Jamie L., 146
Matthews, T. A. K., 635–636, 637, 643
Mattoo, Vinod, 566
Mattsson, Peter, 525, 527
Maurice, M., 185n.15
Max Factor Japan, 442, 446, 447, 451,
    452–453, 456
Mayr, Gerhard, 556, 558, 562, 567
Mazutis, Daina, 68
McBride, Sabina, 680n.5
McCall, William, 689n.40
McDonald, Robert, 283
McDonald's
  Jollibee Foods case study,
    35, 39, 40, 42
  transactional MNE, 669
McGrath, R., 498n.12
McGray, Douglas, 224n.3, 225n.13,
    230n.40, 231nn.42, 44,
    47–48, 233n.65
McKean, Todd, 719
McKee, M., 668n.9
McKinsey & Company
  case study, 461–476
  global survey (2006), 671n.11
  and ING Insurance, 609, 610
McKinsey Global Institute, 476
McKinsey, James (Mac), 461
McKinsey Staff Paper series, 465
McKinsey Yellow Pages, 466
McLean, Andrew, 726n.1
McPherson, J. M., 501t
Medicines for Malaria Venture
    (MMV), 735
Medina, Hector, 146, 162
Meier, Jens Christian, 350, 352
Memorandum of Understanding, 682
Mentalities, 11–14
Menzer, John, 303
Merck, 674–675
Mergers
  joint venture divisions, 570–571
  and strategic alliances, 515
Messmer, E., 84n.55
Metcalf, Ben, 505–506
Mexico
  CEMEX case study, 146
  locally successful firms, 290, 295, 296

Michael, David C., 223, 290
Millar, Steve, 612, 616, 619–622,
    624, 626, 628
Miller, George, 684
Miller, Martin, 238n.137
Mind of the Strategist, The, 465
Ministry of Machinery Industry
    (MMI), 546
Mitchell, Andrew, 237n.125
Mitsubishi, 640
Mlay, Wilfred, 371, 379, 381–382
"Modulated carrier" technology, 421
Mohamed, Marina, 534
Mohney, Doug, 240n.148
Mokita, 754
Monitor Group, 609, 610
Monteiro, F., 503n.19
Montgomerie, Colin, 349
Mooneyham, Stan, 369, 370
Moore, Karl, 2n.2
Moore, Michael, 679, 685
Moral free space, 750
Moretti, Mario, 363
Morishita, Yoichi, 344
Morita, Akio, 326
Morone, J. G., 496n.2, 498n.14
Morrison, David J., 165n.19
Morse, Samuel, 420, 421
Moser, Ted, 165n.19
Mosquera, Aristo Milan,
    714, 716, 717, 718
Motorola
  code of conduct, 749–750, 753
  technology transfer, 585
Mouzas, S., 506n.24
Mr. Clean Magic Eraser, 491, 492
Multicultural teams
  cultural challenges, 384–387
  indirect interventions, 391–392
  managerial strategies, 387–391
Multidimensional perspective, 321–322
Multinational companies, 321–322
Multinational enterprise (MNE)
  cross-border collaboration,
    510–524, 512f
  defined, 1n., 2
  evolutionary pattern, 11–14
  global influence, 3t, 3–4
  globalization forces, 114
  globalization postures, 665–678
  innovation, 408–414
  internationalization prerequisites,
    7–8, 8nn.9–11
  internationalization process, 9f, 9–11
  joint venture strategy, 567–568
  key management groups, 588–600
  local competition, 290–291, 292
  local market success, 301–302
  motivations, 4–7
  operating objectives, 119

  scope, 2
  selected companies, 3, 3t
  trends, 662–665
Multinational enterprise (MNE)
    organizational structure
  administrative heritage, 314, 317–320,
    319f, 320t
  challenges, 330–331
  early models, 314–317, 315f
  managing change, 327–330
  physiological model, 324–327,
    327f, 328f
  transnational organizations, 321–324,
    323f, 324f
Multinational enterprise (MNE) strategies
  competitive advantage tools, 214–216
  emergent theories, 210–211
  flexibility, 213, 213n.3
  global efficiency, 212
  global, 217–218, 219t
  international, 216–219 219t
  multinational, 217, 219t
  multinational industries, 124
  strategic objectives, 211
  strategic tasks, 220–223
  transnational strategy, 218–219, 219t
  worldwide learning, 214–215
Multinational mentality, 11–12
Multitech. See Acer Inc.
Mundie, Craig, 235
Mundt, Kevin A., 165n.19
Murdoch, Rupert, 95, 100–101
Myers, Bryant, 379, 380, 383

N

Nakamura, Kunio, 345
Nanda, Ashish, 698n.3
Napoli, Silvio, 629–630, 631, 632–633,
    635–636, 637–639, 641–645
"National champion," 119
National cultures/differences
  competitive advantage, 211, 214
  key dimensions, 118
National offices, 375, 376
National subsidiary management
  role/responsibilities, 594–597
  transnational organizations, 321
National subsidiary manager, 588
National unit, 656
NEC, 659–560
Neglected diseases, 732–734
Négociants, 129
Negroponte, Nicholas, 224–229,
    231–234, 236–239
Nestlé, 667, 668
Nepotism, 750
Nestlé Canada, 398

NetManager software, 419, 438–440
Networks, 418, 496–509, 499t, 502f, 508t
New Engagement Guide, 461
NGOs, 668, 670–671, 676
Nielsen, Bo Bernhard, 348
Nigeria, 743
Nike
    case study, 679–697
    employment practices, 663, 666, 670
    global opposition movements, 718
    NGO monitoring, 671
Nimgade, Ashok, 419
NineSigma, 492–493
Nipper, Mads, 502
Nishkama karma, 652
"No Sweat" labels, 684
Nobeoka, K., 497n.8
Nohria, N., 498n.15
Nokia
    in China, 301
    mobile cell phones, 674, 675
Nora Holdings Sdn Bhd, 525–531
Nora Research Sdn Bhd (NRSB), 531
Nora-Sakari case study, 520, 525–537
North American Free Trade Agreement
    (NAFTA)
    dirty industries, 670
    trade liberalization, 115
North American Philips (NAP), 332,
    333, 404, 407
Not-invented-here (NIH) syndrome, 433,
    484, 593, 652
Nottage Hill wines, 616, 619, 620, 624,
    625, 626
Novartis, 739
Novo Nordisk Engineering (NNE),
    348, 504

O

O'Connell, Jamie, 34
O'Connor, G. C., 498n.14
Odden, Jake, 686nn.32–35, 687n.36, 691
Ohmae, Kenichi, 307, 465, 515n.2
Ohtsubo, Eumio, 346
"Old boys" network, 318
Olkkola, Aatos, 532
One Firm policy, 461, 464
$100 Laptop case study, 224–243
One Laptop Per Child (OLPC), 224–225,
    231, 233, 238–242
One-pointedness, 647, 651
Oosterveld, Jan, 312, 313
Open invitation networks, 499t
Open networks, 492
Operation Blue Chip, 539, 540–541, 543
"Operation Centurion," 337
"Operation Localization," 343

Organization
    anatomy, physiological, psychological
        model, 324, 325–326
    cultural models, 187–191, 193,
        194f, 195
    internationalization prerequisites, 8
    management questionnaire, 188t
    national differences, 184
    structure, 179
Organization 2005, 442, 449, 453, 460
Orphan Drug Act, 726, 726n.2, 729
Orphaned diseases, Genzyme, 726
Orsted, Hans Christian, 421
Osaka connection, 492
Oswald Cruz Institute (Fiocruz), 735–736
Otis India, 640, 641
Outsourcing
    Nike case study, 680
    strategic alliance, 584
Overlapping consensus, 747

P

Palmisano, Samuel J., 13n.18, 278
Pampers, 654
Panamerican Beverages, 711–712, 714,
    717, 718
Papua New Guinea, 34, 51
Parasitic diseases, 730–731, 732
Parker, M. Philip, 544
Parker, Robert M., 139n.14
Parkhe, A., 506n.24
Parsons, Andrew, 473
Partner selection, 519, 520f
Partnership/fit, 574–576
Partnership offices, 375, 376
Pate, Rickey, 558
Patents, 553–554, 555
Patsalos-Fox, Michael, 472
Paul, Harry W., 128n.1
Paulson, A. S., 496n.2, 498n.14
Pavitt, K., 496n.3
Payphones, 530–531
Peacocke, John, 470–471
Pedersen, Torben, 348
Pekkarinen, Solail, 535
Pepper, John, 447
Performance leveraging, 598–599
Perlmutter, Howard V., 14n.19, 86–95
Peters, Jeff, 470–471
Peters, Thomas "Tom," 464, 465, 515n.3
Peterson, Caitlin, 757n.1
Petroff, A., 79n.25
Pettersson, Bo, 702n.6
Pfeffer, J., 501n.17
Pharmaceutical industry
    AIDS medications, 663
    Genzyme, 727–729

global, 552–554
India, 554–555, 556–557
Mandela lawsuit, 663, 730
Mid Atlantic cluster, 197
Philip, Captain Arthur, 612–613
Philippines
    CEMEX case study, 159–160
    Jollibee Foods case study, 34, 35, 39, 47
Philips, Anton, 332
Philips, Gerard, 332
Philips Electronics
    case study, 331–347
    local innovation, 412, 413
    management structure, 658, 659
    matrix management, 403, 404, 406–407
    organization, 312–313
    strategic leader organization, 656–657
Philips Medical Systems (PMS), 285, 286
Philips of Australia, 333
Philips of Canada, 333
Philips of the United Kingdom, 333
Philips versus Matsushita case study,
    331–347
Phuong, Nguyen Thi Thu, 679
Pierce, Bob, 366, 369
Pierce, Dennis, 232n.54, 234n.81
Piton, Jean-Louis, 128
"Plan Colombia," 710
Plant location decisions, 591
Plasmodium falciparum, 737
Plasmodium vivax, 737
Platform strategy, 308
Poland
    IKEA case study, 699
    locally successful firms, 295
Political distance, 98
Polly Pocket play sets, 176–177
Polycentric firms, 88, 88t, 89–90, 91
Porter, Michael E., 195–209, 210n.1,
    211, 510n.1
Portfolio strategy, 306–307
Portugal
    cluster map, 206f
    ECCO case study, 357–358, 359
Potter, Ed, 723
Poulsen, Kevin, 224n.8, 231n.41,
    232n.58, 233nn.66, 68, 234n.86
Poverty
    common misperceptions, 755–757
    and globalization, 663–664
    worldwide, 755
Power distance, 118, 180, 180t–181t, 185f
Prabhu, Santosh, 438
Practice Bulletins, 465
Practice Development Network (PDNet),
    466, 474, 475
Practice Olympics, 461
Prahalad, C. K., 210n.1, 211, 212, 212f,
    235, 517n.4, 524, 580, 583, 672, 676,
    754, 757

Premier cru, 129
Prescott, J. E., 506n.24
Pringles Prints, 487–488
Procter & Gamble (P&G)
    case study, 442–460
    connect/development innovation,
        487–495, 503, 507
    "Eurobrand" teams, 654–655
    Pampers experiment, 655
    Vicks Vaporub, 645
PRODEM services, 758
Product cycle theory, 5–6, 6n.6
Productivity
    clusters, 199–200
    industrial policy, 209
Project Hope (Health Opportunities
        for People Everywhere), 729–730
Proprietary networks, 491
Prusak, L., 497n.9
Public goods, 200
Public-private relationship, 209
Pugh, D. S., 179n.2, 186n.18
Pyndt, Jacob, 348
"Pyramid of people" model, 184, 185f

Q

"Quality Wines for the World," 616
Quelch, John A., 224
Quella, James A., 165n.19
Questionnaire
    organization model, 188t, 193,
        194f, 195
    regional strategy, 311–312

R

Rachman, Gideon, 133n.8, 138n.9
Railroads, 259–278
Ram, Shivesh, 458–459
Ranbaxy Laboratories Limited, 552,
    556–557, 564, 565
Rangan Exports, 706
Rao, C. R., 440
Ratchet effect, 584
Ratner, Michael, 714, 714n.20
Raw materials, 569
Rawls, John, 747
Readings
    "Building Effective R&D Capabilities
        Abroad," 418, 477–487
    "Clusters and the New Economics of
        Competition," 195–209
    "Collaborate with Your Competitors—
        and Win," 517n.4, 524,
        580–587

"Connect and Develop: Inside Procter
    & Gamble's New Model for
    Innovation," 418, 487–495
"Culture and Organization," 178–195
"Design and Management of
    International Joint Ventures,
    The," 524, 567–580
"Distance Still Matters: The Hard Reality
    of Global Expansion," 95–105
"Finding, Forming, and Performing:
    Creating Networks for
    Discontinuous Innovation,"
    418, 496–509
"How Local Companies Keep
    Multinationals at Bay,"
    223, 290–302
"Local Memoirs of a Global
    Manager," 600
"Managing Differences: The Central
    Challenge of Global Strategy,"
    223, 278–289
"Managing Executive Attention in the
    Global Company," 331, 392–400
"Managing Multicultural Teams,"
    331, 384–391
"Matrix Management: Not a Structure,
    a Frame of Mind," 331, 400–407
"Regional Strategies for Global
    Leadership," 223, 302–313
"Serving the World's Poor, Profitably,"
    676, 754–764
"Tap Your Subsidiaries for Global
    Reach," 600, 653–661
"Tortuous Evolution of the
    Multinational Corporation,
    The," 86–95
"Values in Tension: Ethics Away from
    Home," 676, 743–754
"When You Shouldn't Go Global,"
    105–112
Reardon, M., 420n.1
Recalls, 171, 176, 177–178
Redding, S. G., 186n.18
Reebok, 680, 683
Reebok Human Rights Award, 683
Region/regional
    defining, 310–312
    emergent blocs, 303–304
    forums, 374, 375
    offices, 375, 376
    strategy challenges, challenges,
        312–313
    strategy questionnaire, 311–312
    strategy types, 304–309
Regional Development Centers (RDCs),
    430–432, 433
"Regional Strategies for Global
    Leadership," 223, 302–312
Reich, Robert B., 580n.1
Renault-Nissan partnerships, 514–515

Renmano Wine Cooperative, 614
Research & Development (R&D)
    global strategy, 478–482
    investments, 6
    joint ventures, 570
Research & Development (R&D) sites
    categories, 478, 479–482
    establishing new, 482–486
    global, 477, 478–479
    integrating, 486–487
Research in Motion (RIM)
    case study, 68–85
"Responsibility system," 546
Responsive MNE, 671–673, 678
Retail industry, Mexico, 290
Rhône Poulenc Rorer, 753
Rice, Jerry, 684
Rice, M., 498n.14
Richardson-Vicks, India, 645–646
Ricks, David A., 117n.2
Rio Tinto, 504
Risks, 213
Risk reduction
    cross-border collaboration, 514–515
    joint ventures, 571–572
Robinson, Jancis, 128n.1
Rogers, Ray, 708, 719, 721
Role formalization, 188–189
Romano, B., 81n.33
Ronen, S., 182n.11
Rose, Andrew, 96, 97
Rosenzweig, Philip, 680n.7, 681n.9,
    683nn.17, 18
Rosiello, Rob, 473
Roth, E., 498n.12
Royal Ahold, 111
Royal Philips Electronics, 312–313
Royalty payments, 536
Rudden, E., 210n.1
Rugman, Alan M., 8n.10, 304
"Rugmark," 697–698
Rugmark Foundation, 705
Rugs, IKEA case study, 697–707
Ruola, Julia, 534
Rushford, Greg, 685n.27
Russia
    locally successful firms, 295, 299
    organizational models, 186–187

S

Sahney, Sandeep, 725, 737, 738
Sakari Oy, 525, 527, 532–533
Sakkab, Nabil, 418, 487, 503n.18
Salancik, G., 501n.17
Salter, A., 503n.18
Samsung, 305
Sandell, Vivek, 757n.1

Santos, Jose, 417f
Saro-Wiwa, Ken, 120
Saudi Arabia, 43
Scale economies
    competitive advantage, 211, 214–215
    MNE motivation, 6
Scandinavian management model,
    189–190, 190t
Scanners, GEM, 672
Schaan, Jean-Louis, 538
Scheele, Nick, 308
Schindler, Alfred N., 630, 631, 644
Schindler, Robert, 630
Schneider, S. C., 193n.29
Schneider, Susan, 178
Schindler Holdings Ltd. case study, 629–644
Schoemaker, P., 498n.13, 508n.25
Schotter, Andreas, 601
Schrempp, Jürgen, 106
Schwarz, P., 498n.13
Schwarz, Adam, 682n.16
Schweikert, Tim, 272, 274
Scope economies, 211, 215, 215t
"Screwdriver plants," 120
Search engines, 290
Sellers, Patricia, 687n.39
Selmer, Jan, 189, 189n.25
Serra, José, 736
Services
    BOP demand, 757
    and globalization, 109–110
"Serving the World's Poor, Profitably,"
    676, 754–764
"Seven Spirits of Matsushita," 340, 403, 405
Shanda, 294, 296
Shanghai Automotive Industry Corp.
    (SAIC), 517
Share, Jeff, 29n.16
Shaw, Chris, 561–562
Shenekar, O., 182n.11
Shih, Stan, 53–57, 59, 62–64, 67–68
Shillingford, J., 79n.28
Shu-hung, Cheng, 175
Schindler India case study, 629–644
Shoes, 348–365
Siegel, Jordan, 15
Siemens, case study, 419–441
Siemens, Werner, 420, 421
Siemens Information and Communication
    Networks (ICN), 419, 422, 425–430
Silvio Napoli at Schindler India case
    study, 629–644
Simanis, Erik, 760n.3
Simms, Charis, 760n.3
Singapore, 39–40
Singh, Manmohan, 33, 555
Singh, Mehar Karan, 633, 635–636,
    637–639, 643
Singh, Parvinder, Ranbaxy Laboratories,
    556, 558, 565

Sinha, Pankaj, 637, 638
Sitkin, Sim B., 519n.5
Sjöman, Anders, 697
SK-II Globalization Project, 442–460
Sleeping sickness, 731
Slocombe, Mike, 234n.91
Slovakia
    ECCO case study, 359, 360–361
    locally successful firms, 295
Slums, 756
Slywotzky, Adrian J., 165n.19
Small business services, 757
Smart phones, 68–85
Smart-card ATM, 758
Smartphones, 74–76
Smith, Eliot B., 681n.8
Smith, James F., 164n.18
Smith-Lovin, L., 501t
Socialization
    transnational innovation, 417
    transnational organizations, 324
Societal context, 179
Stevens, J. P., 719
Stockist, 649, 651
Soderstrom, Sulu, 472, 473
Software piracy, 745
Software Publishers Association, 745
Sony, 516
Sørensen, Lars Rebien, 504
Soros, George, 674
South Africa, 663
South Asian Association for Regional
    Cooperation (SAARC), 543
South Korea, 28
Sovereignty at Bay (Vernon), 675
"Sovereignty at bay," 120
Spain
    CEMEX case study, 158–159
    regional strategies, 314–315
Spar, Debora L., 679
Sparks, K., 182n.9
Spector, P. E., 182n.9
Spöerri, Alfred, 631, 632
Sreekanth M., Sai "Charlie," 438
St. George, Anthony, 53
Stages model, 315f, 315n.1, 315–316
Stahl, Lesley, 225n.23
Stalker, G. M., 179n.3, 182n.11
Stamps wine, 616, 620, 624, 625, 626
Starbuck's, 673
Stearns, Richard, 376, 377, 379
Stecklow, Steve, 225n.11, 233n.79
Steffensen, Søren, 349, 350, 352
Stella Artois case study, 244–258
Stevens, O. J., 183n.14, 184
"Stewardship model," 467
Stewart, R., 185n.15, 186n.16
Stick to your knitting, 515, 516
Stiglitz, Joseph, 664
Stopford, John, 315, 315f, 315n.1

Storm over the Multinationals
    (Vernon), 675
Strategic alliances
    building, 519–521, 520f
    challenges, 518
    complexity costs, 517–518
    cooperation with competitors, 580–587
    cross-border collaboration,
        511–512, 512f
    economies of scale, 514–515
    global competition, 513
    industry convergence, 513–514
    management issues, 521–523, 522t
    reevaluation, 523–524
    risks, 516–517
    technology exchanges, 512–513
Strategic competencies, 7–8
Strategic isolation, 393, 396–397
Strategic logic, 574
Strategic vision, 598
"Strategy 2025," 143, 144
Strategy Working Group (SWG), 377
Stropki, John, 15, 19, 24
Structural intervention, 387, 388, 389
Stuckey, John, 470–472
Subsidiaries
    central innovation, 411
    executive attention, 393, 394
    local innovation, 412–413
Sull, D., 497n.10, 503n.19
Sun, Jie, 300
Sun Microsystems, 507
Supervisors, 485–486
Suppliers, 491–492, 499t
Surowiecki, James, 224n.4, 226n.28,
    233nn.69, 75, 77, 234n.82, 83, 85,
    235n.96, 236nn.103–105,
    238nn.140–141
"SURPASS," 430
Survey of Vietnamese and Indonesian
    Domestic Expenditure Levels, 686
Sussick, Ralph, 437
"Sustainability," 671
Svensson, P., 75n.9
Swart, Genevieve, 238n.131
Swartz, Nathan, 363
Swatch project, 632, 641, 642
"Sweatshops," 666
Switzerland, 630
Sybertz, Ted, 732, 737

T

Taiwan
    Acer Inc. case study, 53
    Jollibee Foods case study, 40
Talbot, D., 496n.3
Tallarigo, Lorenzo, 552, 563, 566, 567

Tandon, Atul, 377
Tang, Jun, 300
Tanii, Akio, 344
"Tap Your Subsidiaries for Global Reach,"
    600, 653–661
Target, 666
Taurel, Sidney, 556
Taylor, Frederick, 179n.5
Teams, 384–391
"Tech wreck" recession, 345
Technology
    cross-border collaboration,
        512–513, 516
    entrepreneurial networks, 491
    and globalization, 114–116
    innovation, 490–491
    innovation/learning forces, 122–123
    joint ventures, 571
    local business strategies, 290, 297–298
    localization pressures, 122
    steering committee, 478
    used by poor, 755, 756
    wine industry, 131
Technology transfer
    collaborative ventures, 585–586
    Nora-Sakari joint venture, 536
Telecommunication industry
    AXE digital, 657
    BOP, 758, 760
    Finland, 532
    major equipment vendors, 533
    Malaysia, 526
    Nora Holdings, 525–537
    R&D sites, 482
    Siemens case study, 419–441
    strategic alliances, 515
    timeline, 421
Telekom Malaysia Bhd (TMB), 526
Telephone industry, 527, 530
Teletext, 657
Television, 657
Tempus, 506
Termeer, Henri, 207–208, 725, 726,
    727–730, 732
Terroir, 130
Testament of a Furniture Dealer
    (Kamprad), 701, 702
Thailand
    ECCO case study, 359, 360
    locally successful firms, 295
Thermadyne Holding Corp., 17, 18
Thinghuus, Mikael, 348–349, 350, 365
Thomas Hardy & Sons, 614
Thomke, Stefan, 419
Thompson, Mike, P&G, 459–460
Thorn Electric, 653
Tidd, J., 496n.3
"Tilt the matrix," 336
Timberland, 363–364
Timmer, Jan, 337–338

Tingzon, Manolo "Noli," 34, 36, 48,
    50, 51, 53
To Steal a Book Is an Elegant Offense
    (Alford), 96
Tobacco companies, 668–669, 670
Toley, Sam, 128
Toosbuy, Hanni, 350, 352
Toosbuy, Karl, 348, 350
Top Five Hidden Home Hazards, 170
Torekull, Bertil, 698n.1, 702
"Tortuous Evolution of the Multinational
    Corporation, The," 86–95
Torture Victims Protection Act (TVPA),
    714, 714n.18
Toshiba, 483
Toy industry, 166–177
Toy recalls, 171, 176–178
Toyota, 303, 304, 306, 308–310
Tractor industry
    global export trade, 543, 544
    major Chinese manufacturers, 547
    major vendors, 539
Trade
    barriers, 98, 100
    global liberalization, 115
    gravity theory, 97
    regional, 305
Trade associations, 208
Training, 298
Tran, Steve, 686nn.32–35, 687n.36, 691
Transactional MNE, 669–671, 677
Transformative MNE, 674–675, 678
Transnational
    mentality, 13–14
    organizational characteristics, 321–324
    strategy, 218–219, 219t
    term, 11n.16
Transnational companies
    key decisions, 322
    key organization dimensions, 329–330
    organizational transition, 329
    physiological model, 324–327
Transnational corporation (TNC), 2n.3
Transnational innovation
    barriers, 413–414
    connect/development model,
        489–490, 503
    differentiated coordination, 416
    differentiation, 414–415
    engagement, 494
    interdependence, 415–416
    networks, 491–494
    open model, 488
Transnationality, 124–126
Transparency International, 753
Triad power, 515
Tricon Restaurant International
    (TRI), 103–105
Tripsas, M., 497n.4
Trompenaars, Fons, 118n.3, 501t

Tsai, Jean, 686nn.32–35, 687n.36, 691
Tse, D. K., 186n.18
Tsingtao Brewery, 599
Tuberculosis project, 725, 731, 732, 738
Tuborquia, Dorlahome, 716
Tucker, David, 271, 274
TUI AG, networks, 507–508
Turner, C., 179n.2
Tushman, M., 498n.11

U

Ulnwick, A., 498n.12
"Umbrella contracts," 506n.24
Uncertainty avoidance, 118, 180,
    180t–181t, 185f
Unilever
    matrix management, 403–404, 405, 406
    responsive MNE, 672
    transnational innovation, 414–415
Unilever Shanghai Sales Co., 538
Union Carbide, 668, 670, 746
United Arab Emirates, 43
United Brands, 667
United Kingdom
    organizational chart, 192f
    organizational model, 183f, 183–187,
        185f, 186, 189
    P&G case study, 459, 460
United Nations
    Global Compact, 662, 673
    MNE definition, 2
    model of multinational management, 654
    Universal Declaration of Human
        Rights, 744
United Self-Defense Forces of Colombia
    (AUC), 710
United States
    CEMEX case study, 157–158
    as coordinated federation,
        318–319, 319f
    organizational change model, 327
    organizational chart, 192f
    selected clusters, 201f
    toy industry, 166–167
    wine case study, 130, 132, 141–142, 143
United Steel Workers, 714
Uppsala model, 9, 9f
Uribe Vélez, Álvaro, 710
Utterback, J., 498n.11

V

Vahlne, Jan-Erik, 9n.12
Values, 747
"Values in Tension: Ethics Away from
    Home," 676, 743–754

Van der Klug, Cor, 336–337
Van Reimsdijk, Hendrick, 334, 336
Varadarajan, Tunku, 687n.37
Verbeke, Alain, 304
Vernon, Raymond, 5n.4, 6, 6n.6, 675–676
Vertinsky, I., 186n.18
Verwaltungsrat Ausschuss (VRA), 632
Verzyer, R. W., 496n.2
Vicks Vaporub, 645, 647–651
Vietnam
    Jollibee Foods case study, 43, 47
    Nike case study, 684–685, 686–687,
        692, 697
"Viking Management," 189, 190t
"Village market" model, 184, 185f
Vin de Table, 132
Vins de Pays, 130
Vins Delimités de Qualite Superieure
    (VDQS), 130
Vivaldi, Rogerio, 725, 735, 736–737
Vizir, 655, 657–658
"Voice," 331, 395–396
"Voice over Internet Protocol (IP),"
    420, 441
von Hipple, E., 498n.12
von Pierer, Heinrich, 425, 429

W

Wages, 686–687, 690–692, 693
Wal-Mart International
    Jordanian sweatshops, 666
    regional strategies, 303, 307
Walgenbach, P., 185n.15
Walzer, Michael, 744
Waterman, Robert "Bob," 464,
    465, 515n.3
Wazir, Rafi, 138n.10
Weber, Max, 179n.5
Wehrung, D. A., 186n.18
"Weight," 393, 394–395
Weinberg, S., 82n.40
Weiss, Paul, 94
Welch, Jack, 260, 307
"Welding Experts," 21

"Well-oiled machine" model, 184, 185f
Wesley, David, 707–708
Westney, D. E., 179n.7
Wheatley, Tom, 689
Wheeler, David, 234n.89
"When You Shouldn't Go Global,"
    105–112
White, Rod, 68
Wilkinson, Bruce, 379
Williamson, Peter J., 121n.5, 417f
Wilson, James, 128n.1
Wimm-Bill-Dann (WBD) Foods,
    290, 299–300
Wine industry
    Australia, 612–614
    California, 196–197, 197f
    case study, 128–145
    Chile, 622–623
"Wine-in-a-box" package, 132
"Wireless mesh," 234
Wirth, Dyann, 730
Wirth, Peter, 730, 739–740
Women
    BOP market, 762
    education crisis, 237–238
Women's Information Resource
    Electronic Service (WIRES), 757
Wong, G. Y. Y, 186n.19
Woo, Pam, 680n.7, 681n.9, 683n.17
Woo, Roh Tae, 752
Wood, Richard, 558
Woods, David, 616
Woods, Tiger, 679, 680
World Bank
    demonstrations against, 662
    direct foreign investments, 664, 665
    global alliances, 692, 696
    on global poverty, 663–664
World Economic Forum (Davos), 673
World Health Organization
    neglected diseases list, 732
    pharmaceuticals, 554, 555
World Investment Report, 3t, 4
World Resource Institute, 756
World Trade Organization (WTO)
    demonstrations, 662, 663–664
    trade liberalization, 115

World Vision International (WVI) case
    study, 366–384
World Vision Partnership, 372, 374
Worldwide functional management
    core roles/responsibilities,
        592–594
    transnational organizations, 321
Worldwide functional manager, 588
Wormald, Chris, 76, 84
Wu, Mingdong, 300

X

Xerox
    home-base-augmenting site, 480
    joint ventures, 572–573

Y

Yach, David, 68–69, 85
Yamashita, Toshihiko, 343
Yates, Simon, 226n.24
"Yellow Booklet," 334
Yet2.com, innovation networks, 493
Yoffie, David B., 680nn.4, 6
Yong Zhang, 300
Yoshino, Michael Y., 629
Young, Andrew, 685, 685nn.28, 29,
    686n.31, 718, 718–719, 718n.26
YourEncore, 493
Yuguang, Xie, 175
Yum Brands, 301
Yusof, Nora Asyikin, 531

Z

Zambrano, Lorenzo, 155, 163, 165
Zara, 304–306, 307
Zeng, Ming, 121n.5
Zhiguo, Jin, 599
Zukerman, Ethan, 225nn.15, 18